FOLKSONGS OF BRITAIN AND IRELAND

FOLKSONGS OF BRITAIN AND IRELAND

EDITED BY

PETER KENNEDY

SCHIRMER BOOKS

A Division of Macmillan Publishing Co., Inc.,

New York

Edited by Peter Kennedy

Assisted by Allison Whyte
    Noel Hamilton
    Emrys Cleaver
    Mona Douglas
    Inglis Gundry
    Frank LeMaistre
    Claudie Marcel-Dubois
    John Brune

Musical transcription and guitar chords by Raymond Parfrey

Text copyright © 1975 by Peter Kennedy
Music copyright © 1975 by Folktracks and Soundpost Publications

SCHIRMER BOOKS
A Division of Macmillan Publishing Co., Inc.
866 Third Avenue,
New York, N.Y. 10022

First American Edition 1975
Library of Congress Number 75–7571
Printed in Great Britain

To my parents, Douglas and Helen,
who set me on the road

Preface

I should like to wish you much enjoyment in the use of this book. It represents what I believe to be some of the best versions of songs which are still in the living tradition. However I would like to add some remarks which are prompted by very real twinges of conscience.

As a folk collector I have found that folksinging has survived most successfully in those areas where local collections have *not* been made and published. It seems that any kind of standardisation of a particular song form has been like signing its death warrant, and this has especially been the case in the use of standard versions in the local schools.

It was for this reason that I started recording traditional singers with a tape machine and getting these recordings around before allowing anything to appear in print. However, once there were several versions of a song available, that particular song fortunately seemed to be in a continual state of change as it was passed from person to person. This change may be quite small and unconscious, but always dependent upon the performer's own individual artistry. *To stay alive, folksong must be alive.*

You will see in the note about *Folksong Recordings* that I have stressed the importance of *oral transmission* as a means of learning the songs and this applies particularly to the style of the songs. Again you will see from the sub-title of our book that it is intended as a *Guidebook to the Living Tradition of Folksinging.* I hope that you will continually bear this in mind when using the book and that it will be of value to performers, students, teachers and researchers alike.

Acknowledgements

So many folk have brought this song collection into being, in fact they number thousands and go back many generations, but of our present day folk we should like to acknowledge the help of four groups of people:

Firstly, there are those we call 'the traditional singers', 'the storehouses', who have kept the songs in mind, in many cases for over fifty years, and frequently without much encouragement from their own families or friends. How patient they were with us, delving deep into the past while we were fiddling around with our recording machines. Alas, so many of them have now 'gone on', God rest them. Their names appear in hundreds throughout the various sections of our book, but we would like to single out a few of our main source contributors to whom we are particularly grateful for providing a large number of songs: The Copper Family of Rotting-dean, Sussex; Harry Cox of Catfield in Norfolk; the Findlaters of Dounby on the Orkney mainland; Sheila Gallagher and Conal O'Donnell of Donegal; Adolphus and Eliza Le Ruez of Bonne Nuit on the Island of Jersey; Flora MacNeil (now Mrs Alister MacInnes) of Barra in the Outer Hebrides; the Makem Family in Keady, County Armagh; Jeannie Robertson and the very many members of the Travelling Stewarts in North-east Scotland; John Thomas, the blind Welsh bard; and finally Joe and Winifred Woods of the Isle of Man.

In our second group there are far too many to list even a few. We should like to thank all those who guided us to the 'storehouses' or, with the best intentions, 'informed' on their whereabouts; and all of them for being such wonderfully understanding backroom workers, who appreciate the value of their local traditions. We hope that they will be rewarded by seeing the names of their own particular singers, by their songs coming back into circulation and by hearing younger folksingers quoting their names with reverence. They have helped to maintain the lifeline of our folksong tradition.

Thirdly I would personally like to thank all my fellow tradesmen, the folk collectors, who have helped me to make the recordings, and allowed me to include items from their own collecting or songs which we collected in each other's company: Seamus Ennis, my partner with whom I worked for the BBC Sound Archive; Hamish Henderson of the School of Scottish Studies; my aunt, Maud Karpeles, with whom I followed up some of the families that had sung to Cecil Sharp; Sean O'Boyle who provided a second home for me in Northern Ireland; Patrick Shuldham-Shaw, compatriot worker at Cecil Sharp House; Marie Slocombe, Tim Eckersley and others at the BBC Sound Archive; and finally the Texan, world folk collector Alan Lomax, who initiated the *Folk Songs of Britain* gramophone record series, and the idea for this book as a sequel to his own *Folk Songs of North America* (Cassell, 1960).

Finally I should again like to express my own personal debt of gratitude to the team who worked on the production of this book. The names of the main contributors appear on the title-page, and they are those who have written introductory and background notes to the particular sections: Scottish, Irish, Welsh, Manx, Cornish, French and for the Travellers. None of them, I think, had any idea what a prolonged task it was going to be, and I was frankly very grateful to them all for seeing the job through to its final stages. To them I would add the names of Kenneth Parker and Anne Carter at Cassell, who continually substituted sweet words for curses, and to my wife, Beryl, without whom I am sure it would never have happened at all.

Contents

I SONGS IN SCOTTISH GAELIC

Introduction 19

II SONGS IN IRISH GAELIC

Introduction 71

III SONGS IN WELSH

Introduction 131

IV SONGS IN MANX GAELIC

Introduction 179

V SONGS IN CORNISH

Introduction 205

VI SONGS OF THE CHANNEL ISLANDS

Introduction 247

VII SONGS OF COURTSHIP

Introduction 295

VIII SONGS OF FALSE LOVE AND TRUE

Introduction 343

IX SONGS OF SEDUCTION

Introduction 393

XIII SONGS OF GOOD COMPANY

Introduction 593

XIV SONGS OF DIVERSION

Introduction 641

XV SONGS OF NEWSWORTHY SENSATION

Introduction 691

Introduction 743

Introduction

As I roved out on a May morning
On a May morning right early
I met me love upon my way
O Lord but she was early
  And she sang: Lilt-a-doodle, lilt-a-doodle
  Lilt-a-doodle-dee
  And-she-hidled-on-the-dee
  Hidled-on-the-dee-and-she-landy

This was the verse that became the signature tune for our weekly 'As I Roved Out' Sunday morning BBC radio programmes which ran right through the 1950s. The programmes started with Sarah Makem singing the verse, tape-recorded in her cottage in Keady, Armagh, Northern Ireland, and then the tune of the chorus was taken up by a small orchestra playing an arrangement by Spike Hughes.

The original field recording had been made in 1952 on a portable magnetic tape machine in Sarah's kitchen, and since she could best remember the old songs when she was working, it meant following her around with the microphone, verse by verse, from the kitchen sink to the kitchen range and then back to the sink again:

Her boots were black and her stockings white
And her buckles shone like silver
She had a dark and rolling eye
And her ear-rings tipped her shoulder

None of us will ever forget Sarah's words when she opened the door: 'You're as welcome as the flowers in May.' At first she could only remember fragments, like those first two verses of *As I Roved Out* (No. 121), but then her husband started on the fiddle, her son Jack his pipes, and the neighbours and friends started to move in for a 'ceilidh' (a house-visiting party). Cousin Annie Jane Kelly came in with her dog, stubbed out her cigarette, and gave us her unforgettable performance of *The Magpie's Nest* (No. 182):

For if I was a king, sure, I would make you a queen
I would roll you in my arms where the meadows they are green
Yes, I'd roll you in my heart's content, I will sit you down to rest
'Longsides me Irish colleen in the magpie's nest

All this time, the younger members of the family sat quietly listening, taking it all in, like Tommy Makem, who later went to America and formed a folksong group with the Clancy Brothers. They sat propped up in the corner half asleep as Sarah and Annie Jane started to recall the longer love-songs and broadside ballads like *Derry Gaol* (No. 316):

O, it's after morning, there comes an evening
And after evening another day
And after a false love, there comes a true one
It's hard to hold them that will not stay

The tape-recorder kept going, as one singer sparked off the next, and more and more songs came back into memory; songs that hadn't been thought about for years and songs that otherwise might have lain dormant for many more years. Few, if any of us, in Sarah's kitchen at that time realized just what we were starting in going round taping these songs, nor did we realize

1

Sarah Makem of Keady, Armagh
Photograph: Peter Kennedy

that it probably wasn't the recording of the songs that was half as important as the interest we were awakening in the younger generation.

In retrospect we realize that the broadcast programmes of our collecting trips must have made an immeasurable impact on younger listeners in the 1950s. The old songs were new to most of our listeners, but had a familiar ring that made people say to themselves, 'I'm sure I've heard that somewhere before'. At first the songs were not altogether liked musically and we found that the immediate reaction, particularly from younger listeners, was to ask why anybody should want to listen to these old songs sung by old people who couldn't 'sing' anyway. Yet all the time, those singers' individual way of singing was biting deep into their listeners' consciousness.

In fact, what really made the 'As I Roved Out' programmes go on for week after week in the 1950s with such a high listening audience rating was not so much the songs but the emerging personalities of the singers. In the broadcasts, to give variety to the presentation of the songs, we gave a brief description of the singers and our meeting with them, and before they sang we let the tape run on with some of their conversation and talk. They told us about themselves, their domestic lives and their work as well as what the songs meant to them and why they had remembered them. In so doing they gave us much of their own character and the background struggles from which it had developed.

Most of our singers turned out to be the local 'rebels', refusing to conform to local religious and local political pressures; they were traditionalists and yet at the same time they were often outrageously progressive. They had never accepted without question what they were told or what they read (and indeed many could not read or write) until they had either experienced something for themselves or knew it to match their own personal conviction. So what touched you, when you met them and heard them talking, was their utter sincerity, and when they sang their songs you knew without question that they felt and understood what they were singing about:

> Come down, come down, all off that weary gallows
> For I bear pardon all from the Queen
> I'll let them see that they dare not hang you
> And I'll crown my Willie with a bunch of green

To date, folksongs from Britain have usually appeared in separate collections, either as English, Irish, Scottish or Welsh. Indeed, local nationalism, or regionalism within those areas, has in the past generally been the incentive for their publication and for local collectors and folksong societies to gather material for them. However, these often artificial boundaries of interest have led to the neglect of other local minority and border traditions, while at the same time making it difficult to view the folksong tradition of Britain as a whole.

This volume will, I hope, be breaking new ground with the inclusion of songs in Cornish, Manx Gaelic, Channel Islands French and the various languages of the Travelling People, while at the same time giving examples of both native and 'Anglo' languages to be found in Scotland, Ireland and Wales. From Shetland to the Channel Islands, and from the West of Ireland to East Anglia, there are all sorts of local variations of speech and musical styles. For our purpose we have grouped together in this book all these English and Lowland Scots, Anglo-Irish and Anglo-Welsh areas, and the songs have been arranged according to song types.

Nowadays, national barriers are giving way to a more specialized interest in local songs. In an age of standardization, more and more young singers are looking for regional songs and stories in order to provide themselves with a stronger sense of identity. Within England's boundaries you find a new zest for Manx and Cornish songs, for the French patois songs of the Channel Islands, and for the local songs of the counties, towns and cities. The same is true of Ireland, Scotland and Wales. We have aimed in this book not so much to cater for these special areas, because they require local research, but rather by our careful—and often I hope unexpected—selection from the enormous repertoire of British folksong, to give an overall summary of its richness which will both act as a guide and provide incentive for further study.

*

Being city-born and reared on a very anaemic diet of school and concert performances of folksongs about 'lily-white maidens', when I roved out and went to the West Country in 1950 I was naturally very struck by my first encounters with genuine traditional folksingers, and it was my meeting with a retired shellback sailor in Bristol which changed the course of my life. Although I had already been won over by the lilting rhythms of folkdance music, performances of folksong had always left me cold. So when I first heard a traditional singer roar out his salt-sea shanties with such a strong rhythmic vitality, I knew that the printed page would never contain either his robust and ribald verses nor convey the subtleties of his performance. In fact the importance of the tradition was not so much what he sang but the way that he sang it:

> As I walked down the Broadway
> One evening in July
> I met a maid who asked my trade
> A sailor, John, says I
> And away you, Johnny
> My dear honey
> O, you New York girls
> Can't you dance the polka?

At the Scophony-Baird factory at Wells in Somerset a friend lent me a research prototype of the first domestic magnetic tape recorder, suggesting that I tried to record folk music with it. I went to see the shantyman and recorded his repertoire. Those recordings were sent to the HMV gramophone company and they agreed that he should make a commercial record for them. Next I played them to the BBC and they agreed that my shellback should make some broadcasts. That was how my first folk recordings and broadcasts came to be made and how I started roving out along the roads of Britain; roads that were to lead me along many hundreds of miles of quarter-inch magnetic tape.

Of my first encounters in the West Country, those which left most impression were made around Dartmoor in 1950; in particular my meeting the two brothers from Belstone in Devon, Bill and Harry Westaway, whose father had sung *Widdecombe Fair* to the local antiquarian, Sabine Baring Gould (see *Tom Pearce*, No. 308). Hearing them I soon became aware that they were the last descendants of a noble race of local country bards. Their characters and sharp country wit provided first-rate broadcast value, especially in live programmes, in which you never knew what they might say—or to whom. I feel sure that Frank Gillard, one of Britain's most experienced broadcasters, will never forget the unexpected moments provided by Bill Westaway when Frank was compering a Village Barn Dance programme from the Devon village of South Zeal.

Another veteran of those early BBC West Region broadcasts was the travelling chimney-sweep, Dicky Lashbrook. Dicky journeyed the Devon–Cornwall border in a horse and trap, and when I first met him he was still sleeping rough between jobs, either in an old farmer's barn or under a hedge. At the local barn dances, at which my *Haymakers* band was playing, Dicky delighted in shocking the young ladies with his racy versions of *Blackbirds and Thrushes* (No. 169) and his country courtship duet *Bargain With Me* (No. 194).

Memorable too were the 'follow-up' collecting trips made with my aunt, Maud Karpeles. We were searching out the original families of singers from whom Cecil Sharp had noted down songs in Somerset at the beginning of the century. One of our main difficulties in tracing descendants turned out to be the unfortunate tradition whereby women change their surnames on marriage. Although it was on the whole very depressing to discover how few of the younger members of the family had taken an interest in grandmother's old songs, there were such notable exceptions as Fred Crossman at Huish Episcopi (*The Labouring Man's Daughter*, No. 132) and Edwin Thomas of Allerford (*Bold Reynard*, No. 243).

Before I had started tape-recording songs in the West Country, my spare time had been spent collecting fiddle and pipe tunes and country dances in the North of England. Now when I returned to the North Country again I found the area to be as rich in song as I had previously found it in dances and fiddle music. It was in fact the piper to the Duke of Northumberland, Jack Armstrong, who led me to many of the shepherd singers, such as Jimmy White at Powburn (*The Muckin' o' Geordie's Byre*, No. 257) and Jack Goodfellow at Rennington (*The Bonny Wee Window*, No. 123 and *Jim, the Carter Lad*, No. 228). Further west in Cumberland I found the singing seemed to be mainly in praise of local huntsmen (*Joe Bowman*, No. 252 and *We'll All Go A-Hunting Today*, No. 263). And the rest of England proved to be no less rewarding. Nearly every county is represented by songs in this book, not forgetting the smallest county, Rutland, with Charlie Wilson's *All Jolly Fellows* (No. 241).

A surprisingly large number of the songs in this collection come from Southern England and the Home Counties, now the suburbs of London: from Surrey, Sussex and Kent; but the most rewarding area proved to be East Anglia, and particularly the sparsely populated county of Norfolk. Here I was always rewarded by my visits and re-visits to Harry Cox at Catfield, near Potter Heigham on the Broads. From his repertoire of a hundred or so songs, Harry contributed twenty-one songs to our present collection.

Coverage of England was alternated with collecting trips to Ireland, Scotland and Wales, where I worked in company with the local experts Sean O'Boyle, Hamish Henderson and Emrys Cleaver.

For my first evening of collaboration in Belfast, Sean O'Boyle arranged an eventful 'ceilidh' at which I met such folk stars as 'Granda', Frank McPeake, John McLaverty (*The Doffin' Mistress*, No. 220 and *The Hot Ash-Pelt*, No. 225) and his father, Charles Boyle (*The Greenwood Laddie*, No. 130). It was a wonderful start to what must have been the most intensive coverage two collectors ever accomplished in only a few weeks. Sean was determined to show the visiting Englishman that folksong was far from dead in Ireland. In fact, I remember that as the boxes of tape in the van were used up, they were replaced with crates of ale, in order to save time-wasting journeys to the nearest ale-house!

The insistence of Sean's milkman in Armagh led us to that most productive kitchen in the house of Sarah Makem in Keady, where as well as Sarah's version of *As I Roved Out* (No. 121) we recorded such beautiful songs as *The Forsaken Mother and Child* (No. 154), *The Factory Girl* (No. 221), *The Magpie's Nest* (No. 182) and *Derry Gaol* (No. 316).

Then we combed the hitherto uncharted six counties of Antrim, Armagh, Derry, Down, Fermanagh and Tyrone, and from there plunged into the *gaeltacht* (Gaelic-speaking area). The folk music of Donegal made, I think, the strongest impression on me of any in Britain. From a people who had suffered so much in the past from the suppression of their language, I received the warmest hospitality that I have ever experienced.

One wonders whether it is because of this suppression that they hung on to the songs and music with a greater tenacity and a deeper understanding than elsewhere. Certainly, the outstanding singer in Donegal was over ninety years old. Living in an isolated croft with only her one cow for company, Sheila Gallagher of Gweedore preferred to record her whole repertoire in one five-hour session. I remember that her main concern was to show how many of her love songs should be performed in the fast, rhythmical Donegal style, rather than in the drawn-out lyrical crooning styles of Southern Ireland which were winning so many Irish folksong competitions for a local teenager who had learned the songs from Sheila.

Here we found a large store of mostly unpublished Gaelic material. So we decided to make our collection of Irish Gaelic songs (Nos. 25–48) all from Donegal. Although many of the songs are sung in other parts of Ireland, as in the case of our Scots Gaelic collection, this area alone proved capable of providing a wide range of typical Irish Gaelic song.

My only previous knowledge of Scottish folksong came mainly from my father's family and from tales of his grandfather, David Kennedy, who had taken his family around the world singing Lowland Scots songs to the Scottish communities overseas; and, on the Gaelic side, from great-aunt Marjorie Kennedy Fraser, who had used a portable phonograph recording machine to gather material for the later editions of her *Songs of the Hebrides*. But my personal experience began just over the border in Galloway where I met such fine Scots shepherd-singers as Togo Crawford and heard his *Ca the Yowes to the Knowes* (No. 124) and his local tune for *The Farmer's Boy* (No. 247).

In Aberdeenshire the big singers turned out to be some of the tinker travelling families like the Stewarts, who claimed kinship to the royal family outlawed in Jacobite times. These Stewarts were certainly the aristocrats of Scots Lowland folksinging. One member, Belle Stewart of Blairgowrie, sang us her own *Berryfields of Blair* (No. 339), *The Queen Among the Heather* (No. 141), and the ever-popular Dundee *Overgate* (No. 187); Davie Stewart with his accordion sang us *The Barnyards o' Delgaty* (No. 242), *Rothsay-O* (No. 282) and *Tramps and Hawkers* (No. 358); and Lucy Stewart of Fetterangus sang *The Lady o' the Dainty Doon-by* (No. 179), *Macpherson's Lament* (No. 348), *The Ploughboy* (No. 140), *Poor Wee Jockie Clarke* (No. 236) and *The Ewie wi' the Crookit Horn* (No. 271).

The Gaelic contribution for our Scottish collection (Nos. 1–24) comes to us almost entirely from the singing of Flora MacNeil of Barra, in the Hebrides. To her own large family collection, Flora added a few other Gaelic songs gathered over the years. Once again we are indebted to a single folksinger for her life-long interest and desire to keep the songs in circulation. This unique collection provides a most valuable and varied selection covering a wide range of folksong in Gaelic Scotland.

Although Orkney and Shetland have preserved some Norse influence in their fiddle music, the song tradition appears to be mostly Lowland Scots, brought to the islands by boat from Aberdeenshire. From here we have the three songs: *Yon Green Valley* (No. 168), *Poor Auld Maid* (No. 210), and the local Orkney murder ballad sung by John and Ethel Findlater of Dounby, *The Standing Stones* (No. 332).

Of the singers in the Welsh language, the most prolific in North Wales was blind John Thomas of Corwen (see Nos. 55, 62, 66, 67 and 72) and in the south the largest repertoire came from Ben Phillips of Lochtwrffin in Pembrokeshire (see Nos. 51, 54, 57, 61 and 63). One Welsh-speaking singer in Denbighshire, Tom Edwards, sang both in Welsh (Nos. 52, 56 and 62) and in English (No. 204).

Other songs in English from Wales came from Phil Tanner of Llangennith in the Gower peninsula of South Wales, who has contributed *Young Roger Esquire* (No. 144), *The Oyster*

Girl (No. 234) and *The Parson and the Clerk* (No. 235). The Welsh gipsies, Hywel and Manfrie Wood, also have songs in both English and Welsh and we have included their versions of *Three Men Went a-Hunting* (No. 306) and *Was You Ever See?* (No. 309).

It may come as a surprise to some readers to find songs in Manx Gaelic (Nos. 73–84) and Cornish (Nos. 85–96). In the Gaelic-speaking areas of Scotland and Ireland, and in Welsh Wales, the language is still alive and taught in school, but in the Isle of Man and in Cornwall the last native speakers have gone and the language is having to undergo a rather self-conscious process of revival. It is to assist this revival that I have included this chapter, for singing is one of the best ways of encouraging interest in native language. We are deeply indebted to Mona Douglas for her life-long interest in collecting Manx songs, and to Inglis Gundry and the Federation of Old Cornwall Societies for providing Cornish versions of local folksongs.

My own collecting work in the islands of Jersey, Guernsey, Alderney and Sark covered a period of only a few weeks, but in that short time I found that there were plenty of French songs still sung there and in their folksongs the Islands have preserved speech traditions and versions of songs which have been forgotten in Normandy itself. From the veteran singer Adolphus Le Ruez of Bonne Nuit in Jersey we have seven songs in Jersey-French, as well as his version of the English *The Frog and the Mouse* (No. 294).

*

Before the literary world started to rediscover popular ballads and songs as a distinct body of material among the so-called unlettered folk, there had been a close relationship in minstrelsy between the consciously composed forms and those in general use, or as we say nowadays 'in the public domain'.

The minstrels, that is any of the specialists among a musical community, inherited a repertoire of songs and stories comprising much of the unwritten history and culture of the community. Minstrelsy preserved this tradition by presenting it in the form of sung recitation or narrative, and the stories of new events were borne on the backs of old rhythms, melodies and commonplace phrases. The minstrels, while no doubt sometimes in competition with each other, were more likely to share and maintain the amalgam of poetry and music which belonged to the community as a whole.

The development of printing and improvements in communications produced rapid changes in society, especially the separation of the lettered and the unlettered, resulting in a distinct class of literary practitioners who consciously wrote and composed for a literate and increasingly sophisticated public. During the reigns of the Tudor and Stuart monarchs in the sixteenth and seventeenth centuries, there was still a close relationship between town and country, between squire and tenant, chief and clan, but by the the early eighteenth century, the 'Age of Reason', the literate town-dweller lived in a world almost completely cut off from the people of the countryside. Yet it was the more progressive townsmen who first became curious about their countryside and who discovered, or rediscovered, the value of the traditional songs, stories and music, although it was the sung-stories or ballads which particularly appealed, as poets looked for verse patterns for new compositions.

So began a craze for printed collections of ballads. It started in Scotland with such volumes as Allan Ramsay's *Tea-Table Miscellany* (1724–40), Bishop Percy's *Reliques* (1765), Walter Scott's *Minstrelsy* (1802), and the works of Robert Burns. Burns was himself a collector and supplied a great deal of traditional material to James Johnson for *The Scots Musical Museum* (1787), as well as writing new verses to the old ballad tunes that were running through his head.

The literary interest in these popular ballads of England and Scotland continued through three centuries, leading eventually to the compilation and editing at Harvard of the authoritative volumes of Professor Francis J. Child, *English and Scottish Popular Ballads* (1882–98).

The first wave of interest in balladry concentrated almost wholly on the poetry and texts of the songs, and in the discussions on the possible origins of these anonymous stories, argument was confined to the authorship, form and context of the verse. The concept was that somewhere in earlier history, a poet had written such-and-such a ballad which, having found favour, was transmitted orally by narration or singing. Musical interest in the ballads was almost negligible. The systematic searching for folk melodies was not to come until nearly two hundred years later.

From the middle of the nineteenth century, interest in the melodies of folksongs grew with the increasing popularity of the piano as the musical instrument of the day. In fact some of the first publishers of folk music collections in England were the piano-makers William Chappell and John Broadwood. William Chappell's *National English Airs* (1838) and *Popular Music of the Olden Time* (1858), marked the beginnings of background documentation and musical analysis of English folksongs. Chappell was only thirty years old when his own family published his first collection with the aim 'to give refutation to the popular fallacy that England has no National Music'.

From that time on, English folksong collections appeared with their melodies arranged for the piano. Sea shanties, children's games, seasonal songs and carols extended the field, and songs were gathered from particular regions and counties. All the counties were included in Lucy Broadwood's *English County Songs* (1893).

The number of music collectors had now increased to such an extent that they started to tread on each other's toes. Realizing the importance of working together as a corporate body they began to form separate national folksong societies in England, Wales and in Ireland, publishing annual journals, and those who were collecting were soon benefiting from the shared specialized knowledge of their members.

This second harvest of folksong led to a reappraisal of its importance, as music this time rather than poetry, and music which could make both a national and a universal appeal. This second rediscovery, like the first, was again interpreted as the work of anonymous gifted individuals, a concept of a treasure, literary and musical, being transmitted casually by successive generations of unlettered popular entertainers.

These formalized views have been much modified in the light of a better understanding of the folk process, and folk music is now effectively established in its own right. But it was only just over half a century ago that Cecil Sharp was battling on the platform and in the press for the recognition of folksong as a form distinct from the welter of composed songs, popular or classical. It became for him a particularly bitter argument with his musical antagonists, so much so that in defence he wrote his book *English Folk-Song: Some Conclusions* (1907), which has become a folksong textbook of international renown.

Before the formation of The Folk-Song Society, the musical world in London had recognized only the national songs peculiar to the Irish, Scots, Welsh and other seemingly more volatile races. So when Cecil Sharp and his fellow collectors demonstrated that England also possessed a musical tradition, it was assumed that their work of collecting must have reaped the whole harvest, and it has been a matter of perpetual astonishment to some musicians when still more unrecorded material continues to appear.

Only four composers in Britain really took advantage of the work of Cecil Sharp and his colleagues, and they were four who had had first-hand contact with the tradition by being collectors themselves: George Butterworth, Percy Grainger, E. J. Moeran and of course

Ralph Vaughan Williams. The latter's love of folksong not only enriched his contribution to the world of classical music, but made him an important force in persuading other musicians of its value to music as a whole.* One result of the study of folksong music was that scholars were able to provide companion volumes of tunes for many of the ballads previously collected and published only as poetry. A number of these collections of ballads with tunes—often 'arranged' to their disadvantage—appeared at the beginning of this century, but by far the largest task was undertaken recently by the American Professor Bertrand Bronson, who attempted to gather together all the tunes for each ballad published in Britain and the United States in his *Traditional Tunes of the Child Ballads*.† Unfortunately, this work could not include many of the tunes we have recorded in the field in the flurry of intense activity in Britain in the 1950s and 1960s.

*

Folksong is only one of the many strands making up a folk culture which has, like other biological cultures, evolved as the behaviour pattern of unselfconscious peoples. These include children and other primitives, and also those country folk who still depend on an unconscious process of acquiring their traditional craft skills and lore, such as the oral transmission of music, poetry and stories. Traditional songs and ballads reflect the social conditions and ways of life of a community. Through the refining process of oral transmission, they become intense expressions of generalized feelings which strike with poignancy at the heart of matters. For this reason they form effective vehicles for communicating elemental emotions and simple passions. Used by satirists, lampooners and propagandists, they provide the most potent form of publicity, rivalling the printed word and, with the added power of modern mass-media, can still be a forceful mode of protest, revolt and social comment.

The most effective part of the politically-slanted printed broadsides of the eighteenth and nineteenth centuries were the catchy traditional melodies to which the balladmongers attached their partisan messages. Many were old dance tunes which had already survived because of their capacity to carry meaningful verses and choruses. Often it was an undertone association, for example the bawdiness of the original song, gave a suggestive, salty flavour to a satirical poem or political lampoon. In fact it was this musical suggestiveness that really gave the broadside such a hold over popular songwriters of the period. The appeal of Robert Burns' poetry, for instance, depends a great deal on the rhythms and cadences of the folk airs that inspired so much of his verse, and which have favoured and still favour the makers of 'protest songs'.

*

The word 'folksong' we now accept as having a definite meaning for us today, but it is only in the last two centuries that the word has come to be used, in German as *Volkslied* (Herder: 1773), and creeping gradually into English in the nineteenth century. Over the years the meaning of the word 'folk' has changed considerably. At first they were considered to be unlettered country people, those once called 'peasants', a word which was abandoned to use in only a derogatory sense, and their songs and stories were taken up by poets and authors looking for new literary art forms. It was only at the end of the nineteenth century when local beliefs and customs had come to be known as folklore that the music, both songs and dances, started to attract the attention of composers and musicians, and particularly those working in educational fields.

---

* See his *National Music*, Oxford University Press, 1934.
† Harvard University Press, 1959.

Some countries have never adopted the German word and have found alternative ways of describing their folksongs. In France there are the 'chansons populaires' and the compromise 'chansons folkloriques', while elsewhere folksongs may be called traditional, ethnic, primitive, native or simply songs of a particular country, such as Scottish songs or Irish songs.

At first, the folk were considered to be country people whose local traditions had come to be prized by cultured antiquarians. Then, as technical education became available and industry grew up in the towns, so the folk forsook the country and their own local traditions. The traditions themselves thus became more highly prized, and the need for recording and preserving them grew more urgent every year. Now it looks as though the wheel has turned full circle and the new kind of folk are probably the city-dwellers who have discovered the value of using the old traditions. They, however, are much less concerned about recording and preserving than they are about once again using folksong as an active art form.

Because by their nature they involved so many educational subjects—English Language, Social History, Geography, Politics, Religion, and the emotional aspects of life itself—so it is that folksongs can provide considerable interest among students in schools and colleges as material for study as well as entertainment and relaxation. Folksongs with their infinite variety can be used as an inter-relating as well as a liberal arts subject. In fact this is often found to be the most effective way of introducing folksong to students, rather than as part of the music lesson.

Even as a music subject, probably the best type of introduction is for the students themselves to arrange some kind of off-duty recreational *folk club* activity. Once the songs have become an accepted part of their extra-mural traditions, then workshop type sessions can be arranged for the more serious study of singing technique, group work and the use of the various folk instruments.

A good way to ensure the growth of the folksong tradition in the school or college is to encourage local adaptation, the making of new verses to the old songs, and the making of new songs using the traditional patterns. Folksinging then begins to form a valuable focus for bringing the students together socially as a community, and certain songs come to be used for particular occasions in the academic year.

There are many who rightly question the value of the current revival of interest in folksong. Why bother about the old, sometimes meaningless songs, when there are so many good contemporary songs arriving on the scene each week? These critics are puzzled at the increasing numbers of young people who 'want to become' folksingers and who want first to learn songs of their own national or local tradition and find out more about their lineage.

I think the main reason for this lies in the increasing restraints of standardization imposed upon a rising generation in an urban, welfare society. In folksong they find a music they can perform which will not be an imitation or be bounded by conventions, but can be their own personal creation. As with traditional jazz, folksongs, to be effective, really need to be created every time they are performed. The songs given in this book represent only one version of a song's performance, as part of a living tradition in a constant state of metamorphosis.

The other factor which accounts for its popularity is the ability of folksong to create a community in places where family or local urban life no longer provides this function. An audience shares immediately in the emotions of a folksong performer because a folksinger has evolved his own way with a particular song, it has become part of him, and the real art of the business is the successful communication of his own feelings.

Folksongs can form part of the repertoire of amateur and professional alike. Singers who start for the fun of it, performing for their friends at clubs and parties, often find themselves moving into the realm of professional entertainers. It is then that they begin to feel the need for a deeper understanding of the various performance techniques which can be drawn upon for different types of audiences and locations. The freshness and spontaneity of the performance in front of the smaller, friendly circle now has to be consciously studied and analysed if it is to be retained throughout repeated rehearsals and performances, and particularly performances which may have as an audience only a silent television studio team.

The effectiveness of many of the folksongs comes from their use as a way of telling a story. The unusual rhythms can arouse interest, the familiar tunes can relax, the choruses invite participation, but for the most part folksong audiences find themselves caught up with the almost operatic ability to tell a good tale. In fact it is arguable whether we should think of these songs as music at all, as the tunes are nearly always completely subservient to the story or emotion, rather than forming the basis of any great musical achievement. If he is unaware of these age-old storytelling techniques, the classically trained professional singer meeting folksong for the first time would probably condemn folksong performances as extraordinarily amateurish, using terms like unmusical, tuneless, unpolished, strident, etc., and it may require prolonged contact with the tradition to appreciate some of the subtleties of traditional skills which at first appear as incompetence and artlessness in performance.

It also comes as a surprise to hear singers of storytelling songs and ballads presenting them with a deliberately impersonal style of delivery instead of bringing out important dramatic points and interpreting the story of the song for the audience. The folksinger considers the song significant in its entirety. The listeners are not told what they ought to hear, but are expected to use their imagination and to select those dramatic elements and emotions with which they already have some personal experience.

Another aspect of folksong singing which on first hearing may also seem strange is a kind of embroidery of the vocal line with slides, turns, appoggiatura, glottal stops, etc. Musicians call this 'decoration', but as it forms an essential feature of the singer's technique it cannot be considered only as a decoration of the melody. Since this technique is usually regarded as the province of the unaccompanied singer, it is often called the 'unaccompanied style', which is another not very good term, as it can equally well be used with instrumental accompaniment and, likewise, by a number of singers working in harmony or polyphony.

These techniques are probably most highly developed and therefore most obvious when used by gipsies and street singers. The travelling people were probably the originators of what came to be called 'crooning', although with the travellers this style of performance could be more accurately described as 'decoration'. Other traditional singers use these techniques, but to a much lesser extent and very often to the unsuspecting singer, almost unnoticeably. For examples of the subtleties of the traditional styles one should listen to the recordings of good unaccompanied field singers like Harry Cox, Elizabeth Cronin, Fred Jordan, Thomas Moran, Jeannie Robertson, Belle Stewart and Phil Tanner.

Unaccompanied vocal groups are traditionally part of the folk scene. They do not use the conventional harmonies of the church or concert choir, but instead tend to employ a much more polyphonic extension of unison singing. That is to say, they start together, then depart, and generally resolve, coming together in unison again for the final note of the phrase. This is sometimes called 'glee style', which is perhaps another misnomer, as traditional vocal groups do not use the barber-shop harmonies which are associated with the glee-singers. For examples of traditional harmony, listen to recordings by the Copper family, the McPeake family, Young Tradition and the Watersons.

Singers who use their own self-accompaniment with a guitar, banjo, fiddle, accordion (or what-have-you) have the great advantage of being able to exercise their own control over the balance between voice and instrument, yet they frequently make it more difficult for the listener to hear the story of a song. In order to prevent this kind of war between voice and instrument, folk accompanists have devised all kinds of interesting techniques which can be studied and acquired.

A temptation for self-accompanists is to provide only one main beat, stressing the first beat of every bar. Although this may make a few people happy, banging their feet in sympathy, it is unlikely to help song communication. It is much more effective to avoid the main beat altogether and to fill in all the other places with an 'in-between ripple' of rhythmic syncopation: the 'anacrusis', or approach to the beat, will be found to be more important than the beat itself, which the singer wants his listeners to provide for themselves. In this respect, the technique of providing the 'lilt' is very much like playing for dancing.

Folk guitarists and five-string banjo pickers, now a breed on their own, have devised all kinds of exciting accompanying styles which can add to rather than detract from the songs. They find ways of breaking up the rhythmic pattern and at the same time providing harmonic and polyphonic countermelodies. In addition, they have also found ways of providing a *continuo* in the form of a drone, and this is particularly useful for the many songs in our present collection which are either pentatonic or modal in character.

Working successfully in groups, vocally and instrumentally, naturally depends very much on good teamwork, organized by strong leadership. Family combinations make good folk groups, because each knows what the other can do, or is likely to do, at any given moment. Being close to each other, friends and relations also achieve a unity of rhythm and purpose. It is therefore possible to develop material which is very individual in character, with each member contributing his own part, to make up the whole.

PETER KENNEDY

The Musical Notations of the Songs

In a publication of this kind, part-scientific and part-recreational, inevitably there has to be a compromise. The original field recordings are the best scientific transcription of the tradition; even highly competent musicians will frequently produce quite different transcriptions from the same field recording. Ordinary music notation can only serve as a basic guide to an idiomatic original, so they cannot really be regarded as authentic, for whereas conventional music notations can show the basic essentials of the tune, a really accurate scientific notation of the source singer's performance would mean using some kind of continuous graph tracing of the sound which could follow all the subtleties and idiosyncrasies of the original performance by the traditional singer.

Furthermore, good traditional singers will frequently vary the tune of each verse of their song in order to fit different word metres. Often this is a method of bringing out the words as part of a storytelling technique. Less intentional but just as human are the variations which occur in the first verse, before the singers get into the swing of the 'standard' tune of their song. Most of our transcriptions are hypothetically the standard tunes of subsequent verses matched to the words of the first verse.

Where possible, the original pitch of the song as used by the source singer has been retained, but in certain cases the key has been changed in order to fit the average compass of the human voice. Furthermore, in order to make it easier for accompaniment by fiddles, accordions, guitars and other folk instruments, the use of extreme sharp or flat keys has been avoided.

The chord symbols represent only one of the many possible ways of harmonising the songs. Here again the need for simplicity has restricted the suggested harmonies to chord symbols indicating only major, minor and seventh chords, with an occasional suspension (indicated by the sign: *sus*). Many of our tunes, particularly the Gaelic ones, are pentatonic in origin and are therefore removed from the major-minor system. In these cases the symbols are more arbitrary than ever, but they are offered to those readers who still feel happier with some kind of harmonic guidance.

Metronome marks to indicate speed of performance or the tempo of each song have been omitted on purpose. There is considerable variation in tempos for the same song by different singers in differing locations and a freedom and non-standardisation of performance is much more likely to keep the music alive. Throughout, we have done our best to combine faithfulness to the source singer's performance with a simplicity of notation.

RAYMOND PARFREY

The Translations

There is need to crave our readers' indulgence for some of the translations included in this collection which may seem either to be not very accurate on the one hand, or perhaps not very easy to sing on the other.

Ideally we would like to have provided both a literal and a poetic English translation to each of the non-English songs in the book, but this would have meant an even larger and unwieldy size of book. So we have therefore provided compromise translations, wherever possible placed alongside the original, thus enabling the two to be viewed together.

Whenever possible, of course, we would like the songs to be performed in their original language; in this case the parallel translations will be helpful. However if you do fancy a particular air, and decide you would like to sing it with an English text, then we would like you to feel free to develop our English compromise texts, using as much or as little of our original as you like, in order to produce your own versions.

Folksong Recordings

Sound recordings of most of the original singers from whom the songs in this book were collected are available on both long-playing gramophone records and on standard tape cassettes. This enables those who are learning the songs to get them virtually first-hand from the traditional performers. Learning this way, 'by oral tradition', enables the singer to incorporate all the subtleties of melodic decoration, irregular rhythms and story communication. On the other hand it does not mean that the songs should be slavishly copied from the source performers. Probably the most satisfactory method is to listen to and enjoy the tradition as it has been recorded and then to sing the songs in your own way, and literally 'make them your own'.

TAPE CASSETTES

Standard tape cassettes of most of the songs in each chapter are obtainable from Folktracks, The Centre for Oral Traditions, Dartington Ciderhouse, Totnes, Devon TQ9 6JB.

I	Songs in Scots Gaelic	FSB 001
II	Songs in Irish Gaelic	FSB 003
III	Songs in Welsh	FSB 005
IV	Songs in Manx Gaelic	FSB 007
V	Songs in Cornish	FSB 009
VI	Songs in French	FSB 011
VII	Songs of Courtship	FSB 013
VIII	Songs of False Love and True	FSB 015
IX	Songs of Seduction	FSB 017
X	Songs of Uneasy Wedlock	FSB 019
XI	Songs of Occupations	FSB 021
XII	Songs of Country Life	FSB 023
XIII	Songs of Good Company	FSB 025
XIV	Songs of Diversion	FSB 027
XV	Songs of Newsworthy Sensation	FSB 029
XVI	Songs of the Travellers	FSB 031

LONG-PLAYING DISCS

There is also a series of ten long-playing records, entitled *Folk Songs of Britain*, which is published by Caedmon Records in the USA and by Topic Records in the United Kingdom.

I	Songs of Courtship	Caedmon TC 1142	Topic 12T 157
II	Songs of Seduction	1143	158
III	Jack of All Trades	1144	159
IV	The Ballads (Child Nos. 2–95)	1145	160
V	The Ballads (Child Nos. 110–299)	1146	161
VI	Sailormen and Servingmaids	1162	194
VII	Fair Game and Foul	1163	195
VIII	A Soldier's Life for me	1164	196
IX	Songs of Ceremony	1224	197
X	Songs of Animals, Marvels, etc.	1225	198

BBC SOUND ARCHIVES

Throughout the book there are references giving current BBC numberings. These refer to field recordings which are carefully preserved in the BBC Sound Archive. Except in the cases of those items which have been included in the above-mentioned series, these particular recordings are not commercially available to the general public.

I

Songs in
Scottish Gaelic

Introduction

In the Census Report for 1951, 95 447 people are recorded as being speakers of Scottish Gaelic, the large majority being also English speakers; in 1961 this had dropped to 80 978 Gaelic speakers, a percentage of 1·7 of the total population of Scotland.

The strongholds of Gaelic are the Western Isles and a few remote areas of the mainland, for these areas have proved more conservative, largely because of their remoteness and the relative sparsity of communication with the English-speaking world. But even here, we now find that modern economic pressures cause depopulation and destruction of communities by the demands for centralisation in the industrial south of Scotland. Anglicisation has always had most effect at bridgeheads between the Gaelic and English worlds, such as at a seaport like Stornoway in the Isle of Lewis, where the town is the centre of transport, communications and local government.

Yet Gaelic, although destined to die in the foreseeable future, still retains a remarkable wealth of song, both in the oral tradition (with some examples almost 400 years old), and in manuscript collections and published anthologies.

The earliest private collections, *The Book of Lismore* (early sixteenth century) and *The Fernaig* MS (1688), did not record many of the songs of the ordinary people, but were more concerned with the poetry of the nobility or with that of the collectors' particular friends and relations. Nevertheless, Ossianic ballads are included with them.

It is in the eighteenth century however that we first find collections of non-classical poetry, when there was a marked upsurge of interest in all things pertaining to the past, including folksong. This was a countrywide reaction to the Industrial Revolution, and a way of escape from it.

Equally important as a motivating factor in the development of 'collecting' was the controversy sparked off by the works of James Macpherson, who published Ossianic literature in the 1760s which he claimed to have translated from Gaelic. In fact, he had done far more than translate, and the results bear little resemblance to the original ballads. Though extremely popular at first (testifying to public demand for romantic writing), eventually dispute arose as to the genuineness of his professed originals, and this led to much further study of his sources.

During this period a number of antiquarians formed themselves into an unofficial 'Celtic Group': they had studied together at the University of St Andrews and maintained an academic relationship thereafter. The manuscripts of two members of this group, MacLagan and MacNicol, contain songs of all descriptions, though some are only fragmentary. Printed collections at the end of the century include Patrick MacDonald's *Highland Vocal Airs* (MACDONALD: 1784), and the Gillies' Collection *Sean Dàin* (GILLIES: 1786), which contain texts only.

The early nineteenth century saw further publications, but these were limited to the well-established type of literary poems such as the work of Màiri Nighean Alasdair Ruaidh and Ian Lom (TURNER: 1813 and STEWART: 1804). Perhaps the reason for the partial exclusion of folksong was that some people were still indignantly trying to parry the fierce attacks made by Dr Johnson on the literacy of the Scottish Gael. Yet anyone wishing to prove that Gaelic

19

ora MacNeil of Barra, Outer Hebrides
Photograph: Cassell & Co. Ltd
(by J. D. Hamilton)

literature was not the product of a 'lawless and barbaric people' would surely refrain from citing such songs as *A mhic Iain 'ic Sheumais* (No. 17) as evidence for their defence.*

Later in the century a more liberal view seems to have been taken, and we find collections such as *An Duanaire* (MACPHERSON: 1868), and *An t-Oranaiche* (SINCLAIR: 1879). By this time there was a demand for such books in the Lowlands, especially in Glasgow, a city to which the economic conditions in the Highlands had forced many Gaels. These Highland exiles were forming 'Societies' in an attempt to protect themselves against the non-Gaelic-speaking urban communities amongst whom they lived. At their meetings Gaelic music and communal singing were in demand and this led to a need for printed song-books. Because of their function, these 'Scottish Society Song Books' tended to scoop up, quite uncritically, every sort of song which might prove popular, but *The Gesto Collection* (MACDONALD: 1895) was more discriminating and provides an excellent source for Gaelic song and bagpipe tunes.

Other famous and important publications were the first two volumes of Alexander Carmichael's *Carmina Gadelica* (CARMICHAEL: 1900), to which four further volumes were to be added in later years. Apart from the fifth volume, which contains many secular pieces, these books present mainly religious material, without music, and are not entirely reliable (some of the vocables given do not correspond with those in other versions), but on the whole the text is good and the translations excellent.

The first volume of the now famous *Songs of the Hebrides* (KENNEDY FRASER: 1909) was followed by a second and third in 1917 and 1921 and a fourth volume, *From the Hebrides*, in 1925. These books, the fruits of much labour, have long been the cause of controversy, and it is still debatable whether their appearance has done more harm than good. Marjory Kennedy Fraser was not only a folksong collector, but also a musician searching for basic melodies from which she could develop concert performances; certainly she and her collaborator, Kenneth MacLeod, aimed their collection at the concert platform and the drawing-room musician. Nevertheless, they must be thanked for the vast storehouse of texts and tunes they have given us.

Two collections of this time deserving special mention are Miss Frances Tolmie's contributions to No. 16 of the *Journal of the Folk-Song Society* (JFSS: 1911) and, for texts only, *The MacDonald Collection* (MACDONALD/MACDONALD: 1911). Since these publications in the early years of the century, the most important books on the subject have been *Orain Luaidh* (CRAIG: 1949), *Folksongs and Folklore of South Uist* (SHAW: 1955) and *Hebridean Folksongs* (CAMPBELL/COLLINSON: 1969).

As conditions in Gaelic literature and culture vary considerably from those in other countries of Western Europe, a definition of what 'folksong' means in a Gaelic context has to be made. Before the eighteenth century, distinctions could be drawn between the Bardic school of poetry and what, for want of a better term, we call folk poetry. Bardic poetry was an offshoot of Irish classical poetry, and as regards metre and subject matter conformed to its disciplines. Entrance to the 'craft' was more or less limited by birth and confined to those of a high social standing.

Yet poetry composed outside the Bardic tradition cannot be said to be folk poetry or folksong in the normal sense of the terms: 'folksong' implies certain conditions of composition, and many Gaelic songs are 'folk' only in their method of transmission. Gaelic society before the eighteenth century was still largely illiterate, and this had led to the development of an oral tradition of a higher intellectual standard than that in other parts of the country. So we find songs which would have been classed as 'literature' in a literate society being carried along

---

* CAMPBELL: 1862. *Language, Poetry and Music of the Highland Clans.*

in a fashion which such a society would use only for 'folk' or less sophisticated poetry. *Ailein Duinn* (No. 1) and *Fhir an Leadain Thlàth* (No. 12) are not 'folk' in the same sense as *A Fhleasgaich Oig is Ceanalta* (No. 13), but are surely more conscious products of a single artist.

Admittedly these more sophisticated products may derive their poetic drive from the same emotional storehouse as less artistic works, but the intensity of this drive and, on occasions, the complexity of the finished songs mark them off as different from, say, such Lowland Scots outpourings as the Bothy Ballads of Buchan and Aberdeenshire.

This is not a surprising distinction when one considers that there must have been intelligent people with poetic skills outside the strictly preserved hierarchical Bardic system. They were forced to compose their work in the only other tradition open to them—the oral—and the works of the later poets, like Duncan Bàn MacIntyre, are a testimony to how superfluous a knowledge of writing could be to the composition, but not the survival, of poetry.

The material that we have left to us today in the oral tradition has been conditioned by the changing tastes of generations of Gaelic speakers and singers. A song, however good in a literary sense, had also to pass a 'popularity test' to ensure its survival, and this is the reason why so many old songs are steadily disappearing today: they no longer satisfy the Gaelic public, which is hardly surprising when one considers the vast social and economic differences which exist between the society which gave them birth and that of today.

Alongside the songs which appear to have some literary merit there also survive songs which are more truly 'folk' in inspiration and conception, for example, *Mo Nighean Donn á Còrnaig* (No. 19). There would appear to be no obvious difference in the musical status of the two types of song, and simple folksongs like *Mo Nighean Donn nan Gobhar* (No. 20) have tunes just as complex and musical as those of more literary songs like *A Mhic Dhùghaill 'ic Ruairidh* (No. 16). However, songs of the *Orain Mór* type usually have a quite distinctive and sophisticated type of music which matches the elevated style of the words very well.

In the eighteenth century we find a different picture altogether. The Bardic school of poetry and its accompanying structure had disappeared and a new literary school developed. Yet no valid distinction can be drawn in literary terms between the so-called 'literary' poetry of the eighteenth century and contemporary folksong. Eighteenth-century poets, like Rob Donn, Uilleam Ros and Duncan Bàn, composed within a tradition which was essentially oral. The mere fact of literacy, in the case of poets like Alasdair Mac Mhaighstir Alasdair, does little to exclude their work from this tradition, though it does lead to the inclusion and assimilation of elements hitherto foreign to it, and probably cut off from it by any but literary sources (for example, the use of classical mythology as a frame of reference in both Uilleam Ros and Mac Mhaighstir Alasdair).

It is certainly possible to trace a strain of poetry in the works of all the eighteenth-century poets which would not be carried on in the oral tradition, however much it may be based in it. This can be a result of sheer length, as in Duncan Bàn's *Moladh Beinn Dòbhrainn* or Mac Mhaighstir Alasdair's *Birlinn Chlann Raghaill*. At the same time it is important to note that all writers of the eighteenth century wrote work which followed the pattern of the oral tradition. There are many examples of this: Duncan Bàn's *Oran Seacharan Seilge* (MacLeod: 1952); Mac Mhaighstir Alasdair's *Agus ho Mhórag* (MacDonald: 1924); Uilleam Ros's *Oran Cumhaidh* and *Cuachag nan Craobh* (Calder: 1937). Whether this was done consciously, as in the case of Mac Mhaighstir Alasdair and Uilleam Ros, who actually took over folksongs and remade them to suit their own tastes and times, or whether it was an unconscious process, as seems probable in the work of Duncan Bàn and Rob Donn, the fact remains that the new 'literary' school regarded the oral tradition as being both significant and as socially acceptable as the written tradition. This was also true of the eighteenth-century collectors who copied the works of living, known authors as readily as they collected those of unknown 'folk' authors, and recorded them in the same manuscripts as part of the same tradition. Neither is any distinction felt today on the part of the modern folksinger who regards, say, *Oran Seacharan Seilge* as just as much a part of his repertoire as any of the songs in our collection.

In fact the songs chosen for this collection, though by no means representative of those which are most popular in Gaelic Scotland today, do provide a cross-section of the sort of material still extant in Scottish Gaelic.

In the past many collectors have made much of the remoteness of Gaelic folksong, and they have been over-sentimental and romantic in their approach to editing their material. One would almost believe that it was regarded as some sort of literary virtue that these songs should present a totally different set of attitudes and way of life from the collectors' own experience. In fact this is not a virtue of the songs, but a reminder that any literature must reflect the society which created it and ensured its continued existence. Having admitted that the Gaelic society was radically different, for better or worse, from its English counterpart, one must accept that a reference to a thatched house, for instance (as in *A Phiùthrag 's a phiuthar*, No. 22), is a reference to a simple, ordinary everyday domestic thing, without all the romantic connotations and associations which may have gathered since the thatched house disappeared.

Besides the danger of romanticising the songs themselves, there is the enduring preconceived notion of 'Celtic gloom'. This attitude is commented upon by Miss Amy Murray, herself a bit of a romantic, in CELTIC REVIEW, vol. II:

> Real sorrows are plenty in the Outer Isles, and they have their poignant utterance; there is a quality of sadness, moreover, in many lovely Gaelic airs which is more elemental than human. We read our own vain longings and world-weariness and regrets into them, even as into the voices of the wind and wave; then we say the folk-music of the Gael is altogether sad.

The songs in our collection deal with a wide range of subjects, including all the most important aspects of domestic life. To those who encounter these songs for the first time perhaps the most moving will be the Love Laments such as *Ailein Duinn* (No. 1). Love is indeed the most popular theme, and appears as the main subject of most of our songs. Some are straightforward love songs, like *Caolas eadar mi 's Iain* (No. 6), whilst others combine love with a secondary theme, and we can only describe this type today as being the Heroic Love Songs. Virtues in a man were prowess at sea, in hunting or in battle, and praise for these qualities is implied in Flora MacNeil's version of *Chunnaic mise mo leannan* (No. 8), but is perhaps more explicit in other versions of the same song.

Another important branch of the love-song group are the Pregnancy Songs, where the girl laments her position and often wishes her lover to return to her, the girl scarcely ever bearing her lover any ill-will for deserting her. Indeed these songs often end on a note of admirable forgiveness and well-wishing. Occasionally indifference is feigned but even then the disguise is pretty thin, as in the lines in *Chunnaic mise mo leannan* (No. 8):

Ach cha ruigeadh e leas e	But he needn't have really troubled
Cha robh mise 'n trom dhéidh air	For him I didn't care so much

Frequently love songs are placed in a pastoral background, as in *Mo Nighean Donn nan Gobhar* (No. 20). This group, the Pastoral Love Songs, appears to have developed into a literary convention during the nineteenth century, when we find Glasgow 'exile' poets still composing in this vein in spite of having spent the best part of their adult lives in the city.

The Pastoral Love Poetry has a fairly close relation to Exile Poetry in general (see SINCLAIR:

1879, pp. 39 and 55), but pure Exile Poetry does occur, as *Fàth mo Mhulaid a Bhith Ann* (No. 11).

Of course straightforward lament and praise also exist, as in *Cairistìona* (No. 5) and *Faca sibh Raghaill na Ailein* (No. 10). Praises especially seem to owe their existence to the social structure, and can be seen frequently to belong to the class of public Clan Poetry rather than as personal comments. Examples of this kind of poetry are *Fliuch an Oidhche* (No. 14) and *Beinn a' Cheathaich* (No. 2), which are both in praise of the clan MacNeil of Barra. Laments, perhaps naturally enough, tend to be more personal, but the influences of the clan system cannot be overlooked.

Also very much part of the clan system are the Flyting Songs, which are conversations between two members (usually women) of different clans, each praising her own and making disparaging, if not downright insulting, remarks about the other's clan and chief. Flyting Songs can be found in CRAIG: 1949, pp. 1, 20 and 80.

A less common type is the Topical or Local Event Songs. The only example included here is perhaps rather untypical: *Co Sheinneas an Fhìdeag Airgid?* (No. 9). A great exponent of this in the eighteenth century was Rob Donn, who could develop the most trivial occurrence into a theme of universal interest. As time went on, the accent came to be placed more on the humorous aspects of such local events. Of course, there may have been a body of humorous verse in the same vein in the early period too, but this has not survived, and indeed one would hardly expect poetry which demands a knowledge of topical affairs to last very much after the events which inspired it. The only humorous poetry which remains from the early period is contained in the Matchmaking Songs, some of which appear to have been more or less extemporarily composed on the formulaic frame, or, in early examples, in the puirt-a-beul (mouth-music) tradition. The Matchmaking Songs contain a good percentage of fun, as in *Sean Duine cha ghabh mi idir* (No. 23), though some can also be considered as more serious love poetry.

Nearly all the Matchmaking Songs, however, share the same functions as the Labour Songs (for examples of milking songs see SHAW: 1955, pp. 157–64). Apart from songs whose content is directly concerned with their function, there seems to be no fixed relationship between songs about a particular subject. Examples are to be found of the saddest of subjects in songs which were used as waulking* songs, such as *Chan e Caoidh Mhic Shiridh* (No. 7), *A Bhean Iadach* (No. 3) and *Cairistìona* (No. 5). As such they must have a well-established rhythmic pattern, which the singers find in no way incongruous with such sad topics. The function of a song would seem to be of relative unimportance, but it is perhaps because of the functions that these songs have survived to the present day, and may have caused various changes in the songs themselves.

Metrically the songs of the non-Bardic tradition belong to a stressed system, and not to a syllabic one. The structure of songs of the waulking song type has been discussed by Mr James Ross (EIGSE, vol. 7). The most common metre outside this system is the four line stanza, where the last stressed word of each of the first three lines and a word in the middle of the last line all rhyme, and where the last stressed word in every verse should rhyme. A good example of this metre is *Fhir an Leadain Thlàth* (No. 12).

In approach, most Gaelic poetry can be said to be highly personal; of this collection, only one song—*Fliuch an Oidhche* (No. 14)—is not written in the first person. In Nos. 2, 9, 10, 17 and 21 the personal element is confined to the first lines, and seems to serve the purpose of an introduction: it gives the singer a part in the action, and personalises the comment in the song.

---

* 'Waulking' (Gaelic: 'luadh') is the process of fulling the cloth by pounding the material against a board and stretching it with the hands and feet.

Possibly the intention behind this was to make the song more effective, by giving the singer more authority from his being a participant or first-hand reporter.

Perhaps this apparent immediacy of the songs is responsible in part for the limited use made of imagery. Only one poem in our collection can be said to have any extended imagery at all, and there can hardly be a more frequently used image in Gaelic poetry than that of the tree representing a young chief, which we find in *O Chraobh nan Ubhal* (No. 21). This is a recurrent image in the work of Màiri Nighean Alasdair Ruaidh, and is to be found also in poetry of the Bardic school. *Ailein Duinn* (No. 1) also has some effective, though not sustained, imagery, as in the lines:

O gur mise th'air mo sgaradh?	What is it that so torments me?
Gu bheil do leabaidh anns an fheamainn	That your bed should be the seaweed
Gur iad na ròin do luchd faire	None but seals to be your mourners
Do choinnlean àrd na reultan geala	Stars on high to be your candles
'S do cheòl fìdhle gaoir na mara	The murmuring sea your song of passing

Cairistìona (No. 5) contains a very exotic image, which is not easy to comprehend or assess, and *Fhir an Leadain Thlàth* (No. 12) also has some striking images. But what one finds more remarkable is the great realism of most Gaelic folksongs. This does not mean that a song is packed with background information, but the realistic details are carefully selected to give maximum emotive and descriptive value with the minimum of words. This can lead to most effective conciseness and highly colourful emotive descriptions. To take an example, the following lines from *Chan e Caoidh Mhic Shiridh* (No. 7) deal with the fairly mundane topic of an unmade bed:

Tha do leabaidh gun chàradh	Upon your bed that's not made ready
'S fhad' o'n dh'fhàg thu i fuar	Cold you left it long ago
Cha téid mi g'a càradh	I'll not trouble now to make it
Tha thu ghràidh ro fhad' bhuam	Love, too far away from me

In these two couplets the writer seems to convey both the impression of the coldness of the bed, lately warm, and her own reaction to the idea of making it after her lover's death. The bed is again used in *A Bhean Iadach* (No. 3) where it has the added poignancy of being a bed shared by the drowning woman's husband.

A similar selection of significant detail can be seen in even the smallest impressionistic pictures, as in *Chunnaic mise mo leannan* (No. 8):

Chunnaic mis' e dol seachad	I did see him going past me
Air each glas nan ceum eutrom	Upon the grey horse treading lightly

where the choice of the horse's lightness of foot serves to emphasise the nobility of the rider (that is, it was not a carthorse that he rode) and also to give the impression of how easily he could pass by without even deigning to notice her.

This careful selection of detail is sometimes accompanied by a very effective choice of words. Several examples of sensuous phrases can be found in the songs presented here. A good example is the very concise description the woman gives of the blankets in *A Bhean Iadach* (No. 3):

Ann ad phlaideachan	In your blankets
Mìne, bàna	Soft and snow-white

or the line from *Ailein Duinn* (No. 1):

Leathanach a'bhroillich bhàinghil	Skin like snow MacLean, my own one

Often this sensuous quality can be found combined with a delicate antithesis, as in these lines from CRAIG: 1949, p. 23:

Uisdein 'Ic Iain Mhòir a Tunord	Hugh, son of Iain Mor from Tunord
'S aotrom do cheum, trom do bhuille	Light your step, heavy your blow

One may be tempted to cast aside many very effective lines in Gaelic folksong because they appear to be mere copies of other lines in other songs. A discussion of these formulaic phrases can be found in EIGSE, vol. 8. They are too frequent to be overlooked, as a comparison of these references will show. For instance you may compare CRAIG: 1949, pp. 39 and 100 with *Faca sibh Raghaill na Ailein?* (No. 10) for similar descriptions of sea prowess, and the lines on hunting in CRAIG on pp. 60, 67–8, 77 and 82.

Several theories have been put forward to account for the similarity of these phrases, one being that the texts are in fact corrupt and that singers have confused lines from one song with those from another. This seems improbable when one considers the variations which do exist, some phrases, for instance, demanding an adaptation to another metrical pattern.

In this respect, C. M. Bowra makes a remark relevant to all oral poetry:

> The task of composition, which is treated with such care and seriousness, is helped, as in all oral poetry, by the existence of formulas, of ready-made phrases, which a man is entitled and even expected to use when he makes a song. They are respected because they have been tested by time and have proved their worth, and though they may not meet every possible need or challenge, they are undeniably useful in handling recurrent themes.—(BOWRA: 1952, p. 48.)

There is nothing second-rate about poetry which uses these formulas. The criterion should be not so much whether the lines are original as whether they are effective in the context of the song. It can happen that an over-enthusiastic use of such formulas can break up the unity of a song, and give it so many branches that it becomes difficult to follow the main theme. This occurs in a song in CRAIG: 1949, p. 81, where no less than five elements are introduced, each of which has only the most tenuous connection with the other.

One must also beware of too readily condemning Gaelic folksong for a lack of unity. Sometimes, as is the case in *Ailein Duinn* (No. 1), the song-maker is only shifting the approach to the same central theme. The unity of a poem which deals with a single event or set of circumstances lies in the singleness of the occasion which gave rise to that poem; a poem dealing with several different occasions or emotions is unified by the fact that they are all the experiences of the song-maker. This is the case with *Chan e Caoidh Mhic Shiridh* (No. 7). At first reading the story may seem to be disjointed, with its sudden jump from describing the dead body to describing the unmade bed. Admittedly there is no attempt at a unity of time or space, but the dominant theme is still maintained. At first the reader may be disconcerted by this leaping around from reaction to reaction, but the effect is quite in keeping with this particular theme. The revulsion the song-maker feels at the idea of making her dead brother's bed and her lingering look out to see if by some miracle his boat might appear are both part of the feeling of great loss she is experiencing. Thus they are relevant to the song, which is in fact an exploration of these feelings rather than a lament in the normal sense.

In *Cairistìona* (No. 5), however, the transition in line nine is perhaps more difficult to account for or to understand. Although we can appreciate that some venture is doomed to failure because Cairistìona is not alive, we cannot quite appreciate what this venture is, and what connection it has with Cairistìona.

In some, apparently later, songs the unity is more consciously contrived, as in *Fàth mo*

Mhulaid a Bhith Ann (No. 11), where the listener travels a full circle in his or her imagination to arrive with added emotion back 'fo bharraibh chruaidh nam beann'. In *Co Sheinneas an Fhìdeag Airgid?* (No. 9) a different technique is applied in the repetition of the opening line at the end of the poem. This is a well-worn device in Bardic poetry, where a 'dùnadh' of some sort was obligatory, though its use is not at all common outside that tradition. One or two other examples do exist (see CRAIG: 1949, p. 73, *Mi'm aonar air àird an aisig*).

However, the majority of Gaelic songs make no attempt at formal unity, and it may well be that the writers of these songs did not consider unity as important as we do today, and what emotional unity there is is more or less accidental. Although the texts we have today are perhaps not always complete, or have gathered lines from other songs, this process of give-and-take must always have existed to some extent. Some songs, for instance, would seem now to be fragments of longer versions which have existed earlier in written form (as, for example, the song in CRAIG: 1949, p. 67). Other versions of the same song in publications or on record are listed in the notes to each of the songs in this collection.

PRONUNCIATION OF SCOTTISH GAELIC

Consonants

Simple consonants *b*, *f*, *m*, *n*, *p*, *r*, are pronounced more or less as in English. Both broad and slender forms of *c* are as in Irish, as is the slender form of *d* and *t*. The broad form of *d* and *t* have no close equivalent in English as they are pronounced by the same method as the distinctive broad *l*, *ll* and *nn* of Scottish Gaelic: by placing the tongue against the top front teeth and producing the sound with as little an explosive sound as possible. Without these 'thick' sounds of *l* and *nn* and the softening of *d* and *t*, no one can hope to come anywhere near the correct Gaelic pronunciation, as the pronunciation of the consonants colours all the vowels around them. In Scottish Gaelic the broad and slender *s* sound is irregular; when broad, it is pronounced as in English (*so*, etc.), and this is also the case with slender *s* preceding *g*, *m*, *p*, *r*, and *t*: it is otherwise pronounced as *sh*.

Consonant clusters

l, ll BROAD	as described above
l SLENDER	French *le* or Southern *l*ink
ll SLENDER	mi*ll*ion
nn BROAD	as described above
nn SLENDER	pi*n*ion
mn BROAD	*mr*
cn BROAD	*cr*
l followed by b, bh, g, m or p	a 'svarabhakti', or intrusive, vowel is pronounced after the *l*, though it is unwritten; this vowel reproduces the vowel immediately preceding the *l*, which may be either broad or slender.
m followed by l or r	'svarabhakti' vowel
r followed by b, bh, g or m	'svarabhakti' vowel

Aspirated consonants

ch BROAD	lo*ch*
ch SLENDER	English *h*ue but with more friction
chd BROAD	*ch* (*d* not sounded)
dh, gh BROAD	initially and finally pronounced in the same part of the throat as *ch*, but with a *g* sound (in effect, like a baby's gurgle)

dh, gh	medially silent
dh, gh SLENDER	initially, medially and finally as *y* in *y*es
bh BROAD and SLENDER	initially and finally as *v*
	medially either as *w* or silent
ph BROAD and SLENDER	always *f*
sh BROAD	English *h*
sh SLENDER	*h* in *h*ue

Vowels

WRITTEN IN GAELIC	DESCRIPTION	GAELIC	MEANING	PRONUNCIATION
a, ai	short, open a	gl*a*s	grey	gl*a*ss
à, ài, eà	long, open a	f*a*g	leave	f*a*g
e, ea, ei	short e	f*ea*r	man	f*e*rry
é, eu	long e	d*e*?	what?	d*ay*
i, io	short i	m*i*	I	m*e*
ì, ìo	long i	sg*i*th	tired	sk*i*
o, oi	short open o	s*o*raidh	farewell	s*o*rry
ò, òi, eò, eòi	long open o	*o*l	drink	*a*ll
ó	long closed o	m*o*r	large	m*o*re
u, ui, iu	short u	f*ui*l	blood	f*oo*l
ao, aoi	not found in English: the nearest equivalent is the southern English pronunciation of bird, curl etc., where the *r* disappears and an almost diphthongized vowel is produced. It is always a long vowel in Gaelic.			

Diphthongs

ua, uai   either (1) *u* and obscure vowel, e.g. nuair (when), pron. as American 'newer' without the *y* sound after the *n*.

          or (2) *u* and *a* (usually precedes an *n* or *m* sound) e.g. uaine (green)

ia   short *i* and obscure vowel e.g. *ia*r (west), pron. *ea*r

Spoken diphthongs also occur in vowels which precede the consonant clusters *ll* and *nn* (broad only). These vowels are written as single vowels, but their sound is a diphthong which moves from the sound of the simple vowel to an *oo* sound, as in English *ow*l.

      e.g. gleann, donn, grunnd   thall, toll, null

Diphthongs may also be written as two separate vowel clusters divided by 'silent' consonantal clusters *dh, gh, th* and *bh*.

      e.g. nighean (pron. neon)   odhar (pron. oar)
           phiuthar (pron. fewer)   cobhar (pron. core)

Obscure vowel

Generally speaking, the obscure vowel (as in English th*e*) is used when the Gaelic spelling has a single or monosyllabic *a* (for example, the definite article *a*n is pronounced more as *i*n than as *A*nn). There are, however, exceptions to this rule. The obscure vowel is also used for the ending -ean or -an in plural words.

Stress

With very few exceptions, the stress falls on the first syllable of Gaelic words, e.g. *nighean.*

1 AILEIN DUINN
DARK-HAIRED ALAN

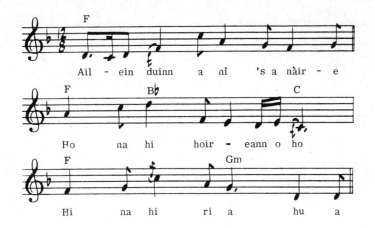

Ail - ein duinn a nì 's a nàir - e

Ho na hi hoir - eann o ho

Hi na hi ri a hu a

1 Ailein duinn a nì 's a nàire
   Ho na hi hoireann o ho
   Hi na hi ri a hu a

2 'S goirt 's gur daor a phàigh mi màl dhut
   Chorus

3 Cha chrodh laoigh 's cha chaoraich bhàna

4 Cha bu chlachan 's cha bu chàis' e

5 Ach an luchd a thaom am bàta

6 Bha m'athair oirre 's mo thriùir bhràithrean

7 'S laoigh mo chuim a rinn mi àrach

8 Chan e sin gu léir a chràidh mi

9 Ach am fear a ghlac air làimh mi

10 Leathanach a'bhroillich bhàinghil

11 A thug o'n chlachan Di-màirt mi

12 Fhaoileag bheag thu, fhaoileag mhar' thu

13 Thig a nall is innis naidheachd

14 Càit an d'fhàg thu na fir geala?

15 Dh'fhàg mi iad 's an eilein mhara

16 Cùl ri cùl is iad gun anail

17 O gur mise th'air mo sgaradh

18 Gu bheil do leabaidh anns an fheamainn

19 Gur iad na ròin do luchd faire

20 Do choinnlean àrd na reultan geala

21 'S do cheòl fìdhle gaoir na mara

1 Dark-haired Alan, my dearest jewel
   Ho na hi hoireann o ho
   Hi na hi ri a hu a

2 Endless grief the rent it cost me
   Chorus

3 'Twas neither sheep nor even cattle

4 Neither cheese nor even ballast

5 But the load the ship took with her

6 Brothers three and my own father

7 Gone my child grown to manhood

8 As if this wasn't all my burden

9 One to whom my heart was given

10 Skin like snow, McLean, my own one

11 Took me from the church on Tuesday

12 Seagull, seagull from the ocean

13 Come to me and tell me plainly

14 Where you left my own, those fair ones?

15 Left alone with sea surrounding

16 Back-to-back, no longer breathing

17 What is it that so torments me?

18 That your bed should be the seaweed

19 None but seals to be your mourners

20 Stars on high to be your candles

21 The murmuring sea your song of passing

2 BEINN A' CHEATHAICH
THE MISTY MOUNTAIN

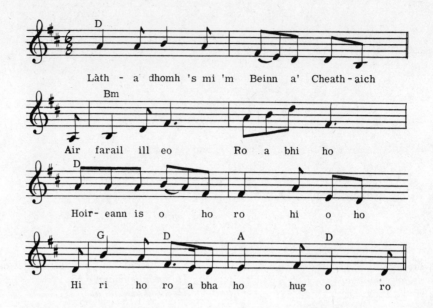

Làth - a dhomh 's mi 'm Beinn a' Cheath - aich

Air farail ill eo   Ro a bhi ho

Hoir- eann is o ho ro hi o ho

Hi ri ho ro a bha ho hug o ro

1 Làtha dhomh 's mi 'm Beinn a' *Air farail ill eo* [Cheathaich *Ro a bhi ho* *Hoireann is o ho ro hi o ho* *Hi ri ho ro a bha ho hug o ro*	1 Once upon the misty mountain *Air farail ill eo* *Ro a bhi ho* *Hoireann is o ho ro hi o ho* *Hi ri ho ro a bha ho hug o ro*
2 Ruagbhail nan caorach 's 'ga faighinn	2 Rounding up the sheep to fold them
3 Gun deach bàta Chlann Nìll seachad	3 The McNeil galley she was passing
4 Gun cheann cumaidh aig a h-astar	4 Nothing holding back her journeying
5 Le dà mhac Iain 'ic a'Phearsain	5 With two sons of Ian McPherson
6 Murchadh Mór á ceann a'chlachain	6 And big Murdoch from the townland
7 Ruairidh òg an t-oighre maiseach	7 With young Roderick, heir so handsome
8 Steach a dùthaich Mhic'ill'Eathain	8 From McLean's land she was coming
9 Steach gu Cìosamul an aigheir	9 To merry Kismul she was heading
10 Far am faighte chuirm ri gàbhail	10 Where there is the finest feasting
11 Fìon a dh'oidhche gu làtha	11 Wine there is from night till morning

3 A BHEAN IADACH
THE JEALOUS WOMAN

A bhean ud thall, *hu go* 'N cois na tràgh - ad, hu go

Sìn do chas dhomh, hao ri ho ro Sìn do làmh dhomh, hu go

1 A bhean ud thall, *hu go*
'N cois na tràghad, *hu go*
Sìn do chas dhomh, *hao ri ho ro*
Sìn do làmh dhomh, *hu go*

2 Sìn do chas dhomh, *hu go*
Sìn do làmh dhomh, *hu go*
Feuch an dean mi, *hao ri ho ro*
Buille snàmh dheth, *hu go*

3 Feuch an dean mi
Buille snàmh dheth

4 Nach truagh leat fhéin
Bean 'ga bàthadh?

5 Cha truagh, cha truagh
'S beag mo chas dhi

6 'S ann a bhios mi
Nochd 'nad àite

7 Ann ad phlaideachan
Mìne, bàna

8 Thoir soraidh bhuam
Gu m'thriùir phàisdean

9 Fear dhiubh bliadhna
'S fear a dhà dhiubh

10 'S fear eile dhiubh
'N aois a thàlaidh

11 Soraidh eile
Gu m'thriùir bhràithrean

12 Thig iad an seo
Moch am màireach

13 'S gheibh iad mise
Air mo bhàthadh

14 'S mo chuailein donn
Feadh an t-sàile

15 'S mo bhainne chìoch
Feadh na làthchadh

1 O woman there, *hu go*
Beside the shore, *hu go*
Reach out your leg, *hao ri ho ro*
Reach out your hand, *hu go*

2 Reach out your leg, *hu go*
Reach out your hand, *hu go*
See if I'm able, *hao ri ho ro*
To swim a stroke, *hu go*

3 See if I'm able
To swim a stroke

4 Have you pity for
A wife that's drowning?

5 None at all
Care little for her

6 In your place
Tonight I will be

7 In your blankets
Soft and snow-white

8 Bid farewell to
My three children

9 One a year old
Two the other

10 And the third
Still being suckled

11 Another farewell to
My three brothers

12 They'll be here
Tomorrow morning

13 And they'll find me
Lying drowned

14 My brown curls
In the salt sea

15 And my breast's milk
Among the sea mud

4 BHEIR MO SHORAIDH THAR GHUNNAIDH
TAKE MY FAREWELL OVER GUNNA

1 Bheir mo shoraidh thar Ghunnaidh
Gu Muile nam mór bheann
Hug oireann o ro hu bha ho
Mo nighean donn bhòidheach
Hug oireann o ro hu bha ho

1 Take my farewell over Gunna
O'er to Mull, the land of mountains
Hug oireann o ro hu bha ho
Mo nighean donn bhòidheach
Hug oireann o ro hu bha ho

2 Far an cluinnear a'chuthag
Air gach bruthach ro'Bhealltainn

2 Where the cuckoo is heard calling
On each hill before May morning

3 Chì mi'm bàta 's i tighinn
Is Iain 'ga seòladh

3 There I see the boat arriving
At the helm I see young Ian

4 Cum dìreach i Iain
Cum tioram i Dhòmhnaill

4 Keep her straight on course, Ian
Keep her safe and dry, Donald

5 I an ciste chaoil chumhaig
Air a dùnadh 's a tàirneadh

5 She is in a narrow coffin
It is closed, held down with nails

6 'S truagh nach robh mi 's an fhiabhras
Mun do chuir mi riamh t'eòlas

6 O that I'd been in a fever
Before I ever got to know you

5 CAIRISTIONA
CHRISTINA

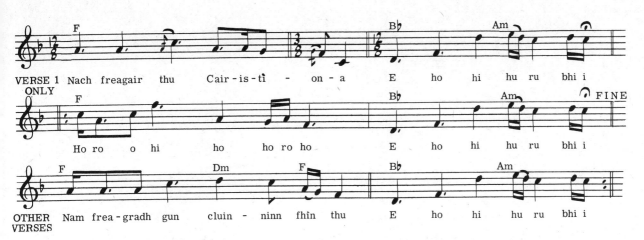

VERSE 1
ONLY
Nach freagair thu Cair-is-tì - on-a E ho hi hu ru bhi i

Ho ro o hi ho ho ro ho E ho hi hu ru bhi i FINE

OTHER
VERSES
Nam frea-gradh gun cluin - ninn fhìn thu E ho hi hu ru bhi i

1 Nach freagair thu Cairistìona?
  E ho hi hu ru bhi i
  Ho ro o hi ho ho ro ho
  E ho hi hu ru bhi i

2 Nam freagradh gun cluinninn fhìn thu

3 Thug mi bliadhn' an cùirt an rìgh leat

4 Ged theirinn e thug mi trì ann

5 Chì mi luingeas air Caol Ile

6 'S iad ag iarraidh Cairistìona

7 Chan ann gu banais a dhèanamh

8 Gus a cur 's an talamh ìseal

9 Sìos fo leacainn gu dìlinn

10 Turus a thug mi Ghleann Comhain

11 'N fhairge trom 's an caolas domhain

12 Chan fhaod mi mo leum a thomhas

13 Ged dh'fhaodadh cha dean mi gnothach

14 Cha bhi Cairistìona romham

1 Will you answer, Christina?
  E ho hi hu ru bhi i
  Ho ro o hi ho ho ro ho
  E ho hi hu ru bhi i

2 If you'd answer, I would hear you

3 A year at Court I was with you

4 Three years myself I did spend there

5 Ships I see in the sound of Islay

6 They are seeking for Christina

7 Not to make a wedding for her

8 In deep clay they're going to lay her

9 Down below the slabs forever

10 To Glencoe I once did journey

11 The waves were high and deep the channel

12 I cannot judge my leap in distance

13 And if I could I would gain nothing

14 Christina for me'll not be waiting

6 CAOLAS EADAR MI IS IAIN
'TWIXT IAN AND ME'S A STRETCH OF WATER

1 Caolas eadar mi is Iain
Hao ri ri 's na hao ri e ho
Cha chaol a th'ann ach cuan domhain
Hao ri ri ri i ibh o
O na hao ri o hao ri e ho

2 'S truagh nach tràghadh e ro'latha
'S nach biodh ann ach loch no abhainn

3 'S truagh nach robh mi 's an t-òg gasda
Mullach beinne guirme caise

4 'S gun duine beò bhith tighinn faisg oirnn
Ach mar gum pòsamaid fo'n altair

1 'Twixt Ian and me's a stretch of water
Hao ri ri 's na hao ri e ho
No narrow strait, but a mighty sea
Hao ri ri ri i ibh o
O na hao ri o hao ri e ho

2 If only 'twould dry before to-morrow
And only be a lake or river

3 If I could be with that fine fellow
Upon the top of a steep green mountain

4 No living soul near us be coming
As if we'd married before the altar

7 CHAN E CAOIDH MHIC SHIRIDH
'TIS NOT LAMENTING O'ER MAC SIRIDH

1 Chan e caoidh Mhic Shiridh
  Dh'fhàg an dìl' air mo ghruaidh
  Hu o ro hu o
  Chall a hi o hi o
  Hu o ra hu o

2 Chan e caoidh mo leannain
  Ged a dh'fhanadh e bhuam

3 Ach a'caoidh mo bhràthar
  Chaidh a bhàthadh 's a'chuan

4 'S duilich leam do chùl chlannaich
  Bhith 's an fheamainn 'ga luadh

5 'S duilich leam do gheal dheudan
  Bhith 'gan reubadh 's a'chuan

6 Tha do leabaidh gun chàradh
  S' fhad' o'n dh'fhàg thu i fuar

7 Cha téid mi 'ga càradh
  Tha thu ghràidh ro fhad' bhuam

8 'S trie mo shùil air an Rubha
  Bho'n bhruthach ud shuas

9 Feuch am faic mi seòl bréidgheal
  Làtha gréine 's a'chuan

---

1 'Tis not lamenting o'er Mac Siridh
  That on my cheeks the tears remain
  Hu o ro hu o
  Chall a hi o hi o
  Hu o ra hu o

2 'Tis not lamenting o'er my sweetheart
  Though he's the one would stay away

3 It is lamenting o'er my brother
  For he's the one that's drowned at sea

4 I'm sad to think your hair so curly
  With the seaweed drifts about

5 I'm sad to think your teeth so pearly
  By the seas are torn apart

6 I see your bed that's not made ready
  As cold you left it long ago

7 I'll not trouble now to make it
  Love, too far away from me

8 Oft my eye's fixed on the headland
  From the hillside there above

9 To see a cloth-white sail I'm waiting
  One sunny day upon the sea

8 CHUNNAIC MISE MO LEANNAN
I DID SEE MY OWN TRUE-LOVER

Na ho ro hi hoireannan
Ho ro chall eile
Na ho ro hi hoireannan

Na ho ro hi hoireannan
Ho ro chall eile
Na ho ro hi hoireannan

1 Chunnaic mise mo leannan
'S cha do dh'aithnich e fhéin mi

1 I did see my own true-lover
And he did not notice me

2 Chunnaic mis' e dol seachad
Air each glas nan ceum eutrom

2 I did see him going past me
Upon the grey horse treading lightly

3 Cha d'fhidir 's cha d'fharraid
'S cha do ghabh e bhuam sgeula

3 He never paid attention to me
He never asked the news of me

4 Ach cha ruigeadh e leas e
Cha robh mise 'n trom dhéidh air

4 But he needn't have really troubled
For him I didn't care so much

5 'S iad mo ghaol-sa Clann Dòmhnaill
Sin an còmhlan nach tréig mi

5 My love is for the clan McDonald
They're the troop which won't forsake me

6 Fir nan calpannan troma
Chùl donna, cheum eutrom

6 Men with legs so strong and sturdy
Dark of hair and light of step

7 Luchd nan claidheanan geala
Chìte faileas ri gréin dhiubh

7 Men with swords of whitest metal
Glistening brightly in the sun

9 CO SHEINNEAS AN FHIDEAG AIRGID?
O WHO WILL PLAY THE SILVER WHISTLE?

VERSE 1 Co shein - neas an fhìd - eag air - gid?

Ho ro hu a hu ill eo

Hi ri liu hill eo Hi ri liu hill eo

OTHER VERSES Mac mo Rìgh - sa dol gu fair - ge

1 Co sheinneas an fhìdeag airgid? *Ho ro hu a hu ill eo* *Hi ri liu hill eo* *Hi ri liu hill eo*	1 O who will play the silver whistle? *Ho ro hu a hu ill eo* *Hi ri liu hill eo* *Hi ri liu hill eo*
2 Mac mo Rìgh-sa dol gu fairge	2 My king's son to sea is going
3 Deanamh deas gu tighinn a dh'Alba	3 To Scotland he prepares his coming
4 Air long mhór air bhàrr na fairge	4 Upon a large ship o'er the ocean
5 Air long mhór nan trì chrann airgid	5 The ship that has three masts of silver
6 Sreangannan dha'n t-sìoda Fhrangach	6 With ropes so light of French silk woven
7 Ulagan òir air gach ceann dhiubh	7 Upon each end are golden pulleys
8 Nuair thig mac mo Rìgh gu fearann	8 When my king's son ashore has landed
9 A'cur fàilt' air Mac'ic Ailein	9 He will welcome the son of Alan
10 'S air Mac Dhòmhnaill Mhór na Ceapaich	10 Big MacDonald come from Keppoch
11 'S air Mac Dhomhnaill Dhuibh Loch Abar	11 Dark MacDonald from Lochabar
12 Nuair thig mac mo Rìgh-sa dhachaidh	12 When my king's son comes back home
13 Cha b'e biadh dha breachdan teine	13 No girdle scones will food be for him
14 Ach bacastair gu deanamh arain	14 But loaves of bread a cook be baking
15 Teàrlach òg nan gorm shùil meallach	15 Young Charles with eyes so blue enticing
16 Fàilte, fàilte, mùirn is cliù dhut	16 Welcome to you, your fame and honour
17 Fìdhleireachd is rogha ciùil dhut	17 Fiddles and choice tunes attend you
18 Co sheinneas an fhìdeag airgid?	18 O who will play the silver whistle?
19 Co chanadh nach seinninn fhìn i?	19 Who'd say I'll not myself be playing?

10 FACA SIBH RAGHAILL NA AILEIN?
HAVE YOU SEEN RONALD OR ALAN?

1 Faca sibh Raghaill na Ailein?
Ro hol ill eo
Ro hol ill eo
Na idir Iain òg mo leannan?
Laoidh leo ho ro
Trom o ro cho
Fair ail ill eo

2 Na idir Iain òg mo leannan
Ro hol ill eo
Ro hol ill eo
Stiùireamaiche 's fheàrr ri gaillean
Laoidh leo ho ro
Trom o ro cho
Fair ail ill eo

3 Stiùireamaiche 's fheàrr ri gaillean

4 Bheireadh tu i slàn gu cala

5 Fad 's a mhaireadh stagh na tarrainn

6 Na buill chainbe ri cruinn gheala

7 Na giuthas o's cionn na mara

1 Have you seen Ronald or Alan?
Ro hol ill eo
Ro hol ill eo
Or young Ian, my sweetheart?
Laoidh leo ho ro
Trom o ro cho
Fair ail ill eo

2 Or young Ian, my sweetheart?
Ro hol ill eo
Ro hol ill eo
In storms the best of helmsmen
Laoidh leo ho ro
Trom o ro cho
Fair ail ill eo

3 In storms the best of helmsmen

4 You'd bring her safe to harbour

5 As long as stays and nails are lasting

6 And canvas against the white masts holding

7 While timbers stay above the water

11 FATH MO MHULAID A BHITH ANN
BEING HERE HAS CAUSED MY SORROW

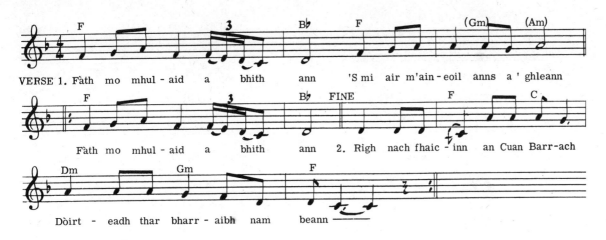

VERSE 1. Fàth mo mhul-aid a bhith ann 'S mi air m'ain-eoil anns a' ghleann

Fàth mo mhul-aid a bhith ann 2. Rìgh nach fhaic-inn an Cuan Barr-ach

Dòirt-eadh thar bharr-aibh nam beann

1 Fàth mo mhulaid a bhith ann
   'S mi air m'aineoil anns a'ghleann
   Fàth mo mhulaid a bhith ann

2 Rìgh nach fhaicinn an Cuan Barrach
   Dòirteadh thar bharraibh nam beann

3 Gaoth an iar le cruaidh fhrasan
   Tighinn 'na lasan o'n tìr thall

4 Luingis bhàn a'snàmh gu h-aotrom
   Mar an fhaoilinn null 's a nall

5 Co tha sud ach an long fhada
   Tuinn 'ga sadail 's i 'na deann

6 Mo thriùir bhràithrean, ceist nan gillean
   Glan an iomairt o'n taobh thall

7 Fear 'ga h-allsadh, fear 'ga stiùireadh
   Am fear òg ri h-iùil 's a 'chrann

8 Iùbraich bhàin na diùlt dhomh 'n t-aiseag
   Cha toir cas mi dh'Innis Gall

9 Dh'fhuarainn Eige agus Canaidh
   Null gu Barraidh ghlas nan tonn

10 Is trom an ionndrainn th'air mo shiubhal
   Cha tog fìdheall e no cainnt

11 Fuaim na h-abh 'gam shìor-éigheachd
   Thugainn m'eudail gu d'thìr dhaimh

12 O ghréin ud shuas, gur beag an t-iongnadh
   Glòir na faoilte bhith mu d'cheann

13 Thu a'triall o'n ghleann 's an oidhche
   Null gu coibhneas a'chuain thall

14 Nam bu leam do thriall 's na speuraibh
   Nàil, cha bhiodh mo cheum cho mall

15 Ach pògaidh tusa nochd Cuan Bharraidh
   'S mis' fo bharraibh chruaidh nam beann

16 Fàth mo mhulaid a bhith ann
   'S mi air m'aineoil anns a'ghleann

1 Being here has caused my sorrow
   For in the glen I am a stranger
   Being here has caused my sorrow

2 O to see the streams of Barra
   Pouring o'er the tops of hillsides

3 The west wind brings the showers so powerful
   Coming in gusts from distant headlands

4 Vessels of white they're sailing lightly
   To and fro, just like the seagulls

5 What is there but the long ship sailing
   Buffeting waves as she goes swiftly?

6 The best of men are my three brothers
   Their journey across was done so neatly

7 One at the sails and one at the steering
   The youngest from the mast is guiding

8 Ship of white, do not refuse to ferry me
   I cannot walk to the Western Islands

9 I'd pass to windward of Eigg and Canna
   Over to Barra, grey with breakers

10 In my heart I'm heavy with longing
   No fiddle nor speech will ease my burden

11 The sound of the ocean ever calling
   Come back, my dearest, to your homeland

12 O sun above, 'tis little wonder
   The glory of joy that does surround you

13 Moving from the glen at evening
   O'er to the kind and distant ocean

14 Could I but take your skyward journey
   Indeed my step would not be tardy

15 Tonight you'll kiss the sea of Barra
   While I'm below unfriendly mountains

16 Being here has caused my sorrow
   For in the glen I am a stranger

12 FHIR AN LEADAIN THLATH
LAD OF LOVELY HAIR

Fhir an lead-ain thlàth Dh'fhàg thu mi fo bhròin

Fhir chùl dual-aich chleach-daich 'S bòidh-che snuadh ri fhaic-inn

Tha do ghaol an tas-gaidh 'N seòm-ar glaist' 'nam fheòil

Fhir an leadain thlàth
Dh'fhàg thu mi fo bhròin

Lad of lovely hair
You've left me in despair

1 Fhir chùl dualaich chleachdaich
  'S bòidhche snuadh ri fhaicinn
  Tha do ghaol an tasgaidh
  'N seòmar glaist' 'nam fheòil
  Chorus

1 Lad of twisting curls
  So beautiful to view
  Your love is kept in store
  Imprisoned inside me
  Chorus

2 Tha do ghruaidh mar shuthain
  An gàrradh nan ubhal
  'S binne leam na chuthag
  Uirghill do bheòil

2 Like the berry is your cheek
  That in the orchard grows
  The cuckoo's not so sweet
  As the sound upon your lips

3 An toiseach a'gheamhraidh
  'S ann a ghabh mi geall ort
  Shaoil leam gum bu leam thu
  'S cha do theann thu 'm chòir

3 When winter first began
  I pledged myself to you
  I thought that you were mine
  But you never came my way

4 Fhir an leadain laghaich
  'S tu mo rùn 's mo roghainn
  Nan sguireadh tu thaghail
  'S an tigh 's am bi'n t-òl

4 Lad of pleasing hair
  My chosen heart's desire
  If you'd only cease to call
  Upon the house of drink

5 Fhir an leadain chraobhaich
  B'òg a rinn thu m'aomadh
  Thug thu mi o m'dhaoine
  A fhuair mo shaothair òg

5 Lad of flowing hair
  So young I was ensnared
  You took me from my own
  From them who had me reared

6 'N gàire rinn mi'n uiridh
  Chuir mo cheum an truimead
  'S mise tha gu duilich
  'S muladach mo cheòl

6 The laughter of last year
  Has weighed my every step
  Now I'm the one who's sad
  And sorrowful is my tune

7 Fhir an leadain thlàth
  Dh'fhàg thu mi fo bhròn
  Tha mi trom an dràsd'
  'S e sin fàth mo bhròin

7 Lad of lovely hair
  You've left me in despair
  With child I'm heavy now
  The cause of all my grief

40

13   A FHLEASGAICH OIG IS CEANALTA
O LAD SO YOUNG AND GENTLE THEE

A fhleasgaich òig is ceanalta
'S tu leannan nan deas ghruagach
Do ghaol a rinn mo shàrachadh
'S tha bhlàth sin air mo shnuadh-sa

1 Shiùbhlainn fada, fada leat
  Siùbhlainn deas is tuath leat
  Is shnàmhainn an cuan Rònach leat
  'S ri m'bheò cha toirinn fuath dhut
  Chorus

2 Gur binn thu na na filidhean
  Gur sìobhalt' leam do ghluasad
  Co chunnaic riamh air ùrlar thu
  Nach dùraigeadh bhith suas riut?

3 Cha phòiteir 's chan fhear daoraich thu
  Bhios daonnnan am measg buairidh
  Sàr chompanach mu'n bhotul thu
  'S chan fhaicear sprochd na gruaim ort

4 'S ged bheireadh Rìgh Seòras àite dhuinn
  Cho àrd 's a th'aig duin'uasal
  Gum b'fheàrr leam bhith air àirigh leat
  An coill 'na tràth 's na luachrach

5 Chan Ileach tha 'na leannan dhomh
  Chan Aranach 's cha Tuathach
  Ach 's ann an Ros a dh'àraicheadh
  Fear àrd an leadain dualaich

6 Chan iongnadh mi bhith muladach
  'S lionn dubh bhith air mo ghruaidhean
  Chaidh innseadh dhomh le fothail
  Gun tug nighean a'ghobha bhuam thu

O lad so young and gentle thee
To all the girls their sweetheart be
Your love has so oppress-ed me
How pale I'm worn 'tis plain to see

1 Far, far away I'd go with thee
  I'd journey north and south with thee
  I'd swim the Rona sea with thee
  Through life I'd not disfavour thee
  Chorus

2 To hear more sweet than poets thee
  Your movements have much grace for me
  Whoe'er on ballroom floor saw thee
  Who would not wish to nearer be

3 Neither drinker nor a drunkard thou
  Who could be drawn into a row
  With a bottle spends a friendly hour
  Never seen being coarse or sour

4 Although King George a house would give
  As grand as those where nobles live
  In a cot with you I'd rather be
  In the wood of grass and reed and tree

5 He's not from Islay is my dearest
  Nor from Arran or North Uist
  But 'twas in Ross where he was reared
  The upright man with curling hair

6 No wonder I am sad and sair
  Marked on my cheeks is dark despair
  When I was told with hasty glee
  The blacksmith's girl took you from me

14 FLIUCH AN OIDHCHE
WET IS THE NIGHT

Fliuch an oidh - che, hu ill o ro

Nochd 's gur fuar i, o hi a bho

Ma thug Clann Nìll, hu ill o ro

Druim a' chuain orr', boch oir - eann o

VARIANT FOR SECOND LINE:

1 Fliuch an oidhche, *hu ill o ro*
  Nochd 's gur fuar i, *o hi a bho*
  Ma thug Clann Nìll, *hu ill o ro*
  Druim a'chuain orr', *boch oireann o*

2 Ma thug Clann Nìll, *hu ill o ro*
  Druim a'chuain orr', *o hi a bho*
  Luchd nan seòl àrd, *hu ill o ro*
  'S nan long luatha, *boch oireann o*

3 Luchd nan seòl àrd
  'S nan long luatha

4 'S nam brataichean
  Dearg is uaine

5 'S nan gunnachan
  Glasa cruadhach

6 'S iomadh sgeir dhubh
  Ris 'n do shuath i

7 Agus bàirneach
  Ghlas a bhuain i

1 Wet is the night, *hu ill o ro*
  Cold is the eve, *o hi a bho*
  If Clan McNeil, *hu ill o ro*
  Set out to sea, *boch oireann o*

2 If Clan McNeil, *hu ill o ro*
  Set out to sea, *o hi a bho*
  Men of tall sails, *hu ill o ro*
  And swift ships, *boch oireann o*

3 Men of tall sails
  And swift ships

4 And of banners
  Red and green

5 And of guns
  Grey and hard

6 Many a dark reef
  Did she brush

7 And grey limpets
  Did she gather

15 GED IS GRIANACH AN LATHA
ALTHOUGH THE DAY IT MAY BE SUNNY

Ged is grian-ach an làth-a O Hao ri ri ho ro

Hu - ra bho ro ho ho Hao ri ri ho

1 Ged is grianach an làtha, o *Hao ri ri ho ro* *Hura bho ro ho ho* *Hao ri ri ho*	1 Although the day it may be sunny *Hao ri ri ho ro* *Hura bho ro ho ho* *Hao ri ri ho*
2 Gur beag m'aighear ri bhòidhchead, o	2 Little joy for me its beauty
3 'S mi ri coimhead a'chaolais, o	3 As I'm watching o'er the channel
4 'S gun mo ghaol-sa 'ga sheòladh, o	4 And my love is not there sailing
5 Ach nam faicinn thu tighinn, o	5 But if I should see you coming
6 'S mi gu rachadh 'nad chòmhdhail, o	6 I would go to you and meet you
7 'S mi gu rachadh 'nad choinneamh, o	7 I would go to meet your coming
8 Air mo bhonnan gun bhrògan, o	8 On my feet no shoes be wearing
9 'S cheart aindheoin luchd diùmbaidh, o	9 In spite of those so disapproving
10 'S mi gun dùraigeadh pòg dhut, o	10 To give you a kiss I would be wanting
11 Ged a chuirte mi 'm sheasamh, o	11 Though it means I would be standing
12 Air an t-seisean Di-dòmhnaich, o	12 On the repentance stool on Sunday
13 Ann am fianais na cléire, o	13 There in front of all the clergy
14 'S gun ach léine 'gam chòmhdach, o	14 With only a shirt to wear for clothing

16 A MHIC DHUGHAILL 'IC RUAIRIDH
SON OF DOUGAL, SON OF RORY

A Mhic Dhùgh - aill   'ic   Ruair - idh

Chuir am buair - eadh   fo m'   chéill - sa

Chuir   an   tain - ead   mo   ghruaidh - ean

'S a dh'fhàg mo ghru - ag   air   droch   ghréidh - eadh

1 A Mhic Dhùghaill 'ic Ruairidh
Chuir am buaireadh fo m'chéill-sa
Chuir an tainead mo ghruaidhean
'S a dh'fhàg mo ghruag air droch ghréidheadh

2 Chuir an tainead mo ghruaidhean
'S a dh'fhàg mo ghruag air droch ghréidheadh
Is diùmbach mise dha m'phiuthair
Nighean bhuidhe an fhuilt steudaich

3 Is diùmbach mise dha m'phiuthair
Nighean bhuidhe an fhuilt steudaich

4 Is cha bhuidheach mi dha m'mhàthair
Is òg a chàirich i bhreug orm

5 Mo mhìle beannachd aig m'athair
'S e nach gabhadh droch sgeul orm

6 Mo mhìle mollachd aig a'bhuachaille
Bha ri uallach na spreidhe

7 Chaidh a dhùsgadh nam balach
Moch ro' làtha mus d'éirich

8 'S ann a' dìreadh a'ghàrraidh
Leig thu ghràidh a'cheud éigh as'd

9 'S ann a'teàrnadh a'bhruthaich
Fhuair thu'm brùthadh a léir thu

10 Gu robh fuil do chuim chùbhraidh
A'drùdhadh ro' d'léinidh

11 Is ged a dh'òl mi ghaoil pàirt dhi
Cha do shlànaich do chreuchdan

12 Is truagh nach robh mi an Sasunn
Am Beul-feirst n'an Dùn Eideann

13 Na tìr nam fear dubha
Na'n Còige Mhutha na h-Eireann

1 Son of Dougal, son of Rory
Who disturbed my peace of mind
Who made my cheeks so hollow
And left my head of hair unkempt

2 Who made my cheeks so hollow
And left my head of hair unkempt
With my sister I'm so annoyed
The girl with golden hair in curls

3 With my sister I'm so annoyed
The girl with golden hair in curls

4 With my mother I am displeased
Young was I when she slandered me

5 But a thousand blessings on my father
For he would hear no ill of me

6 But a thousand curses on the cowherd
The very one who was there herding cattle

7 The one who then did rouse the young men
Who had not risen before the daybreak

8 The time when you did climb the wall
The time that you let out the first cry

9 It was the time when you went down the bank
That you received the fatal hurtful blows

10 The blood from your sweet body ran
Through your shirt was seeping through

11 And even though I sucked some blood
Still your wounds they did not heal

12 It is a pity I was not in England
In Belfast or in Edinburgh

13 In the land among the dark men
Or in the Irish province of Munster

44

14 Mun do chuir mi ort grabadh
   Moch 's a'mhadainn 's tu 'g éirigh

14 Before ever I came to speak to you
   In the morning early before you rose

15 Mun do chuir mi riamh iùil ort
   A lùb ùir a'chùil cheutaich

15 Before that ever I got to know you
   O fresh youth with the comely hair

17 A MHIC IAIN 'IC SHEUMAIS
SON OF JOHN, SON OF JAMES

1 A Mhic Iain 'ic Sheumais
  Tha do sgeul air m'aire
  Air fair al ill eo
  Air fair al ill eo
  Làtha Blàr na Féithe
  Bha feum air mo leanabh
  Hi ho hi ri ibh o hi eileadh hi o
  Hi ri ibh o ro hao o hi ho

1 Son of John, son of James
  Your story's on my mind
  Air fair al ill eo
  Air fair al ill eo
  The battle day of Féithe
  Needed was my child
  Hi ho hi ri ibh o hi eileadh hi o
  Hi ri ibh o ro hao o hi ho

2 Làtha Blàr na Féithe
  Bha feum air mo leanabh
  Air fair al ill eo
  Air fair al ill eo
  Làtha Blàr a'Chéitein
  Bha do léine ballach
  Hi ho hi ri ibh o hi eileadh hi o
  Hi ri ibh o ro hao o hi ho

2 The battle day of Féithe
  Needed was my child
  Air fair al ill eo
  Air fair al ill eo
  The battle day of Céitein
  Then your shirt was stained
  Hi ho hi ri ibh o hi eileadh hi o
  Hi ri ibh o ro hao o hi ho

3 Làtha Blàr a'Chéitein
  Bha do léine ballach

3 The battle day of Céitein
  Then your shirt was stained

4 Bha fuil do chuirp uasail
  Air uachdar an fhearainn

4 Your noble body's blood
  Lying upon the ground →

45

5 Bha fuil do chuirp chùbhraidh
A'drùdhadh ro'n anart

5 Your sweet body's blood
Through the linen soaking

6 Bha mise 'ga sùghadh
Gus na thùch air m'anail

6 Sucking it was I
Till I choked for breath

7 Mu Mhac Iain 'ic Sheumais
Duine treubhach smearail

7 Son of John, son of James
Man of courage strong

18 MILE MARBHAISG AIR A'GHAOL
A THOUSAND CURSES ON LOVE

1 Mìle marbhaisg air a'ghaol
Ho hi ri ri ri ri u
Asam fhìn a thug e chlaoidh
Ho hi u a ho hug o
Ho i u a ho i u
Hao ri u a ho hu go

1 A thousand curses now on love
Ho hi ri ri ri ri u
That from me sapped all strength away
Ho hi u a ho hug o
Ho i u a ho i u
Hao ri u a ho hu go

2 Asam fhìn a thug e chlaoidh
Ho hi ri ri ri ri u
Sgoilt e mo chrìdhe 'nam chom
Ho hi u a ho hug o
Ho i u a ho i u
Hao ri u a ho hu go

2 That from me sapped all strength away
Ho hi ri ri ri ri u
Within my body broke my heart
Ho hi u a ho hug o
Ho i u a ho i u
Hao ri u a ho hu go

3 Sgoilt e mo chrìdhe 'nam chom

3 Within my body broke my heart

4 Dh'fhuasgail e falt far mo chinn

4 Loosed the hair from off my head

5 Cha téid mi le Mac a'Mhaoir

5 With the factor's son I will not go

6 Na idir le Mac an t-Saoir

6 Nor will I with the joiner's son

7 B'annsa fear an leadain duinn

7 For me the one with dark brown hair

8 Mharbhadh feadag is cearc fhraoich

8 Who'd kill the plover and moorhen too

9 Is earba bheag nan gearra chas caol

9 The little deer with the slender legs

19 MO NIGHEAN DONN A CORNAIG
MY DARK-HAIRED MAID FROM CORNAIG

B'olc an sgeul a chual-a mi

Di - luain an déidh Di - dòmh - naich

Mo nighean donn á Còrn - aig

Gu robh thu buidhe bòidh - each—

Mo nighean donn á Còrn - aig

1 B'olc an sgeul a chuala mi
Di-luain an déidh Di-dòmhnaich
Mo nighean donn á Còrnaig
Gu robh thu buidhe bòidheach
Mo nighean donn á Còrnaig

2 'Nuair bha càch 's an t-searmon
Chaidh na cealgairean dha'n mhòintich

3 Bha do chualein slaodadh riut
'S do léine chaol 'na stròicean

4 Gu robh do ghùn an taice riut
'S do bhreacan glaic 'na aonar

5 An deoch a bha gu d'bhanais
Air t'fhalaire a dh'òladh

6 'S truagh nach robh mi'n taice
Ris na balaich rinn an dò-bheart

7 Tha claidheamh fada caol agam
'S gu feuch mi lùths mo dhòrn air

1 The tale I heard was sorrowful
On the Monday following Sunday
My dark-haired maid from Cornaig
You were both fair and lovely
My dark-haired maid from Cornaig

2 When the others were at the service
The villains went to the hillside

3 The hair of your head was tangled
And your petticoat torn in tatters

4 Your dress was lying near you
Alone in a ditch your plaid shawl

5 The drink meant for your wedding day
Instead was drunk at your funeral

6 O that I were not nearer
The men who did such violence

7 For I've a fine long sword
I'll test my strength of arm with

20 HO MO NIGHEAN DONN NAN GOBHAR
O MY DARK-HAIRED GOAT-HERD MAIDEN

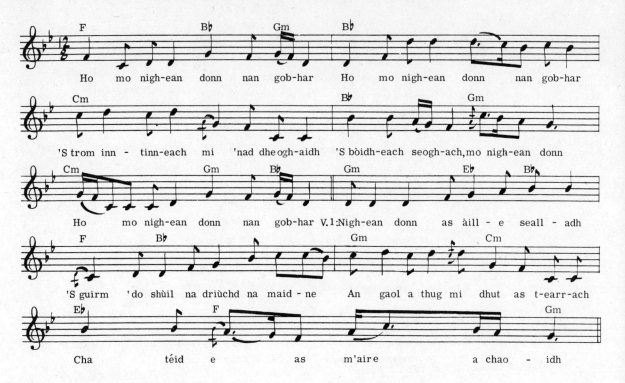

*Ho mo nighean donn nan gobhar
Ho mo nighean donn nan gobhar
'S trom inntinneach mi 'nad dheoghaidh
'S bòidheach seoghach, mo nighean donn
Ho mo nighean donn nan gobhar*

1 Nighean donn as àille sealladh
'S guirm 'do shùil na driùchd na maidne
An gaol a thug mi dhut as t-earrach
Cha téid e as m'aire a chaoidh
Chorus

2 Nighean donn bha ris na gamhna
Bha mi uair 's bu mhór mo gheall ort
Dhut a thigeadh dhol do'n dannsa
Le gùn 's srann aige dha'n t-sìod

3 Dol do'n chlachan Di-dòmhnaich
'S geal do stocainn 's dubh do bhrògan
'S truagh a Rìgh nach mi bha còmh' riut
Ged nach pòsamaid a chaoidh

*O my dark-haired goat-herd maiden
O my dark-haired goat-herd maiden
For you my heart is beating heavy
You're wondrous wise, my dark-haired maid
O my dark-haired goat-herd maiden*

1 Dark-haired maid, so fair appearing
Your eye more bright than dew each morning
The love I gave you in the springtime
From my mind will ne'er diminish
Chorus

2 Dark-haired maid your calves attending
Once for you I had great longing
How well you looked when you went dancing
From your dress the silk was rustling

3 Going to church upon a Sunday
Black your shoes and white your stockings
How I wish that I were with you
Even though we'd never marry

48

21 O CHRAOBH NAN UBHAL
O TREE OF APPLES

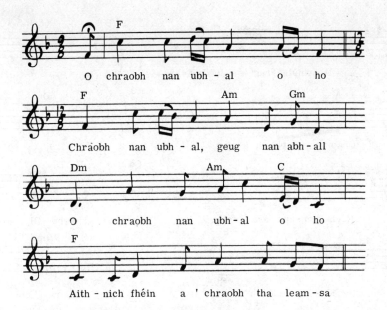

O chraobh nan ubh - al   o   ho

Chràobh   nan   ubh - al,   geug   nan   abh - all

O   chraobh   nan   ubh - al   o   ho

Aith - nich   fhéin   a ' chraobh   tha   leam - sa

O chraobh nan ubhal o ho
Chraobh nan ubhal, geug nan abhall
O chraobh nan ubhal o ho

O tree of apples, o ho
Tree of apples, branch of apples
O tree of apples, o ho

1 Aithnich fhéin a'chraobh tha leam-sa
  Chorus

1 Well I know which tree is mine
  Chorus

2 Chraobh as mùtha 's as mìlse ùbhlan

2 The biggest tree with sweetest apples

3 Chraobh nan ubhal, gu robh Dia leat

3 Apple tree, may God be with you

4 Gu robh 'n àird an ear 's an iar leat

4 East and West, may they be with you

5 Gu robh gach gealach agus grian leat

5 Every sun and moon be with you

22 A PHIUTHRAG 'S A PHIUTHAR
O LITTLE SISTER

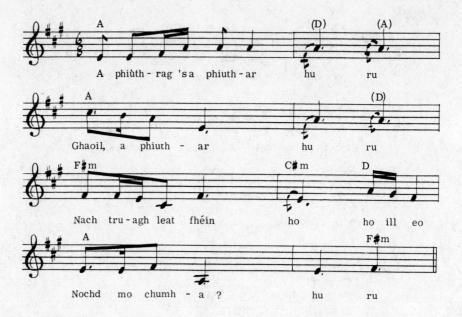

A phiùth-rag 's a phiuth-ar   hu   ru

Ghaoil, a phiuth-ar   hu   ru

Nach tru-agh leat fhéin   ho   ho ill eo

Nochd mo chumh-a?   hu   ru

1 A phiùthrag 's a phiuthar, *hu ru*
  Ghaoil, a phiuthar, *hu ru*
  Nach truagh leat fhéin, *ho ho ill eo*
  Nochd mo chumha? *hu ru*

2 Nach truagh leat fhéin, *hu ru*
  Nochd mo chumha? *hu ru*
  Mi'm bothan beag, *ho ho ill eo*
  Iosal cumhag, *hu ru*

3 Mi'm bothan beag
  Iosal cumhag

4 Gun sgrath dhìon air
  Gun lùb tughaidh

5 Ach uisge nam beann
  Sìos 'na shruth leis

6 Héabhal mhór
  Nan each dhruimfhionn

1 Little sister, sister, *hu ru*
  My love, my sister, *hu ru*
  Can you not pity, *ho ho ill eo*
  My grief tonight? *hu ru*

2 Can you not pity, *hu ru*
  My grief tonight? *hu ru*
  Small my dwelling, *ho ho ill eo*
  Low and narrow, *hu ru*

3 Small my dwelling
  Low and narrow

4 No roof of turf
  No thatch entwined

5 But hillside water
  Like a running stream

6 Mighty Heaval
  With white-maned horses

23 SEAN DUINE CHA GHABH MI IDIR
AN OLD MAN'S NOT FOR ME AT ALL

Air fa laoidh leo Ho ro gheall — aidh eil — e

Air fa laoidh leo Sean duine cha ghabh mi id - ir

Air fa laoidh leo
Ho ro gheallaidh eile
Air fa laoidh leo

1 Sean duine cha ghabh mi idir
Chorus

2 Cha tig e mach gun am bata

3 Saoilidh e gur geòidh na cearcan

4 Saoilidh e gur siùcair sneachda

5 Saoilidh e gur caoraich creagan

6 Saoilidh e gur e ghrian a'ghealach

Air fa laoidh leo
Ho ro gheallaidh eile
Air fa laoidh leo

1 An old man's not for me at all
Chorus

2 He'll not come out without his stick

3 He will think that hens are geese

4 He will think that snow is sugar

5 He will think that rocks are sheep

6 He will think the sun's the moon

24 THUG MI 'N OIDHCHE GED B'FHAD' I
I SPENT THE NIGHT, ALTHOUGH 'TWAS LONG

1 Thug mi 'n oidhche ged b'fhad' i
O hu a leo ho ro
Chaidh an cadal a dhìth orm
Ho ro hi ri linn a
Ho ro hi ri linn a
Ho ro hu ill eo o ro ho

1 I spent the night, although 'twas long
O hu a leo ho ro
Long past sleep, I went without it
Ho ro hi ri linn a
Ho ro hi ri linn a
Ho ro hu ill eo o ro ho

2 Chaidh an cadal a dhìth orm
O hu a leo ho ro
'S mi ri feitheamh nam bràithrean
Ho ro hi ri linn a
Ho ro hi ri linn a
Ho ro hu ill eo o ro ho

2 Long past sleep, I went without it
O hu a leo ho ro
As I waited for the brothers
Ho ro hi ri linn a
Ho ro hi ri linn a
Ho ro hu ill eo o ro ho

3 'S mi ri feitheamh nam bràithrean

3 As I waited for the brothers

4 Bh'anns a'phàirce taobh shìos dhìom

4 Who were in the fields below me

5 Gum b'e sud na fir fhurail

5 These they were such worthy fellows

6 Fhuair an t-urram 's a b'fhiach e

6 Who were honoured and deserved it

7 Thig an claidheamh sìos faraibh

7 The sword becomes you, slung beside you

1 AILEIN DUINN
DARK-HAIRED ALAN

Flora MacNeil: *Folk Songs of Britain*, vol. I, CAEDMON
TC1142/TOPIC 12T157

Printed versions
SINCLAIR: 1879, p. 414
TGSI: vol. XXXVII, p. 91
AN DEO-GREINE: vol. II, p. 92; vol. XIII, p. 170

Compare
JFSS: 1911, No. 16, p. 224: *Shiubhlainn, shiubhlainn*
(Skye), 1900
KENNEDY FRASER: 1909, vol. I, p. 84; and 1925, p. 106:
Harris Love Lament
JEFDSS: 1943, p. 149, *coll.* M. Shaw Campbell (S.
Uist), 1933

The singer is lamenting not so much the drowning of her family—brothers, father and son—as the loss of her husband, her greater grief. The song is a dramatic one in which the approach is shifted several times. First the singer enumerates the tragedies which have struck her; then she describes, very concisely, her husband and by implication their relationship. She moves her stance to address a seagull, who was likely to have first-hand knowledge of the disaster, and seeks news of her family from it. The bird can only confirm the worst, and she ends her lament by considering the position of her dead husband's body in the sea in terms of life.

The song is written in the simple single-line metre and has no reduplication. It is an extremely well-wrought composition, with unity and artistry in style and content alike. It is one of the very few Gaelic folksongs which indulges in slight romanticism—in the passage where the singer addresses the seagull. Gaelic folksong is not given to such flights of fancy as one might imagine from a reading of Kennedy Fraser's *Songs of the Hebrides*, and normally imaginative passages of this sort have a very clear practical purpose, as in these lines from CRAIG: 1949, p. 48:

'S truagh nach robh mi fad seachdain	It is a pity I was not for a week
An riochd a'gheòidh no na lachann	In the shape of a duck or a goose
No na faoileige glaiseadh	Or the grey seagull
'S mi gu snàmhainn cuan farsuinn	I would swim a wide ocean
Go ruiginn an caisteal	Until I reached the castle
'S gun tugainn a mach as	And I would take out of it
Mac as òige chlann Lachlainn	The youngest son of Lachlan's children

Flora MacNeil learned this lament from her mother; she told us that Tuesday is still the traditional day for weddings on the Isle of Barra.

2 BEINN A' CHEATHAICH
THE MISTY MOUNTAIN

Flora MacNeil: *Folk Songs of Britain*, vol. VI, CAEDMON
TC1162/TOPIC 12T194

Printed versions
KENNEDY FRASER: 1909, vol. I, p. 80: *Kismul's Galley*
CAMPBELL/COLLINSON: 1969, text p. 150, music pp.
335–6

This is an impressionistic view of clan life. The singer praises the clan Nìll's ship and crew as they sail into Kismul, the centre of clan activity, where hospitality, a great heroic virtue, abounded in the form of wine both day and night. The song is remarkable for the enthusiasm it has for a social system in which the singer, apparently, does not take part except as a hardworking onlooker (he or she was busy at the sheep when the ship passed). It must date from a period when the clan system was in full swing and totally accepted as the status quo—probably early seventeenth century at the very latest.

The tune has a fine rhythm, and it is interesting to compare this version with the one used for *Kismul's Galley* by Kennedy Fraser. Flora MacNeil learned her version from her mother and said that it was often used as a waulking song in Barra.

3   A BHEAN IADACH
THE JEALOUS WOMAN

Flora MacNeil, rec. P. Kennedy, 1967

Printed versions
MacDonald: 1901, p. 44
MacFadyen: 1902
JFSS: 1911, No. 16, p. 205: *Bean Mhic A' Mhaoir, coll.*
  F. Tolmie (Skye), 1854
O'Muirgheasa: 1915, pp. 380, 451 and 452
Kennedy Fraser: 1917, vol. II, p. 56*ff*
Morison: 1935, p. 37
Andersson: 1952, p. 47
Craig: 1949, p. 1

Shaw: 1955, p. 254
MacLagan Manuscript (University of Glasgow),
  No. 119
Creighton and MacLeod: 1964, p. 158
An Gaidheal: 1871–3, vol. II, p. 165
An Deo-greine: 1914, vol. X, p. 10
An Gaidheal: 1926, vol. XXI, p. 9; 1927, vol. XXII,
  p. 88
Gairm: vol. IV, p. 328: Nova Scotia version from
  Sydney Post Record

This song is supposed to be composed by a woman in danger of drowning by being cut off by the rising tide. She appeals to another woman on the shore to help her, but she refuses, saying that she herself wishes to sleep with the drowning woman's husband. The drowning woman then goes on to send her farewell to her young children, and visualizes her family's discovery of her dead body the next day. The emotions of a wife and mother facing death are most realistically portrayed. (An excellent version of the events leading up to the situation can be found in Shaw: 1955, p. 254.)

The song is not entirely self-explanatory, and yet the story behind it provides an effective emotional build-up. Verse used in narrative in this way has a very long history in Gaelic (very early examples occur in the *Táin Bó Cuailnge*) and in these early examples the poetry was generally used to heighten the drama of a situation rather than simply to narrate events. As recited poetry this particular art form was used frequently in the nineteenth century for performances at 'ceilidhs', and so on. (See MacFadyen: 1902 for examples.)

Flora MacNeil learned the song from her mother, and it is widely known in the Western Isles. There are several published variants of both words and music, all apparently related despite some marked differences in character of the various tunes. A version has been recorded as far afield as Nova Scotia, where a Gaelic-speaking community still preserves songs in the oral tradition. An Irish version is also known, which gives this song an extraordinary geographical range. The theme, too, can be discerned outside the Gaelic tradition as it is reminiscent of the Anglo-Scots ballad *Binnorie* (Twa Sisters; Child No. 10).

The song employs the broken-line metre, and was used occasionally for waulking. The tune, which uses a wide range of effective intervals, is well suited to the sad but rather philosophical acceptance of approaching death.

4   BHEIR MO SHORAIDH THAR GHUNNAIDH
TAKE MY FAREWELL OVER GUNNA

Flora MacNeil, rec. P. Kennedy, 1967

Printed version
MacLeod: 1934

Compare
Kennedy Fraser: 1909, vol. I, p. 119
Gairm: vol. IV, p. 239

In a fairly straightforward lament for a lover, the poet first bids farewell to Mull, where he has heard the cuckoo call. The cuckoo is perhaps used as an image of death here, as there seems to have been an old superstition associating its call with death in some areas (see Martin: 1934, pp. 104 and 424); this may well explain the appearance of this verse in an elegy. Next the narrator moves more directly to his subject, incidentally changing the end rhyme as he changes his approach, and he visualizes the funeral ship coming with his sweetheart aboard in her coffin. Carrying the coffin on board ship seems to have been a fairly common practice (see *Cairistiona* (No. 5)), and indeed most communications of any nature had to be carried out by sea in the Western Isles. In the last verse the poet simply states that he regrets ever having known her, presumably because of the great sorrow her death has caused him.

The fifth version of a song in Gairm: vol. IV, p. 239, resembles the last verse, and the tunes and the general tone of the two songs are very similar.

Flora MacNeil learned her version from Donald MacPherson of Barra who heard it in Mull.

5 CAIRISTIONA
CHRISTINA

Flora MacNeil, *rec.* P. Kennedy, 1967: GAELFONN GLA
2002; ETHNIC FOLKWAYS LIBRARY FE 4430; COLUMBIA
KL 4946

Printed versions
CRAIG: 1949, p. 87
GAIRM: vol. 1, p. 45
CAMPBELL/COLLINSON: 1969, text p. 54, music pp.
251–4

The maker of this song was Cairistìona's foster-mother, and it was composed as a lament on her death. In this version first the nobility of Cairistìona is stressed by mentioning that she spent some time in the King's court. This did not mean the King of Scotland, but more likely one of the great clan chiefs like MacDonald or MacLeod. (For this use of the word 'righ' see the Praise Poem to Dòmhnall Gorm of Sleat in GAIRM: vol. II, p. 239.) Then the story moves to the funeral ships waiting to carry off Cairistìona so that she can be placed in the earth, ships which might have carried her to her happy wedding. At verse ten there are changes in both the approach and the rhyme of the song and the full significance of the image is perhaps lost in our version. CRAIG: 1949, however, is slightly different, and suggests that some misfortune befell Cairistìona while she was in Glencoe, and that her foster-mother intends to fight for justice to be done by her there.

The dating of the song depends very much on the social milieu it represents, and it would thus appear an early one. The idea of fosterage is an old one, and the CRAIG: 1949 version's suggestion of justice being sought from MacLeod would certainly point to a period when the clan system was well established and accepted. The date, on these grounds, can hardly be later than the seventeenth century, though one would hesitate to make it much earlier than this because of the symmetry and simplicity of the refrain (see EIGSE: vol. 7, p. 233), though this may of course be deceptive.

The song, though it may seem quite unsuited to the purpose, has been heard by Flora MacNeil being used as a waulking song, and yet it has not suffered from this use by becoming over-rhythmical. However, she regards this song as a very sad love lament and as one of the oldest and most effective of all Gaelic songs. Her eldest daughter has taken the name. It was, she says, a particular favourite of Father John MacMillan: 'Whenever I visited him at his home, Tamara, overlooking one of the most beautiful beaches in Barra, he would ask for this, saying that there was a sob in the chorus and that was how it should be sung.'

6 CAOLAS EADAR MI IS IAIN
TWIXT IAN AND ME'S A STRETCH OF WATER

Flora MacNeil, *rec.* P. Kennedy, 1967

Compare
CRAIG: 1949, p. 9
CARMICHAEL: 1954, vol. V, p. 44

A simple love song of wishful thinking rather than passion in which the girl expresses her hope that all the natural obstacles between her and her lover can be removed and that they can soon be together. The direct and sincere honesty with which she confesses her love is endearing. The wish expressed in verse three to be with him on the top of a high rocky mountain is consistent with the impression conveyed in other songs that love-making was preferable out of doors. This can be seen from the version in CRAIG: 1949 of *Fliuch an oidhche* (No. 14):

Bu thric a laigh	mi fo d'earradh	Often I lay under your clothes
Ma tha, chan ann	aig a'bhaile	If so, it was not in the village
An lagan uaigneach	an cluain a'bharraich	But in a lonely dell, in the branchy retreat
Do lamh fo m'cheann	t'aodach faram	Your hand under my head, your clothes over me
'S mi fo chirb do	bhreacain bhallaich	As I lay under the edge of your tartan plaid
Gaoth nan ard bheann	draghadh fairis	As the wind of the high hills
Uisge fìorghlan	fuarghlan, fallain	Drenched over fresh, clear, cold wholesome water
O theang' an fhéidh	a nì langan	From the tongue of the deer which bells

Probably this attitude developed from the use of natural imagery to give the telling of the love-making more intensity and power. A possible connection too is that very often the lovers in these songs were not married and a clandestine affair was much less likely to be discovered if it was conducted outside. Note, however, that the author of *Seathan, Mac Righ Eireann* (CARMICHAEL: 1954, vol. V, p. 66) still seems to think it pleasant to make love outside even though the couple appear to be married.

The melody of the song has an effective wide range, and the rhythm would imply that it has been used for waulking, though the single-line unit with end rhyme on the last stressed word has not been utilized and used for reduplication. This could have been done with this song with none of the loss of rhyme which occurs in *Thug mi 'n oidhche ged b'fhad' i* (No. 24). Flora MacNeil said this song is not widely known in Barra and that she had never heard it outside the island.

7 CHAN E CAOIDH MHIC SHIRIDH
'TIS NOT LAMENTING O'ER MAC SIRIDH

Flora MacNeil, *rec.* P. Kennedy, 1967

Printed versions
MacDonald: 1911, pp. 172 and 174
JFSS: 1911, No. 16, p. 202, *Cumha Bhraithrean, coll.*
  F. Tolmie (Ross-shire), 1870
Murray: 1920, p. 148

Craig: 1949, p. 48
Celtic Review: vol. IV, p. 247
Campbell/Collinson: 1969, text p. 120, music pp. 311–13
Compare
Kennedy Fraser: 1917, vol. II, p. xvi

The singer starts by defining the source of her grief, and as a side effect of it she gives a very clear picture of how deep a relationship there was between her and her dead brother. In verse four she moves to a very emotive though realistic description of the sea's effect of disintegrating his body. Straight from this she moves to her own revulsion from going to make his bed, which he has left unmade. She finishes by indicating that she keeps looking out for his ship, thus implying the continuation of emotional hope in the face of rational despair.

The verse phrase has a lovely shape, building up to a climax at the end of the first line of the couplet and gradually curving downwards, and the refrain helps to maintain movement and rhythmic variety in the song as a whole.

Flora MacNeil explained that Mac Siridh was a chief of a sept of the MacKinnon clan. She learned this version from her aunt, Mary Gillies, but had also heard a Skye version from a friend which has variations in both the verses and in the chorus, which went:

> Hu oro hu o ho ro ho hi o hi ho
> Hu oro hu o

8 CHUNNAIC MISE MO LEANNAN
I DID SEE MY OWN TRUE-LOVER

Flora MacNeil, *rec.* P. Kennedy, 1967

Printed versions
Gillies: 1786, p. 245
TGSI: 1878–9, vol. VIII, p. 115; 1908–10, vol. XXVI, p. 240
Sinclair: 1879, p. 504
MacFarlane: 1908, p. 8
MacDonald: 1911, p. 49

Kennedy Fraser: 1917, vol. II, p. xxii
Craig: 1949, p. 34
Gairm: vol. IV, pp. 47–9
Shaw: 1955, p. 228
Creighton and MacLeod: 1964, p. 190

A girl, ignored by her lover, begins by describing how he has passed by her on his noble horse. She pretends indifference to him and takes refuge from his unfaithfulness in the unfailing reliability of the clan McDonald, which she praises with obvious pride.

This is used as a waulking song, and several versions of both tune and words have been collected. There were in fact possibly two different songs at one time which have become confused, or the text given by Flora MacNeil may only be part of a longer song. Her version, however, well illustrates the metre based on the couplet with internal rhyme (verse one, *leannan/aithnich*). The rhyme between the last stressed word in every line is maintained, though this is not always the case with songs of this type.

According to this version the date of the song would appear to be fairly early for the clan system is seen to be still in operation. This is borne out by the version in Craig: 1949, where references to Auldearn and possibly Inverlochy pinpoint the date to the period of the Montrose wars in the mid-seventeenth century.

The drive of this song lies mainly in the lively well-established rhythmic pattern and from the rather unusual change in timing in the last line of the verse which lends a syncopated effect to the whole song.

Flora MacNeil learned her version from her mother but said she had heard it elsewhere with a variety of tunes.

9 CO SHEINNEAS AN FHIDEAG AIRGID?
O WHO WILL PLAY THE SILVER WHISTLE?

Flora MacNeil, *rec.* P. Kennedy, 1967

Other recorded version
CELTIC CX (No. 2)

Printed versions
KENNEDY FRASER: 1909, vol. I, p. 134
CRAIG: 1949, p. 35
CELTIC REVIEW: vol. I, pp. 147–9
CAMPBELL/COLLINSON: 1969, text p. 136, music pp. 325–6

This Jacobite song welcomes Prince Charles to Scotland. Just what the significance of the silver whistle was is not now known, but it may have been some sort of signal. The exact description of Prince Charles' ship can be compared to other Praise Poems where the ship is described in equally enthusiastic terms (as in CRAIG: 1949, p. 12). This gives the whole poem an elevation and a feeling of regality which is further sustained by the reference to the fact that Prince Charles' food was out of the ordinary, and finer than the common man's fare. The respect shown to the Prince in the song and the anticipation with which he is expected are consistent with the rather romantic and certainly tenacious affection which the Highlands in general had for him.

The melody is more wistful than rousing or passionate. The phrases in the second two lines of the refrain have a soaring effect which offsets the quicker movement of the verse line.

Flora MacNeil told us that on Barra itself you may hear a number of different versions of this song.

10 FACA SIBH RAGHAILL NA AILEIN?
HAVE YOU SEEN RONALD OR ALAN?

Flora MacNeil, *rec.* P. Kennedy, 1967

Printed version
CAMPBELL/COLLINSON: 1969, text p. 90, music pp. 284–6

Compare
MACMILLAN: 1930, vol. II, p. 21
CRAIG: 1949, p. 114

This is a poem praising a young sailor whose prowess at sea is extolled in rather exaggerated terms: as long as a single piece of the ship remains above water, Iain will manage to bring her to harbour safely. It is perhaps worth noting here that ability at sea was no mean virtue in a place where one's existence could depend on the sea for food, and where the only form of transport was by ship.

Flora MacNeil told us she never heard anyone except her mother sing this song and that it was always used as a Work Song for the various repetitive tasks that were required: churning butter, waulking and also for rowing a boat. The tempo of the song was adapted to suit the particular occupation.

11 FATH MO MHULAID A BHITH ANN
BEING HERE HAS CAUSED MY SORROW

Flora MacNeil, *rec.* P. Kennedy, 1967

Printed versions
KENNEDY FRASER: 1917, vol. II, p. 225
MACMILLAN: 1930, vol. I, p. 12
MACKINNON: 1939, p. 60
O LOCHLAINN: 1948, p. 11

AN GAIDHEAL: vol. XXXVI, p. 16
CELTIC REVIEW: vol. IX, p. 248

Compare
KENNEDY FRASER: 1909, vol. I, p. 124

This song of exile is obviously written by someone who misses very much the call of the sea while she is imprisoned in a strange landlocked glen. She first visualizes the home scene, her brothers coming to meet her to ferry her across to Barra. Then she describes the call of the sea and realises that the sun will reach Barra that very night, while she is unable to travel with it, but must remain among the hills.

The song may be regarded as a late composition, as the earlier song writers were not exiled as much as later Gaels and their reaction did not become quite so sentimental as the Glasgow Gael did during the nineteenth century.

Flora MacNeil first heard this Exile's Song from the late Father John MacMillan of Barra who was himself a well-known local bard. She obtained the verses twelve to fifteen from him when she visited him in Glasgow shortly before he died: 'The words were so beautiful that I asked him to recite them to me from his bed in the nursing home.'

12 FHIR AN LEADAIN THLATH
LAD OF LOVELY HAIR

Flora MacNeil, *rec.* P. Kennedy, 1967

Printed versions
MacKenzie: 1841, p. 385; 1907 ed., p. 423
Celtic Magazine: vol. IV, p. 80

A love song, in which the girl praises and describes her lover. He has deserted her, although she is pregnant by him, but this does not prevent her loving him, and, in common with the folk tradition, she bears him no grudge for leaving her in this position. There is a large body of pregnancy songs in Gaelic folksong, but this one is perhaps rather different from most in that it is a much more 'literary' product, with a wide use of descriptive images. The adjectives, rather more frequent than in most folksongs, are used as much for their sound value as for their meaning (for example, the first line, where 'dualaich' and 'chleachdaich' both mean practically the same thing).

The verse pattern is more in keeping with later folksong, for earlier forms tend to use either a single-line unit or couplets. Since it has no function as a labour song, it may be concluded that it probably dates from the nineteenth century, but it is a considerably better composition than most products of that period. This late dating tends to be confirmed by the attitude to drink displayed in verse four, for early songs regard it as a virtue to drink and a true stamp of nobility and manliness, as these lines show:

Tadhlaidh m'eudail	Mac'ic Ailein ort	My dear Mac'ic Ailein will visit you
Marcraich nan each	cruidhtheach seanga	The rider of the slender well-shod horses
Poiteir an fhìona	air gach carraig dhiubh	The drinker of wine on every headland
Chan e na caird	ach na gallain	Not pints, but gallons, full hogsheads upended
Togsaidean làn	air an ceannaibh	And all that everyone else would drink
'S na dh'òladh càch	phàigheadh Ailein e	Ailein would pay for it

The tune of the song, which matches the words so well, is beautiful in its sweeping simplicity. It demands a wide range and makes use of interesting intervals. Flora MacNeil said she never heard the song outside Barra.

13 A FHLEASGAICH OIG IS CEANALTA
O LAD SO YOUNG AND GENTLE THEE

Flora MacNeil, *rec.* P. Kennedy, 1967

Printed versions
MacDonald: 1911, p. 222
Gairm: vol. VII, p. 143

This straightforward love song is popular with Gaelic singers. The girl praises her young man. He can do no wrong in her eyes, and even though he has left her, the fault, she implies, lies with 'nighean a'ghobha'.

The metre is a four line stanza with internal rhyme, as in f*ada*/d*eas*, R*ònach*/bh*eò*, and so on. There is consistent end rhyme between lines two and four, as in t*uath*/f*uath*, ghl*uasad*/s*uas*. This metre was to become very popular during the nineteenth century, when poets seemed to develop a remarkable fluency in this art of 'vowel music'. The song probably dates from the reign of King George III (1740–1820), as indicated in verse four.

Flora MacNeil first heard it from an old man at a 'ceilidh' in Barra. She asked her mother about it and this is the version her mother sang to her.

14 FLIUCH AN OIDHCHE
WET IS THE NIGHT

Flora MacNeil, *rec.* P. Kennedy, 1967

Printed versions
MacDonald: 1911, p. 258
JFSS: 1911, No. 16, p. 211: *Coisìch A Rùin, coll.* F. Tolmie (Skye), 1870
Kennedy Fraser: 1925, p. 84
Craig: 1949, p. 36

This version of the song is a song of clan praise, with a description of Clann Nìll at sea in their ships. Other versions (MacDonald: 1911; Craig: 1949) are longer, and contain several other additional elements. The song was used for waulking and possibly also for rowing.

It has the broken-line metre which many songs of this type have, as *A Phiùthrag 's a Phiuthar* (No. 22). When this is the case, the natural line seems to be broken into two halves by a short chorus, and there is thus a complete disregard for the syntactical relationships within the line, and even the more closely related lines can be interrupted by the chorus, as 'brataichean Dearg is uaine' (banners red and green). It may be that the line was not originally intended to be sung to this sort of tune and had therefore to be adapted to it. There are, however, several other examples of this broken line, but none with a comparable melody with shorter lines designed to fit it.

Flora MacNeil says that this was usually the very first song that her mother would sing when she was taking part in a 'luadh' or gathering for waulking.

15 GED IS GRIANACH AN LATHA
ALTHOUGH THE DAY IT MAY BE SUNNY

Flora MacNeil, *rec.* P. Kennedy, 1967

The girl in the song is determined to show her love for her sailor, in spite of the danger that she may be called to account by the Kirk Session. The emotions ring true and one finds sympathy for one who was prepared to face the clergy for the sake of a kiss.

The metre is interesting. While the melody only demands a single line pattern, the verse unit should really be couplets because of the internal rhyme (*là*tha/m'*ai*ghear, ch*ao*lais/gh*ao*l-sa). There seems to be some disintegration at lines five, six, seven and eight, but the pattern is re-established after line nine. This may indicate an adaptation of the words to a tune not originally their own. Here the reverse of the confusion which has occurred in *Thug mi 'n oidhche ged b'fhad i* (No. 24) is apparent.

The tune is rather gentle for such bold statements as lines nine onwards, but it is well suited to the overall character of the song and especially to the rather wistful atmosphere of the opening lines in which she wishes she could see her lover's ship approaching. Note that the first 'o' of the refrain is phrased as the last note of the verse, thus leaving a symmetrical chorus of the ABA structure. This might appear a rather artificial arrangement, as does the division of the second and third lines of the chorus where the musical phrase has no break.

Flora MacNeil believed this to be originally a Skye song but said she never heard anyone sing it except her mother: 'The story behind this song is that of an illicit love affair. The singer is unhappily married and is watching for the one she really loves for whom she would risk the penalty for unfaithfulness.'

16 A MHIC DHUGHAILL 'IC RUAIRIDH
SON OF DOUGAL, SON OF RORY

Flora MacNeil, *rec.* P. Kennedy, 1967

Printed version
GILLIES: 1786, p. 298

Compare
MURRAY: 1920, p. 146

Preserved in the island of South Uist, this fine narrative song is of a girl whose lover has been killed. The opening verses are concerned with the emotional tensions within the girl's own family, whom, apart from her father, she seems to resent. Next she moves to telling how the youths were roused by the shepherd early in the morning, presumably either as she was eloping with her lover or as he was stealing away from visiting her. The youths fire on him, and he is fatally wounded. Even though the girl drinks his blood in an attempt to save him, he dies and she wishes she had been far away rather than have been the cause of his death, for in the last verse she seems to blame herself for having delayed him.

The metre is a common enough one in waulking songs, but in this case there is no chorus, a fact which speaks strongly against its ever having been used for waulking. The basis of the metre is the couplet with internal rhyme, and end rhyme with the last word in every verse. The last couplet in the first verse forms the first couplet in the next.

The date of the song is difficult to ascertain. The reference to blood-drinking is not helpful here, as there is an example as late as 1774 (in *Ailein Duinn o hi shiùbhlainn leat*, CRAIG: 1949, p. 107). Probably it is used here as a literary motif, to give the effect of heightened emotions and stress (see CRAIG: 1949, p. 107 and JFSS: 1915, No. 19, p. 67).

17 A MHIC IAIN 'IC SHEUMAIS
SON OF JOHN, SON OF JAMES

Flora MacNeil, *rec.* P. Kennedy, 1967

Other recorded version
Scottish Gaelic and Scots Folk Songs, SCHOOL OF
SCOTTISH STUDIES DISCS A 003/4

Printed versions
CRAIG: 1949, p. 2
OLIVER/SMITH: 1949

SINCLAIR: 1879, p. 131
School of Scottish Studies Booklet, University of
Edinburgh, p. 29
JFSS: 1911, No. 16, p. 255, *coll.* F. Tolmie (N. Uist),
1870
MACDONALD: 1895, p. 58, Appendix
KENNEDY FRASER: 1921, vol. III, p. xvi

This song was composed about the son of John, son of James by his foster-mother (for the story of its composition, see JFSS: 1911, p. 255*ff*). She praises his bravery in battle and is passionately involved when he is wounded. The reference to blood-drinking here is one of the earliest dateable examples, and it seems more readily accounted for than many of the apparently later ones, for here the warrior is wounded in battle, and the nurse may simply be trying to stop the blood pouring from his wounds by sucking them, much as a dog naturally licks its own wounds to heal them. In *Ailein Duinn o hi Shiùbhlainn Leat* (see CRAIG: 1949, p. 107 and JEFDSS: 1951, p. 67), which is from the eighteenth century, the man has been drowned, and the blood-drinking motif seems much more unnatural and artificial. It is interesting to note that the motif also appears in Lowlands Scots in the ballad *The Dowie Dens o' Yarrow* (Child, No. 214):

> She kiss'd his cheek, she kaim'd his hair
> As oft she did before, O
> She drank the red blood frae him ran
> On the dowie houms o' Yarrow

The song seems to date from about 1601, the date of the Battle of Carinish in North Uist, which was fought by the clans MacLeod and MacDonald.

Flora MacNeil's version, with its stirring tune used for waulking, has some fine syncopation in the long chorus. The verse pattern AB, BC, CD, etc., is used, but the unit is the couplet with internal rhyme, and since a single end-rhyme is not maintained throughout the song, only every second verse (starting with verse one) will have end-rhyme between lines one and three, though the rhyme in lines two and four is constant throughout the song. It is worth noting that here we have a fully developed rhyming couplet which can be dated quite confidently to the early seventeenth, if not the late sixteenth, century. This indicates that the couplet was accepted as a metre in the oral tradition as early as any other metre. Whatever 'literary' influence there may have been on the song, it must be conceded that it would not be accepted in the Bardic tradition. Obviously the composer was not trained in the Bardic school of poetry. Not only was the narrator a nurse, but the fact that she was a woman at all would have debarred her from this honour. The song does not survive at all in the written word: the earliest version is in SINCLAIR: 1879, and this was written about 275 years after the composition of the song. This leads one to question the certainty with which James Ross (EIGSE: vol. 7, p. 237) claims that:

> The appearance of the fully-fashioned couplet with aicill rhyming stress must be taken to show literary influence as revealing that the notion of regular poetic stress common in modern Scottish Gaelic and Irish poetry came into the oral tradition from the literary, and not vice versa as is usually thought.

Flora MacNeil believed this song to have been made by the stepmother of the son of John, son of James after he had been killed in the Battle of Carinish. She heard it from her aunt, Mary Gillies, who told her that the song came originally from Eriskay, whence came *Son of John, Son of James*. It is sometimes known as *The Eriskay Lament* and sung as such, but Flora MacNeil heard it used as a work song for waulking.

18 MILE MARBHAISG AIR A'GHAOL
A THOUSAND CURSES ON LOVE

Flora MacNeil, *rec.* P. Kennedy, 1967

Printed versions
MacCallum: 1821, p. 215
MacDonald: 1911, p. 266
Craig: 1949, p. 191

Flora MacNeil learned this song from her aunt, Mary Gillies. It starts as a comment on the effects of love on a girl, who goes on to refuse to accept either the ground-officer's or the joiner's sons as husbands. She does this because she prefers the young noble who goes out hunting to any of them. This disparagement of tradesmen and professional men is fairly common in Gaelic folksong, and it seems to be that such quiet stay-at-home employments were rather looked down upon as being unmanly (see Craig: 1949, pp. 15–16 and 28–9).

This is a waulking song with single lines and end-rhyme. The lines are used in pairs, with the verse pattern AB, BC, CD, etc. The tune is extremely lively and very suitable to the rather lighthearted way in which she casts aside the two youths as prospective husbands.

19 MO NIGHEAN DONN A CORNAIG
MY DARK-HAIRED MAID FROM CORNAIG

Flora MacNeil, *rec.* P. Kennedy, 1967

Other recorded version
J. C. M. Campbell: Columbia DB 191

Printed versions
MacDonald: 1895, p. 24; Appendix
Kennedy Fraser: 1917, vol. II, p. 140
Craig: 1949, p. 108
TGSI: vol. XXXVII, p. 88

This song is a lament for a girl who was assaulted and murdered on the moor only a day or two before her wedding, while the rest of the village was in church. It describes the significant details of the murder, and in verse five expresses very well the sense of loss and waste of a young life. A parallel is drawn between the funeral celebrations and the wedding which she might have celebrated had she lived. Finally the song-maker wishes he could avenge her death.

It is a difficult song to date. The references to 'claidheamh' (sword) and to the 'bhreacan' (tartan plaid) as a woman's garment tend to indicate an earlier milieu, probably late seventeenth or early eighteenth century. The use of the word 'ghùn' to describe the woman's dress is also an indication of lateness, as the very early songs always describe women as wearing the 'còta' or 'léine'.

Although she has only ever heard this song in Barra, Flora MacNeil wonders whether it may come originally from the Island of Tiree, where there is a place called Còrnaig.

20 HO MO NIGHEAN DONN NAN GOBHAR
O MY DARK-HAIRED GOAT-HERD MAIDEN

Flora MacNeil, *rec.* P. Kennedy, 1967

Other recorded version
Neiliann MacLennan, Gaelfonn GMA 1101

Compare
Sinclair: 1890–2, vol. I, p. 252

Here is a song of the pastoral love poetry school, in which the poet describes a girl for whom he has an affection against her natural background, whether it be tending the goats, as in the refrain, or going to the dance or to church.

The date of the song is probably the eighteenth century, as the presence of goats suggests. Goats were still common when Dr Johnson visited the islands in 1775. Yet from the general appearance and style of the song one might feel justified in placing it at the end of the century.

Flora MacNeil learned this song from her mother when she was a young girl and has not heard it except at home.

21 O CHRAOBH NAN UBHAL
O TREE OF APPLES

Flora MacNeil, *rec.* P. Kennedy, 1967

Other recorded version
Rena Maclean, FOLKWAYS P. 430

Printed versions
LEODHAIS: 1938, p. 65
ANDERSSON: 1952, p. 42
CARMICHAEL: 1954, vol. V, pp. 2 and 6

CAMPBELL/COLLINSON: 1969, text p. 144, music pp. 329–32

Compare
LINGUAPHONE: 1950: *Gaelic Folksongs from the Island of Barra*, Linguaphone Institute for Scotland, p. 36: *Ruairidh MacKinnon*

This is a Praise Poem in which the young chief addressed (probably MacKay of Islay) is eulogised in the image of an apple tree. This is a very common image in both folk-poetry and bardic poetry, and is a favourite of Màiri Nighean Alasdair Ruaidh. It is not often that an image in folk poetry is as extended as this, but the invocation of the natural elements of sun and moon lend this blessing an additional power.

The song appears to be of fairly early origin, possibly early seventeenth century or even earlier, for its subject is within the framework of the clan system.

It may at one time have been used as a waulking song, for the rhyme scheme is of this rhythm type, that is, single lines with ending rhyme. Note the change in rhyme in verse three which occurs when a new approach to the subject is being made.

The tune employed depends for its appeal on the use made of grace-notes, which would seem to be more an integral part of the tune than mere decorations. Note that the 'o' at the beginning of the refrain is used as a link between verse and chorus, so that there is no real break between them.

Flora MacNeil said that this must have been one of the first songs she ever heard as it was one of her mother's particular favourites.

22 A PHIUTHRAG 'S A PHIUTHAR
O LITTLE SISTER

Flora MacNeil, *rec.* P. Kennedy, 1967

Other recorded version
Kitty MacLeod and group, COLUMBIA KL 4946

Printed versions
KENNEDY FRASER: 1909, vol. I, p. 38
CRAIG: 1949, p. 4

There is a story about this song that it is a girl's cry for help to her sister after being carried off by the fairies to Heaval, a hill in Barra (see KENNEDY FRASER: 1909, vol. I, p. 38*ff*). From the text as given by Flora MacNeil, however, all that can be definitely stated is that the singer is in some uncomfortable if not dangerous plight, and that she is seeking the aid, or at least the sympathy, of her sister.

It may be a waulking song, as it conforms to the metrical and vocable pattern of such functional songs, and a version is given in CRAIG: 1949, though the story there would appear to be of a very realistic and human murder rather than a vague fairy elopement.

The date of this text is not easy to ascertain, though the description of the thatchless house, which implies the thatched house as being the norm, certainly makes it no later than the eighteenth century. The version in CRAIG: 1949 would tend to confirm this, as it refers to writing as being one of the accomplishments of the murdered shepherdess; this could hardly have been the case at any point in the seventeenth century.

There is, however, a completely different song beginning with the same line in CARMICHAEL: 1954, vol. V, p. 56. This appears to fit the same metrical and vocable pattern, and may in fact be an older song whose words were supplanted by more modern ones.

The music of the song depends very much on the use of grace-notes which vary to suit the cadences of the words, and there is a fluidity of tempo within a fairly strict rhythmic pattern.

Flora MacNeil learned the song from a first cousin of her mother's, Mrs Mary Johnstone, who was born on the now uninhabited island of Mingulay.

23 SEAN DUINE CHA GHABH MI IDIR
AN OLD MAN'S NOT FOR ME AT ALL

Flora MacNeil, *rec.* P. Kennedy, 1967

Compare
SCHOOL OF SCOTTISH STUDIES: 1960, p. 34: *Bodachan cha phòs mi*

This song is humorous at the expense of the failings that old age brings a man; it is lighthearted and fanciful, with no malicious intent.

It is a waulking song, with single lines with end-rhyme. It cannot be dated with any certainty, but seems unlikely to be any older than the eighteenth century, as the earlier surviving poetry tends to have a more serious flavour.

The music is well in keeping with the words, for it races along very lightly and breathlessly, with a strong, but not compulsive, rhythmic pattern.

Flora MacNeil said that this song was often used to accompany the folding of the tweed at the completion of the waulking. Such songs are known as *Orain Basaidh*, and those taking part would frequently be expected to add a verse or two extempore. Versions of the song, she added, were sung in many of the other islands besides Barra.

24 THUG MI 'N OIDHCHE GED B'FHAD' I
I SPENT THE NIGHT, ALTHOUGH 'TWAS LONG

Flora MacNeil, *rec.* P. Kennedy, 1967

Printed version
LINGUAPHONE: 1950: *Gaelic Folksongs from the Island of Barra*, Linguaphone Institute for Scotland, p. 36

'This song was often sung by my mother and her friends when a number of them were gathered together and also for the waulking.' Flora MacNeil.

This would appear to be a fragment of a longer song but we have so far been unable to trace any other versions of it outside Barra.

Here again we have the waulking song rhythm. The metre is interesting in that it is sung to the verse pattern AB, BC, CD, etc. Yet a close look at the rhymes reveals that it was not built for this pattern, but for individual fixed couplets. Only three verses have internal rhyme, while the others have no rhyme at all, as in:

Chaidh an cadal a dhìth orm   Long past sleep, I went without it
'S mi ri feitheamh nam bràithrean   As I waited for the brothers

This would indicate that singers have extended the use of this AB, BC verse pattern beyond songs adapted, or adaptable, to it, possibly simply to lengthen the song for waulking.

Bibliography

ANDERSSON: 1952
Otto Andersson, *On Gaelic Folk Music from the Island of Lewis*, Budkavlen no. XXXI: Utgiuen av Forlaget Bro., Finland, 1952. Study of musical structure of songs Andersson collected on a short trip to the Isle of Lewis. Some interesting versions in Gaelic and English with music in staff notation.

BAPTIE: 1902
Charles Robertson Baptie, *Orain Ghaidhlig*: J. & R. Parlane, Paisley, 1902. 12 Gaelic songs.

BOULTON: 1913
Harold Boulton, *Songs of the Four Nations*: music arranged by Arthur Somervell, J. B. Cramer, London, 1913. Attempts to bring together 'national songs' of England, Scotland, Ireland and Wales, all with English words but also some verses given in original Cornish, Scots, Irish, Manx Gaelic and Welsh.

BOWRA: 1962
C. M. Bowra, *Primitive Song*: World Publishing, New York, 1962, Weidenfeld & Nicolson, London, 1963. A description of and discussion on the culture of primitive peoples up to the present day. Valuable background to the origins of song.

BROADWOOD: 1934
JEFDSS—Journal of the English Folk Dance & Song Society—1934, pp. 138–46. Contains 'Eleven Gaelic Folk Songs' from Lucy Broadwood Collection mainly from literary sources. An article about her contribution to the collection and study of Gaelic traditional song by Ethel Bassin appears in *Scottish Studies*, 1965, vol. 9, part 2, pp. 145–52, entitled 'Lucy Broadwood 1858–1929'.

BROWN AND MERRYLEES: 1883
Colin Brown and James Merrylees, *The Thistle*: Wm. Collins & Sons & Co., London and Glasgow, 1883. Mainly Lowland Scots songs, but does include several Gaelic airs without words.

CALDER: 1937
George Calder, *Orain Ghaidhealach le Uilleam Ros* (*Gaelic Songs by Uilleam Ros*): Oliver & Boyd, Edinburgh, 1937. Gaelic texts with English translations.

CAMERON: 1932
Rev. Hector Cameron, *Na Bàird Thirisdeach* (*The Tiree Bards*); Aeneas MacKay, Stirling 1932. Local Tiree collection of Gaelic texts only. Of special interest for modern folk-poetry of the humorous school.

CAMPBELL: 1816/18
Alexander Campbell, *Albyn's Anthology*; Oliver & Boyd, Edinburgh; vol. I 1816, vol. II 1818. Gaelic texts, English translations; some of the melodies 'touched up'; includes original compositions and some melodies without their words.

CAMPBELL: 1862
Donald Campbell, *A Treatise of the Language, Poetry and Music of the Highland Clans*; D. R. Collie & Son, Edinburgh, 1862. Versions of several Gaelic folksongs written in a 'phonetic' script with English translation; song texts reliable but contains somewhat over-imaginative theories in the treatise.

CAMPBELL: 1872
J. F. Campbell, *Leabhar na Féinne* (*Heroic Gaelic Ballads*); Spottiswood, London, 1872. Heroic ballads belonging to the Ossianic tradition; collected between 1512 and 1871. Gaelic texts only.

CAMPBELL/COLLINSON: 1969
J. L. Campbell, *Hebridean Folksongs; A Collection of Waulking Songs made by Donald MacCormick in Kilphedir in South Uist in 1893*. Oxford University Press, London, 1969. Tunes transcribed from recordings by Francis Collinson. Collection from two sources. Texts of 37 waulking songs collected by Donald MacCormick in S. Uist in 1893 and field recordings made by John Lorne Campbell and his wife Margaret Fay Shaw from 1937 (for detailed review see *Folk Music Journal*: 1969, p. 352).

CARMICHAEL: 1900–
Alexander Carmichael, *Carmina Gadelica*: vols. I & II. T. & A. Constable, Edinburgh, 1900. 2nd ed. Oliver & Boyd, Edinburgh, 1928. Vol. III ed. Watson; Oliver & Boyd, 1940. Vol. IV ed. Watson; Oliver & Boyd, 1941. Vol. V ed. Angus Matheson: Oliver & Boyd, 1954. Vol. VI ed. Angus Matheson; Oliver & Boyd, 1971 (contains index). The first four volumes contain mainly religious texts but the fifth has a wider selection and contains versions of our songs (texts only). The last three volumes were edited posthumously. Vol. II contains a glossary and list of reciters. Vol. VI contains glossaries, subject and name indexes etc. A large collection of texts given in Gaelic and English (on facing pages) taken down from oral recitation in the Highlands. Mainly from the Outer Hebrides from about 1860 until the turn of the century. A great deal of important background information is contained in these six volumes.

CELTIC MAGAZINE: 1876–88
The Celtic Magazine: A monthly periodical devoted to the Literature, History, Antiquities, Folklore, Traditions, ed. Alexander MacKenzie (vols. I–XI) and Alexander MacBain (vols. XII & XIII): A. & W. MacKenzie, Inverness, 1876–88. A magazine of Celtic studies which occasionally contained Gaelic songs.

CELTIC MONTHLY: 1893–1917
The Celtic Monthly: A magazine for Highlanders, ed. John MacKay: Archibald Sinclair, Glasgow, 1893–1917. A magazine which also occasionally published Gaelic songs.

CELTIC REVIEW: 1904–16
The Celtic Review, ed. Prof. MacKinnon and Miss E. C. Carmichael: T. & A. Constable, Edinburgh, London and Dublin, 1904–16. A quarterly journal for Celtic scholars which occasionally contained Gaelic songs and notes about them. Miss Carmichael was a Gaelic pupil of Prof. MacKinnon and daughter of Alexander Carmichael, and became Mrs Watson, wife of the editor of *Carmina Gadelica*, vols. III and IV. (See CARMICHAEL: 1900–71.)

COLLINSON: 1966
Francis Collinson, *The Traditional and National Music of Scotland*; Routledge & Kegan Paul, London, 1966. Not a music collection but a general discussion on the music of both Gaelic and Lowland Scotland. A useful background study to all types of Scots music.

COMUNN GAIDHEALACH LEODHAIS: 1938
An Comunn Gàidhealach Leodhais: *Eilean Fraoich* (*Lewis Gaelic Songs and Melodies*): Stornoway, 1938. A collection of songs from the Isle of Lewis with Gaelic texts only and music in sol-fa notation.

CRAIG: 1949
K. C. Craig, *Orain Luaidh Màiri Nighean Alasdair*; Alasdair Matheson & Co. Ltd., Glasgow, 1949. 147 songs of the 'waulking' type, from S. Uist, given as collected, in Gaelic only. An important source book which endorses the strength of the oral

tradition well into the twentieth century. Texts are both full and reliable but it is sometimes difficult to relate positions of refrains to the texts.

CREIGHTON AND MACLEOD: 1964
Helen Creighton and Calum MacLeod, *Gaelic Songs in Nova Scotia*, Bulletin 198. Anthropological Series 66, National Museum of Canada; Roger Duhamel, Queen's Printer & Controller of Stationery, Ottawa, Canada, 1964. 93 songs in Gaelic with English translations collected by Helen Creighton, who has had 4 books of English song collections published (1932, 1940, 1950 and 1962). Gaelic editor was Major Calum MacLeod of St Francis Xavier University, Antigonish.

DEO-GREINE: 1906–22
GAILIG: 1923–4
GAIDHEAL: 1924–6
An Deo-Greine: The Monthly Magazine of An Comunn Gàidhealach, 1906–22, continued as *Gailig*, 1923–4 and as *An Gaidheal*, 1924–6. Contains a few songs, especially in earlier numbers. Also previously unpublished prize-winning song collections from the Scottish Mods (music festivals).

DUN: 1780
Finlay Dun, *Orain na h-Albain*: Wood & Co., Edinburgh, n.d. (*c.* 1780). Gaelic texts; English translation; also original compositions; arranged for piano accompaniment but basic tunes are preserved in the vocal line. The preface comments upon the modality of Gaelic folk melodies.

EIGSE: 1939
Eigse: A Journal of Irish Studies, vols. 7 & 8. Colm O Lochlainn for the National University, Dublin; Three Candles, Dublin, 1939. Of particular interest are the writings of James Ross on the various metres used in Gaelic folksongs, especially those of the 'waulking' type.

FRASER: 1816
Captain Simon Fraser of Knockie, *The Airs and Melodies Peculiar to the Highlands of Scotland and the Isles* 'for piano, harp, organ or violincello'; Mackenzie, Inverness, 1816, rev. ed. Hugh Mackenzie, 1874. Melodies of songs only, as words 'objectionable in point of delicacy or loyalty' (in this way many Jacobite songs have not survived in print).

GAIDHEAL: 1871–7
An Gaidheal, Paipeir Naidheachd agus Leabhar-Sgeoil: Mac-Neacail & Co., Glasgow, 1871–7 (6 vols.). Monthly magazine for Highlanders which contained some good versions of songs, many with music written in sol-fa notation.

GAIDHEAL: 1924–6 [see DEO-GREINE: 1906–22]
GAILIG: 1923–4 [see DEO-GREINE: 1906–22]
GAIRM: 1952–
Gairm, ed. D. S. Thomson and Finlay J. MacDonald: A. Learmonth, Stirling, 1952– (continuing). Quarterly all-Gaelic magazine which has printed some good versions of folksongs, some with music, particularly in earlier numbers.

GILLIES: 1786
John Gillies, *Sean Dàin agus Orain Ghaidhealach*; Perth, 1786. Known as 'The Gillies Collection'. Gaelic texts only; wide range of early reliable versions 'transmitted from Gentlemen in the Highlands of Scotland'.

GIVEN: 1930
Jennie Given, *Clàrsach a'Ghlinne* (*The Harp of the Glen*); Paterson, Glasgow & London, 1930. 25 popular Gaelic folksongs with both Gaelic and English words with melodies.

INVERNESS COLLECTION: 1806
Co-chruinneachadh Nuadh do dh' Oranaibh Gàidhealach (editor not named); Eòin Young, Inverness, 1806. Pibrochs, laments, quick-steps and marches of the Highlands of Scotland arranged for the pianoforte.

JFSS: 1899–1931
Journal of the Folk-Song Society: London (35 vols.), 1899–1931.

KENNEDY FRASER: 1909–25
Marjory Kennedy Fraser and Kenneth MacLeod, *Songs of the Hebrides*, Boosey, London: vol. I 1909, vol. II 1917, vol. III 1921; *From the Hebrides*: Patersons, Glasgow, 1925. A wide-ranging collection of Gaelic songs with elaborate background information relevant to most of the songs. Stylised piano arrangements and romanticized English translations mean that these collections must be used with caution.

MACCALLUM: 1821
Duncan MacCallum, *Co-chruinneacha Dhàn, Orain etc.*; James Fraser, Inverness, 1821. (Editor anonymous, but thought to be MacCallum.) Gaelic texts only; mostly original compositions but does include some good folksong texts.

MACDONALD: 1776
Ranald MacDonald, *Comh-Chruinneachadh Orannaigh Gaidhealach*: Duncan, Glasgow, 1776. 2nd ed. (Rev. Patrick Turner) 1809. Known as 'The Eigg Collection', it contains a wide range of Gaelic song texts; no English translations. One of the earliest printed sources.

MACDONALD: 1784
Patrick MacDonald, *A Collection of Highland Vocal Airs*: Edinburgh, *c.* 1784. Early source of Highland vocal airs, dances and bagpipe music in staff notation.

MACDONALD: 1821
Ranald MacDonald, *Orain le Raoghall Donullach Maille ri co-chruinneacha dàin, Orain etc. le ughdairean eugsamhuil*; James Fraser, Inverness, 1821. Mainly original compositions but does include some valuable folksong texts—no music.

MACDONALD: 1894
Archibald MacDonald, *Uist Bards*; Rev. Archibald Sinclair, Glasgow, 1894. Also known as 'The Uist Collection'. Collection of works of well-known and lesser-known Gaelic poets from the islands of N. and S. Uist, but also containing a few versions of folksongs. No music. Gaelic texts only.

MACDONALD: 1895
Keith Norman MacDonald, *The Gesto Collection of Highland Music*; Oscar Brandsetter, Leipzig, 1895. Collection of mainly Gaelic music; not all have words, but melodies are well preserved. Also contains bagpipe music arranged for piano.

MACDONALD: 1900
Keith Norman MacDonald, *MacDonald Bards from Mediaeval Times*; Norman MacLeod, Edinburgh, 1900. Discussion in English on the history of Gaelic literature from early times with particular reference to the works of MacLean Sinclair. Translations are given to most of the quoted examples.

MACDONALD: 1901
Keith Norman MacDonald, *Puirt-a-Beul* (or mouth music) suitable for Dances, etc.: Alexander MacLaren, Glasgow, 1901. Collection of mouth-music with tunes given in sol-fa notation. Gaelic words only. Also includes some waulking songs.

MACDONALD/MACDONALD: 1911
Rev. Archibald MacDonald and Rev. Alexander MacDonald, *The MacDonald Collection of Gaelic Poetry*; Inverness, 1911. Large and reliable collection of Gaelic songs of all types with complete texts in Gaelic only. Introduction less trustworthy. Mostly collected in S. Uist and Benbecula, and all relating to the Clan Donald.

MACDONALD: 1924
Rev. A. MacDonald (ed.), *The Poems of Alexander MacDonald* (*Mac Mhaighstir Alasdair*): Northern Counties Newspaper & Printing & Publishing Co., Ltd., Inverness, 1924.

MACFADYEN: 1902
John MacFadyen, *Sgeulaiche nan Caol*; Rev. Archibald Sinclair, Glasgow, 1902. A book of 'readings' suitable for general entertainment at *ceilidhs*. It is not a song collection but a selection of short poems.

Bibliography

MACFARLANE: 1813
Peter MacFarlane, *Co-chruinneachadh de dh'Orain agus de Luinneagaibh thagha Ghae'lach*; T. Stewart, Edinburgh, 1813. Gaelic texts only; useful minor source with variety of material, but most can be found elsewhere.

MACFARLANE: 1894–1909
Malcolm MacFarlane, *An Uiseag*: 1894; *An Lòn-dubh*: 28 Gaelic Songs; Paisley, 1908; *An Smeòrach, Am Bru-dhearg*; Aeneas MacKay, Stirling, 1909. Small collections with a wide variety of types of Gaelic song arranged for use by schools and choirs.

MACFARLANE: 1908
Malcolm MacFarlane, *Binneas nam Bàrd* (*Bardic Melody*); Aeneas MacKay, Stirling, 1908. Good general collection of Gaelic words and music of songs of the more popular type.

MACKENZIE: 1841
John MacKenzie, *Sàr-Obair nam Bàrd Gaelach*; MacGregor, Polson, Glasgow, 1841; Edinburgh, 1865, etc. Numerous editions with diverse page numbering. Gaelic texts only but notes on texts and lives of authors are given in English. Reliable texts but not all the information trustworthy. Valuable especially for more literary poetry.

MACKENZIE: 1962
Mrs Eila MacKenzie, 'Seven Gaelic Songs', contributed to JEFDSS: 1962, pp. 122–8 from the islands of Mull and Skye.

MACKENZIE: 1964
Annie M. MacKenzie, *Orain Iain Luim*; Oliver & Boyd, Edinburgh, 1964. A collection of the works of Iain Lom, the 17th-century poet. Gaelic texts given with translations. Of interest as a comparison with contemporary Gaelic folksong.

MACKINNON: 1939
Lachlan MacKinnon, *Cascheum nam Bàrd*; Northern Counties Newspaper, Inverness, 1939. General anthology of Gaelic poetry containing only a few folksong texts. Gaelic words only.

MACLAGAN MANUSCRIPT
MacLagan Collection, University of Glasgow Library. Contains many versions of Gaelic songs preserved in a hand-written manuscript of the late 18th century. No music noted but the song texts are good ones.

MACLEOD: 1908
Malcolm MacLeod of Farlane, *Modern Gaelic Bards*; Aeneas MacKay, Stirling, 1908. Mainly original works of 19th-century writers but does contain several popular folksong texts. Gaelic words with English translations. No music.

MACLEOD AND WHITEHEAD: 1908
Malcolm MacLeod and Fr. W. Whitehead, *Songs of the Highlands*; Logan, Inverness, 1908. Wide variety of more popular type of Gaelic songs with both Gaelic and English texts and music.

MACLEOD: 1916
Iain MacLeod, *Bàrdachd Leódhais* (*Lewis Bards*); Alexander MacLaren, Glasgow, 1916. Collection of local poetry from the Isle of Lewis containing work of recognized and folk poets as well as some older folk poetry. Gaelic texts only.

MACLEOD: 1952
Angus MacLeod (ed.), *Orain Dhonnchaidh Bhain* (*Songs of Duncan Ban MacIntyre*), Scottish Gaelic Texts Society; Oliver & Boyd, Edinburgh, 1952. A collection of the works of Duncan Ban MacIntyre with translations and notes. This popular poet had both a 'folk' and literary output. No music.

MACMILLAN: 1929/30
Rev. John MacMillan of Barra, *Gaelic Songs of the Isles of the West*: Boosey, London. Vol. I 1929, vol. II 1930. Folksongs mainly from the Isle of Barra; Gaelic and English words with music arranged by F. W. Lewis. Staff notation.

MACPHERSON: 1868
Donald MacPherson, *An Duanaire*; MacLachlan & Stewart, Edinburgh, 1868. Gaelic texts only but containing valuable and reliable folksong material of an early date.

MARTIN: 1934
Martin Martin, *A Description of the Western Isles of Scotland, 1695*: Aeneas MacKay, Stirling, 1934. A travelogue of the Hebrides at a time when many of the older songs were being composed. It therefore sheds light on the life-style which gave rise to the songs.

MOFFAT: 1922
Alfred Moffat, *The Minstrelsy of the Scottish Highlands*: Bayley & Ferguson, London, 1922. Comprehensive collection of Gaelic songs of the more popular type, Gaelic texts, English translations and music in staff notation.

MORISON: 1935
Duncan Morison, *Ceòl Mara* (*Songs of the Isle of Lewis*): J. & W. Chester, London, 1935. Small but valuable collection of Lewis songs. Gaelic and English words and music in staff notation.

MORRISON: 1913
Angus Morrison, *Orain nam Beann*: Alexander McLaren, Glasgow, 1913. Collection of popular Gaelic songs, including editor's own compositions and arrangements of older material.

MURRAY: 1920/36
Amy Murray, *Father Allan's Island*: New York, 1920; the Moray Press, Edinburgh, 1936. Contains 26 authentic transcriptions of traditional Gaelic songs collected in the Isle of Eriskay but mainly a memoir of personal collecting experiences; Gaelic texts, English translations and music, most with only one or two verses.

O LOCHLAINN: 1948
Colm O Lochlainn, *Deoch Slàinte nan Gillean. Dòrnan Oran a Barraidh*: Three Candles, Dublin, 1948. Collection of more modern folksongs from the Isle of Barra; Gaelic words and music in staff notation.

O MUIRGHEASA: 1915
Enri O Muirgheasa (Henry Morris), *Céad de Cheoltaibh Uladh*: Gill, Dublin, 1915. Songs in Irish Gaelic which provide a useful comparison.

OLIVER/SMITH: 1949
John W. Oliver and J. C. Smith, *A Mhic Iain 'ic Sheumais*; Oliver & Boyd, Edinburgh & London, 1949. An anthology of Scots Gaelic.

PATTISON: 1860
Thomas Pattison, *Twelve Gaelic Songs*: J. Muir Wood, Glasgow, n.d. (about 1860). 2 vols. Gaelic and English words and music in staff notation; contains a few good folksong texts.

PATTISON: 1868
Thomas Pattison, *The Gaelic Bards and Original Poems*: Archibald Sinclair, Glasgow, 1868. Consists almost entirely of English translations of Gaelic poems of the 17th and 18th centuries, only two Gaelic versions included. No music.

ST COLUMBA COLLECTION: 1953
A'Choisir Chiùil (*The St Columba Collection of Gaelic Songs*): Bayley & Ferguson, London & Glasgow, 1953. Collection of popular Gaelic folksongs arranged for choral performance with regularised melodies and rhythms but containing some good Gaelic texts. No English translations.

SCHOOL OF SCOTTISH STUDIES: 1960
Gaelic and Scots Folktales, Gaelic and Scots Folksongs, Scottish Instrumental Music. University of Edinburgh, 1960. A booklet which accompanies recordings of texts and songs.

SCOTTISH GAELIC STUDIES: 1926–
Scottish Gaelic Studies, ed. John MacDonald, M.A. (vols. I–VIII) and Derick S. Thomson (vol. IX), University of Aberdeen, Celtic Department: B. H. Blackwell, Oxford, from 1926. Produced spasmodically, this periodical occasionally includes songs, usually with English translations.

Bibliography

SCOTTISH STUDIES: 1957–
Scottish Studies, School of Scottish Studies: Oliver & Boyd, Edinburgh, from 1957. Published twice yearly by the School of Scottish Studies of Edinburgh University; important background material but few texts of Gaelic folksongs.

SHAW: 1943–4
Margaret Shaw Campbell in JEFDSS: 1943, pp. 149–56. Six Gaelic songs collected in S. Uist and Barra, 1929–39. Also JEFDSS: 1944, pp. 190–6. Seven more Gaelic songs collected in S. Uist as above.

SHAW: 1955
Margaret Fay Shaw: *Folksongs and Folklore of South Uist*: Routledge & Kegan Paul, London, 1955. Contains a wide variety of songs and carefully edited background material. Reliable Gaelic texts, though often regrettably short, with useful English translations and notes. Music in staff notation.

SINCLAIR: 1879
Archibald Sinclair, *An t-Oranaiche* (*The Gaelic Songster*): Sinclair, Glasgow, 1879. Comprehensive collection containing reliable and very complete texts free of 'touching up'. No music or translations.

SINCLAIR: 1890
Rev. A. MacLean Sinclair, *Co-chruinneachadh Ghlinn-a-Bhaird* (*The Glenbard Collection of Gaelic Poetry*): Haszard & Moore, Charlottetown, Canada, 1890. More of a literary than 'folk' collection of Gaelic texts but does include some folksongs.

SINCLAIR: 1890/2
Rev. A. MacLean Sinclair, *The Gaelic Bards from 1411–1715*: Haszard & Moore, Charlottetown, Canada. Vol. I 1890, vol. II 1892. A comprehensive study of early Gaelic literature of all types; especially valuable for wide range of clan poetry of elegy and eulogy types.

SINCLAIR: 1898–1900
Rev. A. MacLean Sinclair, *Na Baird Leathanach* (*The MacLean Bards*): Haszard & Moore, Charlottetown, Canada, 1898. 2nd ed. (vol. II) 1900. Deals specifically with the poetry and history of one particular clan but does contain some texts in Gaelic only.

SINTON: 1906
Rev. Thomas Sinton, *The Poetry of Badenoch*: Northern Counties Publishing, Inverness, 1906. Local collection with Gaelic texts and English translations. Interest lies more in being a local study rather than for the folk poetry texts, which are mostly rather slight.

STEWART: 1804
Alexander and Donald Stewart, *Cochruinneacha Taoghta de Shaothair nam Bard Gaelach* (*A Choice Collection of the Works of the Highland Bards*): Stewart, Glasgow, 1804. Collected in both Highlands and Islands, useful early source covering literary and folk poetry. Gaelic texts only.

STEWART: 1884
Charles Stewart, *The Killin Collection of Gaelic Songs*: MacLachlan & Stewart, Edinburgh, 1884. Contains a wide variety of types of Gaelic song with translations and music arranged for piano. Airs stylised.

TGSI: 1871–
Transactions of the Gaelic Society of Inverness, 1871. Papers presented to the Society some of which, particularly in the earlier volumes, contain versions of folksongs otherwise unrecorded; usually Gaelic texts only.

TOLMIE: 1911
Frances Tolmie's 'Collection of Gaelic Songs' in JFSS: 1911, No. 16. Complete issue JFSS: 1913, No. 17, pp. 351–2. JEFDSS: 1948, pp. 141–4: article on Frances Tolmie by Rose Ethel Bassin. JEFDSS: 1961, pp. 91–2. The Tolmie Collection contains reliable versions of both texts and music.

TURNER: 1813
Patrick Turner, *Comhchruinneacha do dh'Orain Taghta Ghàidhealach*: T. Stewart, Edinburgh, 1813. Reliable early source with some long versions of songs. Gaelic texts only.

WATSON: 1932
Professor William J. Watson, *Bàrdachd Ghàidhlig* (specimens of Gaelic Poetry 1550–1900): A. Learmonth, Stirling, 1932. Comprehensive anthology of all types of Gaelic poetry from many areas. Some excellent versions of folksongs authoritatively presented; Gaelic texts only, but includes notes.

WATSON: 1934
James Carmichael Watson, *Gaelic Songs of Mary MacLeod*: Glasgow, 1934; 2nd ed. Oliver & Boyd, Edinburgh, 1965. Collection of works of a 17th-century poetess which show a relationship between this type of clan poetry and that of the 'folk authors'. Contains translations, but no music.

WHYTE: 1898
Henry (Fionn) Whyte, *The Celtic Lyre*: John Grant, Edinburgh, 1898. Collection of more popular type of Gaelic song most of which can be found elsewhere. Gaelic and English words with music in staff and sol-fa notation.

II

Songs in Irish Gaelic

Introduction

The oldest Irish tune we know would seem to be at least 400 years old.* It exists under the title *Callino* in a manuscript of the end of the sixteenth century (preserved in the library of Trinity College, Dublin). However, a complete form of what is indubitably the same title occurs in a book printed in London in 1565 as *Calen o Custure Me*. This expression occurs again in Shakespeare's *Henry V*, and it puzzled Shakespearean scholars for more than 300 years until at last the late Professor Gerard Murphy realised that it was simply a rendering in English of the Irish song-title *Cailín ó Chois tSiúire Mé* (see EIGSE: vol. 1).

In an article in *Féilscríbhinn Torna* (Cork University Press, 1947) Professor Aloys Fleischmann has gathered together most of the references to Chant in early Irish manuscripts. The majority are in Latin, since Irish had not yet become a written language, and the author concludes that Chant was brought to Ireland very shortly after the introduction of Christianity.

But it must be admitted that some of the references to musicians and singers which we find in early Irish tales are, indeed, as ancient as the sagas themselves. For instance, one of the oldest texts which is easily available is a law-text called *Crith Gablach* (edited by Professor D. A. Binchy, and published at the Stationery Office, Dublin). This text must have been compiled no later than the beginning of the eighth century, although some of the strata contained therein are undoubtedly much older, and it contains references to 'cruitti' (harpers), 'cuislennaig' (pipers) and 'cornairi' (horn-players). References to 'dord' (bass-singing) and another type of singing called 'andord' are to be found in one of the most famous Old Irish sagas: that of the elopement of Deirdre with the sons of Uisnech. This tale is more difficult to date, but it seems to have been compiled in the ninth century at the latest, and possibly much earlier.

From these earliest references to singing, chanting and music-making we see that music was an integral part of life for the Irish at all times, and one could certainly cite a long list of references to music in contemporary and later tales. Suffice it to say that by the late twelfth century, Giraldus Cambrensis, a Welsh-Norman ecclesiastic who made a tour of Ireland with the Anglo-Norman invaders, made favourable comments on the musical attributes of the Irish.

Even so, we know nothing of specific Irish tunes until the beginning of the seventeenth century, when the last schools of Bardic Poetry were disintegrating. This Bardic or Court Poetry, which had held the stage until then, was basically syllabic. In it there was no regularity of stressed syllables, such as would make for easy setting to a tune, but instead each line was required to have only a certain number of syllables, the favourite number being seven. Thus theoretically each line could have any number of stressed syllables, from one to seven, and in any order. As well as this all-important number of syllables to be contained in each line each particular kind of metre, and there were many of them, had to include a certain amount of

---

* We know practically nothing of the origins of our folk music; if we did, the music would not really be folk music, which must emanate from the people and not from a sophisticated composer. But it is tempting to hear traces of Gregorian Chant in many Irish Gaelic religious tunes, as for example in *Is Maith An Bhean Muire Mhór*, *Gabham Molta Bríde*, *Seacht Subhailcí na Maighdine Muire*, *An Bhainis Phósta I gCána*, and even *Deus Meus Adiuva Me*. There is no question of the words of these songs being old, but the music could very well be our oldest folk music.

heila Gallagher of Gweedore, Co. Donegal
Photograph: Peter Kennedy

metrical ornaments. These varied from metre to metre and included the various kinds of rhyme: final and internal, consonance, alliteration, etc. We know that the harp was used to accompany these encomiums as they were recited or chanted by the bards to their lords, but the irregular stress meant that they could not be sung to tunes with a regular rhythm.

As has been noted above, the last schools producing these poets broke up in the seventeenth century, and the advent of Oliver Cromwell in the year 1649 finally put paid to any chances of survival this type of poetry may have had; from now on there were no more nobles in Ireland and the court poets had lost their raison d'être.

Ever since Cromwell's time we have had in Irish a prosody based on regularity of stress in each line, such as would be suitable for singing. The number of syllables in each line was not in the least important and could vary from line to line. As one would expect, however, in the better poems it did not vary very much.

The origin of these stressed metres is quite difficult to explain. The great German scholar Kuno Meyer thought that they had evolved from English exemplars, but unfortunately many of these Irish metres have no counterparts in English. The Irish scholar Osborn Bergin rejected this theory and instead claimed that they had evolved from the looser types of Bardic Poetry. When one adds to this the fact that internal rhymes, although not much used by the Bardic poets, already existed in Middle Irish (tenth and eleventh centuries), and also the great changes that must have occurred in beginning to write poems for the people instead of the nobles, one must admit that in all probability Bergin was on the right track.

Undoubtedly this stressed verse was being practised long before the Bardic Schools came to their end, but we do not possess any definite examples of the new verse forms in this period, most probably because it was looked on as an inferior form of prosody suitable only for the masses, and therefore not worthy of being written down and preserved, as was Bardic Poetry. But it should be remembered that many of the first exponents of the new metres were also skilled in composing in the older Bardic Poetry metres. Nor should it be forgotten that the typical Ulster form in stressed poetry, 'Trí Rann agus Amhrán', as practised by, say, Séamus Dall MacCuarta, differs very little from the examples, late and loose as they may be, in the Bardic Poetry contained in that excellent collection of love poetry *Dánta Grádha* (edited by O Rathile).

The vast majority of the native Irish, until the middle of the seventeenth century, spoke only the Irish language. English, from its introduction by the Anglo-Norman invaders near the end of the twelfth century up to this time, was spoken only in the Pale, a district in and around Dublin, and in the bigger towns, and not at all in the country districts. But at the end of this period Cromwell came over and took the lands from the Catholic Irish and gave them to imported Protestant Scots and English. This marked the beginning of the end for the Irish language, and the ensuing religious persecutions resulted in native emigrations. Even though Catholics had achieved emancipation by the middle of the nineteenth century, the famine added another impetus to emigration. So while it was gradually losing ground during the seventeenth and eighteenth centuries, the famine quickened the rate of deterioration of the language to such an extent that today not much more than 60 000 people speak Irish as an everyday language, although there are more native speakers of Irish than that scattered all over the English-speaking parts of Ireland. The Gaeltacht, the Irish-speaking part of Ireland, is almost all to be found in the west in the counties of Donegal, Mayo, Galway, Kerry and Cork; the exception is a pocket of Irish speakers in County Waterford.

Three of the greatest collectors of Irish folk music—Bunting, Joyce and Petrie—all published at different times collections called *Ancient Music of Ireland*, but we have no reason for thinking that the music those collections contained was in fact of great antiquity.

Introduction

Most of the earliest Irish airs are found in print, not in manuscript. Playford's *Dancing Master*, for instance, published in England in the seventeenth century, contains some Irish airs, though they are not specified as Irish, and the earliest publication of specifically Irish airs was issued in Dublin in 1726 by John and William Neale.

Two periods of English ballad opera in the eighteenth century resulted in the publication of many Irish airs. In 1728 Charles Coffey's *Beggar's Wedding* was performed. Coffey was Irish and all the tunes contained in this score are Irish. As for the second period, there are many Irish airs in William Shield's *Poor Soldier*, produced in 1782.

Towards the end of the eighteenth century there was a definite surge of nationalism, cultural as well as political, with its centre in the city of Belfast, and some cultured patriots decided that it was high time to organize a gathering of the fast-disappearing harpers in the city, the main object being to note their repertoire of airs. The Festival was arranged for July 1792. Ten harpers took part, and the person engaged to note their various repertoires was a young organist later to become famous as the first collector of Irish music, Edward Bunting. In contrast to the young Bunting, only eighteen years old, the harpers were all elderly, most of them over seventy years of age, while the eldest was no less than ninety-seven. Of the ten harpers who participated, six were blind, while they were all, no doubt, the very last members of their profession.

Bunting now decided to make the collecting and preserving of Irish airs the main business of his life. Four years later, in 1796, he published his first collection of sixty-six airs. In the year 1802 he toured Munster and Connaught collecting tunes, and since he knew no Irish himself he took with him one Patrick Lynch, an Irish-speaking schoolmaster from County Down, to note the words of the tunes he was collecting. This was the first occasion on which it was realized just how important a part of the folksong words are. Bunting's second collection, published in 1809, contained seventy-seven airs, while his third and last volume, published in 1840, contained 151 melodies.

In the years 1841 to 1843 over a hundred Irish tunes were published in *The Citizen*, a Dublin monthly, by its music editor, Henry Hudson. Hudson was intensely attracted to Irish music from an early age, and he was collecting or copying folk tunes when he was only fourteen years old. When he died in 1889 he left behind a lot of unpublished material, over 700 tunes which he had collected or copied, and over one hundred of his own compositions based on genuine folksong models.

The next specialist, William Forde, who was born in Cork, was a great collector and probably knew more about Irish music than any other scholar before or since. He toured parts of Connaught in the early 1840s and took back a valuable collection of tunes he noted in the most musical parts of that province. He then began to compare all the known versions of each air, but his proposed publication met with financial difficulties and all Forde's work and collections remain in manuscript.

The great collector, George Petrie, who was born in Dublin in 1789 of Scottish ancestry, was talented in many fields: among others painting, letters, archaeology. But throughout his life Irish music remained his prime interest. In 1855 he published his *Ancient Music of Ireland*, which contained 147 airs, each with valuable notes. He died in 1866, but three important volumes of his collection were published posthumously. In 1877 F. Hoffmann published 196 airs from Petrie's collection, but without his valuable notes. In 1882 a further thirty-nine airs were published, this time along with the notes made by Petrie. In 1905 Sir Charles Stanford published his *Complete Petrie Collection* of 1582 tunes, once again without Petrie's notes. Stanford edited the collection from Petrie's manuscripts, which contained 2148 tunes.

Most of the material in the manuscripts of two other great collectors, John Edward Pigot (1822–71) and James Goodman (1828–96), is as yet unpublished, but they each preserved about 2000 airs.

One of Petrie's most generous contributors of traditional airs was Patrick Weston Joyce (1827–1914). After Petrie's death Joyce had to think of publishing on his own account, and his *Ancient Music of Ireland*, containing one hundred previously unpublished airs, was issued in 1873. He published a second volume in 1888, and in 1909 he published his *Old Irish Folk Music and Songs*, which contained over 800 airs, half of which were taken from the manuscripts of Pigot and Goodman, mentioned above.

In the early years of this century A. Martin Freeman made a collection of songs in west Cork, and it has been issued in vol. VI of the *Journal of the Folk Song Society*. Also deserving special mention are the various publications of Carl Hardebeck, and Mrs Costello's collection of Connaught songs, *Amhráin Mhuighe Seóla*. Many others, too numerous to mention, have done their bit for Irish folk music, the more important ones being Donal O'Sullivan, Sean O'Boyle, Séamus Ennis, Seán Og O Tuama, and Liam de Noraidh.

In addition to the many thousands of tunes contained in the above-mentioned publications and manuscripts, more than a thousand airs have been collected by the Irish Folklore Commission, some in manuscript and some on record; as yet very few of these have seen the light of publication.

Undoubtedly folksongs are still being composed today, in an unconscious way and without formal training in either poetry or music, and the unsophisticated folk poets are never too discerning in choosing tunes for their songs. They just choose any good tune they happen to hear, whether it is native or not. A present-day example in our collection is *Séimidh Eoghainín Duibh* (No. 46), where the tune is a version of the Scottish tune *Kelvin Grove*. But this tendency had already started over 200 years ago, as can readily be seen in articles published by Proinsias O Ceallaigh in the early issues of *Ceol*.

In their passage from generation to generation, both the words and the music undergo many minute changes, with the result that we may find a number of versions of a single song. This is true of all countries, but it has happened in no other country more than in Ireland, where, for example, a whole book has been written about all the versions of one of our songs, *Dónall Óg* (No. 31). This book, by Seosamh O Duibhginn, would have been even more interesting if it had been possible to compare all the versions of the tune as well as all the versions of the words. Many of our most popular folksongs could be similarly treated, for example *An Draighneán Donn* (No. 32) and *Tiocfaidh An Samhradh* (No. 48).

Many great Irish songs, however, belong to the tradition of harpers which died out in the eighteenth century. These songs are to be found only in the very earliest publications and manuscripts, and as a consequence they have not changed from the form in which they were composed and therefore hardly merit the title of folksong. We usually know the names of the composer and poet, although quite a few were very old even when they were first written down. (Excellent examples of this type of music can be heard on Gael-Linn record CEF 015 *Ceol Na nUasal*, which features Seán O Riada, Seán O Sé, and Ceoltóirí Cualann.) The notion of a harper depending on patrons is a curious survival of the Bardic tradition, where the poets composed poems in syllabic verse for the nobles. Not only did these harpers compose tunes for their patrons, but many of them also composed the words to go with the music, particularly Carolan. A curious feature of Carolan (1670–1738), the last of the great harper-composers, was the way in which his compositions show the influence of Corelli and Geminiani. (An excellent biography of Carolan, together with all his compositions, has been written by Donal O'Sullivan.)

In between the two types of song just mentioned—the unsophisticated folksong of today and the early patron-music—we find the type, especially in the eighteenth century, where a poem by a more or less sophisticated poet is married to an already existing air. Often these airs were not of Irish origin, but we look upon them nowadays as being Irish. This was particularly the case with the Munster poets (as will be clear from Proinsias O Ceallaigh's articles in *Ceol*). The fact that some of these 'better' poems became popular is proved by the fact that many versions of them are to be found.

It will come as no surprise that much of the best in folk poetry in Britain is to be found in Irish Gaelic. As Donal O'Sullivan says:

> One finds in the best of these songs a beauty and tenderness beyond the ordinary; a deep and passionate sincerity; a naturalness which disdains all artifice; a feeling for poetical expression unusual in folk songs; all combined with a mellifluous assonance which makes them eminently singable.

The great majority of the songs in the repertoire of the average folksinger in Irish is made up of love songs. Everyone agrees that the loveliest melodies in Irish folksong occur in this type of song. Some are of the joys of love, some complain of the life of a 'mal-mariée', but it must be admitted that the vast majority have that indefinable plaintive quality so typical of the Gael.

A single line from *Bríd Óg ní Mháille* (No. 27) may illustrate some of these qualities:

Níl ní ar bith is áille ná'n ghealach os cionn a' tsáile	There's nothing more lovely than the moon o'er the waters

Note the excellent imagery mixed with stark realism of this lover's lament from *Dónall Óg* (No. 31):

Bhain tú soir 'gus bhain tú siar dom	From me you've stolen East and likewise West
Bhain tú romham is bhain tú mo dhiaidh dom	You took my past and my future besides
Bhain tú an ghealach is bhain tú an ghrian dom	The sun and moon, you've taken them away
'S is ró-mhór m'eagla gur bhain tú Dia dom	To take my God from me I'm most afraid

Less exalted but perhaps more typical of the general run of love songs is this verse from *Is Fada O Bhaile A D'Aithneoinn* (No. 37):

Is fad' ó bhaile a d'aithneoinn féin do shiúl	It's far from home I'd know you by your walk
Do chúl dubh daite faoi hata glan éadrom úr	Your dark head of hair beneath a clean new hat
Bhíodh blas na meala 'ach mhaidin ar phóig mo rún	The taste of honey every morning on your kiss
Roimhe Shamhain gan amhras beidh faire orm féin le cumhaidh	By Hallowe'en it's certain I'll be dying from grief

Although most of the songs in our collection are love songs, many of these are basically laments, and the two types have become so inextricably mixed up in Irish that it is practically impossible to tell the one from the other. There are two laments contained here: *Séamus Mac Murchaidh* (No. 44) is deservedly popular over a wide area of the northern half of Ireland, while *Bríd Bhán* (No. 26) is entirely local and is confined to north-west Donegal.

Ever since the penal days, when intending priests had to go to the Continent to receive an education, emigration has been an almost integral part of Irish life, and has given rise to many beautiful songs: *Slan Le Maigh, Bán-Chnoic Eireann Oighe* and *Aird A' Chumhaing*, for example. Farewells included in this collection are *Bríd Bhán* (No. 26) and *An t-Oileán Úr* (No. 42). Once again we have a genre of 'sad' song, not far removed from the lament.

The plaintive quality of many Irish tunes lends itself admirably to adoption for use with religious verse, although most of the collections and manuscripts mentioned above contain fine examples of tunes associated only with religious verse. Indeed, one cannot help wondering if this type of music, *Gabham Molta Bríde*, *Seacht Subhailcí na Maighdine Muire*, etc., is not the oldest type of essentially vocal music that we possess. One wonders even, on hearing the *Tantum Ergo* sung to that most peaceful air *Pé in Eirinn I*, if some airs are not basically sacred, and the secular versions known all over Ireland are only secondary.

'Suantraighe' (sleep-music) was one of the three main types of music of ancient Ireland. In some of the Old Irish tales, *Orgainn Denna Ríg*, for example, we read of the harper helping his king by putting his enemies to sleep with the music of his harp. Plenty of examples of this are found, as in *Déirín Dé* and *Do Chuirfinn-se Fhéin*.

There are not many nursery rhymes in Irish. The nearest thing we have to them are simply children's songs, usually with quite attractive and lively tunes, for example *Beidh Aonach Amárach*, *Túirne Mháire* and *Is Trua Gan Peata An Mhaoir Agam*.

Just as scarce as the above category are songs of occupation. Those that do exist treat of the rural occupations we would expect to meet in the Gaeltacht, such as churning, herding, milking, spinning, and so on.

No doubt drinking songs exist in every community, and Irish certainly has its fair share. Their lively rhymes adequately answer the charge that Irish music has nothing to offer but sad, slow melodies, and excellent examples are *Preab san Ol*, *An Crúiscín Lán* and *Táim In Arrears*.

Some humorous songs are known all over Ireland, and every Irish-speaking area has its version of *An Seanduine Dóighte* and *Amhrán na mBréag*, to take only two examples. However, many such songs are entirely local, and their humour is not easily seen if they are taken too far from their place of origin. One such example is *Séimidh Eoghainín Duibh* (No. 46).

Contrary to what one might expect, Irish does not contain many airs of a ringing, martial character; most of the rousing patriotic songs that do exist have English words only. Patriotic songs in Irish are usually originally love songs with the lyrics changed. This could well be guessed by the uninitiated for not only are the airs slow and plaintive but many of the titles are simply names of various females, no doubt the names of the original love songs, for example *Róisín Dubh*, *Síle Ní Ghadhra* and *Caitlín Ní Uallacháin*.

In considering the various types of song available in the Irish language, two important absences must be noted. There are no carols in the Irish language, nor has there ever been a reference to any. Even stranger is the absence of boating-songs, so common in Lowland Scots and Gaelic, and the absence of references to dancing.

Ich am of Irlaunde	Gode sire, pray ich thee
ant of the holy londe	come ant daunce wyt me
of Irlaunde	in Irlaunde

This frequently quoted carol can be dated to the fourteenth century, but the earliest reference in the Irish language to dancing does not occur until the end of the sixteenth century. There are no references whatsoever to such a pastime in the older literature, while the words in the modern language appear to be loan-words from English and French. It seems pretty certain that the *Reel* is of Scottish origin, while the *Hornpipe* possibly originated in England and the *Jig* (giga) may have had Continental roots. It would seem then that dancing was first introduced into Ireland not long after the Anglo-Norman conquest, after which the Irish soon adapted it, like other cultural imports, so that it became an integral part of their way of life.

PRONUNCIATION OF IRISH GAELIC

The pronunciation of Irish Gaelic is extremely intricate, so the following hints have been very much simplified.

Consonants

Most consonants have two distinct pronunciations. When followed by *a, o, u* they are known as broad consonants, and when followed (or preceded) by *e* and *i* they are known as slender consonants. (For the sake of simplicity we will ignore the differences between broad and slender *b, f, m, p* and *r*.)

c SLENDER	as *k* in *k*ing
	e.g. cill (kill)
c BROAD	as *c* in *c*ord
	e.g. corc (cork)
d SLENDER	as *j* in *j*am
	e.g. dear (jar)
d BROAD	as *d* in *d*one
	e.g. donn (done)
g SLENDER	as *g* in *g*ive
	e.g. geas (gas)
g BROAD	as *g* in *g*ood
	e.g. goll (gull)
s SLENDER	as *sh* in *sh*ow
	e.g. seal (shall)
s BROAD	as *s* in *s*ame
	e.g. soc (sock)
t SLENDER	as *ch* in *ch*ase
	e.g. tinn (chin)
t BROAD	as *t* in *t*ar
	e.g. toll (tulle)
l and ll SLENDER	both *ll* as in mi*ll*ion (in initial position)
l BROAD	as *l* in *l*aid
n and nn SLENDER	both *n* as in mi*n*ion (in initial position)
n BROAD	as *n* in no*n*e
bh, mh SLENDER	*bhi* as English *v*
	bh, mh as *v* in *v*ital
bh, mh BROAD	as *w* in *w*et
	e.g. bhun (won)
ch SLENDER	as *h* in *h*uge
	e.g. chiú (hue)
ch BROAD	as Scots lo*ch* or Anglo-Irish lou*gh* or rarely as *h* in *h*at
dh, gh SLENDER	sounds as *y* in (English) *y*es or else is silent
dh, gh BROAD	as *g* in Spanish a*g*ua or North German sa*g*en
fh	always silent
ph	as English *f*
sh	as *h* in *h*at or rarely as *ch* (slender)
th	as *h* in *h*at

Initial consonant clusters

mb	pron. *m*
gc	pron. *g*
nd	pron. *n*
bhf	pron. *bh*
ng	pron. as in si*ng*
bp	pron. *b*
ts	pron. *t*
dt	pron. *d*

Vowels

short a, ea	as *h* in *h*at
short e	as *e* in matter or merry
short i	as *i* in sk*i*ll
short o	as *o* in g*o*t or d*o*ne
short u	as *u* in f*u*r
long a	as *a* in f*a*ther
long é, éa, éi	as *a* in s*a*y
long í, ío, ao, aoi	as *ee* in s*ee*
long o	as in (English) *a*wl or *o*we
long ú	as in thr*ou*gh

In the following phonetic example, the first verse of *An Bhanaltra* (No. 25), everything should be pronounced just as in English. Vowels followed by an *h* are the short vowels of above. (*lh* is pronounced as *ll* in mi*ll*ion and *ny* as the *n* in mi*ni*on.)

Original	*Phonetic*
Is deas a' fear i mbaile mé	iss hass eh far eh ma-leh may
Níl dúil agam i mí-ghreann	nyeel dool uggum eh mee-ran
Is deas a' fear i mbaile mé	iss jass eh far eh ma-leh may
Níl dúil agam i síor-chainnt	nyeel dool uggum eh sheer-hainch
Nuair a théid fir a' bhaile 'mach	noor eh hedge fir eh wa-leh mach
A dh'amharc fá n-a ndíobháil	a ga-work fa-na nyee-wilh
Pillim-s' ar an bhanaltra	pilh-ims err eh wanaltra
'Gus bogaim daoith' an cliabhán	guss bugg-emm dee-hin klee-wan

25 AN BHANALTRA
THE NURSEMAID

1 Is deas a' fear i mbaile mé
  Níl dúil agam i mí-ghreann
  Is deas a' fear i mbaile mé
  Níl dúil agam i síor-chainnt
  Nuair a théid fir a' bhaile 'mach
  A dh'amharc fá n-a ndíobháil
  Pillim-s' ar an bhanaltra
  'Gus bogaim daoith' an cliabhán

1 When I'm at home I am a nice man
  For rumour-mongers I don't much care
  When I'm at home I am a nice man
  And gossip too's not my affair
  When all the local lads go sporting
  Devilment is in the air
  Then I go back to my old nursemaid
  And I rock the cradle for her

2 'S a mhíle mh'anam ar maidin thú
  'S arís ag teacht na h-oíche
  Níl uair den lá 'á bhfeicim thú
  Nach ort a bím ag smuainteamh
  Míl' uair go mb'fhearr liom agam thú
  Ná ba na Mumhan 'gus bainne acu
  O is a Dhia, nach trua mo scarúint leat
  'S gur ionnat atá mo chroí 'stigh

2 You're my dearest in the morning
  Then again at night you're dear
  And at times you're out of seeing
  For you I'm waiting to appear
  A thousand times I wish I had you
  Than all the milk of a Munster cow
  O God, what pity we are parting
  When I'm so set upon you now

3 Ní theachaidh síol i dtalamh riamh
  Comh maith leis an mhin eorna
  Níthear uisce beatha dó
  'Gus ceanglann sé 'n grá pósta
  Tá cuid a théid 'un peacaidh leis
  'Gus cuid a théid 'un carthannais
  Agus bheir sé ar na cailleachaí
  Bheith i meidhir insa chlúdaigh

3 No seed that e'er was sown on farmland
  Is half as good as barley grains
  And whisky that is made from barley
  Binds the bliss of marriage bands
  It makes some people turn to sinning
  Others better every day
  It even makes the old hags alter
  In the corner full of play

26 BRID BHAN
FAIR BRIDGET

Ní h-ion-ann liom-sa 'sliabh 's an bhai - le 'tá 'mo dhiaidh

Is, a Dhia, gan mé a - ríst ann ____

Gan mé sa teach mhór 'tá deán-ta'r thaobh an róid

A - gus mé bheith ann gan bhó gan chao-ra ____

Ní bheinn in bhur gcró a - nois ar theacht an Domh - naigh

Bheadh an t Aif - reann do mo chóir 's mo dhaoi - ní

Is dá mba liom-sa Éir' a - nu-as ó Loch Éir - ne

Gur i dTeil - ionn a b'fhearr liom có - naí

1 Ní h-ionann liomsa 'sliabh 's an bhaile 'tá 'mo dhiaidh
Is, a Dhia, gan mé aríst ann
Gan mé sa teach mhór 'tá deánta 'r thaobh an róid
Agus mé bheith ann gan bhó gan chaora
Ní bheinn in bhur gcró anois ar theacht an Domhnaigh
Bheadh an tAifreann do mo chóir 's mo dhaoiní
Is dá mba liomsa Éir' anuas ó Loch Éirne
Gur i dTeilionn a b'fhearr liom cónaí

2 A Bhríd Bhán, a rún, glac misneach bheas mór
Is ná cluintear níos mó thú ag éagaoint
'S nach bhfuil ní ar an domhan dá bhfaca tú le feabhas
Nach mbeidh againn insa bhaile úd 'mbeidh muid
Caoirigh 'gus gabhair, caiple 'gus buaibh
Agus uain mhaith' go bhfuighimist féar daof'
Nach ró-dheas an áit seo i dtoradh 'gus i ngráin
'Gus an bradán ar an abhainn ag léimnigh

3 Tá na caoirigh 'nseo gan dóigh, crupán ar na buaibh
Agus galar ar na gabhair sna h-altaibh
Méadaíonn sé mo bhrón, níl anseo ach móin
Is a' chíb dhubh ní airímse ina féar í
A' méid bradáin agus éisc dár shnámh 'gcuan Teilinn 'riamh
Agus taradh siad aniar faoin gharraí
Ni thabarfainn thart mo shúil le tuirse 'gus le cumhaidh
O tháinig mé in bhur gclúid ghránna

*

1 This place is not a patch on the place that I've left
And, O God, if only I were back there
To be in the big abode that's built beside the road
Even if I'd neither any sheep nor cattle
Nor dwelling in your shed, when Sunday comes
I'd rather the Mass were for me and my people
If only Ireland was mine from here to Lough Erne
It's in Teelin that I'd most want to be living

2 Fair Bridget, my dear, take heart and be of good cheer
And don't let us hear you so lamenting
And you shall have nothing but the best
As that which you have in your own dwelling
There are sheep and goats, some horses and some cows
And there are good lambs for their grazing
It's a fine place for fruit and for the grain to grow
And we've even got some salmon in the river leaping

3 These sheep look like nothing, and the cattle look unhealthy
For the goats, they look diseased and have got some swellings in their joints
What's more my luck is worse with nothing here but turf
The coarse growth couldn't be called grazing
And if all the fish that ever swam in Teelin Bay
Were to come over and land upon my garden
I wouldn't even turn my eyes with weariness and sorrow
Since the first time I reached your ugly corner

27 BRID OG NI MHAILLE
BRIDGET O'MALLEY

'Bhríd Óg Ní Mháil-le 's tú d'fhág mo chroí crái-te

Tá— ar-rain-gea-cha'n bháis ag gabháil fríd cheart-lár mo chroí

Tá na míl-te fear i ngrá le d'éa-dan ciúin nái-reach

Is go dtug tú barr breácht' ar thír Oir-ghiall má's fíor

1 'Bhríd Óg Ní Mháille, 's tú d'fhág mo chroí cráite
Tá arraingeacha 'n bháis ag gabháil fríd cheart-lár
mo chroí
Tá na mílte fear i ngrá le d'éadan ciúin náireach

Is go dtug tú barr breácht' ar thír Oirghiall má's fíor

2 Níl ní ar bith is áille ná'n ghealach os cionn a' tsáile

Ná bláth bán na n-áirní bíos a' fás ar an droighean

O siúd mar bíos mo ghrá-sa, 'na trillsí le breáchta
Béilín meala na páirte nach ndearn ariamh claon

3 Is tuirseach 's is brónach a chaithims' an Domhnach
Mo hata 'n mo dhorn liom 's mé ag osnaíl go trom
Mé 'g amharc ar na bóithre a mbínn 's mo ghrá'
gabháil ann
'Nois ag fear eile pósta is mo h-och nach í 'n fheall

4 Nach mise 'tá thíos leis a' phósadh seó 'dhéanamh

'S nach gcodlaím aon oích' ach ag osnaíl go trom
O nár fhágaidh mé 'n saol seo go rabh mé 's mo
chéad-searc
Ar an aon leabaidh sínte 's mo lámh faoi n-a cionn

5 Is buachaill deas óg mé 'tá ag triall 'un mo phósta
'S ní buan i bhfad beo mé mur' bhfaghaidh mé mo
mhian
A chuisle is a stóirín, deán réidh 'gus bí romham-sa
Cionn deireannach den Domhnach ar Bhóithrín
Droim Sliabh

1 O Bridget O'Malley, you've left me heartbroken
And the arrows of death, they are piercing my hea

There are thousands in love with your modest co
plex
And you're the beauty of Oriel without any doub

2 There's nothing more lovely than the moon o'er t
wat
Or the sloe-tree's white blossom as it grows in the
w
O that's how my love is, illumined with beauty
With those lovely lips of honey that ne'er told a li

3 My Sunday is sad and it leaves me so weary
With my hat in my hand I keep sighing alone
I keep looking at the places where my love and I
wande
But now she's married to another and I can only
make m

4 I'm much the worse off since she made that poor
marria
And I stay awake at nights making sighs all the ti
May I never leave this world till I get my fair dar

Stretched out by my side with our bodies entwine

5 I'm just a young fellow going off to be married
I sooner would die unless my love marries me

O dearest, my darling, be ready and waiting
Be there late on Sunday on the road to Drumslee

82

28 AN CAILIN GAELACH
THE IRISH GIRL

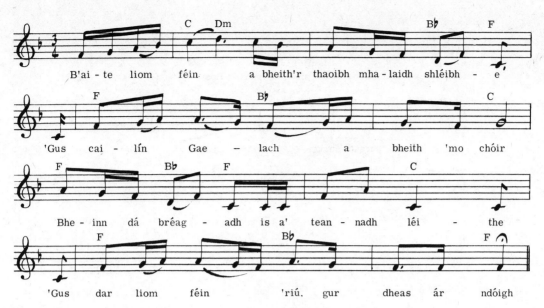

B'ai - te liom féin a bheith'r thaoibh mha-laidh shléibh - e

'Gus cai - lín Gae - lach a bheith 'mo chóir

Bhe - inn dá bréag - adh is a' tean-nadh léi - the

'Gus dar liom féin 'riú, gur dheas ár ndóigh

---

1 B'aite liom féin a bheith 'r thaoibh mhalaidh shléibhe
 'Gus cailín Gaelach a bheith 'mo chóir
 Bheinn dá bréagadh is a' teannadh léithe
 'Gus dar liom féin 'riú gur dheas ár ndóigh

2 'G éirí domh féin ar maidin an lae ghil
 'S mé ag gabháil fán choill chraobhaigh is mé ag
 seoladh bó
 Tharlaigh domh 'n spéirbhean 'na suí ar a' léana
 'S a fallaing léithe is í lán de chnódhann'

3 D'fhiafair mé daoithe go ciúin 's go céillí
 An nglacfaidh tú póg uaim, a stór mo chroí?
 D'fhoscail sí a béilín 'gus labhair sí Béarla
 Sé dúirt sí: *Pray, sir, and let me be*

4 'S maith an airí ar na buaibh a sanntú
 'Gus bheinnse dá seoladh amuigh sa lá
 Im agus bainne ghil ar theacht an tsamhraidh
 'S mar gheall ar bhólacht a phóstar mná

1 If I could spend my time on a bright hillside
 With nobody near but an Irish colleen
 I would be courting her with fond embraces
 And wouldn't that be a fine way to be

2 Once after rising on a bright and clear morning
 Going through the wood with my mother's cows

 Who should I see there but my darling fairy
 With her gathering of nuts in her outspread shawl

3 I asked her gently and very politely
 My darling, a kiss will you accept from me?
 She answered gently and spoke in English
 And said: Pray, sir, and let me be

4 Isn't it a great thing to have plenty of cattle?
 To drive and herd them every day
 Fresh milk and butter all through the summer
 And even get husbands for many's the maid

29 CHUAIGH ME 'NA ROSANN
I WENT TO VISIT THE ROSSES

Chuaigh mé 'na Ros-ann ar cuairt

Gur bhreath-naigh mé uaim an spéir

Is thart fá na h-oil-eáin ó thuaidh

Mar ei-lit ag-us cú 'na diaidh

1 Chuaigh mé 'na Rosann ar cuairt
Gur bhreathnaigh mé uaim an spéir
Is thart fá na h-oileáin ó thuaidh
Mar eilit agus cú 'na diaidh

2 Sé dúirt gach duine fá'n chuan
Nuair a tharlaigh mé anuas fá'n chéidh
Nach maith a aithním ar do ghruaim
Gur fear thú a bhfuil a' tóir 'do dhiaidh

3 Casadh dom a' cailín deas óg
Ach má casadh 'sí a labhair go géar
Má's fear thú a bhain do mhnaoi óig
Cha mholaim rómhór do *thrade* (cheird)

4 Chonnaic mé fear ar thír mór
'S é ag siúl gan bhróg inné
Is dóigh liom gur thusa 'n fear óg
'S go bhfuil ort an tóir 'do dhiaidh

5 D'fhreagair mé 'n ainnir dheas óg
Ghlac sí go mór mo scéal
Stad de do mhagadh níos mó
Nó ní duine den tseort sin mé

6 Ach suigh thus' anall 'e mo chóir
Is bí thus' ar aon nós liom féin
Nó rachaidh mé os coinne do shrón'
Amach go tír mór le léim

7 Thit muid i dtuirse 's i mbrón
Is d'fhiafraigh an óig-bhean díom
Cá bhfuigheas muid gloine le h-ól
A thógfas an brón d'ár gcroí?

1 I went to visit the Rosses
The sky was all I could find
Chased was I round by the islands
Like a doe with a hound behind

2 The people by the harbour were saying
When I happened to go down by the quay
I can tell by your look of doom
That you are a man being pursued

3 I met with a charming young lady
But she was the one who spoke plain
If you're tied to another young woman
I don't have respect for your trade

4 I saw a man yesterday on the mainland
He was walking without any shoes
I think that you must be that young man
And that you are a man being pursued

5 I answered the charming young lady
And she soon accepted my tale
Please don't make fun of me further
For I'm not like that man at all

6 Come over and sit down beside me
And you behave just like you're me
Or I'll go straight away and I'll leave you
To the mainland with only one leap

7 We fell into sadness and weariness
And the young girl to me she did say
Where can we get some good drink here
That will all our grief take away?

8   Tá teach beag ar leath-taoibh an róid
    Agus coinníonn sé i gcónaí braon
    Gabh thusa 'gus rappail an bord
    'S ní dhíolfaidh do phócaí aon phingin

8   There's a little house down by the roadside
    Where they always keep a drop of good beer
    If you go and rap-tap on the table
    You won't need a penny to spare

9   Tharlaigh muid 'steach i dtoigh 'n óil
    Agus b'fhaiteach go leor mé le suí
    Ar eagla go dtiocfadh an tóir
    Is go mbainfí an óig-bhean díom

9   We happened to enter the tavern
    And I was too shy to sit down
    For fear my pursuers might enter
    And away with the young girl might run

10   Nuair a fuair muid gach ní mar ba chóir
    Is mheas mé gur chóir dúinn suí
    Sé dúirt sí: Bí thus' ag gabháil cheoil
    'S ní dhíolfaidh do phócaí aon phingin

10   When we'd had all that we wanted
    That we could now sit down I did think
    What she said then was: Give us some music
    And you won't have to pay for our drinks

11   Cha rabh mis' i bhfad ag gabháil cheoil
    Gur chruinnigh go leor 'un toigh'
    Achan fhear is a ghloine 'n a dhorn
    Le comhmóradh a thabhairt don dís

11   Before I was long at the music
    A good crowd had soon gathered in
    Each man in his hand held a tankard
    And toasted the pair of us then

12   Bhí biotáilte fairsing go leor
    A rabh beagán dá ól sa tír
    'S dá dtarraingeoinn-se galún Uí Dhomhnaill
    B'fhurast mo scór a dhíol

12   Spirits in plenty were flowing
    Although in the district were scarce
    And though I drew a gallon of Donell's
    It was easy to pay for my share

13   Nuair a lig muid dúinn tuirse is brón
    Sé d'fhiafraigh an óig-bhean díom
    Cá mbíonn tú 'do chónaí sa lá
    Nuair nach gcoinníonn tú cró duit féin?

13   When we're rid of sadness and weariness
    The young girl had a thought in her mind
    Where do you live all the daytime
    Since you haven't a house of your own?

14   Bím-se seal 'dtoigh an óil
    Cha deánaim-se lón don phingin
    A' meid údaidh a shaothraím sa lá
    A chathamh le spórt san oích'

14   I spend much of the day in the tavern
    And none of my money goes far
    All that I earn in the space of a day
    At night spend on sport in the bar

15   Má's fear thú a leanas don ól
    Cha mholaim rómhór do *thrade*
    Nó chan iarrfainn ar dhuine de do sheort-sa
    Toiseacht le buaidhreadh an tsaoil

15   If you are a man fit for drinking
    I do not have respect for your trade
    And I would not ask one of your likeness
    To take on such worldly cares

16   Is fearr dúinn fanacht go fóill
    Go ndeánaidh muid lón don phingin
    Is go rabh againn an t-ór
    Is cuidiú d'ár gcóir aríst

16   We'd better wait for a while now
    Till we have enough money saved
    And when we have plenty of pennies
    We will have help with us again

17   Le fanacht go ndeánaidh muid lón
    Caithfear cuid mhór d'ár saol
    Is fearr dúinn toiseacht go h-óg
    'S beidh cuidiú d'ár gcóir aríst

17   If we wait till we've saved enough money
    We shall have to wait most of our time
    It's better to start out as youngsters
    And then we'll have help down the line

18   Do leithéid char casadh go fóill
    Dom i mbealach ná i ród 'mo thriall
    'S dá mbeinn-se i mBéal-an-Átha Mór
    Gheobhainn cailíní óg' ar phingin

18   I've never met one of your likeness
    If any of the roads that I go
    And only if I were in Ballinamore
    Could I find such a pretty young girl

30 DONALL O MAOLAINE
DONALD O'MULLEN

Ea-dar Cai-seal a-gus Úr-choill a ca-sadh domh an cúi-lín

'Sí a' teacht go ciúin céil-lí fá mo choin-ne sa ród —

Rug mé greim cúl uir-thi a-gus leag mé ar an driúcht í

A-gus d'fhág mé a croí dún-ta ai-ci is í 'sil-eadh na ndeor

1 Eadar Caiseal agus Úr-choill a casadh domh an cúilín
  'S í a' teacht go ciúin céillí fá mo choinne sa ród
  Rug mé greim cúl uirthi agus leag mé ar an driúcht í
  Agus d'fhág mé a croí dúnta aici is í 'sileadh na ndeor

2 O seachtain ón lá sin a casadh domh an páiste
  'S í a' teacht go ciúin céillí fá mo choinne sa ród
  Rug sí greim láimh' orm agus chuir sí romham fáilte
  Caidé mar tá do shláinte agatsa 'óganaigh óig?

3 Seo litir ó m'athair agus beannacht ó mo mháthair
  'S bí a' teacht liom 'na h-áite feasta níos mó
  Gheobhaidh tú na táinte agus maoin-chruth gan áireamh
  Is mise ar láimh leat maidin 'gus neóin

4 O, leoga, a pháiste, ba doiligh liom a rá leat
  Sin athrú nach ndeánfainn ar dhá mhíle bó
  Ach a b'é go bhfuil mé dálta le bliain mhór agus ráithe
  Le níon Sheoin Mhic Daibhid i gConndae Mhuigh Eo

5 O deán thusa a' méid sin is ní miste liom féin é
  Ní folamh 'tá Eirinn nó tá d'athrú le fáil
  Ach gur inis tú do'm bhéal-sa gur mheall tú na céadtaí
  'S go nglacfá mé 'mo léinidh gidh nach folamh atáim

6 'S a Rí Mhóir na páirte dá mbeadh agam páiste
  Caidé dheánfainn 'dhíobháil athara do mo leanbhán óg?
  Mise Dónall Ó Maoláine 's ná ceil ar fhearaibh Fáil mé
  Is gheobhaidh tú ar an tSliabh Bhán mé i gConndae Mhuigh Eo

7 'S ar an bhaile seo tá'n cúilín, sí Máire dheas mhúinte í
  Sí an bruinneal í is uaisle 'á dtáinig ó mhnáibh
  Sí mo shearc í, sí mo rún í, sí m'annsacht 'ach uair í
  Sí an samhradh is an fuacht í eadar Nollaig is Cáisc

1 Between Caiseal and Úrchoill I encountered a maiden
Coming quietly and steadily towards me on the road
And by the hair I caught her and upon the dew I laid her
And I left her there crying with her eyes full of tears

2 O again a week later I met the young child
Coming quietly and steadily towards me on the road
And by the hand she caught me and she welcomed me kindly
And how are you keeping, young man of my heart?

3 Here's a letter from my father and a blessing from my mother
We'll be together for ever if you'll come now with me
Your herds will be plentiful, your wealth will be bountiful
Every morning and evening I will be by your side

4 O indeed, my dear child, I'm afraid I must tell you
That I cannot do this, not for two thousand cows
For I've already been promised for a full year and season
To John Davidson's daughter in the County Mayo

5 O take yourself away off and don't think I'm bothered
For Ireland's not deserted, I'll soon find one more
You told me yourself of the hundreds you'd beguiled
That you'd take me in my nightshirt though I'm far from poor

6 O Almighty King of Heaven, if only I'd a child
Who would I have to father it alone?
I'm Donald O'Mullen, don't ever deny it
You will find me on Slieve Bán in the County Mayo

7 In this town there's a maiden, she's quiet and she's gentle
She the most noble lady of any living being
She's my darling, my sweetheart, and my dear one forever
She's both summer and winter, from Christmas to Spring

31 DONALL OG
YOUNG DONALD.

A Dhó-naill Óig, má théir thar far-rai-ge

Beir mé féin leat 's ná deán dom dear-(a)-mad

Beidh ag-at féi-rín lá aon-aigh 'gus mar——(a)-gaidh

Ag-us níon Rí Gréi——ge mar chéi-le lea-pa 'gat

1 A Dhónaill Óig, má théir thar farraige
Beir mé féin leat 's ná deán dom dear(a)mad
Beidh agat féirín lá aonaigh 'gus mar(a)gaidh
Agus níon Rí Gréige mar chéile leapa 'gat

2 Gheall tú dom-sa ní nach dearn tú
Fáinne óir a chur ar 'ach méar domh

Seisreach óir fána hanlaí airgid
Agus muileann siúchra ar 'ach sruth in Éirinn

3 B'fhurast dom aithne nach tú bhí i ndán dom
Chuir tú amach mé oíche na báistí
Bhain truisle dom-sa ag giall na bearnadh
Char dhúirt tú Dia liom 's char chraith tú lámh
liom

4 Bhain tú soir 'gus bhain tú siar dom
Bhain tú romham is bhain tú mo dhiaidh dom
Bhain tú 'n ghealach is bhain tú an ghrian dom
'S is ró-mhór m'eagla gur bhain tú Dia dom

1 Young Donald, mine, if you should go away
Then take me too, don't leave me here to wait
A gift I'll give at the fair on market day
And the Greek king's daughter with you to stay

2 The promise made you never did uphold
That on every finger you would place a ring of
gold
A golden plough with shafts of bright silver
On every Irish stream to stand a sugar-mill

3 'Twas soon I saw that you were not my maid
You sent me out at night in all the rain
I almost tumbled on entering the land
Not even: Bless you, did you say or shake my
hand

4 From me you've stolen East and West likewise
You took my past and my future besides
The sun and moon, you've taken them away
To take my God from me I'm most afraid

32 AN DRAIGHNEAN DONN
THE BLACKTHORN TREE

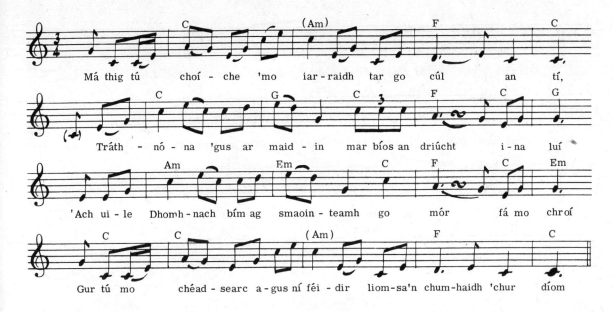

Má thig tú choí - che 'mo iar - raidh tar go cúl an tí,

Tráth - nó - na 'gus ar maid - in mar bíos an driúcht i - na luí

'Ach ui - le Dhomh - nach bím ag smaoin - teamh go mór fá mo chroí

Gur tú mo chéad - searc a - gus ní féi - dir liom-sa'n chum-haidh 'chur díom

1 Má thig tú choíche 'mo iarraidh tar go cúl an tí

Tráthnóna 'gus ar maidin mar bíos an driúcht ina luí

'Ach uile Dhomhnach bím ag smaointeamh go mór fá mo chroí

Gur tú mo chéad-searc agus ní féidir liomsa 'n chumhaidh 'chur díom

2 Fear gan chéill a bheadh ag dréim leis an chaor 'bheadh ard

Is caor íseal lena thaoibh air a leagfadh sé lámh

Gidh gurb ard an crann caorthainn bíonn sé searbh ina bharr

'Gus fásfaidh sméara 's bláth sugh craobh ar an chrann is ísle bláth

3 Síleann gach óigbhean gur leo féin mé nuair a ólaim lionn

Nuair a shuím síos bím ag smuainteamh ar a comhrá liom

Com is míne fá dhó ná'n síoda 'tá ar Shliabh Uí Fhloinn

'Gus tá mo ghrá-sa mar bhláth na n-áirní ar an Draighneán Donn

1 If you ever come to look for me, come around to the backyard door

Either in the night or in the morning, while the dew is still lying o'er

Every Sunday I remind myself and remember more and more

That you are my first and only love and it makes me feel sore

2 Only a fool would want the berry from the top of a lofty tree

While all the time beside them is a low one just in reach

Though the rowan tree is highest, its topmost berries are not sweet

While raspberries and strawberries bloom on the lowest trees

3 All the girls they think I'm theirs when I drink some ale and beer

When I sit down I'm thinking it's her words I like to hear

Her waist is twice as lovely as the silk of Slieve Eileen

And my love is like the sloe flower upon the blackthorn tree

33 EIRIGH 'S CUIR ORT DO CHUID EADAIGH
ARISE AND PUT ON YOUR CLOTHES

1 Eirigh 's cuir ort do chuid éadaigh
Go mbearraidh mé féin do chúl
Go dté muid 'soir easpag na hÉirne
Go gceangaltar mé 'gus tú
Bhí grá 's cion agam féin ort
A chuid 'en tsaol éalaigh liom
'S nach duine dona gan chéill
A scarfadh ó chéile sinn

2 Cuirimse croí ar a' phósadh
'S ar bhuachaillí óga an tsaoil
Nárbh fhearr dófa cailín deas óg acu
Ná bean agus puntaí léi
Oíche mhór fhada sa gheimhreadh
Nár dheas bheith 'súgradh léi
'Bhfarras a' chailleach 'srannfaí
'S í 'tarraingt a' plaincead léi

3 Dé Máirt a rinneadh mo chleamhnas
Mo chreach 's m'amhgar géar
Ghlac mise comhairle mo mhuintir
'S pairt mhór do m'aimhleas é
Pósadh mise gan amhras
Ar shamhailt do mhnaoi gan scéimh
'S níl aon chailín dá gcasfaí sa ghleann damh
Nach rachainn 'un cainte léi

1 Arise an' go 'n' put on your clothes
That I myself may trim your hair
To the Bishop of Erne, we'll go before him
That you and I may become a pair
I have got a love but I long for you
Fly away with me, my pride and joy
Only a fool and a senseless person
Would try to separate us, girl from boy

2 I've put my heart upon our marriage
And on all the young men of the world
For wouldn't a young girl be better for them
Than a woman with plenty of gold
On one of those long nights in winter
'Twould be nice to be hugging her tight
Than down beside some snoring old hag
Pulling the blankets around at night

3 Tuesday was the day that we married
I wished it had not come so soon
From my own people I'd taken advice
For that was what caused my undoing
Though true in the end I was married
To a woman with not even a smile
And there wasn't a girl through the valley
With whom I would not chat awhile

90

4 Nuair a théimse 'un Aifrinn Dé Domhnaigh
'Sé fhiafraíos gach óigfhear daom
'Chormaic, an bhfuil tusa pósta?
Ná an airíonn tú an óige 'choích'?
'Sé abraim is deirim féin leofa
Go n'aireochainn go mór fa-raor
'S an méid agaibh atá gan pósadh
Gur agaibh atá spórt an tsaoil

5 Ach gheobhaidh mé hata 'gus bróga
Agus éireochaidh mé óg arais
Agus rachaidh mé amach go Gleann Domhain
Sin an áit a bhfuil mórán ban
Go bhfaghaidh mé cailín deas óg ann
A shiúlas a' ród go glan
'S nárbh fhearr liomsa leis na mná móra
Ná cailleach Ghleann Domhain 's a ba

4 When to Mass I go on a Sunday
The young men to me they will say
Cormack, is it true that you're married
D'you feel your youth slipped away?
I speak and it's this that I tell them
O indeed, it is true what I say
And all those among you that didn't get wed
You can sport through the world as you may

5 But I'll get a hat and a pair of boots
And I will get back my youth again
And I will go down to Glendowan
Where women in plenty do reign
Till I find the young girl that will suit me just right
Who'll neatly walk up country roads
And would that I'd rather have all the big girls
Than Glendowan's old hag and her cows

34 EIRIGH SUAS A STOIRIN
RISE UP, MY DARLING

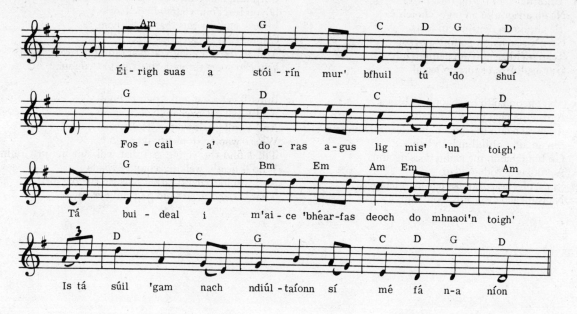

Éi- righ suas a stói-rín mur' bfhuil tú 'do shuí

Fos- cail a' do- ras a-gus lig mis' 'un toigh'

Tá bui- deal i m'ai- ce 'bhéar-fas deoch do mhnaoi'n toigh'

Is tá súil 'gam nach ndiúl-taíonn sí mé fá n-a níon

1 Éirigh suas a stóirín, mur' bfhuil tú 'do shuí
Foscail a' doras agus lig mis' 'un toigh'
Tá buideal i m' aice 'bhéarfas deoch do mhnaoi'n toigh'

Is tá súil 'gam nach ndiúltaíonn sí mé fá n-a níon

2 Nuair a éirím 'mach ar maidin agus dhearcaim uaim siar
'Gus dhearcaim ar a' bhail' úd a bhfuil agam le ghabháil ann
Titeann na deora ina sróite liom síos
Agus nímse míle osna bíos cosúil le cumhaidh

3 I ngleanntán na coilleadh beothorthaí is lag brónach a bím
O Dhomhnach go Domhnach 's mé ag cathamh mo shaoil
Mé a' feitheamh 'ach tráthnóna cé rachadh 'n ród nó thiocfadh 'un tí
Is gan aon ní ar a' domhan mhór a thógfadh mo chroí

4 Nach aoibhinn don éanlaith a éiríos gach lá
'S a luíos aríst ar an aonchraoibh amháin?
Ní h-é sin domh féin 's do mo chéad mhíle grá

Is i bhfad i bhfad ó chéile bíos ár n-éirí gach lá

1 Rise up, my darling, if you're still in bed lying
Open the door that I might come and recline
By my side I've a bottle that I've brought for
your mother
And I hope she'll allow it that you shall be mine

2 When I rise in the morning and look o'er the path-way
And I look at the place where I'll spend the long day

The tears fall in streams down my two cheeks like rain
And many's the time that I sigh for that maid

3 In the thick wooded glen I live there in sorrow

From Sunday to Sunday spending time on my own

The coming and going I watch o'er the road-way

And nothing in this wide world will lift up my load

4 It's great for the birds that rise up every morning
And roost with each other on the same bush or spray
But that's not how it is for both me and my true-
love
For it's far from each other that we rise every day

35 GARDAI 'N RI
THE KING'S OWN GUARDS

1 Rachaidh mise suas le Gárdaí 'n Rí
  Agus bhéarfaidh mis' anuas ar láimh liom í
  Nach mise chuirfeadh cluain ar a báin-chnios mín
  Agus bhéarfaidh mé go Tuaifín í grá mo chroí
  Tógaigí suas ar ghruaidh-mhín an iomair' í
  Lasadh ina gruaidh agus buaidh gach duine léi
  'Ghiolla 'tá gan gruaim a chuirfeadh cluain ar an iomataí
  Nach é mo scéal truaighe mar luaidheadh mise leat

1 I will go away on up there with the King's Own Guards
  I'll return with her in hand and down again we'll march
  I'll praise her beauty highly with no talk of war
  And a visit made to Tuaifín will be my love's reward
  Lift her high upon the shoulders of the soldiers in the park
  With the blushes shining on her cheeks she captures every
  O perfect one, who does possess, so many of the arts [heart
  What a pity that I trusted you and gave to you my heart ➤

93

2 Níl mise tinn agus níl mé slán
Is ró-mhór m'osna is ní fhéadaim a rá

Nuair a smuaintím ar an uair úd a bhí mé is tú, 'ghrá

Guala ar ghualainn agus lámh ar láimh

3 Galar claoite 'choíche 'n grá

'S mairg ar a mbíonn sé oíche ná lá
Gidh gur cruaidh 'n rud a' snaidhm 's nach scaoiltear é
go bráth
O is, a chomrádaí díleas, go dté tú slán

2 I can say that I'm not ill and yet I am not well
And, though I'm sighing far too much, I know I cannot
tell
When I think, dear love, upon the times when first in
love we fell
When side by side and hand in hand, together with my
girl

3 O love it is a conquering disease that makes us weep and
wail
O pity all its sufferers who nights and days turn pale
Though the true-love's knot is very hard it never will
decay
My dearest friend, we wish you health and safety on
your way

36 IN AIMSIR BHAINT AN FHEIR
AT THE CUTTING OF THE HAY

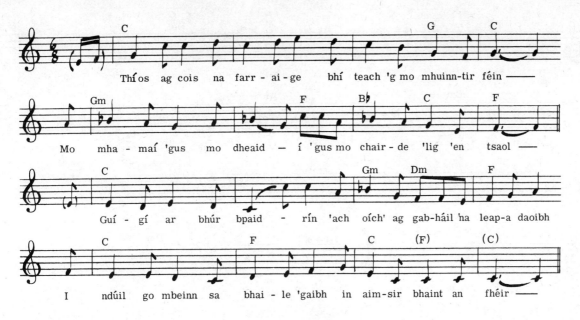

1 Thíos ag cois na farraige bhí teach 'g mo mhuinntir féin

Mo mhamaí 'gus mo dheaidí 'gus mo chairde 'lig 'en tsaol

Guígí ar bhúr bpaidrín 'ach oích' ag gabháil 'na leapa daoibh

I ndúil go mbeinn sa bhaile 'gaibh in aimsir bhaint an fhéir

2 A chailíní is a chailíní, nach trua libh mo scéal
Mise gabháil thar farraige 's gan cead a philleadh 'e choích'

3 Rachaidh mé go h-Albain 's ní phillfidh mé go h-éag
Tiocfaidh mé 'na bhaile agus beidh mé brúite tinn

1 It's down beside the sea I'd be, where all my people dwell

My mother and my father too and all my friends as well

When you're going into your bed at night a prayer for me do say

That home I'll be amongst my friends for the cutting of the hay

2 Come all you girls of every age O pity my sad plight
That I should now be going abroad with no return in sight

3 Then off to Scotland I will go and there I must remain
And when I do return again I will be bruised with pain

37 IS FADA O BHAILE A D'AITHNEOINN
IT'S FAR FROM HOME I'D KNOW YOU

1 Is fad' ó bhaile a d'aithneoinn féin do shiúl
Do chúl dubh daite faoi hata glan éadrom úr
Bhíodh blas na meala 'ach aon mhaidin ar phóig mo
rún
Roimhe Shamhain gan amhras beidh faire orm féin
le cumhaidh

2 Nuair a éirím ar maidin is théim go cúl an toigh'
Is amharcaim le fada ar an taoibh úd a bhfeicinn mo
mhian
Ach 'nois tá mé réidh leis go ndeántar dom cónair
chaol
Is go bhfásann an neantóg 's an féar glas fríd lár mo
chroí

3 A shúil is glaise ná'n coiscreach nuair is úire a bláth
Scéal cinnte go gcaoinfinn gan staonadh dá gcluinfinn
do dháil
Feara Éireann 's dá mbeadh siad cruinn ar aon chnoc
amháin
A ghrá, dá bhféadfainn, 's tú féin 'bheadh agam ar
láimh

4 Tabhair mo mhallacht do d'athair 's do do mháthair
féin
Nach dtug beagán tuigse duit-se le mo lámh a léamh
Go moch ar maidin a chuirfinnse chugat brí mo scéil
Fá mo leithscéal a ghlacadh go gcasfaí duit in uaigneas
mé

1 It's far from home I'd know you by your walk
Your dark head of hair beneath a clean new hat
The taste of honey every morning on your kiss

By Hallowe'en it's certain I'll be dying from grief

2 When I arise each morning and behind the house I go
I look with longing where my true-love used to stroll

I'm finished now forever till in my narrow grave laid
low
Till through my heart the nettles and grasses green
do grow

3 O eye more green than grass or reed that's fresh
in growth
I'd cry unceasing if I heard you were betrothed

If all the men in Ireland were gathered on one hill

'Tis you, my dear, from choice your hand
I would choose still

4 To your father and your mother, curses on them both

Not teaching you to read the letters that I wrote
Early in the morn I'd send the meaning of my moan
Excusing my long absence till we meet again alone

38 IS IOMAIDH COISCEIM FADA
MANY'S A LONG FOOTSTEP

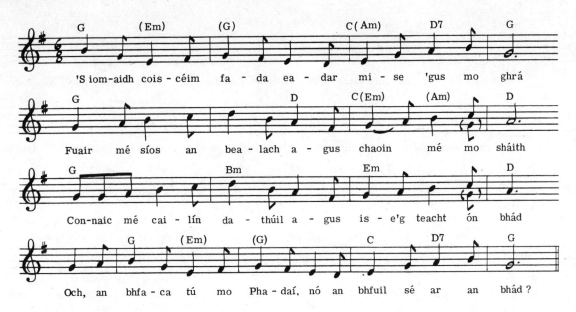

'S iom-aidh cois-céim fa - da ea - dar mi - se 'gus mo ghrá

Fuair mé síos an bea - lach a - gus chaoin mé mo sháith

Con-naic mé cai - lín da - thúil a - gus is - e'g teacht ón bhád

Och, an bhfa - ca tú mo Pha - daí, nó an bhfuil sé ar an bhád?

1 'S iomaidh coiscéim fada eadar mise 'gus mo ghrá
Fuair mé síos an bealach agus chaoin mé mo sháith

Connaic mé cailín dathúil agus ise 'g teacht ón bhád

Och, an bhfaca tú mo Phadaí nó an bhfuil sé ar an bhád?

2 'S iomaidh coiscéim fada eadar mise 'gus mo ghrá
Labhair an cailín dathúil liom: Tá Padaí ar an bhád
'S iomaidh cailín deas, monuar, a tífidh sé ar an bhád
O, is mé bhí cúrtha cráite nuair a mhoithigh mé mo sháith

3 'S iomaidh coiscéim fada eadar mise 'gus mo ghrá
Tháinig mé 'na bhaile nó ní rabh sé ar an bhád

Shuigh mé cois na tineadh agus chaoin mé mo sháith

O, is mairg gan mé in Albain ná'n Sasain go bráth

1 Many's a long footstep lies between my love and I
It's down the road I went alone and there my fill did cry
'Twas there I met a lovely girl just coming from the boat
O did you see my Paddy there or is my love afloat?

2 Many's a long footstep lies between my love and I
Your Paddy he is on the boat, the girl I met replied
It's many a pretty girl, alas, upon the boat he'll see
O I was broken-hearted when all this was clear to me

3 Many's a long footstep lies between my love and me
So I returned back home for him on the boat I could not see
I sat down beside the peat fire and there I wept and cried
O I wish I were in Scotland now or in England till I die

97

39 MA THEID TU 'UN AONAIGH
WHEN YOU GO TO THE FAIR

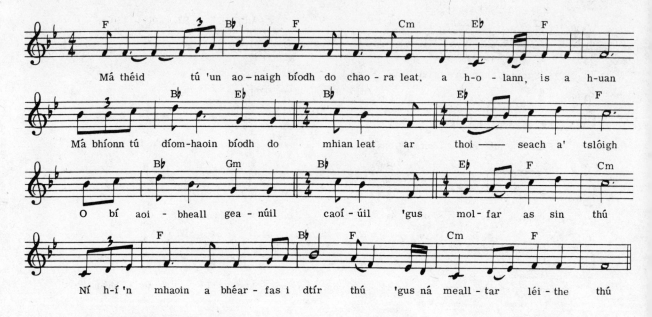

Má théid tú 'un ao-naigh bíodh do chao-ra leat, a h-o-lann, is a h-uan

Má bhíonn tú díom-haoin bíodh do mhian leat ar thoi——seach a' tslóigh

O bí aoi-bheall gea-núil caoí-úil 'gus mol-far as sin thú

Ní h-í 'n mhaoin a bhéar-fas i dtír thú 'gus ná meall-tar léi-the thú

1 Má théid tú 'un aonaigh bíodh do chaora leat, a
h-olann, is a h-uan
Má bhíonn tú díomhaoin bíodh do mhian leat ar
thoiseach a' tslóigh
O bí aoibheall geanúil caoíúil 'gus molfar as sin thú

Ní h-í 'n mhaoin a bhéarfas i dtír thú 'gus ná
mealltar léithe thú

2 Oró annsacht cérbh annsa leat fear eil' agat ná mé

'S gur tú 'n planta beag a shanntaigh mé i dtoiseach
mo ré
Thug mé *fancy* duit gan amhras mar bhí mé óg gan
chéill
'S focal cainnte ná rabh insa chionn údaí a mholfadh
duit ach mé

3 Teacht an earraigh ceannóchad talamh's dheánfad
fárus beag domh féin
'S beidh mo mhuinntir a shíormholadh domh gur
críonn' a rinn mis' é
Níl ach moladh ar mhná'n domhain agus beidh mo
mhian agam féin
Ní h-í an mhaoin atá mé a shanntú, ach a cáilíocht
'sa méin

4 A cheád-searc, sa chéad searc cá gcodlann tú san
oích'
Nó nach léir duit na saighde atá a' polladh in mo
chroí
Tá ní éigin a' mo bhuaradh, 's an fhearthainn a' mo
chloí
Agus mé 'g éisteacht le h-éanacha na coilleadh 'g
gabháil a luí

1 When you go to the fair, take your sheep with you,
along with her wool and her lamb
If you're single have your sweetheart too, in the
forefront of the van
Be always pleasant and jolly, for that you will get
praise
For it's not the riches that matter most, don't think
along those ways

2 O darling one, though dearer to you is some other
man than me
You're the only one I treasure out of all the girls
I've seen
I fell for you completely when I was weak and young

Don't heed those people praising you unless it's
from my tongue

3 Next spring I'll buy some farmland and for myself
a house I'll build
My parents they'll be praising me for being so very
skilled
Praise all the girls in all the world and I will have
my choice
It's not her riches that I crave but her looks and
mindful voice

4 O my true love, O my true love, at night where do
you rest?
O can't you see the arrows that come piercing
through my breast?
I'm troubled now in every way and the rain makes
me depressed
And I'm listening to the woodland birds as they fly
back to their nests

40 MAIRE CHONNACHT AGUS SEAMUS O DONAILL
CONNAUGHT MARY AND JAMES O'DONNELL

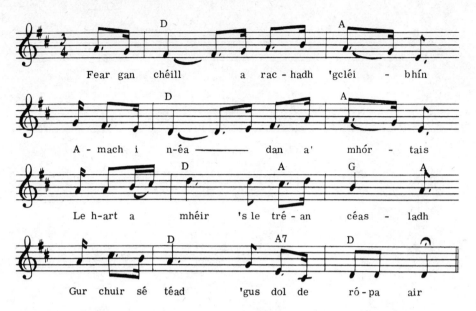

Fear gan chéill a rac-hadh 'gcléi - bhín

A - mach i n-éa — dan a' mhór - tais

Le h-art a mhéir 's le tré - an céas - ladh

Gur chuir sé téad 'gus dol de ró - pa air

1 Fear gan chéill a rachadh 'gcléibhín
Amach i n-éadan a' mhórtais
Le h-art a mhéir 's le tréan céasladh
Gur chuir sé téad 'gus dol de rópa air

1 Only a fool would go out in a sieve
Out in the teeth of a roaring gale
And with skilled hands and strong rowing
Succeed in getting a rowlock rope round

2 Tharraing 'na dhiaidh é go bun a' mhéile
'S cá bhfuil a' té a bheadh 'na dheoidh air
Gan a thabhairt do aoinneach 'ár beathaíodh 'n
Nár fhliuch a ladhar ariamh san ócáid?   [Éirinn

2 To the edge of the sand-bank he pulled it after
And who is there who'd blame him for that
For not giving it to anyone born in Ireland
Who never his hands that time got wet?

3 Más lag nó láidir a' chaill a' t-adhmad
Nach maith an áit a chur sa tséipeal
A chrochadh i n-áirde os coinn' An Ardrí
Le bheith 'guí go bráth ar son na gcréatúr

3 Whether the loss of the wood was great or not
Isn't the chapel the right place
Hung up above the High King's altar
For ever to pray for the sake of the creatures

4 Dearc, a Mháire, ar na fir a fágadh
'S gan lucht a dtarrthála i nÉirinn
Nach gol go cráite ba chóir a dheánamh
'S chan bheith 'gáirí fán éadáil?

4 Look, Mary, on the men who were left there
With no one in Ireland to save them
Should we not be bitterly crying
And not about their loss be laughing?

5 Dá mbeifeá i nArainn taobh 'stuigh de dhá bhliain
Tífeá adhmad saor go leor ann
Muic-fheoil shásta 's síoda Spáinneach
'S ba bheag a b'fhearrde do thír mór é

5 If you were to go to Aran within two years
You would see plenty of cheap timber there
Spanish silk and satisfying bacon
Though little good it would do on the mainland

6 Sé dúirt Naomh Pádraig gur mhíle b'fhearr dúinn
Ag tógáil grágáin fríd a' mhóinidh
Ná a' tógáil adhmad le h-ordú báillidh
'S a chur in Teampall na Róimhe

6 Saint Patrick said 'twas a thousand times better
For us to drag tree-stumps through the bog-lands
Than to lift wood by bailiff's orders
Putting it into the old church of Rome

41 NION A' BHAOILLIGH
O'BOYLE'S DAUGHTER

Bhí mé oí - che taoibh 'stigh Fhéil' Brí - de

Ar fai - re thíos ar a' Mhul - lach Mhór

'Gus thar-laigh naí domh a dtug mé gnaoi daoi

Mar bhí sí caoí - úil lách á - lainn óg

Sí go cinn - te a mhea - raigh m'in - tinn

'Gus Liaigh na bhFiann ó ní leigheas - fadh mé

'Gus tá mo chroí 'stigh ina mhí - le pío - sa

Mar nach bhfaighim cead sí-neadh le n-a brol-lach glé - gheal

1 Bhí mé oíche taoibh 'stigh Fhéil' Bríde
   Ar faire thíos ar a' Mhullach Mhór
   'Gus tharlaigh naí domh a dtug mé gnaoi daoi
   Mar bhí sí caoíúil lách álainn óg
   Sí go cinnte a mhearaigh m'intinn
   'Gus Liaigh na bhFiann ó ní leigheasfadh mé
   'Gus tá mo chroí 'stigh ina mhíle píosa
   Mar nach bhfaighim cead síneadh le n-a brollach
                                        glé-gheal

2 A chailín donn deas a chuaidh i gcontabhairt
   Druid anall liom agus tabhair domh póg
   Nó is leat-s' a shiúlfainn cnoic is gleanntáin
   'S go Baile an Teampaill 'á mbíodh sé romhainn
   Ach anois ó tá mise cúrtha cráite
   'S gur lig mé páirt de mo rún le gaoith
   A Rí atá i bParrthas, deán domh fárus
   I ngleanntán álainn le n-a taoibh

3 Is fada an lá breá ó thug mé grá duit
   Is mé 'mo pháiste bheag óg gan chéill
   'S dá mbíodh mo mhuintir uilig i bhfeirg liom
   Nár chuma liom-sa, a mhíle stór?
   O a mhíle grá, tá cách a rá liom
   Gur den ghrá ort a gheobhaidh mé bás
   Is níl a'n lá margaidh 'á mbeidh sna Gearailtigh
   Nach mbeidh cúl feamainneach is mis' ag ól

1 One evening near St Bridget's feast-day
   I went to a wake down in Mullaghmore
   I fell in love with a young girl I met there
   She was so gentle my heart she stole
   It was she who set my mind a-straying
   And the cure of the Fianna can't give me rest
   My heart is broken in a thousand pieces
   Since I can't recline on her snow-white breast

2 O dark-haired darling who braved such danger
   Come over closer and a kiss give me
   With you I'd walk o'er hills and valleys
   To Ballintemple if that could be
   But since I'm troubled and so tormented
   And have made known to you just what's in my mind
   O King of Heaven, make me a dwelling
   In a beautiful glen with her alongside

3 It's a long fine day since first we were lovers
   And I was only just a senseless child
   And if all my people were angry with me
   What shall I care if with you I bide
   O my dearest, they all do tell me
   That from my love for you I shall surely die
   And not a market-day I'll be in Gearailtigh
   I'll not be drinking with my long-haired bride

42 AN t-OILEAN UR
THE NEW-FOUND ISLAND

1 Rinne mé smuainteamh in m'intinn is lean mé dó go cinnte
   Go rachainn ó mo mhuintir anonn 'un Oileáin Úir
   Tá mé 'g iarraidh impí ar an Ard-Rí 'tá 's mo chionn-sa
   Mo shábháil ar gach dáinséar go gcríochnaí mé mo shiúl

2 Shiúl mé fiche míle 's níor casadh orm Críostaí
   Capall, bó, ná caora dheánfadh inghilt ar an fhéar
   Ach coillte dlúth' is gleanntáin agus búirtheach beithidhigh allta
   Fir is mná gan toint' orthu a chasfainn fá mo mhéar

3 Tharlaigh 'steach i dtoigh mé is casadh orm daoiní
   D'fhiafraigh siad cárbh as mé nó'n tír 'nár tógadh mé
   Labhair mé leof' i mBéarla gur tógadh mé in Éirinn
   Láimh le Loch Eirne i gCoillidh Lios na bhFraoch

4 Bhí cailleach insa chlúdaigh is í ina suí go súgach
   D'éirigh sí go lúfar agus chraith sí liom lámh
   Sé d'bheatha fear do thíre ar' bhfaca mé de dhaoiní
   Nár tógadh mis' in Éirinn i mBaile Lios Béal Atha

5 Nuair a chonnaic mé na daoiní is ansin a rinne mé smaointe
   Gur méanar dá mbeinn in Éirinn 's mé sínte faoi chlár
   Nó sin an áit a bhfuighfinn a' t-aos óg bheadh laghach aoibhinn
   A chaithfeadh liom an oíche 'gus páirt mhór den lá

1 In my mind I made a plan and followed it complete
  To go and leave my people and travel to Amerikay
  The great high King above me, on him I'll try and entreat
  To protect me from all dangers, till I come home again

2 Twenty miles or more I walked, no passing Christian saw
  Neither horse, nor cow, nor sheep did I find grazing there
  Through thick woods and valleys, midst wild beasts that roar
  Where men and women I saw there with not one stitch to wear

3 Into one house I chanced to go, and met some people there
  They asked where I came from, and where I had been reared
  In English I did speak to them, saying in Ireland was I born
  'Twas in the wood of Lisnavree, quite close to fair Lough Erne

4 I saw an old lady in the corner, sitting quietly at her ease
  To her feet she quickly tumbled, and grasped me by the hand
  Of all the people I have met, you're to me most welcome here
  From Ireland I have also come, Lisbellaw was my home town

5 When I saw those people there, 'twas then my thoughts began
  O to be in Ireland, when I do pass away
  For that's the place to find young people who are generous to a man
  Who'd spend the time of night with me and a great part of the day

43 'S ORO LONDUBH BUI
O MY BLACKBIRD GAY

Bhí mé lá breá 'gab-háil an bót-thar 'S ó-ró lon-dubh buí —
Ca-sadh 'n gru-a-gach éa-drom óg dom 'S ó-ró grá mo chroí —

1 Bhí mé lá breá 'gabháil an bóthar
  'S óró londubh buí
  Casadh 'n gruagach éadrom óg dom
  'S óró grá mo chroí

2 D'fhiafraigh sé dom-s' ar níon dom an óig-bhean
  Dúirt mé féin gurbh í mo bhean phóst' í

3 D'iarr sé iasacht bliain nó dhó orm

  Cha deánaim sin ach dheánfaidh mé 'n cóir leat

4 Gabh thusa 'n t-ísleacht 's rachaidh mise an t-ardán
  Cé bith againn a leanfas sí bíodh sí go deo aige

5 Chuaigh seisean a' t-ísleacht 's chuaigh mise 'n t-ardán
  Lean sí 'n gruagach, 's aige bhí an óige

6 D'imigh sí uaim ar feadh trí ráithe
  Tháinig sí chugam, Máire gan náire

7 D'fhiafraigh sí dom-sa caidé mar bhí 'n tsláinte
  Mar is olc le mo charaid 's mar is maith le mo
                                    namhaid

8 Caidé dheánfá thusa dá bhfuighinn-se bás uait?
  O, chuirfinn síos i gcónair faoi chlár thú

9 Nuair a chuala mise na briathra breátha
  Luigh mé siar agus rinne mé an bás úd

10 Chuaigh beirt 'na coilleadh fá dhéin an adhmaid
   Leath-mhaide cuilinn is leath-mhaide fearna

11 Chuir sí síos i gcónair chaol mé
   In gcéad slata den tsacadh ba ghránna

1 Down the road I went, the sun was shining brightly
  O my blackbird gay
  Met a fine young man, he was stepping lightly
  O my heart, my joy

2 And he said to me: Is this girl your daughter?
  She's my wedded wife, this I quickly answered

3 For a year or two, d'you think that you could
                                    lend her?
  That I cannot do, but a chance I'll give you

4 Down the low road go, I will take the steeper
  Whichever one she takes, forever he may keep her

5 He went down the low, I went down the high one
  She did follow him because he was the younger

6 Nine months of the year she from home did stay
  Home again she came, shameless Mary

7 Then she asked me this: How was my health faring?
  As my friends dislike, for my friends quite well,
                                    thanks

8 Now what would you do, if on you I snuffed it?
  I'd put you underground in a sealed coffin

9 Fine words such as these coming from my wifie
  I sat back and took my ease, made as if I'd snuffed it

10 Two men sent for wood, down into the forest
   Half a load of alders, half a load of holly

11 She buried me down below, in a narrow coffin
   A hundred yards of shroud, made of filthy sacking

12 Tógaigí suas ar mur nguailnibh go h-ard é
   Is caithigí sa pholl is deise don tsráid é

13 Nuair a mhoithigh mé féin na briathra gránna
   D'éirigh mé suas go lúfar láidir

14 Fan! Fan! Ligigí síos mé
   Go n-insidh mé scéal beag eil' ar na mná daoibh

15 Is minic a chuaigh bó mhaith thaire 'n teorainn

   Is phill sí aríst sa dóigh a ba chóir daoithe

16 Ach 'a b'é gur bean a bhí in mo mháithrín
   D'inseoinn scéal beag eil' ar na mná daoibh

17 Scéal beag inniu is scéal beag amárach
   Is scéal beag eil' 'ach aon lá go cionn ráithe

12 Lift the old boy high, up upon your shoulders
   Throw him out the yard, in the handiest hollows

13 When I heard her saying words so very ugly
   I rose up from the dead very strong and sturdy

14 Wait, wait, put me down, let me from my coffin
   I'll tell to you a tale, all about the women

15 Many's the time I've known good cows cross the
                                              border
   And come back again in just the way they ought to

16 A woman such as that was my own dear mother
   Women's tales I'll tell, all about each other

17 A story for today and another for tomorrow
   A tale for every day for another quarter

44 SEAMUS MAC MURCHAIDH
JAMES MC MURROUGH

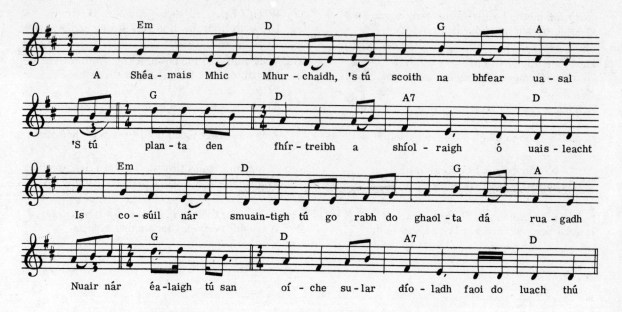

A Shéa - mais Mhic Mhur - chaidh, 's tú scoith na bhfear ua - sal
'S tú plan - ta den fhír - treibh a shíol - raigh ó uais - leacht
Is co - súil nár smuain - tigh tú go rabh do ghaol - ta dá rua - gadh
Nuair nár éa - laigh tú san oí - che su - lar dío - ladh faoi do luach thú

1 A Shéamais Mhic Mhurchaidh, 's tú scoith na bhfear uasal
   'S tú planta den fhír-treibh a shíolraigh ó uaisleacht
   Is cosúil nár smuaintigh tú go rabh do ghaolta dá ruagadh
   Nuair nár éalaigh tú san oíche sular díoladh faoi do luach thú

2 Thíos i lag an tsean-toigh 'tá an tsean-chailleach ghruama
   A d'údaraigh an fheall agus fuair faill lena dheánamh
   Char thuig sí mo chanúint is cha chanfainn léi Béarla
   Ach m'annsacht an bhean dubh atá i ngleanntán an tsléibhe

3 Is trua gan mé 'mo fhraochóig ar thaoibh mhalaidh shléibhe
   Nó mar ghas beag den raithnigh faoi loinnir na gréine
   Nó 'mo lon dubh is mo chionn liom i gCoillidh Dhún Réimhe
   Nó dallann na ballaí mé 'tá ag dalladh na spéire

4 Is trua nach b'é cogadh is a cúrsa 'gabháil i gcampaí
   'Gus Séamas Mhac Murchaidh i dtús air mar cheannphort
   Sé nach dtabharfadh urraim do bhodach an Bhéarla
   Ach sé bhéarfadh an urraim do lucht siúlta na hEireann

5 A Mháire mhín mhodhúil, a d'ordaigh don bhás mé
   Triall chuig mo thórramh agus cóirigh faoi chlár mé
   Dá mba rogha leat mo phósadh nár chóra é ná ar tharlaigh?
   Agus Rí geal na Gloíre go bhfóiridh orm an tráth seo

6 Tiocfaidh cóiste tréan láidir as Ard Macha fá mo choinne
   Agus sluaighte á ghárdáil an Márta seo chugainn
   Beidh claidheamh in gach láimh leo gan trácht ar na gunnaí
   Is gur in íochtar na sráide 'tá an bás fá mo choinne

7 Triallfaidh mo thórramh tráthnóna Dé hAoine
   Nó maidin Dé Domhnaigh má's mian liom fríd na bóithre
   Tiocfaidh Neilidh agus Nóra agus óig-mhná na tíre
   Beidh mé 'g éisteacht lena nglórthaí faoi na fóide is mé sínte

1 O James Mc Murrough, you're the best of all nobles
  You're a drop of the true blood descended from high rank
  You never once thought of your friends being all banished
  When you ne'er did turn tail on the eve of betrayal

2 Down by the old house there's a gloomy old matron
  Who agreed to the treachery and got the chance to betray him
  My language she knew not and English I'd speak not
  The dark girl's my darling that lives in the glenside

3 Would I were a blueberry on the side of a mountain
  Or a shoot of red bracken 'neath the sun's shining rays
  Or a blackbird that's living in the wood of Dunreevy
  For the walls that shut sky out are leaving me dazed

4 Would it were war-time as we march to our quarters
  With James Mc Murrough in front as our General
  For he'd pay no respects to the servants of English
  Instead he would honour the travellers of all Ireland

5 O Mary, so gentle, who sent me to my ending
  O come to my funeral and get ready my coffin
  To marry'd have been happier than that which did happen
  May the bright King of Glory deliver me this time

6 They'll send a strong carriage from Armagh to collect me
  With soldiers for guarding it coming on Tuesday
  They'll each have a sword on, as well as their rifles
  At the end of the street, there death will be waiting

7 My funeral will be held on next Friday evening
  I'll go through the roads lined with people on Sunday
  Nelly and Nora will come and the girls of the country
  I'll hear them all speaking o'er the grave where I'm lying

45 AN SEANDUINE DOIGHTE
THE BURNT-OUT OLD FELLOW

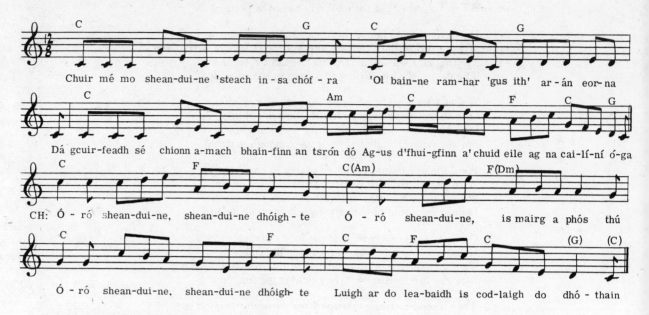

Chuir mé mo shean-dui-ne 'steach in-sa chóf-ra 'Ol bain-ne ram-har 'gus ith' ar-án eor-na

Dá gcuir-feadh sé chionn a-mach bhain-finn an tsrón dó Ag-us d'fhui-gfinn a' chuid eile ag na cai-lí-ní ó-ga

CH: Ó - ró shean-dui-ne, shean-dui-ne dhóigh-te Ó - ró shean-dui-ne, is mairg a phós thú

Ó - ró shean-dui-ne, shean-dui-ne dhóigh-te Luigh ar do lea-baidh is cod-laigh do dhó - thain

1 Chuir mé mo sheanduine 'steach insa chófra
'Ol bainne ramhar 'gus ith' arán eorna
Dá gcuirfeadh sé chionn amach bhainfinn an tsrón
Agus d'fhuígfinn a' chuid eile ag na cailíní óga   [dó
Óró sheanduine, sheanduine dhóighte
Óró sheanduine, is mairg a phós thú
Óró sheanduine, sheanduine dhóighte
Luigh ar do leabaidh is codlaigh do dhóthain

2 Dá bhfuigheadh mo sheanduine gach ní mar ba chóir
Greamannaí ime agus greamannaí feola   [dó
Iochtar na coinneoige 's préataí rósta
Bhainfeadh sé geatair' as cailíní óga

3 Chuir mé mo sheanduine go sráid Bhaile 'n Robá
Cleite ina hata agus buclaí na bhróga
Bhi triúr á mhealladh agus ceathrar á phógadh
Agus chuala mé 'nGaillimh gur imigh sé leofa

4 Chuaigh mé 'un tsiopa 'a dhíol mo chuid móna
'A dh'iarraidh tobaca 'gus clárachaí cónra
'S ar a philleadh 'na bhaile domh tuirseach tráthnóna
Fuair mé mo sheanduine i gclúdaigh na móna

1 I put my old man right into the coffer
To drink buttermilk and barley-bread scoffer
If he'd stick out his head I'd snap off his nose
Leave the rest of his body for all the young girls
O my old man O pity I fed you
O my old man O pity I wed you
O my old man O pity I bed you
Sleepin' your sleep for ever and ever

2 If my old man he got what he wanted
A few bites of meat and a dollop of butter
The fat of the churn and some roasted potatoes
Wouldn't he sport among all the young ladies?

3 To Ballinrobe street I sent my old fellow
Buckled-up shoes and a hat with a feather
Three were enticing him, kissing him four of them
And they told me in Galway he went off with all of
                                                     them

4 I went to the store to get all my turf in
Looking for baccy and planks for a coffin
When I got home and felt like a mourner
I got my old man, stuck him down in the corner

5 Dá bhfeicfeá mo sheanduine ar uair a' mheán oíche
   A chos ar a' bhac is é ag deargadh a phíopa
   Naoi n-uibhe circe bheith bruithte sa ghríosaigh
   'S mur' ndéanfadh sé ansin é ní dheánfadh sé choíche

5 If you were to see my old man about midnight
   His foot on the hob and getting his pipe 'light
   Nine of the hen's eggs boiled in the firelight
   If he didn't do it then right, he'll never do it now right

6 Chuir mé mo sheanduine siar go tír iarthair
   An aít a rabh míle agus fice do liamhain
   Chup a chuid earraidh agus shín a chuid 'iallbhach
   Agus thainig sé chugam na bhromastin bliana

6 I sent my old man to the west of the country
   Where there were whores one thousand and twenty
   His genitals lessened and his jaws became bony
   And he came back to me like a newly-born pony

7 Dá bhfeicfinn mo sheanduine báidhte i bpoll móna
   Bhéarfainn 'na bhaile é 'gus dhéanfainn a thórramh
   Chuirfinn glas ar a' doras is an eochair 'mo phóca
   Is shiúlfainn amach leis na buachaillí óga

7 If I found my old fellow drowned in a bog-hole
   Then I'd fetch him home and I'd yell in his lug-hole
   I'd lock up the door and I'd pocket the key-o
   And all the young fellows would walk out with me-o

46 SEIMIDH EOGHAININ DUIBH
DARK-HAIRED JIMMY OWEN

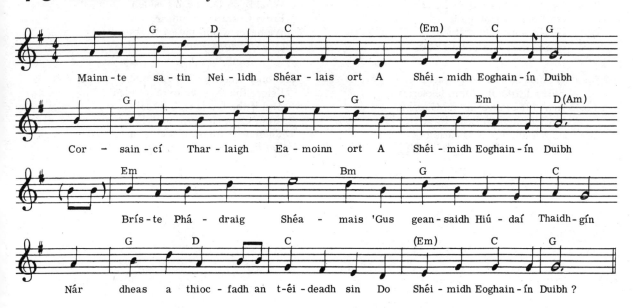

1 Mainnte satin Neilidh Shéarlais ort
   A Shéimidh Eoghainín Duibh
   Corsaincí Tharlaigh Éamoinn ort
   A Shéimidh Eoghainín Duibh
   Bríste Phádraig Shéamais
   'Gus geansaidh Hiúdaí Thaidhgín
   Nár dheas a thiocfadh an t-éideadh sin
   Do Shéimidh Eoghainín Duibh?

1 Nellie Charles' satin mantle on you
   Dark-haired Jimmy Owen
   Terry Edwards' neck'chief on you
   Dark-haired Jimmy Owen
   Paddy James' pair of breeches
   And Hughie Taggart's woollen Guernsey
   Wouldn't all those clothes look fine
   On dark-haired Jimmy Owen? ➔

2 Mainnte báinín Shiúsaidh Phadabháin ort
Bheiste chnáibe Shéamais Chnagadáin ort
Léinidh Sheáin 'Ic tSiolgadáin
Sobhestar Mhánais Mhiolgadáin
Anuas go cnámh a' smiolgadáin
Ar Shéimian Eoghainín Duibh

3 Dá mbeifeá i lár an aonaigh 'gainn
Agus curca geal 'en tsíoda ort
Bheadh cailíní na tíre
I riocht a chéile 'chíoradh
Cé acu sin a shnaidhmfeadh leat
A Shéimidh Eoghainín Duibh

4 Is trua nach rabh tú san ár againn
Sula dtáinig clann na Spáinne 'ugainn
Nó dá mbeifeá leis an Dálach
On Chorrshliabh go Cionn tSáile
Ní chascórtaí go bráth sinn
A Shéimidh Eoghainín Duibh

5 O bhíomar seal i n-éineacht
Sula ndeárnadh orainn léirscrios
Ach 'a b'é gur chaill na Gaedhil
O Chorcaigh go Loch Eirne
Ní bheadh aon rí ar Eirinn
Ach Shéimidh Eoghainín Duibh

2 Susie Gallagher's white wool dress on you
Seamus Cavanagh's waistcoat on you
Sean McSheehan's linen shirt
Manus McMeehan's sou'wester
Pulled down to the collar-bone
On dark-haired Jimmy Owen

3 If we had you in the market-place
A fine bright hat of silk upon you
All the girls for miles around
Would fight like wild cat and hound
Which one you'd marry she'd be found
O dark-haired Jimmy Owen

4 Would you had been in battle with us
Before the Spaniards came upon us
Would you had been beside O'Donnell
From Corraslieve unto Kinsale
We never would have been put down
O dark-haired Jimmy Owen

5 O once when we were all united
Before the days we were invaded
And if the Gaels had not fallen
From Cork city to Lough Erne
There would not be a king of Ireland
But dark-haired Jimmy Owen

47 THÍOS I DTEACH A' TORRAIMH
DOWN AT THE WAKE-HOUSE

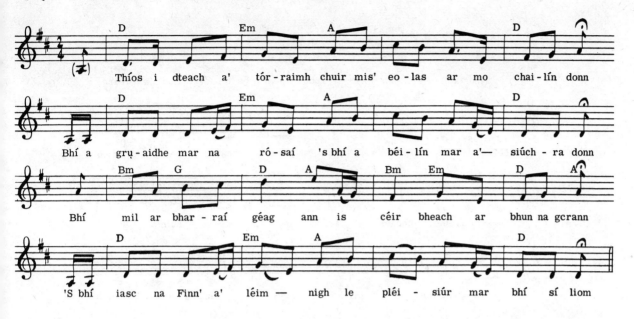

Thíos i dteach a' tór-raimh chuir mis' eo-las ar mo chai-lín donn

Bhí a gru-aidhe mar na ró-saí 's bhí a béi-lín mar a'— siúch-ra donn

Bhí mil ar bhar-raí géag ann is céir bheach ar bhun na gcrann

'S bhí iasc na Finn' a' léim — nigh le pléi-siúr mar bhí sí liom

1 Thíos i dteach a' tórraimh chuir mis' eolas ar mo
chailín donn
Bhí a gruaidhe mar na rósaí 's bhí a béilín mar a'
siúchra donn
Bhí mil ar bharraí géag ann is céir bheach ar bhun na
gcrann
'S bhí iasc na Finn' a' léimnigh le pléisiúr mar bhí
sí liom

2 Bhí mé lá go ceolmhar ar mo sheol 'gus mé i gcionn
a' toigh'
A' síor-ghabháil don cheol 's a' cur na mbréag in iúl
do ghrá mo chroí
Ní chreidfeadh sí mo ghlórthaí nó shíl sí gur dá
mealladh bhínn
Tá mé óg go leor i gcónaí is ní phósfaidh mé ach
mian mo chroí

3 Is binn agus is ceolmhar a labhras 'ach éan i dtom

Is deas an uile sheort ann 's is ró-dheas mo chailín
donn
Is aici a fuair mis 'eolas ar mhórán 's ar thuilleamh
grinn
Nach deas a' rud sugh na h-eorna bheith dá h-ól
agus a' teannadh linn

1 Down at the wake-house, where I first met that
brown-haired girl of mine
Her cheeks they were like roses, her lips they were
like Spanish wine
On each branch top there was honey there, beeswax
beneath each tree
And the fish of the Finn did leap for joy because
she was with me

2 Light-heartedly at my loom I work when e'er I am
at home
And many's the sweet song I'd sing, to win her for
my very own
She never would believe me, but thought some
harm on my part
But a young man I will always be and wed the only
love of my heart

3 So noisily and sweetly do the birds sing in the tops
of every tree
Though all the world is fair enough, it's not as fair
as my love to me
From her I learnt a lot of things, concerning all the
joys of life
The whisky it is fine to drink when she's cuddled
by my side

48 TIOCFAIDH AN SAMHRADH
THE SUMMER WILL COME

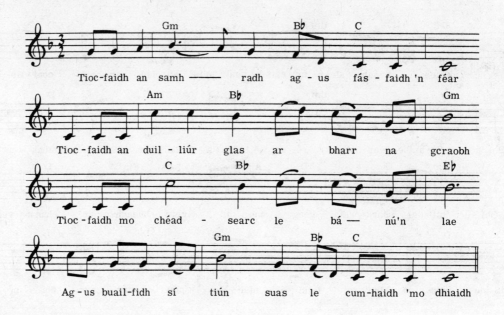

1 Tiocfaidh an samhradh agus fásfaidh 'n féar
Tiocfaidh an duilliúr glas ar bharr na gcraobh
Tiocfaidh mo chéad-searc le bánú 'n lae
Agus buailfidh sí tiún suas le cumhaidh 'mo dhiaidh

2 Is óg 's is óg a chuir mé dúil i ngreann
Dheánfainn súgradh le mo rún le fonn
Níl baile cuain ar bith 'á ngluaisfinn ann
Nach bhfuighinn maighdean óg dheas ar bhuideal
rum

3 Scairt mé 'réir ag an doras thall
Scairt mé 'ríst ar mo rún go teann
'Sé dúirt a mamaí liom nach rabh sí ann
Nó gur éalaigh sí 'réir leis an bhuachaill dhonn

4 Tá 'n oíche seo dorcha agus beidh go lá
Le ghabháil 'na mhuilinn suas a dh'iarraidh mná
Ionns' ar Thadhg Ó Gionnaile nach bhfuil aige ach í
Go bhfaghaidh muid Máire uaidh faoina láimh

1 The summer will come and the grass turn to hay
Green leaves will come on the tops of each spray
My true love will come at the dawn of the day
And she'll strike up a tune to drive sorrow away

2 When I first took to sport I was very very young
To play with my sweetheart was plenty of fun
Not a town with a harbour, there wasn't a one
Where I couldn't get a young girl for a bottle of rum

3 Last night did I call at yonder door over there
I called for my love both loudly and clear
And her mother she told me that she wasn't there
She had gone off last night with the lad with brown
hair

4 The night it is dark and it will be till day
For going up to the mill in search of a maid
To tackle Tim Gunnell who with his daughter does
But we'll get Mary from him and take her away   [stay

5 Tá ceathrar agus fich' acu ar aon *rank* amháin

    Sí mo bhean féin acu an bhean is fearr
    Tá blas na meal' uirthi agus boladh breá
    O sí 'n *posy* álainn í 'tá doiligh 'fháil

6 Shiúl mé thoir agus shiúl mé thiar
    Shiúl mé Corcaigh 'gus Baile Átha Cliath

    Shiúl mé 'n baile seo faoi dhó le bliain
    Ag iarraidh mo stóirín 'bhain daom mo chiall

7 'Gus plóid ar an fharraige nach b'í 'tá mór
    Sí 'tá gabháil eadar mé is mo mhíle stór
    D'fhág sí ar a' bhaile seo mé a' deánamh bróin
    'S gan dúil lena feiceáil go Samhain Úr

8 Slán ag m'athair 's ag mo mháthair ó
    'Gus slán ag mo dheirfiúr is gan agam ach í
    Má théim-se thar farraige, rud a rachas mé
    Cuirfidh mé *fortune* ionns' ar a' féirín ó

5 There are four and twenty of them and each one the
                        same
    But my own sweetheart is the best I could name
    She tastes of sweet honey and smells like the rain
    She's the prettiest little posy yet the hardest to obtain

6 I walked east and west and I walked up and down
    Through Cork I have walked and I've walked Dublin
                        town
    Once this year already I have walked this town round
    My darling took my sense away and now can't be
                        found

7 Ah cursed be the sea, for it is widest of all
    And goes between me and my own dearest girl
    She left me in this town a-grieving full sore
    With no hope of seeing her until the next fall

8 Farewell to my father and to my mother adieu
    Farewell to my sister who is all I have too
    If I go across the sea, one thing I must do
    I will send home a fortune, my darling, to you

25 AN BHANALTRA
THE NURSEMAID

Hudie Devaney, Ranafast, Donegal, *rec.* P. Kennedy
  and S. O'Boyle, 1953: BBC 19969
Other recorded version
Kitty Gallagher, Gweedore, Donegal, 1947: BBC 12053

Compare
COSTELLO: 1919, p. 33
O'SULLIVAN: 1960, p. 17

An unusual mixture of lullaby, love song and drinking song, this has a lively air more commonly associated with another Donegal song *Fuígfidh Mise An Baile Seo.* The words 'A's nach deas an fear i mbaile mé' occur in the Connaught version of *Bean an tSeanduine* (COSTELLO: 1919, p. 33) which has other similarities in the words. A version of the first verse also occurs in *An Leanb Aimhréidh* (O'SULLIVAN: 1960, p. 17).

> He was a rakish kind of a fellow: here, there and everywhere. And he had a lover in every town and every place. In the last verse, he says, there never was a better seed than barley sold in the land. It's cut and dried and whisky made of it. He praises the whisky in the song, what whisky could do: make the old crippled women jump around through the house when they get a sup of it.—HUDIE DEVANEY.

26 BRID BHAN
FAIR BRIDGET

Conal O'Donnell, Ranafast, Donegal, *rec.* P. Kennedy,
  London, 1962
Other recorded version
Anne Donegan, Teelin, 1953: BBC 19358

Printed version
O MUIRGHEASA: 1915, no. 59, pp. 111 and 266 n.

The tune of this song, one of the finest airs to be found in Donegal, has not appeared in any collections, but the words are given in O MUIRGHEASA: 1915.

> She was from Teelin [a small townland beside the sea] in south Donegal, and she got married to a man 'in the mountain', as they would say in that part of the country. He came from Meenawanne,* between Carrick and Ardara.
>   She went to live at Meenawanne, and it was a heartbreak for her to leave Teelin and start a new life. She composed so many verses, and he composed so many verses, but she had the last word in the last verse.
>   As far as I know from the old people, she came back to her own place in the end. They don't like to hear this song where she went to live, but the Teelin people very much enjoy it.—CONAL O'DONNELL.

27 BRID OG NI MHAILLE
BRIDGET O'MALLEY

Conal O'Donnell, Ranafast, Donegal, *rec.* P. Kennedy,
  1962
Other recorded version
Hudie Devaney, *rec.* P. Kennedy and S. O'Boyle, 1953:
  BBC 19970

Printed versions
THE SHAMROCK (February 1872)
HARDEBECK: 1939. Government Publications (M.103),
  Dublin

Conal O'Donnell tells that a friend of his, Owen O'Donnell, happened to be a Gaelic teacher in County Mayo and took a fancy to this song, and brought it back to Donegal where it has become very popular. It is the oft-repeated story of the young man who has lost his love to another. He bemoans her marriage, and laments his own forthcoming one.

> This girl left him in his pain. I would say that he took it very bad when he didn't succeed in getting her. He tells about the change that took place in himself.—CONAL O'DONNELL.

> There's one verse in this song where he says: 'There is nothing more beautiful than the moon over the sea or the white blossom, and my love is like that with her golden tresses and her honey-mouth that has never deceived anybody.'—HUDIE DEVANEY.

* Meenawanne = Mín a' Bainne. 'Mín' means a piece of flat ground on the mountainside that was good for grazing milk-cows. 'Chíb' in verse 3, line 4, is the sour grass which grows on the mountains. The old people could tell from the teeth of the cattle when they had been grazing on it for too long.

28 AN CAILIN GAELACH
THE IRISH GIRL

Conal O'Donnell, Ranafast, Donegal, *rec.* P. Kennedy,
London, 1962
Other recorded version
Hudie Devaney, Ranafast, Donegal, *rec.* P. Kennedy
and S. O'Boyle, 1953: BBC 19970

Printed version
O BAOIGHILL: 1944, p. 8

My brother was in Tory Island collecting old stories and folklore and he came across John Tom [Dougan] and he got this one down on the 'Ediphone' recording machine and I learned it off that.—CONAL O'DONNELL.

He'd love to be out on the side of the hill with an Irish colleen. One morning, as he was going to the fields to collect his cattle home, he saw this beautiful girl sitting on the lane-way, and he spoke to her and asked for a kiss, and she said, as it's given in song [in English]: 'Pray sir, let me be.'—HUDIE DEVANEY.

Seamus Ennis said that the song is also known from its first line as *Mallaigh Shleibhe*. 'Gaelach' means 'Irish', but 'Gaolach' (same pronunciation) is 'friendly' (cf. 'gaol' meaning 'kinship' and, in Scots Gaelic, 'love').

In this song there is a reference to nuts, which, in the lingua franca of love songs, would refer to the virginity or otherwise of the girl. The song also owes its great popularity to the implication that the young man is rebuffed by an English-speaking girl and would much prefer an Irish-speaking girl in the same situation.

29 CHUAIGH ME 'NA ROSANN
I WENT TO VISIT THE ROSSES

William Rodgers, Baile Thiar, Tory Island, Donegal,
rec. Noel Hamilton, 1967
Other recorded version
Conal O'Donnell, Ranafast, Donegal, *rec.* P. Kennedy,
1962

Printed versions
AN GAODHAL (1888); Irisleabhar na Gaedhilge (1894/1902) tune supplied but different
O'MUIRGHEASA: 1915, p. 347; notes about Peter Walsh, p. 231
FAINNE AN LAE: 1923

I hear that they're giving the old bar in Arranmore the title of this song. That it's going to be christened to attract the tourist. And that's where this song was composed. It was Peadar Breatnach, the poet from Finntown, who wrote the song over a hundred years ago, and he went in there to get a drink. All the poets had a drink and it seems that this girl who was in the bar comes in to the whole of this song. He pretends that he is in the bar talking to her, taking a liking to her, in love with her, having a chat with her, and he has her in love with him, and he has her making a bargain with him as well as doing it himself.—CONAL O'DONNELL.

The song was composed by Peadar Breatnach (or Peter Walsh), a tailor from Ballinamore, Glenfinn, in central Donegal. It describes his exploits on one of the islands in the Rosses, probably Arranmore, the only big island, and how the girl he met did not approve of all his 'pastimes'.

30 DONALL O MAOLAINE
DONALD O'MULLEN

Recorded version
Conal O'Donnell, Glenties, Donegal, *rec.* P. Kennedy
and S. O'Boyle, 1953: BBC 20151

Printed versions
HARDEBECK: 1937. Government Publications (M.32)
O'SULLIVAN: 1960, p. 166

The way Máire John told me the story you would swear that you could see Donall coming along and meeting this girl and the promises that were made. Afterwards, it seems, her father found out she was going to have a child and then they met again and she told her story. She told her story and he had another story ready about another girl that he liked.—CONAL O'DONNELL.

This song, generally known in Munster as *Eamonn Mágáine*, would seem to be about 250 years old. Many versions of the words with only slight variations have been printed, mostly in periodicals which are now out of print. The tunes printed elsewhere, in HARDEBECK: 1937 and O'SULLIVAN: 1960, are different from the one here.

31 DONALL OG
YOUNG DONALD

Mrs Kitty Rodgers, Baile Thiar, Tory Island, Donegal,
  rec. Noel Hamilton, 1967

Printed version
O DUIBHGINN: 1960: contains most texts ever collected
  but not all music versions

This is one of the most intense love songs in the Irish language: a young girl's lament for her lover, Young Donald. The song is extensively distributed throughout Ireland (and also in Scotland) and has been well covered in the book by Seosamh O Duibhginn devoted to the song.

  The printed text includes the most important verses in this version of the song from Mrs Kitty Rodgers, one of the best singers in Tory Island, who also provided *Tiocfaidh an Samhradh* (No. 48).

32 AN DRAIGHNEAN DONN
THE BLACKTHORN TREE

James Meenan, Baile Thiar, Tory Island, Donegal, *rec.*
  Noel Hamilton, 1967

Printed versions
COSTELLO: 1919, pp. 71–4
O'SULLIVAN: 1960, p. 49
O TUAMA: 1960, vol. VIII, p. 5

This song is generally associated with Connemara, where it enjoys the greatest popularity, but it can still be heard in versions from other localities, including Donegal. The versions which appear in COSTELLO: 1919, O'SULLIVAN: 1960 and O TUAMA: 1960 are all variants of one great tune. Most versions have the words spoken by a girl, but our version is instead descriptive of the fair sex.

33 EIRIGH 'S CUIR ORT DO CHUID EADAIGH
ARISE AND PUT ON YOUR CLOTHES

Conal O'Donnell, Ranafast, Donegal, *rec.* P. Kennedy,
  London, 1962
Other recorded version
Hudie Devaney, Ranafast, Donegal, *rec.* P. Kennedy
  and S. O'Boyle, 1953: BBC 19971

Printed versions
O MUIRGHEASA: 1915, p. 104: *Buaidheadh an phosta*
O BAOIGHILL: 1944, p. 28

Because of a dream he has had, the singer exhorts his lover to rise and hurry off with him to get married. As seems so frequently the case in Donegal folksong, there is a reference to the Erne, which seems always to have been the lover's idea of Utopia.

  There was a man in this town long ago and he didn't get the girl he wanted. Later on in life he got married to an elderly woman. This night, when he was lying in his bed, the one he was in love with in his young days came to him in his dream, and told him to get up and that she'd cut his hair from him and dress him up, that the two of them would go off to the bishop and get married, and he'd leave the old one and come along with her.—HUDIE DEVANEY.

34 EIRIGH SUAS A STOIRIN
RISE UP, MY DARLING

Hudie Devaney, Ranafast, Donegal, *rec.* P. Kennedy
  and S. O'Boyle, 1953: BBC 19971
Other recorded version
Conal O'Donnell, *rec.* P. Kennedy, London, 1962

Printed version
O BAOIGHILL: 1944, p. 30: Ranafast version with tune
  written in the Dorian mode

English was the new thing at one time, and somebody would possibly learn a little phrase of it, and then they thought it would put special flavour into the song, so they made use of it.

He's on his own and he's coming to look for this woman's daughter, and he hopes he won't be refused, but he doesn't get her. He's all the time looking back to the time when he first went to look for her.

Well this is one of Máire John's. It describes how marriages were in the Gaelic-speaking places or the poor parts of Ireland.

Marriages in them days was more or less a bargain. A man didn't move out to look for a wife until he was a good age and then he came along and he had somebody with him to more or less coax the father and mother to agree by giving him the daughter. In this song this man came along and he says, 'Rise up my darling, that's if you're in bed', and then he mentions about having a bottle of whisky and that they would have a dram and he hoped that she wouldn't refuse him by giving the daughter. There we can see the whole thing bargained up, which was a true story in them days.

Then we can see the girl in a lonely place. Perhaps in the depths of the mountain and her crying her eyes out. There she's dropping tears and everything and she there in the glens, her very lonely and nobody to come on a Sunday evening, not even to cheer her up or anything like that then she looks and she hears the birds so happy and her so lonely.

I think it's a very sad song and it's a very true song. I still can see the picture of this girl being led away into marriage and then her heart breaking and may be not in love with that man at all but just by the way her father and mother coaxed her into it.

I've witnessed some of these things myself in my young days and I've heard so many stories about them. And I'd say this song is very true.—CONAL O'DONNELL.

35 GARDAI 'N RI
THE KING'S OWN GUARDS

Conal O'Donnell, Ranafast, Donegal, *rec.* P. Kennedy,
London, 1962
Other recorded version
Hudie Devaney, Ranafast, Donegal, *rec.* P. Kennedy
and S. O'Boyle, 1953: BBC 19970

Printed versions
O BAOIGHILL: 1944, p. 34
AN TULTACH: October 1936: contains another Donegal
version

There was no such thing, you know, before my father's time, as there is now, when they're meeting girls at dances. The old people had great command on the young people and they wouldn't let them from their doorsteps, as they are now. It became a very common thing for them to meet their coming wife at the fairs and wakes. The only ceilidhing in the houses would be at marriages.

In cases where a man used to let the years get a grip of him, somebody would mention to him, 'There's a girl in such a place that no-one bothers his head with her, and I think she'd make a match for you.'

A team of men would be picked out, then and there, a few bottles of whisky would be bought and shibeen poteen, and they would set out on their journey. And maybe they would describe themselves as the 'King's Own Guard', you know, just to put a polish on it. (They weren't quite so slow in those days as we might think they were!)

It sounds like a few, just egging on this man that's going to be left on the shelf and telling him about a girl on the mountain top. 'And wouldn't it be a grand thing if we just marched up there to the top of the mountain and put our case?'

They'd let everybody go to bed, and then they'd march up to the house and rap at the door. The man of the house would answer and the woman of the house would be whimpering to get the daughter up out of her bed.

Well then, the men would set about praising the man of the house, telling him about all the fine land he has, about all the money that he has, and how good a match he could make for his daughter.

And so it was that the father and mother would have the last word, and not the daughter at all. That was very common in this part of the country.

After the men had given the man's side of it all, the father wouldn't let his daughter go without giving her something, maybe three or four bullocks, if they were up in a mountainy place, or else some sheep or money.—CONAL O'DONNELL.

36 IN AIMSIR BHAINT AN FHEIR
AT THE CUTTING OF THE HAY

Sheila Gallagher, Gweedore, Donegal, *rec.* P. Kennedy
and S. O'Boyle, 1953: BBC 20145

> He was going to Scotland but he would rather be home to cut the hay. He wanted the girls to say their prayers for him, so he could be home at the hay-cutting time.—SHEILA GALLAGHER.

The tune used for this song is that of a dance tune, a hornpipe called *The Cuckoo's Nest*. A song version in English, recorded in Ireland, is *The Magpie's Nest* (No. 182), which is sung like this one, with a lilting dance rhythm to the chorus.

The same tune is also used in Ireland in a slower and more lyrical manner for songs such as *An Splealadóir*.

37 IS FADA O BHAILE A D'AITHNEOINN
IT'S FAR FROM HOME I'D KNOW YOU

James Meenan, Baile Thiar, Tory Island, Donegal, *rec.*
Noel Hamilton, 1967
Other recorded version
Kitty Gallagher, Gweedore, Donegal, 1947: BBC 12053

Although this song has been heard in other parts of Donegal, for some unaccountable reason it has never before appeared in print and, considering the effectiveness of both the words and the tune, this is surprising.

A girl sings of her lost love. She tells of all the things that remind her of him, and feels that she will most certainly die before the next Hallowe'en. And should she hear that he has become betrothed to another, she would cry without stopping. For her, he was the only possible choice:

Feara Eireann 's dá mbeadh siad cruinn' ar aon chnoc amháin If all the men in Ireland gathered on one hill
A ghrá, dá bhféadfainn, 's tú féin 'bheadh agam ar láimh 'Tis you, my dear, from choice, I'd choose still

In the last verse she curses his parents that they did not teach him to read, so that he could read the love-letters in which she would send her excuses.

38 IS IOMAIDH COISCEIM FADA
MANY'S A LONG FOOTSTEP

Sheila Gallagher, Gweedore, Donegal, *rec.* P. Kennedy
and S. O'Boyle, 1953: BBC 20144

> Paddy went on the boat, and she met this girl coming off the boat, and she asked the girl, 'Was Paddy on the boat?' She said, 'Yes, Paddy's on the boat and you'll never see him more.'—SHEILA GALLAGHER.

This would seem to be a fragment of a longer song, so far untraced; and because Sheila Gallagher seemed to mix some of her lines this text has been slightly edited to make sense of it.

The song was sung in a style consisting of a series of jerky statements, giving the story of the girl's realisation of her loss, in an atmosphere that seems to bring to life the feeling of her problem—in which direction she should take another step. It was quite clear from Sheila Gallagher's performance that this was an important characteristic of the song and not just the hesitation of a singer of over ninety years of age.

39 MA THEID TU 'UN AONAIGH
WHEN YOU GO TO THE FAIR

Conal O'Donnell, Ranafast, Donegal, *rec.* P. Kennedy, London, 1962
Other recorded version
Hudie Devaney, Ranafast, Donegal, *rec.* P. Kennedy and S. O'Boyle, 1953: BBC 19969

Printed versions
O MUIRGHEASA: 1915, p. 88*ff* (version from Monaghan and from an Edinburgh MS)
AN LÓCHRANN: 1908

This love song is a conversation between a boy and a girl in which he is telling her that she must marry for love and not for riches. Hudie Devaney told of an old lady who quoted the last verse of this song on her deathbed. These were the last words that she said before she passed away.

Hudie Devaney gave a translation of the last verse into English:

> True-love, is it possible that you sleep at night
> Can you not see the spears that are piercing through my heart
> There's something worrying me and the pain is terrible
> And I am suffering listening to the birds in the wood going to rest.

The song seems to be native of Ulster, other versions having been collected in County Monaghan as well as in Donegal. The song has probably remained popular because its subject concerns the all-important matter of money. In marriage in Donegal, suitors were refused or accepted according to whether or not they would bring much wealth into the marriage.

> I've heard this from Maire John and the old people. It would happen that there would be a man left in the house all alone and somebody would come along and give him a bit of advice: 'It's about time you done something, you're going to be left alone, there's nobody going to be looking after you. Why not go over to such and such a place, to Mickey's daughter or Barney's daughter and she's getting old as well.' And he'd agree and the next thing a night would be arranged unknown to the girl and her father and mother and they would wait until everybody was in bed in case somebody would be ceilidhing in another house as they went there. It was mostly at daybreak or around two or three in the morning.
>
> They would walk in and tell their business. The mother would go up and shake the daughter out of bed and she'd come down and for her parents' sake she'd agree, but not in her heart. It was the case of the father bargaining something with the man that come asking for the daughter: 'I'll give you a few cows or so much money.'
>
> Then a few days after that they would get married and in them days it was mostly at night that they got married about seven or eight o'clock at night. They were a kind of a shy crowd, you know! Especially as there were more maids than bachelors.—CONAL O'DONNELL.

The song is also known as *Dá mBéadh Lán Na Páirce Báin Agam.*

40 MAIRE CHONNACHT AGUS SEAMUS O DONAILL
CONNAUGHT MARY AND JAMES O'DONNELL

Conal O'Donnell, Ranafast, Donegal, *rec.* P. Kennedy, London, 1962

Printed versions
Maire: *Rann na Feirste* n.d. (words only)
HAMILTON: 1973, p. 9

This song is local to the Ranafast area of west Donegal and concerns the problem caused by a lot of timber that came drifting into the area, floating in from the Atlantic. It was composed as a conversation between a Ranafast O'Donnell and a woman who came to Ranafast from County Galway or Mayo and became known locally as Mary Connaught. She sings the first pair of verses, he sings the middle pair, and Mary has the last word in verses 5 and 6.

> When the timber came ashore, the priest more or less took the timber from the people that had got it ashore in order to make use of it for roofing the chapel. As far as I could hear, they said that Mary of Connaught was too much for him in the song. She had the last word.—CONAL O'DONNELL.

The tune of this song is the air of a well-known Connaught song *Cuaichín Ghleann Néifín* (O'TUAMA: 1955), and is also used for *Chaith Mé Seacht Seachtainí I Mainistir Na Búille*, recorded by Máire Ní Scolaí for GAEL-LINN.

> I've heard the old people in Ranafast talking about her. That she lived in Kencasslagh where the chapel has been built.
>
> So she came from Connaught in them early days. People moved until they got some place—after the Battle of Kindale they were on the move. And that's how they came into these poor parts. It's not that there were land there around Kencasslagh or parts of the Rosses but it was rocky and mountainy and there was nothing there but cliffs but in any case they made land. As the man said they made land out of the rocks and they quarried these stones and boulders and everything so it seems Mary Connaught took up her residence in Kencasslagh.

So there was a priest there and he fancied where she was living for to build a chapel there so she didn't agree with the priest and there were an argument and a quarrelling all like this between herself and the priest. But they say she was gifted in the tongue. She was an able person and could hold her own with them whether it be clergy or lay people or whoever they would be. That's how she came into it—being gifted in composing songs and verses and everything like that.

So in them days anyhow there were hardly any such thing as anybody being the owner of where they lived. They just took up residence there and the priest more or less fancied this spot. And not that he commandeered it or anything but he tried to come to an agreement with her. But she wouldn't agree by having the chapel there. She more or less called it her own homeplace.

In any case the priest took advantage of the place and he built the chapel and they say that she had potatoes growing there where the graveyard is now. And they say that the potatoes grew up after him making the chapel and she was able to dig up the potatoes in the graveyard that she had planted before they started building.—CONAL O'DONNELL.

41 NION A' BHAOILLIGH
O'BOYLE'S DAUGHTER

Conal O'Donnell, Ranafast, Donegal, *rec*. P. Kennedy, London, 1962
Other recorded version
Hudie Devaney, Ranafast, Donegal, *rec*. P. Kennedy and S. O'Boyle, 1953: BBC 19968

Printed versions
O BAOIGHILL: 1944, p. 46: the Ranafast version
DE NORAIDH: 1965, p. 37: Munster version
Compare
First verse: COSTELLO: 1919, p. 4: *Mo Mhuirnín Bhán*, a Connaught song

The beginning of February this wake was in Mullaghmore ('mullagh' means 'height' and 'more' is 'big'). He describes the house where it was, and how he happened to be there, how this girl was in, and that he took a fancy to her (this word 'fancy' was used in Gaelic).

They weren't in sorrow all the time at these wakes you know. They had plenty of fun on their own. The old people that was in the house, if it was an old person that was dead, especially. You used to have to enjoy yourselves and they had all sorts of tricks. It's dying out now, the keening over the dead.

Anyway this young man happened to be at the wake and he took a fancy to this girl. He describes everything about her, her hair, her neck, her figure, her charms, her speech. She has him carried away in such a way that he'll never forget her. But in the end he doesn't get her, but he doesn't forget her good looks.

The song gives the whole story there, as you might see a townland from the top of a mountain.—CONAL O'DONNELL.

This is typical of love songs still to be found all over the Gaeltacht. The first verse is widely distributed, yet the song itself would seem to belong to Donegal, as much by its title as by anything else, since O'Boyle is more common as a name in Donegal than in other parts of the Gaeltacht.

The place-names do not help us much in determining the origin, for both Mullaghmore and Ballintemple are common in many parts of Ireland. Liaigh na bhFiann was the magic all-healing well at Tara.

42 AN t-OILEAN UR
THE NEW-FOUND ISLAND

Sheila Gallagher, Gweedore, Donegal, *rec*. P. Kennedy and S. O'Boyle, 1953: BBC 20149
Other recorded version
Conal O'Donnell, Ranafast, Donegal, *rec*. P. Kennedy, London, 1962

Printed version
O MUIRGHEASA: 1915, no. 79, pp. 139 and 293

When emigration started, especially in the famine time, they went away to what they call The New(found) Island: that's the only way they had of describing the place we now call America.

This man was travelling across the New Island. He went through strange places where he met them naked and all such as that, and wild animals and so on. And then it was Heaven to him when he walked into this certain house and made himself known. The old lady in the corner got up and spoke to him in Gaelic and shook him by the hand. She came from Lough Erne in County Fermanagh.

I heard the song from Marie John in Ranafast. Maire wouldn't be tired telling you the story of this song. She could pity that man and what he went through and how small was the world and how he then made the second thought that he wasn't going to stay there.—CONAL O'DONNELL.

The place-names in the song seem very much corrupted. Énrí O Muirgheasa remarks on this in *Céad de Cheoltaibh Uladh* and explains that it is because the song has travelled beyond its native district.

43 'S ORO LONDUBH BUI
O MY BLACKBIRD GAY

Mary Doohan, Baile Thiar, Tory Island, Donegal, *rec.*
  Noel Hamilton, 1967
Other recorded versions
Sheila Gallagher, Middle Dore, 1943: BBC 20148
Tomás O Súilleabháin, GAEL-LINN CEOLTA EIREANN
  CEF 001

Printed versions
GAELIC JOURNAL: July 1892, Dunamanagh, County
  Tyrone: fifty-four lines, or twenty-six verses
GAELIC JOURNAL: March 1902, Tory Island: sixty-eight
  lines or thirty-four verses
O MUIRGHEASA: 1915, no. 44, pp. 89 and 250: composite
  text from above
COSTELLO: 1919, p. 67: a Connaught version, it has the
  refrain 'Thugamar féin an samradh linn'
O BAOIGHILL: 1944, p. 24: (seven verses only)

This song has been described as a sort of 'chanson de la mal-mariée' in reverse. A man whose wife has left him for a younger man and then comes back to him feigns death to see how well she will bury him.

44 SEAMUS MAC MURCHAIDH
JAMES McMURROUGH

Eamonn Doogan, Baile Thiar, Tory Island, Donegal,
  rec. Noel Hamilton, 1967

This is a lament for a man who was hanged in Armagh for having abducted a young girl. Some of the verses are spoken by this man himself, the first is addressed to him by someone else, while another person talks about him in the third person.

This is and was a very popular song all over Ulster and as a result both words and music have been published often in Irish periodicals, although the song does not appear in any of the well-known collections. For those who can read Gaelic there is more about this eighteenth-century Irish outlaw in *Pádraic O Conaire agus Aistí Eile* by Seosamh Mac Grianna. (There is an orchestral arrangement by Redmond Friel of another tune, called *Séamus 'ac Mhurchaidh*, on the GAEL-LINN record CEF 001.)

45 AN SEANDUINE DOIGHTE
THE BURNT-OUT OLD FELLOW

Conal O'Donnell, Ranafast, Donegal, *rec.* P. Kennedy
and S. O'Boyle, 1953: BBC 20151
Other recorded version
Sheila Gallagher, Gweedore, Donegal, *rec.* P. Kennedy
  and S. O'Boyle, 1953: BBC 20145

Printed versions
AN CLAIDHEAMH SOLUIS: 26th September 1908
AN tULTACH: July 1928
AR AGHAIDH: September 1936
O'SULLIVAN: 1960, p. 74

Probably this song was, in origin, a straightforward complaint by a young wife against her aged husband, but it has developed into a rather comic and sometimes scurrilous list of the old man's incapacities, and this no doubt accounts for its widespread popularity. There are probably more versions of this song than any other in the Irish language, and it is certainly by far the most popular 'chanson de la mal-mariée' in Irish.

The places mentioned in our north-west Donegal version are in the counties of Mayo and Galway, but the song is generally taken to be of Munster origin. The tune that is nearly always used for it is a variant of that which was used for the Scottish *The Campbells are Coming*.

46 SEIMIDH EOGHAININ DUIBH
DARK-HAIRED JIMMY OWEN

Conal O'Donnell, Ranafast, Donegal, *rec.* P. Kennedy,
London, 1962

When I was small, going through some of the neighbouring houses, where they would be ceilidhing at night, we got an old man or an old woman singing one of these songs. We wouldn't maybe take any notice of the songs, but the old people always went into these songs through a conversation, a conversation that would lead on to them singing the song.

Some conversations would arise, for instance, about relations of relations in the townland: marriages, deaths, and so on, like that. There was such and such in a marriage, and so forth. I'll give you an example about a particular person.

This mother just had the one boy and naturally enough she thought the world of him, as every mother would do when she had only the one child and him to be a boy. She thought more of him than if she had a full family, and with the result that all the neighbouring women round about got sick listening to her praising her little Jimmy. And if she saw another boy about little Jimmy's height, and him to have a new pair of trousers or wearing something new—O, it wasn't fitting that boy at all, it would fit little Jimmy far better.

Everything was all right until this neighbouring boy got a pair of trousers, and little Jimmy's mother made out that they were far too big for this boy, and she more or less said they wouldn't fit anybody but her little Jimmy. And he got very annoyed about his new trousers and he told somebody about it, and there happened to be a poet in the neighbourhood and he got to hear about it, and he composed a song rigging out little Jimmy with all the queer things that was ever worn round the neighbourhood from leggings to headgears like old sou'westers.

The song was very popular, it was sung by young and old, but it's an old story said by the people that eventually it got to little Jimmy's ears, and, as he grew up, he left the neighbourhood in disgust.—CONAL O'DONNELL.

This is an entirely local song from west Donegal, which is typical of how such amusing and rather malicious satire comes to be made as an internal comment on members of the community. Like all such satires, of course, it goes a bit farther than the truth, and little Jimmy's mother is accused of coveting even women's apparel for young Jimmy.

This is another example of a local tune which has become well known through its popularity in Scotland, where it was used for the song *Kelvin Grove* (see *An Seanduine Dóighte*, No. 45, which uses the tune of *The Campbells are Coming*). The words of *Kelvin Grove* were composed in the early 1800s by Thomas Lyle and were probably a reworking of the traditional song *The Shearing's Not For You*.

47 THIOS I DTEACH A' TORRAIMH
DOWN AT THE WAKE-HOUSE

Hudie Devaney, Ranafast, Donegal, *rec.* P. Kennedy
 and S. O'Boyle, 1953: BBC 19968
Other recorded version
Sheila Gallagher, Middle Dore, 1953: BBC 20146

Printed version
AN tULTACH: August 1928

Down at the wake-house, that's to say a house where some man or woman had died, he happened to see this fair damsel and fell in love with her, and, like all the rest, he didn't manage to get her. He only saw her at the wake and never saw her afterwards.

He was a weaver. He said he wanted to have the girl at home so that he could sit at one end of the house, at the loom and weave, and keep singing and telling stories to his lover while she'd be working through the house.—HUDIE DEVANEY.

48 TIOCFAIDH AN SAMHRADH
THE SUMMER WILL COME

Kitty Rodgers, Baile Thiar, Tory Island, Donegal, *rec.*
 Noel Hamilton, 1967
Other recorded version
Conal O'Donnell, Ranafast, Donegal, *rec.* P. Kennedy,
 London, 1962

Printed versions
AN CLAIDHEAMH SOLUIS: 1903
AN tULTACH: May, 1928
AN CAMAN: 1934
HARDEBECK: 1950. Government Publications (M. 164),
 Dublin
O FRIGHIL: 1952. Government Publications (M.177),
 Dublin
HAMILTON: 1973, p. 2

It tells you how everything looks: grass growing, the colour of it, the leaves on the trees, everything budding up and shining. 'From my heart out, I'll sing this tune,' and then he goes back to his very young days, how he would make love to the girls, and everybody wanted to see him coming. He describes himself well here: his charms and how he was liked in places.

But at the end—and I think that's the nicest part—the mother appeared and told him he's too late. She went last night with another man. And then he comes back to tell you how everything looked different from the beginning. Now the night is dark and there's a storm at sea.

I can still remember the deep voice of the man I heard singing this song. He used to kind of hum it through his nose. He had a great hum to it. I have heard this song spoiled by singers who have never heard it properly sung. They leave out the hum and it's as though the leaves have come off the trees.—CONAL O'DONNELL.

This is one of the best-known and most haunting of sad Irish love-songs to be found in the Gaeltacht areas of Donegal. A number of versions, some with music, have already been published but have long since gone out of print.

Bibliography

ALLINGHAM: 1852
William Allingham, 'Irish Ballad Singers and Irish Street Ballads', an article in *Household Words*, vol. IV, No. 94, pp. 361–8, London, 1852.

AN CAMÁN: 1931–4
An Camán (published annually), Dublin, 1931–4. One of many short-lived periodicals in Irish, it contained short stories and words of songs, including a version of No. 48.

AN CLAIDHEAMH SOLUIS: 1899–1918
An Claidheamh Soluis, The Gaelic League Weekly, Dublin, 1899–1918. Contained a mixture of stories, essays, words of songs, including versions of Nos. 45 and 48. This periodical continued as *Fáinne an Lae*, 1918–19 and 1922–30 (q.v.).

AN GAODHAL: 1884–1904
An Gaodhal, New York, U.S.A., 1884–1904. Contains mixture of stories and songs, including a version of No. 29.

AN LOCHRANN: 1907–13
An Lóchrann: Kerry People, Tralee, Kerry, 1907–13 and with breaks of a few years in other places until 1931. Contains a mixture of stories and songs, including a version of No. 39.

AN tULTACH: 1924–
An tUltach, Ulster Gaelic League Monthly, Dundalk, Louth, 1924– (continuing). A number of Irish songs from Northern Ireland have been published in this periodical.

AR AGHAIDH: 1931–70
Ar Aghaidh, Connaught Press, Galway, 1931–70. A similar but smaller periodical to the previous item which concentrates more on Connaught Irish. Includes a version of No. 45.

BOULTON: 1913
Harold Boulton, *Songs of the Four Nations*: music arranged by Arthur Somervell, J. B. Cramer, London, 1913. Attempts to bring together 'national songs' of England, Scotland, Ireland and Wales, all with English words but also some verses given in original Cornish, Scots, Irish, Manx Gaelic and Welsh.

BREATHNACH: 1920
An tAthair P. Breathnach, *Ar gCeól Féinig*: Browne & Nolan, Dublin, 1920.

BREATHNACH: 1934
An tAthair P. Breathnach, *Ceól Ar Sínsear*: Browne & Nolan, Dublin, 1934. Two useful collections of songs in Irish from Southern Ireland. Music is written in tonic sol-fa only.

BREATHNACH: 1963
Breandán Breathnach: *Ceol Rince na hEireann*: Government Publication M.223, Dublin, 1963. A collection of dance music transcribed from oral transmission over a period of 20 years.

BREATHNACH: 1971
Breandán Breathnach, *Folk Music and Dances of Ireland*, Talbot Press, Dublin, 1971. A short illustrated history of Irish dancing and music.

BUNTING: 1796/1809/1840
Edward Bunting, *Ancient Irish Music*, first collection 1796, second collection 1809; *The Ancient Music of Ireland*, 1840. Bunting's first collection of 66 tunes, published in London, contained no words and was pirated by a Dublin publisher. His second volume contained both words and translations and was likewise used as the basis for Thomas Moore's *Irish Melodies*. *The Ancient Music of Ireland* contained 151 tunes. About 300 Irish folksongs appeared in the three collections. (See also O'SULLIVAN: 1927–39.)

CEOL: 1963
Ceol, Dublin, 1963– (continuing), published irregularly, edited by B. Breathnach. A periodical devoted exclusively to Irish music containing articles, dance music and songs in both Irish and English.

COSTELLO: 1919
Mrs E. Costello, 'Amhráin Mhuighe Seóla', *Journal of the Irish Folk-Song Society*: London, 1919 (also Three Candles Press, Dublin). 80 songs collected in Galway and Mayo with notes and translations, music in staff notation, including versions of Nos. 25, 32, 41 and 42.

DE NORAIDH: 1965
Liam de Noraidh, *Ceol ón Mumhain*: An Clóchomhar, Dublin, 1965. Contains 42 songs in Irish recorded in the 1940's in Southern Ireland. Music, in staff notation, includes a version of No. 41.

EIGSE: 1939
Éigse, A Journal of Irish Studies, edited by Colm O Lochlainn: Three Candles Press, Dublin, 1939– (continuing). A learned journal of mainly Irish studies but also containing some articles about and words of Irish folksongs.

FAINNE AN LAE: 1898–1900
Fáinne An Lae, edited by Brian O Dubhghaill, Dublin, 1898–1900. Contains a miscellany of articles in Irish.

FAINNE AN LAE: 1918–19 and 1922–30
Fáinne an Lae, Gaelic League Weekly, Dublin, 1918–19 and 1922–30. Continuation of *An Claidheamh Soluis*, 1899–1918. A periodical containing a mixture of stories, essays and words of songs, including a version of No. 29.

GAELIC JOURNAL: 1882–1909
Irisleabhar Na Gaedhilge (The Gaelic Journal), Dublin, 1882–1909. Contains mainly articles but includes some songs.

GRAVES: 1895
Alfred Percival Graves, *The Irish Song Book*: Sealy, Bryers and Walker, Dublin, 1895. A comprehensive collection using Irish titles but words in English. Music in staff notation.

GRAVES AND WOOD: 1897
A. P. Graves and Charles Wood, *Irish Folk Songs*: Boosey, London, 1897.

GRAVES: 1928
Alfred Percival Graves, *The Celtic Song Book*: Ernest Benn, London, 1928. (Representative Folk Songs of the Six Celtic Nations.) Contains 30 Irish songs in English with composed words.

HAMILTON: 1973
Nollaig O hUrmoltaigh (Noel Hamilton), *Ceolta Uladh*, vol. I: Queen's University, Belfast, 1973. Contains 11 Irish songs from Ulster with music in staff notation, including a version of Nos. 40 and 48.

HANNIGAN AND CLANDILLON: 1904/27
Margaret Hannigan and James Clandillon, *Londubh an Chairn*: Gaelic League, Dublin, 1904. 3 vols. Reprinted as *Songs of the Irish Gaels*: Oxford University Press, London, 1927. A valuable collection of 75 songs in both tonic sol-fa and staff notation with notes and translations.

HARDEBECK: 1908
Carl G. Hardebeck, *Seóda Ceóil*: Pigott & Co. Ltd., Dublin, 1908 (3 parts). Collection of traditional songs and a few composed by Hardebeck with piano accompaniment.

Bibliography

HARDEBECK: 1937

Carl G. Hardebeck, *Fiunn Fiadh Fuinidh*: Government Publications Nos. M.28 and M.32. Dublin, 1937 (2 parts). Two small collections of Irish songs with piano accompaniment, the second of which contains a version of No. 30.

HARDEBECK: 1936–52

Carl G. Hardebeck, Various Government Publications: Dublin, 1936–52. M.9–11; 17; 25; 27; 37; 42–4; 49; 51; 82; 149; 163; 165–6. A number of individual pieces each published with piano accompaniment, M.103 (1939) and M.164 (1950), are versions of Nos. 27 and 48.

HAYWARD: 1925

H. Richard Hayward, *Ulster Songs and Ballads*: Duckworth, London, 1925. A collection of songs in English mainly from the North of Ireland.

HENEBRY: 1928

Richard Henebry, *A Handbook of Irish Music*: Cork University Press, Cork and Longmans Green & Co., London, 1928. A study of mainly instrumental music, particularly violin, in which the author tried to show that the musical scale in Ireland differed from the well-tempered scale adopted elsewhere.

HENRY: 1924

Sam Henry, *Songs of the People*: Northern Constitution, Coleraine, Co. Derry, N. Ireland, 1924. Over 800 songs were published in the local Derry newspaper. Many were contributed by readers but it was Henry's diligent research and background notes that gave interest to each contribution.

HUGHES: 1904

Pádraig Mac Aodh O Néill (Herbert Hughes), *Songs of Uladh* (Ulster): Hughes & Campbell, Belfast, 1904. A small collection of Anglo-Irish songs from Ulster, music in staff notation.

HUGHES: 1909–36

Herbert Hughes, *Irish Country Songs*: Boosey, London, 1909–36. 4 vols. About 20 songs in each album collected in the northern counties of Ireland.

JFSS: 1899–1931

Journal of the Folk-Song Society: London (35 vols.), 1899–1931. Nos. 23, 24, 25, 1920–1. 'Eighty-four Irish Gaelic Songs' collected by A. Martin Freeman in Ballyvourney, Co. Cork. Music in staff notation with notes of other versions, translations and bibliography.

JIFSS: 1904–37

Journal of the Irish Folk-Song Society: London, 1904–37.

JOYCE: 1909

P. Weston Joyce, *Old Irish Folk Music and Songs*: University Press, Dublin, 1909. 842 Irish Airs and Songs, edited with annotations for the Royal Society of Antiquaries of Ireland of which Joyce was the President. Most of the music previously unpublished but some are versions of songs already in *Ancient Music of Ireland* (1873) and *Irish Peasant Songs in the English Language* (1906), both published by McGlashan & Gill, Dublin.

LLOYD: 1902–8

Joseph Lloyd and others, *Cláirseach na nGaedheal*: Gaelic League, Dublin, 1902–8 (5 parts). Each part, originally sold for threepence, gave some 50 songs of which a few were harmonised for voices.

MOFFAT: 1903

Alfred Moffat, *The Minstrelsy of Ireland*: Augener, London, 1903. A collection of popular Irish songs with piano accompaniment which has some useful annotations and historical information attached to the tunes.

MORTON: 1970

Robin Morton, *Folksongs Sung in Ulster*: Cork, 1970. 50 songs in English, music in staff notation, with notes.

O BAOIGHILL: 1944

Seán O Baoighill, *Cnuasacht de Cheoltaibh Uladh*: Comaltas Uladh a d'Foillsigh, 1944. Contains 25 songs collected in Donegal, in both staff notation and tonic sol-fa, but with no background information, and contains versions of Nos. 28, 34, 35, 41 and 42.

O'DALY/MANGAN: 1849

John O'Daly, *The Poets and Poetry of Munster*: A Selection of Irish Songs with poetical translations by James Clarence Mangan: Dublin, 1849. There were several later additions with considerable alterations in the contents. The second series 'with metrical translations by Erionnach [George Sigerson],' 1860. The 4th and 5th editions were published by James Duffy, Dublin, 1884. Irish texts and unharmonised airs give valuable examples of the florid Munster ornamentation of simple tunes in staff notation, and together with short biographies of Irish hedge-schoolmasters and peasant poets etc. make this book of especial interest.

O DUIBHGINN: 1960

Seosamh O Duibhginn, *Dónall Og*: An Clóchomhar, Dublin, 1960. Contains only one version of the music of this song (No. 31) but a large number of variant texts.

O FRIGHIL: 1952

Réamonn O Frighil: *Tiocfaidh an Samhradh*: Government Publication M.177, Dublin, 1952. A version of No. 48 with piano accompaniment.

O LOCHLAINN: 1939

Colm O Lochlainn, *Irish Street Ballads*: Three Candles, Dublin, 1939. Over 100 songs, words, music and annotations collected in many different parts of Ireland (including the North). All in English and many having equivalents in England and Scotland. Illustrated with woodcuts from the original broadsheets.

O LOCHLAINN: 1965

Colm O Lochlainn, *More Irish Street Ballads*: Three Candles, Dublin, 1965. A further 100 songs, all again in the English language.

O MUIRGHEASA: 1915

Enrí O Muirgheasa (Henry Morris), *Céad de Cheoltaibh Uladh*: Gill, Dublin, 1915. The texts of 100 songs in Ulster Irish with notes but no music.

O MUIRGHEASA: 1934

Enrí O Muirgheasa, *Dhá Chéad de Cheoltaibh Uladh*: Government Publications, Dublin, 1934. Words of 200 songs in Ulster Irish with only 6 tunes quoted in tonic sol-fa.

O'NEILL: 1910

Captain Francis O'Neill, *Irish Folk Music*: Regan Printing House, Chicago, 1910. A dissertation on the traditional songs and their variants containing a good many notes on the Gaelic.

O'SULLIVAN: 1927–39

Donal O'Sullivan, *The Bunting Collection*: Irish Folk-Song Society, London, 1927–39 (6 parts). A carefully edited selection from the first two Bunting collections including translations and background notes to songs with references to other versions.

O'SULLIVAN: 1952

Donal O'Sullivan, *Irish Folk Music and Song*: Three Candles, Dublin, 1952. Small reasonable history, no music examples.

O'SULLIVAN: 1958

Donal O'Sullivan, *Carolan*: Routledge & Kegan Paul, London, 1958. 2 vols. A study in depth of one of the last great Irish harpers with over 200 examples of his musical compositions.

O'SULLIVAN: 1960

Donal O'Sullivan, *Songs of the Irish*: Browne & Nolan, Dublin, 1960. A good collection of all kinds of songs in Irish, with notes and translations. 80 songs in staff notation, including Nos. 25, 30, 32 and 45.

O TUAMA: 1955–64

Seán Og O Tuama, *An Chóisir Cheoil*: Education Company of Ireland, Dublin, 1955–64. Vols. I–XI. 10–11 songs in Irish in each volume, music in staff notation and tonic sol-fa, but with no background information. Contains versions of No. 32 and 40.

Bibliography

PETRIE: 1855/1877/1882
George Petrie, *The Petrie Collection of the Ancient Music of Ireland*: M. H. Gill, Dublin, 1855. *Ancient Music of Ireland from the Petrie Collection*: Pigott, Dublin, 1877. *Music of Ireland*: M. H. Gill, Dublin, 1882.

PETRIE COLLECTION: 1902–5
George Petrie, *The Complete Petrie Collection*: ed. C. V. Stanford (3 parts) Boosey, London, 1902–5. Full details of the collection are given in JEFDSS: 1946, pp. 1–12 together with a list of tunes appearing in the 1855 and 1882 volumes.

RIMMER: 1969
Joan Rimmer, *The Irish Harp*: Mercier Press, Cork, 1969. A useful history of the harp in Ireland.

THE SHAMROCK: 1866–1901
The Shamrock, Dublin, 1866–1901. Consists mainly of articles but the issue for February 1872 contained a version of No. 27.

TREOIR: 1969
Treoir, bi-monthly magazine of Comhaltas Ceoltóirí Eireann (Irish Traditional Music, Song and Dance), Dublin. Mainly domestic information about the Society but occasionally contains songs and music.

WALSH: 1913
Rev. Patrick Walsh (An tAthair P. Breathnach), *Fuinn na Smól*: Browne & Nolan, Dublin, *c.* 1913. 7 parts in one, contains about 130 songs with Irish words and music in tonic sol-fa but with no background information. (See also BREATHNACH: 1934.)

WALSH: 1915–22
Rev. Patrick Walsh (An tAthair P. Breathnach), *Songs of the Gael*: Browne & Nolan, Dublin, 1915–22. 4 vols. Anglo-Irish songs in tonic sol-fa with no background notes.

ZIMMERMAN: 1966
Georges-Denis Zimmerman, *Irish Political Street Ballads and Rebel Songs (1780–1900)*: La Sirène, Geneva, Switzerland, 1966. A most valuable study of Anglo-Irish political balladry with 100 examples of texts, mostly with tunes in staff notation, and a useful bibliography.

III

Songs in Welsh

Introduction

The coming of the Celts to the British Isles occurred in the early part of the first millennium BC, and even though it is difficult to be precise about their movements it is generally agreed that the Late Bronze and Early Iron Age people were Celtic speaking, and that by the sixth century AD the Welsh language had developed.

Unfortunately, little can be gleaned about Celtic music during the pre-Christian era, but there are references to the Celtic poets or bards who sang odes in the land of Gaul which testify that music was an important element in Celtic civilisation. The language of the Gauls, Galeg—a descendant of the Celtic mother-tongue—can be called the sister language of Goedeleg, which was the tongue spoken by the Celts of Ireland, and from which developed Hen Wyddeleg (Old Irish), Manaweg (Manx) and Gaeleg (the Gaelic of Scotland). Another sister language was Brythoneg, spoken by the Celts of the main island of Britain, and from which developed Cymraeg (Welsh), Cernyweg (Cornish) and Llydaweg (Breton). It is interesting and significant to note that the leading terms used by the Welsh tribesmen to describe the skills of poets and musicians are of purely Celtic origin, for example 'bardd' (poet), 'prydydd' (maker), 'cerddor' (musician), 'crwth' (crowd).

In the tenth-century Laws of Hywel Dda, a prince who convened a conference which standardized the laws throughout Wales, there is evidence to substantiate the importance of music in the lives of the Cymry, and the references to the Penkerdd (Chief of Song) and Bardd Teulu (Bard of the Household) show clearly the importance of those responsible for music and poetry—an importance which can only be explained by a continual growth in the function of music and poetry in the lives of the Cymry throughout the centuries.

Giraldus Cambrensis in the twelfth century affords further evidence of the musical awareness of the Welsh in his references to their superb skill in part singing. Nothing however is written of the music of the Middle Ages, except a strange notation of string music ('cerdd dant') in the Penllyn manuscript. (See JONES, WILLIAMS AND PUGH: 1870 and CROSSLEY-HOLLAND: 1942.)

Nevertheless it is known that the bardic and musical tradition flourished in Wales up until the Tudor period. Indeed the bardic tradition had developed into an elaborate system of classical poetry and had produced a substantial body of literature—a major factor in the existence of a literature which extends in an unbroken tradition from about the middle of the sixth century to the present day.

However the disappearance of the 'uchelwr' or nobleman in Tudor times was a severe blow to the Bardic tradition, and marked the end of what may be fairly described as the Golden Age of mediaeval Welsh poetry. As far as the musical tradition was concerned the effect was disastrous, for it was almost completely lost, and no record of Welsh music exists before 1742.

This is not to say that the 'gwerin' (the people of Wales) had become silent. On the contrary the song was taken from the 'llys' (court) to the tavern, fair and mart, and the numerous harpers of this period were also well versed in the Bardic tradition already referred to. The music of these popular harpers included songs which were related to the traditional Welsh holidays, the matin carols of Christmas for instance, as well as numerous original songs, but unfortunately little was committed to writing.

In the eighteenth century the Methodist Revival proved to be an influence which nearly killed the folksinging of Wales as it did the popular Anterliwt (Interlude). The singing of

Thomas of Llangwm, Corwen,
erionethshire
Photograph: Peter Kennedy

popular songs was deemed to be an exercise in vulgarity, and the joys of singing, dancing and playing games no better. For generations the 'gwerin' was, for the most part, silent under a mantle of respectability and too reticent to express its feelings and experiences in its old songs.

The first attempt to collect and publish harp tunes was made in the nineteenth century by the celebrated Welsh harpers who became famous in London. The three most eminent of these were John Parry Rhiwabon, the celebrated blind harper, John Parry (Bardd Alaw) and Edward Jones (Bardd y Brenin). According to Edward Jones the tunes were collected from hearing them being played by 'venerable harpers' in North Wales (see GWYNN WILLIAMS: 1932). Many of these were based on old melodies and dance tunes and arranged as variations for the harp, and many became popular later as excellent songs, such as those arranged by Brinley Richards (RICHARDS: 1879). Others were used as Penillion airs in the traditional Bardic style of North Wales.

This distinctive feature of Welsh music—'canu gyda'r tannau' (singing with harp strings) —deserves a word of explanation. It is considered to be more of the Bardic tradition than of the folk class, and has been practised in Wales for centuries (see GWYNN WILLIAMS: 1932). Strictly speaking it is the singing of extemporised verses or set poems to an original counterpoint woven around some well-known melody played by the harper. The singer does not start with the harper's melody, but fits in his verse in such a way as to end with it. The style is typically Welsh, and is particularly suited to the genius of the Welsh language.

This type of singing is very much in vogue in Wales today, and is one of the greatest joys in the music-making of the Welsh. There are now plenty of young harpers preparing themselves to meet the popular demand. Penillion singers have their own National Society, and a national festival is held annually to foster the art. So popular has been its musical development in recent years that groups and choirs are formed to sing a prepared counterpoint in unison or in parts. This particular style is well suited to, and is a wonderful expression of the Welshman's love of poetry, and indeed has been exploited by professional musicians (see CLEAVER: 1968).

Wales has a store of folksongs, a rich inheritance of melodies which were on the point of being lost for ever but for the formation of the Welsh Folk Song Society at the beginning of this century. From 1908 hundreds of these lovely old tunes and their variants have been collected. Discarded by singers and musicians at one period, they now are an essential part in the activities of groups and choirs, professional singers and composers, and are taught in the schools. In short, they are an essential part of the music-making of Wales.

The Welsh folksongs proper are usually much shorter and less highly developed in form than those of Ireland and Scotland, and show very little ornamentation. In spite of their notable simplicity, the wealth and variety of Welsh folksongs prompted the English musician, Sir Richard Terry, to describe the Welsh folksong as 'second, I think, to none—unless it be Irish'. Dr J. Lloyd Williams, the first editor of the Journal of the Welsh Folk Song Society, said of the typical folk tune:

> The melodies were simple, devoid of modulation or chromatics, and without vocal difficulties, but they were frequently beautiful in form and most expressive in spirit. In the best examples, the harmony of word and note, of musical and rhetorical accent, is so perfect that it is difficult to decide whether the music is an attempt to express the words or whether the two grew up together in intimate union. As to their origin, we know that certain of them, very few in number it is true, were composed; some of the others may be communal for aught we know, it matters little which. It is certain that most if not all of them have been modified by the singing of successive generations till they have assumed their present form.*

* Vol. I, part I, p. 19.

Introduction

Many of the characteristic tunes are in the Dorian mode, or as Dr Alfred Daniell thinks (JWFSS: vol. I, part 2), in a scale which is some kind of a 'quasi-Dorian recitative Mode . . . full of quarter tones and augmented or grave intervals'. This scale, seemingly, is the basis of the Welsh 'hwyl' so characteristic of the style of the old Welsh preacher, a word now frequently used outside Wales to denote the gusto of the Welsh singing felt even at a Welsh rugby match. The majority of melodies however are in the major or minor (Modern and Aeolian), certainly the minor—although less used than the major—is a great favourite with the Welsh singer.

The words of the most lyrical Welsh folk tunes have a unique and specific feature in that they reflect the complex principles of 'cynghanedd', the elaborate system of consonantal and vocalic harmony found in Welsh verse written in strict metre (assonance and alliteration in English poetry faintly resemble it).

The first real attempt to collect folksongs proper in Wales was made by Maria Jane Williams of Aberpergwm in the Neath Valley (WILLIAMS: 1844). These were songs 'collected among the peasantry of the districts of Gwent and Morgannwg'. The following year saw the publication of *The Cambrian Minstrels* by John Thomas (Ieuan Ddu) (THOMAS: 1845). Both attempts contained beautiful unpublished folk tunes. Clearly there was a wealth of material among the people in the valleys and glens of South Wales. Not before the beginning of this century however did Wales take seriously the collecting and singing of its folksongs. The work started with an enthusiastic group of young students from the University College of North Wales, Bangor, in 1906. They formed a society called the Canorian (Songsters). Their leader was Dr J. Lloyd Williams, a lecturer in Botany, who was given responsibility for music at the college and who became the great pioneer of the folksong movement in Wales. It was he who sent the young enthusiasts home to their respective districts during vacations intent on collecting the old songs of the people. So successful were they that a movement was started by influential people connected with the University College of North Wales to found a society which would collect and study Welsh folksongs. Consequently the Welsh Folk Song Society was formed in 1908, and its first journal was published in 1909 with Dr J. Lloyd Williams as editor. He was succeeded by W. S. Gwynn Williams, the present editor. The four published volumes completed to date contain hundreds of songs and variants from all districts of North and South Wales in both staff and sol-fa notation, with notes on sources and singers.

The songs selected for this book are more recent in period and do not as a whole possess the quality of the older traditional songs already published: some of them are evidently and consciously intentional, in contrast to the spontaneity of some of the older songs handed down by oral tradition, but some are certainly old and traditional in style and character. Others are 'family versions' in the sense that they were noted or recorded from the singing of people who could remember previous generations singing them, and these represent the old folk style of singing of the last century. Although the tradition of folk singing is slowly dying, these recent field recordings prove that it still lingers on, and even today the young people of Wales are in more modern performances, very conscious of the true native characteristics of the old folksongs.

PRONUNCIATION OF WELSH

Welsh is phonetic, and the majority of letters and combinations of letter have one sound. With few exceptions, Welsh letters are pronounced as in English.

Consonants

b, d, h, l, m, n, p, s, t, w, i (like *y* in *yes*) as in English.

The following have English sounds but they are not always represented by the same letters:

c	as *k* in *k*itten. (There is no k in Welsh.)
dd	as *th* in see*the*
f	as *v* in *v*ow
ff, ph	as *f* in *f*air
g	as *g* in *g*um
ng	*ng* in lo*ng*; *ng* in Ba*ng*or and da*ng*os are as in li*ng*er
s	as *s* in *s*ing and *c* in dan*c*e
th	as *th* in *th*rong
si	as *sh* in *sh*op

The following have different sounds from the English:

r	strong and more like the Scottish *r*
rh	*r* softened
ll	this is difficult: it should be produced by placing the tongue in the same position as *l* and emitting breath rather sharply
ch	like the German *ch* in ma*ch*en
mh, nh and ng	almost like *m*, *n* and *ng* in English, but with an emission of breath.

Vowels

long a	as *a* in r*a*ther
short a	as *a* in s*a*t
long e	as *a* in m*a*te, but it is an open consonant
short e	as *e* in s*e*t
long i	as *ea* in s*ea*m
short i	as *i* in sl*i*m
long o	as *o* in h*o*me, but it is an open consonant
short o	as *o* in sh*o*t
long w	as *oo* in m*oo*d
short w	as *oo* in s*oo*t
u	in South Wales this is pronounced like the short *i*; in North Wales it is more obscure or guttural
y	has two sounds: one is like the short *i*, and the other like *u* in f*u*n

Diphthongs

ai, ae, au	as *aye*
oi, oe, ou	as *oy* in j*oy*
iw, uw, yw	as *eu* in *eu*logy
aw	as *aow* in mi*aow*
ei, eu, ey	as *y* in th*y*
ow	as *ow* in l*ow*; sometimes like *ow* in c*ow*

The circumflex is used to denote the long vowel when words of one syllable have two meanings, e.g. glan, glân, mor, môr.

Emphasis

The emphasis is nearly always on the penultimate syllable in polysyllabic words.

The following example of emphasis is the first verse from *Bwmba* (No. 54), in which an accent is shown in polysyllabic words:

Original	*Phonetic*
Pan roeddwn i gynt yn fachgen	Pan roédd-wn i gynt yn fách-gen
Bwmba, bwmba, bwmba didl dei	*Bwm-ba, bwm-ba, bwm-ba di-dl déi*
Heb feddwl fowr am angen	Heb fédd-wl fowr am áng-en
Fe roddes fy mryd ar ferched glân	Fe róddes fy mryd ar férched glân
I hala'r byd yn llawen	I há-la'r byd yn lláw-en

49 AMBELL I GAN
AN OCCASIONAL SONG

1 Ambell i gân a geidw fy mron
   Rhag suddo i lawr dan ambell i don
   Mae'r awel mor siriol, mor swynol, mor lân
   Diolchaf o galon am ambell i gân

2 Ambell i gân dry d'wllwch y nos
   Mor olau â'r dydd, mor siriol â'r rhos
   Caddugawl anobaith gymylau fel gwlân
   Y troant os gallaf gael ambell i gân

3 Ambell i gân rydd nerth yn y fraich
   A'r ysgwydd i gario amal i faich
   A grym anawsterau falurir yn lân
   Os gallaf gael canu ambell i gân

4 Ambell i gân a gaf yn y byd
   Ond teithiaf i wlad fydd yn ganu i gyd
   Ac wedi im adael yr anial yn lân
   Gobeithiaf gael canu nid ambell i gân

1 Sometimes a song it doth keep my breast
   From sinking right under those many wave-crests
   So charming, so sweet, and so fair is the tongue
   I'm always so thankful for the occasional song

2 Sometimes a song will turn darkness of night
   Into day that's as light as the moorland so bright
   When the dark clouds, like wool, above me do form
   They'll all disappear with my occasional song

3 Sometimes a song the arm will make strong
   Also my shoulder to carry loads on
   But the power of obstruction will be overcome
   If I can but give you an occasional song

4 An occasional song makes the world roll along
   When I am a-travelling to a land that's all song
   And when from the wilderness completely I've gone
   I hope I'll sing more than an occasional song

50 AR BEN WAUN TREDEGAR
ON THE FENS OF TREDEGAR

Ar ben Waun Tre-de-gar mae ei-rin a chnau

Ar ben Waun Tre-de-gar mae fal-e ym mis Mai

Ar ben Waun Tre-de-gar mae ffrwyth-e o bob rhyw

Ar ben Waun Tre-de-gar mae nghar-iad i'n byw

1 Ar ben Waun Tredegar mae eirin a chnau
Ar ben Waun Tredegar mae fale ym mis Mai
Ar ben Waun Tredegar mae ffrwythe o bob rhyw
Ar ben Waun Tredegar mae nghariad i'n byw

2 Fy nghariad a 'notws i wylad y nos

Fy nghariad a wedws, do, lawer gair crôs
Fy nghariad a 'nodws i edrych yn llon
Fy nghariad a dorrws fy nghalon i bron

3 Mae heb ei thorri eto ond mae'n glwyfus iawn o hyd
Wrth feddwl am y bachgen sy 'mhell dros y byd
Mae digon o fechgyn yn agos ac ymhell

Ond beth dâl am hynny, mae nghariad i'n well?

4 Chwi ferched ieuainc hawddgar na charwch ddim
ond un
Gochelwch gael eich denu gan grechyn teg ei lun
Mae cariad fel y moroedd yn chwyddo fyth i'r lan
Mae'r ferch sy'n caru'n gywir yn canu clychau'r llan

1 On the fens of Tredegar there are damsons and nuts
On the fens of Tredegar there are apples in May
On the fens of Tredegar there are all kinds of fruit
On the fens of Tredegar there my sweetheart she
stays

2 My sweetheart at night-time she made me just watch
her
My sweetheart spoke many's the word that was cross
My sweetheart she made me pretend to look happy
My sweetheart she's nearly my heart broke away

3 It isn't quite broken but it's still very painful
When I think of the lad who's far o'er the deep
Though there're plenty of young men in every
direction
What matter that when my love's the most sweet?

4 You young loving maidens, love none but one only

Beware the attractions of a good-looking swell
My love's like the waves that break on the sea-shore
The girl who loves truly will ring the church bell

136

51 AR LAN Y MOR
BESIDE THE SEA

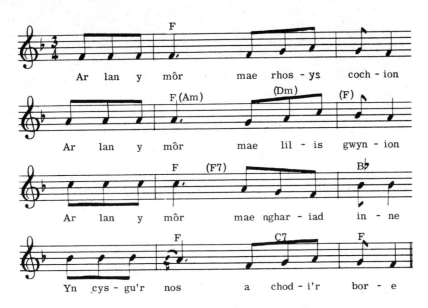

Ar lan y môr mae rhos - ys coch - ion

Ar lan y môr mae lil - is gwyn - ion

Ar lan y môr mae nghar - iad in - ne

Yn cys - gu'r nos a chod - i'r bor - e

1 Ar lan y môr mae rhosys cochion
Ar lan y môr mae lilis gwynion
Ar lan y môr mae nghariad inne
Yn cysgu'r nos a chodi'r bore

2 Oer yw'r rhew ac oer yw'r eira
Oer yw'r tŷ heb dân yn y gaea'
Oer yw'r eglwys heb ddim ffeirad
Oer wyf innau heb fy nghariad

3 Dacw'r tŷ a dacw'r talcen
Lle ces i nosweithiau llawen
Ar y lloft uwchben y gegin
Gyda'r ferch â'r rhuban melyn

4 Mae gen i fuwch â dau gorn arian,
Mae gen i fuwch sy'n godro'i hunan
Mae gen i fuwch sy'n llanw'r stwcau
Fel mae'r môr yn llanw'r baeau

1 Beside the sea there are red roses
Beside the sea there're lovely lilies
Beside the sea my sweetheart lives
Asleep at night and awake at morning

2 Cold is the frost and cold the snowfall
Cold the house without fire in winter
Cold is the church without a vicar
Cold am I also without my lover

3 Yonder's the home and yonder the building
Where I've spent many a happy evening
In the loft there above the kitchen
With the girl with the yellow ribbon

4 I've a cow with two horns of silver
I've a cow milks herself on her own
I've a cow that fills the pails up
Just like the sea which fills the seashore

52 BACHGEN IFANC YDWYF
I AM A YOUNG MAN

Bach-gen if-anc yd—wyf Yn dech-rau cod-i 'mhen—

Yn nydd—iau fy ienc-tyd Yn ca—ru lod-es wen—

Ei char-u a'i chof-leid—io A gof-yn idd-i hi—

A leic-iai yn ei chal-on fach Gael bach-gen fel my-fi?—

1. Bachgen ifanc ydwyf
   Yn dechrau codi 'mhen
   Yn nyddiau fy ienctyd
   Yn caru lodes wen
   Ei charu a'i chofleidio
   A gofyn iddi hi
   A leiciai yn ei chalon fach
   Gael bachgen fel myfi?

2. Rwy'n fachgen i gymydog
   Rwy'n fachgen i neb o bell
   Rwy'n cynnig fy hunan i chwi
   Does genny ddim sydd well
   Does genny ddim tai na thiroedd
   Nag arian chwaeth ar log
   Ond byw trwy fodd ar 'wyllys Duw
   Yn llawen fel y gog

3. Yn debyg i'r golomen
   Sy'n pigo'r gwenith gwyn
   Mae honno mor ddiniwed
   Na wnaiff hi ddrwg i ddim
   Ond pan ddaw'r saethwr heibio
   A 'nelu dan ei bron
   Dim chwaneg o sôn amdani, Syr
   Heblaw hwdiwch, pluwch hon

1. I am a young man
   About to take notice
   In the days of my youth
   Courting a fair maid
   Loving and caressing
   And then asking her
   Would she in her little heart
   Have a young man like me?

2. I'm a son of a neighbour
   And of none far away
   I offer myself to you
   I have nothing better
   Neither land nor houses
   Or money on interest
   But I'm living by God's will
   As happy as the cuckoo

3. I am like the dove
   Who picks ripening wheat
   She is so innocent
   That she will harm nothing
   But when the hunter comes shooting
   And aims at her bosom
   No more mention of her, Sir
   Except, here, take this

53 Y BACHGEN MAIN
THE LANKY LAD

Fel yr oedd-wn i'n rhod-io'r gae-af Dydd Mawrth diw-edd-af o ddydd-iau'r byd

Mewn lle is-el dan goed-wig daw-el Lle clywn ryw ddwy'n ym-gom-io 'nghyd

Nes-u wnes i'n nes nes at-ynt Nes oedd-wn i yn y lle a'r man

A phwy oedd yn — o yn ym-gom-io Ond f'ann-wyl gar-iad gyd-a'i mam

1. Fel yr oeddwn i'n rhodio'r gaeaf
   Dydd Mawrth diweddaf o ddyddiau'r byd
   Mewn lle isel dan goedwig dawel
   Lle clywn ryw ddwy'n ymgomio 'nghyd
   Nesu wnes i'n nes nes atynt
   Nes oeddwn i yn y lle a'r man
   A phwy oedd yno yn ymgomio
   Ond f'annwyl gariad gyda'i mam

2. Ai ti sydd yna fy annwyl eneth?
   Gyda mi a'th ddwylaw'n rhydd
   Yn lân dy drwsiad a hardd dy osodiad
   A minnau am dy fatsio sydd
   Cei fowntio'th geffyl fy nghangen gynnil
   A gweision sifil iawn i'w trin
   A golud bydol sef aur melynion
   Ac arian gloywon wrth dy glin

3. Pe cawn i rannau gwledydd India
   Sidan Persia aur Peru
   Gwell genny'r mab 'rwyf yn ei garu
   'Rwyf am sefyll iddo'n *driw*
   O ai fel yna rwyt ti'n darparu
   Cei gweirio'th wely ar bigau'r drain
   Oni choeli 'm geiriau bydd chwerw'r chwarae
   Os mentri gyda'r bachgen main

4. Gyda'r bachgen main mi fentraf
   Mam a d'wedyd i chwi'r gwir
   Gadawa' i'r moddion i'r cybyddion
   A mentraf gyda blodau'r sir
   Ei wyneb purwyn a'i wallt melyn
   Ac ar ei rudd y mae dwy ros
   A gwyn fyd y ferch a fyddo
   Yn ei freichiau'n cysgu'r nos

1. As I was out walking in winter
   On Tuesday, the last day of the year
   In a quiet forest beside a low covert
   I heard two women talking there
   And as I approached them much closer
   Until by that place I drew near
   And who was it talking together
   With her mother, my own dearest dear

2. Is it thou who art there, O my dearest?
   Our hands are not joined, but you're near
   Your dress is so fine, you're the fairest
   I'm longing to marry you, dear
   You may mount horses, my precious
   Kind servants to look after thee
   Burning gold, the wealth of the worldly
   And bright silver to your knee

3. If I should own parts of all India
   Persian satins and gold of Peru
   I'd still like the boy of my choosing
   And wish to stay faithful and true
   If that is the way you're intending
   You can lie on a bed of sharp thorns
   Believe me or words will turn bitter
   If you dare go with that lanky young lad

4. With that lanky lad, mother, I'll venture
   I must tell you what is the truth
   For I must leave physic to misers
   And go with the flowers of the field
   His clean face and hair of the fairest
   On his cheeks two roses add charms
   And blessed be the girl who'll be with him
   And sleeping at night in his arms

54 BWMBA
BOOMBA

Pan roedd-wn i gynt yn fach — gen Bwm-ba, bwm-ba, bwm-ba did-l dei

Heb fedd - wl fowr am ang — en Fe rodd-es fy mryd ar fer - ched glân

I hal - a'r byd yn llaw - en CH: Bwm - ba, bwm - ba, bwm - ba did-l dei

Bwm - ba, bwm - ba bei - bo Fe rodd - es fy mryd ar

fer - ched glân, I hal - a'r byd yn llaw - en

1 Pan roeddwn i gynt yn fachgen
   Bwmba, bwmba, bwmba didl dei
   Heb feddwl fowr am angen
   Fe roddes fy mryd ar ferched glân
   I hala'r byd yn llawen
   Bwmba, bwmba, bwmba didl dei
   Bwmba bwmba bei bo
   Fe roddes fy mryd ar ferched glân
   I hala'r byd yn llawen

2 O'r diwedd fe briodes
   À'r lana' ferch a welais
   Fe fuase'n well imi, wir ddyn byw'
   Briodi â Gwyddeles

3 Ni alle hi weu na gwnio
   Na golchi'n lân na stilio
   Na rhoddi clwtyn ar ryw hen fritsh
   Fe haedde'r *witsh* ei chico

4 Fe gane wrth fynd i'r gwely
   Fe lefe beth wrth godi
   Eistedde i lawr o flaen y tân
   'Se awr yn rhy fach iddi grafu

1 When I was a raw and a rakish elf
   Boomba, boomba, boomba all the day
   Little did I to better myself
   For I lost my heart to the pretty little girls
   For the merriest life in the world-o
   Boomba, boomba, boomba diddle day
   Boomba boomba die-do
   For I lost my heart to the pretty little girls
   For the merriest life in the world-o

2 To one of those girls I soon got hooked
   Better for me if I never had looked
   Better for me if I never had lived
   Or plumped for an Irish maid-o

3 Spin not, knit not, neither could she sew
   Cleaning clothes she did not know
   To patch my pants she would not try
   She's a witch and fit to be kicked-o

4 She'd sing before she'd fall asleep
   Morning came she'd up and weep
   Before the fire she'd sit and stretch
   And scratch for an hour or more-o

5 O'r diwedd fe ddaeth Ange'
  Ymaflodd yn ei sodle'
  A thyna fel aeth y *bitsh* o'r byd
  A thyna 'i gyd oedd eisie'

5 Now at last her turn to go
  For Death came in and laid her low
  And that's the tale of my old bitch
  And the end was the best of all-o

55 Y CEFFYL DU
THE BLACK HORSE

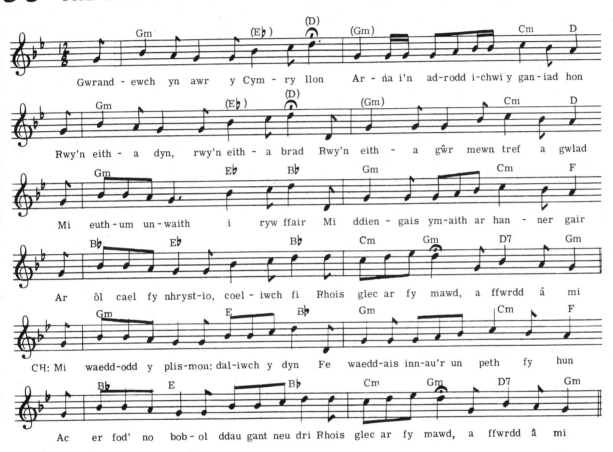

Gwrand - ewch yn awr y Cym - ry llon   Ar - na i'n ad-rodd i-chwi y gan-iad hon

Rwy'n eith - a dyn, rwy'n eith - a brad Rwy'n eith - a gŵr mewn tref a gwlad

Mi euth - um un - waith i ryw ffair Mi ddien - gais ym-aith ar han - ner gair

Ar ôl cael fy nhryst-io, coel - iwch fi Rhois glec ar fy mawd, a ffwrdd â mi

CH: Mi waedd-odd y plis-mon: dal-iwch y dyn Fe waedd-ais inn-au'r un peth fy hun

Ac er fod' no bob - ol ddau gant neu dri Rhois glec ar fy mawd, a ffwrdd â mi

1 Gwrandewch yn awr, y Cymry llon
  Arna i'n adrodd ichwi y ganiad hon
  Rwy'n eitha dyn, rwy'n eitha brad
  Rwy'n eitha gŵr mewn tref a gwlad
  Mi euthum unwaith i ryw ffair
  Mi ddiengais ymaith ar hanner gair
  Ar ôl cael fy nhrystio, coeliwch fi
  Rhois glec ar fy mawd, a ffwrdd â mi
  Mi waeddodd y plismon: daliwch y dyn
  Fe waeddais innau'r un peth fy hun
  Ac er fod'no bobol ddau gant neu dri
  Rhois glec ar fy mawd, a ffwrdd â mi

1 You joyous Welshmen, listen I pray
  And hear the words of this song I say
  I'm quite a traitor, I'm quite a man
  I'm quite a fellow in country and town
  Once I took myself to a fair
  Say half a word and I'd fly from there
  Having been trusted, I'll tell to thee
  With a click of my thumb, away with me
  The policeman he shouted: O catch that man
  And I myself shouted the very same thing
  Although there were people, two hundred or three
  With a click of my thumb, away with me →

2 Mi brynais geffyl gan ryw ddyn
A hwnnw'n *rogue* fel fi fy hun
Cynigiais iddo ddeugain punt
Am geffyl *sound* heb dorri ei wynt
Y dyn a ddwedodd chwi wyddoch y drefn
A pharodd i minnau fynd ar ei gefn
Rhois innau sbardun i'r hen geffyl du
A chlec ar fy mawd, a ffwrdd â mi

3 Mi dwyllais y bwtcher ar ryw dro
O hanner dafad a hanner llo
Ac er fod y bwtcher yn hen fachgen cwic
Ond dangosais iddo bertiach tric
Rhois i'r hen fachgen ddau lygad du
A chlec ar fy mawd a ffwrdd â mi

4 Mi es am frecwast i'r Cwc Siop
Ces yno *steaks* a *mutton chops*
Ac yno bum yn brysur iawn
Am ennyd fer yn brysur iawn
Daeth bechgyn eraill at y bwrdd
A minnau'r pen arall yn mynd i ffwrdd
Tra'n tendio rhain bu gwraig y tŷ
Rhois glec ar fy mawd, a ffwrdd â mi

5 Mi es i'r siop am ddillad ar fy hynt
A phrynais yno werth dwy bunt
Fe ddwedais wrtho y talwn yn ffri
A'r gwas ddanfonodd ef gyda mi
Ond wrth imi basio heibio yr Harp
A'r bachgen nid oedd yn hanner siarp
Fe safodd yn ôl ddau gam neu dri
Rhois glec ar fy mawd a ffwrdd â mi

2 I purchased a horse which I got from a man
The man was a rogue, just such as I am
For it I offered him forty pounds
If it weren't chesty, but perfectly sound
Then said the man: You know what to do
So I got on the horse to see if 'twere true
In the old black horse I dug my heels
With a click of my thumb, away with me

3 Once in a while the butcher I'd cheat
Of half a calf or half a sheep
Although the butcher's a fine smart lad
A clever trick I showed him I had
Two black eyes I gave him, you see
And a click of my thumb and away with me

4 For breakfast I went into the cook-shop
There I had steak and mutton chops
The time I was there I was busying along
Busy indeed for I didn't stay long
To the end of the table some other boys came
And I at the other end going away
And whilst the waitress attended to these
With a click of my thumb, away with me

5 I called at the shop to get clothes on my way
They came to a total of two pounds to pay
I told him that I would pay so free
But he sent the assistant along with me
And as we were passing along by The Harp
The boy he wasn't just half enough sharp
He stayed behind me a step, two or three
With a click of my thumb, away with me

56 Y DERYN DU
THE BLACKBIRD

Y der - yn du sy'n rhod — io'r gwled - ydd

Hi a ŵyr yr hen a'r new - ydd

A roi di gyng - or i — fach - gen - nyn

Sydd yn cur - io ers gwell na blwydd - yn

A roi di gyn - gor i mi ?

1 Y deryn du sy'n rhodio'r gwledydd
Hi a ŵyr yr hen a'r newydd
A roi di gyngor i fachgennyn
Sydd yn curio ers gwell na blwyddyn
A roi di gyngor i mi?

2 O dyro'n nes fachgennyn gwrando
Gael gwybod beth sydd yn dy flino
Pa un ai'r byd sy'n troi'n dy erbyn
Neu curio rwyt am gariad rhywun
A fynni di gyngor gen i?

3 O nid y byd sy'n troi'n fy erbyn
Na churio rwyf am gariad rhywun
Ond gweld y merched glan yn ymballu
Nis gwn pa le 'droi 'mhen i garu
A roi di gyngor i mi?

4 A fynni di yr hen wraig weddw
Sydd â'i chôd yn llawn yn ymyl marw
A'i gwartheg duon yn y buches
Fe wna honno iti fawrles
A fynni di honno i ti?

1 O in our country there dwells the blackbird
Who knows the old and who knows the new
Will you give a young lad some advising
Who has been pining for more than a year
Will you give advice to me?

2 O my young lad, will you come closer
That I may hear and heed your part
Whether the world has turned against you
Or whether you're longing for someone's heart
Will you take advice from me?

3 It's not the world that's turned against me
Nor am I longing for any girl's heart
But it's seeing all those pretty girls disappearing
That I'm confused where to play my part
Will you give advice to me?

4 O would you have an old widowed woman
On the brink of death with money in her purse
And in the barn some fine black cattle
To you she'd be of the greatest use
Will you take that one for thee?   ⟶

5 Ni fynnaf i mo'r hen wraig weddw
Sydd â'i chôd yn llawn yn ymyl marw
A'i gwartheg duon yn y buches
I lanc tylawd dyw hon ddim fawrles
Ni fynna i mo honno i mi

6 Wel, fynni dithau ferch tafarnwr
Sydd â'i phen yn llawn o synnw'r
A'i chwrw a'i bîr a'i chwarter parod
Yn derbyn arian bob pen diwrnod
A fynni di honno i ti?

7 Ni fynnaf i mo ferch tafarnwr
Sydd â'i phen yn llawn o synnw'r
Pan fo'r pwrs yn brysur lluchio
A llawer ceiniog ddrwg fydd ynddo
Ni fynna'i mo honno i mi

8 Wel, fynni di y lân wnyddes
Sydd gyda'i nodwydd fain a'i phinces
Ti gei dy grys yn lân bob amser
Fy fyddai honno'n well na llawer
A fynni di honno i ti?

9 Ni fynnaf i mo'r lân wnyddes
Sydd gyda'i nodwydd fain a'i phinces
Pan fo arnaf eisie nythio
Fe fydd y wynthrew ar ei dwylo
Ni fynna'i mo honno i mi

10 Wel, fynni di ferch yr hwsmon
Sydd yn gangen lawen dirion
Dyry arian i'r cornelau
A neidia naid am naid i tithau
A fynni di honno i ti?

11 Wel, ffarwel bellach iti aderyn
Wel, dyma'r ferch rwyf yn ei mofyn
Tra llong ar fôr a gro mewn afon
Ni fynnaf byth ond merch yr hwsmon
Ffarwel, ffarwel i ti

5 I do not want the old widowed woman
On the brink of death with money in her purse
And her brown cattle in the milk-shed
To a poor lad like me she'd offer little
I will not take that one for me

6 O would you have the innkeeper's daughter
Whose head is filled with common sense
With her quarts of beer all standing ready
And counting the money at the long day's end
Will you take that one for thee?

7 I do not want the innkeeper's daughter
Whose head is filled with common sense
When the bags of money grow old and dusty
There'll be many bad pennies between her and me
I will not take that one for me

8 O would you have the handsome seamstress
With her case of pins and her needles fine
From her a clean shirt you'll ne'er be wanting
O she'll be better than most for thee
Will you take that one for thee?

9 I do not want the handsome seamstress
With her case of pins and her needles fine
For when that I shall need to winnow
With hoar frost her hands will be stiffened
I'll not take that one for me

10 O would you have the bailiff's daughter
She's the most happy and gentlest branch
She puts her money in the neatest corners
She'll welcome thee if you give her the chance
Will you take that one for thee?

11 Then I'll bid farewell to you, O blackbird
For she's the girl I wish to love
While there's ships on the sea and stones on the sea-b
The bailiff's daughter, I'll have none but she
Fare-thee-well, farewell to thee

57 DYWETSE'R HEN DDYN WRTH EI FERCH
THE OLD MAN SAID TO HIS DAUGHTER DEAR

Dywet-se'r hen ddyn wrth ei ferch O dac - w'r hen fab tir - ion

O dyn - a le braf i ti gynn - al tai Os med - ri ar dy gal — on

O dyn - a le braf i ti gynn - al tai Os med - ri ar dy gal — on

1 Dywetse'r hen ddyn wrth ei ferch
O dacw'r hen fab tirion
O dyna le braf i ti gynnal tai
Os medri ar dy galon
O dyna le braf i ti gynnal tai
Os medri ar dy galon

2 Braf yw'r tai a theg yw'r tir
A dweud y gwir amdano
Fy annwyl dad, na ddigiwch ddim
Ni fynna'i ddim o'r henddyn
(Repeat the last two lines)

3 Ti gei gyda'r henddyn ddigon o dai
Cei aur, cei arian ddigon
A da a defaid o bob rhyw
Beth na gewn ni gan feibion

4 Mae'n well gen' i gael buwch neu ddwy
O'r siort rwyf i'n eu mofyn
A godro'r ddwy'r un pryd i'm pec
Na gwrando ar glec yr henddyn

5 Ti gei fynd i'r gwely gwyn
O bluf yr adarn gwyllt'on
A phluf tylluan a phluf y dryw
Beth na gewn ni gan feibion

6 Mae'n well gen' i fyned i wely o frwyn
A cha'l mab mwy i'm hoedran
Na mynd i'r gwely gwyn o bluf
A chyda'r henddyn druan

7 Ti gei eistedd ar ei glin
Cei yfed gwin a chwrw
Ag o ba les fydd gwin i mi
Ar glin yr hen fab gweddw

1 The old man said to his daughter dear
There's a gentle old bachelor there-o
And property fine for you to share
If your heart would only care-o
And property fine for you to share
If your heart would only care-o

2 The houses are large and the land's not bad
To tell you the truth it's my plan-o
O father dear, please don't get mad
But I shall not wed the old man-o
(Repeat the last two lines)

3 With the old man you'll have houses galore
Silver and gold in the store-o
Cows and sheep of every sort
A young one would never have more-o

4 One cow or two's enough for me
The sort that I prefer-o
To go and milk them both in one peck
Than suffer the old man's jaw-o

5 But you could sleep in a nice white bed
With wild birds' feathers made-o
With feather of owl and feather of wren
You'll not get with a young jade-o

6 A bed of straw would suit me right
With one that's nearer my span-o
Than a bed of feathers soft and white
And stuck with this poor old man-o

7 You could sit on the old man's lap
And drink of his wine and beer-o
What good his wine or beer to me
In the lap of a worn old man-o

58 Y FARN A FYDD
THE JUDGEMENT

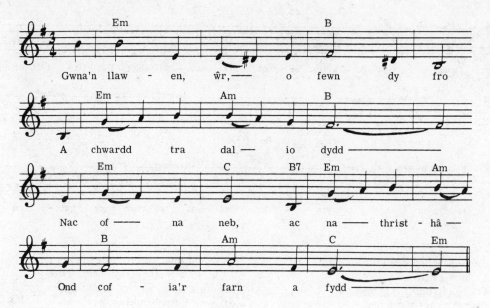

Gwna'n llaw - en, wr,—— o fewn dy fro

A chwardd tra dal—io dydd ————

Nac of——na neb, ac na——thrist-hâ——

Ond cof—ia'r farn a fydd

1 Gwna'n llawen, ŵr, o fewn dy fro
  A chwardd tra dalio dydd
  Nac ofna neb, ac na thristhâ
  Ond cofia'r farn a fydd

2 Mwynhâ bob pleser, myn dy chwant
  Na ffrwyna'r trachwant rhydd
  Mewn rhwysg a gloddest treulia'th dda
  Ond cofia'r farn a fydd

3 Diystyra grefydd a phob da
  A phoera'n wyneb ffydd
  Oddi wrth foesoldeb ymbellhâ
  Ond cofia'r farn a fydd

4 Myn bob difyrrwch ym mhob man
  Gwna'n ddiddan yn dy ddydd
  Mewn gwin a gwleddoedd llawenhâ
  Ond cofia'r farn a fydd

5 Na wrando ar un cyngor cu
  Na'r ymresymu sydd
  Dirmyga'r ddeddf, a thòr bob darn
  Ond cofia'r farn a fydd

6 Cais bob llawenydd, na lwfrhâ
  Ymhoewa, rhodia'n rhydd
  Gwna orchymynion Duw yn sarn
  Ond cofia'r farn a fydd

7 Y farn, y farn, y farn a fydd
  O, ryfedd ddydd a ddaw
  Y farn, y farn, y farn a fydd
  A' th ddyry'n brudd mewn braw

1 Make merry, O man, in your demesne
  And laugh while the day goes on
  Be a-feared of none and be not sad
  But remember the trial to come

2 Pursue all joys, follow desire
  And let your passions run
  In pomp and pleasure spend yourself
  But remember the trial to come

3 Religion ignore and all that's good
  The face of faith you shun
  From moral code estrange yourself
  But remember the trial to come

4 On every hand partake of joy
  For all your time have fun
  With food and wine make merry withal
  But remember the trial to come

5 Heed not to reason's single voice
  Nor advice from a kindly one
  Despise the law and break each bond
  But remember the trial to come

6 Seek all happiness, be not afraid
  But inhibitions shun
  God's laws break up in little bits
  But remember the trial to come

7 The trial, the trial, the trial to come
  A wondrous day that's near
  The trial, the trial, the trial to come
  'Twill make you so sad with fear

59 FFARWELIWCH, RWY'N MADAL A'M GWLAD
FAREWELL, FOR I'M LEAVING MY LAND

Ffar - wel - iwch, rwy'n ma-dal â'm gwlad —— Mae mwr-iad am fyn - ad i'r môr ——

Ffar - wel - iwch, fy mam a fy nhad —— Sy'n teim-lo fy hir-aeth ar ôl ——

Ffar - wel - iwch, mewn hedd-wch mwyn hardd —— Chwi - or - ydd a brod-yr yng - hyd ——

Mae am-can a bwr-iad y bardd —— Am fyn - ad i bell - ter y

byd —— Am fyn - ad i bell - ter y byd ——

Ffarweliwch, rwy'n madal â'm gwlad	Farewell, for I'm leaving my land
Mae mwriad am fynad i'r môr	Intending to go off to sea
Ffarweliwch, fy mam a fy nhad	Farewell to my mother and father
Sy'n teimlo fy hiraeth ar ôl	Who feel such longing for me
Ffarweliwch, mewn heddwch mwyn hardd	In gentle sweet peace it's fare thee well
Chwiorydd a brodyr ynghyd	My sisters and brothers, the both
Mae amcan a bwriad y bardd	The purpose and plan of the poet
Am fynad i bellter y byd	Is to go to the ends of the world
Am fynad i bellter y byd	*Is to go to the ends of the world*

60 FY MORWYN FFEIN I
MY FINE MAID

Ble rwyt ti'n myn — ed, fy mor — wyn ffein i?

Mynd ar ôl y gwarth — eg, O Syr, d'wed — odd hi

Dou ros — yn coch, a dou ly — gad du

Yn y baw a'r llac - a, O Syr, d'wed - odd hi

1 Ble rwyt ti'n myned, Fy morwyn ffein i?
Mynd ar ôl y gwartheg, O Syr, d'wedodd hi
Dou rosyn coch, a dou lygad du
Yn y baw a'r llaca, O Syr, d'wedodd hi

1 Where are you going, my fine maid?
Going after the cows, O sir, she said
Two rosy cheeks and two dark eyes
In the mud and the mire, O sir, she said

2 A ga i ddod gyda thi, Fy morwyn ffein i?
Fel bo chi'n dewis, O Syr, d'wedodd hi

2 May I come with you, my fine maid?
Just as you wish, O sir, she said

3 A ga i un cusan, Fy morwyn ffein i?
Beth ydy hwnnw, O Syr, d'wedodd hi

3 May I have a kiss, my fine maid?
And what is that, O sir, she said

4 A ga i dy briodi, Fy morwyn ffein i?
Os bydd mam yn folon, O Syr, d'wedodd hi

4 Then may I marry you, my fine maid?
If mother is willing, O sir, she said

5 Beth wnawn i am arian, Fy morwyn ffein i?
Gyda chi mae'r arian, O Syr, d'wedodd hi

5 What'll we do for money, my fine maid?
You've got the money, O sir, she said

6 Myfi bia'n arian, Fy morwyn ffein i
Myfinne bia'm hunan, O Syr, d'wedodd hi

6 My money's my own, my fine maid
And I own myself, O sir, she said

61 Y GWCW
THE CUCKOO

O'r Gw - cw,—— O'r Gw - cw,—— ble bu - ost ti cyd

Cyn dod i'r gym - dog - aeth ti ae - thost yn fud ?

Cyn dod i'r gym - dog - aeth ti ae - thost yn fud ?

1 O'r gwcw, O'r gwcw, ble buost ti cyd
   Cyn dod i'r gymdogaeth ti aethost yn fud?
   Cyn dod i'r gymdogaeth ti aethost yn fud?

2 Ti gollaist dy amser bythefnos ymron
   Ti ddest yn y diwedd a'th ganiad yn llon
   Ti ddest yn y diwedd a'th ganiad yn llon

3 Mi godais fy aden yn uchel i'r gwynt
   Gan feddwl bod yma dair wythnos ynghynt

4 Nid unrhyw gamsynied paid meddwl mor ffôl
   Ond oerwynt y gogledd a'm cadwodd yn ôl

5 Mae'n well iti dreial byw'r gaea' ffordd hyn
   Yng Ngelltydd Alltyrodyn neu elltydd
   Gwaralltryn

6 Mae Gelltydd Alltyrodyn yn llawer rhy hyll
   Mae Dai Penrhiwceule'n mynd yno â'i ddryll

7 Os hapnith fy ngweled neu glywed fy llais
   Fe'm saetha yn union yn syth dan fy ais

8 Fe ganodd y gwcw do Ebrill a Mai
   A phart o Mehefin, ffarwel i bob rai

9 Yn awr trwy derfynu, ffarwel i chwi oll
   Cyn dôf yma nesa' bydd canoedd ar goll

10 Bydd llawer gwrandawr yn isel ei ben
   Cyn rhoddaf fy nghaniad ar frigyn y pren

1 O cuckoo, O cuckoo, what's kept you so long
   In gaining this country before you were dumb?
   In gaining this country before you were dumb?

2 By nearly a fortnight thou didst lose your time
   Thou hast come at last now with your joyful song
   Thou hast come at last now with your joyful song

3 'Twas raising my wings up so high in the wind
   For three weeks before I ought to have been

4 Don't be foolish to think some mistake
   But the cold North wind kept me and made me so
   late

5 Why could you not shelter away from the wind?
   From the Alltyrodyn Forest or else from
   Gwaralltryn

6 The Alltyrodyn Forest's forbidding and grim
   Dai Penrhiwceule goes there with his gun for the
   game

7 If he happens to see me or my voice he should know
   He will straightaway shoot me in under the bone

8 The cuckoo is singing from April to May
   Goodbye to you everyone, then in June flies away

9 In one hour she's gone and it's farewell everyone
   And when she returns there'll be hundreds have
   gone

10 Many a listener's head will lay down
   Before you'll be singing upon a tree's bough

62 GWENNO FWYN
GENTLE GWEN

Gwen - no fwyn, Gwen - no fwyn Sgub - ar'r tŷ yn lân

A thyrd â'r gad - air freich - iau mlaen Mi fynn - wn gan - u cân

Dyr - o fawn - en ar y tân A gol - au'r gan - nwyll frwyn

Tra bydd - af in - nau'n rhoi mewn hwyl Hen dan - nau'r del - yn fwyn

CH:O Gwen - no fwyn, O Gwen - no, O dyr - o gân i mi

Tra bydd - i di'n rhoi tro i'r uwd Rhôf in - nau gân i - ti

1 Gwenno fwyn, Gwenno fwyn
  Sgubar'r tŷ yn lân
  A thyrd â'r gadair freichiau mlaen
  Mi fynnwn ganu cân
  Dyro fawnen ar y tân
  A golau'r gannwyll frwyn
  Tra byddaf innau'n rhoi mewn hwyl
  Hen dannau'r delyn fwyn
  O Gwenno fwyn, O Gwenno
  O dyro gân i mi
  Tra byddi di'n rhoi tro i'r uwd
  Rhôf innau gân iti

1 Gentle Gwen, O gentle Gwen
  O sweep the house out clean
  And bring the armchair up this way
  I'd like to have a sing
  Put a peat-turf on the fire
  The rush-candle light the hearth
  Whilst I myself will get tuned up
  Th'old strings of the gentle harp
  Gentle Gwen, O gentle Gwen
  O sing a song to me
  And whilst you stir the porridge pot
  A song I'll sing to thee

2 Gwenno fwyn, Gwenno fwyn
  Weli di Johnny Bach
  Mae'n chwerthin arnat yn ei grud
  Fel pe bai'n angel bach
  Dyro gusan ar ei rudd
  A sua ef i'w hun
  Does neb anwylach yn y byd
  Os nad wyt ti dy hun
  O Gwenno fwyn, O Gwenno
  O dyro gân i mi
  A thra bo ti'n cusanu John
  Rhôf innau gân iti

3 Gwenno fwyn, Gwenno fwyn
  O mor hapus yw
  Cael bwyd a thân a chalon lân
  A chornel glân i fyw
  O bopeth da sydd yn y byd
  Y gorau gennyf i
  Yw cefni ar y bydau blin
  A rhedeg atat ti
  O Gwenno fwyn, O Gwenno
  O dyro gân i mi
  Tra byddi di'n rhoi tro i'r uwd
  Rhôf innau gân iti

4 Gwenno fwyn, Gwenno fwyn
  Mor hapus yw fy myd
  Cael gweithio a chanu bob yn ail
  Fel hyn o hyd o hyd
  Rwyf i yn frenin ar fy nhŷ
  A phen a chalon iach
  A chan fy mod i'n frenin, Gwen
  Rwyt ti'n frenhines fach
  O Gwenno fwyn, O Gwenno
  O dyro gân i mi
  Tra byddi di'n rhoi tro i'r uwd
  Rhôf innau gân iti

2 Gentle Gwen, O gentle Gwen
  O look at little John
  He's smiling in his crib at you
  As if an angel born
  Place a kiss upon his cheeks
  And lull him off to sleep
  There's no one dearer in the world
  Excepting you, my sweet
  Gentle Gwen, O gentle Gwen
  O sing a song to me
  And while you're kissing little John
  A song I'll sing to thee

3 Gentle Gwen, O gentle Gwen
  O how good it is for me
  With food and fire and honest heart
  A corner clean to live
  All that's in the world so good
  What I love best to none
  To turn our backs on a troubled world
  To you, my dear, I run
  Gentle Gwen, O gentle Gwen
  O sing a song to me
  And while you stir the porridge pot
  A song I'll sing to thee

4 Gentle Gwen, O gentle Gwen
  O the world it goes so fine
  Turn about to work and sing
  It's like this all the time
  I am the king of my own house
  With head and heart so keen
  And just as I am king, my Gwen
  So you're a little queen
  Gentle Gwen, O gentle Gwen
  O sing a song to me
  And while you stir the porridge pot
  A song I'll sing to thee

63 HEN LADI FOWR BENFELEN
A BUXOM OLD BLONDE

1 Hen ladi fowr benfelen yn dwad i 'dre o'r ffair

Gynigodd i mi goron am ladd yr wrglo' wair

Tw-dl-rei-di-lym-bi-dym
Tw-dl-rei-di-lym-bi-dym
Tin-ddi-weu
Tin-ddi-eu
Tin-ddi-o

2 Wel we tonnen ar ei chanol, digon o le i sinco llong

Mae gofyn cael bachgen handy cyn mentro miwn i hon

3 Ond mae genny bladyr handy ond bod 'i blân hi'n fain

A chlwt yn cario carreg, ac yn baglan fel y train

4 Dywedodd yr hen ladi a ddowch chi lan i'r tŷ

I mi gael talu'r goron addewes i i chi

5 Ond yn lle talu'r goron fe dalodd i mi bunt

A dyna fel yr oedd hi'n yr hen amseroedd gynt

1 An old lady, blonde and buxom, home from the fair she came

Offered me a crown of money to cut the meadow full of hay

Tw-dl-rei-di-lym-bi-dym
Tw-dl-rei-di-lym-bi-dym
Tin-ddi-weu
Tin-ddi-eu
Tin-ddi-o

2 Like the button on her middle there's room to sink a wave

'Twould take a handy fellow, to enter 'twould be brave

3 For I've got a scythe so handy, its point is wearing thin

A rag to carry my stone along 'twould trip one like a train

4 To the house come, said the lady, I'll give to you your due

And so that I may offer thee the crown I promised you

5 Instead of paying the crown to me she gave one pound in gold

And that is how it used to be in the glorious days of old

152

64 YR HEN WR MWYN
THE GENTLE OLD MAN

P'le bu-och chi neith-iwr? Yr hen ŵr mwyn Yr hen ŵr mwyn-a'n fyw

Wel, bûm yn pys-got-a, Be-ti Ffi-dl a-di a-ti Ffi-dl a-di a-ti O O

1 P'le buoch chi neithiwr?
Yr hen ŵr mwyn
Yr hen ŵr mwyna'n fyw
Wel, bûm yn pysgota, Beti
Ffidl adi ati
Ffidl adi ati O
Wel bûm yn pysgota, Beti
Ffidl adi ati
Ffidl adi ati O

2 Beth a ddaliasoch?
Wel, samwn wedi marw, Beti

3 P'le ddarfu chi wlychu?
Wedi syrthio i Lyn y Felin, Beti

4 Pam 'rych chi'n crynu?
Wel, dim ond yr annwyd, Beti

5 Beth pe baech chi'n marw?
Wel, dim ond fy nghladdu, Beti

6 P'le mynnech chi'ch claddu?
Wel, dan garreg yr aelwyd, Beti

7 Beth wnewch chi fan honno?
Wel, gwrando'r uwd yn berwi, Beti

1 Where were you last night?
Gentle old man
Gentlest old man alive
Well, I went out fishing, Betty
Fiddle-addy-atty
Fiddle-addy-atty-O
Well, I went out fishing, Betty
Fiddle-addy-atty
Fiddle-addy-atty-O

2 What did you catch, then?
Well, I caught a dead salmon, Betty

3 Where did you get wet, then?
After falling in the mill-pond, Betty

4 Why are you trembling?
Well, it's only with the cold, Betty

5 What if you die, then?
Well, it's only to bury me, Betty

6 Where will you be buried?
Well, it's under the hearthstone, Betty

7 What would you do there?
Well, listen to the porridge boil, Betty

65 LISA LAN
FAIR LIZA

Fy nghang-en law —— en, fy nghow-lad glyd

Ty-di yw'r lan-a sy'n y byd

Ty-di sy'n per-i poen a chur—— Ty-di sy'n dwyn fy nghal-on i

LAST VERSE O Lis-a, ddoi —— di i'm dan-fon i

I roi fy nghorff mewn dae-ar ddu ?

Go-beith-io doi di f'an-wyl-yd ffrind Hyd lan y bedd, lle rwyf yn mynd

1 Fy nghangen lawen, fy nghowlad glyd
Tydi yw'r lana sy'n y byd
Tydi sy'n peri poen a chur
Tydi sy'n dwyn fy nghalon i

2 Pan fyddwy'n rhodio gyda'r dydd
Fy nghalon fach sy'n mynd yn brudd
Wrth glywed cân yr adar mân
Daw hiraeth mawr am Lisa lân

3 Pan fyddwy'n rhodio yn yr ardd
Ym mysg y blodau sydd yn hardd
Yn torri'r mwyn friallu mân
Daw hiraeth mawr am Lisa lân

4 Pan fyddwy'n rhodio gyda'r hwyr
Fy nghalon fach a dodd fel cŵyr
Wrth glywed swn y tannau mân
Daw hiraeth mawr am Lisa lân

1 My branch of joy, my armful warm
In all the world you have most charm
'Tis you that's caused both grief and pain
'Tis you that's stole my heart away

2 As I go walking at the dawn of day
My heart is sad, no longer gay
The little birds, I hear their song
For Liza comes a yearning strong

3 When in the garden I do stray
Among the flowers so sweet and gay
I cut the little prim-e-rose
For Liza fair my yearning grows

4 When I go walking at the close of day
My poor heart melts like wax away
I hear the sound of tiny strings
For Liza fair my yearning springs

5 O Lisa, ddoi di i'm danfon i
  I roi fy nghorff mewn daear ddu?
  Gobeithio doi di f'anwylyd ffrind
  Hyd lan y bedd, lle rwyf yn mynd

5 O Liza, come to me I crave
  And place my body in some dark grave
  I hope you'll join me, my dearest dear
  Unto the grave for I'm going there

66 LODES LAN
FAIREST MAID

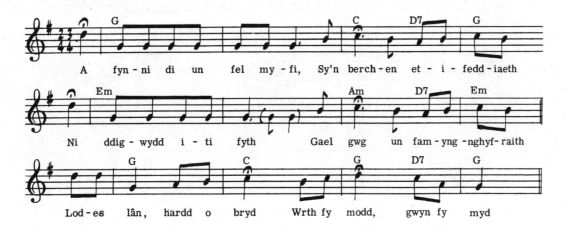

A fyn-ni di un fel my-fi, Sy'n berch-en et-i-fedd-iaeth

Ni ddig-wydd i ti fyth Gael gwg un fam-yng-nghyf-raith

Lod-es lân, hardd o bryd Wrth fy modd, gwyn fy myd

1 A fynni di un fel myfi
  Sy'n berchen etifeddiaeth?
  Ni ddigwydd iti fyth
  Gael gwg un fam-yng-nghyfraith
  Lodes lân, hardd o bryd
  Wrth fy modd, gwyn fy myd

1 O will you have one such as me
  Inheriting from my father?
  For then you need not see the frown
  On the face of my mother-in-law
  Fairest maid, so fine of form
  Luck is mine, so glad I'm born

2 Mae gennyf balas hardd i'th ddwyn
  A gardd o amryw flodau
  Cei dithau rodio ymysg y rhain
  A dewis unrhyw liwiau

2 I've a beautiful place where I'll take thee
  A glade with many flowers
  And you can walk among them all
  To choose their many colours

3 Os digwydd imi fynd ryw ddydd
  I hela'r ysgyfarnog
  Cei dithau, ferch, O, geffyl hardd
  I hela y llwynogod

3 And should I have to go one day
  To hunt the hare or such
  Then you shall have a stallion white
  'Pon him to chase the fox

4 Cei hefyd bâr o gotten shoes
  A gown o'r mwslin gore
  A morwyn deg i gyrlio'th wallt
  Os mynni hwyr a bore

4 Likewise a pair of cotton shoes
  A gown of muslin warm
  The fairest maid to curl your hair
  If needs be night and morn

67 MAE 'NGHARIAD I'N FENWS
MY LOVE SHE'S A VENUS

1. Mae 'nghariad i'n Fenws
   Mae 'nghariad i'n fain
   Mae 'nghariad i'n dlysach
   Na blodau y drain
   Fy 'nghariad yw'r lana
   A'r fwyna'n y sir
   Nid ran mod i'n brolio
   Ond d'wedyd y gwir

2. Wych eneth fach siriol
   Sy'n lodes mor lân
   A'i gruddiau mor writgoch
   A'i dannedd mân, mân
   A'i dau lygad siriol
   A'i dwy ael fel gwawn
   Fy nghalon a'i carai
   Pe gwyddwn y cawn

1. My love she's a Venus
   My love's got a fine form
   My love she is prettier
   Than the flowers of the thorn
   My love she's the fairest
   Tenderest of all fruit
   It's not that I'm boasting
   Just telling plain truth

2. She's so dear and so cheerful
   A maiden so sweet
   With cheeks red and rosy
   And teeth neat as neat
   Her two bright eyes shining
   Two lids soft as down
   My heart it does love her
   If I knew she'd be mine

68 Y MARCH GLAS
THE GREY HORSE

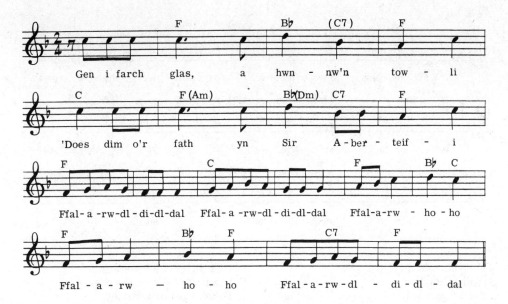

Gen i farch glas, a hwn - nw'n tow - li

'Does dim o'r fath yn Sir A - ber - teif - i

Ffal - a - rw - dl - di - dl - dal Ffal - a - rw - dl - di - dl - dal Ffal - a - rw - ho - ho

Ffal - a - rw — ho - ho Ffal - a - rw - dl — di - dl — dal

1 Gen i farch glas, a hwnnw'n towli
  'Does dim o'r fath yn Sir Aberteifi
  Ffal-a-rwdl-didl-dal
  Ffal-a-rwdl-didl-dal
  Ffal-a-rw-ho-ho
  Ffal-a-rw-ho-ho
  Ffal-a-rwdl-didl-dal

2 Gen i gyfrwy' newy' o grô'n ochor mochyn
  Ffrwyn dwbwl rains, a gwarthol, a sbardun

3 Gen i het silc o siop Aberhonddu
  Phrisiwn i fawr roi sofren amdani

4 Gen i got fain o waith teiliwr Llundain
  Stitshoi'n dynn oboiti fy nghefen

1 I have a grey horse, a handsome trotter
  There's none like him anywhere in Cardigan
  Fal-a-roodle-diddle-dal
  Fal-a-roodle-diddle-dal
  Fal-a-roo-ho-ho
  Fal-a-roo-ho-ho
  Fal-a-roodle-diddle-dal

2 I have a new saddle made out of pig-skin
  Double-reined mouth-bit, a spur and a stirrup

3 I have a silk hat from a shop in Brecon
  I would not change it, not even for a sovereign

4 I have a slim coat from a London tailor
  That is stitched tight, all around my tail

69 Y FERI LWYD
THE GREY MARI

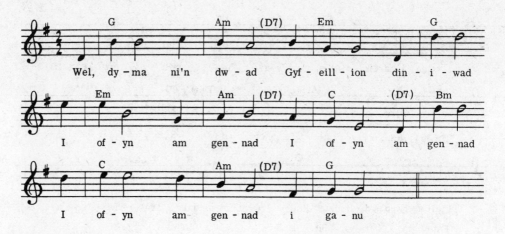

1 Wel, dyma ni'n dwad Gyfeillion diniwad I ofyn am gennad I ofyn am gennad I ofyn am gennad i ganu	1 Well, here we are coming You harmless good friends To ask your permission To ask your permission To ask your permission this evening
2 Beth ydyw y twrw Y ffusto a'r curo? A beth yw eich ewyllys A beth yw eich ewyllys A beth yw eich ewyllys nos heno?	2 What is all this fussing With knockings and trampings? What are your wishes What are your wishes What are your wishes this evening?
3 Y Feri Lwyd lawen A'i chwt ar i chefan Sy' yma â'i miri Sy' yma â'i miri Sy' yma â'i miri nos heno	3 The merry Grey Mari With her tail behind her Is here, merry and jolly Is here, merry and jolly Is here, merry and jolly this evening
4 Os ydyw y Feri Yn addo i'r cwmpni I ymddwyn yn deidi Heb gnoi na thraflyngcu Caiff ddyfod i'r cwmpni nos heno	4 If only the Mari Will promise the company To keep her behaviour Not biting or gulping We'll allow you this company this evening
5 Mae'r Feri yn addo I uno 'n y cwmpni Heb gnoi na thraflyngcu Ond dyplu y miri Wrth ganu baleti nos heno	5 The Mari she promises To join in the company Without biting or gulping And to double the merriment By the singing of ballads this evening
6 Ond beth am y Pwnsh A'r procar a'r Judi I ddifa y cysur A'r tanllwyth i'r cwmpni A'r tanllwyth i'r cwmpni nos heno?	6 But what if the Punch And poker and Judy That spoils all comfort Rakes the fire of the company Rakes the fire of the company this evening?

7 Mae'r Feri yn addo
  Fod Pwnsh a'r hen Judi
  I sefyll yn llonydd
  Ac ymddwyn yn deidi
  A gatal y tanllwyth i'r cwmpni nos heno

7 The Mari she promises
  That Punch and old Judy
  Will stand in position
  Prepared to behaviour
  Keep the fire for the company this evening

8 Mae'r cwmpni yn fishi
  Yn doti y llestri
  A'r dishan yn deidi
  Cyn acor drws iddi
  Cyn acor i'r Feri nos heno

8 The company is busy
  Preparing the dishes
  The cake getting ready
  To open the door up
  To open to the Mari this evening

9 Mae'r Feri yn rhewi
  A'i thrâd bron â fferru
  Wrth aros i'r cwmpni
  I acor drws iddi
  I acor i'r Feri nos heno

9 The Mari is perishing
  Her feet they are freezing
  Through waiting for the company
  To open the door up
  To open to the Mari this evening

10 Mae'r cwmpni yn fishi
   Yn doti y llestri
   A'r dishan yn deidi
   Cyn acor drws iddi
   Cyn acor i'r Feri nos heno

10 The company is busy
   Preparing the dishes
   The cake getting ready
   To open the door up
   Tc open to the Mari this evening

11 Fe ddotiff y Feri
   Y dishan yn deidi
   Ym mola y Feri
   Ynghenol y miri
   Ond acor drws iddi nos heno

11 The Mari she'll put it
   The cake that is ready
   Inside Mari's belly
   In the midst of the jollity
   Only open the door up this evening

12 Yr ydym yn acor
   Y clocon am noson
   O ganu a dawnsio
   A'r crwth a'r hen delyn
   Pob croeso i'r Feri nos heno

12 We'll open now for you
   The fastenings this evening
   For singing and dancing
   For fiddling and harping
   All welcome to the Mari this evening

13 Pob croeso i'r Feri
   I ganu faint fyn hi
   Ynghenol y twrw
   Wrth rannu y cwrw
   Pob croeso i'r Feri nos heno

13 All welcome the Mari
   To sing as she wishes
   With plenty of jollity
   With drinking of beer
   All welcome to the Mari this evening

14 Wel, dyma ni'n mynad
   A'n pena i'r gweirad
   A Duw ŵyr cyn bellad
   A Duw ŵyr cyn bellad
   A Duw ŵyr cyn bellad nos heno

14 Well here we are leaving
   With heads pointing downwards
   Only God knows how far
   Only God knows how far
   Only God knows how far this evening

70 ROWN I'N RHODIO MYNWENT EGLWYS
WAND'RING THROUGH THE CHURCHYARD

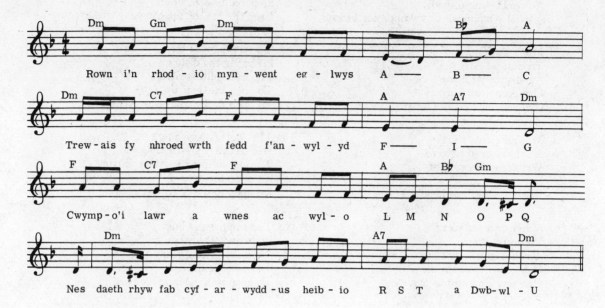

1 Rown i'n rhodio mynwent eglwys
A – B – C
Trewais fy nhroed wrth fedd f'anwylyd
F – I – G
Cwympo'i lawr a wnes ac wylo
L – M – N – O – P – Q
Nes daeth rhyw fab cyfarwyddus heibio
R – S – T a Dwbwl-U

2 Cwympo'i lawr a wnes ac wylo
Nes daeth rhyw fab cyfarwyddus heibio
Cwyd dy ben a phaid ag wylo
Ti gei gariad newydd eto

3 Nid wyf fi ond gwan obeithio
Na cha i gariad newydd eto
Ond mawr drueni sy arna' i weled
Ddodi pridd ar fab mor laned

1 I was wand'ring through the churchyard
A – B – C
My foot caught my true-love's gravestone
F – I – G
Fell to the ground and cried my eyes out
L – M – N – O – P – Q
Till a helpful man came by and saw me
R – S – T and *W*

2 Fell to the ground and cried my eyes out
Till a helpful man came by and saw me
Lift your head and stop your weeping
You shall soon have another true-love

3 I am still but faintly hoping
I'll not have another true-love
But I'm sad to see this happening
Earth being thrown on a youth so handsome

71 TAFARN Y RHOS
THE TAVERN ON THE MOOR

Pan oedd-wn yn dy-fod o Daf-arn y Rhos
My - fi a'm cwm-pein-i am get-yn o'r nos
Yn dyf-od tua char-tre, tua thre at fy ngwraig
Mi gef-ais i daf-od mewn geir-iau Cym-raeg

1 Pan oeddwn yn dyfod o Dafarn y Rhos
  Myfi a'm cwmpeini am getyn o'r nos
  Yn dyfod tua chartre, tua thre at fy ngwraig
  Mi gefais i dafod mewn geiriau Cymraeg

2 O coda, Gwen, coda, ac agor y ddôr
  Mae yna'n lled gynnes, mae yma'n lled ô'r
  A'r tô yn diferu dip-dap ar fy mhen
  Gwn, gwn na ddymunech ddim drwg imi, Gwen

3 O na wna', O na wna', a choelia fy ngair
  Dy le di sydd deilwng mewn towlod o wair
  A phob sotyn meddw'r un fel â thydi

  Yn gwario pob ceiniog heb gownt am dy dŷ

4 O coda, O coda, ac agor imi
  Mae gen i ffon gollen neu ddwy yn y tŷ
  Os na chaf fi'r rheiny caf bolyn clawdd gardd
  Mi a'i plygaf yn ddwbwl yn grô's ar dy war

5 O coda 'ngŵr annwyl, mi godaf ar ffrwst
  Breuddwydio'r own 'smeitin a dweud trwy fy
  Gan daflu'r cwerylon nis gwn i ba le   [nghwsg
  Mae'r tegell yn berwi, o dowch i gael tê

6 Cydwledda a wnaethom o amgylch y bwrdd
  Ein gofid a'r helynt hedasant i ffwrdd
  Cyfamod a wnaethom i fyw yn gytun
  Mae'r tegell yn berwi, dwy galon yn un

1 When I did come from the inn on the moor
  At midnight, myself, my friends and a score
  Coming home to my home, to my wife and who else
  I'd a piece of her mind that was spelled out in Welsh

2 O get up, Gwen, get up, and open the door
  There it's quite warm, but here it's quite raw
  The roof is drip-dripping, on my head it does spill
  Gwen, Gwen, you'd not wish me to come to some ill?

3 I wouldn't, I wouldn't, believe what I say
  The place where you should be's up there on the hay
  And with all those drunkards who've been on the
                                              roam
  Spending the money without thought of home

4 O get up, O get up, open up for your spouse
  There's one or two hazel-sticks there in the house
  If I don't get them, from the hedge I've a cane
  And over your shoulders I'll bend it again

5 I'll get up, dear husband, I'll get up with one leap
  For some time I've been dreaming and talked in my
  Throwing out quarrels to where I know not   [sleep
  Come, the kettle it's boiling, the tea's in the pot

6 We feasted at table, together, we two
  Our worries and troubles away from us flew
  In harmony living, a truce it was signed
  To love one another, two hearts and one mind

72 TREN O'R BALA I FFESTINIOG
THE BALA–FFESTINIOG TRAIN

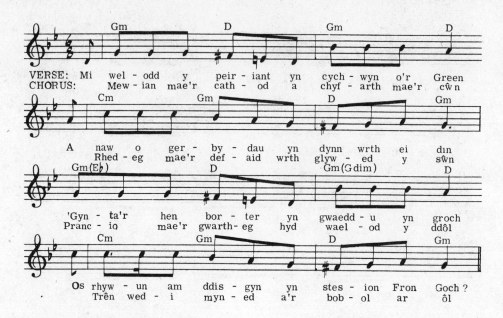

VERSE: Mi wel-odd y peir-iant yn cych-wyn o'r Green
CHORUS: Mew-ian mae'r cath-od a chyf-arth mae'r cŵn

A naw o ger-by-dau yn dynn wrth ei din
Rhed-eg mae'r def-aid wrth glyw-ed y sŵn

'Gyn-ta'r hen bor-ter yn gwaedd-u yn groch
Pranc-io mae'r gwarth-eg hyd wael-od y ddôl

Os rhyw-un am ddis-gyn yn stes-ion Fron Goch?
Trên wed-i myn-ed a'r bob-ol ar ôl

1 Mi welodd y peiriant yn cychwyn o'r Green
A naw o gerbydau yn dynn wrth ei din
'Gynta'r hen borter yn gwaeddu yn groch
Os rhywun am ddisgyn yn stesion Fron Goch?
Mewian mae'r cathod a chyfarth mae'r cŵn
Rhedeg mae'r defaid wrth glywed y sŵn
Prancio mae'r gwartheg hyd waelod y ddôl
Tren wedi myned a'r bobol ar ôl

2 Bloeddio yn Saesneg roedd cry' siop y parc
We're goin' for the trip and there for a lark
Ond pan oedd yn rhedeg ar gae Llechwedd Hên
Druan o'r cryddyn fe gollodd y trên
(Chorus with changing last line)
Trên wedi myned a'r cryddyn ar ôl

3 Pobol Llidiardai sy'n myned am dro
Pobol Rhyd Ucha' a William y go'
Bydd 'dolau'r hen geffyla' yn hynod o rad
Ar ôl i'r tren fyned i redeg trwy'r wlâd
Trên wedi myned a'r bobol ar ôl

4 Dafydd y Garn yn chwys ac yn faw
Rhedeg i ore' dan godi ei law
A ydyw hi'n amser cael ticed 'rhen ffrind?
Atebodd y porter mae'r trên newydd fynd
Trên wedi myned a Dafydd ar ôl

1 He saw the old engine start off from the Green
Nine carriages following, close on her heels
The old porter shouts out with a very loud voice
Anyone here for the station, Fron Goch?
The screeching of cats and the barking of dogs
The scattering of sheep at the noise of the cogs
The cows in the meadow prance away down the lane
The train it is gone and the people remain

2 Shouting in English was the cobbler of Park Shop
We're going for the trip and there for a lark
He ran across fields beside Llechwedd Hen
Sorry old cobbler but you've missed the train
(Chorus with changing last line)
The train it is gone, but the cobbler remains

3 Most of the Llidiardai are out for the trip
Most of Rhyd Ucha and William, the smith
For the shoes of the horses much less will we pay
Since the train's leaving to trot through this way
The train it is gone and the people remain

4 Sweaty and dirty, comes David from Garn
He's running his fastest and waving his arms
Can't wait for the ticket: Come on, my old friend
No need, says the porter: The train has just went
The train it is gone and it's David remains

5 Emwnt Gelligerrig yn rhedeg ei lais
  Gofyn i ryw hen hogyn o Saes
  Tell me the bachgen and don't be so mên
  To tell to hen ffarmwr what time was the trên
  Trên wedi myned ag Emwnt ar ôl

6 Morris Abersanno yn cychwyn o'r tŷ
  Ar y cyfeiriad i'r stesion am dri
  Ond pan oedd yn rhedeg ar gae Cefen Glâs
  Druan o Forris fe gollodd y râs
  Trên wedi myned a Morris ar ôl

5 Edmund Gelligerrig, his voice he did throw
  Asks an old Englishman: When did it go?
  Come now, old fellow, don't be so naïve
  And tell an old farmer: what time did it leave?
  The train it is gone and it's Edmund remains

6 Morris Abersanno shot out of his door
  To make three o'clock the station before
  But as he was running across Cefen Glas
  Woe to old Morris, the race he had lost
  The train it is gone and it's Morris remains

49 AMBELL I GAN
AN OCCASIONAL SONG

Watcyn o Feirion, Bala, Merionethshire, *rec.* E. Cleaver, 1954

Printed version
JWFSS: 1956–7, vol. V, part I, p. 13

The minor-keyed tune of this song is reminiscent of the melodic phrases frequently found in Welsh melody and hymn tunes. It has been said of the Welshman that he is happiest when he grieves, and the Welsh certainly revel in this type of minor tune and their joy in the serious and grievous mood is reflected in many of the best hymn tunes, such as *Aberystwyth* by Joseph Parry.

Watcyn o Feirion was an expert in the art of Penillion singing and learned this song from Evan Jones of Trawsfynydd, a well-known tenor in Merionethshire. Jones learned it from his father and it became well known in the district from his family's singing of it.

50 AR BEN WAUN TREDEGAR
ON THE FENS OF TREDEGAR

Sam Davies, 'Sam y Delyn' (Sam the harp), Pontrhydyfen, near Neath, Glamorganshire, *coll.* Rev. Gomer M. Roberts.

Printed versions
JWFSS: 1910, vol. I, pt. 2, pp. 78–80: *Cariad i Notws* (from between Merthyr Tydfil and Hirwaun, Glamorganshire)
JWFSS: 1952, vol. IV, part 2, p. 54: Sam Davies version

This is an example of Hen Benillion (Old Stanzas), which were single stanzas of repetitive lines frequently sung to well-known tunes. (The next song, *Ar Lan y Môr* (No. 51), is also an example of this kind.) The stanzas are repetitive but the second half of each line varies in thought and increases in its interest to a climax in the last line.

These songs were exceedingly popular in Wales, especially in the Vale of Glamorgan, and this particular one was sung in the taverns when Sam Davies was a youngster about sixty years ago. The words in the second verse are local Glamorganshire Welsh dialect:

notws = nododd (from 'dodi'), to compel (gorfododd); wedws = ddywedodd; dorrws = dorrodd

51 AR LAN Y MOR
BESIDE THE SEA

Ben Phillips, Lochtwrffin, Pembrokeshire, *rec.* E. Cleaver and S. Ennis, 1953: BBC 20192

Printed versions
JWFSS: 1937, vol. III, part 3, pp. 125–6
GWYNN WILLIAMS: 1963, no. 100, p. 132

On the BBC recording Ben Phillips sang the first verse:

Ar lan y môr mae rhosys cochion	Beside the sea there are red roses
Ar lan y môr mae lilis gwynion	Beside the sea there are lovely lilies
Ar lan y môr mae glân rhosynnau	Beside the sea there are beautiful roses
Ar lan y môr mae nghariad innau	Beside the sea my sweetheart lives

A variant, *Hen Benillion* (T. H. Parry Williams) printed by J. D. Lewis & Son, Gwasg Gomer, Llandyssul, 1940, p. 90, No. 343 and p. 92, No. 351, reads thus:

Ar lan y môr mae carreg wastad	Beside the sea a rock is standing
Lle bûm yn siarad gair â'm cariad	Where once my love and I were loving
O amgylch hon fe dyf y lili	About the rock there grows the lily
Ac ambell gangen o rosmari	Beside it also grows some rosemary
Yng nglan y môr mae cerrig gleison	Beside the sea are bluish pebbles
Yng nglan y môr blodau'r meibion	Beside the sea are silver brambles
Yng nglan y môr mae pob rhinweddau	Beside the sea is truth excelling
Yng nglan y môr mae nghariad innau	Beside the sea my love is dwelling

The 'triad' formula is well known in Welsh literature, the triad being the three ideas expressed, and the third idea being the climax or contrast. They are the single traditional stanzas type referred to as Hen Benillion (Old Stanzas). The particular version noted from Pembrokeshire however is interesting in as much that the formula ascends a third with every idea with a different twist in the phrases.

52 BACHGEN IFANC YDWYF
I AM A YOUNG MAN

Tom Edwards, Bryneglwys, Denbighshire, *rec.* P. Kennedy and E. Cleaver, 1954: BBC 22425

Printed versions
JWFSS: 1952, vol. IV, part 2, p. 23: *Ffarwel i Ddociau Lerpwl* (version with chorus from Pembrokeshire)
DE LLOYD: 1931: *Cân Ffarwel, Ferched Llanwennog* (collected in Cardiganshire)

The tune of this song will be familiar as it is the one used (transferred into even-time) for the American minstrel song *O Susannah*. In this six-eight, or uneven, time it was much used throughout England for quadrilles, country and morris dancing.

Other versions of the song have farewell verses and the young man is represented as a sailor. The Pembrokeshire version was in fact known to be sung at sea by sailors.

53 Y BACHGEN MAIN
THE LANKY LAD

Ellis Thomas, Corris, Merionethshire, *rec.* S. Ennis, 1953: BBC 20198

Printed versions
WILLIAMS: 1844: *Callyn Serch*
THOMAS: 1927

Y Bachgen Main is one of a group of popular Welsh ballads relating the tragic love affairs of young maidens (e.g. *Y Ferch o Gefn Ydfa* and *Y Ferch o Sger*). The tune used is also popular for a number of ballads, of which the most well known is *Y Ferch o Blwy Penderyn*. The tune has been used as a signature tune for a television serial version of Richard Llewellyn's *How Green Was My Valley*. The words of the song are also sung to different tunes and there is also an old carol tune with the same title.

Ellis Thomas (1879–1956) who also sang *Lisa Lan* (No. 65) learned his songs from his father, the local blacksmith. Ellis himself worked as a 'rock man' in the slate quarries.

54 BWMBA
BOOMBA

Ben Phillips, Lochtwrffin, Pembrokeshire, *rec.* S. Ennis, 1952: BBC 19068
Other recorded version
Andrew Thomas, Pembrokeshire, 1953: BBC 20195

Printed versions
JWFSS: 1922, Vol. II, part 3, no. 128, p. 194: *Pan Oeddwn i Gynt yn Fachgen* (from Llanwddyn, Merionethshire)
JWFSS: vol. IV, part 2, p. 60: *Cân yr Hen Wyddeles* (version from Andrew Thomas)
GWYNN WILLIAMS: 1961, no. 60, p. 67

'Ben Bach' (Little Ben) Phillips was a great exponent of Welsh folksongs, and had a wonderful repertoire. He possessed a sweet tenor voice, with a pronounced Pembrokeshire dialect, and his was an excellent example of the old style of singing. Listening to him, well-known songs took on a different image and every song was something personal to him.

The song gives a humorous account of a young man who married without much thought, then repented when he found out that his wife was a good-for-nothing. It is a type of ballad, often found in country districts, of the Llofft Stabal (Stable Loft) class. The stable loft was the room above the shippen where the farmhands used to sleep in the old days. Local lads would get together in the winter evenings for a sing-song, and extemporise verses alluding to comical incidents that had happened to someone in the company, or to someone they knew in the vicinity. There is much jollity in singing this type of song with its chorus and nonsense syllables.

This version is also noted with slight differences from the singing of Andrew Thomas (JWFSS, vol. IV), as shown above. (See JWFSS: vol. II, part 3, p. 194 and vol. IV, part 2, p. 60 for a different tune, a minor version, quite as jolly but with different words, from Llanwddyn, Merionethshire).

55 Y CEFFYL DU
THE BLACK HORSE

John Thomas, Llangwm, Denbighshire, *rec.* P. Kennedy
and E. Cleaver, 1954

This humorous song is not old, but is an excellent example of popular folk singing in Wales (in the vicinity of Bala, North Wales, in this instance) where the well-known Tai'r Felin party kept alive the tradition of 'caneuon y werin' (the people's songs)—'by the people, of the people, to the people'—in the 'Noson Lawen' (sing-song gatherings) and concerts. John Thomas and his singing partner, Bob Roberts 'Tai'r Felin', were the two star exponents of these songs in the Tai'r Felin party. So popular were these two old singers amongst the 'gwerin' of Wales in the 1920s and 1930s that an Old People's Home in Bala has been dedicated to the memory of John Thomas, and a bust of Bob Roberts erected outside his home, Tai'r Felin. Both represent the culture of a generation of Welsh people, possibly the last, who contrived and sang a song and a stanza spontaneously and without self-consciousness, inspired by sad or humorous events which were part and parcel of their daily lives. This song is another example of the Welsh 'hwyl' in the minor key.

56 Y DERYN DU
THE BLACKBIRD

Tom Edwards, Bryneglwys, Denbighshire, *rec.* P.
Kennedy and E. Cleaver, 1954: BBC 22426

Printed versions
JWFSS: 1911, vol. I, part 3, no. 1, p. 123
GWYNN WILLIAMS: 1961, no. 24, p. 31

Tom Edwards, an old Ballad singer who lived in a little cottage on his own in Bryneglwys, Denbighshire, was a farm hand, and spent much of his time singing in local taverns for his beer. His kind of robust voice, typically North Welsh in quality, is often found in the mountainous areas of North Wales. A reticent man, in the joy of singing he could, as someone commented, be heard for miles. It is sad to think that he died of malnutrition.

This song of the question and answer type was very popular in both North and South Wales. The form of conversing with a bird has a literary tradition in Wales, dating from the classical period of Dafydd ap Gwilym. It was called 'canu llatai' ('llatai' = love-messenger) and describes the love-struck poet sending the bird with messages of love to his sweetheart. The folk ballad was known to have been sung by Dic Dywyll (Blind Dick), alias Richard Williams, a very famous singer, in the streets of Caernarvon in the 1830s, and the words have been frequently printed in ballad form. They were written some 200 years ago by David Jones, a mole-catcher of Llandyssul, Cardiganshire.

There are several variants of the tune, four of which are printed in JWFSS. The song has also been recorded from John Thomas.

57 DYWETSE'R HEN DDYN WRTH EI FERCH
THE OLD MAN SAID TO HIS DAUGHTER DEAR

Ben Phillips, Lochtwrffin, Pembrokeshire, *rec.* S. Ennis,
1952: BBC 19069

Printed version
JWFSS: 1941, vol. III, part 4, pp. 189–90

The version published in JWFSS comes from the Jennie Williams collection of folksongs of the counties of Cardigan, Carmarthen and Pembroke. The version collected in Aberystwyth contains some different verses which mention pink shoes, silk stockings and worsted garters with silver buckles which the rich old man gives to his daughter. She has however no respect for these riches but prefers a plain garter, stockings of sheep's wool and a leather shoe to fit her foot. The love of a young man is more precious to her than all the riches of her rich old man!

The tune used for this song might well be an old dance air, for several of the other rhythmical songs we have encountered are sung to old Welsh dance tunes. The inner rhyme of the Welsh 'triban' (triad) is noticeable in some of the verses, in the second stanza, for example:

Braf yw'r tai a theg yw'r *tir*   The houses are large and the land's not bad
A dweud y *gwir* amdano   To tell you the truth it's my plan-o

58 Y FARN A FYDD
THE JUDGEMENT

Mrs G. Megan Tibbott, Aberystwyth, Cardiganshire, *coll.* E. Cleaver

Printed version
JWFSS: 1954, vol. IV, part 4, p. 91

Mrs Tibbott learned this and many other Welsh folksongs from her father, Arthur Wellesley Jones, a former Welsh Board of Health Inspector, who died in 1937. He learned most songs from his father, but this tune in fact was sung to him by his mother, Mary Jones of Pontweli, Llandyssul, Cardiganshire. Although born in Pontypridd, Glamorganshire, she was brought up at the old family home at Panteg, Felindre, Drefach, near Llandyssul, and died in 1910 at the age of sixty.

Mrs Tibbott doubts whether her father knew more than four verses of the song or the name of its composer. She herself discovered quite recently that the author was a certain Ebenezer Thomas (Eben Fardd), a local schoolmaster (1802–63). In the opening line Mrs Tibbott's father sang, 'Gwna'n llawen, ŵr, ynghylch dy fro.'

59 FFARWELIWCH, RWY'N MADAL A'M GWLAD
FAREWELL, FOR I'M LEAVING MY LAND

Lewis Howel, Pontrhydyfen, Glamorganshire, *coll.* Rev. Gomer M. Roberts

Printed version
JWFSS: 1953, vol. IV, part 3, p. 71

Farewell songs of this type were popular in different parts of Wales and were great favourites amongst soldiers and sailors. It strikes the characteristic 'hiraeth' note of the Welshman (the nearest meaning in English is 'longing'). Here it means the sailor's sadness on leaving his home and his family. Stanzas in the other farewell songs consist of local names of favourite sweethearts. These farewell songs are very beautiful in form and expression. Notice the continual change from major to minor, and the effective upward run on the word 'byd' at the end with the repetitive descent to the tonic.

The one traditional stanza has a flavour of the Glamorganshire dialect.

60 FY MORWYN FFEIN I
MY FINE MAID

Andrew Thomas, Pencnwc, Fishguard, Pembrokeshire and Ben Phillips, Lochtwrffin, Mathry, Pembrokeshire, *rec.* E. Cleaver and S. Ennis, 1953: BBC 20194

Printed versions
JWFSS: 1925, vol. II, part 4, no. 133, pp. 223–4: *B'le 'rwyt ti yn myned?*

JWFSS: 1930, vol. III, part 1, no. 44, p. 76: *B'le 'rwyt ti yn myned?*
GWYNN WILLIAMS: 1961, no. 62, p. 69: the version in JWFSS: 1925
GWYNN WILLIAMS: 1963, no. 122, p. 154: the version in JWFSS: 1930

This song is a Welsh equivalent of the English *Where are you going to, my Pretty Maid?*

The version published in JWFSS: 1925 was said to have been popular in Pembrokeshire and parts of Carmarthenshire; that in JWFSS: 1930 was noted from an old man at Glynneath, Glamorganshire. The two tunes are quite different and show how popular were the words in many different areas at one time.

Local influences also show variations in some of the verses. The question and answer of the last two verses were sung:

Beth yw dy ffortiwn . . .	What is thy fortune . . .
Dim ond a welwch . . .	Only what you see . . .
Yna ni'th briodaf . . .	Then I will not marry you . . .
Ni ofynnais ichwi . . .	I did not ask you . . .

In the South Wales dialect 'dau' (two) is pronounced 'dou'. 'Gwedodd' in the second version is the colloquial form of 'dwedodd'.

61 Y GWCW
THE CUCKOO

Andrew Thomas, Pencnwc, Fishguard, Pembrokeshire, *rec.* E. Cleaver and S. Ennis, 1953: BBC 20195
Printed versions
JWFSS: 1954, vol. IV, part 4, no. 21, p. 33 and no. 58, p. 93: *The Cuckoo*

JWFSS: 1910, vol. I, part 2, no. 1, pp. 128 and 206: *Cerdd y Gog Lwydlas*; also recorded from Ben Phillips, Pembrokeshire: BBC 19068
Gwyn Williams: 1963, no. 98, p. 130

The words of this song are given in *Hanes Plwyf Llandysul* (The History of the Parish of Llandyssul). In Cardiganshire it is stated that the song was composed by Daniel Jones, a local bard and mole-catcher, and later revised by Thomas Humphries, another local bard. The following verses were contributed from Llandyssul:

Mae crydd yn byw hefyd wrth fron Gwaralltryn
Dyw wiw imi dreio byw'r gaeaf ffordd hyn

Mae hwnnw fel filain a'i elfen am ladd
Pe gallwn ymguddiwn o'i olwg fel gwadd

Cyn elot ar gerdded dwed ble rwyt yn mynd
Eglura'r dirgelwch i ambell hen ffrind

Ddaw neb i dy ganlyn, d'oes undyn mor ffôl
Cei eto lawn groeso pan ddelot yn ôl

O gadw'r dirgelwch caf heddwch fy hun
Ffolineb o'r mwyaf yw dweud wrth un dyn

Ffarweliwch mewn heddwch ar ddiwedd y gôl
Os byw fyddaf eto retyrnaf yn ôl

A shoemaker also lives by the slopes of Gwaralltryn
It's no use my trying to live this way in the winter

He is like a villain keen on killing
If I could I would hide from his sight like a mole

Ere thou goest away, say, where dost thou go?
Explain the mystery to some of your friends

No one will follow thee, none is so foolish
Thou wilt again get a full welcome when thou returnest

By keeping the secret I get peace myself
It is most unwise to tell any man

Bid farewell in peace at the end of the journey
If I shall live I shall return again

Ben Phillips in Pembrokeshire had the following:

Mae'r gwcw yn canu ar frigyn y pren
A chanu wnaf inne' wrth fadel â Gwen
A chanu wnaf inne' wrth fadel â Gwen

Pan ddelwyf 'ma nesa'i ro'i 'nghaniad ar bren
By idd llawer gwran dawr yn sel ei ben
By idd llawer gwran dawr yn sel ei ben

The cuckoo is singing on the branch of a tree
And I shall also sing when parting with Gwen
And I shall also sing when parting with Gwen

Before I come here next to give my song from a tree
Many a listener's head will have been laid low
Many a listener's head will have been laid low

62 GWENNO FWYN
GENTLE GWEN

John Thomas, Llangwm, Corwen, Denbighshire and Tom Edwards. Bryneglwys, Denbighshire, *rec.* E. Cleaver and P. Kennedy, 1954

The words of this song were composed by Mynyddog in 1866 and the tune is well known as that of the American minstrel song *Nelly Bly*:

1 Nelly Bly, Nelly Bly
Bring de broom along
We'll sweep the kitchen clean, my dear
And hab a little song
Poke de wood, my lady lub
And make de fire burn
And while I take my banjo down
Just gib de mush a turn

Heigh, Nelly, ho, Nelly
Listen lub to me
I'll sing to you, play to you
A dulcem melody

2 Nelly Bly hab a voice
   Like de turtle dove
   I hears it in de meadow
   And I hears it in de grove
   Nelly Bly hab a heart
   Warm as cup of tea
   And bigger dan de sweet potato
   Down in Tennessee

3 Nelly Bly shuts her eye
   When she goes to sleep
   And when she wakens up again
   Her eyeballs gin to peep

   De way she walks she lifts her foot
   And den she puts it down
   And when it falls dere's music dar
   In dat part of de town

4 Nelly Bly, Nelly Bly
   Nebber, nebber sigh
   Nebber bring de teardrop to
   De corner ob your eye
   For de pie is made ob pumkins
   And de mush is made ob corn
   An dere's corn and pumpkins plenty, lub
   A-lying in de barn

63 HEN LADI FOWR BENFELEN
A BUXOM OLD BLONDE

Ben Phillips, Lochtwrffin, Mathry, Pembrokeshire, *rec.*
E. Cleaver and S. Ennis, 1953: BBC 19069

A song containing the 'double entendre' erotic imagery of 'mowing the meadow' provides a good example of the type of seduction ballads which, at one time, must have been more common in the Welsh language. It is sung to a variant of the well known *Tôn y Melinydd*.

64 YR HEN WR MWYN
THE GENTLE OLD MAN

Mrs Gaerwen Jones, Cerrig-y-drudion, Denbighshire, *coll.* E. Cleaver

Printed versions
JWFSS: 1956–7, vol. V, part 1, p. 18

JWFSS: 1910, vol. I, part 2, nos. 10–11, pp. 81–4
BENNETT: 1896, p. 84
GWYNN WILLIAMS: 1961, nos. 19–20, pp. 26–7: two versions

This song is a variant of an old singing game which must have been very popular throughout Wales. The late J. Lloyd Williams, the editor of the Journal of the Welsh Folk Song Society, received a large number of variants from all parts of the country. It was known to have been sung in the streets in Glamorgan, and in the 'Noson Lawen' in Anglesey. David Lloyd George, the one-time Prime Minister, remembered it being sung by children when he was a boy at Llanystumdwy, Caernarvonshire. There are about four variants quoted in the JWFSS and another in BENNETT: 1896. The late Lady Herbert Lewis quotes an example published in *Manx Ballads and Music* entitled *My Henn Ghooiney Mie*, the tune being 'sung by the old woman, the old man's answer being spoken . . . the last verses being strikingly similar to those of the Welsh form: "What if thou should'st die, my good old man", etc.' (see JWFSS: 1925, vol. II, pt. 4, pp. 198–9).

The idea and the tune must be very old. Even though there is a great variation in the question and answer in different localities, in all the Welsh versions the last questions and answers are the same.

The first part should be sung very slowly with mock pathos. The pitied old man, however, is in a rollickingly light-hearted mood in his answers, even in the last two verses when he refers to his death and his burial.

The version noted here is a recent find, with yet another variation in the stanzas. It was sung by Mrs Jones, who heard it from her father, and it was a singing game popular with the children in the neighbourhood sixty years ago. Mr Emrys Jones of Cerrig-y-drudion won the first prize in the Pwllheli National Eisteddfod in 1955 when he sang it, unaccompanied, in the Folk Song competition.

65 LISA LAN
FAIR LIZA

Ellis Thomas, Corris, Merionethshire, *rec.* E. Cleaver
and S. Ennis, 1953: BBC 20198
Printed versions
JWFSS: 1909, vol. I, part 1, no. 20, pp. 37–9

JWFSS: 1925, vol. II, no. 4, p. 272
GWYNEDDON DAVIES: 1923, vol. II: an Anglesey version
GWYNN WILLIAMS: 1961, no. 8, p. 16: from JWFSS: 1909

Perhaps this is the most widespread, both in North and South Wales, of all Welsh folksongs. The version given here is similar to the one noted in Anglesey by Mrs Gwyneddon Davies, which has the flattened seventh. Here the flattened seventh is only used sparingly: in the last verse, where it is used to give a special melodic effect. In England this type of tune is used mainly for ballads such as *Barbara Allen*.

The version contributed to the JWFSS: 1909 also contained a flattened seventh and further 'hen benillion' (old stanzas):

Bûm yn dy garu lawer gwaith
Do lawer awr mewn mwynder maith
Bûm yn dy gusanu Lisa gêl
Yr oedd dy gwmni'n well na'r mêl

I loved thee dearly many a time
Aye, many an hour in joy sublime
I kissed thee freely, Lisa fair
Oh honey sweet, beyond compare

Fy nghangen lân, fy nghowlad glyd
Tydi yw'r lanaf yn y byd
Tydi sy'n peri poen a chri
A thi sy'n dwyn fy mywyd i

My fairest branch, my armful warm
In all the world you have most charm
'Tis you that's caused both tears and pain
'Tis you that's stole my life away

66 LODES LAN
FAIREST MAID

John Thomas, Llangwm, Corwen, Denbighshire, *rec.*
E. Cleaver and P. Kennedy, 1954

Printed version
THOMAS: 1927

Oral tradition produces variants of folksongs, but often awaits the personal imprint of the true folksong exponent to make its impact. This is an example of such a song. When first seen in print, in THOMAS: 1927, it makes little impression, but when heard from John Thomas with his characteristic pauses and his choice of a few different notes to point the words, what seemed quite ordinary on paper becomes a living thing. The ad-lib style of some of the old singers was part of their artistry and often transformed a simple song into a moving experience. Thus the appeal of this song, as in the case of many similar simple ones, is in observing the pauses and to endear the words by ad-libbing.

67 MAE 'NGHARIAD I'N FENWS
MY LOVE SHE'S A VENUS

John Thomas, Llangwm, Corwen, Denbighshire, *rec.*
E. Cleaver and P. Kennedy, 1954: BBC 20190
Other recorded version
Fragment, *rec.* S. Ennis, 1952

Printed version
JWFSS: 1922, vol. II, part 3, pp. 193 and 218

This love song has a typical flavour both in tune and words. The tune is mainly in the minor key, but makes an effective change to the major in the third and fourth bars. The two verses are an excellent example of Welsh euphony with the long vowels making a good sound for 'singing out'.

An Anglesey version of the song uses another well-known tune in the major key and shows some variation in the first verse.

68 Y MARCH GLAS
THE GREY HORSE

Mrs G. Megan Tibbott, Aberystwyth, Cardiganshire, *coll.* E. Cleaver and S. Ennis, 1953

Printed versions
JWFSS: 1954, vol. IV, part 4, no. 68
Gwynn Williams: 1963, no. 111, p. 144

According to Mrs Tibbott this song was sung near the borders of southern Cardiganshire and in the parish of Llangeler in Carmarthenshire. In the local dialect of south Cardiganshire, it describes a fop of a man and the different parts of his attire. There were many more verses, but Mrs Tibbott could only remember four.

The tune is effective, and does suggest the trotting of the horse. 'Towli' is a dialect form of 'taflu', and in this context is used to describe a horse trotting: 'Oboiti' is a dialect form of 'oddeutu' = 'around about'.

69 Y FERI LWYD
THE GREY MARI

Margaretta Thomas, Nantgarw, Caerphilly, and from Llangynwyd, Maesteg, Glamorganshire, *rec.* P. Kennedy, 1956: *Folk Songs of Britain*, vol. IX, Caedmon TC 1224/Topic 12T 197
Other recorded versions
Margaretta Thomas, *rec.* Llangynwyd, 1947 (song only): BBC 12110
Margaretta Thomas, *rec.* P. Kennedy, Llangynwyd, 1956 (with talk about custom): BBC 23514

Printed versions
Roberts: 1852: gives full account of custom with verses
JWFSS: 1909, vol. I, part 1, p. 30: *Canu Cwnsela*
Gwynn Williams: 1927: T. Bassett, Llansantffraid-ar-Lai, Glamorganshire
Llangollen MS: 1858: Roberts (1852)
Williams: 1938: arranged for four voices SSAA
Gwynn Williams: 1961, no. 4, p. 12: version from JWFSS: 1909

William Roberts (1852) suggests that this Christmas custom is a relic of the ancient festival of Balaam's Ass, the flight of Mary into Egypt (hence 'Mari lwyd' meaning 'blessed Mary'). It is now thought, less romantically, to mean only 'grey mare' and to be related to the similar Hooden Horse and Old Tup ceremonies found in parts of England.

The 'Mari lwyd' itself is represented by a man covered by a white sheet. He holds a broomstick on which is mounted the skull of a horse's head decorated with bells and jingles. The horse is accompanied by a party of four or five men, sometimes including the two characters of Punch and Judy.

The Mari Lwyd Party go round the farms and houses at Christmas and New Year. They sing outside and the families inside the house make their answer in song. Many of the verses in the old days were improvised (this is still done at Llangynwyd) but Mrs Margaretta Thomas sang us the verses she remembered sung at Nantgarw from 1880 to 1920.

J. H. Davies in JWFSS states that at one time 'this type of song was common all over Wales. There is a large collection of the Anglesey ones in the British Museum'.

Verse one is sung by the Feri outside the house. The doors are locked and they are not allowed in until after a series of questions and answers. During verse three the Mari makes a loud gnashing of teeth by working the jaws of the horse's skull. During verse five Punch is heard tapping the stones outside with a poker, while Judy is busy sweeping the doors and windows with a brush. Should those inside not succeed in keeping the doors and windows fastened, Punch and Judy would come in and rake the fire and sweep the dirt all over the house.

After verse twelve, when everything inside the house was ready, the door would be unlocked and the Mari would be admitted. Verse thirteen was then sung by all the company and a loaf of cake and a gallon of beer offered to the visiting party.

There was great merriment, the singing of ballads and love songs, such as *The Maid of Cefn Ydfa* and *The Maid of Sker*, dancing to the fiddle and harp and after some hours the Feri would sing her farewell (verse fourteen) at the door.—Margaretta Thomas.

70 ROWN I'N RHODIO MYNWENT EGLWYS
WAND'RING THROUGH THE CHURCHYARD

Mrs T. R. Jones, Bronnant, Aberystwyth, Cardiganshire,
coll. Rachel Thomas at Abertridwr, Caerphilly,
Glamorganshire
Other recorded version
Frances Mon Jones, 1953: BBC 21844

Printed versions
JWFSS: 1925, vol. I, part 4, nos. 168 and 170, pp. 71
and 192
GWYNN WILLIAMS: 1961, no. 68, p. 75: *Mynwent Eglwys*
GWYNN WILLIAMS: 1963, no. 116, p. 149: *Pan own i'n
rhodio Mynwent Eglwys* (sung by sailors along the
shores of Cardigan Bay).

Rachel Thomas was singing a variant of this Welsh cradle song at a recital of Welsh song, prose and poetry at Abertridwr, Caerphilly. Mrs T. R. Jones came up to her after the recital and sang her mother's version. It is a combination of lullaby and a method of teaching the English alphabet with which her mother used to rock the children to sleep some sixty years ago. There are other examples of Welsh songs used for teaching numbers and also the tonic sol-fa.

71 TAFARN Y RHOS
THE TAVERN ON THE MOOR

Sam Davies, Pontrhydyfen, Glamorganshire, *coll.* Rev.
Gomer M. Roberts

Printed version
JWFSS: 1953, vol. IV, part 3, pp. 72–3: two variants

This is an example of a conversational ballad in which the singers recite the words in a singing style, with a syllable to every note. The story is all-important: the tune simply follows the words phrase by phrase in a free and easy manner.

The Rev. Gomer Roberts remembered Sam Davies at the age of 77 singing this kind of sobering up song with gusto to the accompaniment of the harp played by his son. He also noted a different tune with similar words, but for dialectical differences, from his old uncle who lived in Llandybie, Carmarthenshire. According to the Rev. Thomas Levi (*Y Traethodydd*, 1869, p. 31) the words were written by Siôn Levi from the Swansea Valley.

72 TREN O'R BALA I FFESTINIOG
THE BALA–FFESTINIOG TRAIN

John Thomas, Llangwm, Denbighshire, *rec.* P. Kennedy
and E. Cleaver, 1954: BBC 22337

John Thomas sang this song with his typical Welsh 'hwyl'. It was a treat to watch him in his rocking chair smiling through the humorous ballad, and he imbued it with his typical colouring of some of the notes, the words, the old place-names and the names of the old characters.

The words of these ballad-type tunes were all-important to the old singers, the music being only a means of expressing the meaning and the spirit of the words. An example of the Stable Loft type, it shows the old custom among country folk in Wales to be always ready to sing a song with topical allusions to incidents concerning local characters: in this one, in connection with the advent of the first train running from Bala to Ffestiniog. Notice the mixing of broken English with the Welsh.

The tune is typically Welsh in its minor idiom. To follow John Thomas' style, the first verse is to be taken rather slowly in the ad-lib fashion, and the chorus quickens its tempo to resemble a fast-moving train with the people running after it to catch up.

Bibliography

BENNETT: 1896
Nicholas Bennett, *Alawon Fy Ngwlad* (*The Lays of my Land*):
Phillips & Son, Newtown, 1896. 2 vols. Consists of nearly 500
Welsh airs, also of biographical notes on Welsh harpers and
Penillion singers, a collection of recorded, but previously un-
published melodies. Many were taken from the LLEWELYN
ALAW MSS, 1858 (see below).

BLAKE: 1954
Loïs Blake, *Welsh Folk Dance and Costume*: Gwynn Publishing,
Llangollen, 1954. This is the only book ever written dealing
solely with Welsh folk dance and Welsh costume.

BODWIGEN MS
Robert A Huw of Bodwigen, Anglesey, *Musica neu Beroriaeth*:
British Museum, Add. MS 14905. 'The music of the Britons as
settled by a Congress or Meeting of Masters of Music by order
of Gruffydd Ap Cynan, Prince of Wales, about A.D. 1100'—a
note in B.M. Addit MS 14905. 'The Ms. was wrote by Robert
ap Huw . . . in Charles 1st time'. A kind of tablature not understood or sung. (See GWYNN WILLIAMS: 1932, pp. 30–4.)

BOULTON: 1913
Harold Boulton, *Songs of the Four Nations*: music arranged by
Arthur Somervell, J. B. Cramer, London, 1913. Attempts to
bring together 'national songs' of England, Scotland, Ireland
and Wales, all with English words but also some verses given in
original Cornish, Scots, Irish, Manx Gaelic and Welsh.

CLEAVER: 1968
Emrys Cleaver, *Musicians of Wales*: John Jones, Ruthin, 1968.
An account of the lives and work of the major musicians of
Wales in the 19th century (and into the 20th), with special
reference to nationalistic composers.

CROSSLEY-HOLLAND: 1942
Peter Crossley-Holland, 'Secular Homophonic Music in Wales
in the Middle Ages'; an article in *Music and Letters*, 1942. Results
of research undertaken to decipher the strange music of the
Bodwigen MS. (see above).

CROSSLEY-HOLLAND: 1968
Peter Crossley-Holland, 'Welsh Folk Song Tonality', an article
in JWFSS: 1968, vol. V, part 2, p. 2. 'An attempt to form an
objective picture of the main tonal limits within which Welsh
Folk Song melody moves and has its being.'

DAVIES: 1919
Hubert Davies, *Caneuon Gwerin Cymru* (*Welsh Folk Songs*):
Hughes, Cardiff, 1919. 11 Welsh folksongs with piano accom-
paniment in staff and sol-fa notation.

DE LLOYD: 1931
David de Lloyd, *Forty Welsh Traditional Tunes*: Oxford
University Press, London, 1929. '40 Welsh Traditional Tunes'
issued by the Cardiganshire Antiquarian Society arranged
for 2 voices and piano. A very useful song book in both staff and
sol-fa notation.

GWYNEDDON DAVIES: 1914/23/24
Grace Gwyneddon Davies, *Alawon Gwerin Môn* (*Folk Songs of
Anglesey*): Hughes, Cardiff. Vol. I 1914, vol. II 1923, vol. III
1924. Welsh traditional folksongs collected in Anglesey for
voice and piano in staff notation. With English words. Vol. I
has 7 songs, vol. II 6 songs and 1 variant, and vol. III 6 songs.

GWYNN WILLIAMS: 1927
W. S. Gwynn Williams, *Old Welsh Folk Songs*: Gwynn Publishing, Llangollen, 1927. A collection of 12 songs arranged for
voice and piano with English translations. The songs are thought
to be among the oldest Welsh music extant. The collection contains modal types which are characteristic of the ancient vocal
Welsh music. The introduction provides a concise history of
Welsh traditional music.

GWYNN WILLIAMS: 1932
W. S. Gwynn Williams, *Welsh National Music and Dance*:
Gwynn Publishing, Llangollen, 4th ed. 1932; Schirmer, U.S.A.
and Curwen, London, 1953 (latest ed. 1971). The only standard
work on the history and character of Welsh national music and
dance. The work contains very important chapters on Welsh
traditional songs, instruments and dances from pre-Christian
times.

GWYNN WILLIAMS: 1946
W. S. Gwynn Williams, *Old Welsh Ballads*: Gwynn Publishing,
Llangollen, 1946. A collection of 7 of the most popular Welsh
'Ballads' for SA and piano or SATB, with Welsh and English
words.

GWYNN WILLIAMS: 1958
W. S. Gwynn Williams, *Eleven Welsh Folk Songs*: Gwynn
Publishing, Llangollen, 1958. 11 characteristic Welsh traditional songs first published in JWFSS: 1909–58; arranged for
voice and piano with both Welsh and English words.

GWYNN WILLIAMS: 1961/3
W. S. Gwynn Williams, *Caneuon Traddodiadol Y Cymry*
(*Traditional Songs of the Welsh*): Gwynn Publishing, Llan-
gollen. Book I 1961, book II 1963. Selected from the JWFSS.
These are most useful volumes both for the singer and student.
Book I consists of 74 traditional Welsh folksongs with notes on
their character and sources. Book II has 50 songs as above with
an extract from 'Remarks of the Tonality of some Welsh
melodies' (Alfred Daniel) and 'Notes on Welsh metres' (T.
Gwynn Jones).

JWFSS: 1909–71
Journal of the Welsh Folk Song Society, ed. J. Lloyd Williams,
W. S. Gwynn Williams, 1909–71 (intermittently). The Journal
consists of hundreds of songs and variants from aural, MS and
published sources, which are given in both staff and sol-fa
notation.

JENKINS KERRY MS
John Jenkins Kerry, *Jenkins Kerry Manuscript*: National
Library of Wales, Aberystwyth. The earliest manuscript collection of Welsh folksongs, written at the end of the 18th and the
beginning of the 19th centuries.

JONES: 1784
Edward Jones, *Musical and Poetical Relicks of the Welsh Bards*:
London, 1784. 'Musical and Poetical Relicks of the Welsh
Bards, preserved by tradition and authentic manuscripts from
remote antiquity; never before published'. It also contains
variations for the harp, harpsichord, violin and flute. It was
reprinted several times.

JONES: 1802
Edward Jones, *The Bardic Museum*: A. Strahan, London, 1802.
'The second volume of the musical, poetical and historical
relicks of the Welsh Bards and Druids'. The volume contains
about 60 airs with new basses and variations for traditional
instruments.

JONES, WILLIAMS AND PUGH: 1801–70
Owen Jones (Myfyr), Edward Williams (Iolo Morganwg) and

William Owen Pugh, *The Myvyrian Archaeology of Wales*: S. Rousseau, London. Vols. I and II 1801, vol. III 1807 (2nd ed. in one volume Gee, Denbigh, 1870). Material collected out of ancient manuscripts.

LEWIS: 1914
Mrs Herbert Lewis, *Folk Songs collected in Flintshire and the Vale of Clwyd*: Hughes, Cardiff and Wrexham, 1914. Contains 12 songs in Welsh only (with no translations into English), and two songs in English. Arranged for voice and piano with comparative notes and details of sources.

LLANGOLLEN MS: 1858
'Orpheus', *The Llangollen Manuscript from the Llangollen Eisteddfod, 1858*: National Library of Wales, Aberystwyth, 1858. 'Orpheus' was the unknown competitor who sent his collection to the Llangollen Eisteddfod of 1858. The other competitor who won the first prize was Llewelyn Alaw (see following entry). Both are very valuable early collections of Welsh folksongs.

LLEWELYN ALAW: 1858
Llewelyn Alaw, *Collection of the Llangollen Eisteddfod*: National Library of Wales, Aberystwyth, 1858. The other collection of unpublished folksongs sent to the Llangollen Eisteddfod 1858.

LLOYD WILLIAMS AND JONES: 1920/3/4
J. Lloyd Williams and L. D. Jones, *Welsh Folk Songs*: Hughes, Cardiff; vol. I 1920, vol. II 1923, vol. III 1924. Three volumes of Welsh folksongs arranged for schools for two or three voices with piano accompaniment. They contain 36 songs with English and Welsh words.

LLOYD WILLIAMS: 1928
J. Lloyd Williams, *Hwiangerddi Cymraeg (Welsh Lullabies)*: Hughes, Cardiff, 1928. 12 old Welsh lullabies with piano arrangement. Welsh words and English translations. A collection used for infants and junior schools.

LLOYD WILLIAMS: 1948
J. Lloyd Williams, *Manuscript Collection*: National Library of Wales, Aberystwyth. J. Lloyd Williams, first editor of the *Journal of the Welsh Folk Song Society*, died in 1948 and his family donated his unpublished material to the National Library.

MORGANWG MS
Iolo Morganwg (1747–1826), *Llanofer Manuscript*, MS 59 (1800c), National Library of Wales, Aberystwyth, MS C2. An early MS of old Welsh songs and folklore, including descriptions of entertainment very common in Glamorganshire known as 'stable-loft gatherings'.

MORRIS: 1700–79
Richard Morris, *Manuscript Collection and Listing*, British Museum Add. MS 14992. Ballads, carols and songs with a list of tunes from about 1717.

MORRIS: 1762–90
Richard Morris (son), *Manuscript Listing*, British Museum Add. MS. 14939. List of tunes sung by Welsh minstrels and harpists.

MYNYDDOG: 1866/70/77
Caneuon Mynyddog (Songs of Mynyddog): Hughes, Cardiff, vol. I 1866, vol 2 1870, vol. 3 1877. A poet and a singer, Mynyddog published three volumes which consisted of popular Welsh songs rather than traditional folksongs.

OWAIN: 1873
John Owain (Owain Alaw), *Gems of Welsh Melody*: Hughes, Wrexham, and Simpkin Marshall, London, 1873. 'A selection of popular Welsh songs with English and Welsh words.' Also Penillion singing, Welsh national airs, ancient and modern. It is one of the well-known works and one of the earliest collections.

PARRY: 1839/48
John Parry (Bardd Alaw), *The Welsh Harper*: D'Almaine, London, 1839, 2nd ed. 1848. An extensive collection of Welsh music including most of the contents of the three volumes published by the late Edward Jones ... 'and of the late Mr Parry of Ruabon'. The second volume contains 'Two Hundred Welsh Airs, chiefly selected from MS. collections'.

PARRY AND WILLIAMS: 1742
John Parry (of Ruabon) and Evan Williams, *Antient British Music*: Mickleborough, London, 1742. This volume contains 24 airs set for the harp, harpsichord and other instruments. It has also 'An Historical Account of the Rise and Progress of Music among the Antient Britons'. It is the first recorded published work of Welsh National music.

PARRY: 1752–61
John Parry (of Ruabon), *A Collection of Welsh, English and Scotch Airs*: John Johnson, London, 1752 and/or 1761. 'A collection of Welsh, English and Scotch airs with new variations.'

RICHARDS: 1879
Brinley Richards, *The Songs of Wales*: 4th ed. Boosey, London, 1879. This volume of 64 Welsh airs arranged as songs with piano accompaniment is one of the most popular song books ever published in Wales. It has Welsh and English words. Music in staff notation only. (A revised version by E. T. Davies and S. Northcote was published by Boosey in 1959.)

ROBERTS: 1852
W. Roberts, *Crefydd Yr Oesau Tywyll*: Carmarthen, 1852. In this book we have a full account of *Y Feri Lwyd* (No. 69).

ROBERTS: 1938
Mervyn Roberts, *Chwe Chân Werin Gymreig (Six Welsh Folk Songs)*: Gwynn Publishing, Llangollen, 1938. Arranged for voice and piano with Welsh words and English translations. Also arranged for SA and SSA.

THOMAS: 1845
John Thomas (Ieuan Ddu), *Y Caniedydd Cymreig (The Cambrian Minstrel)*: Dr Jones, Merthyr Tydfil, 1845. A collection of 140 songs, 40 of which are recorded and the remainder composed by John Thomas himself. It contains about 24 unpublished folksongs.

THOMAS: 1862
John Thomas (Pencerdd Gwalia), *Welsh Melodies for the Voice*: vols. I and II, Addison, Hollier Lucas, 1862; vol. III Lamborn Cock, 1870; vol. IV J. B. Cramer, 1874. Welsh and English words. A collection of 49 airs in all, arranged for voice, also harmonized for four voices, with harp and piano accompaniment.

THOMAS: 1927
Philip Thomas, *Alawon Gwerin Cymru*: Hugh Evans, Liverpool, 1927. Published for the Welsh Summer School, Llanwrtyd. This collection contains 41 Welsh folksongs for voice in sol-fa notation, with Welsh words only.

VAUGHAN THOMAS: 1928/50
D. Vaughan Thomas, *Ten Welsh Folk Songs*: USA, 1928; Gwynn Publishing, Llangollen, 1950. Ten authentic Welsh folksongs arranged for voice and piano. Staff and sol-fa notation. Good selection and well arranged.

WILLIAMS: 1844
Maria Jane Williams, *Ancient National Airs of Gwent and Morgannwg*: William Rees, Llandovery and D'Almaine, London, 1844. This volume is the first published collection of traditional Welsh folksongs. These 43 songs with Welsh words are arranged for the harp or piano.

WILLIAMS: 1938
Mari Lwyd (Blessed Mary), arr. Grace Williams for SSAA: Gwynn Publishing Co., Llangollen, 1938. Arrangement of the song associated with the *Mari Lwyd* custom (see No. 69).

IV

Songs in
Manx Gaelic

Introduction

The Isle of Man is situated almost at the centre of the British Isles and is roughly oval in outline, its greatest length being thirty-three miles and its greatest width twelve miles, while its total area is 227 square miles. A central ridge of mountains runs from north-east to south-west, with a break at the valley running east to west between Douglas, the capital of the Island, and Peel, the main centre of Manx fishing. From this central ridge the rivers flow down long, deep glens to the sea on either side, and it is among the people of this glen and upland country that the folksongs have been longest preserved in general use, though the fisher-crofters of the coastal districts and villages have also been good sources of folk material —songs, dances and stories. The total population of the island even today is only about 50 000 (the 1961 census showed it at 48 150), and when the bulk of the folksongs were collected it was considerably less.

The island has many antiquities. There are traces of Neolithic man and of early Pictish art, but the basic race in historical times was that of the Gaelic Celt. Later this amalgamated with the Norse, owing more to Norse settlement than to the many Viking raids with which the Norse-Manx period began, and even today these two basic types, and the mixture resulting from their union, are easily recognisable among the population, though the strains have been modified during the last 100–150 years by immigration. The influence of the Norse language, however, is scarcely traceable except in place-names, the Manx language remaining almost purely Gaelic. The earliest form of religion seems to have been the Druidism practised in ancient Ireland, and several figures of the old Irish pantheon are well known in Manx folklore. In fact one, Mananan, is traditionally the first ruler of the island, and part of the annual Tynwald, or law-giving ceremony, is officially stated to be in memory of a tribute paid to him. Many relics of this early religion survive in Manx folklore and song and even in Manx law, which includes 'breast laws' similar to those of Druidism.

Politically this island has always been independent, and it still is, though it no longer rules the Hebridean Isles as during the long Norse-Manx period, when the Kings of Man and the Isles flew the Viking Ship as their ensign and rendered only a token fealty to the King of Norway and the Pope, who took the island under his protection at the request of King Magnus of Man for a token payment of ten marks. Christianity has been practised in the island from the fifth century, and much of the folklore is connected with Christian relics, customs and legends, but it is always pervaded by a strong influence from the earlier Druidic religion.

The rulership of the island has passed through many hands in the course of its history, but never since Norse-Manx days have its overlords been closely concerned with the life of the people. In a sense it has been an occupied country for centuries, with two distinct communities, and it is the Gaelic-speaking native Manx community which has preserved its folklore and songs. Of recent years the line of demarcation has been less pronounced, but it is still there. Today Queen Elizabeth II is Lord of Man and the island is part of the British Commonwealth of Nations; it still enacts its own laws, is governed by its own Tynwald under its own independent Constitution, and is different in many respects from any other part of the British Isles.

Manx Gaelic, the language in which the songs are composed, is a branch of the ancient

m Taggart of Grenaby, Isle of Man
Photograph: Manx Press

Gaelic once common currency in Ireland, Scotland and Man. Although it has developed many differences of idiom and intonation, and retained some old forms lost in the other two branches, there is still sufficient similarity for a Manx Gaelic speaker to follow the drift of a conversation in Irish or Scottish Gaelic, and to be understood to about the same extent when speaking. In the fishing voyages to Ireland and the Hebrides which were part of the Manx annual routine until the first decade of this century, the fishermen found no difficulty about communicating with the Gaelic speakers of either country.

Until well within living memory Manx Gaelic was the everyday speech of the countryfolk. Up to the end of the nineteenth century it was used regularly in church and in the law courts, and most businessmen needed to use it to some extent. Only since the first decade of the present century has it debilitated as the general means of communication, first being superseded by an ephemeral Anglo-Manx dialect and more recently by standard English; and it is perhaps significant that in neither of these forms of speech have any folksongs been composed by the people, though one or two 'concert' songs composed and printed in the dialect, such as *A Manx Wedding* and *The Pride of Purt-le-Murra*, have become very popular.

The passing of the Anglo-Manx dialect, which was evoked by the transition from Gaelic to English, can hardly be regretted as it was never a full means of expression and is now generally regarded as a medium for broad comedy only. But the near loss of our beautiful and expressive Manx Gaelic, due mainly to the adoption of an alien educational system, has come to be regarded by Manx people as a grave deprivation. There is today a strong movement for its revival, particularly successful among the younger generation. Many Gaelic classes are well supported, there are social gatherings of Gaelic speakers, church services are conducted in the old language and Gaelic concerts are organized quite frequently, and in these concerts the folksongs are featured in solo and choral arrangements and also in community singing.

We are fortunate in that the bulk of the songs were collected when the language was only starting to decline. Less fortunately many of the tunes were noted by the chief collectors of the nineteenth century without their accompanying words, or with only fragments of them. These collectors were Dr Clague of Castletown, Deemster Gill and his brother Mr W. H. Gill, who were jointly responsible for the first important publications of Manx folksongs, *Manx National Songs* (GILL: 1896) and *Manx National Music* (GILL: 1898), the latter being a collection of over 200 airs arranged for piano but without words beyond the titles. At much the same period Mr A. W. Moore, Speaker of the House of Keys and a fluent Manx Gaelic speaker, was busy noting songs and stories on his own account, and his *Manx Ballads and Music*, published in Douglas (MOORE: 1896), contains much the largest printed collection of song-words (including an Ossianic fragment noted in 1789), but only forty-three airs, of which some are only slightly different versions of the same tune.

Three volumes of the *Journal of the Folk Song Society* (nos. 28, 29 and 30: 1924–6) were devoted almost entirely to the printing and criticism of Manx folksongs from the Clague Collection and other sources. Edited by Miss A. G. Gilchrist, these are recommended to anyone wishing to make a more extensive study of the subject.

The present revival of general interest in Manx Gaelic has led to Manx folksongs being sung in their original language once more, instead of in an English translation, and a few new songs have been composed in the Gaelic and a number of hymns for use in Gaelic church services. These new Gaelic words are almost invariably fitted to tunes already well known, though some of them are traditional.

Introduction

PRONUNCIATION OF MANX GAELIC

Manx Gaelic, though identical in structure and fairly close in intonation to the Gaelic of Northern Ireland and the Scottish Isles, has one advantage for the non-Gaelic-speaker or singer: it was first written down by men who were not familiar with the language and literature of the other Gaelic countries but had received the standard English education of their day, and so they tried to write the Gaelic words phonetically according to the pronunciation of English instead of using standard Gaelic orthography. This is regarded by Gaelic scholars as a grave defect in Manx, but it is certainly helpful to anyone not a native speaker who tries to speak or sing in the language. In the songs it will be found that the air follows closely the natural stress of the Gaelic words, so if the following few rules are taken as a guide a reasonably good pronunciation of the song words should be achieved by a non-Manx-speaking singer.

Consonants

b, f, j, k, m, p, q, v and w as in English.

c	always hard, as in *c*at and never as in city
ch	without cedilla as in Scots lo*ch*
	with cedilla as in *ch*erry
d, dd	as *th* in *th*y
dd	when flanked by slender vowels, as *z*
l, ll, n	often have the slender sound, as *l*ya, *n*ya
bb	when in the middle of a word, as *v*
t, d	when initial, as *th* or *dh*
y	always as in th*e* as used in conversation, never as *y* in th*y*. When occurring at the end of a word, as in Manx 'foalsey' (false) it makes the final syllable sound like a short *a*: 'fawlsa'

Vowels

a (long)	as in English *ah*
a (short)	as in *a*dd
aa (or ae), eh	as in m*ay*
ee	as in s*ee*
e	as in *e*gg
i	as in *i*f
o	as in *o*f
u	as in *u*nless
iw	eeoo
ui	ooee
au	aeoo
ou	as in th*ou*
iu (or eu)	as in *you*

73 ARRANE Y BLIEH
THE GRINDING SONG

O ta'n cor - key mie son beisht as dooin - ney

T'eh jan - noo cheh as la - jer ooil - ley

As ayns coon - lagh cor - key mie dy lhie

CH: O yn mwyl - lin, mwyl - lin - O As yn ar - roo, ar - roo noa

As ta'n grine veg cor - key goll gys y vwyl - lin ————

1 O ta'n corkey mie son beisht as dooinney
T'eh jannoo cheh as lajer ooilley
As ayns coonlagh corkey mie dy lhie
O yn mwyllin, mwyllin-o
As yn arroo, arroo noa
As ta'n grine veg corkey goll gys y vwyllin

2 O ta'n curnaght mie son berreen as arran
Mie lesh caashey eeym as sollan
T'eh mie ayns y thie as mie ayns keeill
(Chorus with changing last line)
As ta'n grine veg curnaght goll gys y vwyllin

3 O ta'n grine veg oarn ny share ny ooilley
T'eh ynrican oarn ta mee goaill son folliu
Ta oarn cur bioys er ny ching ayns cree
As ta'n grine veg oarn ersooyl gys y vwyllin

1 O the oats are great for human and cattle
It keeps them warm and gives them mettle [cuddle
And in the straw for the bedding is the best place to
O a-millin', millin'-o
An' the corn, the corn is new
An' the little oat grain is a-goin' to the mill-o

2 O the wheat is good for bread and cake baking
It's good with cheese and salt and butter
It's good at home and it's good in the chapel
(Chorus with changing last line)
An' the little wheat grain is a-goin' to the mill-o

3 O the grain of the barley is the best of any
And it's only from barley I'll take my tally
It cheers and it banishes melancholy
An' the little barley grains are a-goin' to the mill-o

74 ARRANE Y LHONDHOO
THE SONG OF THE BLACKBIRD

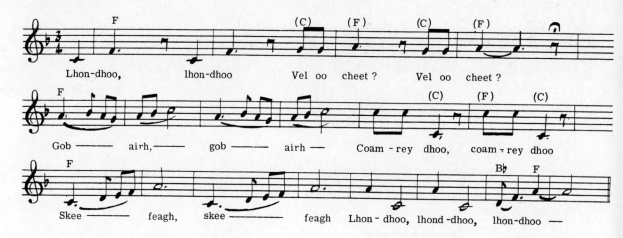

1 Lhondhoo, lhondhoo
Vel oo cheet? Vel oo cheet?
Gob airh, gob airh
Coamrey dhoo, coamrey dhoo
Skee feagh, skee feagh
Lhondhoo, lhondhoo, lhondhoo

2 Tar bieau, tar bieau
Lhondhoo, lhondhoo
Laa liauyr, laa liauyr
Keirys dhoo, keirys dhoo
Skee feagh, skee feagh
Lhondhoo, lhondhoo, lhondhoo

1 Blackbird, blackbird
Will you come? Will you come?
Golden beak, golden beak
Coat o' black, coat o' black
Weary waiting, weary waiting
Blackbird, blackbird, blackbird

2 Come quickly, come quickly
Blackbird, blackbird
Long day's, long day's
Dusk darkens, dusk darkens
Weary waiting, weary waiting
Blackbird, blackbird, blackbird

75 ARRANE NY NIEE
THE WASHING SONG

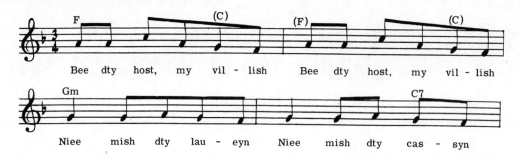

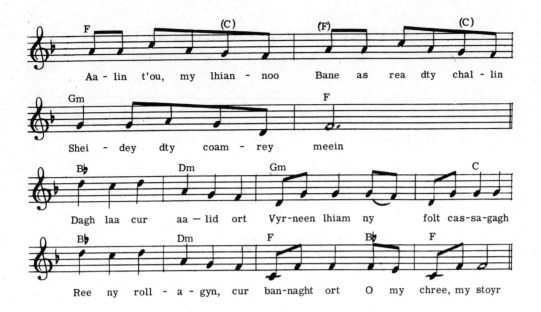

Aa-lin t'ou, my lhian-noo Bane as rea dty chal-lin
Shei-dey dty coam-rey meein
Dagh laa cur aa—lid ort Vyr-neen lhiam ny folt cas-sa-gagh
Ree ny roll-a-gyn, cur ban-naght ort O my chree, my stoyr

1 Bee dty host, my villish
Bee dty host, my villish
Niee mish dty laueyn
Niee mish dty cassyn
Aalin t'ou, my lhiannoo
Bane as rea dty challin
Sheidey dty coamrey meein
Dagh laa cur aalid ort
Vyrneen lhiam ny folt cassagagh
Ree ny rollagyn, cur bannaght ort
O my chree, my stoyr

2 Chooid nagh gaase 'sy voghrey
Lhig eh gaase 'syn keeiraght
Niee mish dty laueyn
Niee mish dty cassyn
Chooid nagh gaase ec munlaa
Lhig eh gaase 'syn oie
Cur ort dy chooilley grayse
Dagh laa cur niartys ort
Vyrneen lhiam ny folt cassagagh
Ree ny rollagyn, cur bannaght ort
O my chree, my stoyr

1 Hush-a-bye, my darling
Hush-a-bye, my darling
Hands now I'll wash them
Feet now I'll wash them
Handsome you, my young one
Fair and smooth your body
Clothes made of silk so fine
Each day puts beauty on you
Darling sweet, with hair a-curling
King of stars, blessings on you
O my heart, my joy

2 At morn that which grows not
By the twilight's growing
Hands now I'll wash them
Feet now I'll wash them
At noon that which grows not
By the night-time's growing
And puts on every grace
Each day puts strength upon you
Darling sweet, with hair a-curling
King of stars, blessings on you
O my heart, my joy

76 ARRANE NY SHEEAGHYN TROAILTAGH
THE SONG OF THE TRAVELLING FAIRIES

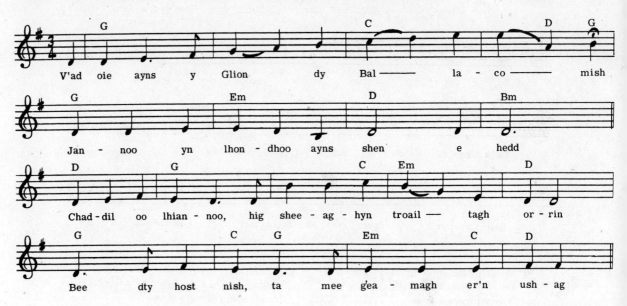

V'ad oie ayns y Glion dy Bal — la - co — mish
Jan - noo yn lhon - dhoo ayns shen e hedd
Chad - dil oo lhian - noo, hig shee - ag - hyn troail — tagh or - rin
Bee dty host nish, ta mee g'ea - magh er'n ush - ag

1 V'ad oie ayns y Glion dy Ballacomish
Jannoo yn lhondhoo ayns shen e hedd
Chaddil oo lhiannoo, hig sheeaghyn troailtagh orrin
Bee dty host nish, ta mee g'eamagh er'n ushag

2 V'ad oie ayns Glion Rushen dy reagh ny sleityn
Jannoo yn shirragh ayns shen e hedd

3 V'ad oie er ny creggyn Kione ny Spainagh
Jannoo y foillan ayns shen e hedd

4 Hig ad gys Gordon, agh ayns shen, cooie
Jannoo yn dreean veg y hedd
Chaddil oo lhiannoo, ny gow-jee aggle Adhene
Bee dty host nish, ta mee g'eamagh er'n ushag

1 One night in the glen, in the glen of Ball'comish
The blackbird will come to build her own nest
Sleep, little child, the fairies will come to us
Hush now, my baby, the bird I will call

2 One night in Glen Rushen high in the mountains
The falcon will come to build her own nest

3 One night on the rocks of Spanish Headland
The seagull will come to build her own nest

4 They'll come to Gordon, but there so conveniently
There will the little wren build her own nest
Sleep, little child, of Those People don't be 'feared
Hush now, my baby, the bird I will call

77 ARRANE NY VLIEAUN
THE MILKING SONG

Cur dty vain - ney, cur dty vain - ney Choud as mish ta goaill ar - rane

Lhig yn curn nish roie har - rish Lesh dty vain - ney, my voa veen

Ban-naght Jee mish cur orts nish Ayr as Mac as Spyr - ryd Noo

As Moir - rey Ban - nit bish - ee Dty vain - ney, my voa

1 Cur dty vainney, cur dty vainney
Choud as mish ta goaill arrane
Lhig yn curn nish roie harrish
Lesh dty vainney, my voa veen
Bannaght Jee mish cur orts nish
Ayr as Mac as Spyrryd Noo
As Moirrey Bannit bishee
Dty vainney, my voa

2 Mie dty vainney, mie dty vainney
Lesh kay son yn eeym
Jean dty chooidshare dy chur dou palchey
As yiow uss tooilley oarn
Chorus

1 Give your milk, cow, give your milk
Whilst I sing my song to you
Let the milk-churn fill and spill
With your milk, my dear old cow
Blessings of God I'll put upon you
Father, Son and Holy Ghost
And also Blessed Mary
Give more milk, my cow

2 Yours is good milk, fine and healthy
From the butter there'll be cream
Do your best to give me plenty
Then your barley share you'll gain
Chorus

78 HELG YN DREEAN
HUNT THE WREN

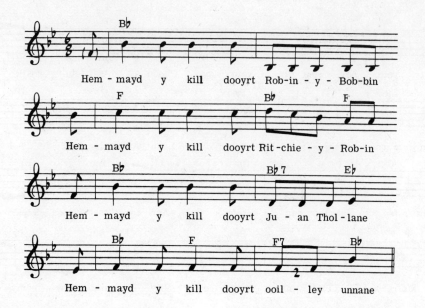

Hem - mayd y kill dooyrt Rob-in - y - Bob-bin

Hem - mayd y kill dooyrt Rit -chie - y - Rob-in

Hem - mayd y kill dooyrt Ju - an Thol - lane

Hem - mayd y kill dooyrt ooil - ley unnane

1 Hemmayd y kill *dooyrt Robin-y-Bobbin*
Hemmayd y kill *dooyrt Ritchie-y-Robin*
Hemmayd y kill *dooyrt Juan Thollane*
Hemmayd y kill *dooyrt ooilley unnane*

2 Cre'n fa shen? *dooyrt Robin-y-Bobbin*
(*etc.*)

3 Dy helg y dreean

4 C'raad t'eh? C'raad t'eh?

5 Soie ayns y crouw

6 Kys yiowmayd geddyn?

7 Ceau clagh, ceau clagh

8 Nish t'eh marroo

9 Crenaght ymmyrk eh?

10 Ayns sleod ymleyder

11 Crenaght coagyr eh?

12 Harrish y voain

13 Crenaght neemayd g'ee eh?

14 Lesh meir ain

15 Quoi hig yinnair?

16 Yn Ree as Ven-rein

17 Sooillyn y doal, *dooyrt Robin-y-Bobbin*
Lurgyn y croobagh, *dooyrt Ritchie-y-Robin*
Scrobbag ny moght, *dooyrt Juan Thollane*
Crauyn y moddee, *dooyrt ooilley unnane*

18 Dreean, dreean, Ree n'eeanlee
Laa'll Steoain marroo ayns y connee
Ga t'eh beg e cleinney mooar
Cur dooin jough, ven-thie, dy liooar'

1 Let's go to the wood, *said Robin-the-Bobbin*
Let's go to the wood, *said Ritchie-the-Robin*
Let's go to the wood, *said Juan Thollane*
Let's go to the wood, *said everyone*

2 Why do we go there? *said Robin-the-Bobbin*
(*etc.*)

3 To hunt the wren

4 Where is he? Where is he?

5 Sitting in the bush

6 How'll we get him?

7 Throw a stone, throw a stone

8 Now he is dead

9 How to carry him?

10 In the brewer's sledge

11 How to cook him?

12 Over the turf

13 How'll we eat him?

14 With our fingers

15 Who'll come to dinner?

16 The King and the Queen

17 Eyes to the blind, *says Robin-the-Bobbin*
Legs to the lame, *says Ritchie-the-Robin*
Crop to the poor, *says Juan Thollane*
Bones to the dogs, *says everyone*

18 The wren, the wren, the king of the birds
St. Stephen's day he's caught in the furze
Although he is small, his family's great
Give us plenty of drink, woman, plenty to eat

HOP-TU-NAA
HOP-TU-NAA

1 Ta shenn oie houney, *hop-tu-naa*
Ta'n eayst soil shean, *trol-la-laa*
Hop-tu-naa as trol-la-laa
Ta shenn oie houney, *hop-tu-naa*

2 Kellagh as kiark, *hop-tu-naa*
Shibbyr y gounee, *trol-la-laa*
Hop-tu-naa as trol-la-laa
Kellagh as kiark, *hop-tu-naa*

3 Cre'n gauin gow mayd?
Yn gauin beg breck

4 Kerroo ayns y phot
Vlayst mee yn vroit

5 Scold mee my scoarnagh
Roie mee gys y chibbyr

6 Diu mee my haie
Eisht cheet ny yei

7 Veeit mee poul kayt
Ren eh scryssey

8 Roie mee gys Nalbin
Cre naight ayns shen?

9 Yn cheeaght va traaue
Ny cleain va cleiee

10 Va ben aeg giarey caashey
Yn skynn va geyre

11 Yiare ee e mair
Lhap ee 'sy clooid

12 Ghlass ee eh 'sy choir
Ren eh sthock as stoyr

13 Three kirree keeir, *hop-tu-naa*
Va ec Illiam yn Oe, *trol-la-laa*
Hop-tu-naa as trol-la-laa
Three kirree keeir, *hop-tu-naa*
(*Spoken*)
My ta shiu cur veg dou
Cur eh dou nish
Son ta mish laccal goll thie
Lesh soilshey yn eayst
Hop-tu-naa

1 'Tis old Hollantide, *hop-tu-naa*
The moon shines bright, *trol-la-laa*
Hop-tu-naa as trol-la-laa
'Tis old Hollantide, *hop-tu-naa*

2 Cock and hen, *hop-tu-naa*
Sup of the heifer, *trol-la-laa*
Hop-tu-naa as trol-la-laa
Cock and hen, *hop-tu-naa*

3 What heifer shall we take?
The little spotted one

4 Quarter in the pot
I tasted the broth

5 I scalded my throat
I ran to the well

6 I drank my fill
Then coming back

7 I met a pole-cat
He grinned at me

8 I ran to Scotland
What news was there?

9 The plough was ploughin'
The harrows harrowin'

10 A girl was cutting cheese
The knife was sharp

11 She cut off her finger
She wrapped it in a cloth

12 Locked it in a chest
It made stock and store

13 Three brown sheep, *hop-tu-naa*
Had Will, the grandson, *trol-la-laa*
Hop-tu-naa as trol-la-laa
Three brown sheep, *hop-tu-naa*
(*Spoken*)
If you give me anything
Give it me soon
For I want to go home
With the light of the moon
Hop-tu-naa

80 NY KIRREE FO NIAGHTEY
THE SHEEP ARE 'NEATH THE SNOW

Lurg geu-rey dy niagh-tey as ar-ragh dy rio

Va ny shenn chir-ree mar-roo, agh eay-in beg-gey vio

O gir-ree shiu my voch 'llyn, as gow shiu da'n clieau

Ta ny kir — ree fo niagh — tey, cha dowin as va'd rieau

1 Lurg geurey dy niaghtey as arragh dy rio
Va ny shenn chirree marroo, agh eayin beggey vio
O girree shiu my voch'llyn, as gow shiu da'n clieau
Ta ny kirree fo niaghtey, cha dowin as v'ad rieau

2 Shoh dooyrt Nicholas Raby, as eh 'sy thie ching
Ta ny kirree fo niaghtey ayns Braaid Farrane-fing

3 Shoh dooyrt Nicholas Raby, goll seose er y lout
Dy row my shiaght vannaght er my ghaa housane
muilt

4 Kirree t'ayms ayns y Laggan, kirree-goair er Clieau
Rea
Kirree keoi 'sy Coan-y-Chistey cha jig dy bragh veih

5 Dirree mooinjer Skeeyll Lonan, as hie ad er-y-chooyl
Hooar ad ny kirree marroo ayns Laggan Varoole

6 Dirree mooinjer Skeeyll Lonan, as Skeeylley-Chreest
neesht
As hooar ad ny kirree beggey ayns Laggan Agneash

7 Ny muilt ayns y toshiaght, ny reaghyn 'sy vean
Eisht ny kirree trome-eayin cheet geiyrt orroo shen

8 'Streih lhiams son my chirree, cha vel monney bio
Agh ynrican eayin dy chur y sluight fo

9 Ta mohlt aym son y Nollick as jees son y Chaisht

As ghaa ny tre elley son yn traa yioyms baase

1 After a winter of snow-fall and a spring-time of frost
The young lambs were living but the old sheep were
O rise up, my shepherds, and go to the hill [dead
The sheep are 'neath snow as deep as can be

2 Thus spoke Nicholas Raby and he sick at home
The sheep are 'neath snow in the Braid Farrane-fing

3 Thus spoke Nicholas Raby going up to the loft
On my two thousand wethers be my seven blessings
tossed

4 There are sheep in the Laggan, goats and sheep on
Clieau Rea
Wild sheep in Coan-y-Chistey that will ne'er come
away

5 The Lonan folk rose and so soon they did go
And they found the dead sheep in the Laggan
Varoole

6 The Lonan folk rose and the folk of Lezayre

And they found the young sheep in the Laggan
Agneash

7 The wethers were in front and the rams in between
And sheep heavy in lamb behind them were seen

8 How I grieve for my sheep for not many of them live
For there's only the lambs to put under to breed

9 There's a wether for Christmas and for Easter there's
two
And two or three more for the time when I'm
through

81 SHIAULL ERSOOYL
SAIL AWAY

Shiaull er - sooyl, my vaa - tey, vaa — tey braew

Shiaull er - sooyl, my vaa - tey, vaa — tey braew

Choud as t'an tid - ey gym - myr - key lesh Ta me goaill - ar - rane lesh choraa jesh

Shiaull er - sooyl, my vaa - tey, vaa — tey braew

Shiaull ersooyl, my vaatey, vaatey braew	Sail away, my vessel, vessel brave
Shiaull ersooyl, my vaatey, vaatey braew	Sail away, my vessel, vessel brave
Choud as t'an tidey gymmyrkey lesh	So long as the tide does bear us along
Ta me goaillarrane lesh choraa jesh	In fine voice are we lifting our song
Shiaull ersooyl, my vaatey, vaatey braew	Sail away, my vessel, vessel brave

82 SNIEU, QUEEYL, SNIEU
SPIN, WHEEL, SPIN

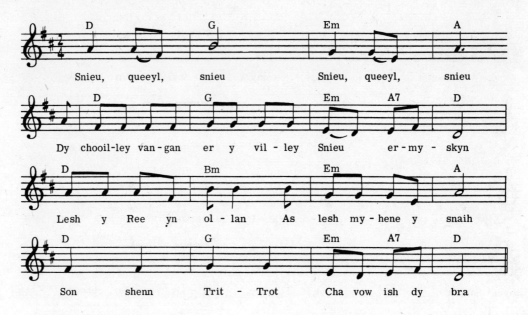

D	G	Em	A

Snieu, queeyl, snieu   Snieu, queeyl, snieu

D	G	Em	A7	D

Dy chooil-ley van-gan er y vil-ley   Snieu er-my-skyn

D	Bm	Em	A

Lesh y Ree yn ol-lan   As lesh my-hene y snaih

D	G	Em	A7	D

Son   shenn   Trit - Trot   Cha vow ish dy bra

1 Snieu, queeyl, snieu
Snieu, queeyl, snieu
Dy chooilley vangan er y villey
Snieu er-my-skyn
Lesh y Ree yn ollan
As lesh myhene y snaih
Son shenn Trit-Trot
Cha vow ish dy bra

1 Spin, wheel, spin
Spin, wheel, spin
Every branch upon the tree
Spin above for me
With the King the wool-man
With myself the spool-man
So old Trit-Trot
He'll ne'er have her always

2 Snieu, queeyl, snieu
'Rane, queeyl, 'rane
As dy chooilley chlea er y thie
Snieu er-my-hon
Lesh y Ree yn ollan bane
As lesh myhene y snaih
Son shenn Trit-Trot
Cha vow ish dy bra

2 Spin, wheel, spin
Sing, wheel, sing
Every slate upon the house
Spin above for me
With the King the white wool
With myself the spool-man
So old Trit-Trot
He'll ne'er have her always

3 Snieu, queeyl, snieu
'Rane, queeyl, 'rane
As dy chooilley tonn er y traie
Snieu er-my-hon
Lesh y Ree yn ollan keear
As lesh myhene y snaih
Son tra vees y Fidder cheet
Cha vow ish dy bra

3 Spin, wheel, spin
Run, wheel, run
Every wave upon the shore
Spin alone for me
With the King the grey wool
With myself the spool-man
So that when the weaver comes
He'll ne'er have her always

83 TE TRAA GOLL THIE
IT'S TIME TO GO HOME

Te traa goll thie, as goll dy lhie Ta'n stoyll foym grein‑nagh mee roym
Shen cow‑rey dooid dy ghleas — hagh Te tayrn dys traa ny liab‑bagh —

1 Te traa goll thie, as goll dy lhie
  Ta'n stoyll foym greinnagh mee roym
  Shen cowrey dooid dy ghleashagh
  Te tayrn dys traa ny liabbagh

2 My Ghuillyn vie, shegin dooin goll thie
  Ta'n dooie cheet er y chiollagh
  Te geignagh shin dy gholl dy lhie
  Te bunnys traa dy ghraa, Oie‑vie

1 It's time to go home and go to rest
  My stool is making me want to rise
  This is a sign that we should move
  Drawing us nearer to bed-time

2 Come, my good lads, for we must away
  Darkness draws in upon the hearth
  Telling us all we must go to rest
  The time for saying Good Night

84 TROILT Y VOIDYN MOIRREY BANNEE
JOURNEY OF THE BLESSED VIRGIN MARY

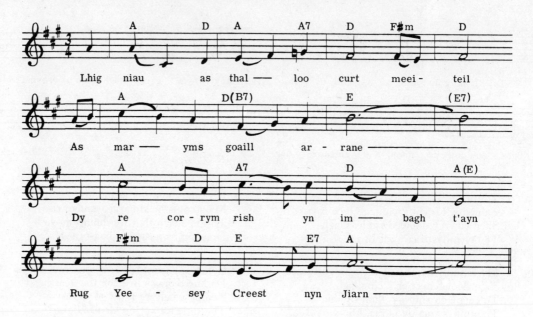

Lhig niau as thal—loo curt meei-teil

As mar—yms goaill ar-rane

Dy re cor-rym rish yn im—bagh t'ayn

Rug Yee—sey Creest nyn Jiarn

1 Lhig niau as thalloo curt meeiteil
   As maryms goaill arrane
   Dy re corrym rish yn imbagh t'ayn
   Rug Yeesey Creest nyn Jiarn

2 She ish yn Voidyn crauee va
   Bannit erskyn dagh ben
   Ghow jurnaa liauyr as doggeragh
   Dys Balley Bethlehem

3 She shoh va'n boayl hug Jee my-ner
   As chiare ad e rolaue
   Dy re ayn ruggagh Chiarn ny Shee
   Dy vannaghey sheelnaue

4 Ard gloyr da Jee 'syn yrjey-heose
   As er y thalloo, shee
   Aigney-mie Yee da slane sheelnaue
   Myr shoh va'n ainleyn guee

1 Let earth and heaven combine together
   And join with me in song
   For unto us upon this day
   Lord Jesus Christ was born

2 Unto his own Virgin mother
   Blessed above all other women
   A long and weary journey going
   To the town of Bethlehem

3 This was the place that God made known
   And with his hand provided
   There the Prince of Peace was born
   Blessing to all mankind

4 Glory give to God the highest
   Peace on earth to reign
   Goodwill of God to all mankind
   Thus were the angels praying

73 ARRANE Y BLIEH
THE GRINDING SONG

Margaret Quayle, Glen Aldyn, Lezayre, *coll.* Mona
Douglas, 1925
Other recorded version
Joan Owen, 1958: BBC 24012

Printed versions
DOUGLAS: 1957, no. 6, p. 24 (arrangement by Arnold
Foster)

JFSS: 1918, no. 21, p. 19: refrain only noted by Dr
Clague (from *Mannin*, November, 1916) where the
tune is related to *Lilliburlero*, *The Blue-eyed Stranger*
and *The Mill, Mill O* by Anne Gilchrist
JFSS: 1926, no. 30, p. 313: *Yn Oabbyr Vwyllin*

The refrain of this song was first noted by Dr Clague from the singing of Joseph Crellin of Colby, and versions of the song have been heard in other parts of the island.

Margaret Quayle, who lived in the parish of Lezayre all her life, and was related to the miller's family at Milntown Mill, said that it was sung by millers both at Milntown and at Ballure. As both these mills are near Ramsey, it would probably mean that the song was used more recently as an occupational song in the north of the island.

Although Anne Gilchrist (JFSS: 1918) has related the song to various dance tunes, as it is sung by Margaret Quayle it has a slow pace perfectly in tempo with the sound of millstones in action.

74 ARRANE Y LHONDHOO
THE SONG OF THE BLACKBIRD

Tom Taggart, Grenaby, Malew, *coll.* Mona Douglas,
1924
Other recorded version
Joan Owen, 1958: BBC 24012

Printed versions
JFSS: 1924, no. 28, p. 150: another blackbird song with
the tune from the Clague Collection *Yn Eeanleyder as
y Lhondhoo*
GRAVES: 1928, p. 159. No source given
DOUGLAS: 1957, no. 4, p. 16 (arrangement by Arnold
Foster)

The imitation of birds in song must at one time have been popular in the Gaelic-speaking areas and is still to be heard in the Hebrides. The blackbird is also the subject of song in Wales and in Ireland, where the Blackbird Song is also used for dancing. The bird in the Manx blackbird tune seems to sound most like that of the thrush but, of course, the blackbird is a bird renowned as an imitator of other bird calls.

Musical imitations of bird songs are characteristic features of Manx folksong. They are usually prefixed by a little story in which the bird speaks, tells a secret or makes a complaint, and then the song attempts to combine the characteristic notes of the bird with the Gaelic words it is supposed to use. The blackbird is a particular favourite, but other birds imitated are the snipe, grouse, corncrake, cuckoo and yellowhammer. The story is that when the blackbirds got married they agreed between themselves that they would take turns looking after the young when they appeared. But when the young really did come into the nest Father Blackbird was off on his own occasions and poor Mother Blackbird was left sitting on the nest all day. So this was the song she sang calling to her mate to come back.

Tom Taggart, of Grenaby, Malew, who sang the *Arrane y Lhondhoo*, was a fiddler as well as a singer, and he knew many songs. He was a tailor by trade and used to make suits for most of the local men, but he also worked occasionally on neighbouring farms and was noted for his successful treatment of sick animals, which was based on herbs plus a few effective charms. He always sang to a sick horse or cow while treating it, sometimes sitting by the patient and singing all through the night. Besides *Arrane y Lhondhoo* he knew other bird songs and stories.

75 ARRANE NY NIEE
THE WASHING SONG

James Kelly, Ballachrink, Lonan, *coll.* Mona Douglas,
1921

James Kelly said that this was the song the women always used to sing when washing their babies. He maintained that they learned it first from the fairies, who had been heard singing it as they washed their own babies in the early morning in the Awin Ruy, a small river near his farm. The words seem to be a kind of incantation for the child to grow in beauty and strength.

James Kelly, who had lived on the farm at Ballachrink all his life, had been brought up there with two old uncles who spoke only Gaelic. When he was a young man taking farm produce to Douglas he liked to take with him someone who spoke better English than himself to deal with the customers, but when he sang this for us he was in his eighties and spoke English fluently, though he still preferred and felt easier in the Gaelic.

76 ARRANE NY SHEEAGHYN TROAILTAGH
THE SONG OF THE TRAVELLING FAIRIES

Caesar Cashin, Peel, *coll.* Mona Douglas, 1930
Other recorded version
Joan Owen, 1958: BBC 24012

Printed versions
DOUGLAS: 1957, no. 1, p. 4 (arrangement by Arnold Foster)
JFSS: 1924, no. 28, p. 164: *Arrane y Clean-lhannoo* (a cradle song)

Caesar Cashin, who had a fruit and sweet shop in Peel when the song was noted from him, was really a Dalby man and had been fishing out of the Niarbyl. He said that there used to be a little dance after each verse imitating the movements of the particular birds named: blackbird, falcon, seagull and wren. These birds are probably invoked in order to protect the sleeping child from any fairy mischief.

Another version of the song which was noted in Arbory by the late William Cubbon, curator of the Manx Museum, has a verse and chorus mainly in English:

In the Glion [glen] of Balla Comish
The Lhondhoo [blackbird] will build her nest

Sleep thee, my baby
Sleep thee, my graihagh [loving] baby
Sleep thee, my baby
And thou'll get the birdie

77 ARRANE NY VLIEAUN
THE MILKING SONG

Mrs Faragher, Kerro Glass, Kirk Michael, *coll.* Mona Douglas, 1929

Printed version
JFSS: 1926, no. 30, p. 312: Mrs Faragher, *c.* 1919: *Churning Song*

This milking song is fairly well known in the north of the island. The words are very practical: the milker asks the cow to give milk while she sings, and promises that if the cow gives plenty, with good cream for butter, she will get her share of barley. In the refrain the singer puts the blessing of the Trinity on her cow, and invokes the Blessed Mary to increase her milk yield.

Mrs Faragher, a farmer's wife living on the hillside above the village, was one of the last native Gaelic speakers in the Kirk Michael area. She sang a churning song, as well as this milking song, and said that both were sung while milking or churning as a matter of course when she was a girl.

78 HELG YN DREEAN
HUNT THE WREN

James Kelly, Ballachrink, Lonan, *coll.* Mona Douglas, 1921
Other recorded versions
Joe and Winifred Woods, Douglas, *rec.* Leslie Daiken, 1958 (sung in English): BBC 25617
Rec. P. Kennedy, London, 1965
Printed versions
BARROW: 1820
CHAMBERS: 1826: a Scottish version
MASON: 1877, p. 47: *The Cutty Wren* (Carmarthenshire)
MOORE: 1891: full account of custom and song
ECKENSTEIN: 1906: a comparative study as a nursery rhyme
JWFSS: 1911, vol. I, part 3, pp. 99–113: a paper on the custom in Wales contributed by Llew Tegid with five music examples

JFSS: 1916, vol. XXVII, no. 3: a paper on the custom in Ireland
WILLIAMS: 1923, p. 184: *Richat and Robet*: English version from Gloucestershire
JFSS: 1914, no. 18, p. 75: three English versions from Somerset, Yorkshire and Oxfordshire
JFSS: 1916, no. 20, p. 291: an Irish version from Horncastle's *Music of Ireland* (1844) with further notes
JFSS: 1924, no. 28, p. 177: tunes only from the Clague Collection and BARROW: 1820, with notes on custom by Anne Gilchrist and Lucy Broadwood
HENRY: 1924, no. 744: *The Cricketty Wee*
GRAVES: 1928, p. 176 from BARROW: 1820
GILL: 1932: account of custom from three sources
FMJ: 1969, p. 346: *I'm going to the Woods*, coll. J. Baldwin (Berkshire)

On a certain day of the year [26th December], a wren was caught and killed. It was carried round from house to house, by a singing procession of men or boys, in a decorated receptacle from house to house. Its feathers, in exchange for food or coins, being distributed to be worn as protective charms or luck-bringing amulets, or to be kept in the houses or fishing boats for the same purpose. The body of the bird was afterwards buried to the singing of dirges, formerly in the churchyard with subsequent circular dances, but latterly on the seashore or in any convenient piece of waste ground.

The above, condensed from accounts written by Waldron (1731), Mrs Bullock (1816) and Train (1845), was published in *A Second Manx Scrapbook* (1932) by W. Walter Gill.

In the Isle of Man the wren was usually carried about in a small box made of coloured paper and gaily decorated with ribbons or paper streamers, tinsel or foil, or else it was suspended by a leg from the junction point of two hoops of willow or other flexible wood with their ends fastened together to form two circles, and intersecting each other at right angles, the decorations being similar to those of the box. Bunches of such greenery as could be got at that time of the year, often holly or ivy, were sometimes fixed round the receptacle; this must have formerly been an essential part of the equipment, for its technical name was always 'the bush' or 'the wren bush'.

Dr John Clague (1842–1908), who was a fellow collector of Gill's, gives further interesting accounts in his *Manx Reminiscences* (1911) which was printed posthumously in parallel pages of Manx-Gaelic and English. He quotes the Manx legend that during the Irish rebellion, when English soldiers and Manx Fencibles were in Ireland, the noise made by the wren on the end of a drum woke a sleeping sentry and thus saved them from being taken unawares; this was the reason for hunting the wren on St Stephen's Day.

Clague describes the ceremonial carrying of the wren. The bird was placed on a stick between two boys, on a fir-branch tied with ribbons. A third boy was covered with a net, his face was blackened and a bunch of leeks tied together served as a tail. He carried a long pole for a stick and kept time with the tune with heavy stamping. (This was also done by a shepherd of Adderbury, Oxfordshire, also a morris dancer, who sang a version of the song called *Richard to Robin*, noted by Janet Blunt in JFSS: 1914, no. 18, p. 77.)

The Wren Song is also still sung in Ireland where there is a similar ceremony.

> The Wren, the wren, the king of all birds
> St Stephen's Day, was caught in the furze
> Although he is little, his family's great
> I pray you good landlady, give us a treat

The song was first published in Horncastle's *Music of Ireland* (1844) and an account of the custom given in *Folk Lore*: 1916, vol. XXVII, no. 3. There is a version called *The Cricketty Wee* in HENRY: 1924, no. 744.

There are Scottish variants in CHAMBERS: 1826 and also in the Buchan MS, vol. I, pp. 166(a)–7(b), which begins:

> Where are ye gain? quoth Hose to Mose
> Where are ye gain? quoth Johnny Rednose
> And where are ye gain? quoth brethren three
> To shoot the wren, quo' Wise Willie

A number of Welsh variants appear in JWFSS: 1911, vol. I, part 3, pp. 99–113, together with an account of the custom by Llew Tegid. A Breton version is given in M. Luzel's *Chansons Populaires de la Basse Bretagne* (Paris, 1971).

A version called *The Cutty Wren* sung in English in Carmarthenshire is published in Mason's *Nursery Rhymes and Country Songs* (1908):

> O where are you going? says Milder to Malder
> O I cannot tell, says Festel to Fose
> We're going to the woods, says John the Red Nose
> We're going to the woods, says John the Red Nose
>
> O what will you do there?
> We'll shoot the Cutty Wren
>
> O how will you shoot her?
> With arrows and bows
>
> O that will not do
> With cannons and guns
>
> O how will you bring her home?
> On four strong men's shoulders
>
> O that will not do
> In waggons and carts
>
> O what will you cut her up with?
> With knives and with forks
>
> O that will not do
> With hatchets and cleavers
>
> O how will you boil her?
> In kettles and pots
>
> O that will not do
> In cauldrons and pans

> O who'll have the spare ribs?
> We'll give them to the poor

A Yorkshire version does not contain the shooting but the bird is just found:

> I fun'a bird's nest says Robin a-bobbin
> What will we do wi' ut?
> We'll tak' ut to keepers
> What shall we get for it?
> Three ha-pence a piece
> What shall we do wi'ut?
> We'll go and get drunk

There always seems to be great trouble getting it into the cart or, in this case, a 'cab':

> How shall we get home?
> We'll hire a cab
> How shall we get in?
> We'll tumble in
> How shall we get out?
> Same way we got in

An Oxfordshire version elaborates on the cooking:

> How shall us cook her?
> We'll buy a furnace
> We must hire a cook
> What shall us gie her?
> We must gie her the feathers
> That won't be enough
> We must gie her the bones
> The feathers will choke her
> The feathers *have* choked her
> So the poor cook is dead!

For the significance of this song see Lina Eckenstein's *Comparative Studies in Nursery Rhymes* (1906) and JFSS: 1916, no. 20. Manx versions are given in JFSS: 1924, no. 28.

79 HOP-TU-NAA
HOP-TU-NAA

Children at Lezayre, *coll.* Mona Douglas, 1925
Other recorded version
Joe and Winifred Woods, *rec.* P. Kennedy, London, 1965

Printed versions
JFSS: 1924, no. 28, p. 174: three tunes from the Moore and Clague Collections

JFSS: 1926, no. 30, p. 312: Mona Douglas's version
MOORE: 1896
MacLAGEN: *Games of Argyleshire*. Folklore Society, 1900

Just as the wren hunting ceremony and song (see *Helg yn Dreean*, No. 78) mainly survives in the western parts of the British Isles, so it is with the Hallowe'en customs.

In the Celtic areas this was really their New Year and it may well be that *Hop-tu'-naa* is simply the Manx equivalent of the Scots term 'Hogmanay'. There has been as much unconvincing theorising about the Manx term as there has been about the Scots.

The Hogmanay rhymes are similar:

> Hogmanay, trollolay
> Give us your white bread and none of your grey

Nowadays the Manx children are heard singing an anglicised form of the Gaelic rhyme on Bonfire Night (5th November) and in some areas they preserve the Hallowe'en custom of carrying turnip lanterns. Previously the proper date had been 11th November, the eve of Hollantide, or 'Laa Houney' as it is called in Manx. (According to Moore the day itself was called 'Sauin', 'Souin' or 'Yn Tauin', corresponding with the Irish and Scots Gaelic 'Samhain').

The 12th November, which was 1st November in the old-style calendar, was, according to Anne Gilchrist, the day in the Isle of Man for the yearly hiring and paying of rents; it was also the largest fair day in the year.

Joe and Winnie Woods sang the English rhyme, which probably evolved as being the nearest sounds in English to the Gaelic words, the non-Gaelic-speaking younger generation imitating the rhymes heard from the older Gaelic speakers:

> Hop-tu-naa, hop-tu-naa
> Jeannie the witch went over the house
> To get the sticks to lather them out
> Hop-tu-naa, hop-tu-naa

80 NY KIRREE FO NIAGHTEY
THE SHEEP ARE 'NEATH THE SNOW

John Matt Mylechreest, Thaloo Hogg, Lonan, *coll.*
  Mona Douglas, 1929
Other recorded version
Joan Owen, 1958: BBC 24012

Printed versions
JFSS: 1924, no. 28, pp., 117–20: four versions
DOUGLAS: 1928, no. 5, p. 13
GRAVES: 1928, p. 170: from MS. of J. F. Crellin of
  Orrisdale

Unlike *Hop-tu-naa* (No. 79) and *Helg yn Dreean* (No. 78), of which there are many variants in English, *Ny Kirree fo Niaghtey* was always sung in the Gaelic by the country singers who still remembered the song.

John Matthew Mylechreest, known throughout Lonan parish as John Matt, was an old shepherd-crofter, a friend of mine from early childhood. He lived with his sister, Christian, in the Thalloo Hogg, a small croft, and had sheep on most of the hills round about, his own fields being on the edge of the mountain. He had only one arm, having lost the other in an accident while working on the construction of the Snaefell mountain railway, but he was very active and capable, and after his sister died he lived alone and looked after himself until well on in his eighties. He was a great story-teller, and also knew quite a few songs and dances. He knew all the places mentioned in *Ny Kirree fo Niaghtey* and would tell how the song was 'made on' Nicholas Colcheragh, or Raby as he was called, 'before the Murrays [the Dukes of Atholl] came to Mann', by a young lad living in Raby who was a wonderful singer and fiddler, and how after the great storm and the loss of his flocks Raby himself died, so the tale went. John himself had worked for most of his life all around Raby, and had lived for a time at the Laggan Agneash, a croft at the foot of Snaefell.

81 SHIAULL ERSOOYL
SAIL AWAY

Margaret Quayle, Glen Aldin, Lezayre, *coll.* Mona
  Douglas, 1925
Other recorded version
Joe Woods, *rec.* P. Kennedy, London, 1965, from
  Mary Ledley, Dalby, 1935

Joe Woods, who sang us a version of this song, said there was a romantic idea about the song being sung 'by an old man who came out of the sea in a coracle from Ireland', but he himself understood it to be a fisherman's song. He told us more about the superstitions connected with the herring fishing on the West Coast:

In June a boat goes out to sea with the sun, and there was quite a ceremony about it.

If the fisherman lost the first fish as he was hauling in his line, it was unlucky. If the first herring caught was a milt herring and had a roe it was lucky. To be a 'third' boat, especially on the first day of the season, was unlucky, so very often they lashed two boats together so that there was only first and second.

First thing on a Monday morning you must not turn back, no matter what you'd forgotten, or else things would go against you all the week. If you were on your way to the quay and you met a parson or a woman, you must turn your back at once, and stay at home for that night, or you would have bad luck. A fisherman must never call a parson or priest anything except 'a black coat'.

82 SNIEU, QUEEYL, SNIEU
SPIN, WHEEL, SPIN

Mrs Callow, Cardle Veg, Maughold, *coll.* Mona Douglas,
  1918–20

Printed versions
JFSS: 1924, no. 28, p. 111: with an associated folk tale;
  the versions are from Clague and Moore
DOUGLAS: 1928, no. 8, p. 22 (arrangement by Arnold
  Foster)

Mrs Callow, a farmer's wife who was about seventy-five when she sang this, was herself a capable spinner and knew many songs and stories. To her the ancient sea-god and first King of Man, Mananan mac Leirr, was no meaningless name out of a forgotten past but a living presence for ever about us: a song like *The Lament of the Seal-woman's Lover* related a tragedy that might happen to any island man even today.

This song has been noted as part of a fable called *The Lazy Wife* (MORRISON: 1911 and JFSS: 1924, no. 28, p. 111) which is a version of *Rumpel-Stiltskin* (German), *Whippity Stoorie* (Scots), *Trwtyn-Tratyn* (Welsh), and so on. A. W. Moore noted a version of the song with a story in which the lazy wife and husband are King and Queen, as in the English *Tom Tit Tot*.

The Queen gives a woman the task of spinning some wool within a given time, and if she does not do so she will become the Queen's slave. Finding the job impossible, the woman calls upon the branches of the tree overhead to help her.

83 TE TRAA GOLL THIE
IT'S TIME TO GO HOME

Tom Taggart, Grenaby, Malew, *coll.* Mona Douglas,
1924

Printed versions
JFSS: 1924, no. 28, p. 186: from the Clague Collection
DOUGLAS: 1928, no. 12, p. 32 (arrangement by Arnold
Foster)
GRAVES: 1928, p. 179: from the Clague Collection

This song is the Manxman's equivalent of the Scots *Auld Lang Syne* or, to be more exact, the various Scots parting songs such as *The Last Guid Night* or *Goodnight and Joy be with you*. It was the last song at a Christmas Eve carol-singing or Oie'll Voirrey (Mary's Eve). It was sung in the churches and again in the taverns after the drinking of hot spiced ale.

Tom Taggart was a well-known fiddler, singer and story-teller and a fine native speaker of Manx Gaelic. Although a fiddler in the traditional manner, the fiddle he played upon was, in fact, a cello. He was a great Methodist and led the singing on Sundays in the little Kerrowkiel Chapel on the slopes of South Barrule, but he also played for local gatherings. He seemed to harbour a slightly guilty feeling on that account and once said, 'The old fiddle has never what you could call sinned to, girl, but she's fond of a lively tune now and then, I'm admitting.' Besides his musical activities, Tom was something of a local 'charmer' and his cures of sick animals, and people too, were famous through the south of the island.

84 TROILT Y VOIDYN MOIRREY BANNEE
JOURNEY OF THE BLESSED VIRGIN MARY

Printed versions
Words from FARGHER: 1891 (see below); tune from Tom
Kermode (Clague Collection)
JFSS: 1925, no. 29, p. 259: from the Clague Collection
and given as *Joseph's Carol*

Although the word 'carval' is said to be 'carol' adapted as a loan word, the Manx carvals are by no means always Christmas carols as known in England, but rather more long religious poems sung to old folk tunes. Many of them have verses which celebrate the Nativity of Christ, as do the verses selected from this one. They were very popular in the eighteenth and early nineteenth centuries, and were always written down—in fact some of the old manuscript carval books still survive. They were sung mainly at the Oie'll Voirrey services, which provided a sort of contest of skill for the composers and singers. A book called *Carvalyn Ghailckagh*, compiled from manuscript sources, was printed, with translations into English, by Clucas and Fargher, Douglas, in 1891, the editor being the head of the firm, John Christian Fargher, who was a fluent Gaelic speaker and who used the language habitually in his business.

Bibliography

BARROW: 1820
J. Barrow, *The Mona Melodies*: Mitchell's Music Library, London, 1820. 12 traditional tunes set to English words and arranged for voice with piano accompaniment. Only four copies known of which two are in the British Museum.

BOULTON: 1913
Harold Boulton, *Songs of the Four Nations*: music arranged by Arthur Somervell, J. B. Cramer, London, 1913. Attempts to bring together 'national songs' of England, Scotland, Ireland and Wales, all with English words but also some verses given in original Cornish, Scots, Irish, Manx Gaelic and Welsh.

CHAMBERS: 1826/70
Robert Chambers, *Popular Rhymes of Scotland*: Edinburgh, 1826 and 1870. The first collection of Scots nursery rhymes, it contains interesting texts of songs which were connected with annual customs and children's games, but only six tunes are included.

CLAGUE: 1911
Dr John Clague (posthumous), *Manx Reminiscences*: Douglas, I.O.M., 1911. Written in Manx Gaelic and English. Includes origins of hunting the wren (No. 78) custom. (A new edition is in preparation by Yn Cheshaght Ghailckagh.)

CLAGUE: 1913-17
Dr John Clague, MS collection of songs in *Mannin* Journal of the Manx Language Society, Douglas, I.O.M., 1913-17. Reproductions of a number of airs from the Clague MS collection in the Manx Museum Library but none which are not included in the Folk-Song Journals (see JFSS: 1924-6).

CREGEEN: 1910
Archibald Cregeen, ed. J. J. Kneen, *Cregeen's Manx Dictionary*: Brown & Sons, Douglas, I.O.M. Reprinted and edited for the Manx language Society. Contains many folk sayings and rhymes, and many quotations connected with the custom of hunting the wren (No. 78).

CUBBON: 1952
William Cubbon, *Island Heritage*: Faulkner & Sons, Manchester, 1952. Mainly provides historical background, but does contain some references to folklore and customs.

DERBY: 1914
Thomas Derby, *Manx Minstrelsy*: Pamphlet in Manx Museum, Douglas, I.O.M., 1914 (off-print from the Transactions of the Manchester Literary Club, vol. XL, 1913-14, pp. 307-23). A brief survey of the better-known Manx folksongs with airs from GILL: 1896.

DOUGLAS: 1928
Mona Douglas, *Manx Folk Songs*: Set I, Stainer & Bell, London, 1928. 12 traditional songs in both English and Manx with piano arrangements by Arnold Foster.

DOUGLAS: 1929
Mona Douglas, *Manx Folk Songs*: Set II, Stainer & Bell, London, 1929. 12 more songs as above.

DOUGLAS: 1949
Mona Douglas, *Folk Song and Dance in Mann with notes on collection and revival of dances*. Proceedings of Scottish Anthropological and Folklore Society, vol. IV, No. 1, 1949.

DOUGLAS: 1957
Mona Douglas, *Manx Folk Songs*: Set III, Stainer & Bell, London, 1957. 12 more songs in English and Manx with piano arrangements by Arnold Foster.

DOUGLAS: 1966
Mona Douglas, *This is Ellan Vannin again*: I.O.M. Times Press, Douglas, I.O.M., 1966. Background stories of songs and singers.

ECKENSTEIN: 1906
Lina Eckenstein, *Comparative Studies in Nursery Rhymes*: Duckworth, London, 1906. Includes essays on those associated with customs, numbers, chants of the creed, and sacrificial hunting, including the robin and the wren.

FMJ: 1965-
Folk Music Journal: English Folk Dance and Song Society, London (from 1965). Continuing the work of JFSS (Journal of the Folk-Song Society), 1889-1931 and JEFDSS (Journal of the English Folk Dance and Song Society), 1932-64.

FARGHER: 1891
J. C. Fargher, *Carvalyn Ghailckagh*: Clucas & Fargher, Douglas, I.O.M., 1891. Carvals in Manx with English translations. This is the most complete collection of the words of the carvals but contains no music.

GILCHRIST: 1922
A. G. Gilchrist, *Manx Carvals and an old Christmas custom*. *The Choir*, No. 156, December, 1922. Contains an account of the Oie 'll Voirrey service held in parish churches on Christmas Eve with notes of some of the carvals and musical notation of four of them.

GILL: 1895
W. H. Gill, *Manx Music: Mona's Herald*. Report of a lecture given to the Sidcup Literary and Scientific Society, Kent, on 22 March 1895 entitled 'Pictures from Manxland' illustrated by his daughter.

GILL: 1896
W. H. Gill, *Manx National Songs*: Boosey, London, 1896. 51 airs set to English words which frequently have no previous connection. Arranged for voice and piano.

GILL: 1898
W. H. Gill, *Manx National Music*: Boosey, London, 1898. 138 airs arranged for the piano (no words) selected from CLAGUE MS (1913-17). Manx Gaelic titles usually but not invariably given.

GILL: 1929/32/34
W. W. Gill, *A Manx Scrapbook*: Arrowsmith, Bristol. Vol. I 1929, vol. II 1932, vol. III 1934. Field section of The Isle of Man Natural History and Antiquarian Society, Douglas. Scholarly treatment of dialect, folklore, personal names, etc.

GRAVES: 1928
Alfred Percival Graves, *The Celtic Song Book*: Ernest Benn, London, 1928. (Representative Folk Songs of the Six Celtic Nations.) 30 Irish songs in English, 20 Scots songs, 10 in Scots Gaelic, 22 Manx songs in Manx and English, 32 Welsh in Welsh and English, 12 Cornish songs in English, and 30 Breton songs with composed words. The Manx songs are printed either with their original Gaelic words and English translations under the airs or with composed English words.

HENRY: 1924
Sam Henry, *Songs of the People*: Northern Constitution, Coleraine, Co. Derry, N. Ireland, 1924. Over 800 songs were published in the local Derry newspaper. Many were contributed by readers but it was Henry's diligent research and background notes that gave interest to each contribution.

Bibliography

Isherwood: 1897
Rev. H. Isherwood, 'Notes on Manx Melody', article in the *Isle of Man Examiner*, 1897. A detailed discussion in 18 sections on the characteristics and modal content and definitives of Manx folksongs.

JEFDS: 1911–31
Journal of the English Folk Dance Society: London, Mona Douglas: 'Ceremonial Folk Song, Mumming and Dance in the I.O.M.', 1928, 2nd series No. 2, pp. 17–21.

JEFDSS: 1932–64
Mona Douglas: 'Manx Folk Dances: their Notation and Revival': *Journal of the English Folk Dance and Song Society*: London, vol. III, No. 2, 1937, pp. 110–16. Contains brief details of 14 complete dances and another 5 that are noted but incomplete. Mona Douglas, 'A Chiel' among 'em: Memories of a Collector on the Isle of Man', 1958, pp. 156–9.

JFLS: 1878– (continued)
Journal of the Folk-Lore Society: The Folk-Lore Society, London.
1878–82 The Folk-Lore Record; 1883–9 The Folk-Lore Journal; 1890–1957 Folk-Lore; 1958– Folk-lore.
Mona Douglas: 'Animals in Manx Folklore'. 1928, pp. 209–20.

JFSS: 1899–1931
Journal of the Folk-Song Society: London (35 vols.), 1899–1931. No. 28 1924, No. 29 1925 and No. 30 1926 contain a critical selection by Anne Gilchrist of songs and tunes from the Clague MS collection with further material collected by Mona Douglas, Sophia Morrison and others. 127 songs with Manx and English index (in No. 30). The most complete source collection which is supplemented by items of later collection by others.

JWFSS: 1909–
Journal of the Welsh Folk Song Society: 1909– (continued intermittently).

Jackson: 1955
Kenneth Jackson, *Contributions to the study of Manx Phonology*: Nelson, London, 1955. Concerned with the Manx Gaelic language and therefore helpful in respect of pronunciation of the words of the songs.

Lyon: 1909
Dr James Lyon, 'Manx Folksong' in *The Manx Quarterly*: S. K. Broadbent, Douglas, I.O.M. Text of an adjudication address at the Manx Music Festival, 1909. The author claimed to have studied Manx folksong for 25 years and suggested its use as a basis for modern compositions.

Manx Museum Library Collection
Contains the Clague Manuscript Collection, publications of the Manx Society (45 vols.), index to Gill's Manx scrapbooks and the papers of Mona Douglas and other collectors, and is the best source for research.

Mason: 1877/1908
Miss M. H. Mason, *Nursery Rhymes and Country Songs*: Metzler, London, 1877. Second edition without illustrations and with additional notes, 1908. Over 50 folksongs of great variety mainly from her own Mitford family in Northumberland, also from Broadwood in Sussex, with piano accompaniments.

Moore: 1891
A. W. Moore, *Folklore of the Isle of Man*: Brown & Sons, Douglas, I.O.M., 1891. Contains full account of the custom of hunting the wren (No. 78), together with words and music of song. (Reprinted by the Manx Museum, 1972.)

Moore: 1896
A. W. Moore, *Manx Ballads and Music*: Douglas, I.O.M., 1896. 45 airs mostly with piano accompaniment. Manx traditional words with English translations. Long scholarly introduction taking little account of the oral tradition.

Moore: 1902
A. W. Moore, *History of the Isle of Man*: Fisher Unwin, London, 1902. 2 vols. Useful and reliable history.

Morrison: 1911
S. Morrison, *Manx Fairy Tales*: David Nutt, London, 1911.

Morrison: 1924
Sophia Morrison and Edmund Goodwin, *A Vocabulary of the Anglo-Manx Dialect*: Oxford University Press, London, 1924. Contains folk-sayings and rhymes, but no musical notations or songs.

Paton: 1939
C. I. Paton, *Manx Calendar Customs*: Folklore Society, London, 1939. Contains the words of some folksongs connected with customs.

Quayle: 1914
J. E. Quayle, *Choral Variations on Carval Abban Rushen*: The Manx Society, Douglas, I.O.M., 1914.

Quayle: 1945
J. E. Quayle, Paper on 'Manx Folk Music' (read 1937): Proceedings of the I.O.M. Natural History and Antiquarian Society, 1945, vol. 4, p. 240. Contains personal reminiscences of the collectors Clague and Gill and a critical study of available collections.

Williams: 1923
Alfred Owen Williams, *Folk Songs of the Upper Thames*: Duckworth, London, 1923. Over 300 folksongs (words only) noted mainly in Berkshire, Gloucestershire, Oxfordshire and Wiltshire. Interesting introduction about rural life, more fully covered by Williams in *Round About the Upper Thames* (Duckworth, 1922). Further unpublished texts in Swindon Reference Library. See FMJ: 1969 'Alfred Williams: A Symposium'.

V

Songs in Cornish

Introduction

Cornwall might be called the musical Cinderella of the Celtic family. While all the other five languages resound in song, ancient Cornish can show the words of only a few, and those without their music. We have to rely mainly on songs collected since the English language became adopted, or on modern Cornish compositions and translations.

One does not have to seek far for the reasons for this loss of the native tongue, which had happened by the end of the eighteenth century. In area Cornwall is only about a tenth of the size of Ireland or Wales and does not have the advantage, like Man, of being an island. I have heard Irishmen blame England for retarding their industries, but Cornwall might complain of the exact opposite: that through her wealth of tin she was the first part of Britain to be industrialized. Holding a central position at a gathering of sea lanes in days before road transport, it was no wonder she was the earliest to lose her language, at a time when folk music was not collected anywhere.

Some surprising examples of old Cornish literature have been preserved: the *Passion Poem* and other smaller pieces; the five Mystery Plays (which none of the other Celtic countries can boast); the three fifteenth-century *Ordinalia*, which last three days in performance (*Origo Mundi* 2846 lines, *Passio* 3242 lines and *Resurrectio* 2646 lines), the *Gwryans an Bys* or *Origo Mundi* written down by William Jordan in 1611, and the saint's play *Bewnans Meryasek* of about 1504.

Antiquarian interest in the language started, just as it was dying out, when Borlase (1754) and Pryce (1790) published their Cornish-English vocabularies and the Hon. Daines Barrington made Dolly Pentreath notorious as the last Cornish speaker. But though the following letter was written in 1776, a year before Dolly died, its writer, William Bodener, lived till 1789. He spells out the Cornish words in an English way, interlining them with his own translation:

Bluth vee Ewe try Egence a pemp,
My age is three score and five,
thearra vee dean Boadjack an poscas,
I am a poor fisherman,
me rig desky Cornoack termen me vee mawe,
I learned Cornish when I was a boy,
me vee de more gen cara vee a pemp dean moy en cock,
I have been to sea with my father and five other men in the boat,
me rig scantlower clowes Eden ger Sowsnack Cowes en cock,
and have not heard one word of English spoke in the boat,
rag sythen warebar.
for a week together.
No rig a vee biscath gwellas lever Cornoack,
I never saw a Cornish book,
me rig deskey Cornoack mous da more gen tees coath.
I learned Cornish going to sea with old men.
Nag es moye vel pager pe pemp en dreav nye
There is not more than four or five in our town
el clappia Cornoack leben.
can talk Cornish now.

n Casley of Morvah, St Just, Cornwall
Photograph: Peter Kennedy

But in spite of the interest of such people as Lhuyd, Borlase and Pryce in the eighteenth century and Davies Gilbert and Edwin Norris in the nineteenth, it was left to the twentieth century to inaugurate a real revival. This was led by Gwas Myghal, the first Grand Bard of the Cornish Gorsedd, and his successor, Mordon, who published dictionaries, edited the Cornish texts and invented a system of unified spelling, now generally adopted, as well as writing much in the language himself. Another pioneer who ought to be mentioned was Caradar, who helped Mordon edit the texts and who was an excellent scholar and teacher; we now owe him much. A generation has grown up of people (however few) who can write and speak a little in the old tongue, becoming bards by examination.

At the present time we are glad to report that music is coming to be valued more highly in Cornwall; for if one wants to re-pronounce a lost language, music is one of the ways in which one can get the feel of it on the tongue and the sound of it in one's ears. Mordon's successor, Talek, to whom we are indebted for most of the translations included in this chapter, may not be a musician and yet his way of speaking the language is perhaps more musical than his predecessor's. And his bardic successor, Gunwyn, is particularly interested in music and has published a collection of hymns in Cornish.

In the carols we catch glimpses of a much older England preserved in Cornwall:

> Come you here, Mother, and you shall see
> My hands are fast nail'd to the root of the tree
> And my feet, Mother, are fast nail'd thereby
> A realice sight, Mother, for you to see.

('Realice', a word unknown even to Strattman and Bradley's Middle English Dictionary, is thought by Dr Anthony Petti to mean 'royal; it is probably a variant of "realiche", an early Middle English word from the Old French "reál" + "lic"—an Old English adjectival suffix.')

In the sphere of carols our tradition has been specially healthy, for with the coming of the English language the carols have replaced in popular favour the Mystery Plays. We know of no carols in ancient Cornish or any Mystery Plays performed in English. But if we remember that the carol was originally a song-dance, we have not far to look for a link with the mediaeval drama. Sometimes the more regular stanza-forms of the plays are replaced by a lighter, more dance-like measure which looks as if it was intended for music:

> Fleghes ebbrow   Boys of Israel
> dvn yn vn rew   come in one row
>   scon hep lettye   quick! don't linger!
> er byn ihesu   off to meet Him
> neb yv guyr dev   who is true God
>   ow tos the'n dre   a-come to town

(The spelling has been adapted by Norris after the MS; the translation attempts to imitate the rhythm of the original.)

The Wesleyan conquest of Cornwall at the end of the eighteenth century fostered carol-composition at the expense of secular folk music, but Baring Gould in the 1880s collected variants of the same words and tunes in east Cornwall as have been found in all other parts of the English-speaking world. It is a pity he did not have more opportunity of searching further west, for it was from St Ives that he received the tune for *An Eos Whēk* (No. 89), a song that is believed to have originally had Cornish words.

At the time when Cornwall fully adopted it, the English language was in its golden age, and since Cornwall was by then a remote district we discover Elizabethanisms lingering there long after they had died out in London. Thus allusions to the 'three-men's songs' of Shakespeare's time turn up in BOTTRELL: 1870. Mordon seems to have confused the term 'three-men's song' with the catch, which is listed separately by Bottrell. Surely the term refers only to a piece sung by a male trio in three-part harmony, as dated from the twelfth century Rondellus, not necessarily in the form of a canon, though including such when in three parts. That the Cornish, like everyone else in Tudor times, were addicted to three-men's songs seems warranted by CAREW: 1602 in his reference to John Dory: 'Moreover the prowess of one Nicholas son of a widow near Foy, is descanted upon in an old three-men's song namely how he fought bravely at sea, with John Dory. . . .' Mordon regarded the following old Cornish rhyme as a possible three-men's song and it was set as a three-part catch by Michael Cardew (the spelling has been unified):

An lavar coth yu lavar gwyr	Still true the ancient saw will stand
byth dorn re ver dhe'n tavas re hyr	Too long a tongue too short a hand
mar den hep tavas a-gollas y dyr	The tongueless man, though, lost his land

In 1698 Tonkin recorded a 'fisherman's catch given to me by Capt. Noel Cater of St Agnes' (the spelling is as the original):

A Mi a Moaz, a mi a Moaz, a mi a Moaz in Goon Glaze	As I was going, as I was going, as I was going on blue plain
Mi a Clouaz, a Clouaz a Clouaz a Troz, a Troz, a Troz an' Pysgaz miniz	I heard, heard, heard the sound, the sound, the sound of the little fishes
Bez mi a trouviaz un Pysg brawze Naw Losia	but I found one great fish with nine tails
Olla Boble in Porthia ha Marazjowan Ne mi or Dho Gan Zingy	All the people in St Ives and Marazion could never keep hold of it

BOTTRELL: 1870 spoke of *Here's a Health to the Barley Mow* as a three-men's song and described the practice, in the memory of his time, as a habit of 'sober old folks' while the youngsters were 'corantan' around in their lively dances, or as a musical interlude between spells of a long droll-tale to give the speaker time to drain his cup and breathe awhile.

But whether the Cornish of the last few centuries derived their music from their own Celtic sources, or whether the itinerant droll-teller who brought his pack of ballads round the villages had picked them up from London or Plymouth, the 'old men' knew how to make their own use of them. The dramatic tradition lingered through the presence in their midst of the playing-places and rounds (as at St Just and Gwennap). The Christmas folk-play of St George, which is common everywhere, was not the only 'guise-dance' or 'guise-dance droll' as these homespun plays were called. At Newlyn they had one called *David and Goliath*, and from West Penwith came *Duffy and the Devil* (BOTTRELL: 1870). BARING GOULD: 1890 in his note on *The Lovers' Tasks* describes the little farm-house charade-opera, which also took place during the twelve days of Christmas. A girl sits on a chair while a young man, who represents her dead fiancé, goes out of the room. He returns as a ghost singing the first part of the song:

Thou must buy me, my Lady, a cambrick shirt
As every grove rings with a merry antine
And stitch it without any needlework
O and thou shalt be a true lover of mine

Only if she can fulfil a number of impossible tasks like this will he cease to haunt her. She replies that she will do this if he also performs another set of impossible tasks, which she gives him ('Thus was he baffled').

At every village feast-day or 'feria' there was probably some 'furry dance', even if the main survival is at Helston and only a tune recorded for the Bodmin Riding. Then there were the May Day celebrations such as that at Padstow, and the midsummer bonfire, though no tunes have been recovered for us to dance round the blaze. The tin-mines we know must certainly have often echoed with song; the tinners at any rate became the best composers of carols, which they used to practise below ground.

Like Prospero's island, Cornwall was a land 'full of noises, sounds and sweet airs' attributed to the small people, piskies, and knockers of the mines:

> Many strange stories we have, more especially among the miners, of Fairies, or, as they call them, Piskys, Small People, &c; of the discovering mines to them, playing on Musick very sweetly in them, Dancing in Rings and Circles . . . (Tonkin: c. 1727)

They were said to make their instruments from reeds and shells. On calm moonlit nights fishermen overheard the revels of the small people in their cliff gardens and listened to the strange music 'resounding along the shore from sawn to carn' (BOTTRELL: 1870).

The mill-house or inn was the local club for dancing and harvest songs, and millers developed a special talent for playing the 'crowd' (the early form of fiddle). Time for dancing the old ballads was also beaten out on the other 'crowd' or 'croder' (a drum made from a sieve rind covered with sheepskin). At Altarnun Church there is a representation of bagpipes, and it would be strange if Cornwall, alone of the Celtic countries, had never had such. The Helston Furry Dance was at one time accompanied by pan-pipes (an odd link with Rumanian folk music that might have a common ancestor among the Phoenicians). The old drolls also speak of many sorts of harps of different sizes.

No doubt Cornwall, like every other part of the world, has had a chequered musical history, for all the elements I have mentioned never seem to have flourished at the same time. Indeed many of her songs, especially the carols, have migrated overseas to America and, with *Cousin Jack*, to south Australia. The Cinderella of the Celtic musical world has therefore a remarkable tradition of her own which surely gives her a place, if a late one, in the combined celebrations of British music.

PRONUNCIATION OF CORNISH

The loss of the spoken language is not the prime cause of the difficulty in pronunciation today. Any indication of a uniform method of speaking and spelling Cornish from the Middle Ages till the eighteenth century would have been detectable by comparison with dialect survivals and other languages. But it is clear from the varieties of spelling from Middle to Late Cornish that there were changes throughout the centuries, as with all living languages. There must also have been differences of pronunciation from district to district, as there are in the dialect today.

Modern speakers do not all talk alike. At the annual Cornish Evensong, you may hear the First Lesson read in Welsh-Cornish, the Second in London-Cornish and the sermon in something that perhaps sounds more authentic. However, music is a great leveller of accents, and the singer who follows the rules given below may be recognizable even to a fifteenth-century ghost.

long a	(1) as in f*air* or French t*ê*te
	e.g. gl*ā*s (blue)m br*ā*s (strong)
	(2) as in f*a*ther or Italian open *a*
	d*a* (good), m*a*r (if)
	(H*a* (and) may be sung long when accented or lengthened)
short a	(1) as in p*a*n (usually in an accented position)
	e.g. p*a*n (when)
	(2) as the obscure vowel *a* in *a*dore or mort*a*l
	e.g. *a* (by itself) or ha when not accented (or in unaccented end syllables)
ay	as in Sp*ai*n
	e.g. Sp*ay*n
	(but Cornish m*ay* as in m*y*)
c	always hard, as in *c*at
dh	voiced *th* as in *th*en
long e	(ea in Late Cornish) as in t*a*ke
	e.g. t*ē*k (fair)
ea	t*ea*g as t*ē*k but could be pronounced t*ee*g
short e	(1) as in m*e*t
	e.g. *e*f (he), m*e*s (but)
	(2) obscure vowel when unaccented, e.g. mell*e*n as in mel*o*n
er	same vowel as above but lengthened, e.g. m*er*gh as in h*er*
ew	as in d*ew*
f	tends to be voiced and to sound like a *v*
g	always hard, as in *g*et
gh	unsounded, except at the end of a word
	e.g. mer*gh* (horses) when it sounds as in Scots lo*ch*
gwr	the *w* can be omitted
long o	(1) as in m*aw*s, d*aw*s
	e.g. m*ō*s (go), d*ō*s (come)
	(2) when vowel is alone, or in final unclosed position, as *oh* in t*o*ne
	e.g. *o* (was), a-dhe-dr*o* (around)
short o	(1) as in *o*live
	e.g. *o*ll (all)
	(2) obscure when in unaccented position
	e.g. col*o*n (heart) sounds like col'n
	(But singing may turn (2) into (1))
ou	as *oo* in m*oo*n
ow	(1) as in h*ow*. When a monosyllable or accented, pronounced *eoo* rather than *aoo*
	e.g. *ow* (my), p*ow* (country)
	(2) when followed by a hyphen, or it is an unaccented end syllable, sounds *oh*
	e.g. *ow*-tevy (a-growing), fett*ow* (gear)
r	usual West Country sound
s	at end of word, usually pronounced *z*
	but less preference for *z* in west Cornwall than in the east (near to Devon)
th	always unvoiced as in *th*in (see *dh* for *th*en: this distinction in spelling is not found in the original texts)
long u	as in m*oo*n
	e.g. l*ū* (army)
short u	as in p*u*p
	p*u*p (every)
ü	e.g. a wr*ü*k (did) sounded *ee* with lips rounded

w	may stand for *oo*
wh	e.g. *whȳ* (you) pronounced *hw*ee, but most speakers omit the *h*
wr	leave out the *w*
long y	as *ee* sound in m*ea*l, kn*ee*
	e.g. *mȳl* (thousand), *nȳ* (we)
short y	(1) as in *in*
	e.g. *yn*
	(2) obscure when standing alone
	e.g. *y* r*ēs* (should) rather like *e*rase

The obscure vowels mentioned above are unaccented forms of the shortened vowels preceding them, though they all amount to the same *er* vowel. When singing them however it may often be acceptable to restore them from the (2) to the sound (1), e.g. 'myttyn' (morning) would be spoken as 'mitten', but could be sung to sound 'mittin'.

Other vowels and consonants not given in the above list are pronounced as in English.

85 BRYN CAMBRON
CAMBORNE HILL

Mōs war-van bryn Cam-bron, dōs trē —— Mōs war-van bryn Cam-bron, dōs trē ——

Y whor-tas an vergh, —————— an ro-sow ēth a-dro ——————

Mōs war-van bryn Cam-bron, dōs trē ——

1 Mōs war-van bryn Cambron, dōs trē
Mōs war-van bryn Cambron, dōs trē
Y whortas an vergh, an rosow ēth adro
Mōs war-van bryn Cambron, dōs trē

2 Hȳ a wrük gwysca lodrow yū gwyn
Hȳ a wrük gwysca lodrow yū gwyn
Hȳ lodrow yū gwyn, rak ny's tevo na hen
Mōs war-van bryn Cambron, dōs trē

1 Goin' up Camborne Hill, comin' down
Goin' up Camborne Hill, comin' down
The 'osses stood still, the wheels went around
Goin' up Camborne Hill, comin' down

2 White stockin's, white stockin's she wore
White stockin's, white stockin's she wore
White stockin's she wore, for she had no more
Goin' up Camborne Hill, comin' down

86 CAN CALA ME
MAY DAY SONG

Om - ü - neugh - whȳ hag om - ü - nya gwren - nȳ

Rag hedh - yū de - vedh - ys yū Hāf

Pleth e - son - nȳ ow - mōs, oll om - ü - nya myn - nyn - nȳ

Yn an myt - tyn low - en mȳs Mē

(5) Sen Jo - ry plē - ma — O plē - ma - va, O?

Yn mēs yn ȳ scath - hȳr — Oll war an mōr sal, O —

(6) A - van y - nȳj an scowl — A - whe - syth a goth —

Dhe Vod - ryp Es - se - ly Yth e - sa da - vas gōth, O

Mer - wys yn hy kew — hȳ, O

212

1 Omüneugh-whȳ hag omünya gwren-nȳ
Rag hedhyū devedhys yū Hāf
Pleth eson-nȳ ow-mōs, oll omünya mynnyn-nȳ
Yn an myttyn lowen mȳs Mē

2 Gans son rak löwenhē, Adieu dhe'n Gwaynten gay
Yss yū lowenek an edhenyk hag ow-cana hȳ

3 An tüs yowynk Padstow y halsens mar mynsens
Y halsens güthyl gorhel, ha y owra gans owr

4 Benewennow Padstow y halsens mar mynsens

Y halsens güthyl garlont gans rosennow gwyn ha rüth

5 *Sen Jory plēma*
O, plēma-va, O?
Yn mēs yn ȳ scath-hȳr
Oll war an mōr sal, O

6 *Avan y-nȳj an scowl*
Awhesyth a goth
Dhe Vodryp Essely
Yth esa davas gōth, O
Merwys yn hy kew-hȳ, O

7 Yn-sol, Mēster ——, ha lowena dhysojȳ
Ha splan yū an venen poran yū rybos-sȳ

8 Yn-sol, Mēstres ——, dha vysow re bo a owr
Ha ro dhyn hanaf coref may kennyn da lowr

9 Yn-sol, Mestresyk ——, oll mēs a'gas gwelyow
An rosen rüth ha'n gwyn yn agas chambour scullys
'vȳth

10 Yn-sol, Mēster ——, mȳ ath wor lowr yn ta
Ün sols üs genes, mȳ a vyn y vōs dhymmovȳ

11 Yn-sol, Mestresyk ——, oll yn dha bows wer
Ty yu arlodhes del servya'n vyghternes mar dēk

12 Plēma an dūs yowynk a-dal omma donsya?

'Ma rē anedha yn Pow Saws, rē erel yn Frynk

13 Yn-sol, Mēster ——, ha hēth dhym dha dhorn
Y fȳth dhysojȳ moren vew ha mȳl püns gensy-hȳ

14 Yn-sol, Mestresyk ——, ha scull oll 'dha vlejyow
Nyns yū mes agensow agan blejyow a scullsyn-nȳ

15 Yn-sol, Mēster ——, dha gledha ryp dha denewan
Dha vergh üs y'n marghtȳ ow-quaytya mōs dhe-vēs

16 Dew lemmyn genough-why, bedhens agas cher da

Y tün namoy dh'agas gweles ken bledhen aral y'n
chȳ-ma

1 Unite and unite and let us all unite
For summer is a-come in today
And whither we are going we all will unite
In the merry Morning of May

2 With the merry ring, adieu the merry Spring
How happy is the little bird that merrily doth sing

3 The young men of Padstow they might if they would
They might have built a ship and gilded her with
gold

4 The young women of Padstow they might if they
would

They might have made a garland with the white rose
and the red

5 *O, where is St. George*
O, where is he, O?
He's out in his long boat
All on the salt seas, O

6 *Up flies the kite*
Down falls the lark, O
Aunt Ursula Birdhood
She had an old yowe
And she died in her own park, O

7 Rise up, Mr ——, and joy you betide
And bright is your bride that lies by your side

8 Rise up, Mrs ——, and gold be your ring
And give to us a cup of ale the merrier we shall sing

9 Rise up, Miss ——, all out of your bed
Your chamber shall be strewed with the white rose
and the red

10 Rise up, Mr ——, I know you well and fine
You have a shilling in your purse and I wish it was
in mine

11 Rise up, Miss ——, all in your gown of green
You are as fine a lady as wait upon the Queen

12 Where are those young men that now here should
dance?
Some they are in England and some they are in
France

13 Rise up, Mr ——, and reach me your hand
And you shall have a lively lass with a thousand
pounds in hand

14 Rise up, Miss ——, and strew all your flowers
It is but a while ago since we have strewed ours

15 Rise up, Mr ——, with your sword by your side
Your steed is in the stable awaiting for to ride

16 Now we fare you well and we bid you all good
cheer
We'll call no more unto your house before another
year

87 CAN WASSEL
WASSAIL SONG

Na-de-lek yū gyl-lys ha'n bled-hen noweth ow-tōs

Y-ger-eugh dar-ra-jow h'a-ber-veth gwren dōs

CH: Gans a-gan Was-sel Was-sel, Was-sel, Was-sel

Low-e-e-na dh'a-gan jol-yf Was-sel

1 Nadelek yū gyllys ha'n bledhen noweth ow-tōs
Ygereugh darrajow h'aberveth gwren dōs
Gans agan Wassel
Wassel, Wassel, Wassel
Lowena dh'agan jolyf Wassel

2 A vēstres ha mēster, owth-esedha yn chȳ
Rag drē lȳs nȳ mebyon y travalyn-nȳ

3 An chȳ cōth ma hagar dynerghy nȳ a vyn
Ny rēs dheugh kedryna ūsadow üs dhyn

4 Otta nȳ y 'n lē-ma, yn ün rew nȳ a sēf
Mebyon Wassel fest jollyf gans cogen y 'n lüf

5 Nȳ a wayt agas avallennow bōs spēdys dhe dhōn
Drȳ newodhow mōs arta omma pan ōn

6 Nȳ a wayt agas barlys bōs spēdys yn tēk
Ma 'gas bo lanwes gans helder mar plēk

7 A vēstres ha mēster, fatel yllough hepcor
Orth lenwel agan cogen a sȳder ha cor'

8 A vēstres ha mēster, yn esedhys attēs
Whyleugh agas pors ha reugh nebes, mȳ a 'th pȳs

9 Bennath warnough lemmyn ha bewnans fest hȳr
Aban veugh mar güf h'agas helsys mar vür

1 Now Christmas is over and the New Year begin
Pray open your doors and let us come in
With our wassail
Wassail, wassail, wassail
And joy come to our jolly wassail

2 Good mistress and master, sitting down by the fire
Whilst we poor wassail boys are travelling the mire

3 This ancient old house we'll kindly salute
It is the old custom you need not dispute

4 We are here in this place, we orderly stand
We're the jolly wassail boys with a bowl in our hand

5 We hope that your apple trees will prosper and bear
And bring forth good tidings when we come next year

6 We hope that your barley will prosper and grow
That you may have plenty and more to bestow

7 Good mistress and master, how can you forbear
Come fill up our bowl with cider and beer

8 Good mistress and master, sitting down at your ease
Put your hands in your pockets and give what you
please

9 I wish you a blessing and a long time to live
Since you've been so free and so willing to give

214

88 DUS HA MY A GAN DHYS
COME AND I WILL SING YOU

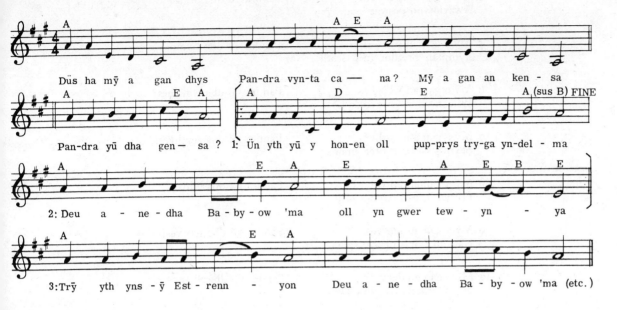

Düs ha mȳ a gan dhys   Pan-dra vyn-ta ca — na?   Mȳ a gan an ken-sa

Pan-dra yū dha gen — sa?   1: Ün yth yū y hon-en oll   pup-prys try-ga yn-del-ma

2: Deu a - ne - dha   Ba - by-ow 'ma   oll yn gwer tew-yn - ya

3: Trȳ yth yns-ȳ Est-renn - yon   Deu a-ne-dha   Ba-by-ow 'ma (etc.)

1 Düs ha mȳ a gan dhys   Pandra vynta cana?
  Mȳ a gan an kensa   Pandra yū dha gensa?
  Ün yth yū y honen oll pupprys tryga yndelma

2 Düs ha mȳ a gan dhys   Pandra vynta cana?
  Mȳ a gan an nessa   Pandra yū dha nessa?
  Deu anedha Babyow 'ma oll yn gwer tewynya
  Ün yth yū y honen oll pupprys tryga yndelma

3 Düs ha mȳ a gan dhys   Pandra vynta cana?
  Mȳ a gan an tressa   Pandra yū dha dressa?
  Trȳ yth yns-ȳ Estrennyon
  Deu anedha Babyow 'ma oll yn gwer tewynya
  Ün yth yū y honen oll pupprys tryga yndelma

*

1 Come and I will sing you   What will you sing to me?
  I will sing you one-O   What is your one-O?
  One is one and all alone, and forever will remain so

2 Come and I will sing you   What will you sing to me?
  I will sing you two-O   What is your two-O?
  Two of them are lily-white babes, cloth-ed all in green-O
  One is one and all alone, and forever will remain so

3 Come and I will sing you   What will you sing to me?
  I will sing you three-O   What is your three-O?
  Three of them are strangers
  Two of them are lily-white babes, cloth-ed all in green-O
  One is one and all alone, and forever will remain so

4 My a gan an peswera   Pandra yū dha beswera?
   Awayloryon peswar 'ma

5 Mȳ a gan an pympes   Pandra yū dha bympes
   Pymp an Trethor yn ȳ Scath

6 Mȳ a gan an whēghes   Pandra yū dha whēghes?
   Whēgh yū 'n Gwaytyer Lowen

7 Mȳ a gan an seythves   Pandra yū dha seythves?
   Seyth yn Ebren Stēr ymons

8 Mȳ a gan an ēthves   Pandra yū dha ēthves?
   Ēth yū 'n Ēth Arghel Mür

9 Mȳ a gan an nawves   Pandra yū dha nawves?
   Naw an Lōr a dewyn splan

10 Mȳ a gan an degves   Pandra yū dha dhegves?
   Dēk Gorhemmynadow Dew

11 Mȳ a gan an ünnegves   Pandra yū dha ünnegves?
   Ünnek mōs a wrons dhe 'n nēf

12 Düs ha mȳ a gan dhys   Pandra vynta cana?
   Mȳ a gan an deudhekves   Pandra yū dha dheudhekves?

   Deudhek yū Ebestely
   Ünnek mōs a wrons dhe'n nēf
   Dēk Gorhemmynadow Dew
   Naw an Lōr a dewyn splan
   Ēth yū 'n Ēth Arghel Mür
   Seyth yn Ebren Stēr ymons
   Whēgh yū 'n Gwaytyer Lowen
   Pymp an Trēthor yn ȳ Scath
   Awayloryon peswar 'ma
   Trȳ yth yns-ȳ Estrennyon
   Deu anedha Babyow 'ma oll yn gwēr tewynya
   Ün yth yū y honen oll pupprys tryga yndelma

4 I will sing you four-O   What is your four-O?
    Four is the Gospel Preachers

5 I will sing you five-O   What is your five-O?
    Five is the Ferryman in the boat

6 I will sing you six-O   What is your six-O?
    Six is the charming waiters

7 I will sing you seven-O   What is your seven-O?
    Seven is the seven stars in the sky

8 I will sing you eight-O   What is your eight-O?
    Eight is the eight Archangels

9 I will sing you nine-O   What is your nine-O?
    Nine is the moonshine, clear and bright

10 I will sing you ten-O   What is your ten-O?
    Ten is the Ten Commandments

11 I will sing you eleven-O   What is your eleven-O?
    'Leven is the 'leven a-going to Heaven

12 Come and I will sing you   What will you sing to me?
    I will sing you twelve-O   What is your twelve-O?
    Twelve is the Twelve Apostles
    'Leven is the 'leven a-going to Heaven
    Ten is the Ten Commandments
    Nine is the moonshine, clear and bright
    Eight is the eight Archangels
    Seven is the seven stars in the sky
    Six is the charming waiters
    Five is the Ferryman in the boat
    Four is the Gospel Preachers
    Three of them are strangers
    Two of them are lily-white babes, cloth-ed all in green-O
    One is one and all alone, and forever will remain so

89 AN EOS WHEK
THE SWEET NIGHTINGALE

Ow hüf co-lon gwra dōs   A ny glew-yth y'n cōs

An ē-os ow ca-na pür whēk? —

A ny glew-yth hȳ lēf   A wo-les a sēf

Y'n nan-sow ow ca-na mar dēk? —

Y'n nan-sow ow ca-na mar dēk? —

1 Ow hüf colon gwra dōs
A ny glewyth y'n cōs
An ēos ow cana pür whēk?
A ny glewyth hȳ lēf
A woles a sēf
Y'n nansow ow cana mar dēk?
Y'n nansow ow cana mar dēk?

1 My sweetheart, come along
Don't you hear the fond song
The sweet notes of the nightingale flow?
Don't you hear the fond tale
Of the sweet nightingale
As she sings in the valley below?
As she sings in the valley below?

2 Na fyll, Betty gēr
Na vyth yn awher
Dha gelorn y'n degaf dhe'th vos
Ty a glew orth an gan
A'n ēos mar splan
Ow-whybya aberveth y'n cōs

2 Pretty Betty, don't fail
For I'll carry your pail
Safe home to your cot as we go
You shall hear the fond tale
Of the sweet nightingale
As she sings in the valley below

3 Ogh, gas dhymmo crēs
Mȳ, y'n degaf gans ēs
Kē dhe gerdhes, ny vynnaf-vȳ mōs
Dhe glewes an gan
Kyn fo vyth mar splan
An ēos ow-whybya y'n cōs

3 Pray let me alone
I have hands of my own
Along with you, sir, I'll not go
For to hear the fond tale
Of the sweet nightingale
As she sings in the valley below

4 Esēth dhymmo, sür
Genef-vȳ yn lür
Yn mysk an bryally y'n lan
An lēf tȳ a glew
A-woles y'n sclew
A'n ēos y'n nansow a gan

4 Pray sit yourself down
With me on the ground
On this bank where the primroses grow
You shall hear the fond tale
Of the sweet nightingale
As she sings in the valley below

5 Acordys yns-ȳ
  A dhemedhy defrȳ
  Ha dystough dhe 'n eglos dhe vōs
  Namoy hȳ ny scon
  Dhe gemeres y dhorn
  Ha kerdhes y'n nans ryb an cōs

5 The couple agreed
  To be married with speed
  And soon to church they did go
  No more she's afraid
  For to walk in the shade
  Or to sit in the valley below

90 GLAW, KESER, ERGH OW-CUL YMA
IT RAINS, IT HAILS AND SNOWS AND BLOWS

1 Hedhyu y whandrys nep deugans myldȳr
  Y whelys chȳ bȳghan tēk oll y'n forth vür
  Ma na 'n welys-vȳ nefra kens
  Ma na 'n welys-vȳ nefra kens

1 Forty long miles I've travelled this day
  I saw a fine cottage all on the highway
  Which I never had seen before
  Which I never had seen before

2 Y kerdhys dhe 'n darras ha bonkya fest dūr
  Y clewys nep moren terlemmel war lür
  Ha: P 'yū ena?, y crȳas glew
  Ha: P 'yū ena?, y crȳas glew

2 I boldly stepped up and I knocked on the door
  I heard a fine lassie skip over the floor
  And she boldly cried: Who's there?
  And she boldly cried: Who's there?

3 Glaw, keser, ergh ow-cül yma
  Mayth ōf-vy glyp dhe 'n oll nessa
  Hag y praydha gas dhym mōs ajȳ?
  Hag y praydha gas dhym mōs ajȳ?

3 It rains, it hails and snows and blows
  And I am wet through to all my clothes
  And I pray will you to let me in?
  And I pray will you to let me in?

→

4 Henna ny ȳl bynytha bōs
Ow honen oll yth-esof y 'n vōs
Kē gerdhes alemma ytho
Kē gerdhes alemma ytho

4 O let you in that never can be
There's no one in the house but me
So I pray you be gone from my door
So I pray you be gone from my door

5 Ow heyn-vȳ del y 'n trelys rak mōs
Y talleth gwyns ow-quetha a 'n nōs
Hȳ a 'm gelwys arta trē
Hȳ a 'm gelwys arta trē

5 As I did turn my back to go
The stormy winds began to blow
And she called me back again
And she called me back again

6 Dysk dha lyp ha 'n segh omgweth
Ha kē y 'n gwely, yn cosel groweth
Hag yn-scath ena mȳ a vȳth
Hag yn-scath ena mȳ a vȳth

6 Take off your wet, put on some dry
Go into the bed and quietly lie
And so quick-e-ly I shall be there
And so quick-e-ly I shall be there

7 An nos-na y cusksyn orth bōth agan brȳs
Ha ternos nȳ ēth dhe 'n eglos a-brȳs
Hȳ a dhedhewys bōs ow hēr
Hȳ a dhedhewys bōs ow hēr

7 That night we slept in sweet content
And on the next day to church we went
And she promised to be my dear
And she promised to be my dear

8 Mes pan esen arta ow-tōs dhe 'n chȳ
An venen-ma mȳ a 's asas-hȳ
Ha nefra dȳ arta nyns ȳth
Ha nefra dȳ arta nyns ȳth

8 But when returning home from church
I left this lady in the lurch
And I never went there any more
And I never went there any more

9 Deugh oll tüs yowynk yn lē may feugh
Bayeugh oll moronyon byth a welough
Hag y whrons dheugh gelwel trē
Hag y whrons dheugh gelwel trē

9 Come all young men where e'er you be
Kiss all the maids that ever you see
And they'll call you back again
And they'll call you back again

91 'MA GRUN WAR 'N GELYNEN
THE HOLLY BEARS A BERRY

'Ma grün war'n ge — lyn - en, 'ga lyū - ȳ lēth - wyn

Ha Jē - sus ō may - lyes yn dyl - las owr - lyn

Ha Mam ō an Vagh - teth Ma - rȳa Mam Dew

Ha gwe - dhen an gwel - la An ge - lyn - en ' yū Ke - lyn, ke - lyn

Ha gwe - dhen an gwel - la An ge - lyn - en yū

1 'Ma grün war 'n gelynen, 'ga lyū-ȳ lēthwyn
Ha Jēsus ō maylyes yn dyllas owrlyn
Ha Mam ō an Vaghteth
Marȳa Mam Dew
Ha gwedhen an gwella
An gelynen yū
Kelyn, kelyn
Ha gwedhen an gwella
An gelynen yū

2 'Ma grün war 'n gelynen, 'ga lyū-ȳ gwelswer
Ha Jēsus ō crowsys, ȳ Vam yn awhēr

3 'Ma grün war 'n gelynen, 'ga lyū-ȳ gosrüth
Ha Jēsus yū 'gan Sylw'as, y vernans mar drüth

4 'Ma grün war 'n gelynen, 'ga lyū-ȳ glowdhū
Ha Jēsus ō marow, dredho nȳ a vew

1 Now the holly bears a berry as white as any milk
And Mary bore Jesus who was wrapped up in silk
And Mary bore Jesus Christ
Our Saviour for to be
And the first tree of the greenwood
It was the holly
Holly, holly
And the first tree of the greenwood
It was the holly

2 Now the holly bears a berry as green as the grass
And Mary bore Jesus who died on the cross

3 Now the holly bears a berry as red as the blood
And Mary bore Jesus who died on the rood

4 Now the holly bears a berry as black as the coal
And Mary bore Jesus who dies for us all

92 HAL-AN-TOW
HAL-AN-TOW

Rob - in Hood ha Jow - an Vȳghan An dheu res ēth dhe'n fēr, O

Ha nȳ 'wra mōs dhe'n gel - ly - wyk wēr Pyth 'wrel - lons e - na dhe vȳr - as, O

Rag helgh - ya yorgh, O Rag helgh - ya yorgh ha da

CH:Hal - an - tow, fest ca - bū - ly, O ——

Rak nȳ a sēf dyw - orth an tarth a'n jēth, O

Ha rag dhe he - dhes Hāf dhe drē An Hāf ha'n sper - nen wyn, O

Rag Hāf üs ow - tōs, O Ha Gwāf üs ow - mōs. O

1 Robin Hood ha Jowan Vȳghan
An dheu res ēth dhe 'n fēr, O
Ha nȳ 'wra mōs dhe 'n gellywyk wēr
Pyth 'wrellons ena dhe vȳras, O
Rag helghya yorgh, O
Rag helghya yorgh ha da
Hal-an-tow, fest cabūly, O
Rak nȳ a sēf dyworth an tarth a'n jēth, O
Ha rag dhe hedhes Hāf dhe drē
An Hāf ha 'n spernen wyn, O
Rag Hāf üs ow-tōs, O
Ha Gwāf üs ow-mōs, O

1 Robin Hood and Little John
They both are gone to Fair, O
And we will go to the merry greenwood
To see what they do there, O
And for to chase, O
To chase the buck and doe
Hal-an-Tow Jolly Rumble, O
For we are up as soon as any day, O
And for to fetch the summer home
The summer and the May, O
For summer is a come, O
And winter is a gone, O

2 Plēma an Spanyer-na
  A wra fās mar vrās, O?
  Y whrons ȳ dybry an blüven goth
  Ha nȳ a dheber an golȳth. O
  Yn oll an tȳryow
  Py lē yth yllyn, O

2 Where are those Spaniards
  That make so great a boast, O?
  They shall eat the grey goose feather
  And we will eat the roast, O
  In every land, O
  The land where'er we go

3 'Wos Sen Jory an marrek-na
  Sen Jory ef o marrek, O
  Yn mysk pup oll yn Crystyoneth
  Sen Jory yū an gwella, O
  Yn oll an tȳryow
  Py lē yth yllyn, O

3 As for that good knight St George
  St George he was a knight, O
  Of all the knights in Christendom
  St George he is the right, O
  In every land, O
  The land where'er we go

4 Durson' An Mary Moses
  Hag oll hȳ nell ha nerth, O
  Ha danvon crēs dhyn yn Kernow
  Ha dēth ha nōswyth ynweth, O
  Ha danvon crēs dhe Gernow
  Ha bys vynary, O

4 God bless Aunt Mary Moses
  And all her power and might, O
  And send us peace in Merry England
  Both day and night, O
  And send us peace in Merry England
  Both now and evermore, O

93 JOWAN BON
JOHN THE BONE

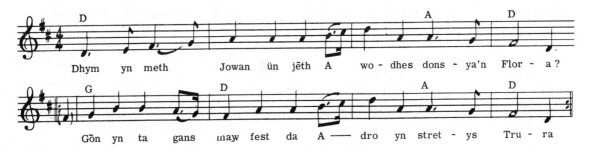

Dhym yn meth Jowan ün jēth A wo-dhes dons-ya'n Flor-a?
Gōn yn ta gans maw fest da A — dro yn stret-ys Tru-ra

1 Dhym yn meth Jowan ün jēth
  A wodhes donsya 'n Flora?
  Gōn yn ta gans maw fest da
  Adro yn stretys Trura

1 John said to me one day
  Can you dance the Flora?
  Yes, I can with a nice young man
  Through the streets of Trura

2 Jowan Bon, ef ē yn hens
  Pan dhēth erbyn y Sally
  Un bay dhedhy a wrüg-e rȳ
  Dywwyth, tergwyth, gensy

2 John the Bone was marching on
  When he met with Sally Dover
  He kissed her once and he kissed her twice
  And he kissed her three times over

94 PELEA ERA WHY MOAZ, MOES FETTOW TEAG?
WHERE ARE YOU GOING TO, MY PRETTY MAID?

1 Pelēa era whȳ mōaz, moes fettow tēag
   Gen ackas pedden dew ha ackas blew mellen?
   Mōas than ventan, *sarra wēage*
   Sarra wēage
   Sarra wēage
   Rag delkiow seve gwra moesse tēag

2 Ra ve mōaz gena whȳ, moes fettow tēag?
   Grew mena whȳ, *sarra wēage (etc.)*

3 Fatla gwra ve ackas gorra whȳ en dōar?
   Me veddn sefuall arta

4 Fatla gwra ve ackas drȳ whȳ gen flo?
   Me veden e thone

5 Pew veda whȳ gowas rag seera rag as flo?
   Whȳ ra bose ye seera

6 Pendre vedda whȳ geal rag lednow rag as flo?
   E sera veath trēhar

1 Where are you going to, my pretty maid
   With red rosy cheeks and curling black hair?
   I'm going a-milking, sir, she said
   Sir, she said
   Sir, she said
   For roving in the dew makes the milkmaids fair

2 May I go along with you, my pretty maid?
   Yes, if you like, *sir, she said (etc.)*

3 What if I lay you down, my pretty maid?
   Then I'll get up again

4 What if there's a child, my pretty maid?
   Then you shall father it

5 What'll you do for a cradle, my pretty maid?
   My brother's a carpenter

6 What'll you do for clothing, my pretty maid?
   I can make them myself

95 TRELAWNY

TRELAWNY

Gans cle-dha da yn dorn yū lēl Gwȳr, low-en an go-lon

Yth as-won Mygh-tern Jam-ys fēl Pandr' wrel-lo Ker-new-on

Yū ord-nys lē ha prȳs an-cow? Tre-law-ny dōs dh'y fȳn?

Mes ü-gans mȳl an düs Ker-now Goth-fos an pra-ga 'vyn

'Ver-ow Tre-law-ny brās? 'Ver-ow Tre-law-ny brās?

Ot-om-ma ü-gans mȳl Ker-now A woff-yth oll an cās

1 Gans cledha da yn dorn yū lēl
Gwȳr, lowen an golon
Yth aswon Myghtern Jamys fēl
Pandr' wrello Kernewon
Yū ordnys lē ha prȳs ancow?
Trelawny dōs dh'y fȳn?
Mes ügans mȳl an düs Kernow
Gothfos an praga 'vyn
A vew Trelawny brās?
'Verow Trelawny brās?
Otomma ügans mȳl Kernow
A woffyth oll an cās

1 A good sword and a trusty hand
A merry heart and true
King James's men shall understand
What Cornish men can do
And have they fixed the where and when?
And shall Trelawny die?
Here's twenty thousand Cornishmen
Will know the reason why
And shall Trelawny live?
Or shall Trelawny die?
Here's twenty thousand Cornishmen
Will know the reason why →

2 Yn meth ən Capten, bew ȳ wōs
Gwas jolyf yn mysk cans
Tour Loundres kyn fē Carrek Lōs
Y'n dylerfsen dewhans
Nȳ a drēs Tamar, tȳr dhe dȳr
Bȳ 'ny vyth Havren let
Ha scōth ryp scōth, cowetha gwȳr
Pyu orthyn-nȳ a set?

2 Out spake the captain brave and bold
A merry wight was he
Though London Tower were Michael's hold
We'll set Trelawny free
We'll cross the Tamar, land to land
The Severn is no stay
Then one and all and hand in hand
And who shall bid us nay?

3 Devedhys bys yn Fōs Loundres
Gwel dēk dhyn, nȳ a grȳ
Deugh mes, ownegyon oll, deugh mes
Gwell ōn agesough-why
Trelawny yū avel felon
Fast yn cargharow tyn
Mes ügans mȳl a Gernewon
Gothfos an kēn a vyn

3 And when we come to London wall
A pleasant sight to view
Come forth, come forth, ye cowards all
Here are better men than you
Trelawny he's in keep in hold
Trelawny he may die
But twenty thousand Cornish bold
Will know the reason why

96 AN WEDHEN WAR AN VRE
THE TREE ON THE HILL

War - ben ün vrē yth es - a gwe-dhen Byth ny we-lough gwe-dhen an par

An we-dhen war an vrē, hag an vrē o stak Hag an gwer-wels ow-te-vy a-dhe - dro

Hag an gwer-wels ow-te-vy a-dhe - dro, a sōs Hag an gwer-wels ow-te-vy a-dhe - dro

Hag an gwer-wels ow-te-vy a-dhe - dro, a sōs Hag an gwer-wels ow-te-vy a-dhe - dro

1 Warben ün vrē yth esa gwedhen
Byth ny welough gwedhen an par
An wedhen war an vrē hag an vrē o stak
Hag an gwerwels ow-tevy a-dhe-dro
Hag an gwerwels ow-tevy a-dhe-dro, a sōs
Hag an gwerwels ow-tevy a-dhe-dro
Hag an gwerwels ow-tevy a-dhe-dro, a sōs
Hag an gwerwels ow-tevy a-dhe-dro

1 Now on a hill there was a tree
Such a tree you never did see
The tree on the hill and the hill stood still
And the green grass grew all around
And the green grass grew all around, my boys
And the green grass grew all around
And the green grass grew all around, my boys
And the green grass grew all around

2 Ha war an wedhen-na 'th esa scoren
Byth ny welough scoren an par
An scoren war an wedhen
Hag an wedhen war an vrē hag an vrē o stak
Hag an gwerwels ow-tevy a-dhe-dro
Hag an gwerwels ow-tevy a-dhe-dro, a sōs (etc.)

3 Ha war an scoren-na 'th esa baren . . .

4 Ha war an varen-na 'th esa delen . . .

5 Ha war an dhelen-na 'th esa nȳth . . .

6 Aberth y'n nȳth-na 'th esa oy . . .

7 Aberth y'n oy-na 'th esa edhen . . .

8 Ha war an edhen-na 'th esa askel . . .

9 Ha war an askel-na 'th esa plüven . . .

10 Ha war an blüven-na 'th esa whannen . . .
Byth ny welough whannen an par
An whannen war an blüven
Hag an blüven war an askel
Hag an askel war an edhen
Hag an edhen y'n oy
Hag an oy yn an nȳth
Hag an nȳth war an dhelen
Hag an dhelen war an varen
Hag an varen war an scoren
Hag an scoren war an wedhen
Hag an wedhen war an vrē, hag an vrē o stak
Hag an gwerwels ow-tevy a-dhe-dro

2 Now on that tree there was a branch
Such a branch you never did see
The branch on the tree
The tree on the hill and the hill stood still
And the green grass grew all around
And the green grass grew all around, my boys (etc.)

3 Now on that branch there was a twig . . .

4 Now on that twig there was a leaf . . .

5 Now on that leaf there was a nest . . .

6 Now in that nest there was an egg . . .

7 Now in that egg there was a bird . . .

8 Now on that bird there was a wing . . .

9 Now on that wing there was a feather . . .

10 Now on that feather there was a flea
Such a fine flea you never did see
The flea on the feather
And the feather on the wing
And the wing on the bird
And the bird in the egg
And the egg in the nest
And the nest on the leaf
And the leaf on the twig
And the twig on the branch
And the branch on the tree
And the tree on the hill and the hill stood still
And the green grass grew all around

85 BRYN CAMBRON
CAMBORNE HILL

John Thomas, Camborne, *rec.* P. Kennedy, and Skinners
  Bottom Glee Singers, Redruth, *rec.* P. Kennedy, 1956:
  BBC 23654

Cornish words by Talek and Ylewyth
Printed version
GUNDRY: 1966, p. 53: Thomas version

This is a song which can be readily dated, as it refers to the occasion of Christmas Eve, 1801, when Richard Trevithick's steam locomotive first carried a load of passengers up a hill from Weath to Camborne Beacon. The wheels were turned around by the engine while the 'osses stood still and looked on, as everyone else did, in amazement.

It has been said that the attendants bandaged their legs with white flannel to prevent the steam from harming them, but the white stockings may refer to the girls at the fuse factory who wore them. Alternatively, it may describe the spurts of steam which shot out of the pistons or to the painting of the wheels by Trevithick to measure her speed and distance.

The song is a parody on *Jack Hall* (No. 322), the ballad about the chimney-sweep burglar who was brought up Tyburn Hill on a cart to be hanged. (*Admiral Benbow* and *The Irish Famine Song* also use this as a matrix.)

86 CAN CALA ME
MAY DAY SONG

Cornish words by Talek and Ylewyth

Blue Ribbon Hobby Horse Team, Padstow, *rec.* P.
  Kennedy and A. Lomax 1954: *Folk Songs of Britain*,
  vol. IX, CAEDMON TC 1224/TOPIC 12T 197
Other recorded versions
BBC 1083, 9499, 9500 (1944); Columbia World Library
  SL 206
Printed versions
BARING GOULD MS: B. H. Watts (1860): B.G. (1891)
CHAMBERS: 1864, vol. I, p. 547: *The Old May Song*
  (Swinton, Manchester)
HUNT: 1881, p. 474: words noted in 1865
BARRETT: 1891, no. 4, p. 6: *The Old May Song*
BARING GOULD: 1895: with notes on the custom

JOURNAL OF THE ROYAL INSTITUTE OF CORNWALL: 1913,
  no. 60: Article by Peter Thurstan
JFSS: 1916, no. 20, p. 274, *coll.* Sharp, 1914, pp. 328–
  39: Article by L. Broadwood with notes on custom and
  its significance
DEVON AND CORNWALL NOTES AND QUERIES: 1922, vol.
  XII, part iv
DUNSTAN: 1929, p. 26: includes second version (Mr
  Tonkin)
JEFDSS: 1939, pp. 229–34: article on Hobby Horses
  by Violet Alford
REEVES: 1960, no. 104, p. 205: from BARING GOULD:
  1889 and 1895
GUNDRY: 1966, pp. 14–17: seven recordings of the tune
  (1860–1960)

The May Day Song has been sung at Padstow from time immemorial, with only a few short breaks. Whether it was originally Cornish or English is a moot point. The expression 'icumen today' (wrongly annotated 'a-come unto day') seems to take the English words back to the time of *Sumer is icumen in* (*c.* 1240). The Celts were Christians before the Anglo-Saxons, so this ancient May festival, though surviving in a Celtic country, might have been brought by pagan invaders. But it might equally well be so old that it belonged to the Celts before they were converted, and the word 'icumen' might simply show the age of the first translation from Cornish to English.

'Oss, Oss, Wee Oss' is the cry that goes up from a united body of Padstow townspeople. ('Wee Oss' is thought to mean 'Our Horse'.) The horse is in fact a most fearsome-looking object which makes you think immediately of African witch-doctor maskings. A man inside the horse carries on his shoulders a heavy hoop about six feet in diameter which is covered with a black-painted canvas 'skirt'. A black and white and red painted mask with a tall-pointed hood conceals the man's face. Fastened to the hoop are a hobby-horse head and tail. The horse is preceded by a sailor known as 'The Teaser' who carries a painted club.

Accordions strike up and, as the horse and teaser dance and sway, the townspeople sing *The May Day Song*. Occasionally the horse makes for a young unmarried girl and catches her under his 'skirt'. Formerly the horse was covered in wet tar and the carrier kept a bag of soot under the skirt to squirt over her. They say that the girl who is so caught will be married by Christmas.

However, the excitement at Padstow really begins at midnight as May Eve gives way to May Day, and as the church clock strikes twelve the horse comes out of his winter stable for the first time. Coming out of the public house, followed by his 'Ossy Choir', they follow a traditional route through the streets and gardens stopping outside certain houses to sing special verses of *The Night Song*:

1   Rise up Mrs —— we wish you well and fine
     For Summer is a-come unto day
   You have a shilling in your purse and I wish it were in mine
     In the merry morning of May

2 Rise up Mr —— wed gold be your ring
   And give to us a cup of ale and the merrier we will sing

3 Rise up Miss —— all in your smock of silk
   And all your body under as white as any milk

4 Rise up Mr —— and joy you betide
   And bright be that bonny bride that lays by your side

5 Rise up Master —— and reach out your hand
   And you shall have a lively lass and a thousand pounds in hand

Just as it is getting light, the young men of Padstow go out and steal greenery from the squire's plantation and decorate the town. A Maypole stands in the main square from which flags are strung out in all directions. At about ten o'clock not only does 'The Old Oss' perambulate the town with his accompanying Teaser and musicians but there is a rival horse known as 'The Blue Ribbon' with its own accompanying team.

Formerly the horse used to go to a small hamlet about a mile out of the town and be submerged or 'drink' from a pool after which the spectators were sprinkled, but this part of the ceremony has been discontinued since about thirty years ago. When it returned there was a much longer song performed to the slower tune. The horse lay down on the ground as though dead and verses, which resemble the Helston Hal-an-tow, were sung. Nowadays this death sequence is repeated at frequent intervals during the procession through the town and each time after the song about St George and Ursula Birdhood the Teaser bangs the club against the horse. It leaps up with renewed energy and the accompanying Mayers sing the 'Unite' verses.

There has been much speculation about Aunt Ursula and her old ewe. In previous years, 'the Teaser' has not been dressed as a sailor but as a man-woman, a man dressed as a woman, and like the 'Old Tup' in other parts of the country the horse itself may well have started as an old ewe (see *The Ram Song*, No. 304).

To delve deeper into the mention of Ursula is to become involved in the work of Oskar Schade, friend of the Grimm brothers, who studied the legends of St Ursula and concluded that the British princess was a Christianised form of the Earth-mother who was worshipped as the goddess of fertility by the Europeans. Schade saw traces of this in the civic processions of the Middle Ages which still survive, such as the plough and ship-drawing festivals in Britain and the Continent (the *Up Helly-Aa* in Shetland being an example).

At Minehead, also on the north coast of the West Country peninsula, the local hobby horse is shaped like a ship and is known as the 'Sailor's Horse'. The mention of the 'building of a ship' in the Padstow Song may bear out the theory that at one time the so-called hobby horse was a ship.

Lucy Broadwood in JFSS: 1916, no. 20, p. 330, details the findings of Oskar Schade and that of a Lithuanian, Leopold von Schroeder. She traces the common elements in folk rites and processions: St George (or, in the earlier pagan forms, the old woman), the waggon or ship laden with good things, the attendants with clubs or rods, the throwing of soot or blackening of faces, the immersing in water, the rude jest, the songs and the quête (collecting).

Padstow is a place connected with well-worship. There is in fact a St George's Well and many other wells in the vicinity. The place name may well derive from the word 'pid' which carries implications both of roots of water and of an estuary.

In southern Germany and Austria around the Innsbruck area, on Shrove Tuesday youths called 'Hutler' armed with whips and dirty brooms accompany the 'Fastnacht 'srösslein' ('Shrove Tuesday little horse'), and chase the spectators. 'Hutler' means 'hoodeners' and implies that they are both 'hatted' and 'protectors' (Robin Hood we regard as a guardian, for instance). In parts of Kent in southern England there were formerly hooden horses who went round the houses looking like the Welsh Feri Lwyd (see No. 69) or the Midland Old Tup. Hoodening may possibly derive from Woden who always appeared as a hat-wearer. 'Birdhood' may thus refer to the hood formerly worn by the Teaser at Padstow.

In Brittany *Le Cheval Mallet*, a wooden horse wreathed in flowers, dances round the may-tree and the Batonnier sings a ceremonial song. At Padstow the may-tree was sometimes as high as ninety feet and was erected by the local ship-wrights to the accompaniment of pistol-firing.

A similar carol called *The Old May Song* was at one time sung at Swinton, near Manchester. It was printed in CHAMBERS: 1861, and contains six verses with an almost identical tune.

All in this pleasant evening together come are we
   For the summer springs so fresh and green and gay
We'll tell you of a blossom that buds on every tree
   Drawing nigh unto the pleasant month of May

Rise up the master of this house, put on your chain of gold,
   For the summer springs so fresh and green and gay
We hope you're not offended, with your house we make so bold
   Drawing nigh unto the pleasant month of May

Rise up the mistress of this house, with gold all on your breast
And if your body be asleep I hope your soul's at rest

Rise up the children of this house in all your rich attire
For every hair upon your head shines like a silver wire

Rise up the fair maid of the house, put on your gay gold ring
And bring to us a can of beer the better we shall sing

So now we're going to leave you in peace and plenty here
We shall not sing this song again until another year

A second carol sung at Swinton, known as *The New May Carol*, had ornate verses about the beauties of nature, and was sung to a tune very like the *St George and Aunt Ursula* verses of the Padstow May Day Song.

87 CAN WASSEL
WASSAIL SONG

Cornish words by Talek and Ylewyth

Harold Tozer and the Truro Wassail Bowl Singers, *rec.* P. Kennedy, Malpas, 1957: BBC 25653
Other recorded versions
Charlie Bate, Padstow, *rec.* P. Kennedy, 1956: *Folksongs of Britain*, vol. IX, CAEDMON TC 1224/TOPIC 12T 197
Joe Thomas, Constantine, *rec.* P. Kennedy, 1956: BBC 23654
Printed versions
SANDYS: 1833 (Gloucestershire)
CHAPPELL: 1838, p. 160: As SANDYS, with account of the custom
BROADWOOD: 1843/90, p. 14 (Sussex)
DIXON: 1846 and BELL: 1857 (Gloucestershire)
SUMNER: 1888, p. 9 (Somerset)

BROADWOOD: 1893, p. 14 (Yorkshire)
BARING GOULD: 1895: Grampound (Cornwall)
SHARP AND MARSON: 1904–9, vol. V, no. 127, p. 70: *New Year's Song* (Somerset)
JFSS: 1914, no. 18, p. 28: *coll.* C. Sharp, Redruth (Cornwall); 1915, no. 19, pp. 210–13 (Lancashire and Yorkshire)
WILLIAMS: 1923, p. 116 (Wiltshire)
KIDSON AND MOFFAT: 1929 (Yorkshire)
JFSS: 1929, no. 33, p 132: four versions (Cornwall)
DUNSTAN: 1929, p. 132: Truro version (Cornwall)
JEFDSS: 1952, p. 17: article on Percy's unpublished version (Staffordshire)
GUNDRY: 1966, p. 56: Version from Joe Thomas (Cornwall)

The Truro 'Wassail Boys', up to the time when this recording was made, had maintained an unbroken tradition of wassailing around Truro and district between Christmas and the New Year. Into the wooden Wassail Bowl, which they carry from door to door, goes a wide variety of alcoholic drinks and coins donated by the householders and landlords of public houses on whom they call.

'The Boys' consisted on this occasion of Harold Tozer (aged 52) lead singer, Thomas Jewel (aged 64) bass and Albert Jose (aged 67) descant. Mr Tozer started going round with the Wassail Boys at the age of sixteen and the other two began ten years prior to the year of the recording.

The custom of Christmas and New Year wassailing is still practised from Cornwall in the extreme south-west to Yorkshire in the north-east of England. In fact wassailing has been recorded in the same areas of England where May carols are sung, thus outlining the main areas of Anglo-Saxon survivals of pagan ritual.

The word 'wassail' comes from Anglo-Saxon 'wes' (be) and 'hal' (whole) and indicates a toast: 'Be of good health'. Like mumming, carol singing and maying, the custom involves house to house visiting with the partaking of food and drink to bring good luck to both visitors and visited. In most cases the wassailers take with them some kind of emblem of good luck such as a wassail bowl, box, vessel, bough or other evergreen branches and seasonal flowers.

One of the earliest wassails was a Saxon toasting cry sung in the English camp on the eve of the Battle of Hastings by the Anglo-Norman poet (d. 1080) quoted by Sir James Ramsay in *Foundations of England*, vol. ii:

Bublie crient e weissel
E latcome e drencheheil
Drinc Hindrewart e Drintome
Drinc Helf, e drinc tome

Rejoice and wassail
Pass the bottle and drink healthy
Drink backwards and drink to me
Drink half and drink empty

Although Bishop Thomas Percy, after publication of his famous *Reliques of Ancient English Poetry*, collected a variety of old ballads (thirty-three were published by Francis James Child) which were sent to him, there was only one occasion when Percy himself noted a local song. When he was vicar of Easton Maudit in Northamptonshire (about 1760) he noted the words of a 'Staffordshire wassel song' (Percy's unpublished papers in Harvard University Library):

We have been walking among the leaves so green
And hither we are coming so stately to be seen
With our wassel, our jolly wassel
All joys come to you and to our wassel bowl

Good master and good mistress, as you sit by the fire
Remember us poor wassellers that travel in the mire
With our wassel, our jolly wassel
All joys come to you and to our wassel bowl

Our bowl is made of the mulberry tree
And soe is your ale of the best barley

Pray rise up master Butler and put on your golden ring
And bring to us a jug of ale, the better we shall sing

Our purse it is made of the finest calves skin
We want a little silver to line it well within

Good Mr X, good Mist(ress) if that you are but willing
Send down two of your little boys to each of us a shill(ing)

We'll hand a silver napkin upon a golden spear
And come no more a wassiling untill another year

The bowl of these wassailers was mulberry. Later versions have rosemary (Bramley and Stainer), white maple tree (VAUGHAN WILLIAMS: 1908), elderberry bough (Gower, South Wales) and ashen tree (Sharp). Cecil Sharp contended that this took us back to the period when all common domestic vessels were made of wood and when there was an ecclesiastical edict against the use of wooden vessels for the Holy Communion.

In some cases the carrying of greenery accompanied the singing of the song. A Yorkshire version in BROADWOOD: 1893 (*English County Songs*) says, 'The children carry green boughs and wave them over their heads asking for a New Year's gift'. At Camborne in Cornwall, the local carol party was accompanied by a small child dressed in evergreens who was known as Lucy Green:

Here we come a-wassailing long with our Lucy Green
And here we come a-wandering as fair to be seen
Love and joy come to you and to your wassail too
And God send you a happy New Year
(see JFSS: 1929, no. 33, p. 132)

Dr Dunstan in his *Christmas Carols* (1925) prints a West Yorkshire version sung by children with blackened faces, decked with and carrying greenery, who sang:

Pier, Tier, Wessel
And a jolly wessel

In Yorkshire too, at Whitby, until a few years ago, an image of the Saviour was placed in a box surrounded by evergreens and flowers and each house visited was allowed to take one sprig out of the 'wessel' box. All these would seem to be survivals of the bearing of the Christmas vessel-cup.

There are numerous European equivalents of these various English wassails. For example the Roumanian Calusari dancers carry with them a pole decorated on the top with silver objects, and they always have with them some garlic to act as potent magic. Similar words are sung in France by youths going from house to house during Advent and at Christmas time (*Chants Pop. du Bas-Quercy*, 1889), and in Greece children sing a similar wassail song varying little from one sung by their forefathers two thousand years ago (BROADWOOD: 1843).

88 DUS HA MY A GAN DHYS
COME AND I WILL SING YOU

Cornish words by Talek and Ylewyth

Fred Horrell, Launceston, *rec.* P. Kennedy, 1950
Other recorded version
Ben Baxter, Southrepps, Norfolk, *rec.* S. Ennis, 1955:
  BBC 22156

Printed versions
CHAMBERS: 1826/42, p. 50: Scots version
SANDYS: 1833, p. 135
LONGMAN'S MAGAZINE: 1889
BROADWOOD: 1893, p. 157: *The Twelve Apostles* (Dorset)
  and *Green Grow the Rushes O* (Eton College); variations
  of the song, pp. 158–9
BARING GOULD: 1889–1905, no. 78: *The Dilly Song*
BARING GOULD: 1895, p. 62: nursery rhyme
SHARP AND MARSON: 1904–9, vol. IV, no. 87, p. 22:
The Dilly Song (Somerset)

ECKENSTEIN: 1906: discusses symbolism in nursery
  rhyme
JFSS: 1918, no. 21, p. 24, *coll.* F. Keel, Buckinghamshire
UDAL: 1922, p. 81 (Dorset)
WILLIAMS: 1923, p. 286: *The One O* (Oxfordshire)
GRAVES: 1928, p. 267: Baring Gould version
JEFDSS: 1964, p. 257: L. Broadwood letters
GUNDRY: 1966, p. 37: *coll.* H. E. Piggott, Truro, 1910
NOTES AND QUERIES: series 4, ii, p. 599; iii, p. 90; Series
  6, i, p. 481; ii, p. 255

SHARP AND KARPELES: 1917/32, vol. II, no. 207, p. 283:
  five versions *The Ten Commandments*
PEACOCK: 1965, pp. 785 and 800 (Canada)

This song is generally well known as *Green Grow the Rushes O* in its popular community form. In the West Country Baring Gould and Cecil Sharp both called this song *The Dilly Song* and found it common to the area. The name 'dilly' probably derived as a description of its chorus of vocables but Baring Gould gave the Welsh 'dillyn' (= pretty or gay) describing a festal song as a possible derivative. Both quote Scots, Flemish, Breton, Moravian, Greek, Hebrew and Medieval Latin versions of the song. Gilbert and Sullivan used the West Country version as a basis for their *I Have a Song to Sing-O* in *The Yeomen of the Guard*, according to Leslie Baily.*

* Leslie Baily: *The Gilbert and Sullivan Book*, 1952, p. 290.

As to how the song came to be included in the Jewish Passover Service, Cecil Sharp quotes Simrock's German folksong description of a peasants' drinking song changed by monks into an ecclesiastical song being taken up by German Jews in the latter half of the sixteenth century. Jewish authorities on the other hand describe it as a Hebrew nursery rhyme. The symbolism of the nursery rhyme versions are discussed by ECKENSTEIN: 1906. Lucy Broadwood gives variations of the twelve numbers and references for a more detailed study of its history.

89 AN EOS WHEK
THE SWEET NIGHTINGALE

Cornish words by Gelvynak

Skinner's Bottom Glee Singers, Redruth, *rec.* P. Kennedy, 1956: BBC 23654
Other recorded version
Charlie Bate, Padstow, *rec.* P. Kennedy, 1956
Printed versions
Dr Arne's opera *Thomas and Sally* (1761)
DIXON: 1846 and BELL: 1857: version taken from miners in Germany and Truro
BARING GOULD: 1889–1905: tune from St Ives
JFSS: 1906, no. 3, p. 72; *Come, Come Pretty Maids, coll.* W. P. Merrick, Sussex

JFSS: 1918, no. 21, p. 5: *Well Met, Pretty Maid, coll.* F. Keel, Surrey
JFSS: 1919, no. 22, p. 91: A. H. Fox Strangways' note about Dr Arne's opera
WILLIAMS: 1923, p. 45: *To Milk in the Valleys Below* (Wiltshire)
HENRY: 1924, *Songs of the People*, no. 47: *The Valley Below* (Donegal, Ireland)
DUNSTAN: 1929, p. 47: version from BELL
GUNDRY: 1966, p. 20: version from BELL, with tune from BARING GOULD; Cornish words

One of the most beautiful of all folksongs, this has come down to us in a strangely roundabout way, and it is perhaps touched up in places. The first person who thought of putting it on paper was Robert Bell, author of *Ancient Poems, Ballads and Songs, of the Peasantry of England*, 1857. He heard it in Germany in 1854 from four Cornish singers employed as lead miners near the town of Zell. 'Cap'n' John Stocker, their leader, said that:

> the song was an established favourite with the lead miners of Cornwall and Devonshire, and was always sung on the pay-days and at the wakes, and my own grandfather, who died thirty years before at the age of a hundred years, used to sing the song and say that it was very old. The tune is plaintive and original.

It was said to be a 'translation from the ancient Cornish tongue'.

Unfortunately Bell failed to get down either words or music from the Cornish lead miners and their 'plaintive and original' tune may not have been the one we know. He relied for his copy of the words on a gentleman of Plymouth who

> was obliged to supply a little here or there, but only when a bad rhyme, or rather none at all, made it evident what the real rhyme was. I have read it over to a mining gentleman at Truro, and he says it is pretty near the way we sing it.

So much for the English words, which are those we now know. The melody we know was first given to Baring Gould by Mr E. F. Stevens, of The Terrace, St. Ives, who claimed that it had run in his head 'any time these eight and thirty years'. Baring Gould later collected the song 'always to the same air' from 'a good many old men in Cornwall'.

Baring Gould questioned Bell's date for the song (seventeenth century) on the grounds that Bickerstaff had written some similar verses for Arne's opera *Thomas and Sally*, but the author of an eighteenth-century ballad opera might easily have based some verses on an already existent folksong. In any case Arne's music has no resemblance to the tune given here, which certainly might be as old as Purcell's time.

90 GLAW, KESER, ERGH OW-CUL YMA
IT RAINS, IT HAILS AND SNOWS AND BLOWS

Cornish words by Talek and Ylewyth

Joe Thomas, Constantine, *rec.* P. Kennedy, 1956: BBC 23654
Other recorded versions
Billy Pennock, Goathland, Yorkshire, *rec.* P. Kennedy, 1953
Reg Gulliford, Coombe Florey, Somerset, *rec.* P. Kennedy, 1957
Printed versions
HERD: 1769: *Let me in this ae Night* (Scots)
KIDSON: 1891, no. 1, p. 58: *Forty Miles* (also in KIDSON AND MOFFAT: 1927, p. 64)
JFSS: 1899, no. 1, p. 18: *The Cottage by the Wood*, *coll.* K. Lee, Shropshire
DUNCAN MS: p. 407: *Open the Door* (Aberdeenshire)

HAMMOND MS: 1905: four versions (Dorset and Hants)
Cf. GREIG: 1909–14, no. 139: *Rap at the Door* (Aberdeenshire)
JFSS: 1918, no. 21, p. 19: *Cottage near a Wood*, *coll.* F. Keel, Surrey; three versions, *coll.* A. G. Gilchrist, Lancashire and Sussex
SHARP (School Series): VII, 1922, p. 14: *Forty Long Miles* (Somerset)
HAMER: 1973, p. 22: Harry Scott (Bedfordshire)

LEACH: 1965, p. 134: *Love Let Me In* (Labrador)

Compare
REEVES: 1958, p. 96: *Cold Blow and a Rainy Night*, *coll.* C. Sharp, Kent

It rains, it hails and snows and blows
And I am wet through to all my clothes
And I pray will you to let me in

Joe Thomas only remembered verses 3 to 5 and 7 to 8, but knew that there were other verses he could not remember at the time of recording. The remaining verses have been taken from other versions recorded by Peter Kennedy in the West Country.

This was a favoured theme for traditional love poetry in many countries and our particular song was well distributed through both England and Scotland. In other songs with this same theme the young man after being refused entry is allowed to go on his way. Perhaps the best of these was one recorded in Aberdeenshire by Gavin Greig, given here in full:

1 The last time I came o'er the muir
It was to see my love to be sure
It was to see my love to be sure
And she bade me rap at the door, door
And she bade me rap at the door, door
It was to see my love to be sure
And she bade me rap at the door, door
And she bade me rap at the door

2 Open the door and let me in
Coming to see you I've broken my shin
And the pain it feels wondrous sore

3 Broken your shin, how sorry am I
I can't find out the way for to cry
But I will find out the way by and by
And I'll tease you ten times more

4 Tell your father and your mother too
That I'm your lover come to court you
And I pray you to open the door

5 If I were to open the door to you
It would only be for a minute or two
My father and mother they'd you endure
And they'd beat me wondrous sore

6 O my lad I'm up to your tricks
For you have beguiled five or six
And I myself will not be the next
You may stand and rap at the door

7 If I've beguiled six or seven
Eight or nine, ten or eleven
You yourself will make a round dozen
So I'll rap no more at your door

8 The trees are high, the leaves are green
The days are past that we have seen
There's another in the place where you should have been
So you may stand and rap at the door

9 If the trees are high, the leaves are not shaken
Although I'm slighted, I'm not heartbroken
As long's there's another true love to be gotten
I'll rap no more at your door

10 O young man, I value you not
Altho' the hangman had your coat
And yourself in a bottomless boat
With the Devil to row you ashore

91 'MA GRUN WAR 'N GELYNEN
THE HOLLY BEARS A BERRY

Cornish words by Tyrvab (W. Daniel Watson)

Skinner's Bottom Glee Singers, Redruth, *rec.* P. Kennedy, 1956: BBC 25653
Other recorded versions
Peter Jones, Herefordshire, *rec.* M. Karpeles and P. S. Shaw, 1952: BBC 18619
John Thomas, Camborne, *rec.* P. Kennedy, 1956

Printed versions
SYLVESTER: 1861
HUSK: 1868: Wadsworth broadside, Birmingham, *c.* 1710
SHARP: 1911, no. 7, p. 17: *The Holly and the Ivy* (Gloucestershire)
JFSS: 1929, no. 33, p. 111: *Cherry, Holly and Ivy* (Cherry Tree carol with 'holly' refrain from Camborne); p. 113: two other versions from Camborne
DUNSTAN: 1929, p. 89: broadside version with French tune; p. 123: St Day carol (now the *Holly Bears a Berry*)

The song was translated into Cornish by Tyrvab (W. Daniel Watson), one of the earliest Cornish bards to be initiated (in 1928), who died in 1959. He was gardener to the Penzance Borough (Morrab). He learned his Cornish from Gwas Myghal and, being a natural linguist, learnt Breton also. He used to talk with Breton fishermen in the Morrab Gardens at Penzance. He collected hundreds of Cornish dialect words which Mordon used in his dictionary.

Tyrvab did not accept Mordon's unified spelling, but for the sake of uniformity the words appear here as in *Lyver Hymnys ha Salmow*, with kind permission of the Editors.

92 HAL-AN-TOW
HAL-AN-TOW

Cornish version by Talek and Ylewyth

Joe Thomas, Constantine, *rec.* P. Kennedy, 1956
Other recorded versions
BBC 1083 (n.d.), 6797 (1943) and 25951 (1959)
Printed versions
DIXON: 1846: words from SANDYS: 1846
SANDYS: 1846: specimens of Cornish dialect
BELL: 1857: specimens of Cornish dialect

BARING GOULD: 1889–1905, no. 24, p. 50
BARING GOULD: 1895
GRAVES: 1928, p. 265: version from BARING GOULD
DUNSTAN: 1929, p. 30: version from SANDYS: 1846 adapted by R. Morton Nance
REEVES: 1960, no. 62, p. 147: version from BARING GOULD: 1895 and 1905, with extensive notes
GUNDRY: 1966, p. 12: version *coll.* Cleak and Jenkin: 1962

Like the Furry Dance, the Hal-an-Tow is also performed at Helston on 8th May by a procession, now of school children, into the country to gather flowers and branches, accompanied by Robin Hood and other characters from the old May Games, to whom are added St Michael (the patron saint) and the Dragon. It was originally a dance-song, but the steps are lost and the custom lapsed from about a century ago till 1930 when it was revived. The oldest surviving version was published by SANDYS: 1846 (reprinted GUNDRY: 1966). It has more variety than the tune printed here, which shows how distinctions get smoothed down to repetitions by popular favour.

The meaning of the title is disputed. According to one theory it is 'heave on the rope', an adaptation by Cornish sailors from the Dutch 'Haal aan het touw' ('tow' is pronounced to rhyme with 'cow' in Helston today). Others think it might refer to the heel and toe dance of *The Monk's March*, which is still danced in the English Cotswold morris tradition.

Mordon evidently inclined to this view, for he writes that it

> has every sign of being a processional morris dance even to the slow part at the beginning of the chorus in which, when its steps were still known and used, the dancers in characteristic morris dance style would have spread out sideways for a few steps, waving their handkerchiefs before forming into line as before.

But it seems a pity with such a Cornish-sounding title to despair of finding a link with the old language. In 1660 Nicholas Boson of Newlyn said that there the may-pole was set up by men singing 'Haile an Taw and Jolly Rumbelow'. It looks from this as though 'tow' in the seventeenth century rhymed with 'awe' rather than 'cow'. (In Cornish 'Hal an to' (taw) would appear to mean 'Hoist the roof'.)

93 JOWAN BON
JOHN THE BONE

Cornish words by Talek and Ylewyth

Skinner's Bottom Glee Singers, Redruth, *rec.* P. Kennedy, 1956: *The Flora Dance*, BBC LP 23654

Printed versions
GILBERT: 1823: tune only ('a specimen of Celtick Musick')
CHAPPELL: 1838: reference to the tune
DUNSTAN: 1929, p. 31: *The Helston Furry, Flurry, Flora or Faddy Dance*

The Helston Furry Dance, as performed annually on the 8th May at Helston, is wordless, but here we have a Cornish translation (by Talek and Ylewyth) of some English words that were sung to the tune in the neighbouring town of Truro.

A Jon Bon was Member of Parliament for Helston and reeve of the town early in the fourteenth century, though Sarah Dover is unknown in its records.—MORDON.

94 PELEA ERA WHY MOAZ, MOES FETTOW TEAG?
WHERE ARE YOU GOING TO, MY PRETTY MAID?

Cornish words (1698) adapted by Talek

Dicky Lashbrook, Launceston, *rec.* P. Kennedy, 1950: BBC 17796 (1952)
Other recorded versions
Fred Jordan, Wenlock, Shropshire, *rec.* P. Kennedy, 1952: BBC 18696
Albert Beale, Kenardrington, Kent, *rec.* M. Karpeles and P. Kennedy, 1954: BBC 21157

Printed versions
PRYCE: 1790: Cornish version sung in 1698
BOULTON: 1913, no. 11, p. 58: *Where be going? contrib.* by Baring Gould
JFSS: 1921, no. 25, p. 332, *coll.* M. Freeman, County Cork, Ireland
GUNDRY: 1966, p. 42: Cornish version of *Seventeen Come Sunday* (from St Ives)

Compare
As I Roved Out (No. 121) and *Rolling in the Dew* (No. 189)

One of the few old Cornish songs that have come down to us, it is given here with the original Late Cornish spelling.

The Cornish verses were sung by Edward Chirgwin at Carclew in 1698 and sent by Thomas Tonkin of Trevaunan to Pryce for his Collection of Proverbs, Rhimes, etc. in his *Archaeologia Cornu-Britannica*. Most people know the English form *Where are you Going to, My Pretty Maid?* so they will be tempted to agree with Mordon in believing that this example must have been a Cornish translation made in the seventeenth century. But the same song appears in other Celtic languages, so that this 1698 version may well be the oldest we possess in writing, and it would be equally admissible to maintain that it was originally Cornish.

95 TRELAWNY
TRELAWNY

Cornish words by Talek

John Casley, Morvah, *rec.* P. Kennedy, 1956
Other recorded version
Skinner's Bottom Glee Singers, Redruth, *rec.* P. Kennedy, 1956: *The Miner's Song*, BBC 23654

Printed versions
DIXON: 1846 AND BELL: 1857
OLD CORNWALL, 1925: *Miner's Song*
DUNSTAN: 1929, pp. 17–18: two versions *Trelawny*
GUNDRY: 1966, p. 54: *Trelawny* with *The Miner's Song* (entitled *Wheal Rodney*)

Everything about the origin of *Trelawny*, words and tune alike, is baffling. According to DIXON: 1846:

The song has been handed down traditionally since 1688 and has never appeared in print except in a work of limited circulation edited by the late Davies Gilbert.

According to DUNSTAN: 1929, the refrain (omitted by Dixon) is the only original part and the verses he gives (differing little from Dixon's) were a 'restoration' written about 1835 by the Rev. R. S. Hawker.

According to Hawker and Dixon the Trelawny referred to was the Bishop of Bristol and later Exeter who was committed to the Tower in 1688, but according to Gwas Myghal the chorus originated when Bishop Trelawny's grandfather was imprisoned in the Tower for contempt of the House of Commons in the reign of Charles I.

In keeping with all this, there is no settled translation into Cornish. Mordon was dissatisfied with Gwas Myghal's (DUNSTAN: 1929) and the present version (first published in GUNDRY: 1966) is by Talek, incorporating most of Mordon's amendments.

The tune seems not to have been originally connected with Trelawny but with Frederick, Duke of York (1763–1827) when he was celebrated in a popular skit which has been recorded in a children's singing game:

> O the brave old Duke of York
> He had ten thousand men
> He marched them halfway up the hill
> And he marched them down again . . .

Whatever the origin of the tune (and it may come from the French *Petit Tambour*) it has been a favourite maid-of-all-work in Cornwall for some time, being adapted to mumming:

> Oh, a mumming we will go, will go, etc.

or to mining:

1 O the farmers go around the fields
  Their legs tied up with straw
  The miners they go underground
  And never miss a blaw

> *O a-minin' we will go, my boys*
> *A-minin' we will go*
> *With picks and shovels in our 'ands*
> *A-minin' we will go*

2 Now I and Cap'n Franky
  Got up to go to bal
  We started for Wheal Rodney
  Where there was work for all

3 Said I to Cap'n Franky
  What trebbut shall us 'ave
  Thirtain shellen and foorpence
  But foorteen us did crave

4 Us had feftain foot of 'Saafety'
  Of candles foortain pound
  And that was our materyal
  For woorkin' underground

5 Now us had luck at laast, boys
  the knackers shawed us wheer
  To shut the rock and raise the tin
  And started us off feer

6 Then us had jolly times, boys
  And plenty for to ait
  So us left a bit for Bucca
  Who put us 'pon our fait

7 We all worked at Wheal Easy
  And when the bal was scat
  We all lived in the engine house
  And made the best of that

8 Last Monday was Faste Monday
  We 'ad a bit to (spare) spend
  We took the maidens to the fair
  And now we've nought to lend

9 We 'ad a sturt last Monday
  And ordered mutton stew
  Paid landlord Jan for nine months beer
  And that was overdue

10 And when we're up we're up
  And when we're down we're down
  And when we're only 'alfway up
  We're neither up nor down

96 AN WEDHEN WAR AN VRE
THE TREE ON THE HILL

Cornish words by Talek who took similar Breton songs into account

John Casley, Morvah, Cornwall, *rec.* P. Kennedy, 1956: BBC 23654
Other recorded versions
Christy Purcell, Belfast, N. Ireland, *rec.* P. Kennedy and S. O'Boyle, 1952: *The Tree in the Bog*, BBC 18586
Seamus Ennis, Dublin, *rec.* P. Kennedy: *The Rattling Bog*
Clifford Yeldham, Thaxted, Essex, *rec.* J. Hyman, 1962: *The Tree in the Wood*, BBC 29820

Printed versions
MASON: 1877, p. 26: *The Tree in the Valley* (Devon)
BARING GOULD: 1889, no. 104, p. 220: *The Everlasting Circle* (Devon)
BROADWOOD: 1893, p. 174: from MASON: 1877 (Devon)
SHARP MS: 1904: seven versions noted (two published)
SHARP: 1904–9, vol, IV, no. 93, p. 44: *The Tree in the Wood* (Somerset)
JWFSS: 1909, vol. 1, no. 23, p. 40: *Ar y Bryn Daeth Pren* (Merionethshire, Wales)

GREIG: 1909–14, vol. I, p. 87 (Scotland)
SHARP: 1916, p. 124: another version from Somerset
WILLIAMS: 1923, p. 182: *Down in the Lowlands* (Wiltshire)
REEVES: 1958, no. 104, p. 211: further two versions from SHARP: 1904 (Somerset)
REEVES: 1960, no. 36, p. 101: BARING GOULD: 1889 and 1905 version and extensive notes
JFSS: 1909, no. 13, p. 276: *The Tree in the Valley*, coll. Gardiner and Guyer (Hampshire) with notes about Breton, Danish, Swiss and Welsh
GUNDRY: 1966, p. 57: John Casley version

NEWELL: 1884–1903, p. 111: American children's version
SHARP AND KARPELES: 1917–32, vol. II, no. 206, p. 281: three versions (N. Carolina and Virginia)
CREIGHTON AND SENIOR: 1940, p. 34: *The Tree in the Bog* (Nova Scotia)
LEACH: 1965, p. 268: *The Stump* (Labrador)
JAFL: VIII, 87

In some West Country versions of *The Tree Song* the story completes that of *The Everlasting Circle*. In fact this was the title given to the song when it was published in Baring Gould's two early editions of *Songs of the West*. (It was omitted in the later edition revised by Cecil Sharp in 1905):

> And out of this feather was made a fine bed . . .
> And all with this bed a lad did lie . . .
> And all with this lad a maiden she did sleep . . .
> And all in this maiden a baby did grow . . .
> And out of this baby a boy did grow . . .
> And the boy he did lay in the ground an acorn . . .
> And out of this acorn did grow a great tree

Another version taken down by Baring Gould had a different ending:

> And out of the baby there grew a fine lawyer . . .
> And then from the lawyer there came a fine parson . . .
> And out of the parson there sprang a black devil . . .

Another version ends on:

> All on this feather there was a colour . . .

A broadside by Pitts of Seven Dials (n.d.) has 'feather, bed, maid and man' as the final sequence.
Baring Gould makes comparison with a Breton version *Ar parc caer* (The fair field) (published in F.M. Luzel: *Chansons Populaires de Basse-Bretagne*, Paris, 1890). Anne Gilchrist (JFSS: 1909, no. 13, p. 277) later drew attention to a similar French version *Le Bois Joli* with a polite ending:

> Au quatre coin de Paris
> Devinez ce qu'il y a
> Il y a un bois
> Un petit bois joli, Mesdames,
> Il y a un bois
> Un petit bois joli, il y a

The final verse ends with a message inside the yolk:

> Et dedans ce petit jaune
> Il y a ecrit
> Votre serviteur, Mesdames
> Il y a ecrit
> Votre serviteur je suis!

A Danish version *Langt udi skoven* (Long out in the wood) is published in *Danmarks Melodier* where it is described as a Sang-Renise (Rigmarole-type song). A Swiss version *Dert unde-n-i-der On Dert steit a Birliboum* (in *Kinderlied und Kinderspiel im Kanton Bern*, G. Zuricher) begins with the tree and ends with the pip within the core.

A Welsh version *Ar y bryn daeth pren* (JWFSS, vol. I, no. 1) ends (translated):

> The bed from the feathers
> The feathers from the chicken
> The chicken from the egg
> The egg from the nest
> The nest on the branch
> The branch on the tree
> The tree on the earth
> And the earth on nothing

The Welsh versions conform to the Celtic patterns of internal assonantal rhyme and one might draw the conclusion that the Breton and Welsh forms are the oldest. Perhaps John Casley's ancestors sang the song in Cornish.

John Casley, like his father from whom he learned this song, is a farmer and church organist. His father played in the local church for forty-six years and when recorded John had already been at it for forty. He has also been chapel organist for sixty-seven years and played trombone in Pendeen band for twenty-five. Apart from the Second World War, when he was in the Home Guard, he has never missed a Sunday.

Johnny said this song was known 'right through Pendeen' (district). As a boy, he recalled, he used to meet the rest of the lads outside the church and they would have a sing-song of just these sorts of songs.

Bibliography

Baring Gould: 1889–1905
Rev. S. Baring Gould and Rev. H. Fleetwood Sheppard, *Songs and Ballads of the West*: Patey & Willis, London (4 parts) 1889–91. Methuen, London (4 parts), 1891–4; (1 vol.) 1895; revised edition, 1905. Details are given by E. A. White in JEFDSS: 1937, p. 143 and 1946, p. 67. When reprinted in four parts this collection, mainly from Devon and N. Cornwall, comprised 110 songs 'collected from the mouths of the people'. Texts were modified and in some cases completely rewritten and the same applied to tunes. However, in the revised edition, under the musical editorship of Cecil Sharp and with the adding of the name of the Rev. F. W. Bussell, one of the original collectors, many original texts and tunes were restored. For further comment on this publication see Dean-Smith: JEFDSS: 1950, p. 41.

Baring Gould: 1895
Rev. S. Baring Gould, *A Book of Nursery Songs and Rhymes*: Methuen, London, 1895. An early collection of diversionary songs for children.

Baring Gould Ms: 1889–95
Rev. S. Baring Gould. Manuscript in Plymouth City Library.

Barnicoat: 1927
Ben Barnicoat, *Old Cornish Carols*: F. T. Nettlinghame, Polperro, Cornwall, 1927. Transcribed from MSS 'written and collected' by Barnicoat's grandfather, Francis Woolcock, of Tregoney, who died in 1888. Barnicoat's harmonies are less doctored than are those of HEATH: 1889 and WARMINGTON: 1912. MSS so far have not been traced.

Barrett: 1891
William A. Barrett, *English Folk Songs*: Novello, London, 1891. 54 songs with piano arrangements. An early publication using the term 'collected folk song'; most of the songs published elsewhere; exact details of origins not given and Barrett not nationally accepted as reputable collector or arranger.

Bell: 1857 (see Dixon: 1846 and Bell: 1857)

Bottrell: 1870/1873/1880
William Bottrell, *Traditions and Hearthside Stories of West Cornwall*: first series W. Cornish, The Library, Green Market, Penzance, 1870; second series, Beare & Son, Penzance, 1873; third series, *Stories and Folklore of West Cornwall*: F. Rodda, Penzance, 1880. A valuable source of Cornish folklore with many references to songs.

Boulton: 1913
Harold Boulton, *Songs of the Four Nations*: music arranged by Arthur Somervell: J. B. Cramer, London, 1913. Attempts to bring together 'national songs' of England, Scotland, Ireland and Wales, all with English words but also some verses given in original Cornish, Scots, Irish, Manx Gaelic and Welsh.

Broadwood: 1843
Rev. John Broadwood, *Old English Songs*: (privately printed) Balls & Co., London, 1843. 16 songs, collected in Surrey and Sussex by the Rev. John Broadwood of Lyne near Horsham. Arrangements by G. A. Dusart of Worthing. Said to be the 'first collection of folksong airs for their own sake'.

Broadwood: 1890
Rev. John Broadwood, *Sussex Songs (Popular Songs of Sussex)*: Stanley, Lucas & Weber, London, 1890. 26 songs (including the 16 in BROADWOOD: 1843) collected by Broadwood and arranged by H. F. Birch Reynardson.

Broadwood: 1893
Lucy Broadwood and J. A. Fuller-Maitland, *English County Songs*: Cramer, London, 1893. Important early publication containing 92 songs collected in nearly every county of England. Most have little relevance to their district origins but some local and in dialects of their locality. Scholarly presentation with straightforward piano accompaniments. For article about editor see JEFDSS: 1948, p. 136 and 1950, p. 38.

Carew: 1602
Richard Carew of Antonie, *Survey of Cornwall*: London, 1602. Reprinted, London, 1953.

Chambers: 1826/70
Robert Chambers, *Popular Rhymes of Scotland*: Edinburgh, 1826 and 1870. The first collection of Scots nursery rhymes, it contains interesting texts of songs which were connected with annual customs and children's games, but only six tunes are included.

Chambers: 1864
Robert Chambers, *The Book of Days*: W. and R. Chambers, London, 1864. This 'Miscellany of Popular Antiquities' contains references to annual customs in Britain including the May Day ceremonies at Padstow in Cornwall.

Chappell: 1838
William Chappell, *National English Airs*: Chappell and Simpkin Marshall, London, 1838. One volume containing 245 tunes arranged for piano and the other historical references, annotations and details of sources. Much of the reference is to printed works and MSS in the library of Edward Rimbault which was later dispersed. This work was superseded twenty years later by *Popular Music of the Olden Time* (1858).

Courtney: 1890
M. A. Courtney, *Cornish Feasts and Folklore*: Penzance, 1890. Contains rhymes, charms, games and ballads, some of which are copied from earlier books. No music. Miss Courtney was also the author of *Glossary of Words used in West Cornwall*, which was revised and printed in *The Folk-Lore Society Journal*, 1886–7.

Creighton and Senior: 1940
Helen Creighton and Doreen H. Senior, *Twelve Folk Songs from Nova Scotia*: Novello, London, 1940. Piano accompaniments by Miss Senior to 5 songs already published in Helen Creighton's *Songs and Ballads from Nova Scotia*, 1932, and 7 songs not previously published.

Dean-Smith: 1954
Margaret Dean-Smith, *A Guide to English Folk Song Collections (1822–1952)*: University of Liverpool, 1954. A useful index of published songs under titles, alternative titles and first lines, with some full descriptions of important books with historical annotations and an introduction which traces the development of collecting and publication of folksong in England over a period of 130 years.

Dixon: 1846 and Bell: 1857
James Henry Dixon, *Ancient Poems, Ballads and Songs of the Peasantry*: Percy Society, London, vol. 42, 1846. Robert Bell (title as above): J. W. Parker, London, 1857. By agreement with Dixon, Bell's publication was a revision and enlargement and editing by Bell of Dixon's collection and notes. Most of the material was collected in West Yorkshire and on Tyneside.

Bibliography

DUNCAN MS: 1905–11
James Duncan (1848–1917). MS collected *c.* 1905–11. Aberdeen University Library. Consists of two notebooks, the first containing 800 tunes with words of first verse, and the second giving texts of over 350 songs all supplied by a Mrs Gillespie. For obituary by Lucy Broadwood see JFSS: 1918, No. 21, p. 41.

DUNSTAN: 1929
Ralph Dunstan, *The Cornish Song Book*: A. W. Jordan, Truro and Reid Brothers, London, 1929; Lodenek Press, Padstow, Cornwall, 1974. Contains 11 songs with Cornish words, 72 with English words collected in Cornwall or songs associated with Cornwall, and 48 carols. Aimed to provide a selection of music for 'community singing wherever Cornishmen (and Cornish women) forgather the world over'.

DUNSTAN: 1932
Ralph Dunstan, *Cornish Dialect and Folk Songs*: A. W. Jordan, Truro and Reid Brothers, London, 1932; Lodenek Press, Padstow, Cornwall, 1972. A sequel to *The Cornish Song Book* containing 37 songs.

ECKENSTEIN: 1906
Lina Eckenstein, *Comparative Studies in Nursery Rhymes*: Duckworth, London, 1906. Includes essays on those associated with customs, numbers, chants of the creed, and sacrificial hunting, including the robin and the wren.

GILBERT: 1822
Davies Gilbert, *Some Ancient Christmas Carols*: John Nichols, London, 1822; 2nd ed., London, 1823. 8 carols with interesting folk harmonies. Three folksongs and two dances were added in the second edition. All these have been reprinted in GUNDRY: 1966.

GRAVES: 1928
Alfred Percival Graves, *The Celtic Song Book*: Ernest Benn, London, 1928. Representative Folk Songs of the Six Celtic Nations. 30 Irish songs in English, 20 Scots songs, 10 in Scots Gaelic, 22 Manx songs in Manx and English, 32 Welsh in Welsh and English, 12 Cornish songs in English, and 30 Breton songs with composed words.

GREIG: 1909/14
Gavin Greig, *Folk Songs of the North-East*: The Buchan Observer, Peterhead, Scotland. Vol. I 1909, vol. II 1914. Folklore Associates, Pennsylvania, USA, 1963. Greig was an Aberdeenshire schoolmaster and an accomplished musician who noted the words and tunes of over 3,000 songs. His manuscripts, extending over 90 volumes, are deposited in the library of King's College, Aberdeen.

GUNDRY: 1966 (i)
Inglis Gundry, *Canow Kernow*. Federation of Old Cornwall Societies, 1966. Soundpost Publications, Dartington Institute of Traditional Arts, Totnes, Devon, 1972. Over 60 songs, carols, shanties and dance tunes collected in Cornwall. Some songs published with versions in Cornish. This collection brings together songs from BARING GOULD: 1889–1905, GILBERT: 1822, JFSS and those in *Old Cornwall* (published by The Federation of Old Cornwall Societies) and field recordings made by Peter Kennedy in Cornwall in 1956.

GUNDRY: 1966 (ii)
Inglis Gundry, *Now Carol We*: Oxford University Press, London, 1966. 12 carols from an old MS written out by John Hutchens for Davies Gilbert about 1825. Arranged for unaccompanied mixed voices. This MS was discovered only recently in the possession of Gilbert's great grand-daughter and contained carols that were sent to Gilbert too late for inclusion in GILBERT: 1822.

HAMER: 1973
Fred Hamer, *Green Groves*: EFDS Publications, London, 1973. 38 songs, words and melodies (chord symbols). A further selection published posthumously. As in Hamer's *Garners Gay*, no exact details of locations, dates or comparative notes to songs.

HAMMOND AND GARDINER MSS: 1905–9
H. E. D. Hammond (1866–1910), R. F. F. Hammond (1868–1921) and Dr George Gardiner (1852–1910) collected mainly in Dorset and Hampshire. Their manuscripts, deposited in the Vaughan Williams Memorial Library at Cecil Sharp House, London, have been indexed by Frank Purslow, who has also edited three books drawn from them.

HEATH: 1889
R. H. Heath, *Cornish Carols*: R. H. Heath (organist, Redruth), printed by C. G. Roder, Leipzig: Redruth, 1889. Collection as sung in the Redruth district, but some of the melodies to these carols may well be composed rather than based on the traditional tunes. Also the harmonies may well be Heath's own rather than the ones which were sung locally.

HENRY: 1924
Sam Henry, *Songs of the People*: Northern Constitution, Coleraine, Co. Derry, N. Ireland, 1924. Over 800 songs were published in the local Derry newspaper. Many were contributed by readers but it was Henry's diligent research and background notes that gave interest to each contribution.

HERD: 1769/76
David Herd, *The Ancient and Modern Scottish Songs, Heroic Ballads, etc.*: Dickson & Elliot, Edinburgh, 1769; (2 vols.) 1776. Paterson, Edinburgh, 1870. New 2-vol. edition, 1973, Scottish Academic Press. Early Scots source material. Herd's original MS, in the British Museum, served as basis for many of Robert Burns's songs as well as for Sir Walter Scott's *Minstrelsy of the Scottish Border*.

HUNT: 1881
Robert Hunt, *Popular Romances of the West of England*: London, 1881; Chatto & Windus, London, 1930. 'Drolls, traditions and superstitions of Old Cornwall' with illustrations by George Cruikshank. The only song is the words of the Padstow May Song (No. 86) given in the Appendix, but the book is a veritable compendium of folk-lore and legends.

HUSK: 1868
William Henry Husk, *Songs of the Nativity*: John Camden Hotten, London, 1868. 80 carols including those from SYLVESTER: 1861. Preface owes much to SANDYS: 1833.

JAFL: 1888–
Journal of American Folklore, now published by University of Pennsylvania.

JEFDSS: 1932–64
Journal of The English Folk Dance and Song Society: London (32 vols), 1932–64.

JFSS: 1899–1931
Journal of the Folk-Song Society: London (35 vols.), 1899–1931.

JWFSS: 1909–71
Journal of the Welsh Folk Song Society, ed. J. Lloyd Williams, W. S. Gwynn Williams, 1909–71 (intermittently). The Journal consists of hundreds of songs and variants from aural, MS and published sources, which are given in both staff and sol-fa notation.

JENNER: 1904
Henry Jenner, *A Handbook of the Cornish Language*: London, 1904. Mainly about the last survival of the language but also containing some account of Cornish history and literature.

KIDSON: 1891
Frank Kidson, *Traditional Tunes*: C. Taphouse, Oxford, 1891. Texts and melodies (without accompaniment) mainly from Yorkshire. Later published with piano accompaniment in KIDSON AND MOFFAT: 1926 and 1927. Many texts filled out from broadsides. For article about Frank Kidson see JEFDSS: 1948, p. 127. Reissued by S. R. Publishers, 1970.

KIDSON AND MOFFAT: 1926
Frank Kidson and Alfred Moffat, *A Garland of English Folk Songs*: Ascherberg, Hopwood & Crew, London, 1926. 60 songs

collected by Kidson, mainly in Yorkshire, with piano accompaniments by Moffat; most previously published in KIDSON: 1891.

KIDSON AND MOFFAT: 1927
Frank Kidson and Alfred Moffat, *Folk Songs from the North Countrie*: Ascherberg, Hopwood & Crew, London, 1927. A further 60 songs with piano accompaniment, published one year after the collector's death. The foreword by Lucy Broadwood provides information about the collector. See also *Frank Kidson: portrait*, JEFDSS: 1948, pp. 127–35.

KIDSON AND MOFFAT: 1929
Frank Kidson, Ethel Kidson and Alfred Moffat, *English Peasant Songs*: Ascherberg, Hopwood & Crew, London, 1929. 'Third and last Selection of Sixty Folk Songs from the Frank Kidson Collection.' Compiled by his niece with piano accompaniments by Moffat. See KIDSON AND MOFFAT: 1926 and 1927.

LEACH: 1965
MacEdward Leach, *Folk Ballads and Songs of the Lower Labrador Coast*: National Museum of Canada, Ottawa, 1965.

LHUYD: 1707
Edward Lhuyd, *Archaeologia Britannica*: Oxford, 1707. Observations on language and local customs, etc., made during travels through Britain, including Cornwall.

MASON: 1877/1908
Miss M. H. Mason, *Nursery Rhymes and Country Songs*: Metzler, London, 1877. Second edition without illustrations and with additional notes, 1908. Over 50 folksongs of great variety mainly from her own Mitford family in Northumberland, also from Broadwood in Sussex, with piano accompaniments.

NEWELL: 1884/1903
W. W. Newell, *Games and Songs of American Children*: Harper Bros., New York, 1884; new and enlarged edition 1903.

OLD CORNWALL: 1925
Federation of Old Cornwall Societies.

PEACOCK: 1965
Kenneth Peacock, *Songs of the Newfoundland Outports*: National Museum of Canada, Ottawa, 1965.

PRYCE: 1790
William Pryce, *Archaeologica Cornu-Britannica* (*An Essay to Preserve the Ancient Cornish Language*): Sherborne, Dorset, 1790. Contains the original Cornish words to *Pelēa era whȳ moāz, moes fettow tēag?* (No. 94) which were sung at Carclew in 1698.

REEVES: 1958
James Reeves, *The Idiom of the People*: Heinemann, London, 1958. Words of 115 folksongs from Cecil Sharp MSS (about 40 printed for the first time) selected as examples of 'English Traditional Verse'. Introduction concerned with the Folk Song Movement in England; Sharp as a collector; text revisions, description of the MSS, the popular idiom; and a detailed consideration of certain songs.

REEVES: 1960
James Reeves, *The Everlasting Circle*: Heinemann, London, 1960. 142 texts from the MSS of Baring Gould, Hammond and Gardiner considered as 'English traditional verse'. Introduction concerned with Baring Gould as a collector and his MSS; Hammond and Gardiner; varieties of folksong; the theme of fertility and a discussion on the lingua franca of English traditional song.

SANDYS: 1833
William Sandys, *Christmas Carols: Ancient and Modern*: Beckley, London, 1833. These carols came mainly from Cornwall. The tunes, limited in number, show similar folk harmony to GILBERT: 1822. Contains long introduction on history of Christmas and carol-singing.

SANDYS: 1846
William Sandys (pseud. Uncle Jan Treenoodle), *Specimens of Cornish Provincial Dialect*: London, 1846. Contains a selection of songs and other pieces connected with Cornwall, including earliest printed record of *Hal-an-tow* (No. 92).

SHARP MS: 1903–23
Cecil Sharp (1859–1924), foremost collector of English folksongs and folkdances, was the founder of The English Folk Dance Society and for many years a member of The Folk-Song Society.(In 1932 these two societies amalgamated as The English Folk Dance and Song Society.) For a full account of his life-work and publications see *Cecil Sharp* by A. H. Fox-Strangways (Oxford University Press, London, 1933), revised by Maud Karpeles (Routledge & Kegan Paul, London, 1967). Words, songs, tunes and dance notes in Cecil Sharp's autograph are in the Library of Clare College, Cambridge. There are also photostat copies in the Harvard University Library and the New York Public Library, and microfilm copies in the libraries of the University of California and in the library at Cecil Sharp House, London, the headquarters of The English Folk Dance and Song Society. Cecil Sharp's own collection of books was left to the EFDSS and formed the beginnings of the specialist library at Cecil Sharp House.

SHARP AND MARSON: 1904–9
Cecil J. Sharp and Rev. Charles L. Marson, *Folk Songs from Somerset*: Simpkin Marshall, London, and Barnicott, Taunton, Somerset. Vol. I 1904, vol. II 1905, vol. III 1906, vol. IV 1908, vol. V 1909. The most important single collection of English folksong, later edited as the *Selected Edition* (1916–21). Introduction concerning singers and style most valuable.

SHARP (School Series): 1908–36
Cecil J. Sharp, NOVELLO'S SCHOOL SONGS, Sets I and II: *Folk-Songs from Somerset*, 1908; Sets III and IV: *Various Counties*, 1909; Set V: *Folk-Songs from Somerset*, 1910; Set VI: *Folk-Songs for Schools*, 1912; Sets VII and VIII: 1922; Set IX: 1925; Set X: 1936.

SHARP: 1911
Cecil J. Sharp, *English Folk Carols*: Novello (Simpkin), London; Barnicott & Pearce, Taunton, Somerset. 21 carols with piano accompaniment mostly from W. Midlands.

SHARP: 1916/21
Cecil J. Sharp, *English Folk Songs: Selected Edition*: Oliver Ditson, New York, 1916. Novello, London, 1921. 2 vols. 100 songs of which all but 18 from Somerset previously published in SHARP AND MARSON: 1904–9. 12 of the songs, not previously published, were variants. Introduction (and notes to songs) are of great value as they post-date by 14 years his *English Folk Song, Some Conclusions*.

SHARP AND KARPELES: 1917/32
Olive Dame Campbell and Cecil J. Sharp, *English Folk Songs from the Southern Appalachians*: Putnam, New York, 1917. Cecil J. Sharp and Maud Karpeles (2 vols.), Oxford University Press, London, 1932.

SUMNER: 1888
Heywood Sumner (editor and illustrator), *The Besom Maker and other Country Folk Songs*: Longmans Green, London, 1888. Texts and melodies (without accompaniments). Mainly an illustrated 'gift book' (with decoration which is reminiscent of Laurence Housman) of country songs sung 'at harvest suppers by the old folk who do not change their tune to the times'. No details of sources but includes 9 songs which, although some are fragmentary, were undoubtedly most carefully noted.

SYLVESTER: 1861/76
Joshua Sylvester (pseudonym), *A Garland of Christmas Carols*: John Camden Hotten, London, 1861. *Christmas Carols and Ballads*: 1876.

UDAL: 1922
John Symonds Udal, *Dorsetshire Folk-Lore*: Stephen Austin, Hertford, 1922. J. Stephens-Cox, St Peter Port, Guernsey, 1970. Contains a long 'fore-say' by William Barnes, 'The Dorset Poet'. A mixture of material including words of about 20 songs.

VAUGHAN WILLIAMS: 1908
Ralph Vaughan Williams, *Folk Songs from the Eastern Counties*: Novello, London, 1908. 15 songs from Essex, Norfolk and Cambridgeshire most already in JFSS: 1906, No. 8.

WARMINGTON: 1912
T. N. Warmington, *Old Christmas Carols and Anthems*: Warmington, Carbis Bay, Cornwall, 1912. 2 vols. Similar collection to HEATH: 1889 but as sung in the St Ives district. Harmonies may be his own rather than those sung locally.

WILLIAMS: 1865
Robert Williams, Canon of St Asaph, *Lexicon Britannicum*: Llandovery, Carmarthenshire, Wales, 1865. A dictionary in which the words are elucidated by copious examples from survivals of Cornish works.

WILLIAMS: 1923
Alfred Owen Williams, *Folk Songs of the Upper Thames*: Duckworth, London, 1923. Over 300 folksongs (words only) noted mainly in Berkshire, Gloucestershire, Oxfordshire and Wiltshire. Interesting introduction about rural life, more fully covered by Williams in *Round About the Upper Thames* (Duckworth, 1922). Further unpublished texts in Swindon Reference Library. See *Folk Music Journal*: 1969, 'Alfred Williams: A Symposium'.

VI

Songs of the
Channel Islands

Introduction

Generally speaking the folksongs and dances of the Channel Islands are those of Normandy. This does not make them any the less distinct or interesting. The Islands remained British in 1204 when King John lost control of Normandy but until comparatively recent times there was close communication with the mainland of France, particularly Normandy, and the language was basically the same as that of Normandy. The Islanders although of old Norman stock were, almost anomalously, ever loyal subjects of the English Crown. However, to this day the Islands are still known in French as Les Îles Anglo-Normandes (the Anglo-Norman Islands) and the reigning Monarch of England is still to Islanders Notre Duc (Our Duke) as it was in those far-off days when the King of England was likewise Duc de Normandie.

This century has seen the gradual but sure decline of the Norman-French language and, with it, the way of life and much that was traditional in each of the four islands of Jersey, Guernsey, Alderney (Auregny) and Sark (Sercq). For various reasons anglicization has been proceeding apace for many years, to the prejudice of very much of the insular character of the people and their fundamentally Norman folklore and customs, and much has been lost under the designation of progress.

Very few Norman songs and dances have survived through collection and publication in Normandy. As exceptions one may mention the ballads, drinking songs and love songs of the sixteenth century known as *Vaux de Vire*, published at Caen in 1875 under the title of *Vaux de Vire d'Olivier Basselin et de Jean Le Houx*, being reproduced from earlier editions of 1858 and 1811, though the earliest record of these dated back to 1670. Another work of reference, also containing old Norman songs, was Jean Fleury's *La Littérature orale de la Basse-Normandie*, 1883. In the Channel Islands in the nineteenth century songs were occasionally published in annuals such as *L'Almanach de la Chronique de Jersey*. These songs were handed down orally and were still popular till the turn of the present century. They were sung chiefly at family gatherings in the winter-time, and on occasions of revelry all the year round such as at wedding feasts. At the end of communal plough days, after the chief evening meal, the rest of the soirée was given to dancing and singing, followed by only a brief night's rest before returning to the plough at dawn the following day.

However, most of the Island songs and dances had fallen into disuse very much earlier. One great cause was the puritanical legislation which accompanied the establishment of Calvinism in the Islands at the time of the Reformation. Several statutes were passed in the sixteenth and early seventeenth centuries forbidding profane songs, dances and all 'illicit games'. Culprits had to do penance with their heads bared in Church in sight of the whole congregation, holding a lighted torch and with legs and feet clad in a winding sheet. In 1785 these severe restrictions were supplemented by a further decree forbidding hotel keepers (except on fête days) to allow dancing on their premises after ten o'clock. Many of the islanders became fiercely Calvinistic, austerity was the order of the day and any form of revelry was frowned upon. Traces of Calvinism still exist to this day among the more conservative and truly native populations of Jersey, Guernsey and Sark (there are very few real ('Auregnais') Alderney people left).

In 1787 John Wesley paid a visit to the Islands, and persuaded a section of the populace to become his followers. In spirit they cordially agreed that singing and dancing savoured of

247

phus and Eliza Le Ruez of Bonne Nuit,
sey

Photograph: Peter Kennedy

papacy, and between repressive legislation on the one hand and arbitrary convictions on the other, much of the native 'joie de vivre' was crushed out of existence. Strangely enough, though much of folksong and dance disappeared, in common with many of the old customs, the vernacular has remained as virile as ever and to this day much folklore has survived through oral tradition.

The French songs of the Channel Islands must have undergone changes over the years, but it is remarkable how well preserved most of them are in their 'pure' renderings. They are often found to be the same as those which have been carried to Canada by Frenchmen from Normandy and the western provinces of France. As in Normandy the songs in the Islands were sung mostly in French, that is to say in one form or another of French, but Norman dialect modifications were quite common and some indeed were entirely in the Norman-French. Each island having its own separate dialect or 'parler' of Norman-French, it follows that a particular song such as for example *Man Bouonhomme est bein malade* (No. 110) was sung in part to different words according to the island.

It must be remembered that the great majority of the inhabitants of the Islands, in common with the country people elsewhere, were illiterate well into the nineteenth century. Thus very few songs or poems have been put on paper. The first published efforts in versification in Norman-French did not take place until the early nineteenth century. There is thus a gap between, for instance, nineteenth-century writers and the few early writers such as Maistre Wace, a twelfth century son of Jersey whose poems such as *Le Roman de Rou*, *Le Roman de Brut*, were written in Old Norman-French—with similar words and expressions used in the Channel Islands 'parlers' of today.

Quite apart from the Old French or Norman-French words, most singers nowadays tend to use modern French 'adaptations'. By such modifications the sequence of the tale is often jumbled and lost, the sense obscure or even unintelligible, and many survivals of the present day have lost their original meaning: a verse may start off in the first person singular and a few lines later be altered to the second or third person, either singular or plural.

As regards the subjects with which these songs deal, the most common theme concerns aspects of love. It is interesting that a number of the so-called love songs would once have been considered by earlier generations elsewhere as suggestive or vulgar, but the Island folk did not mean or see anything harmful in giving voice to such ribald material. However there are still some people in the Islands, particularly the womenfolk, who show their downright disapproval. It is therefore quite surprising that any of these down-to-earth songs should have survived the combined pressure of puritanical legislation and a strict puritanical outlook. Songs about national or local events are of course also common, whilst a few deal with some topic long since forgotten, thus making little sense to present-day singers and audiences. Quite often, songs have survived because of their popular tuneful appeal, whilst others with verses composed during the last hundred years or so were set to tunes of the older folksongs.

This collection of songs is of great interest historically, sociologically and musicologically. It consists of songs entirely in French in the main belonging to the classical roots of traditional French song. It is a case of survival on the spot and not, as in the case of French songs in Canada, a migration of a repertoire from its native soil. In a population which is becoming more and more English in manners and language, the survival of these songs is a remarkable fact. Up till the First World War there was more Norman-French spoken than English, whereas today the reverse is the case.

Most of these singers being already elderly people, a somewhat linear style is very similar to the French peasant style, that is that of the older country people singing collected pieces which have remained for a long time in their memory and which have been transmitted orally to them by their ancestors.

The melodies are syllabic in style and of fairly narrow range, only occasionally going outside the octave and restricting themselves often to the sixth or fifth. The songs are strophic in form and monodic in performance. One particularly interesting kind found in this collection is that of songs of repetitive enumerations called 'randonnée' (for example No. 115). This type still exists in French peasant songs where it has often become a children's song or nursery rhyme. There are also songs whose texts carry refrains of meaningless words (No. 105) and others whose refrains have their separate texts and music (No. 97).

This collection lends itself to comparison with similar French folksongs in original manuscript and in recordings made in French country districts during the last thirty years, particularly those of the National Museum of Popular Arts and Traditions in Paris (referred to in the notes as MATP). Such a comparison reveals the presence of three groups of songs in the Channel Islands collections.

GROUP I

A Comparison with Norman Songs—Nos. 97, 99, 100, 105, 109, 110, 111, 112, 118.

This grouping does not necessarily mean that in France these songs are found only in Normandy —one can see that on reading the notes, but with few exceptions Basse-Normandie (or Lower Normandy) alone produces this type. The nine songs in our collection which make up this group come for the most part from Jersey, but are also found in Guernsey and Sark.

GROUP II

A Comparison with Songs of Western France—Nos. 98, 101, 113, 115, 117, 119, 120.

'Western France' in this definition is from Upper Brittany (roughly the country to the west of a line St. Brieuc–Vannes and the coastal strip as far south as the Spanish border). There are comparisons to be made also with certain regions of Central France, especially Berry and the Nivernais, and some even more distant relationships. Our seven songs from this group come for the most part from Guernsey.

GROUP III

A Comparison with French Songs in General—Nos. 102, 103, 104, 106, 107, 108, 114, 116.

This third category lumps together the songs which are French in root or tradition but which are not or can no longer be located in a particular region of France. The eight songs of this type come from the three islands, Jersey, Guernsey, and Sark.

J'ai Perdu Ma Femme (No. 103) has not been found in the contemporary French folksong repertoire, but it is clearly in the French tradition.

In France these songs were still well-known to country folk until only a few decades ago, and in fact it could be said that this collection from the Channel Islands represents a sample of the classical songs of the French Romantic period.

97 AU BORD D'UNE FONTAINE
'TWAS THERE BESIDE A FOUNTAIN

Au bord d'u - ne fon - tai - ne   Je me suis re - po - sé - e

Je me suis re - po - sée   Au bord d'u - ne fon - tai - ne

Je me suis re - po - sée   Les cot - il - lons sont lourds dans l'sac - que

Les   cot - il - lons   sont   lourds

1 Au bord d'une fontaine
Je me suis reposé-e
Je me suis reposée
Au bord d'une fontaine
Je me suis reposée
Les cotillons sont lourds dans l'sac-que
Les cotillons sont lourds

2 Au bord d'une fontaine
Je me suis reposé-e
Je me suis reposée
Et l'eau était si claire
Que je me suis baignée

3 Et l'eau était si claire
Que je me suis baigné-e
Que je me suis baignée
Avec des feuilles de chêne
Je me suis essuyée

4 Et l'eau était si claire
Que je me suis baigné-e
Que je me suis baignée
Dessus la plus haute branche
Le rossignol chantait

5 Dessus la plus haute branche
Le rossignol chantait-e
Le rossignol chantait
Chant-e, bel-e rossignol
Et toi qui a le coeur gai

1 'Twas there beside a fountain
'Twas there I took my rest, Sir
'Twas there I took my rest
'Twas there beside a fountain
'Twas there I took my rest
These petticoats weigh heavy in the wash-bag
These petticoats weigh so

2 'Twas there beside a fountain
'Twas there I took my rest, Sir
'Twas there I took my rest
And the water was so clear
That a-bathing I didst go

3 And the water was so clear
That a-bathing I didst go, Sir
That a-bathing I didst go
With leaves from the oak-tree
I used to dry myself

4 And the water was so clear
That a-bathing I didst go, Sir
That a-bathing I didst go
From the very topmost branch
The nightingale was singing

5 From the very topmost branch
The nightingale was singing, Sir
The nightingale was singing
Sing on, pretty nightingale
You're the one with the happy heart

98 AU LOGIS DE MON PERE
'TWAS AT MY FATHER'S HOUSE

Au lo - gis de mon pè — re Au bas - le Mont Quer - vaux

Il y a - t - un pom - mier doux et doux et doux Il y a - t - un pom - mier doux

1 Au logis de mon pè-re
Au bas-le Mont Quervaux
Il y a-t-un pommier doux et doux et doux
Il y a-t-un pommier doux

2 Et les feuilles en sont ver-tes
Au bas-le Mont Quervaux
Et le fruit en est doux et doux et doux
Et le fruit en est doux

3 C'est trois filles de prix-e
Au bas-le Mont Quervaux
Qui sont endormies dessous et sous et sous
Qui sont endormies dessous

4 La plus jeune s'y levai-e
Au bas-le Mont Quervaux
Elle dit: Ma sœur, il est jour et jour et jour
Elle dit: Ma sœur, il est jour

5 Non, ce n'est pas le jour-e
Au bas-le Mont Quervaux
C'est le feu des armées, armées, armées
C'est le feu des armées

6 Ce sont nos amants doux-e
Au bas-le Mont Quervaux
Qui sont à combattre pour nous et nous et nous
Qui sont à combattre pour nous

1 'Twas at my father's house, Sir
Down there at Mont Quervaux
There's an apple tree so sweet as sweet as sweet
There's an apple tree so sweet

2 And the leaves they are so green, Sir
Down there at Mont Quervaux
And the fruit it is so sweet as sweet as sweet
And the fruit it is so sweet

3 They are three champion girls, Sir
Down there at Mont Quervaux
They're sleeping there below, below, below
They're sleeping there below

4 The youngest she arose, Sir
Down there at Mont Quervaux
Said: Sister, it is light, a-light, a-light
Said: Sister, it is light

5 O no it's not daylight, Sir
Down there at Mont Quervaux
It is the army's fire, a-fire, a-fire
It is the army's fire

6 It is our own sweethearts, Sir
Down there at Mont Quervaux
They're fighting for ourselves, ourselves, ourselves
They're fighting for ourselves

99 BELLE ROSE
LOVELY ROSIE

J'ai cueil - li la bel - le ro - se J'ai cueil - li la bel - le ro - se

Qui pen - dait au ro - sier blanc Bel - le Ro - se

Qui pen - dait au ro - sier blanc Bel - le Ro - se, rose au blanc

1 J'ai cueilli la belle rose
J'ai cueilli la belle rose
Qui pendait au rosier blanc
Belle Rose
Qui pendait au rosier blanc
Belle rose, rose au blanc

2 Je l'apportis à ma mère
Je l'apportis à ma mère
Entre St Jean et St Ouën
Belle Rose
Entre St Jean et St Ouën
Belle rose, rose au blanc

3 Je n'y rencontris personne
Que le rossignol chantant

4 Qui disait dans son langage
Mariez-vous, fille de quinze ans

5 A quel âge m'y marirai-je?
Moi qui n'a pas encore quinze ans

6 Vous couch'rez avec ma mère
Avec moi le plus souvent

7 Je n'couche poin-t-avec les hommes
Que j'n'épouse auparavant

1 I did pluck the lovely rose
I did pluck the lovely rose
Hanging from the white rose bush
Lovely Rosie
Hanging from the white rose bush
Lovely Rosie, rose of white

2 I did take it unto my mother
I did take it unto my mother
Between St Jean and St Ouën
Lovely Rosie
Between St Jean and St Ouën
Lovely Rosie, rose of white

3 Not a soul did I encounter
Just a nightingale singing

4 He was saying in his language
Girl of fifteen, go an' get married

5 At what age should I marry?
Me, no more than fifteen years old

6 You will sleep with my mother
And often as not with me

7 I do not sleep with men at all
Unless I'm already married

100 BITCHON-BITCHETTE
BITCHON-BITCHETTE

Ha Bit - chon - Bit - chette Tu sor - ti - ras d'dans mes choux

Il faut al - ler cher - chi le loup Pour ve - nir man - gi Bit - chette

Le loup n'veurt pon man - gi Bit - chette Bit - chette n'veurt pon sor - ti des choux

Ah mais, tu sor - ti - ras, Bit - chon - Bit - chette

Ah mais, tu sor - ti - ras de ces choux - là

1 *Ha, Bitchon-Bitchette*
Tu sortiras d'dans mes choux
Il faut aller cherchi le loup
Pour venir mangi Bitchette
Le loup n'veurt pon mangi Bitchette
Bitchette n'veurt pon sorti des choux
Ah! mais, tu sortiras, Bitchon-Bitchette
Ah! mais, tu sortiras de ces choux-là

2 *Ha, Bitchon-Bitchette*
Tu sortiras d'dans mes choux
Il faut aller cherchi le tchian
Pour venir mord'e le loup
Le tchian n'veurt pon mord'e le loup
Le loup n'veurt pon mangi Bitchette
Bitchette n'veurt pon sorti des choux
Ah, mais, tu sortiras, Bitchon-Bitchette
Ah, mais, tu sortiras de ces choux-là

1 *Ha, Bitchon-Bitchette*
You must come from my cabbage patch
We must set off to find the wolf
To come and eat Bitchette
The wolf it will not eat Bitchette
Bitchette won't leave the cabbage patch
Ah, but you will come out, Bitchon-Bitchette
Ah, but you will come from the cabbage patch

2 *Ha, Bitchon-Bitchette*
You must come from my cabbage patch
We must set off to find the dog
To come and bite the wolf
The dog it will not bite the wolf
The wolf it will not eat Bitchette
Bitchette won't leave the cabbage patch
Ah, but you will come out, Bitchon-Bitchette
Ah, but you will come out from the cabbage patch

3 Il faut aller cherchi le bâton
 Pour venir battre le tchian
 L'bâton n'veurt pon batt' le tchian
 Le tchian n'veurt pon mord'e le loup (*etc.*)

4 Il faut aller cherchi du feu
 Pour brûler le bâton
 Le feu n'veurt pon brûler l'bâton
 Le bâton n'veurt pon batt' le tchian (*etc.*)

5 Il faut aller cherchi de l'ieau
 Pour dêteindre le feu
 L'ieau n'veurt pon dêteindre le feu
 Le feu n'veurt pon brûler l'bâton (*etc.*)

6 Il faut aller cherchi un vieau
 Pour venir béthe l'ieau
 Le vieau n'veurt pon béthe l'ieau
 L'ieau n'veurt pon dêteindre le feu (*etc.*)

LAST Il faut aller cherchi le bouochi
 Pour venir tuer le vieau
 Le bouochi veurt bein tuer le vieau
 Le vieau veurt bein béthe l'icau
 L'ieau veurt bein dêteindre le feu
 Le feu veurt bein brûler le bâton
 Le bâton veurt bein batt' le tchian
 Le tchian veurt bein mord'e le loup
 Le loup veurt bein mangi Bitchette
 Bitchette n'veurt pon sorti des choux
 Ah ha, té v'là sortie, Bitchon-Bitchette
 Ah ha, té v'la sortie d'dans mes choux

3 We must set off to find the stick
 To come and beat the dog
 The stick it will not beat the dog
 The dog it will not bite the wolf (*etc.*)

4 We must set off to find some fire
 To come and burn the stick
 The fire it will not burn the stick
 The stick it will not beat the dog (*etc.*)

5 We must set off to find some water
 To come and quench the fire
 The water will not quench the fire
 The fire it will not burn the stick (*etc.*)

6 We must set off to find the calf
 To come and drink the water
 The calf it will not drink the water
 The water will not quench the fire (*etc.*)

LAST We must set off to find the butcher
 To come and kill the calf
 The butcher will gladly kill the calf
 The calf will gladly drink the water
 The water will gladly quench the fire
 The fire will gladly burn the stick
 The stick will gladly beat the dog
 The dog will gladly bite the wolf
 The wolf will gladly eat Bitchette
 Bitchette won't leave the cabbage patch
 Ah ha, you've come from there, Bitchon-Bitchette
 Ah ha, you've come from out my cabbage patch

101 LE BON MARAIN
THE SEAMAN FINE

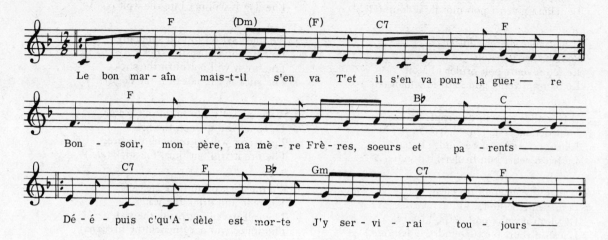

Le bon mar-aîn mais-t-il s'en va T'et il s'en va pour la guer — re

Bon - soir, mon père, ma mè - re Frè - res, soeurs et pa - rents ——

Dé - é - puis c'qu'A - dèle est mor-te J'y ser-vi - rai tou - jours ——

1 Le bon maraîn mais-t-il s'en va
T'et il s'en va pour la guer-re
Le bon maraîn mais-t-il s'en va
T'et il s'en va pour la guer-re
Bonsoir, mon père, ma mè-re
Frères, soeurs et parents
Dé-épuis c'qu'Adèle est mor-te
J'y servirai toujours
(*Last two lines may be repeated as chorus*)

1 The seaman's fine but goes away
Goes away unto the war
The seaman's fine but goes away
Goes away unto the war
Goodbye, papa, mama
Brothers, sisters and all
Now that Adèle she is dead
I'll serve for all my time
(*Last two lines may be repeated as chorus*)

2 Le bon maraîn mais-t-il s'en va
Z'et trouver l'son capitain-e
Le bon maraîn mais-t-il s'en va
Z'et trouver son capitain-e
Bonsoir, mon capitain-e
Donnez-moi mon congé
Dé-épuis c'qu'Adèle est mort-e
J'y servirai toujours

2 The seaman's fine but goes away
In search of his cap-i-tain
The seaman's fine but goes away
In search of his cap-i-tain
Good evening, cap-i-tain
Give to me my discharge
Now that Adèle she is dead
I'll serve for all my time

3 Le bon maraîn mais-t-il s'en va
Z'et à la rencont' d'Adèle
Le bon maraîn mais-t-il s'en va
Z'et à la rencont' d'Adèle
Adèle n'est pas d'ici
Elle n'est pas de retour
Son corps est dans la tomb'le
Son âme au Paradis

3 The seaman's fine but goes away
And goes to meet Adèle
The seaman's fine but goes away
And goes to meet Adèle
Adèle she is not here
And never will return
Her body's in the grave
Her soul's in paradise

4 Le bon maraîn lui a répondu-le
Comm-e brave homme de guerr-e
Le bon maraîn lui a répondu-le
Comm-e brave homme de guerr-e
Regrettant mon Adèl-e
Donnez-moi mon congé
Puis tu pren'ra les armes
Tu seras officier

4 The seaman fine to him replied
As any brave man of war
The seaman fine to him replied
As any brave man of war
So lamenting my dear Adèle
Give to me my discharge
Then you can take arms
Flag-officer you'll be

102 LA FILLE DE L'AVOCAT
THE LAWYER'S DAUGHTER

Au jar-din de mon père O rap-toup-toup-ca-ma-rad'-rap sa

Au jar-din de mon pè-re ——— Il y a-t-un o-ran-ger

O - O - O - O Il y a-t-un o-ran - ger

1 Au jardin de mon père
  O, rap-toup-toup-ca-ma-rad'-rap-sa
  Au jardin de mon pè-re
  Il y a-t-un oranger
  O-o-o-o
  Il y a-t-un oranger

2 Il y craît des oranges
  Il y craît des oran-ges
  Je ne sais qui les tchillera

3 Marguerite prit son échelle
  Dans l'orang' elle monta

4 Elle cueilla les plus jaunes
  Les vertes elle les laissa

5 Marguerite prit son panier
  Prit son panier à son bras

6 S'en fut avaû la ville
  L'premier qu'elle rencontra

7 Combien les vends-tu, belle?
  O, fille de l'avocat

8 Six sous la d'mi-douzaine
  O, fille de l'avocat

9 Courage, courage, ma fille
  Là, tu n'en mourras pas

1 In my father's garden
  Oh, rap-toup-toup-ca-ma-rad'-rap-sa
  In my father's garden
  There is an orange tree
  Oh-oh-oh-oh
  There is an orange tree

2 Some oranges grow there
  I wonder who will pick them

3 Marguerite fetched her ladder
  Climbed in the orange tree

4 She picked the ripest ones
  The green she left behind

5 Marguerite fetched her basket
  Her basket on her arm

6 She went off through the town
  The first man she did meet

7 How much are they, my beauty
  Oh daughter of the lawyer

8 Sixpence half a dozen
  Oh daughter of the lawyer

9 Be brave, be brave, my beauty
  There now, you won't die of it

103 J'AI PERDU MA FEMME
I DID LOSE MY WIFE

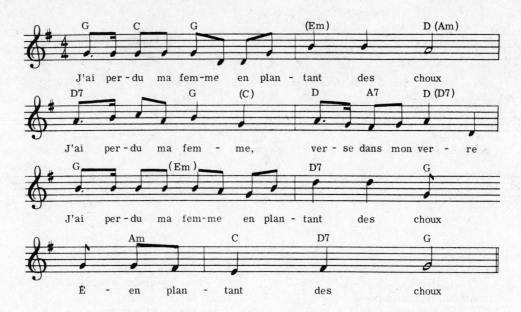

J'ai per-du ma fem-me en plan-tant des choux

J'ai per-du ma fem - me, ver-se dans mon ver - re

J'ai per-du ma fem-me en plan-tant des choux

É - en plan - tant des choux

1 J'ai perdu ma fem-me en plantant des choux
J'ai perdu ma femme, verse dans mon verre
J'ai perdu ma fem-me en plantant des choux
É-en plantant des choux

2 On me l'a ramenée au bout de huit jours
On me l'a ramenée, verse dans mon verre
On me l'a ramenée au bout de huit jours
É-au bout de huit jours

3 Tiens, voilà ta fem-me toi, mari jaloux
Tiens, voilà ta femme, verse dans mon verre
Tiens, voilà ta fem-me toi, mari jaloux
É-toi, mari jaloux

4 Je ne la veux pas-se, gardez-la pour vous
Je ne la veux pas, verse dans mon verre
Je ne la veux pas-se gardez-la pour vous
Mais, gardez-la pour vous

5 J'ai-t-une servante qui me sert de tout
J'ai-t-une servante, verse dans mon verre
J'ai-t-une servante qui me sert de tout
É-qui me sert de tout

6 Elle balaie ma chambr' et fait mon lit bien doux
Elle balaie ma chambre, verse dans mon verre
Elle balaie ma chambr' et fait mon lit bien doux
Et fait mon lit bien doux

7 Elle fait bien autre chose mais je n'dirai pas tout
Elle fait bien autre chose, verse dans mon verre
Elle fait bien autre chose mais je n'dirai pas tout
Mais je n'dirai pas tout

1 I did lose my wife as I was planting greens
I did lose my wife, come fill up my glass
I did lose my wife as I was planting greens
As I was planting greens

2 Brought her back they did to me at eight days past
Brought her back they did to me, come fill up my glass
Brought her back they did to me at eight days past
At eight days past

3 There, here she is again your wife, you jealous spouse
There, here she is again your wife, come fill up my glass
There, here she is again your wife, you jealous spouse
You jealous spouse

4 I don't want her, you can have her for yourself
I don't want her, you can have her, come fill up my glass
I don't want her, you can have her for yourself
For yourself

5 I've a servant girl of mine who does for me
I've a servant girl of mine, come fill up my glass
I've a servant girl of mine who does for me
Who does for me

6 She does sweep my room for me, my bed makes nice
She does sweep my room for me, come fill up my glass
She does sweep my room for me, my bed makes fine
My bed makes fine

7 Other things she does as well, but I won't tell
Other things she does as well, come fill up my glass
Other things she does for me, but I won't tell
But I won't tell

104 JEAN, PETIT COQ
JOHN, LITTLE LAD

Introduction to song (almost recited):
L'aut' jour un homme vint à ma porte
Qui s'appelle mon cousin

CHORUS: Got - ton vi - ton vi - tai - ne gen - ti - se Jean, pe - tit coq, o coq - o - no - vis

VERSE 2: Vint un hom - me à — ma por - te Qui s'ap - pel - le mon cou - sin

Et à cause du pa - ren - ta - ge Je l'fis en - trer au lo - gis

1 (Spoken) L'aut' jour un homme vint à ma porte
Qui s'appel-le mon cousin
Gotton viton vitai-ne genti-se
Jean, petit coq, o coq-o-no-vis

2 Vint un homme à ma por-te
Qui s'appel-le mon cousin
Et à cause du parenta-ge
Je l'fis entrer au logis

3 Et à cause du parenta-ge
Je l'fis entrer au logis
Je l'fis faire une couocha-de
Tout au pied de notre liet

4 Je l'fis faire une couocha-de
Tout au pied de notre liet
Mais pendant toute la nui-te
Ma femme n'y pouvait dormi

5 Mais pendant toute la nui-te
Ma femme n'y pouvait dormi
Elle s'y tourne et se retour-ne
Elle s'y glisse au pied du lit

6 Elle s'y tourne elle s'y tour-ne
Elle s'y glisse au pied du lit
Je la trouve dans la cave
Dans les bras d'mon p'tit cousin

7 Je la trouve dans la cave
Dans les bras de mon cousin
Je me suis 'crié-t-: Au diable
Quels parents j'avais, ceux-ci

1 (Spoken) One day a man came up to my door
Who called himself my cousin
Come on, get on, get along with your part
John, little lad, O light of my heart

2 Up to my door there came a man
Who called himself a cousin of mine
On account he was a relation of mine
Into the house I made him come

3 On account he was a relation of mine
Into the house I made him come
To sleep I made him lay his head
Down at the foot of our own bed

4 To sleep I made him lay his head
Down at the foot of our own bed
Throughout the length of the long night through
My wife she was so short of sleep

5 Throughout the length of the long night through
My wife she was so short of sleep
She tosses and turns and turns again
To the foot of the bed did quietly creep

6 She tosses and turns and turns again
To the foot of the bed did quietly creep
Down in the cellar I found her there
Wrapped in the arms of my cousin dear

7 Down in the cellar I found her there
Wrapped in the arms of my cousin dear
It's: Go to the devil, I did cry
What kind of relations are these of mine

105 JEAN, PETIT JEAN
JOHN, LITTLE JOHN

1 Jean, petit Jean, lui prit sa hache
O rou-pé-ta-fli-pé-ta-fli-pé-ta-flap
Jean, petit Jean, lui prit sa hache
Et s'en allait fagoter du bois
S'en allait fagoter du bois

2 Quand il revint 'vièrs les onze heures
Il trouva sa femme couochie

3 Il trouva sa femme couochie
Et un gros mâle entre ses bras

4 Jean, petit Jean, prit son souper
La chatte lui happait son lard

5 Là, si j'endgeule souvent la chatte
Je craindrais qu'elle me grimerait

1 John, little John, he took his axe
O rou-pé-ta-fli-pé-ta-fli-pé-ta-flap
John, little John, he took his axe
And off he went to bundle some wood
And off he went to bundle some wood

2 When he returned about eleven
He found his wife had gone to bed

3 He found his wife had gone to bed
In her arms a great big chap

4 John, little John, he took his tea
The cat she snatched his bacon away

5 There, if I scold the cat too free
Then I'm afraid she may scratch me

106 MA MERE M'ENVOIE-T-AU MARCHE
MY MOTHER SENDS ME TO MARKET

VERSE 2: Ma mère me ren-voie-t-au mar-ché Pour un coq a-che-ter

Mon coq dit: Ko-ro-ko-ko Et ma poule dit: Ki-ri-ki-ki Ki-ri-ki-ki, Ko-ro-ko-ko

Et ce n'est pas la peine d'al-ler au mar-ché, mes-da-mes Pour un coq a-che-ter

1 Ma mère m'envoie-t-au marché
Pour une poule acheter
Ma poule dit: *Kiri-ki-ki*
Ce n'est pas la peine d'aller au marché, mesdames
Pour une poule acheter

1 My mother sends me to market
In order to buy a hen
My hen says: *Chick-a-chick-chick*
Ladies, it's not worth going to market
In order to buy a hen

2 Ma mère me renvoie-t-au marché
Pour un coq acheter
Mon coq dit: *Koro-ko-ko*
Et ma poule dit: *Kiri-ki-ki*
Kiri-ki-ki, Koro-ko-ko
Et ce n'est pas la peine d'aller au marché, mesdames
Pour un coq acheter

2 My mother again sends me to market
In order to buy a cock
My cock says: *Cock-a-doodle-do*
And my hen says: *Chick-a-chick-chick*
Chick-a-chick-chick, Cock-a-doodle-do
Ladies, it's not worth going to market
In order to buy a cock

3 une cane
Couac-couac-couac

3 a duck
Quack-quack-quack

4 une dinde
Glou-glou-glouc

4 a turkey
Clu-clu-cluck

5 Ma mère me renvoie-t-au marché
Pour une âne acheter
Mon âne dit: *Hi-han*
Et ma dinde dit: *Glou-glou-glouc*
Et ma cane dit: *Couac-couac-couac*
Et mon coq dit: *Koro-ko-ko*
Et ma poule dit: *Kiri-ki-ki*
Kiri-ki-ki, Koro-ko-ko
Couac-couac-couac
Et *Glou-glou-glouc*
Et *Hi-han*
Et ce n'est pas la peine d'aller au marché, mesdames
Pour une âne acheter

5 My mother again sends me to market
In order to buy an ass
My ass says: *Hee-haw*
And my turkey says: *Clu-clu-cluck*
And my duck says: *Quack-quack-quack*
And my cock says: *Cock-a-doodle-do*
And my hen says: *Chick-a-chick-chick*
Chick-a-chick-chick, Cock-a-doodle-do
Quack-quack-quack
And *Clu-clu-cluck*
And *Hee-haw*
Ladies, it's not worth going to market
In order to buy an ass

107 MADELEINE
MADELEINE

1 En passant par chez nous
La belle zigue-zigue, la belle zigue-zon
En passant par chez nous
La belle zigue-zigue, la belle zigue-zon
N'oubliez pas Ma-de-leine
La bri-ga-don-dai-ne
N'oubliez pas Ma-de-lei-ne
Aux oiseaux, aux oiseaux

2 Il y a du pain, du vin chez nous
Et de l'eau à la fontai-ne

3 Madeleine est un beau nom
C'est la fille du capitai-ne

4 Dans le régiment, je sais
Est un officier qu'elle ai-me

5 Mais c'qui est encore plus beau
C'est le cœur de Madelei-ne

1 When passing by our home
O beautiful zinger-zinger, beautiful zinger-zong
When passing by our home
O beautiful zinger-zinger, beautiful zinger-zong
Do not forget our Ma-de-lei-ne
The brig-a-dier-a-dier
Do not forget our Ma-de-lei-ne
Fly a-way, fly a-way

2 There's bread and wine at home with us
And some water at the fountain there

3 Madeleine's a pretty name
She that is a captain's daughter

4 In the regiment well I know
It is an officer she loves

5 More than that and better still
It is the heart of Madeleine

108 MALBROUCK
MARLBOROUGH

1 Malbrouck s'en va-t-en dguèr-re
Mironton-mironton-mirontai-ne
Malbrouck s'en va-t-en dguèr-re
J'ne sais quand i' r'vi'ndra
J'ne sais quand i' r'vi'ndra
J'ne sais quand i' r'vi'ndra

2 Il reviendra-z-à Pâques
Ou à la Trinité

3 La Trinité se pas-se
Malbrouck ne revient pas

4 Madame à sa tour mon-te
Si haut qu'ell' peut monter

5 Elle aperçoit son pa-ge
Tout de noir habillé

6 Beau page, ah mon beau pa-ge
Quelles nouvelles apportez?

7 Aux nouvelles que j'appor-te
Vos beaux yeux vont pleurer

8 Quittez vos habits ro-ses
Et vos satins brochés

9 Monsieur Malbrouck est mor'-re
Est mort et enterré

10 J'l'ai vu porté en ter-re
Par quatre-z-officiers

11 L'un portait son grand cuiras-se
L'autre son bouclier

12 L'un portait son grand sab-re
L'aut-re ne portait rien

13 A l'entour de sa tom-be
Romarin l'on planta

14 Sur la plus hau-te bran-che
Le rossignol chanta

15 On vit voler son â-me
A travers des lauriers

16 Chacun mit ventre à ter-re
Et puis se releva

17 Pour chanter les victoi-res
Que Malbrouck rempor-ta

18 La cérémonie fai-te
Chacun s'en fus s'coucher

19 Je n'en dis pas davanta-ge
Car, en voilà assez

1 Marlborough he's gone to the war
Mironton-mironton-mirontai-ne
Marlborough he's gone to the war
I don't know when he'll be back
I don't know when he'll be back
I don't know when he'll be back

2 He will be back at Easter
Or else at Trinity

3 The Trinity's gone by now
Marlborough he's not come back

4 The lady climbs up to her tower
As high as she can go

5 There she sees her page-boy
And he's dressed all in black

6 Fine page, O my fine page-boy
What news have you brought to me?

7 The news that I have brought you
Your beautiful eyes will weep

8 Leave off your pinks in clothing
Your brocades of satin too

9 Mr Marlborough he is dead now
He's dead and in his tomb

10 I saw him laid in the ground
By four of the officers there

11 One of them carried his breast-plate
The other he carried his shield

12 One of them carried his long sword
The other one nothing at all

13 All around by his gravestone
They planted rosemary

14 Upon the uppermost branch
A nightingale he sang

15 One saw his soul fly away
And through the laurels pass

16 They all laid flat on the ground
And then got up again

17 To sing of all the victories
That Marlborough's carried away

18 The ceremony being over
They all went to their beds

19 I've not told you the best part
Because enough's been said

109 MARGUERITE
MARGUERITE

Mar-gue-rite se pro-mè-ne le long de son jar-din——

Le long de son jar-din sur le bord de l'î-le

Le long de son jar-din sur le bord de l'eau Sur le bord du vais-seau———-seau—

LAST TIME

1 Marguerite se promè-ne le long de son jardin
Le long de son jardin sur le bord de l'î-le
Le long de son jardin sur le bord de l'eau
Sur le bord du vaisseau

2 Elle aperçoit une bar-que de bien trente matelots
De bien trente matelots sur le bord de l'î-le
De bien trente matelots sur le bord de l'eau
Sur le bord du vaisseau

3 Le plus jeune des tren-te chantait-t-un-e chanson
Chantait-t-une chanson sur le bord de l'î-le
Chantait-t-une chanson sur le bord de l'eau
Sur le bord du vaisseau

4 La chanson que tu chan-tes j'aimerais bien la savoir
J'aimerais bien la savoir sur le bord de l'î-le
J'aimerais bien la savoir sur le bord de l'eau
Sur le bord du vaisseau

5 Embarquez dans ma bar-que, je vous l'apprendrerai
Je vous l'apprendrerai sur le bord de l'î-le
Je vous l'apprendrerai sur le bord de l'eau
Sur le bord du vaisseau

6 Quand elle fut dans la bar-que elle s'y mit à pleurer
Elle s'y mit à pleurer sur le bord de l'î-le
Elle s'y mit à pleurer sur le bord de l'eau
Sur le bord du vaisseau

7 N'y pleurez pas, ma bel-le, c'est de l'argent prêté
C'est de l'argent prêté sur le bord de l'î-le
C'est de l'argent prêté sur le bord de l'eau
Sur le bord du vaisseau

1 Marguerite she is walking along her garden side
Along her garden side on the island's shore
Along her garden side on the water's edge
By the side of the ship

2 There she beheld a vessel full thirty sailors aboard
Full thirty sailors on the island's shore
Full thirty sailors on the water's edge
By the side of the ship

3 The youngest of the thirty singing he was a song
Singing he was a song on the island's shore
Singing he was a song on the water's edge
By the side of the ship

4 The song that you are singing I'd like to know it well
I'd like to know it on the island's shore
I'd like to know it on the water's edge
By the side of the ship

5 Come on board my vessel, I will teach it you
I will teach it you on the island's shore
I will teach it you on the water's edge
By the side of the ship

6 Once on board the vessel she began to cry
She began to cry on the island's shore
She began to cry on the water's edge
By the side of the ship

7 Do not cry, my beauty, the money is only lent
The money is only lent on the island's shore
The money is only lent on the water's edge
By the side of the ship

110 MAN BOUONHOMME EST BEIN MALADE
MY OLD MAN IS VERY ILL

Man bouon-homme est bein ma - lade Je n'sai pon tchi dgiâbl' qu'il a

En grand dan - gi dé mouo - thi En grand dan - gi dé mouo - thi

J'l'ai - mais tant, man bouon - hom - me J'l'ai - mais tant, man mar - i

JERSEY VERSION

1 Man bouonhomme est bein malade
  Jé n'sai pon tchi dgiâbl' qu'il a
  En grand dangi dé mouothi
  En grand dangi dé mouothi
  J'l'aimais tant, man bouonhomme
  J'l'aimais tant, man mari

2 I'm'a d'mandé pouor du pain
  J'm'en fus don li'en cherchi
  À la carre dé nouot' armouaithe
  À un crôtîn d'pain mouaîsi

3 I'm'démandit pouor dé l'ieau
  J'm'en fus don li'en cherchi
  À la carre dé not' louogis
  À un canné d'ieau pouôrrie

4 I'm'démandit pouor d'la méd'cinne
  J'm'en fus don li'en cherchi
  Quand j'èrvîns dé la ville
  Man pouôrre bouonhomme 'tait pâssé

5 Quand j'vîns à vaie tch'est
  Qu'mes pathents avaient fait
  I'l'avaient mîns dans iun
  D'mes touos bouons lîncheurs
  Tout d'suite jé m'dêpêchis
  Et jé l'mîns dans iun d'mes pus vièrs

6 Quand j'l'eus bein èrpatchi dans l'lîncheu
  Jé l'mîns sus ma vielle chiviéthe
  Et j'men fus bein vite ava l'côti
  Et jé l'bîndis là ava

JERSEY VERSION

1 My old man is very ill
  I don't know what the devil's wrong
  I think that he will die
  I think that he will die
  I loved him so, my old man
  I loved him so, husband mine

2 For some bread he asked me for
  So I went and got him some
  From the corner of the chest
  From a crust of mouldy bread

3 He told me that he needed water
  So I went and got him some
  From the corner of our home
  From a brook with water rank

4 He asked me for some medicine
  So I went and got him some
  When I came back from the town
  My poor man was passed and gone

5 When I came to see what was
  That my parents they had done
  They had put him into one
  Of my very best of sheets
  Immediately I hurried then
  And put him in my older ones

6 When I'd well-wrapped him in the sheet
  I laid him on my old wheelbarrow
  Quickly I went down the slope
  And I slung him 'way down there

SARK VERSION overleaf ➔

MAN BOUONHOMME EST BEIN MALADE

SARK VERSION

1 Man mari est bein malade
  Et je n'sais pas qu'est-ce qu'il a

2 Je m'en fus-t-en Guer-ne-sie
  De Lundi au Mercredi

3 Mais quand j'ervins il 'tait mort
  Et encore ensev-eli

4 Je happis mes p'tites ciselettes
  Point à point je l'décousis

5 Mais quand j'appraichis p'tite gorgette
  Je craignais qui n'me mordisse

6 Je l'happis par le gros orté
  Je l'env'yis avaû l'côti

7 Je priyis tous les corbins
  De v'ni prier auprès d'li

SARK VERSION

1 Husband of mine he's very ill
  What can it be I do not know

2 I did go to Guern-e-sey
  Monday up till Wednesday

3 When I returned I found him dead
  And all ready to be laid

4 I took up my scissors small
  Step by step I stitched him all

5 When I reached the little throat
  I was scared he'd bite like a dog

6 By the big toe I took hold
  Down the side I threw him o'er

7 To all the crows I did cry
  That they'd come and pray nearby

111 MON PERE IL ME MARIE
MY FATHER HE MARRIED ME OFF

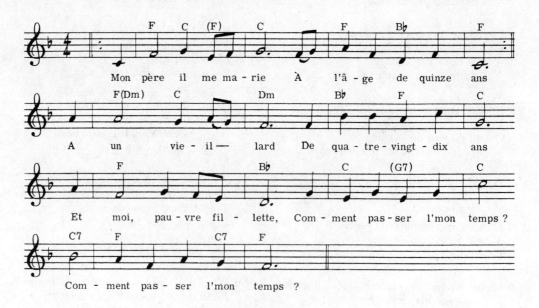

Mon père il me ma - rie À l'â - ge de quinze ans
A un vie - il — lard De qua - tre - vingt - dix ans
Et moi, pau - vre fil - lette, Com - ment pas - ser l'mon temps ?
Com - ment pas - ser l'mon temps ?

1 Mon père il me marie
  À l'âge de quinze ans
  Mon père il me marie
  À l'âge de quinze ans
  À un vieillard
  De quatre-vingt-dix ans
  Et moi, pauvre fillette
  Comment passer l'mon temps?
  Comment passer l'mon temps?

2 La première nuit d'mes noces
  Avec lui fallut coucher
  La première nuit d'mes noces
  Avec lui fallut coucher
  Il me tourna le dos
  Et se mit à ronfler
  Et moi pauvre fillette
  Comment passer l'mon temps?
  Comment passer l'mon temps?

3 Le lendemain d'mes noces
  Je suis chez mon père, je m'en vas
  Le lendemain d'mes noces
  Je suis chez mon père, je m'en vas
  Bonjour, chers père et mère
  Que l'beau jour vous y soit donné
  Vous m'avez donné un homme
  Qui n'y vaut rien du tout
  Qui n'y vaut rien du tout

4 Oh, tais-toi, belle fillette
  C'est un vieux riche marchand
  Oh, tais-toi, belle fillette
  C'est un vieux riche marchand
  On dit qu'il est malade
  Et l'on croit même qu'il en mourra
  C'est toi qui seras l'héritière
  De tout ce qu'il aura
  De tout ce qu'il aura

5 Au diable soient les richesses
  Si le plaisir n'y est pas
  Au diable soient les richesses
  Si le plaisir n'y est pas
  J'estime mieux les jeunes hommes
  À mon conten-te-ment
  Que ce vieux riche marchand
  Avec toutes ses richesses
  Avec toutes ses richesses

1 My father he married me off
  At the age of fifteen years
  My father he married me off
  At the age of fifteen years
  To an old man
  Of ninety years of age
  And me, poor lass am I
  How shall I spend my time?
  How shall I spend my time?

2 The first night I was wed
  With him I had to lie
  The first night I was wed
  With him I had to lie
  He turned his back to me
  And he began to snore
  And me poor lass am I
  How shall I spend my time?
  How shall I spend my time?

3 The day that followed that
  To my father I did go
  The day that followed that
  To my father I did go
  Good day to you, pa and ma
  I wish you a very fine day
  You've given to me a man
  Who is worth nothing at all
  Who is worth nothing at all

4 O quiet, my pretty lass
  He is an old merchant rich
  O quiet, my pretty lass
  He is an old merchant rich
  They say that he is ill
  And perhaps may even die
  It's you will be the heir
  Of all that he does own
  Of all that he does own

5 To the devil with all the riches
  If the pleasure is not there
  To the devil with all the riches
  If the pleasure is not there
  I much prefer young men
  For my own happiness
  Than this old merchant rich
  With all his riches great
  With all his riches great

112 MON PERE M'A DONNE-Z-UN MARI
MY FATHER A HUSBAND'S GIVEN ME

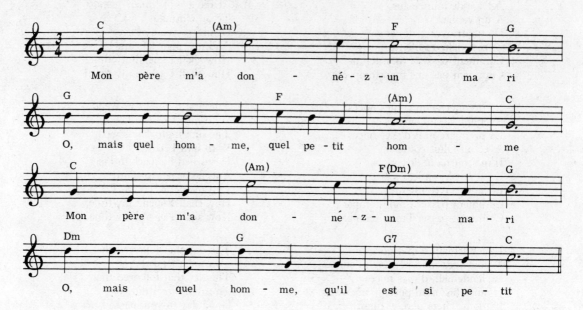

Mon père m'a don - né - z - un ma - ri

O, mais quel hom - me, quel pe - tit hom - me

Mon père m'a don - né - z - un ma - ri

O, mais quel hom - me, qu'il est si pe - tit

1 Mon père m'a donné-z-un mari
  O, mais quel hom-me, quel petit hom-me
  Mon père m'a donné-z-un mari
  O, mais quel hom-me, qu'il est si petit

2 La première nuit je couche après lui

3 Je l'ai perdu-e dans la paille

4 Je l'ai assis sur une assiette

5 Le chat l'a pris pour une souris

6 O chat, O chat, c'est mon mari

1 My father a husband's given me
  O what a fellow, what a small fellow
  My father a husband's given me
  O what a fellow, so little is he

2 The very first night I slept with him

3 I did mislay him in the bedding

4 I sat him down upon a platter

5 For a mouse the cat did mistake him

6 O cat, O cat, he is my husband

113 LE PETIT COUTURIER
THE LITTLE DRESSMAKER

C'é - tait un p'tit cou - tu - rier Lam - tid - lam - tid - lam - et - dée - dée

C'é - tait un p'tit cou - tu - rier Qui é - tait mu - ni d'ai - guil - les

1 C'était un p'tit couturier
Lam-tid-lam-tid-lam-et-dée-dée
C'était un p'tit couturier
Qui était muni d'aiguilles
Qui était muni d'aiguilles

2 S'en fut en hôtellerie
Pour y boire et y manger-e

3 Et dans cette hôtellerie-là
Y'avait deux jolies filles

4 La p'tite fille faisait d'l'amour
Et la grande hantait mari-e

5 Couche avec moi, p'tit couturier
Je t'y donnerai cent louis-e

6 Ah, vraiment non, j'n'y coucherai pas
Quand tu m'en donnerais mille

7 J'ai mon honneur à garder
Aussi bien que les filles

8 Sors d'ici, p'tit couturier
Sur le pavé de ville

9 Quand il fut sur le pavé
Il tremblait la guenille

10 Ah, si j'm'y revoyais en paix
Jamais ne réfuserais fille

11 Car elles m'ont trop bien joué
Avec toutes leurs aiguilles

1 It was a little dressmaker
Lam-tid-lam-tid-lam-et-dée-dée
It was a little dressmaker
Who was supplied with needles
Who was supplied with needles

2 To a tavern he did go
To have some food and drink there

3 And there were in this hotel
There were two lovely damsels

4 The smallest girl she did make love
And the largest to look for a husband

5 Sleep with me, little dressmaker
I'll give you a hundred sovereigns

6 Ah, truly no I won't do so
Even if you gave a thousand

7 I have my honour for to keep
As well as that of the damsels

8 Get out of here, little dressmaker
For you the streets of the town

9 Once he was out on the street
His knees began to tremble

10 Ah, if I were back at peace
I ne'er would refuse a damsel

11 But they have tricked me very much
With all their pointed needles

114 LE PETIT NAVIRE
THE LITTLE CORVETTE

C'é - tait un pe - pe - tit na - vi - re C'é-tait un pe - pe - tit na - vi - re

Qui n'a - vait ja - ja - ja-mais na - vi - gué

Qui n'a - vait ja - ja - ja-mais na-vi-gué Ah oui, ah oui

CH: Si la pi - quette est bon - ne et en y bu - vant tou - jours

C'est le rév - eil à traî - ner ra - vi en nos a - mours —

Les ma - te - lots pon - pon - pon-pon, la belle Eu-gé-nie pon - pon

Sont em - bras - sés, sont em - bras - sés: Nos ri - ches cou - leurs —

Bra-con-nier — p'tit meu - nier, — pous-sons-nous car-ré-ment de la terre —

Car-ré - ment, dé - lié - ment, pous - sons-nous de l'agré - ment

Pous-sa - sons-nous glac-glac, glac-glac Pous-sons-nous de l'agré - ment

1 C'était un pe-pe-tit navi-re
C'était un pe-pe-tit navi-re
Qui n'avait ja-ja-jamais navigué
Qui n'avait ja-ja-jamais navigué
Ah oui, ah oui
Si la piquette est bon-ne et en y buvant toujours
C'est le réveil à traîner ravi en nos amours
Les matelots pon-pon-pon-pon, la belle Eugénie pon-pon
Sont embrassés, sont embrassés : Nos riches couleurs
Braconnier, p'tit meunier, poussons-nous carrément de la terre
Carrément, déliément poussons-nous de l'agrément
Poussa-sons-nous glac-glac, glac-glac
Poussons-nous de l'agrément

2 Au bout de cinq à six semaines
Les vivres vinrent, vinrent, vinrent-t-à manquer
Ah oui, ah oui

3 On tira à la courte paille-e
Pour savoir qui, qui, tchi sera mangé
Ah oui, ah, oui

*

1 It was a lit-little corvette
It was a lit-little corvette
That never ne-ne-never sailed away
That never ne-ne-never sailed away
Ah yes, ah yes
If that the wine be good and plenty of drinking time
It's in the morning lingers enraptured with our love
The sailors go : pom-pom, pom-pom, lovely Eugénie pom-pom
Hugging they are, they are : Our colours fine
Poacher lad, miller small, push ourselves steadily from the land
Steady there, quickly now, push ourselves out in all truth
Let's push ourselves out : glac-glac, glac-glac
Push ourselves out with one accord

2 When five or six weeks they had ended
The victuals came, came, came very scarce
Ah yes, ah yes

3 Men with short straws they did draw lots
To know just who, who, who'd be eaten
Ah yes, ah yes

115 SI J'AVAIS LES SOULIERS
IF ONLY I'D THE SHOES

1 O, si j'avais les souliers que Maman m'avait don-nés
O, si j'avais les souliers que Maman m'avait don-nés
Mes souliers sont de cuir doux
O, radieux donc, ma mignon-ne
Mes souliers sont de cuir doux
Radieux donc mes amours

2 O, si j'avais les belles bliouques que Maman m'avait
données
O, si j'avais les belles bliouques que Maman m'avait
données
Mes belles bliouques sont d'argent fin
O, radieux donc, ma mignon-ne
Mes belles bliouques sont d'argent fin
Et mes souliers sont de cuir doux
Radieux donc mes amours

3 les bels bas
Mes bels bas sont de soie bleue

4 les jarretières
Mes jarretières sont tout entières

5 les tchulottes
Mes tchulottes vont de botte en botte

6 la chemise
Ma chemise est toil-e fine

7 le gilet
Mon gilet est si bien fait

8 la cravate
Ma cravate est zic et zac

1 O, if only I'd the shoes that Mama had given me
O, if only I'd the shoes that Mama had given me
My new shoes of softest hide
O how smart, my sweetheart
My new shoes of softest hide
How smart I'm now, O my loves

2 O, if only I'd the fine buckles that Mama had given
me
O, if only I'd the fine buckles that Mama had given
me
My fine buckles shining bright
O how smart, my sweetheart
My fine buckles shining bright
And my new shoes of softest hide
How smart I'm now, O my loves

3 fine long hose
My fine long hose of bluest silk

4 knee-garters
My knee-garters all complete

5 pant'loons
My pant'loons stretch from toe to toe

6 chemise
My chemise of finest lawn

7 waistcoat
My waistcoat that's so well cut

8 cravat
My cravat is zig-a-zag

9 O, si j'avais la casquette que Maman m'avait donnée
   O, si j'avais la casquette que Maman m'avait donnée
   Ma casquette est ric et rac
   Et ma cravate est zic et zac
   Mon gilet est si bien fait
   Et ma chemise est toile fine
   Mes tchulottes vont de botte en botte
   Et mes jarretières sont tout entières
   Mes bels bas sont de soie bleue
   Et mes belles bliouques sont d'argent fin
   Mes souliers sont de cuir doux
   O radieux donc, ma mignon-ne
   Mes souliers sont de cuir doux
   Radieux donc mes amours

9 O, if only I'd the tip-top that Mama had given me
   O, if only I'd the tip-top that Mama had given me
   My tip-top is all skew-whiff
   And my cravat is zig-a-zag
   My waistcoat that's so well cut
   And my chemise of finest lawn
   My pant'loons stretch from toe to toe
   And my knee-garters all complete
   My fine long hose of bluest silk
   And my fine buckles shining bright
   My new shoes of softest hide
   O how smart, my sweetheart
   My new shoes of softest hide
   How smart I'm now, O my loves

116 LES TROIS DEMOISELLES ET LE CORDONNIER
THE THREE DAMSELS AND THE COBBLER

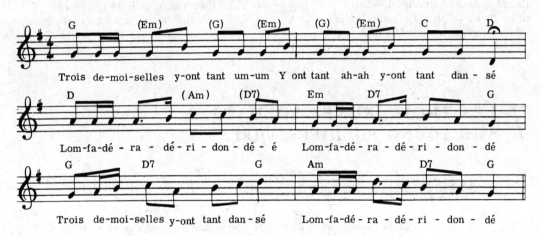

Trois de-moi-selles y-ont tant um-um Y ont tant ah-ah y-ont tant dan-sé
Lom-fa-dé-ra-dé-ri-don-dé-é Lom-fa-dé-ra-dé-ri-don-dé
Trois de-moi-selles y-ont tant dan-sé Lom-fa-dé-ra-dé-ri-don-dé

1 Trois demoiselles y-ont tant um-um
   Y-ont tant ah-ah y-ont tant dansé
   Lom-fa-dé-ra-dé-ri-don-dé-é
   Lom-fa-dé-ra-dé-ri-don-dé
   Trois demoiselles y-ont tant dansé
   Lom-fa-dé-ra-dé-ri-don-dé

1 There were three damsels so um-um
   So ah-ah and they danced so much
   Lom-fa-dé-ra-dé-ri-don-dé
   Lom-fa-dé-ra-dé-ri-don-dé
   There were three damsels danced so much
   Lom-fa-dé-ra-dé-ri-don-dé

2 Elles ont dépensé leurs um-um
   Et leurs ah-ah et leurs souliers
   Elles ont dépensé leurs souliers

2 They soon wore out their dance um-um
   And their dance ah-ah and their dancing shoes
   They soon wore out their dancing shoes

3 Elles ont été chez le cor um-um
   Et le cor ah-ah et le cordonnier
   Elles ont été chez le cordonnier

3 Then they went to the cobb-um-um
   And the cobb-ah-ah and the cobb-e-ler
   Then they went to the cobb-e-ler

4 Pouvez-vous nous fair-e des um-um
   Et des ah-ah et des souliers?
   Pouvez-vous nous faire des souliers?

4 Can you make for us these um-um
   And these ah-ah and these dance-shoes?
   Can you make for us these dancing shoes? →

273

5 Ah, vraiment oui, si vous um-um
  Et si vous ah-ah et si vous l'voulez
  Ah, vraiment oui, si vous l'voulez

5 Indeed, ah yes, if you um-um
  And if you ah-ah and if you do wish
  Indeed, ah yes, if you do wish

6 Combien nous ferez-vous um-um
  Ferez-vous ah-ah ferez-vous payer?
  Combien nous ferez-vous payer?

6 How much shall we need um-um
  And we need ah-ah and we need to pay to you?
  How much shall we need to pay to you?

7 À chaque point-z-un doux um-um
  Et un doux ah-ah et un doux baiser
  À chaque point-z-un doux baiser

7 For every stitch a sweet um-um
  And a sweet ah-ah and a sweet kiss I'll need
  For every stitch a sweet kiss I'll need

8 Ah, je n'aime point ces cor um-um
  Et ces cor ah-ah et ces cordonniers
  Ah, je n'aime point ces cordonniers

8 Ah, I don't much like these cobb-um-um
  And these cobb-ah-ah and these cobb-e-lers
  Ah, I don't much like these cobb-e-lers

9 Ils ont toujours les braies um-um
  Et les braies ah-ah et les braies brâlées
  Ils ont toujours les braies brâlées

9 They always have such stick-um-um
  And such stick-ah-ah and such sticky breeches
  They always have such sticky breeches

117 LES TROIS JEUNES SOLDATS
THE YOUNG SOLDIERS THREE

1 Trois jeunes soldats revenant de guerre
  Trois jeunes soldats revenant de guerre
  Bien habil'-yés, très mal chaussés
  Sans savoir où aller loger

1 Young soldiers three coming back from war
  Young soldiers three coming back from war
  They were well dressed but badly shod
  Not knowing where they could put up

2 Ils se trouvaient chez une jeune hôtesse
  Ils se trouvaient chez une jeune hôtesse
  Hôtesse, avez-vous du vin blanc?
  Ah oui, soldats, pour de l'argent

3 Pour de l'argent nous n'en avons pa'e
  Pour de l'argent nous n'en avons pa'e
  Nous vous donnerons nos vêtements
  Notre équipage et nos chevaux

4 Les trois soldats se mirent-t-en tab-le
  Les trois soldats se mirent-t-en tab-le
  À rire, à boire et à manger
  La jeune hôtesse à soupirer

5 Qu'avez-vous don' notre belle hôtesse?
  Qu'avez-vous don' notre belle hôtesse?
  Qu'avez-vous don' chère jeune hôtesse
  À soupirer tant de douleur?

6 Il y a sept ans, mon mari est en guerre
  Il y a sept ans, mon mari est en guerre
  Oui, il y a sept ans qu'il est parti
  Et je crois bien qu'c'est ici lui

7 J'avais reçu de fausses lettres
  J'avais reçu de fausses lettres
  Qu'il était mort et enterré
  Et, moi, je me suis r'mariée

8 Oh, qu'as-tu don' fait, méchante femme?
  Qu'as-tu don' fait, méchante femme?
  Je n't'avais l'ssi que deux enfants
  Et maintenant y'en voilà quatre

9 Si j'y conn'issais le père
  Ah, si j'y conn'issais le père
  Je tuerais père, mère et enfants
  Et au bataillon je m'en r'tour'ais

10 J'attends le temps pour qu'ils m'appellent
   J'attends le temps pour qu'ils m'appellent
   Adieu, ma belle, et mes enfants
   Je vais rejoindre mon régiment

2 They were at the inn of a hostess young
  They were at the inn of a hostess young
  Hostess young, have you white wine?
  Ah, soldiers, yes, if money you have

3 As for money we have not any
  As for money we have not any
  We'll give to you our soldiers' clothes
  Equipment and our horses too

4 The soldiers three sat down to table
  The soldiers three sat down to table
  They laughed, they drank and they did eat
  The hostess young how she did sigh

5 What have you then our lovely hostess?
  What have you then our lovely hostess?
  What have you then dear hostess young
  That you do sigh with so much grief?

6 It's seven years my husband's at war
  It's seven years my husband's at war
  Yes, seven years since he went away
  And I believe that here he is

7 I have received some letters falsely
  I have received some letters falsely
  That he was dead and had been buried
  And, as for me, I have re-married

8 O what have you done, you wicked woman?
  O what have you done, you wicked woman?
  I left you only children two
  And now I see that there are four

9 If I could know who was their father
  If I could know who was their father
  I'd father, mother, children kill
  And I'd return to the battalion

10 I'll wait my time for them to call me
   I'll wait my time for them to call me
   Farewell, my dear, and my children too
   I'm going to rejoin my regiment

118 LES TROIS JEUNES TAMBOURS
THE YOUNG DRUMMERS THREE

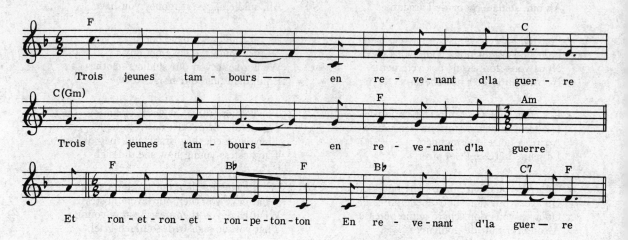

1 Trois jeunes tambours en revenant d'la guer-re

Trois jeunes tambours en revenant d'la guerre

Et ron-et-ron-et-ron-pe-ton-ton
En revenant de la guerre

2 Le plus jeune des trois à sa bouche une ro-se

3 La fille du roi étant à sa fenê-tre

4 Joli tambour, veux-tu m'donner ta ro-se?

5 Ah, vraiment non, tu n'es pas assez ri-che

6 J'ai trois vaisseaux qui flottent sur les eaux-e

7 Un chargé d'or et l'autre d'argenteri-e

8 Et le troisième pour y prom'ner ma mi-e

9 Joli tambour, tu peux avoir ma ro-se

10 Ah, vraiment oui, je vous en remerci-e

11 Car par chez nous y'en a d'aussi joli-es

1 Young drummers three they're coming back from war

Young drummers three they're coming back from war

Ta-rum-ta-rum-ta-rum-pe-ti-tum
Coming back from war

2 Youngest of the three had in his mouth a flower

3 The daughter of the king was watching at her window

4 Handsome drummer boy, would'st give to me your flower?

5 Ah, no, indeed, you're not rich enough

6 Three ships have I, a-sailing on the water

7 One filled with gold, the other filled with silver

8 As for the third, she'll carry off my own one

9 Handsome drummer boy, you can enjoy my flower

10 How kind indeed, I'll thank you for your offer

11 All around my home, there's some there just as lovely

19 VER-DU-RON, VER-DU-RO-NET'-O
VER-DU-RON, VER-DU-RO-NET'-O

Ver-du - ron, ver-du -ro -net'- o   Ver-du - ron, don - don

Que fais-tu là, la Bel - le? Pê - chez-vous du pois - son?

Ver-du-ron, ver-du-ro-net'-o
Ver-du-ron, don-don

1 Que fais-tu là, la Bell-e?
  Pêchez-vous du poisson?
  Chorus

2 Ah non, dit-elle, la Bell-e
  Je suis tombée dans l'fond

3 Que donnerez-vous, la Bell-e?
  Nous vous retirerons

4 Je n'suis qu'une simple fill-e
  Je n'ai rien-z-à donner

5 Qu'un baiser sur ma bouche
  Ou deux s'il vous en plaît

6 Quand la belle fut tirée
  Elle court pour la maison

7 Mit la tête à la fenêtre
  Chantant-z-un-e chanson

Ver-du-ron, ver-du-ro-net'-o
Ver-du-ron, don-don

1 What are you doing there, beauty?
  Catching yourself some fish?
  Chorus

2 Ah no, says she, the beauty
  I have tumbled to the bottom

3 What will you give us, beauty
  If we come and pull you out?

4 I am just a simple maiden
  I have nothing I can give

5 Only a kiss upon my mouth
  Or two for you, if it pleases

6 When the beauty was pulled out
  She did run towards the house

7 Through the window put her head
  And this the song she sang them

120 LE VINGT-CINQUIEME DU MOIS D'OCTOBRE
THE TWENTY-FIFTH OF OCTOBER

1 Le vingt-cinquième du mois d'Octob'e
  Le vingt-cinquième du mois d'Octob-re
  Pour Gilbatare j'allons partir-e
  Par quatre-vingt navires de guer-re
  Par quatre-vingt navires de guerre

2 Ah, quand on vint d'un peu-s-au large
  Ah, quand on vint d'un peu-s-au lar-ge
  On s'aperçut d'un grand navi-re
  Faisant sur nous en grande furi-e
  Faisant sur nous en grande furie

3 Il a tiré trois coups de canon
  Il a tiré trois coups de cano-ne
  Le premier coup qu'il a tiré-e
  Ils ont tiré sur notre arriè-re
  Ils ont tiré sur notre arrière

4 Le deuxièmc coup qu'ils ont tiré
  Le deuxième coup qu'ils ont tiré-e
  Ils ont tiré sur not' grand mât
  Sans jamais aucun mal nous fai-re
  Sans jamais aucun mal nous faire

1 The twenty-fifth of the October month
  The twenty-fifth of the October month
  For Gibraltar we set sail
  With eighty ships all men-of-war
  With eighty ships all men-of-war

2 And when we'd sailed a little way out
  And when we'd sailed a little way out
  We sighted there a very large ship
  Bearing down upon us with fury great
  Bearing down upon us with fury great

3 She fired at us three shots of cannon
  She fired at us three shots of cannon
  The very first shot that she did fire
  They caught us on our quarters aft
  They caught us on our quarters aft

4 The second shot that they fired upon us
  The second shot that they fired upon us
  They fired upon our mainmast tall
  But no harm on us befell
  But no harm on us befell

5 Le troisième coup qu'ils ont tiré
 Le troisième coup qu'ils ont tiré-e
 Le capitaine s'est écrié-e
 Y-a-t-il quelqu'un d'nos hommes blessé-e?
 Y-a-t-il quelqu'un d'nos hommes blessé?

6 Ah oui, ah oui, cher capitaine
 Ah oui, ah oui, cher capitai-ne
 Il y a là-bas le cont'e-maîtr-e
 Ah, cont'e-maître, ah mon grand ami-e
 Ah, cont'e-maître, ah mon grand ami

7 N'as-tu pas le regret d'mourir?
 N'as-tu pas le regret d'mouri-re?
 Tout le regret que j'ai't'au monde
 C'est de quitter ma chère blond-e
 C'est de quitter ma chère blonde

8 Ta chère blonde, j'envierai à la chercher
 Ta chère blonde, j'envierai à la chercher-e
 Par quatre soldats de la Marine
 Qui s'en vont sur la mer jolie-e
 Qui s'en vont sur la mer jolie

5 The third shot that they fired upon us
 The third shot that they fired upon us
 The captain he did call out and asked
 Have any of our men been wounded?
 Have any of our men been wounded?

6 Ah yes, ah yes, dear cap-i-tain
 Ah yes, ah yes, dear cap-i-tain
 Down there there is the bosun's mate
 Ah bosun's mate, ah, my good friend
 Ah, bosun's mate, ah, my good friend

7 Do you not sorrow that you're dying?
 Do you not sorrow that you're dying?
 All the sorrow I have in the world
 To leave my dearest fair one behind
 To leave my dearest fair one behind

8 Your dearest fair one, I'll send for her
 Your dearest fair one, I'll send for her
 It's by four soldiers of the Marines
 For they are sailing on the lovely sea
 For they are sailing on the lovely sea

97 AU BORD D'UNE FONTAINE
'TWAS THERE BESIDE A FOUNTAIN

John Gallienne, Torteval, Guernsey, *rec.* P. Kennedy,
1957: BBC 23844
Other recorded version
Jack Hacquoil, La Botellerie, St Ouen, Jersey, *rec.* P.
Kennedy, 1960: 'En revenant des noces', BBC 26235

Printed versions
MacCulloch: 1903: *coll.* Edith Carey (Guernsey)
Doncieux/Tiersot: 1904, p. 467. Comparative study of
this song

Compare
Leclerc/Lefebvre: *c.* 1930, p. 28
MATP: 50.8.15; 53.1.46/47

It's a chap who was coming back from a wedding one night. He couldn't go home, so he had a good rest by a fountain by a stream and in the morning he wake up and wipe the eyes; he was full, you know, by having been on the booze, we'll say, the night before.

He had a good wash by the stream and he rubbed himself with leaves, instead of taking linen, and there was a bird on the top of the tree who was always whistling.—John Gallienne.

We find here the classic French song generally entitled *A la claire fontaine* (The clear fountain) or *En revenant des noces* (Returning from the wedding). It was published in *Brunettes et petits airs tendres* by Christophe Ballard in 1704, but in the tradition of the French countryside it is sung to a much older trumpet tune. This musical style, heroic in feeling, is also found in well-known versions of this song in French-speaking Canada and numerous traditional versions exist in France, especially in the West and in Normandy, and the song has been the subject of a thorough study (Doncieux/Tiersot: 1904).

It is interesting to compare our version with two Norman versions. One collected in 1950 in the Orne at Tinchebray by C. Marcel-Dubois and M. Andral (MATP: 50.8.15) and the other at Beaumont-Hague (La Manche) by the Ethnology Laboratory of Caen at about the same period (MATP: 53.1.46 and 47). The musical and literary parallels with the Guernsey version can be discerned here, but the refrain of the latter version seems to be peculiar to the Channel Islands. This probably originates from a combination with the refrain of a marching song from Lower Berry: *Derrière chez mon père y'a-t-un beau moulin* (Behind my father's house there is a fine windmill), with the refrain 'Les godillots sont lourds dans le sac, les godillots sont lourds' (Barbillat/Touraine: 1931, vol. 4, p. 96.) However, we know that French songs during their migration or their evolution have very often changed and the refrains have become accidentally adapted. An example of this occurs in the version of the song from Upper Normandy which has this kind of adapted refrain with meaningless words (Leclerc/Lefebvre: 1930, p. 28).

John Gallienne, when he recorded our Guernsey version, nearly always sang the chorus twice. At first it seemed that he was singing 'les cotillons' (petticoats) in the chorus but as he continued it was difficult to detect whether or not he was singing 'les godillots' as in the Lower Berry version.* In any case he did not know the meaning of the word but simply tried to sing it the way he had heard it.

Further verses of the song, noted in Guernsey, were gathered by Edith Carey:

6   Le mien n'est pas de même   Mine is not the same
    Il est bien affligé   He is greatly grieved

7   Pierre, mon ami, Pierre   Peter, my friend, Peter
    A la guerre est allé   To the war has gone

8   Pour un bouton de rose   For a rose-bud
    Que je lui refusai   Which I refused of him

9   Je voudrais que la rose   I wish that the rose
    Fut encore au rosier   Were still on the tree

10   Et que mon ami Pierre   And my friend Peter
    Fut ici à m'aimer   Was here to love me

In Jersey we recorded another version of the song, entitled *En revenant des noces*. It was sung by Jack Hacquoil:

1   En revenant des noces   On returning from the wedding
    Je me suis reposé   I took a rest
    Qu'elle était si belle   She was so lovely
    Que je me suis baigné   That I did bathe
      Oui, je l'attends, je l'attends, je l'attends   Yes, I will wait, I will wait, I will wait
      Que mon coeur aime   One my heart likes
      Oui, je l'attends, je l'attends, je l'attends   Yes, I will wait, I will wait, I will wait
      Celle que mon coeur aime tant   One my heart likes so much

* According to Rousseau, 'godillots' is an old word for hob-nailed boots. It is a word still known in modern French.

98 AU LOGIS DE MON PERE
'TWAS AT MY FATHER'S HOUSE

Adolphus Le Ruez, Bonne Nuit, Jersey, *rec.* P. Kennedy,
1957: BBC 23841

Printed versions
MILLIEN: 1910, vol. II, p. 8: *Le Pommier doux*
MARCEL-DUBOIS collection, 1940 (Les Mauges version)
CANTELOUBE: 1951, vol. I, p. 343

Compare
BOURGEOIS: 1931, p. 26: *Auprès de ma blonde* (Poitou, Vendée)
D'INDY AND TIERSOT: 1890, vol. I, p. 134: *Au Jardin de mon père* (Languedoc, Ardèche)

> It was in a war, you see, and these girls had sheltered under an apple tree, and the youngest said to her sister in the early morning: 'Sister it's getting daylight,' and the other sister says: 'It's the fire from the armies and it's our lovers that are fighting for us.'—ADOLPHUS LE RUEZ.

This song belongs to the same family as *Au Pommier doux* (The sweet apple-tree) which is one of the great songs of the Romance period of France, with its origin probably going back to the twelfth century. It is well known in French-Canada where there are more than twenty versions and it has also been noted in High Brittany. It is still well known in Normandy, the country of the apple trees. Indeed it is pretty widely scattered, being known in the north and east of France, in the Ardennes, Champagne and in Burgundy and also in the Nivernais (MILLIEN: 1908, vol. II, p. 8) which would indicate other links with the Anglo-Norman repertoire (see No. 115). It was also still sung until recently in Les Mauges in Anjou and in the province of La Vendée (Marcel-Dubois collection, 1940).

99 BELLE ROSE
LOVELY ROSIE

Adolphus Le Ruez, Bonne Nuit, Jersey, *rec.* P. Kennedy,
1957: BBC 23840
Other recorded version
George Le Feuvre, St Ouen, Jersey, *rec.* P. Kennedy,
1960: BBC 26235

Printed version
CAREY: 1908, p. 14: *Belle Rose au rosier b'ianc* (eleven verses) (Jersey)

Compare
MADELAINE: 1907, p. 359: *Une Bocaine trop confiante*
DUCHON: 1926: *J'ai cueilli la blanche rose*
MORAND: 1936, p. 27: *Ronde de la Rose*
MATP: 1950, 50.8.18 (Marcel-Dubois/Andral collection)

Verses 1–5 were sung by Adolphus Le Ruez and verses 6–7 were added, to a slight variation of the tune, by George Le Feuvre. Verse 2 refers to two of the parishes in Jersey. Further verses collected by Edith Carey:

6	Hélas comment me marirai-je,	Alas how will I marry
	Moi qui suis baisse pour un an?	I who am a servant for a year?
7	Combien gagnez-vous, ma belle	How much do you earn, my lovely
	Combien gagnez-vous par an?	How much do you earn a year?
8	Je gagne bien cent pistoles,	I earn 100 coins
	Cent pistoles en argent blanc	100 coins in white silver
9	Venez avec moi, ma belle,	Come with me, my lovely,
	Vous en aurez bien autant	You will have as many
10	Je ne vais avec personne	I am not going with anyone
	Si l'on ne m'épouse avant	If he does not marry me before
11	Si l'on ne me mène à l'église	If I am not taken to the Church
	Par devant tous mes parents	In the presence of all my relatives

Belle Rose should be compared with two songs from Lower Normandy, one, *Là-Haut sur la montagne*, collected in the region of Argentan by C. Marcel-Dubois and M. Andral in 1950 (MATP: 50.8.18), the other, in old Norman, *Une Bocaine trop confiante* noted as being from the Bocage (MADELAINE: 1907, p. 359). In effect, we seem to be concerned with a comparison between the two songs: the same literary theme and musical analogies occur in the first and the same theme of the nightingale as a messenger of love in the second. The same subject and musical style are also to be found in a Round from Ille et Vilaine called *Ronde de la Rose* in which the last verse of each couplet is 'Belle Rose, belle rose du printemps' (MORAND: 1936, p. 27) and they occur also in a Bourbon song written down at Arfeuilles (Allier) by P. Duchon about 1925, where repeated lines in each couplet are '. . . Belle rose et rose et blanc, belle rose . . . belle rose du printemps'.

100 BITCHON-BITCHETTE
BITCHON-BITCHETTE

Adolphus Le Ruez, Bonne Nuit, Jersey, *rec.* P. Kennedy,
1957: BBC 23841
Printed versions
BUJEAUD: 1895, vol. 3, p. 46; *Ah! Tu sortiras, Biquette*
(no music)

DELARUE: 1934–47, vol. 3, p. 56: *Biquette ne veut pas
sortir du chou*

BARBEAU: 1962, p. 167: *Biquette* (Canada)
Compare
MATP: 1950 53.1.7 (Argentan), coll. Marcel-Dubois/
  Andral
CAEN ETHNOLOGY LABORATORY: 1952

It was a nanny-goat that had strayed in the cabbages, you see, and this man said to the nanny-goat: I'll
soon clear you out from there. But the nanny-goat, she was called Bitchon Bitchette, she refused to move.
Then he said: Well then, I'm going to get the wolf to eat you. When he came to the wolf the wolf wouldn't
eat it. Then he said: I'll get the dog to bite the wolf but the dog wouldn't bite the wolf, so then he got a stick
to beat the dog but the stick wouldn't beat the dog. Then he summoned the fire to burn the stick, but the fire
wouldn't burn the stick either. Then eventually he got some water to put out the fire, but the water wouldn't
put out the fire. Then after that, he said: I'll get a calf to drink you, but the calf wouldn't drink the water.
So then after that he summoned the butcher and asked the butcher to kill the calf.

Well the butcher agreed to kill the calf, and the calf drank the water, the water put out the fire, the fire
burned the stick, the stick beat the dog, the dog bit the wolf and the wolf chased Bitchon Bitchette out of
the cabbages.—ADOLPHUS LE RUEZ.

This is certainly a Norman-French dialect version of the repetitive song well known to all French children *Biquette
ne veut pas sortir du chou* (The little goat does not want to come out of the cabbage patch), a children's marching song
found in rural France, particularly in the Nivernais. In fact it is found practically all over France. For example there
is the often quoted Languedoc version *La chanson de Bricou*. The way the song repeats and builds up extends beyond
Europe. One can also compare it with the English nursery rhyme *The Old Woman and the Pig* and *The House that
Jack Built*. See also *Si j'avais les souliers* (No. 115).

With its subject, the story of a goat, this piece can also be compared with a Norman song collected in 1950 in the
region of Argentan by C. Marcel-Dubois and M. Andral and also in 1952 by the Ethnographic Laboratory of Caen in
the region of Alençon (MATP: 53.1.7).

101 LE BON MARAIN
THE FINE SEAMAN

John Gallienne, Torteval, Guernsey, *rec.* P. Kennedy,
1957: BBC 23844
Other recorded version
Sark male chorus acc. accordion, *rec.* 1938: BBC 1835

Printed version
MORAND: 1936, p. 24: *C'était un jeune marin*

It's a sailor, you know, who'd been in a warship into the war. He had a girl, you know, and she died—she got
buried and he didn't know—that's what it is.—JOHN GALLIENNE.

Sometimes John Gallienne sang the last two lines twice as a chorus.

A version of the song was collected by Simone Morand about 1930 in the canton of Hédé, about 40 km south of
St Malo, and it was thought to be typical of that particular region.

In the Channel Islands the song was still sung in Jersey up to about 1914 and in Sark up to about 1957.

102   LA FILLE DE L'AVOCAT
THE LAWYER'S DAUGHTER

John Gallienne, Torteval, Guernsey, *rec.* P. Kennedy,
1957: BBC 23844

Printed versions
DONCIEUX/TIERSOT: 1904, p. 259, no. 19
YOUNG: 1956 (Canada)

The history of this romantic song has been studied by Doncieux and goes back to the sixteenth century. Originally it was thought that it originated in Artois but local variants have been noted elsewhere, for example in Gascony.

The more commonly used title for the classic romance is *La fille aux oranges* (The orange girl) and in that it is the son, not the daughter, of the lawyer who is the hero of the story and seduces Marguerite.

A French-Canadian version, with a similar tune to the Guernsey variant, has been collected at L'Islet in Quebec province.

103   J'AI PERDU MA FEMME
I DID LOSE MY WIFE

Ernest Sauvage (of Jersey), *rec.* P. Kennedy in Guernsey,
1957: BBC 23838
Other recorded versions
Jack Le Feuvre, Sark, *rec.* P. Kennedy, 1957
Also *rec.* Sark, 1938: BBC 1834

> She got hidden under the cabbages, I couldn't find her. She went under with another chap and after a certain
> time he brought her back and I said to him: Keep her for yourself, I've got one, better than I had before!—
> JACK LE FEUVRE.

A drinking song with saucy undertones in the ancient tradition which seems to belong only to the Channel Islands. In each Island it is sung with local dialect words, but generally there is little variation of words or tune. The allusion to kale or cabbage-growing is characteristic of the agricultural tradition of the Channel Islands.

104   JEAN, PETIT COQ
JOHN, LITTLE LAD

Adolphus Le Ruez, Bonne Nuit, Jersey, *rec.* P. Kennedy,
1957: BBC 23841

Printed version
ROLLAND: 1883, vol. 1, p. 70: *Le Mari Bénit* (1724)

Known in all the Channel Islands, with local variations in the verses, *Jean, Petit Coq* is still popular with the older folk in some parts of Normandy. At one time it was probably sung only in French but over the years it has developed with a mixture of French and Norman French.

In the course of time, the refrain has probably lost the original meaning. The first word, for example, was used as a pet name for 'Marguerite'. Adolphus Le Ruez pronounces the last word of the first line as 'Gentille'.

The first half of the song is given in the past tense and the last half in the present. Note also in the fourth verse the unusual use of 'n'y' for 'ne', and in the fifth and sixth verses 's'y' for 'se'.

105 JEAN, PETIT JEAN
JOHN, LITTLE JOHN

George Le Moigne, Guernsey, *rec.* P. Kennedy, 1957:
BBC 23839

Printed version
UDRY: 1930, p. 201: *V'là p'tit Jean qui prend sa serpe*

A Norman-French version of the song is quoted in French collections as originating from the Seine estuary. A similar 14-stanza version (UDRY: 1930) seems to go back to the middle of the nineteenth century. This version contains a number of words in local dialect.

106 MA MERE M'ENVOIE-T-AU MARCHE
MY MOTHER SENDS ME TO MARKET

Adolphus Le Ruez, Bonne Nuit, Jersey, *rec.* P. Kennedy,
1957: BBC 23840
Printed versions
ARNAUDIN: 1912, p. 179

CANTELOUBE: 1951, vol. II, p. 392
YOUNG: 1956, p. 96: *En allant au marché* (Canada)

This song, reminiscent of *The Farmyard Song*, is known in all the Channel Islands and is still popular in Normandy and elsewhere in France. Versions recorded in French-Canada are particularly close to this version from Jersey.

107 MADELEINE
MADELEINE

Jack Le Feuvre, Sark, *rec.* P. Kennedy, 1957
Other recorded version
Sark, male chorus acc. accordion, *rec.* 1938: BBC 1834

Also called in Jersey *En passant par chez nous*, this was at one time one of the most popular folksongs sung in the Channel Islands. In France, where it has been widely sung in children's holiday camps, it is also known as *Sur la route de Dijon*, and the girl's name is Marjolaine.

108 MALBROUCK
MARLBOROUGH

George Le Feuvre, Jersey, *rec.* P. Kennedy, 1960: BBC
26235

Printed versions
TRÉBUCQ: 1896, p. 98: Poitou (Vendée), twelve verses
CAREY: 1908, p. 11: Channel Islands

A burlesque song referring to John Churchill, first Duke of Marlborough (1650–1722), which has been very popular in the Islands as in Normandy and elsewhere in France for 250 years.

George Le Feuvre begins with the first verse in Jersey Norman-French, thereafter singing the next eighteen verses in French. The song is often rendered in this way in a mixture of French and Norman-French.

The tune of *Malbrouck* was adapted in England to the words of *For he's a jolly good fellow* and *We won't go home till morning* and has been much used for country dancing (for example the dance collected by Cecil Sharp, *Country Dance Book*, part 1: Novello, London, 1909). In France it was used by the Huguenots as a requiem on the death of the Duke of Guise in 1563 (*Le Chansonnier Huguenot*, vol. II, p. 253):

> Qui veut ouir chanson?
> C'est du grand Duc de Guise
> Et bon, bon, bon, bon
> Di, dan, di, dan, bon
> C'est du grand Duc de Guise
> Qu'est mort et enterré

Just as the Huguenots burst into song at the death of the tyrant Duke of Guise, so also was there a song born in 1722 to celebrate the death of France's natural foe, for in France the fear of the Duke of Marlborough was similar to that in England a hundred years later towards Napoleon or 'Boney', the bogey man of the nursery.

In fact the Duke of Marlborough did not die on the battlefield but at home in bed after a protracted illness.

109 MARGUERITE
MARGUERITE

Jack Le Feuvre, Sark, *rec.* P. Kennedy, 1957: BBC 23842
Other recorded version
Sark, male chorus acc. accordion, *rec.* 1938: BBC 1835
Printed versions
FLEURY: 1883, p. 247: *Sur le bord de l'Île* (Lower Normandy)
LECLERC/LEFEBVRE: *c.* 1930, p. 16 (Hague and Val de Saire)

Compare
MATP: 1956, 56.10.23 (Île de Noirmoutier) coll. Marcel-Dubois/Andral

Well, she saw a boat with about thirty hands of crew. The youngest was singing a song and she asked him if he could learn it to her. But when she got on board she started crying and he said there was no need for her to start crying because it was only money lent.—JACK LE FEUVRE.

There are many other versions in Normandy and all over France of this song in the ancient French tradition. The Norman versions are almost identical to the present one from Sark but contain more verses. At one time a number of other tunes and refrains were sung in the Islands and in some versions the girl's name is given as Catherine.

110 MAN BOUONHOMME EST BEIN MALADE
MY OLD MAN IS VERY ILL

Adolphus Le Ruez, Bonne Nuit, Jersey, *rec.* P. Kennedy, 1957: BBC 23841
Other recorded versions
Sark, Male chorus acc. accordion, *rec.* 1938: BBC 1836
Philip Hamon/Hilary Carré, Sark: *Mon mari est bien malade*: BBC 23838
Printed version
L'Assemblée d'Jèrriais Bulletin No. 30 (1960), p. 475:

Man Buonhomme est bein malade: Jersey, Sark and Normandy versions (words only)
LECLERC/LEFEBVRE: 1930, p. 72 (Normandy)
CANTELOUBE: 1951, vol. III, p. 332
Compare
FLEURY: 1883, p. 359: *La Femme qui a perdu son Mari* (Lower Normandy)

The story is that she had a husband and she was very fond of him. She went to Guernsey from the Monday to the Wednesday. When she came back he was dead and laid out. Well she took her scissors and started on sewing him. When she came to the throat part she was afraid he might bite her, so she stopped, caught hold of him by the big toe and threw him down the cliff. And she prayed all the crows to come and pray by him.—HILARY CARRÉ.

She went to town to buy him some medicine that was needed, d'ye see? Then, when she got back, the poor old chap had died and her parents had put him in one of her best sheets. And she put on one of the old sheets and took out her best one. Then she hitched him up in a barrow, went down the cliff side and tipped him over.—ADOLPHUS LE RUEZ.

This is one song that has always been rendered entirely in the Norman-French language either in Jersey or Sark and also, of course, in various parts of Normandy. The version from Lower Normandy has sixteen verses.

111 MON PERE IL ME MARIE
MY FATHER HE MARRIED ME OFF

Adolphus Le Ruez, Bonne Nuit, Jersey, *rec.* P. Kennedy, 1957: BBC 23840

Compare
PUYMAIGRE: 1881, vol. 2, p. 26 (Metz)
D'INDY/TIERSOT: 1890–1900, vol. 2, p. 80 (Vivarais)
LECLERC/LEFEBVRE: 1930, p. 62 (Normandy)
CANTELOUBE: 1951, vol. II, p. 385 (Saintonge),
   p. 416 (Charente); vol. IV, p. 114 (Champagne), p. 373 (Brittany)

MATP (coll. Marcel-Dubois/Andral):
   44.2.35 (Les Mauges)
   50.8.16 (Frênes, Orne)
   52.24.130 (Île de Batz, Léon)
   52.24.160 (Morlaix)

D'HARCOURT: 1956, p. 261 (Quebec, Canada)
BARBEAU: 1962, p. 387: *Quand l'amour n'y est pas*

It's a young girl of fifteen that her father insisted that she should marry an old man of ninety because he was rich, he was a rich merchant, you see.
   She did marry the old chap and she went to bed with the old chap, of course, and he turned his back to her and started snoring. So the next morning she went up to her father and mother and said: 'Good morning, father and mother,' she said, 'may the day be restful and pleasant for you,' she said, 'but you have given me a man that is useless altogether.' And the old father said: 'Hush, my dear little one, he's a very rich merchant and people say he's dying and you'll be the heir, you'll have all his money.' So all the girl answered: 'To the devil with all the money if the pleasure's not there.'—ADOLPHUS LE RUEZ.

This kind of song, so popular in the Channel Islands, is also widespread throughout France. It is found in the west right down to the Pyrenees, and in the centre, notably at Puy-de-Dôme, Indre and Creuse. Examples are recordings made by Marcel-Dubois and Andral in 1940 at Les Mauges and in 1952 on the Île de Batz and at Morlaix.
   In Normandy, there is a comparable song, *Rosette se marie à un vieillard de 90 ans.* (Rosette marries a ninety-year-old) noted in 1950 at Frênes and one with a refrain 'Ah m'n enfant', called *Mon père m'a mariée à l'age de 15 ans* (My father married me off at the age of fifteen), from Champagne. One from the Charente is called *Voici le jour venu où Rosette se marie* (Here's the day when Rosette must marry).

112 MON PERE M'A DONNE-Z-UN MARI
MY FATHER A HUSBAND'S GIVEN ME

Jack and Reg Hacquoil, La Botellerie, St Ouen, Jersey, *rec.* P. Kennedy, 1960: BBC 26235

Printed versions
FLEURY: 1883, p. 350: *Le Mari brûlé* (Lower Normandy)
CANTELOUBE: 1951, vol. IV, p. 216 (Touraine)
MATP: 53.1.43 (Beaumont-Hague, La Manche)

Another *mal-mariée* but this time it is the husband's extreme shortness in height which is held against him. Once again we find this particular song is especially popular in Touraine where it is similar to the Jersey version. In Lower Normandy, it is known as *Le mari brûlé* (The husband burnt alive). Versions similar to the Jersey version were collected in 1952 by the Caen Ethnographic Laboratory in the region of Beaumont-Hague in La Manche.

113 LE PETIT COUTURIER
THE LITTLE DRESSMAKER

Jack Le Feuvre, Sark, *rec.* P. Kennedy, 1957: BBC 23842

Printed version
BNP MSS: 1855, vol. IV, p. 11 (words); vol. V, p. 206 (music); coll. Rousselet (Loudéac)

YOUNG: 1956, p. 51 (Canada)

It's a man who went to an hotel to stay and there was two girls living there and one was making love with him and the other one was jealous and so he got chucked out of the hotel.—JACK LE FEUVRE.

This story of the little tailor was particularly popular in the nineteenth century and is still sung to the present day on the north coast of Brittany in the region of Loudéac. It has also survived in Canada.
   In the manuscripts of the Bibliothèque Nationale we read that tailors and dressmakers had little respect in the country districts of Brittany. The country people always belittled them when they spoke of dressmakers or 'Cousous': 'J'avons le couturier chez nous, sauf votre respect' (We have the tailor at home, begging your pardon).

114 LE PETIT NAVIRE
THE LITTLE CORVETTE

John Gallienne, Torteval, Guernsey, *rec.* P. Kennedy,
  1957: BBC 23839

Printed version
DAVENSON: 1946, p. 327: *La courte Paille* (fifteen verses)

This is an old but very well-known French folksong found in the repertoire of the old deep-sea sailors. Its history probably goes back to at least the sixteenth century and the song is found along both the Atlantic and Mediterranean coasts of France.

John Gallienne learnt this song about 1900. Although he seemed unsure of the words and only remembered three verses, his chorus is of particular interest. Perhaps it is borrowed from some other French naval song or it may well be that the song itself was originally a drinking song and other versions have lost this refrain.

4 Le sort tomba sur le plus jeune
   Qui n'avait ja-, ja-, jamais navigué

   The lot it fell to the youngest one
   Who had ne-ne-never been to sea

5 Il monta à la grande hune
   Et puis il se, se, se mit à prier

   He climbed up to the main top mast
   And there he knee-knee-kneeled to pray

6 On le mangea à la sauc' blanche
   Avec des sal-, sal-, salsifis pas cuits

   They ate him up with white sauce
   And with some sal-sal-salsify uncooked

7 Ils eurent la délicatesse
   De mettre, sa, sa, sa part de côté

   They had the good manners
   To put hi-hi-his share aside

8 Si cette histoire vous amuse
   Nous allons la, la, la recommencer

   Now if this story did make you smile
   We'll be-be-begin it again

9 Si au contraire ell' vous ennuie
   Nous allons la, la, la laisser d'côté

   But if instead it did annoy you
   We'll leave it there-there-there aside

An English version of this song, said to have been written by Thackeray, is the story of *Little Billee*, which begins:

There were three men of Bristol City
They stole a ship and went to sea
There was gorging Jack and guzzling Jimmy
And also little boy Billee

115 SI J'AVAIS LES SOULIERS
IF ONLY I'D THE SHOES

Jack de la Mare, Rocquaine, Guernsey, *rec.* P. Kennedy,
  1957: BBC 23844

Printed versions
MACCULLOCH: 1903, p. 572 (words only)
MATP: 1915, 50.1.105, coll. M. Barbeau

D'HARCOURT: 1956: 2 versions, nos. 155 and 155b
  (Canada)
PEACOCK: 1965, p. 96: 2 verses *Si J'avais le bateau*
  (Canada)

Compare
COIRAULT: 1959, vol. 3, for a study of the repetitive cumulative *randonnée* folksong in France

This song bears witness to the strong connections between the Channel Islands and the west of France as versions can still be heard right down to the present day in Anjou, Aunis, Saintonge, Poitou, Les Landes, and even as far as Ariège. In Central France it can be heard in Berry and Nivernais. The refrains may vary but do not greatly alter the rhythm or melodic style. For example, in Berry:

Mes souliers sont rouges
Adieu ma mignonne
Mes souliers sont rouges
Adieu mes amours

My shoes are red
Goodbye my pet
My shoes are red
Goodbye my loves

And in Anjou:

Mes souliers sont rouges
Or, adieu ma maîtresse
Mes souliers sont rouges
Or, adieu mes amours

My shoes are red
So, goodbye my mistress
My shoes are red
So, goodbye my loves

Mes talons sont ronds	My heels are round
Adieu capitaine	Goodbye Captain
Mes talons sont ronds	My heels are round
Adieu Mousaillon	Goodbye Mousaillon

The song has also crossed to Canada where Dr Marius Barbeau found it at Beauharnois in the cantons east of Quebec in 1915. Marguerite and Raoul d'Harcourt have published two Canadian versions (D'HARCOURT: 1956), one from Montreal and the other from St. Rémy.

A Guernsey version was noted without tune by Sir Edgar MacCulloch and appears in his collection edited by Edith Carey (MACCULLOCH: 1903):

First verse: Si j'avais le chapeau
Que ma mie m'avait donné
Mon chapeau est bel et beau

Chorus: Adieu ma mignonne
Adieu donc mes amours

Last verse: Si j'avais les souliers
Que ma mie m'avait donnés
Mes souliers sont de cuir doux
Mes blancs bas sont de demas
Mes culottes de bottes en bottes
Ma cravate est ric et rac
Mon corselet est fort bien fait
Ma casaque est zic et zac
Et mon chapeau est bel et beau

116 LES TROIS DEMOISELLES ET LE CORDONNIER
THE THREE DAMSELS AND THE COBBLER

Jack Le Feuvre, Sark, *rec.* P. Kennedy, 1957: BBC
23842

Compare
FLEURY: 1883, p. 353: *Le petit Marcelot*

Trois demoiselles they went to a dance and they broke their shoes, the soles came off. So they went to the cobbler to have their shoes repaired. He said: 'Yes, I can repair your shoes' and they said: 'How much are you going to charge?' He replied: 'Every stitch a kiss.' So they said they didn't like those cobblers because their trousers were always sticky with wax.—JACK LE FEUVRE.

This song, at one time widely sung in the Islands, is well known in France. A version was selected and appears in French School and College anthologies under the title *Les trois filles sur un rocher* (Three girls on a rock) but the song is also sometimes known as *Le Cordonnier* (The cobbler). Marcel-Dubois points out a rather distant resemblance to the song *Le petit matelot* (The little sailor) of which one version was collected in Lower Normandy (FLEURY: 1883).

117 LES TROIS JEUNES SOLDATS
THE YOUNG SOLDIERS THREE

Jack De La Mare, Rocquaine, Guernsey, *rec.* P. Kennedy, 1957
Other recorded version
George Le Moigne, Perelle, Guernsey: BBC 23839

Printed version
D'HARCOURT: 1956, p. 318, 2 versions (Gaspé, Canada)

First noted in France in the eighteenth century this song arrived in Guernsey in two versions, both with a very complete text. Jack de la Mare's version concerns three soldiers, whereas the second has only one, *Pauvre soldat, revenant de guerre*. Both employ a number of Norman French words.

The song was published in an almanack in Guernsey in 1842 and in Jersey in 1844 and in recent times has been found in France, in the west in Saintonge, Poitou, Angoumois and in Upper Brittany. It has also been noted in the Alps in the south-east, the Metz region in the east, again in Nivernais, and also many times in French Canada. In France it is generally known under the title *Le retour du soldat* (The return of the soldier) or *Le retour du marin* (The return of the sailor).

118 LES TROIS JEUNES TAMBOURS
THE YOUNG DRUMMERS THREE

Elizabeth Guille (of Sark), *rec.* P. Kennedy, Guernsey,
  1957: BBC 23839
Other recorded version
Sark, male chorus acc. accordion, 1938: BBC 1836

Printed versions
BNP MSS: 1855, vol. II, p. 445 (Artois, Pas de Calais)
MacCulloch: 1903 (Guernsey)
Davenson: 1946, p. 333: *Joli Tambour*

A song which once was well known in all the Channel Islands and has been noted in Normandy, Île de France and La Vendée. In France it has become popular in schools in the version published by Davenson. The following verses not sung by Mrs Guille are needed to complete the story between verses 4 and 5:

<table>
<tr><td>A</td><td>Ô fille du roi, veuillez être ma femme</td><td>Oh princess, be my wife</td></tr>
<tr><td>B</td><td>Mon joli tambour, demandez à mon père</td><td>My handsome drummer, ask my father</td></tr>
<tr><td>C</td><td>Ô Sire le roi, donnez-moi votre fille</td><td>Oh Sire, your Majesty, give me your daughter</td></tr>
</table>

119 VER-DU-RON, VER-DU-RO-NET'-O
VER-DU-RON, VER-DU-RO-NET''-O

Morrison Torode, St Peter, Guernsey, *rec.* P. Kennedy,
  1957: BBC 28344

Printed version
Young: 1956, p. 35 (Canada)

In France this song is well known under the title *La fille au cresson* (The watercress girl). In Nivernais it is sung in a version very similar to our present one from Guernsey. It would appear to go back at least to the beginning of the eighteenth century when it was included in pedlars' chapbooks and broadsides, as well as in the collections of dance songs of the period.

120 LE VINGT-CINQUIEME DU MOIS D'OCTOBRE
THE TWENTY-FIFTH OF OCTOBER

George Le Moigne, Perelle, Guernsey, *rec.* P. Kennedy,
  1957: BBC 23839
Other recorded version
Jack Le Feuvre, Sark, *rec.* P. Kennedy, 1957: BBC 23842

Printed version
Marcel-Dubois/Andral coll. 1956 (Périgord)
Compare
Marcel-Dubois/Andral coll: 1954, pp. 230–45

This sailor's lament brings to life a particular tragedy, a naval battle or a wreck which has left its mark on the French people. It may well be linked with the Siege of Gibraltar. The date quoted at the beginning of the song varies in local versions: 'Le vingt-cinq du mois de mars', 'Le dix octobre', 'Le dix-huit du mois dernier', and in the Sark version 'Le vingt-sixième d'octobre'. It has been noted several times in western France: in La Vendée in 1911 and Périgord, in the Île de Noirmoutier, in 1956. We can also compare it with the lament of L'Hilda sung in 1951–3 in the Île de Batz in Upper Léon (Marcel-Dubois/Andral: 1954, pp. 230–45).

Bibliography

ARNAUDIN: 1912
Félix Arnaudin, *Chants populaires de la Grande-Lande*: Paris-Bordeaux, 1912. Noteworthy collection gathered on the spot from the rural areas of the Landes at the beginning of the 20th century and here presented with authoritative and full references. 196 songs; dialect words with translation and music, melodies only; notes on the singers.

BNP MSS: 1855
Poésies populaires de la France: Paris, Bibliothèque Nationale, 1855. Files bringing together documents (information, words, music) as a result of the official inquiry into folksongs and popular poetry undertaken in 1852 by Minister Fortoul. These sources have been much used and exploited by the authors of works on folksong.

BARBEAU: 1937
Marius Barbeau, *Romancero du Canada*: Macmillan, Toronto, Canada, 1937. Contains 50 songs; words and music—melodies only; notes on location for each song, interpretation, the circumstances and origins, and study of the rhythmic formulas and musical analyses.

BARBEAU: 1962
Marius Barbeau, *Le Rossignol y chante*: Musée National du Canada, 1962. Collected and recorded on Lower St Lawrence River and in Nova Scotia, between 1916 and 1918, and later in 1922, by this pioneer collector of French songs in Canada. Contains 161 songs; words and music—melodies only; notes on interpretation and dates of collection; historical notes on the songs.

BARBEY: 1901
Jeanne-Marie Barbey, 'Chansons du Morbihan' (in *Revue des traditions populaires*, vol. 16, 1901, pp. 231–2). A valuable document. Contains 2 songs; words and music—melodies only; no commentary.

BARBILLAT/TOURAINE: 1931
Emile Barbillat and Laurian Touraine, *Chansons populaires dans le Bas-Berry*: Châteauroux, Edition 'Gargaillon', 1931. 5 vols. These collections provide a good basic repertoire for the region. Vol. 1, 50 *rondes*; vol. 2, 64 love songs; vol. 3, 58 shepherdesses' songs; vol. 4, 65 soldiers' songs; vol. 5, 97 'light airs'. Words and music—melodies only; no commentary.

BOURGEOIS: 1931
Georges Bourgeois, *Vieilles chansons du Bocage Vendéen*: Bossonet, Paris, 1931. A major work, the product of on-the-spot inquiries. Contains 75 songs; words and music—melodies only; notes on sources; comparative commentary on the songs and their origins.

BUJEAUD: 1863–95
J. Bujeaud, *Chants et chansons populaires des Provinces de l'Ouest, Poitou, Saintonge, Aunis et Angoumois*: Niort, 1863–95. 3 vols. Source work. Excellent, authoritative documentation on the songs of these districts in the middle of the 19th century. About 540 songs of which 300 were published with words and music—melodies only; introduction on the circumstances in which they were collected and a commentary on each song.

CANTELOUBE: 1951
Joseph Canteloube, *Anthologie des chants populaires français*: Durand, Paris, 1951. 4 vols. Very useful collection. Extensive choice of songs from every district of France. The Auvergne songs were collected by the editor on the spot. Contains about 1,400 songs; words, in both dialect and standard French, with music—melodies only; brief running commentary region by region.

CAREY: 1908
Edith F. Carey, *A Link with the Past (Souvenir Normand)*: Labey & Blampied, Jersey, 1908. Important local collection with descriptions of customs, 6 dances and 8 songs with music.

COIRAULT: 1956–63
Patrice Coirault, *Formation de nos chansons folkloriques*: Paris, 1956–63. 5 vols. Important work of scholarship, historically orientated, discussing each song individually. Contains 72 songs; words and some musical notation—melodies only; comparative notes on songs.

DAVENSON: 1946
Henri Davenson, *Le Livre des chansons*: Neuchâtel, Switzerland, 1946. A work on the history of French song with a rather theoretical introduction followed by learned commentary on each of the songs reproduced. Contains 139 songs; words and music—melodies only; coverage is world-wide.

DELARUE: 1934–47
Paul Delarue, *Recueil de chants populaires du Nivernais* (Coll. Ligue de l'Enseignement): Nevers, Paris, 1934–47. 7 vols. A serial work of reference, providing admirable documentation on the songs and word-of-mouth literature in Nevers. Many examples are reproduced from Achille Millien's MSS. Contains about 50 songs; words and music—melodies only; commentaries on informants and collecting as well as different versions of each song, its origins and its purpose.

D'HARCOURT: 1956
Marguerite and Raoul D'Harcourt, *Chansons folkloriques françaises au Canada*: Laval University, Quebec, 1956. Interesting work providing a musicological survey of a selection of songs set down by Marius Barbeau in the first decades of the 20th century. The songs are grouped under literary headings. Contains 190 songs; words and music—melodies only; comprehensive notes on sources; explanatory and comparative commentary on the songs.

D'INDY AND TIERSOT: 1890/1900
Vincent d'Indy and Julien Tiersot, *Chants populaires du Vivarais*: Durand et Fils, Paris, 1890 and 1900. 2 vols. Musical anthology based on songs collected locally. Vol. 1, 77 songs; vol. 2, 50 songs. Words and music, arranged for piano; commentary on the songs with explanatory notes on the words.

DONCIEUX AND TIERSOT: 1904
Georges Doncieux and Julien Tiersot, *Le Romancero populaire de la France*: Lib. Emile Bouillon, Paris, 1904. Source work; historical study of the different versions of the words of great French songs, complete with musicological notes. Contains 44 songs; words and music—melodies only, comparative and critical commentary on each version.

DUCHON: 1926
Paul Duchon, *Chansons populaires du Bourbonnais*: Ed. Roudanez, Paris, 1926. Collection of piano arrangements of songs, but basically good source material. Contains 31 songs; words and music; concise notes on origin and interpretation.

FLEURY: 1883
Jean Fleury, *La Littérature orale de la Basse-Normandie*: Maisonneuve, Paris, 1883. Early work but still a good reference

book. Contains 60 songs; words and very occasionally music—melodies only; some commentary on the songs.

LECLERC AND LEFEBVRE: 1930

Léon Leclerc and René Lefebvre, *Chansons populaires du Pays Normand*: Paris, *c.* 1930. An outstanding collection, the product of research undertaken, around the turn of the century, into the folksong tradition in rural Normandy by two natives of Honfleur. Contains 40 songs; words and music, with piano arrangements.

LUZEL: 1971

F. M. Luzel, *Chants et chansons populaires de Basse-Bretagne*: Maisonneuve et Larose, Paris, 1971. 4 vols of the new edition of the 1868–90 collection. Classic collection of Breton songs considered in terms of their words only. Contains about 420 songs, words only; different versions of the same song with translation; no commentary.

MATP

Collections du Musée National des Arts et Traditions populaires: Paris. The Department of Ethnomusicology of the National Museum of Folk Arts and Traditions—which includes a research record library—studies and houses several thousand recordings of traditional folk music from France and the French sphere of influence (Canada, Louisiana, French Switzerland etc.). The Museum's library contains several hundred books and articles on French folk music.

MACCULLOCH: 1903

Sir Edgar MacCulloch (ed. Edith F. Carey), *Guernsey Folklore*: Eliot Stock, London, 1903. Contains descriptions of old customs, weather lore, proverbs, superstitions, songs and children's games.

MADELAINE: 1907

A. Madelaine, *Au bon vieux temps (récits, contes et légendes de l'ancien Bocage normand, jeux, vieilles chansons, 20 airs notés)*: Delesques, Caen, 1907. A good selection of stories, fairy-tales, games, old songs and legends from the old Normandy Bocage. Contains 20 songs; words and music—melodies only; no commentary.

MARCEL-DUBOIS AND ANDRAL: 1954

Claudie Marcel-Dubois and Maguy Andral, 'Musique populaire vocale de l'Ile de Batz' (in *Arts et traditions populaires*, July–Sept. 1954, pp. 193–250): Paris, 1954. The results of an ethnomusicological expedition undertaken in three stages from 1951–3. Collection of songs with full musical settings based on recordings made on the island by the editors. Original documents for a limited area. 20 songs; words, translations and music—melodies only; notation for every verse. Study of the district, the singers and the songs, with notes on the circumstances of performance.

MILLIEN: 1906/10

Achille Millien, *Chants et chansons populaires (Coll.: Littérature orale et traditions du Nivernais)*: E. Leroux, Paris, 1906–10. 2 vols. Source documentation on the Nevers district concerning oral literature and songs. Reproduced in part in the series of instalments published for schools by Delarue. Contains about 400 songs; words and music—melodies only; different versions of the text with annotations.

MORAND: 1936

Simone Morand, *Chansons d'Ille et Vilaine*: Rennes, 1936. Small collection of songs from Upper Brittany gathered and set to music by a good musician. Contains 12 songs; words and music—melodies only; no commentary.

MOULLE: 1909–13

Edouard Moullé, *52 chants anciens, recueillis en Normandie*: Rouart, Lerolle et Cie, Paris, 1909–13. 3 vols. Collection of musical settings of songs which are pleasant to sing and have previously been collected in the district. Contains 52 songs; words and music arranged for the piano; no commentary.

PEACOCK: 1965

Kenneth Peacock, *Songs of the Newfoundland Outports*: National Museum of Canada, Ottawa, 1965. 3 vols.

POUEIGH: 1926

Jean Poueigh, *Chansons populaires des Pyrénées françaises*: Paris, 1926. Admirable work presenting the results of a sponsored inquiry undertaken from 1918–23 in the French Pyrenees and specially in the Ariège; most of the songs have been collected in the places cited by the author and taken down aurally, others have been gathered from various archives. Contains 350 songs in dialect; words and melodies; some arrangements for various instruments.

PUYMAIGRE: 1881

A. de Puymaigre, *Chants populaires recueillis dans le pays messin*: Paris, 1881. 2 vols. Important work giving extensive coverage to the poetry and the literary content of the songs of the Metz district. Notes on the distribution of the songs. Vol. 1, 77 songs; vol. 2, 123 songs; words and some tunes—melodies only; notes on text and on text variations.

ROLLAND: 1883

Eugène Rolland, *Recueil de chansons populaires*: Paris, 1883. 5 vols. Varied selection (18th-century songs, local songs, etc.). Collected at second-hand. Vol. 1, 200 songs; vol. 2, 226 songs, vol. 3, 32 songs; vol. 4, 32 songs; vol. 5, 28 songs. Words and music—melodies only; no notes on the songs.

TREBUCQ: 1896

Sylvain Trébucq: *La chanson populaire en Vendée*: Paris, 1896. 150 songs, 110 of which have melodies.

TREBUCQ: 1912

Sylvain Trébucq, *La chanson populaire et la vie rurale des Pyrénées à la Vendée*: Bordeaux, 1912. 2 vols. Admirable work based on local inquiries and archive research undertaken in the first decade of the 20th century. The songs form part of a study in depth of the characteristic of the folksong and traditions of the region under consideration. About 300 songs, half of them with musical notation—melodies only; notes on the origins and dates of collection and on the songs.

UDRY: 1930

Albert Udry, *Les vieilles chansons en patois de tous les pays de France*: Paris, 1930. Good popular work grouping by Department songs previously collected and in some cases published by various authors; from about 1841 to around 1925. Contains 96 songs; words and music—melodies only; concise information on interpretation and songs.

YOUNG: 1956

R. S. Young, *Vieilles chansons de Nouvelle France*: Quebec, Canada, 1956. Selection of French songs from Canada gathered there by the author in 1953–4. The whole collection is housed in the Folklore Archives in Quebec. Contains 50 songs; words and music—melodies only; brief notes on informants.

VII

Songs of
Courtship

Introduction

> As Johnny walk-ed out, one midsummer's morn
> He soon became quite weary and sat down beneath a thorn
> 'Twas there he spied a pretty fair maid, as she was passing by
> And young Johnny followed after with his long and wishing eye

'As I roved out . . .' or 'As I walked out . . .'—these are the classic 'openings' for the English and Anglo-Irish courtship ballads, and are certainly influenced by both Irish Gaelic (see 'S Óró Londubh Buí: O My Blackbird Gay, No. 42) and Welsh (Y Bachgen Main: The Lanky Lad, No. 53). A good example of a song demonstrating transition from Irish Gaelic into English is Easter Snow (No. 128):

> At twilight in the morning, as I roved out upon the dew
> With my morning cloak around me, intending all my flocks to view
> I spied a lovely fair one, she was a charming beauty bright
> And I took her for Diana, or the evening star that rules the night

The air is popular in Donegal and the west coast of Ireland as a fiddle tune, and the English words would seem to be the work of a 'hedge schoolmaster' or local poet with a good working knowledge of both languages.

In this chapter there are twelve songs from different parts of England and another twelve from Ireland, Scotland and Wales: six being Anglo-Irish, five Lowland Scots, and one recorded in the English-speaking Gower peninsula in South Wales. Most are seriously romantic but six are cast in a lighter comic vein (Nos. 127, 129, 131, 135, 138 and 139).

Examples of other 'As I roved out' romantic courtship songs here are The Long and Wishing Eye (No. 134), whose opening stanza is reproduced above, Next Monday Morning (No. 137), The Ploughboy (No. 140) and The Spotted Cow (No. 142).

These most common type of courtship songs are often known as 'The True-Lovers' Discussion', as they take the form of an argument between two lovers in which the power of true love triumphs over their differences of wealth and upbringing, as in Come Write Me Down the Powers Above (No. 126):

> O it's not your gold would me entice
> To leave my friends for your advice
> I never intend to marry at all
> Nor be at any young man's call
>
> So he picked up his hat, he was going away
> She said: Don't go, young man, but stay
> Stay, O stay, my heart is true
> I never will wed any man but you

The same technique is used by Colin with his Phoebe in another English true-lovers' discussion (No. 125) in which the girl feels herself young at scarce sixteen and Colin comforts her with this thought:

> Never mind what the world say, for it all proves a lie
> We are not alone, there's that couple hard by
> Let them judge of our actions, be you cheerful, my dear
> For no harm is intended to my Phoebe I'll swear

295

Phoebe and Joe Smith at Woodbridge, Suffolk

Photograph: Peter Kennedy

Songs of Courtship

Sometimes a third party, the observer of the discussion, steps forward and questions the girl, trying to tell her that she is far too young to get married at the age of fifteen, to which she gives her determined reply of *Next Monday Morning* (No. 137):

> O you talk like a man without sense, without skill
> Three years now I've tarried against my own will
> I have made a vow that I mean to fulfil
> I'm going to get married next Monday morning

In *The Mountain Stream* (No. 136), a Lowland Scots song with pastoral verses recorded in Ireland, the girl is prepared to wait awhile rather than face her parents, who might threaten her with confinement in a dark dungeon should they find out she was in love with a rover:

> If you'll call around and frequent my parents
> Lest a hasty marriage should produce a foe
> I'll stay at home for another season
> By the mountain stream where the moorcock crows

The romantic picture of the Scottish country lassie by the mountain stream, kilted and bare-foot, is well portrayed in two songs from the Lowlands, *The Queen Among the Heather* (No. 141) and *Ca the Yowes to the Knowes* (No. 124):

> For it's been to me a happy day
> The day I spied my rovin' fancy
> She was herding her yowes oot ower the knowes
> And down amongst the curlin' heather

The father of one of these particular shepherdesses was cheerfully tricked into giving away his daughter and some of his land when her suitor accosted him:

> Good morning to you, old man, you're counting your flock
> Could you spare me a ewe-lamb for to keep up my stock
> And grass for to feed it on yonder green lea?
> Ca the yowes to the knowes, Molly and me

121 AS I ROVED OUT

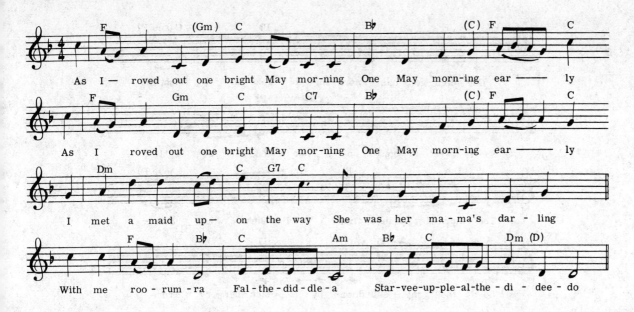

As I — roved out one bright May mor-ning One May morn-ing ear ——— ly

As I roved out one bright May mor-ning One May morn-ing ear ——— ly

I met a maid up — on the way She was her ma-ma's dar - ling

With me roo - rum - ra Fal - the - did - dle - a Star-vee-up-ple-al-the - di - dee - do

1 As I roved out one bright May morning
One May morning early
As I roved out one bright May morning
One May morning early
I met a maid upon the way
She was her mama's darling
With me roo-rum-ra
Fal-the-diddle-a
Star-vee-upple-al-the-di-dee-do

2 Her shoes were black and her stockin's white
And her hair shines like the silver
She has two nice bright sparkling eyes
And her hair hangs o'er her shoulder

3 What age are you, my pretty fair maid?
What age are you, my darling?
She answered me quite modestly
I'm sixteen years next Monday morning

4 And will you come to my mama's house?
The moon shines bright and clearly
O, open the door, and let me in
And dada will not hear us

5 She took me by the lily-white hand
And led me to the table
There's plenty of wine for soldiers here
As far as they can take it

6 She took my horse by the bridle rein
And led him to the stable
There's plenty of hay for a soldier's horse
As far as they are able

7 And she went up and dressed the bed
And dressed it soft and easy
And I went up to tuck her in
Crying: Lassie, are you comfort-able?

8 I slept in the house till the break of day
And in the morning early
I got up and put on my shoes
Crying: Lassie, I must leave you

9 And when will you return again
Or when will we get married?
When cockle shells make silver bells
That's the time we'll marry

122 BLACKBERRY GROVE

One Mich-ael-mas morn-ing I woke in a fright —
So I went to get up — be-fore it was light
The morn-ing being fine I thought I would roam —
So I took my-self down by a black-ber-ry grove

1 One Michaelmas morning I woke in a fright
So I went to get up before it was light
The morning being fine I thought I would roam
So I took myself down by a blackberry grove

2 To moisten my mouth one or two of them took
But to get up the others I wanted a hook
As I was a-walking O there did I see
A fair pretty maid milking under a tree

3 I stepped up to her and made this reply
One penn'orth o' milk for I'm very dry
She says: My kind sir, just look all around
Don't you see how my milk it lies spilled on the ground?

4 You see the black cow that's got a white tail
She's kicked down my milk and has brindled my pail
She's kicked down my milk which I have for to sell
And what to do for it no means can I tell

5 And then if perchance I do meet with a friend
Who'll lend me a shilling, I'll pay him again
I pulled out my shillings by one, two and three
And said: My dear jewel, come hither to me

6 And here are some shillings before we do part
And in a short time you'll be my sweetheart
I pulled out my shillings by one two and three
And said: My dear jewel, come hither to me

123 THE BONNY WEE WINDOW

Now there was a young lass —— and her name it was Nell ——
In a snug lit-tle cot wi' her gran-ny did dwell ——
Now the hoose was bit wee —— and the win-dow was less ——
It had but four loz-ens —— and yin wan-ted gless ——
'Twas a bon-ny wee win-dow, —— the hand-some wee win-dow
The bon-ni-est wee win-dow —— that ev-er I saw ——

1 Now there was a young lass and her name it was Nell
In a snug little cot wi' her granny did dwell
Now the hoose was bit wee and the window was less
It had but four lozens and yin wanted gless
'Twas a bonny wee window, the handsome wee window
The bonniest wee window that ever I saw

2 Now it happened one night, Granny went to her bed
And Johnny, the blithest young lad that Nell had
Came ower the hill, his true-love to see
In under the window right planted got he
At the bonny wee window . . .

3 Now the twa lovers hadna got very much said
When Granny cries: Nelly, come unto your bed
I'm comin', dear Granny, young Nelly did say
So, fare thee well, Johnny, come back the next day
To the bonny wee window . . .

4 Now Nelly, dear Nelly, dinna tak it amiss
Before I gang away you maun grant me a kiss
So to get a bit kiss, Johnny put his heid through
For what wouldna love make a fond lover do?
At the bonny wee window . . .

5 It's twa kisses got Johnny and sweet were the smacks
But for his dear life could he get his heid back
He wrugg-ed, he tugg-ed, he bawled and he bang
When Nelly's loud laughter all through the hoose rang
At the bonny wee window . . .

6 Granny she heard the noise, jumped oot on the floor
And seizin' the poker made away for the door
And at poor Johnny's back sic a thump she laid on
Another like that would have broke his back-bone
Wi' his heid through the window . . .

7 Johnny reekin' wi' heat and smartened with pain
He wrugg-ed, he tugg-ed with might and wi' main
Till the lintels gaed wa' and the window did break
But, O, the best half o't stuck fast to his neck
'Twas a bonny wee window . . .

124 CA THE YOWES TO THE KNOWES

Good mor-ning to you, fair maid, you're tend-ing your flock

What brings you so ear-ly un-to this green spot?

My fai-ther's in the fields —— and he's wait-ing for me

To ca the yowes to the knowes, —————— Mol-ly and me

1 Good morning to you, fair maid, you're tending your flock
   What brings you so early unto this green spot?
   My faither's in the fields and he's waiting for me
   To ca the yowes to the knowes, Molly and me

2 My faither's a shepherd, herds sheep on yon hill
   If you get his sanction I'll be at your will
   And if he does grant it, right glad I will be
   To ca the yowes to the knowes, Molly and me

3 Good morning to you, old man, you're counting your flock
   Could you spare me a ewe-lamb for to keep up my stock
   And grass for to feed it on yonder green lea?
   Ca the yowes to the knowes, Molly and me

4 Gang doon to yon burnside and choose your ain lamb
   You can get it as easy as any man can
   And grass for to feed it on yonder green lea
   Ca the yowes to the knowes, Molly and me

5 Tommy stepped forward, caught Molly by the hand
   And right before her aul' faither the couple did stand
   Saying: This is the ewe-lamb that I asked from thee
   Ca the yowes to the knowes, Molly and me

6 O Tommy, O Tommy, it's you've me beguiled
   It's little did I think that you meant my own child
   But since I have said it say: Well then, let it be
   Ca the yowes to the knowes, Molly and me

7 A peck of gold thou shalt have, it will sleek with my one
   And if that won't do then I'll heap with my hand
   And yon fleecy flocks a' that feed on yon lea
   I will sign them all over to Molly and thee

125 COLIN AND PHOEBE

Well, well, dear-est — Phoe-be, and why in such — haste?

Through fields and through mea — dows all day have I chased

In — search of the fair one, who doth me dis — dain

And — who will re-ward me And who will re-ward me for all my past pain?

1 Well, well, dearest Phoebe, and why in such haste?
Through fields and through meadows all day have I
In search of the fair one, who doth me disdain   [chased
And who will reward me
And who will reward me for all my past pain?

2 Go, go, boldest Colin, how dare you be seen
With a burden like me and not scarcely sixteen?
To be seen with the fair one, I am so afraid
That the world would soon call me
That the world would soon call me: No longer a maid

3 Never mind what the world say, for it all proves a lie
We are not alone, there's that couple hard by
Let them judge of our actions, be you cheerful, my
For no harm is intended   [dear
For no harm is intended to my Phoebe I'll swear

4 Say, say, boldest Colin, and say what you will   [skill
You may swear, lie and flatter, and prove your best
And before I will be conquered, I will let you to know
That I will die a virgin
That I will die a virgin, so I pray let me go

5 Come, come, dearest Phoebe, such thoughts I now have
I come here to see if tomorrow you'd wed
But since you so slighted me, I will bid you adieu
And will go and seek some other girl
And will go and seek some other girl more kinder than
                                                      you

6 Stay, stay, dearest Colin, just one moment stay
I will venture to wed if you mean what you say
Let tomorrow first come, love, and in church you will
That the girl you thought cruel   [find
That the girl you thought cruel will always prove kind

126 COME WRITE ME DOWN THE POWERS ABOVE

Come write me down the — powers a - bove

That first cre - a - ted a man to love

For I have a dia - mond in my eye

Where all my — joy and fan - cy lies

1 Come write me down the powers above
That first created a man to love
For I have a diamond in my eye
Where all my joy and fancy lies

2 Now, I'd give her gold, and I'd give her pearls
If only she'd fancy to be my girl
And all such costly robes she'd wear
If only she'd fancy to be my dear

3 O, it's not your gold would me entice
To leave my friends for your advice
I never intend to marry at all
Nor be at any young man's call

4 Then, go your way you scornful dame
Since you prove false, I will prove the same
For I don't care, but I shall find
Some other fair maid to my mind

5 So he picked up his hat, he was going away
She said: Don't go, young man, but stay
Stay, O stay, my heart is true
I never will wed any man but you

6 So to church they went that very next day
And were married by asking, as I've heard say
So now that girl she is his wife
She will prove his comfort day and night

127 THE COUNTRY COURTSHIP

SHE: O, when shall we — get mar-ried —— O, when shall we — get mar-ried —

O, when shall we — get mar-ried —— John-ny, me own true love? ——

HE: As soon as time comes, to be sure As soon as time comes, to be sure —

As soon as time comes, to be sure Sure-ly the wench is mad? ——

1 SHE: O, when shall we get married
O, when shall we get married
O, when shall we get married
Johnny, me own true love?

HE: As soon as time comes, to be sure
As soon as time comes, to be sure
As soon as time comes, to be sure
Surely the wench is mad?

SHE: And can't we get married sooner
And can't we get married sooner
And can't we get married sooner
Johnny, me own true love?

HE: Wha's want to get married tonight var
Wha's want to get married tonight var
Wha's want to get married tonight var
Surely the wench is mad?

2 O what shall I wear to the wedding?

Thee wold print frock an' thee yepron

And can't I wear anything better?

Wha's want to wear silks and satins var?

3 O, what will you wear to the wedding?

Me best smock coat an' me breeches

And can't you wear something smarter?

Wha's want top-hat an' gaiters var?

4 O, who shall we ask to the wedding?

Thee feyther, an' mother, an' sister

O, can't we ask anyone better?

Wha's want princes an' queens var?

5 O, where shall we sleep then together?

We'll sleep in the pig-stye, to be sure

And can't we sleep anywhere better?

Wha's want to sleep in a palace var?

6 O, what shall we 'ave for the dinner?

Chaties, an' cabbage, an' bycon, an' baens

And can't we have anything better?

Wha's want roast beef and plum-pudding var?

7 O, when shall we 'ave any children?

As soon as time comes, to be sure

And can't we have any sooner?

Wha's want children tonight var?

8 O, how shall we go to the wedding?

Thee's got two fine legs to walk wi' I

And can't we have carriage and pair?

Thee'll tak' me arm an' we'll walk like this

128 EASTER SNOW

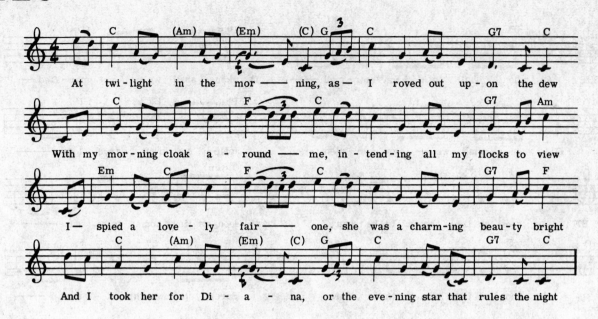

At twilight in the morning, as I roved out upon the dew
With my morning cloak around me, intending all my flocks to view
I spied a lovely fair one, she was a charming beauty bright
And I took her for Diana, or the evening star that rules the night

1 At twilight in the morning, as I roved out upon the dew
  With my morning cloak around me, intending all my flocks to view
  I spied a lovely fair one, she was a charming beauty bright
  And I took her for Diana, or the evening star that rules the night

2 I being so much surprised with her, it being the forenoon of the day
  To see so fair a creature, coming o'er the bank to Sweet Lough Rea
  Her snow-white breast lay naked, and her cheeks they were a rosy red
  And my heart was captivated by the two black eyes rolled in her head

3 As I approached this fair maid, said I: My joy and heart's delight
  My heart it is enamoured by your exceeding beauty bright
  To heal my lovesick passion, if you'll consent along with me to go
  I'll roll you in my morning cloak and bring you home to Easter Snow

4 Said I: My lovely Peggy, sit you down awhile by me
  And cast your eye around you, some pastime you may see
  The gentle hares a-hunting, the fields are decorated so
  The valley sounds melodiously by the sporting plains of Easter Snow

5 Said I: My lovely Peggy, sit you down awhile by me,
  You'll see the fox a-hunted by the best nobilitie
  The gentlemen well mounted, and the huntsmen crying: Tally-Ho
  So gloriously we'll pursue the chase from Sweet Lough Rea to Easter Snow

6 She says: Young man, excuse a simple maiden of the moor
  Forbear such splendid eloquence for one who is so poor
  My heart is not my own to give, nor can I it bestow
  'Tis pledged to one who lives and loves far from Easter Snow

129 THE GREASY COOK

I fell in love with a grea-sy cook And that I can't de-ny

I fell in love with a grea-sy cook And I'll tell you the rea-son why

And I'll tell you the rea-son why

1 I fell in love with a greasy cook
And that I can't deny
I fell in love with a greasy cook
And I'll tell you the reason why
And I'll tell you the reason why

2 Plum-puddin', roast-beef but plenty
Plum-puddin' and roast beef
And when my belly was empty
She would give to me relief
She would give to me relief

3 I kindly was invited
Some supper for to take
And kindly I did accept it
All for my stomach's sake
All for my stomach's sake

4 Now after tea was over
The cupboard she got the keys
One pocket she crammed with butter
And the other she crammed with cheese
And the other she crammed with cheese

5 We had not been there very long
About an hour or more
Her master smelling of the cheese
Came rap-tap at the door
Came rap-tap at the door

6 I'd been a-sitting at supper
I'd nowhere for to go
So I crawled up the chimney
As black as any crow
As black as any crow

7 I had not been there very long
A-sitting at me ease
The fire melted my butter
And likewise toasted my cheese
And likewise toasted my cheese

8 Every drop that fell in the fire
It caused the old fire to rear
The old woman looked up at the chimbley top
And swore the old devil was there
And swore the old devil was there

9 Her master got to the chimbley top
A bucket of water let fall
And I came tumbling after
My butter and cheese and all
My butter and cheese and all

10 The dogs they barked, the children screamed
Up flew the windows all
The old woman cried out: Well done, well done
There go butter and cheese and all
There go butter and cheese and all

130 THE GREENWOOD LADDIE

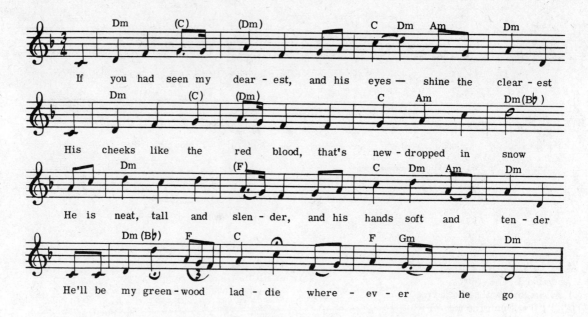

1 If you had seen my dearest, and his eyes shine the clearest
   His cheeks like the red blood, that's new-dropped in snow
   He is neat, tall and slender, and his hands soft and tender
   He'll be my greenwood laddie where-ever he go

2 My parents, my darling, they slight you with scorn
   Because you have no riches wrapped up in store
   But the more that they slight you, the more I'll invite you
   To be my greenwood laddie, till time is no more

3 For if I had the wealth of the East or West Indies
   Or I had the gold of the African shore
   Or if I could gain thousands I'd lie on your bosom
   You'd be my greenwood laddie whom I'll always adore

4 It's down yonder bower I've spent many's the long hour
   A-pulling the flowers by yon clear winding shore
   It was his stolen kisses caused my fondest wishes
   He'll be my greenwood laddie and the boy I adore

131 HARRY THE TAILOR

Young Har - ry, the tai - lor, 'bout twen - ty years old

He be - gan to grow ratt - lin' cour - ag - eous and bold

He told his old moth - er with - out an - y jest

A wife he would have then so well as the rest

And sing: Fal - the - ral - lad - dy - O   Fal - the - ral - lad - dy - O

Fal - the - ral - lad - dy - O   Fal - the - lie - day

1 Young Harry, the tailor, 'bout twenty years old
He began to grow rattlin' courageous and bold
He told his old mother without any jest
A wife he would have then so well as the rest

And sing: Fal-the-ral-laddy-O
Fal-the-ral-laddy-O
Fal-the-ral-laddy-O
Fal-the-lie-day

2 He got up one morning, before it was day
From his house to the farmer's he did run away
Where she was a-working her dairy alone   [own
He got bobbin' and playin' but 'twas not with his

3 I'll tell you the truth, let him say what he may
He came here a little before it was day
Where Dolly, the dairymaid, makin' her cheese
He began for to play and to tickle her knees

4 She gave him a shove, and straightway he fell
From the house of the dairy right into the well
Young Harry cried out with such pitiful sound
Or else, my dear Dolly, then I shall be drowned

5 Then William, the farmer, he did then come in
And up in the bucket he pulled him again
He says: You young rascal, and how came you here?
It was: Thou shoved me in, sir, I vow and declare

6 The farmer got up in a passion at that
And said: You young rascal, what have you been at?
The basin of buttermilk at him he threw
Which made him look sair and damn well blue

7 Young Harry went home like a poor drowned rat
And told his old mother what he had been at
Wi' slaps on his cheeks and a terrible fall
If this is your courtin', the devil take all

132 THE LABOURING MAN'S DAUGHTER

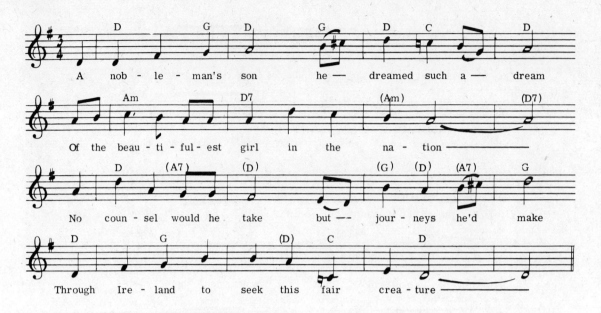

1 A nobleman's son he dreamed such a dream
Of the beautiful-est girl in the nation
No counsel would he take but journeys he'd make
Through Ireland to seek this fair creature

2 'Twas seven long years he'd searched here and there
Till he came to the place where he'd meet her
He opened the door and she stood on the floor
She was only a labouring man's daughter

3 I never have seen you but once in my life
And that was in a dream you lay by me
But now I'm beside you, by the look in your eyes
I know that you ne'er will deny me

4 O what's your desire, pray tell me, kind sir
That you're so afraid of denial?
Although I am poor, no scorn I'll endure
Do not put me under any such trial

5 No scorn will I bring, nor any such thing
And he took out a ring as a token
O love is a thing which does hang on a string
And between us it ne'er will be broken

133 THE LION'S DEN

In Lon-don ci-ty there lived a la-dy Who was po-ssessed of a vast est-ate

And she was court-ed by men of hon-our Lords, Dukes and Earls on her did wait

There was two bro-thers who be-came lo-vers And both ad-mir-ed this la-dy fair

And both to gain her, they did en-dea-vour And how to please her, was all their care

1 In London city there lived a lady
Who was possessed of a vast estate
And she was courted by men of honour
Lords, Dukes and Earls on her did wait
There was two brothers who became lovers
And both admir-ed this lady fair
And both to gain her, they did endeavour
And how to please her, was all their care

2 The older one, who being a Captain
The greater part of his love did make
The younger one said that he would venture
His life and fortune for her sweet sake
Now she said: I'll find a way to try them
And see which of them will the sooner start
And he that will behave the bravest
Will be the governor of my heart

3 She ordered her coachman for to get ready
For to get ready at the break of day
The lady and her two warlike heroes
To the Tower Hill they did ride away
And when she came to the Tower Hill
She threw her fan into the lions' den
Saying: He who wishes to gain my favour
Will bring me back my fan again

4 Out bespoke then the older brother
So distress-ed all in his mind
To hostile danger I am no stranger
And to face my foes I am still inclined
But here where lions and wild beasts are roarin'
For to go in with them I do not approve
So therefore, madam, for fear of danger
Some other champion must gain your love

5 Out bespoke then the younger brother
In a voice of thunder both loud and high
To hostile danger I am no stranger
I'll bring you back, love, your fan or die
He took his sword and went in among them
The lions fawned and fell at his feet
And then he stooped for the fan and got it
He said: Is this it, my darling sweet?

6 The lady being in her coach sat weeping
Thinking that he would be the lions' prey
This gallant action it being over
Then to the lady he made his way
But when she saw her brave hero coming
And unto him was no harm done
With open arms she did embrace him
Saying: Take the prize, love, you so dearly won

134 THE LONG AND WISHING EYE

As John-ny walk-ed out,——— one —— mid —— sum-mer's morn

He soon be-came quite wea-ry and sat down be-neath a thorn

'Twas there he spied a pret-ty fair maid, as she was pass-ing by

And young John-ny foll-owed af —— ter with his long and wish-ing eye

CHORUS: With his long and wish-ing eye, brave boys With his long and wish-ing eye

1 As Johnny walk-ed out, one midsummer's morn
He soon became quite weary and sat down beneath a thorn
'Twas there he spied a pretty fair maid, as she was passing by
And young Johnny followed after with his long and wishing eye
With his long and wishing eye, brave boys
With his long and wishing eye
And young Johnny followed after
With his long and wishing eye

2 Good morning, gentle shepherd, have you seen my flock of lambs
Strayed away from their fold, strayed away from their dams
O have you seen the ewe-lamb, as she was passing by
Has she strayed in yonder meadow where the grass grows very high?
Where the grass grows very high, brave boys
Where the grass grows very high
Has she strayed in yonder meadow
Where the grass grows very high?

3 O yes, O yes, my pretty fair maid, I saw them passing by
  They went down in yonder meadow and that is very high
  Then turning round so careless-lie and smiling with a blush
  And young Johnny followed after, and hid all in a bush
  And hid all in a bush, brave boys (etc.)

4 She searched the meadow over, no lambs could she find
  Oft'times did she cross that young man in her mind
  Then turning round, she shouted: What's the meaning of your plan?
  Not knowing that young Johnny was standing close at hand
  Was standing close at hand, brave boys (etc.)

5 The passions of young Johnny's love began to overflow
  He took her up all in his arms, his meaning for to show
  They sat down in the long grass and there did sport and play
  The lambs they were forgotten, they hopped and skipped away
  They hopped and skipped away, brave boys (etc.)

6 'Twas the following morning this couple met again
  They joined their flocks together to wander o'er the plain
  And now this couple's married, they're joined in wedlock's bands
  And no more they'll go a'roving in searching for young lambs
  In searching for young lambs, brave boys (etc.)

135 MADAM, WILL YOU WALK?

O will you ac-cept of a new sil-ver pin To pin up your hair and your fine mus-e-lin ?

Ma-dam, will you walk ? Ma-dam, will you talk with me ?

No, I won't ac-cept of a new sil-ver pin To pin up my hair and my fine mus-e-lin

Neith-er will I walk Neith-er will I talk with you

CODA: When you could, you would not Now you will, you shall not So fare thee well My Cath-er-ine Sue

1 O will you accept of a new silver pin
To pin up your hair and your fine mus-e-lin?
Madam, will you walk?
Madam, will you talk with me?

No, I won't accept of a new silver pin
To pin up my hair and my fine mus-e-lin
Neither will I walk
Neither will I talk with you

2 Will you accept of the key of my heart
To bind us together and to never never part?
Madam, will you walk?
Madam, will you talk with me?

No, I won't accept of the key of your heart
To bind us together and to never never part
Neither will I walk
Neither will I talk with you

3 Will you accept of the key of my des'
And all the money that I possess?
Madam, will you walk?
Madam, will you talk with me?

Yes, I will accept of the key of your des'
And all the money that you possess
Then I will walk
Then I will talk with you

Coda:
When you could, you would not
Now you will, you shall not
So fare thee well
My Catherine Sue

136 THE MOUNTAIN STREAM

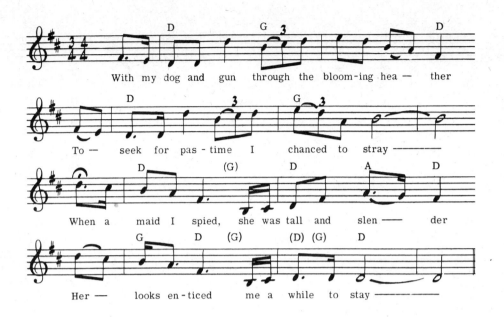

With my dog and gun through the bloom-ing hea — ther
To — seek for pas-time I chanced to stray —
When a maid I spied, she was tall and slen — der
Her — looks en-ticed me a while to stay —

1 With my dog and gun through the blooming heather
To seek for pastime I chanced to stray
When a maid I spied, she was tall and slender
Her looks enticed me a while to stay

2 Says I: My fair maid, I own I love you
Tell me your name and your dwelling also?
Excuse my name, sir, you'll find my dwelling
By the mountain stream where the moorcocks crow

3 If you'd consent and go with a rover
My former raking I would leave aside
I'm doomed to love you, so don't prove cruel
But do consent and become my bride

4 If my parents knew that I loved a rover
It's great affliction I would undergo
In a dungeon dark they would close confine me
By the mountain stream where the moorcocks crow

5 O it's crimson coloured all her features
She stood awhile but was not dismayed
Then here's my hand, love, I'll pledge my honour
And it's I'll prove true till I meet my grave

6 If you'll call around and frequent my parents
Lest a hasty marriage should produce a foe
I'll stay at home for another season
By the mountain stream where the moorcocks crow

7 Then I'll bid adieu to Scotch hills and valleys
To yon mountain streams and yon flowery vales
And when we meet, love, we'll embrace each other
And I'll pay attention to your love-sick tales

8 It's hand in hand, we will roam together
And I'll escort you to the plains below
Where the linnet changes his notes more pleasant
By the mountain stream where the moorcocks crow

137 NEXT MONDAY MORNING

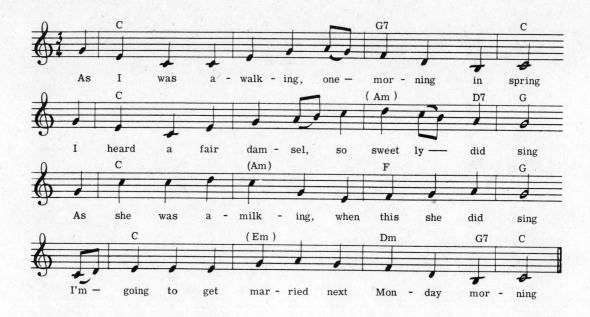

As I was a-walk-ing, one — mor-ning in spring

I heard a fair dam-sel, so sweet-ly — did sing

As she was a-milk-ing, when this she did sing

I'm — going to get mar-ried next Mon-day mor-ning

1 As I was a-walking, one morning in spring
I heard a fair damsel, so sweetly did sing
As she was a-milking, when this she did sing
I'm going to get married next Monday morning

2 O where is your dwelling, fair maid, I recall?
I dwell in yon house, I'm the fairest of all
I dwell in yon cot at the foot of yon hill
And I'm going to get married next Monday morning

3 O fifteen years old is too young for to marry
A year or two longer I'll have you now tarry
For young men are false, their vows to fulfil
So put off your wedding next Monday morning

4 O you talk like a man without sense, without skill
Three years now I've tarried against my own will
I have made a vow that I mean to fulfil
I'm going to get married next Monday morning

5 So next Sunday night, I mean to prepare
To comb out my locks and to curl up my hair
And six pretty fair maids, so neat and so trim
Shall dance at my wedding next Monday morning

6 So next Monday night when I go to my bed
So close to my true-love I will lay my head
If a maid I remain when I rise again
I shall wish I had never a-seen Monday morning

7 So next Monday morn when I put on my rings
Now my husband he gave me two far finer things
Two precious jewels he gave my adorning
So I shall be his bride next Monday morning

138 NO SIR

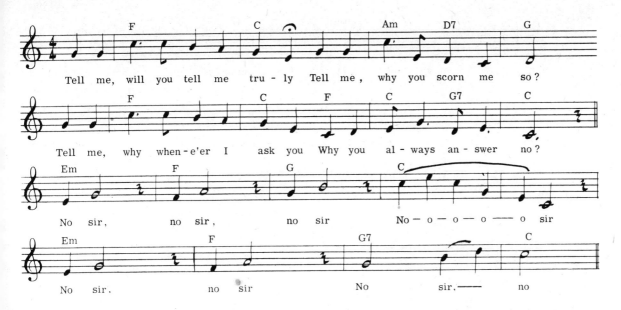

Tell me, will you tell me tru-ly Tell me, why you scorn me so?

Tell me, why when-e'er I ask you Why you al-ways an-swer no?

No sir, no sir, no sir No — o — o — o — o sir

No sir. no sir No sir,—— no

1 Tell me, will you tell me truly
Tell me, why you scorn me so
Tell me, why whene'er I ask you
Why you always answer no?
No sir, no sir, no sir
No-o-o-o-o sir
No sir, no sir,
No sir, no

2 My father was a Spanish merchant
And before he went to sea
Told me to be sure and answer
No to all you said to me

3 If when walking in the garden
Plucking flowers all wet with dew
Tell me, would you be offended
If I walked and talked to you?

4 If when walking in the garden
I should ask you to be mine
And should tell you that I loved you
Would you then my heart decline?

5 In the garden we were sitting
And her blushes she did show
Tell me would you be offended
If one kiss I did bestow?

6 Madam, may I tie your garter
Would you let me make so free
If I should be a little bolder
Would you think it wrong of me?

7 If to bed we went together
I would stay till cocks do crow
When I'd say: It's time to leave you
Would you ever let me go?

139 OLD GREY BEARD

VERSE 1: A dot-tered auld carl cam' ower the lea

Ha, – ha, — but I would nae hae him ————

He cam' ower the lea and a' to court me

Wi' his grey — beard new — ly sha - ven

2 - 6: My mo-ther tell'd me to — op - en the door

Ha, – ha, — but I would nae — hae him ————

I — op - ened the door and he tot - tered in ower

Wi' his grey beard new - ly sha - ven

1 A dottered auld carl cam' ower the lea
Ha, ha, but I would nae hae him
He cam' ower the lea and a' to court me
Wi' his grey beard newly shaven

2 My mother tell'd me to open the door
I opened the door and he tottered in ower

3 My mother tell'd me to gie him a chair
I gied him a chair and he sit on the flair

4 My mother tell'd me to gie him some meat
I gied him some meat but he'd nae teeth to eat

5 My mother tell'd me to gie him a drink
I gied him a drink and he began to wink

6 My mother tell'd me to gie him a kiss
If you like him so well, you can kiss him yoursel'

140 THE PLOUGHBOY

As I was a - wander-ing in the month of sweet May

I — heard a young plough-boy to whis-tle and to say

And aye as he was lam-ent-ing these words — he did say

There's no life like the plough-boy in the month of sweet May

1 As I was a-wandering in the month of sweet May
   I heard a young ploughboy to whistle and to say
   And aye as he was lamenting these words he did say
   There's no life like the ploughboy in the month of sweet May

2 The lark is a bonny bird and flies off her nest
   She mounts the morn air with the dew on her breast
   She flies o'er the ploughboy, she whistles and she sings
   And at eve she returns with the dew on her wing

3 Early one morning the ploughboy arose
   Whistling and singing to his horses as he goes
   He met a pretty fair maid, he met her in the lane
   One question he asked her and he thought it was no shame

4 One question he asked her: he would take her to the fair
   To buy her some ribbons for to tie up her hair
   Now this fair maid being young and foolish to the fair she would not go
   Saying: I don't want your ribbons, I can buy myself a bow

5 Then walking and talking down by yon shady grove
   With no-one to listen but the young turtle dove
   He threw his arms around her neck and brought her to the fair
   And he bought her the ribbons for to tie back her hair

6 And as they returned from the fair unto the town
   The meadows were mowed and the grass it was cut down
   The nightingale she whistled upon the hawthorn spray
   And the moon was a-shining upon the new-mown hay

7 Good luck unto the ploughboys wherever they may be
   They will take a winsome lass for to sit upon their knee
   And with a jug of beer, boys, they'll whistle and they'll sing
   And the ploughboy is as happy as a prince or a king

141 THE QUEEN AMONG THE HEATHER

For it's up a wide and a lone—ly glen

It was shed by ma-ny's a lof-ty—moun-tain

It being on-to the bu-sy haunts—of men

It be-ing the first—day—that I—went out a-hunt-ing

1 For it's up a wide and a lonely glen
  It was shed by many's a lofty mountain
  It being onto the busy haunts of men
  It being the first day that I went out a-hunting

2 For it's been to me a happy day
  The day I spied my rovin' fancy
  She was herding her yowes oot ower the knowes
  And down amongst the curlin' heather

3 For her coat was white and her goon was green
  Her body it being long and slender
  Wi' her cast-doon looks and her well-fared face
  It has oft-times made my heart to wander

4 For it's I've been to balls where they were bust-eye
                                        and braw
  And it's I've been to London and Balquither
  And the bonniest lassie that e'er I saw
  She was kilted and bare-fitted amongst the heather

5 Says I: My lass, will you come with me
  And sleep wi' me in a bed of feathers?
  I'll gie you silks and scarlets that will mak' you shine
  If you'll be my queen amongst the heather

6 She said: My lad, your offer's fair
  And I really think you're all for laughter
  For it's you being the son of a high squire man
  And me but a poor humble shepherd's dochter

7 But it's her I sought and it's her I got
  And with her I intend to be contented
  Fare you well, fare you well to your heathery hill
  Fare you well, fare you well, my song it is ended

142 THE SPOTTED COW

One morn-ing in the month — of May

As from — my cot I strayed —

Just at the dawn — ing of — the morn

I met with a charm-ing maid —

1 One morning in the month of May
  As from my cot I strayed
  Just at the dawning of the morn
  I met with a charming maid

2 My pretty maid, now whither you stray
  So early, tell me now?
  The maid replied: Kind sir, she cried
  I have lost my spotted cow

3 So, no longer weep, no longer mourn
  Your cow is not lost, my dear
  I saw her down in yonder grove
  Come, love, and I'll show you where

4 O, I must confess you very kind
  Very kind, said she
  It's there you're sure the cow to find
  Come, sweetheart, walk with me

5 Then in the grove we spent the day
  And thought it passed too soon
  At night we homeward made our way
  When brightly shone the moon

6 Next day we went to view the plough
  Across the flowery vale
  We clasped and kissed each other there
  And love was all the tale

7 So, if I should cross the flowery glen
  Or go and view the plough
  She'd come and call me: Gentle swain
  I have lost my spotted cow

143 WHEN A MAN'S IN LOVE

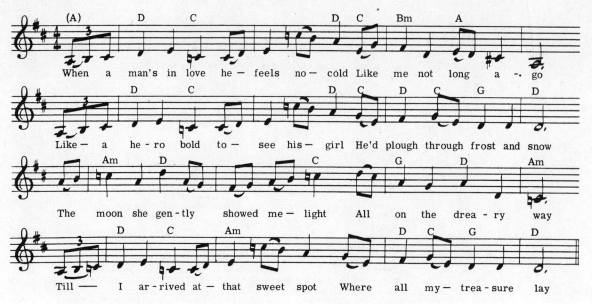

When a man's in love he — feels no — cold Like me not long a - go

Like — a he - ro bold to — see his — girl He'd plough through frost and snow

The moon she gen - tly showed me — light All on the drea - ry way

Till — I ar - rived at — that sweet spot Where all my — trea - sure lay

1 When a man's in love he feels no cold
Like me not long ago
Like a hero bold to see his girl
He'd plough through frost and snow
The moon she gently showed me light
All on the dreary way
Till I arrived at that sweet spot
Where all my treasure lay

2 I rapped at my love's window saying
My dear, are you within?
And speedily she unlocked the door
And slyly I stepped in
Her hand so soft, her breath so sweet
Her tongue did gently glide
I stole my arm around her waist
And I asked her to be my bride

3 Take me to your chamber, love
O, take me to your bed
Take me to your chamber, love
To rest my weary head
To take you to my chamber, love
My parents would not agree
But sit you down by yon bright fire
And I'll sit close by thee

4 Many a night I've courted you
Against your parents' will
But you never yet said you'd be my bride
But now, my girl, sit still
To-night I have to cross the sea
To far Columbia's shore
And you will never, never see
Your youthful lover more

5 Many a cold and stormy night
I came to visit you
When tossed about with cold winter wynds
And wet with the morning dew
Tonight our courtship's at an end
Between my love and me
So now farewell, my favourite girl
A long farewell to thee

6 Are you going to leave me here?
Or what else can I do?
I would break through every tie of love
To come along with you
Perhaps my parents might forget
But I'm sure they must forgive
For from this moment I'm content
Along with you to live

7 Don't talk of going away, my love
These words do break my heart
Come let us go and married be
Before that we do part
Then with a kiss the ring was closed
And the wedding it's come on
From courtship's cares they are released
These two are joined in one

144 YOUNG ROGER ESQUIRE

Young Ro - ger Es - quire —— came a - court - ing of late
To a rich far - mer's daugh - ter called beau - ti - ful Kate
She had fine prec - ious clo - thing, she'd jewels and rich **rings**
And — she for her for - tune had ma - ny fine things
And she for her for - tune had five thous - and pound
With rich rings and jew - els With rich rings and jew - els And a piece of fine ground

1 Young Roger Esquire came a-courting of late
To a rich farmer's daughter called beautiful Kate
She had fine precious clothing, she'd jewels and rich rings
And she for her fortune had many fine things
And she for her fortune had five thousand pound
With rich rings and jewels
With rich rings and jewels
And a piece of fine ground

2 The day being appointed and the money laid down
Was not that a fine fortune of five thousand pounds
If I marry your daughter I'll need the grey mare
Young Roger he swore that he would have his fair share
Young Roger he swore by his long curling hair
I'll not wed your daughter
I'll not wed your daughter
Without the grey mare

3 Then spoke up her father and thus say-ed he
I thought that you lov-ed my daughter indeed
The money again shall return to my purse
But as I have got her my daughter's no worse
But as I have got her thus far in my care
You shall not have my daughter
You shall not have my daughter
Nor yet the grey mare

4 Then twelve months being over and a little above
Young Roger Esquire met Katie his love
Saying: Katie, loving Katie, O don't you know me?
Such a man of your likeness I chance for to see
Such a man of your likeness with curling long hair
That once came a-courting
That once came a-courting
My father's grey mare

5 Says Roger to Katie them words I'll deny
And the truth of the story I will on you try
I'm now very sorry for what I have done
I thought that your father had lost a good son
I thought that your father would have made no dispute
But to give me his daughter
But to give me his daughter
And the grey mare to boot

121 AS I ROVED OUT

Seamus Ennis, Dublin, *rec.* P. Kennedy and A. Lomax, 1951: *Folk Songs of Britain,* vol. I, CAEDMON TC1142/ TOPIC 12T157

Other recorded versions
Sarah Makem, Keady, Armagh, *rec.* P. Kennedy and S. O'Boyle, 1952: BBC 18474
Paddy Doran, Belfast, *rec.* P. Kennedy and S. O'Boyle, 1952: BBC 18580
Mary McGarvey, Donegal, *rec.* S. Ennis, 1954: BBC 21837
Thomas Moran, Mohill, Co. Leitrim, *rec.* S. Ennis, 1954: BBC 22035
John McLaverty, Belfast, *rec.* P. Kennedy and S. O'Boyle, 1952: BBC 22336
Peter Jones, Bromsash, Ross-on-Wye, Herefordshire, *rec.* M. Karpeles and P. Shuldham-Shaw, 1952: BBC 18620
Charlie Scamp, Chartham Hatch, Canterbury, Kent, *rec.* P. Kennedy, 1954: BBC 19965
Ben Baxter, Southrepps, Norfolk, *rec.* S. Ennis, 1955: BBC 22157
Harry Cox, Catfield, Yarmouth, Norfolk, *rec.* P. Kennedy, 1956: BBC 22915

Printed versions
JOHNSON: 1790: *A Waukrife Minnie, coll.* Robert Burns, Nithsdale, Scotland
BARING GOULD: 1889: no. 73: *On a May Morning so early,* words rewritten (Devon)

FORD: 1899: *My Rolling Eye* (Perthshire, Scotland)
JFSS: 1901, no. 3, p. 92: *coll.* Merrick (Surrey)
JFSS: 1905, no. 6, p. 9: *coll.* Sharp (Somerset)
JFSS: 1913, no. 17, p. 291: *coll.* Butterworth (Sussex), *coll.* R. Vaughan Williams
JFSS: 1918, no. 21, p. 7: *coll.* F. Keel (Surrey)
SHARP MS: 1904-23: twenty-four variants (England)
GARDINER MS: 1905-9: four variants (Hampshire)
HAMMOND MS: 1905-6: three variants (Somerset and Dorset)
SHARP AND MARSON: 1905, vol. II: words adapted (Somerset)
BUTTERWORTH: 1912, p. 16 (Sussex)
KIDSON AND MOFFAT: 1927, p. 2 (Yorkshire)
HENRY: 1924, no. 152: *Come over the Burn;* no. 793: *As I gaed over a Whinny Knowe* (N. Ireland)
REEVES: 1958, p. 126: original words, *coll.* Sharp (Sussex)
REEVES: 1960, p. 238: original words, *coll.* Baring Gould (Devon)
PURSLOW: 1968, p. 104: *coll.* Gardiner (Hampshire)
HAMER: 1973, p. 75 (Lincolnshire)

SHARP AND KARPELES: 1917/1932, no. 11, p. 156 (Virginia)
COX: 1925, p. 394 (Virginia)
EDDY: 1939, p. 188 (Ohio)
CREIGHTON AND SENIOR: 1950, p. 164 (Nova Scotia)
PEACOCK: 1965, p. 284

A good leading question to persuade an English or Irish country singer to launch into what you hope may be a good traditional song, and one with a good tune, is to ask him if he knows any old love songs beginning with 'As I roved out' or 'As I walked out'. Although there are at least a score of other Courtship Ballads which could employ such an opening, the chances are that you will be treated to a version of this song.

This love song has a question and answer pattern which is found in the older type of Anglo-Scots 'riddling' ballads. In fact there is a Scots ballad, *The Trooper and the Maid* (Child: no. 299), of similar theme from which the Anglo-Irish form may well derive. A similar courtship duet also appears in the Seduction Song *Rolling in the Dew* (No. 189) and in *Where are you going to, my Pretty Maid?* of which we have a Cornish version (No. 94).

The age of our incomparable maiden is given as 'sixteen Monday morning', but other versions, and that used as a convenience title by scholars, have 'seventeen come Sunday'. It is a classic encounter, with the stage just right for rural romance: a bright May morning, the girl with shining hair hanging down over her shoulders, and the boy invited to return later when the moon shines bright and clearly. In the lingua franca of British folksong 'she leads his horse to the stable'.

122 BLACKBERRY GROVE

Ted Lambourne, North Marston, Bletchley, Buckinghamshire, *rec.* S. Ennis, 1952: BBC 18140

Printed versions
BARING GOULD AND SHEPPARD: 1895, p. 25: words only
HAMMOND MS: 1905, no. 101: George Roper (Dorset)
BARING GOULD AND SHARP: 1906, no. 51: *One Michaelmas Morn*

A young labouring lad wakes up late. Remembering he has a long way to travel to get to his next job, he has no time for breakfast. He is already hot and sweating as he sets off on his journey. Going through Blackberry Grove, he picks some of the ripe berries to moisten his mouth, and we can easily visualise his lips purple with berry juice when suddenly his attention is caught by the sight of the cool milkmaid, dressed all in white, in sad lamentation under a tree.

Seamus Ennis, who sang *As I Roved Out* (No. 121), collected *Blackberry Grove* from a window-cleaner in Buckinghamshire. Ted Lambourne had learned it as a child from an old man who was now 'gone on'. The vivid picture portrayed in the song caught his fancy and it has always remained in his mind.

Michaelmas was an important time in the country calendar, for it was then that the farm labourers moved to new employment. This therefore was a day when a young man could have a lot of money in his pocket and it was also the occasion when a young milkmaid could well afford to arrange for one of her cows to kick over the bucket and spill all the precious milk. This was the clever trick she used to hook the lad she wanted before he left the district.

123 THE BONNY WEE WINDOW

Jack Goodfellow, Rennington, Northumberland, *rec.*
P. Kennedy, 1954: BBC 22444

GREIG: 1909–14, no. cxxiii
ORD: 1930, p. 99

Printed versions
FORD: 1899, p. 20: eleven verses without tune (Scotland)

RANDOLPH: 1946, vol. I, p. 431: seven variants: words only (Missouri, USA)

In the spring, the laugh is on young Johnny who succeeds in getting his head stuck in a bonny wee hole in the bonny wee window. The panes are called 'lozens' in Scots and this particular window conveniently lacked one of its 'lozens'.
     The rest of the story is given in the three final verses which we quote from a Scots version from FORD: 1899:

As soon as the window in ruins did lie
Auld granny let out such a horrible cry
It alarmed a' the neighbours; Lad, lass, man and wife
And caused poor Johnny to rin for his life

O'er hill and o'er dale he pursued his way hame
Like a bear that was hunted, ne'er lookin' behin'
And the neighbours they followed wi' clamour and squeals
While some o' them hunted their dogs at their heels

Frae the bonny wee window . . .

As he ran frae the window . . .

When Johnny got hame, wi' a hatchet did he
Frae his wooden gravat syne set himsel' free
But he wow'd that the de'il micht tak' him for his ain
If he e'er kissed a lass through a window again

Be she ever sae bonny, or live wi' her granny
Or the bonniest wee lassie that ever he saw

The various embarrassments of young lovers, the predicaments and awkward places in which they land themselves, are popular subjects for Courtship Songs, particularly in the Scottish lowlands and north-east Scotland. There are also two English examples in this chapter: *The Greasy Cook* (No. 129) and *Harry the Tailor* (No. 131). In these songs the chimney flue, the water well and the window pane respectively bring a symbolic sexual significance into otherwise apparently innocent humorous ditties.
     Jack Goodfellow learned this song at South Ord in Berwickshire, Scotland, the place where he was born in 1892.

124 CA THE YOWES TO THE KNOWES

Togo Crawford, Mossdale, Kirkcudbrightshire, *rec.* P.
Kennedy, 1954: BBC 21486 and 22879

FORD: 1899, p. 225: *Lovely Molly* (with tune)
GREIG: 1909–14, no. 1: *Lovely Mollie*
HENRY: 1924, no. 175: *The Yowe Lamb*
DUNCAN MS: W. 141; M. 100: *Lovely Molly*

Printed versions
JOHNSON: 1789: contains an air collected by Robert Burns
CHRISTIE: 1876, vol. I, p. 148: *Ca the Ewes to the Fauld,
Jamie, wi me*

As Molly was milking her yowes on a day
Willie came to her and thus he did say
As your fingers so nimble, will ye gang wi me?
And we'll ca the yowes ower the knowes, Molly and me

It was the fine air to this song which Robert Burns sent to Johnson's Scots Musical Museum, which has made one version of the tune perhaps better known than the original words.
     Certainly the song is a classic and deserves more attention. The above is the first verse from the Northern Ireland version in the Sam Henry collection which has a fine triple-time tune and similar words to the version in this volume.
     Tommy's problem here is how to get Molly away from her father when she tells him he only has to 'ask Daddy':

My father's a shepherd herds sheep on yon hill
If you get his sanction I'll be at your will

Tommy finds the answer all right. All he has to do is to talk to him in a language he will understand, the technical language of sheep:

Ye'll gae doon to the buchts where the yowes stand ane and a'
And ye'll wile the best ewe lamb that is among them a'
He went down to the chamber where his true lovie lay
And in spite of a father he's ta'en her away

Pox be on you, Johnnie, for ye hae me beguiled
Ye sought but ae ewe lamb and ye've taken my child
But since I once said it, e'en so let it be
Come ca the yowes to the knowes, Johnnie, wi' me

Gavin Greig points out that the word 'ca' is not the vernacular form of 'call' but is a Scots word meaning 'to drive'.

125 COLIN AND PHOEBE

Harry Cox, Catfield, Norfolk, *rec.* P. Kennedy, 1954
Printed versions
KIDSON: 1891, p. 73: two traditional variants of the tune published 'original', dated 1755
GARDINER MS: 1906–9, no. 323 (Hampshire) and no. 1366 (Sussex)

SHARP MS: 1909, vol. V: two variants (Somerset)
GILL: 1917, p. 2
KIDSON AND MOFFAT: 1926, p. 106: another tune
HAMMOND MS: 1906: one variant (Dorset)

PEACOCK: 1965, p. 510: *Bold Escallion and Phoebe* (Canada)

The most dangerous moment in the act of courtship always seems to be when one of the couple appears to have made the irrevocable decision never to marry. This is the cruel test which leads to a happy result. In this case it is Phoebe who tells Colin that she wishes to opt out of their friendship:

> That I will die a virgin
> So I pray let me go

Fair enough. Colin had only come to ask Phoebe to marry him the very next day. He has been slighted so he is not going to waste any more time on Phoebe. That does the trick. Phoebe is not so heartless after all:

> That the girl you thought cruel
> Will always prove kind

Kidson mentions that he came across the 'original' in a twenty-four page folio *The New Ballads sung by Mr Lowe and Miss Stevenson at Vauxhall London 1755*. The song is called *Corydon and Phoebe: A Dialogue*. In the third verse of the version given here there is 'a couple hard by', in Kidson's traditional version there is 'a cottage' and in the published 'original' it is 'chaste Cythia' who is near by.

Harry Cox, from whom this song was recorded, sings 'Colin' as 'Col-yeen', pronouncing it rather like the Irish word 'colleen'; in the Kidson versions the name is Corydon.

126 COME WRITE ME DOWN THE POWERS ABOVE

Cecilia Costello, Birmingham, *rec.* P. Kennedy, 1951: BBC 17034
Other recorded version
Jim, John, Bob and Ron Copper, Rottingdean, Sussex: BBC 17986
Printed versions
BARING-GOULD MS: 1891, no. 133: *The Scornful Dame* (Devon)
JFSS: 1899, no. 1, p. 22: *Wedding Song* (Kate Lee from the Copper family, Sussex)

SHARP AND MARSON: 1904–9, vol. III: two versions (Somerset)
JEFDSS: 1954, p. 149: two-part transcription of the Copper variant
HAMMOND MS: 1905–7: two variants (Dorset)
GARDINER MS: 1907: variant (Hampshire)
PURSLOW: 1972, p. 17: *coll.* Hammond (Dorset)

PEACOCK: 1965, p. 571: *Oh Write me down, ye Powers above*: six verses (Newfoundland, Canada)

> Come write me down the powers above
> That first created a man to love

Sussex singers, such as the Copper family, call this song *The Wedding Song*, and for good reason, as we discover. Like *Colin and Phoebe* (No. 125) it is concerned with the age-old courtship problem of Colin getting Phoebe to make up her mind.

An appeal for recognition from Heaven is made by a young man who cannot get his 'scornful dame' into the marrying mood. He promises all the usual things—gold, pearls and costly robes—but she replies that this is not her main interest. All he has to say is that he will go off and find another girl. He picks up his hat (that's the part that does it) and she agrees in the Canadian version to marry him the very next day, as quickly as that:

> My roving days are gone and passed
> My joy and comfort has come at last
> How happy, happy I shall be
> Since God has found his love for me

127 THE COUNTRY COURTSHIP

Edwin Cox and Harry Stephens, Wool, Dorset, *rec.* P. Kennedy, 1954: BBC 21496–7

Other recorded version
Fanny Rumble and Albert Collins, Tilshead, Wiltshire, *rec.* P. Kennedy, 1954: *What Shall I Wear to the Wedding, John?* BBC 21493

Printed versions
D'URFEY: 1719
Wit's Cabinet (1731): *The Clown's Courtship*
CHAPPELL: 1858, p. 87
ROXBURGHE: 1871–93, c. 20, f. 10, vol. IV: *Quoth John to Joan*
HERD: MS XLVII: *Nichol o' Cod*
HERD: 1769: *Reckle Mahudie*
HALLIWELL: 1849: *My dear Nicholas Wood*
JFSS: 1905, no. 6, p. 58: *Joan to Jan, coll.* C. Sharp, Devon

SHARP MS: 1908 and 1912: sent by Baring Gould (Devon)
WILLIAMS: 1923, p. 168: *When Shall we get Married?* (Gloucestershire)
JFSS: 1931, no. 35, p. 257: *My Old Sweet Nichol, coll.* E. J. Moeran, Norfolk, 1924: variant from HERD: 1769
OPIE: 1951, p. 74
REEVES: 1958, p. 221: from SHARP: 1908 (Devon). In the MS the title is *Nickety Nod*: the song was preceded by a dance
HAMER: 1967, p. 30: *When Shall we get Married, John?* (Bedfordshire)
HAMER: 1973, p. 60: *When Shall we get Married?* (Lancashire)

LOMAX: 1960, p. 315: *Buffalo Boy:* a composite variant of *The Mountaineer's Courtship* from the Stoneman family and Sam Hinton (USA)

The village tailor and undertaker of Wool in Dorset combined to sing this dialogue which they had learned from their respective uncles.

> EDWIN COX: 'My uncle sang this as *The Lady from London*, and it'd been handed down from ages. I had on a black crinoline dress, red shawl, a kind of bonnet, parasol and veil. I wore my wife's shoes as I take the same size as 'er, number seven.'
> HARRY STEPHENS: 'I had on a smock frock, brown leggings, a red tie and a billy-cocked hat.'
> EDWIN COX (prompting): 'And a bit of straw in his mouth.'

According to William Chappell the variant of this song, *Quoth John to Joan*, is 'certainly as old as the time of Henry VIII'.

> Quoth John to Joan, wilt thou have me?
> I prithee now wilt? And I'se marry with thee
> My cow, my calf, my house, my rents
> And all my lands and tenements
> O say my Joan, say my Joan, will not that do?
> I cannot come every day to woo

Cecil Sharp had great difficulty in noting a survival of this *Joan to Jan* at Meshaw in Devon. William Nott, the old man who sang it, said, 'It is very difficult to sing, for you must show the two voices', as in:

> I long to be married, says Joan to Jan
> I have no boots for to get married in
> An old pair of bootlegs will do
> O what an 'orrid thing for to get married in
> Good as other poor folks, says Joan to Jan

Stockings, breeches, waistcoat, jacket and necktie follow, and in the final verse:

> I've no hat to be married in
> An old bee butt will do, says Joan to Jan

A Scottish version *Reckle Mahudie* (HERD: 1769) has a dialogue between a mother and her miserly son for whom she is trying to find a wife:

> Where will we get a wife to you
> My auld son, Reckle Mahudie?
>
> Wha but Maggie a-yont the burn
> She'll make a wife right gudie

> I fear she'll be but a sober wife
> My auld son, Reckle Mahudie
>
> I believe you'd hae me seek a king's dochter
> But foul fa' me if I dudie

Another version *Nichol o' Cod* (*Songs from David Herd's manuscripts*), has the last line:

> I think the auld runt be gane mad

The song may also be sung solo by the girl, instead of as a dialogue as in *My Old Sweet Nichol* collected in Norfolk by the Irish composer E. J. Moeran:

> O when shall we get married?
> My old sweet Nichol did say
> O we'll get married o' Sunday
> For I think that is wonderful good

128 EASTER SNOW

Brigid Tunney, Belleek, County Fermanagh, N. Ireland,
  rec. P. Kennedy and S. O'Boyle, 1952: BBC 18527
Other recorded version
Played as an air on the fiddle by John Doherty, Donegal,
  Ireland, *rec.* P. Kennedy and S. O'Boyle, 1953: BBC
  19535

Printed versions
PETRIE COLL: 1902–5: *Iseart Nuadhain* (1851)
HENRY: 1924: no. 66: *Wester Snow*

CREIGHTON: 1961, p. 43: three verses *The Easter Snow*
  (New Brunswick, Canada)

As a result of the suppression of the Irish language, a parallel tradition has grown up in English which makes use of an existing repertoire of Irish tunes. Many, often unbeknown to their performers, contain political significance, or started their life within the tradition of political allegory, the girl being the symbol of Ireland.

Whether or not *Easter Snow* contains this element, it does have an interesting courtship conversation between a highly eloquent shepherd and 'a simple maiden of the moor'. He wants her to watch the fox-hunting by the well-mounted nobility, but she asks him to 'forbear such splendid eloquence for one who is so poor' and tells him:

> My heart is not my own to give
> Nor can I it bestow
> 'Tis pledged to one who lives and loves
> Far from Easter Snow

Easter Snow would appear to be a townland in Roscommon called Estersnowe, previously the Gaelic *Iseart Nuadhain*, which is the title given to the tune in the Petrie collection. Lough Rea (pron. 'Ray'), also mentioned in the song, separates Roscommon and Longford.

129 THE GREASY COOK

Harry Cox, Potter Heigham, Norfolk, *rec.* P. Kennedy,
  1953: DTS LFX 4 (1965)
Other recorded versions
John McLaverty, Belfast, N. Ireland, *rec.* P. Kennedy
  and S. O'Boyle, 1952: BBC 18376
Leslie Johnson, Fittleworth, Sussex, *rec.* R. Cooper,
  1954, *The Cook's Choice*: BBC 22762
Sam Larner, Winterton, Norfolk, 1959, *Butter and
  Cheese and All*: BBC LP 26076

Printed versions
GARDINER MS: 1905: variant (Somerset)
WILLIAMS: 1923, p. 108 (Oxfordshire and Berkshire)
SEEGER AND MACCOLL: 1960, p. 99: *Butter and Cheese
  and All*
STUBBS: 1970, p. 38 (Sussex)

GREENLEAF: 1933, p. 108 (Newfoundland, Canada)
PEACOCK: 1965, p. 251 (Newfoundland, Canada)

It's a pity you should tease me so
Or tempt me for to sing
You know it never lay in my power
To do any such a thing
To do any such a thing

But since that you do plague me so
I'll see what I can do
And when I come to the chorus
You must all help me too
We must all help him too

So goes one set of opening verses for this Courting-in-the-Kitchen-type song which enjoys widespread popularity in England and Ireland. One Northern Ireland performer closed the song with:

So all you sporting bachelors
A-courtin' cooks do go
Take your fill in pocket alone
For fear you overthrow
For fear you overthrow

For if you don't you'll surely rue
'Twill prove your downfall
For I was thrown out in the middle of the night
My butter and cheese and all
Butter and cheese and all

130 THE GREENWOOD LADDIE

Charles Boyle, Belfast, N. Ireland, *rec.* P. Kennedy and
S. O'Boyle, 1952: BBC 18404
Other recorded version
Robert Cinnamond, Belfast: BBC 24842

Printed version
JOYCE: 1909, no. 633, p. 322: *The Greenwood Lad* (tune
only)

> You muses assist me, there's none can resist me
> Only that fair one whom I do adore
> And while others do tease me, he's the young man can please me
> And he's my Greenwood Laddie whom I'll always adore

Robert Cinnamond had this opening to a song, which may well have originated as a translation from Irish. Charles Boyle learned the song from his mother in Belfast, who said it was sung regularly in the mills and factories in Belfast in her younger days.

The song tells us that the young lad was too poor to get her parents' permission for marriage, but his green-ness may well have a deeper political significance beyond that of unfulfilled love.

131 HARRY THE TAILOR

Harry and Bill Westaway, Belstone, Devon, *rec.* P. Kennedy, 1950; Bill Westaway, 1952: BBC 17793

Printed versions
SHARP MS: 1904–9: two variants (Somerset)
VAUGHAN WILLIAMS: 1908: *The Cobbler and the Tailor*
(Cambridgeshire)

A sudden fit of courtship courage sends hapless Harry off to visit his darling, Dolly the dairymaid, but to dampen his ardour Dolly shoves him in the well. Not believing that young ladies like Dolly could do such a thing, he accuses his rescuer, the infuriated farmer, who then throws a basin of buttermilk over him. Returning home 'like a poor drowned rat', Harry decides that courtship is not for him.

The tune used for this song, sometimes known as *The Chapter of Donkeys* (or *Accidents*), is used for a number of other similar songs. As *Swaggering Boney* it is the tune used for a Cotswold morris dance. It is well known among country singers in England as the tune for *Joe Muggins* (or *I don't mind if I do*). Ralph Vaughan Williams noted a tune for the song in Cambridgeshire and used it for a variant of *The Cunning Cobbler* (No. 197).

132 THE LABOURING MAN'S DAUGHTER

Frederick Crossman, Huish Episcopi, Somerset, *rec.* P. Kennedy, 1950
Other recorded version
Lal Smith (Irish tinker), Belfast, N. Ireland, *rec.* P. Kennedy and S. O'Boyle, 1952: BBC 18304 (middle verses omitted)

Printed versions
SHARP MS: six variants (Somerset)
SHARP AND MARSON: 1904–9, vol. I, no. 36: *A Cornish Young Man* (Somerset)

KIDSON AND MOFFAT: 1926, p. 118: *The Knight's Dream* (Yorkshire)
JFSS: 1905, no. 6, p. 53: Cecil Sharp's variant from Mr Crossman's father and words from a broadside by Jackson (Birmingham)
HAMMOND MS: 1906: variant (Dorset)
JFSS: 1906, no. 9, p. 273 (Yorkshire)
PEACOCK: 1965, p. 540: *Knight and Labourman's Daughter* (Newfoundland, Canada)

> For love is, my dear, like a stone in a sling
> And it's hard to believe all that's spoken
> So you take up this ring and this guinea in gold
> And between us never let it be broken

This was the last verse noted by Cecil Sharp from Frederick Crossman's father, who had the same name. After fifty years there seems to be little variation in the tune in one generation but there are marked differences in the words. This is probably due to the fact that the son remembers it being sung by an old man from a neighbouring village and was not aware that his father knew the song at all.

A broadside version quoted by Cecil Sharp gives three further verses:

If I should consent your bride for to be
Your parents would both be offended
Besides they would always be frowning on me
Because you are highly descended

As for father and mother I've none in this world
I've none but myself and a brother
And as to my friends they will not frown on me
So we can but love one another

So now he has gained his joy and delight
They're living in great joy and plenty
A labouring man's daughter has married a knight
Heaven protect them both together

133 THE LION'S DEN

Teresa Maguire, Belfast, N. Ireland, *rec.* S. O'Boyle, 1955: *Folk Songs of Britain*, vol. VIII, CAEDMON TC 1164/TOPIC 12T196: BBC LP 24842

Other recorded version
Robert Taylor, Hilltown, County Down, N. Ireland, *rec.* P. Kennedy and S. O'Boyle, 1953: BBC 19592

Printed versions
CHRISTIE: 1881, vol. II, p. 126 (Aberdeenshire, Scotland)
SHARP AND MARSON: 1904–9, vol. III, no. 56: *The Bold Lieutenant*, two variants (Somerset)
HAMMOND MS: 1908: one variant (Dorset)

GREIG: 1914, no. 68: *In Roslyn Isles there Lived a Lady* (fifteen verses)
JFSS: 1916, no. 20, p. 258: *coll.* C. Sharp, Somerset
HENRY: 1924, no. 474: *The Glove and the Lions* (N. Ireland)
ORD: 1930, p. 393

CREIGHTON: 1932, p. 87: *Lion's Den* (Canada)
CREIGHTON: 1962, p. 34: *The Lady's Fan* (Canada)
KARPELES: 1971, p. 140: three versions (Newfoundland, Canada)

Cecil Sharp believed this song to be based on a folk tale which probably preceded the account of an actual incident in France in the sixteenth century, as given by Seigneur de Brantome in 1666. Schiller used the incident as the basis for *Der Handschuh* (1797) and later Robert Browning followed him with *The Glove*, one of his dramatic romances.

Writing in the JFSS, Lucy Broadwood drew attention to the fact that the British traditional texts end with happy marriage, but in the literary versions the hero throws his glove in the lady's face.

Leigh Hunt, who composed a ballad called *The Glove and the Lions*, also had this ending:

She dropped her glove to prove his love
Then looked at him and smiled
He bowed and in a moment leaped
Among the lions wild
The leap was quick; return was quick
He soon regained his place
Then threw the glove, but not with love
Right in the lady's face.

But in one of the Scots traditional versions there are two final verses:

It was not long till the King got notice
Two of his lions they were slain
He was not in the least displeased
But gave him honour for the same

He has raised him from a Third Lieutenant
And made him Admiral of the Blue
So the next day they both got married
See what the power of love can do

Lions were kept at the Tower of London from the time of Henry III down to 1834.

134 THE LONG AND WISHING EYE

George Spicer, Copthorne, Sussex, *rec*. P. Kennedy and M. Plunkett, 1956: BBC LP 23093

Other recorded version
Edwin Thomas, Allerford, Somerset, *rec*. P. Kennedy and M. Karpeles, 1952, *Midsummer's Morning*: BBC 17782

Printed versions
SHARP MS: 1904–14: six variants
GARDINER MS: 1905–9: six variants (Cornwall, Hampshire and Sussex)

HAMMOND MS: 1905: one variant (Somerset)
JOYCE: 1909, p. 180: *Searching for Young Lambs* (Ireland)
HENRY: 1924, no. 548: *One Morning Clear* (N. Ireland)
REEVES: 1958, p. 148: *coll*. C. Sharp, Devon, 1904

CREIGHTON AND SENIOR: 1950, p. 133 (Nova Scotia, Canada)

As I walked out one midsummer's morn
There did I hide myself under a thorn
And there I saw a fair pretty maid, I saw her to pass by
Whilst young Johnny followed after with a long and wishing eye

This was the first verse as sung by Ernest Thomas of Allerford near Minehead in Somerset. Although Cecil Sharp collected six versions of the song in Somerset, none were published. Gardiner also collected six in Cornwall, Hampshire and Sussex. Under the title *Searching for Young Lambs*, Joyce printed a four-verse family version from County Limerick in Ireland. He described it as a 'pleasing little peasant pastoral'.

Good morrow, gentle shepherd, have you seen any lambs?
This morning a pair strayed away from their dams
If you have seen them pass you by, come tell to me, I pray
That those innocent lambs from their dams no farther stray

The artful Johnny is not so much helping her to find the young lambs as sending her off to a nearby field of long green grass where he can observe her from his hiding place in the nearby hawthorn hedge.

135 MADAM, WILL YOU WALK?

Lottie Chapman, North Waltham, Hampshire, *rec*. R. Copper, 1955: BBC 21860: *The Silver Pin*

Other recorded version
Mr and Mrs John Mearns, Aberdeen, *rec*. A. Lomax, 1951: BBC 2145

Printed versions
HALLIWELL: 1849, p. 21: contains a note about the keys of Canterbury (Yorkshire)
MASON: 1877, p. 27: *Madam I Present You with Six Rows of Pins* (Northumberland)
BURNE: 1884: *The Disdainful Lady* (Shropshire)
BARING GOULD: 1889, no. 22: *Blue Muslin* (Devon)
BROADWOOD: 1893, p. 32: *I Will Give You the Keys of Heaven* (Cheshire, Yorkshire and from BARING GOULD)
GOMME: 1894–8: singing game variants, *There Stands a Lady on the Mountain*
DUNCAN MS: 1900: *When I Was Young I Was Well Beloved* (Scotland)
SHARP: 1902, no. 59, p. 126: *coll*. Broadwood (Cheshire)
SHARP MS: 1904–18: five variants (Somerset)
GARDINER MS: 1905–9: six variants, nos. 62, 49, 986, 1248, 1267, 1357 (Hampshire)

HAMMOND MS: 1905–6: one variant, no. 52 (Somerset); two variants, nos. 563, 565 (Dorset)
SHARP AND MARSON: 1904–9, vol. III, no. 63: *The Keys of Heaven* (Somerset)
GILLINGTON: 1909: singing game variants, *The Keys of Heaven* (Surrey); *Lady on the Mountain* (Isle of Wight); *There Stands a Lady in the Ocean* (Hampshire)
SHARP: 1921, vol. II, p. 110: *The Keys of Canterbury*
UDAL: 1922, p. 135: words only (Dorset)
WILLIAMS: 1923, pp. 80–1: two variants, *If You Will Walk With Me* (Gloucestershire and Wiltshire)
JFSS: 1923, no. 27, p. 92: two variants, *coll*. Hammond, *O Madam I Will Give to Thee* (Somerset)
JEFDSS: 1961, p. 77: the present variant from Lottie Chapman
HAMER: 1967, p. 80: *The Little Row of Pins* (Cambridgeshire)
PURSLOW: 1968, p. 71: *coll*. Hammond (Somerset)

NEWELL: 1903, p. 51 (USA)
SHARP AND KARPELES: 1917–32, no. 92: six variants, *The Keys of Heaven* (USA)

I'll gie to you a pennyworth o' preens
To fasten up your flounces and aither bonny things
If you'll walk, if you'll talk
If you'll walk wi' me

I'll gie to you a yellow hairy muff
To keep you han'ies warm when the weather's cold and rough

I'll gie to you a cosy armchair
To rest your sellie in, when your banes are all unsair

330

But I'll gie to you the keys o' my hairt
And frae you, I'll never never pairt

So runs the Scots duet version sung to us by Mr and Mrs John Mearns in Aberdeenshire. A Northumbrian question and answer version presents her with 'six rows of pins':

Madam, I present you with six rows of pins
The very first offering my true love brings

Madam I present you with a little silver bell
To call up your servants when you're not well

Madam I present you with a pretty golden watch
To hang by your side when you go to church

A Devonshire version, *Blue Muslin* (pronounced mous-el-ine), collected by Baring Gould before the turn of the century, was sung as a question and answer and then the whole was sung again in the reverse order:

O will you accept the mus-e-lin so blue
To wear all in the morning and to dabble in the dew?

O will you accept of the pretty silver pin
To pin your golden hair with the fine mus-e-lin?

O will you accept of a pair of shoes of cork
The one is made in London, the other's made in York?

O will you accept of the keys of Canterbury
That all the bells of England may ring and make us merry?

O will you accept of a kiss from loving heart
That we may join together and never more may part?

A Yorkshire version from Masham collected by Lucy Broadwood has the following:

I will give you the keys of heaven
To lock the gates when the clock strikes seven

In many areas children have used the song as a two team singing game. A Somerset singer at Combe Florey sang Henry Hammond a version in which the chorus was danced to a polka step:

If you will be my bride, my joy and my dear
If you'll go a-walking with me anywhere

136   THE MOUNTAIN STREAM

Denis Cassley, Glenshesk, Antrim, N. Ireland, *rec.* P. Kennedy and S. O'Boyle, 1953: BBC 20022

Other recorded versions
Brigid Tunney, Belleek, Fermanagh, N. Ireland, *rec.* P. Kennedy and S. O'Boyle, 1952: BBC 18526
Paddy Tunney (Brigid's son), *Folk Songs of Britain*, vol. I, CAEDMON TC1142/TOPIC 12T157
Jean Thompson, Blairgowrie, Perthshire, Scotland, *rec.* P. Kennedy, 1961

John Doherty (fiddle tune), *Where the Moorcocks Crow*, *rec.* P. Kennedy and S. O'Boyle, Donegal, 1953: BBC 19579

Printed version
HENRY: 1924, no. 32 (Coleraine, County Derry, N. Ireland)

Although the above versions have been recorded in Northern Ireland, it is thought that the song originates in Scotland, probably in Ayrshire; it has much in common with songs like *The Corncrake* (*among the whinny knowes*) which come from there.

However Sam Henry, who published a County Derry version from the Houston Collection, added a note that it had been composed by a roving sportsman in honour of a young lady at Letterban in Northern Ireland.

137 NEXT MONDAY MORNING

Harry Cox, Catfield, Norfolk, *rec.* P. Kennedy, 1953: DTS LFX 4 (1965)

Other recorded version
Thomas Moran, Mohill, Leitrim, Ireland, *rec.* S. Ennis, 1954: BBC 22036

Printed versions
SHARP AND MARSON: 1904–9, vol. I, no. 3: *The Sign of the Bonny Blue Bell* (Somerset)
JOYCE: 1873, no. 17: *I'm Going to Get Married on Sunday* (Ireland)

JFSS: 1905, no. 6, p. 51: *At the Sign of the Bonny Blue Bell*, *coll.* C. Sharp, Somerset, 1904; Newcastle broadside
HAMMOND MS: 1907: two variants, 739, 907 (Dorset)
JFSS: 1931, no. 35, p. 260: *As I was a-Walking One Morning in Spring*, *coll.* E. J. Moeran, Norfolk, 1926

CREIGHTON AND SENIOR: 1940, p. 25: *I'm Going to get Married* (Nova Scotia, Canada)
PEACOCK: 1965, p. 559 (Newfoundland, Canada)

This song is a word of advice to a young girl who apparently decided to get married at the age of twelve. She has already waited three years and does not intend to postpone the wedding day any more:

> If a maid I remain when I rise again
> I shall wish I had never a-seen Monday morning

Though there is no indication in the song, the day could well be Whit Monday or Easter Monday and the preparations take place on the Sunday. An Irish version however has the wedding on the Sunday.

138 NO SIR

Emily Bishop, Bromsberrow Heath, Herefordshire, *rec.* P. Kennedy, 1952: BBC 18678

Other recorded versions
James Copper, Rottingdean, Sussex, *rec.* P. Kennedy, 1951: BBC 16063
Albert Beale, Kenardington, Kent, *rec.* M. Karpeles and P. Kennedy, 1954: *No John, no*
Sam Larner, Winterton, Norfolk, *rec.* P. Kennedy, 1958

Printed versions
SHARP MS: 1903–13: eight variants
HAMMOND MS: 1906–7: two variants, nos. 417, 880 (Dorset)

SHARP AND MARSON: 1904–9, vol. IV, no. 94: *O No John* (Somerset)
GARDINER MS: 1909: one variant (Wiltshire)
JFSS: 1913, no. 17, p. 300: *coll.* C. Sharp (Somerset; Kent)
REEVES: 1958, no. 68, p. 162: composite text of four variants, *coll.* C. Sharp; also a discussion on the song, pp. 33–7
PURSLOW: 1965, p. 63: two Dorset variants, *coll.* Hammond, *No, Sir, No*
HAMER: 1973, p. 58 (Lancashire)
LOMAX: 1960, p. 314: *Uh-uh No* (USA)

O No John, the version published by Cecil Sharp in *Folk Songs from Somerset* in 1908, was republished again in Novello's *School Songs* and in volume two of the *Selected Edition of English Folk Songs* in 1921. As a result of its popularity Sharp's version has become a 'national song'.

In fact Cecil Sharp only used two of the original verses, as they were sung to him by William Wooley of Bincombe, Somerset, for 'the rest of the song was coarse and needed considerable revision'. Apart from the need for making the song suitable for schoolchildren, there was another reason for his decision. He did not recognise the song as being distinct from *Madam, will you walk?* (No. 135), which he called *The Keys of Heaven* and of course from other songs and children's singing game versions such as *Twenty Eighteen, Ripest Apples* and *On Yonder Hill there Stands a Lady*.

It is easy now, in the light of all the many song versions recorded in England and America, to recognise separate identities, but even so there are plenty of 'mixed' versions.

139 OLD GREY BEARD

Jeannie Robertson, Aberdeen, Scotland, *rec.* P. Kennedy, 1953: *Folk Songs of Britain*, vol. I, CAEDMON TC1142/TOPIC 12T157

Printed versions
RAMSAY: 1724: *The Young Lass contra Auld Man*
HERD: 1776: *The Carle he came o'er the Croft*
JOHNSON: 1853, vol. IV, no. 416
BELL: 1857, p. 237 (Northumberland)
MASON: 1877/1908, p. 33: *There was an A'd Man cam' over the Lea* (Northumberland)
KIDSON: 1891, p. 92: *An Auld Man he courted me* (N. Yorkshire)
FORD: 1899, p. 141: *The Carle he cam' over the Croft*
SHARP MS: 1904–21: four variants *My Mother Bid Me*

GARDINER MS: 1908: one variant (Hampshire)
GRAHAM: 1910, p. 10: *I'll Not Have Him* (Lancashire)
DUNCAN MS: 1911: one version (Aberdeenshire)
GREIG: 1914, p. 149: five variants *The Auld Carle*
WILLIAMS: 1923, p. 73: *The Old Grey Man* (Wiltshire)
JEFDSS: 1937, p. 130: *The Old Man from Lee* (Essex)
PURSLOW: 1965, p. 65: Gardiner variant *Old Grey Beard a'-wagging* (Hampshire)

SHARP AND KARPELES: 1917–32, vol. II, no. 108, p. 93: five variants *My Mother Bid Me* (USA)
COX: 1925, p. 489: *The Old Man who Came over the Moor* (USA)
JAFL: ccviii, p. 158 (Kentucky)

The song gives us the views of the young girl whose marriage has been arranged by her parents. No doubt the man is rich, but certainly he is old and unacceptable, and in the final verse the girl offers him to her mother:

> My mother tell'd me to gie him a kiss
> Ha, ha, but I would nae hae him
> If you like him so well, you can kiss him yoursel'
> Wi' his grey beard newly shaven

140 THE PLOUGHBOY

Lucy Stewart, Fetterangus, Aberdeenshire, Scotland, *rec.* P. Kennedy and H. Henderson, 1955

Other recorded versions
Jim O'Neill, Markethill, County Armagh, N. Ireland, *rec.* P. Kennedy and S. O'Boyle, 1952: BBC 18481
Lily Cook, Lewes, Sussex, *rec.* R. Copper, 1954: BBC 22736
Jim Copper, Rottingdean, Sussex, *rec.* P. Kennedy, 1951
Bob and Ron Copper, *rec.* P. Kennedy, 1955: *The Lark in the Morning*, EFDSS LP 1002
Paddy Tunney, Belleek, Fermanagh, N. Ireland, *rec.* P. Kennedy, London, 1958

Printed versions
KIDSON: 1891, p. 145: *The Pretty Ploughboy*
BARING GOULD: 1895, p. 58
SHARP: 1905–18: two variants

GARDINER: 1906–7: two variants (Hampshire)
HAMMOND: 1905: one variant (Dorset)
JFSS: 1906, no. 9, p. 272: Kidson; and an Edinburgh broadside, 1778
VAUGHAN WILLIAMS: 1908, p. 18 (Essex)
SHARP AND MARSON: 1904–9, vol. V, no. 105: *The Lark in the Morn* (Somerset)
WILLIAMS: 1923, p. 236: *The Ploughboys* (Wiltshire)
KIDSON AND MOFFAT: 1926, p. 18; and KIDSON AND MOFFAT: 1927
REEVES: 1960, no. 81, p. 172: two variants (words only) *The Lark in the Morn*, coll. Hammond, Dorset, 1905; and Gardiner, Hampshire, 1906
PURSLOW: 1965, p. 51: Hammond variant *The Lark in the Morning*

> The lark in the morn she arises from her nest
> She ascends all in the air with the dew upon her breast
> And with the pretty ploughboy she'll whistle and she'll stay
> And at night she'll return to her own nest again

So runs a Sussex version of the song. As is so often the case, the appeal of a song may come from one particular verse, in which the symbolism sets the scene.

> When his day's work is over O then what will he do?
> It's all from his work, to some country wake he'll go
> And with his pretty sweetheart he'll whistle and he'll sing
> And at night he will return with his love home again

141 THE QUEEN AMONG THE HEATHER

Jeannie Robertson, Aberdeen, Scotland, *rec.* P. Kennedy, 1953: BBC 21093

Other recorded versions
Charlie Gillies, Angus, Scotland, *rec.* S. Ennis, 1953: *Up a Wide and Lonely Glen*: BBC 19018
Also from Duncan Burke, Perth, and Lucy Stewart, Fetterangus, Aberdeen, Scotland: *rec.* P. Kennedy and H. Henderson, 1955
Belle Stewart, Blairgowrie, Perthshire, *rec.* P. Kennedy, 1955

Printed versions
GREIG: 1909–14, no. 44: *Far up yon Wide and Lofty Glens* (Scotland)
MacColl: 1953, p. 75 and BUCHAN: 1962, p. 112: Jessie Murray, Banff, Scotland: *Skippin Barfit thro the Heather*

Compare
HENRY: 1924, no. 177: *O'er the Moor among the Heather* (N. Ireland)
O LOCHLAINN: 1965, no. 6, p. 12: *Doon the Moor* (N. Ireland)

> She barefoot was and homely clad
> And she was wearing neither hat nor feather
> Her plaid hung neatly roond her waist
> As she tripped o'er the blooming heather
> Doon the moor
> Doon the moor among the heather

So runs a Northern Ireland version of another 'heathery' song. Perhaps this was one of the traditional songs which inspired Robert Tannahill of Paisley, Scotland, to write *The Braes of Balquidder* and Frank McPeake in more recent years in Belfast to fashion his *Wild Mountain Thyme*:

> Will you go, lassie, go?
> And we'll all go together
> To pull wild mountain thyme
> All around the blooming heather
> Will you go, lassie, go?

142 THE SPOTTED COW

Harry Cox, Catfield, Norfolk, *rec.* P. Kennedy, 1953: DTS LFX 4 (1965); BBC 22915 (1956)

Other recorded versions
Jim Copper, Rottingdean, Sussex, *rec.* P. Kennedy, 1951
Bob Copper, Rottingdean, Sussex, 1955: BBC 21546
George Attrill, Fittleworth, Sussex, *rec.* R. Copper, 1954: BBC 22739

Printed versions
VOCAL LIBRARY: 1822, no. 1402, p. 517: *One Morning*
BARING GOULD: 1889, no. 74 (Devon)
KIDSON: 1891, p. 70: two variants of tune (Yorkshire)
SHARP MS: 1904–6: five variants (Somerset)
GARDINER MS: 1907–9: three variants (Hampshire)
HAMMOND MS: 1905: one variant (Somerset)
WILLIAMS: 1923, p. 71 (Wiltshire)
PURSLOW: 1968, p. 108: *coll.* Hammond (Somerset)

> My pretty maid, now whither you stray
> So early tell me now?
> The maid replied: Kind sir, she cried
> I have lost my spotted cow

What more heart-rending a situation is there than the sight of a gentle milkmaid, a symbol of undefiled purity, crying for the loss of her spotted cow, the symbol of female fertility? Although few versions have ever been published, the song has a currency which has outlived the milkmaids themselves.

Kidson notes that the words are on broadsides and also in Fairburn's *Everlasting Songster* (c. 1825).

143 WHEN A MAN'S IN LOVE

Michael Gallagher, Belleek, Fermanagh, N. Ireland, *rec.* P. Kennedy and S. O'Boyle, 1953: BBC 20025

Other recorded versions
Paddy Tunney (nephew of Michael Gallagher): *Folk Songs of Britain*, vol. I, CAEDMON TC1142/TOPIC 12T157
Winnie Ryan (tinker), Belfast, N. Ireland, *rec.* P. Kennedy and S. O'Boyle, 1952: BBC 18306
Sarah Makem, Keady, Armagh, N. Ireland, *rec.* P. Kennedy and S. O'Boyle, 1952: BBC 18412
Elizabeth Cronin, Cork, Ireland, *rec.* S. Ennis, 1952: BBC 19026

Thomas Moran, Mohill, *rec.* S. Ennis, 1954, Co. Leitrim, Ireland: BBC 22036 (1954)
Robert Cinnamond, Belfast, N. Ireland, *rec.* S. O'Boyle, 1955: BBC 24840

Printed versions
O'NEILL: 1903, p. 29: tune only (Ireland)
HENRY: 1924, no. 211 (Derry, N. Ireland)

CREIGHTON AND SENIOR: 1950, p. 214 (Nova Scotia, Canada)
LOMAX: 1960, p. 146 (Nova Scotia, Canada)
KARPELES: 1971, p. 194: two versions (Newfoundland, Canada)

> For a boy in love he feels no cold
> Like me some time ago
> Like a hero bold through frost and snow
> For to meet my girl I'll go
> O will you come to my parlour?
> O then will you come to my room?
> O will you come to some silent place
> Where I'll wait you each afternoon?

As sung by a seventeen-year-old Irish tinker girl, this song took on all the intensity of a modern popular love ballad. Her version, sung in a characteristic nasal style, used all the ornamental embellishments of the street-singer which have passed into the techniques of the popular crooner.

A fine variety of tunes are used to carry this story of a country courtship. In Nova Scotia Helen Creighton heard it to the *Lazarus* or *Star of the County Down* tune. Our tune has a characteristic, typical of modal tunes, in that the third tends to be uncertainly major or minor. There is also a halfway pause on the seventh in marked contrast to the more usual pause on the fifth note of the scale.

144 YOUNG ROGER ESQUIRE

Phil Tanner, Llangennith, Glamorganshire, Wales: BBC 13387 (1949): EFDSS LP 1005

Printed versions
BARING GOULD: 1889, no. 51: words re-cast (Devon)
KIDSON: 1891, p. 79: two variants of words (Yorkshire)
GARDINER MS: 1906–7: two variants (Hampshire)
GREIG: 1909–14, vol. II, lxvii: one-verse fragment (Aberdeen)
KIDSON AND MOFFAT: 1927, p. 6 (Yorkshire)
HENRY: 1924, no. 90 (N. Ireland)
PURSLOW: 1965, p. 40: from GARDINER: 1907 (Hampshire)

Other references
POUND: 1922, p. 80: *My father's Grey Mare* (Nebraska, USA)
FLANDERS AND BROWN: 1932, p. 62: *Gay Jemmie, the Miller* (Vermont, USA)
GREENLEAF: 1933, p. 59 (Newfoundland, Canada)
EDDY: 1939, p. 172 (Ohio, USA)
GARDNER AND CHICKERING: 1939, p. 392 (Michigan, USA)
BELDEN: 1940, p. 235 (Kansas, USA, from MS)
PEACOCK: 1965, p. 278 (Newfoundland, Canada)
JAFL: no. 12, p. 251: seven verses (Massachusetts, USA) from MS
JAFL: no. 35, p. 372 (Ohio, USA)

> I thought that your father
> Would have made no dispute
> But to give me his daughter
> And the grey mare to boot

This song only just gets into this chapter because Young Roger was not really courting the beautiful farmer's daughter but was instead after her father's grey mare!

The second verse in Kidson and that following verse three help to complete the story:

> The glittering money and beauty likewise
> Did tickle his fancy and dazzle his eyes
> Which caus-ed young Roger to tell of his mind
> And unto his lover be constant and kind
> That no other woman should ere be his bride
> For thou art my jewel
> For thou art my jewel
> My jewel and pride

Then Roger that rascal was turned out of door
And bid to begone and come there no more
Then Roger he tore his locks of long hair
And he wished he'd never stayed for the grey mare
Then Roger he tore his locks of long hair
And he wished he'd never stayed
And he wished he'd never stayed
For the grey mare

Bibliography

This bibliography has been divided into two sections. Books published in Britain and Ireland appear first, followed by those published abroad, both in alphabetical order

BARING GOULD: 1889–1905
Rev. S. Baring Gould and Rev. H. Fleetwood Sheppard, *Songs and Ballads of the West*: Patey & Willis, London (4 parts) 1889–91. Methuen, London (4 parts) 1891–4; (1 vol.) 1895; revised edition 1905. Details are given by E. A. White in JEFDSS: 1937, p. 143, and 1946, p. 67. When reprinted in four parts this collection, mainly from Devon and N. Cornwall, comprised 110 songs 'collected from the mouths of the people'. Texts were modified and in some cases completely rewritten and the same applied to tunes. However, in the revised edition, under the musical editorship of Cecil Sharp and with the adding of the name of the Rev. F. W. Bussell, one of the original collectors, many original texts and tunes were restored. For further comment on this publication see Dean-Smith: JEFDSS: 1950, p. 41.

BARING GOULD MS: 1889–95
Rev. S. Baring Gould. Manuscript in Plymouth City Library.

BARING GOULD AND SHEPPARD: 1895
Rev. S. Baring Gould and Rev. H. Fleetwood Sheppard, *A Garland of Country Song*: Methuen, London, 1895. 50 songs with much edited text compounded from various sources; detailed notes about songs, particularly those associated with customs, and comparative texts given. The introduction gives a history of folksong collecting from 1843.

BARING GOULD AND SHARP: 1906
Rev. S. Baring Gould and Cecil J. Sharp, *English Folk Songs for Schools*: Curwen, London, 1906. 53 songs from collections of both editors 'designed to meet the requirements of the Board of Education'—who that year had recommended the inclusion of National or Folk Songs in the school curriculum, and 'dedicated to T. R. H. Prince Edward and Prince Albert of Wales'.

BROADWOOD: 1893
Lucy Broadwood and J. A. Fuller-Maitland, *English County Songs*: Cramer, London, 1893. Important early publication containing 92 songs collected in nearly every county of England. Most have little relevance to their district origins but some are in the dialects of their locality. Scholarly presentation with straightforward piano accompaniments. For article about editor see JEFDSS: 1948, p. 136, and 1950, p. 38.

BURNE: 1884
Charlotte S. Burne, *Shropshire Folk-lore*: Trubner, London, 1884. In addition to local folk-lore there are accounts of Morris dance and Mummers play with song, a number of ballads and carols, wassail songs, some children's games and 'choral games'.

BUTTERWORTH: 1912
George Butterworth, *Folk Songs from Sussex*: Augener, London, 1912. 11 songs with piano arrangements collected by Butterworth and Francis Jekyll with names of singers and sources given in short preface. (For other songs noted by Butterworth see JFSS: 1913, No. 17.)

CHAPPELL: 1858/9
William Chappell, *Popular Music of the Olden Time*: Cramer, Beale & Chappell, London, vol. I 1858, vol. II 1859; Dover Publications, New York, 1965. Includes most of material from *National English Airs* (1838) but more has been added from other sources with particular reference to the ballads in the Pepys and Roxburghe collections. For further comment see Dean-Smith's *Guide* and JEFDSS: 1950, p. 38.

CHRISTIE: 1876/81
William Christie, *Traditional Ballad Airs*: Edmonston and Douglas, Edinburgh, vol. 1 1876, vol. II 1881. Dean Christie noted down songs mainly in Aberdeenshire. This book combines his own collecting with publication of tunes and words from many other collections, both published and unpublished, including Percy, Scott, Jamieson, Motherwell, Kinloch, Sharpe and Buchan. Also contains a few original compositions.

COURTNEY: 1890
M. A. Courtney, *Cornish Feasts and Folklore*: Penzance, 1890. Contains rhymes, charms, games and ballads, some of which are copied from earlier books. No music.

DEAN-SMITH: 1954
Margaret Dean-Smith, *A Guide to English Folk Song Collections (1822–1952)*: University of Liverpool, 1954. A useful index of published songs under titles, alternative titles and first lines, with some full descriptions of important books with historical annotations and an introduction which traces the development of collecting and publication of folksong in England over a period of 130 years.

DUNCAN MS: 1905
James Duncan (1848–1917). MS collected *c.* 1905–11. Aberdeen University Library. Consists of two notebooks, the first containing 800 tunes with words of first verse, and the second giving texts of over 350 songs all supplied by a Mrs Gillespie. For obituary by Lucy Broadwood see JFSS: 1918, No. 21, p. 41.

D'URFEY: 1698–1720
Thomas D'Urfey, *Wit and Mirth (or Pills to Purge Melancholy)*: London, 1698–1720. First edition printed with airs was in two vols. (1698). Further editions increased to 6 vols. (1720). This was the earliest publication to contain both words and music of a large number of English and Scots folksongs.

FMJ: 1965–
Folk Music Journal: English Folk Dance and Song Society, London (from 1965). Continuing the work of JFSS (*Journal of the Folk-Song Society*): 1889–1931 and JEFDSS (*Journal of the English Folk Dance and Song Society*): 1932–64.

FORD: 1899–1904
Robert Ford, *Vagabond Songs and Ballads of Scotland*: Gardiner, Paisley, Scotland, 1899–1901; new edition 1904. A comprehensive collection of songs and ballads, containing a number of bothy ballads', but only a few for which he provides the music. Important in that it covers the wide range of songs that were current up to the end of the century, particularly those sung by 'the travellers'.

GARDINER: 1909
George B. Gardiner, *Folk Songs from Hampshire*: Novello, London, 1909. 16 songs collected by Gardiner and his musical associates, Gamblin, Balfour Gardiner and Guyer and arranged by Gustav (von) Holst.

GARDINER MS: 1905–9
For further details about Gardiner's work see *The George Gardiner Folksong Collection* in FMJ: 1967, p. 129 and introduction to PURSLOW: 1968. (See also under HAMMOND)

GILL: 1917
W. H. Gill, *Songs of the British Folk*: Curwen, London, 1917.
GILLINGTON: 1909/13
Alice E. Gillington, *Old Singing Games: Hampshire, Isle of Wight, Surrey*: Curwen, London, 1909. *Dorset, Wilts and New Forest*: Curwen, London, 1913.
GOMME: 1894–8
Alice B. Gomme, *The Traditional Games of England, Scotland and Ireland* (as Part I of *Dictionary of British Folk-Lore*): David Nutt, London. Vol. I 1894, vol. II 1898. Dover Publications, New York, 1964. A 1000-page collection of games arranged alphabetically with music for those that were sung.
GRAHAM: 1910
John Graham, *Dialect Songs of the North*: Curwen, London, 1910. 15 songs from Lancashire, Cheshire, Westmorland and Cumberland collected by Graham with piano accompaniments by Percy E. Fletcher.
GREIG: 1909/14
Gavin Greig, *Folk Songs of the North-East*: The Buchan Observer, Peterhead, Scotland. Vol. I 1909, vol. II 1914. Folklore Associates, Pennsylvania, USA, 1963. Greig was an Aberdeenshire schoolmaster and an accomplished musician who noted the words and tunes of over 3,000 songs. His manuscripts, extending over 90 volumes, are deposited in the Library of King's College, Aberdeen.
HALLIWELL: 1842/9
J. O. Halliwell, *The Nursery Rhymes of England*: Percy Society Publications, London, 1842. Vol. IV, and several subsequent editions. (It was reissued in 1970 by Bodley Head.) *Popular Rhymes and Nursery Tales*: London, 1849 (a sequel to the above). Words of nursery rhymes 'collected from oral tradition'.
HAMER: 1967
Fred Hamer, *Garners Gay*: EFDS Publications, London, 1967. 50 songs, words and melodies (chord symbols) mainly collected in Bedfordshire but also from other counties of England. No exact locations or dates given of informants or comparative notes to songs, but contains hitherto unpublished local songs and songs connected with local customs.
HAMER: 1973
Fred Hamer, *Green Groves*: EFDS Publications, London, 1973. 38 songs, words and melodies (chord symbols). A further selection published posthumously. As in Hamer's *Garners Gay*, no exact details of locations, dates or comparative notes to songs.
HAMMOND AND GARDINER MSS: 1905–9
H. E. D. Hammond (1866–1910), R. F. F. Hammond (1868–1921) and Dr George Gardiner (1852–1910) collected mainly in Dorset and Hampshire. Their manuscripts, deposited in the Vaughan Williams Memorial Library at Cecil Sharp House, London, have been indexed by Frank Purslow, who has also edited three books drawn from them (see below).
HENRY: 1924
Sam Henry, *Songs of the People*: Northern Constitution, Coleraine, Co. Derry, N. Ireland, 1924. Over 800 songs were published in the local Derry newspaper. Many were contributed by readers but it was Henry's diligent research and background notes that gave interest to each contribution.
HERD: 1769/76
David Herd, *The Ancient and Modern Scots Songs, Heroic Ballads*: Dickson and Elliot, Edinburgh, 1769; (2 vols.) 1776. Paterson, Edinburgh, 1870. New 2-vol. edition, 1973, Scottish Academic Press. Early Scots source material. Herd's original MS, in the British Museum, served as basis for many of Robert Burns's songs as well as for Sir Walter Scott's *Minstrelsy of the Scottish Border*.
JEFDSS: 1932–64
Journal of The English Folk Dance and Song Society: London (32 vols.), 1932–64.

JFSS: 1899–1931
Journal of the Folk-Song Society: London (35 vols.), 1899–1931.
JOHNSON: 1787–1853
James Johnson, *The Scots Musical Museum*: 6 vols. Edinburgh, 1787–1803; 4 vols. with notes by William Stenhouse and David Laing, Edinburgh, 1853. This was the beginning of systematic documentation of Scots songs to which Robert Burns contributed material of his own collecting which he restored by re-writing amplification of the texts.
JOYCE: 1873/1906
P. Weston Joyce, *Ancient Music of Ireland*: McGlashan & Gill, Dublin, 1873. Longmans Green, Dublin and New York, 1906.
JOYCE: 1909
P. Weston Joyce, *Old Irish Folk Music and Songs*: University Press, Dublin, 1909. 482 Irish Airs and Songs, edited with annotations for the Royal Society of Antiquaries of Ireland of which Joyce was the President. Most of the music previously unpublished but some are versions of songs already in *Ancient Music of Ireland* (1873) and *Irish Peasant Songs in the English Language* (1906).
KIDSON: 1891
Frank Kidson, *Traditional Tunes*: C. Taphouse, Oxford, 1891. Texts and melodies (without accompaniment) mainly from Yorkshire. Later published with piano accompaniment in KIDSON AND MOFFAT: 1926 and 1927. Many texts filled out from broadsides. For article about Frank Kidson see JEFDSS: 1948, p. 127. Reissued by S. R. Publishers, 1970.
KIDSON AND MOFFAT: 1926
Frank Kidson and Alfred Moffat, *A Garland of English Folk Songs*: Ascherberg, Hopwood & Crew, London, 1926. 60 songs collected by Kidson, mainly in Yorkshire, with piano accompaniments by Moffat; most previously published in *Traditional Tunes* (1891). A further 60 songs were selected for a second volume by Kidson and Moffat (1927).
KIDSON AND MOFFAT: 1927
Frank Kidson and Alfred Moffat, *Folk Songs from the North Countrie*: Ascherberg, Hopwood & Crew, London, 1927. A further 60 songs with piano accompaniment, published one year after the collector's death. The foreword by Lucy Broadwood provides information about the collector. See also *Frank Kidson: portrait*, JEFDSS: 1948, pp. 127–35.
MACCOLL: 1953
Ewan MacColl, *Scotland Sings*: Workers Music Association, London, 1953. 100 songs and ballads divided into 'muckle' (i.e. great songs or ballads), 'Orra' (hero) folk and rebels, Kissin's nae sin, ploo lads, pipes and drums, drinking, shuttle and cage, muckle toons (urban), children's songs and lullabies.
MASON: 1877/1908
Miss M. H. Mason, *Nursery Rhymes and Country Songs*: Metzler, London, 1877. Second edition without illustrations but with additional notes, 1908. Over 50 folksongs of great variety mainly from her own Mitford family in Northumberland, also from Broadwood in Sussex, with piano accompaniments.
O'NEILL: 1903
Captain Francis O'Neill, *Music of Ireland*: Lyon & Healey, Chicago, 1903.
OPIE: 1951
Iona and Peter Opie, *The Oxford Dictionary of Nursery Rhymes*: Oxford University Press, London, 1951. 550 rhymes and jingles with literary and historical background information.
ORD: 1930
John Ord, *Bothy Songs and Ballads*: Alexander Gardner, Paisley, Scotland. The standard work on the 'bothy ballads' of N.E. Scotland; 'bothy' meaning farm cottage or hut used by hands, ploughmen, shepherds and farm-servants, and the

ballads, although including folksongs found elsewhere, being mainly those describing, and often complaining about, local farm life.

PETRIE COLLECTION: 1902-5
George Petrie, *The Complete Petrie Collection*: ed. C. V. Stanford, 3 parts, Boosey, London, 1902-5. Full details of the collection are given in JEFDSS: 1946, pp. 1-12, together with a list of tunes appearing in the 1855 and 1882 volumes.

PURSLOW: 1965
Frank Purslow, *Marrowbones*: EFDS Publications, London, 1965. A series of pocket-size publications initiated by Peter Kennedy in order to make available the songs collected by Hammond and Gardiner in the care of the EFDSS library. This selection contains 100 songs, provided with chord symbols over the melodies.

PURSLOW: 1968
Frank Purslow, *The Wanton Seed*: EFDS Publications, London, 1968. A second selection from Hammond and Gardiner again containing 100 songs.

PURSLOW: 1972
Frank Purslow, *The Constant Lovers*: EFDS Publications, London, 1972. A third selection in which the type-size has been increased and the number of songs reduced to 78.

RAMSAY: 1724-40
Allan Ramsay, *The Tea-Table Miscellany*: Edinburgh, 1724 (1 vol.); London, 1733 (3 vols.); London, 1740 (4 vols.). Collection of words only which was so successful that it ran into 18 editions covering about 500 'old' songs, as well as some newly composed by himself and 'some ingenious young gentlemen'. The tunes used must have been well-known at the time as they are given only by name.

REEVES: 1958
James Reeves, *The Idiom of the People*: Heinemann, London, 1958. Words of 115 folksongs from Cecil Sharp MSS (about 40 printed for the first time) selected as examples of 'English Traditional Verse'. Introduction concerned with the Folk Song Movement in England; Sharp as a collector; text revisions, description of the MSS; the popular idiom; and a detailed consideration of certain songs.

REEVES: 1960
James Reeves, *The Everlasting Circle*: Heinemann, London, 1960. 142 texts from the MSS of Baring Gould, Hammond and Gardiner considered as 'English traditional verse'. Introduction concerned with Baring Gould as a collector and his MSS; Hammond and Gardiner; varieties of folksong; the theme of fertility and a discussion on the *lingua franca* of English traditional song.

ROXBURGHE: 1871-93
Roxburghe Ballads (about 1540-1790): 7 vols. Vols. I-II ed. William Chappell, Ballad Society, London, 1871-80; vols. III-VII ed. J. W. Ebsworth, Hertford, 1883-93.

SEEGER AND MacCOLL: 1960
Peggy Seeger and Ewan MacColl, *The Singing Island*: Mills Music, London, 1960. 96 English and Scots folksongs arranged for 'the post-war folk revival' mainly from Scotland under headings: Children, Courting, Men at Work, On the Road, Sailors, Barrack Room, Rovin' Boys and Flash Girls, Historical and Fill up your Glass.

SHARP: 1902
Cecil J. Sharp, *A Book of British Song*: John Murray, London, 1902. 78 songs published before Sharp started collecting. They are listed under National, Soldier and Sailor, Country, Humorous, Old English and Old Scottish, starting with *God Save the King* and *Rule Britannia* and finishing with *Auld Lang Syne*. Only two Welsh and two Irish national songs are included.

SHARP MS 1903-23
Cecil Sharp (1859-1924), foremost collector of English folk-

songs and folkdances, was the founder of The English Folk Dance Society and for many years a member of The Folk-Song Society. (In 1932 these two societies amalgamated as The English Folk Dance and Song Society.) For a full account of his life-work and publications see *Cecil Sharp* by A. H. Fox-Strangways (Oxford University Press, London, 1933), revised by Maud Karpeles (Routledge & Kegan Paul, London, 1967). Words, songs, tunes and dance notes in Cecil Sharp's autograph are in the Library of Clare College, Cambridge. There are also photostat copies in the Harvard University Library and the New York Public Library, and microfilm copies in the libraries of the University of California and in the library at Cecil Sharp House, London, the headquarters of The English Folk Dance and Song Society. Cecil Sharp's own collection of books was left to the EFDSS and formed the beginnings of the specialist library at Cecil Sharp House.

SHARP AND MARSON: 1904-9
Cecil J. Sharp and Rev. Charles L. Marson, *Folk Songs from Somerset*: Simpkin Marshall, London and Barnicott, Taunton, Somerset. 5 vols. Vol. I 1904, vol. II 1905, vol. III 1906, vol. IV 1908, vol. V 1909. The most important single collection of English folksong, later edited as the *Selected Edition* (1916-21). Introduction concerning singers and style most valuable.

SHARP: 1916/21
Cecil J. Sharp, *English Folk Songs: Selected Edition*: Oliver Ditson, New York, 1916; Novello, London, 1921. 2 vols. 100 songs of which all but 18 from Somerset previously published in SHARP AND MARSON: 1904-9. 12 of the songs, not previously published, were variants. Introduction (and notes to songs) are of great value as they post-date by 14 years his *English Folk Song, Some Conclusions* (1907).

STUBBS: 1970
Ken Stubbs, *The Life of a Man*: EFDS Publications, London, 1970. 50 songs, texts and melodies (chord symbols). Many from our same source singers, but includes a wide variety from Home Counties (Surrey, Sussex mainly and some from Kent) with some important variant versions and some hitherto unpublished songs. Biographical notes about singers.

UDAL: 1922
John Symonds Udal, *Dorsetshire Folk-Lore*: Stephen Austin, Hertford, 1922; J. Stephens-Cox, St Peter Port, Guernsey, 1970. Contains a long 'fore-say' by William Barnes, 'The Dorset Poet'. Like BURNE: 1884 and LEATHER: 1912-70, this is a mixture of material including the words of about 20 songs.

VAUGHAN WILLIAMS: 1908
Ralph Vaughan Williams, *Folk Songs from the Eastern Counties*: Novello, London, 1908. 15 songs from Essex, Norfolk and Cambridgeshire; most already in JFSS: 1906: No. 8.

VOCAL LIBRARY: 1822
The Vocal Library: Sir Richard Phillips, London, 1822. Contains words of nearly 2,000 songs, including many without known authors and described as 'the largest collection of English, Scottish and Irish songs ever printed in one volume selected from the best authors between the age of Shakespeare, Jonson and Cowley and that of Dibdin, Wolcot and Moore'.

WILLIAMS: 1923
Alfred Owen Williams, *Folk Songs of the Upper Thames*: Duckworth, London, 1923. Over 300 folksongs (words only) noted mainly in Berkshire, Gloucestershire, Oxfordshire and Wiltshire. Interesting introduction about rural life, more fully covered by Williams in *Round About the Upper Thames* (Duckworth, 1922). Further unpublished texts in Swindon Reference Library. See FMJ: 1969 'Alfred Williams: A Symposium'.

BELDEN: 1940
H. M. Belden, *Ballads and Songs Collected by the Missouri*

Folklore Society: University Studies XV (No. 1), Columbia, Missouri, USA, 1940.

CHILD: 1882–98
Francis James Child, *The English and Scottish Popular Ballads*: Houghton Mifflin, Boston, USA. 5 vols. (10 parts), 1882–98. Dover Publications Reprint, New York, 1965.

COX: 1925
John Harrington Cox, *Folk Songs of the South*: Harvard University Press, Cambridge, Mass., USA, 1925. Dover Publications Reprint, New York, 1967 (released 1968). 185 songs collected in West Virginia (29 with tunes). Introduction describes collecting methods and identifies informants. Notes, references to other versions and other data given with texts of songs.

CREIGHTON: 1932
Helen Creighton, *Songs and Ballads from Nova Scotia*: Dent, Toronto, Canada, 1932. Dover Publications Reprint, New York, 1966. 150 songs, gathered mainly in the vicinity of Halifax, written down by the author and afterwards checked with recordings. First of four published collections.

CREIGHTON AND SENIOR: 1940
Helen Creighton and Doreen H. Senior, *Twelve Folk Songs from Nova Scotia*: Novello, London, 1940. Piano accompaniment by Miss Senior of 5 songs already published in CREIGHTON: 1932 and 7 songs not previously published.

CREIGHTON AND SENIOR: 1950
Helen Creighton and Doreen Senior, *Traditional Songs from Nova Scotia*: Ryerson Press, Toronto, Canada, 1950. 100 songs and 36 ballads collected in the Maritimes with additional variants of both tunes and texts in many instances. An important and well documented collection with versions of many of the songs in this book.

CREIGHTON: 1962
Helen Creighton, *Maritime Folk Songs*: Ryerson Press, Toronto, Canada, 1962. Michigan State University Press, East Lansing, Michigan, USA, 1962. 169 songs which were published with a companion gramophone record (Folkways 4307). There was also an earlier record called *Folk Music from Nova Scotia* (Folkways 4006).

EDDY: 1939
Mary O. Eddy, *Ballads and Songs from Ohio*: J. J. Augustin, New York, 1939.

FLANDERS AND BROWN: 1932
Helen Hartness Flanders and George Brown, *Vermont Folk Songs and Ballads*: Stephen Daye, Brattleboro, Vermont, 1932.

GARDNER AND CHICKERING: 1939
Emelyn E. Gardner and Geraldine J. Chickering, *Ballads and Songs of Southern Michigan*: University Press, Ann Arbor, Michigan, USA, 1939.

GREENLEAF: 1933
Elizabeth Bristol Greenleaf and Grace Yarrow Mansfield, *Ballads and Sea Songs from Newfoundland*: Harvard University Press, Cambridge, Mass., USA, 1933.

JAFL: 1888–
Journal of American Folklore now published by University of Pennsylvania.

KARPELES: 1934/1971
Maud Karpeles, *Folksongs from Newfoundland*: Oxford University Press, London, 1934. 2 vols.; Faber & Faber, London, 1971. 30 songs (with piano accompaniments) were published in 1934 and 90 songs, 150 tunes including variants (with no accompaniments) in 1971. All collected during 1929–30.

LOMAX: 1960
Alan Lomax, *Folk Songs of North America*: Cassell, London, 1960.

NEWELL: 1884/1903
W. W. Newell, *Games and Songs of American Children*: Harper Bros., New York, 1884; new and enlarged edition 1903.

PEACOCK: 1965
Kenneth Peacock, *Songs of the Newfoundland Outports*: National Museum of Canada, Ottawa, 1965. 3 vols.

POUND: 1922
Louise Pound, *American Ballads and Songs*: Charles Scribner's Sons, New York, 1922.

RANDOLPH: 1946–50
Vance Randolph and Floyd C. Shoemaker, *Ozark Folk Songs*: State Historical Society, Columbia, Missouri, USA, 1946–50. 4 vols.

SHARP AND KARPELES: 1917/32
Olive Dame Campbell and Cecil J. Sharp, *English Folk Songs from the Southern Appalachians*: Putnam, New York, 1917. Cecil J. Sharp and Maud Karpeles (2 vols.), Oxford University Press, London, 1932.

VIII

Songs of
False Love and True

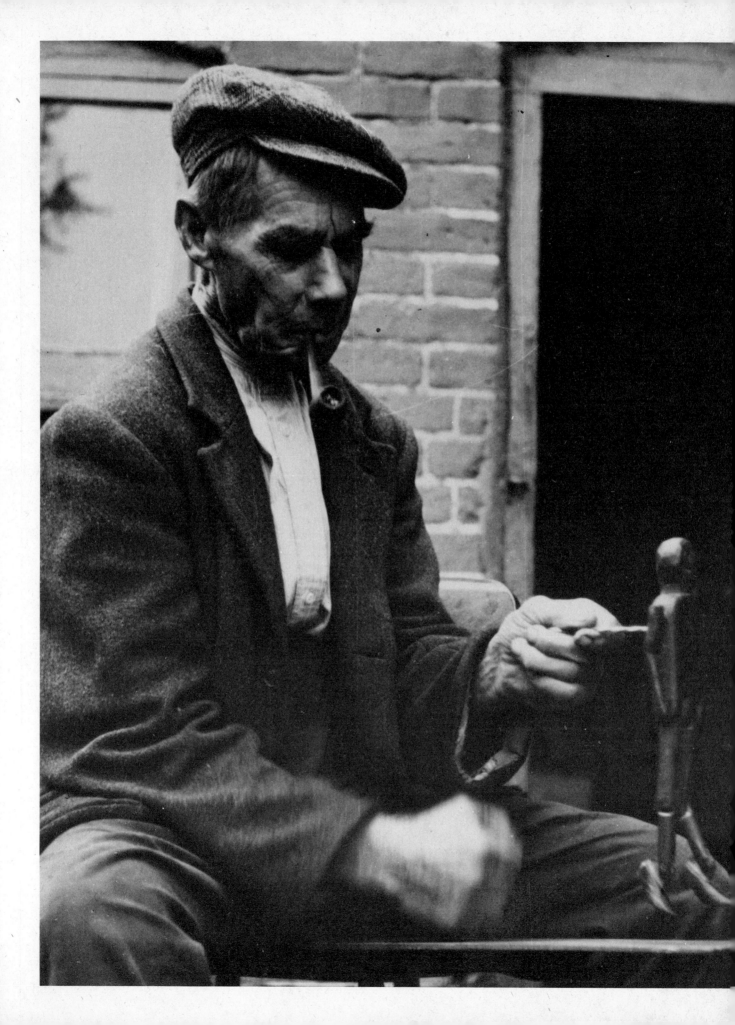

Introduction

> Green grows the laurel, soft falls the dew
> Sorry was I, love, when parting from you
> But at our next meeting I hope you'll prove true
> And we'll join the green laurel and the violet so blue

Wearing a flower or, as in *All Round My Hat* (No. 145), green willow, were demonstrative symbols of faithfulness and chastity, and many of our love songs make use of the symbols of flowers and trees. Over the years the early significances have been forgotten and the symbols have sometimes changed their meanings. Green laurel has stood for young love, or fickleness, but also faithfulness, and has even been associated with Irish political loyalty. The violet in *Green Grows the Laurel* (No. 158) is a symbol of truth, but in *The Seeds of Love* (No. 167) it is added to the flower catalogue as another that does not last, and a young girl is advised to wait until after the first blooms are over:

> For the grass that you oft'times have trampled underfoot
> Give it time it will rise again

A similar warning is given in *Going to Mass Last Sunday* (No. 155):

> For there's a tree in my father's garden, and it goes by the name of rue
> While young men steal as young men will, then young men will ne'er prove true
> While young men steal as young men will, and the fruits will go to decay
> For the sweetest flowers will blossom and fade, and their beauty soon fade away

The tree features in many of our love songs, for example the palm tree in *The Forsaken Mother and Child* (No. 154):

> For the taller that the palm tree grows, the sweeter is the bark
> And the fairer that a young man speaks, the falser is his heart

and in various versions of *The Nobleman's Wedding* (No. 164) there are similar *green colour* verses, also a verse about the bark separation:

> But I stole you away from your true-lover Johnny
> It's then I separated the bark from the tree

The tallness of the tree occurs frequently as in *The Forsaken Mother and Child* and *The False Young Man* (No. 153), and even the sturdiness of the oak is in question in *Deep in Love* (No. 149):

> I leaned my back against an oak
> Thinking it being some trustive tree
> But first it bent and then it broke
> And so did my false love and me

Like *The Seeds of Love*, this same song features 'the prickly rose', but suggests plucking the flowers while they are still green:

> I put my hand into the bush
> Thinking the sweetest rose to find
> I pricked my finger to the bone
> And left the sweetest rose behind

> If roses are such prickly flowers
> They ought to be gathered when they are green
> For controlling of an unkind love
> I'm sure strives hard against the stream

Cox of Catfield, Yarmouth, Norfolk
Photograph: Peter Kennedy

The heights of love are likened to the tops of trees and mountains and the depths of love to the roots of the trees and, of course, to the sea, as in *Deep in Love* (No. 149):

> I saw a ship sailing on the sea
> She sailed as deep as she could be
> But not so deep as in love I am
> I care not whether I sink or swim

Ten of the songs in this chapter of heartaches have been recorded in England, three in Scotland and eleven in Ireland. As in the 'Songs of Courtship', the Irish influence is strong in love songs in English, and once again the tradition may well have come from Irish Gaelic; compare the Irish Gaelic song *An Draighneán Donn:* The Blackthorn Tree (No. 32), in which false love is compared to the bitterness of the wild berries like the sloe and the rowan:

> Though the rowan tree is highest, its topmost berries are not sweet
> While raspberries and strawberries bloom on the lowest trees

The Irish colour of green appears with significance in many of the songs in this chapter: *All Round my Hat* (No. 145); *Deep in Love* (No. 149); *Green Bushes* (No. 156); *Green Grass it Grows Bonny* (No. 157); *The Nobleman's Wedding* (No. 164); *Yon Green Valley* (No. 168); and it appeared in *The Greenwood Laddie* (No. 130) in the last chapter. In these songs there may be either a meaning of young and false love or there may be the significance of Ireland, or even the double symbolism with both meanings implied.

145 ALL ROUND MY HAT

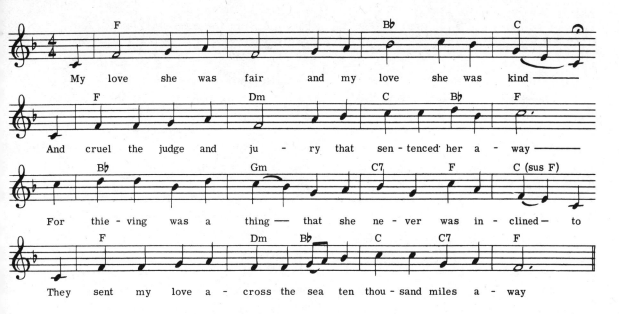

My love she was fair and my love she was kind

And cruel the judge and ju - ry that sen - tenced her a - way

For thie - ving was a thing — that she ne - ver was in - clined — to

They sent my love a - cross the sea ten thou - sand miles a - way

1 My love she was fair and my love she was kind
  And cruel the judge and jury that sentenced her away
  For thieving was a thing that she never was inclined to
  They sent my love across the sea ten thousand miles away

  All round my hat I will wear the greenie willow
  All round my hat for a year and a day
  And if anyone should question me the reason for my wearing it
  I'll tell them my own true love is ten thousand miles away

2 I bought my love a golden ring to wear upon her finger
  A token of our own true love and to remember me
  And when she returns again we'll never more be parted
  We'll marry and be happy for ever and a day

3 Seven, seven long years my love and I are parted
  Seven, seven long years my love is bound to stay
  Seven long years I'll love my love and never be false-hearted
  And never sigh or sorrow while she's far, far away

4 Some young men there are who are preciously deceitful
  A-coaxing of the fair young maids they mean to lead astray
  As soon as they deceive them, so cruelly they leave them
  I'll love my love for ever though she's far, far away

146 A BLACKSMITH COURTED ME

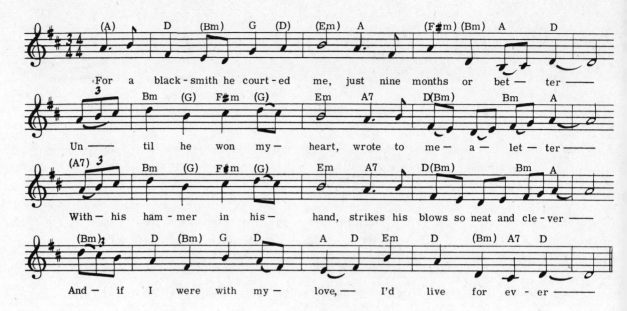

For a black-smith he court-ed me, just nine months or bet-ter

Un-til he won my-heart, wrote to me a let-ter

With-his ham-mer in his-hand, strikes his blows so neat and cle-ver

And-if I were with my-love,-I'd live for ev-er

1 For a blacksmith he courted me, just nine months or better
Until he won my heart, wrote to me a letter
With his hammer in his hand, strikes his blows so neat and clever
And if I were with my love, I'd live for ever

2 Now he talks about going abroad, fighting for strangers
And he'd better stay at home, and keep from all dangers
For you stay at home with me, my dearest jewel
And you stay at home with me, and don't prove cruel

3 My true love's gone across the sea, gathering fine posies
My true love's gone across the sea, with his cheeks like roses
I'm afraid that broiling sun will spoil his beauty
And if I was with my love, I would do love's duty

4 For it's once I had gold in store, they all seemed to like me
And now I'm low and poor, they all seem to slight me
For there ain't no belief in a man, nor your own brother
So it's: Girls, whenever you love, love one each other

147 THE BONNY LABOURING BOY

As I strolled out one morn — ing All in — the bloom - in' spring —

I heard a love — ly maid com - plain And grie - vi - ous did — she sing —

How cruel — were — her par - ents They did her so - an - noy —

And they would not let her mar — ry The bon - ny labour - ing boy —

1 As I strolled out one morning
All in the bloomin' spring
I heard a lovely maid complain
And grie-vi-ous did she sing
How cruel were her parents
They did her so annoy
And they would not let her marry
The bonny labouring boy

2 Young Johnny was her true-love's name
As you may plainly see
Her parents they employed him
Their labouring boy to be
To harrow, plough and sow the seed
Upon her father's land
And soon she fell in love with him
As you may understand

3 She courted him for twelve long months
But little did she know
That her cruel parents
Did prove her overthrow
They watched them close one evening
Down in a shady grove
A-pleadin' their joys together
In the constant bonds of love

4 Her father step-ped up to her
And took her by the hand
He swore he'd send young Johnny
Unto some foreign land
He locked her up in her bedroom
Her comfort to annoy
And he kep' her there to weep and mourn
For her bonny labouring boy

5 Her mother came next morning
And unto her did say
Your father his intent is not
To see you thrown away
So boldly she made answer
Unto her did reply
It's singly I will still remain
For my bonny labouring boy

6 His cheeks are like the roses red
His eyes as black as sloes
He's mild in his behaviour
Wherever he may go
He's manly, neat and handsome
His skin as white as snow
For the sake of my parents' malicy
With my labouring boy I'll go

7 So come fill your glasses to the brim
And let them go merrily round
Here's health to every labouring boy
That plough and till the ground
For when his work is over
It's home he goes with joy
Then happy is the girl who gets
The bonny labouring boy

148 THE CUCKOO

1 The cuckoo is a pretty bird, he sings as he flies
He brings us glad tidings and tells us no lies
He sucks little birds' eggs to make his voice clear
And sings to us sweetly three months of the year
Cuckoo in April, cuckoo in May
Cuckoo in June and July flies away

2 A-walking and a-talking and a-walking went I
To meet my true-lover, he'll come by and by
To meet him in the meadows it is my delight
Then I'll go a-walking from morning to night

3 For meeting is a pleasure and parting is a grief
And a false-hearted lover's far worse than a thief
A thief will but rob you and take all you've saved
But an inconstant lover will turn you to the grave

348

149 DEEP IN LOVE

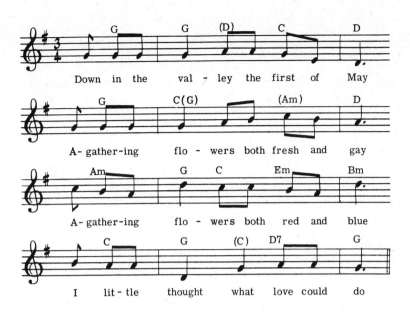

Down in the val-ley the first of May

A-gather-ing flo-wers both fresh and gay

A-gather-ing flo-wers both red and blue

I lit-tle thought what love could do

1 Down in the valley the first of May
A-gathering flowers both fresh and gay
A-gathering flowers both red and blue
I little thought what love could do

2 Where love is planted there it grows
It buds and blossoms most like a rose
It has a sweet and pleasant smell
No flower on earth can it excel

3 I put my hand into the bush
Thinking the sweetest rose to find
I pricked my finger to the bone
And left the sweetest rose behind

4 If roses are such prickly flowers
They ought to be gathered when they are green
For controlling of an unkind love
I'm sure strives hard against the stream

5 I leaned my back against an oak
Thinking it being some trustive tree
But first it bent and then it broke
And so did my false love and me

6 I saw a ship sailing on the sea
She sailed as deep as she could be
But not so deep as in love I am
I care not whether I sink or swim

7 Thousands and thousands all on this earth
I think my love carries the highest show
Surely she is some chosen one
I will have her or I'll have none

8 But now she's dead and in her grave
Poor girl I hope that her heart's at rest
We will wrap her up in some linen strong
And think of her now she's dead and gone

150 THE DELUDED LOVER

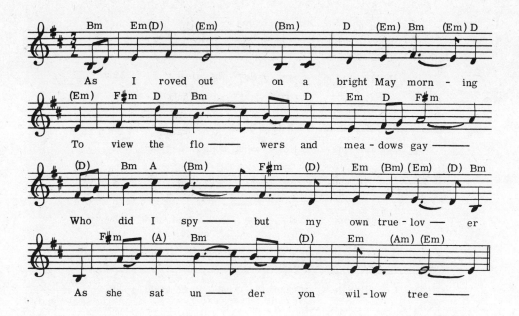

1 As I roved out on a bright May morning
To view the flowers and meadows gay
Who did I spy but my own true-lover
As she sat under yon willow tree

2 I took off my hat and I did salute her
I did salute her courageously
But she turned around and the tears fell from her
Saying: False young man, you have deluded me

3 For to delude you, how can that be, my love?
It's from your body I am quite free
I'm as free from you as a child unborn
And so are you, my dear Jane, from me

4 Three diamond rings, sure, I own I gave you
Three diamond rings to wear on your right hand
But the vows you made, love, you went and broke
And married the lassie that had the land   [them

5 If I married the lassie that had the land, my love
It's that I'll rue until the day I die
Where misfortune falls, sure, no man can shun it
I was blind-folded I'll ne'er deny

6 For at night when I go to my silent slumber
The thoughts of my true-love run in my mind
When I turn around to embrace my darling
Instead of gold, sure, it's brass I find

7 But I wish the Queen would call home her armies
From England, Ireland, from Amerikay and Spain
And every man to his wedded woman
In hopes that you and I may meet again

151 DOWN BY BLACKWATERSIDE

One morn-ing fair, I took the air Down by Black - wa - ter - side

O, then, gaz - ing all a - round — me —— 'Twas an Ir — ish girl I spied

1 One morning fair, I took the air
  Down by Blackwaterside
  O, then, gazing all around me
  'Twas an Irish girl I spied

2 So red and rosy were her cheeks
  And coal-black was her hair
  I caught her by her lily-white hands
  And I asked her to be my dear

3 All through the middle of the night
  We slept till the daylight clear
  Then the young man arose and put on his clothes
  Saying: Fare-thee-well, my dear

4 That's not the promise you made to me
  Down by Blackwaterside
  The promise I made is a promise I'll keep
  For I never intend to lie

5 Go home to your father's garden
  Go home and cry your fill
  And think of your own misfortune
  That you brought of your own free will

6 There's not a girl in this wide world
  That would prove more loyal and true
  When the fishes will fly and the seas run dry
  Sure, 'tis then that I'll marry you

152 THE FALSE BRIDE

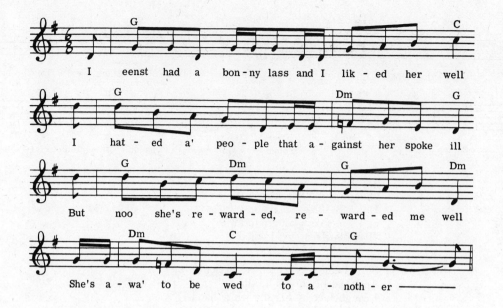

I eenst had a bon-ny lass and I lik-ed her well

I hat-ed a' peo-ple that a-gainst her spoke ill

But noo she's re-ward-ed, re-ward-ed me well

She's a-wa' to be wed to a-noth-er

1 I eenst had a bonny lass and I lik-ed her well
I hated a' people that against her spoke ill
But noo she's rewarded, rewarded me well
She's awa' to be wed to another

2 When I saw my bonny lass to the church go
Wi' young men and maidens she cut a fine show
And I followed on wi' my hairt full o' woe
To see my love wed to another

3 When I saw my bonny lass pass the church stile
I tramped on her goon but I didna it spoil
And she turned aroon and she gie me a smile
Young man, ye are troubled for nothing

4 When I saw my bonny lass in yon church stand
Wi' gold rings on her fingers and gloves in her
                                                    hand
I wished him that had her much houses and land
For the lass, I did want the best for her

5 O the minister that married them gi'ed a loud cry
If there's any objectors then let them draw nigh
I thocht in my ain mind objections hae I
But the lass, I didna want to affront her

6 When marriage was over and going home to dine
I filled up the glasses with brandy and wine
And I drank to the bonny lass that should hae been
Though it wasna my fortune to get her   [mine

7 When drinking was over and we sat down to meat
I sat down beside her but little could I eat
But I lo'ed her company much better than meat
Though it wasna my fortune to get her

8 When supper was over and going home to bide
I put on my hat and I bid them good night
I reached o'er the table, gave a kiss to the bride
And spoke to the bridegroom beside her

9 You can keep her and hold her for all your great
                                                    prize
For many's the time that she's laid by my side
She's lain in my bed ne'er eenst, twice or thrice
She's only my old sheen now you've got her

10 O the folk in the forest they a' laughed at me
How many blae'berries grows in the salt sea?
Then I turned right aroon wi' grief in my e'e
As many ships as sails in the forest

153 THE FALSE YOUNG MAN

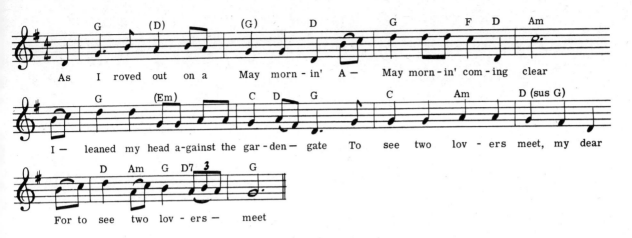

As I roved out on a May morn-in' A— May morn-in' com-ing clear
I— leaned my head a-gainst the gar-den— gate To see two lov-ers meet, my dear
For to see two lov-ers— meet

1 As I roved out on a May mornin'
A May mornin' coming clear
I leaned my head against the garden gate
To see two lovers meet, my dear
For to see two lovers meet

2 For to see two lovers meet, my dear
And to hear what they might say
That I may know a little of their minds
Before I'd go on my way, my dear
Before I'd go on my way

3 It's sit you down on the grass, he said
On this pleasant grass so green
For it's been three-quarters of a year or more
Since together we have been, my dear
Since together we have been

4 O I'll not sit on the grass, she said
Neither now or at any other time
For I've heard that you're going with another young
And your heart's no longer mine, she said   [girl
And your heart's no longer mine

5 For when your heart was mine, she said
And your head lay upon my breast
You would make me believe with all your deceit
That the sun would rise in the west, my dear
That the sun would arise in the west

6 I'll not believe what an old man says
For his days'll not be long
And I'll not believe what a young man says
For he's promised to many's the one, she said
For he's promised to many's the one

7 For he's promised to many's the one, she said
And many's the false story he will tell
But when that he's gained a pretty girl's heart
It's adieu, pretty girl, farewell, he'll say
Adieu, pretty girl, farewell

8 I will climb a high, high tree
And I'll rob the wild bird's nest
And I'll come down with whatever I do get
To the arms that I love best, he said
To the arms that I love best

9 J it stands for my love John
T it stands for Tom
W stands for sweet William, dear
But Johnny is the fairest one, she said
But Johnny is the fairest one

154 THE FORSAKEN MOTHER AND CHILD

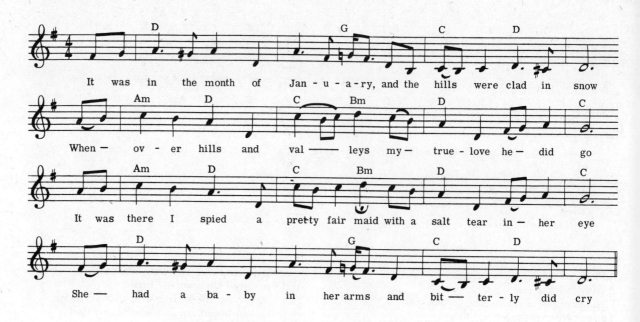

It was in the month of Jan-u-a-ry, and the hills were clad in snow

When — ov-er hills and val — leys my — true-love he — did go

It was there I spied a pretty fair maid with a salt tear in — her eye

She — had a ba-by in her arms and bit — ter-ly did cry

1 It was in the month of January, and the hills were clad in snow
  When over hills and valleys my true-love he did go
  It was there I spied a pretty fair maid with a salt tear in her eye
  She had a baby in her arms and bitterly did cry

2 How cruel was my father that barred the door on me
  And cruel was my mother this dreadful crime to see
  Cruel was my own true-love to change his mind for gold
  And cruel was that winter's night that pierced my heart with cold

3 For the taller that the palm tree grows, the sweeter is the bark
  And the fairer that a young man speaks, the falser is his heart
  He will kiss you and embrace you, till he thinks he has you won
  Then he'll go away and leave you, all for some other one

4 So, all you pretty fair maids, a warning take by me
  And never try to build your nest on top of a high tree
  For the leaves they will all wither and the branches will decay
  And the beauties of a false young man will all soon fade away

5 O hush, my little baby boy, and lay closer to my breast
  How little does your father know this night we're in distress
  He kissed me and embraced me till he had my favour gained
  Then went away and left me, in sorrow, grief and shame

6 I'll go down to yon lonely valley and upon my knees I'll fall
  And there unto Almighty God for mercy I will call
  She kissed her baby's cold white lips and laid him by her side
  She raised her eyes to Heaven, then both laid down and died

155 GOING TO MASS LAST SUNDAY

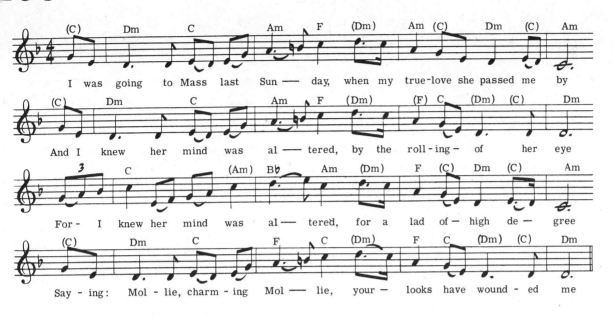

I was going to Mass last Sun — day, when my true-love she passed me by

And I knew her mind was al — tered, by the roll-ing- of her eye

For- I knew her mind was al — tered, for a lad of- high de — gree

Say - ing: Mol - lie, charm - ing Mol — lie, your — looks have wound - ed me

1 I was going to Mass last Sunday, when my true-love she passed me by
And I knew her mind was altered, by the rolling of her eye
For I knew her mind was altered, for a lad of high degree
Saying: Mollie, charming Mollie, your looks have wounded me

2 For I'll send my love a bottle, and I'll fill it to the brim
Saying: Drink, my charming Mollie, our courtship's at an end
Saying: Drink, my charming Mollie, let the bottom stand for me
For one guinea it lies in a wager, that married we'll never be

3 For it's never court with a pretty girl, with a dark and a rolling eye
Just kiss her and embrace her, for I'll tell you the reason why
Just kiss her and embrace her, till you cause her heart to yield
For there's never a faint-hearted soldier that has gained the battlefield

4 For there's some do court in earnest, and others that court in fun
And it's some will court a new true-love, for to draw the old love on
And it's some will court a new true-love, for to keep their mind at rest
And it's when their back it is turn-ed, they'll court whom they love the best

5 And it's when they're tired of walking, all night to the break of dawn
They'll tell them loving stories, they'll go home for to weep and mourn
They'll tell them loving stories, they'll go home and cry their fill
For you never need be blaming anyone, when it's all of your own free will

6 For there's a tree in my father's garden, and it goes by the name of rue
While young men steal as young men will, then young men will ne'er prove true
While young men steal as young men will, and the fruits will go to decay
For the sweetest flowers will blossom and fade, and their beauty soon fade away

156 GREEN BUSHES

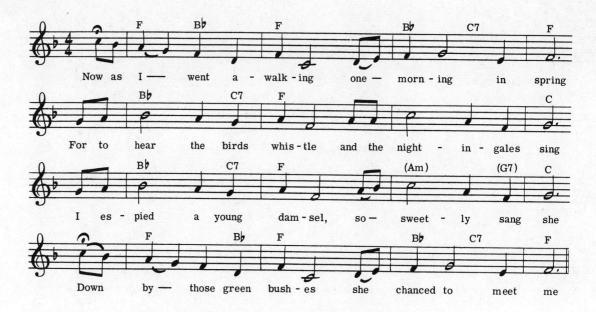

1 Now as I went a-walking one morning in spring
  For to hear the birds whistle and the nightingales sing
  I espied a young damsel, so sweetly sang she
  Down by those green bushes she chanced to meet me

2 O why are you waiting, my sweet pretty maid?
  I'm waiting for my true-love, so softly she said
  May I be your true-love and will you agree
  To leave those green bushes and tarry with me?

3 I'll buy for you beavers and a fine silken gown
  I'll buy for you petticoats and flounces all round
  I'll buy you fine clothing and rich you shall be
  If you'll forsake your own darling and get married to me

4 O away with your beavers and your fine silken hose
  For I ne'er was so poor as to marry for clothes
  But if you'll prove constant to you I'll prove true
  I'll forsake my own darling and get married to you

5 O let us be going, kind sir, if you please
  Love, let us be going from out under these trees
  For yonder he's coming my true-love I see
  Down by those green bushes where he thinks he'll meet me

6 And when he came there and he found she was gone
  He looked all around him like a man quite forlorn
  Saying: She's gone with some other, she's false unto me
  So adieu to green bushes forever, said he

7 I'll be like some schoolboys, spend my whole time in play
  No false-hearted young girl to stand in my way
  Untroubled at night I can slumber and snore
  So farewell to green bushes, I will see you no more

157 GREEN GRASS IT GROWS BONNY

I won-der what is keep-ing my true-love to-night

I — won-der what is keep-ing him — out — of my sight

Lit-tle he — knows all the — pain I en-dure

He would not stay from me this night I am sure

1 I wonder what is keeping my true-love tonight
  I wonder what is keeping him out of my sight
  Little he knows all the pain I endure
  He would not stay from me this night I am sure

2 O, love, are you not coming my pain to advance
  Or, love, do you wait on a far better chance
  Or have you but a sweetheart laid by you in store
  Or are you coming to tell me you love me no more?

3 Love, I'm not coming your pain to advance
  Or, love, do I wait on a far better chance
  Or have I but a sweetheart laid by me in store
  But I'm coming to tell you: I love you no more

4 I have gold in my pocket and love in my heart
  But I can't love a maiden that has got two sweethearts
  I love you just lightly like the dew on the thorn
  That falls down at night and goes away in the morn

5 Green grass it grows bonny, spring water runs clear
  I weary, I weary, when I think of you, dear
  You were my first in true love, but it's now do I rue
  The fonder I loved you, the falser you grew

6 Come, all young maidens, take a warning from me
  Never build your nest on the top of the tree
  The roots they will wither, the branches decay
  Like that false-hearted young man, they will soon fade away

158 GREEN GROWS THE LAUREL

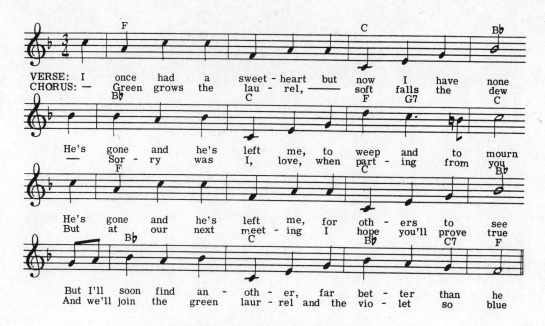

VERSE: I once had a sweet-heart but now I have none
CHORUS: — Green grows the lau-rel, — soft falls the dew

He's gone and he's left me, to weep and to mourn
— Sor-ry was I, love, when part-ing from you

He's gone and he's left me, for oth-ers to see
But at our next meet-ing I hope you'll prove true

But I'll soon find an-oth-er, far bet-ter than he
And we'll join the green laur-rel and the vio-let so blue

1 I once had a sweetheart but now I have none
He's gone and he's left me, to weep and to mourn
He's gone and he's left me, for others to see
But I'll soon find another, far better than he

Green grows the laurel, soft falls the dew
Sorry was I, love, when parting from you
But at our next meeting I hope you'll prove true
And we'll join the green laurel and the violet so blue

2 He passes my window both early and late
And the looks he gives at me would make my heart break
The looks he gives at me a thousand would kill
Though he hates and detests me, I love that lad still

3 I wrote him a letter in red rosy lines
He wrote back an answer all twisted and twined
Saying: Keep your love-letters and I will keep mine
You write to your love and I'll write to mine

4 Now I oft'times do wonder why maidens love men
And oft'times I wonder why young men love them
But from my own knowledge I will have you to know
That the men are deceivers wherever they go

159 A HEALTH TO ALL TRUE-LOVERS

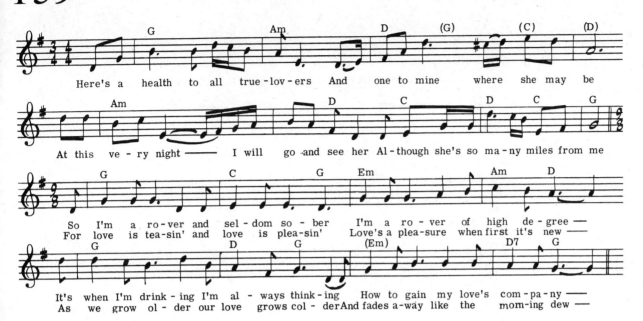

Here's a health to all true-lov-ers And one to mine where she may be
At this ve-ry night —— I will go and see her Al-though she's so ma-ny miles from me

So I'm a ro-ver and sel-dom so-ber I'm a ro-ver of high de-gree ——
For love is tea-sin' and love is plea-sin' Love's a plea-sure when first it's new ——

It's when I'm drink-ing I'm al-ways think-ing How to gain my love's com-pa-ny ——
As we grow ol-der our love grows col-derAnd fades a-way like the morn-ing dew ——

1 Here's a health to all true-lovers
And one to mine where she may be
At this very night I will go and see her
Although she's so many miles from me
So I'm a rover and seldom sober
I'm a rover of high degree
It's when I'm drinking I'm always thinking
How to gain my love's company
ALTERNATIVE CHORUS
For love is teasin' and love is pleasin'
Love's a pleasure when first it's new
As we grow older our love grows colder
And fades away like the morning dew

2 The night being dark, as dark as a dungeon
And not a star looked to appear
For I am tired of my long journey
Into the arms that I love so dear

3 When I arrived at my love's window
Sure I placed my foot upon a stone
And I whispered softly in through the window
Are you asleep, my love, are you alone?

4 She raised her head from her snow-white pillow
And she clasped her hands upon her breast
Saying: Who is there at my bedroom window
Disturbing me from my good night's rest?

5 It is your own, your true-love, darling
Rise up quickly and let me in
For I am tired of my long journey
And my clothes are wet, love, unto the skin

6 Then she arose in all great splendour
For to let her own true-lover in
Sweet kisses then did embrace each other
Till that long night it was nearly in

7 The cocks are crowing and I must be going
O'er the Belfast mountains I have to cross
For over them I will roam with pleasure
For late last night I've been with my lass

160 IN SHEFFIELD PARK

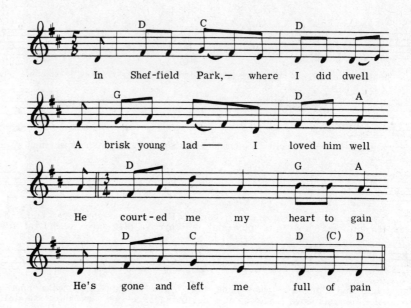

In Shef-field Park,— where I did dwell

A brisk young lad —— I loved him well

He court-ed me my heart to gain

He's gone and left me full of pain

1 In Sheffield Park, where I did dwell
A brisk young lad I loved him well
He courted me my heart to gain
He's gone and left me full of pain

2 I went upstairs to make the bed
And lay me down and nothing said
My mistress came and to me said
What is the matter with you, my maid?

3 O mistress, mistress, thou little know
What pain and sorrow I undergo
It's put your hand on my left breast
My fainting heart can take no rest

4 My mistress turned away with speed
Some help, some help, I will go seek
No help, no help, no help I crave
Young William has stolen my heart away

5 Then write a letter to my love with speed
Ask him the question that he can read
And bring me an answer without delay
For he has stolen my heart away

6 She took the letter immediately
He read it over while she stood by
But as soon as he did her question learn
Into the fire threw it to burn

7 What a foolish one this girl must be
To think I love no-one but she
Man was not made for one alone
It's my delight to hear her moan

8 Her mistress returned without delay
And found her maid as cold as clay
Beware, young maids, don't love in vain
For love has broken her heart in twain

9 We'll gather green grass all for your bed
And a flowery pillow for your head
And the leaves that blow from tree to tree
Shall be the covering over thee

161 THE IRON DOOR

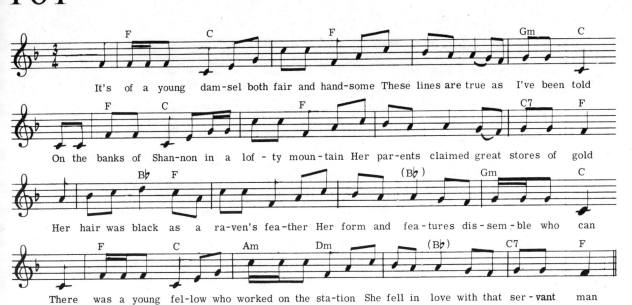

It's of a young dam-sel both fair and hand-some These lines are true as I've been told

On the banks of Shan-non in a lof-ty moun-tain Her par-ents claimed great stores of gold

Her hair was black as a ra-ven's fea-ther Her form and fea-tures dis-sem-ble who can

There was a young fel-low who worked on the sta-tion She fell in love with that ser-vant man

1 It's of a young damsel both fair and handsome
These lines are true as I've been told
On the banks of Shannon in a lofty mountain
Her parents claimed great stores of gold
Her hair was black as a raven's feather
Her form and features dissemble who can
There was a young fellow who worked on the station
She fell in love with that servant man

2 As Mary Ann and her love were walking
Her father heard them and nearer drew
As these two lovers were truly talking
In anger home her father flew
To build a dungeon was his intention
To part true love he's contrived a plan
He swore an oath too vile to mention
He would part this fair one from her servant man

3 He built a dungeon of bricks and mortar
With a flight of steps it was underground
The food he gave her was bread and water
And only a chair for her was found
Three times a day he cruelly beat her
Unto her father she then began
Saying: If I have transgressed, my own dear father
I'll live and die for my servant man

4 Young Edwin found her habitation
It was well secured by an iron door
He vowed in spite of all the nation
He'd gain her freedom or rest no more
It's after leisure he told with pleasure
How he'd gain releasement for Mary Ann
He gained her object, he found his treasure
She cries: My faithful young servant man

5 Says Edwin: Now I have found my treasure
I will be true to my love likewise
And for her sake I will face her father
For to see me here it will him surprise
When her cruel father brought bread and water
To call his daughter he then began
Said Edwin: Enter, I've freed your daughter
Aye and I will suffer, your servant man

6 As soon as he found that his daughter had vanished
Then like a lion then he did roar
He says: From Ireland you shall be banished
With my broad sword I will spill your gore
I grieve, said Edwin, it's at your leisure
Since I have freed her, do all you can
Forgive your daughter, I'll die with pleasure
The one in fault was your servant man

7 Soon as he found him so tender-hearted
Then down he fell on the dungeon floor
Saying: True-lovers shall never be parted
Since love can enter an iron door
So they were joined to be parted never
To roam in riches this young couple can
And now young Mary Ann rules with pleasure
To live forever with her servant man

162 LOCKS AND BOLTS

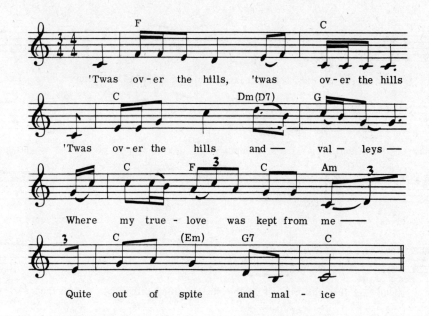

'Twas ov-er the hills, 'twas ov-er the hills
'Twas ov-er the hills and — val - leys —
Where my true-love was kept from me —
Quite out of spite and mal - ice

1 'Twas over the hills, 'twas over the hills
   'Twas over the hills and valleys
   Where my true-love was kept from me
   Quite out of spite and malice

2 I went unto her father's house
   Enquiring for my jewel
   They answered me: She's not at home
   She's at her uncle's house keeping

3 I went unto her uncle's house
   Enquiring for my jewel
   They answered me: She is not here
   Which proved to my heart so cruel

4 This fair maid hearing of his voice
   Put her head out of the window
   She says: My dear, you're welcome here
   But locks and bolts do hinder

5 He stood a moment all in amaze
   All in amaze and humour
   Till at length he drew, in a passion flew
   And the door he broke asunder

6 Her uncle's servant he being at home
   Soon after he did follow
   He said: Young man, you must quit this room
   Or in your own blood wallow

7 He took his true-love all by the hand
   And his sword all in the other
   Said he: If you have more right than I
   Take one and fight the other

8 And now this couple in wedlock joined
   They do adore each other
   They oft'times think all on that day
   When the door he broke asunder

163 MY DARLING PLOUGHMAN BOY

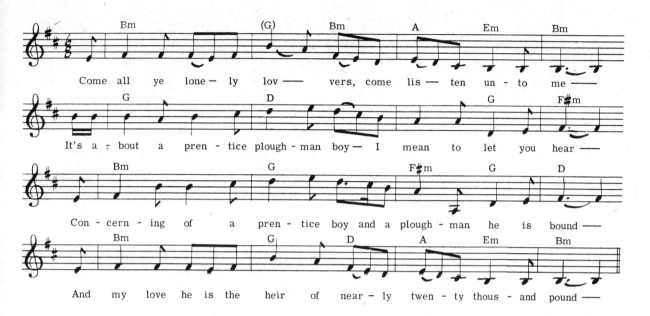

Come all ye lone—ly lov——vers, come lis—ten un-to me——

It's a—bout a pren-tice plough-man boy— I mean to let you hear——

Con-cern-ing of a pren-tice boy and a plough-man he is bound——

And my love he is the heir of near-ly twen-ty thous-and pound——

1 Come all ye lonely lovers, come listen unto me
It's about a prentice ploughman boy I mean to let you hear
Concerning of a prentice boy and a ploughman he is bound
And my love he is the heir of nearly twenty thousand pound

2 Down in my father's garden when first my love met me
He threw his arms around my neck and embraced me tenderly
We both sat down upon the ground for to complete our joy
Go where ye will and I love him still, he's my darling ploughman boy

3 The sticks and leaves are well pulled down, on them I'll make my bed
The greenwood piles are well pulled down below my weary head
The reaper bush will be my guide and for once my heart decoy
Go where ye will and I love him still, he's my darling ploughman boy

4 Now since I'm not inclin-ed to tell to you his name
He is the laddie and the man, the lad that I lo'e well
But when he sings, the valley rings, and he makes my heart full o' joy
Go where ye will and I love him still, he's my darling ploughman boy

164 THE NOBLEMAN'S WEDDING

I — once was in — vi - ted — to a no - ble — man's — wed - ding

And — all that were there were — to sing just one — song

The — first one to — sing was — the bride's for - mer — lov - er

The — song —— that — he sang was of days that were gone

1 I once was invited to a nobleman's wedding
And all that were there were to sing just one song
The first one to sing was the bride's former lover
The song that he sang was of days that were gone

2 How can you sit at another man's table
How can you drink of another man's wine
How can you lie on another man's pillow
You being so long a true-love of mine?

3 The bride she was seated at the head of the table
Hearing those words she remembered so well
Verse after verse, she could bear it no longer
Till down at the foot of the table she fell

4 One request, one request, from you that I'm asking
The first and the last, this favour shall be
And that is the first night to lie with my mother
All the rest of my days I will lie beside thee

5 Sighing and sobbing, she arose from the table
Sighing and sobbing, she went to her bed
Early next morning when her husband awakened
He went to 'brace her and found she was dead

6 O Molly, lovely Molly, cruel-hearted Molly
I loved you better than you'll ever love me
But I stole you away from your true-lover Johnny
It's then I separated the bark from the tree

165 OUR WEDDING DAY

I loved a wee las - sie when I was but young

And I own she be - guiled — me with her flat - ter - ing tongue

I — own she be — guiled — me and that well I — know

I — lost my wee dar - ling by court - ing too slow

1 I loved a wee lassie when I was but young
And I own she beguiled me with her flattering
tongue
I own she beguiled me and that well I know
I lost my wee darling by courting too slow

2 Her eyes shone like the stars on a clear frosty night
And when I looked on her my heart filled with
delight
All day I dote on her and at night I would dream
I was rolled in the arms of my comely young dame

3 My young love said to me: My mother won't mind
Nor my father slight you for your lack of kind
As she went away from me, this did she say
It will not be long, love, to the next market day

4 As my young love stepped from me and she went
through the fair
How fondly I watched her, move here and move
there
And then she went home with her geese and her
And that was the last that I saw of my dear   [gear

5 Last night in sweet slumber she gently came in
So softly came she that her feet made no din
Laid her soft hand upon me and this did she say
It will not be long, love, until our wedding day

6 Then according to promise at midnight I arose
But all that I found was the down-folded clothes
The sheets they lay empty 'twas plain for to see
For it's out of the window with another went she

7 Last night as I entered my lonely room door
The stars gave me light and the moon gave me more
A voice it spoke to me sad tidings of woe
I'd lost my wee darling through courting too slow

8 I own that I loved her as dear as my life
I had no other notion but to make her my wife
Till a young man, a stranger, a-courting her came
And he soon gained the favour of my comely young
dame

9 I will list in the Army, a soldier I'll be
And I'll go my bread-earning in some strange
counterie
I will fight amongst the heathens more honour to
gain
For my poor heart is broken by my comely young
dame

10 On a Saturday night men do tend to their wives
And the lads to their lasses as dear as their lives
But my poor heart lies bleeding for the girl I adore
I will pray for her welfare, what can I do more?

166 RAMBLE-AWAY

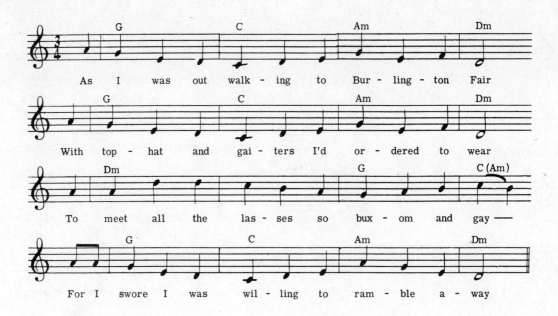

As I was out walk-ing to Bur-ling-ton Fair

With top-hat and gai-ters I'd or-dered to wear

To meet all the las-ses so bux-om and gay ——

For I swore I was wil-ling to ram-ble a-way

1 As I was out walking to Burlington Fair
With top-hat and gaiters I'd ordered to wear
To meet all the lasses so buxom and gay
For I swore I was willing to ramble away

2 And the very first step that I took to the fair
I saw pretty Nancy a-combing her hair
I tipped her the wink, and she rolled a dark eye
Thought I to myself, I'll be there by and by

3 The very first step that I took in the dark
I took this girl, Nancy, to be my sweetheart
She smiled in my face and these words she did say
Are you the young fellow called Ramble-away?

4 I said: Pretty Nancy, don't smile in my face
For I've not very long for to stay in this place
She packed up her clothes, farewell Burlingtonshire
She swore she would ramble she didn't care where

5 My father and mother, they're both gone along
And when they return I will sing them a song
The song it will tell how their daughter's astray
She'll be gone on her travels with young Ramble-away

6 The summer is over and the winter is past
And pretty young Nancy grew stout round her waist
Her shoes wouldn't lace nor her apron strings tie
You see what you've done with your Ramble-away?

7 The autumn has passed and the winter has come
And the pretty girl Nancy's a lovely fine son
She huddled him and cuddled him and these words
she did say
Grow up like your father and ramble away

8 Come, all you young maidens, wherever you be
With those jolly young fellows don't make over free
And come all you young ramblers, and mind you take
Or else you'll get brambled at Burlington Fair   [care

167 THE SEEDS OF LOVE

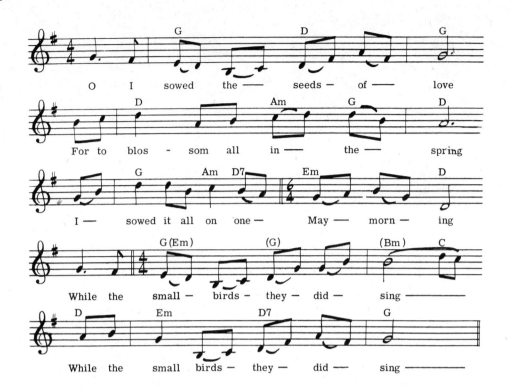

1 O I sowed the seeds of love
   For to blossom all in the spring
   I sowed it all on one May morning
   While the small birds they did sing
   While the small birds they did sing

2 O I locked my garden gate
   And I choosed for to keep the key
   Till some young man came a-courting me
   And he stole my heart away
   And he stole my heart away

3 O the gardener was standing by
   And I asked him to choose for me
   He chose me the violet, the lily and the pink
   All those flowers I refused all three
   All those flowers I refused all three

4 O the violet I did not like
   Because it would fade so soon
   But the lily and the pink I fairly overlooked
   And I vowed I would stay till June
   And I vowed I would stay till June

5 For in June there grows a red red rose
   And that is the flower for me
   Oft'times have I pluck-ed at the red rose bud
   Till I gain-ed the willow tree
   Till I gain-ed the willow tree

6 O the willow tree will twist
   And the willow tree it will twine
   And so will that false and deluded young man
   That once stole the heart of mine
   That once stole the heart of mine

7 O come all you fair young maids
   A warning take by me
   For the grass that you oft'times have trampled underfoot
   Give it time it will rise again
   Give it time it will rise again

168 YON GREEN VALLEY

For a young man court — ed me ear-nest-lie

It was with his wish — es I did com-ply

It was his false vows and his flat-ter-ing tongue

He be-guil-ed me, love, when I was young

1 For a young man courted me earnest-lie
It was with his wishes I did comply
It was his false vows and his flattering tongue
He beguil-ed me, love, when I was young

2 In yon green valley we both went down
Where the pretty small birds come whistling round
Changing their notes from tree to tree
As the sun arose on yon green val-ley

3 As I sat down by my love's right hand
He swore by heaven, by sea and land
That the rising sun he would never see
If ever he proved false to me

4 For eleven long months he proved true and kind
But a short time after he changed his mind
He changed his mind to a high degree
And he bad' farewell to yon green val-ley

5 O hold him fast, don't let him go
For he is mine and that well he knows
Don't you mind of the promise you made to me
As the sun arose on yon green val-ley?

6 I mind of the promise I made to you
But I'll have nothing more to do with you
My father's counsel I must obey
So it's goodbye, darling, I must away

7 O if he's gone then I wish him well
For to get married as I hear tell
My innocent babe I may tender care
Of his false promise let him beware

8 O am I married, or am I free
Or am I bound, love, to marry thee?
And a single life is the best I see
A contented mind bears no sla-ve-ry

145 ALL ROUND MY HAT

Harry Westaway, Belstone, Devonshire, *rec.* P. Kennedy, 1951

Printed versions
CHAPPELL: 1838, no. 22, p. 43; no. 126, p. 108
CHAPPELL: 1858, p. 666 (as above)
John Ashton, *Modern Street Ballads*, 1888, p. 173
BARING GOULD: 1895, p. 26 (London)
HAMMOND MS: 1906: one version (Dorset)
GILLINGTON: 1911: one verse only as dance song
(Hampshire)

JOYCE: 1909, p. 47: one verse only
JFSS: 1927, no. 31, p. 38; notes about song
JFSS: 1930, no. 34, p. 202: *Nobleman's Wedding* and
further notes about song

CREIGHTON AND SENIOR: 1950, p. 126: two versions, one
verse only (Nova Scotia, Canada) and CREIGHTON:
1962, p. 80

> All round my hat I will wear the greenie willow
> All round my hat for a year and a day
> And if anyone should question me the reason for my wearing it
> I'll tell them my own true love is ten thousand miles away

Our first true-lovers' song is perhaps one of the most popular of all English love songs. A street hawker is lamenting that his girl friend, a London flower-seller, has been caught for thieving and sentenced to transportation to Australia, ten thousand miles away. The refrain commemorates the time when true-lovers wore demonstrative tokens to indicate their pledges of faithfulness and chastity. In one English love song, *The Lily*, collected by Clive Carey, the wearer began to show signs of weariness of the burden:

> I wore the green willow for full one season
> But I do not intend to wear it for long
> Because this green garland it does not become me
> Although I am forc-ed to wear it now

Ashton tells us that as a 'humorous ballad' this street song was popular in the 1830s, and he gives it in cockney dialect:

> 'Twas going of my rounds in the streets I did miss her
> Oh I thought she was an hangel just come down from the sky

In his version the singer breaks into speech in the same manner as in *Villikens and his Dinah*:

> She'd a nice wegitable countenance, turnip nose
> Reddish cheeks and carroty hair (etc.)
> And never a woice more louder and more sweeter
> Vhen she cried: Buy my primroses, my primroses come buy

Chappell gives the tune under the title *The Budgeon is a Fine Trade* (a 'budge' being cockney slang for a thief who slips into people's houses after dark to steal clothing).

146 A BLACKSMITH COURTED ME

Phoebe Smith, Woodbridge, Suffolk, *rec.* P. Kennedy, 1956: BBC 23099

Other recorded versions
Charlie Scamp, Chartham Hatch, Canterbury, *rec.* P. Kennedy, 1954: BBC 19965
Tom Willett, Paddock Wood, Kent, 1962: TOPIC 12 T 84

Printed versions
JFSS: 1901, no. 3, p. 131: *Our Captain Cried*, *coll.* W. Percy Merrick, Sussex
SHARP MS: 1904–8: three variants
HAMMOND MS: 1905: Wimborne, Dorset, *coll.* H. Hammond: two Vaughan Williams tunes (as in JFSS: 1913, no. 17)
JFSS: 1906, no. 8, p. 202: Mrs Verrall, Monksgate, Horsham, Sussex, *coll.* R. Vaughan Williams: *Our Captain Calls*
JFSS: 1907, no. 11, pp. 97–9: note about tune by Anne Gilchrist and Lucy Broadwood
JFSS: 1913, no. 17, p. 279: Mr Verrall, Horsham, *coll.* George Butterworth: *The Blacksmith*: three other tunes *coll.* R. Vaughan Williams, Essex and Herefordshire

JFSS: 1927, no. 31, p. 17: *The Shoemaker*, Somerset, *coll.* Cecil Sharp
JFSS: 1930, no. 34, p. 206: *With the Hammers in my Hand*, *coll.* H. Hammond, Dorset; two Vaughan Williams tunes
GARDINER MS: 1908–9: two variants (Hampshire)
BUTTERWORTH: 1912, no. 2, p. 4: variant from Mr Verrall (JFSS: 1913, no. 17)
Arrangement by Gustav Holst of variant *coll.* George Gardiner, Hampshire: *The Blacksmith*, CURWEN 50618
REEVES: 1958, no. 71, p. 165: *Our Captain Cried All Hands*, *coll.* C. Sharp, 1904, p. 233: fragment (in Appendix)
PURSLOW: 1972, p. 62: *Our Captain cried*, *coll.* Gardiner

JAFL: vol. xxxv, pp. 357–8
HUNTINGTON: 1964, p. 99: *The Captain Calls All Hands*; Huntington suggests the song is related to *The Bold Privateer*, KIDSON: 1891
PEACOCK: 1965, p. 416: *Our Captain Calls* (Canada)

An interesting song, in that there are really two forms: *The Blacksmith*, from the girl's point of view, and *Our Captain Calls*, from the man's viewpoint:

> Our captain calls all hands on board tomorrow
> Leaving my dear to mourn in grief and sorrow
> Dry up those briny tears and leave off weeping
> So happy we may be at our next meeting

This was the first verse sung to Ralph Vaughan Williams by Mrs Verrall, formerly of Monksgate, Horsham, Sussex in 1904. Vaughan Williams liked the air and decided to adapt it. He used it as a hymn tune to the words of Bunyan's *Pilgrim* ('He who would valiant be'), and for English churchgoers ever since it has been a favourite; the tune was named *Monksgate*.

Because of the existence of men's verses and women's verses in the various collected versions, it can be surmised that at one time the song existed in an extended form as a duet-type love song. In our four-verse version we have only the point of view of the girl who has been left behind while her blacksmith goes off 'fighting for strangers'; other versions supply the men's viewpoint.

147 THE BONNY LABOURING BOY

Harry Cox, Catfield, Norfolk, *rec.* P. Kennedy, 1953: DTS LFX 4 (1965); BBC 22915 (1956)

Other recorded version
Jennie Davison, Antrim, N. Ireland, *coll.* S. Ennis, 1954: 21839

Printed versions
JFSS: 1902, no. 4, p. 206: *coll.* Lucy Broadwood (Surrey and Hertfordshire); words from *Such* balladsheet (two verses)
JFSS: 1907, no. 11, p. 110: *coll.* H. Hammond, Dorset
SHARP MS: 1906: one version (Somerset); 1921: one variant (Herefordshire)

GARDINER MS: 1907–9: two variants (Hampshire and Surrey)
HAMMOND MS: 1907: one variant (Dorset)
HENRY: 1924, no. 576 (Derry), eight verses
PURSLOW: 1965, p. 9: Hammond variant as in JFSS: 1907, no. 11

GARDNER AND CHICKERING: 1939, p. 180 (Indiana via Michigan, USA)
PEACOCK: 1965, p. 564 (Newfoundland, Canada)
KARPELES: 1971, p. 216 (Newfoundland)

> My parents thought to have me wed unto a lord or peer
> I being the only heiress of five thousand pounds a year
> But on one true love I've placed my heart my one and only joy
> For him I'll range the world all o'er, my bonny labouring boy

This song is often quoted as the classic English folksong and it enjoys widespread popularity in southern England as well as in Northern Ireland. The reason may lie in the words which express the thoughts of so many young lovers in the defiance of parents and riches for thwarting the course of true love.

It is much printed on broadside ballad sheets and these include further conversation verses between the mother and daughter. One verse not sung by Harry Cox tells how the girl eventually fled to Plymouth in Devon and got married:

Nine hundred pounds and all my clothes I took that very night
And with the lad that I adored to Plymouth did take flight
And there I did get marr-i-ed to my love and only joy
In peace and comfort here I live with my bonny labouring boy

148 THE CUCKOO

Charlie Phillips, Symondsbury, Dorset, *rec.* P. Kennedy, 1951

Other recorded versions
Bill Westaway, Belstone, Devon, *rec.* P. Kennedy, 1952: BBC 17794
Reg Gulliford, Combe Florey, Somerset, *rec.* P. Kennedy, 1957
Caroline Hughes, Blandford, Dorset, *rec.* P. Kennedy, 1968

Printed versions
HERD: 1769, vol. II, p. 180
HALLIWELL: 1842, p. 99 (two verses given in dialect)
BARRETT: 1891, p. 81 (no source given)
BARING GOULD AND SHEPPARD: 1895: two variants (Devon)
DUNCAN MS: 1900: two variants *To a Meeting One Evening* (Aberdeenshire)
JFSS: 1902, no. 4, p. 205: *Some Rival has Stolen my True Love Away* (Surrey); p. 308: *The Americans that Stole my True Love Away* (Sussex)
SHARP MS: 1903: seven variants (Somerset), three variants (Gloucestershire, Sussex and Warwickshire)
SHARP AND MARSON: 1904–9, vol. III, no. 72, p. 48: two sources (Somerset)

HAMMOND MS: 1905: seven variants (Somerset, Dorset)
JFSS: 1907, no. 11, p. 90: *coll.* Hammond, Dorset
GARDINER MS: 1907–8: five variants (Hampshire)
HAMMOND: 1908, p. 24 (Dorset)
JFSS: 1908, no. 12, p. 223: Percy Grainger, *The Merry King*, Sussex
BUTTERWORTH: 1912, p. 12 (Sussex)
JFSS: 1918, no. 21, p. 14: one verse only *coll.* F. Keel, Surrey
WILLIAMS: 1923, p. 165 (Wiltshire)
HENRY: 1924, no. 479 (no source given)
REEVES: 1960, p. 79: four variants (Devon and Hampshire)
PURSLOW: 1968, p. 32: *coll.* Hammond (Somerset)

SHARP AND KARPELES: 1917–32, vol. II, p. 177: thirteen variants (Kentucky, N. Carolina and Virginia, USA)
BELDEN: 1940, p. 473 (Missouri, USA)
RANDOLPH: 1946, vol. I, p. 271 (Ozark, USA)
CREIGHTON AND SENIOR: 1950, p. 143 (Nova Scotia, Canada)
BROWN: 1952, vol. III, p. 271 (N. Carolina, USA)
JAFL: vol. XXX, p. 346

It's a merry king of old England that stole my love away
And it's I in old England no longer can stay
I'll swim the wide ocean all on my bare breast
For to find out my true-love whom I do love best

And it's when I have found her my own heart's delight
I will be as true to her by day as by night
I will be as true to her as a true turtle dove
And I'll never at any time prove false to my love

These are the opening verses of a 'turtle dove' song which includes many of the same stanzas as *The Cuckoo* printed here. In fact it is possible that at one time both birds were included (they represented constancy and inconstancy) in one ballad concerning Edward IV and his 'princely wooing of the fair maid of London' (see JFSS: 1908, no. 12, p. 225, note by Lucy Broadwood).

Not included in our version are the final verses:

The grave it will rot you and will bring you to the dust
There's not one in twenty that a young girl can trust
They will kiss you and court you, and swear to be true
And the very next moment they'll bid you adieu.

So come all you pretty maidens take a warning from me
And never set your mind on a sycamore tree
For the green leaves they will wither and the roots will decay
And the beauty of a fair maid will soon fade away

149 DEEP IN LOVE

Mrs Gladys Stone, Fittleworth, Sussex, *rec.* R. Copper, 1954: BBC 22740

Printed versions

JOHNSON: 1787–1803, vol. VI, p. 582: *In Yon Garden*
LOGAN: 1869, p. 336: *Picking Lilies* (from a chap book *c.* 1782)
CHRISTIE: 1876: vol. I, p. 226: *The Prickly Rose*
BARING GOULD MS: 1889–91: three variants (Devon and Cornwall)
BARING GOULD: 1889, no. 86: *A Ship came Sailing* (Cornwall)
DUNCAN MS: 1900: *My Heart it is Sair* (Aberdeenshire)
SHARP MS: 1904–6: two variants (Somerset)
HAMMOND MS: 1905: two variants, nos 98, 522 (Dorset)
GARDINER MS: 1906–9: two variants, nos. 566, 643 (Hampshire) and no. 1385 (Sussex)
SHARP AND MARSON: 1904–9, vol. III, no. 66: *O Waly Waly* (Somerset)

HUGHES: 1909, vol. I, p. 68: *Must I go Bound?* (Derry)
JFSS: 1923, no. 27, p. 69: *Deep In Love coll.* Hammond, Dorset
HENRY: 1924, no. 218: two variants giving man's and woman's viewpoint: *Must I go Bound?* (N. Ireland)
JEFDSS: 1954, p. 161: article by J. W. Allen with complete list of references of variants of this song
REEVES: 1958, no. 108, p. 218: *Waly Waly* (from SHARP)
REEVES: 1960, no. 30, p. 89: *Deep in Love* (from HAMMOND)
PURSLOW: 1965, p. 23: *coll.* Hammond, Dorset

SHARP AND KARPELES: 1917–32, vol. II, p. 76: four variants *The Brisk Young Lover* (Appalachians, USA)
COX: 1925, p. 142: *Maggie Goddon* (Virginia, USA)

> There was three worms on yonder hill
> They neither could not hear or see
> I wish I'd been but one of them
> When first I gained my liberty

Mr Bartlett of Wimborne, Dorset, who sang these verses to the collector Henry Hammond in 1905, believed the song to be an answer to *The Cuckoo* song (No. 148). The song is perhaps best known in England from the outstanding version beginning 'The water is wide' collected by Cecil Sharp in Somerset, to which he gave the Scots title *O Waly Waly*. This was not the name used by his informants but he believed that the song was a variant of the Scots song of this title. Also incorporating verses of the song is the ballad *Jamie Douglas* of which there are fifteen versions in Child. Other versions collected since are most frequently called *Down in the Meadows, Must I be Bound* or *The Prickly Rose*. A broadside version dating from about 1766 in the British Museum calls it *The Unfortunate Swain*. (Details of the many versions can be found in the article on *O Waly Waly* by J. W. Allen in JEFDSS: 1954, p. 161.)

> Down in a meadow fair and gay
> Plucking a rose the other day
> Plucking a rose both red and blue
> I little thought what love can do

There is much in common too between our song and *There is a Tavern in the Town* or *Died for Love*. In fact the opening verse given at the head would seem to belong more to *Died for Love* than *Deep in Love*. Then there is another related song *The Effects of Love*:

> O love is hot and love is cold
> And love is dearer than any gold
> And love is dearer than anything
> Unto my grave it will me bring

The Scots version collected by James Duncan starts with this opening verse:

> My heart it is sair and very very sair
> But there's none shall hear my melody
> I die for love but I daur-na tell
> A bonny bonny laddie deceiv-ed me

It also includes the *Deep in Love* stanza 'I leant my back against an oak', after which it is similar to our version. In our first verse it is (as in *Died for Love*) an orange instead of a willow tree and following our verse five Duncan heard:

> My friends they conveyed me to yon church
> Before yon priest for to appear
> My lips said: Yes at their request
> But my heart it said: O no, my love's nae here

150   THE DELUDED LOVER

Michael Gallagher, Belleek, Fermanagh, N. Ireland, *rec.* P. Kennedy and S. O'Boyle, 1953: BBC 20023: *As I roved out*

Other recorded versions
Brigid Tunney, Belleek, Fermanagh, N. Ireland, *rec.* P. Kennedy and S. O'Boyle, 1953: BBC 20026
Mary McGarvey, Donegal, Ireland, *rec.* S. Ennis, 1954, *The Briar and the Rose*: BBC 21999

> Yes, all your vows, love I know I got them
> My faith and troth, dear, and my right hand
> And all those promises, you went and broke them
> And you married a girl for the sake of land

This fine song about former lovers who are full of regret, recorded from members of the Tunney family in Northern Ireland, was also sung by Mary McGarvey of Donegal, where it was entitled *The Briar and the Rose*. In spite of all sorts of promises ('three diamond rings' in our version) to his former lover, the soldier has married another woman; she presumably has also married and is now also regretful:

> But every night when I go to my bed
> The thoughts of you, love, runs in my head
> When I turn round to embrace my darling
> I find the briar where the rose should lie

(In our version, instead of the rose and briar, which denote true and false love, we have gold and brass, with their implications of wealth and poverty in the strength of love.) Now she hopes that the Queen will not only recall her soldiers but, in so doing, will also call them away from women they have married while abroad:

> But if the Queen would call off her men
> Through England, Ireland, France and Spain
> And take every man from his wedded woman
> Sure, the Lord might send me my true-love again

151   DOWN BY BLACKWATERSIDE

Winnie Ryan, Belfast, N. Ireland, *rec.* P. Kennedy and S. O'Boyle, 1952: BBC 18551

Other recorded versions
Paddy and Mary Doran, *rec.* P. Kennedy and S. O'Boyle, 1952: BBC 18579
Also *rec.* Puck Fair, Killorglin, Kerry, Ireland, 1947: BBC 13383

Printed versions
JOHNSON: 1787–1803, vol. IV, p. 410: *I am too Young*
BARING GOULD: 1889, no. 23: *The Squire and the Fair Maid*, partly rewritten; not in revised edition, 1905
SHARP MS: 1903/5: two variants *The Squire and the Maid* (Somerset)
JFSS: 1909, no. 13, p. 296: *Abroad as I was Walking*, coll. Gamblin, Hampshire

JFSS: 1913, no. 17, p. 281: *Down by the Greenwood Side*, coll. G. Butterworth, Sussex
REEVES: 1958, no. 28, p. 106: *Down by a Riverside*, coll. C. Sharp, Somerset (contains verses of *Captain Thunderbolt*)
REEVES: 1960, no. 1, p. 41: *Abroad as I was Walking*, coll. Gardiner, Hampshire; no. 124, p. 247: *The Squire and the Fair Maid*, coll. S. Baring Gould, Devon (complete ballad version in extended metre)
SHARP AND KARPELES: 1917/1932, no. 180: three variants *The Irish Girl* (Virginia and N. Carolina, USA); first variant is mixed with *Going to Mass Last Sunday* (No. 155)
PEACOCK: 1965, pp. 503, 551: *Blackwater Side* (Canada)

As *The Squire and the Fair Maid*, a ballad version of this song from Ireland has been collected in England's West Country. Our version from Irish travelling tinkers contains fewer stanzas and gains much from its concise statement. Although mainly concerned with its accusations of false behaviour, in some respects it could also be classed as a seduction ballad. In fact extra seduction verses from *Captain Thunderbolt* (or *Down by the Shannon Side*) are included in the version which Cecil Sharp noted from Mrs Overd, Hambridge, Somerset, in 1904 (see REEVES: 1958).

It is interesting to compare our version with the very full text noted by the Rev. Baring Gould from two singers, John Hoskins and James Parsons, on Dartmoor before the turn of the century:

1 As I was walking out one day
   Down by a river's side
   I heard two lovers in discourse
   A squire and his fair bride
   You are so comely, sir, she said
   And have a ready tongue
   I would you were my bride, fair maid
   Nay sir, I am too young

2 The younger you are the better you are
   The better you are for me
   I vow and swear and do declare
   I'll marry none save thee
   He took her by the lily-white hand
   To talk with her awhile
   He took her by the lily-white hand
   And led her o'er the stile

3   He led her to some wedding room
She kissed his ruddy cheeks
She stroked his flowing, flaxen hair
No word then might he speak
And in the beginning of the night
They both had jest and play
And the remainder of the night
Close to his breast she lay

4   The night being gone, the day come on
The morning shined clear
The youth arose, put on his clothes
And said: Farewell, my dear
Is this the promise that you made
All by the river-side?
You promised me you'd marry me
Make me your lawful bride

5   If I to you a promise made
That's more than I can do
Man loveth none so easy won
So ever fond as you

Go get you where are gardens fair
There sit and cry your fill
And when you think on what you've done
Then blame your forward will

6   There is a herb in your garden
Some people call it rue
When fishes fly as swallows high
Then young men will prove true
She went all then to her garden
She sat her down to cry
Was ever found on God's good ground
One crossed in love as I?

7   Was ever girl in city or town
So used as I have been?
Was ever girl so used as I
For wearing a gown of green
Sing lullaby, sing lullaby
For that alone I'm able O
Whilst others roam, I stay at home
At home and rock the cradle O

The transfer of the English ballad to the location of Blackwaterside probably came about because of similarity with another song, *The Lovely Irish Maid*. This version recorded from the Cronin family opened with the following verses:

As I went out one morning 'twas early as I strayed
It being in the merry month of May the birds sang in the shade
It being in the merry month of May the fields were decked with pride
With the primroses and daisies down by Blackwaterside

And scarcely had I gone a mile when it's there by chance I spied
Two lovers talked as they did walk down by Blackwaterside
And as he twined her in his arms those words to her did say
It's in America I'll prove true to my lovely Irish maid

When you are in America some Yankee maid you'll find
You will have sweethearts of your own more pleasing to your mind
You will forget those promises and those to me you made
So stay at home, love, do not roam from your lovely Irish maid

When I am in America, some Yankee girls I'll see
They must be very handsome to remind me still of thee
O there's not a flower on yon green lawn or growing in the glade
But will remind me still of thee, my lovely Irish maid

152 THE FALSE BRIDE

Lucy Stewart, Fetterangus, Aberdeenshire, Scotland, *rec.* P. Kennedy and H. Henderson, 1955

Other recorded versions
Louis Hooper, Hambridge, Somerset: BBC 4039 (1942)
Harry Cox, Catfield, Norfolk: BBC 17231 (1945)
Jim Copper, Rottingdean, Sussex, *rec.* P. Kennedy, 1951: *The Week before Easter*
Bob Copper, Rottingdean, Sussex: BBC 17990 (1952); *Folk Songs of Britain*, vol. I. CAEDMON TC1142/TOPIC 12T157
John Connell, Cork, Ireland, *rec.* S. Ennis, 1952: BBC 19024
Jeannie Robertson, Aberdeenshire, Scotland: BBC 29543 (1964)

Printed versions
Broadside, *c.* 1685 by John White, Newcastle upon Tyne: *The Forlorn Lover*
(1773): New Pantheon Concert No. 14: *The False Nymph*
ROXBURGHE: 1871, c. 20, f. g., vol. III, p. 672: *The Forlorn Lover, The Despairing Lover*
CHRISTIE: 1881, vol. II, p. 134: *It Hasna been my Lot to get Her* (Buchan, Scotland)
BARING GOULD AND SHEPPARD: 1895, no. 97: (words modified) *The False Lover* (Devon)
JFSS: 1899, no. 1, p. 23: James Copper, Sussex, *The Week before Easter* (tune varies halfway through song)

SHARP MS: 1904–11: nine variants (Somerset and Gloucestershire)
SHARP AND MARSON: 1904–9, vol. I, no. 20: *The False Bride* (Somerset)
JFSS: 1905, no. 6: three variants, *coll.* Sharp, Somerset
RYMOUR: 1906: *I loved a Lass*
GARDINER MS: 1907: variant (Hampshire)
HAMMOND MS: 1907: variant (Dorset)
DUNCAN MS: 1909: *The Forsaken Bridegroom* (Aberdeenshire, Scotland)
GREIG: 1909–14, no. 24: *The False Bride* (Aberdeenshire, Scotland)
ORD: 1930, p. 175: *It wasna my Fortune to Get Her* (Aberdeenshire, Scotland)
O LOCHLAINN: 1939, no. 86, p. 170: *The Lambs on the Green Hills* (Dublin, Ireland)
JEFDSS: 1944, p. 185: two variants (Banffshire, Scotland, and Kent)
SEEGER AND MACCOLL: 1960, p. 31: *I loved a Lass* (from RYMOUR: 1906)

PEACOCK: 1965, p. 441: *The False Maiden* (Canada)
KARPELES: 1971, p. 126: three versions (Newfoundland, Canada)

The earliest printed version would seem to be on a broadside by John White, Newcastle upon Tyne, during the reign of James II (1685–8). It was called *The Forlorn Lover* and was directed to be sung 'to a pleasant new tune':

> How a lass gave her lover three slips for a Teaster
> And married another a week before Easter

It has sixteen stanzas and begins 'A week before Easter'. It is remarkable that these opening verses are still employed by Sussex singers such as the Copper family of Rottingdean:

> The week before Easter the morn bright and clear
> The sun it shone brightly and keen blew the air
> I went up in the forest to gather fine flowers
> But the forest won't yield me no roses

> The roses are red, the leaves they are green
> The bushes and briars are pleasant to be seen
> Where the small birds are singing and changing their notes
> Down among the wild beasts in the forest

In the last verse, as sung by the Sussex singers, the broken-hearted former lover gives warning that he will put an end to his life:

> So dig me my grave, both long, wide and deep
> And strew it all over with roses so sweet
> That I might lay down there and take a long sleep
> And that's the right way to forget her

But one of our Scots singers, Jeannie Robertson, had two final death verses, the first implying that the bride herself was also dead, the last substituting lilies for roses:

> She has broken my hairt and forever left me
> She has broken my hairt and forever left me
> But it's not once or twice that she's laid with me
> For she's dead and she canna deny it

> So I'll lay doon my heid and I'll tak a long sleep
> Yous can cover me over by lilies so sweet
> Yous can cover me over by lilies so sweet
> For that's the only way I'll ever forget her

Songs of False Love and True

153 THE FALSE YOUNG MAN

Mary Murphy, Draperstown, Derry, N. Ireland, *rec.* P. Kennedy and S. O'Boyle, 1953: BBC 19975

Other recorded versions
Frank McPeake, Belfast, 1952: *The Verdant Braes of Skreen*, BBC 18294
Frank and Francis McPeake (with Uillean pipes): *Folk Songs of Britain*, vol. I, CAEDMON TC1142/TOPIC 12T157

Printed versions
CHRISTIE: 1876, vol. I, p. 198: *The Fause Young Man* (Banffshire, Scotland)
SHARP MS: 1904–9, vol. I: two variants *J stands for Jack and T stands for Thomas*
VAUGHAN WILLIAMS: 1908, p. 16: *As I Walked Out* (Essex)
GARDINER MS: 1908/9: two variants (Hampshire) *T stands for Thomas*
HUGHES: 1909, vol. I, p. 1: *The Verdant Braes of Skreen*, three verses (Derry, N. Ireland)

HENRY: 1924, no. 593: *My Love John* (Down, N. Ireland)
ORD: 1930, p. 174: *The Fause Young Man* (N.E. Scotland)
O LOCHLAINN: 1965, no. 8, p. 16: *The Verdant Braes of Skreen* (Ireland)
JFSS: 1906, no. 8, p. 152: *As I Walked Out*, coll. Vaughan Williams, Essex
JFSS: 1927, no. 31, p. 25: *T for Thomas*, coll. C. Sharp, Gloucestershire
PURSLOW: 1968, p. 109: *coll.* Gardiner (Hampshire)

WYMAN AND BROCKWAY: 1916, p. 50 (Kentucky, USA)
SHARP AND KARPELES: 1917/32, vol. II, no. 94, p. 51: ten variants (Kentucky, Virginia and N. Carolina, USA)
KORSON: 1949, p. 29 (Pennsylvania, USA)
MOORE: 1964, p. 60: one verse only (Oklahoma, USA)
FOWKE: 1965, no. 15, p. 42 (Ontario, Canada)

> I will never believe a man any more
> Let his hair be white, black or brown
> Save he were on the top of a high gallows tree
> And swearing he'd wish to come down

So runs the last verse of a fine Buchan version collected by Dean William Christie from the singing of Old Janet, who died in 1866 at Buckie in Banffshire.

A third person leans over a garden gate and listens to the argumentative exchange of two lovers: he asks her to sit down, she refuses, complaining of his unfaithfulness and his ability with words, so much so that she will never believe any man at all, young or old.

The conversational form suggests that at one time it may have formed part of a longer classical ballad. In fact the song has much in common with *As I cam Down by yon Castle Wall* (JOHNSON: 1787, no. 326) and *Young Hunting* (Child, no. 68).

154 THE FORSAKEN MOTHER AND CHILD

Sarah Makem, Keady, Armagh, N. Ireland, *rec.* P. Kennedy and S. O'Boyle, 1952: BBC 18535 (four verses only): *The Month of January*

Other recorded version
Caroline Hughes, Blandford, Dorset, *rec.* P. Kennedy, 1968

Printed versions
VOCAL LIBRARY: 1822, no. 1409, p. 521: *Twas one winter's evening*

HUGHES: 1909: *The Fanaid Grove* (Donegal) 'adapted by the editor'
PURSLOW: 1968, p. 33: *coll.* Gardiner (Hampshire)

MACKENZIE: 1928, p. 166: *The Fatal Snowstorm* (Nova Scotia, Canada)
PEACOCK: 1965, p. 447 (Newfoundland, Canada)

> Now come all you feeling people
> You come listening to my song
> Don't you trust yourself to no young man
> To your heart don't grieve no pain
> They'll kiss, they'll coax, they'll cuddle you
> And they'll call to you their bride
> And they'll leave you, like my first love left me
> With sorrows, grief and pain

This was the 'Come all ye' verse sung by the English gipsy, Caroline Hughes.

A mother and baby are forsaken and shut out in the cold winter's snow by both parents as well as by the father of the little child. Although sung in the Victorian Music Halls as a melodramatic tear-jerker, when this sort of song is sung in an impersonal, non-dramatic manner by traditional singers its beauty is apparent.

Sarah Makem, mother of Tommy Makem, who teamed up with a well-known popular Irish folksong group, The Clancy Brothers, learned this song at a dance near Derrynoose in County Armagh, Northern Ireland. Her third and fourth verses are floating 'false lover' stanzas more frequently found in such songs as *The Cuckoo* (No. 148) and *The False Young Man* (No. 153).

A song with the same theme is *Mary of the Wild Moor*, where there is a subsequent development in the last verse in which the baby is saved:

The father in grief pined away
And the child to its mother went soon
There's no-one lives there to this day
The cottage to ruins is gone
The villager points out the cot
Where the wild rose droops over the door
'Twas there Mary died by the house of her pride
With the wind that blew across the wild moor

155 GOING TO MASS LAST SUNDAY

Winnie Ryan, Belfast, N. Ireland, *rec.* P. Kennedy and
S. O'Boyle, 1952: BBC 18583

Other recorded versions
Una Douglas, Belfast: *My Charming Molly, rec.* P. Kennedy and S. O'Boyle, 1952: BBC 18541
Robert Cinnamond, Belfast: *Down in Yonder Valley, rec.*
S. O'Boyle, 1955: BBC 24835

Printed versions
GILL: 1917, p. 87: *Lovin' Hannah*

HENRY: 1924, no. 615: *Farewell Ballymoney*; no. 625:
Dark-eyed Molly O
JFSS: 1927, no. 31, p. 16: *Meeting is a Pleasure, coll.*
C. Sharp, London, 1909

SHARP AND KARPELES: 1917–32, vol. II, no. 180, p. 254:
variant *The Irish Girl* (Virginia, USA)
RANDOLPH: 1946–50, vol. IV, p. 232: *Black-eyed Mary*
LOMAX: 1960, p. 209: *Lovin' Hannah* (Kentucky, USA)
PEACOCK: 1965, p. 465: *In Courtship there Lies Plenty*
(Newfoundland, Canada)

Down in yonder valley, there dwells my heart's delight
I will roll her in my arms unto the dawn of light
I will roll her in my arms and I'll make her heart to feel
For a false-hearted soldier he never gained the field

As I went to Mass last Sunday my darling she passed me by
I knew her mind was chang-ed by the rolling of her eye
I knew her mind was chang-ed to a lad of high degree
O my lovely Molly, O married we will never be

Robert Cinnamond of Belfast sung the preliminary 'Down in yonder valley' verse preceding the 'Going to Mass last Sunday' which is remembered by the older singers. It brings in the vivid picture of the false-hearted soldier who can never succeed in battle unless he strikes deep at the heart.

This is certainly one of the most outstanding love songs in the English language. A beautiful Kentucky version, *Lovin' Hannah*, recorded from the Ritchie family, appears in Alan Lomax's *Folk Songs of North America* (LOMAX: 1960, p. 209). Although Cecil Sharp collected from the Ritchie family during the First World War he only came across one version in Virginia which he included under the heading of *The Irish Girl*. He did however hear a fragment from an old man in the Marylebone Workhouse in London in 1909 and immediately recognized the tune as Irish:

O meeting is a pleasure between you, my love, and I
And it's down in yonder valley I'll meet you by and by

American versions such as *Lovin' Hannah* have 'I rode to Church last Sunday' with 'Church' rather than 'Mass'. 'Church' is also found in the two Northern Ireland versions which were published in *The Northern Constitution* by Sam Henry. Recent recordings in Northern Ireland however have all favoured the Catholic 'Mass'. Since both 'Church' and 'Mass' have been collected in different localities close to each other, the words are obviously interchangeable, so that it would not be unauthentic to change the word for different audiences to bring more power to an already potent love song.

156 GREEN BUSHES

Thomas Moran, Mohill, Leitrim, Ireland, *rec.* S. Ennis, 1954: BBC 22038

Other recorded versions
Kathleen Devaney, Galway, Ireland, 1947: BBC 12611
Cecilia Costello, Birmingham, *rec.* P. Kennedy, 1951
John Stickle, Lerwick, Shetland, *rec.* P. Shuldham-Shaw, 1952: BBC 18624
Bill Sebbage, Fittleworth, Sussex, *rec.* R. Copper, 1954: BBC 22740
Tune played on fiddle by Billy Pennock, Goathland, Yorkshire, *rec.* P. Kennedy, 1953: BBC 21492

Printed versions
BARING GOULD: 1889–1905: two variants (Devon)
JOYCE: 1873, pp. 23–6 (Ireland)
BARING GOULD: 1889, no. 43: amended text (Devon)
KIDSON: 1891, p. 47 (Yorkshire)
BROADWOOD: 1893, p. 170 (Devon)
PETRIE: 1902–5, pp. 369–70
SHARP MS: 1903–23: eleven variants
SHARP AND MARSON: 1904–9, no. 34, p. 16 (Somerset)
GARDINER MS: 1905: four variants (Hampshire and Surrey)

HAMMOND MS: 1905: four variants (Dorset and Worcestershire)
GILLINGTON: 1911, p. 4: New Forest gipsy variant (Hampshire)
HENRY: 1924, no. 143 (Antrim, N. Ireland)
ORD: 1930, p. 147: chapbook variant (Scotland)
JFSS: 1915, no. 19, p. 177 (Kent). See also notes on song pp. 178–80
JFSS: 1929, no. 33, p. 112 (Cornwall)
JFSS: 1930, no. 34, p. 209 (Dorset)
REEVES: 1960, p. 133: set of words from BARING GOULD
PURSLOW: 1965, p. 38: from HAMMOND (Dorset)
HAMER: 1967, p. 42 (Bedfordshire)

SHARP AND KARPELES: 1917–32, vol. II, p. 155 (Virginia, USA)
FLANDERS AND BROWN: 1932, p. 246 (Vermont, USA)
CREIGHTON: 1932, p. 38 (Nova Scotia, Canada)
GREENLEAF: 1933, p. 67 (Newfoundland, Canada)
CREIGHTON AND SENIOR: 1940, p. 20 (as 1932)
MEREDITH AND ANDERSON: 1967, p. 173 (Australia)
KARPELES: 1971, p. 244 (Newfoundland)

> As I was out a-walking one morning in June
> To view those green fields and meadows in bloom
> I spied a young lassie so sweetly sang she
> Down by the green bushes where he thinks to meet me

So sang Mrs Costello of Birmingham, whose family went there from Ireland. Although the song is often regarded as purely Irish in both words and tune, it is also popular in many parts of England and Scotland and has been much printed on broadsides. The song was sung by Mrs Fitzwilliam in Buckstone's play *The Green Bushes* (1845) and it was published in Duncombe's *Musical Casket* and other collections at the time. Since then the words have often been credited to J. B. Buckstone, with the music composed by E. F. Fitzwilliam, but we can presume that it was traditional long before it was used by Buckstone.

A young man encounters a young damsel waiting for her sweetheart, and the song is in the form of a duet between them. He offers riches and fine clothing, but she only wants constancy. Seeing her true-love arriving, her new lover escorts her from the place. The penultimate verse gives a vivid description of the former lover's arrival and his forlorn expression. Some versions describe him as looking like 'some lambkin' or 'very sheepish' until in the final verse he realizes his freedom:

> I'll be like some schoolboys, spend my whole time in play
> No false-hearted young girl to stand in my way

157 GREEN GRASS IT GROWS BONNY

Mary McGarvey, Donegal, Ireland, *rec.* S. Ennis, 1954: BBC 21831: *The Dew and the Thorn*

Other recorded versions
Seamus Ennis, Dublin, Ireland, 1949: *I Wonder what is keeping My True Love Tonight*, BBC 13767
Jimmy McBeath, Elgin, Morayshire, Scotland, *rec.* A. Lomax, 1951: BBC 26506

Printed versions
GREIG: 1909–14, nos. 84, 87: *The Rue and the Thyme*
ORD: 1930, p. 187: *The Rose and the Thyme*

> Aye but I am sorry and it's aye but I am sad
> Aye but I am sorry when I'm thinking on my lad
> The green grass is a-growing and the water's running clear
> Aye but I am sorry when I'm thinking on my dear

So runs Jimmy McBeath's introductory verse to this song, which he calls *The Laddie wi' the Dark and Rolling Eye*.

> Once I did love you but now I do disdain
> I will for the world, aye, it's love you once again
> You look sae unco sigh, my love, when I did pass you by
> Farewell unto the laddie wi' the dark and rolling eye

In Jimmy's version there is a verse about love-letters which was not sung by Mary McGarvey:

> He sends me a letter saying that he was stout and strong
> I sent to him another saying that I had heard his song
> But it's keep to your love-letters and I will keep to mine
> I will write to my sweetheart and you can write to thine

Ord has a version which brings in the rose and thyme as well as the rue:

> My love sent me a letter that he was lying bad
> I sent him another I did not him regard
> He sent me another wi' the red rose so fine
> But I sent him another wi' the rue and the thyme
>
> Keep ye the red rose, love, and I'll keep my thyme
> Drink ye to your true love and I'll drink to mine
> I'll eat when I'm hungry and drink when I'm dry
> And rest when I'm wearied, contented am I

Gavin Greig had a nine-verse version sent him by James Mackie of Strichen, which included these verses:

> I can love little or I can love long
> I can love an old one till a new one comes home
> I only said I loved him for to keep his mind at ease
> And when his back is to me I shall love whom I please
>
> I loved him I loved him, but now I disdain
> The more that I loved him the prouder he grew
> The saucier he gaed and the prouder he grew
> And now I can tell him it's time for to rue

158 GREEN GROWS THE LAUREL

Robert Cinnamond, Belfast, N. Ireland, *rec.* P. Kennedy and S. O'Boyle, 1955: BBC 24839

Other recorded versions
Lal Smith, Belfast, N. Ireland, *rec.* P. Kennedy, 1952: BBC 18302
Jack Fuller, Sussex, *rec.* P. Kennedy, 1952: BBC 18717
Dodie Chalmers, Turriff, Aberdeenshire, Scotland, *rec.* S. Ennis, 1952: BBC 18784

Printed versions
SHARP MS: 1903–8: three variants (Somerset and Gloucestershire)
GARDINER MS: 1907: two variants (Hampshire)
HUGHES: 1909, p. 91 (N. Ireland)
GREIG: 1909–14, lxx
HENRY: 1924, no. 165: two variants *Green Grow the Rushes*; also nos. 479, 624: *The Cuckoo* and *I am a Wee Laddie* (both have 'Green grows the laurel' chorus)

ORD: 1930, p. 182
GILLINGTON: 1911, no. 3, p. 8: gipsy variant
KIDSON AND MOFFAT: 1929, p. 60
JFSS: 1904, no. 5, p. 246: *coll.* F. Kidson, Yorkshire
JFSS: 1914, no. 18, p. 70: *coll.* C. Sharp, Gloucestershire

FLANDERS AND BROWN: 1932, p. 113 (Vermont, USA)
CREIGHTON: 1932, p. 40: *I Wrote my Love a Letter* (Canada)
BELDEN: 1940, p. 490 (Missouri, USA)
RANDOLPH: 1946, vol. I, p. 273 (Ozarks, USA)
LOMAX: 1960, p. 332 (Utah, USA)
PEACOCK: 1965, p. 454 (Canada)
FOWKE: 1965, no. 44, p. 110: *I once loved a Lass* (Ontario, Canada)

> O come all you pretty fair maids take a warning by me
> Don't you ever look up, love, to the top of a tree
> Where the green leaves may wither and those flowers will decay
> And the beauty of a fair maid will soon fade away

This was the first verse sung by a teenage tinker girl in Ireland who said that the song was very popular among the travelling people. It is also popular with Scottish tinkers, and it appears in Alice Gillington's collection of gipsy songs from the New Forest area of southern England. Jack Fuller, a gipsy who travels mainly in Sussex and Kent, used the chorus of the song for verses which are popular among the Fullers, Smiths, and other gipsy families who travel this area.

> I met a pretty damsel when her age was sixteen
> She was as good looking as a young fairy queen
> I walked her, I talked her, I led her astray
> For she changed the green laurels for the violets so gay
>
> For the first one I met he was a page boy
> I gave him ten shillings to call him my joy
> I gave him ten shillings and a thousand times more
> But since we have parted it's cost me ten more

For the second one I met she was a *beau* tart
Her eyes in the middle shone like the blue stars
I gave her a wink and I called her away
And we'll change the green laurels for the violets are gay

As love symbolism, green laurels imply innocence and fickleness, whereas violets stand for truth and constancy. Some versions have:

Green grow the rushes and the tops of them sma'
For love is a thing that will conquer us a'

and in another, other plants are introduced:

The tulip may wither and the lily it will die soon
But the red rose will flourish in the sweet month of June

Other versions change orange and blue for green laurels and Anne Gilchrist believed this showed the song to have had political significance at the time of the 1688 Rebellion, pointing out the reference to the green laurel tree as the symbol of Irish liberty in *McKinnon's Dream*, and the orange and blue in the Orange song *Protestant Boys*. Orange and blue suggest a union of English and Irish Protestants, changing the emblem of the rebels for that of their own combined order.

The song is not always sung from a woman's point of view, and the gender can be easily reversed throughout the song. In the last verse, for instance, Dodie Chalmers sang:

I oft-times do wonder why young men love maids
And I oft-times do wonder why young maids love men
But by my experience, well, I ought to know
Young maids are deceivers wherever they go

159 A HEALTH TO ALL TRUE-LOVERS

Jimmy McKee, Armagh, N. Ireland, *rec.* P. Kennedy
and S. O'Boyle, 1952: BBC 18410

Other recorded versions
Mary Doran, Belfast, N. Ireland, *rec.* P. Kennedy and
S. O'Boyle, 1952: BBC 18304
Willie Mathieson, Turriff, Aberdeenshire, Scotland, *rec.*
S. Ennis, 1952, *I'm a Rover, Seldom Sober*: BBC 18789
Belle Stewart, Blairgowrie, Perthshire, Scotland, *rec.* P.
Kennedy, 1961

Printed versions
ORD: 1930, p. 89: *Hearken Ladies and I will Tell You*
(Scotland)

HENRY: 1924, no. 580: *Farewell Darling*; no. 722: *Sweet Bann Water* (N. Ireland)
SEEGER AND MACCOLL: 1960, p. 24: tinkers at Blairgowrie, Perthshire, Scotland
REEVES: 1960, p. 179: *Love it is Pleasing, coll.* Hammond, Dorset

Other reference
LOMAX: 1960, p. 136: *Love is Pleasin', coll.* Ritchie from an Irish girl in New York

First comes night and then comes morning
Then comes the end of another day
First comes young ones and then comes old ones
And so we pass our time away

Willie Mathieson sang this one-verse fragment as a song separate from the nine-stanza performance of his version of the song with its chorus 'I'm a rover, seldom sober'. He ended with these last two verses:

The cocks may cra' and the birds may whistle
The burns may rin through about the brae
But remember, lass, I'm a plooman laddie
And thos aboon, love, I must obey

Noo, my love, I must go and leave thee
To climb the hills that are far above
But to o'er climb them the greatest pleasure
Seeing I've been there with my own true-love

Jimmy McKee and other singers use the 'Love is teasing' chorus to the song, but this chorus may possibly be borrowed from another song.

When I was young, love, and in full blossom
All young men then came surrounding me
When I was young, love, and well behav-ed
A false young man came a-courting me

I left my father, I left my mother
I left my brothers and sisters too
I left my home and my kind relations
Forsaked them all for the love of you

I never thought that my love would leave me
Until one morning when he came in
He drew up a chair and sat down beside me
And then my troubles, O, they did begin

So girls beware of your false young lovers
Never mind what the young men say
They're like a star on a foggy morning
You think they're near when they're far away

160 IN SHEFFIELD PARK

Enos White, Axford, Hampshire, *rec.* R. Copper, 1955:
  BBC 21857
Other recorded version
Ben Butcher, Popham, Hampshire, *rec.* R. Copper, 1955:
  BBC 21862
Printed versions
HAMMOND MS: 1905: two variants (Somerset, Dorset)

GARDINER MS: 1906: two variants (Hampshire)
SHARP MS: 1906–21: four variants (Somerset)
GILLINGTON: 1907, p. 14: *In Sheffield Park* (Hampshire)
JFSS: 1923, no. 27, p. 74: *In Yorkshire Park*, coll.
  Hammond, Dorset
PURSLOW: 1968, p. 105: *coll.* Gardiner (Hampshire)
SHARP AND KARPELES: 1917–32, no. 101: *Brisk Young
  Lover* version A (Georgia, USA)

There is a tavern in the town
Where my love goes and sits him down
He takes another girl on his knee
And tells her what he doesn't tell me

It's grief to me and I'll tell you why
Because she has more gold than I
But in needy time her gold shall fly
And she shall have no more than I

These are two verses of the widespread *Died for Love* which has been collected in many parts of England. Its verses are sometimes intermingled with *Deep in Love* (No. 149) and sometimes the same title is used for our present song in which a young girl is dying for her love. She is a broken-hearted servant girl who, while in the process of making the beds, is found lying on one of them. Her mistress offers to help with her love affair by taking a letter to her lover, but her young man takes the letter and throws it in the fire.

There is a similar song, *In Jersey City*, which may well be a parody on *In Sheffield Park*. It is sung by country singers and it is also popular in the British Army, where it is performed to a rather sentimental Victorian tune. In this song the girl is in love with a butcher boy and she is found by her father hanging by a rope. Mrs Barnes, of Chideock, Dorset, sang:

In Jersey City where I do dwell
The butcher boy whom I loved so well
He courted me both night and day
And now with me he will not stay

Jack Le Feuvre of Sark, one of the Channel Islands, had a sailor's version of the song:

1 O mother dear, you do not know
  What pains and sorrows I do undergo
  Bring me a chair for to sit down
  And pen and ink to write it down

2 She ran upstairs to make her bed
  She laid on it, not a word she said
  Her mother ran upstairs to see
  But the door was locked, asleep was she

3 When her father return-ed home
  And asking for his daughter dear
  He ran upstairs and the door he broke
  And found her hanging by a rope

4 He took his knife and cut her down
  And on her breast these words were found
  O foolish girl, so foolish I
  To hang myself for a sailor boy

The Army song, generally known as *Died for Love*, is certainly a version of *In Jersey City*, in turn probably based on *In Sheffield Park*, and it includes some of the *Tavern in the Town* verses:

1 A soldier young and bold was he
  Who courted in society
  This soldier was so bold and gay
  He led a little girl astray

2 O when her apron strings hung low
  He courted her in rain and snow
  But when those strings refused to meet
  He passed her by upon the street

3 Her father came back late one night
  And found the house without a light
  He went upstairs to go to bed
  When a sudden thought entered his head

4 He rushed into his daughter's room
  And found her hanging from a beam
  He took a knife and cut her down
  And on her breast these words he found

5 I wish my baby had been born
  Before my troubles had begun
  So dig my grave and dig it deep
  And put white lilies at my feet

6 They dug her grave both wide and deep
  They put white lilies at her feet
  And on her breast they laid a dove
  To signify she died of love

7 Now all you soldiers bear in mind
  A true girl's love is hard to find
  So if you find one good and true
  Don't change the old love for the new

161 THE IRON DOOR

Lily Cook, North Chailey, Sussex, *rec.* R. Copper, 1954: BBC 22735: *Her Serving Man*

Other recorded version
Bert Edwards, Little Stretton, Shropshire, *rec.* P. Kennedy, 1952: BBC 18700

Printed versions
SHARP MS: 1906–9: four variants
HAMMOND MS: 1906: variation (Dorset)
BROADWOOD: 1908, p. 37 (Sussex)
JFSS: 1902, no. 4, p. 220: two variants *The Young Servant Man, coll.* Lucy Broadwood, Sussex; and Percy Merrick, Surrey
JFSS: 1905, no. 7, p. 97: five tunes (Herefordshire, Norfolk, Sussex, Essex and Surrey)

JFSS: 1907, no. 10, p. 55: *coll.* Gardiner, Hampshire
JFSS: 1927, no. 31, p. 27: *The Daughter in the Dungeon, coll.* Sharp, Oxfordshire
HENRY: 1924, no. 668: *Love Laughs at Locksmiths* (N. Ireland)
O LOCHLAINN: 1965, no. 61, p. 122: *The Young Serving Man* (Ireland)
STUBBS: 1970, p. 28: *The Cruel Father* (Sussex)

CREIGHTON: 1932, no. 84, p. 181: *Since Love can Enter an Iron Door* (Nova Scotia, Canada)
CREIGHTON: 1962, p. 54 (Nova Scotia, Canada)
PEACOCK: 1965, p. 590 (Newfoundland, Canada)

> True lovers shall ne'er be parted
> Since love can enter an iron door

A version from Northern Ireland in the Henry collection is appropriately entitled *Love Laughs at Locksmiths*, and Cecil Sharp had *The Daughter in the Dungeon* from Oxfordshire. It has also been called *The Two Affectionate Lovers*.

It seems to have been equally popular in both England and Ireland and should be classed as Anglo-Irish since the young damsel in question lived with her parents on the banks of a river Shannon, of which there are at least six in Ireland (running through the counties of Clare, Limerick, Galway, Tipperary, Leitrim and Roscommon).

162 LOCKS AND BOLTS

George Maynard, Copthorne, Sussex, *rec.* P. Kennedy and M. Plunkett, 1955: BBC 23093

Printed versions
SHARP MS: 1906–9: four variants (Somerset)
GARDINER MS: 1906–8: four variants (Hampshire)
JEFDSS: 1963, p. 192: George Maynard version (Sussex)
SHARP AND KARPELES: 1917–32, vol. II, no. 80, p. 17: five variants *Locks and Bolts* (Appalachians, USA)
SANDBURG: 1927, p. 149: *I Dreamed Last Night of my True Love* (Iowa, USA)

BREWSTER: 1940, p. 300: *Locks and Bolts* (Indiana, USA)
BELDEN: 1940, p. 168: two verses only (Missouri, USA)
RANDOLPH: 1946, p. 413: two variants, *I Dreamed of my True Lover* (Missouri, Arkansas, USA)
ARNOLD: 1950, p. 62 (Alabama, USA)
BROWN: 1952, p. 285 (North Carolina, USA)
HENRY: 1938, p. 253 (Georgia and Tennessee, USA)
THOMPSON: 1939, p. 399 (New York, USA)
JAFL: 1949, p. 236 (Kentucky, USA)
JAFL: 1952, p. 13 (Kentucky via Wisconsin, USA)

Although both Cecil Sharp and George Gardiner noted four versions each in Somerset and Hampshire respectively, no British Isles version had hitherto been published in printed collections or journals until our version was recorded from George Maynard in 1955. In the United States, on the other hand, where the song was also collected by Cecil Sharp, versions have since appeared in numerous publications.

163 MY DARLING PLOUGHMAN BOY

Jimmy McBeath, Elgin, Morayshire, Scotland, *rec.* A. Lomax, 1951: *Folk Songs of Britain*, vol. I. CAEDMON TC1142/TOPIC 12T157

Other recorded version
Frank Steele, Whitehills, Banffshire, *rec.* S. Ennis, 1952: BBC 18128

Printed versions
SHARP AND MARSON: 1904–9, vol. IV, no. 102, p. 62: *The Bonny Lighter Boy* (three verses) (Somerset)
ORD: 1930, p. 328: *My Bonnie Sailor Boy* (three verses)

Perhaps because of its delightful tune, this song was a favourite in the bothies of north-east Scotland. In our version it is about a ploughman boy, but in Ord's collection we find a bothy version featuring a sailor. Cecil Sharp came across a version of the song in Somerset, again about a sailor, but in this case its title was *The Bonny Lighter Boy*. His informant could only remember four lines of the first verse: 'It's of a brisk young sailor lad / and he a prentice bound / And she a merchant's daughter / with fifty thousand pound.'

The second verse in the Somerset version is similar, but another verse brings in a cruel father element:

> Her father, he being near her, he heard what she did say
> He cried: Unruly daughter, I'll send him far away
> On board a ship I'll have him pressed, I'll rob you of your joy
> Send him where you will, he's my love still
> He's my bonny lighter boy.

164 THE NOBLEMAN'S WEDDING

Joe Heaney, Carna, Galway, Ireland, *rec.* P. Kennedy, London, 1959

Other recorded versions
Dodie Chalmers, Turriff, Aberdeenshire, Scotland, *rec.* S. Ennis, 1952: *The Orange and the Blue*: BBC 18782–3
Belle Stewart, Blairgowrie, Perthshire, Scotland, *rec.* P. Kennedy, 1961
Conal O'Donnell, Ranafast, Donegal, *rec.* P. Kennedy, 1965

Printed versions
PETRIE: 1855: three variants, including the JOYCE variant
SHARP MS: 1904–7: two variants *Down in the Meadow* (Somerset)
GARDINER MS: 1907–9: two variants (Hampshire); one variant (Sussex)
HAMMOND MS: 1906: one variant (Dorset) (see JFSS: 1930, no. 34)
JOYCE: 1909, p. 224 (Joyce gave this variant to Petrie)
HENRY: 1924, no. 60: *The Bark and the Tree* (N. Ireland)
GREIG: 1914, no. 24, p. 1: *Orange and Blue* (words only) (Scotland)

ORD: 1930, p. 132: *The Unconstant Lover* (Scotland)
JFSS: 1927, no. 31, p. 4: *Down in my Garden, coll.* Sharp, Somerset
JFSS: 1930, no. 34, p. 202: *All Round my Hat, coll.* Hammond, Dorset
REEVES: 1958, p. 110: *Down in my Garden, coll.* Sharp, Somerset
REEVES: 1960, p. 44: *All Round my Hat, coll.* Hammond, Dorset
PURSLOW: 1965, p. 61: *coll.* Hammond, Dorset

SHARP AND KARPELES: 1917–32, vol. II, no. 105, p. 83: *The Awful Wedding* (Georgia, USA)
KARPELES: 1934, vol. II, p. 135: from Mrs Lucy Heaney, Newfoundland, Canada
GREENLEAF: 1933, p. 155 (Newfoundland, Canada)
BELDEN: 1940, p. 165: *The Faultless Bride*, from MS (Missouri, USA)
JAFL: no. 24, p. 339: *The Love Token*, from MS (Maine, USA)
PEACOCK: 1965, p. 691: four variants (Canada)
KARPELES: 1971, p. 124 (Newfoundland)

> Come all you young men that go a-courting
> This is a warning take by me
> If ever you go down between the grove and the valley
> Never venture between the bark and the tree

So runs a verse from one Northern Ireland version of the song. Another from Donegal mentions the wearing of coloured garments, and this has sometimes created confusion between this song and *All Round my Hat* and *Here's a Health to All True Lovers* (or *The Orange and the Blue*):

> Now I will wear a suit of deep mourning
> Suits of deep mourning I will wear two or three
> And then I will wear my own wedded garment
> And I'll try not to go between the bark and the tree

These three suits are further explained by the following verses from the north-east Scotland version *Orange and Blue*:

> First I'll put on a coat of green velvet
> This I will wear for one month or two
> And then I'll put on the green and the yellow
> And aye and aye after the orange and blue

> If anyone should ask me, should ask me, should ask me
> Why I do wear such a costly array
> It's I will quickly tell them why I wear it
> Because my true love lies cold in the clay

Our version was given to Joe Heaney by his father, Patrick Heaney, at home in Carna just before he died in 1937:

> I heard him singing that since I was knee high but only picked up bits of it. There's more of it than that. He sang at night. He'd go through them one after the other. Never stop singing. Never. He was always singing or humming. Always. Never stopped. I was ten years old when he died. I had very few of them learned. He was a small farmer, that's all. Very small. The land there is hopeless. It is hard to believe that anyone can exist there.—JOE HEANEY.

165 OUR WEDDING DAY

Francis McPeake, Belfast, N. Ireland, *rec.* P. Kennedy, 1953: *Folk Songs of Britain*, vol. I. CAEDMON TC1142/ TOPIC 12T157

Other recorded versions
Robert Cinnamond, Belfast, N. Ireland, *rec.* S. O'Boyle, 1955: *The Comely Young Dame*, BBC 24839-41
Brigid Tunney, Belleek, Co. Fermanagh, N. Ireland, *rec.* P. Kennedy and S. O'Boyle, 1952: *Out of the Window*; also from Paddy Tunney, her son, *rec.* P. Kennedy, 1958

Printed versions
HUGHES: 1909-36, vol. I, p. 46: adapted text *She Moved through the Fair* (Donegal, Ireland)
HENRY: 1924, no. 24: *The Star of Benbradden* (Derry, N. Ireland); no. 141: *Out of the Window* (Derry, N. Ireland); no. 149: *Pining Day and Daily*; no. 534: *Our Wedding Day*; no. 709: *If I were a Fisher*

> She stepped away from me and she went through the fair
> And fondly I watched her move here and move there
> And then she went homewards with one star awake
> As the swan in the evening moves over the lake

The three verses published in HUGHES: 1909-36 as *She Moved through the Fair* have a fine version of the tune, collected as an instrumental fiddle tune in County Donegal. The published words were said to be adapted by Padraig Colum from the old ballad, but they in fact depart very little from other recorded versions.

One of the five versions in the Sam Henry Collection also brings in the swan:

> At the foot of Benbradden clear waters do flow
> There dwells a wee damsel her breast white as snow
> Her cheeks are like roses, her neck's like the swan
> She's the Star of Benbradden I would she were mine

Paddy Tunney, on the Fermanagh-Donegal border, sings:

> She went away from me and moved through the fair
> Where hand-slapping dealers' loud shout rent the air
> The sunlight about her did sparkle and play
> Saying: It will not be long, love, till our wedding day
>
> When dew falls on meadow and moss fills the night
> When glow off the Grecian hearth throws the half-light
> I'll slip from the casement, and we'll run away
> And it will not be long, love, till our wedding day

166 RAMBLE-AWAY

Alec Bloomfield, Framlingham, Suffolk, *rec.* P. Kennedy, 1952: *Burlington Fair*

Printed versions
BARING GOULD MS: 1891, no. 151 (Devon)
KIDSON: 1891, p. 150: *Brocklesby Fair* (Yorkshire; Brocklesby is in Lincolnshire)
SHARP AND MARSON: 1904-9, vol. III, no. 78, p. 62: *Brimbledon Fair* (adapted words from the two variants *coll.* Sharp, Somerset)

GARDINER MS: 1905: two variants (Hampshire)
HAMMOND MS: 1905-7 (Dorset)
KIDSON AND MOFFAT: 1927: as above (Yorkshire)
JFSS: 1927, no. 31, p. 22: *Brimbledown Fair*, *coll.* Sharp, Somerset
REEVES: 1960, p. 93: *Young Ramble Away* (*Tavistock Street*), *coll.* Baring Gould, Devon; *Derry Down Fair*, *coll.* Hammond, Dorset

> Come all you young maidens wherever you be
> With those jolly young fellows don't make over free
> And come all you young ramblers and mind you take care
> Or else you'll get brambled at Burlington Fair

Broadside versions of this song call it *Birmingham Fair*, and the various other names used in the different versions are probably all corruptions of Birmingham which is neither easy nor very poetic in sound when sung. Thus we have Brocklesby, Brimbledon, Brimbledown and our Burlington. In this book we have also *The Birmingham Boys* (No. 195), which was sung as *Burnham Boys*.

167 THE SEEDS OF LOVE

George Maynard, Copthorne, Sussex, *rec.* P. Kennedy and M. Plunkett, 1956: BBC 23092

Other recorded versions
Bill Squires, Holford, Somerset, *rec.* P. Kennedy and M. Karpeles, 1952: BBC 17778
Gabriel Figg, West Chiltington, Sussex, *rec.* P. Kennedy, 1958 and J. Hyman, 1965: BBC 29821

Printed versions
CAMPBELL: 1816, vol. I, p. 40 (Roxburghshire, Scotland)
CHAPPELL: 1838, p. 93: fragment (Lancashire)
CHAPPELL: 1858–9, p. 520: collated variant
DIXON: 1846: words only
BELL: 1857: words only
JOYCE: 1873, no. 74 (Ireland)
BRUCE AND STOKOE: 1882 (Northumberland)
BARING GOULD: 1889, no. 108: *Shower and Sunshine* (omitted in revised edition 1905)
BROADWOOD: 1893, p. 58 (Northamptonshire; also Sussex, Surrey and West Country versions of tune)
SHARP: 1903–22: twenty-seven variants, six published in JFSS
SHARP MS: 1903–22: twenty-seven variants, six published in JFSS
SHARP AND MARSON: 1904–9, vol. I, no. 1, from John England (Hambridge, Somerset)
GARDINER MS: 1905–7: three variants (Hampshire)
HAMMOND MS: 1905–6: seven variants (Dorset)
GREIG: 1909–14, no. xvii (Aberdeenshire)
MERRICK: 1912, p. 34: with violin (Sussex)
BUTTERWORTH: 1912, no. III, p. 6: *Sowing the Seeds of Love* (Sussex)
CAREY: 1915, p. 16: *The Red Rose-bud* (Surrey and Sussex)
WILLIAMS: 1923, p. 86: words only (Wiltshire)
JFSS: 1901, no. 3, p. 88: *coll.* Merrick, Sussex
JFSS: 1902, no. 4, p. 209: four variants, *coll.* Broadwood, Surrey and Sussex
JFSS: 1905, no. 6, p. 23: four variants, *coll.* Sharp, Somerset
JFSS: 1914: no. 18, p. 93: one variant, *coll.* Sharp, Somerset
JFSS: 1927, no. 31, p. 19: two variants, *coll.* Sharp, Warwickshire and Somerset
REEVES: 1958, p. 194: five variants with a discussion (Warwickshire)
JEFDSS: 1959, p. 202: version noted by C. Sharp from Jim Squires, Bill Squires's father, in 1904
REEVES: 1960, p. 229: various versions of *The Sprig of Thyme* and BARING GOULD MS: *Dead Maid's Land* (Devon)
HAMER: 1967, p. 14 (Bedfordshire)

> I'll forsake all faded flowers
> I'll forsake all false young men
> Just give to me the man that's been trodden underfoot
> Give him time he will rise again

This verse, sung by Gabriel Figg at West Chiltington, Sussex, gives us the key to this famous English love song in which the flowers in the garden are likened to the various handsome young men when they first come into bloom. The lady asks a gardener to choose the various flowers she has planted, but all of them seem to lack necessary lasting qualities.

Our version makes no mention of thyme whereas many of those collected not only contain verses about it, but are actually entitled *The Sprig of Thyme*. Since the thyme verses are frequently mixed with other verses concerning seeds it is difficult to decide whether we have two distinct songs or not. James Reeves gives some interesting early broadside versions of the song and discusses this question in *The Everlasting Circle*, pp. 229–38 (REEVES: 1960). It is rather remarkable that the song is not more common in Ireland, Scotland or America.

168 YON GREEN VALLEY

Bruce Laurenson, Bressay, Shetland, *rec.* P. Shuldham-Shaw, 1952: BBC 18648

Printed versions
GREIG: 1909–14, xlv, p. 57: words only, *A Young Man Courted me all in the Sly*, from Annie Shirer, Kininmouth, Scotland

CREIGHTON: 1962, p. 86: four variants (Canada)

> In yon green valley we both went down
> Where the pretty small birds come whistling round
> Changing their notes from tree to tree
> As the sun arose on yon green vall-ey

This song was collected from a retired sailor on the Isle of Bressay in Shetland. Brucie Laurenson was blind, but he had always had a good strong voice and a good memory for songs. Thus it was that as a young man he had been used as a shantyman on board sailing ships.

What is remarkable is that this fine English love song had not previously appeared in any published collections in Britain before it was recorded from Mr Laurenson by Patrick Shuldham-Shaw in Shetland in 1952. In 1951 Helen Creighton recorded a version in Nova Scotia and in 1954 she recorded three other versions in New Brunswick:

Songs of False Love and True

I will sing one verse of his yellow hair
His rosy cheeks are uncompared
His dark blue eyes so entic-ed me
As the sun rose o'er the green vall-ee

I will sing one verse and I'll sing no more
Of the false young man I so adored
I will change my mind like the wavering wind
I will dote no more upon false mankind

Bibliography

This bibliography has been divided into two sections. Books published in Britain and Ireland appear first, followed by those published abroad, both in alphabetical order

BARING GOULD: 1889–1905
Rev. S. Baring Gould and Rev. H. Fleetwood Sheppard, *Songs and Ballads of the West*: Patey & Willis, London (4 parts) 1889–91. Methuen, London (4 parts) 1891–4; (1 vol.) 1895; revised edition 1905. Details are given by E. A. White in JEFDSS: 1937, p. 143, and 1946, p. 67. When reprinted in four parts this collection, mainly from Devon and N. Cornwall, comprised 110 songs 'collected from the mouths of the people'. Texts were modified and in some cases completely re-written and the same applied to tunes. However, in the revised edition, under the musical editorship of Cecil Sharp and with the adding of the name of the Rev. F. W. Bussell, one of the original collectors, many original texts and tunes were restored. For further comment on this publication see Dean-Smith: JEFDSS: 1950, p. 41.

BARING GOULD MS: 1889–95
Rev. S. Baring Gould. Manuscript in Plymouth City Library.

BARING GOULD AND SHEPPARD: 1895
Rev. S. Baring Gould and Rev. H. Fleetwood Sheppard, *A Garland of Country Song*: Methuen, London, 1985. 50 songs with much edited text compounded from various sources; detailed notes about songs, particularly those associated with customs, and comparative texts given. The introduction gives a history of folksong collecting from 1843.

BARRETT: 1891
William A. Barrett, *English Folk Songs*: Novello, London, 1891. 54 songs with piano arrangements. An early publication using the term 'collected folk song'; most of the songs published elsewhere; exact details of origins not given and Barrett not nationally accepted as reputable collector or arranger.

BELL: 1857
See DIXON: 1846 AND BELL: 1857

BROADWOOD: 1893
Lucy Broadwood and J. A. Fuller-Maitland, *English County Songs*: Cramer, London, 1893. Important early publication containing 92 songs collected in nearly every county of England. Most have little relevance to their district origins but some are in the dialects of their locality. Scholarly presentation with straight-forward piano accompaniments. For article about editor see JEFDSS: 1948, p. 136, and 1950, p. 38.

BROADWOOD: 1908
Lucy Broadwood, *English Traditional Songs and Carols*: Boosey, London, 1908. 39 songs mainly from Surrey-Sussex border with informative preface and brief notes about singers with comparative transcriptions made by phonograph cylinder recordings.

BRUCE AND STOKOE: 1882
Rev. J. Bruce and J. Stokoe, *Northumbrian Minstrelsy*: Society of Antiquaries, Newcastle-upon-Tyne, 1882. Texts and 130 melodies (without accompaniments) collected by Melodies Committee of the Society with copious and invaluable notes to songs, information about small-pipes as well as a list of current tunes forming a 'Minstrels Budget' between Part 1: Songs and Part 2: Small-pipe tunes.

BUTTERWORTH: 1912
George Butterworth, *Folk Songs from Sussex*: Augener, London, 1912. 11 songs with piano arrangements collected by Butterworth and Francis Jekyll with names of singers and sources given in short preface. (For other songs noted by Butterworth see JFSS: 1913, No. 17.)

CAMPBELL: 1816/18
Alexander Campbell, *Albyn's Anthology*: Oliver & Boyd, Edinburgh; vol. I 1816, vol. II 1818.

CAREY: 1915
Clive Carey, *Ten English Folk Songs*: Curwen, London, 1915. 8 songs from Surrey and Sussex, and 2 from Yorkshire with collector's own piano accompaniment.

CHAPPELL: 1838
William Chappell, *National English Airs*: Chappell & Simpkin Marshall, London, 1838. One volume containing 245 tunes arranged for piano and the other historical references, annotations and details of sources. Much of the reference is to printed works and MSS in the library of Edward Rimbault which was later dispersed. This work was superseded twenty years later by *Popular Music of the Olden Time* (1858).

CHAPPELL: 1858/9
William Chappell, *Popular Music of the Olden Time*: Cramer, Beale & Chappell, London, vol. I 1858, vol. II 1859; Dover Publications, New York, 1965. Includes most of material from *National English Airs* (1838) but more has been added from other sources with particular reference to the ballads in the Pepys and Roxburghe collections. For further comment see Dean-Smith's *Guide* and JEFDSS: 1950, p. 38.

CHRISTIE: 1876/81
William Christie, *Traditional Ballad Airs*: Edmonston and Douglas, Edinburgh, vol. I 1876, vol. II 1881. Dean Christie noted down songs mainly in Aberdeenshire. This book combines his own collecting with publication of tunes and words from many other collections, both published and unpublished, including Percy, Scott, Jamieson, Motherwell, Kinloch, Sharpe and Buchan. Also contains a few original compositions.

DEAN-SMITH: 1954
Margaret Dean-Smith, *A Guide to English Folk Song Collections (1822–1952)*: University of Liverpool, 1954. A useful index of published songs under titles, alternative titles and first lines, with some full descriptions of important books with historical annotations and an introduction which traces the development of collecting and publication of folksong in England over a period of 130 years.

DIXON: 1846 AND BELL: 1857
James Henry Dixon, *Ancient Poems, Ballads and Songs of the Peasantry of England*: Percy Society, London, No. 62, 1846. Robert Bell (title as above): J. W. Parker, London, 1857. By agreement with Dixon, Bell's publication was a revision, enlargement and editing by Bell of Dixon's collection and notes. Most of the material was collected in West Yorkshire and on Tyneside.

DUNCAN MS: 1905–11
James Duncan (1848–1917). MS collected *c.* 1905–11. Aberdeen University Library. Consists of two notebooks, the first containing 800 tunes with words of first verse, and the second giving texts of over 350 songs all supplied by a Mrs Gillespie. For obituary by Lucy Broadwood see JFSS: 1918, No. 21, p. 41.

FMJ: 1965–
Folk Music Journal: English Folk Dance and Song Society, London (from 1965). Continuing the work of JFSS (*Journal of the Folk-Song Society*): 1889–1931 and JEFDSS (*Journal of the English Folk Dance and Song Society*): 1932–64.

GARDINER: 1909
George B. Gardiner, *Folk Songs from Hampshire*: Novello, London, 1909. 16 songs collected by Gardiner and his musical associates, Gamblin, Balfour Gardiner and Guyer, and arranged by Gustav (von) Holst.

GARDINER MS: 1905–9 (see also under HAMMOND)
For further details about Gardiner's work see *The George Gardiner Folksong Collection* in FMJ: 1967, p. 129 and introduction to PURSLOW: 1968.

GILL: 1917
W. H. Gill, *Songs of the British Folk*: Curwen, London, 1917.

GILLINGTON: 1907
Alice E. Gillington, *Eight Hampshire Songs*: Curwen, London, 1907. Songs arranged by Miss Gillington with piano accompaniments. No preface or notes to songs.

GILLINGTON: 1911
Alice E. Gillington, *Songs of the Open Road*: Williams, London, 1911. The earliest English publication devoted to gipsy songs and dance tunes. 16 songs and 9 dances collected in Hampshire and the New Forest mostly from a family called Lee. Music arranged for piano by Dowsett Sellars.

GREIG: 1909/14
Gavin Greig, *Folk Songs of the North-East*: The Buchan Observer, Peterhead, Scotland. Vol. I 1909, vol. II 1914. Folklore Associates, Pennsylvania, USA, 1963. Greig was an Aberdeenshire schoolmaster and an accomplished musician who noted the words and tunes of over 3,000 songs. His manuscripts, extending over 90 volumes, are deposited in the Library of King's College, Aberdeen.

HALLIWELL: 1842/9
J. O. Halliwell, *The Nursery Rhymes of England*: Percy Society Publications, London, 1842. Vol. IV, and several subsequent editions. (It was reissued in 1970 by Bodley Head.) *Popular Rhymes and Nursery Tales*: London, 1849 (a sequel to the above). Words of nursery rhymes 'collected from oral tradition'.

HAMER: 1967
Fred Hamer, *Garners Gay*: EFDS Publications, London, 1967. 50 songs, words and melodies (chord symbols) mainly collected in Bedfordshire but also from other counties of England. No exact locations or dates given of informants or comparative notes to songs, but contains hitherto unpublished local songs and songs connected with local customs.

HAMMOND: 1908
H. E. D. Hammond, *Folk Songs from Dorset*: Novello, London, 1908. 16 songs previously published in JFSS: 1907: No. 11, 11 with piano accompaniments by Cecil Sharp. For further details about Hammond's collecting work see *The Hammond Brothers Folk Song Collection* in FMJ: 1968, p. 236 and introductions to PURSLOW: 1965 and 1968.

HAMMOND AND GARDINER MSS: 1905–9
H. E. D. Hammond (1866–1910), R. F. F. Hammond (1868–1921) and Dr George Gardiner (1852–1910) collected mainly in Dorset and Hampshire. Their manuscripts, deposited in the Vaughan Williams Memorial Library at Cecil Sharp House, London, have been indexed by Frank Purslow, who has also edited three books drawn from them (see PURSLOW 1965, 1968 and 1972).

HENRY: 1924
Sam Henry, *Songs of the People*: Northern Constitution, Coleraine, Co. Derry, N. Ireland, 1924. Over 800 songs were published in the local Derry newspaper. Many were contributed by readers but it was Henry's diligent research and background notes that gave interest to each contribution.

HERD: 1769/76
David Herd, *The Ancient and Modern Scots Songs, Heroic Ballads*: Dickson & Elliot, Edinburgh, 1769; (2 vols.) 1776. Paterson, Edinburgh, 1870. New 2-vol. edition, 1973, Scottish Academic Press. Early Scots source material. Herd's original MS, in the British Museum, served as basis for many of Robert Burns's songs as well as for Sir Walter Scott's *Minstrelsy of the Scottish Border*.

HUGHES: 1909–36
Herbert Hughes, *Irish Country Songs*: Boosey, London, 1909–36. 4 vols. Vol. I 1909, vol. II 1915, vol. III 1935, vol. IV 1936. About 20 songs in each album collected in the northern counties of Ireland.

JEFDSS: 1932–64
Journal of The English Folk Dance and Song Society: London (32 vols.), 1932–64.

JFSS: 1899–1931
Journal of the Folk-Song Society: London (35 vols.), 1899–1931.

JOHNSON: 1787–1853
James Johnson, *The Scots Musical Museum*: 6 vols. Edinburgh, 1787–1803; 4 vols. with notes by William Stenhouse and David Laing, Edinburgh, 1853. This was the beginning of systematic documentation of Scots songs to which Robert Burns contributed material of his own collecting which he restored by re-writing amplification of the texts.

JOYCE: 1873/1906
P. Weston Joyce, *Ancient Music of Ireland*: McGlashan & Gill, Dublin, 1873. Longmans Green, Dublin and New York, 1906.

JOYCE: 1909
P. Weston Joyce, *Old Irish Folk Music and Songs*: University Press, Dublin, 1909. 842 Irish airs and songs, edited with annotations for the Royal Society of Antiquaries of Ireland of which Joyce was the President. Most of the music previously unpublished but some are versions of songs already in *Ancient Music of Ireland* (1873) and *Irish Peasant Songs in the English Language* (1906).

KIDSON: 1891
Frank Kidson, *Traditional Tunes*: C. Taphouse, Oxford, 1891. Texts and melodies (without accompaniment) mainly from Yorkshire. Later published with piano accompaniment in KIDSON AND MOFFAT: 1926 and 1927. Many texts filled out from broadsides. For article about Frank Kidson see JEFDSS: 1948, p. 127. Reissued by S. R. Publishers, 1970.

KIDSON AND MOFFAT: 1926
Frank Kidson and Alfred Moffat, *A Garland of English Folk Songs*: Ascherberg, Hopwood & Crew, London, 1926. 60 songs collected by Kidson, mainly in Yorkshire, with piano accompaniments by Moffat; most previously published in *Traditional Tunes* (1891). A further 60 songs were selected for a second volume by Kidson and Moffat (1927).

KIDSON AND MOFFAT: 1927
Frank Kidson and Alfred Moffat, *Folk Songs from the North Countrie*: Ascherberg, Hopwood & Crew, London, 1927. A further 60 songs with piano accompaniment, published one year after the collector's death. The foreword by Lucy Broadwood provides information about the collector. See also *Frank Kidson: portrait*, JEFDSS: 1948, pp. 127–35.

KIDSON AND MOFFAT: 1929
Frank Kidson, Ethel Kidson and Alfred Moffat, *English Peasant Songs*: Ascherberg, Hopwood & Crew, London, 1929. 'Third and last Selection of Sixty Folk Songs from the Frank Kidson Collection.' Compiled by his niece with once again piano accompaniments by Moffat. (See KIDSON AND MOFFAT: 1926 and 1927.)

LOGAN: 1869
W. H. Logan, *A Pedlar's Pack*: Paterson, Edinburgh, 1869.

MERRICK: 1912
W. Percy Merrick, *Folk Songs from Sussex*: Novello, London, 1912. 15 songs, all from one singer, previously in JFSS: 1901, No. 3 and 1904, No. 5, with piano accompaniments by R. Vaughan Williams, two songs, *The Unquiet Grave* and *The Seeds of Love* (167), with violin *ad lib*. The last song was arranged by Albert Robins.

O LOCHLAINN: 1939
Colm O Lochlainn, *Irish Street Ballads*: Three Candles, Dublin, 1939. Over 100 songs, words, music and annotations collected in many different parts of Ireland (including the North). All in English and many having equivalents in England and Scotland. Illustrated with woodcuts from the original broadsheets.

O LOCHLAINN: 1965
Colm O Lochlainn, *More Irish Street Ballads*: Three Candles, Dublin, 1965. A further 100 songs, all again in the English language.

ORD: 1930
John Ord, *Bothy Songs and Ballads*: Alexander Gardner, Paisley, Scotland. The standard work on the 'bothy ballads' of N.E. Scotland; 'bothy' meaning farm cottage or hut used by hands, ploughmen, shepherds and farm-servants, and the ballads, although including folksongs found elsewhere, being mainly those describing, and often complaining about, local farm life.

PETRIE COLLECTION: 1902–5
George Petrie, *The Complete Petrie Collection*: ed. C. V. Stanford, 3 parts, Boosey, London, 1902–5. Full details of the collection are given in JEFDSS: 1946, pp. 1–12 together with a list of tunes appearing in the 1855 and 1882 volumes.

PURSLOW: 1965
Frank Purslow, *Marrowbones*: EFDS Publications, London, 1965. A series of pocket-size publications initiated by Peter Kennedy in order to make available the songs collected by Hammond and Gardiner in the care of the EFDSS library. This selection contains 100 songs, provided with chord symbols over the melodies.

PURSLOW: 1968
Frank Purslow, *The Wanton Seed*: EFDS Publications, London, 1968. A second selection from Hammond and Gardiner again containing 100 songs.

PURSLOW: 1972
Frank Purslow, *The Constant Lovers*: EFDS Publications, London, 1972. A third selection in which the type-size has been increased and the number of songs reduced to 78.

REEVES: 1958
James Reeves, *The Idiom of the People*: Heinemann, London, 1958. Words of 115 folksongs from Cecil Sharp MSS (about 40 printed for the first time) selected as examples of 'English Traditional Verse'. Introduction concerned with the Folk Song Movement in England; Sharp as a collector; text revisions, description of the MSS; the popular idiom; and a detailed consideration of certain songs.

REEVES: 1960
James Reeves, *The Everlasting Circle*: Heinemann, London, 1960. 142 texts from the MSS of Baring Gould, Hammond and Gardiner considered as 'English traditional verse'. Introduction concerned with Baring Gould as a collector and his MSS; Hammond and Gardiner; varieties of folksong; the theme of fertility and a discussion on the *lingua franca* of English traditional song.

ROXBURGHE: 1871–93
Roxburghe Ballads (about 1540–1790): 7 vols. Vols. I–II ed. William Chappell, Ballad Society, London, 1871–80; vols. III–

VII ed. J. W. Ebsworth, Hertford, 1883–93.

RYMOUR: 1906–28
Miscellanea of the Rymour Club: Edinburgh, 1906–28. Versions of folksongs and contains nursery rhymes with their tunes collected mainly in the Lowlands by members of the club.

SEEGER AND MACCOLL: 1960
Peggy Seeger and Ewan MacColl, *The Singing Island*: Mills Music, London, 1960. 96 English and Scots folksongs arranged for 'the post-war folk revival' mainly from Scotland under headings: Children, Courting, Men at Work, On the Road, Sailors, Barrack Room, Rovin' Boys and Flash Girls, Historical and Fill up your Glass.

SHARP MS 1903–23
Cecil Sharp (1859–1924), foremost collector of English folksongs and folkdances, was the founder of The English Folk Dance Society and for many years a member of The Folk-Song Society. (In 1932 these two societies amalgamated as The English Folk Dance and Song Society.) For a full account of his life-work and publications see *Cecil Sharp* by A. H. Fox-Strangways (Oxford University Press, London, 1933), revised by Maud Karpeles (Routledge & Kegan Paul, London, 1967). Words, songs, tunes and dance notes in Cecil Sharp's autograph are in the Library of Clare College, Cambridge. There are also photostat copies in the Harvard University Library and the New York Public Library, and microfilm copies in the libraries of the University of California and in the library at Cecil Sharp House, London, the headquarters of The English Folk Dance and Song Society. Cecil Sharp's own collection of books was left to the EFDSS and formed the beginnings of the specialist library at Cecil Sharp House.

SHARP AND MARSON: 1904–9
Cecil J. Sharp and Rev. Charles L. Marson, *Folk Songs from Somerset*: Simpkin Marshall, London and Barnicott, Taunton, Somerset. 5 vols. Vol. I 1904, vol. II 1905, vol. III 1906, vol. IV 1908, vol. V 1909. The most important single collection of English folksong, later edited as the *Selected Edition* (1916–21). Introduction concerning singers and style most valuable.

STUBBS: 1970
Ken Stubbs, *The Life of a Man*: EFDS Publications, London, 1970. 50 songs, texts and melodies (chord symbols). Many from our same source singers, but includes a wide variety from Home Counties (Surrey, Sussex mainly and some from Kent) with some important variant versions and some hitherto unpublished songs. Biographical notes about singers.

VAUGHAN WILLIAMS: 1908
Ralph Vaughan Williams, *Folk Songs from the Eastern Counties*: Novello, London, 1908. 15 songs from Essex, Norfolk and Cambridgeshire most already in JFSS: 1906, No. 8.

VOCAL LIBRARY: 1822
The Vocal Library: Sir Richard Phillips, London, 1822. Contains words of nearly 2,000 songs, including many without known authors and described as 'the largest collection of English, Scottish and Irish songs ever printed in one volume selected from the best authors between the age of Shakespeare, Jonson and Cowley and that of Dibdin, Wolcot and Moore'.

WILLIAMS: 1923
Alfred Owen Williams, *Folk Songs of the Upper Thames*: Duckworth, London, 1923. Over 300 folksongs (words only) noted mainly in Berkshire, Gloucestershire, Oxfordshire and Wiltshire. Interesting introduction about rural life, more fully covered by Williams in *Round About the Upper Thames* (Duckworth, 1922). Further unpublished texts in Swindon Reference Library. See FMJ: 1969 'Alfred Williams: A Symposium'.

ARNOLD: 1950
Byron Arnold, *Folksongs of Alabama*: University of Alabama

Press, Tuscaloosa, Alabama, USA, 1950.

BELDEN: 1940
H. M. Belden, *Ballads and Songs Collected by the Missouri Folklore Society*: University Studies XV (No. 1), Columbia, Missouri, USA, 1940.

BREWSTER: 1940
Paul G. Brewster, *Ballads and Songs of Indiana*: University Folklore Publications No. 1, Bloomington, Indiana, USA, 1940.

BROWN: 1952–62
Frank C. Brown, *Collection of North Carolina Folklore*: vol. II Ballads; vol. III Songs; vols. IV and V Tunes. Duke University Press, Durham, N. Carolina, USA, 1952–62.

CHILD: 1882–98
Francis James Child, *The English and Scottish Popular Ballads*: Houghton Mifflin, Boston, USA. 5 vols. (10 parts), 1882–98. Dover Publications Reprint, New York, 1965.

COX: 1925
John Harrington Cox, *Folk Songs of the South*: Harvard University Press, Cambridge, Mass., USA, 1925. Dover Publications Reprint, New York, 1967 (released 1968). 185 songs collected in West Virginia (29 with tunes). Introduction describes collecting methods and identifies informants. Notes, references to other versions and other data given with texts of songs.

CREIGHTON: 1932
Helen Creighton, *Songs and Ballads from Nova Scotia*: Dent, Toronto, Canada, 1932. Dover Publications Reprint, New York, 1966. 150 songs, gathered mainly in the vicinity of Halifax, written down by the author and afterwards checked with recordings. First of four published collections.

CREIGHTON AND SENIOR: 1940
Helen Creighton and Doreen H. Senior, *Twelve Folk Songs from Nova Scotia*: Novello, London, 1940. Piano accompaniment by Miss Senior of 5 songs already published in CREIGHTON: 1932 and 7 songs not previously published.

CREIGHTON AND SENIOR: 1950
Helen Creighton and Doreen Senior, *Traditional Songs from Nova Scotia*: Ryerson Press, Toronto, Canada, 1950. 100 songs and 36 ballads collected in the Maritimes with additional variants of both tunes and texts in many instances. An important and well documented collection with versions of many of the songs in this book.

CREIGHTON: 1962
Helen Creighton, *Maritime Folk Songs*: Ryerson Press, Toronto, Canada, 1962. Michigan State University Press, East Lansing, Michigan, USA, 1962. 169 songs which were published with a companion gramophone record (Folkways 4307). There was also an earlier record called *Folk Music from Nova Scotia* (Folkways 4006).

FLANDERS AND BROWN: 1932
Helen Hartness Flanders and George Brown, *Vermont Folk Songs and Ballads*: Stephen Daye, Brattleboro, Vermont, USA, 1932.

FOWKE: 1965
Edith Fowke, *Traditional Singers and Songs from Ontario*: Folklore Associates, Pennsylvania and Burns & MacEachern, Ontario, Canada. 62 songs from 10 traditional singers with musical transcriptions by Peggy Seeger. Songs in the collection are on the following records: Folkways FM 4005, 4018, 4051 and 4052; Folk Legacy FSC 10; Prestige INT 25014; Topic 12T140.

GARDNER AND CHICKERING: 1939
Emelyn E. Gardner and Geraldine J. Chickering, *Ballads and Songs of Southern Michigan*: University Press, Ann Arbor, Michigan, USA, 1939.

GREENLEAF: 1933
Elizabeth Bristol Greenleaf and Grace Yarrow Mansfield, *Ballads and Sea Songs from Newfoundland*: Harvard University Press, Cambridge, Mass., USA, 1933.

HENRY: 1938
Mellinger E. Henry, *Folksongs from the Southern Highlands*: J. J. Augustin, New York, 1938.

HUNTINGTON: 1964
Gale Huntington, *Songs the Whalermen Sang*: Barre Publishers, Barre, Mass., USA, 1964.

JAFL: 1888–
Journal of American Folklore now published by University of Pennsylvania.

KARPELES: 1934/1971
Maud Karpeles, *Folksongs from Newfoundland*: Oxford University Press, London, 1934 (2 vols.); Faber & Faber, London, 1971. 30 songs (with piano accompaniments) were published in 1934 and 90 songs, 150 tunes including variants (with no accompaniments) in 1971. All collected during 1929–30.

KORSON: 1949
George Korson, *Pennsylvania Songs and Legends*: University Press, Philadelphia, Penn., USA, 1949.

LOMAX: 1960
Alan Lomax, *Folk Songs of North America*: Cassell, London, 1960.

MACKENZIE: 1928
W. Roy Mackenzie, *Ballads and Sea Songs from Nova Scotia*: Harvard University Press, Cambridge, Mass., USA, 1928.

MEREDITH AND ANDERSON: 1967
John Meredith and Hugh Anderson, *Folk Songs of Australia*: Ure Smith, Sydney, 1967.

MOORE: 1964
Ethel Moore and Chauncey O. Moore, *Ballads and Folk Songs of the Southwest*: University of Oklahoma, Norman, Oklahoma, USA, 1964.

PEACOCK: 1965
Kenneth Peacock, *Songs of the Newfoundland Outports*: National Museum of Canada, Ottawa, 1965. 3 vols.

RANDOLPH: 1946–50
Vance Randolph and Floyd C. Shoemaker, *Ozark Folk Songs*: State Historical Society, Columbia, Missouri, USA, 1946–50. 4 vols.

SANDBURG: 1927
Carl Sandburg, *The American Songbag*: Harcourt Brace, New York, 1927.

SHARP AND KARPELES: 1917/32
Olive Dame Campbell and Cecil J. Sharp, *English Folk Songs from the Southern Appalachians*: Putnam, New York, 1917. Cecil J. Sharp and Maud Karpeles (2 vols.), Oxford University Press, London, 1932.

THOMPSON: 1939
Harold W. Thompson, *Body, Boots and Britches*: J. B. Lippincott, Philadelphia, USA, 1939.

WYMAN AND BROCKWAY: 1916
Loraine Wyman and Howard Brockway, *Lonesome Tunes (Folk Songs from the Kentucky Mountains)*: H. W. Gray, New York 1916.

IX

Songs of
Seduction

Introduction

> O yes, I got some excellent good skills
> O yes, I got some excellent good skills
> Now come along with me
> Down to yonder shady tree
> I'll catch thee a small bird or two
> > *Three Maidens to Milking did go*: No. 191

Perhaps the greatest surprise in the recent folksong revival in England has been for the English themselves to discover how many of their folksongs are down-to-earth love songs which have survived the puritan Victorian era. Most of the songs in this chapter have been recorded in England; of the half-dozen from Scotland and Ireland, two are certainly of English origin.

Whereas in the two previous chapters of love songs the Irish influence has been strong, now the Irish symbolism of flowers and trees changes to English pictures of bird-hunting in the greenwoods and cornfields, and in *The Little Ball of Yarn* (No. 180) young maidens are advised:

> You birds of early dawn
> When you're playing all in the corn
> Take care you do not come to any harm
> For the blackbird and the thrush
> They come warbling around the bush
> So keep your hand upon your little ball of yarn

The best known of the seduction ballads will probably be *The Foggy Foggy Dew* (No. 174). Its revival popularity started in the United States with a recording of two verses by the American poet, Carl Sandburg, later carried back across the Atlantic in the three-verse recordings made by Burl Ives and Josh White. Even the English composer Benjamin Britten used these same three verses (the first, middle and last stanzas of our version) and the Sandburg tune for a vocal and piano arrangement. The words of our nine-stanza version seem quite a literary piece compared to the five-stanza traditional variants normally found in English counties. Phil Hammond sang them to the Sandburg tune, which was used by the Norfolk tree-feller from whom he heard it, but as a variation from an almost too well-known tune we have fitted the words to a traditional Sussex air. Harry Cox (see the Notes to the song) sang the five stanzas to the tune best known from its *Banks and Braes* use by Robert Burns.

The Foggy Foggy Dew is still widely sung in Ireland and has also been used there for a political parody concerned with the Easter Rising. In fact it may have originated there, and its title have derived from an anglicization of Irish Gaelic.

James Reeves, in trying to discover the significance of the title, suggests 'fogge', the 'Middle English for coarse, rank grass of the kind which grows in marshes and bogs where the atmosphere would be damp and misty', and this, as in *Rolling in the Dew* (No. 189), would represent maidenhead, and the dew would imply virginity or chastity. 'Foggy Dew' may be an English tongue's best attempt at the sound of the Gaelic, and derive from 'Oroce dhu' meaning a black or dark night. Robert Graves proposed a theory that it stood for the black pestilence of the church and that the girl was really being protected from entering a nunnery. There seems no end to what can be interpreted from the lines of folksongs.

liam Rew of Sidbury, Sidmouth, Devon
Photograph: Peter Kennedy

Another song, also sung in Ireland, is *The Magpie's Nest* (No. 182). In England, we find it as *The Cuckoo's Nest*, used as a hornpipe for stepdancing and for the Morris Dances of the Cotswolds; bawdy words to the tune are also sung in Scotland. *The Little Ball of Yarn*, another song recorded in Ireland, favourite of gipsies and tinkers, and also found in both England and Scotland, would be equally at home in Chapter XVI, 'Songs of the Travelling People', like the third song recorded in Ireland, *The Bold English Navvy* (No. 171) which is also common to England and Scotland and a favourite with the Travellers.

Two of the three songs recorded in Scotland, *The Overgate* (No. 187) and *She Was a Rum One* (No. 190) are both Dundee localizations based on *As I Roved Out* (No. 121), and there is a similar English song, *The Brewer Laddie* (or *Bilberry Town*) in the Hammond collection from Dorset. The third Scots song, *The Lady o' the Dainty Doon-by* (No. 179), perhaps more ballad than song, is a good example of a seduction song in the Lowland Scots style. In fact it is quoted by Professor Child in his notes to Ballad No. 290 in his collection.

One song, *The Nightingales Sing* (No. 185), will be of particular interest to American readers as it has been widely noted in the United States and Canada. When I first heard it sung by the Cantwell family, near Oxford, I recognized at once that here was a tune that quite apart from the words could gain great popularity. It happened rapidly; a friend, Bob Gale, wrote new words for a kind of imitation dialect song, *Dorset is Beautiful*, and his words have now spread almost as rapidly among modern folksingers as the traditional ones.

169 BLACKBIRDS AND THRUSHES

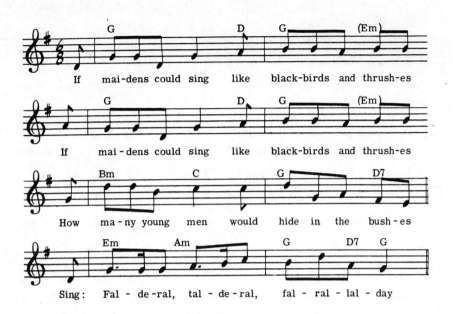

If mai-dens could sing like black-birds and thrush-es

If mai-dens could sing like black-birds and thrush-es

How ma-ny young men would hide in the bush-es

Sing: Fal - de -ral, tal - de -ral, fal - ral - lal - day

1 If maidens could sing like blackbirds and thrushes
  If maidens could sing like blackbirds and thrushes
  How many young men would hide in the bushes
  Sing: Fal-de-ral, tal-de-ral, fal-ral-lal-day

2 If maidens could run like hares on the commons
  If maidens could run like hares on the commons
  How many young men would take horse and ride hunting

3 If maidens could swim like fish in the water
  If maidens could swim like fish in the water
  How many young men would undress and dive after

4 If maidens could dance like rushes a-growin'
  If maidens could dance like rushes a-growin'
  How many young men would get scythes and go mowing

5 If maidens could sleep like sheep on the mountains
  If maidens could sleep like sheep on the mountains
  How many young men would lie down beside them

170 BLOW THE CANDLE OUT

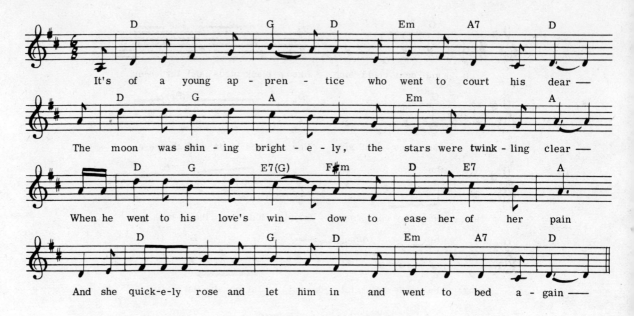

It's of a young ap - pren - tice who went to court his dear —

The moon was shin - ing bright - e - ly, the stars were twink - ling clear —

When he went to his love's win — dow to ease her of her pain

And she quick-e-ly rose and let him in and went to bed a - gain —

1 It's of a young apprentice who went to court his dear
The moon was shining bright-e-ly, the stars were twinkling clear
When he went to his love's window to ease her of her pain
And she quick-e-ly rose and let him in and went to bed again

2 My father and my mother in yonder room do lay
They are embracing one another and so may you and I
They are embracing one another without a fear or doubt
Saying: Take me in your arms, my love, and blow the candle out

3 My mother she'd be ang-e-ry if she should come to know
My father he'd be angry too, to prove my overthrow
I wouldn't forfeit five guineas now that they should find me out
Saying: Take me in your arms, my love, and blow the candle out

4 O when your baby it is born you may dandle it on your knee
And if it be a baby boy then name it after me
For when nine months are over my apprenticeship is out
I'll return and do my duty and blow the candle out

5 Now six months they were over, six months and a day
He wrote his love a letter that he was going away
He wrote his love a letter without a fear or doubt
Saying he never should return again to blow the candle out

6 Come, all you pretty young local girls, a warning take by me
And don't be quick to fall in love with everyone you see
For when they're in their prenticeship they'll swear their time is out
Then they'll leave you, as mine left me, to blow the candle out

171 THE BOLD ENGLISH NAVVY

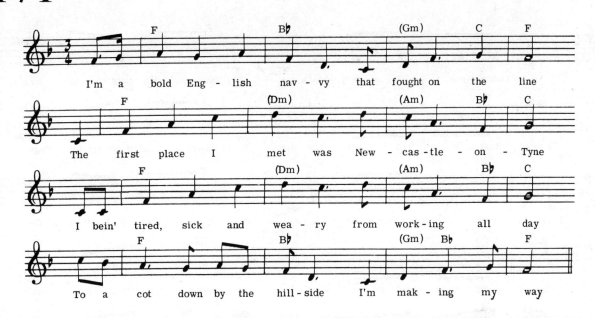

I'm a bold Eng - lish nav - vy that fought on the line

The first place I met was New - cas - tle - on - Tyne

I bein' tired, sick and wea - ry from work - ing all day

To a cot down by the hill - side I'm mak - ing my way

1 I'm a bold English navvy that fought on the line
The first place I met was Newcastle-on-Tyne
I bein' tired, sick and weary from working all day
To a cot down by the hillside I'm making my way

2 O I first had me supper and then had a shave
For courtin' this fair maid I highly prepared
Th'ould stars in the sky as the moon it shone down
And I hit for the road with my navvy boots on

3 I knocked at my love's window, my knock she did
And out of her slumber she woken so slow   [know
I knocked there again and she said: Is that John?
And I quickly replied: With my navvy boots on

4 O she opened the window and then let me in
'Twas into her bedroom she landed me then
Th'ould night it being cold and the blankets rolled on
And I slept there all night with my navvy boots on

5 O then early next morning at the dawn of the day
Said I to my true love: It's time to go away
Sleep down, sleep down, you know you've done wrong
For to sleep here all night with your navvy boots on

6 O he bent down his head with a laugh and a smile
Saying: What could I do, love, in that little while?
And I know if I done it, I done it in fun
And I'll do it again with my navvy boots on

7 O then six months being over and seven at the least
When this pretty fair maid got stout round the waist
For eight months being over when nine comes along
And she handed him a young son with his navvy
                                          boots on

8 O come all you pretty fair maids take a warning, she
Don't ever leave a navvy go into your bed   [said
For when he'll get warm and think upon yon
Sure, he'll jump on your bones with his navvy boots
                                          on

172 THE COACHMAN'S WHIP

I once took a job as a coach-man — My mo-ney was paid in ad - vance —

I — then took a trip down to Lon - don — From there I crossed o - ver to France

There I met a charm - ing young la - dy — Who 'dressed me and said with a smile —

Young man, I'm in need of a coach-man To drive me in old-fash - ioned style

O she was such a charm - ing young la - dy — And a la - dy of high-est re - nown —

And I being a dash - ing young coach-man — I drove her ten times round the town

1 I once took a job as a coachman
My money was paid in advance
I then took a trip down to London
From there I crossed over to France
There I met a charming young lady
Who 'dressed me and said with a smile
Young man, I'm in need of a coachman
To drive me in old-fashioned style
O she was such a charming young lady
And a lady of highest renown
And I being a dashing young coachman
I drove her ten times round the town

2 She then took me down in the cellar
She filled me with whisky so quick
I hadn't been there many moments
When she asked for a look at my whip
She held it, she viewed it a moment
And she then laid it down with a smile
Young man, by the look and the length of your slash
We could drive the best part of ten mile

3 She bid me get up to the chaise-box
So I climbed right up to the seat
Three swishes I gave with my cracker
And drove her straight down the High Street
I handled my whip with good judgement
Until I was up to her ways
But the very first turn that I gave on the wheel
I broke the main spring of her chaise

4 When my mistress grew tired or grew weary
She'd call me to stop for a rest
She'd shout for her serving-maid, Sally
The girl that I loved second-best
Sally, we've got a good coachman
He understands driving in style
While the spring on the chaise's repairing
I'll let him drive you for a while

173 FIRELOCK STILE

So come all young men, come lis - ten a - while

I'll tell you what hap - pened at Fire - lock Stile

When a stump of a nail catched hold of her clothes

She fell down and she did ex - pose

Her old rump - a - tump too - ral loo - ral lad - die - dy

Rump - a - tump too - ral loo - ral day

1 So come all young men, come listen awhile
I'll tell you what happened at Firelock Stile
When a stump of a nail catched hold of her clothes
She fell down and she did expose
Her old rump-a-tump tooral looral laddie-dy
Rump-a-tump tooral looral day

2 A gay young buck was standing by
The sight of her quim that dazzled his eye
She said: Young man, I feel amazed
To see a young gentleman stand and gaze
On my rump-a-tump . . .

3 She said: Young man, if you mean what you say
Twenty bright guineas in gold were to pay
Twenty bright guineas in gold for to pay
And then, young man, you may fiddle away
On my rump-a-tump . . .

4 That very soon he gave consent
And into the woods together they went
While he pre-formed and she pre-tuned
The boy and the beauty kept time to the tune
On her rump-a-tump . . .

5 Now six weeks being over, as I have been told
She gave him some fire to keep him from cold
To keep him from cold by night and by day
And he cursed the young damsel that learned him
On her rump-a-tump . . .   [to play

6 Now all young men, come listen awhile
I've told you what happened at Firelock Stile
Or else, like me, you'll rue the day
You go into the woods for to learn to play
On her rump-a-tump . . .

174 THE FOGGY FOGGY DEW

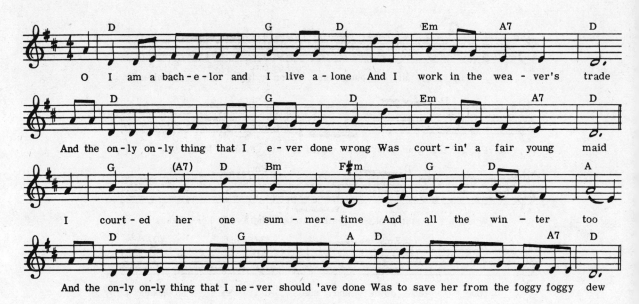

1 O I am a bachelor and I live alone
  And I work in the weaver's trade
  And the only only thing that I ever done wrong
  Was courtin' a fair young maid
  I courted her one summer-time
  And all the winter too
  And the only only thing that I never should 'ave done
  Was to save her from the foggy foggy dew

2 I got that tired of living alone
  I says to her one day
  I've a nice little crib in my old shack
  Where you might safely lay
  You'll be all right in the summer-time
  And in the winter too
  And you'll lay right warm and take no harm
  Away from the foggy foggy dew

3 I don't think much of this old shack
  And I shall lonely be
  With only that poor old Cyprus cat
  To keep me company
  There's a cricket singing on the hearth
  And what can that thing do
  If the night turn raw and the fire won't draw
  To keep me from the foggy foggy dew?

4 One night she come to my bedside
   Time I laid fast asleep
   She puts her head down on my bed
   And she starts in to weep
   She yelled and she cried, she well near died
   She say: What shall I do?
   So I hauled her into bed and I covered up her head
   To save her from the foggy foggy dew

5 Says I: My dear, lay close to me
   And wipe away them tears
   Then I hauled her shift up over her head
   And I wrapped it round her ears
   We was all right in the winter-time
   And in the summer too
   And I held her tight that live-long night
   To save her from the foggy foggy dew

6 Now lay you still, you silly young fool
   And don't you feel afraid
   For if you want to work with me
   You got to learn your trade
   I learned her all that summer-time
   And all the winter too
   And truth to tell she learned that well
   She saved us from the foggy foggy dew

7 One night I laid there good as gold
   And then she say to me
   I've got a pain without my back
   Where no pain ought to be
   I was all right in the summer-time
   And in the winter too
   But I've took some ill or a kind of chill
   From laying in the foggy foggy dew

8 One night she start to moan and cry
   Says I: What's up with you?
   She say: I never should 'ave been this way
   If that hadn't 'ave been for you
   I got my boots and trousers on
   I got my neighbour too
   But do what we would, we couldn't do no good
   And she died in the foggy foggy dew

9 So I am a bachelor, I live with my son
   And we work in the weavin' trade
   And every time I look in his face I can see
   The eyes of that fair young maid
   It remind me of the summer-time
   And of the winter too
   And the many many nights she laid in my arms
   To save her from the foggy foggy dew

175 THE GAME OF CARDS

As I was a-walk-ing one mid-sum-mer's morn-ing

I heard the birds whis-tle and the night-in-gales play

And there did I spy a beau-ti-ful mai-den

As I was a-walk-ing all on the high-way

And there did I spy a beau-ti-ful mai-den

As I was a-walk-ing all on the high-way

1 As I was a-walking one midsummer's morning
I heard the birds whistle and the nightingales play
And there did I spy a beautiful maiden
As I was a-walking all on the highway
And there did I spy a beautiful maiden
As I was a-walking all on the highway

2 O where are you going, my fair pretty lady?
O where are you going so early this morn?
She said: I'm going down to visit my neighbours
I'm going down to Leicester, the place I was born
(*Repeat last two lines of each verse*)

3 It's: May I come with you, my sweet pretty darling?
May I go along in your sweet compan-ie?
Then she turned her head and smiling all at me
Saying: You may come with me, kind sir, if you please

4 We hadn't been walking but a few miles together
Before this young damsel began to show free
She sat herself down, saying: Sit down beside me
And the games we shall play shall be one, two and three

5 I said: My dear lady, if you're fond of the gaming
   There's one game I know I would like you to learn
   The game it is called: The Game of All Fours
   So I took out my pack and began the first turn

6 She cut the cards first and I fell a-dealing
   I dealt her a trump and myself the poor jack
   She led off her ace and stole my jack from me
   Saying: Jack is the card I like best in your pack

7 Since I dealt them last time, it's your turn to shuffle
   And my turn to show the best card in the pack
   Once more she'd the ace and the deuce for to beat me
   Once again I had lost when I laid down poor jack

8 So I took up my hat and I bid her: Good morning
   I said: You're the best that I know at this game
   She answered: Young man, if you'll come back to-morrow
   We'll play the game over and over again

176 THE HASELBURY GIRL

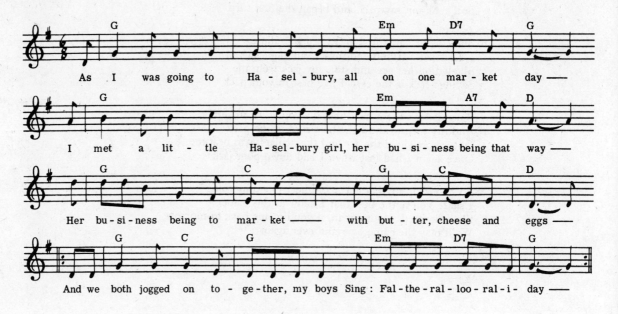

As I was going to Ha-sel-bury, all on one mar-ket day —
I met a lit-tle Ha-sel-bury girl, her bu-si-ness being that way —
Her bu-si-ness being to mar-ket — with but-ter, cheese and eggs —
And we both jogged on to-ge-ther, my boys Sing: Fal-the-ral-loo-ral-i-day —

1 As I was going to Haselbury, all on one market day
  I met a little Haselbury girl, her business being that way
  Her business being to market, with butter, cheese and eggs
  And we both jogged on together, my boys
  Sing: Fal-the-ral-looral-i-day

2 As we were jogging along the road, chatting side by side
  I spied this pretty fair maid's garter come untied
  And fearing she should lose it, I unto her did say
  My love, your garter is coming untied
  Sing: Fal-the-ral-looral-i-day

3 Now if you tie it up for me, rewarded you shall be
  Then if I tie it up for you, come under yonder tree
  Whilst tying up her garter, such a wonderful sight did I see
  My hand did slip right up to her hip
  Sing: Fal-the-ral-looral-i-day

4 Now since you've had your way to-day, pray tell to me your name
  Likewise your occupation, from where and whence you came
  My name is Jack the Rover, from Dub-i-lin Town I do come
  And I live alongside of the Ups and Downs
  Sing: Fal-the-ral-looral-i-day

5 Returning home from the market, her butter it being all sold
  And a-losing of her maidenhead, it made her blood run cold
  O it's gone, it's gone, so let it go, it's gone to the lad I adore
  And he lives alongside of the Ups and Downs
  And I'll never see him any more

177 THE JOLLY TINKER

1 A noted London lady
   O she loved a tinker-man
   But she couldn't get in his company
   But a little now and then
      And I'll be bound she couldn't
   Fol-the-rol-the-diddle-diddle
   Whack-fol-the-day
   Fol-the-rol-the-diddle-diddle
   Whack-fol-the-day

2 She wrote to him a letter
   And she sent it with a friend
   She said: My jolly tinker
   I've some kettles for you to mend
      And I'll be bound she had

3 She wrote to him another
   And she sealed it with a stone
   She said: My jolly tinker
   I can never lay alone
      And I'll be bound she couldn't

4 The tinker he came down the lane
   And on the door did knock
   O have you got some pots and pans
   With rusty holes to block?
      And I'll be bound she had

5 She brought him through the kitchen
   She brought him through the hall
   The cook cried: It's the devil
   He is going to block us all
      And I'll be bound he could

6 She brought him up the stairs
   For to show him what to do
   She fell on the feather-bed
   And he fell on it too
      And I'll be bound he did

7 She took up a frying pan
   And he began to knock
   Just to let the servants know
   That he was hard at work
      And I'll be bound he was

8 She put her hand into her purse
   And she pulled out twenty pound
   O take this money, tinker-man
   And we'll have another round
      And I'll be bound they did

9 I've been a jolly tinker now
   For forty years or more
   And such a rusty hole as that
   I've never blocked before
      And I'll be bound he hadn't

178 THE KNIFE IN THE WINDOW

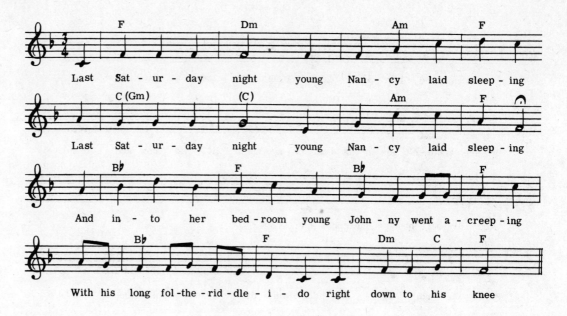

Last Sat - ur - day night young Nan - cy laid sleep - ing

Last Sat - ur - day night young Nan - cy laid sleep - ing

And in - to her bed - room young John - ny went a - creep - ing

With his long fol -the -rid-dle - i - do right down to his knee

1 Last Saturday night young Nancy laid sleeping
Last Saturday night young Nancy laid sleeping
And into her bedroom young Johnny went a-creeping
With his long fol-the-riddle-i-do right down to his knee

2 He said: Lovely Nancy, may I come to bed to you?
He said: Lovely Nancy, may I come to bed to you?
She smiled and replied: John, I'm afraid you'll undo
me
*With your long fol-the-riddle-i-do right down to your
knee*

3 His small clothes fell from him and into bed tumbled
His small clothes fell from him and into bed tumbled
She laughed in his face when his breeches he fumbled
With his long fol-the-riddle-i-do right down to his knee

4 My breeches fit tight, love, I cannot undo them
My breeches fit tight, love, I cannot undo them
She smiled and replied: John, you must take a knife
to them
*With your long fol-the-riddle-i-do right down to your
knee*

5 My knife will not cut, love, it ain't worth a cinder
My knife will not cut, love, it ain't worth a cinder
She smiled and replied: John, there's two on the
window
*With your long fol-the-riddle-i-do right down to your
knee*

6 He picked up the knife and he unrest his breeches
He picked up the knife and he unrest his breeches
The knife it was sharp and it cut through the stitches
With his long fol-the-riddle-i-do right down to his knee

7 All the long night how they rolled and they tumbled
All the long night how they rolled and they tumbled
Before daylight i' the morning Nancy's nightgown he
crumpled
With his long fol-the-riddle-i-do right down to his knee

8 Now nine months being past, it fell on a Sunday
Now nine months being past, it fell on a Sunday
A child it was born with a knife-mark in the window
With a long fol-the-riddle-i-do right down to his knee

179 THE LADY O' THE DAINTY DOON-BY

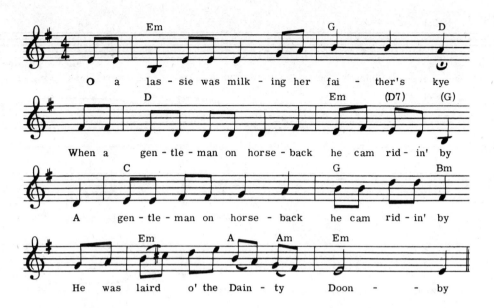

O a las-sie was milk-ing her fai-ther's kye
When a gen-tle-man on horse-back he cam rid-in' by
A gen-tle-man on horse-back he cam rid-in' by
He was laird o' the Dain-ty Doon - - by

1 O a lassie was milking her faither's kye
When a gentleman on horseback he cam ridin' by
A gentleman on horseback he cam ridin' by
He was laird o' the Dainty Doon-by

2 O lassie, O lassie, what would I gie
For tae lie ain nicht wi thee
To lie with me would never never dee
For you're laird o' the Dainty Doon-by

3 He took her by the lily-white hand
He laid her doon war the grass grew lang
'Twere a lang lang time ere he picked her up again
He says: You're lady o' the Dainty Doon-by

4 It happened to be on a fine summer's day
Her faither he had some money for to pay
Her faither having some money for to pay
To the laird o' the Dainty Doon-by

5 Good morning, sir, and how dee ye do?
How is your dochter, Jannity, noo?
How is your dochter, Jannity, noo
Since I laid her in the Dainty Doon-by?

6 O my dochter, Jannity, she's nae very well
My dochter, Jannity, she kowks at her tail
My dochter, Jannity, is lookin' unco pale
May the de'il wi ye, Dainty Doon-by

7 He took her by the lily-white hand
He placed the keys in tae her hand
He showed her through the rooms, twenty-one
He says: You're lady o' the Dainty Doon-by

8 O said the aul' man, it's fit will I dee
I, said the aul' wife, I'll dance until I dae
O, said the aul' man, O I think that I'll dance ta
Since she's lady o' the Dainty Doon-by

180 THE LITTLE BALL OF YARN

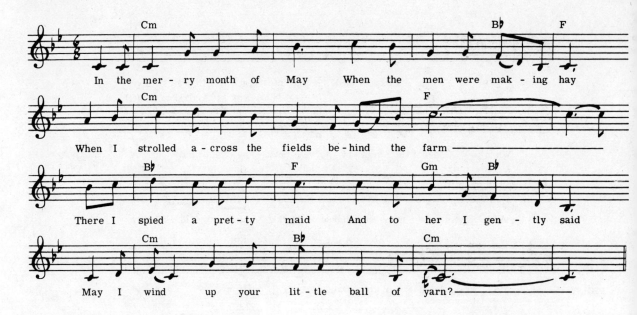

In the mer-ry month of May When the men were mak-ing hay

When I strolled a-cross the fields be-hind the farm

There I spied a pret-ty maid And to her I gen-tly said

May I wind up your lit-tle ball of yarn?

1 In the merry month of May
When the men were making hay
When I strolled across the fields behind the farm
There I spied a pretty maid
And to her I gently said
May I wind up your little ball of yarn?

2 O no, kind sir, said she
You're a stranger unto me
And no doubt you have some other lady charm
O no, my turtle dove
You're the only girl I love
May I help with your little ball of yarn?

3 In the middle of the green
Where I knew we couldn't be seen
Not intending to do her any harm
Sure, it was to my surprise
When I looked into her eyes
Then I wound up her little ball of yarn

4 It was nine months from that day
When I met her on her way
And she had a little baby on her arm
Now I said: My pretty miss
Now you did not expect this
When I wound up your little ball of yarn?

5 You birds of early dawn
When you're playing all in the corn
Take care you do not come to any harm
For the blackbird and the thrush
They come warbling around the bush
So keep your hand upon your little ball of yarn

181 THE LONG PEGGIN' AWL

As I was—a-walk-ing one mor-ning in May
I— met a pret-ty fair maid, her gown it-a was gay
I step-ped up to her, and back she did fall
She want to be played with the long peg-gin' awl

1 As I was a a-walking one morning in May
   I met a pretty fair maid, her gown it-a was gay
   I step-ped up to her, and back she did fall
   She want to be played with the long peggin' awl

2 I said: Pretty fair maid, will you travel with me?
   Unto foreign countries, strange things for to see
   And I will protect you, what e'er may befall
   And follow your love with his long peggin' awl

3 Then home to her parents, she then went straightway
   And unto her mother, these words she did say
   I'll follow my true-love, whate'er may befall
   I'll follow my love with his long peggin' awl

4 O daughter, O daughter, how can you say so?
   For young men are false, you very well know
   They'll tell you fine things, and the devil and all
   And leave you big-bellied with the long peggin' awl

5 O mother, O mother, now do not say so
   Before you were sixteen, you very well know
   There was father and mother and baby and all
   You followed my dad for his long peggin' awl

182 THE MAGPIE'S NEST

For if I was a king Sure, I would make you a queen

I would roll you in my arms Where the mea-dows they are green

Yes, I'd roll you in my heart's con-tent I will sit you down to rest

'Long — sides me I-rish col-een In the mag-pie's nest

CH: Skid-dly-id-le-dad-dle-did-dle-di-dle-da-dle-dum

Di-di-dle-da-dle-dum-dad-dle-did-dle-di-dle-dum

Skid-dly-id-le-dad-dle-did-dle-da-dle-did-dle-di-dle-dum

I will l'ave you down to rest in the mag-pie's nest

1 For if I was a king
  Sure, I would make you a queen
  I would roll you in my arms
  Where the meadows they are green
  Yes, I'd roll you in my heart's content
  I will sit you down to rest
  Longsides me Irish colleen
  In the magpie's nest
  (CHORUS: Mouth music at quicker tempo)
  Skiddly-idle-daddle-diddle-didle-dadle-dum
  Di-didle-dadle-dum-daddle-diddle-didle-dum
  Skiddly-idle-daddle-diddle-dadle-diddle-didle-dum
  I will l'ave you down to rest in the magpie's nest

2 For the magpie's nest
  It is a cottage neat and clean
  It stands 'longside the Shannon
  Where the meadows they are green
  But I never met a colleen
  With such beauties blest
  Like the little Irish fairy
  In the magpie's nest

3 For I have wandered all through Kerry
  I have wandered all through Clare
  From Dublin down to Galway
  From there to God knows where
  But I never met a colleen
  With such beauties blest
  Like the little Irish fairy
  In the magpie's nest

183 THE MAID OF AUSTRALIA

As I walked down by the Hawkes-bor-ough Banks

Where the maids of Aus-tra-lia do play their wild pranks

Be-neath a green shad-y bow-er I sat my-self down

Where the birds sang so gai-ly en-chant-ed all around

In the for-est, the nat-ive Aus-tra-li-a

In the for-est, the nat-ive Aus-tra-li-a Where the mai-dens are hand-some and gay ——

1 As I walked down by the Hawkesborough Banks
Where the maids of Australia do play their wild pranks
Beneath a green shady bower I sat myself down
Where the birds sang so gaily enchanted all around
In the forest, the native Australia
In the forest, the native Australia
Where the maidens are handsome and gay

2 As I sat a-viewin' this beautiful scene
When a pretty fair damsel I happened to see
She must be going swimming or so it would seem
For she laid down her clothing beside the clear stream
By the stream of her native Australia
By the stream of her native Australia
Where the maidens are handsome and gay

3 She stripped off her clothing, before me she stood
  As naked as Venus that rose from the flood
  She blushed with confusion and smiling said she
  For these are the clothes that Australia gave me
  The day I was born in Australia
  The day I was born in Australia
  Where the maidens are handsome and gay

4 Now she dived in the water without fear or dread
  Her beautiful limbs she exceedingly spread
  Her hair hung in ringlets, the colour was black
  Sir, said she, you will see how I float on my back
  On the stream in me native Australia
  On the stream in me native Australia
  Where the maidens are handsome and gay

5 Now bein' exhausted she came to the brink
  Assistance, kind sir, for I surely shall sink
  As quick as the lightnin' I took hold of her hand
  My foot slipped and we fell on the sand
  Then I entered the bush of Australia
  Then I entered the bush of Australia
  Where the maidens are handsome and gay

6 Now we frolicked together in the highest of glee
  In the finest Australia you ever did see
  The sun it went down and the clouds did resign
  Then I left the fair maid of Australia
  Then I left the fair maid of Australia
  Then I left the fair maid of Australia
  Just as the sun went down

7 Now six months being over and nine being come
  This pretty fair maid she brought forth a fine son
  O where was his father? He could not be found
  And she cursed the hour that she lay on the ground
  In her native, the plains of Australia
  In her native, the plains of Australia
  Where the maidens are handsome and gay

184 THE NEW-MOWN HAY

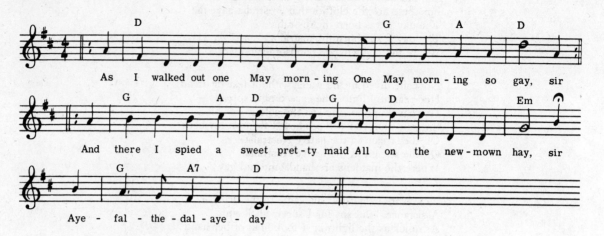

As I walked out one May morn-ing One May morn-ing so gay, sir

And there I spied a sweet pret-ty maid All on the new-mown hay, sir

Aye - fal - the - dal - aye - day

1 As I walked out one May morning
One May morning so gay, sir
As I walked out one May morning
One May morning so gay, sir
And there I spied a sweet pretty maid
All on the new-mown hay, sir
Aye-fal-the-dal-aye-day
And there I spied (etc.)

2 Suppose I prove another pretty maid
In the dew all on the ground, sir?
Suppose I prove another pretty maid
In the dew all on the ground, sir?
But the answer that she give to me
You'll spoil my maiden gown, sir
Aye-fal-the-dal-aye-day
But the answer (etc.)

3 I have a cock in my father's yard
That never trod on hens, sir *(etc.)*
Well he claps his wings and he never flies
Don't you think you're just like him, sir?

4 Will you step up to my father's yard
Where it is walled all round, sir? *(etc.)*
And you shall have your will of me
And thirty thousand pound, sir

5 Whenever you meet with another pretty maid
In a market, fair or town, sir *(etc.)*
Never mind her flannel petticoats
Nor the spoiling of her gown, sir

185 THE NIGHTINGALES SING

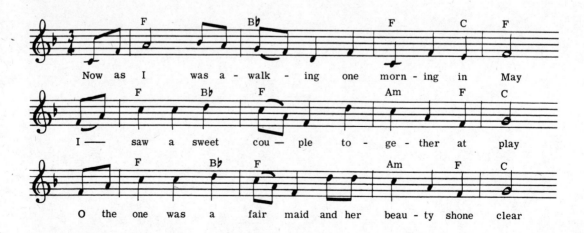

Now as I was a - walk - ing one morn - ing in May

I — saw a sweet cou — ple to - ge - ther at play

O the one was a fair maid and her beau - ty shone clear

And the o - ther was a sol - dier and a brave gren - a - dier

CHORUS: But they kissed so sweet and com - for - ting as they pressed to each o - ther

They went arm - ing a - long the road like sis - ter and bro - ther

They went arm - ing a - long the road till they came to a spring

Then they both sat down to - ge - ther just to hear the night - in - gales sing

1 Now as I was a-walking one morning in May
I saw a sweet couple together at play
O the one was a fair maid and her beauty shone clear
And the other was a soldier and a brave grenadier

But they kissed so sweet and comforting as they pressed to each other
They went arming along the road like sister and brother
They went arming along the road till they came to a spring
Then they both sat down together just to hear the nightingales sing

2 Then out of his knapsack he drew a long fiddle
And he played to her such merry tunes that she ever did hear
And he played to her such merry tunes, caused the valleys to ring
Hark, hark, replied the fair maid, how the nightingales sing

3 O come, said the soldier, 'tis time to give o'er
O no, says the fair maid, please play one tune more
I do like your playing and the touching of the long string
And to see the pretty flowers grow, hear the nightingales sing

4 Now as I'm going to India for seven long years
Drinking wines and strong whisky instead of strong beers
But if I ever return again, it will be in the spring
Then we'll both sit down together, love, and hear the nightingales sing

5 Now, said the fair maid, come, soldier, marry me
O no, replied the soldier, how ever can that be?
For I've a nice little wife at home in my own count-e-rie
And she is the smartest little woman that your eyes ever seen

186 THE NUTTING GIRL

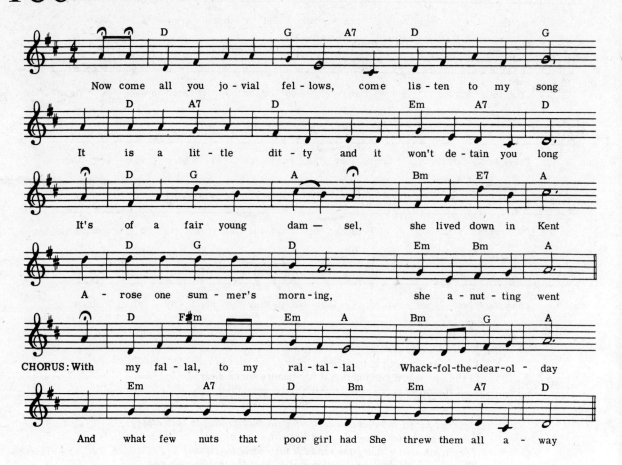

Now come all you jo-vial fel-lows, come lis-ten to my song

It is a lit-tle dit-ty and it won't de-tain you long

It's of a fair young dam — sel, she lived down in Kent

A - rose one sum-mer's morn-ing, she a-nut-ting went

CHORUS: With my fal - lal, to my ral - tal - lal   Whack-fol-the-dear-ol - day

And what few nuts that poor girl had   She threw them all a - way

1 Now come all you jovial fellows, come listen to my song
It is a little ditty and it won't detain you long
It's of a fair young damsel, she lived down in Kent
Arose one summer's morning, she a-nutting went

With my fal-lal, to my ral-tal-lal
Whack-fol-the-dear-ol-day
And what few nuts that poor girl had
She threw them all away

2 It's of a brisk young farmer, was ploughing of his land
He called unto his horses, to bid them gently stand
As he sit down upon his plough, all for a song to sing
His voice was so melodious, it made the valleys ring

3 It's of this fair young damsel, she was nutting in a wood
His voice was so melodious, it charmed her as she stood
In that lonely wood, she could no longer stay
And what few nuts she had, poor girl, she threw them all away

4 She then came to young Johnny, as he sit on his plough
She said : Young man, I really feel I cannot tell you how
He took her to some shady broom, and there he laid her down
Said she: Young man, I think I feel the world go round and round

5 Now, come all you young women, take warning by my song
If you should a-nutting go, don't stay from home too long
For if you should stay too late, to hear the ploughboy sing
You might have a young farmer, to nurse up in the spring

187 THE OVERGATE

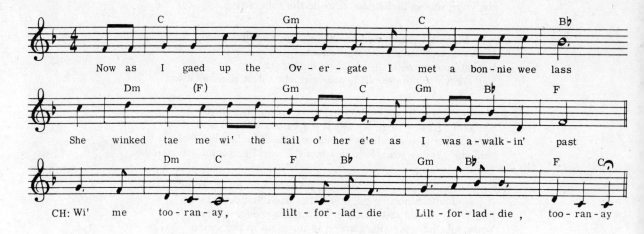

Now as I gaed up the Ov-er-gate I met a bon-nie wee lass

She winked tae me wi' the tail o' her e'e as I was a-walk-in' past

CH: Wi' me too-ran-ay, lilt-for-lad-die Lilt-for-lad-die, too-ran-ay

1 Now as I gaed up the Overgate I met a bonnie wee lass
   She winked tae me wi' the tail o' her e'e as I was a-walkin' past
   Wi' me too-ran-ay, lilt-for-laddie
   Lilt-for-laddie, too-ran-ay

2 Noo, I asked her if she'd tak a glass, she said she'd like it fine
   Says I: I'm ower frae Auchtermuchty tae the market wi' some swine

3 Noo, I took her tae a sittin' room, a wee bit doon the burn
   It's true what Robbie Burns said: A man was made to m'urn

4 She'd four hot pies and porter, she swallid them baith galore
   She ate and drank as much hersel' as an elephant or a score

5 O, then we baith get up the stair to hae a contented night
   When an a'ful knock cam to the door at the breakin' o' the light

6 O, it was a big fat bobby, he got me by the top o' the hair
   And he give me the whirlijig right doon to the foot o' the stair

7 Noo, I get up the stair again, I was seekin' oot my claes
   You'd better gang oot o' this, young man, or I'll gie ye sixty days

8 Says I: I've lost my waistcoat, my watchchain and my purse
   Says she: I've lost my maidenhead and that's a damn sight worse

9 O noo, I'll go back to Auchtermuchty an' contented I will be
   With a-breakin' o' my five pound note wi' a lassie in Dundee

188 REMEMBER THE BARLEY STRAW

So it's of a jol-ly old far — mer, lived in the West Count - er - ie —

He had the fin - est daugh — ter, that ev - er my eyes did see —

He had a love — ly daugh - ter, so come - ly kind and free —

And — ma-ny a gal - lant nob-le-man, they sought her com - pa - nie —

1. So it's of a jolly old farmer, lived in the West Count-e-rie
   He had the finest daughter, that ever my eyes did see
   He had a lovely daughter, so comely kind and free
   And many a gallant nobleman, they sought her comp-a-nie

2. 'Tis of a rich young squire, was living at close by
   And he vowed he wouldn't be easy, until he'd had a try
   So he dressed himself as a tinker, and travelled on his way
   Until he came to the farmer's house, was standing at close by

3. O have you got any kettles, any pots or pans to mend
   Or have you got any lodgings, my being a single man?
   O no, replied this pretty fair maid, not thinking any harm
   O you can stay with us all night, if you sleep in our old barn

4. So after tea was over, she went to make his bed
   The tinker following after, which stole her maidenhead
   The tinker being nimble, jumped up and barred the door
   And she slept all night in the tinker's arms, amongst the barley straw

5. Now since you've slept with me all night, don't think me none the worse
   He put his hand in his pocket, and pulled out a heavy purse
   Here's fifty pound I will give you, to pay the nurse's fee
   And if ever I come this way again, fair maid, I'll marry thee

6. So now you cannot marry me, pray tell to me your name
   Likewise your occupation, and where and whence you came
   He whispered softly in her ear: O call me Davie Shaw
   And if ever I come this way again, remember the barley straw

7. Now six months being over, and nine months being come
   This pretty little fair maid was the mother of a son
   The old man cried: O daughter dear, who has done you this harm?
   I'm afraid it was the old tinker that slept in our old barn

419

189 ROLLING IN THE DEW

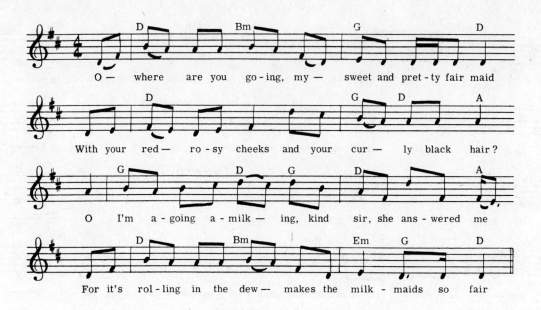

O — where are you go-ing, my — sweet and pret-ty fair maid

With your red — ro-sy cheeks and your cur — ly black hair?

O I'm a-going a-milk — ing, kind sir, she ans-wered me

For it's rol-ling in the dew — makes the milk-maids so fair

1 O where are you going, *my sweet and pretty fair maid*
With your red rosy cheeks and your curly black hair?
O I'm a-going a-milking, *kind sir, she answered me*
For it's rolling in the dew makes the milk-maids so fair

2 O shall I go along with you, *my sweet and pretty fair maid*
With your red rosy cheeks and your curly black hair?
Why surely you can please yourself, *kind sir, she answered me*
For it's rolling in the dew makes the milk-maids so fair

3 Supposing I should lay you down, *my sweet (etc.)*
Then you'd have to pick me up again, *kind sir, (etc.)*

4 Supposing I should dirt your gown . . . .?
Why surely it would wash again . . .

5 Supposing you should be with child . . .?
Then you would be the father of it . . .

6 What would you do for linen . . .?
My father he's a linen-draper . . .

7 What would you do for a cradle . . .?
Why my brother he's the basket-maker . . .

8 Supposing I should go to sea . . .?
Then I would follow after you . . .

9 Supposing I should jump overboard . . .?
Then the devil would jump after you . . .

190 SHE WAS A RUM ONE

As I strolled out one clear moon-light
One clear moon-light in win-ter
It was there I met a pret-ty fair maid
And — I fell in be-hind her
CHORUS: She was a rum one Fol-the-did-dle-di-do-day
But a bon-ny one Fol-the-did-dle-di-do

1 As I strolled out one clear moonlight
One clear moonlight in winter
It was there I met a pretty fair maid
And I fell in behind her
She was a rum one
Fol-the-diddle-di-do-day
But a bonny one
Fol-the-diddle-di-do

2 She walk-ed up and she walk-ed down
And I kept close behind her
And I asked of her the reason why
That she could'na step no wider

3 Go away, go away, you foolish young man
And stop such foolish talking
For it does not suit young men, she said
To pick up young women's walking

4 I am a chlochter to my trade
My friends they call me rare-o
If you'll tell me where your trouble lies
I'll clean you nate and fair-o

5 My trouble lies between my thighs
And e'er it is abidin'
It tickles me baith night and day
And it keeps me from my stridin'

6 He laid her down upon a bank
Till he provided the plaster
She jump-ed up upon her feet
And she walk-ed all the faster

7 She's gi'ed to me my winter's beef
Besides my winter's fuellin'
Far better than that she's gi'ed to me
Was a stable for my stallion

191 THREE MAIDENS TO MILKING DID GO

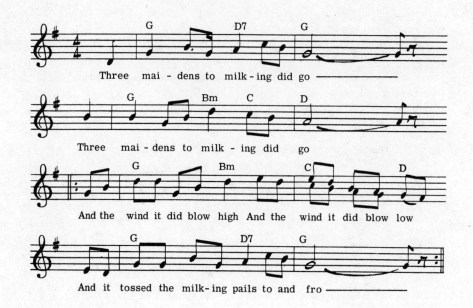

Three mai - dens to milk - ing did go —

Three mai - dens to milk - ing did go

And the wind it did blow high And the wind it did blow low

And it tossed the milk-ing pails to and fro —

1 Three maidens to milking did go
Three maidens to milking did go
And the wind it did blow high
And the wind it did blow low
And it tossed the milking pails to and fro
And the wind it did blow high
And the wind it did blow low
And it tossed the milking pails to and fro

2 I met with a man I knew well
I met with a man I knew well
And I kindly asked of him
If he 'ad got any skills
For to catch me a small bird or two

3 O yes, I got some excellent good skills
O yes, I got some excellent good skills
Now come along with me
Down to yonder shady tree
I'll catch thee a small bird or two

4 And away to the woods they did go
And away to the woods they did go
He tapp-ed at the bush
And the little birds flew out
Right into her lily-white breast

5 Here's luck to the blackbird and thrush
Here's luck to the blackbird and thrush
It's a bird of one feather
And we'll all flock together
Let the people say little or much

6 Here's luck to the jolly dragoon
Here's luck to the jolly dragoon
We'll ramble all day
And at night we'll spend our play
And go home by the light of the moon

192 UP TO THE RIGS

Up Lon-don ci-ty I took my way It was up Cheap-side I chanced to stray

When a fair pret-ty girl there I did meet And with kis-ses her then I did greet

For I was up to the rigs Down to the jigs Up to the rigs of Lon-don town

1 Up London city I took my way
It was up Cheapside I chanced to stray
When a fair pretty girl there I did meet
And with kisses her then I did greet
For I was up to the rigs
Down to the jigs
Up to the rigs of London town

2 She took me to some house of fame
And boldly she did enter in
Loudly for supper she did call
Thinking I was going to pay for it all

3 The supper o'er, the table cleared
She called me her jewel and then her dear
The waiter brought white wine and red
While the chamber-maid prepared the bed

4 Between the hours of one and two
She asked me if to bed I'd go
Immediately I did consent
And along with this pretty girl I went

5 Her cheeks was white and her lips was red
And I kissed her as she laid in bed
But soon as I found she was fast asleep
Out of the bed then I did creep

6 I searched her pockets and there I found
A silver snuff box and ten pound
A gold watch and a diamond ring
I took the lot and I locked me lady in

7 Now all young men wherever you be
If you meet a pretty girl you use her free
You use her free but don't get *pied* [drunk]
But remember me when I was up Cheapside

169 BLACKBIRDS AND THRUSHES

Dicky Lashbrook, Kelly, Devon, *rec.* P. Kennedy, 1950 and 1952: BBC 17796

Other recorded versions
Louis Hooper, Hambridge, Somerset, *rec.* D. Cleverdon, 1942: BBC 4014
Harry List, Swefling, Suffolk, *rec.* P. Kennedy and A. Lomax, 1953. This version includes verses of *The Knife in the Window* (No. 178)
Charles Boyle, Belfast, N. Ireland, *rec.* P. Kennedy and S. O'Boyle, 1952: BBC 18405

Printed versions
SHARP MS: 1903–6: five variants (Somerset)
SHARP AND MARSON: 1904, vol. I, two versions nos. 10 and 11, pp. 20, 22: *Hares on the Mountains* (Somerset)
JFSS: 1905, no. 6, p. 40: three variants, *coll.* Sharp, Somerset

BARING GOULD AND SHARP: 1906, no. 18: version for schools
HAMMOND MS: 1906–7: four variants (Dorset)
SHARP AND MARSON: 1906, vol. III, no. 77, p. 60: *O Sally my Dear* (rewritten verses of *The Knife in the Window*)
WILLIAMS: 1923, p. 224: *If Pretty Maids could Sing* (Wiltshire)
REEVES: 1958, no. 38, p. 119: original texts of three variants as well as original verses of *O Sally my Dear*, with verses of this song following
REEVES: 1960, no. 63, p. 150: *coll.* Hammond, Dorset. Probably another fragment of *The Knife in the Window* with verses of this song added
O LOCHLAINN: 1965, no. 50, p. 100: composed Irish Gaelic verses added

This was the first of a number of songs of seduction recorded from a Cornishman, Dicky Lashbrook, a travelling chimney sweep. Before he died, Dicky was living near the river Tamar which divides Devon and Cornwall. He had only three verses for this song, but other singers tack these verses on to another seduction ballad, *The Knife in the Window* (No. 178). For example, Harry List in Norfolk sang:

> If maidens were sheep and would lie on the mountains
> Look how the young men they would go and lie with them
> *Sing: Fal the ral doodle, Jack, fal the ral day*
>
> O, if maidens were blackbirds, they would build in the bushes
> Look how the young men they could spoil their young nestlings
>
> O, if maidens were moor-hens, they could build in the rushes
> Look how the young men they could use their short brushes

Harry List then went on to sing verses like those in our version of *The Knife in the Window* (No. 178):

> So it's early in the morning. Young Johnny went creeping
> Right into the bedroom where Polly lay sleeping

The rest of the verses were similar to those sung by another Norfolk singer, Harry Cox. Cecil Sharp also found this same combination of verses and separated them out as two distinct songs. He found them in Somerset and called the song *O Sally my Dear. The Knife in the Window* verses were, in his case, preceding rather than following the *Blackbirds and Thrushes* verses:

> If blackbirds was blackbirds as thrushes was thrushes
> How soon the young men would go beating the bushes
>
> Should young women be hares and race round the mountain
> Young men'd take guns and they'd soon go a-hunting
>
> Should young women be ducks and should swim round the ocean
> Young men would turn drakes and soon follow after

Baring Gould and Cecil Sharp included this song in *English Folk Songs for Schools* (1906) with an additional 'educational' verse composed for the occasion:

> But the young men are given to frisking and fooling
> I'll let them alone and attend to my schooling
> *With ri fol de dee, cal al de day, ri fol i dee*

In Northern Ireland an effective version was sung by Charles Boyle, father of the collector Sean O'Boyle. He had heard it from street-singer Alec McNicholl in North Street, Belfast, and said that his friend, the German composer Carl Hardebeck, had incorporated the air in a piano piece, *Irish Air and Old Highland Melody* included in *Preludes and Pieces Part III* (Pigott, Dublin). Boyle had a fourth verse which he refrained from recording for the BBC:

> Ach, if all the young ladies were trees in the valleys
> Then all the young men would creep up on their bellies
> *Ri fol dol lol, fol diesel dum doo*

P. Kearney's song *The Bold Phenian Men* uses the Irish variant of the tune. Colm O Lochlainn includes a further version from Ireland in *More Irish Street Ballads*, pointing out that the song was often attributed to Samuel Lover (1797–1865) because of its inclusion in his novel *Rory O'More*.

170 BLOW THE CANDLE OUT

Edgar Button, Theberton, Leiston, Suffolk, *rec.* P. Kennedy, 1953: BBC 23100; HMV 7EG 8288

Other recorded versions
Harry Baxter, Southrepps, Norfolk, 1955: BBC 22019
Jimmy Gilhaney, Orkney, *rec.* P. Kennedy, 1955: *Folk Songs of Britain*, vol. II, CAEDMON TC1143/TOPIC 12T158

Printed versions
D'URFEY: 1720, vol. VI, p. 342: *The London Prentice*
GARDINER MS: 1907: two variants (Hampshire)
DUNCAN MS: 1900: *The London Apprentice*

SHARP MS: 1904–8: two variants (Somerset)
ORD: 1930, p. 95: five verses, words only
PINTO AND RODWAY: 1957, no. 131, p. 366: D'Urfey version
O LOCHLAINN: 1965, no. 74, p. 146: air from PETRIE: 1902, words from Dublin broadside by Brereton, Ireland
PURSLOW: 1968, p. 14: *coll.* Gardiner (Hampshire)

LOMAX: 1960, no. 160, p. 312 (Missouri, USA)
COMBS: 1925, p. 161: *The Jolly Boatsman* (Kentucky, USA)

Considering the widespread popularity of this classic folksong with country singers in England, Ireland and Scotland, it seems extraordinary that it is not included in any of the well-known collections. Although two variants were collected by Cecil Sharp, they were not included in *The Idiom of the People*. However, James Reeves did select a parallel broadside collected by Sharp, called *The Devil's in the Girl* (REEVES: 1958, no. 27, p. 104) which must have been a well-known pipe tune for London theatre-goers at some time. We had it from Walter Sealey, Ash Priors, Somerset, in 1957:

> It's of a lusty gentleman returning from his play
> He knock-ed at his true-love's door that night with her to stay
> She quickly let this young man in and called him her delight
> Saying: Take me in your arms, my love, and bide till morning light
>
> The maid she was a crafty jade and to her love did say
> O what did please you best, my love, while you were at the play?
> He says, My dear, I learnt a tune, forget it I never shall
> It's called, a very pretty tune: The Devil's in the Girl

171 THE BOLD ENGLISH NAVVY

Lal Smith, Belfast, N. Ireland, *rec.* P. Kennedy and S. O'Boyle, 1952: BBC 18303; *Folk Songs of Britain*, vol. II, CAEDMON TC1143/TOPIC 12T158

Other recorded versions
Jimmy McBeath, Elgin, Morayshire, Scotland, *rec.* P. Kennedy, 1956
John Stickle, Baltasound, Unst, Shetland: *The Moon Shining Brightly*, *rec.* P. Shuldham-Shaw, Lerwick, Shetland, 1952: BBC 18623

Printed versions
GREIG: 1909–14, xxxii, p. 51: words only *The Courtin' Coat*
REEVES: 1958, no. 53, p. 139: *The Kettle Smock, coll.* Sharp, Somerset, 1907

This song appears only in collectors' manuscripts; in England, in both the Sharp and Hammond collections, as *The Kettle Smock*, and in Scots, in the Greig collection, as *The Courtin' Coat*. A fine fragment of *The Courtin' Coat* was recorded by Patrick Shuldham-Shaw from Shetlander John Stickle, from the island of Unst:

> The moon shining brightly, when shavin' my beard
> Nae better for courtin' could I be prepared
> The moon shining brightly once laved me along
> And here I arrived wi' my courtin' coat on
>
> Who's that at my window who gave a loud knock?
> Who's that at my window who wakened me up?
> Who's that at my window, O, is it you John?
> And here you've arrived wi' your courtin' coat on
>
> All night we did sport and all night we did play
> Courtin' the hours as the night rolls away
> When early next morning she says to me: John
> You'll think what you did wi' your courtin' coat on
>
> All that I've done, lassie, and do not chide me
> It was not for courtin' that I came to thee
> When a man's doon in his spirits and thinks upon yon
> He canna lie up wi' his courtin' coat on

172 THE COACHMAN'S WHIP

Recorded version
Chris and Tom Willett, Paddock Wood, Kent, *rec.* P.
  Kennedy, 1963

Printed version
PINTO AND RODWAY: 1957, no. 173, p. 453: *The Jolly
  Driver* (from a Nottingham broadside)

Compare
REEVES: 1960, no. 68, p. 156: *I am a Coachman: coll.*
  Hammond, 1906 (Dorset)

> I am a coachman out on the high road
> A-kissing and courting is all my mode
> I kiss them, I court them, I lie by their side
> And when I am tired, I get up and ride

This was one of three verses forming 'a catalogue of trades each with its metaphorical sexual significance' (REEVES: 1960), in a song collected by Henry Hammond in Dorset in 1906. The other verses concerned secondly a blacksmith (or perhaps it should have been a tinker) whose delight was 'the stopping of holes' and thirdly a fisherman who 'tried for a boy but did get a wench'.

    A Nottingham broadside called *The Jolly Driver* has a verse which sums up the potential qualities of the coachman:

> I understand all kinds of servitude
> And every fashion so tight
> If you hire me as your coachman
> I am a safe driver by night

The broadside version also includes a second verse not sung by the Willett family, in which the lady strikes her bargain:

> Up came a lady of fashion
> And thus unto me did say
> If I hire you as a coachman
> You must drive me by night and by day
> Ten guineas a month I will give you
> Besides a bottle of wine
> If you keep me in plenty of drink
> I will drive you in a new fashion style

173 FIRELOCK STILE

Harry Cox, Catfield, Norfolk, *rec.* P. Kennedy, 1953:
EFDSS LP 1004 (1965)

> So come all young men, come listen awhile
> I'll tell you what happened at Firelock Stile
> When a stump of a nail catched hold of her clothes
> She fell down and she did expose . . .

We tend nowadays to think of prostitutes frequenting only the city streets, but when towns were not so large it was often in the lanes leading out into the country that they could be found. The old-fashioned stile was a wooden 'stepping over' place where the footpath crossed the boundary fence or hedge of two fields. Here was a place where a prostitute could display her charms without getting booked for indecent exposure!
    The fire referred to in this song, and the name Firelock, was a description of the discomfort brought upon the unfortunate male victim some six weeks after his apparently innocent rural encounter.

> Now six weeks being over, as I have been told
> She gave him some fire to keep him from cold
> To keep him from cold by night and by day
> And he cursed the young damsel that learned him to play

    What at first hearing seems like a good honest piece of bawdry extolling the pleasures of the sexual act turns out to be a solemn warning of the dangers of contracting venereal disease.

427

174 THE FOGGY FOGGY DEW

Phil Hammond, Morston, Blakeney, Norfolk, *rec.* P. Kennedy, 1952: BBC 18704: words

Other recorded versions

Mark Fuller and Luther Hills, East Dean, Sussex, *rec.* P. Kennedy, 1953: BBC 18714: tune

Marcella Hurley, Cork, Ireland, 1947: BBC 12490

Sam Bennett, Ilmington, Warwickshire, *rec.* P. Kennedy, 1950

Alec Bloomfield, Framlingham, Suffolk, *rec.* P. Kennedy, 1952

Harry Cox, Catfield, Norfolk, *rec.* P. Kennedy, 1953: BBC 21479; EFDSS LP 1004

Edgar Button, Leiston, Suffolk, *rec.* P. Kennedy, 1956

Charlie Wills, Bridport, Dorset, *rec.* P. Kennedy, 1957

Printed versions

BUNTING: 1840, p. 109: tune only *Air thaobh na carraige baine* (Ireland)

PETRIE: 1855, p. 143

KIDSON: 1891, p. 165: tune, from 1825 MS, like *Banks and Braes* (Yorkshire); also in KIDSON AND MOFFAT: 1927

SHARP MS: 1893–1914: eight variants (Somerset), one variant (Devon)

GREIG MS: 1904–8: ten variants, including version called *Boodie Bo* (Aberdeenshire)

SHARP AND MARSON: 1904–9, vol. I, no. 17, p. 34: three verses rewritten (Somerset)

HAMMOND MS: 1905–6: two variants (Somerset), two variants (Dorset)

JFSS: 1901, no. 3, p. 134: one verse only, *coll.* P. Merrick, Sussex, 1900

JFSS: 1909, no. 13, p. 295: tune only, *coll.* R. Vaughan Williams, Hampshire

JOYCE: 1909, no. 58, p. 31 (Ireland)

HENRY: 1924, no. 694: parody on a song called *Upside Down* (Ireland)

KIDSON AND MOFFAT: 1927, p. 78: rewritten text of five verses (Yorkshire)

PINTO AND RODWAY: 1957, no. 231, p. 577: from Nottingham broadside

REEVES: 1958, no. 33, p. 111: composite version from SHARP (six verses); for a full discussion on the song see pp. 43–57

JEFDSS: 1958, p. 152: transcription of Harry Cox version with comments by A. L. Lloyd and P. S. Shaw referring to James Reeves's theories

SHARP AND KARPELES: 1917–32, vol. II, no. 137, p. 174 (Virginia, USA)

COMBS: 1925, p. 214 (Kentucky, USA)

SANDBURG: 1927, p. 14, and *The Weaver*, p. 460

HENRY: 1938, p. 182 (Tennessee, USA)

THOMPSON: 1939, p. 421 (New York, USA)

RANDOLPH: 1946–50, vol. I, p. 394 (Missouri, USA)

MORRIS: 1950, p. 160 (Florida, USA)

LOMAX: 1960, no. 43, p. 89: Harry Cox; no. 44, p. 90 from SANDBURG, with middle verse added

HUBBARD: 1961, p. 115 (Utah, USA)

FOWKE: 1965, no. 43, p. 108 (Ontario, Canada)

PEACOCK: 1965, p. 518 (Newfoundland, Canada)

> When I was an old bachelor, I followed a roving trade
> And all the harm that ever I done I courted the servant maid
> I courted her one summer season and part of the winter too
> And many a time I rolled my love all over the foggy dew

Harry Cox sang his version of the song to a variant of the tune which Robert Burns used for *Ye Banks and Braes of Bonny Doon*.* Frank Kidson heard a Yorkshire singer use the same tune, and in 1891 he remarked on how Burns had used it. When Cecil Sharp published a Somerset version in 1904 he included an 'exception' tune for its own interest, but at the same time wrote that the *Banks and Braes* tune was the more usual in the Somerset area. He did not feel able to publish the words as they had been collected, and his collaborator, Charles Marson, wrote three rather literary verses which incorporated only a few of the original lines. Later Cecil Sharp noted an American version in Virginia and the text was published. In fact, both his American and his Somerset informants had sung versions of the words similar to those sung by Harry Cox:

> One night as I laid in my bed a-taking my balm of sleep
> This pretty fair maid came to me and how bitterly she did weep
> She wept, she mourned, she tore her hair, crying: Alas what shall I do?
> For this night I resolved to sleep with you, for fear of the foggy dew
>
> Now all the first part of the night how we did sport and play
> And all the later part of the night, she in my arms did lay
> And when broad daylight did appear, she cried: I am undone
> Oh hold your tongue, you silly young girl, for the foggy dew is gone
>
> Supposing that you should have one child, it would make you laugh and smile
> Supposing that you should have another, it would make you think awhile
> Supposing that you should have another, another, another one too
> It would make you leave off these foolish young tricks and think of the foggy dew
>
> I loved that girl with all my heart, loved her as I loved my life
> And in the other part of the year I made her my lawful wife
> I never told her of her faults, yet never intend to do
> Yet many a time as she winks and smiles, I think of the foggy dew

* See further notes about this song in the introduction to this chapter.

175 THE GAME OF CARDS

Charlie Wills, Morcombelake, Bridport, Dorset, *rec.* P. Kennedy, 1952

Other recorded versions
Harry Westaway (six verses) and Bill Westaway (one verse), Belstone, Devon, *rec.* P. Kennedy, 1952: *As I Walked Out*, BBC 17794
Wally Fuller, Laughton, Sussex, *rec.* P. Kennedy, 1952: BBC 18719
Ben Baxter, Southrepps, Norfolk, *rec.* S. Ennis, 1955: BBC 22156
Sam Larner, Winterton, Norfolk, *rec.* P. Kennedy, 1958: *Game of All Fours*

Tom Willett, Paddock Wood, Kent, *rec.* P. Kennedy, 1963

Printed versions
SHARP MS: 1904–8: four variants (Somerset)
GARDINER MS: 1905–9: four variants (Hampshire), one variant (Surrey)
REEVES: 1960, no. 2, p. 43: seven verses *All Fours* from GARDINER (Hampshire)
PURSLOW: 1965, p. 35: *The Game of All Fours* (from GARDINER)

As I walked out on a midsummer's morning
To view the fields and the meadows so gay
There I saw a sweet young damsel
As I was walking on the highway
 Ri-fol-the-diddle-dol ri-fol-the-diddle-dol
 Ri-fol-the-diddle-dol ri-fol-the-day

Then he said my dear how far are you going?
How far are you going so early in the morn?
I'm going down to my next door neighbour
Down in Cullompton where I was born

Then he said my dear are you fond of the gaming
One game of yours I should like to learn
And that would be a game of all fours
I will pick you three two one

These were the first three verses recorded from Harry Westaway, Belstone, near Okehampton, Devon. Harry and Bill Westaway, who came of a famous singing family from whom Baring Gould collected *Widdecombe Fair* (*Tom Pearce*, No. 308), both sang the song. In their version they sang Cullompton, a local market town on the other side of Exeter from Belstone, as the birthplace. This was our first hearing of a song which had hitherto never appeared in any published collection.

Of the four unpublished versions collected by Cecil Sharp, two have tunes which are variants of that sung by Charlie Wills, the most common tune for the song. When asked if he knew any songs commencing 'As I walked out . . .' Wally Fuller, a Sussex gipsy, made various attempts, during which other songs were started, until he finally landed a fine version of this song.

176 THE HASELBURY GIRL

Harry Cox, Catfield, Norfolk, *rec.* P. Kennedy, 1953

Other recorded versions
Bill Lowne, Cley-on-Sea, Norfolk, *rec.* S. Ennis, 1953: BBC 22173 (*The Happisburgh Girl*)
George Maynard, Copthorne, Sussex, *rec.* P. Kennedy, 1956: BBC 23092 (*The Aylesbury Girl*)
Tom Willett, Paddock Wood, Kent, *rec.* P. Kennedy, 1953 (*The Salisbury Girl*)

Printed versions
D'URFEY: 1719
SHARP MS: 1903–6: two variants (Somerset)

HAMMOND MS: 1905–7: three variants (Dorset)
GARDINER MS: 1908: two variants *Jack The Rover* (Hampshire)
PINTO AND RODWAY: 1957, no. 110: *The Maid of Tottenham* (Totnam), from *Choyce Drollery: Songs and Sonnets*, ed. J. W. Ebsworth (R. Roberts), Boston, Lincolnshire, 1886
REEVES: 1958, no. 41, p. 123: *The Hazelbury Girl*, coll. Sharp, Somerset
PURSLOW: 1965, p. 97: *The Ups and Downs*, coll. Gardiner, Hampshire

A number of English market towns claim ownership of this very daring little milkmaid. In an early broadside she comes from Tottenham (Middlesex) and elsewhere she is either from Aylesbury (Buckinghamshire) or Salisbury (Wiltshire). In Norfolk however she comes from the little coastal village of Happisburgh between Cromer and Yarmouth. Happisburgh is pronounced Hais'bury, so it fits well as a substitution for Aylesbury. In Somerset, where Cecil Sharp collected two versions, it was naturally Haselbury because there is such a village: to give it its full name, Hazelbury Plucknett.

The name given to the milkmaid on demand by the young man in the song *Jack The Rover* is also used as a title for the song. He also says that he comes from Dublin town and that he lives alongside the 'Ups and Downs' and this too is a title which is used in some versions.

177 THE JOLLY TINKER

Billy Dickeson, Morston, Norfolk, *rec.* P. Kennedy,
  1952: BBC 18703 (three verses only)

Other recorded versions
Thomas Moran, Mohill, Leitrim, Ireland, *rec.* S. Ennis,
  1954: BBC 22013; *Folk Songs of Britain*, vol. II, CAED-
  MON 1143/TOPIC 12T158
Jimmy McBeath, Elgin, Morayshire, Scotland, *rec.* A.
  Lomax, 1953

Printed versions
ROXBURGHE: 1871–93, vol. III, no. 230: *Room for a
  Jovial Tinker* and *Old Brass to Mend*
PINTO AND RODWAY: 1957, no. 156 (from ROXBURGHE)

> Here is a Tinker full of mettle
> The which can mend pot, pan or Kettle
> For stopping of holes is his delight
> His work goes forward day and night
> If there be any women brave
> Whose Coldrons need of mending have
> Send for this Tinker, ne'er deny him
> He'll do your work well if you try him
> A proof of him I'll forthwith show
> 'Cause you his workmanship may know

So runs the 'build-up' given to this next 'sonnet' in the Roxburghe Collection, fourteen verses, of which the last gives the moral:

> You merry tinkers, every one, that hear this new made sonnet
> When as you do a Lady's work, be sure you think upon it
> Drive home your nails to the very head, and do your work profoundly
> And then, no doubt, your Mistresses will pay you for it soundly

> *With hey, ho, derry derry down, with hey trey, down, down, derry*

178 THE KNIFE IN THE WINDOW

Harry Cox, Catfield, Norfolk, *rec.* P. Kennedy, 1953:
  EFDSS LP 1004: *Nancy and Johnny*

Other recorded version
Harry List, Swefling, Suffolk, *rec.* P. Kennedy and A.
  Lomax, 1953 (version which includes verses of *Black-
  birds and Thrushes* (No. 169))

Printed versions
SHARP MS: 1906–7: three variants (Somerset), one
  variant (Oxfordshire)
SHARP AND MARSON: 1904–9, vol. III, no. 77, p. 60:
  O Sally my Dear (verses rewritten) (Somerset)
REEVES: 1958, no. 38, p. 119: *Hares on the Mountains*
  (original verses collected by SHARP)

> Sally, my dear, shall I come to bed to you
> She laugh and reply: I'm afraid you'll undo me
>
> O Sally, my dear, why I will not undo you
> She laugh and reply: You may come to bed to me
>
> Sally my dear I cannot undo my breeches
> She laugh and reply: Take a knife and rip stitches
>
> O Sally, my dear, I cannot undo them
> She laugh and reply: There's a knife in the window
>
> Now he took off his breeches and into bed tumbled
> I leave you to guess how the young couple fumbled

These five verses, noted by Cecil Sharp from a Somerset singer, were followed by three verses of *Blackbirds and Thrushes* (No. 169). This same association of the two songs was also heard from Harry List in Suffolk. Needless to say Cecil Sharp, when he published *Sally my Dear*, wrote that the words 'had of necessity to be somewhat altered', and a completely rewritten text was published in his Somerset collection and also in the selected edition of *English Folk Songs*, vol. II, 1921. The words of the original *Knife in the Window* song therefore remained unpublished until they were included under *Hares on the Mountains* in REEVES: 1958.

179 THE LADY O' THE DAINTY DOON-BY

Lucy Stewart, Fetterangus, and Jeannie Robertson, Aberdeen, Scotland, *rec.* P. Kennedy and H. Henderson, 1955

Other recorded versions
Davie Stewart, Dundee, Angus, Scotland, *rec.* A. Lomax, 1954
Jeannie Robertson, Aberdeen, Scotland, *rec.* P. Kennedy, London, 1958: BBC 27809

Printed versions
HERD: 1776, vol. II, p. 232: *The Dainty Downby*
KINLOCH: 1827, no. 363 *The Laird O'Keltie*; vol. V, no. 145 *The Laird O' The Dainty Downby*
HECHT: 1904, p. 221: as in HERD: 1776
GREIG: 1909, no xxv, p. 29: words only *Dainty Doon-Byes* and several variants *Parks o'Keltie*

In writing the notes to *The Wylie Wife of the Hie Toun Hie* Professor Child remarks that the denouement is similar to this present song which he had seen in Herd's manuscript and published in *Scottish Songs*, and also in Kinloch's manuscripts (Child, no. 290). The theme is that of the farmer's daughter who is seduced by the young laird. The farmer goes to pay his rents and the laird asks him about his daughter who has recently become unwell. When the laird learns that he is discovered he makes her his lady and all ends happily.

Here are the last four verses as they appear in Herd's manuscript:

When this lassie before this young laird came
Her lover baith grew pale and wan
O Marg'ret, Marg'ret, you've laid with a man
Since you was in the Dainty Downby

O kind sir, you may well understand
Since you made me to be at your command
You made me to be at your command
And wo to your Dainty Downby

O Marg'ret, Marg'ret if I be the man
If I be the man that has done ye the wrong
I shall be the man that will raise you again
Since you was in the Dainty Downby

Then he has call'd upon his vassals all
He has call'd on them baith great and small
Then he has made her there, before them all
The Lady of the Dainty Downby

180 THE LITTLE BALL OF YARN

Winnie Ryan, Belfast, N. Ireland, *rec.* P. Kennedy and S. O'Boyle, 1952: BBC 18590

Other recorded versions
Charlie Wills, Morcombelake, Bridport, Dorset, *rec.* P. Kennedy, 1950

Tom Willett, Paddock Wood, Kent, 1963

Printed version
HUGILL: 1961, p. 533: shanty version

O don't ever go out too early in the morning
For the blackbird and the thrush
They come warbling round the bush
Keep your hand upon your little ball of yarn

Winnie Ryan, a young tinker girl of seventeen, sang this at a gathering of travellers on the outskirts of Belfast. She admitted that she had forgotten much of the story so we have substituted a collated text from another traveller, Tom Willett, an English gipsy from Kent, and Charlie Wills, a retired Dorset shepherd.

Winnie started with a 'Come all ye' verse, but only remembered the second line which she repeated again in her last verse.

Stanley Hugill in his collection includes the song as a shanty and remarks that winding up tarry lengths of yarn was a regular job in the old square-riggers and that this is really the origin of the expression 'to spin a yarn'.

181 THE LONG PEGGIN' AWL

Harry Cox, Catfield, Norfolk, *rec.* P. Kennedy, 1953; *Folk Songs of Britain*, vol. II, CAEDMON TC1143/Topic 12T158

Printed versions
REEVES: 1960, no. 21, p. 73: two variants *The Cobbler* (Hampshire)

SHARP AND KARPELES: 1917–32, no. 100: *The Shoemaker* (North Carolina, USA)
COX: 1925, no. 171, p. 491: *The Cobbler's Boy* (Ohio, USA)
LOMAX: 1960, no. 144, p. 283: *Peg an' Awl* (sung by The Carolina Tar Heels)

I'll follow my true-love, whate'er may befall
I'll follow my love with his long peggin' awl

James Reeves comments that the regard for the cobbler's awl, with which the cobbler makes the sewing holes in leather, as phallic 'has been commonplace since at least the Middle Ages'. A. L. Lloyd in his book on English folksong used this song as a typical example of English eroticism. Harry Cox himself enjoyed singing the song in female company— after he had first been granted the go-ahead.

George Gardiner collected two versions of another cobbler song in Hampshire, about which Reeves made his commentary. Cecil Sharp came across a version of this same song in North Carolina and John Harrington Cox in Ohio. In it a cobbler's boy who has obtained his freedom meets a pretty girl and regrets that he has lost most of his cobbler's wax:

> I am a merry cobbler and lately gained my freedom
> I set my affections on her, a fair young damsel pretty
> *Must I use my awl for my derry derry down*
> *Must I use my awl for my dear O?*
> *Ring-ting-ting, ring-a-ting-a-ting*
> *O you are my dear O*
>
> Five pounds I have in gold and that is all my treasure
> Besides an old greatcoat and a jolly bit of leather
>
> O zounds I've lost my wax, I dunno what's become of it
> It's no use to swear or vex, for here lies some of it

Another cobbler song, in an American survival, can be found in LOMAX: 1960; entitled *Peg an' Awl*, it is recorded by The Carolina Tar Heels:

> They've invented a new machine [three times] Peg an' Awl
> The prettiest little thing you ever seen
> *Peggin' shoes is all I done*
> *I'll throw away my pegs, my pegs, my pegs, my awl*

182 THE MAGPIE'S NEST

Annie Jane Kelly, Keady, Armagh, N. Ireland, *rec.* P. Kennedy and S. O'Boyle, 1952: BBC 18475

Other recorded version
Folk Songs of Britain, vol. I, CAEDMON TC1142/TOPIC 12T157

Printed versions
FORD: 1899, p. 157: *The Bonnie Brier Bush* (rewritten by Robert Burns, Lady Nairne)

HUGHES: 1909–36, vol. II, p. 26: one verse only (Dublin)

Compare
The Cuckoo's Nest: Jeannie Robertson and John Strachan, Aberdeenshire, Scotland: *Folk Songs of Britain*, vol. II, CAEDMON TC1143/TOPIC 12T158

PEACOCK: 1965, p. 259: 'Chin Music' (Newfoundland, Canada)

> Some like the lassies that's gay weel dressed
> And some like the lassies that's techt aboot the waist
> But it's in amang the blankets that I like best
> To get a jolly rattle at the cuckoo's nest

In its instrumental version as a dance tune, this mouth-music jingle is called *The Cuckoo's Nest*, and it is well known as a hornpipe in England, Ireland and Scotland. John Strachan sang his verse and afterwards commented, 'It was always realistic, you know, with their verses, and they were bloody clever often.' His verse, three more from Jeannie Robertson and the hornpipe played on the tin-whistle can be heard on the CAEDMON/TOPIC records *Folk Songs of Britain*.

> There is a thorn bush in oor kell-yard
> There is a thorn bush in oor kell-yard
> At the back of thorn bush there stands a lad and lass
> But they're busy, busy hairing at the cuckoo's nest
>
> It is thorned, it is sprinkled, it is compassed all round
> It is thorned, it is sprinkled, and it isn't easy found
> She said: Young man, you're plundering; I said it wasnae true
> I said it wasnae true
> But I left her with the makings of a young cuckoo
>
> It's hi the cuckin, ho the cuckin, hi the cuckoo's nest
> It's hi the cuckin, ho the cuckin, hi the cuckoo's nest
> I'll gie onybody a shilling and a bottle o' the best
> If they'll ramble up the feathers o' the cuckoo's nest

The version of *The Magpie's Nest* given in this collection, with its subtle change from lyrical to dance rhythm, must be heard to be appreciated. These patter dance-rhythm refrains were aptly described by one singer in Northern Ireland as 'courantes'. Certainly the effectiveness of the song lies in the contrast between the slower lyrical treatment of the verse in contrast to the faster dance-beat of its 'courante'.

183 THE MAID OF AUSTRALIA

Harry Cox, Catfield, Norfolk, *rec.* P. Kennedy, 1953: BBC 22195 (five verses)

Other recorded version
Folk Songs of Britain, vol. II, Caedmon TC143/Topic 12T158

Printed versions
JEFDSS: 1958, p. 149: Harry Cox version with comment by A. L. Lloyd about the theme of miscegenation

not being common in Australia. (In JEFDSS: 1959, p. 219, John Meredith disagrees with A. L. Lloyd and cites examples in Australian songs)
Seeger and MacColl: 1960, p. 22: from Sam Larner, Winterton, Norfolk

Peacock: 1965, p. 276 (Newfoundland, Canada)

> As I walked down by the Hawkesborough Banks
> Where the maids of Australia do play their wild pranks

The Hawkesbury River reaches the sea north of Sydney at Broken Bay, New South Wales. To date the song seems only to have been heard in Norfolk and has not come to light in Australia.

In commenting on Harry Cox's version of the song, when it was published in the JEFDSS: 1958, A. L. Lloyd remarked on the unusual theme of miscegenation which he himself had never encountered in Australia. This produced a remarkable fund of examples in the next issue of the *Journal* which were submitted by the Australian collector and authority John Meredith from New South Wales. Here are some of the titles of songs and recitations containing this theme which he mentioned: *Gooniwindi Song, King Billy Song, Warrego Lament*, a bawdy version of *Waltzing Matilda, Black Alice, Sam Holt, Black Velvet, The Convict and the Australian Lady, The Bastard from the Bush, The Shearer's Lament, The Man from Thargomindah, Jacky Jacky and his Lubra Mary*, etc.

184 THE NEW-MOWN HAY

William Rew, Sidbury, Sidmouth, Devon, *rec.* P. Kennedy and W. Humphries, 1954

Printed versions
Sharp MS: 1905–8: three variants
Gardiner: 1909, Hampshire
JFSS: 1909, no. 13, p. 257: *The Baffled Knight*, coll. R. Vaughan Williams, Hampshire; only two verses printed

Reeves: 1958, no. 14, p. 79; Sharp: composite version
Purslow: 1968, p. 8: *All under the new-mown Hay*, coll. Hammond, 1906 (Hampshire)

Karpeles: 1971, p 237 (Newfoundland, Canada)

> I asked if I should lay her down
> All on the new mown hay, sir
> The answer that she gave to me
> I'm afraid it will not do, sir
> *Sing Fol-the-dol, aye, day*

This song, of which the above is a variant, has much in common with *Blow Away the Morning Dew* and *The Baffled Knight* (Child, no. 112), the latter seeming to be an older form of our song. Vaughan Williams submitted a version, which he collected in Hampshire, to which he ascribed the title *The Baffled Knight* and included as verses 5 and 7:

> When she came to her father's house
> The house that's walled all round, O
> She did go in and shut the door
> And shut me out behind, O

> When you met with me, kind sir
> You thought you'd met with a fool, O
> So take your Bible under your arm
> And run along to school, O

However, even though the theme is similar, the ballad *The Baffled Knight* is really distinct from our song. The best-known form of it was published by Cecil Sharp as *Blow Away the Morning Dew*. A recording of a Herefordshire version may be heard on *Folk Songs of Britain*, vol. V.

> There was a shepherd and he kept sheep upon a hill
> And he would go each morning all for to drink his fill
> So it's blow the windy morning,
> Blow the winds-i-o
> Clear away the morning dew
> And sweet the winds shall blow

185 THE NIGHTINGALES SING

Raymond and John Cantwell, Standlake, Oxfordshire, *rec.* P. Kennedy, 1956: BBC 23537; *The Soldier and the Lady: Folk Songs of Britain*, vol. II, CAEDMON TC1143/ TOPIC 12T158

Other recorded versions
Walter Hayne, Abbotsbury, Dorset, *rec.* P. Kennedy, 1950: BBC 22437 (1954)
George Attrill, Fittleworth, Sussex, *rec.* R. Copper, 1954: BBC 22737

Printed versions
SHARP MS: 1904: eight variants *The Bold Grenadier*
HAMMOND MS: 1905–7: five variants (Dorset and Somerset)
GARDINER MS: 1906: *Nightingales Sing* (Hampshire)
JFSS: 1930, no. 34, p. 194: two tunes *The Grenadier and the Lady*, coll. Hammond, Dorset
REEVES: 1958, no. 17, p. 85: *The Bold Grenadier*, coll. Sharp, Somerset (Kentucky verses collected by Sharp are given for comparison)
PURSLOW: 1965, p. 60: *coll.* Hammond (Dorset)
STUBBS: 1970, p. 16: *The Bold Privateer* (Sussex)

WYMAN AND BROCKWAY: 1916, p. 68: six verses (Kentucky, USA)
SHARP AND KARPELES: 1917/1932, no. 145: *The Nightingale* (Tennessee, USA)
SANDBURG: 1927, p. 136: *One Morning in May* (Pine Mountain, Virginia, USA)
CAMBIAIRE: 1934, p. 92
SCARBOROUGH: 1937, p. 310 (Virginia, USA)
HENRY: 1938, p. 200 (Tennessee, USA)
BELDEN: 1940: four variants and a fragment (Missouri, USA)
RANDOLPH: 1946–50, vol. I, p. 266: from MS (nine verses from Missouri, and from Arkansas, USA)
MORRIS: 1950, p. 360: (from Florida, with four verses from Ireland via Florida, USA)
FLANDERS AND OLNEY: 1953, p. 164 (Massachusetts, USA)
LOMAX: 1960, no 198, p 382: *The Wild Rippling Water*, cowboy version with composite text (Texas, USA)
PEACOCK: 1965, p. 600: *The Soldier and the Lady* (Newfoundland, Canada)
KARPELES: 1971, p. 232: *The Nightingale* (Newfoundland, Canada)

> As I was out a-walking one morning in June
> I met a happy couple enjoying a spoon
> The one was a lady and her beauty shone clear
> Whilst the other was a soldier in the bold Grenadiers
>
> They hadn't been there long before he put his arm around her middle
> And out from his knapsack he drew a long fiddle
> And played such a tune, me boys, that caused the valleys for to ring
> Hark, hark, cried the lady, how the nightingales sing

These were the first and third verses of the version recorded in the bar of the Ilchester Arms at Abbotsbury in Dorset. Walter Hayne agreed to sing the song providing I also sang a song. So I sang one verse of Harry Cox's *The Pretty Ploughboy*, which I had recently heard for the first time. Walter sang one verse of *Nightingales* and stopped for me to sing the second verse of *Ploughboy*. So we went on, verse by verse, against the background of the pub radio. After I had passed this test Walter was prepared to sing many other songs. After this initiation into collecting, I never looked back.

186 THE NUTTING GIRL

Cyril Poacher, Blaxhall, Woodbridge, Suffolk, *rec.* P. Kennedy, 1953: BBC 19881: *Folk Songs of Britain*, vol. II, CAEDMON TC1143/TOPIC 12T158

Other recorded version
George Attrill, Fittleworth, Sussex, *rec.* R. Copper, 1954: *The Nutting Maid*, BBC 22739

Printed versions
BARING GOULD: 1895, no. 83: *A Nutting We Will Go* 'words toned down somewhat' (Devon)

JFSS: 1901, no. 3, p. 127: *The Nut Girl*, coll. Merrick, Sussex
SHARP MS: 1904: one variant, music only (Somerset)
GARDINER MS: 1905–6: two variants (Hampshire)
HAMMOND MS: 1906: one variant (Dorset)
MOERAN: 1932, no. 1, p. 2: *Nutting Time* (Suffolk)
PURSLOW: 1972, p. 1: *coll.* Hammond (Dorset)
HAMER: 1973, p. 12 (Essex)

> Now Young Johnny left his horses, likewise he left his plough
> And he took her to some shady grove his courage for to show
> Then he took her round her middle so small and gently laid her down
> She said: My dear, I think I see the world go round and round
>
> He went back to his horses to finish off his song
> He said: My pretty fair maid, your mother will think you long
> But she flung her arms all round his neck as they went o'er the plain
> And she said: My dear, I should like to see the world go round again

These are two of the seven verses sung by George Attrill at Fittleworth in Sussex which extend the worldly erotic sequence of this most popular of country seduction ballads.

The tune of the song enjoys as much popularity as the words. It was used for Morris and Country Dances in England, and it has also been used with the words of many other songs. Bunting collected it from a harper in 1792 (BUNTING: 1840) and Samuel Lover used it in his *Low-Backed Car*. It is used for the tune of a Yorkshire hunting song, *Howgill Lads* (BBC 22449–50), and a *Mowing Match Ballad* (BBC 18136) sung by Becket Whitehead, Delph, Lancashire.

187 THE OVERGATE

Belle Stewart, Blairgowrie, Perthshire, Scotland, *rec.* P. Kennedy and H. Henderson, 1954

Other recorded versions
Jimmy McBeath, Elgin, Morayshire, Scotland, *rec.* A. Lomax, 1953: BBC 21089
Jeannie Robertson, Aberdeen, Scotland, *rec.* P. Kennedy, 1953: BBC 27810

Printed versions
FORD: 1899, p. 99: *My Rolling Eye* (the travelling singer took his name Rolling Eye from the song)
JFSS: 1913, no. 17, p. 292: *My Rolling Eye* (as above); tune only compared to *As I Roved Out*
REEVES: 1960, no. 8, p. 55: *Bilberry Town*, coll. Hammond, Dorset
PURSLOW: 1965, p. 11: *The Brewer Laddie* (*Bilberry Town*, as above)

For as I gaed doon the Overgate I met a bonny wee lass
For she winked tae me with the tail o' her e'e as I went walking past
   Ricky doo dum day doo dum day, ricky ricky doo dum day

I asked her what her name might be, she said: Jemima Rose
And I live in Blaeberry Lane at the foot o' the Buchan Close

I asked her what was her landlady's name, she said it was Mrs Bruce
And with that she invited me to come awa' to the hoose

As we went up the windin' stair, them bein' long and dark
For I slipped my money from my inside pooch and I tied it to the tail of my sark

We scarcely had got in the hoose when she took me tae a room
It was there we pulled a bottle oot, and then we baith sat down

But a'nicht long I dreamed I was lying in the airms o' Jemima Rose
But when I wokened I was lying on my back at the foot o' the Buchan Close

Come a' ye jolly ploo men lads that gang oot for a walk
Just slip your money frae your inside pooch and tie it to the tail o' your sark

Jeannie Robertson sang these words to *The Overgate* (BBC 27810) with a 'Ricky doo dum day' chorus, but she also sang a version similar to the one from Belle Stewart which has a 'Roving eye' chorus (BBC 21089):

     Wi' my rovin' eye
     Fal-the-doo-a-die
     My rovin'-di-dum-derry
     Wi' my rovin' eye

Belle Stewart had other verses which at some time or other had been improvised about the various characters working at a particular farm:

     Noo there is a maid upon oor fairm, she is a dainty dame
     She milks the kye at early morn, gin thither times there's crame

     O there is a cattle-man on the fairm, he has a wooden leg
     He dairts aboot frae burn to byre a-seekin' ilka egg

     There is a man upon the fairm, Will Garthell is his name
     He'll tak' ilka pint you'll gie em but he will pay for nane

The song may well be based on *As I Roved Out* (No. 121) with words improvised and added as the occasion required.

188 REMEMBER THE BARLEY STRAW

Harry Cox, Catfield, Norfolk, *rec.* P. Kennedy, 1953:
BBC 16416 (1947)

Other recorded versions
Ben Baxter, Southrepps, Norfolk, *rec.* S. Ennis, 1955:
BBC 22421
Bill Lowne, Cley, Norfolk, *rec.* S. Ennis, 1955: BBC
22173
Jeannie Robertson, Aberdeen, Scotland, *rec.* P. Kennedy,
1953: *Davie Faa*, BBC LP 27809 (1963)

Printed versions
BARING GOULD: 1895, no. 98: *The Barley Straw* (Devon);
text entirely rewritten
SHARP MS: 1905–7: two variants, *The Tinker* (Somerset)
and *Kitty will You Go with Me*
GARDINER MS: 1907: one variant (Hampshire)

The location of the song varies, but Jeannie Robertson had the idea that the song was about James V of Scotland and how he 'went a-roving' as a young man. This is the popular belief in connection with the ballad *The Gaberlunzie* or *Beggar Man* (CHILD, no. 279). Her title she gives as *Davie Faa*, for this is the name the tinker calls himself in her version:

> The bonny lassie blushed and O but she thocht shame
> It's since you've the wills o' me, come tell to me your name
> He whispered in the lassie's ear, they ca' me Davie Faa
> And I'll mind upon the happy nicht amongst the pile o' stra'

Bill Lowne substituted a *Haselbury Girl* (No. 176) verse:

> Now since you've had your way, young man, pray tell to me your name
> And likewise your vocation and where and whence you came
> My name is Johnny the Rover, from Dublin town I came
> I live at the side of the ups and downs and you'll never see me again

189 ROLLING IN THE DEW

Leslie Johnson, Fittleworth, Sussex, *rec.* R. Copper,
1954: BBC 22762

Other recorded versions
Shirley Collins, Hastings, Sussex, *rec.* P. Kennedy, 1954
George Maynard, Copthorne, Crawley, Sussex, *rec.*
P. Kennedy and M. Plunkett, 1956: BBC 23093

Printed versions
HALLIWELL: 1842, p. 336: fragment *Rolling in the Dew*
FORD: 1899, p. 149: six variants, *Where are you going to,
my pretty fair maid?*
HECHT: 1904, p. 155: (Perthshire) *King Hearted Nancy*
SHARP AND MARSON: 1904–9, vol. II, no. 35: *Dabbling in
the Dew*; words rewritten by Marson (Somerset)
SHARP MS: 1904–14: sixteen variants (West Country)
BARING GOULD AND SHARP: 1906, no. 23: *Dabbling in the
Dew*: rewritten for school use
HAMMOND MS: 1906–7: one variant (Somerset), two
variants (Dorset)

GARDINER MS: 1906–9: five variants (Hampshire,
Somerset, Surrey and Wiltshire)
BUTTERWORTH: 1912, no. 9: *Roving in the Dew* (Sussex)
LEATHER: 1912, p. 205: *The Milkmaid's Song* (Hereford-
shire)
JFSS: 1913, no. 17, pp. 282–6: seven variants, *coll.*
Butterworth, Jekyll, Sussex; Vaughan Williams,
Cambridgeshire, Herefordshire and Sussex; Sharp,
Gloucestershire and Shropshire
SHARP: 1916–21: revised text using Halliwell variant
REEVES: 1958, no. 24, p. 100: original Sharp text,
Somerset, 1909
REEVES: 1960, no. 27, p. 85: Hammond, Dorset, 1906
JEFDSS: 1963, p. 191: George Maynard variant
GUNDRY: 1966, p. 28: *coll.* Baring Gould (Cornwall)
PURSLOW: 1972, p. 80: *coll.* Gardiner (Hampshire)

> Shall I carry your pail then?
> O no sir, I'll carry it myself
>
> Suppose I was to kiss you?
> That would be no harm, sir

> Suppose I was to run away?
> Then I must run the faster
>
> Suppose I was to run too fast?
> O the devil would fetch you back again

These are variant verses collected by Cecil Sharp to this milkmaid song, of which he came across a total of sixteen variants in the West Country.

Baring Gould had a verse for clothing:

> What should we have to clothe him in?
> Sir, I can weave and also spin

and George Butterworth had a further verse to do with footwear:

> What will you do for boots then?
> My brother is a shoemaker

436

190 SHE WAS A RUM ONE

Davie Stewart, Dundee, Angus, Scotland, *rec.* P. Kennedy, 1956

Other recorded version
Jeannie Robertson, Aberdeen, Scotland, *rec.* P. Kennedy, 1953: BBC 21090 (subsequently withdrawn)

Printed version
GREIG: 1907, vol. II, 112 ii (tune only)

Compare
REEVES: 1960, No. 8, p. 55: *Bilberry Town, coll.* Hammond, Dorset, 1906
PURSLOW: 1965, p. 11: Hammond version, *The Brewer Laddie*

Gavin Greig collected a tune for this song though, doubtless because of the somewhat clinical character of the story line, the words were not noted. It certainly seems to be related to *As I Roved Out* (No. 121) and the many songs which follow the same theme and pattern such as *The Overgate* (No. 187). One that seems so akin that it may well be a variant of the same song is *The Brewer Laddie* which was popular in England as well as Scotland. A version collected by Henry Hammond in Dorset uses a similar chorus, but the verses of the song are clearly based on *As I Roved Out*.

191 THREE MAIDENS TO MILKING DID GO

Fred Hewett, Mapledurwell, Hampshire, *rec.* R. Copper, 1955: BBC 21860

Printed versions
CHRISTIE: 1881, vol. II, p. 256: tune only (from BUCHAN: 1828) *A Young Maid A-Milking Did Go* with new words for *Her Kiss Was Soft*
KIDSON: 1891, p. 73: *Three Maidens A-Milking Did Go* (Yorkshire)
BARING GOULD: 1895, No. 90: *The Blackbird;* text rewritten by Baring Gould, with two original verses given in the notes
BARING GOULD: 1905, No. 90, p. 184: *The Blackbird in the Bush;* original words restored but modified, with a reference to a Welsh version of the tune in the notes.
GARDINER MS: 1904, Nos. 35 and 141 (Somerset), 798 and 845 (Hampshire; four variants)
HAMMOND MS: 1905, No. 266 (Dorset, published by Purslow)
SHARP MS: 1906–23: nine variants

JFSS: 1910, No. 15, p. 93: *Three Pretty Maidens Milking Did Go, coll.* Wyatt-Edgell, Devon
WILLIAMS: 1923, p. 229: *Three Maidens A-Milking Would Go* (Gloucestershire); REEVES: 1958 believes the text to be slightly edited
JFSS: 1927, No. 31, p. 22: *Three Maidens A-Walking Did Go, coll.* Sharp, Oxfordshire, 1923; (the last song he collected)
KIDSON AND MOFFAT: 1927, p. 62: rewritten text by Annie Gilchrist with two traditional verses
PINTO AND RODWAY: 1957, No. 230: nine verses *Three Maidens A-Milking Would Go* from a University of Nottingham Library broadside collection
REEVES: 1958, No. 102, p. 208: *Three Maids A-Milking, coll.* Sharp, Somerset, 1907
REEVES: 1960, No. 131, p. 259: original verses *coll.* Baring Gould, Devon, 1890
JEFDSS: 1961, p. 75: Fred Hewett's version
PURSLOW: 1965, p. 2: *The Bird in the Bush, coll.* Hammond, Dorset, 1905

> Here's a health to the blackbird in the bush
> Likewise to the bonny wood-doe
> If you'll go along with me
> Unto yonder flow'ring tree
> I will catch you a small bird or two

This was the only verse retained when the song was published after it had been noted by Baring Gould at Widdecombe in Devon in 1890 from Roger Hannaford, who called it *The Blackbird*. To publish it at all Baring Gould found it necessary to write an entirely different ballad retaining only the third verse as the first of his new set of words. However in the revised edition of *Songs of the West* under the musical editorship of Cecil Sharp and under the title *The Blackbird in the Bush* the song was printed very nearly in its original form.

According to James Reeves the feminine symbolism of the milk pail is traced to the seventeenth century, but he believes the song to be of a much earlier origin. The Nottingham broadside in PINTO AND RODWAY: 1957 contains this verse:

> Then he set her up against a green tree
> And he beat the bush and the bird flew in
> A little above my love's knee

192   UP TO THE RIGS

Charlie Wills, Morcombelake, Bridport, Dorset, *rec*. P. Kennedy, 1952: *Folk Songs of Britain*, vol. II, CAEDMON TC1143/TOPIC 12T158

Other recorded versions
Harry Cox, Catfield, Norfolk, *rec*. P. Kennedy, 1953: BBC 21482
Thomas Moran, Mohill, County Leitrim, Ireland, *rec*. S. Ennis, 1954: BBC 22038

Printed versions
GARDINER MS: 1907: two variants (Hampshire)
SHARP MS: 1907–8: three variants (Somerset)
JFSS: 1924, No. 28: *In London Streets I Went Astray*; from the Clague Collection, no text (Isle of Man)
JFSS: 1931, No. 35: *London Town, coll*. E. J. Moeran from Harry Cox, Norfolk, 1927
REEVES: 1958, No. 80, p. 180: *The Rigs of London Town, coll*. Sharp, Gloucestershire, 1908
STUBBS: 1970, p. 74 (Sussex)

> Now she thought by me she'd work her will
> Times she frisk-ed, I laid still
> And as soon as she had got to sleep
> Out of bed I gently creep

Harry Cox sang this verse with sheer delight, for he has always regarded the big cities as being full of tricksters, both men and women. He had been to London on a few occasions and prided himself that he had never been tricked. So when he sang the song he performed it with the conviction of one who could have been the actor in the story.

Bibliography

This bibliography has been divided into two sections. Books published in Britain and Ireland appear first, followed by those published abroad, both in alphabetical order

BARING GOULD: 1889–1905
Rev. S. Baring Gould and Rev. H. Fleetwood Sheppard, *Songs and Ballads of the West*: Patey & Willis, London (4 parts) 1889–91. Methuen, London (4 parts) 1891–4; (1 vol.) 1895; revised edition 1905. Details are given by E. A. White in JEFDSS: 1937, p. 143, and 1946, p. 67. When reprinted in four parts this collection, mainly from Devon and N. Cornwall, comprised 110 songs 'collected from the mouths of the people'. Texts were modified and in some cases completely re-written and the same applied to tunes. However, in the revised edition, under the musical editorship of Cecil Sharp and with the adding of the name of the Rev. F. W. Bussell, one of the original collectors, many original texts and tunes were restored. For further comment on this publication see Dean-Smith: JEFDSS: 1950, p. 41.

BARING GOULD MS: 1889–95
Rev. S. Baring Gould. Manuscript in Plymouth City Library.

BARING GOULD AND SHARP: 1906
Rev. S. Baring Gould and Cecil J. Sharp, *English Folk Songs for Schools*: Curwen, London, 1906. 53 songs from collections of both editors 'designed to meet the requirements of the Board of Education'—who that year had recommended the inclusion of National or Folk Songs in the school curriculum, and 'dedicated to T. R. H. Prince Edward and Prince Albert of Wales'.

BUNTING: 1840
Edward Bunting, *The Ancient Music of Ireland*: 1840. Bunting's third collection of folksongs contained 151 tunes.

BUTTERWORTH: 1912
George Butterworth, *Folk Songs from Sussex*: Augener, London, 1912. 11 songs with piano arrangements collected by Butterworth and Francis Jekyll with names of singers and sources given in short preface. (For other songs noted by Butterworth see JFSS: 1913, No. 17.)

CHRISTIE: 1876/81
William Christie, *Traditional Ballad Airs*: Edmonston & Douglas, Edinburgh, vol. I 1876, vol. II 1881. Dean Christie noted down songs mainly in Aberdeenshire. This book combines his own collecting with publication of tunes and words from many other collections, both published and unpublished, including Percy, Scott, Jamieson, Motherwell, Kinloch, Sharpe and Buchan. Also contains a few original compositions.

DEAN-SMITH: 1954
Margaret Dean-Smith, *A Guide to English Folk Song Collections (1822–1952)*: University of Liverpool, 1954. A useful index of published songs under titles, alternative titles and first lines, with some full descriptions of important books with historical annotations and an introduction which traces the development of collecting and publication of folksong in England over a period of 130 years.

DUNCAN MS 1905–11
James Duncan (1848–1917). MS collected *c.* 1905–11. Aberdeen University Library. Consists of two notebooks, the first containing 800 tunes with words of first verse, and the second giving texts of over 350 songs all supplied by a Mrs Gillespie. For obituary by Lucy Broadwood see JFSS: 1918, No. 21, p. 41.

D'URFEY: 1698–1720
Thomas D'Urfey, *Wit and Mirth (or Pills to Purge Melancholy)*: London, 1698–1720. First edition printed with airs was in 2 vols. (1698). Further editions increased to 6 vols. (1720). This was the earliest publication to contain both words and music of a large number of English and Scots folksongs.

FMJ: 1965–
Folk Music Journal: English Folk Dance and Song Society, London (from 1965). Continuing the work of JFSS (*Journal of the Folk-Song Society*): 1889–1931 and JEFDSS (*Journal of the English Folk Dance and Song Society*): 1932–64.

FORD: 1899–1904
Robert Ford, *Vagabond Songs and Ballads of Scotland*: Gardiner, Paisley, Scotland, 1899–1901; new edition 1904. A comprehensive collection of songs and ballads, containing a number of 'bothy ballads', but only a few for which he provides the music. Important in that it covers the wide range of songs that were current up to the end of the century, particularly those sung by 'the travellers'.

GARDINER: 1909
George B. Gardiner, *Folk Songs from Hampshire*: Novello, London, 1909. 16 songs collected by Gardiner and his musical associates, Gamblin, Balfour Gardiner and Guyer, and arranged by Gustav (von) Holst.

GARDINER MS: 1905–9 (see also under HAMMOND)
For further details about Gardiner's work see *The George Gardiner Folksong Collection* in FMJ: 1967, p. 129 and introduction to PURSLOW: 1968.

GREIG: 1909/14
Gavin Greig, *Folk Songs of the North-East*: The Buchan Observer, Peterhead, Scotland. Vol. I 1909, vol. II 1914. Folklore Associates, Pennsylvania, USA, 1963. Greig was an Aberdeenshire schoolmaster and an accomplished musician who noted the words and tunes of over 3,000 songs. His manuscripts, extending over 90 volumes, are deposited in the Library of King's College, Aberdeen.

GUNDRY: 1966
Inglis Gundry, *Canow Kernow*. Federation of Old Cornwall Societies, 1966. Soundpost Publications, Dartington Institute of Traditional Arts, Totnes, Devon, 1972. Over 60 songs, carols, shanties and dance tunes collected in Cornwall. Some songs published with versions in Cornish.

HALLIWELL: 1842/9
J. O. Halliwell, *The Nursery Rhymes of England*: Percy Society Publications, London, 1842. Vol. IV, and several subsequent editions. (It was reissued in 1970 by Bodley Head.) *Popular Rhymes and Nursery Tales*: London, 1849 (a sequel to the above). Words of nursery rhymes 'collected from oral tradition'.

HAMER: 1967
Fred Hamer, *Garners Gay*: EFDS Publications, London, 1967. 50 songs, words and melodies (chord symbols) mainly collected in Bedfordshire but also from other counties of England. No exact locations or dates given of informants or comparative notes to songs, but contains hitherto unpublished local songs and songs connected with local customs.

HAMER: 1973
Fred Hamer, *Green Groves*: EFDS Publications, London, 1973. 38 songs, words and melodies (chord symbols). A further selec-

tion published posthumously. As in Hamer's *Garners Gay*, no exact details of locations, dates or comparative notes to songs.

HAMMOND AND GARDINER MSS: 1905–9

H. E. D. Hammond (1866–1910), R. F. F. Hammond (1868–1921) and Dr George Gardiner (1852–1910) collected mainly in Dorset and Hampshire. Their manuscripts, deposited in the Vaughan Williams Memorial Library at Cecil Sharp House, London, have been indexed by Frank Purslow, who has also edited three books drawn from them (see PURSLOW: 1965, 1968 and 1972).

HECHT: 1904

Hans Hecht, *Songs from David Herd's Manuscript*: William Hay, Edinburgh, 1904. (See HERD: 1769–76.)

HENRY: 1924

Sam Henry, *Songs of the People*: Northern Constitution, Coleraine, Co. Derry, N. Ireland, 1924. Over 800 songs were published in the local Derry newspaper. Many were contributed by readers but it was Henry's diligent research and background notes that gave interest to each contribution.

HERD: 1769/76

David Herd, *The Ancient and Modern Scots Songs, Heroic Ballads*: Dickson & Elliot, Edinburgh, 1769; (2 vols.) 1776. Paterson, Edinburgh, 1870. New 2-vol. edition, 1973, Scottish Academic Press. Early Scots source material. Herd's original MS, in the British Museum, served as basis for many of Robert Burns's songs as well as for Sir Walter Scott's *Minstrelsy of the Scottish Border*.

HUGHES: 1909–36

Herbert Hughes, *Irish Country Songs*: Boosey, London, 1909–36. 4 vols. Vol. I 1909, vol. II 1915, vol. III 1935, vol. IV 1936. About 20 songs in each album collected in the northern counties of Ireland.

HUGILL: 1961

Stan Hugill, *Shanties of the Seven Seas*: Routledge & Kegan Paul, London, 1961.

JEFDSS: 1932–64

Journal of The English Folk Dance and Song Society: London (32 vols.), 1932–64.

JFSS: 1899–1931

Journal of the Folk-Song Society: London (35 vols.), 1899–1931.

JOYCE: 1909

P. Weston Joyce, *Old Irish Folk Music and Songs*: University Press, Dublin, 1909. 842 Irish airs and songs, edited with annotations for the Royal Society of Antiquaries of Ireland of which Joyce was the President. Most of the music previously unpublished but some are versions of songs already in *Ancient Music of Ireland* (1873) and *Irish Peasant Songs in the English Language* (1906).

KIDSON: 1891

Frank Kidson, *Traditional Tunes*: C. Taphouse, Oxford, 1891. Texts and melodies (without accompaniment) mainly from Yorkshire. Later published with piano accompaniment in KIDSON AND MOFFAT: 1926 and 1927. Many texts filled out from broadsides. For article about Frank Kidson see JEFDSS: 1948, p. 127. Reissued by S. R. Publishers, 1970.

KIDSON AND MOFFAT: 1926

Frank Kidson and Alfred Moffat, *A Garland of English Folk Songs*: Ascherberg, Hopwood & Crew, London, 1926. 60 songs collected by Kidson, mainly in Yorkshire, with piano accompaniments by Moffat; most previously published in *Traditional Tunes* (1891). A further 60 songs were selected for a second volume by Kidson and Moffat (1927).

KIDSON AND MOFFAT: 1927

Frank Kidson and Alfred Moffat, *Folk Songs from the North Countrie*: Ascherberg, Hopwood & Crew, London, 1927. A further 60 songs with piano accompaniment, published one year after the collector's death. The foreword by Lucy Broadwood provides information about the collector. See also *Frank Kidson: portrait*, JEFDSS: 1948, pp. 127–35.

KINLOCH: 1827

George R. Kinloch, *Ancient Scottish Ballads*: Longman, London and Edinburgh, 1827. Probably inspired by Sir Walter Scott's collections, this was an important ballad and song publication with tunes.

LEATHER: 1912

Mrs E. M. Leather, *Folk-Lore of Herefordshire*: Jakeman & Carver, Hereford, and Sidgwick & Jackson, London, 1912; S.R. Publishers, E. Ardsley, Wakefield, Yorkshire, 1970. Like Burne's *Shropshire Folk-lore* (1884), this contains mainly folklore, but includes 23 songs, dances, mummers, ballads and carols. For further details about the collector see JFSS: 1928, No. 32, pp. 29–30.

MOERAN: 1932

E. J. Moeran, *Six Suffolk Folk Songs*: Curwen, London, 1932. Collected and arranged with piano accompaniments by Moeran, who also collected songs in his own native Kerry, in Ireland. The two areas are compared in JEFDSS: 1948, pp. 152–4 'Some Folk Singing of To-day'.

O LOCHLAINN: 1939

Colm O Lochlainn, *Irish Street Ballads*: Three Candles, Dublin, 1939. Over 100 songs, words, music and annotations collected in many different parts of Ireland (including the North). All in English and many having equivalents in England and Scotland. Illustrated with woodcuts from the original broadsheets.

O LOCHLAINN: 1965

Colm O Lochlainn, *More Irish Street Ballads*: Three Candles, Dublin, 1965. A further 100 songs, all again in the English language.

ORD: 1930

John Ord, *Bothy Songs and Ballads*: Alexander Gardner, Paisley, Scotland. The standard work on the 'bothy ballads' of N.E. Scotland; 'bothy' meaning farm cottage or hut used by hands, ploughmen, shepherds and farm-servants, and the ballads, although including folksongs found elsewhere, being mainly those describing, and often complaining about, local farm life.

PETRIE: 1855/77/82

George Petrie, *The Petrie Collection of the Ancient Music of Ireland*: M. H. Gill, Dublin, 1855. *Ancient Music of Ireland from the Petrie Collection*: Pigott, Dublin, 1877. *Music of Ireland*: M. H. Gill, Dublin, 1882.

PINTO AND RODWAY: 1957

V. de Sola Pinto and A. E. Rodway, *The Common Muse*: Chatto & Windus, London, 1957; Penguin Books, London, 1965. An anthology of Popular British Ballad Poetry from the 15th to the 20th century. In two parts: the first 'Amatory' and the second 'General'. 245 texts from England, Ireland and Scotland with an introduction mainly about street balladry.

PURSLOW: 1965

Frank Purslow, *Marrowbones*: EFDS Publications, London, 1965. A series of pocket-size publications initiated by Peter Kennedy in order to make available the songs collected by Hammond and Gardiner in the care of the EFDSS library. This selection contains 100 songs, provided with chord symbols over the melodies.

PURSLOW: 1968

Frank Purslow, *The Wanton Seed*: EFDS Publications, London, 1968. A second selection from Hammond and Gardiner again containing 100 songs.

PURSLOW: 1972

Frank Purslow, *The Constant Lovers*: EFDS Publications, London, 1972. A third selection in which the type-size has been increased and the number of songs reduced to 78.

REEVES: 1958
James Reeves, *The Idiom of the People*: Heinemann, London, 1958. Words of 115 folksongs from Cecil Sharp MSS (about 40 printed for the first time) selected as examples of 'English Traditional Verse'. Introduction concerned with the Folk Song Movement in England; Sharp as a collector; text revisions, description of the MSS; the popular idiom; and a detailed consideration of certain songs.

REEVES: 1960
James Reeves, *The Everlasting Circle*: Heinemann, London, 1960. 142 texts from the MSS of Baring Gould, Hammond and Gardiner considered as 'English traditional verse'. Introduction concerned with Baring Gould as a collector and his MSS; Hammond and Gardiner; varieties of folksong; the theme of fertility and a discussion on the *lingua franca* of English traditional song.

ROXBURGHE: 1871–93
Roxburghe Ballads (about 1540–1790): 7 vols. Vols. I–II ed. William Chappell, Ballad Society, London, 1871–80; vols. III–VII ed. J. W. Ebsworth, Hertford, 1883–93.

SEEGER AND MACCOLL: 1960
Peggy Seeger and Ewan MacColl, *The Singing Island*: Mills Music, London, 1960. 96 English and Scots folksongs arranged for 'the post-war folk revival' mainly from Scotland under headings: Children, Courting, Men at Work, On the Road, Sailors, Barrack Room, Rovin' Boys and Flash Girls, Historical and Fill up your Glass.

SHARP MS 1903–23
Cecil Sharp (1859–1924), foremost collector of English folksongs and folkdances, was the founder of The English Folk Dance Society and for many years a member of The Folk-Song Society. (In 1932 these two societies amalgamated as The English Folk Dance and Song Society.) For a full account of his lifework and publications see *Cecil Sharp* by A. H. Fox-Strangways (Oxford University Press, London, 1933), revised by Maud Karpeles (Routledge & Kegan Paul, London, 1967). Words, songs, tunes and dance notes in Cecil Sharp's autograph are in the Library of Clare College, Cambridge. There are also photostat copies in the Harvard University Library and the New York Public Library, and microfilm copies in the libraries of the University of California and in the library at Cecil Sharp House, London, the headquarters of The English Folk Dance and Song Society. Cecil Sharp's own collection of books was left to the EFDSS and formed the beginnings of the specialist library at Cecil Sharp House.

SHARP AND MARSON: 1904–9
Cecil J. Sharp and Rev. Charles L. Marson, *Folk Songs from Somerset*: Simpkin Marshall, London and Barnicott, Taunton, Somerset. 5 vols. Vol. I 1904, vol. II 1905, vol. III 1906, vol. IV 1908, vol. V 1909. The most important single collection of English folksong, later edited as the *Selected Edition* (1916–21). Introduction concerning singers and style most valuable.

SHARP: 1916/21
Cecil J. Sharp, *English Folk Songs: Selected Edition*: Oliver Ditson, New York, 1916; Novello, London, 1921. 2 vols. 100 songs of which all but 18 from Somerset previously published in SHARP AND MARSON: 1904–9. 12 of the songs, not previously published, were variants. Introduction (and notes to songs) are of great value as they post-date by 14 years his *English Folk Song, Some Conclusions* (1907).

STUBBS: 1970
Ken Stubbs, *The Life of a Man*: EFDS Publications, London, 1970. 50 songs, texts and melodies (chord symbols). Many from our same source singers, but includes a wide variety from Home Counties (Surrey, Sussex mainly and some from Kent) with some important variant versions and some hitherto unpublished songs. Biographical notes about singers.

WILLIAMS: 1923
Alfred Owen Williams, *Folk Songs of the Upper Thames*: Duckworth, London, 1923. Over 300 folksongs (words only) noted mainly in Berkshire, Gloucestershire, Oxfordshire and Wiltshire. Interesting introduction about rural life, more fully covered by Williams in *Round About the Upper Thames* (Duckworth, 1922). Further unpublished texts in Swindon Reference Library. See FMJ: 1969 'Alfred Williams: A Symposium'.

BELDEN: 1940
H. M. Belden, *Ballads and Songs Collected by the Missouri Folklore Society*: University Studies XV (No. 1), Columbia, Missouri, USA, 1940.

CAMBIARE: 1934
Celestin Pierre Cambiare, *East Tennessee and Western Virginia Mountain Ballads*: Mitre Press, London, 1934.

COMBS: 1925
Josiah H. Combs, *Folk Songs du Midi des États-Unis*: Les Presses Universitaires de France, Paris, 1925. *Folk Songs of the Southern United States* edited by D. K. Wilgus (annotated English edition) as 19th volume of American Folklore Society's Bibliographical Special Series. University of Texas Press, Austin, Texas, USA, 1967.

COX: 1925
John Harrington Cox, *Folk Songs of the South*: Harvard University Press, Cambridge, Mass., USA, 1925. Dover Publications Reprint, New York, 1967 (released 1968). 185 songs collected in West Virginia (29 with tunes). Introduction describes collecting methods and identifies informants. Notes, references to other versions and other data given with texts of songs.

FLANDERS AND OLNEY: 1953
Helen Hartness Flanders and Marguerite Olney, *Ballads Migrant in New England*: Farrar, Straus & Young, New York, 1953.

FOWKE: 1965
Edith Fowke, *Traditional Singers and Songs from Ontario*: Folklore Associates, Pennsylvania and Burns & MacEachern, Ontario, Canada. 62 songs from 10 traditional singers with musical transcriptions by Peggy Seeger. Songs in the collection are on the following records: Folkways FM 4005, 4018, 4051 and 4052; Folk Legacy FSC 10; Prestige INT 25014; Topic 12T140.

HENRY: 1938
Mellinger E. Henry, *Folksongs from the Southern Highlands*: J. J. Augustin, New York, 1938.

HUBBARD: 1961
Lester A. Hubbard, *Ballads and Songs from Utah*: University of Utah, Salt Lake City, USA, 1961.

KARPELES: 1934/71
Maud Karpeles, *Folksongs from Newfoundland*: Oxford University Press, London, 1934 (2 vols.); Faber & Faber, London, 1971. 30 songs (with piano accompaniments) were published in 1934 and 90 songs, 150 tunes including variants (with no accompaniments) in 1971. All collected during 1929–30.

LOMAX: 1960
Alan Lomax, *Folk Songs of North America*: Cassell, London, 1960.

MORRIS: 1950
Alton C. Morris, *Folksongs of Florida*: University of Florida, Gainesville, Florida, USA, 1950.

PEACOCK: 1965
Kenneth Peacock, *Songs of the Newfoundland Outports*: National Museum of Canada, Ottawa, 1965. 3 vols.

RANDOLPH: 1946–50
Vance Randolph and Floyd C. Shoemaker, *Ozark Folk Songs*:

State Historical Society, Columbia, Missouri, USA, 1946–50. 4 vols.

SANDBURG: 1927
Carl Sandburg, *The American Songbag*: Harcourt Brace, New York, 1927.

SCARBOROUGH: 1937
Dorothy Scarborough, *A Song Catcher in the Southern Mountains*: Columbia University Press, New York, 1937.

SHARP AND KARPELES: 1917/32
Olive Dame Campbell and Cecil J. Sharp, *English Folk Songs from the Southern Appalachians*: Putnam, New York, 1917. Cecil J. Sharp and Maud Karpeles (2 vols.), Oxford University Press, London, 1932.

THOMPSON: 1939
Harold W. Thompson, *Body, Boots and Britches*: J. B. Lippincott, Philadelphia, USA, 1939.

WYMAN AND BROCKWAY: 1916
Loraine Wyman and Howard Brockway, *Lonesome Tunes (Folk Songs from the Kentucky Mountains)*: H. W. Gray, New York, 1916.

X

Songs of
Uneasy Wedlock

Introduction

> If I had a hundred sovereigns, I would give them with goodwill
> To put my wife away twelve months upon the treading-mill
> And if the devil would but take her, I'd thank him for his pains
> So it's hang me in my garters before I wed again
>
> *The Scolding Wife*: No. 214

> Before we was married, we 'ad lots o' quids
> But now that we's married, we got lots o' kids
> But yus, I loves 'im, I can't denies it
> I goes wiv 'im wherever 'e goes
>
> *He Comes down our Alley*: No. 203

Of the twenty-four songs in this chapter, fifteen are voiced by the men and nine are from the woman's point of view (thirteen recorded in England, six in Ireland, four in Scotland and one in Wales). Of the men's songs, four (Nos. 197, 200, 201 and 206) of them could also be classed as seduction songs, but in this chapter their encounters are with unfaithful married women.

In these four songs the story is always related from the husband's point of view and the women always get caught. For example, in No. 197 the butcher puts the cunning little cobbler in the bull-pen and then pins a ticket on his back saying: 'This cobbler to the bedroom goes, mending ladies' shoes.' In No. 200 a drover threatens to burn the cupboard in which a groggy old tailor is hiding while his wife hastens to tell him it contains a game-cock. He kicks the cupboard out of doors and declares: 'I've cooked your game-cock.' In song No. 201 the injured male party 'swore and tore' at his 'darling wife Hannah', and told her to 'hop it and take her piano' and he advises all young married men to tune their own pianos. In the fourth song, No. 206, a mole-catcher charges ten pounds to the farmer who has been tilling his ground and the farmer laughingly works this out to be 'tuppence a time'.

> So come all you young fellows and mind what you're at
> For fear you'll get caught in a mole-catcher's trap

These are what Vaughan Williams called examples of the type of Chaucerian *rough fun* as occurs, for example, in 'The Clerk of Oxenforde'. They are also the *mal-mariée* in French folk-song (see *J'ai perdu ma femme*, No. 103; *Jean, petit coq*, No. 104; *Jean, petit Jean*, No. 105; *Mon père il me marie*, No. 111, and *Mon père m'a donné-z-un mari*, No. 112).

In the case of *Rap-Tap-Tap* (No. 211), the farmer's servant man gets away with his enjoyment of the farmer's wife by telling the farmer that he has been looking after his affairs:

> So when my master did come home
> O he asked me what I had done
> I told him I'd minded his business
> Just as well as if he was at home

There are four *toil and strife* songs complaining of married life by the husbands (Nos. 193, 204, 214 and 215) and four of complaint by the wives (Nos. 202, 203, 207 and 213).

The Linen Song (No. 205), which takes more the form of a courtship song, has been included here because of its hint of impending domestic strife. It could in fact be sung by a young husband whose heart still misses a beat at the sight of his darling young wife, busy with a different domestic duty for each day of the week. An acceptance of the domestic scene, but more a case of events overtaking the husband in double measure, is the song *The One Thing or the Other* (No. 209):

> We live in peace and unity, right well content together
> In our daily occupation at the one thing or the other

The Birmingham Boys (No. 195) is a warning to wives not to be unfaithful and spend their husband's money while he is away at sea, and two other songs, both voiced by the husbands, regret the unfaithfulness of their wives. In *The Deserted Husband* (No. 198) the wife goes off with a neighbour, and in *Rocking the Cradle* (No. 212) the husband is left at home to look after the baby that's none of his own.

Another warning to wives intending unfaithfulness is given in the story of *The Old Woman of Blighter Town* (No. 208). She asks the doctor to give her something to 'drive her old man blind', and he keeps her quiet, recommending 'marrowbones'; her husband cunningly accepts the medicine, pretends blindness and asks his wife to take a run at him, to push him in the river, saying that since he cannot see her, he might as well drown:

> The old woman got back a pace or two   She was up to her neck in water, boys
> And took a race at him   And loudly she did bawl
> The old man he popped a little one side   He put his hands all over his eyes
> Headlong the old woman went in   Saying: I can't see thee at all

> The old woman she did squabble about
> And nearly reached the brim
> The old man took a girt long pole
> And pushed her further in

A sequel to this is *The Dumb Wife* (No. 199), the story of a husband who decides to go to the doctor about his wife:

> To the doctor he did her bring and they cut her clattering strings
> And gave her the liberty of her tongue, tongue, tongue
> Her tongue began to sing, and her clatter began to ring
> And it sounded in his ears like a drum, drum, drum

And so, of course, he has to go back to the doctor again, and he offers him 'fifty pounds in gold to have her dumb, dumb, dumb':

> But it's past the power of man, let him do whate'er he can
> For to make a scolding wife hold her tongue, tongue, tongue

A desperate widow looking for a new husband provides a good conversation piece. In *Bargain with Me* (No. 194) she makes her advances to Billy Boy, who has come to her seeking service, but Billy does not agree to marry her until he has checked up on her and found out (a) where he will sleep, (b) the whereabouts of her late husband, (c) where her husband was buried and (d) how long he has been dead.

The loneliness of the spinster with her 'candle burning dim' is dramatically conveyed by *The Poor Auld Maid* (No. 210):

> The time passes by with the clock's dull tick
> And the wearisome purr of the cat
> It seems that I've lived since the ark came down
> On the top of Mount Ararat

One of the most unusually racy, also perhaps one of the oldest songs in the chapter, is *The Crab-fish* (No. 196), which first appeared in print in the seventeenth century. At that time crab themes were popular in English prose and the crab was thought to possess powers of fertility, when brought into contact with the genitals. However, in our song, the crab took on devilish powers and gave the old wife a nip you-can-guess-where and caught her husband by the nose:

> Wife, wife, wife you must be going mad
> That you don't know the devil from an old sea crab

The last song in this chapter, one of the most beautiful of our folksongs, popular in England, Ireland and Scotland, is a lament of early marriage, *Young and Growing* (No. 216). In our version the 'bairney boy' was married at sixteen, had a son at seventeen and was dead at the age of eighteen, but in some versions he was married as young as twelve:

> So come all you pretty fair young maids a warning take from me
> And never build your nest in the top of any tree
> For the green leaves they will wither and the roots they will decay
> While the blushes of your bairney boy are fading away

193 THE BALD-HEADED END OF THE BROOM

O love it is a fun-ny fun-ny thing It af-fects both young and old

It's like a plate of burn-ing hot ash And man-y's the man that is sold

It makes you feel like a fresh-wat-er eel Caus-es your head to — swell

To lose your mind through true-love is blind And it emp-ties your poc-ket-book as well

So boys, I say, from the girls keep a-way And give them lots of room

For, when that they are wed, they will beat you on the head With the bald-headed end of the broom

1 O love it is a funny funny thing
It affects both young and old
It's like a plate of burning hot ash
And many's the man that is sold
It makes you feel like a fresh-water eel
Causes your head to swell
To lose your mind through true-love is blind
And it empties your pocket-book as well

So boys, I say, from the girls keep away
And give them lots of room
For, when that they are wed, they will beat you on the
With the bald-headed end of the broom   [head

2 When a man is gone on a pretty little girl
He'll talk to her as gentle as a dove
He'll spend all his money and he'll call her his honey
All for fun and love
When his money's all spent and his clothes all rent
He'll find that the old story's true
That a mole in the arm's worth two in the leg
And what is he going for to do?

3 With a wife and sixteen half-starved kids
You'll find it is no fun
When the butcher comes round to collect up his bill
With his dog and double-barrelled gun
With a cross-eyed baby on each knee
And a wife with a plaster on her nose
You'll find true-love doesn't run so very smooth
When you have to wear those pawnshop clothes

4 So now, my boys, take my advice
And don't be in a hurry to wed
You'll think you're in clover till the honeymoon
And then you'll wish you were dead   [is over
When the rents are high and the children cry
For want of a hash to chew
He'll call on his son to load up his gun
And shoot his old mother-in-law

194 BARGAIN WITH ME

Where are you go-ing to, my boy, Bil-ly boy

Where are you go-ing, O, Bil-ly, me boy

Where are you go-ing, for ev-er-more, here be-low

Down in the mea-dows, so gay, so gay?

1 Where are you going to, my boy, Billy boy
Where are you going, O, Billy, me boy
Where are you going, for evermore, here below
Down in the meadows, so gay, so gay?
(Spoken) *I'm going to seek service, missus*

2 Then, bargain with me, O, my boy, Billy boy
Bargain with me, O, Billy, me boy
Bargain with me, for evermore, here below
Down in the meadows, so gay, so gay
What will 'ee give me, missus?

3 O dree pound and ten, O, my boy, Billy boy
Dree pound and ten, O, Billy (*etc.*)
Who shall I slape wi', missus?

4 O, slape with the chap, O, my boy, Billy boy
Slape with the chap, O, Billy (*etc.*)
He'll poke, missus

5 Then slape with the maid, O, my boy, Billy boy
Slape with the maid, O, Billy (*etc.*)
For shame, missus

6 Then slape with me, O, my boy, Billy boy
Slape with me, O, Billy (*etc.*)
Where's maister to, missus?

7 O, dead, O, dead, O, my boy, Billy boy
Dead, O, dead, O, Billy (*etc.*)
How long 'ave 'im been dead, missus?

8 O, seven long years, O, my boy, Billy boy
Seven long years, O, Billy (*etc.*)
Where was 'im buried to, missus?

9 Down yonder churchyard, O, my boy, Billy boy
Yonder churchyard, O, Billy (*etc.*)
Then I'll marry you, missus

195 THE BIRMINGHAM BOYS

In Bir-ming-ham town there lived a man And he had such a lov-e-ley wife
And so dear-ly she loved com-pa-ny As dear-ly as she loved her life, boys, life
As dear-ly as she loved her life

1 In Birmingham Town there lived a man
And he had such a lov-e-ley wife
And so dearly she loved company
As dearly as she loved her life, boys, life
As dearly as she loved her life

2 And this poor man he goes to sea
His living for to get
And where he spent one penny, she spent two
And it's all for the wants of wit, boys, wit
And it's all for the wants of wit

3 When this poor man came home from sea
It being late in the night
Enquiring for his own dear wife
Was his joy and his heart's delight, boys, light
Was his joy and his heart's delight

4 O she's just gone to her sister's O
Shall I go fetch her in?
Saying: O my dear, I will go myself
And ask myself to drink, boys, drink
And ask myself to drink

5 As he was a-going along the road
He heard such a dis-a-mal noise
And who should it be but his own dear wife
Along with the Birmingham boys, brave boys
Along with the Birmingham boys

6 So this poor man stood thinking
His heart was nearly broke
Then he went back and sent the maid
While he prepared a rope, boys, rope
While he prepared a rope

7 Then she came jumping, skipping in
Gave him such a joyful kiss
Saying: You're welcome home, kind husband dear
Long time you have been missed, boys, missed
Long time you have been missed

8 So we'll bar the door so neat and snug
And let us go to bed
For the pain that do lay in my breast
I can no longer rest, boys, rest
I can no longer rest

9 So he took a stick and he beat her so
Till she was wonderful sore
O forbear, forbear, she cried, husband dear
I'll never do so no more, no more
I'll never do so no more

10 For if you do I'll make you rue
And curse the hour you were born
For deceiving of your husband dear
I'll make you wear the horn, boys, horn
I'll make you wear the horn

11 So come all you women in Birmingham
And listen unto me
And don't you spend your money a-waste
When your husband is on the sea, boys, sea
When your husband is on the sea

196 THE CRAB-FISH

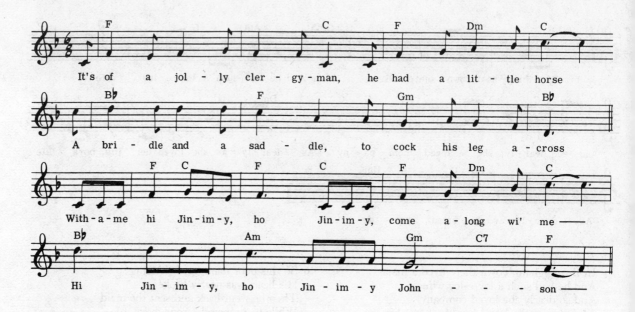

It's of a jol-ly cler-gy-man, he had a lit-tle horse

A bri-dle and a sad-dle, to cock his leg a-cross

With-a-me hi Jin-im-y, ho Jin-im-y, come a-long wi' me

Hi Jin-im-y, ho Jin-im-y John - - son

1 It's of a jolly clergyman, he had a little horse
A bridle and a saddle, to cock his leg across
With-a-me hi Jin-im-y, ho Jin-im-y, come along wi' me
Hi Jin-im-y, ho Jin-im-y Johnson

2 And as he was a-riding, a-riding by the brook
He saw a little man with a fishing-rod and hook

3 O fisherman, O fisherman, O fisherman, said he
Have you got a little crab-fish that you will sell
to me?

4 O yes sir, O yes sir, O yes sir, said he
The finest in the basket I will sell to thee

5 So he took the little crab-fish, he took him by the
horns
He slung him on his back and he toddles him off
home

6 But when he got it home, boys, he couldn't find a
dish
So he popped it in a pot, boys, that wasn't used for
fish

7 And when his wife got out of bed in the middle of
the night
The naughty little crab-fish it gave her such a bite

8 She shouted to her husband and quick-e-ly he arose
And the naughty little crab-fish it caught him by
the nose

9 It's: Husband, O husband, as sure as I was born
The devil's in the charlie, a-sticking up his horn

10 Wife, wife, wife, you must be going mad
That you don't know the devil from an old sea crab

11 Then one got a stick and t'other got a broom
And they chased the poor old crab-fish all around
the room

12 They kicked him on the head, they kicked him on
the side
They jumped upon his back, boys, until the poor
crab died

197 THE CUNNING COBBLER

1 This is just a little story but the truth I'm going to tell
It does concern a butcher who in Dover town did dwell
Now this butcher was possessed of a beautiful wife
But the cobbler he loved her as dearly as his life
Singing: fol-the-riddle-i-do
Fol-the-riddle-day

2 Now this butcher went to market for to buy an ox
And then the little cobbler, sly as any fox
'E put on his Sunday coat and courtin' he did go
To the jolly butcher's wife because 'e loved her so

3 Now when the little cobbler stepped into the butcher's shop
The butcher's wife knew what he meant and bade him for to stop
O, says he: Me darling, have you got a job for me?
The butcher's wife, so cunning, says: I'll go up and see

4 Now she went to the bedroom door and gave the snob a call:
I have got an easy job if you have brought your awl
And if you do it workmanlike some cash to you I'll pay
O thank you, said the cobbler, and began to stitch away →

453

5 But as the cobbler was at work a knock come on the door
  The cobbler scrambled out of bed and laid upon the floor
  O, said she, me darling, what will me husband say?
  But then she let the policeman in along with her to play

6 But the butcher came from market in the middle of the night
  The policeman scrambled out of bed and soon got out of sight
  The butcher's wife so nimbly locked the bedroom door
  But in her fright she quite forgot the cobbler on the floor

7 But the butcher soon found out when he laid down in bed
  Something here is very hard, the butcher smiled and said
  She says: It is me rolling pin, the butcher he did laugh
  How came you for to roll your dough with a policeman's staff?

8 Now the butcher threw the truncheon underneath the bed
  There he cracked the pepper-pot and hit the cobbler's head
  The cobbler cried out: Murder; said the butcher: Who are you?
  I am the little cobbler who goes mending ladies' shoes

9 If you are the little cobbler, come along with me
  I'll pay you for your mending before I've done with thee
  He put him in the bull-pen, the bull began to roar
  The butcher laughed to see the bull a-roll him o'er and o'er

10 Now early in the morning just as people got about
  The butcher mopped his face with blood, and then he turned him out
  He pinned a ticket to his back and on it was the news
  This cobbler to the bedroom goes, mending ladies' shoes

198 THE DESERTED HUSBAND

I'm as trou-bled a young man, my friends, as ev-er you did see —

Since I mar-ried this dam-sel, her age it was scarce twen-ty-three —

I'm sor-ry to say I mar-ried this false-mind-ed one —

For she left me a-lone and went off with an-oth-er young man —

1 I'm as troubled a young man, my friends, as ever you did see
   Since I married this damsel, her age it was scarce twenty-three
   I'm sorry to say I married this false-minded one
   For she left me alone and went off with another young man

2 The day we were wed, she said, I went on the spree
   A neighbour next door, she swore, was better than me
   He came in every night and stayed dancing till morning away
   And the pair left me there to fare the best that I may

3 Three months we were wed when this damsel I took her to town
   Expenses I paid, on the way I gave her a crown
   I met with a friend and he took me in for a drain
   And while we were there, the pair made off in the train

4 When I found she was gone, like a madman I rushed through the square
   Crying out: Ochone, and trying to tear out my hair
   A neighbour named Ned stuck out his head at the door
   Saying: Did your wife go away, will she ne'er come back any more?

5 I've an acre of land and a dandy fine pig and a cow
   A duck and a drake but no-one to take care of them now
   I'll sell them all out for now I am tired of my life
   And says each man to Dan: Go along and look for your wife

199 THE DUMB WIFE

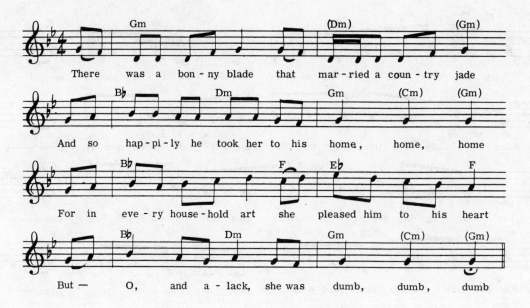

1 There was a bonny blade that married a country jade
And so happily he took her to his home, home, home
For in every household art she pleased him to his heart
But O, and alack, she was dumb, dumb, dumb

2 She could brew and she could bake, she could sew and she could make
She could sweep the house so clean with her broom, broom, broom
She could wash and she could wring and do any kind of thing
But still she complained she was dumb, dumb, dumb

3 To the doctor then he went for to give his wife content
Saying: Doctor, cure my wife of the mumb, mumb, mumb
O that's the easiest part that belongs unto my art
For to make a woman speak that is dumb, dumb, dumb

4 To the doctor he did her bring and they cut her clattering strings
And gave to her the liberty of her tongue, tongue, tongue
Her tongue began to sing and her clatter began to ring
And it sounded in his ears like a drum, drum, drum

5 To the doctor John did go for to see whether or no
He'd undo all the work that he'd done, done, done
For my wife she's turned a scold and with her tongue I cannot hold
I'd give you fifty pounds in gold to have her dumb, dumb, dumb

6 I did freely undertake for to make your wife to speak
'Twas a thing that was most easily done, done, done
But it's past the power of man, let him do whate'er he can
For to make a scolding wife hold her tongue, tongue, tongue

200 THE GAME-COCK

In fair Lon-don town a young dam-sel did dwell

With her wit and her beau-ty none could her ex-cel

Her wit and her beau-ty none could her ex-cel

And her hus-band he was a bold dro - ver

Fal - the - ral - loo - ral - i - day

1 In fair London town a young damsel did dwell
  With her wit and her beauty none could her excel
  Her wit and her beauty none could her excel
  And her husband he was a bold drover
  Fal-the-ral-looral-i-day

2 A groggy old tailor he liv-ed close by
  And all on the fair damsel he cast a sly eye
  Ten guineas I'll give if I can with you lay
  For your husband he is a bold drover

3 The bargain was made and upstairs they did run
  And they hopped into bed, soon the music begun
  They huddled, they cuddled, they both fell asleep
  And they never once thought of the drover

4 In the middle of the night the old drover returned
  And he knocked at the door with the palm of his hand
  O hide me, O hide me, the old tailor he cried
  For I hear the loud knock of the drover

5 There's a rustic old cupboard hangs over the door
  And it's there you can get in, so snug and secure
  Then I will go down and I'll undo the door
  And I'll let in my husband, the drover

6 She undone the door and her husband walked in
  With her kiss and her compliments she welcomed
                                                        him in
  Your kiss and your compliments now I don't give a
  I will strike up a light, said the drover   [pin

7 O husband, dear husband, there's no firestuff
  And if you come to bed, you'll be quite warm enough
  There's a rustic old cupboard hangs over the door
  And this night I will burn, said the drover

8 O husband, dear husband, now grant my desire
  For the cupboard is too good to be burned by the fire
  In it I've a game-cock I do so much admire
  Then I'll fight your game-cock, said the drover

9 So in half the old cupboard went down on the floor
  And he kicked it, he knocked, it went o'er and o'er
  Heels over lugs and right out of the door
  And away run the groggy old tailor

10 He knocked the old cupboard well down on the floor
   He kicked it, he knocked, it went o'er and o'er
   Heels over lugs and right out of the door
   And I've cooked your game-cock, said the drover

457

201 THE GERMAN MUSICIANER

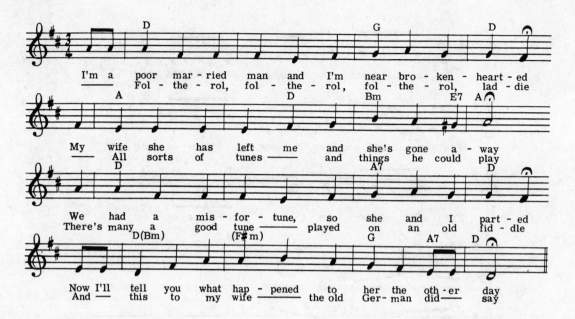

I'm a poor mar-ried man and I'm near bro-ken-heart-ed
Fol-the-rol, fol-the-rol, fol-the-rol, lad-die

My wife she has left me and she's gone a-way
All sorts of tunes and things he could play

We had a mis-for-tune, so she and I part-ed
There's many a good tune played on an old fid-dle

Now I'll tell you what hap-pened to her the oth-er day
And this to my wife the old Ger-man did say

1 I'm a poor married man and I'm near broken-hearted
My wife she has left me and she's gone away
We had a misfortune, so she and I parted
Now I'll tell you what happened to her the other day
Women are weak, they should mind their possessions
I think now with grief, mad me it will send
For she's gone away with a German Musicianer
Who goes about crying: Pianos to mend

Fol-the-rol, fol-the-rol, fol-the-rol, laddie
All sorts of tunes and things he could play
There's many a good tune played on an old fiddle
And this to my wife the old German did say

2 It happened one day this old German Musicianer
Came through our streets crying: Pianos to mend
My wife's piano being out of condition
Straightway the boy for the old German did send
He knocked at the door and he said most politely
I think, ma'am, it's here you are needing repairs
Please, ma'am, I've called to mend your piano
All right, said my wife: Will you please walk upstairs?

3 She took him upstairs, showed him her piano
And with the old German seemed greatly amused
And when he had seen it, he said to my Hannah
I think, ma'am, your music's not very much use
He touched it, he handled it, both over and under
Sharp as a needle, as light as a cork
With all sorts of tools he pulled it asunder
And rattled away with his old tuning fork

4 When I came home she told me the story
And said the old German had been there all day
He'd worked very hard to mend her piano
And do what she would he'd not taken her pay
I thought it was strange when she told me the story
And said the old German was ever so kind
Would you ever believe that this old German sausage
Before going away left his trade-mark behind?

5 I swore and I tore at my darling wife Hannah
With grief and with rage I'm sure no one can tell
I told her to hop it and take her piano
And likewise to take the old German as well
So come all young married men, don't take too much
For all women want is to handle your pilf   [spooning
So if ever your wife's piano wants tuning
Just take my tip, boys, and tune her yourself

202 GRAT FOR GRUEL

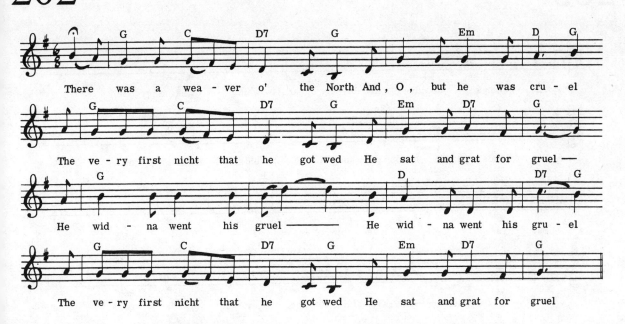

There was a wea-ver o' the North And, O, but he was cru-el

The ve-ry first nicht that he got wed He sat and grat for gruel —

He wid-na went his gruel ———— He wid-na went his gru-el

The ve-ry first nicht that he got wed He sat and grat for gruel

1 There was a weaver o' the North
And, O, but he was cruel
The very first nicht that he got wed
He sat and grat for gruel
He widna went his gruel
He widna went his gruel
The very first nicht that he got wed
He sat and grat for gruel

2 There is nae a pot in a' the hoose
That I can mak your gruel
O the washing pot it'll dae wi me
For I mun hae ma gruel
For I mun hae ma gruel
I canna went ma gruel
O the washing pot it'll dae wi me
For I mun hae ma gruel

3 There is nae a spoon in a' the hoose
That ye can sup your gruel
O the gairden spade it'll dae wi me
For I mun hae ma gruel
For I mun hae ma gruel
I canna went ma gruel
O the gairden spade it'll dae wi me
For I mun hae ma gruel

4 She gaed ben the hoose for cakes and wine
She brocht them on a truel
O gae awa, gae awa with your fol-de-rols
For I mun hae ma gruel
For I mun hae ma gruel
I canna went ma gruel
O gae awa, gae awa with your fol-de-rols
For I mun hae ma gruel

5 Come, all young lassies, tak' my advice
And never marry a weaver
The very first nicht that he got wed
He sat and grat for gruel
He widna went his gruel
He widna went his gruel
O the very first nicht that he got wed
He sat and grat for gruel

459

203 HE COMES DOWN OUR ALLEY

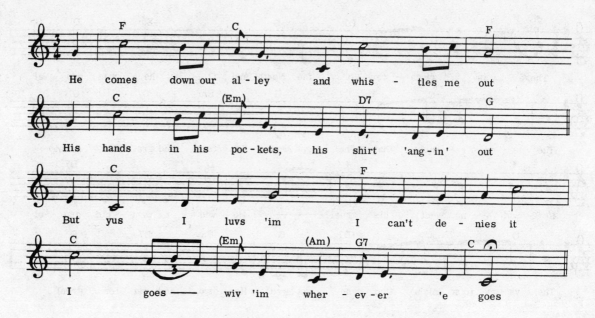

1 He comes down our alley and whistles me out
His hands in his pockets, his shirt 'angin' out
But yus I luvs 'im
I can't denies it
I goes wiv 'im
Wher'ever 'e goes

2 He bought me an 'ankerchief, red white and blue
Outside the pawnshop 'e tore it in two

3 O I like an apple and I like a pear
And I like a feller with nice curly hair

4 'E took me to the public and ordered me stout
Before I could drink it, 'e'd ordered me out

5 Before we was married, we 'ad lots o' quids
But now that we's married, we got lots o' kids

204 I WISHED TO BE SINGLE AGAIN

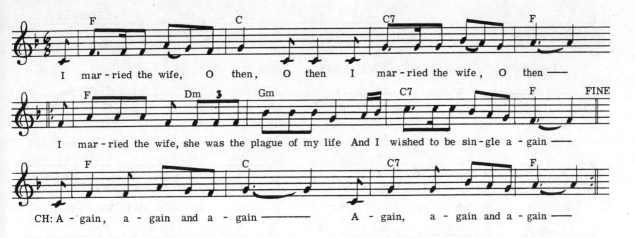

I married the wife, O then, O then I married the wife, O then —

I married the wife, she was the plague of my life And I wished to be single again —

CH: A-gain, a-gain and a-gain —— A-gain, a-gain and a-gain ——

1 I married the wife, O then, O then
I married the wife, O then
I married the wife, she was the plague of my life
And I wished to be single again

Again, again and again
Again, again and again
I married the wife, she was the plague of my life
And I wished to be single again

2 O when I was single, O then, O then
O when I was single, O then
O when I was single, my pockets did jingle
And the world it went merrily then

3 My wife took a fever, O then, O then
My wife took a fever, O then
My wife took a fever, I hope it won't leave her
For I long to be single again

4 My wife she died, O then, O then
My wife she died, O then
My wife she died and I laughed till I cried
I was glad to be single again

5 I went to the funeral then, O then
I went to the funeral then
The band did play and I danced all the way
For joy to be single again

6 I walked from the grave-side, O then, O then
I walked from the grave-side, O then
I walked from the grave-side and saw a maid pass by
And I wished to be married again

7 I married another, O then, O then
I married another, O then
I married another, she was worse than the other
And I longed for the old one again

8 Now all you old men who have wives, O then
And all you young men who have none
Be kind to the first for the next will be worse
And you'll long for the old one again

Again, again and again
Again, again and again
Be kind to the first or the next will be worse
And you'll long for the old one again

205 THE LINEN SONG

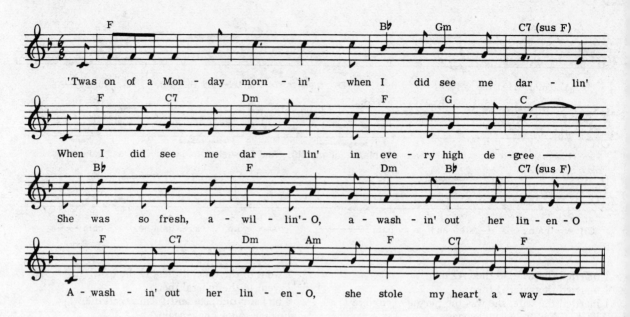

'Twas on of a Mon - day morn - in' when I did see me dar - lin'

When I did see me dar ——— lin' in eve - ry high de -gree ———

She was so fresh, a - wil - lin'- O, a - wash - in' out her lin - en - O

A - wash - in' out her lin - en - O, she stole my heart a - way ———

1 'Twas on of a Monday mornin' when I did see me darlin'
   When I did see me darlin' in every high degree
   She was so fresh, a-willin'-O, a-washin' out her linen-O
   A-washin' out her linen-O, she stole my heart away

2 'Twas on of a Tuesday mornin' when I did see me darlin'
   When I did see me darlin' in every high degree
   She was so fresh, a-willin'-O, a-wringin' out her linen-O
   A-wringin' out her linen-O, she stole my heart away

3 'Twas on of a Wednesday mornin' when I did see me darlin'
   When I did see me darlin' in every high degree
   She was so fresh, a-willin'-O, a-dampin' down her linen-O
   A-dampin' down her linen-O, she stole my heart away

4 'Twas on of a Thursday mornin' when I did see me darlin'
   When I did see me darlin' in every high degree
   She was so fresh, a-willin'-O, an-ironin' out her linen-O
   A-ironin' out her linen-O, she stole my heart away

5 'Twas on of a Friday morning when I did see me darlin'
   When I did see me darlin' in every high degree
   She was so fresh, a-willin'-O, a-foldin' up her linen-O
   A-foldin' up her linen-O, she stole my heart away

6 'Twas on of a Saturday mornin' when I did see me darlin'
   When I did see me darlin' in every high degree
   She was so fresh, a-willin'-O, an-airin' out her linen-O
   An-airin' out her linen-O, she stole my heart away

7 'Twas on of a Sunday mornin' when I did see me darlin'
   When I did see me darlin' in every high degree
   She was so fresh, a-willin'-O, a-wearin' all her linen-O
   A-wearin' all her linen-O, she stole my heart away

206 THE MOLE-CATCHER

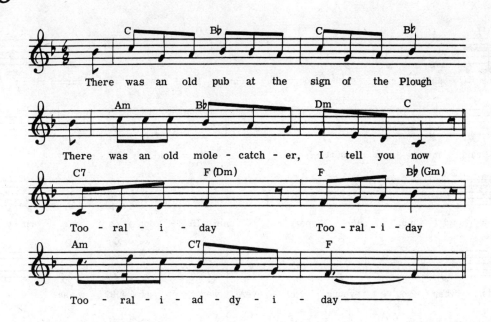

There was an old pub at the sign of the Plough
There was an old mole-catch-er, I tell you now
Too-ral-i-day   Too-ral-i-day
Too-ral-i-ad-dy-i-day

1 There was an old pub at the sign of the Plough
There was an old mole-catcher, I tell you now
Too-ral-i-day
Too-ral-i-day
Too-ral-i-addy-i-day

2 He had an old wife, she was buxom and gay
And she and another young farmer would play

3 The mole-catcher jealous of the very same thing
He stood in the brewhouse and watched 'em go in

4 To see the young farmer nip over the stile
It caused the mole-catcher to give such a smile

5 He knocked at the door and it's thus he did say
O where is your husband, good woman, I pray?

6 He's catching of moles, you need have no fear
So little she thought the mole-catcher was there

7 She went up the stairs and she give him the sign
The mole-catcher smiling he followed behind

8 When the young farmer was at the top of his sport
The mole-catcher came in and caught hold of his coat

9 You villain, he cried, what have you been at?
I think I have caught you in my old mole-trap

10 I'll make you pay dearly for tilling my ground
And the sum of the money shall be ten pound down

11 Ten pound, laughed the farmer, O sure I don't mind
For that won't amount t'above tuppence a time

12 So come all you young fellows and mind what
you're at
For fear you'll get caught in a mole-catcher's trap

207 NEVER WED A' AULD MAN

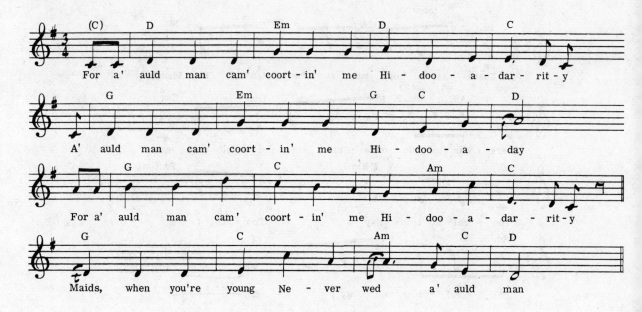

For a' auld man cam' coort-in' me Hi-doo-a-dar-rit-y
A' auld man cam' coort-in' me Hi-doo-a-day
For a' auld man cam' coort-in' me Hi-doo-a-dar-rit-y
Maids, when you're young Ne-ver wed a' auld man

1 For a' auld man cam' coortin' me
Hi-doo-a-darrity
A' auld man cam' coortin' me
Hi-doo-a-day
For a' auld man cam' coortin' me
Hi-doo-a-darrity
Maids, when you're young
Never wed a' auld man

2 For when we went to the church
I left him in the lurch
When we went to the church
Me being young
When we went to the church
I left him in the lurch

3 For when we went to owr tea
He started teasin' me
When we went to owr tea
Me being young
When we went to owr tea
He started teasin' me

4 When we went to owr bed
He lay as he was dead
When we went to owr bed
Me being young
When we went to owr bed
He lay as he was dead

208 THE OLD WOMAN OF BLIGHTER TOWN

There was an old wo-man of Bligh-ter Town In Bligh-ter Town did dwell —

She lov-ed her old man dear-ly — But an-oth-er man twice as well —

Sing: Tit-ty-fol-ol, sing: Tit-ty-fol-ol Sing: Tit-ty-fol-ol — ri — tay —

Ri-tit-ty-fol-ol — ri-tit-ty-fol-ol Ri-tit-ty-fol-ol — ri — tay —

1 There was an old woman of Blighter Town
In Blighter Town did dwell
She lov-ed her old man dearly
But another man twice as well
Sing: Titty-fol-ol, sing: Titty-fol-ol
Sing: Titty-fol-ol-ri-tay
Ri-titty-fol-ol-ri-titty-fol-ol
Ri-titty-fol-ol-ri-tay

2 She went unto a doctor's shop
A doctor's shop so fine
Can you tell me the very best thing
That'll drive me old man blind?

3 He told her to get some marrowbones
And scrape them fine and small
And rub it in her old man's eyes
Till he can't see at all

4 The old man he being cunning and crafty
And up to those tricks before
He took one of those marrowbones
Saying: I can't see you at all

5 Early the next morning
Before the break of day
He said: Dear wife, I'll drown myself
If you'll show me the way

6 She took him to the riverside
And led him to the brim
He said: Dear wife, get back a pace
And push me headlong in

7 The old woman got back a pace or two
And took a race at him
The old man he popped a little one side
Headlong the old woman went in

8 She was up to her neck in water, boys
And loudly she did bawl
He put his hands all over his eyes
Saying: I can't see thee at all

9 The old woman she did squabble about
And nearly reached the brim
The old man took a girt long pole
And pushed her further in

10 Now my song is ended
And, gentlemen, don't you think
Bain't I a very good singer
And don't I deserve a drink?

465

209 THE ONE THING OR THE OTHER

1 At the age of twenty-one, I was in the prime of life
Me mother often told me to go and choose a wife
To go and choose a wife, I knew little about the bother
At the same time I was thinking on the one thing or the other
Mush-a-whack-a-row-di-dow-now
Right-fol-di-daddy
Mush-a-whack-a-row-di-dow-now
Right-fol-di-dee

2 I went to a wee girl that I for sometime knew
To tell her what me mother was advising me to do
What d'you earn? cries the sister; What d'you earn? cries the mother
And to cut the story short, says I: It's the one thing or the other

3 Now we have got married, we lead a happy life
I'm her loving husband, and she's my loving wife
We live in peace and unity, right well content together
In our daily occupation at the one thing or the other

4 A year passed away, and we never knew a care
But now the people say that we're going to have an heir
It's a son, cries the sister; It's a daughter, cries the mother
And to cut the story short, says I: It's the one thing or the other

5 'Twas on a Monday morning, just as me story runs
'Twas on a Monday morning, when first I heard the twins
It was on a Monday morning my grief I couldn't smother
As I listened to the squalling of the one thing and the other

210 THE POOR AULD MAID

In a lone-ly gar-ret an — auld maid sat

Wi' her can-dle burn-ing — dim

While stretch-ed at her feet lay an auld tam cat

As grey — as Meth-u-sa-lem

1 In a lonely garret an auld maid sat
Wi' her candle burning dim
While stretched at her feet lay an auld tam cat
As grey as Methusalem

2 The wintry winds they ravage and roar
The trees they crack and mourn
While this poor maid stretched oot on the floor
And sang in a dolorous tone

3 No gentle tap ever comes tae my door
Nor a kindly hand to caress
Nor ever a footstep crosses me floor
Tae lighten me loneliness

4 The time passes by with the clock's dull tick
And the wearisome purr of the cat
It seems that I've lived since the ark came down
On the top of Mount Ararat

5 My cheeks are growing grizzled and my hair's turn-
And the sight of my eyes nearly spent   [ing grey
And my chance of getting wed it's as far far away
As the stars in the firmament

6 Come all you that cling to your true-lovers' arms
Take warning by what I have said
For the lonie-somest life in a' this world
Is the life of a poor auld maid

211 RAP-TAP-TAP

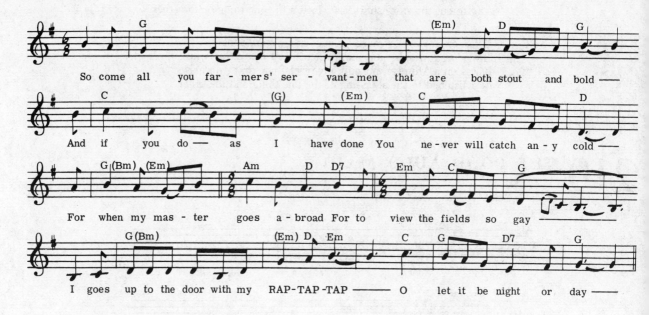

So come all you far-mers' ser-vant-men that are both stout and bold —

And if you do — as I have done You ne-ver will catch an-y cold —

For when my mas-ter goes a-broad For to view the fields so gay —

I goes up to the door with my RAP-TAP-TAP —— O let it be night or day ——

1 So come all you farmers' servant-men
That are both stout and bold
And if you do as I have done
You never will catch any cold
For when my master goes abroad
For to view the fields so gay
I goes up to the door with my *rap-tap-tap*
O let it be night or day

2 'Twas every Thursday afternoon
My master to market did go
He asked me to mind his bus-i-ness
As servants always do
As soon as my master's back was turned
I went toddling out of the barn
I went up to the door with my *rap-tap-tap*
For sure I thought no harm

3 O no harm at all, my mistress said
And she asked me to go in
When I complained of the belly-ache
She gave to me some gin
I took it and I drank it down
But not a word did I say
For I thought I would come with my *rap-tap-tap*
So upstairs we went straightway

4 O there we lay in sport and play
For half an hour or more
My mistress she was so fond of the sport
I thought she'd never give o'er
O you've won my heart for ever, Jack
Your master's no man for me
For he can't come with his *rap-tap-tap*
Not half so well as thee

5 So when my master did come home
O he asked me what I had done
I told him I'd minded his bus-i-ness
Just as well as if he was at home
He gave to me some beer to drink
But not a word did he know
That I'd been there with my *rap-tap-tap*
If he had he'd a never done so

212 ROCKING THE CRADLE

It was the oth-er night, sure, I chanced to go ro-ving —

Down by the clear ri-ver I jog-ged a-long —

I — heard an old man mak-ing sad lam-en-ta-tion —

A-bout rock-ing the cra-dle and the child not his own —

Hi — ho, hi-ho, my lad-die, lie ai-sy —

For per-haps your own dad-dy might ne-ver be known —

I'm see-in' and sigh-in' and rock-in' the cra-dle —

And nurs-in' the bab-bie that's none of my own —

1 It was the other night, sure, I chanced to go roving
Down by the clear river I jog-ged along
I heard an old man making sad lamentation
About rocking the cradle and the child not his own

Hi-ho, hi-ho, my laddie, lie aisy
For perhaps your own daddy might never be known
I'm seein' and sighin' and rockin' the cradle
And nursin' the babbie that's none of my own

2 When first that I married your inconstant mother
I thought myself happy to be blessed with a wife
But for my misfortune, sure I was mistaken
She proved both a curse and a plague on my life

3 She goes out every night to a ball or a party
And leaves me here rockin' the cradle halone
The innocent laddie he calls me his daddie
But little he knows that he's none of me own

4 Now come all you young men that's inclined to get married
Now take my advice and let the wee-men halone
For by the law Harry, if ever you marry
They'll give you a bab-bie and swear it's your own

469

213 RUE THE DAY

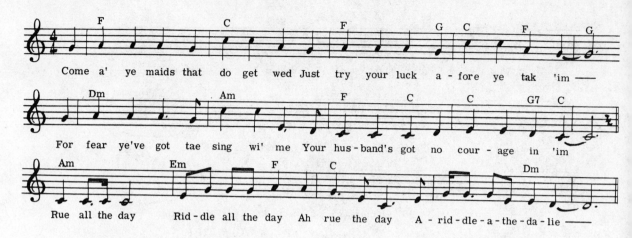

Come a' ye maids that do get wed Just try your luck a-fore ye tak' 'im —
For fear ye've got tae sing wi' me Your hus-band's got no cour-age in 'im
Rue all the day Rid-dle all the day Ah rue the day A-rid-dle-a-the-da-lie —

1 Come a' ye maids that do get wed
Just try your luck afore ye tak' im
For fear ye've got tae sing wi' me
Your husband's got no courage in 'im
Rue all the day
Riddle all the day
Ah rue the day
A-riddle-a-the-da-lie

2 Seiven lang years I've made his bed
An' sax o' them I've lain aside 'im
But afore I lie sae lang again
I'd burn the bed frae a' aboot 'im

3 All kinds o' food it's he has got
All kinds o' meat's been provided for 'im
Fae the oyster pie tae the ile o' rue
But naethin' wid pit courage in 'im

4 Wi' my twa een I winkit at 'im
Wi' my twa knees I patit at 'im
Wi' the nails o' ma taes I scratcht 'is shins
But naethin' wid pit courage in 'im

5 Wi' a' ma hairt I wish 'im dead
An' in 'is coffin I'd quickly lay 'im
An' then I'd try anither instead
That the neist may have mair courage in 'im

214 THE SCOLDING WIFE

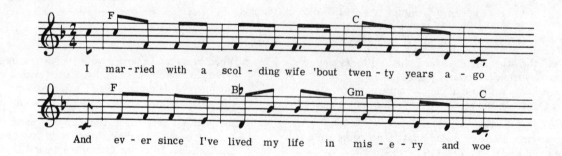

I mar-ried with a scol-ding wife 'bout twen-ty years a-go
And ev-er since I've lived my life in mis-e-ry and woe

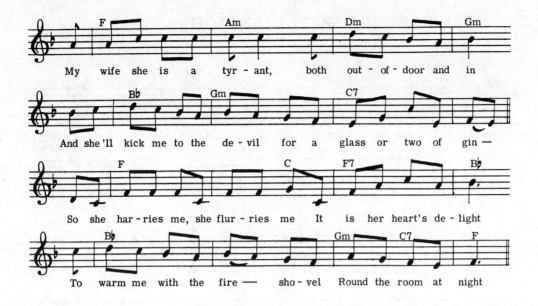

My wife she is a tyr - ant, both out - of - door and in

And she'll kick me to the de - vil for a glass or two of gin —

So she har - ries me, she flur - ries me It is her heart's de - light

To warm me with the fire — sho - vel Round the room at night

1 I married with a scolding wife 'bout twenty years ago
And ever since I've lived my life in misery and woe
My wife she is a tyrant, both out-of-door and in
And she'll kick me to the devil for a glass or two of gin

So she harries me, she flurries me
It is her heart's delight
To warm me with the fire-shovel
Round the room at night

2 When her gets up in the morning, she walks out to take a dram
While I dress myself and go to work, as quiet as any lamb
I dare not for to grumble, nor neither for to groan
For I know well the moment I tell, it's the poker when I come home

3 When I come home at tea-time, with patience I must stop
While she does drink her cup of tea, I must drink the slop
She'll eat cake and biscuits, and for me it's stale bread
And if I make to mention, then she gives me the aching head

4 O ten o'clock each evening, when I'm just going to bed
'Tisn't five minutes on the pillow that I do lay my head
When in there pops her wagsman and he open makes the door
He kicks me out the bedroom and I lie on the floor

5 If I had a hundred sovereigns, I would give them with goodwill
To put my wife away twelve months upon the treading-mill
And if the devil would but take her, I'd thank him for his pains
So it's hang me in my garters before I wed again

215 THE WEARING OF THE BRITCHES

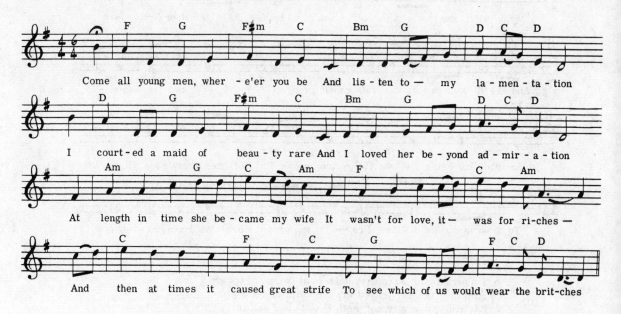

Come all young men, wher-e'er you be And lis-ten to— my la-men-ta-tion

I court-ed a maid of beau-ty rare And I loved her be-yond ad-mir-a-tion

At length in time she be-came my wife It wasn't for love, it— was for ri-ches—

And then at times it caused great strife To see which of us would wear the brit-ches

1 Come all young men, wher-e'er you be
And listen to my lamentation
I courted a maid of beauty rare
And I loved her beyond admiration
At length in time she became my wife
It wasn't for love, it was for riches
And then at times it caused great strife
To see which of us would wear the britches

2 O Paddy Keane it is my name
My height it is five foot eleven
And my wife she is not so big
She only measures four foot seven
How often we do fight and bawl
With nothing going but rogues and witches
Her head comes often to the wall
But still she swears she'll wear the britches

3 I am a tailor to my trade
At cutting-out I am quite handy
And all the money that I earn
She lives it out on tay and brandy
The hedges I have nearly stripped
I've left them short of rods and switches
Her hide with blows I have left black
But still she swears she'll wear the britches

4 And if I go to seek some friend
Or to the ale-house for a noggin
My drunken wife she follows me
Swearin', cursin', like a dragon
She yells: Come home, you drunken sot
And don't go spending all our riches
For to protect what you have got
I will show who wears the britches

5 One morning at the tay and eggs
Contented sitting by the fire
She threw the tay-pot at me legs
She made me lape and then retire
How often I do sigh and moan
I may go hobbling on my critches
I wish I'd broken me collar-bone
The day I let her wear my britches

6 One day my wife was taken ill
'Twas seven weeks before she snuffed it
I pretended to be very sad
I sighed and cried but only bluffed it
And now she's dead and laid to rest
She'll break no plates or cups or dishes
For now at last her tongue lies still
And she must wear the wooden britches

7 So now young men, wher-e'er you be
Ne'er marry a maid if she's enchanting
For if you do, when she is young
With the young men she'll be gallivanting
Now my advice to any young man
Is to marry for love and work for riches
If you can't get a girl with a civil tongue
That'll give you l'ave to wear your britches

472

216 YOUNG AND GROWING

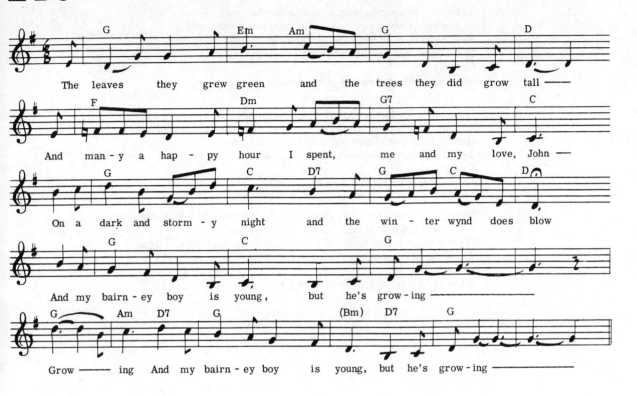

The leaves they grew green and the trees they did grow tall —

And man-y a hap-py hour I spent, me and my love, John —

On a dark and storm-y night and the win-ter wynd does blow

And my bairn-ey boy is young, but he's grow-ing —

Grow — ing And my bairn-ey boy is young, but he's grow-ing —

1 The leaves they grew green and the trees they did grow tall
And many a happy hour I spent, me and my love, John
On a dark and stormy night and the winter wynd does blow
And my bairney boy is young, but he's growing
Growing
And my bairney boy is young, but he's growing

2 O father, dear father, you've done to me what's wrong
You've married me to this bonny boy and I fear he's rather young
His age is sixteen, aye, and I am twenty-one
Ah my bairney boy is young, but he's growing
Growing
Ah my bairney boy is young, but he's growing

3 O daughter, dear daughter, don't mind what people say
For he will be a man to you, when you are old and grey
He will be a man to you when I am dead and gone
He's your bairney boy, he's young, but he's growing
Growing
He's your bairney boy, he's young, but he's growing

4 As I strolled out one evening down by the college wall
I saw four and twenty college boys all playing at bat and ball
It's there I spied my own love John, the fairest of them all
He's my bairney boy, he's young, but he's growing
Growing
He's my bairney boy, he's young, but he's growing

5 At the age of sixteen, sure, he was a married man
At the age of seventeen he was the father of a son
At the age of eighteen, sure, the grass grew over his grave
Cruel death has put an end to his growing
Growing
Cruel death has put an end to his growing

6 O we made for him a shroud which was made with green and gold
And while we was a-making it, sure, the tears they did downflow
Once'd I'd a sweetheart but now I have got none
And we'll rear up his son while he's growing
Growing
And we'll rear up his son while he's growing

7 So come all you pretty fair young maids a warning take from me
And never build your nest in the top of any tree
For the green leaves they will wither and the roots they will decay
While the blushes of your bairney boy are fading
Fading
While the blushes of your bairney boy are fading

193 THE BALD-HEADED END OF THE BROOM

Martha Gillen, Antrim, N. Ireland, *rec.* S. O'Boyle and
S. Ennis, 1954: BBC 21839

Other recorded version
Lee Monroe Presnell, North Carolina: FOLK LEGACY
FSA 23

> When the rents are high and the children cry
> For want of a hash to chew
> He'll call on his son to load up his gun
> And shoot his old mother-in-law

Songs about uneasy wedlock are no doubt popular for two reasons: firstly to act as a safety valve for the problems of the married, and secondly to act as a warning to youngsters to put off 'the day' as long as it is practicable. Our first song seems to combine both these aspects. It starts with a verse stating that true-love is blind, then paints the picture of a wife and sixteen half-starved children and the butcher coming round to collect his bill. It ends with the warning: 'don't be in a hurry to wed'.

194 BARGAIN WITH ME

Dicky Lashbrook, Kelly, Lifton, Devon, *rec.* P. Kennedy,
1950: BBC 17796 (1952): *Billy Boy*
Other recorded version
Duncan McPhee, Blairgowrie, Perthshire, Scotland:
Tam Buie (tune: *The Campbells Are Coming*), *rec.* H.
Henderson and P. Kennedy, 1955

Printed versions
BUCHAN: 1828, vol. II, p. 241: *O Faer ye Gaun Will Boy?* (tune: *Laird o' Cockpen*)
DUNCAN MS: *The Rigwiddy Carlin* (tune: *Kenmure's On and Awa*)
GARDINER MS: 1907, No. 946: *The Hiring Song* (Hants)
HENRY: 1924, No. 478: *Magherafelt Hiring Fair* (*Tam Bo*)
JEFDSS: 1966, p. 78: Duncan version

1 Crying: Fee wi me, Tam Buie, Tam Buie
Fee wi me, wi ma heart to my joy
Fee wi me, wi ma heart to my joy
And sic a wanton poor widow was I
(*spoken*) What's the pay, you ol' bitch?

2 Twenty broad shillings. . . .
(*spoken*) What's for tea, you ol' bitch?

3 Tea an' toast. . . .
(*spoken*) What's for supper, you ol' whore?

4 Porridge and milk. . . .
(*spoken*) Wha'll I sleep you ol' bitch

5 Why, ye can sleep wi' the bairnies. . . .
(*spoken*) Ach no, they'll piss on the tail o' my shirt

6 Why, ye can sleep wi' mysel'
(*spoken*) You han't got a big enough. . . .

7 Why, six inches'll do. . . . etc.

Nineteen-year-old Duncan McPhee had to be held over a camp fire and roasted by a crowd of his young tinker friends before he would sing his version of the song to *The Campbells Are Coming* tune. His father had first heard it at a 'peats-cutting' at Tomintoul in Banffshire.

In a Northern Ireland version the wages are higher, the diet different and the comforts of 'a loft full of rats' are offered. The mistress gives the hireling little alternative:

1 Would you hire with me, Tam Bo?
(*spoken*) What wages, mistress?

2 Two pounds five. . . .
(*spoken*) Too little wages, mistress

3 Then two pounds ten. . . .
(*spoken*) What diet, mistress?

4 Sowans and eels. . . .
(*spoken*) Too slippy diet, mistress

5 Then potatoes and beef. . . .
(*spoken*) Where will I lie, mistress?

6 You'll lie in the loft. . . .
(*spoken*) The rats might eat me, mistress

7 You'll lie wi the weans. . . .
(*spoken*) The weans might kick me, mistress
etc.

The first publication of the song, as far as we know, is in Peter Buchan's *Ancient Ballads and Songs of the North of Scotland* in 1828, sung to the tune of *The Laird o' Cockpen*, but one would suspect that it goes back at least a hundred years before that, if not two hundred. It is the type of dialogue song that was popular in the seventeenth century. A very similar type of dialogue with spoken responses is the song, *The Good Old Man*.

195 THE BIRMINGHAM BOYS

Harry Cox, Catfield, Norfolk, *rec.* P. Kennedy, 1953:
  BBC 21481: *The Burningham Boys*

Printed versions
SHARP MS: 1904: *There Was a Man in Dover* (Somerset)
HAMMOND MS: 1905–7: three variants (Dorset), one
  variant: *The Man of Dover* (Somerset)

JFSS: 1910, No. 15, p. 85: *coll.* Vaughan Williams,
  Norfolk
JFSS: 1922, No. 26, p. 8: *In Burnham Town*, *coll.*
  Moeran from Harry Cox
PURSLOW: 1968, p. 74: *coll.* Hammond (Dorset)

Come all you girls in Birmingham Town
A warning take by me
And never spend your husband's money
While he's away at sea, boys, sea
While he's away at sea

For if you do they'll make you rue
And curse the hour you were born
For cuckolding of your husbands dear
They'll make you wear the horns, boys, horns
They'll make you wear the horns

These are the last two warning verses from Harry Cox. He sang 'in Burnham Town', but he was quite ready to agree that the town meant Birmingham because, as he said, the things that happen in the song would only happen in a big city like that. However, there are four Burnhams in Norfolk: Burnham Overy, Burnham Norton, Burnham Thorpe (where Nelson was born) and Burnham Market. Burnham Market was once an important town but now it is a small village, situated on the most northerly stretch of Norfolk coast between Hunstanton and Wells.

196 THE CRAB-FISH

Harry Cox, Catfield, Norfolk, *rec.* P. Kennedy, 1952
Printed versions
Bishop Percy *Folio*, c. 1620–50, vol. 4: *The Sea Crabbe*
SHARPE: 1823, Part 2, p. 10: *The Crab* (Scots version); a
  footnote says the song is founded on the story *Le
  Moyen de Parvenir*

SHARP MS: 1904–21: two variants (Somerset)
JFSS: 1905, No. 6, p. 28: *coll.* Sharp, Langport,
  Somerset: five verses only
SHARP AND MARSON: 1906, vol. III, No. 59: journal
  version edited; note the remarks on emphatic gestures
  made by the singer

We have a written record of this song in the seventeenth century, and it is still popular in all-male communities when occasions are ripe for bawdy songs. It appeared in Bishop Percy's *Folio Manuscript* in 1620, but because of English prudery it has not appeared since in print. John Masefield drew attention to its existence when he was working on sea songs in 1906.

Like other ballads of the 'mal-mariée' type, such as *The Cunning Cobbler* (No. 197) and *The Game-Cock* (No. 200), it seems likely to be either French in origin or in imitation of French balladry (at any rate this is a chance to disown it as an English composition). Gershon Legman has drawn attention to similar sea-crab themes in prose-tales which appear in several collections of the seventeenth century. They always end too with what he calls 'vagina dentata', the clutching of the wife's pubis and the husband's nose (Antoine d'Ouville: *L'Elite des Contes*, Rouen, 1680; Jouaust's reprint, Paris, vol. I, p. 181).

The final verses which are sung at the Eels Foot, Leiston, Suffolk are:

I started with a song and I finished with a ditty
There was a baby born he'd a crabfish on his titty

Now I've finished with my story although it was sad
This was the end of that poor old crab

197 THE CUNNING COBBLER

George Spicer, Copthorne, Sussex, *rec.* P. Kennedy,
  1956: BBC 23093: *Folk Songs of Britain*, vol. II,
  CAEDMON TC1143/TOPIC 12T158

Other recorded version
Alec Bloomfield, Framlingham, Suffolk, *rec.* P. Kennedy,
  1952

Printed versions
JFSS: 1906, No. 8, p. 156: *The Cobbler*, *coll.* R. Vaughan
  Williams (Essex)
JFSS: 1909, No. 13, p. 253: two versions, *coll.* G.
  Gardiner (Hampshire)
PINTO AND RODWAY: 1957, No. 176, p. 459: from a
  Nottingham broadside
PURSLOW: 1972, p. 15: *The Cobbler and the Butcher*, *coll.*
  Gardiner

(*spoken*) Come gather round my merry lads a tale to you I'll tell
(*sung*)   Concerning of a butcher who in London town did dwell

George Spicer always starts this song by speaking the first line and then going into song by the time the second is reached. His Kent version, of course, has Dover as the town, but other versions favour London.

Vaughan Williams, in submitting this song to the JFSS, remarked on its modernity, because it introduces a police-man, and says, 'It is a modern example of the kind of rough fun which we find in Chaucer's "Clerk of Oxenforde".'
An extra verse can be sung between verses five and six:

> The cobbler lay a-shivering and was frightened for to move
> The butcher's wife said: O my dear, my darling and my love
> Thought the cobbler how he'd treat her if she was his own wife
> O I really think the bed will fall, I fear upon my life

Alec Bloomfield begins verse six as follows:

> A rap-a-tat come at the door, it put them in a fright
> The policeman scrambled down the stairs and soon was out of sight

And he has an extra verse at the end:

> Now the people they got frightened to see the cobbler run
> His coat and breeches were so torn he nearly showed his bum
> He ran so fast he hit his wife he knocked her on the floor
> He swore to her he wasn't going a-mending any more

198 THE DESERTED HUSBAND

Seamus Ennis, Dublin, Ireland, *rec.* P. Kennedy, 1958
The Deserted Wife, rec. 1949: BBC 13768

> I'm sorry to say I married this false-minded one
> For she left me alone and went off with another young man

The Irish Gaelic tradition of internal assonantal rhyme is maintained in this English song from Ireland. It is sung in a speaking voice, each phrase being recited in a short sharp burst with pauses between them.
This song of the deserting young wife, or the deserted husband, is somewhat unusual. The tradition of British love songs is that it is generally the husband who leaves the girl in the lurch. Perhaps the whole point of this song is its comic reversal or parody on the usual ballad of masculine unfaithfulness.

199 THE DUMB WIFE

Billy Wells, Bampton, Oxfordshire, *rec.* P. Kennedy, 1952

Other recorded versions
Willie Mathieson, Turriff, Aberdeenshire, *rec.* A. Lomax, 1951
Frank McPeake, Belfast, N. Ireland, *rec.* P. Kennedy, 1952

Printed versions
D'URFEY: 1698–1720: vol. III, p. 276: *There Was A Bonny Blade*
CHAPPELL: 1858–9, p. 120: *I Am The Duke of Norfolk*
FORD: 1899, p. 30 (Perthshire, Scotland): has a note about earlier versions in the Maitland MSS in the Pepysian Library and University of Cambridge Library

JOYCE: 1909, p. 196: *Dumb, Dumb, Dumb* (Ireland)
GREIG: 1914, vol. II, xiii
EDDY: 1939, p. 214 (Ohio, USA)
RANDOLPH: 1946–50, vol. III, p. 119 (Missouri, USA)
KORSON: 1949, p. 56 (Pennsylvania, USA)
MORRIS: 1950, p. 380: two variants (Florida, USA)
BROWN: 1952, p. 453: two variants (N. Carolina, USA)
SFLQ: vol. V, p. 181 (Indiana, USA)
JAFL: No. 57, p. 282: variant reprinted (Indiana, USA)
JAFL: No. 62, p. 62 (Pennsylvania, USA)
JAFL: No. 66, p. 48: for references (New York, USA)

> Now the best advice I could give, let her die or let her live
> Is to get the oil of hazel that is *strong, strong, strong*
> And every time she frowns, give her a good dressing down
> That will make a scolding woman hold her *damn long tongue*

This was the last verse which used to be sung by Shepherd Hayden at Bampton, from whom Billy Wells probably learned his version of the song.
'Jinkey' Wells, who died in 1953, was Dancer, Fiddler and Fool for The Morris Dancers of Bampton-in-the-Bush. A tribute to him together with transcriptions of him playing and talking can be found in JEFDSS: 1956, pp. 1–15.

200 THE GAME-COCK

Harry Cox, Catfield, Norfolk, *rec.* P. Kennedy, 1956:
DTS LFX 4 and BBC 22914: *The Groggy Old Tailor*

Other recorded versions
Charlie Chettleburgh, Winterton, Norfolk, 1947: *The Bold Drover*
Frank Cole, North Waltham, Basingstoke, Hampshire, *rec.* R. Copper, 1955

Printed versions
BARING GOULD MS: 1889: *The Bold Trooper* (Devon)
JFSS: 1931, No. 35, p. 274: *The Groggy Old Tailor*, coll. E. J. Moeran, Norfolk, from Charlie Chettleburgh
PURSLOW: 1965, p. 6: *The Bold Trooper*, coll. G. Gardiner, Hampshire
PEACOCK: 1965, p. 243: *Bold Trooper* (Canada)

> O husband, dear husband, now grant my desire
> For the cupboard is too good to be burned by the fire
> In it I've a game-cock I do so much admire
> Then I'll fight your game-cock said the drover

Cobblers and tailors have the worst reputation for getting into married ladies' bedrooms, but in the songs they get discovered. In this song it is a 'groggy old tailor' who pays ten guineas for his pleasure, and the lady's husband is a bold drover. In the Hampshire version collected by George Gardiner he is a bold trooper and gets his revenge on the tailor by taking the tailor's scissors from his pocket and cutting off his ears. This is additional payment for his night's lodging:

> He put his hand in his pocket and pulled out his shears
> And off on the table he cut his two ears
> Saying, for my night's lodging I've paid very dear
> And away ran the poor croppy tailor

201 THE GERMAN MUSICIANER

Harry Cox, Catfield, Norfolk, *rec.* P. Kennedy, 1956:
DTS LFX 4 (1965)

Compare
Thomas Moran, Co. Leitrim, Ireland, *rec.* S. Ennis, 1954: *The Wonderful German Musician*
Charlie Wills, Morcombelake, Dorset, *rec.* P. Kennedy, 1954: *The German Clockmaker*

> Fol-the-rol, fol-the-rol, fol-the-rol, laddie
> All sorts of tunes and things he could play
> There's many a good tune played on an old fiddle
> And this to my wife the Old German did say

The popularity of the German bands in England was almost certainly the reason for a number of ballads about Germans, whose tunes imitated the oom-cha-cha rhythm of the bands.

One of these which is popular with traditional singers is *The German Clockmaker*. Here are the words recorded from Charlie Wills in Dorset:

1 A Germany Clockmaker to England once came
Ingleberg Snook was the old German's name
And old clocks and watches he'd mend
He'd put them right, nine times out of ten
(*With his too-ra-lum, too-ra-lum, too-ra-lum day*) etc.

2 He met an old lady in Kemonsway Square
She told him her clock was out of repair
He followed her off, to the lady's delight
In about a five minutes he had her clock right

3 They sat down to tea and so easy they got
All of a sudden they heard a loud knock
In walked her husband with a hell of a shock
To see this white German winding his wife's clock

4 His wife he did scold her, he said: Mary Anne
Why did you take in such an innocent man?
He the German made promise no more in his life
He'd wind up the clock of another man's wife

Another is *The Wonderful German Musician* recorded from Thomas Moran of County Leitrim:

1 O a wonderful musician once in Germany did dwell
His name quite unpronounceable, impossible to spell
He could play on any instrument no matter how great or small
O this beautiful musician he could play upon them all

> *A big drum, a kettle drum, a fiddle, flute or piccolo*
> *Piano, harp, harmonica and many more besides*
> *A French horn, a sax-horn, drums, beans, bones, tamborines*
> *Bassoons enough to size*

2 Well he only had a little room upon the second floor
A very little room it was indeed you may be sure
He had no chairs, or table, no cradle or no bed
Well, he said, he didn't want them for, of course, he had instead

3 Well, the neighbours used to grumble for his making such a din
At daybreak every morning to practise he'll begin
And sometimes out of slumbers she wakens in a fright
O for often he'd be playing in the middle of the night

202 GRAT FOR GRUEL

Jimmy McBeath, Elgin, Moray, Scotland, *rec.* Alan
Lomax, 1951: *Folk Songs of Britain*, vol. III, Caedmon
TC1144/Topic 12T159: *Gruel*

> Come, all young lassies, tak' my advice
> And never marry a weaver
> The very first nicht that he got wed
> He sat and grat for gruel

Grat is the Lowland Scots form of *greet*, meaning 'to cry'. Gruel is a semi-liquid food made of oatmeal and water, otherwise known as porridge.

This is a portrait of the weaver who is so worn out at his loom and set in his habits that before he thinks of the charms of his new bride he calls out for his plate of porridge. The song is made on a variant of the tune of *The Northamptonshire Poacher* (No. 258).

203 HE COMES DOWN OUR ALLEY

Betty Redshaw, London, *rec.* P. Kennedy, 1954
Other recorded versions
Phil Hamond, Morston, Holt, Norfolk, *rec.* P. Kennedy, 1952: *Still I Love Him*, BBC 18702
Jimmy Davidson, Bellingham, Northumberland, *rec.* P. Kennedy, 1954: *Canny Laddie*, BBC 20614

Lucy Stewart, Fetterangus, Aberdeenshire, and Charlotte Higgins, Blairgowrie, Perthshire, Scotland, *rec.* P. Kennedy and H. Henderson, 1954: *When I Was Single*

> When I was single I wore a black shawl
> And now since I've married I've got none at all
> *Still I love him, can't deny it*
> *I'll go with him wherever he goes*

This was the first verse and chorus from Lucy Stewart in Aberdeenshire. The song, which now seems to be widespread in England, Ireland and Scotland, was not known by the public until it was recorded from Phil Hamond in Norfolk and broadcast in 1952. Its airing on the radio brought in a letter from a listener in London who had heard it sung by children in the poorer districts of Liverpool and Birkenhead during the Second World War:

O I like an apple and I like a pear
And I like a sailor with nice curly hair
O gee I love 'im, I can't deny it
I'll be with 'im whe'ver he goes

He takes me to the pictures, he saves me a seat
And when I get there he says: Stand on your feet

He stands on the corner and whistles me out
He shouts: Oo-ey, oo-ey, are you coming out?

There's meat in the oven and cakes on the shelf
And if you don't like them, I'll eat them me-self

In Durham and Northumberland the miners' wives have added their verses:

> He gets up in the morning, he chops me the sticks
> Lights me the fire up and gangs oot at six
> *But still I love him, cannie laddie*
> *I'll gang wiv him wherever he gangs*
> He warks in the pityard for twelve bob a week
> Comes hame on the Saturdays as full as a leech

At Yarmouth in Norfolk the fishwives have theirs:

My back is a-breaking, my fingers are sore
Guttin' the herrin' he bring to the shore

If he's gone to Heaven, he'll come to no harm
If he's gone down below then he'll keep himself warm

> The storm is a-ragin', his boat isn't in
> T'others won't tell me what's happened to him

Our present London version Betty Redshaw learned from her sailor grandfather whose family lived alongside the River Thames at Gravesend in Kent. He kept a notebook of all the old songs and shanties he heard from the sailors who came into the London docks.

204 I WISHED TO BE SINGLE AGAIN

Recorded version
Tom Edwards, Bryneglwys, Corwen, Denbighshire, Wales, *rec.* P. Kennedy and E. Cleaver, 1954: BBC 22425

Printed versions
DUNCAN MS: 1904: *When I Was A Young Man, O Then* (Aberdeenshire)
SHARP MS: 1909: one variant (Somerset)
WILLIAMS: 1923, p. 111: *Once I Was Single* (Oxfordshire)

> Once I was single, O then
> Once I was single, O then
> When I was single my pockets did jingle
> And I long to be single again

This song is widely sung and known in all parts of Britain, which is perhaps the reason why it has appeared in few collections. Tom Edwards was a Welsh-speaker and sang nearly all his songs in Welsh, but this was one he had picked up in English and liked singing for its infectious rhythm in, what was for him, a strange tongue.

205 THE LINEN SONG

Fred Perrier, Shrewton, Wiltshire, *rec.* P. Kennedy, 1954: BBC 21493: *Twas on of a Monday Morning*
Printed versions
SHARP MS: 1904–9: three variants (Somerset)
GARDINER MS: 1909: one variant, *The Smoothing Iron* (Sussex)

SHARP AND MARSON: 1904–9, vol. V, No. 113, p. 29: *Drivin' Away At The Smoothing Iron* (Somerset)
SHARP: 1916/1921, No. 32: *Dashing Away With The Smoothing Iron* (Somerset) (this version also published for schools)
SANDBURG: 1927, p. 117: *Hanging Out The Linen Clothes* (California, USA)

> Twas on a Monday morning
> When I beheld my darling
> O she was fair and she was free
> In every high degree

> Yes she was neat and willing O
> A-picking up her linen clothes
> And driving away at the smoothing iron
> She stole my heart away

Cecil Sharp collected three versions of the song in Somerset. For this one he had 'a-picking up' on Monday, 'a-soaping of' on Tuesday, 'a-starching of' on Wednesday, 'a-hanging out' on Thursday, 'a-rolling down' on Friday, 'ironing of' on Saturday, and 'a-wearing of' on Sunday. In another version, which he published for use in schools, the last lines were 'Dashing away with the smoothing iron She stole my heart away'.

Carl Sandburg obtained his version from friends in San Francisco, California. His verses had 'a-hanging out', 'a-taking in', a-ironing', 'a-mending', 'a-folding', etc. His verses consisted of four lines instead of the eight of our English versions and he claimed that 'Grandmothers of the present generation of Californians sang this over wash-tubs and ironing-boards, over the needles as they stitched and hemmed.'

William Chappell printed the air of the song in *Ancient English Melodies* (No. 126) as 'a Somersetshire tune, the original of *All Round My Hat*'. In fact it seems only to have been collected from Somerset singers. Fred Perrier learned his version when he was working as a ploughboy in Somerset in 1897 from an old man who called him 'Ploughshare Joe'.

206 THE MOLE-CATCHER

Alec Bloomfield, Benhall, Framlingham, Suffolk, *rec.* P. Kennedy, 1905

Other recorded version
Harry Cox, Catfield, Norfolk, *rec.* P. Kennedy, 1953

Printed versions
BARING GOULD: 1905, No. 45, p. 90: *coll.* H. Fleetwood Sheppard, Devon: text rewritten
GARDINER MS: 1906–8 (Hampshire)

HAMMOND MS: 1906, No. 667 (Dorset)
JFSS: 1910, No. 15, p. 87 three variants, tunes only, *coll.* R. Vaughan Williams: F. W. Jekyll and G. S. Kaye-Butterworth, Norfolk
REEVES: 1960, No. 93, p. 191, *coll.* G. Gardiner, 1906
PURSLOW: 1972, p. 61: *coll.* Gardiner (Hampshire)

> A mole-catcher am I, and that is my trade
> I potters about wi' my spunt and my spade
> On a moonshiny night
> O 'tis my delight
> A-catching o' moles

Baring Gould copied this verse from an early Garland in the British Museum. He found the rest of the words had been ripped out, probably, he says, for the same reason that prevented him taking down the words from an old singer at South Brent in Devon, and when he published it in the revised edition of *Songs of the West* (1905) he 'supplemented with fresh words' as he felt that the original words were 'very gross'.

Five years later Ralph Vaughan Williams contributed three tunes which had been noted in Norfolk by himself and others to the JFSS: 1910 with the remark that 'the words are unsuitable for this Journal'.

Harry Cox learned his version of the song from a man known as Old Buck, the local innkeeper.

Alec Bloomfield, a gamekeeper who has recorded many fine versions of East Anglian folksongs which he learnt from his father, was the person who introduced us to the pub at Blaxhall where we have filmed and recorded so many fine performances by traditional singers.

George Gardiner collected five versions in Hampshire. One published by James Reeves (1960) has an interesting ending on which Reeves comments: ' "At the sign of the Cross" is probably a euphemism for the support of bastard (i.e. cross-bred) children, just as "the sign of the Plough" implies fornication.'

> So now the young farmer must live at the last
> For he spent all his money at the Sign of the Cross
>
> He spent all his money, I cannot tell how
> I dare him hang up at the Sign of the Plough

207 NEVER WED A' AULD MAN

Jeannie Robertson, Aberdeen, Scotland, *rec.* P. Kennedy, 1953: BBC 21088–9: *Maids When You're Young*; *Folk Songs of Britain*, vol. II, CAEDMON TC1143/TOPIC 12T158
Other recorded version
Sam Larner, Winterton, Norfolk, *rec.* P. Kennedy, 1958
Printed versions
HERD: 1870, Appdx pp. 63–4: *Scant Love*; *Want of Love*
KIDSON: 1891, 1927, p. 92: *An Auld Man He Courted Me* (Yorkshire)
PETRIE: 1902: version from JOYCE (Ireland)
SHARP MS: 1904–12: one variant, Somerset, 1904, one variant, Essex, 1912

GARDINER MS: 1907: two variants (Hampshire)
HAMMOND MS: 1907–8: one variant (Dorset), one variant (Wiltshire)
JOYCE: 1909, no. 228, p. 111: *An old Man he courted me* (Ireland)
GREIG: 1914, vol. II, No. 149 (Scotland)
JFSS: 1906, No. 9, p. 273: tune only, *Maids, While You Live, Never Wed An Auld Man*, coll. T. C. Smith, Yorkshire, 1888
SEEGER AND MACCOLL: 1960, p. 34: Sam Larner version (Norfolk)
PURSLOW: 1965, p. 66: *An Old Man Came Courting Me*, coll. George Gardiner, Hampshire
HUBBARD: 1961, p. 156 (Utah, USA)
FOWKE: 1965, no. 10, p. 32: *An old Man he courted me* (Ontario, Canada)

When this old man comes to bed
He lays like a lump of lead
　Maids when you're young never wed an old man
When this old man goes to sleep
Out of bed I do creep
　Into the arms of some jolly young man

A young man is my delight
He'll kiss you day and night
　Maids when you're young never wed an old man
I wish this old man'd die
I'd soon make his money fly
　Into the arms of my jolly young man

The song seems equally well-known in Scotland and England. The last verse, which Jeannie omits in uncertain company, is frequently sung as a chorus after every other verse among friends who appreciate the song. Sam Larner the Norfolk singer, who also recorded a version, has a similar chorus:

> For they've got no fal-loo-ral, fal-liddle, fal-loo-ral
> They've got no fal-looral fal liddle all day
> They've got no fal-loo-rum, they've lost their ding doo-rum
> So maids when you're young never wed an old man

In the last verse when she has crept into the arms of her 'jolly young man', it becomes 'and I found his. . . .'

208 THE OLD WOMAN OF BLIGHTER TOWN

Frank Hillier, Okeford Fitzpaine, Dorset, *rec.* P. Kennedy, 1959

Other recorded versions
Harry Cox, Catfield, Yarmouth, Norfolk, *rec.* P. Kennedy, 1953: *Old Woman in Yorkshire*
Mary Connors and Paddy Doran, Belfast, N. Ireland, *rec.* P. Kennedy and S. O'Boyle, 1952: *The Blind Man He Can See*, BBC 18584
Thomas Moran, Mohill, County Leitrim, Ireland, *rec.* S. Ennis, 1953: *Old Woman in Our Town*, BBC 22013
Jack Weafer, Wexford, *rec.* S. Ennis, 1955: *Old Woman Of Dover*, BBC 22373

Printed versions
SHARP MS: 1905–21 (Somerset and Herefordshire)
GREIG: 1914, No. xiii: *The Wily Auld Carle* (Scotland)
HENRY: 1924, No. 174: *The Aul Man and the Churnstaff*
HUGHES: 1936, vol. IV: *Tigaree Torum Orum* (N. Ireland)
REEVES: 1958, No. 99, p. 204: Sharp versions
JEFDSS: 1959, p. 197: *There Was An Old Lady in Our Town*, coll. Cecil Sharp and Maud Karpeles, Herefordshire, 1921
PURSLOW: 1965, p. 55: *Marrowbones*, coll. H. Hammond, Dorset, 1906

SHARP AND KARPELES: 1917–32, vol. I, No. 55, p. 348: three variants *The Rich Old Lady* (N. Carolina and Virginia, USA)
COX: 1925, p. 464 (W. Virginia, USA)
SCARBOROUGH: 1937, p. 239 (Virginia, USA)
NEELY AND SPARGO: 1938, p. 151: *The Old Woman from Slab City* (Illinois, USA)
CHAPPELL: 1939, p. 79 (N. Carolina, USA)
EDDY: 1939, p. 90 (Ohio, USA)
LINSCOTT: 1939, p. 255: *The Old Woman in Dover* (Maine, USA)
BELDEN: 1940, p. 238 (Missouri, USA)
BREWSTER: 1940, p. 281 (Indiana, USA)
LOMAX: 1941, p. 176 (Texas, USA)
RANDOLPH: 1946–50, vol. IV, p. 248 (Arkansas, USA)
OWENS: 1950, p. 207: *The Old Woman From Ireland* (Texas, USA)
BROWN: 1952, p. 450: two variants (N. Carolina, USA)
LOMAX: 1960, No. 274, p. 512: *The Rich Old Lady* (Texas, USA)
LEACH: 1965, p. 283: *A Cruel Life* (Labrador, Canada)
PEACOCK: 1965, p. 261: *Eggs and Marrowbones* (Newfoundland, Canada)

> There was an old woman in Yorkshire
> In Yorkshire she did dwell
> She loved her husband dearly
> And the lodger twice as well

Harry Cox, who called the woman's 'other man' 'the lodger', had the location of his song as Yorkshire. Dover is also favoured, but as with so many of these songs there are almost as many towns housing the old woman as there are versions of the song. The same might also be said about the final verses. Harry's version:

> So now my song is ended
> And I can't sing no more
> My old woman is drownded
> And I am safe on shore

But a Scottish version *The Aul Man and the Churnstaff*, contributed from Northern Ireland by Sam Henry, gives the old woman another chance:

> O when he thought she'd got enough
> He pulled her to dry lan'
> Saying: I think the notion's oot o' your heid
> O' ha'in' anither man

Cecil Sharp came across a *Ram Song* (No. 304) type ending in the West Country:

> So there's an end to my song, Sir
> And I can sing no more
> And they that say I can, Sir
> Be a lying son of a whore

209 THE ONE THING OR THE OTHER

Michael Gallagher, Belleek, County Fermanagh, N.
Ireland, *rec*. P. Kennedy and S. O'Boyle, 1953: BBC
20024: *The Twins*

Printed version
SHARP MS: 1903 one variant (Somerset)

PEACOCK: 1965, p. 313: *One Thing and the Other*
(Newfoundland, Canada)

This appears on Irish broadsides with several other verses. The last two verses in the Newfoundland variant, which comment on the arrival of twins, are unusual:

> Some people they do murmur and perhaps they have a cause
> Me wife soon brought me twins and then it was too late to pause
> I'm obliged to run for doctor Dunn when in come me mother
> O what have she got? says she, said I. . . .

> Some people they do murmur and grumble at their state
> But if she brought me ten times two I couldn't help my fate
> So now defy and now supply and help give one another
> And I hope I pleased you all with the. . . .

210 THE POOR AULD MAID

Johina Leith, Stenness, Orkney, *rec*. P. Kennedy, 1955:
BBC 22650: *The Old Maid's Lament*

Other recorded version
John Findlater, Dounby, Orkney, *rec*. P. Kennedy, 1955

Compare
GREIG: 1914, No. 17: *The Auld Maid's Lament*

> Come rich man, come poor man, come wise man or come witty
> Come any man at all that would marry me for pity
> *O dear me, what would I do*
> *If I die an old maid in a garret*

So runs the last verse of a similar song, *The Old Maid in the Garret*, which has been recorded in England and Scotland as well as in America.

> I can cook and I can sew, I can keep the house right tidy
> Rise up in the morning and get the breakfast ready
> But there's nothing in this wide world would make me half so cheery
> As a wee fat man that would call me his own dearie

This type of song is frequently performed at special gatherings, not so much for the pathos of the forgotten unmarried as a warning for the future to the young men and maids not to delay too long.

In the final verse of *The Old Maid in the Garret* she says that if she cannot get a man she will surely get a parrot, and the parrot and cat both seem to feature in these 'old maid' songs (see GREIG: 1914).

> And noo she maun live in a wee bit garret
> Withoot ony frien' but a cat and a parrot

211 RAP-TAP-TAP

Harry Cox, Catfield, Norfolk, *rec*. P. Kennedy, 1953
Other recorded version
Sid Load, Southrepps, Norfolk, *rec*. S. Ennis, 1955:
BBC 22020: *The Farmer's Servant*

Printed versions
GARDINER MS: 1905: one variant (Hampshire)
HAMMOND MS: 1906: one variant (Dorset)
PURSLOW: 1965, p. 73: Gardiner (Hampshire)

> So when my master did come home
> O he asked me what I had done
> I told him I'd minded his business
> Just as well as if he was at home

> He gave to me some beer to drink
> But not a word did he know
> That I'd been there with my *rap-tap-tap*
> If he had he'd a never done so

This song, with its theme of minding the master's business and employing the 'tap-tap-tap' chorus of door-knocking, became popular in post-war years as *The Thing* (to the tune of *The Lincolnshire Poacher*).

212 ROCKING THE CRADLE

John Doherty, Glenties, Donegal, Ireland, *rec*. P. Kennedy and S. O'Boyle, 1953: BBC 19533

Other recorded versions
Seamus Ennis, Dublin, Ireland, 1949: BBC 13774
Gwen Harris, Pembrokeshire, Wales, *rec*. S. Ennis, 1953: BBC 20188

Thomas Moran, Mohill, Co. Leitrim, Ireland, *rec*. S. Ennis, 1954: BBC 22023
Robert Cinnamond, Belfast, N. Ireland, *rec*. S. O'Boyle, 1955: BBC 24839
LOMAX: 1960, p. 375: S. Ennis variant *The Old Man's Lament*
PEACOCK: 1965, p. 478: *The Milkman's Lament* (Canada)

If ever I was single once more to my glory
No element of pleasure would e'er me invoke
I'd rather be a slave in wild New Guinea
Than married to a drunkard, to deceit be a cloak

Crying. . . . My baby lie easy
She leaves me in sorrow alas to bemoan
Weeping and wailing and rocking the cradle
Pleasing the child that is none of my own

Also sometimes known as *Baby Lie Easy* or *Weeping and Wailing*, from its chorus, versions of this song have circulated among the student communities of colleges and universities.
There is a belief in Ireland that the tune of this song was the lullaby sung to the Christ child by the Virgin Mary.

213 RUE THE DAY

Lucy Stewart, Fetterangus, Aberdeenshire, Scotland, *rec*. P. Kennedy and H. Henderson, 1955

Printed versions
SHARP MS: 1904: three variants (Somerset)
HAMMOND MS: 1906: one variant (Dorset)
REEVES: 1958: No. 67, p. 160: *O Dear O, coll*. Cecil Sharp, Somerset
PURSLOW: 1968, p. 82: *coll*. Hammond (Dorset)

As I was walking one midsummer morning
To view the fields and the leaves a-springing
There was two birds upon the tree
Sounding their notes and sweetly singing

O dear O, what shall I do?
My husband's got no courage in him

I saw two maidens standing by
And one of them her hands was wringing
And all of her conversation were
My husband's got no courage in him

My husband's admired wherever he go
And everyone looked well upon him
By his hands and feet and well-shaped eye
But still he got no courage in him

To 'rue the day' is to regret or repent. Rue, the bitter-tasting evergreen plant, was not only a symbol of chastity but was also regarded as an aphrodisiac. In this song we have a reference to oyster pie and oil of rue which were believed to have powers of sexual stimulation.
Although Cecil Sharp collected three versions of the song in Somerset, until the words were reproduced by James Reeves in *The Idiom of the People* the song had remained unpublished.

214 THE SCOLDING WIFE

Bill Westaway, Belstone, Devon, *rec*. P. Kennedy, 1950
Other recorded version
Charlie Wills, Bridport, Dorset, *rec*. P. Kennedy, 1959

Compare
SHARP AND MARSON: 1904–9, vol. IV, no. 101, p. 60: *The brisk young Bachelor* (Somerset)
GARDINER: 1909, p. 29: *The scolding Wife* (Hampshire)

When I come home to supper just ready for a drop
My wife has drained the kettle dry and all I get is slop
And if to her I say a word, the poker is my doom
Her tongue is full of scolding as I'm chased around the room
O she hurries me, she worries me, it is her whole delight
To chase me with the fire shovel round the house at night

This was one of the verses sung by Charlie Wills in Dorset which was not sung by Bill or Harry Westaway, the two Dartmoor folk singers from whom we also heard the song. Between verses 4 and 5 Charlie had a verse which brought help in the shape of a policeman to the scene of the crime:

The neighbours heard me yelling and it put them in a fright
So they went and called the policeman, he came running through the night
He heard me calling: Murder, and he soon broke down the door
And there they found her beating me as I lay upon the floor

215 THE WEARING OF THE BRITCHES

Joe Tunney, Belleek, County Fermanagh, N. Ireland, *rec.* P. Kennedy, London, 1958: *Folk Songs of Britain*, vol. III, Caedmon TC1144/Topic 12T159: *The Tailor by Trade*

Other recorded version
Patrick Keown, Garrison, County Fermanagh, N. Ireland, *rec.* P. Kennedy and S. O'Boyle, 1952: BBC 18525: *The Wearing of the Breeches*

Printed versions
Joyce: 1873, p. 58
Sharp MS: 1903: *The Tailor by his trade* (Somerset)
Reeves: 1958, No. 98, p. 203: Sharp version

Compare
Williams: 1923, p. 268: *The Struggle for the Breeches*: a duologue; not the same song (Wiltshire)

I am a tailor by my trade
In buttoning-up I am quite handy
And all the money I do earn
My drunken wife lays out in tea and brandy

Or if I go to seek a friend
Or for to take a noggin
My drunken wife she follows me
A-cursing like a dragon

Cecil Sharp collected a three-verse fragment of this tailor song in Somerset with a 'right fal lal laddie' type of chorus. Joe Tunney, from a famous singing family, heard his version from Patrick Keown. Joe is a melodeon player and was already playing the tune of the song as an Irish jig at local dances.

216 YOUNG AND GROWING

Mary McGarvey, Donegal, N. Ireland, *rec.* S. Ennis, 1954: BBC 21999: *The trees they did grow tall*

Other recorded versions
Seamus Ennis, Dublin, 1949: *The Bonnie Boy*, BBC 13767
Pat Kelly, Newry, Co. Down, N. Ireland, *rec.* P. Kennedy and S. O'Boyle, 1953, *The Trees Are Growing Tall*: BBC 20020
Sidney Richards, Curry Rivel, Somerset, *rec.* P. Kennedy and Maud Karpeles, 1952: *The Trees They Do Grow High*: BBC 17779

Printed versions
Johnson: 1792, vol. IV: *Lady Mary Ann*, with notes by Stenhouse
Maidment: 1824
Christie: 1881, vol. ii, p. 212: *Young Craigston*, with details of supposed origin
Baring Gould: 1895, No. 4: *The Trees They Are So High*, from various singers, Devon and Cornwall
JFSS: 1902, No. 4, p. 214: *coll.* Lucy Broadwood, Surrey, 1896
Sharp MS: 1904–21: twelve variants
Sharp and Marson: 1904–9, vol. II, No. 15: *The Trees They Do Grow High*, from Harry Richards, uncle of Sidney Richards (Somerset)
JFSS: 1905, No. 6, p. 44: Harry Richards version, *coll.* Sharp (music of each verse transcribed); also another variant (Somerset)
JFSS: 1905, No. 7, p. 95 (Devon); two variants *coll.* H. A. Jeboult, Somerset

JFSS: 1906, No. 8, p. 206: *coll.* R. Vaughan Williams, Sussex
JFSS: 1906, No. 9, p. 274: *coll.* Frank Kidson, W. Yorkshire; *coll.* Rev. Capel-Cure, Dorset
Gardiner: 1906–9: three variants (Hampshire), one variant (Wiltshire)
Broadwood: 1908 (Sussex)
JFSS: 1915, No. 19, p. 190: *coll.* Lucy Broadwood, Hertfordshire, and two variants *coll.* Anne Gilchrist, Lancashire
Kidson and Moffat: 1929, p. 10: *My Bonny Lad Is Young* (Yorkshire)
Ord: 1930, p. 112: *My Bonny Laddie's Lang, Lang A'Growing*
JEFDSS: 1951, p. 86 (Nova Scotia, Canada)
JEFDSS: 1956, p. 20: Pat Kelly variant (County Down)
Reeves: 1958, No. 96, p. 200: *Still Growing*, collated from two texts in Sharp
Reeves: 1960, No. 134: *The Trees They Are So High*, from Baring Gould
Sturgis and Hughes: 1919, p. 3 (Vermont, USA)
Sharp and Karpeles: 1932, vol. I, p. 410 (Kentucky, USA)
Creighton and Senior: 1950, p. 108 (Nova Scotia, Canada)
Flanders and Olney: 1953, p. 196 (Connecticut, USA)
Creighton: 1962, p. 100 (Nova Scotia, Canada)
Peacock: 1965, p. 677 (Newfoundland, Canada)
Meredith and Anderson: 1967, p. 177 (Australia)
Karpeles: 1971, p. 122 (Newfoundland)

At thirteen he married was, a father at fourteen
And then his face was white as milk, and then his grave was green
And the daisies were outspread and the buttercups of gold
O'er my pretty lad so young now ceased growing

When this verse was published in *Songs of the West* the age of the boy was modified to seventeen and the girl to eighteen 'in deference to the opinion of those who like to sing the song in a drawing-room or at a public concert'. Another version collected by Lucy Broadwood in Surrey has the ages of the boy as twelve with the girl 'scarcely thirteen'.

There is no doubt that the Baring Gould version from the West Country, from which the above verse is taken, shows the signs of touching-up by a literary hand, particularly in the extended ornate coda of each verse. Yet there is no admission of his 'improvements' either in his manuscripts or in the notes to the published collection. Here is another of his verses by way of example:

To let the lovely ladies know they may not touch and taste
I'll bind a bunch of ribbons red about his little waist
But the raven hoarsely croaks and I shiver in my bed
Whilst my pretty lad so young now ceased growing

Bibliography

This bibliography has been divided into two sections. Books published in Britain and Ireland appear first, followed by those published abroad, both in alphabetical order

BARING GOULD: 1889–1905
Rev. S. Baring Gould and Rev. H. Fleetwood Sheppard, *Songs and Ballads of the West*: Patey & Willis, London (4 parts) 1889–91. Methuen, London (4 parts) 1891–4; (1 vol.) 1895; revised edition 1905. Details are given by E. A. White in JEFDSS: 1937, p. 143, and 1946, p. 67. When reprinted in four parts this collection, mainly from Devon and N. Cornwall, comprised 110 songs 'collected from the mouths of the people'. Texts were modified and in some cases completely re-written and the same applied to tunes. However, in the revised edition, under the musical editorship of Cecil Sharp and with the adding of the name of the Rev. F. W. Bussell, one of the original collectors, many original texts and tunes were restored. For further comment on this publication see Dean-Smith: JEFDSS: 1950, p. 41.

BARING GOULD MS: 1889–95
Rev. S. Baring Gould. Manuscript in Plymouth City Library.

BARING GOULD AND SHARP: 1906
Rev. S. Baring Gould and Cecil J. Sharp, *English Folk Songs for Schools*: Curwen, London, 1906. 53 songs from collections of both editors 'designed to meet the requirements of the Board of Education'—who that year had recommended the inclusion of National or Folk Songs in the school curriculum, and 'dedicated to T. R. H. Prince Edward and Prince Albert of Wales'.

BROADWOOD: 1908
Lucy Broadwood, *English Traditional Songs and Carols*: Boosey, London, 1908. 39 songs mainly from Surrey–Sussex border with informative preface and brief notes about singers with comparative transcriptions made by phonograph cylinder recordings.

BUCHAN: 1828
Peter Buchan, *Ancient Ballads and Songs of the North of Scotland*: Edinburgh, 1828. 2 vols. His first collection was *Gleanings of Scotch, English and Irish Scarce Old Ballads* (1825). He was a diligent collector who corresponded with Sir Walter Scott. This collection contains Scots versions of folksongs such as *The Hiring Song* (see No. 194).

CHAPPELL: 1858/9
William Chappell, *Popular Music of the Olden Time*: Cramer, Beale & Chappell, London, vol. I 1858, vol. II 1859; Dover Publications, New York, 1965. Includes most of material from *National English Airs* (1838) but more has been added from other sources with particular reference to the ballads in the Pepys and Roxburghe collections. For further comment see Dean-Smith's *Guide* and JEFDSS: 1950, p. 38.

CHRISTIE: 1876/81
William Christie, *Traditional Ballad Airs*: Edmonston & Douglas, Edinburgh, vol. I 1876, vol. II 1881. Dean Christie noted down songs mainly in Aberdeenshire. This book combines his own collecting with publication of tunes and words from many other collections, both published and unpublished, including Percy, Scott, Jamieson, Motherwell, Kinloch, Sharpe and Buchan. Also contains a few original compositions.

DEAN-SMITH: 1954
Margaret Dean-Smith, *A Guide to English Folk Song Collections (1822–1952)*: University of Liverpool, 1954. A useful index of published songs under titles, alternative titles and first lines, with some full descriptions of important books with historical annotations and an introduction which traces the development of collecting and publication of folksong in England over a period of 130 years.

DUNCAN MS: 1905–11
James Duncan (1848–1917). MS collected *c.* 1905–11. Aberdeen University Library. Consists of two notebooks, the first containing 800 tunes with words of first verse, and the second giving texts of over 350 songs all supplied by a Mrs Gillespie. For obituary by Lucy Broadwood see JFSS: 1918, No. 21, p. 41.

D'URFEY: 1698–1720
Thomas D'Urfey, *Wit and Mirth* (or *Pills to Purge Melancholy*): London, 1698–1720. First edition printed with airs was in 2 vols. (1698). Further editions increased to 6 vols. (1720). This was the earliest publication to contain both words and music of a large number of English and Scots folksongs.

FMJ: 1965–
Folk Music Journal: English Folk Dance and Song Society, London (from 1965). Continuing the work of JFSS (*Journal of the Folk-Song Society*): 1889–1931 and JEFDSS (*Journal of the English Folk Dance and Song Society*): 1932–64.

FORD: 1899–1904
Robert Ford, *Vagabond Songs and Ballads of Scotland*: Gardiner, Paisley, Scotland, 1899–1901; new edition 1904. A comprehensive collection of songs and ballads, containing a number of 'bothy ballads', but only a few for which he provides the music. Important in that it covers the wide range of songs that were current up to the end of the century, particularly those sung by 'the travellers'.

GARDINER: 1909
George B. Gardiner, *Folk Songs from Hampshire*: Novello, London, 1909. 16 songs collected by Gardiner and his musical associates, Gamblin, Balfour Gardiner and Guyer, and arranged by Gustav (von) Holst.

GARDINER MS: 1905–9 (see also under HAMMOND)
For further details about Gardiner's work see *The George Gardiner Folksong Collection* in FMJ: 1967, p. 129 and introduction to PURSLOW: 1968.

GREIG: 1909/14
Gavin Greig, *Folk Songs of the North-East*: The Buchan Observer, Peterhead, Scotland. Vol. I 1909, vol. II 1914. Folklore Associates, Pennsylvania, USA, 1963. Greig was an Aberdeenshire schoolmaster and an accomplished musician who noted the words and tunes of over 3,000 songs. His manuscripts, extending over 90 volumes, are deposited in the Library of King's College, Aberdeen.

HAMMOND AND GARDINER MSS: 1905–9
H. E. D. Hammond (1866–1910), R. F. F. Hammond (1868–1921) and Dr George Gardiner (1852–1910) collected mainly in Dorset and Hampshire. Their manuscripts, deposited in the Vaughan Williams Memorial Library at Cecil Sharp House, London, have been indexed by Frank Purslow, who has also edited three books drawn from them (see PURSLOW: 1965, 1968 and 1972).

HENRY: 1924
Sam Henry, *Songs of the People*: Northern Constitution,

Coleraine, Co. Derry, N. Ireland, 1924. Over 800 songs were published in the local Derry newspaper. Many were contributed by readers but it was Henry's diligent research and background notes that gave interest to each contribution.

HERD: 1769/76
David Herd, *The Ancient and Modern Scots Songs, Heroic Ballads*: Dickson & Elliot, Edinburgh, 1769; (2 vols.) 1776. Paterson, Edinburgh, 1870. New 2-vol. edition, 1973, Scottish Academic Press. Early Scots source material. Herd's original MS, in the British Museum, served as basis for many of Robert Burns's songs as well as for Sir Walter Scott's *Minstrelsy of the Scottish Border*.

HUGHES: 1909-36
Herbert Hughes, *Irish Country Songs*: Boosey, London, 1909-36. 4 vols. Vol. I 1909, vol. II 1915, vol. III 1935, vol. IV 1936. About 20 songs in each album collected in the northern counties of Ireland.

JEFDSS: 1932-64
Journal of The English Folk Dance and Song Society: London (32 vols.), 1932-64.

JFSS: 1899-1931
Journal of the Folk-Song Society: London (35 vols.), 1899-1931.

JOHNSON: 1787-1853
James Johnson, *The Scots Musical Museum*: 6 vols. Edinburgh, 1787-1803; 4 vols. with notes by William Stenhouse and David Laing, Edinburgh, 1853. This was the beginning of systematic documentation of Scots songs to which Robert Burns contributed material of his own collecting which he restored by re-writing amplification of the texts.

JOYCE: 1873/1906
P. Weston Joyce, *Ancient Music of Ireland*: McGlashan & Gill, Dublin, 1873. Longmans Green, Dublin and New York, 1906.

JOYCE: 1909
P. Weston Joyce, *Old Irish Folk Music and Songs*: University Press, Dublin, 1909. 842 Irish airs and songs, edited with annotations for the Royal Society of Antiquaries of Ireland of which Joyce was the President. Most of the music previously unpublished but some are versions of songs already in *Ancient Music of Ireland* (1873) and *Irish Peasant Songs in the English Language* (1906).

KIDSON: 1891
Frank Kidson, *Traditional Tunes*: C. Taphouse, Oxford, 1891. Texts and melodies (without accompaniment) mainly from Yorkshire. Later published with piano accompaniment in KIDSON AND MOFFAT: 1926 and 1927. Many texts filled out from broadsides. For article about Frank Kidson see JEFDSS: 1948, p. 127. Reissued by S. R. Publishers, 1970.

KIDSON AND MOFFAT: 1926
Frank Kidson and Alfred Moffat, *A Garland of English Folk Songs*: Ascherberg, Hopwood & Crew, London, 1926. 60 songs collected by Kidson, mainly in Yorkshire, with piano accompaniments by Moffat; most previously published in *Traditional Tunes* (1891). A further 60 songs were selected for a second volume by Kidson and Moffat (1927).

KIDSON AND MOFFAT: 1927
Frank Kidson and Alfred Moffat, *Folk Songs from the North Countrie*: Ascherberg, Hopwood & Crew, London, 1927. A further 60 songs with piano accompaniment, published one year after the collector's death. The foreword by Lucy Broadwood provides information about the collector. See also *Frank Kidson: portrait*, JEFDSS: 1948, pp. 127-35.

KIDSON AND MOFFAT: 1929
Frank Kidson, Ethel Kidson and Alfred Moffat, *English Peasant Songs*: Ascherberg, Hopwood & Crew, London, 1929. 'Third and last Selection of Sixty Folk Songs from the Frank Kidson Collection.' Compiled by his niece with once again piano accompaniments by Moffat. (See KIDSON AND MOFFAT: 1926 and 1927.)

ORD: 1930
John Ord, *Bothy Songs and Ballads*: Alexander Gardner, Paisley, Scotland. The standard work on the 'bothy ballads' of N.E. Scotland; 'bothy' meaning farm cottage or hut used by hands, ploughmen, shepherds and farm-servants, and the ballads, although including folksongs found elsewhere, being mainly those describing, and often complaining about, local farm life.

PETRIE COLLECTION: 1902-5
George Petrie, *The Complete Petrie Collection*: ed. C. V. Stanford, 3 parts, Boosey, London, 1902-5. Full details of the collection are given in JEFDSS: 1946, pp. 1-12 together with a list of tunes appearing in the 1855 and 1882 volumes.

PINTO AND RODWAY: 1957
V. de Sola Pinto and A. E. Rodway, *The Common Muse*: Chatto & Windus, London, 1957; Penguin Books, London, 1965. An anthology of Popular British Ballad Poetry from the 15th to the 20th century. In two parts: the first 'Amatory' and the second 'General'. 245 texts from England, Ireland and Scotland with an introduction mainly about street balladry.

PURSLOW: 1965
Frank Purslow, *Marrowbones*: EFDS Publications, London, 1965. A series of pocket-size publications initiated by Peter Kennedy in order to make available the songs collected by Hammond and Gardiner in the care of the EFDSS library. This selection contains 100 songs, provided with chord symbols over the melodies.

PURSLOW: 1968
Frank Purslow, *The Wanton Seed*: EFDS Publications, London, 1968. A second selection from Hammond and Gardiner again containing 100 songs.

PURSLOW: 1972
Frank Purslow, *The Constant Lovers*: EFDS Publications, London, 1972. A third selection in which the type-size has been increased and the number of songs reduced to 78.

REEVES: 1958
James Reeves, *The Idiom of the People*: Heinemann, London, 1958. Words of 115 folksongs from Cecil Sharp MSS (about 40 printed for the first time) selected as examples of 'English Traditional Verse'. Introduction concerned with the Folk Song Movement in England; Sharp as a collector; text revisions; description of the MSS; the popular idiom; and a detailed consideration of certain songs.

REEVES: 1960
James Reeves, *The Everlasting Circle*: Heinemann, London, 1960. 142 texts from the MSS of Baring Gould, Hammond and Gardiner considered as 'English traditional verse'. Introduction concerned with Baring Gould as a collector and his MSS; Hammond and Gardiner; varieties of folksong; the theme of fertility and a discussion on the *lingua franca* of English traditional song.

SEEGER AND MACCOLL: 1960
Peggy Seeger and Ewan MacColl, *The Singing Island*: Mills Music, London, 1960. 96 English and Scots folksongs arranged for 'the post-war folk revival' mainly from Scotland under headings: Children, Courting, Men at Work, On the Road, Sailors, Barrack Room, Rovin' Boys and Flash Girls, Historical and Fill up your Glass.

SHARP Ms 1903-23
Cecil Sharp (1859-1924), foremost collector of English folksongs and folkdances, was the founder of The English Folk Dance Society and for many years a member of The Folk-Song Society. (In 1932 these two societies amalgamated as The English Folk Dance and Song Society.) For a full account of his life-work and publications see *Cecil Sharp* by A. H. Fox-Strangways

(Oxford University Press, London, 1933), revised by Maud Karpeles (Routledge & Kegan Paul, London, 1967). Words, songs, tunes and dance notes in Cecil Sharp's autograph are in the Library of Clare College, Cambridge. There are also photostat copies in the Harvard University Library and the New York Public Library, and microfilm copies in the libraries of the University of California and in the library at Cecil Sharp House, London, the headquarters of The English Folk Dance and Song Society. Cecil Sharp's own collection of books was left to the EFDSS and formed the beginnings of the specialist library at Cecil Sharp House.

SHARP AND MARSON: 1904-9
Cecil J. Sharp and Rev. Charles L. Marson, *Folk Songs from Somerset*: Simpkin Marshall, London and Barnicott, Taunton, Somerset. 5 vols. Vol. I 1904, vol. II 1905, vol. III 1906, vol. IV 1908, vol. V 1909. The most important single collection of English folksong, later edited as the *Selected Edition* (1916-21). Introduction concerning singers and style most valuable.

SHARP: 1916/21
Cecil J. Sharp, *English Folk Songs: Selected Edition*: Oliver Ditson, New York, 1916; Novello, London, 1921. 2 vols. 100 songs of which all but 18 from Somerset previously published in SHARP AND MARSON: 1904-9. 12 of the songs, not previously published, were variants. Introduction (and notes to songs) are of great value as they post-date by 14 years his *English Folk Song, Some Conclusions* (1907).

SHARPE: 1823/80
Charles Kirkpatrick Sharpe, *A Ballad Book*: private circulation, Edinburgh, 1823; Blackwood, Edinburgh, 1880.

WILLIAMS: 1923
Alfred Owen Williams, *Folk Songs of the Upper Thames*: Duckworth, London, 1923. Over 300 folksongs (words only) noted mainly in Berkshire, Gloucestershire, Oxfordshire and Wiltshire. Interesting introduction about rural life, more fully covered by Williams in *Round About the Upper Thames* (Duckworth, 1922). Further unpublished texts in Swindon Reference Library. See FMJ: 1969 'Alfred Williams: A Symposium'.

BELDEN: 1940
H. M. Belden, *Ballads and Songs Collected by the Missouri Folklore Society*: University Studies XV (No. 1), Columbia, Missouri, USA, 1940.

BREWSTER: 1940
Paul G. Brewster, *Ballads and Songs of Indiana*: University Folklore Publications No. 1, Bloomington, Indiana, USA, 1940.

BROWN: 1952-62
Frank C. Brown, *Collection of North Carolina Folklore*: vol. II Ballads; vol. III Songs; vols. IV and V Tunes. Duke University Press, Durham, N. Carolina, USA, 1952-62.

CHAPPELL: 1939
Louis W. Chappell, *Folk-Songs of Roanoke and the Albemarle*: Ballad Press, Morgantown, W. Virginia, USA, 1939.

COX: 1925
John Harrington Cox, *Folk Songs of the South*: Harvard University Press, Cambridge, Mass., USA, 1925. Dover Publications Reprint, New York, 1967 (released 1968). 185 songs collected in West Virginia (29 with tunes). Introduction describes collecting methods and identifies informants. Notes, references to other versions and other data given with texts of songs.

CREIGHTON AND SENIOR: 1950
Helen Creighton and Doreen Senior, *Traditional Songs from Nova Scotia*: Ryerson Press, Toronto, Canada, 1950. 100 songs and 36 ballads collected in the Maritimes with additional variants of both tunes and texts in many instances. An important and well documented collection with versions of many of the songs in this book.

CREIGHTON: 1962
Helen Creighton, *Maritime Folk Songs*: Ryerson Press, Toronto, Canada, 1962. Michigan State University Press, East Lansing, Michigan, USA, 1962. 169 songs which were published with a companion gramophone record (Folkways 4307). There was also an earlier record called *Folk Music from Nova Scotia* (Folkways 4006).

EDDY: 1939
Mary O. Eddy, *Ballads and Songs from Ohio*: J. J. Augustin, New York, 1939.

FLANDERS AND OLNEY: 1953
Helen Hartness Flanders and Marguerite Olney, *Ballads Migrant in New England*: Farrar, Straus & Young, New York, 1953.

FOWKE: 1965
Edith Fowke, *Traditional Singers and Songs from Ontario*: Folklore Associates, Pennsylvania and Burns & MacEachern, Ontario, Canada. 62 songs from 10 traditional singers with musical transcriptions by Peggy Seeger. Songs in the collection are on the following records: Folkways FM 4005, 4018, 4051 and 4052; Folk Legacy FSC 10; Prestige INT 25014; Topic 12T140.

HUBBARD: 1961
Lester A. Hubbard, *Ballads and Songs from Utah*: University of Utah, Salt Lake City, USA, 1961.

JAFL: 1888–
Journal of American Folklore now published by University of Pennsylvania.

KARPELES: 1934/1971
Maud Karpeles, *Folksongs from Newfoundland*: Oxford University Press, London, 1934 (2 vols.); Faber & Faber, London, 1971. 30 songs (with piano accompaniments) were published in 1934 and 90 songs, 150 tunes including variants (with no accompaniments) in 1971. All collected during 1929-30.

KORSON: 1949
George Korson, *Pennsylvania Songs and Legends*: University Press, Philadelphia, Penn., USA, 1949.

LEACH: 1965
MacEdward Leach, *Folk Ballads and Songs of the Lower Labrador Coast*: National Museum of Canada, Ottawa, 1965.

LINSCOTT: 1939
E. H. Linscott, *Folk Songs of Old New England*: Macmillan, New York, 1939.

LOMAX: 1941
John and Alan Lomax, *Our Singing Country*: Macmillan, New York, 1941.

LOMAX: 1960
Alan Lomax, *Folk Songs of North America*: Cassell, London, 1960.

MEREDITH AND ANDERSON: 1967
John Meredith and Hugh Anderson, *Folk Songs of Australia*: Ure Smith, Sydney, 1967.

MORRIS: 1950
Alton C. Morris, *Folksongs of Florida*: University of Florida, Gainesville, Florida, USA, 1950.

NEELY AND SPARGO: 1938
Charles Neely and John W. Spargo, *Tales and Songs of Southern Illinois*: George Banta, Menasha, Wisconsin, USA, 1938.

OWENS: 1950
William A. Owens, *Texas Folk Songs*: Texas Folk-Lore Society, Dallas, Texas, USA, 1950.

PEACOCK: 1965
Kenneth Peacock, *Songs of the Newfoundland Outports*: National Museum of Canada, Ottawa, 1965. 3 vols.

RANDOLPH: 1946-50
Vance Randolph and Floyd C. Shoemaker, *Ozark Folk Songs*: State Hist. Soc., Columbia, Missouri, USA, 1946-50. 4 vols.

Bibliography

SFLQ: 1937
Southern Folklore Quarterly: University of Florida, Gainesville, Florida, USA, 1937–.

SANDBURG: 1927
Carl Sandburg, *The American Songbag*: Harcourt Brace, New York, 1927.

SCARBOROUGH: 1937
Dorothy Scarborough, *A Song Catcher in the Southern Mountains*: Columbia University Press, New York, 1937.

SHARP AND KARPELES: 1917/32
Olive Dame Campbell and Cecil J. Sharp, *English Folk Songs from the Southern Appalachians*: Putnam, New York, 1917. Cecil J. Sharp and Maud Karpeles (2 vols.), Oxford University Press, London, 1932.

STURGIS AND HUGHES: 1919
Edith B. Sturgis and Robert Hughes, *Songs from the Hills of Vermont*: G. Schirmer, New York, 1919.

XI

Songs of
Occupations

Introduction

> I'm a roving jack of many a trade
> And every trade of all trades
> And if you wish to know my name
> They call me Jack-of-all-trades

Here are some of the songs of pleasure and complaint as voiced by the working people of the towns and villages of Britain. Some of them like the cobblers and tailors have already been featured in our previous chapter, taking advantage of the wives of uneasy wedlock, or suffering themselves from a scolding wife, and here again we find them boasting their valour with the ladies:

> It's arise, girls, arise, wake up and open your eyes
> Go and fetch me some ale that I might swallow
> I can climb up to the top without a ladder or a rope
> And it's there you will hear me: Halloa
>
> *Sweep, Chim-nie Sweep*: No. 240

> So Johnny went into this castle so great
> And entered this lady's room, gay room
> She gave him a chair and bad' him sit there
> Crying: You're welcome, young man, with your brooms
>
> *Green Brooms*: No. 223

The most renowned of country tradesmen is the miller (see *The Jolly Miller*: No. 229), who claims to have advantages over both farmers and shopkeepers, as well as a hold over the local squire, and, of course, the bonny local lasses:

> Aye an' gently stepping o'er the limbs
> She heard the milly's clattering din
> And softly said: May I come in
> And shelter from the rain-O?
>
> *The Buchan Miller*: No. 218

In the old days the miller's livelihood often depended on taking his toll out of every bushel that he ground. In *The Miller's Last Will* (No. 232) an old miller is on his deathbed and calls his three sons to his bedside to ask them how they would organize the toll, if they inherited the mill. The first son says he'd take one peck, the second half a bushel, but the old boy gives the mill to the youngest son, who tells him he'd 'take the lot and swear to the sack':

> And now the old man is dead and gone
> And the youngest son is carrying on
> But if any corn to grind you've got
> Don't take it to him or he'll take the lot

In times of great stress, particularly during the Napoleonic wars, the tradesmen could not find work and farmers and tradesmen alike were convinced the others were profiteering. At that time two somewhat similar 'hard times' songs came into being in England:

> Come all brother tradesmen that travel alone
> O pray come and tell me where the trade is all gone
> Long time I have travelled and cannot find none
> And it's O, the hard times of old England
> In old Eng-e-land very hard times
>
> *The Hard Times of Old England*: No. 224

MacDonald of Pitgaveny, Elgin,
Morayshire
Photograph: Peter Kennedy

> Now the very best plan that I can find
> Is to pop them all up in a high gale of wynd
> And when they get up, the cloud it will bu'st
> And the biggest old rascal come tumbling down first
>   Singing: Honesty's all out of fashion
>   These are the rigs of the time
>   *The Rigs of the Time*: No. 237

Probably the happiest tradesman at this particular time was the beggar:

> For when a beggar's tired he can sit him down and rest

The beggar, the song *A-Beggin' I Will Go* (No. 217) says, could always sleep the night in a hollow tree, which also serves as an open-air pulpit for a soldier and a sailor to offer up a series of prayers:

> Now the next thing we'll pray for will be some good beef
> Said the sailor to the soldier: We'll eat with relief
> For where we get one pound I hope we'll get ten
> And never, never go hungry, cried the soldier: Amen
>   *The Soldier and the Sailor*: No. 239

In *The Parson and the Clerk* (No. 235), while the parson is delivering his sermon of religious and moral principles, the clerk keeps up a continuous flow of mumbled comments on what really happens in life:

> O never sigh for that dross called gold
> For blessed is the man that is poor
> Nor cast ye away the loaves of bread
> Nor fishes from the door
> For, I grieve to say it is my fate
> To drive a carriage-and-pair in the park
> With a thousand a year, said the Parson
> O give it to me, said the Clerk
> *Amen*
> There's no pride about me, said the Clerk

In another duologue, there is a comparison of pleasures, clothing, food and drink, in the two occupations of *The Husband-Man and the Servant-Man* (No. 226), with the latter eventually confessing that the former has the more important calling.

A drinking song, *When Jones's Ale Was New* (No. 287), in Chapter XIII, introduces the ploughman, blacksmith and other tradesmen. In previous chapters there are also two songs that tell of the blacksmith: *A Blacksmith Courted Me* (No. 146) and *Twankydillo* (No. 286), but the arrival of the threshing machine brought a new kind of husbandry and teamwork as we see in *The Machiner's Song* (No. 231):

> The man who made her he made her so well
> He made every cog and wheel to tell
> While the big wheel runs the little one hums
> And the feeder sits above the drum

On the rough roads the carters, carriers and wagoners cheerfully braved all kinds of weather:

> My father was a carrier many years ere I was born
> He used to rise at daybreak and go his round each morn
> He would often take me with him especially in the Spring
> When I loved to sit upon the cart and hear me father sing
>   *Jim, the Carter Lad*: No. 228

When first I went a-wagonin', a-wagonin' did go
I filled my parents' hearts full of sorrow, grief and woe
And many were the hardships that I did undergo
The Jolly Wagoner: No. 230

Then along came machines again and teams of Irishmen with cauldrons of boiling pitch left the fields to work on smoothing over the rough surface of the roadways with *The Hot Ash-Pelt* (No. 225):

'Tis lately gone six months ago, since I came to Bandon Town
Where I helped me Uncle Barney for to cut the harvest down
But sure now I wear a guernsey and around me waist a belt
I'm the gaffer o'er the boys that makes the hot ash-pelt

There were also other travelling teams of quarrymen and miners:

All our delight, boys, is to split the rocks in time
Our pleasure it is more than that in working underground
Six Jolly Miners: No. 238

Children who were employed in the towns to sell the evening newspapers were a familiar sight, bicycling along or standing at street corners in a ragged jacket of their father's, several sizes too large:

O poor wee Jockie Clarke, he sells *The Evening Star*
He whistles and he sings as he pedals through the glar
And by all your paper-sellers he's the best in a' the lot
If he'd only mak' a jacket oot his faither's auld coat
Poor Wee Jockie Clarke: No. 236

Songs of some of the street vendors can be found in later chapters, such as *The Little Beggarman* (No. 345); *The Roving Journeyman* (No. 353); *Sweet Blooming Lavender* (No. 356), and *The Travelling Candyman* (No. 359). In this chapter, there is the pedlar, Wandering Jack, who cries:

Needlecases, will you buy one? You will buy one I'm sure
Won't you buy a case o' needles from Jack that's so poor?
Needlecases: No. 233

There are two Irish songs concerned with the linen mill, or *factory*, workers. First a courtship of a hard-working young mill girl, *The Factory Girl* (No. 221) and the other, from Belfast, was sung in disapproval of a new overseer:

O do you know her or do you not, this new doffin' mistress we have got
Anne-Jane Brady was our doffer's name and she helped her doffers at every frame
The Doffin' Mistress: No. 220

A song popular in England, Ireland, and Scotland describes an encounter with a girl pickpocket selling shellfish, *The Oyster Girl* (No. 234):

I've travelled through Ireland, through Scotland and through France
But never was I, in all my life, served out by such a dance
For the English girls are certain, if you give them half a chance
They will teach you the way to sell oysters

Laziest of all workers, so the song said, was the offshore fisherman who was so particular about having just the right conditions to go out fishing:

O me dad was a fisherman bold and he lived till he grew old
For he opens the pane and he pops out the flame, just to see how the wind do blow
If the flame don't flicker 'e'd know that there's not enough wind do blow
But if that silly old flame blow out, then there's too much wind to go
The Candlelight Fisherman: No. 219

217 A-BEGGIN' I WILL GO

1 Of all the trades in England the beggin' is the best
For when a beggar's tired, he can sit him down and rest
And a-beggin' I will go-o-o
And a-beggin' I will go

2 I've a poke for me m'ale and another for me rye
I've a bottle by me side, to drink when I am dry

3 I've a poke for me salt, and another for me malt
I've a pair of little crutches, you should see how I can halt

4 I've been a-beggin' seven years with me ol' wooden leg
For lame I've been, since I was born, and so I'm forced to beg

5 In a hollow tree I pass the night, and there I pay no rent
Providence provides for me, and I am well content

218 THE BUCHAN MILLER

I am a mil-ler to my trade And that fu' well you ken - O

I am a mil-ler to my trade And that fu' well you know ———

I am a mil-ler to my trade And mo-ny's the bag o' m'ale I've made

And court-ed mony a bon-ny maid A - mong the bags o' m'ale - O

1 I am a miller to my trade
And that fu' well you ken-O
I am a miller to my trade
And that fu' well you know
I am a miller to my trade
And mony's the bag o' m'ale I've made
And courted mony a bonny maid
Among the bags o' m'ale-O

2 It's merrily gangs the wheel aroond
That grinds the p'ase and corn-O
It's merrily gangs the wheels aroond
That mak the stanes to go
It's merrily gangs the wheels aroond
And when the corn is ripe and soond
I'll be the happiest man aroond
Among the bags o' m'ale-O

3 It happened on a wintry night
I start to l'ave the lane-O
It happened on a wintry night
My lassie she passed by
Aye an' gently stepping o'er the limbs
She heard the milly's clattering din
And softly said: May I come in
And shelter from the rain-O?

4 Says I: My lass, you're welcome here
Come in and dry your claes-O
Said I: My lass, you're welcome here
And that fu' well you know
Said I: My lass, you're welcome here
Now here's some news that I would speir
If you'll consent to be my dear
Among the bags o' m'ale-O?

5 That night she named the waddin' day
Among the bags o' m'ale-O
That night she named the waddin' day
O that fu' well you know
And tho' the waddin's by lang syne
And now we hae two bairnies fine
And some o' them are sometimes playing
Among the bags o' m'ale-O

219 THE CANDLELIGHT FISHERMAN

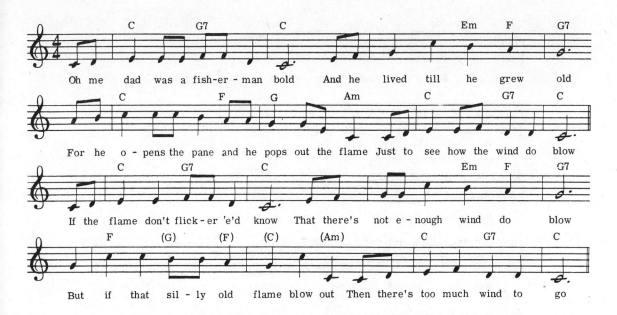

Oh me dad was a fish-er-man bold And he lived till he grew old

For he o-pens the pane and he pops out the flame Just to see how the wind do blow

If the flame don't flick-er 'e'd know That there's not e-nough wind do blow

But if that sil-ly old flame blow out Then there's too much wind to go

1 O me dad was a fisherman bold
And he lived till he grew old
For he opens the pane and he pops out the flame
Just to see how the wind do blow
If the flame don't flicker 'e'd know
That there's not enough wind do blow
But if that silly old flame blow out
Then there's too much wind to go

2 And often he'd say to me
You'd be wise before you go
Do you open the pane and pop out the flame
Just to see how the candle do blow

3 When the north wind rough did blow
Then I lay right snug below
But I opens the pane and I pop out the flame
Just to see how the wind do blow

4 When the wind come out of the east
You'll be looking for snow and sleet
But I opens the pane and I pop out the flame
Just to see how the wind do blow

5 When the wind back into the west
That'll come a rough in at best
But I opens the pane and I pop out the flame
Just to see how the wind do blow

6 When the south wind soft do blow
It's then I love to go
And I opens the pane and I pop out the flame
Just to see how the wind do blow

7 And my poor wife say to me
We shall starve if you don't go
So I opens the pane and I pop out the flame
Just to see how the wind do blow

8 Now all you fishermen bold
If you live till you grow old
Do you open the pane and pop out the flame
Just to see how the wind do blow

220 THE DOFFIN' MISTRESS

1 O do you know her or do you not
This new doffin' mistress we have got?
Anne-Jane Brady was our doffer's name
And she helped her doffers at every frame
Raddie-right-fol-ra
Raddie-right-fol-ra

2 On Monday morning when she came in
She hung her clothes on the highest pin
She turned around for to view her frames
Shouting: Damn you, doffers, tie up your ends

3 Tie up our ends we will surely do
For Anne-Jane Brady, but not for you
We'll tie up our ends and we'll leave our frames
And wait for Anne-Jane Brady to return again

221 THE FACTORY GIRL

As I | went a - walk — ing, | one fine sum - mer's morn - ing

The birds | on the bran - ches they sweet - ly — did sing ——

The lads | and — the las — ses to - geth - er were sport - in'

Go — ing down to - yon fac — tory, their work to be - gin ——

As I went a-walking, one fine summer's morning
The birds on the branches they sweetly did sing
The lads and the lasses together were sportin'
Going down to yon factory, their work to begin

I spied a wee damsel, more fairer than Venus
Her skin like the lily, not one could excel
Her cheeks like the red rose that grew in yon valley
She's my own only goddess, she's a sweet factory girl

I stepp-ed up to her, it was for to view her
When on me she cast a proud look of disdain
Stand off me, stand off me, and do not insult me
For although I'm a poor girl, I think it's no shame

I don't mean to harm you, I'm sure I would scorn it
But grant me one favour: Pray where do you dwell?
Kind sir, you'll excuse me, for now I must leave you
For yonder's the sound of the factory bell

5 I have lands, I have houses adorn-ed with ivy
I've gold in my pocket and silver as well
And if you go with me, a lady I'll make you
So try and say yes, my dear factory girl

6 O love and sensation rules many a nation
To many a young girl perhaps you'd look well
I am a poor girl, without home or relations
And besides I'm a hard-working factory girl

7 It's true I did love her but now she won't have me
And all for her sake I'll go wander awhile
Over high hills and valleys where no one shall know me
I'll mourn for the sake of my factory girl

8 Now this maid's she got married and become a great lady
Become a great lady of fame and renown
She may bless the day and the bright summer's morning
She met with the squire and upon him did frown

9 Well now to conclude, and to finish these verses
This couple got married, and both are doing well
So, lads, fill your glasses, and drink to the lasses
Till we hear the sweet sound of the factory bell

222 FAGAN THE COBBLER

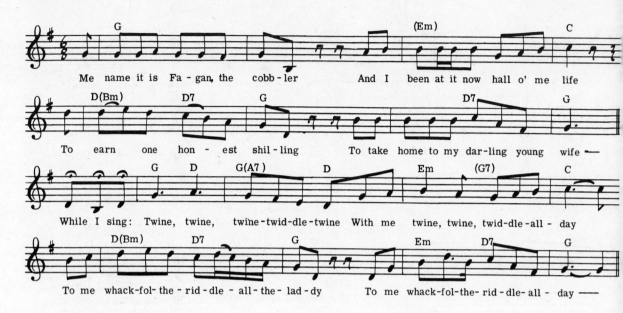

Me name it is Fa-gan, the cobb-ler   And I been at it now hall o' me life

To earn one hon-est shil-ling   To take home to my dar-ling young wife —

While I sing: Twine, twine, twine-twid-dle-twine With me twine, twine, twid-dle-all - day

To me whack-fol-the - rid-dle - all-the-lad-dy   To me whack-fol-the- rid-dle-all - day —

1 Me name it is Fagan, the cobbler
And I been at it now hall o' me life
To earn one honest shilling
To take home to my darling young wife

While I sing:
Twine, twine, twine-twiddle-twine
With me twine, twine, twiddle-all-day
To me whack-fol-the-riddle-all-the-laddy
To me whack-fol-the-riddle-all-day

SPOKEN: Now I'll tell you how I made me fortune . . .

2 It's thirty long years have I travelled
Earned me living by carrying me pack
With me 'ammers, me awls and me pinchers
I carried them all on me back
While I sing (*etc.*)

SPOKEN: Now I'll tell you about the old woman . . .

3 My wife she started drinking
And she's drinking her pints by the score
O I know she's a-spending all my money
By the way that she chatters her jaw

SPOKEN: Now I'll tell you how I sorted her out . . .

4 It was early one dark winter's evening
When the moon she was hiding her light
I carelessly strolled by the river
And I carelessly bid her: Good night

SPOKEN: Now here's the happy consequentials . . .

5 My wife she's turned a teetotaller
And she swears she won't mop any more
For now she's a-saving all my money
She's putting it by in galore

223 GREEN BROOMS

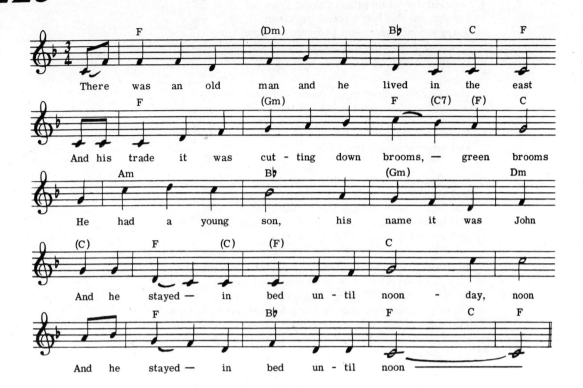

1 There was an old man and he lived in the east
   And his trade it was cutting down brooms, green brooms
   He had a young son, his name it was John
   And he stayed in bed until noon-day, noon
   And he stayed in bed until noon

2 The father arose and up to John goes
   And swore he would burn his room, gay room
   If he didn't rise and sharpen his knives
   And go down to the wood to cut brooms, green brooms
   And go down to the wood to cut brooms

3 So Johnny went on down through the green wood
   Till he came to a castle of fame, fame, fame
   He spied a maid and stood at the gate
   Crying: Fair maid, do you want any brooms, green brooms
   Fair maid, do you want any brooms?

4 This lady being up in her window so high
   She spied this young man so terribly neat, neat, neat
   She said to her maid: Go down to the gate
   And call in this young man with his brooms, green brooms,
   And call in this young man with his brooms ➜

5 So Johnny went into this castle so great
  And entered this lady's room, gay room
  She gave him a chair and bad' him sit there
  Crying: You're welcome, young man, with your brooms, green brooms
  You're welcome, young man, with your brooms

6 Then to Jack she did say: You're handsome and gay
  Give over your cutting of brooms, green brooms
  And smiling she said: Give over your trade
  And marry this lady in bloom, gay bloom
  And marry this lady in bloom

7 Then Jack gave consent, to this lady's content
  And married they were in her room, gay room
  And Jack blessed the day that he travelled that way
  And became lord of that castle of fame, great fame
  And became lord of that castle of fame

8 So, come all you young blades, whatever your trades
  May you meet with a lady in bloom, gay bloom
  So, boys, will we drink, or what do you think?
  There is nothing like cutting down brooms, green brooms
  There is nothing like cutting down brooms

224 THE HARD TIMES OF OLD ENGLAND

Come — all bro - ther trades - men that tra - vel a - lone —

O, pray come and tell me where the trade is all gone

Long time I have tra - velled and can - not find none

And it's : O, the hard times of old Eng - land ———

In old Eng - e - land ve - ry hard times ———

1 Come all brother tradesmen that travel alone
O pray come and tell me where the trade is all gone
Long time I have travelled and cannot find none
And it's: O, the hard times of old England
In old Eng-e-land very hard times

2 Provisions you buy at the shop it is true
But if you've no money there's none there for you
So what's a poor man and his family to do?

3 If you go to a shop and you ask for a job
They will answer you there with a shake and a nod
So that's enough to make a man turn out and rob

4 You will see the poor tradesmen a-walking the street
From morning till night for employment to seek
And scarcely they've got any shoes to their feet

5 Our soldiers and sailors have just come from war
Been fighting for their queen and the country, 'tis sure
Come home to be starved, better stayed where they were

6 And now to conclude and to finish my song
Let us hope that these hard times they will not last long
I hope soon to have occasion to alter my song
And sing: O, the good times of old England
In old Eng-e-land jolly good times

225 THE HOT ASH-PELT

'Tis — late-ly gone six months a-go since I left sweet Ban-don town

Where I helped me Un-cle Bar-ney for to cut the har-vest down

But, sure, now I wear a Guern-sey and a-round me waist a belt

I'm the gaf-fer o'er the boys that makes the hot ash - pelt

So you may talk a-bout your sol-diers and your sai-lors and the rest

Your tai-lors and your shoe-ma-kers to please the la-dies best

But the de-vil a one of them has got their grais-y hearts to melt

Like the boys a-round the boi-ler ma-king hot ash-pelt

1 'Tis lately gone six months ago since I left sweet Bandon town
Where I helped me Uncle Barney for to cut the harvest down
But, sure, now I wear a Guernsey and around me waist a belt
I'm the gaffer o'er the boys that makes the hot ash-pelt
So you may talk about your soldiers and your sailors and the rest
Your tailors and your shoemakers to please the ladies best
But the devil a one of them has got their graisy hearts to melt
Like the boys around the boiler making hot ash-pelt

2 Now one day a peeler came to me and says he to me: McGuire
  Would you kindly let me light my *duidin* at your boiler fire?
  Then he turns round to the boiler with his coat-tails up so neat
  Now says I: My decent man, you'd better go and mind your beat
  O sure, says he, that'll do for me, for I've got me blooming marks
  And I know you for a dirty pack of Tipperary barks
  Then I drew out from me shoulder and I gave him such a belt
  That I knocked him into the boiler full of hot ash-pelt

3 Well we quickly pulled him out again and put him in a tub
  And with soap and warm water, sure, how we did rub and scrub
  But the devil a bit of tar came off, it stuck on just like stone
  And every rub that we did give, you should hear the peeler groan
  And out of the wetting he did get, he caught a blooming cold
  And for scientific purposes his body has been sold
  And now in the National Museum he's hanging by the belt
  As an example of the dire effects of hot ash-pelt

226 THE HUSBAND-MAN AND THE SERVANT-MAN

Well met, well met, my friend, all — on the high-way rid-ing

So sim-ply to-ge-ther here we stand —

I pray thee tell to me of what cal-ling mayst thou be

Art thou not a ser-vant - man? —

No, no, my bro-ther dear, what — makes thee to en - quire

Of an - y such thing from mine hand? —

In - deed I do not 'frain, but I will tell thee plain

I am a down-right hus - band - man —

In - deed I do not 'frain, — but I will tell thee plain —

I am a down-right hus - band - man —

1 Well met, well met, my friend, all on the highway riding
So simply together here we stand
I pray thee tell to me of what calling may'st thou be
Art thou not a servant-man?
No, no, my brother dear, what makes thee to enquire
Of any such thing from mine hand?
Indeed I do not 'frain, but I will tell thee plain
I am a downright husband-man
Indeed I do not 'frain, but I will tell thee plain
I am a downright husband-man

2 If an husband-man you be, will you walk along with me?
And simply we will see how we stand
For in a very short space, I may take you to a place
Where you may be a servant-man
As for this diligence I give thee many thanks
But nothing do I require from thine hand
But something to show, therefore that I may know
The pleasures of a servant-man

3 O isn't it a nice thing to ride out with the king
Lords, dukes or any such men?
To hear the horn to blow, see the hounds all in a row
That's pleasures for a servant-man
But my pleasure's more than that: to see my oxen fat
And a good stack of hay by them stand
For with my ploughing and my sowing, my reaping and my mowing
That's pleasures for an husband-man

4 The clothes that we do wear they are costly, rich and rare
Our coats they are trimmed with silk all around
Our shirts are white as milk, our stockings made of silk
That's grandeur for a servant-man
As for thy gaudy gear, give I the clothes I wear
Some bushes to ramble among
Give to me a good great coat and in my purse a groat
That's habit for an husband-man

5 And then we do eat such delicate fine meat
Our goose, our capon and our swan
Our pastry's made so fine, we drink sugar in our wine
That's diet for a servant-man
But as for thy cocks and capons, give I some beans and bacon
Some butter and cheese now and then
For in a farmer's house you'll find both brawn and souse
That's living for an husband-man

6 Kind sir, I must confess and grant you your request
So hold up your uppermost hand
Although it is most painful, it is altogether gainful
I wish I had been an husband-man
So, good people all, I'll tell you, great and small
To honour the king of our land
And still maintain forever and do your best endeavour
For to support an husband-man

227 THE IRISH BARBER

O, there was an Ir-ish bar-ber, he had a jol-ly tune
He was al-ways a-sing-ing it from morn-ing un-til noon
And his voice was so mer-ry and his voice it was so sweet
Sure he thought he'd call the peo-ple in from the street
To me fol-the-did-dle-air-o Fol-the-did-dle-air-um
Hi-did-dly-air-um Fol-the-did-dle-an-dy

1 O there was an Irish barber, he had a jolly tune
He was always a-singing it from morning until noon
And his voice was so merry and his voice it was so sweet
Sure he thought he'd call the people in from the street

To me fol-the-diddle-air-o
Fol-the-diddle-air-um
Hi-diddly-air-um
Fol-the-diddle-andy

2 But there was one darned practice he said that he would stop
That he would give no score from out his barber's shop
So he got an old razor, all gapped and all rusty
Swore he'd l'ave it on the first one that come look for trusty

3 So as poor Irish Paddy came down the street that day
  He called into the barber's shop he thought to have a shave
  When he got to the door, then he threw down his hod
  Sure you'll give me a shave for the love and honour I've got

4 For my beard it is growing this many a long day
  There's a ha'penny in my pocket, sure I have for to pay
  I've been tramping the road by day and by night
  With a whisker like this now I sure look a sight

5 Come in, says the barber, and sit on the chair
  It's your old baby whiskers I'll mow to a hair
  Then the barber he began, sure, he lathered like a man
  With his old rusty razor he quickly began

6 Stop, says Paddy, and that very soon
  Stop, roared Paddy, or my poor joy you'll ruin
  But the barber not pitying poor Paddy's case
  Though the tears as big as apples rolled down poor Paddy's face

7 Up leapt Paddy and he run down the street
  'Twas the old widow Murphy he chanced for to meet
  O begorra now, Paddy, you sure got a drop
  When you thought you'd get a shave at the mad barber's shop

8 Now, be Japers, says Paddy, sure this was a t'aser
  I love a good shave with the devil's own razor
  He can lather and can shave all his friends in his seat
  But, be Japers, I'd sooner be shaved by Old Nick

228 JIM, THE CARTER LAD

Me name is Jim, the car-ter lad A jol-ly cock am I

I al-ways am con-ten-ted Be the wea-ther wet or dry ——

I crack me fin-gers at the snow And whis-tle at the rain ——

And I've braved the storm for ma-ny a day And can do so a-gain ——

CHORUS: So it's crack, crack, goes me whip I whis-tle and I sing ——

I sit up-on me wag-on I'm as hap-py as a king ——

My horse is al-ways wil-ling And for me, I'm ne-ver sad ——

There's none can lead a jol-li-er life Nor Jim, the car-ter lad ——

1 Me name is Jim, the carter lad
   A jolly cock am I
   I always am contented
   Be the weather wet or dry
   I crack me fingers at the snow
   And whistle at the rain
   And I've braved the storm for many a day
   And can do so again
   So it's crack, crack, goes me whip
   I whistle and I sing
   I sit upon me wagon
   I'm as happy as a king
   My horse is always willing
   And for me, I'm never sad
   There's none can lead a jollier life
   Nor Jim, the carter lad

2 My father was a carrier
   Many years e'er I was born
   He used to rise at daybreak
   And go his round each morn
   He would often take me with him
   Especially in the spring
   When I loved to sit upon the cart
   And hear me father sing

3 It's now the girls all smile on me
   As I go driving past
   The horse is such a beauty
   As we jog along so fast
   We've travelled many weary miles
   But happy days we've had
   And there's none can use a horse more kind
   Nor Jim, the carter lad

4 Now, friends, I bid you all: Adieu
   'Tis time I was away
   I know my horse will weary
   If I much longer stay
   To see your smiling faces here
   It makes me feel quite glad
   And I know you'll grant your kind applause
   To Jim, the carter lad

229 THE JOLLY MILLER

I am a jol-ly mil——ler come frae the mill o' Sàl-loch ——

And if you do not know— me, my name is Wil-lie Sprott ——

I play up-on— the bag-pipes with mic-kle mirth and glee ——

And I care for no-bo-dy, no not I, and no-bo-dy cares for me ——

1 I am a jolly miller come frae the mill o' S'alloch
   And if you do not know me, my name is Willie Sprott
   I play upon the bagpipes with mickle mirth and glee
   And I care for nobody, no not I, and nobody cares for me

2 First when I come here aboot, I'd too much for to do
   Wi' grindin corn and shearin grass, both late and early too
   But now the harvest's over and I maun mi' my lee
   And I care for nobody, no not I, and nobody cares for me

3 Wi' carrying heavy burdens, my back's inclined to bu'
   Wi' carrying heavy burdens, my back's near broke in two
   But nature has formed the eemost slip for a pinch of the sneeshin bree
   And I care for nobody, no not I, and nobody cares for me

4 My mill's got new machinery, it's somewhat strange to me
   It's of a new construction as ever me eyes did see
   Gin I o' twa o' three roonds o' her and a pinch of the broon drappie
   I'd care for nobody, no not I, and nobody cares for me

5 I'm engaged wi' Doctor Ramsey, he's laird o' a' owr land
   And when that he does call on me I am at his command
   Some people say he's quarrelsome but he never quarrels me
   So I care for nobody, no not I, and nobody cares for me

230 THE JOLLY WAGONER

1 When first I went a-wagonin', a-wagonin' did go
  I filled my parents' hearts full of sorrow, grief and woe
  And many were the hardships that I did undergo

  Sing: Whoa, me lads, sing: Whoa
  Drive on, me lads, hi-o
  Who would not lead the life
  Of a jolly wagoner?

2 It is a dark and stormy night and I'm wet to the skin
  But I'll bear it with contentment, till I gets to the inn
  Where I shall get good liquor and the landlord and his friends

3 The summer has a-come, my lads, the pleasures we shall see
  The blackbird and the thrush, they sings from every tree
  While the martins and the swallows, they fly above me

4 When winter it will come, my lads, and the stormy winds do blow
  We'll make the wheels rattle through the frost and through the snow
  Then every lad will take his lass and sit her on his knee

231 THE MACHINER'S SONG

It's all ve-ry well to have a ma-chine To thrash your wheat and bar-ley clean

To thrash it and win' it, all fit for sale Then go off to mar-ket so brisk and well

Sing-ing: Rum-ble-dum-dai-ry, flair up, Ma-ry And make her old ta-ble shine

1 It's all very well to have a machine
To thrash your wheat and barley clean
To thrash it and win' it, all fit for sale
Then go off to market so brisk and well
Singing: Rumble-dum-dairy, flair up, Mary
And make her old table shine

2 The man who made her he made her so well
He made every cog and wheel to tell
While the big wheel runs the little one hums
And the feeder sits above the drum

3 There's old father Howard the sheaves to put
While old mother Howard she does make up
And Mary she sits and feeds all day
While Johnny he carries the straw away

4 At seven o'clock we do begin
And we generally stop about nine or ten
To have our beer and oil her up
Then off we go till one o'clock

5 Then after a bite and a drink all round
The driver he climbs to his box again
And with his long whip he shouts: All right?
And he drives them round till five at night

232 THE MILLER'S LAST WILL

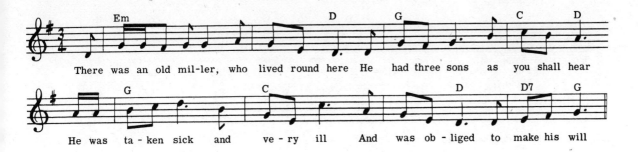

There was an old mil-ler, who lived round here He had three sons as you shall hear

He was ta-ken sick and ve-ry ill And was ob-liged to make his will

1 There was an old miller, who lived round here
He had three sons as you shall hear
He was taken sick and very ill
And was obliged to make his will

2 He called to him his eldest son
Said he: My life is almost done
And if to you these mills I give
Pray tell me what sort of toll you'll take?

3 Father, you know my name is Dick
And out of every bushel I'll take one peck
For from every bushel that I do grind
In that way a good living I shall find

4 You fool, you fool, the old man said
You have not half learned out your trade
And if to you these mills I give
On such a toll no man could live

5 So he called up his second son
Said he: My life is almost done
And if to you these mills I give
Pray tell me what sort of toll you'll take?

6 Father, you know my name is Ralph
And out of every bushel I'll take one half
And from every bushel that I do grind
In that way a good living I shall find

7 You fool, you fool, the old man said
You have not half learned out your trade
And if to you these mills I give
On such a toll no man could live

8 So he called up his youngest son
Said he: My life is almost done
And if to you these mills I give
Pray tell me what sort of toll you'll take?

9 Father, you know I am your boy
And taking a toll is all my joy
But rather than that I'd live in lack
I'll take the lot and swear to the sack

10 Good boy, good boy, the old man said
Thou has well learned thy father's trade
And now to thee these mills I'll give
On such a toll as that any man can live

11 And now the old man is dead and gone
And the youngest son is carrying on
But if any corn to grind you've got
Don't take it to him or he'll take the lot

233 NEEDLECASES

I'm a poor wand'-ring fel-low, my name it is Jack

No shoes to my feet, scarce-ly a rag to me back

My bel-ly's near-ly emp-ty, my feet they are sore

Won't you buy a case o' need-les from Jack that's so poor?

Need-le-cas-es, will you buy one? You will buy one, I'm sure

Won't you buy a case o' need-les From Jack that's so poor?

1 I'm a poor wand'ring fellow, my name it is Jack
No shoes to my feet, scarcely a rag to me back
My belly's nearly empty, my feet they are sore
Won't you buy a case o' needles from Jack that's so poor?

Needlecases, will you buy one?
You will buy one, I'm sure
Won't you buy a case o' needles
From Jack that's so poor?

2 I once had a table all lined with good food
Both of eating and of drinking and of everything that was good
But now I've no table, no friend nor not that
I'm forced to get a crust from the crown on my hat

3 I once was a farmer and followed my plough
Don't you think I'm a charmer, just look at me now
All tattered in rags from the bottom to top
Don't you think that I'm become a poor wandering rag-shop?

4 Now since you won't buy one, I think I must leave
But to leave such a good company it does my 'eart grieve
To leave you, to leave you, but if I should come back
Won't you buy a case o' needles from poor wandering Jack?

234 THE OYSTER GIRL

As I — was a-walk — ing,— up a Lon - don street —
A pret - ty lit - tle oys - ter girl, the first I chanced to meet
Her — clothes they were rag - ged, she'd no shoes up - on her feet
On her head she'd a bas - ket of oys - - - ters —
Her clothes they were rag - ged, she'd no shoes up - on her feet
On her head she'd a bas - ket of oys - - - ters —

1 As I was a-walking, up a London street
A pretty little oyster girl, the first I chanced to meet
Her clothes they were rag-ged, she'd no shoes upon her feet
On her head she'd a basket of oysters
Her clothes they were rag-ged, she'd no shoes upon her feet
On her head she'd a basket of oysters

2 O oysters, O oysters, O oysters, said she
I've got some of the finest oysters that ever you did see
O' tis three a penny I do sell, but four I'll give to thee
For to bargain for the basket of oysters

3 O oyster girl, O oyster girl, O oyster girl, said he
If you've got the finest oysters then I'll buy them all from thee
We'll go to some alehouse and we'll merry, merry be
While we bargain for the basket of oysters

4 O landlord, O landlord, O landlord, said he
Have you got a little private room for the oyster girl and me?
Where we both may sit down and so merry, merry be
While we bargain for the basket of oysters ➝

5 We sat down to supper and it's drinks we had a few
For this pretty little oyster girl she knew a thing or two
She pick-ed my pockets and it's down the stairs she flew
And she left me with her basket of oysters

6 O landlord, O landlord, O landlord, said he
Have you seen that little oyster girl that came along with me?
She hath pick-ed my pockets of eighty pounds and three
And left me with her basket of oysters

7 O yes, sir, O yes, sir, O yes, sir, said he
I've seen that little oyster girl that came along with thee
She hath paid all the reckoning so now you can go free
For to travel with her basket of oysters

8 I've travelled through Ireland, through Scotland and through France
But never was I, in all my life, served out by such a dance
For the English girls are certain, if you give them half a chance
They will teach you the way to sell oysters

235 THE PARSON AND THE CLERK

A par-son preached to his flock one day On the sins of the hu — man race
And the clerk: A - men, a - loud did say With the so-lem-nest tone and face
And the pi - ous clerk, on the quiet, — though Would ven-ture a bit of re - mark
O sin is sweet, said the par-son Then sin for me, said the clerk
A - - - men Then sin for me, said the clerk — LAST VERSE A - - men —

1 A parson preached to his flock one day
On the sins of the human race
And the clerk: Amen, aloud did say
With the solemnest tone and face
And the pious clerk, on the quiet, though
Would venture a bit of remark
O sin is sweet, said the parson
Then sin for me, said the clerk
Amen
Then sin for me, said the clerk

2 O never covet thy neighbour's goods
The parson he said, nor his maid
To rob a man of that what's his
Why a fellow should be afraid
Nor covet ye not no man of sin
I would venture this better to mark
Thy neighbour's wife, said the parson
The slavey for me, said the clerk
Amen
The slavey for me, said the clerk

3 O never sigh for that dross called gold
For blessed is the man that is poor
Nor cast ye away the loaves of bread
Nor fishes from the door
For, I grieve to say, it is my fate
To drive a carriage-and-pair in the park
With a thousand a year, said the parson
O give it me, said the clerk
Amen
There's no pride about me, said the clerk

4 My Christian friends and brethren
You should ever be humble and meek
And never strike a sinful man
When he smiteth you one on the cheek
But turn, my friends, to the erring one
Yes, turn to the sinner so dark
Thy other cheek, said the parson
I'll break his nose, said the clerk
Amen
Yes, land him one, said the clerk

5 O the boys are awfully friv-u-lous
The parson he said with a groan
The boys too oft at Sunday school
Won't let the young hussies alone
I've watched them grin behind their books
And I've seen the boys at their lark
They was kissing that girl, said the parson
I've done it myself, said the clerk
Amen
And they're fond of it too, said the clerk

6 Well now, my sermon, friends, is done
I bid you go work and pray
And don't do all your parson does
But do as your parson say
And be ready to part of all worldly care
I venture this modest remark
Never drink, said the parson
I am awfully dry, said the clerk
Amen
I'm off for a wet, said the clerk
Amen

236 POOR WEE JOCKIE CLARKE

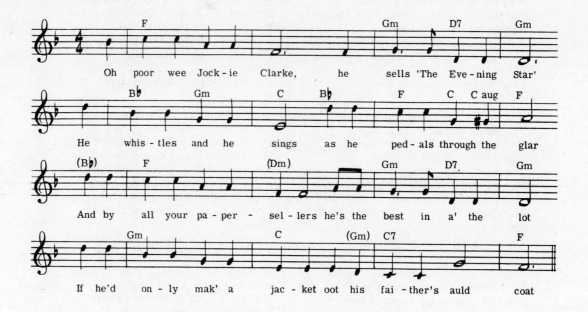

1 O poor wee Jockie Clarke, he sells *The Evening Star*
He whistles and he sings as he pedals through the glar
And by all your paper-sellers he's the best in a' the lot
If he'd only mak' a jacket oot his faither's auld coat

2 O Jockie's faither took a dram, as ye mun understan'
He was a tyrant till his wife and a plague unto the lan'
And oft-times by the neighbours he was called a drunken sot
For his little bits o' bairnies a' neglected an' forgot

3 Here, said Jockie till his mither: Nay, wauld woman, I do think shame
You'd think I'd nae a faither, a mither or a hame
My claes they are sae ragged, nae a heel stitch hae I got
Would you try an' mak' a jacket oot me faither's auld coat?

4 O Jockie's mither she looked doon at her bairney wi' a smile
And said: Me little canny lad, it's hardly worth my while
Now go on and sell your papers and be sure you sell the lot
And I'll try an' mak' a jacket oot your faither's auld coat

5 O the jacket it was made and it was unco' braw
It was a grand protection against the rain and snaw
The pooches in particular, o' Jockie's mind did please
It'd haud a stane o' tatties wi' the greatest o' ease

6 O, said Jockie till his mither: Ah, wauld woman, I do think shame
You'd think I'd baith a faither, a mither and a hame
My claes they are sae neatly, nae a ragged stitch I've got
Since you made me up the jacket oot me faither's auld coat

237 THE RIGS OF THE TIME

O 'tis of an old but-cher, I must bring him in

He charge two shil-lings a pound, — and thinks it no sin

Slaps his thumb on the scale-weights and makes them go down

He swears it's good weight yet it wants half a pound

Sing-ing: Hon-es-ty's all out of fash-ion —

These are the rigs of the time Time, my boys These are the rigs of the time

1 O 'tis of an old butcher, I must bring him in
  He charge two shillings a pound, and thinks it no sin
  Slaps his thumb on the scale-weights and makes them
  go down
  He swears it's good weight yet it wants half a pound

  Singing: Honesty's all out of fashion
  These are the rigs of the time
  Time, my boys
  These are the rigs of the time

2 Now the next is a baker, I must bring him in
  He charge fourpence a loaf and thinks it no sin
  When he do bring it in, it's not bigger than your fist
  And the top of the loaf is popped off with the ye'st

3 No wonder that butter be a shilling a pound
  See the little farmer's daughters, how they ride
  up and down
  If you ask them the reason they'll say: Bone', alas
  There's a French war and the cows have no grass

4 O the next is a publican, I must bring him in
  He charge fourpence a quart, he thinks it no sin
  When he do bring it in, the measure is short
  The top of the pot is popped off with the froth

5 Here's next to the tailor who skimps with our clothes
  And next the shoemaker who pinches our toes
  We've nought in our bellies, our bodies are bare
  No wonder we've reason to curse and to swear

6 Now the very best plan that I can find
  Is to pop them all up in a high gale of wynd
  And when they get up, the cloud it will bu'st
  And the biggest old rascal come tumbling down first

238 SIX JOLLY MINERS

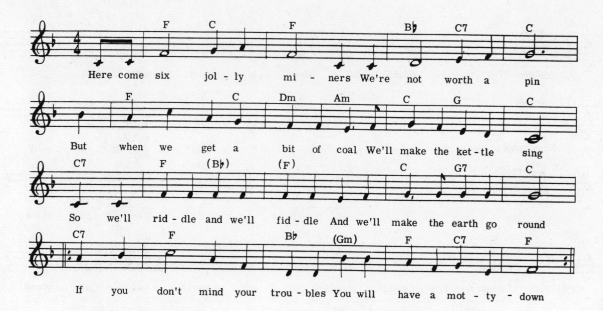

Here come six jol-ly mi-ners We're not worth a pin

But when we get a bit of coal We'll make the ket-tle sing

So we'll rid-dle and we'll fid-dle And we'll make the earth go round

If you don't mind your trou-bles You will have a mot-ty-down

1 Here come six jolly miners
We're not worth a pin
But when we get a bit of coal
We'll make the kettle sing
So we'll riddle and we'll fiddle
And we'll make the earth go round
If you don't mind your troubles
You will have a motty-down
If you don't mind your troubles
You will have a motty-down

2 Two came from Derby
And two from Derby town
The others came from Oughterbridge
And they all came firing down

3 We've travelled all of England
Scotland and Ireland round
And all of our delight
Is in working underground

4 All our delight, boys
Is to split the rocks in time
Our pleasure it is more than that
In working underground

5 We'll call for liquors plenty
And let the drinks go round
Here's health to the jolly miner lad
That works down underground

6 Sometimes we have money
But now we've none at all
And since you have good credit
It's upon you we do call

239 THE SOLDIER AND THE SAILOR

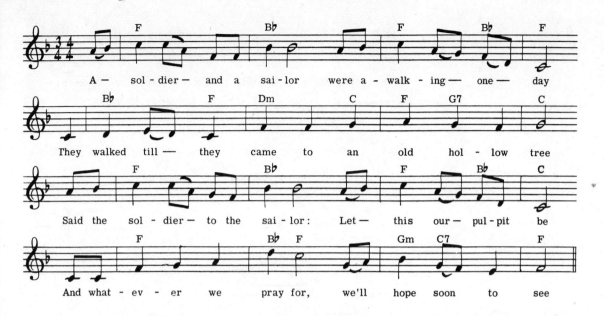

A — sol - dier — and a sai - lor were a - walk - ing — one — day

They walked till — they came to an old hol - low tree

Said the sol - dier — to the sai - lor: Let — this our — pul - pit be

And what - ev - er we pray for, we'll hope soon to see

1 A soldier and a sailor were a-walking one day
They walked till they came to an old hollow tree
Said the soldier to the sailor: Let this our pulpit be
And whatever we pray for, we'll hope soon to see

2 Now the first thing we'll pray for will be some good beer
Said the sailor to the soldier: I wish it was here
For where we get one pint I hope we'll get ten
And never, never want for liquor, cried the soldier: Amen

3 Now the next thing we'll pray for will be some good beef
Said the sailor to the soldier: We'll eat with relief
For where we get one pound I hope we'll get ten
And never, never go hungry, cried the soldier: Amen

4 Now the next thing we'll pray for will be our gracious queen
And may she live as happy and long may she reign
And where she get one man I hope she will have ten
May she never want for bounty, cried the soldier: Amen

5 Now the next thing we'll pray for will be a good wife
And may we live as happy all the days of our life
And if she be a bad one kick her out and out again
May the devil double-treble-trim her, cried the soldier: Amen

240 SWEEP, CHIM-NIE SWEEP

Sweep, chim—nie sweep Is the com-mon—cry I keep—

If you can but right-ly un-der-stand me

With my brush, broom and my rake With my brush, broom and my rake—

See what clean-lie work I make——

With my hoe,—— hoe,—— hoe—— and my hoe

And it's sweep,— chim-nie sweep, for—— me

1 Sweep, chim-nie sweep
Is the common cry I keep
If you can but rightly understand me
With my brush, broom and my rake
With my brush, broom and my rake
See what clean-lie work I make
With my hoe, hoe, hoe and my hoe
And it's sweep, chim-nie sweep, for me

2 Girls came unto the door
I looked as black as any Moor
I am as constant and true as the day
Although my face is black
Although my face is black
I can give as good a smack
And there's no-one, no-one, no-one, there's no-one
And there's no-one shall call me on high

3 It's arise, girls, arise
Wake up and open your eyes
Go and fetch me some ale that I might swallow
I can climb up to the top
I can climb up to the top
Without a ladder or a rope
And it's there you, there you, there you, and there you
And it's there you will hear me: Halloa

4 Now here I do stand
With my hoe all in my hand
Like a soldier that's on the sent-e-ry
I will work for a better sort
I will work for a better sort
And kindly thank them for it
I will work, work, work, and I'll work
And I'll work for none but gent-e-ry

217 A-BEGGIN' I WILL GO

Becket Whitehead, Delph, Yorkshire, *rec.* S. Ennis, 1952: BBC 18136

Printed versions
Playford: *Choyce Ayres*: 1684, Book V; and *Loyal Songs*: 1685
D'Urfey: 1698
Chappell: 1838, pp. 80 and 193: *The Jovial Beggars*
Dixon: 1846 and Bell: 1857: tune of *A-Nutting we will go* (*Nutting Girl*)
Chappell: 1858–9, vol. I, p. 345

Ford: 1899, p. 267: twenty-three verses *The Beggar's Chorus*
Sharp: 1902, No. 61, p. 130: *The Beggar's Chorus*
Greig: 1909, No. 30: *The Beggin'* (Scots)
Williams: 1923, p. 305: one verse (Oxfordshire)
Ord: 1930, p. 381 (Aberdeenshire)
JEFDSS: 1936, pp. 65–8: three variants: Aberdeenshire, *coll.* Rev. J. K. Maconochie, tune and some verses from Ford, and Playford: 1684; note by Anne Gilchrist about James V in disguise
Seeger and MacColl: 1960, p. 49: *To The Begging I Will Go* (Angus)

> Of all the trades in England
> The beggin' is the best
> For when a beggar's tired
> He can sit him down and rest

William Chappell believed that this was sung in 1641 at The Cockpit, Drury Lane, in Brome's comedy *The Jovial Crew* (or *The Merry Beggars*) as a Beggar's Chorus. Ten verses are printed, with a tune almost identical to that sung by Becket Whitehead, in Playford: *Choyce Ayres* and *Loyal Songs*. Here are the first and last:

> There was a jolly beggar
> He had a wooden leg
> Lame from his cradle
> And he was forced to beg

> I fear no plots against me
> I live in open cell
> Then who would be a King
> When beggars live so well

This would seem to be a reference to James V of Scotland travelling in disguise. A Scots version of the song with twenty-three verses contains interesting details of the beggar's preparations for his journeying:

> Afore that I do gang awa
> I'll let my beard grow strang
> And for my nails I winna pare
> For beggars wear them lang

> I'll gang seek my quarters
> Before that it grows dark
> Just when the gudeman's sittin doon
> And new hame frae his wark

> I'll gang to some greasy cook
> And buy frae her a hat
> Wi twa-three inches o the rim
> A-glitterin owre wi fat

> Syne I'll tak oot my muckle dish
> And stap it fu wi meal
> And say: Gudewife, gin ye gie me bree
> I winna seek your kail

> Syne I'll gang tae a turner
> And I'll gar him mak a dish
> And it maun haud three chappins
> For I couldna dae wi less

> And some will gie me breid and beef
> And some will gie me cheese
> And I'll slip oot amang the folk
> And gather the bawbees

Following the popularity of the song in the seventeenth century, the tune was published for instruments to play for dancing, so it may well be that the chorus of beggars in *The Jovial Crew* performed a dance called *The Beggar's Rant*. Further verses which were collected point to this:

> And should there be a marriage
> I'll endeavour to be there
> And I will give my blessing
> Upon the happy pair

> I'll go and buy some instruments
> For I'm sure that they're not scant
> And in among the marriage folk
> I'll dance the beggar's rant

218 THE BUCHAN MILLER

John MacDonald, Elgin, Moray, Scotland, *rec.* P. Kennedy, 1955: *Folk Songs of Britain*, vol. III, Caedmon TC 1144/Topic 12T159

Other recorded version
Lucy Stewart, Fetterangus, Aberdeenshire, Scotland, *rec.* P. Kennedy and H. Henderson, 1955

Printed versions
GARDINER MS: 1906: three variants (Hampshire)

SHARP MS: 1906–7: two variants (Somerset)
REEVES: 1958, No. 63, p. 56: *The Miller and the Lass*, coll. Sharp (Somerset)
PURSLOW: 1972, p. 60, *coll.* Gardiner (Hampshire)

CREIGHTON: 1962, p. 31: *The Miller*; the singer made the mill sound with an elbow and a hand on the table (Nova Scotia, Canada)

In traditional songs the miller is nearly always jolly and contented with his trade. He is of course an essential link in the farm community and his trade is jealously kept within the family (see *The Miller's Last Will*, No. 232).

The miller has a further reputation in the sphere of amorous achievements. In fact this song really falls within the class of those songs of courtship and seduction. The mill itself provides ideal conditions: it is warm and secluded and there are snug places for courtship 'among the bags of meal'.

Lucy Stewart sang two further verses between our fourth and fifth verses:

The lassie laughed an' gied a smile
And said she couldna tell O
The lassie laughed an' gied a smile
And said she couldna tell O
The lassie laughed an' gied a smile
Said she: Young man ye'll wait awhile
When ye hear your mill's a-clatterin din
Ye'll get me tae yersel' O

O I kissed her lips as sweet as honey
As sweet as honey dew O
O I kissed her lips as sweet as honey
As sweet as honey dew O
O I kissed her lips as sweet as honey
Until a tear cam in her e'e
Tae leave ma mammy all for thee
And bide wi' ye for ae O

219 THE CANDLELIGHT FISHERMAN

Phil Hamond, Morston, Holt, Norfolk, *rec.* P. Kennedy, 1952: BBC 18703; *Folk Songs of Britain*, vol. III, CAEDMON TC1144/TOPIC 12T159

This is the story of the self-employed sea fisherman who can suit himself. As Phil Hamond explained: 'He got to turn out of bed in the mornin'—he light the candle—he put it out the window. If the flame blow out there's too much wind for him to go, and if it don't blow out, then there ain't wind enough, so he go back to bed again.'

This same story is also told of fishermen at Mevagissey in Cornwall.

220 THE DOFFIN' MISTRESS

John McLaverty, Belfast, N. Ireland, *rec.* P. Kennedy and S. O'Boyle, 1952: BBC 18375

Other recorded versions
Charles O'Boyle, Belfast, *rec.* P. Kennedy and S. O'Boyle, 1952: *Billy Gillaspie*, BBC 18407
Hugh Quinn, Belfast, *rec.* P. Kennedy, 1954

Printed versions
DUNCAN MS: 1904: *To My Indenture I Was Bound*
GREIG: 1909–14, No. 44 (Aberdeenshire)
HENRY: 1924, No. 739: *Sea Apprentice* (N. Ireland)

Compare
The Apprentice Sailor (or *The 'Prentice Boy*)
Paddy McCluskey, Clough Mills, County Antrim, N. Ireland, *rec.* P. Kennedy and S. O'Boyle, 1953: BBC 20032
Robert Cinnamond, Belfast, *rec.* S. O'Boyle, 1955: BBC 24836

CREIGHTON: 1932, p. 304 (Newfoundland, Canada)
GREENLEAF: 1933, No. 107, p. 214 (Newfoundland, Canada)
PEACOCK: 1965, p. 575: two variants (Newfoundland, Canada)

Hugh Quinn remembered that the last time he heard this sung in the streets of Belfast was in 1894 when he was only ten years old.

A 'doffing mistress' was the woman in charge of a room of mill-workers. When she left the mill to get married, or to take up a more lucrative job in another mill, the mill-workers escorted her home on her last day, singing and gesticulating. While she was having her tea, they sang outside her door and their late doffing mistress made a speech from a top window. Then they dispersed, singing lively airs, in the way that a military band plays brisk and bright music on returning from the funeral of a dead comrade.

Charles Boyle remembered a verse about a spinning master called *Billy Gillaspie*:

> O Billy Gillaspie goes down the pass
> He spreads his feet like an old jackass
> He turns around for to view the frames
> Singing: Damn you doffers, lay up your ends
> Laddie, whack-fol-day
> Laddie, whack-fol-day

The tune of *The Doffin' Mistress* is similar to that used for a Scots-Irish sailor song called *The Apprentice Sailor* or *The 'Prentice Boy*; in fact one could say that this was its matrix. Here are two recorded verses:

> Seven years I'm apprentice bound
> To sail the salt sea round and round
> I never sailed a voyage but one
> Till I fell in love with young Mary Anne
> Fol-the-doo-aye-day
> Fol-the-doo-aye-day

> I bought her ear-rings, I bought her rings
> I bought her many's the precious things
> She took them all and was in no way shy
> And she drank her health to her prentice boy

221 THE FACTORY GIRL

Sarah Makem, Keady, County Armagh, N. Ireland, *rec.* P. Kennedy and S. O'Boyle, 1952: BBC 18536

Other recorded versions
Margaret Barry, Dundalk, County Louth, Ireland, *rec.* P. Kennedy, 1953
Ben Baxter, Southrepps, Norfolk, *rec.* S. Ennis, 1955: BBC 22156

Printed versions
GARDINER MS: 1906: one variant (Hampshire)
HENRY: 1924, No. 127 (County Derry, N. Ireland)
PURSLOW: 1972, p. 29, *coll.* Gardiner (Hampshire)

> It's not for to scorn you, fair maid, I adorn you
> But grant me one favour, love, where do you dwell?
> Kind sir, you'll excuse me, for now I must leave thee
> For yonder's the sound of the factory bell

Sam Henry published nine verses of a Derry version of this song in his column 'Songs of the People' in the *Northern Constitution*, a newspaper published at Coleraine in the 1920s. This version tells how the hard-working factory girl got married to the local squire.

> Now this maid she's got married and became a great lady
> Became a rich lady of fame and renown
> She may bless the day and the bright summer's morning
> She met with the squire and on him did frown

The linen mills in Ireland were the 'factories'. Margaret Barry heard the song in County Cork and believed that it referred to a particular factory above Blackpool.

222 FAGAN THE COBBLER

Albert Richardson, Blaxhall, Woodbridge, Suffolk, *rec.* P. Kennedy, 1953: *Folk Songs of Britain*, vol. III, CAEDMON TC1144/TOPIC 12T159; 16mm ciné film: *Health to the Barley Mow* produced by P. Kennedy, Folk Films, 1968

Other recorded versions
Louis Brown, Burton Bradstock, Dorset, *rec.* P. Kennedy, 1950
Sarah Makem, Keady, County Armagh, N. Ireland, *rec.* P. Kennedy and S. O'Boyle, 1952: *Dick Derby*

Compare
REEVES: 1960: No. 21, p. 73; similar cobbler song, *coll.* Gardiner
GARDNER AND CHICKERING: 1939, p. 935: *My Father's a Lawyer in England* (Michigan, USA)
LOMAX: 1960, p. 134: from GARDNER AND CHICKERING
JAFL: No. 29, p. 187

'Wickets' Richardson generally introduced this song with a short speech. He'd say: 'Ladies and gentlemen, I've sung this song before The Queen and The King and various other public houses.' Then he'd sing One Two Three, remarking 'that's the Overture, ladies and gentlemen'. The chorus of the song he'd act out, using both his shoes: one for the hammer and the other to represent a shoe being repaired. His performance has been recorded visually on film (see above).

Sarah Makem sang a version which was about Dick Derby, the cobbler:

1 O my name is Dick Derby, I'm a cobbler
   I serv-ed my time with old camp
   Some call me an old agitator
   But now I'm resolved to repent

   With my ing-twing of an ing-ting of an aye-doe
   With me ing-twing of an ing-ting of an aye-day
   With my roo-boo-boo, roo-boo-boo randy
   And my lap-stone keeps b'ating away

2 Now there's forty long years I have travelled
   All by the contents of my pack
   My hammers, my awls and my pincers
   I carry them all on me back

3 O my father was hung for sheep stealing
   My mother was burned for a witch
   My sister's a dandy house-keeper
   And I'm a mechanical switch

4 O my wife she's humpy, she's lumpy
   My wife she's the devil, she's black
   And no matter what I may do with her
   Her tongue it goes clicketty-clack

5 It was early one fine summer's morning
   A little before it was light
   I dipped her three times in the river
   And carelessly bid her: Good night

223 GREEN BROOMS

Sean McDonagh, Carna, County Galway, Ireland, *rec.* S. Ennis and A. Lomax, 1951: *Folk Songs of Britain*, vol. III, CAEDMON TC1144/TOPIC 12T159

Other recorded versions
Art O'Keefe, Lisheen, County Kerry, 1947: BBC 11887
Patrick Green, Ballinalee, County Longford, 1947: BBC 12055
Louis Hooper, Hambridge, Somerset, 1942: BBC 4015
Sam Larner, Winterton, Norfolk, 1959: BBC 26076
George Belton, Arundel, Sussex: EFDSS LP1008

Printed versions
D'URFEY: 1720, vol. VI, p. 100: *The Jolly Broom-man* or *The Unhappy Boy Turned Thrifty*
RITSON: 1783
BRUCE AND STOKOE: 1882, p. 98 (Northumberland)

BARING GOULD: 1889, No. 10: edited text (Devon)
STOKOE AND REAY: 1892 (Northumberland)
BROADWOOD: 1893, p. 88 (Norfolk)
JFSS: 1901, No. 3, p. 84: *coll.* W. Percy Merrick, Surrey
SHARP MS: 1903–22: six variants (Somerset)
GARDINER MS: 1905–8: three variants (Hampshire)
SHARP AND MARSON: 1904–9, vol. IV, No. 104 (Somerset)
GREIG: 1909–14, No. 122: *The Broom Cutter* (No. 124 contains further verses) (Aberdeenshire)
WILLIAMS: 1923, p. 152 (Wiltshire)
HENRY: 1924, No. 147 (N. Ireland)
KIDSON AND MOFFAT: 1926, p. 86 (Yorkshire)
REEVES: 1960, No. 56, p. 131: *coll.* G. Gardiner, Hampshire
KARPELES: 1971, p. 230 (Newfoundland)

There was an old farmer lived down in the west
His money and trade was all gone
He had a lazy boy Jack for son
And he lay in bed till noon

The farmer in our version of the song lives in the east, but in other versions collected in England and Ireland we find the west is more favoured. George Gardiner collected a *Green Broom* in Hampshire in which the town where Jack meets the good lady is called Perfume:

Oh a lady I am and a lady by name
I lives in this town of Perfume
And if you'll be married, I'll be your offer
For I fancy both you and your broom

The trade of broom-cutting here is intended to be erotic and for this reason the song could well be classed as a seduction ballad. D'Urfey's *Pills to Purge Melancholy* contained what James Reeves has described as a discreetly suggestive version of fourteen verses. According to Reeves, Baring Gould emended his version for publication in *Songs of the West* so that its meaning was literal rather than metaphorical.

224 THE HARD TIMES OF OLD ENGLAND

Ron Copper, Rottingdean, Brighton, Sussex, *rec.* P. Kennedy, 1955: EFDSS LP 1004

Compare
Harry Cox, Catfield, Norfolk, *rec.* P. Kennedy, 1953: EFDSS LP 1004: *What Will Become of Eng-e-land*

In the repertoire of the outstanding English folksingers there are some songs of outspoken protest. After listening to a large number about the contented lot of the farm labourer and country craftsman, one eventually comes across the song which complains bitterly about the way things are going. Outstanding among these is *The Rigs of the Time* (No. 237), which comments on the trickery of various tradesmen in times of need. *The Hard Times of Old England* may well be a variant. It concerns the tradesmen who are unable to find employment in time of war, but it is not wholly gloomy and ends on an optimistic note: that the hard times will not last long.

It is interesting to note that all the American equivalents of *The Rigs of the Time* have a chorus of 'Hard times' and this in fact is the name by which the song is known across the Atlantic.

Harry Cox had a two-verse fragment of a similar type of song of complaint:

> What will become of Eng-e-land if things go on this way?
> There's many a thousand working man is starving day by day
> He cannot find employment, for bread his children cry
> And hundreds of those children, they now lay in their graves
>
> Some have money plenty, but still they crave for more
> They will not lend a hand to help the starving poor
> They pass you like a dog, and on you cast a frown
> That is the way old Eng-e-land the working man cast down

225 THE HOT ASH-PELT

John McLaverty, Belfast, N. Ireland, *rec.* P. Kennedy
  and S. O'Boyle, 1952: BBC 18310

Other recorded version
Ben Baxter, Southrepps, Norfolk, *rec.* S. Ennis, 1956:
  BBC 23383 (chorus only)

Printed version
MacColl: 1953, p. 148: one verse only *Hot Ashphalt*,
  from his father William Miller (Stirling, Scotland)

Compare
Tune: *Napoleon Crossing the Alps* (march)
Paddy McCluskey (fiddle), Clough Mills, Co. Antrim,
  rec. P. Kennedy and S. O'Boyle, 1953: BBC 21152
John Doherty, Fintown, Donegal, *rec.* P. Kennedy and
  S. O'Boyle, 1953

> Good evening all me jolly lads, I'm glad to see you well
> If you gather all around me, boys, a story I will tell
> For I've got a situation and begorra 'ts a fancy job
> I can whisper: I've the weekly wage of eighteen bob

This was the introductory verse sung by an Irish travelling tinker, at Blairgowrie, Perthshire, Scotland. John McLaverty omitted this introduction and sang only three refrains, but the tinker had a refrain after each of his six verses. 'Peeler' is a slang term for a policeman and 'duidin' is Irish for a small tobacco pipe.

A considerable number of Irish street ballads have been composed to this tune, perhaps the best known ballad being *Let Mister Maguire Sit Down*. There is also a march called *Napoleon Crossing the Alps*.

226 THE HUSBAND-MAN AND THE SERVANT-MAN

Raymond and Frederick Cantwell, Standlake, Oxfordshire, *rec.* P. Kennedy, 1956: BBC 23537

Other recorded versions
Dorchester Mummers, Dorset, 1936: BBC 14290
Fred Crossman, Huish Episcopi, Somerset, *rec.* P.
  Kennedy, 1950
Tom Eveleigh, Eype, Dorset, *rec.* P. Kennedy, 1951:
  BBC 22323
Symondsbury Mummers, Dorset, *rec.* P. Kennedy, 1957:
  The Singing of the Travels, BBC 25509; *Folk Songs of
  Britain*, vol. IX, Caedmon TC1124/Topic 12T197

Printed versions
Broadwood: 1843, No. 13 (Sussex)

Dixon: 1846: note about recitative performance style
Bell: 1857, p. 46 (as Dixon: 1846)
Chappell: 1858, p. 118: *I Am the Duke of Norfolk*
Broadwood: 1890, p. 26 (Sussex)
Broadwood, 1893, p. 144 (Hampshire)
Sharp and Marson: 1904–9, vol. III, No. 71 (Somerset)
Sharp MS: 1907: two further variants
Sharp (School Series): 1912, Set VI: *coll.* Hammond,
  arr. R. Vaughan Williams (Dorset)
Udal: 1922, p. 95: in Mummers Play (W. Dorset)
Williams: 1923, p. 112 (Wiltshire)
JEFDSS: 1952, p. 11: *The Singing of the Travels*
  (Symondsbury Mummers)

> We're to meet our brothers dear all on the highway
> And so solemn I was walking along
> So pray come tell to me what calling yours may be
> And I'll have you for some servant man

So sings St George and his chorus of soldiers in the local folk play performed by Christmas mummers in Dorset. They call the song *The Singing of the Travels*, and while they are singing they march in a circle, first in one direction and then in another, around three other actors who stand in the centre. The three actors represent a countryman called Jan, his wife called Old Bet, and the hobby horse known as Tommy the pony. After singing the first part of the verse, the soldiers stand facing centre while Jan speaks the Servant Man's reply:

> For all thy diligence I give thee many thanks
> Aye, and I'll quit thee as soon as I can
> For I can plough and sow, aye, and reap and mow
> But vain do I know whether you can do so
> To show the pleasure of a servant man

Then his wife, Bet, backs him up by saying 'No Jan'. The song continues in this way verse by verse and ends with a Christmas chant.

Apparently speaking the lines of this song is nothing new. When it was printed in *Ancient Poems and Songs of the Peasantry* for the Percy Society in 1846, Mr Dixon remarked that the song was 'said in a sort of chant or recitative'.

Most collectors have drawn attention to the similarity of the tune used for this song with those used for the May Carols, *The Moon Shines Bright*, and *God Rest Ye Merry Gentlemen*. William Chappell found it to be a version of *St Paul's Steeple*, which was published in Playford's *Dancing Master*, a song appealing for a new steeple to replace the one which came tumbling down when London's St Paul's Cathedral was burnt in 1561. In about 1728 the same tune was used for a song in *The Cobbler's Opera*:

> I am the Duke of Norfolk newly come to Suffolk
> Say shall I be attended or no, no, no
> Good duke, be not offended and you shall be attended
> And you shall be attended now, now, now

227 THE IRISH BARBER

Jack Weafer, Wexford, Ireland, *rec.* London by S. Ennis, 1955: BBC 22373

Compare
SHARP AND MARSON, 1904, vol. II, No. 48: *The Irish Bull*, a similar song (Somerset)
GARDINER MS: 1907: *Pat and the Barber* (Hampshire)

SHOEMAKER: 1931, p. 134 (Pennsylvania, USA)
HENRY: 1938, p. 409 (Tennessee, USA)
BELDEN: 1940, p. 251 (Missouri, USA)
BECK: 1941, p. 225: *Lather and Shave* (Michigan, USA)
CREIGHTON: 1962, p. 136: *Love o' God Razor* (Canada)
MEREDITH AND ANDERSON: 1967, p. 211: *The Love-of-God Shave* (Australia)

There must at some time have been a particular incident at a particular barber's shop which sparked off a whole set of ballads about Irish barbers as a whole. The next most popular to the one given here is called *The Monkey Turned Barber* which appeared on many nineteenth-century broadsides. Cecil Sharp collected a version in Somerset called *The Irish Bull*:

> O I went into the barber's shop it was to get shaved
> Where an old ugly monkey unto all ill behaved
> He lathered and he shaved me and he cut me as you see
> He was dressed like a man, ah, but 'twas a monk-ee

228 JIM, THE CARTER LAD

Jack Goodfellow, Rennington, Northumberland, *rec.* P. Kennedy, 1954: BBC 22443; *Folk Songs of Britain*, vol. III, CAEDMON TC1144/TOPIC 12T159

Other recorded versions
Cornelius Godwin, Ashcott, Somerset, 1938: BBC 1672
Jimmy McBeath, Elgin, Moray, Scotland, *rec.* A. Lomax, 1952
Becket Whitehead, Delph, W. Yorkshire, *rec.* S. Ennis, 1952: BBC 18136

Jim (Harold) Swain, Angmering, Sussex, *rec.* R. Copper, 1954: BBC 22763
George Belton, Arundel, Sussex: EFDSS LP 1008

Printed versions
GREIG: 1909–14, No. 94: *Jim the Carter Lad* (Scotland)
HENRY: 1924, No. 171: *Jim the Carman Lad* (N. Ireland)
HAMER: 1967, p. 68: *Jimmy the Carter Lad* (Cornwall)

This song is still popular and versions have been collected in England, Ireland and Scotland. It gives a vivid picture of the young country carrier sitting upon his wagon caring even more about his horse than the sight of the young girls he passes as he jogs along.

> I never think of politics or anything so great
> I care not for their high talk about the Church or State
> I act aright as man to man and that's what makes me glad
> You'll find there beats an honest heart in Jim the carter lad

229 THE JOLLY MILLER

John Strachan, Fyvie, Aberdeenshire, Scotland, *rec.* A. Lomax, 1951: *Folk Songs of Britain*, vol. III, CAEDMON TC1144/TOPIC 12T159

Printed versions
CHAPPELL: 1838, No. xxii, p. 43
CHAPPELL: 1858, pp. 666–8: *The Budgeon it is a Delicate Trade*

GREIG: 1909–14, No. 41: *The Miller o' Straloch* (Aberdeenshire, Scotland)
SHARP MS: 1909–14 (London and Yorkshire)
GARDINER MS: 1906 (Hampshire)
WILLIAMS: 1923, p. 194: *The Miller of the Dee*; a conversation between a miller and Old King Hal (Oxfordshire)

> I'm nae gien up to drinkin', it never troubles me
> Nor is there one of the female sex would keep my sleep from me
> But there's one thing I am subject to, is a pinch o' the broon Rappee
> And when that I'm deprived o' that, I'm no good company

Gavin Greig noted this verse and identifies the location of the song as Straloch, a property to the north-west of Newmachar station in Aberdeenshire, east of Inverurie and north of Aberdeen. However, this may well be a localized bothy ballad version of an older *Jolly Miller*, in the same way that *The Miller of Dee* may also have been a literary reworking of the same common original.

> There was a jolly miller once lived on the river Dee
> He worked and sang from morn till night, no lark more blithe than he
> And this the burden of his song forever used to be
> I care for nobody, no not I, if nobody cares for me
>
> The reason why he was so blithe he once did thus unfold
> The bread I eat my hands have earned, I covet no man's gold
> I do not fear next quarter-day, in debt to none I be
> I care for nobody, no not I, if nobody cares for me
>
> A coin or two I've in my purse to help a needy friend
> A little I can give the poor and still have some to spend
> Though I may fail, yet I rejoice, another's good hap to see
> I care for nobody, no not I, if nobody cares for me
>
> So let us his example take and be from malice free
> Let everyone his neighbour serve, as served he'd like to be
> And merrily push the can about and drink and sing with glee
> If nobody cares a doit for us, why, not a doit care we

William Chappell believed the song used an older tune, that of *The Budgeon it is a Delicate Trade*, a song about the trade of house-thieving which used cant terms, published in 1725.

> The budgeon it is a delicate trade and a delicate trade of fame
> For when that we have bit the blow we carry away the game
> But if the cully nab us and the lurries from us take
> O then he rubs us to the whit though we are not worth a make

The tune was afterwards introduced into a number of ballad operas including *The Quaker's Opera* (1728); one stanza of *There was a Jolly Miller* was sung in Bickerstaffe's *Love in a Village* (1762) and the song is therefore sometimes attributed to him. The tune was one of those harmonized by Beethoven for George Thompson's collection of *Scotch Songs* (1824). It was included not because it was Scotch but because it was popular.

230 THE JOLLY WAGONER

Fred Jordan, Diddlebury, Wenlock, Shropshire, *rec.* P. Kennedy, 1952: BBC 18696

Printed versions
DIXON: 1846 and BELL: 1857: words only
BARING GOULD: 1895: edited version

SHARP: 1902: No. 25, p. 54, from BARING GOULD AND SHEPPARD: 1895
BARING GOULD AND SHARP: 1906, No. 34: for schools
WILLIAMS: 1923, p. 157: words only (Wiltshire)
KIDSON AND MOFFAT: 1926, p. 44: *The Warbling Waggoner* (Yorkshire)

This is another carrier song like *Jim, the Carter Lad* (No. 228), which has enjoyed widespread popularity in England. In 1835 a parody was made of the song on the ruinous effect of the railways on the highway taverns:

> Along the country roads, alas, but waggoners few are seen
> The world is topsy-turvy turned and all things go by steam
> And all the past is passed away like to a moving dream
> The landlords cry: What shall we do, our business is no more?
> *The railway it has ruined us, who badly fared before*
> *'Tis luck and gold to one or two, but ruin for a score*

231 THE MACHINER'S SONG

Bob and Ron Copper, Rottingdean, Brighton, Sussex,
rec. P. Kennedy, 1955: EFDSS LP 1002 (1963)
Other recorded version
Jim Copper, 1951: *The Threshing Song*, BBC 16067;
Columbia SL 206 (1952)

Frank Bond, North Waltham, Hampshire, *rec.* R. Cop-
per, 1955: *The Chiners Song*, BBC 21862
Printed version
Gardiner MS: 1905–6: two variants (Hampshire)

1 Six o'clock come we now begin
  We usually start twixt nine and ten
  To wind her up and see all things right
  And she'll dress two ricks and a half be night
    Sing Fal the ol ler um
    Fal the lal laddie aye day

2 There's Jimmy Bailey runs a concern
  'E's plenty of coal and wood to burn
  He pulls a lever and makes her grunt
  And the wheels'll keep going round for a month

3 There's Brewer Allan the sheaves to put
  The liveliest gait he must keep up
  Old Chin keeps shipping the bonds all day
  And Butler 'elps her cave-ing away

4 There's big old Hungen and Plumer Hyde
  On the corn rick work and side by side
  They takes it easy, 'tis just like play
  Supplyin' Old Brewer with sheaves all day

5 The 'chine got blocked the other day
  I heard old Jimmy Bailey say
  Here comes Herb Mender so we shan't be long
  Hoppin' along with his cave and prong

6 There's Wickey and Mush a-building the rick
  To see 'em working it is a freak
  They build 'em round and square and flat
  And tops 'em up the shape o' your hat

7 There's Sammy Elmer and Old Tom too
  Hoein' the corn, they got plenty to do
  They got a sack'lifter of great renown
  Who squeezes the handle, to steady her down

8 There's our old Lucy works at 'the Sun'
  If there's ever a nut, well she is one
  I come in to-day, there was no-body here
  She gave me bitter instead of beer

Frank Bond sang these verses to Bob Copper. He called it *The Chiners Song* (pron. 'Sheeners') and believed it to be mainly his own composition, dating from about 1906–7. However the song had previously been collected in Hampshire and it was therefore mainly the substitution of local names which made Frank's contribution. He used a variant of the tune *Richard of Taunton Dene*. Chining ('Sheening'), he told Bob Copper, was the name they always gave to the use of the threshing machine.

One of the best-known accounts of the working of a threshing machine as it travelled from farm to farm is to be found in Thomas Hardy's *Tess of the d'Urbervilles*.

232 THE MILLER'S LAST WILL

William Arken, Boscastle, Cornwall, *rec.* P. Kennedy, 1950
Other recorded versions
Edwin Thomas, Allerford, Somerset, *rec.* P. Kennedy and Maud Karpeles, 1952: BBC 17778
Harry Cox, Catfield, Norfolk, *rec.* P. Kennedy, 1953
Jack Endacott, Chagford, Devon, *rec.* P. Kennedy, 1954: BBC 22323

Printed versions
Dixon: 1846 and Bell: 1857, p. 194
Chappell: 1858–9, p. 773: note to *The Oxfordshire Tragedy* (p. 191) as tune used for this song
Roxburghe: 1871–93, III, 681: *The Miller's Advice to his Three Sons*

Bruce and Stokoe: 1882 (Northumberland)
Baring Gould: 1889, No. 12: sung by a miller (Devon)
Stokoe and Reay: 1892, p. 94 (Northumberland)
Gardiner MS: 1906: one variant (Hampshire)
Greig: 1914, vol. II, No. 41 (Aberdeenshire)
Whittaker: 1921 (Northumberland)
Williams: 1923, p. 192 (Wiltshire)
Purslow: 1965, p. 56: *coll.* Gardiner (Hampshire)

Newell: 1884–1903, p. 103
Sharp and Karpeles: 1917–32, No. 116: two variants (Kentucky and N. Carolina, USA)
Cox: 1925, pp. 450 and 531

There was a miller who had three sons
And knowing his life was almost run
He called them all and asked their will
If that to them he left his mill

The miller reproves the eldest son and the second also for not intending to take enough toll, but the youngest wins his heart by saying:

Father, you know I am your boy
And in taking toll is all my joy
Rather than I'd good living lack
I'd take the whole and forswear the sack

These words from *The Roxburghe Ballads* were quoted in 1858 by William Chappell as still then being sung in the north of England.

In many places the tradition is to imitate the clatter of the mill by working the hands and elbows on the table during the chorus.

233 NEEDLECASES

Arthur Smith, Swinbrook, Burford, Oxfordshire, *rec.*
 P. Kennedy, 1952: BBC 18688

Printed versions
WILLIAMS: 1923, p. 234 (Gloucestershire)

KIDSON AND MOFFAT: 1929, p. 112: *Case of Needles* (Yorkshire)
JEFDSS: 1946, p. 18: first verse only *coll.* Bob Arnold and F. Collinson, Brize Norton (Oxfordshire)
OPIE: 1951, p. 326: *Jack-a-needle*: note about peddling

After singing the first chorus Arthur Smith called out, 'It'll only cost you sixpence, the paper!' and explained that the local pedlars used to sell their pins, at so much for a sheet on which they were fastened, and this was known as 'a paper of pins'. Sometimes the papers had poems or old songs printed on them.

Another version of the tune, also from Oxfordshire, collected by Bob Arnold, a local folksong collector, and submitted by Francis Collinson, may be found in JEFDSS: 1946, p. 18, where the song is compared with the children's choosing game *Jack o' Needles* and also with the tune of the *Spanish Waltz* or *Guaracha*.

234 THE OYSTER GIRL

Phil Tanner, Llangennith, Glamorganshire, Wales, *coll.*
 Maud Karpeles, 1937: BBC 1711

Printed versions
DUNCAN MS: 1904: two variants (Aberdeenshire, Scotland)
SHARP MS: 1904: one variant (Somerset)

GREIG: 1914, vol. II, No. 96: *The Girl and the Oysters* (Aberdeenshire, Scotland)
HENRY: 1924, No. 725: *The Basket of Oysters* (N. Ireland)
KIDSON AND MOFFAT: 1929, p. 108 (Yorkshire)
CHAPPELL: 1939 (N. Carolina, USA)

As I walked up Manchester street
A pretty little oyster girl I happened for to meet
And into her basket so neatly I did peep
To see if she had gotten any oysters

O it's oysters, oysters, oysters, quo' she
If you want any oysters, buy them a' frae me
It's four for a penny but five I'll gie to thee
If you deal in my basket of oysters

We'll go down to yon tavern, yon tavern quo' she
If you want any oysters, buy them a' frae me
And then to the dance hall an hour two or three
Where she laid down her basket of oysters

We danced till my noddle was all in a clew
Then out of my pocket my treasure she drew
And downstairs like lightning this oyster girl flew
And left me her basket of oysters

O it's landlord, landlord, landlord, quo' he
Did you see the little oyster girl was dancin' with me?
She has rifled my pockets and stole my money
And left me a basket of oysters

Oh ho says the landlord that's a fine joke
Since you have got no money you must pop off your coat
For the landlady says she has got it in her book
That she gave you bread and butter to your oysters

I've travelled through England, Ireland and France
And in all my travels I ne'er met such a lass
For the Manchester girls they would learn you how to dance
If you deal in their basket o' oysters

This was *The Basket of Oysters* which appeared in the Irish newspaper the *Northern Constitution*, published at Coleraine, County Derry, contributed by Sam Henry in 1924 as one of *The Songs of the People*. It is here printed in full. The song appeared on numerous ballad sheets printed in England, and is well-known to English country singers.

235 THE PARSON AND THE CLERK

Phil Tanner, Llangennith, Glamorganshire, Wales, *coll.*
Maud Karpeles, 1949: BBC 13385; *Folk Songs of Britain*, vol. X, CAEDMON TC1225/TOPIC 12T198;
EFDSS LP 1005

These religious sermon parodies must have enjoyed a fairly widespread popularity over a long period. Other examples are *The Soldier and the Sailor* (No. 239) and *The Mare and the Foal* (not included in this collection). In the case of the best known, *The Soldier and the Sailor*, the sermon does not take place in church, and the pulpit is 'an old hollow tree'.

236 POOR WEE JOCKIE CLARKE

Lucy Stewart, Fetterangus, Aberdeenshire, Scotland, *rec.* P. Kennedy and H. Henderson, 1955
Other recorded version
Bob Clarke, Whittingham, Northumberland, *rec.* P. Kennedy, 1954: BBC 20629: *Fairther's Old Coat*

Printed version
MacColl: 1953, p. 95: two verses only *Faither's Old Coat* from William Miller, Stirlingshire, Scotland

O poor wee Johnnie Clarke he sells the *News* and *Star*
He whistles and he sings as he pedals through the glar
Among other paper-sellers he's the blithest of the lot
If he only had a jacket not his fairther's auld coat

Bob Clarke in Northumberland played the tune on his googa (jew's harp) and sang four verses similar to those recorded from Lucy Stewart in Scotland. The *News* and the *Star* are the names of Glasgow newspapers and one can be certain that the song must have originated there. The song is sparked off by the sight of the young paper boys wearing coats several sizes too big for them standing on the street corners as the men came from work in the evening.

237 THE RIGS OF THE TIME

J. W. ('Charger') Salmons, Stalham, Norfolk, *rec.* P. Kennedy and A. Lomax: COLUMBIA SL 206 (1950); 'The Windmill', Sutton, Norfolk: BBC 13864 (1947)
Printed versions
WILLIAMS: 1923, p. 104: words only *Here's First to those Farmers* (Berkshire)

American and Canadian versions, entitled *Hard Times*:
LOMAX: 1910, p. 103: words only (Texas); (1938): p. 176 (Oregon)

COX: 1925, p. 511: mixed with a night visiting song (Virginia)
LOMAX: 1934, p. 138 (New Jersey)
HUDSON: 1936, p. 215: words only (Mississippi)
BELDEN: 1940, p. 433 (Missouri)
BROWN: 1952, p. 419 (N. Carolina)
LOMAX: 1960, p. 438: from LOMAX: 1934
PEACOCK: 1965, p. 57: two variants (Canada)

Come listen awhile and I'll sing you a song
Concerning our times but I won't keep you long
For although everybody from each other must buy
We're cheating each other, I can't tell you why

From brother to sister, from father to mother
From uncle to aunt, we're all cheating each other
Dishonesty's grown to be so much in fashion
I believe that this cheating will ruin the nation

Here is another song of complaint like *The Hard Times of Old England* (No. 224), to which this one may well be related; *Hard Times* is the chorus and the title of its American cousins.

Alfred Williams collected a Berkshire version with other verses:

Here's first to the farmers who do sell the corn
And they are as big rogues as ever was born
They are never contented but still they have none
If the land was to yield fifty bushels for one

Now the next rogue I found was a thief in a mill
Out of other folk's bags his own for to fill
And all his delight was in taking of toll
One with a dish and the other with a bowl

And next there's the lawyer, you plainly will see
He'll plead for your case for a very large fee
All day he will talk proving all wrong is right
He'll make you believe that a black horse is white

And next there's the parson, he'll soon have your soul
If you stick to the book you will keep off the dole
He'll give you his blessing and likewise his curse
Put his hand in your pocket and walk off with your purse

And next there's the doctor I nearly forgot
I believe in my heart that he's worst of the lot
He'll tell you he'll cure you for half you possess
And when you are buried he'll take all the rest

Across the Atlantic other tradesmen are brought in, such as merchants, carpenters and fishermen, and in some cases the song has been blended with a love song to include bachelors and widows, young men and maids.

Versions of the song appear on various broadsheets. One such is *Adulterations* (to the tune of *Dennis Bulgruddery*):

The grocer sells ash leaves, and sloe leaves for tea
Ting'd with Dutch pink and virdigris, just like Bohea
What slow poison means, Sloman now has found out
We shall to a T be poisoned no doubt

The milkman, although he is honest he vows
Milks his pumps night and morn quite as oft as his cows
Claps you plenty of chalk in your score—what a bilk
And egad, claps you plenty of chalk in your milk

The baker will swear all his bread's made of flour
But just mention alum, you'll make him look sour
His ground bones and pebbles turn men skin and bone
We ask him for bread, he gives us a stone

A slippery rogue is the cheesemonger, zounds
For with kitchen-stuff oft he his butter compounds
His fresh eggs are laid over the water, we know
For which, faith, he over the water should go

The butcher puffs his tough mutton like lamb
And oft for south down sells an old mountain ram
Bleed poor worn-out cows to pass off for white veal
For which he deserves to die by his own steel

The brewer a chymist is, that is quite clear
For we soon find no hops have hopp'd into his beer
'Stead of malt, he from drugs brews his porter and swipes
So, no wonder that we have so often the drug gripes

The tobacconist smokes us with short cut of weeds
And finds his returns of such trash still succeeds
With snuff of ground grass and dust, oft we are gull'd
And for serving our noses so, his should be pull'd

238 SIX JOLLY MINERS

Louis Rowe, Wortley, Sheffield, Yorkshire, *rec*. P. Kennedy, 1959: BBC 26582; *Folk Songs of Britain*, vol. IX, CAEDMON TC1224/TOPIC 12T197

Other recorded versions
Mrs A. Cosgrave, Newtongrange, Midlothian, Scotland, *rec*. Alan Lomax, 1951
Victor ('Turp') Brown, Cheriton, Hampshire, *rec*. R. Copper, 1957: BBC 26349

Printed versions
LLOYD: 1952: *Six Jolly Wee Miners* (Dumfriesshire, Scotland)
PINTO AND RODWAY: 1957, No. 174, p. 455 (from LLOYD)
REEVES: 1960, No. 92, p. 190: *The Miners*, coll. G. Gardiner, 1905 (Hampshire)
Korson, 1938, *Minstrels of the Mine Patch* (Nova Scotia, Canada)
Korson: 1943, *Coal Dust on the Fiddle* (Pennsylvania, USA)

Louis Rowe described this local begging custom:

As kiddies we used to get a pick, an old shovel, bit of coal, and if we could get some motties [numbered metal pierced tallies which every collier had to exchange for his coal allowance], knee-pads, and black faces, and back-sides-out trousers and shirt pulled through.

We used to go singing from door to door and they would have us singing in the public houses, gathering coppers at Christmas time.

He added that even if only two colliers went round they still sang *Six Jolly Miners*.

A Hampshire version recorded from Victor Brown at Cheriton has the following four verses:

> Six jolly miners, six miners you shall hear
> For they had been a-mining for many a long year
> They travelled England, Ireland and Scotland all around
> But of all their delight was a-working underground
>
> There was one came from Cornwall and two from Derby town
> The other three from Williamsbridge, young lads of high renown
> But of all their delight was to split those rocks in twine
> And it's all for the treasure, my boys, as we does undermine
>
> Sometimes we got money, boys, sometimes we've none at all
> But we can have good credit, my boys, when on it we can call
> We call for liquors merrily and drink our ale all round
> Here's a health to all the jolly miners that works all underground
>
> So 'tis down by the crystal river stream I heard a fair maid sing
> O have you seen my miner, or have you been this way?
> O have you seen my miner? So sweetly sang she
> For of all the trades in England it's a-mining for me.

A Scots version from Mrs A. Cosgrave at Newtongrange included two further verses:

> I'll knit my love a cravat as doggie as can be
> And the colours I'll put in it will fairly tak' his e'e
> The reddles they should go up to him and say: Where did you get that?
> O I got it frae my wee doggie bloke and what d'ye think o' that?
>
> I'll build my love a castle, a castle of high renown
> Neither kings, queens, or earls will pull that castle down
> The king loves the queen and the emperor does the same
> Here's my hand to every wee collier lad that works below the ground

239 THE SOLDIER AND THE SAILOR

Harry Cox, Catfield, Norfolk, *rec.* P. Kennedy, 1953:
  BBC 21483

Other recorded versions
Archie Lennox, Aberdeen, Scotland, *rec.* Alan Lomax,
  1951: *Folk Songs of Britain*, vol. VIII, Caedmon
  TC1164/Topic 12T196
Brigid Tunney, Belleek, County Fermanagh, N. Ireland,
  rec. P. Kennedy and S. O'Boyle, 1952: BBC 18527
Harry Scott, Eaton Bray, Bedfordshire, *rec.* P. Kennedy,
  1958: BBC 18527

Printed versions
Petrie: 1902–5, No. 771: contributed by Joyce (Ireland)
Gardiner MS: 1906 (Hampshire)
JFSS: 1914, No. 18, p. 72: *The Sailor and the Soldier*,
  coll. C. Sharp, Somerset, and Oxfordshire
JFSS: 1931, No. 35, p. 270: one verse only, Harry Cox
  variant *coll.* E. J. Moeran (Norfolk)
Reeves: 1958, No. 85, p. 187: words of C. Sharp version
  (Somerset)
Purslow: 1965, p. 81: *The Soldier's Prayer*, *coll.*
  Gardiner (Hampshire)
Hamer: 1967, p. 22: Harry Scott version (Bedfordshire)

> A soldier and a sailor went walking one day
> Said the soldier to the sailor let's kneel down and pray
> And if we have one prayer, may we also have ten
> May we have a ruddy sermon, said the sailor Amen

This song exists with variations among college students as well as in all three Armed Services:

> The first thing we'll pray for, we'll pray for a boat
> And we don't give a damn if she sink or she float
> And if we have one boat may we also have ten
> May we have a royal Navy, said the sailor Amen

Cecil Sharp believed *The Soldier and the Sailor* to be a modernization of an older song *The Mare and the Foal*. Like *The Hard Times of Old England* (No. 224) and *The Rigs of the Time* (No. 237), *The Mare and the Foal* contains verses of complaint against various tradesmen which are couched in the form of ironic prayers. Here is a version from Suffolk:

The old clerk in this parish I know very well
He often do toll the eight o'clock bell
He went to the alehouse and got a full pot
And forgot the old church for to lock-a-lock lock

A mare and a foal they ran in great speed
The mare from the bible began for to read
Stay, said the foal, before you begin
Whatever you pray for, I'll answer Amen

We'll pray for the millers who grind us our corn
For they are the biggest rogues that ever were born
Instead of one sackful they'll take two for toll
May the devil take the millers, Amen, said the foal

We'll pray for the bakers who bake us our bread
They'll take a small loaf and then hurl it at your head
They'll rip it and squeeze it at every roll
May the devil take the bakers, Amen, said the foal

We'll pray for the tailors for they are no men
They'll buy an old coat and they'll sell it again
They'll rub it and scrub it and darn up a hole
May the devil take the tailors, Amen, said the foal

We'll pray for the publicans who draw us our liquor
Small measure they like, they can fill us the quicker
If you ask them for best beer they'll draw you the small
May the devil take the publicans, Amen, said the foal

We'll pray for the butchers for they are great cheats
They'll buy an old cow and they'll sell it young meat
May their fingers be burnt into cinders of coal
May the devil take the butchers, Amen, said the foal

240 SWEEP, CHIM-NIE SWEEP

Bob and Ron Copper, Rottingdean, Sussex, *rec.* P.
Kennedy, 1955: *Folk Songs of Britain*, vol. III,
CAEDMON TC1144/TOPIC 12T159

Other recorded version
Jim and Bob Copper, 1951: BBC 16062

Printed versions
BARING GOULD: 1889, No. 20: *The Chimney Sweep*
/(Devon)
SHARP MS: 1906: one variant (Somerset)
GARDINER MS: 1906–8: two variants (Hampshire)
HAMMOND MS: 1907: one variant (Dorset)

The first verse of this song appeared in James Catnach's *Cries of London* in about 1815. Baring Gould came across a
version on the edge of Dartmoor at South Brent, and when it was included in the revised edition of *Songs of the West*
Cecil Sharp added a note suggesting that the tune was possibly of French origin because it was similar to one used by
the Savoyard sweeps.

Bibliography

This bibliography has been divided into two sections. Books published in Britain and Ireland appear first, followed by those published abroad, both in alphabetical order

BARING GOULD: 1889–1905
Rev. S. Baring Gould and Rev. H. Fleetwood Sheppard, *Songs and Ballads of the West*: Patey & Willis, London (4 parts) 1889–91. Methuen, London (4 parts) 1891–4; (1 vol.) 1895; revised edition 1905. Details are given by E. A. White in JEFDSS: 1937, p. 143, and 1946, p. 67. When reprinted in four parts this collection, mainly from Devon and N. Cornwall, comprised 110 songs 'collected from the mouths of the people'. Texts were modified and in some cases completely re-written and the same applied to tunes. However, in the revised edition, under the musical editorship of Cecil Sharp and with the adding of the name of the Rev. F. W. Bussell, one of the original collectors, many original texts and tunes were restored. For further comment on this publication see Dean-Smith: JEFDSS: 1950, p. 41.

BARING GOULD: 1895
Rev. S. Baring Gould, *A Book of Nursery Songs and Rhymes*: Methuen, London, 1895. An early collection of diversionary songs for children.

BARING GOULD AND SHEPPARD: 1895
Rev. S. Baring Gould and Rev. H. Fleetwood Sheppard, *A Garland of Country Song*: Methuen, London, 1895. 50 songs with much edited text compounded from various sources; detailed notes about songs, particularly those associated with customs, and comparative texts given. The introduction gives a history of folksong collecting from 1843.

BARING GOULD AND SHARP: 1906
Rev. S. Baring Gould and Cecil J. Sharp, *English Folk Songs for Schools*: Curwen, London, 1906. 53 songs from collections of both editors 'designed to meet the requirements of the Board of Education'—who that year had recommended the inclusion of National or Folk Songs in the school curriculum, and 'dedicated to T. R. H. Prince Edward and Prince Albert of Wales'.

BELL: 1857
See DIXON: 1846 AND BELL: 1857.

BROADWOOD: 1843
Rev. John Broadwood, *Old English Songs*: (privately printed) Balls & Co., London, 1843. 16 songs, collected in Surrey and Sussex by the Rev. John Broadwood of Lyne near Horsham. Arrangements by G. A. Dusart of Worthing. Said to be the 'first collection of folksong airs for their own sake'.

BROADWOOD: 1890
Rev. John Broadwood, *Sussex Songs* (*Popular Songs of Sussex*): Stanley, Lucas & Weber, London, 1890. 26 songs (including the 16 in BROADWOOD: 1843) collected by Broadwood and arranged by H. F. Birch Reynardson.

BROADWOOD: 1893
Lucy Broadwood and J. A. Fuller-Maitland, *English County Songs*: Cramer, London, 1893. Important early publication containing 92 songs collected in nearly every county of England. Most have little relevance to their district origins but some are in the dialects of their locality. Scholarly presentation with straightforward piano accompaniments. For article about editor see JEFDSS: 1948, p. 136, and 1950, p. 38.

BRUCE AND STOKOE: 1882
Rev. J. Bruce and J. Stokoe, *Northumbrian Minstrelsy*: Society of Antiquaries, Newcastle-upon-Tyne, 1882. Texts and 130 melodies (without accompaniments) collected by Melodies Committee of the Society with copious and invaluable notes to songs, information about small-pipes as well as a list of current tunes forming a 'Minstrels Budget' between Part 1: Songs and Part 2: Small-pipe tunes.

CHAPPELL: 1838
William Chappell, *National English Airs*: Chappell & Simpkin Marshall, London, 1838. One volume containing 245 tunes arranged for piano and the other historical references, annotations and details of sources. Much of the reference is to printed works and MSS in the library of Edward Rimbault which was later dispersed. This work was superseded twenty years later by *Popular Music of the Olden Time* (1858).

CHAPPELL: 1858/9
William Chappell, *Popular Music of the Olden Time*: Cramer, Beale & Chappell, London, vol. I 1858, vol. II 1859; Dover Publications, New York, 1965. Includes most of material from *National English Airs* (1838) but more has been added from other sources with particular reference to the ballads in the Pepys and Roxburghe collections. For further comment see Dean-Smith's *Guide* and JEFDSS: 1950, p. 38.

DEAN-SMITH: 1954
Margaret Dean-Smith, *A Guide to English Folk Song Collections* (*1822–1952*): University of Liverpool, 1954. A useful index of published songs under titles, alternative titles and first lines, with some full descriptions of important books with historical annotations and an introduction which traces the development of collecting and publication of folksong in England over a period of 130 years.

DIXON: 1846 AND BELL: 1857
James Henry Dixon, *Ancient Poems, Ballads and Songs of the Peasantry of England*: Percy Society, London, No. 62, 1846. Robert Bell (Title as above): J. W. Parker, London, 1857. By agreement with Dixon, Bell's publication was a revision, enlargement and editing by Bell of Dixon's collection and notes. Most of the material was collected in West Yorkshire and on Tyneside.

DUNCAN MS: 1905–11
James Duncan (1848–1917). MS collected c. 1905–11. Aberdeen University Library. Consists of two notebooks, the first containing 800 tunes with words of first verse, and the second giving texts of over 350 songs all supplied by a Mrs Gillespie. For obituary by Lucy Broadwood see JFSS: 1918, No. 21, p. 41.

D'URFEY: 1698–1720
Thomas D'Urfey, *Wit and Mirth* (*or Pills to Purge Melancholy*): London, 1698–1720. First edition printed with airs was in 2 vols. (1698). Further editions increased to 6 vols. (1720). This was the earliest publication to contain both words and music of a large number of English and Scots folksongs.

FMJ: 1965–
Folk Music Journal: English Folk Dance and Song Society, London (from 1965). Continuing the work of JFSS (*Journal of the Folk-Song Society*): 1889–1931 and JEFDSS (*Journal of the English Folk Dance and Song Society*): 1932–64.

FORD: 1899–1904
Robert Ford, *Vagabond Songs and Ballads of Scotland*: Gardiner,

Paisley, Scotland, 1899–1901; new edition 1904. A comprehensive collection of songs and ballads, containing a number of 'bothy ballads', but only a few for which he provides the music. Important in that it covers the wide range of songs that were current up to the end of the century, particularly those sung by 'the travellers'.

GARDINER: 1909
George B. Gardiner, *Folk Songs from Hampshire*: Novello, London, 1909. 16 songs collected by Gardiner and his musical associates, Gamblin, Balfour Gardiner and Guyer, and arranged by Gustav (von) Holst.

GARDINER MS: 1905–9 (see also under HAMMOND)
For further details about Gardiner's work see *The George Gardiner Folksong Collection* in FMJ: 1967, p. 129 and introduction to PURSLOW: 1968.

GREIG: 1909/14
Gavin Greig, *Folk Songs of the North-East*: The Buchan Observer, Peterhead, Scotland. Vol. I 1909, vol. II 1914. Folklore Associates, Pennsylvania, USA, 1963. Greig was an Aberdeenshire schoolmaster and an accomplished musician who noted the words and tunes of over 3,000 songs. His manuscripts, extending over 90 volumes, are deposited in the Library of King's College, Aberdeen.

HAMER: 1967
Fred Hamer, *Garners Gay*: EFDS Publications, London, 1967. 50 songs, words and melodies (chord symbols) mainly collected in Bedfordshire but also from other counties of England. No exact locations or dates given of informants or comparative notes to songs, but contains hitherto unpublished local songs and songs connected with local customs.

HAMMOND AND GARDINER MSS: 1905–9
H. E. D. Hammond (1866–1910), R. F. F. Hammond (1868–1921) and Dr George Gardiner (1852–1910) collected mainly in Dorset and Hampshire. Their manuscripts, deposited in the Vaughan Williams Memorial Library at Cecil Sharp House, London, have been indexed by Frank Purslow, who has also edited three books drawn from them (see PURSLOW: 1965, 1968 and 1972).

HENRY: 1924
Sam Henry, *Songs of the People*: Northern Constitution, Coleraine, Co. Derry, N. Ireland, 1924. Over 800 songs were published in the local Derry newspaper. Many were contributed by readers but it was Henry's diligent research and background notes that gave interest to each contribution.

JEFDSS: 1932–64
Journal of The English Folk Dance and Song Society: London (32 vols.), 1932–64.

JFSS: 1899–1931
Journal of the Folk-Song Society: London (35 vols.), 1899–1931.

KIDSON AND MOFFAT: 1926
Frank Kidson and Alfred Moffat, *A Garland of English Folk Songs*: Ascherberg, Hopwood & Crew, London, 1926. 60 songs collected by Kidson, mainly in Yorkshire, with piano accompaniments by Moffat; most previously published in *Traditional Tunes* (1891). A further 60 songs were selected for a second volume by Kidson and Moffat (1927).

KIDSON AND MOFFAT: 1927
Frank Kidson and Alfred Moffat, *Folk Songs from the North Countrie*: Ascherberg, Hopwood & Crew, London, 1927. A further 60 songs with piano accompaniment, published one year after the collector's death. The foreword by Lucy Broadwood provides information about the collector. See also *Frank Kidson: portrait*, JEFDSS: 1948, pp. 127–35.

KIDSON AND MOFFAT: 1929
Frank Kidson, Ethel Kidson and Alfred Moffat, *English Peasant Songs*: Ascherberg, Hopwood & Crew, London, 1929. 'Third and last Selection of Sixty Folk Songs from the Frank Kidson Collection.' Compiled by his niece with once again piano accompaniments by Moffat. (See KIDSON AND MOFFAT: 1926 and 1927.)

LLOYD: 1952
A. L. Lloyd, *Come All Ye Bold Miners*: Lawrence & Wishart, London, 1952. 'Ballads and Songs of the Coalfields' is the sub-title.

MACCOLL: 1953
Ewan MacColl, *Scotland Sings*: Workers Music Association, London, 1953. 100 songs and ballads divided into 'muckle' (i.e. great songs or ballads), 'Orra' (hero) folk and rebels, Kissin's nae sin, ploo lads, pipes and drums, drinking, shuttle and cage, muckle toons (urban), children's songs and lullabies.

OPIE: 1951
Iona and Peter Opie, *The Oxford Dictionary of Nursery Rhymes*: Oxford University Press, London, 1951. 550 rhymes and jingles with literary and historical background information.

ORD: 1930
John Ord, *Bothy Songs and Ballads*: Alexander Gardner, Paisley, Scotland. The standard work on the 'bothy ballads' of N.E. Scotland; 'bothy' meaning farm cottage or hut used by hands, ploughmen, shepherds and farm-servants, and the ballads, although including folksongs found elsewhere, being mainly those describing, and often complaining about, local farm life.

PETRIE COLLECTION: 1902–5
George Petrie, *The Complete Petrie Collection*: ed. C. V. Stanford, 3 parts, Boosey, London, 1902–5. Full details of the collection are given in JEFDSS: 1946, pp. 1–12 together with a list of tunes appearing in the 1855 and 1882 volumes.

PINTO AND RODWAY: 1957
V. de Sola Pinto and A. E. Rodway, *The Common Muse*: Chatto & Windus, London, 1957; Penguin Books, London, 1965. An anthology of Popular British Ballad Poetry from the 15th to the 20th century. In two parts: the first 'Amatory' and the second 'General'. 245 texts from England, Ireland and Scotland with an introduction mainly about street balladry.

PURSLOW: 1965
Frank Purslow, *Marrowbones*: EFDS Publications, London, 1965. A series of pocket-size publications initiated by Peter Kennedy in order to make available the songs collected by Hammond and Gardiner in the care of the EFDSS library. This selection contains 100 songs, provided with chord symbols over the melodies.

PURSLOW: 1968
Frank Purslow, *The Wanton Seed*: EFDS Publications, London, 1968. A second selection from Hammond and Gardiner again containing 100 songs.

PURSLOW: 1972
Frank Purslow, *The Constant Lovers*: EFDS Publications, London, 1972. A third selection in which the type-size has been increased and the number of songs reduced to 78.

REEVES: 1958
James Reeves, *The Idiom of the People*: Heinemann, London, 1958. Words of 115 folksongs from Cecil Sharp MSS (about 40 printed for the first time) selected as examples of 'English Traditional Verse'. Introduction concerned with the Folk Song Movement in England; Sharp as a collector; text revisions, description of the MSS; the popular idiom; and a detailed consideration of certain songs.

REEVES: 1960
James Reeves, *The Everlasting Circle*: Heinemann, London, 1960. 142 texts from the MSS of Baring Gould, Hammond and Gardiner considered as 'English traditional verse'. Introduction concerned with Baring Gould as a collector and his MSS; Hammond and Gardiner; varieties of folksong; the theme of

fertility and a discussion on the *lingua franca* of English traditional song.

RITSON: 1783/1810
Joseph Ritson, *Gammer Gurton's Garland or The Nursery Parnassus*: Durham, 1783; London, 1810.

ROXBURGHE: 1871–93
Roxburghe Ballads (about 1540–1790): 7 vols. Vols. I–II ed. William Chappell, Ballad Society, London, 1871–80; vols. III–VII ed. J. W. Ebsworth, Hertford, 1883–93.

SEEGER AND MACCOLL: 1960
Peggy Seeger and Ewan MacColl, *The Singing Island*: Mills Music, London, 1960. 96 English and Scots folksongs arranged for 'the post-war folk revival' mainly from Scotland under headings: Children, Courting, Men at Work, On the Road, Sailors, Barrack Room, Rovin' Boys and Flash Girls, Historical and Fill up your Glass.

SHARP: 1902
Cecil J. Sharp, *A Book of British Song*: John Murray, London, 1902. 78 songs published before Sharp started collecting. They are listed under National, Soldier and Sailor, Country, Humorous, Old English and Old Scottish, starting with *God Save the King* and *Rule Britannia* and finishing with *Auld Lang Syne*. Only two Welsh and two Irish national songs are included.

SHARP MS 1903–23
Cecil Sharp (1859–1924), foremost collector of English folksongs and folkdances, was the founder of The English Folk Dance Society and for many years a member of The Folk-Song Society. (In 1932 these two societies amalgamated as The English Folk Dance and Song Society.) For a full account of his lifework and publications see *Cecil Sharp* by A. H. Fox-Strangways (Oxford University Press, London, 1933), revised by Maud Karpeles (Routledge & Kegan Paul, London, 1967). Words, songs, tunes and dance notes in Cecil Sharp's autograph are in the Library of Clare College, Cambridge. There are also photostat copies in the Harvard University Library and the New York Public Library, and microfilm copies in the libraries of the University of California and in the library at Cecil Sharp House, London, the headquarters of The English Folk Dance and Song Society. Cecil Sharp's own collection of books was left to the EFDSS and formed the beginnings of the specialist library at Cecil Sharp House.

SHARP AND MARSON: 1904–9
Cecil J. Sharp and Rev. Charles L. Marson, *Folk Songs from Somerset*: Simpkin Marshall, London and Barnicott, Taunton, Somerset. 5 vols. Vol. I 1904, vol. II 1905, vol. III 1906, vol. IV 1908, vol. V 1909. The most important single collection of English folksong, later edited as the *Selected Edition* (1916–21). Introduction concerning singers and style most valuable.

STOKOE AND REAY: 1892
John Stokoe and Samuel Reay, *Songs and Ballads of Northern England*: Scott, Newcastle-upon-Tyne and London, 1899 (British Museum Catalogue date). 92 songs with annotations intended as instrumental accompaniment to the songs which previously appeared in BRUCE AND STOKOE: 1882 and before that in DIXON: 1846 and BELL: 1857 in which the names of the tunes were given but the music was not printed.

UDAL: 1922
John Symonds Udal, *Dorsetshire Folk-Lore*: Stephen Austin, Hertford, 1922; J. Stephens-Cox, St Peter Port, Guernsey, 1970. Contains a long 'fore-say' by William Barnes, 'The Dorset Poet'. This is a mixture of material including the words of about 20 songs.

WHITTAKER: 1921
W. Gillies Whittaker, *North Countrie Ballads, Songs and Pipetunes*: Curwen, London, 1921. 47 songs and 11 pipe-tunes. Although stated to be his own personal collection, most of the material had already appeared in DIXON: 1846 and BELL: 1857,

BRUCE AND STOKOE: 1882, and STOKOE AND REAY: 1892. Further information about the musical traditions of N.E. England is given in his *Collected Essays* (Oxford University Press, 1940).

WILLIAMS: 1923
Alfred Owen Williams, *Folk Songs of the Upper Thames*: Duckworth, London, 1923. Over 300 folksongs (words only) noted mainly in Berkshire, Gloucestershire, Oxfordshire and Wiltshire. Interesting introduction about rural life, more fully covered by Williams in *Round About the Upper Thames* (Duckworth, 1922). Further unpublished texts in Swindon Reference Library. See FMJ: 1969 'Alfred Williams: A Symposium'.

BECK: 1941
Earl Clifton Beck, *Songs of the Michigan Lumberjacks*: University Press, Ann Arbor, Michigan, USA, 1941.

BELDEN: 1940
H. M. Belden, *Ballads and Songs Collected by the Missouri Folklore Society*: University Studies XV (No. 1), Columbia, Missouri, USA, 1940.

BROWN: 1952–62
Frank C. Brown, *Collection of North Carolina Folklore*: vol. II Ballads; vol. III Songs; vols. IV and V Tunes. Duke University Press, Durham, N. Carolina, USA, 1952–62.

CHAPPELL: 1939
Louis W. Chappell, *Folk-Songs of Roanoke and the Albemarle*: Ballad Press, Morgantown, W. Virginia, USA, 1939.

COX: 1925
John Harrington Cox, *Folk Songs of the South*: Harvard University Press, Cambridge, Mass., USA, 1925. Dover Publications Reprint, New York, 1967 (released 1968). 185 songs collected in West Virginia (29 with tunes). Introduction describes collecting methods and identifies informants. Notes, references to other versions and other data given with texts of songs.

CREIGHTON: 1932
Helen Creighton, *Songs and Ballads from Nova Scotia*: Dent, Toronto, Canada, 1932. Dover Publications Reprint, New York, 1966. 150 songs, gathered mainly in the vicinity of Halifax written down by the author and afterwards checked with recordings. First of four published collections.

CREIGHTON: 1962
Helen Creighton, *Maritime Folk Songs*: Ryerson Press, Toronto, Canada, 1962. Michigan State University Press, East Lansing, Michigan, USA, 1962. 169 songs which were published with a companion gramophone record (Folkways 4307). There was also an earlier record called *Folk Music from Nova Scotia* (Folkways 4006).

GARDNER AND CHICKERING: 1939
Emelyn E. Gardner and Geraldine J. Chickering, *Ballads and Songs of Southern Michigan*: University Press, Ann Arbor, Michigan, USA, 1939.

GREENLEAF: 1933
Elizabeth Bristol Greenleaf and Grace Yarrow Mansfield, *Ballads and Sea Songs from Newfoundland*: Harvard University Press, Cambridge, Mass., USA, 1933.

HENRY: 1938
Mellinger E. Henry, *Folksongs from the Southern Highlands*: J. J. Augustin, New York, 1938.

HUDSON: 1936
Arthur Palmer Hudson, *Folksongs of Mississippi*: University of N. Carolina, Chapel Hill, N. Carolina, USA, 1936.

JAFL: 1888–
Journal of American Folklore now published by University of Pennsylvania.

KARPELES: 1934/1971
Maud Karpeles, *Folksongs from Newfoundland*: Oxford University Press, London, 1934 (2 vols.); Faber & Faber, London,

1971. 30 songs (with piano accompaniments) were published in 1934 and 90 songs, 150 tunes including variants (with no accompaniments) in 1971. All collected during 1929–30.

LOMAX: 1910/38
John A. Lomax, *Cowboy Songs and other Frontier Ballads*: 1910. Revised ed., 1938. Macmillan, New York.

LOMAX: 1934
John and Alan Lomax, *American Ballads and Folk Songs*: Macmillan, New York, 1934.

LOMAX: 1960
Alan Lomax, *Folk Songs of North America*: Cassell, London, 1960.

MEREDITH AND ANDERSON: 1967
John Meredith and Hugh Anderson, *Folk Songs of Australia*: Ure Smith, Sydney, 1967.

NEWELL: 1884/1903
W. W. Newell, *Games and Songs of American Children*: Harper Bros., New York, 1884; new and enlarged edition 1903.

PEACOCK: 1965
Kenneth Peacock, *Songs of the Newfoundland Outports*: National Museum of Canada, Ottawa, 1965. 3 vols.

SHARP AND KARPELES: 1917/32
Olive Dame Campbell and Cecil J. Sharp, *English Folk Songs from the Southern Appalachians*: Putnam, New York, 1917. Cecil J. Sharp and Maud Karpeles (2 vols.), Oxford University Press, London, 1932.

SHOEMAKER: 1931
Henry W. Shoemaker, *Mountain Minstrelsy of Pennsylvania*: Newman F. McGirr, Philadelphia, USA, 1931.

XII

Songs of
Country Life

Introduction

Who would like a jovial count-e-rie life
Happy am I with my home and wife
People may stare at my hard degree
They say I'm poor, but it just suits me
   ... I'm out with my gun in the morning

The Contented Countryman: No. 245

This might be the song of a present-day city-dweller who has turned his back on the rat race, and its higher wages in favour of life in the country on less money and the discomforts of a more humble dwelling:

For grates we've got none, but a fire on the ground
Chairs we've got none for to sit ourselves down
A three-legged stool is the chiefest of our store
I've a neat little cottage that's ground for the floor
   ... I'm as happy as those that's got fine marble floor

Ground for the Floor: No. 250

Those who move into the country soon discover that their on-the-spot entertainments become the farm environment with its seasonal changes in both weather and scenery and also by the different jobs that go on around the farms:

January is the first month, the sun goes very low
All into some farmer's yards where the cattle feed on straw
The weather being so cold and the snow lays on the ground
We shall see an alteration, before the year comes round

The Months of the Year: No. 256

In the old days farmhands went to the local market to be hired, or 'to fee' as it was called in Scotland and Ireland. Since they were contracted for a full year's work, it was important to try and get onto a good farm, and a wealthy farmer did not always mean a good place:

He promised me, mon, the twa best horse
That treads in a' the country roon
When I get hame tae the Barnyards
There's naething there but skin and bane

The Barnyards o' Delgaty: No. 242

The ploughboys worked in a team and had the opportunity to stand up to the farmer's criticism of their work or lack of it. One day's ploughing and the relationship with the farmer is well described in one of the most popular of English country songs, *All Jolly Fellows* (No. 241):

Our master came to us and thus he did say
What have you been doing this long summer day?
You've not ploughed an acre, I'll swear and I'll vow
And you be idle fellows that follow the plough

The Farmer's Boy (No. 247) is another song with widespread popularity in England. However, instead of the usual English tune, our version comes from Galloway in Scotland.

Included in this chapter is a local composition by a Scots farmworker sung to a traditional

y Lashbrook at Kelly, Lifton, Devon
Photograph: Peter Kennedy

ballad air, in which a girl is singing her praises of *The Roving Ploughboy-O* (No. 260) whom she has followed from farm to farm:

> A champion ploughman, my Geordie-O
> Cups and medals and prizes-O
> On bonny Devronside there are none to compare
> With my jolly roving ploughboy-O

In *The Brisk and Bonny Lass* (No. 244) a farm girl describes the milking, haying and harvesting work done on the farm by the female hands:

> I rise up in the morn so soon my labour to pursue
> And with my yoke and milking-pail I trudge the morning dew
> My cows I milk and then I taste the sweetest nature yields
> And the larks do sing to welcome in down in yon flowery fields

There is a verse about the haymaking time when 'each lad then he will take a lass and dance her on the green', and there is also a vivid description of such a scene at this time of year in *The Merry Haymakers* (No. 255).

Perhaps the most humorous description of country life is given in *The Muckin' o' Geordie's Byre* (No. 257), in which everything that could go wrong, goes wrong, on the day that George McIntyre decided to clean out his cowshed. The trouble starts when he himself trips over a rotten turnip. Turnips are also the feature of a song popular in the Salisbury Plain area in Wiltshire, where the *The Turnip-Hoer* (No. 261) is forever scratching away between the rows of turnips to keep off the flies:

> But there's some delights in harvesting
> And some bein' fond o' mowin'
> And of the jobs that be on a farm
> Give I the turnip-hoeing

A conversation piece between *The Husband-Man and the Servant-Man* (No. 226) in the last chapter, has an equivalent in our songs of country life. It has a similar type of questioning by the local farmer of his thresherman whom he meets on his return from hunting:

> O there was a jolly huntsman went a-huntin' out one day
> He met a jolly thresher all on the highway
> With his flails all o'er his shoulders and his bottles full of beer
> He's as cheery as a lord with ten thousand pounds a year
>
> *The Jolly Thresher*: No. 253

Five hunting songs are given in this chapter, Nos. 243, 246, 251, 252 and 263, while six—Nos. 248, 249, 254, 258, 259 and 262—are concerned with the less legal sport of poaching.

There are two songs of country life in Chapter VIII, Nos. 147 and 163; and in Chapter XI, songs Nos. 228–32 inclusive; in Chapter XIII, No. 267 is a sheepshearing song.

241 ALL JOLLY FELLOWS

'Twas ear-ly one morn-ing at the break of the day

The cock-'rels were a-crow-ing, the far-mer did say

Come rise up, my good fel-lows, come rise with good will

For your hors-es want some-thing their bel-lies to fill

1 'Twas early one morning at the break of the day
The cock'rels were a-crowing, the farmer did say
Come rise up, my good fellows, come rise with good
will
For your horses want something their bellies to fill

2 When four o'clock comes, then up we arise
And into the stable, boys, so merrily fly
With rubbing and scrubbing our horses I vow
And we're all jolly fellows that follows the plough

3 When six o'clock comes, at breakfast we meet [eat
With beef, bread and pork, boys, well heartily we'll
With a piece in our pockets, I'll swear and I'll vow
That we're all jolly fellows that follows the plough

4 Then we harness our horses and away then we go
And trip over the plain, boys, as nimbly as doe
And when we come there so jolly and bold
To see which of us our straight furrow can hold

5 Our master came to us and thus he did say
What have you been doing this long summer day?
You've not ploughed an acre, I'll swear and I'll vow
And you be idle fellows that follows the plough

6 Then I walked back to him and made this reply [lie
We've all ploughed an acre, so you've told a damned
We've all ploughed an acre and I'll swear and I'll vow
And we're all jolly fellows that follows the plough

7 Then he turned himself round and laughed at his joke
It's gone two o'clock, boys, it's time to un-yoke
Unharness your horses and rub them down well
And I'll give you a jug of the very best ale

8 So come all you good fellows wherever you be
Come take my advice and be rul-ed by me
Never fear your own master and then he will vow
That we're all jolly fellows that follows the plough

242 THE BARNYARDS O' DELGATY

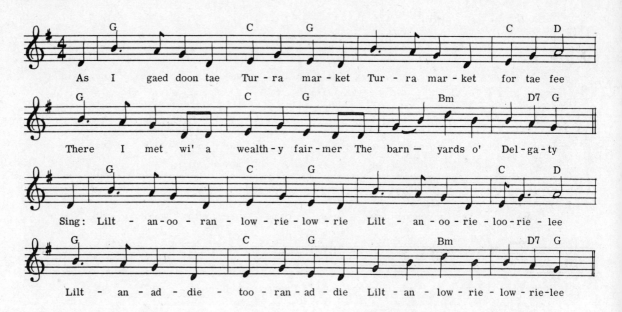

As I gaed doon tae Tur-ra mar-ket Tur-ra mar-ket for tae fee

There I met wi' a wealth-y fair-mer The barn — yards o' Del-ga-ty

Sing: Lilt - an-oo-ran - low-rie-low-rie Lilt - an-oo-rie-loo-rie-lee

Lilt - an-ad-die - too-ran-ad-die Lilt-an-low-rie-low-rie-lee

1 As I gaed doon tae Turra market
Turra market for tae fee
There I met wi' a wealthy fairmer
The barnyards o' Delgaty
Sing: Lilt-an-ooran-lowrie-lowrie
Lilt-an-oorie-loorie-lee
Lilt-an-addie-tooran-addie
Lilt-an-lowrie-lowrie-lee

2 He promised me, mon, the twa best horse
That treads in a' the country roon
When I get hame tae the Barnyards
There's naething there but skin and bane

3 The aul' grey mare sat on her hunkers
The aul' dun horse laid in the grame
And a' that we can whup and cry
They wouldna rise at yokin' time

4 Lang Meg Scott she mak's my bed
You feel the marks upon my shins
She's a course auld tricked wain
She fills my bed wi' prickly whins

5 Then Jean McPherson mak's my brose
Me an' her we canna agree
It's first a mote and syne a knot
And aye anither jilt o' bree

6 I can gae tae the kirk on a Sunday
Mony a bonny lassie I see
Sittin' by her faither's side
For mony a walk she's ta'en wi' me

7 Some can drink and nae be drunk
Ithers can fecht and canna be slain
But I can kiss any durned man's wife
And aye be welcome to my ain

8 The carn'le noo it is burnt oot
There's nae lecht abin the wane
But fare-ye-weel ye Barnyards
Ye'll never catch me here again

243 BOLD REYNARD

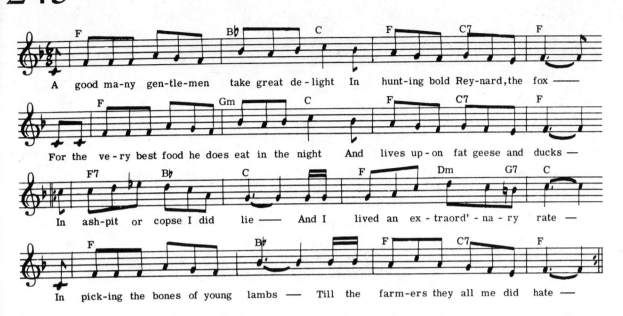

A good ma-ny gen-tle-men take great de-light In hunt-ing bold Rey-nard, the fox —

For the ve-ry best food he does eat in the night And lives up-on fat geese and ducks —

In ash-pit or copse I did lie — And I lived an ex-traord'-na-ry rate —

In pick-ing the bones of young lambs — Till the farm-ers they all me did hate —

1 A good many gentlemen take great delight
In hunting bold Reynard, the fox
For the very best food he does eat in the night
And lives upon fat geese and ducks
In ash-pit or copse I did lie
And I lived an extraord'nary rate
In picking the bones of young lambs
Till the farmers they all me did hate

2 All for my lord's horses and hounds they did send
And the huntsman he swore I must die
They made all the hair on my coat stand on end
And caused me from my young ones to fly
All down Stony Lane they did run me
And I gave them a very good race
When I entered the wood I did rest
Then the dogs they got forward a pace

3 All through the wild woods they gave chase and did
And the gamekeeper saw me go by   [gain
They chased me out into the wild open plain
'Twas then that he fired at my thigh
'Twas in Stony Fields they did kill me
Those bloodthirsty dogs did me follow
They tore my old coat all in pieces
And it caused the glad huntsman to holler

4 O pardon, dear huntsman, for I've spoiled your game
And the keeper has caused me to die
But I've left little brothers of mine to remain
That love little lambs better than I
O now that bold Reynard is dead
We'll go to The Dolphin and dine
And we'll dip his fore-foot in a bumper
And drink our lord's health in good wine

244 THE BRISK AND BONNY LASS

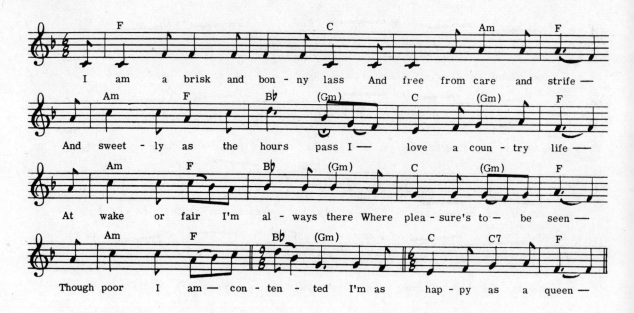

I am a brisk and bon-ny lass And free from care and strife —
And sweet-ly as the hours pass I — love a coun-try life —
At wake or fair I'm al-ways there Where plea-sure's to — be seen —
Though poor I am — con-ten-ted I'm as hap-py as a queen —

1 I am a brisk and bonny lass
And free from care and strife
And sweetly as the hours pass
I love a country life
At wake or fair I'm always there
Where pleasure's to be seen
Though poor I am contented
I'm as happy as a queen

2 I rise up in the morn so soon
My labour to pursue
And with my yoke and milking-pail
I trudge the morning dew
My cows I milk and then I taste
The sweetest nature yields
And the larks do sing to welcome in
Down in yon flowery fields

3 All in the time of haying
When meadows to be seen
Each lad then he will take a lass
And dance her on the green
And when their dance it is all o'er
Then home they will return
With friendship, love and harmony
They'll rest until the morn

4 All in the time of harvest
So cheerful-lie we go
Some with hooks and some with crooks
And some with scythes to mow
And when our corn is free from harm
No further for to roam
It's all away to celebrate and sing
Welcome Harvest Home

5 All in the time of winter
When cattle do eat straw
The cocks do crow to waken me
My eyelids for to draw
When the whistle-lie winds do whistle
And the northerly winds do blow
With joy and sweet contentment
We country lass do know

6 In summer or in winter
We never ought to grieve
For in the time of hardship
Each neighbour should relieve
But still I think of a country life
While others do surpass
So sit me down contented
I'm a happy country lass

245 THE CONTENTED COUNTRYMAN

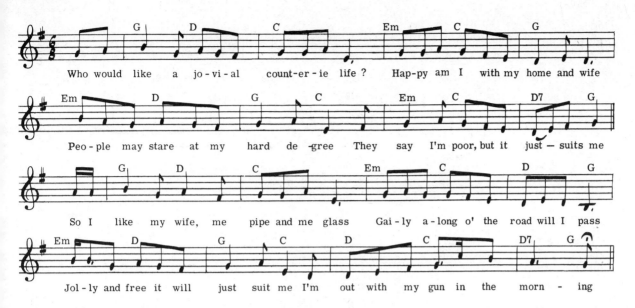

Who would like a jo-vi-al count-er-ie life? Hap-py am I with my home and wife

Peo-ple may stare at my hard de-gree They say I'm poor, but it just — suits me

So I like my wife, me pipe and me glass Gai-ly a-long o' the road will I pass

Jol-ly and free it will just suit me I'm out with my gun in the morn - ing

1 Who would like a jovial count-e-rie life?
  Happy am I with my home and wife
  People may stare at my hard degree
  They say I'm poor, but it just suits me
  So I like my wife, me pipe and me glass
  Gaily along o' the road will I pass
  Jolly and free it will just suit me
  I'm out with my gun in the morning

2 Who would lie in bed when the larks sing high
  And scorn a blue and a cloudless sky?
  Gay as the birds to the fields I go
  Back I return when the sun sinks low

3 My dear little wife as she crosses the stile
  She welcomes me home with a lovin' smile
  Perhaps other women would fairer be
  She is my own and she'll just do me

4 Now the winter may come and the winds can blow
  Safe at home from frost and snow
  By my fireside with my wife I sing
  I would not change for a crown-ed king

5 Happy am I in my little cot
  Contented I'll be with my humble lot
  People they sneer at my low degree
  They say I'm poor, but it just suits me

246 THE E-CHOIN' HORN

1 The ē-choin' horn sounds well in the morn
   To call the brave sportsmen away
   When the cry of the hounds makes a musical sound
   So greatly enlightens the day
   The day
   So greatly enlightens the day

2 We will away to some joys, to hear some brave noise
   Our hounds they will open their throats
   When the fox he breaks cover, hark forward, high
   We will follow their musical notes   [over
   Their notes
   We will follow their musical notes

3 Hedges, gates and stiles causes no denials
   Our horses they leap them so well
   With the crying: Hark forward, hark forward, high
   What pleasures can hunting excel   [over
   Excel
   What pleasures can hunting excel

4 While our hounds are at force, we hold on our horse
   Till the scent of the fox we have gained
   With a high tally-ho and away we will go
   We will gallop him over the plain
   The plain
   We will gallop him over the plain

5 Over mountains he flies, then afterwards dies
   He has led us an excellent chase
   We will take off his brush, then home we will rush
   In order our spirits to raise
   To raise
   In order our spirits to raise

6 With a bottle and friend an evening we'll spend
   We'll crown the brave sports of the day
   And our wives shall at night give us great delight
   And so drive all our sorrows away
   Away
   And so drive all our sorrows away

247 THE FARMER'S BOY

The sun went down, be-yond yon hills A-cross yon drear-y moor

When wear-y and lame, a boy there came Up — to — the far-mer's door

May I ask you, if an-y there be That will give me em-ploy?

To plough and sow, to reap and mow And to be — a far-mer's boy

1 The sun went down, beyond yon hills
Across yon dreary moor
When weary and lame, a boy there came
Up to the farmer's door
May I ask you, if any there be
That will give me employ?
To plough and sow, to reap and mow
And to be a farmer's boy
May I ask you, if any there be
That will give me employ?
To plough and sow, to reap and mow
And to be a farmer's boy

2 And if that thou won't me employ
One thing I have to ask
Will you shelter me, till break of day
From this cold wintry blast?
At break of day I'll trudge away
Elsewhere to seek employ
To plough and sow, to reap and mow
And to be a farmer's boy
At break of day I'll trudge away
Elsewhere to seek employ
To plough and sow, to reap and mow
And to be a farmer's boy

3 My father's dead, my mother's left
With her five children small
And what is worse for mother still
I'm the eldest of them all
Though little I be, I fear not work
If thou wilt me employ
To plough and sow, to reap and mow
And to be a farmer's boy
Though little I be, I fear not work
If thou wilt me employ?
To plough and sow, to reap and mow
And to be a farmer's boy

4 In course of time, he grew a man
The good old farmer died
And left the boy the farm now has
And his daughter for his bride
The boy that was, the farm now has
He thinks and smiles with joy
Of the lucky day he came that way
For to be a farmer's boy
The boy that was, the farm now has
He thinks and smiles with joy
Of the lucky day he came that way
For to be a farmer's boy

248 THE GALLANT POACHER

I and five more a-poach-ing went To kill some game was our in-tent

As through the woods we gai-ly went No o-ther sport we'd try

And the moon shone bright Not a cloud in sight

The keep-er heard us fire a gun And to the spot did quick-ly run

He swore be-fore the ris-ing sun That one of us should die

1 I and five more a-poaching went
To kill some game was our intent
As through the woods we gaily went
No other sport we'd try
And the moon shone bright
Not a cloud in sight
The keeper heard us fire a gun
And to the spot did quickly run
He swore before the rising sun
That one of us should die

2 The bravest shot amongst our lot
'Twas his misfortune to be shot
But his feat will never be forgot
By all those he loved below

3 Come all young lads of high renown
That love good ale and ale that's brown
We'll bring those lofty pheasants down
With powder, shot and gun

4 His memory ever shall be blessed
He rose again to stand the test
Whilst down upon his gallant breast
The crimson blood did flow

5 The youth he sank upon the ground
And in his breast a mortal wound
Whilst through the woods the guns did sound
That took his life away

6 Deep was the wound the keeper gave
No mortal man his life could save
He now lies sleeping in his grave
Until the judgement day

7 His case it makes the heart lament
Our comrades all to gaol were sent
Our enemies seemed fully bent
That there we should remain

8 No more locked up in midnight cells
To hear the turnkeys boast their bells
Those clanging doors we bid farewells
And the rattle of the chains

9 The murderous hand that did him kill
And on the ground his blood did spill
Must wander e'er against his will
And find no resting place

10 Condemned to wander all forlorn
And ever feel the smarting thorn
Be pointed out with the finger of scorn
Condem-ned for to die

249 GAMEKEEPERS LIE SLEEPING

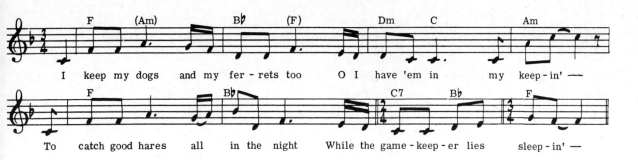

I keep my dogs and my fer - rets too O I have 'em in my keep - in' —

To catch good hares all in the night While the game - keep - er lies sleep - in' —

1 I keep my dogs and my ferrets too
O I have 'em in my keepin'
To catch good hares all in the night
While the gamekeeper lies sleepin'

2 My dogs and I went out one night
For to view their habitation
Up jumped poor puss and away ran she
Straightway to our plantation

3 She had not gone so very far in
Before someone caught her runnin'
So loudly then she cried out: Aunt?
Says I: Uncle's just a-comin'

4 I then pulled out my little pen-knife
O quickly for to paunch her
She turned out to be one of the female kind
O how glad I was I catched her

5 She squeaked, she halloaed, so very loud
I heard someone a-runnin'
Says I to my dogs: It's time we're gone
The gamekeeper is comin'

6 I took this hare to a nearby town
To see what they were a-fetchin'
Five shillings I'll give and another one too
While the gamekeeper lies sleepin'

7 Now I'll go down to some alehouse by
And I'll drink this hare quite mellow
I'll spend a crown and a jolly crown too
And I'll be a hearty bold fellow

250 GROUND FOR THE FLOOR

I've been liv-ing in the wood for a num-ber of years

With my dog and my gun I drove a-way sore — cares

I've a neat — lit-tle cot — tage and the roof is so se-cure —

But if you look un-der-neath you'll find ground for the floor —

Ground for the floor — I'm as hap — py as those that's got fine mar-ble floor —

1 I've been living in the wood for a number of years
With my dog and my gun I drove away sore cares
I've a neat little cottage and the roof is so secure
But if you look underneath you'll find ground for the floor
Ground for the floor
I'm as happy as those that's got fine marble floor

2 My house is surrounded with brambles and thorns
How sweet are those notes of the birds in the morn
I've a guinea in my pocket and plenty more in store
And if you look underneath you'll find ground for the floor

3 For grates we've got none, but a fire on the ground
Chairs we've got none for to sit ourselves down
A three-legged stool is the chiefest of our store
I've a neat little cottage that's ground for the floor

4 My bed's made of straw when I want to repose
To wear upon my back I've but one suit of clothes
It's made out of a good texture and stitched up so secure
I've nothing else to cover me up or keep me from the cold

5 God bless my dear old father, O now he's dead and gone
I hope his soul's in Heaven and never to return
For he left me all his riches as he'd heaped up in store
I've a neat little cottage where there's ground for the floor

251 THE INNOCENT HARE

Sports-men a-rouse, the morn-ing is clear

The larks are sing-ing all in — the air —

Go and tell your sweet lo-ver the hounds are out

Go and tell your sweet lo-ver the hounds are out

Sad-dle your hors-es, your har-ness pre-pare

We'll a-way to some co-ver to seek for a hare

1 Sportsmen arouse, the morning is clear
The larks are singing all in the air
Sportsmen arouse, the morning is clear
The larks are singing all in the air
Go and tell your sweet lover the hounds are out
Go and tell your sweet lover the hounds are out
Saddle your horses, your harness prepare
We'll away to some cover to seek for a hare

2 We searched the woods, the groves all round
The trial being over, the game is found
We searched the woods, the groves all round
The trial being over, the game is found
Then off she springs, through brake she flies
Then off she springs, through brake she flies
Follow, follow, the musical horn
Sing: Follow, hark forward, the innocent hare ➔

3 Our huntsman blows his joyful sound
  Tally-ho, my boys, all over the downs
  Our huntsman blows his joyful sound
  Tally-ho, my boys, all over the downs
  From the woods to the valleys see how she creeps
  From the woods to the valleys see how she creeps
  Follow, follow, the musical horn
  Sing: Follow, hark forward, the innocent hare

4 All along the green turf she pants for breath
  Our huntsman he shouts out for death
  All along the green turf she pants for breath
  Our huntsman he shouts out for death
  Relope, relope, retiring hare
  Relope, relope, retiring hare
  Follow, follow, the musical horn
  Sing: Follow, hark forward, the innocent hare

5 This hare has led us a noble run
  Success to sportsmen every one
  This hare has led us a noble run
  Success to sportsmen every one
  Such a chase she has led us for hours or more
  Such a chase she has led us for hours or more
  Wine and beer we'll drink without fear
  We'll drink a success to the innocent hare

252 JOE BOWMAN

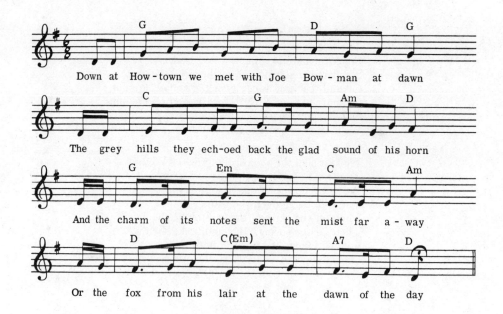

Down at How-town we met with Joe Bow-man at dawn

The grey hills they ech-oed back the glad sound of his horn

And the charm of its notes sent the mist far a-way

Or the fox from his lair at the dawn of the day

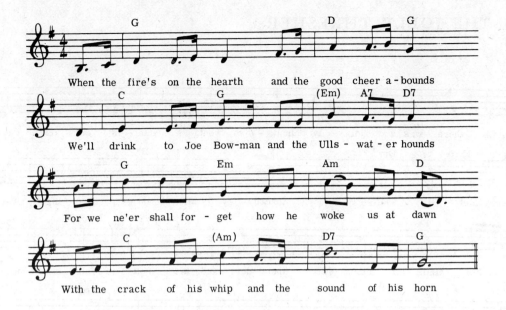

When the fire's on the hearth and the good cheer a-bounds

We'll drink to Joe Bow-man and the Ulls-wat-er hounds

For we ne'er shall for-get how he woke us at dawn

With the crack of his whip and the sound of his horn

1 Down at Howtown we met with Joe Bowman at dawn
The grey hills they echoed back the glad sound of his horn
And the charm of its notes sent the mist far away
Or the fox from his lair at the dawn of the day
When the fire's on the hearth and the good cheer abounds
We'll drink to Joe Bowman and the Ullswater hounds
For we ne'er shall forget how he woke us at dawn
With the crack of his whip and the sound of his horn

2 Then with steps that were light and with hearts that were gay
To a right smittle spot we all hastened away
The voice of Joe Bowman, how it rang like a bell
As he cast off his hounds by the side of Swath Fell

3 The shout of the hunters it startled the stag
When a fox came in view on this lofty Brock Crag
Tally-ho, cries Joe Bowman, the hounds are away
O'er yon hills let us follow their musical bay

4 Master Reynard was anxious his brush for to keep
So he followed the winds of the high mountains steep
By the deep silent tarn and the bright running beck
He hoped by his cunning to give us his check

5 He led us o'er Kitsty, we held to his track
As we hunted, my lads, with the Ullswater pack
They caught up their fox and effected a kill
By the silvery streams of that bonny Ram's Ghyll

6 Now his head's on the crook and the bowl is below
We're gathered round by this fire's warming glow
Our song it is merry and our chorus is high
So we'll drink to all hunters who'll join in the cry

253 THE JOLLY THRESHER

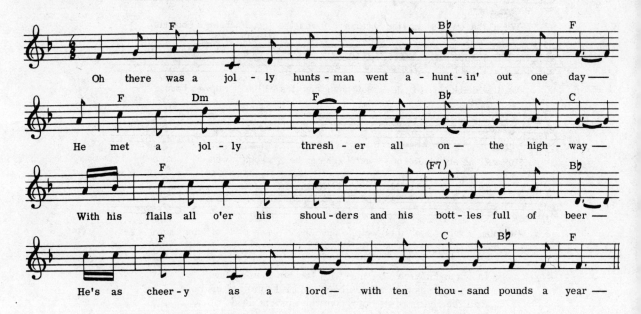

Oh there was a jol-ly hunts-man went a-hunt-in' out one day —

He met a jol-ly thresh-er all on — the high-way —

With his flails all o'er his shoul-ders and his bott-les full of beer —

He's as cheer-y as a lord — with ten thou-sand pounds a year —

1 O there was a jolly huntsman went a-huntin' out one day
  He met a jolly thresher all on the highway
  With his flails all o'er his shoulders and his bottles full of beer
  He's as cheery as a lord with ten thousand pounds a year

2 O I say, my jolly thresher, come tell to me now
  How do you maintain your familie and have but one cow?
  Your pay it is so little and your familie so small
  And how you do maintain them I don't know at all

3 Sometimes I go a-r'apin' and other times I mow
  Sometimes I go a-hedgin' and a-ditchin' I do go
  There's nothing comes amiss to me, I harrow and I plough
  And I earn all me money by the sweat of me brow

4 O me wife and I's agreeable, we're both o' one yoke
  Striving with the world to keep everything in stroke
  We live like two doves although we are but poor
  But we'll thresh away all poverty that calls till our door

5 When I come home at night, O then weary as I be
  The eldest of my seven sons will sit upon me knee
  The rest will gather round me with their prattles and their toys
  And that's all the comfort a poor man enjoys

6 Well done, my jolly thresher, you speak well of your wife
  I'll make you to live happy all the days of your life
  And if you be industrious and of it take good care
  Here's thirty acres of good land for you, your son and heir

254 KEEPERS AND POACHERS

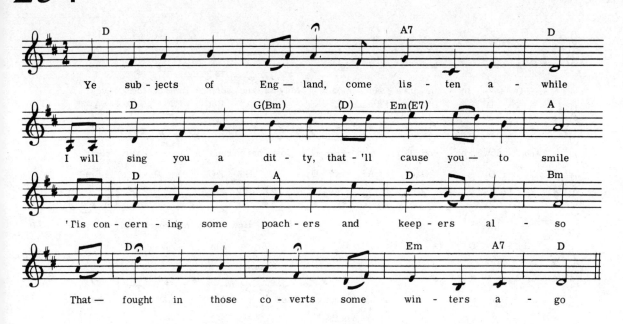

Ye sub-jects of Eng—land, come lis-ten a-while

I will sing you a dit-ty, that-'ll cause you—to smile

'Tis con-cern-ing some poach-ers and keep-ers al-so

That—fought in those co-verts some win-ters a-go

1 Ye subjects of England, come listen awhile
I will sing you a ditty, that'll cause you to smile
'Tis concerning some poachers and keepers also
That fought in those coverts some winters ago

2 Now when we go in, boys, good luck to us all
Our guns they do rattle and the pheasants do fall
But in less than ten minutes twelve keepers we did spy
Get you gone, you bold poachers, how dare you come nigh?

3 Says one to the other: Now what shall we do?
Says one to the other: We all will stand true
So they did agree for to all be as one
And fight those twelve keepers, till the battle was won

4 Now there's one, William Taylor, who won't run away
When five of these keepers all on him did play
Young Taylor being weary, he sit down to rest
Young Taylor was taken, though he fought the best

5 Now the judges and jury to him they did say
If you will confess now, your sweet life we'll save
Oh no, said young Taylor, that won't do at all
Now since you've got me, I will die for them all

6 Now there's none like young Taylor, no never was yet
There is none like young Taylor, no never were yet
Now there's none like young Taylor, you keepers all know
That fought in those coverts some winters ago

255 THE MERRY HAYMAKERS

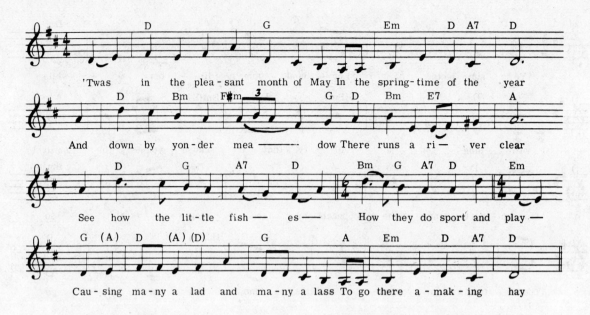

'Twas in the plea-sant month of May In the spring-time of the year

And down by yon-der mea————dow There runs a ri—ver clear

See how the lit-tle fish—es——How they do sport and play—

Cau-sing ma-ny a lad and ma-ny a lass To go there a-mak-ing hay

1 'Twas in the pleasant month of May
In the springtime of the year
And down by yonder meadow
There runs a river clear
See how the little fishes
How they do sport and play
Causing many a lad and many a lass
To go there a-making hay

2 Then in comes that scythesman
That meadow to mow down
With his old leather-ed bottle
And the ale that runs so brown
There's many a stout and a labouring man
Goes there his skill to try
He works, he mows, he sweats, he blows
And the grass cuts very dry

3 Then in comes both Tom and Dick
With their pitchforks and their rakes
And likewise black-eyed Susan
The hay all for to make
There's a sweet, sweet, sweet, and a jug, jug, jug
How the harmless birds do sing
From the morning till the evening
As we were a-haymaking

4 It was just at one evening
As the sun was a-going down
We saw the jolly piper
Come a-strolling through the town
There he pulled out his tapering pipes
And he made the valleys ring
So we all put down our rakes and forks
And we left off haymaking

5 We call-ed for a dance
And we trip-ped it along
We danced all round the haycocks
Till the rising of the sun
When the sun did shine such a glorious light
How the harmless birds did sing
Each lad he took his lass in hand
And went back to his haymaking

256 THE MONTHS OF THE YEAR

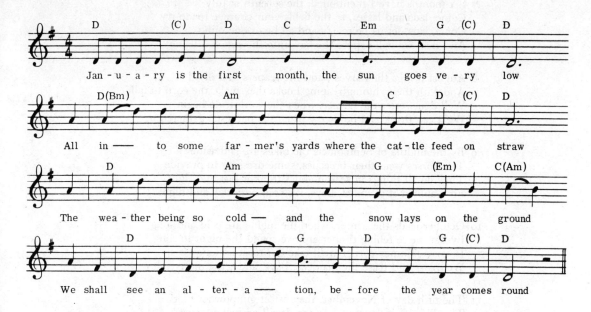

Jan - u - a - ry is the first month, the sun goes ve - ry low

All in — to some far - mer's yards where the cat - tle feed on straw

The wea - ther being so cold — and the snow lays on the ground

We shall see an al - ter - a — tion, be - fore the year comes round

1 January is the first month, the sun goes very low
   All into some farmer's yards where the cattle feed on straw
   The weather being so cold and the snow lays on the ground
   We shall see an alteration, before the year comes round

2 February is the next month, so early in the spring
   The farmer's ploughs are ploughing, it's such a glorious thing
   The little lambs are playing, by their dams they skip and dance
   And I hope all things will prosper that we may leave to chance

3 March being a noted month, above all months of the year
   In preparing for the harvest and in brewing of strong beer
   It's long before the time God knows that we live to see
   Here's a health unto the Queen and the Royal Familie

4 And April is the next month, so early in the morn
   The farmer's rather industrious in sowing of his corn
   With his gallant teams following after in smoothing of the land
   And I hope all things will prosper the farmer takes in hand

5 In May I walk-ed out, for to hear the birds to sing
   Their notes are most delightful, being humble to the King
   It charms my heart to hear them whilst walking on my way
   And each one they have warbling notes as they sit on yonder spray

6 So early in the morning, there comes the summer sun
   The month of June's arriving, the colder nights are gone
   The cuckoo she's a fine bird, she sings as she does fly
   And the more she sings her cuckoo notes, the blue-er comes the sky ➤

7 Six months have I mentioned, the seventh is July
Come, lads and lasses, to the fields your courage for to try
Come, lads, let us be merry and all be of one mind
And then we will expose the hay unto the sun and wynd

8 August brings the harvest, and the reapers first of all
And with their shining reaping hooks they make the corn to fall
Well done, cries the farmer, when the work it do begin
We'll eat, drink and be merry when the harvest's gathered in

9 By the middle of September, the rakes are laid aside
The horses wear their breeches, some dressing to provide
They do all things in season and I think it just and right
For summer it is ended, boys, it's cold both day and night

10 October leads the winter, when the nights are cold and long
By day we're felling timber and we spend the night in song
In cosy chimney corner we'll take our toast and ale
We'll kiss and tease the maidens, boys, and tell a merry tale

11 The fifth day of November, they call it gunpowder plot
They'll keep it down in London, 'twill never be forgot
The trees are stripped of all their leaves, the elm alone is green
The frosts will bite them sharply and not a flower be seen

12 O then comes dark December, the last month of the year
The holly, yew and laurel they fill our hearts with cheer
We sing our Christmas carols as we go from door to door
And at the same time wondering what next year has in store

257 THE MUCKIN' O' GEORDIE'S BYRE

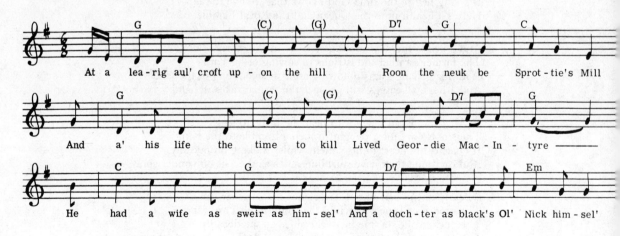

At a lea-rig aul' croft up-on the hill Roon the neuk be Sprot-tie's Mill

And a' his life the time to kill Lived Geor-die Mac-In-tyre

He had a wife as sweir as him-sel' And a doch-ter as black's Ol' Nick him-sel'

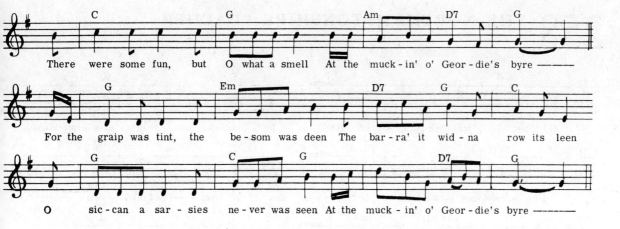

There were some fun, but O what a smell At the muck-in' o' Geor-die's byre —————

For the graip was tint, the be-som was deen The bar-ra' it wid-na row its leen

O sic-can a sar-sies ne-ver was seen At the muck-in' o' Geor-die's byre —————

1 At a lea-rig aul' croft upon the hill
Roon the neuk be Sprottie's Mill
And a' his life the time to kill
Lived Geordie MacIntyre
He had a wife as sweir as himsel'
And a dochter as black's Ol' Nick himsel'
There were some fun, but O what a smell
At the muckin' o' Geordie's byre
For the graip was tint, the besom was deen
The barra' it widna row its leen
O siccan a sarsies never was seen
At the muckin' o' Geordie's byre

2 Now the dochter she had to strae her neeps
The a'l' wife started to swipe the greep
But Geordie fell splite on a rotten neep
At the muckin' o' Geordie's byre
Now ben the greep cam' Geordie's soo
And she stands up and ahint the coo
The coo kick-ed oot and O what a stew
At the muckin' o' Geordie's byre

3 Now the a'l' wife she was booin' doon
The soo was kick-ed on the croon
And shoved her heid i' the wifie's goon
And ben through Geordie's byre
The dochter cam' through the barn door
And she and her mither let oot a roar
To the midden they ran and fell ower the boar
At the muckin' o' Geordie's byre

4 Now the boar he loup-ed the midden dyke
And ower the rigs wi' Geordie's tyke
They baith ran into yon bumbie's bike
At the muckin' o' Geordie's byre
The cocks and hens began to cra'
When Biddy astride the soo they sa'
The postie's sheltie it run awa'
At the muckin' o' Geordie's byre

5 Now a hundred years is passed and mair
The hoose it stands, the hill is bare
The croft's awa' and we'll see nae mair
O' the muckin' o' Geordie's byre
His folks are deid and awa' lang syne
So in case his memory we should tine
We're puttin' a stane to keep us in mind
O' the muckin' o' Geordie's byre

258 THE NORTHAMPTONSHIRE POACHER

(1) When I was bound ap-pren-tice — in fam-er-ous North-amp-ton-shire

I served my mas-ter tru-ly — for se-ven — long year —

Then I took up game-poach-ing — of this you now must hear —

O it's my de-light of a shi-ny night in the sea-son of the year —

(2) My com-pan-ion and I, we was set-ting four or five —

Tak-ing — them up a-gain, we caught the hare a-live —

A game-keep-er stood watch-ing us, for him we did not care —

For — we can wres-tle and fight, my boys, jump o-ver an-y-where —
O it's my de-light of a shi-ny night in the sea-son of the year —

1 When I was bound apprentice in fam-e-rous Northamptonshire
   I served my master truly for seven long year
   Then I took up game-poaching, on this you now must hear
   O it's my delight of a shiny night in the season of the year
   O it's my delight of a shiny night in the season of the year

2 My companion and I, we was setting four or five
   Taking them up again, we caught the hare alive
   A gamekeeper stood watching us, for him we did not care
   For we can wrestle and fight, my boys, jump over anywhere

3 We threw him over our shoulders, and wandered through the town
   We called unto the neighbourhood, and we sold him for a crown
   We sold him for a crown, me boys, but I did not tell you where
   O it's my delight of a shiny night in the season of the year

4 Now here's success to poachers, but I do not think 'tis fair
   Bad luck to every game-keeper, who would not sell his deer
   Good luck to every game-keeper, if he wants to buy a hare
   O it's my delight of a shiny night in the season of the year

259 THE OLD FAT BUCK

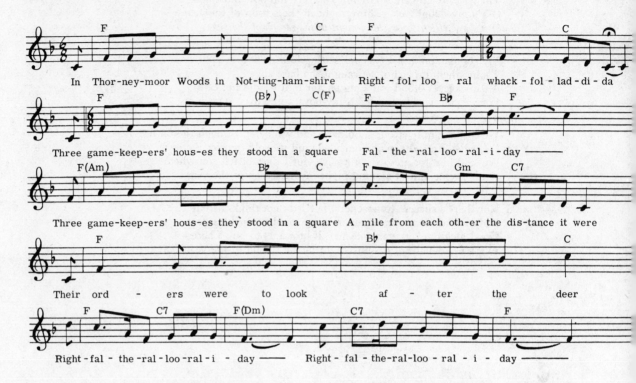

In Thor-ney-moor Woods in Not-ting-ham-shire Right - fol - loo - ral whack - fol - lad - di - da

Three game-keep-ers' hous-es they stood in a square Fal - the - ral - loo - ral - i - day —

Three game-keep-ers' hous-es they stood in a square A mile from each oth-er the dis-tance it were

Their ord - ers were to look af - ter the deer

Right - fal - the - ral - loo - ral - i - day — Right - fal - the - ral - loo - ral - i - day —

1 In Thorneymoor Woods in Nottinghamshire
Right-fol-loo-ral whack-fol-lad-di-da
Three gamekeepers' houses they stood in a square
Fal-the-ral-loo-ral-i-day
Three gamekeepers' houses they stood in a square
A mile from each other the distance it were
Their orders were to look after the deer
Right-fal-the-ral-loo-ral-i-day
Right-fal-the-ral-loo-ral-i-day

2 Now me and my dogs went out one night
The moon and stars were shining bright
Over hedges, ditches, gates and stiles
With my three dogs close after my heels
To catch a fat buck in Thorneymoor Fields

3 Now the very first night we got bad luck
One of my very best dogs got shot
He came to me both bloody and lame
Sorry was I for to see the same
He not being able to follow the game

4 I looked at his wounds and found them slight
'Twas done by some keeper out of spite
I'll take my pikestaff in my hand
I'll search the woods till I find that man
I'll hammer his old hide right well if I can

5 Then I went home and went to bed
And Limping Jack went out in my stead
He searched the woods all round and round
Found a large fat buck lying dead on the ground
'Twas my little dog that gave him his death wound

6 I took my knife and cut the buck's throat
I took a string and I tied the buck's leg
You would have laughed to see Limping Jack
Go trudging along with a buck at his back
He carried it like some Yorkshireman's pack

7 Now we ordered a butcher to skin the game
Likewise an old woman to sell the same
The very first joint we offered for sale
Was to an old woman who sold bad ale
She had us three chaps up to Nottingham Gaol

8 Now Nottingham Sessions were drawing nigh
Where us three chaps have got to be tried
The judge and jury laughed for scorn
That naughty old bugger should be foresworn
For all into pieces she ought to have been torn

9 Now Nottingham Sessions are over and past
Us three blokes got clear at last
Neither bucks nor does shall never go free
For a poacher's life is the life for me
And a poacher I will always be

260 THE ROVING PLOUGHBOY-O

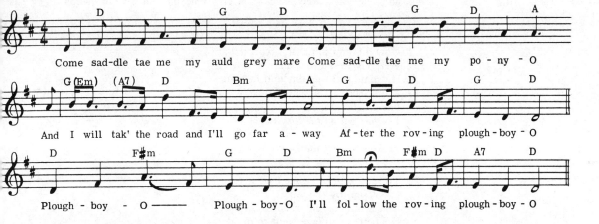

1 Come saddle tae me my auld grey mare
Come saddle tae me my pony-O
And I will tak' the road and I'll go far away
After the roving ploughboy-O
Ploughboy-O
Ploughboy-O
I'll follow the roving ploughboy-O

2 Last night I lay on a fine feather bed
Sheets and blankets sae cosy-O
This night I maun lie in a cold barn shed
Wrapped in the arms o' my ploughboy-O

3 A champion ploughman, my Geordie-O
Cups and medals and prizes-O
On bonny Devronside there are none to compare
With my jolly roving ploughboy-O

4 Sae fare ye well to old Huntley toon
Fare thee well, Drumdelgie-O
For noo I'm on the road and I'm goin' far awa'
After the roving ploughboy-O

261 THE TURNIP-HOER

Now the first job that I work-ed at For Mais-ter Far-mer Varr —

He — come to I one day and he said A first-class tur-nip-ho-er thee 't are

For the flies, the flies The flies got on the tur-nips

It's all me eye and no use to try To keep 'em off them tur-nips

1 Now the first job that I work-ed at
For Maister Farmer Varr
He come to I one day and he said
A first-class turnip-hoer thee 't are
For the flies, the flies
The flies got on the turnips
It's all me eye and no use to try
To keep 'em off them turnips

2 The second place that I went to
I took 'em by the job
And if only an elder son I 'ad
Far better I to 'ave went to quod

3 But there's some delights in harvesting
And some bein' fond o' mowin'
But of all the jobs that be on a farm
Give I the turnip-hoeing

262 VAN DIEMEN'S LAND

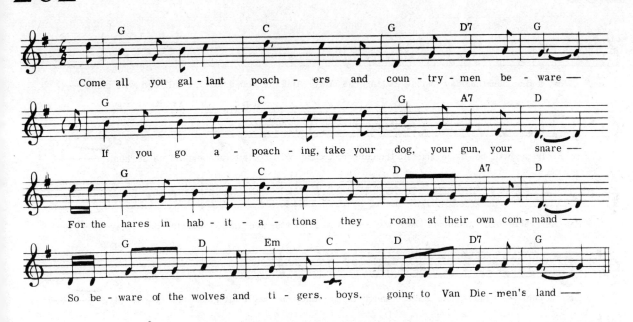

1 Come all you gallant poachers and countrymen beware
If you go a-poaching, take your dog, your gun, your snare
For the hares in habitations they roam at their own command
So beware of the wolves and tigers, boys, going to Van Diemen's Land

2 'Twas poor Jack Brown from Glasgow, Will Guthrie and Munroe
They were three daring poachers, the country well did know
The keeper caught them hunting, all with their guns in hand
They were fourteen years transported unto Van Diemen's Land

3 We had a gallant comrade, Jean Wilson was her name
She used to come along with us for the sharin' o' the game
But the captain fell in love with her and he married her straight by hand
So she gave us the best of treatment, boys, going to Van Diemen's Land

4 It's when we landed on the coast, ten thousand, aye, and more
And when the natives saw us, they began to shout and roar
They marched us from the vessel, boys, it's right up to the strand
So they yok-ed us up like horses, boys, to plough Van Diemen's Land

5 Although the poor of Scotland do labour and do toil
They're robbed of every blessing and produce of the soil
Your proud imperious landlords, if you break from their commands
They'll send you on the British hulks to plough Van Diemen's Land

263 WE'LL ALL GO A-HUNTING TODAY

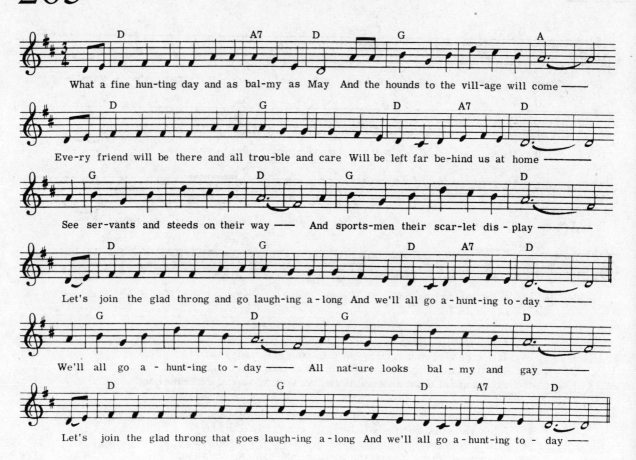

What a fine hun-ting day and as bal-my as May And the hounds to the vill-age will come ———

Eve-ry friend will be there and all trou-ble and care Will be left far be-hind us at home ———

See ser-vants and steeds on their way —— And sports-men their scar-let dis - play ———

Let's join the glad throng and go laugh-ing a - long And we'll all go a - hunt-ing to-day ———

We'll all go a - hunt-ing to - day —— All nat-ure looks bal - my and gay ———

Let's join the glad throng that goes laugh-ing a - long And we'll all go a - hunt-ing to - day ———

1 What a fine hunting day and as balmy as May
And the hounds to the village will come
Every friend will be there and all trouble and care
Will be left far behind us at home
See servants and steeds on their way
And sportsmen their scarlet display
Let's join the glad throng and go laughing along
And we'll all go a-hunting today

We'll all go a-hunting today
All nature looks balmy and gay
Let's join the glad throng that goes laughing along
And we'll all go a-hunting today

2 Farmer Hodge to his dame said: I'm sixty and lame
   Times are hard and my rent I can't pay
   But I don't care a jot if I raise it or not
   For I must go a-hunting today
   There's a fox in the spinney they say
   Let's find her and get her away
   I'll be first in the rush and ride hard for his brush
   For I must go a-hunting today

3 There's a doctor in boots, with a breakfast that suits
   Of strong home-brewed ale and good beef
   His patient in pain said: I've called once again
   To consult you in hope of relief
   To the poor he advice gives away
   To the rich he prescribes and takes pay
   But to all of them said: You will shortly be dead
   If you don't go a-hunting today

4 Then the Judge sits in court and gets wind of the sport
   The lawyers apply to adjourn
   And no witness have come and there's none left at home
   They have followed the hounds and the horn
   Said his worship: Great fines they shall pay
   If they will not our summons obey
   But it's jolly fine sport so we'll close up the Court
   And we'll all go a-hunting today

5 The village bells chime, there's a wedding at nine
   And the parson unites the fond pair
   When he hears the sweet sound of the horn and the hound
   And he knows that it's time to be there
   Saying he: For your welfare I pray
   I regret I no longer can stay
   You're safely made one, I will shortly be gone
   For I must go a-hunting today

6 None are left in the lurch for all friends at the church
   With beadles and clerks and all they
   They're determined to go and to shout: Tally-ho
   And the bell-ringers joined in the fray
   With bridegroom and bride in array
   Each one to each other did say
   Let's join the glad throng that goes laughing along
   And we'll all go a-hunting today

7 There's only one cure for all maladies sure
   That reaches the heart to its core
   That's the sound of the horn on a fine hunting morn
   And where is the heart wishing more
   It turneth the grief into gay
   Makes pain unto pleasure give way
   Makes the weak become strong and the old become young
   So we'll all go a-hunting today

264 WHAT'S THE LIFE OF A MAN?

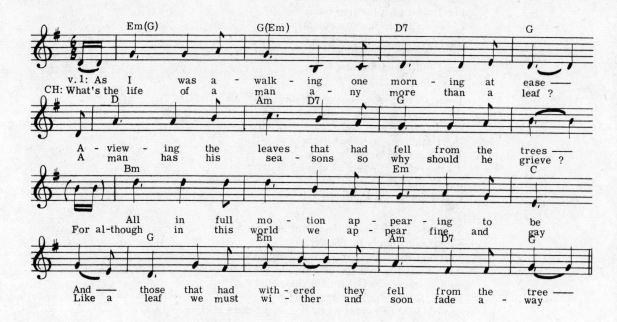

v. 1: As I was a-walk-ing one morn-ing at ease —
CH: What's the life of a man a-ny more than a leaf?

A-view-ing the leaves that had fell from the trees —
A man has his sea-sons so why should he grieve?

All in full mo-tion ap-pear-ing to be
For al-though in this world we ap-pear fine and gay

And — those that had with-ered they fell from the tree —
Like a leaf we must wi-ther and soon fade a-way

1 As I was a-walking one morning at ease
  A-viewing the leaves that had fell from the trees
  All in full motion appearing to be
  And those that had withered they fell from the tree
  What's the life of a man any more than a leaf?
  A man has his seasons so why should he grieve?
  For although in this world we appear fine and gay
  Like a leaf we must wither and soon fade away

2 If you'd a' seen the trees but a few days ago
  How beautiful and green they all seemed to grow
  A frost came upon them and withered them all
  A storm came upon them and down they did fall

3 If you look in the churchyard there you will see
  Those that have passed like a leaf from the tree
  When age and affliction upon them did call
  Like a leaf they did wither and down they did fall

241 ALL JOLLY FELLOWS

Charlie Wilson, Empingham, Rutland, *rec.* P. Kennedy, 1952: BBC 19337

Other recorded versions
Local singers, Ambleside, Westmorland, 1940: BBC 2522
Fred Jordan, Diddlebury, Wenlock, Shropshire, *rec.* P. Kennedy, 1952: BBC 18697
Frank Steele, Whitehills, Banffshire, Scotland, *rec.* S. Ennis, 1952: BBC 18776
Plough Jags, Barrow-on-Humber, Lincolnshire, *rec.* P. Kennedy, 1953: BBC 19028
Enos White, Axford, Hampshire, *rec.* R. Copper, 1955: BBC 21858
Ernest Jeffrey, Wisbech, Cambridgeshire, *rec.* P. Kennedy, 1956: BBC 23622
George Belton, Arundel, Sussex: EFDSS LP 1008

Printed versions
BARRETT: 1891, p. 30: *The Old Farmer* (Sussex)
BROADWOOD: 1893, p. 64: *'Twas Early One Morning* (Oxfordshire and Berkshire)
SHARP MS: 1903–23: eighteen unpublished variants
GARDINER MS: 1904–9: five variants (Hampshire, Somerset and Surrey)
BARING GOULD: 1905 (revised edition), No. 63 (Devon)
HAMMOND MS: 1905–6: three variants (Dorset)
GREIG: 1909–14, No. 158: *The Jolly Fellows who Follow the Plough* (Scotland)
JFSS: 1909, No. 13, p. 278: Gardiner (Hampshire)
WILLIAMS: 1923, p. 207 (Oxfordshire)
KIDSON AND MOFFAT: 1926, p. 54: *We Are Jolly Fellows that Follow the Plough* (Yorkshire)

The ploughmen, those skilled men responsible for the working teams of horses, the power units of the farms, must obviously have been on occasion as temperamental as operatic sopranos. To a farmer a good team of horsemen was of the greatest importance. To get the best out of them he had to be careful not to let slip a wrong word. What he said to them at the end of a morning's work was crucial, and if he made a joke then it must be quite clear that what he had said was intended to be one. Our song really hinges on this. It is certainly the most widespread of the many ploughboy songs which can be heard in most parts of England and north-east Scotland. Wherever it is sung it uses a jaunty tune with a good strong basic rhythm. It is essentially a song for a crowd of men singing in unison. It has also been found to be effective with an accordion accompaniment, as for example when sung by the Plough Jags in Lincolnshire. Originally 'plough jags' were a group of plough hands who went round the farms at Christmas, and especially on Plough Monday (the first Monday after Twelfth Night). They used to take horses and a plough with them. After singing this song they went into the house, one at a time, to perform their special Mummers Play in rhyming verse. If the farmer didn't give them enough money or show enough appreciation they were likely to plough up his best front lawn or his doorstep and then run away.

In Lincolnshire the characters in the plough jag play who sang this song were Tom Fool, Thrashing Blade, Beelzebub, Hopper Joe, Musical Jack, Besom Bet, Hobby Horse, Plough Boy, Dame Jane, Recruiting Sergeant, Lady, Indian King, Doctor and the Foreign Traveller.

242 THE BARNYARDS O' DELGATY

Davie Stewart, Dundee, Scotland, *rec.* P. Kennedy, 1956: *Folk Song Today*, HMV DLP 1143

Other recorded versions
John Strachan, Crichie, Aberdeenshire, Scotland, *rec.* A. Lomax and H. Henderson, 1952: BBC 17811
Frank Steele, Whitehills, Banffshire, Scotland, *rec.* S. Ennis, 1952: BBC 18128: *Turra Market*
Jimmy McBeath, Elgin, Morayshire, Scotland, *rec.* A. Lomax and H. Henderson, 1951: BBC 21538; TOPIC 12T173

Printed version
ORD: 1930, p. 214 (Aberdeenshire, Scotland)

> The breid was thick, the broth was thin
> They brocht them a' like tattie bree
> I chased them all day roun' the plate
> An' a' that I could get was three

The most popular of all the Aberdeenshire bothy ballads, or songs about local farm life, concerns a farm near Turriff, not far from Delgaty Castle, whose reputation inspired this song. John Strachan placed the farm a mile out of Turriff, on the opposite side of the road to where the old market used to be held.

Jimmy McBeath has some other verses to describe the place, which he calls Bairnie:

> It's Bairnie's toon's a coal black hole
> It's nae like my faither's home ava
> They work, they work in double strength
> And that does grieve me worst of all

> It's Bairnie's milk it's by the pint
> And Bairnie's meal it is but raw
> And if ye dinna bile the breid
> The brose they wouldna sup ava

> When I have brok' that steen in hand
> To work my wark, my penny fee
> I would take the gate and the road I've come
> And a better bairnie I will be

The two verses which we suspect account for the popularity of the song beyond its own locality are more concerned with the virility of the farm hands. As John Strachan sung them:

Fan I gang tae the kirk on a Sunday
Mony's the bonny lass that I see
Sittin' by her faither's side
An' winkin' ower the pews tae me

But I can drink an' nae get drunk
I can fecht an' nae get slain
An' I can court ma neighbour's lass
An' aye be welcome to my ain

243 BOLD REYNARD

Edwin Thomas, Allerford, Minehead, Somerset, *rec.* P. Kennedy and Maud Karpeles, 1952: BBC 17782

Tune used for *West Percy Hunt* (composed by John Mowat): BBC 20607

Printed versions
BROADWOOD: 1890, p. 34: *Bold Reynard the Fox* (Sussex)
SHARP MS: 1904: two variants (Devon and Somerset)

HAMMOND MS: 1906: similar to Guyer variant (Dorset)
WILLIAMS: 1923, p. 63: words only, *Bold Reynolds* (in Hampshire Did Dwell), mentioning Alton, Lord Badminton and Lord Lovelock (Wiltshire); two other variants in Williams MS
JEFDSS: 1967, p. 152: *Bold Reynard*, coll. J. F. Guyer, Hampshire, 1908

Edwin Thomas responded to a letter written by Dr Maud Karpeles and published in a north Somerset newspaper, prior to a recording expedition. The object of the expedition was to trace descendants of Somerset singers from whom Cecil Sharp had noted songs between 1903 and 1913, and Mr Thomas was certainly the outstanding discovery on this occasion. He recorded *The Long and Wishing Eye* (No. 134), *The Lost Lady Found* (No. 347), *Young Henry the Poacher* (see No. 248), *Barbara Helen* and a version of *The Miller's Last Will* (No. 232) in which he made the sound of the mill by rolling the back of his knuckles on the table.

Bold Reynard should not be confused with the hunting song *Bold Reynolds* (see JFSS: 1913, No. 17, p. 296: *Bold Reynolds* (in Oxfordshire), coll. Francis Jekyll, Sussex), or with the *Three Jolly Huntsmen* (or *Three Jovial Welshmen*) which has the chorus 'With me hark-tally-ho. . . .'

244 THE BRISK AND BONNY LASS

Mark Fuller and Luther Hills, East Dean, Sussex, *rec.* P. Kennedy, 1952: BBC 18714

Other recorded version
James and Bob Copper, Rottingdean, Sussex, 1951: BBC 16062; COLUMBIA SL 206: *Brisk and Bonny Lad*

Printed versions
BARRETT: 1891, p. 2: *The Country Lass* (Shoreham, Sussex)
JFSS: 1918, No. 21, p. 4: *Harvest Home Song*, coll. Frederick Keel, Fernhurst, Sussex

The Copper family and other Sussex singers today sing this as *The Brisk and Bonny Lad*. With the milkmaid now being replaced by milkmen the song has undergone a change of wording, so that they give a rather unexpected picture of a farm boy with yoke and milking pail trudging the morning dew. It is only when they reach the line 'as happy as a queen' that the listener realizes that a change of sex has taken place.

245 THE CONTENTED COUNTRYMAN

Jim Baldry, Melton, Woodbridge, Suffolk, *rec.* P. Kennedy, 1956: BBC 23100: *Out with my Gun in the Morning*

Printed versions
BROADWOOD: 1843 and BROADWOOD: 1890, p. 24: *A Sweet Country Life* (Sussex)
JFSS: 1914, No. 18, p. 92: *coll.* Sharp (Gloucestershire)
KIDSON AND MOFFAT: 1926, p. 112: *A Poor Man's Wish* (Yorkshire)

Although the theme of the sweet country life is common to a large number of English folk songs, we have so far been unable to trace any other version of this particular song in earlier collections. For a less favourable view of the 'humble cot' see *Ground for the Floor* (No. 250).

Our singer Jim Baldry specialized in songs of country life and his favourites were poaching songs such as *Gamekeepers Lie Sleeping* (No. 249). He also made a memorable recording of the classic *The Northamptonshire Poacher* (No. 258) and sang a drinking song, called *The Irish Familie* (No. 275).

246 THE E-CHOIN' HORN

Bob Copper, Rottingdean, Brighton, Sussex, *rec.* P. Kennedy, 1956
Other recorded version
George Townshend, Lewes, Sussex, *rec.* P. Kennedy, London, 1956: *Glittering Dewdrops*

Printed version
WILLIAMS: 1923, p. 60: *When Morning Stands on Tiptoe* (Gloucestershire and Wiltshire)

> When morning stands on tiptoe, 'twixt mountain and sky
> How sweet 'tis to follow the hounds in full cry
> When the bright sparkling dewdrops the meadows adorn
> How sweet 'tis to follow the echoing horn

Alfred Williams, who considered this 'unsurpassed as a hunting song', only obtained a fragment of a song which has been kept alive by the Copper family for several generations. The Coppers have it as a fox-hunting song, but George Townshend of Lewes calls it *Glittering Dewdrops* and regarded it as a hare-hunting song:

> When puss rose from cover 'twas early in the morn
> O how sweet it is to follow at the sound of the horn

A song with the same title was sung at Covent Garden in 1761 in Dr Arne's operetta, *Thomas and Sally*.

247 THE FARMER'S BOY

Togo and Burns Crawford, Mossdale, Castle Douglas, Kircudbrightshire, Scotland, *rec.* P. Kennedy, 1954: BBC 21488

Other recorded versions
Plough Jags, Barrow-on-Humber, Lincolnshire, *rec.* P. Kennedy, 1953: BBC 19028
Fred Jordan, Wenlock, Shropshire, *rec.* P. Kennedy, 1950

Printed versions
DIXON: 1846 and BELL: 1857, p. 118
BARRETT: 1891, p. 22: *Ye Sons of Albion*
KIDSON: 1891, p. 63: four variants
BROADWOOD: 1893, pp. 120 and 134: three variants (Sussex and Yorkshire)

SHARP MS: 1903–8: four variants (Somerset)
GARDINER MS: 1907 (Hampshire)
KIDSON AND MOFFAT: 1926, p. 100 (Yorkshire)
FLANDERS AND BROWN: 1932, p. 118 (Vermont, USA)
BELDEN: 1940, p. 272 (Wisconsin, USA)
CREIGHTON AND SENIOR: 1950, p. 158 (Nova Scotia, Canada)
HUNTINGTON: 1964, p. 216
JAFL: vol. 51, p. 38: from 1855 MS (Ohio, USA); vol. 52, p. 37 (Kentucky via Wisconsin, USA)
POUND: 1922, p. 69 (England via Wyoming, USA)
STOUT: 1936, p. 27 (Iowa, USA)

Wherever this rather sentimental ballad is performed the words vary hardly at all. Although six or more different tunes have been published for the song in Britain we felt that this fine Scottish one from Galloway should be made more widely known. It was sung to us by two brothers, one a shepherd and the other specializing in land drainage. Both their parents were singers; their father was 'something of a local poet' and their mother 'could play anything on a fiddle and melodeon'.

Their tune is somewhat different and certainly more interesting than the usual *Ye Sons of Albion* which appears in national song books. It has a circular effect obtained by the major opening, and a move towards the minor for the cadence (cf. *Dame Durden*: No. 293).

248 THE GALLANT POACHER

Becket Whitehead, Delph, Yorkshire, *rec.* S. Ennis, 1952: *Poaching Song*, verses 1–3, BBC 18136
Other recorded version
Harry Westaway, Belstone, Devon, *rec.* P. Kennedy, 1950

Printed versions
SHARP MS: 1904–9: two variants (Somerset)
GARDINER MS: 1906: one variant (Somerset) *Botany Bay*, three variants (Hampshire) *Young Henry the Poacher*

> The bravest shot amongst our lot
> 'Twas his misfortune to be shot
> But his feat will never be forgot
> By all those loved below

The words of the first three verses come from a singer on the Yorkshire–Lancashire border, the other seven being supplied by a similar variant from Dartmoor in Devon. Both used the same tune, which is associated with a song called *The Spring Glee* (*When Spring Comes On*) and which bears a resemblance to *Malbrouck s'en Va-t'en Guerre* (or *We Won't Go Home till Morning*)—see No. 108.

249 GAMEKEEPERS LIE SLEEPING

Bob Copper, Rottingdean, Brighton, Sussex, *rec.* P.
Kennedy, 1965: BBC 21547: *I keep my Dogs*
Other recorded versions
Frank Cole, North Waltham, Hampshire, *rec.* R. Copper,
1955: *Dogs and Ferrets*, BBC 21860
Jim Baldry, Melton, Woodbridge, Suffolk, *rec.* P.
Kennedy, 1954: *Hares in the Old Plantation*, BBC
23100
Chris and Tom Willett, Paddock Wood, Kent, *rec.*
P. Kennedy, 1961

Printed versions
KIDSON: 1891: *Hares in the Old Plantations*
GARDINER MS: 1907–8: three variants (Hampshire)
SHARP MS: 1909–11: two variants (Oxfordshire); one
variant (Cambridgeshire)
GILLINGTON: 1911, p. 20: *The Sleeping Gamekeeper*
(from a New Forest gipsy)
WILLIAMS: 1923, p. 110: *I Keep my Dogs and Ferrets too*
(Berkshire and Wiltshire)
JEFDSS: 1961, p. 78: Frank Cole variant (Hampshire)
PURSLOW: 1965, p. 36: two variants from Gardiner
collection (Hampshire)
STUBBS: 1970, p. 82 (Sussex)

My parents they driv' me away from home
Don't you think that was starvation
For I'd a brace of dogs and an 'are-gun too
And I kept them for my sporting

This was the preliminary verse sung by Jim Baldry in Suffolk. Baldry called the song *Hares in the Old Plantation*.
Alfred Williams (WILLIAMS: 1923) points out that the poacher was pleased the hare was a female because it would
be better eating, but it could also be on account of its being more valuable for breeding purposes.

250 GROUND FOR THE FLOOR

Steve Goodall, Basingstoke, Hampshire, *rec.* R. Copper,
1955
Other recorded version
George Maynard, Copthorne, Sussex, *rec.* P. Kennedy
and M. Plunkett, 1956: BBC 23092: *The Sun being set*
Printed versions
BROADWOOD: 1893, p. 96 (Yorkshire and Cambridge-
shire)
BARING GOULD MS: two versions (Devon)

SHARP MS: 1904: one variant (Somerset)
GARDINER MS: 1905–7: one variant (Cornwall), three
variants (Hampshire)
HAMMOND MS: 1906: one variant (Dorset)
WILLIAMS: 1923, p. 153 (Wiltshire)
KIDSON AND MOFFAT: 1926, p. 64
JEFDSS: 1963, p. 185: George Maynard variant

My wants are but simple, I've honey and milk
I'm as happy as those who dress in fine silk
Though I haven't their riches surely I am not poor
I've a neat little cottage with ground for the floor

My cot is surrounded by green leafy trees
And pleasant the hum from the straw hive of bees
My purse holds a guinea and I've got plenty more
I've a neat little cottage but ground for the floor

Ground for the floor,
If you look underneath it, you'll find ground for the floor
This song was popular all over England, from Yorkshire to Cornwall, and Lancashire to Kent.

251 THE INNOCENT HARE

Bob and Ron Copper, Rottingdean, Sussex, *rec.* P.
Kennedy, 1955: EFDSS LP 1002
Other recorded version
Mark Fuller and Luther Hills, East Dean, Sussex, 1952:
Sportsmen Arouse, BBC 18714

Compare
KIDSON AND MOFFAT: 1929: *The Morning Looks Charming* (Yorkshire)

Sportsmen arouse, the morning's fair
The larks are singing all in the air
Go and tell your sweet lover the hounds are out
Follow, follow the musical horn,
Sing: tally, hark forward, the innocent hare

Mark Fuller and Luther Hills, in Sussex, sang an almost identical version of this hare-hunting ballad. *The Morning
Looks Charming*, collected by Frank Kidson from Yorkshire, is a similar song but not a variant of that recorded in Sussex.

252 JOE BOWMAN

John Dalton, Cockermouth, Cumberland, *rec.* P. Kennedy, 1959: BBC 26582

Talk about Joe Bowman by Moore Sedgwick, Sedburgh, Yorkshire, *rec.* P. Kennedy, 1954: BBC 22450

The most renowned huntsman in the Lake District has long remained famous, largely because of the popularity of one of the many songs that were sung about him:

> D'ye ken John Peel with his coat so gay
> D'ye ken John Peel at the break of the day
> D'ye ken John Peel when he's far far away
> With his hounds and his horn in the morning

For this song, John Woodcock Graves used the first part of the tune *Bonnie Annie*, with its stirring chorus:

> For the sound of the horn brought me from my bed
> And the cry of his hounds which he oft-times led
> Peel's view halloo would waken the dead
> Or the fox from his lair in the morning

Perhaps the next most popular of all the John Peel songs which are still chorused in the Lake District is the rather plaintive *John Peel's Echo*:

> Now the horn of the hunter's now silent
> On the banks of the Ellen no more
> O'er in Denton you'll hear his wild echo
> Clear-sounding o'er dark curlew's roar

But if John Peel's memory is immortal, certainly the next most famous hunter in the area, about whom there are also many songs, is Joe Bowman. One of the most amusing is *You'll Never Get in Without*, sung to the tune of the *Cock o' the North* and recorded by Moore Sedgwick. It was made by a Dr Eton after a hunt at Mardale in which Sedgwick's father slept all night with 'Hunty' Bowman when a fox went into a hole and they were waiting there for a crowbar.

In Sedgwick's recorded talk about Bowman he said that:

> He hunted the Ullswater foxhounds for forty years. He was a well-known character in the north of England. I've heard people say that he was as good a man as ever John Peel ever was, was Joe Bowman. A lover of sport, a lover of hounds, and a lover of nature, children and everything, and everything else. He was a real character. He lived at Patterdale [Westmorland] in the Lake District, and he was thought a lot about by everybody.
>
> His songs are sung at every 'do' there is; any hunting songs are sung, you'll always find Joe Bowman's songs are sung. It didn't matter where you go, everybody seemed to like him.
>
> He died in March 1940 and he was eighty-nine years of age when he died. And it was a big funeral too. There was huntsmen representing all the Fell packs, farmers and shepherds came down and I never saw as big a funeral in my life.

253 THE JOLLY THRESHER

Nicholas Hughes, Forkhill, County Armagh, N. Ireland, *rec.* P. Kennedy and S. O'Boyle, 1952: *Hunting Song*, BBC 18485

Other recorded versions
Walter Gales, Sutton, Norfolk, 1947: *The Bold Thrasher*, BBC 13863
James Copper, Rottingdean, Sussex, 1951: *The Labourer*, BBC 16064
Bob and Ron Copper, *rec.* P. Kennedy, 1955: *The Honest Labourer*, EFDSS LP 1002

Printed versions
JOHNSON: 1792, vol. iv, No. 372: contributed by Robert Burns
DIXON: 1846 and BELL: 1857: words only from Newcastle broadside (in ROXBURGHE XXI, vol. vii, p. 329)
BROADWOOD: 1893, p. 68: *The Thresher and the Squire*
STOKOE AND REAY: 1892 (Northumberland)
JFSS: 1901, No. 3, p. 79: *The Thresherman and the Squire*, coll. W. Percy Merrick, Surrey

GARDINER MS: 1905–6: ten variants (Cornwall, Hampshire and Wiltshire)
HAMMOND MS: 1905–7: two variants (Dorset and Hampshire)
JFSS: 1906, No. 8: *The Jolly Thresherman*, coll. R. Vaughan Williams, Sussex
SHARP MS: 1908–22: four variants *Nobleman and Thresherman*
SHARP: 1908–22: four variants *Nobleman and Thresherman*
JFSS: 1909, No. 13, p. 302: two versions coll. Gardiner and Hammond, Hampshire
MERRICK: 1912, p. 6: *The Thresherman and the Squire* (Surrey)
JFSS: 1915, No. 19, p. 200: *The Thresherman* (Westmorland) and another coll. Hammond variant, Dorset
WILLIAMS: 1923, p. 138: *The Nobleman and the Thresher* (Berkshire and Oxfordshire)
HENRY: 1924, No. 117: *As a King Went a-Hunting*; No. 662: *The Jolly Thrasher*
ORD: 1930, p. 48: *The Hedger* (*and Gentleman*)

Nicholas Hughes, who learned the song from his grandmother in Northern Ireland, made it a conversation between a huntsman and a thresher (pron. 'thrasher'), but other versions have a squire or nobleman. In Norfolk, Walter Gales sang:

It's of a nobleman in a village of late
He had a bold thrasher, his family was great
He'd a wife and seven child-e-ren and most of them being small
And nothing but his labours to maintain them all

The Copper family in Sussex call the song *The [Honest] Labourer* and the labourer is met by a gentleman:

A gentleman one evening walking out to take the air
He met with this poor labouring man and solemnly declared
I think you are the thrasher man, yes sir, said he, that's true
How do you get your living just as well as you do?

254 KEEPERS AND POACHERS

George Maynard, Copthorne, Sussex, *rec.* P. Kennedy and M. Plunkett, 1955: BBC 23093: *Bold William Taylor*

Other recorded version
Jasper Smith, Edenbridge, Kent, *rec.* J. Brune, 1964: *Come All You Young Subjects*

Printed versions
JFSS: 1927, No. 31, p. 7: *The Keepers and the Poachers*, *coll.* C. Sharp, Middlesex
JEFDSS: 1963, p. 188: George Maynard variant *Bold William Taylor*
HAMER: 1967, p. 34: *William Taylor* (Bedfordshire)

O, it's all you young keepers come listen awhile
I'll tell you of a story that will cause you to smile
Concerning some keepers, you poachers all know
That fought in these covers some winters ago

A very complete version of this song was noted in 1913 by Cecil Sharp, but because its tune was a variant of the well-known *Villikens and his Dinah* it was not published until after his death when Dr Maud Karpeles contributed it to the JFSS in 1927.

John Brune has recently recorded a variant from a gipsy in Kent who explained that 'all the woods were mined—they'd dug some traps to catch poachers, man-traps, covered with sticks and leaves and there was some sort of signal to tip off the keepers but the poachers slipped through and made off with the pheasants':

O we haven't been in there a scarce half an hour
All the woods they were mined, soon them keepers drawed near
But it's just like young Taylor said: It's my time to call
And our guns they did rattle and pheasants did fall

O stand off, O stand off, you're a false-speaking man
But before I would round I would die on my plan
All the woods they were mined and the keepers also
As we fared through them covers some winters ago

255 THE MERRY HAYMAKERS

Bob and Ron Copper, Rottingdean, Sussex, *rec.* P. Kennedy, 1955: *Folk Songs of Britain*, vol. III, CAEDMON TC1144/Topic 12T159; EFDSS LP 1002

Other recorded versions
Bob Copper, 1951: *The Month of May*, BBC 16067
Sam Larner, Winterton, Norfolk, 1958: *The Merry Month of May*, BBC 26075

Printed versions
D'URFEY: 1719–20: *The Beggar's Wedding*: air 22, *In the Merry Month of June*
DIXON: 1846 and BELL: 1857, p. 171

SHARP: 1902, No. 28, p. 60, Baring Gould
BARING GOULD: 1889, No. 109: words rewritten
GARDINER MS: 1906: one variant, *Haymakers Song* (Hampshire)
HAMMOND MS: two variants, *The Merry Month of May* (Dorset)
BARING GOULD AND SHARP: 1906: rewritten version for school use
WILLIAMS: 1923, p. 187: *The Haymakers* (Gloucestershire)
STUBBS: 1970, p. 40 (Sussex)
PURSLOW: 1972, p. 58, *coll.* Gardiner (Hampshire)

From the beginning of the century English schoolchildren have been treated to the romantic rewriting of the song by the Rev. Baring Gould with its chorus:

The pipe and tabor both shall play
The viols loudly ring
From morn till eve each summer day
As we go hay-making

At first encounter the song might seem over-selfconscious and literary, but with further examination it can be seen to be very much part of our folk tradition.

256 THE MONTHS OF THE YEAR

Bill and Harry Westaway, Belstone, Devon, *rec.* P.
Kennedy, 1950: BBC 17794 (1952)

Printed versions
BARING GOULD: 1889, No. 19: three variants, *The Seasons*, one collected from Belstone, Devon
BARING GOULD: 1905 (revised edition), No. 19: now called *The Months of The Year*
SHARP MS: 1905 (Devon)
HAMMOND MS: 1905 (Somerset and Dorset)

Baring Gould noted down many songs, including *Widdecombe Fair*, from the father of our two singers, Bill and Harry Westaway, who described how he was taken into Okehampton and given some drinks before it was put down on paper. As far as *Widdecombe Fair* is concerned, the Westaways always assumed that Baring Gould wrote it down incorrectly. What happened in fact was that Baring Gould published another version from another singer or, as in the case of *Tom Pearce*, a composite version from a number of sources. Our version is also a composite, compiled from the two Westaway brothers.

Cecil Sharp in the revised edition of *Songs of the West* draws our attention to a French version *Les Douze Mois de l'Année* (in E. de Coussemaker: *Les Chants populaires des Flamands de France*, 1856, p. 133: 1930 ed., p. 129).

257 THE MUCKIN' O' GEORDIE'S BYRE

Jimmy White, Whittingham, Northumberland, *rec.* P.
Kennedy, 1954: BBC 20606

Other recorded version
Jimmy McBeath, Aberdeen, Scotland, *rec.* Alan Lomax,
1951: *Folk Songs of Britain*, vol. IX, CAEDMON TC1224/
TOPIC 12T197

Printed version
MacCOLL: 1953, p. 33: from Jimmy McBeath

This song in Lowland Scots was a favourite of music-hall comedian Willie Kemp and was widely sung on both sides of the Scottish border. It makes use of many Scots words which have now dropped out of use. We are therefore giving a gentlemanly English translation:

1 At a makeshift old cot upon the hill
Around the corner beside Sprott's Mill
For all his life he'd time to kill
Lived Mister George McIntyre
He'd a wife as lazy as he himself
A daughter as black as the devil in hell
There was plenty of fun, but O what a smell
At the cleaning of George's cow-house

The fork was bent, the broom was worn
The barrow it would not roll on its own
And such a pickle never was known
At the cleaning of George's cow-house

2 The daughter for turnips the straw put down
The old wife to sweep the drain begun
But George fell flat on a rotten one
At the cleaning of George's cow-house
Along the drain came George's sow
And she comes up behind the cow
The cow kicked out and O what a row
At the cleaning of George's cow-house

3 The old wife she was bending down
The sow got kicked upon the crown
She shoved her head in the old wife's gown
And went through George's cow-house
The daughter came through the cow-house door
And she and her mother let out a roar
To the dung-heap ran and the pig fell o'er
At the cleaning of George's cow-house

4 The pig he jumped the dung-heap ditch
With George's dog came over the ricks
And both of them into the beehive trips
At the cleaning of George's cow-house
The cocks and hens began to crow
When Biddy they saw astride the sow
The postman shouts: It's a run away show
At the cleaning of George's cow-house

5 Now more has passed than a hundred year
The house still stands but the hill is bare
No more we'll see the cot stand there
Or the cleaning of George's cow-house
His people are long since dead and gone
So in case his memory should decline
We'll put up a stone to remember the time
At the cleaning of George's cow-house

258 THE NORTHAMPTONSHIRE POACHER

Jim Baldry, Melton, Woodbridge, Suffolk, *rec.* P. Kennedy, 1956: BBC 23100

Printed versions

CHAPPELL: 1838, p. 62 and 1859, p. 732: *The Lincolnshire Poacher*
DIXON: 1846 and BELL: 1857 (Lincolnshire)
SHARP MS: 1904–12: four variants (Somerset, Gloucestershire and Yorkshire)
GARDINER MS: 1906: two variants (Hampshire)

HAMMOND MS: 1905: two variants (Dorset)
WILLIAMS: 1923, p. 175: (Northamptonshire in song) *It's My Delight of a Shiny Night* (Gloucestershire)
JFSS: 1901, No. 3, p. 118: *The Northamptonshire Poacher*, coll. W. Merrick, Sussex, 1899
PINTO AND RODWAY: 1957, No. 76, p. 235: *A Shining Night or Dick Daring the Poacher* (Nottingham broadside)
REEVES: 1958, No. 74, p. 170: (Somerset in song) *Poaching Song*, coll. C. Sharp, Gloucestershire, 1908

Although Lincolnshire, Somerset and Leicestershire occur as the location for this most 'fam-e-rous' of poaching songs, more than half the versions from genuine sources favour Northamptonshire. Like *Widdecombe Fair* the song has become widely known as a national song. It therefore comes as a surprise to people not used to the ever-adaptable folksong that there is not one original or right version. For our part, if any county is to claim this song, with our singer we say it is Northamptonshire.

259 THE OLD FAT BUCK

Harry Cox, Catfield, Norfolk, *rec.* P. Kennedy, 1956: BBC 22915

Printed versions

BROADWOOD: 1843, 1890, and 1893, p. 50: *The Nottinghamshire Poacher*, noted by Rev. John Broadwood, Sussex, before 1840
DIXON: 1846 and BELL: 1857, p. 214: *Thonehagh-Moor Woods* (Nottinghamshire)
MASON: 1877, p. 57: Broadwood version, *In Thorney Woods*
BROADWOOD: 1890, p. 12: *The Poacher's Song* (Sussex)

SHARP MS: 1909–21: four unpublished versions
GARDINER MS: 1906–7: two variants (Hampshire)
HAMMOND MS: 1906: one variant (Worcestershire)
JFSS: 1915, No. 19, p. 198: *Thorny Woods*, coll. Lucy Broadwood, Hertfordshire; p. 199: *Thornyholme Woods*, coll. Anne Gilchrist, Sussex, 1907
JFSS: 1922, No. 26: first verse only, *The Old Fat Buck*, coll. E. J. Moeran, 1921, Norfolk
PURSLOW: 1965, p. 88: *Thornaby Woods*, coll. Hammond, Worcestershire, 1906

Unlike *The Northamptonshire Poacher* (No. 258), the location of this song is consistently Nottinghamshire. The woods are thought to be Thorney Wood Chase, part of Sherwood Forest near Newark-on-Trent, which were enclosed about 1790.

260 THE ROVING PLOUGHBOY-O

John MacDonald, Elgin, Moray, Scotland, *rec.* P. Kennedy, 1953: *Folk Songs of Britain*, vol. III, CAEDMON TC1144/TOPIC 12T159

Printed version

SCOTTISH STUDIES: 1961, vol. 5, pt. 2, pp. 202–22 'How a Bothy Song came into being': Hamish Henderson

Compare

GREIG AND KEITH: 1925, p. 128: *The Gypsie Laddie*
ORD: 1930, p. 42: *The Collier Laddie*; p. 411: *The Gypsy Laddie*

This song is a reworking by the singer of a traditional fragment. Because it has similar verses and tune one would conclude that it is a bothy parody of the ballad *The Gipsy Laddie* mentioned by Ord in *Bothy Songs and Ballads* (p. 42). In fact it uses a similar tune to that sung by Jeannie Robertson for *The Gipsy Laddie*.

Variants of the same tune are also used for two other popular Occupational Songs: *The Brewer Lad* and *The Collier Laddie* (the latter touched up by Robert Burns). In a note to the *The Collier Laddie* Ord remarks that in the north-eastern counties of Scotland (Aberdeenshire, Banffshire and Morayshire) 'Ploughman Laddie' is substituted for 'Collier Laddie'. He gives the opening verse:

> I've been East and I've been West
> And I've been in St Johnstone,
> But the bonniest laddie that ever I saw
> Was a ploughman laddie dancing

The Collier Laddie too would seem to be parodied on *The Gipsy Laddie*.

> I'll gie her lands and I'll gie her rents
> And I'll make her a lady,
> I'll make her one of a higher degree
> Than to follow a collier laddie

Another song with a similar tune is *Mormond Braes*, but it could also be a fragment of the same song:

> There's as guid fish into the sea　　　Sae fare ye weel, ye Mormond Braes
> As ever yet was taken　　　　　　　Where aftimes I've been cheery
> I'll cast my line and try again　　　　Fare ye weel, ye Mormond Braes
> I'm only once forsaken　　　　　　　For it's there I've lost my dearie

This in turn could also be part of *The Brewer Lad* which has similar verses:

> She has rambled up, she's rambled down
> She's rambled through Kirkcaldy
> And mony's the time she rues the day
> She jilted her brewer laddie

261　THE TURNIP-HOER

Fred Jordan, Diddlebury, Wenlock, Shropshire, *rec.* P. Kennedy, 1952: BBC 18697

Other recorded versions
Unnamed farmer (Gloucestershire): BBC 754
Fred Perrier (with accordion and chorus), West Lavington, Wiltshire, *rec.* P. Kennedy, 1950: COLUMBIA SL 206
Andrew Curtis, Corfe, Dorset, *rec.* P. Kennedy, 1954: BBC 21477

Fred Perrier, Shrewton, Wiltshire, *rec.* P. Kennedy, 1954: BBC 21493

Printed versions
BROADWOOD: 1893, p. 70: *Turmut-hoeing* (Oxfordshire)
SHARP: 1902, No. 26, p. 56, *coll.* Broadwood
SHARP MS: 1903–6: three unpublished variants
UDAL: 1922, p. 322 (Dorset)

Fred Jordan learned this song from a gamekeeper who came from Buckinghamshire in 1940. The version in *English County Songs* was sent to Lucy Broadwood by a man living in Oxfordshire, but he too came from Buckinghamshire. Yet the song has attached itself to Wiltshire and was adopted as the regimental march of the Wiltshire Regiment (originally the 62nd and 99th Foot), now amalgamated with the Berkshire Regiment in the Duke of Edinburgh's Royal Regiment.

Lucy Broadwood remarked in 1893 that the song was a favourite with soldiers and popular in many counties. Fred Perrier, our Wiltshire singer, in fact learned the song from the soldiers on Salisbury Plain when they first came to train in the fields where he was working in the 1890s.

262　VAN DIEMEN'S LAND

Jimmy McBeath, Elgin, Moray, Scotland, *rec.* Alan Lomax, 1951: *Folk Songs of Britain*, vol. VII, CAEDMON TC1163/TOPIC 12T195: BBC 21533

Other recorded versions
Seamus Ennis, Dublin, Ireland, 1949: BBC 13769 (O Lochlainn version)
Harry Cox, Catfield, Norfolk, *rec.* P. Kennedy, 1953
Robert Cinnamond, Belfast, N. Ireland, *rec.* S. O'Boyle 1955: BBC 24836

Printed versions
JFSS: 1902, No. 4, p. 142: *The Gallant Poachers*, *coll.* Lucy Broadwood, Sussex, 1893
GARDINER MS: 1906: one variant (Hampshire)
HAMMOND MS: 1906: three variants (Dorset)
SHARP MS: 1906: one variant (Somerset)

BROADWOOD: 1908, p. 2
GREIG: 1909–14, No. 14, xxxiii: *The Gallant Poachers* (Scotland)
WILLIAMS: 1923, p. 263: *Poor Tom Brown of Nottingham Town* (Oxfordshire)
ORD: 1930, p. 384: *The Poachers* (Aberdeenshire, Scotland)
O LOCHLAINN: 1939, No. 21, p. 42 (Cashel, Tipperary, Ireland)
PINTO AND RODWAY: 1957, No. 77, p. 236: Catnach broadside
REEVES: 1958, No. 107, p. 217: *Van Dieman's Land*, *coll.* Cecil Sharp, 1906

MACKENZIE: 1928, p. 304 (Nova Scotia, Canada)
CREIGHTON AND SENIOR: 1950, p. 131 (Nova Scotia)
LEACH: 1965, p. 708 (Newfoundland, Canada)

> So all you gallant poachers, give ear unto my song
> It is a bit of good advice, although it is not long
> Throw by your dogs and snares, for to you I'll speak plain
> For if you knew our hardships you would never poach again

This transportation ballad appears on many ballad sheets, and it has been collected in England, Ireland and Scotland. In an English version *Poor Tom Brown of Nottingham Town*, from Henry Burstow of Sussex, the girl's name is Susan Summers. In an Irish version collected by Colm O Lochlainn, Thomas comes from Nenagh and the girl is Peg Brophy.

A Scots version similar to ours, which appears in ORD: 1930 sounds like a letter home:

> The houses that we dwell in here are built of clod and clay
> With rotten straw for bedding, we dare not say them nay
> Our cots are fenced with wire and we slumber when we can
> And we fight the wolves and tigers which infest Van Diemen's land
>
> To see our fellows suffer I'm sure I can't tell how
> Some chained unto the harrow and some unto the plough
> They hooked us out by two and two, like horses in a team
> And a driver standing over us with his long lash and cane
>
> One night in all my slumbers I had a pleasant dream
> I dreamed I was with my dear wife down by some purling stream
> With the children's prattling stories all around me they did stand
> But I awake quite broken-hearted all on Van Diemen's land

Van Diemen's Land was discovered in 1797 and first colonized by British settlers in 1804. Its present name Tasmania does not appear to have come into general use until after the first quarter of the nineteenth century.

After singing the song Jimmy McBeath said:

> That was a poachery. At one time of day they used to transport poachers all the way from this country if they were catched poaching. A lot of men goes and poaches yet and takes rabbits and steals and shoots and shoots anything that they see—to make money out of it. At one time of day—at that time—they used to transport them to the Devil's Island or Van Diemen's Land for all their life, they never got back again—that what they did with the poachers. It was a French ship, a four-masted frigate, used to come round and collect all the convicts—they put them to Van Diemen's Land or the Devil's Island for the rest of their life. They were a'ful cruel at that time. The laws were different.

263 WE'LL ALL GO A-HUNTING TODAY

Miles Wilson, Cockermouth, Cumberland, *rec.* P. Kennedy, 1959: BBC 26583

Other recorded versions
Billy (accordion) and Jack (banjo) Bowman, tune of song: BBC 26583
Neal Pearson, Cambo, Northumberland, tune on the fiddle: BBC 20621

Printed versions
DUNSTAN: 1932, p. 86: *Egloshayle Hunting Song* (Cornwall)
STUBBS: 1970, p. 76 (Sussex)

> We'll all go a-hunting today
> All nature looks balmy and gay
> Let's join the glad throng that goes laughing along
> And we'll all go a-hunting today

Although this fine chorus song is widely sung in hunting circles in England it is not available in current publications. When recording for the BBC, Miles Wilson omitted verses five and six.

264 WHAT'S THE LIFE OF A MAN?

Jim Small, Cheddar, Somerset, *rec.* P. Kennedy, 1950: BBC 14627

Other recorded versions
Jim Copper, Rottingdean, Sussex, *rec.* P. Kennedy, 1951
Gabriel Figg, West Chiltington, Sussex, *rec.* P. Kennedy, 1952

Harry Scott, Eaton Bray, Bedfordshire, *rec.* P. Kennedy, 1958: BBC 26071

Printed versions
SHARP MS: 1904: two variants, *The Fall of the Leaf* (Somerset)
WILLIAMS: 1923, p. 28 (Wiltshire)
STUBBS: 1970, p. 80 (Sussex)

This pastoral reflection on our temporal nature seems to have been widely sung in southern England. Looking at broadside versions we find religious verses added which bring in our Blessed Saviour and the Scriptures:

> Now the season is over and the leaves are all gone
> Back again to the trees they will never return
> But 'tis not so with man, for the Scriptures say plain
> Out of the dust, we must all rise again

> The Scriptures plainly tell us of something besides
> We must stand there in judgement for us to be tried
> Before our Blessed Saviour, both rich and poor stand
> And happy will be they who go to his right hand

Bibliography

This bibliography has been divided into two sections. Books published in Britain and Ireland appear first, followed by those published abroad, both in alphabetical order

BARING GOULD: 1889–1905
Rev. S. Baring Gould and Rev. H. Fleetwood Sheppard, *Songs and Ballads of the West*: Patey & Willis, London (4 parts) 1889–91. Methuen, London (4 parts) 1891–4; (1 vol.) 1895; revised edition 1905. Details are given by E. A. White in JEFDSS: 1937, p. 143, and 1946, p. 67. When reprinted in four parts this collection, mainly from Devon and N. Cornwall, comprised 110 songs 'collected from the mouths of the people'. Texts were modified and in some cases completely re-written and the same applied to tunes. However, in the revised edition, under the musical editorship of Cecil Sharp and with the adding of the name of the Rev. F. W. Bussell, one of the original collectors, many original texts and tunes were restored. For further comment on this publication see Dean-Smith: JEFDSS: 1950, p.41.

BARING GOULD MS: 1889–95
Rev. S. Baring Gould. Manuscript in Plymouth City Library.

BARING GOULD AND SHARP: 1906
Rev. S. Baring Gould and Cecil J. Sharp, *English Folk Songs for Schools*: Curwen, London, 1906. 53 songs from collections of both editors 'designed to meet the requirements of the Board of Education'—who that year had recommended the inclusion of National or Folk Songs in the school curriculum, and 'dedicated to T. R. H. Prince Edward and Prince Albert of Wales'.

BARRETT: 1891
William A. Barrett, *English Folk Songs*: Novello, London, 1891. 54 songs with piano arrangements. An early publication using the term 'collected folk song'; most of the songs published elsewhere; exact details of origins not given and Barrett not nationally accepted as reputable collector or arranger.

BELL: 1857
See DIXON: 1846 and BELL: 1957.

BROADWOOD: 1843
Rev. John Broadwood, *Old English Songs*: (privately printed) Balls & Co., London, 1843. 16 songs, collected in Surrey and Sussex by the Rev. John Broadwood of Lyne near Horsham. Arrangements by G. A. Dusart of Worthing. Said to be the 'first collection of folksong airs for their own sake'.

BROADWOOD: 1890
Rev. John Broadwood, *Sussex Songs* (*Popular Songs of Sussex*): Stanley, Lucas & Weber, London, 1890. 26 songs (including the 16 in BROADWOOD: 1843) collected by Broadwood and arranged by H. F. Birch Reynardson.

BROADWOOD: 1893
Lucy Broadwood and J. A. Fuller-Maitland, *English County Songs*: Cramer, London, 1893. Important early publication containing 92 songs collected in nearly every county of England. Most have little relevance to their district origins but some are in the dialects of their locality. Scholarly presentation with straightforward piano accompaniments. For article about editor see JEFDSS: 1948, p. 136, and 1950, p. 38.

BROADWOOD: 1908
Lucy Broadwood, *English Traditional Songs and Carols*: Boosey, London, 1908. 39 songs mainly from Surrey–Sussex border with informative preface and brief notes about singers with comparative transcriptions made by phonograph cylinder recordings.

CHAPPELL: 1838
William Chappell, *National English Airs*: Chappell & Simpkin Marshall, London, 1838. One volume containing 245 tunes arranged for piano and the other historical references, annotations and details of sources. Much of the reference is to printed works and MSS in the library of Edward Rimbault which was later dispersed. This work was superseded twenty years later by *Popular Music of the Olden Time* (1858).

CHAPPELL: 1858/9
William Chappell, *Popular Music of the Olden Time*: Cramer, Beale & Chappell, London, vol. I 1858, vol. II 1859; Dover Publications, New York, 1965. Includes most of material from *National English Airs* (1838) but more has been added from other sources with particular reference to the ballads in the Pepys and Roxburghe collections. For further comment see Dean-Smith's *Guide* and JEFDSS: 1950, p. 38.

DEAN-SMITH: 1954
Margaret Dean-Smith, *A Guide to English Folk Song Collections* (*1822–1952*): University of Liverpool, 1954. A useful index of published songs under titles, alternative titles and first lines, with some full descriptions of important books with historical annotations and an introduction which traces the development of collecting and publication of folksong in England over a period of 130 years.

DIXON: 1846 AND BELL: 1857
James Henry Dixon, *Ancient Poems, Ballads and Songs of the Peasantry of England*: Percy Society, London, No. 62, 1846. Robert Bell (Title as above): J. W. Parker, London, 1857. By agreement with Dixon, Bell's publication was a revision, enlargement and editing by Bell of Dixon's collection and notes. Most of the material was collected in West Yorkshire and on Tyneside.

DUNCAN MS: 1905–11
James Duncan (1848–1917). MS collected *c*. 1905–11. Aberdeen University Library. Consists of two notebooks, the first containing 800 tunes with words of first verse, and the second giving texts of over 350 songs all supplied by a Mrs Gillespie. For obituary by Lucy Broadwood see JFSS: 1918, No. 21, p. 41.

DUNSTAN: 1929
Ralph Dunstan, *The Cornish Song Book*: A. W. Jordan, Truro & Reid Brothers, London, 1929; Lodenek Press, Padstow, Cornwall, 1974. Contains 11 songs with Cornish words, 72 with English words collected in Cornwall or songs associated with Cornwall, and 48 carols. It is aimed to provide a selection of music for 'community singing wherever Cornishmen (and Cornish women) forgather the world over'.

DUNSTAN: 1932
Ralph Dunstan, *Cornish Dialect and Folk Songs*: A. W. Jordan, Truro and Reid Brothers, London, 1932; Lodenek Press, Padstow, Cornwall, 1972. A sequel to *The Cornish Song Book* containing 37 songs.

D'URFEY: 1698–1720
Thomas D'Urfey, *Wit and Mirth* (*or Pills to Purge Melancholy*): London, 1698–1720. First edition printed with airs was in 2 vols. (1698). Further editions increased to 6 vols. (1720). This

was the earliest publication to contain both words and music of a large number of English and Scots folksongs.

FMJ: 1965–
Folk Music Journal: English Folk Dance and Song Society, London (from 1965). Continuing the work of JFSS (*Journal of the Folk-Song Society*): 1889–1931 and JEFDSS (*Journal of the English Folk Dance and Song Society*): 1932–64.

GARDINER: 1909
George B. Gardiner, *Folk Songs from Hampshire*: Novello, London, 1909. 16 songs collected by Gardiner and his musical associates, Gamblin, Balfour Gardiner and Guyer, and arranged by Gustav (von) Holst.

GARDINER MS: 1905–9 (see also under HAMMOND)
For further details about Gardiner's work see *The George Gardiner Folksong Collection* in FMJ: 1967, p. 129 and introduction to PURSLOW: 1968.

GILLINGTON: 1911
Alice E. Gillington, *Songs of the Open Road*: Williams, London, 1911. The earliest English publication devoted to gipsy songs and dance tunes. 16 songs and 9 dances collected in Hampshire and the New Forest most from a family called Lee. Music arranged for piano by Dowsett Sellars.

GREIG: 1909/14
Gavin Greig, *Folk Songs of the North-East*: The Buchan Observer, Peterhead, Scotland. Vol. I 1909, vol. II 1914. Folklore Associates, Pennsylvania, USA, 1963. Greig was an Aberdeenshire schoolmaster and an accomplished musician who noted the words and tunes of over 3,000 songs. His manuscripts, extending over 90 volumes, are deposited in the Library of King's College, Aberdeen.

GREIG AND KEITH: 1925
Gavin Greig and Alexander Keith, *Last Leaves of Traditional Ballads*: Buchan Club, Aberdeen, 1925. Contains best texts and tunes of the Scottish versions of ballads collected by Greig.

HAMER: 1967
Fred Hamer, *Garners Gay*: EFDS Publications, London, 1967. 50 songs, words and melodies (chord symbols) mainly collected in Bedfordshire but also from other counties of England. No exact locations or dates given of informants or comparative notes to songs, but contains hitherto unpublished local songs and songs connected with local customs.

HAMMOND AND GARDINER MSS: 1905–9
H. E. D. Hammond (1866–1910), R. F. F. Hammond (1868–1921) and Dr George Gardiner (1852–1910) collected mainly in Dorset and Hampshire. Their manuscripts, deposited in the Vaughan Williams Memorial Library at Cecil Sharp House, London, have been indexed by Frank Purslow, who has also edited three books drawn from them (see PURSLOW: 1965, 1968 and 1972).

HENRY: 1924
Sam Henry, *Songs of the People*: Northern Constitution, Coleraine, Co. Derry, N. Ireland, 1924. Over 800 songs were published in the local Derry newspaper. Many were contributed by readers but it was Henry's diligent research and background notes that gave interest to each contribution.

JEFDSS: 1932–64
Journal of The English Folk Dance and Song Society: London (32 vols.), 1932–64.

JFSS: 1899–1931
Journal of the Folk-Song Society: London (35 vols.), 1899–1931.

JOHNSON: 1787–1853
James Johnson, *The Scots Musical Museum*: 6 vols. Edinburgh, 1787–1803; 4 vols. with notes by William Stenhouse and David Laing, Edinburgh, 1853. This was the beginning of systematic documentation of Scots songs to which Robert Burns contributed material of his own collecting which he restored by re-writing amplification of the texts.

KIDSON: 1891
Frank Kidson, *Traditional Tunes*: C. Taphouse, Oxford, 1891. Texts and melodies (without accompaniment) mainly from Yorkshire. Later published with piano accompaniment in KIDSON AND MOFFAT: 1926 and 1927. Many texts filled out from broadsides. For article about Frank Kidson see JEFDSS: 1948, p. 127. Reissued by S. R. Publishers, 1970.

KIDSON AND MOFFAT: 1926
Frank Kidson and Alfred Moffat, *A Garland of English Folk Songs*: Ascherberg, Hopwood & Crew, London, 1926. 60 songs collected by Kidson, mainly in Yorkshire, with piano accompaniments by Moffat; most previously published in *Traditional Tunes* (1891). A further 60 songs were selected for a second volume by Kidson and Moffat (1927).

KIDSON AND MOFFAT: 1927
Frank Kidson and Alfred Moffat, *Folk Songs from the North Countrie*: Ascherberg, Hopwood & Crew, London, 1927. A further 60 songs with piano accompaniment, published one year after the collector's death. The foreword by Lucy Broadwood provides information about the collector. See also *Frank Kidson: portrait*, JEFDSS: 1948, pp. 127–35.

KIDSON AND MOFFAT: 1929
Frank Kidson, Ethel Kidson and Alfred Moffat, *English Peasant Songs*: Ascherberg, Hopwood & Crew, London, 1929. 'Third and last Selection of Sixty Folk Songs from the Frank Kidson Collection.' Compiled by his niece with once again piano accompaniments by Moffat. (See KIDSON AND MOFFAT: 1926 and 1927.)

MACCOLL: 1953
Ewan MacColl, *Scotland Sings*: Workers Music Association, London, 1953. 100 songs and ballads divided into 'muckle' (i.e. great songs or ballads), 'Orra' (hero) folk and rebels, Kissin's nae sin, ploo lads, pipes and drums, drinking, shuttle and cage, muckle toons (urban), children's songs and lullabies.

MASON: 1877/1908
Miss M. H. Mason, *Nursery Rhymes and Country Songs*: Metzler, London, 1877. Second edition without illustrations but with additional notes, 1908. Over 50 folksongs of great variety mainly from her own Mitford family in Northumberland, also from Broadwood in Sussex, with piano accompaniments.

MERRICK: 1912
W. Percy Merrick, *Folk Songs from Sussex*: Novello, London, 1912. 15 songs, all from one singer, previously in JFSS: 1901, No. 3 and 1904, No. 5, with piano accompaniments by R. Vaughan Williams, two songs, *The Unquiet Grave* and *The Seeds of Love* (No. 167), with violin *ad lib*. The last song was arranged by Albert Robins.

O LOCHLAINN: 1939
Colm O Lochlainn, *Irish Street Ballads*: Three Candles, Dublin, 1939. Over 100 songs, words, music and annotations collected in many different parts of Ireland (including the North). All in English and many having equivalents in England and Scotland. Illustrated with woodcuts from the original broadsheets.

ORD: 1930
John Ord, *Bothy Songs and Ballads*: Alexander Gardner, Paisley, Scotland. The standard work on the 'bothy ballads' of N.E. Scotland; 'bothy' meaning farm cottage or hut used by hands, ploughmen, shepherds and farm-servants, and the ballads, although including folksongs found elsewhere, being mainly those describing, and often complaining about, local farm life.

PINTO AND RODWAY: 1957
V. de Sola Pinto and A. E. Rodway, *The Common Muse*: Chatto & Windus, London, 1957; Penguin Books, London, 1965. An anthology of Popular British Ballad Poetry from the 15th to the

20th century. In two parts: the first 'Amatory' and the second 'General'. 245 texts from England, Ireland and Scotland with an introduction mainly about street balladry.

PURSLOW: 1965
Frank Purslow, *Marrowbones*: EFDS Publications, London, 1965. A series of pocket-size publications initiated by Peter Kennedy in order to make available the songs collected by Hammond and Gardiner in the care of the EFDSS library. This selection contains 100 songs, provided with chord symbols over the melodies.

PURSLOW: 1968
Frank Purslow, *The Wanton Seed*: EFDS Publications, London, 1968. A second selection from Hammond and Gardiner again containing 100 songs.

PURSLOW: 1972
Frank Purslow, *The Constant Lovers*: EFDS Publications, London, 1972. A third selection in which the type-size has been increased and the number of songs reduced to 78.

REEVES: 1958
James Reeves, *The Idiom of the People*: Heinemann, London, 1958. Words of 115 folksongs from Cecil Sharp MSS (about 40 printed for the first time) selected as examples of 'English Traditional Verse'. Introduction concerned with the Folk Song Movement in England; Sharp as a collector; text revisions, description of the MSS; the popular idiom; and a detailed consideration of certain songs.

ROXBURGHE: 1871–93
Roxburghe Ballads (about 1540–1790): 7 vols. Vols. I–II ed. William Chappell, Ballad Society, London, 1871–80; vols. III–VII ed. J. W. Ebsworth, Hertford, 1883–93.

SCOTTISH STUDIES: 1957–
Journal of the School of Scottish Studies, University of Edinburgh, published twice a year. Subjects already covered include Classification of Gaelic Folk Song by James Ross and an article by Hamish Henderson about *The Roving Ploughboy* (No. 260).

SHARP: 1902
Cecil J. Sharp, *A Book of British Song*: John Murray, London, 1902. 78 songs published before Sharp started collecting. They are listed under National, Soldier and Sailor, Country, Humorous, Old England and Old Scottish, starting with *God Save the King* and *Rule Britannia* and finishing with *Auld Lang Syne*. Only two Welsh and two Irish national songs are included.

SHARP MS 1903–23
Cecil Sharp (1859–1924), foremost collector of English folksongs and folkdances, was the founder of The English Folk Dance Society and for many years a member of The Folk-Song Society. (In 1932 these two societies amalgamated as The English Folk Dance and Song Society.) For a full account of his life-work and publications see *Cecil Sharp* by A. H. Fox-Strangways (Oxford University Press, London, 1933), revised by Maud Karpeles (Routledge & Kegan Paul, London, 1967). Words, songs, tunes and dance notes in Cecil Sharp's autograph are in the Library of Clare College, Cambridge. There are also photostat copies in the Harvard University Library and the New York Public Library, and microfilm copies in the libraries of the University of California and in the library at Cecil Sharp House, London, the headquarters of The English Folk Dance and Song Society. Cecil Sharp's own collection of books was left to the EFDSS and formed the beginnings of the specialist library at Cecil Sharp House.

STOKOE AND REAY: 1892
John Stokoe and Samuel Reay, *Songs and Ballads of Northern England*: Scott, Newcastle-upon-Tyne and London, 1899 (British Museum Catalogue date). 92 songs with annotations intended as instrumental accompaniment to the songs which previously appeared in BRUCE AND STOKOE: 1882 and before that in DIXON: 1846 and BELL: 1857 in which the names of the tunes were given but the music was not printed.

STUBBS: 1970
Ken Stubbs, *The Life of a Man*: EFDS Publications, London, 1970. 50 songs, texts and melodies (chord symbols). Many from our same source singers, but includes a wide variety from Home Counties (Surrey, Sussex mainly and some from Kent) with some important variant versions and some hitherto unpublished songs. Biographical notes about singers.

UDAL: 1922
John Symonds Udal, *Dorsetshire Folk-Lore*: Stephen Austin, Hertford, 1922; J. Stephens-Cox, St Peter Port, Guernsey, 1970. Contains a long 'fore-say' by William Barnes, 'The Dorset Poet'. This is a mixture of material including the words of about 20 songs.

WILLIAMS: 1923
Alfred Owen Williams, *Folk Songs of the Upper Thames*: Duckworth, London, 1923. Over 300 folksongs (words only) noted mainly in Berkshire, Gloucestershire, Oxfordshire and Wiltshire. Interesting introduction about rural life, more fully covered by Williams in *Round About the Upper Thames* (Duckworth, 1922). Further unpublished texts in Swindon Reference Library. See FMJ: 1969 'Alfred Williams: A Symposium'.

BELDEN: 1940
H. M. Belden, *Ballads and Songs Collected by the Missouri Folklore Society*: University Studies XV (No. 1), Columbia, Missouri, USA, 1940.

CREIGHTON AND SENIOR: 1950
Helen Creighton and Doreen Senior, *Traditional Songs from Nova Scotia*: Ryerson Press, Toronto, Canada, 1950. 100 songs and 36 ballads collected in the Maritimes with additional variants of both tunes and texts in many instances. An important and well documented collection with versions of many of the songs in this book.

FLANDERS AND BROWN: 1932
Helen Hartness Flanders and George Brown, *Vermont Folk Songs and Ballads*: Stephen Daye, Brattleboro, Vermont, USA, 1932.

HUNTINGTON: 1964
Gale Huntington, *Songs the Whalermen Sang*: Barre Publishers, Barre, Mass., USA, 1964.

JAFL: 1888–
Journal of American Folklore now published by University of Pennsylvania.

LEACH: 1965
MacEdward Leach, *Folk Ballads and Songs of the Lower Labrador Coast*: National Museum of Canada, Ottawa, 1965.

MACKENZIE: 1928
W. Roy Mackenzie, *Ballads and Sea Songs from Nova Scotia*: Harvard University Press, Cambridge, Mass., USA, 1928.

POUND: 1922
Louise Pound, *American Ballads and Songs*: Charles Scribner's Sons, New York, 1922.

STOUT: 1936
Earl J. Stout, *Folklore from Iowa*: American Folklore Society, vol. XXIX, New York, 1936.

XIII

Songs of
Good Company

Introduction

Come all you honest labouring men, that work hard all the day
And join with me at the Barley Mow, to pass an hour away
Where we can sing and drink and be merry
And drive away all our cares and worries

When Jones's Ale was New: No. 287

Farm labourers and tradesmen gather together at the local, the pub, or public house, here called The Barley Mow, for their pints of beer, and each one as he comes into the pub is introduced like an actor in a folk drama. In fact it is a kind of 'calling-on' song:

The first to come in was the ploughman, with sweat all on his brow
Up with the lark at the break of day, he guides his speedy plough
He drives his team, how they do toil
O'er hill and valley to turn the soil

In come all the rest of them: tinkers, soldiers, tailors, sailors, including the blacksmith, 'his brawny arms all bare', who is also praised in another popular drinking song:

Here's a health to the jolly blacksmith, the best of all fellows
Who works at his anvil while the boy blows the bellows
Which makes his bright hammer to rise and to fall
There's the Old Cole and the Young Cole and the Old Cole of all

Twankydillo: No. 286

Half of the songs in this chapter are those specifically in praise of drink, and many of these could be classed as Songs of Diversion (see Chapter XIV).

Our first song, *The Barley Mow* (No. 265), is a mouthful, a tongue-twisting cumulative catalogue of drinking companions; it starts with the smallest measure, the nipperkin, works up through the gill, pint, gallon, barrel, and then brings in the landlord, landlady, daughter, slavey, brewer and finally all the company, ending with the tavern itself.

I'll drink one, if you'll drink two
And here's a lad that'll drink with you
And if you do as I have done
You'll be a good companion

To Be a Good Companion: No. 285

This numerical enumeration song requires that each member of the company should contribute a verse and improvise the rhymes and in addition, of course, drink one more pint than the last man. A Scots variation of this is *Tam Broon* (No. 283), which is based on playing card numbers and royals. Another song, *Here's to the Grog* (No. 274), uses all the articles of worn-out clothing: coat, breeches, shirt, boots and tile (hat), whilst others utilize the farmyard (see Nos. 297 and 310 in the next chapter).

O me father had a horse and me mother she'd a mare
Sister Susie had a rabbit and Johnny he'd a hare
So we'd a ride from father's horse
And a gallop from mother's mare
We'd a pie from Susie's rabbit
And a course from Johnny's hare

The Irish Familie: No. 275

593

Scarce and Wickets Richardson at
he Ship Inn, Blaxhall, Suffolk
Photograph: C. M. Allen Ltd

Here again the singer improvises animals and other rhyming articles: bull, cow, pig, sow; buck, doe, tup, ewe; cock, hen, robin, wren; rat, mouse, flea, louse; knife, fork, bottle, cork, and so on.

Difficulty in getting drinks from countries not under British control or during wartime, and still more the threats of invasion and with it perhaps the loss of every kind of drink has been a constant source of worry to the English:

> Then up spake bold Churchill, of fame and renown
> He swears he'll be true to his country and his crown
> For the cannons they shall rattle, and the bullets they shall fly
> Shall fly
> Before that they shall come and drink old England dry
>
> *Drink Old England Dry*: No. 270

Although brandy from France and rum from the West Indies may be difficult to come by, and although there is a scolding wife and a father recently drowned at sea, yet thankfully there is always beer and cider for the punch bowl in which to drown one's sorrows:

> Come all you bold fellows that 'ave to this place come
> And we'll sing in the praise of good brandy and rum
> Let's lift up our glasses, good cheer is our goal
> Bring in the punch ladle, and we'll fathom the bowl
>
> *Bring in the Punch Ladle*: No. 268

The song of the weaver also has this consolatory theme:

> What more pleasure could a boy desire
> Than to sit him down, O, beside the fire?
> And in his hand, O, a jug of punch
> Aye, and on his knee, O, a tidy wench
>
> *The Jug of Punch*: No. 278

That song, and the one about *John Barleycorn* (No. 276), are both sung in the pub at Haxey on the Yorkshire–Lincolnshire border before a kind of annual village all-in Rugby match. This song gives the whole story of how the barley is grown, cut down, thrashed and malted into beer:

> Then they put him into the mashing tub
> Thinking to scald his tail
> And the next thing they called Barleycorn
> They called him home-brewed ale

However, most of the songs in praise of drink also warn of its dangers:

> It is you that makes my friends my foes
> It is you that makes me wear old clothes
> But since you come so near my nose
> It's up you comes and down you goes
>
> *Good Ale*: No. 273

Further detrimental qualities of drink are treated in three story songs: *Farewell to Whisky* (No. 272); *Nancy Whisky* (No. 279); and in *Wild Rover* (No. 288):

> So now I'll give over and I'll lead a new life
> And I'll stop all my ramblings and look for a wife
> I'll pay up back reckonings, put my money in store
> And I never will play the wild rover no more

265 THE BARLEY MOW

Now here's good luck to the gill - pot Good luck to the Bar - ley Mow ———

Here's good luck to the gill - pot Good luck to the Bar - ley Mow ———

The gill - pot, half - a - gill, quar - ter - gill Nip - per - kin and a round bowl.

And here's good luck, good luck Good luck to the Bar - ley Mow ———

1 Now here's good luck to the gill-pot
Good luck to the Barley Mow
Here's good luck to the gill-pot
Good luck to the Barley Mow
The gill-pot, half-a-gill, quarter-gill
Nipperkin, and a round bowl
And here's good luck, good luck
Good luck to the Barley Mow

2 Now here's good luck to the half-a-pint
Good luck to the Barley Mow
Here's good luck to the half-a-pint
Good luck to the Barley Mow
The half-a-pint, gill-pot, half-a-gill, quarter-gill
Nipperkin, and a round bowl
And here's good luck, good luck
Good luck to the Barley Mow

3	pint-pot	9	landlord
4	quart-pot	10	landlady
5	half-a-gallon	11	daughter
6	gallon	12	slavey
7	half a barrel	13	brewer
8	barrel	14	company

LAST And here's good luck to the tavern [*or name of tavern*]
Good luck to the Barley Mow
Here's good luck to the tavern
Good luck to the Barley Mow
The tavern
The company
The brewer
The slavey
The daughter
The landlady
The landlord
The barrel
Half a barrel
The gallon
Half-a-gallon
Quart-pot
Pint-pot
Half-a-pint
Gill-pot
Half-a-gill
Quarter-gill
Nipperkin, and a round bowl
And here's good luck, good luck
Good luck to the Barley Mow

266 BILLY JOHNSON'S BALL

1 Billy Johnson he got married just a twelve-month and a day
And he wrote his friends a letter in which he meant to say
How about six months ago a baby had been sent
And he'd give a ball to celebrate the glorious event
And we'll play: la, la-di-da
Row-di-dow-di-diddle-um
We'll play it on the fiddle
Up and down the middle
Jolly boys, pretty girls
Enough to pl'ase us all
And a regular jollification spree
Was Billy Johnson's Ball

2 He introduced the baby, we kissed it twice around
 Mrs Johnson she became quite overcome, fell fainted on the ground
 They brought her in some water, put a drop o' something in
 And very shortly after, the dancing did begin
 And we played: la (etc.)

3 There was the Jonatese, the Smithatese, there was the Brownatese a score
 The Higginses and Scrovinses and half a dozen more
 In Johnson's room there wasn't room for to dance a single jig
 So we went down and took a larger room at The Tinder-Box and Pig
 And we played: la (etc.)

4 I drank love to the Jonatese, I drank love to the Browns
 I tried to keep on dancing, but there were ups and down
 Johnson he kept dancing with all the girls around
 And Mrs Johnson she grew jealous and she said he was unkind
 Doing the la (etc.)

5 It was in and out and round about, such a ball was never seen
 And now and then we had to stop to have a drink between
 But to tell you how it ended I really am not able
 For I found myself next morning lying underneath the table
 Playing: la (etc.)

267 THE BLACK RAM

1 Come all my jolly boys, and we'll together go
Together with our masters, to shear the lambs and yowes
All in the month of June, of all times in the year
It always comes in season, the lambs and yowes to shear
And then we will work hard, my boys, until our backs do break
Our master he will bring us beer, whenever we do lack

2 Our master he comes round, to see our work's done well
And he says: Shear them close, my boys, for there is but little wool
O yes, good master, we reply, we'll do well as we can
Our captain cried: Shear close, my lads, to each and every man
And at some places still we have this story all day long:
Bend your backs and shear them well, and this is all their song

3 And then our noble captain doth to the master say
Come let us have a bucket of your good ale, I pray
He turns unto our captain, and makes him this reply
You shall have the best of beer, I promise, present-lie
Then with the foamin' bucket pretty Betsy she doth come
And master says: Maid, mind and see that every man has some

4 This is some of our pastime while we the sheep do shear
And, though we are such merry boys, we work hard I declare
And when 'tis night and we are done, our master is more free
And stores us well with good strong beer and pipes of to-bac-cy
And there we sit a-drinkin', we smoke and sing and roar
Till we become far merrier than e'er we were before

5 When all our work is done, and all the sheep are shorn
Then home with our captain, to drink the ale that's strong
It's a barrel then of hum-cap, which we call The Black Ram
And we do sit and swagger, we swear that we are men
And yet before the night is through, I'll bet you half-a-crown
That if you haven't a special care, that Ram will knock you down

268 BRING IN THE PUNCH LADLE

Come all you bold fel-lows that 'ave to this place come

And we'll sing in the praise of good bran-dy and rum

Let's lift up our glass-es,——— good cheer is our goal

Bring in the punch la-dle and we'll fa-thom the bowl

CH: Fa-thom the bowl, fa-thom the bowl

Bring in the punch la-dle and we'll fa-thom the bowl

1 Come all you bold fellows that 'ave to this place come
And we'll sing in the praise of good brandy and rum
Let's lift up our glasses, good cheer is our goal
Bring in the punch ladle and we'll fathom the bowl

Fathom the bowl, fathom the bowl
Bring in the punch ladle and we'll fathom the bowl

2 From France we do get brandy and from Jamaica comes rum
Sweet oranges and lemons from Portugal come
But stout, beer and cider are England's control
Bring in the punch ladle and we'll fathom the bowl

3 O my wife she do come in when I'm taking my ease
She scolds me and grumbles but she'll do as she please
She may scold and may grumble till she's black as the coal
Bring in the punch ladle and we'll fathom the bowl

4 O my father he do lie in the depth of the sea
With no stone at his feet but what matter for he
There's a clear crystal fountain near England does roll
Bring in the punch ladle and we'll fathom the bowl

269 CAMPBELL THE ROVER

On the first day of Ap-ril I shall not for-get

When two Eng-lish blades to - ge-ther they met

They swore they'd play a trick on the first one they'd spy

When Camp-bell the Ro - ver he chanced to ride by

Lad-die fol - de-ral lad-die Lal-lie fol - de-ral - lee

1 On the first day of April I shall not forget
When two English blades together they met   [spy
They swore they'd play a trick on the first one they'd
When Campbell the Rover he chanced to ride by
Laddie fol-de-ral laddie
Lallie fol-de-ral-lee

2 On Campbell the Rover they cast a sly eye
They mounted their horses and rode up alongside
They saluted Campbell and he done the same
And in close conversation together they came

3 They came to an inn where they made a full stop
They asked Campbell in for to have a small drop
Campbell consented and said with a smile
I long for a taste of this draught of sweet ale

4 The tumblers of whisky they followed with wine
Twenty-five shillings it cost them a time
There was more for the horses for oats and for hay
And they planned to leave Campbell the reckoning
to pay

5 Then the two English blades they slipped out one
by one
Leaving Campbell at the table to pay the whole sum
Then in came the landlord to Campbell did say
Your friends they are gone the reckoning you'll pay

6 Never mind them, says Campbell, since they're
gone away
I have plenty of money the reckoning to pay
Sit down here beside me before I will go
I'll tell you a trick that perhaps you don't know

7 I'll tell you a trick that's contrary to law
That two sorts of liquor from one punch I can draw
The landlord being eager to find out the plan
It's down to the lower cellar with Campbell he ran

8 He bored him a hole in a very short space
He then bored another in the very same place
He said to the landlord: Now place your hand there
Till I for a tumbler will run up the stair

9 He mounted his horse and was soon out of sight
The servant came in to see if all was right
He searched the whole house from top to the ground
'Twas down in the lower cellar his master he found

10 Up on the counter they found Campbell had wrote
You're very well paid for the trick that I taught
For the two kinds of liquor the reckoning I've paid
I've left you two bullets for those two English blades

601

270 DRINK OLD ENGLAND DRY

Now come, me brave boys,— as I've told you be-fore

Come drink me brave boys, and we'll bold-ly call for more

For the French they've in-vi-ted us and they say that they will try

Will try They say that they will come and drink old Eng-land dry

CH: Aye, dry, aye, dry, me boys, aye, dry ———

They say that they will come and drink old Eng-land dry

1 Now come, me brave boys, as I've told you before
Come drink, me brave boys, and we'll boldly call for more
For the French they've invited us and they say that they will try
Will try
They say that they will come and drink old England dry

Aye, dry, aye, dry, me boys, aye, dry
They say that they will come and drink old England dry

2 Supposin' we should meet with the Germans by the way
Ten thousand to one we will show them British play
With our swords and our cutlasses, we'll fight until we die
We die
Before that they shall come and drink old England dry

602

3 Then up spake bold Churchill of fame and renown
He swears he'll be true to his country and his crown
For the cannons they shall rattle and the bullets they shall fly
Shall fly
Before that they shall come and drink old England dry

4 Then it's drink, me brave boys, as I've told you before
Come drink, me brave boys, till you cannot drink no more
For those Germans they may boast and shout, but their brags are
My eye   [all my eye
They say that they will come and drink old England dry

271 THE EWIE WI' THE CROOKIT HORN

O the ewie wi' the crookit horn
A' that kenned her could ha'e sworn
That sicca ewie ne'er was born
Here aboots or far awa'

1 O the ewie wi' the crookit horn
A' that kenned her could ha'e sworn
That sicca ewie ne'er was born
Here aboots or far awa'

2 But fid-ye think for a' my keepin'
There cam' a nickim fan I was sleepin'
There cam' a nickim fan I was sleepin'
And stole my ewie horn an a'

3 O gin I had the lad that did it
I hae sworn as weel as said it
Though the de'il himself they should forbid it
I would gie his neck a thraw

4 She'd neither knot nor 'carf or keel
To mark upon her hip or heel
Her crookit horn it did as weel
To ken her ower amang them a'

5 The ewie wi' the crookit horn
The ewie wi' the crookit horn
My ewie wi' the crookit horn
Is taen frae me an sto'en awa

272 FAREWELL TO WHISKY

I'll gang to the ale-hoose, and look for my Jim-my
The day is far spent, and the night's com-in' on
You're sit-tin' there drink-in', and leave me la-men-tin'
So rise up. my Jim-my, and come a-wa' hame

1 I'll gang to the ale-hoose, and look for my Jimmy
  The day is far spent, and the night's comin' on
  You're sittin' there drinkin', and leave me lamentin'
  So rise up, my Jimmy, and come awa' hame

2 Nae mind o' the bairnies, that are at hame greetin'
  Nae meal in the barrow, to fu' their wee wames
  Your siller's near dune, and the stoups toom before ye
  So rise up, my Jimmy, and come awa hame

3 Wha's that at the door, that is speakin' sae kindly
  It's the voice of my wifie, called Jeannie, by name
  Come in by me, dearie, and sit doon beside me
  It's time enough yet, for to gang awa' hame

4 Then Jimmy rose up, and he banged the door open
  Sayin': Cursed be the ale-hoose, that e'er let me in
  And cursed be the whisky, that mak's me so brisky
  So fare thee well, ale-hoose, and I'll awa' hame

273 GOOD ALE

It is   of good ale to you I'll   sing   And   to good ale I'll al-ways cling

I   like my mug filled to the   brim   And   I'll drink all you'd like to   bring

O   good   ale,   thou art my   dar-lin'   Thou art my   joy,   both night   and mor-nin'

1 It is of good ale to you I'll sing
   And to good ale I'll always cling
   I like my mug filled to the brim
   And I'll drink all you'd like to bring
   O good ale, thou art my darlin'
   Thou art my joy, both night and mornin'

2 It is you that helps me with my work
   And from a task I'll never shirk
   While I can get a good home brew
   And better than one pint I like two

3 I love you in the early morn
   I love you in daylight, dark or dawn
   And when I'm weary, worn or spent
   I'll turn the tap and ease the vent

4 It is you that makes my friends my foes
   It is you that makes me wear old clothes
   But since you come so near my nose
   It's up you comes and down you goes

5 And if all my friends from Adam's race
   Was to meet me here all in this place
   I could part from all without one fear
   Before I'd part from my good beer

6 And if my wife should me despise
   How soon I'd give her two black eyes
   But if she loved me as I love thee
   What a happy couple we should be

7 You have caused me debts that I've often swore
   I never would drink strong ale any more
   But you for all that I'll forgive
   And I'll drink strong ale as long as I live

274 HERE'S TO THE GROG

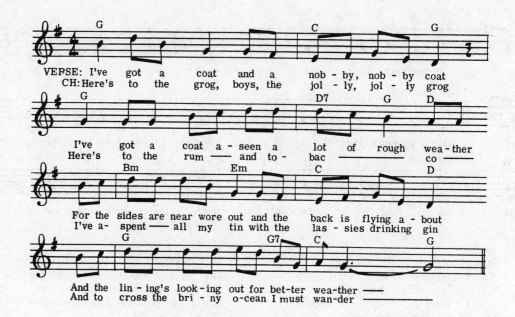

VERSE: I've got a coat and a nob-by, nob-by coat
CH: Here's to the grog, boys, the jol-ly, jol-ly grog

I've got a coat a-seen a lot of rough wea-ther
Here's to the rum — and to-bac co

For the sides are near wore out and the back is flying a-bout
I've a-spent — all my tin with the las-sies drinking gin

And the lin-ing's look-ing out for bet-ter wea-ther —
And to cross the bri-ny o-cean I must wan-der —

1 I've got a coat and a nobby, nobby coat
   I've got a coat a-seen a lot of rough weather
   For the sides are near wore out and the back is flying about
   And the lining's looking out for better weather

Here's to the grog, boys, the jolly, jolly grog
Here's to the rum and tobacco
I've a-spent all my tin with the lassies drinking gin
And to cross the briny ocean I must wander

2 I've got me breeches, me nobby, nobby breeches
   I've got breeches a-seen a lot of rough weather
   For the pouch is near wore out and the seat's all flying about
   And me knees are looking out for better weather

3 I've got a shirt and a nobby, nobby shirt
   I've got a shirt a-seen a lot of rough weather
   For the collar's near wore out and the sleeves are flying about
   And me tail's looking out for better weather

4 I've got me boots, me nobby, nobby boots
   I've got boots a-seen a lot of rough weather
   For the bottoms' near wore out and the heels flying about
   And me toes are looking out for better weather

5 I've got a tile, a nobby, nobby tile
   I've got a tile a-seen a lot of rough weather
   For the brim it is wore out and the crown is flying about
   And the lining's looking out for better weather

275 THE IRISH FAMILIE

O me fa-ther had a horse And me mo-ther she'd a mare

Sis-ter Su-sie had a rab-bit And John-ny he'd a hare

So we'd a ride from fa-ther's horse And a gal-lop from mo-ther's mare

We'd a pie from Su-sie's rab-bit And a course from John-ny's hare

So the more we have to drink And the mer-ri-er we shall be

For we all — do be - long — To an Ir-ish fa-mi-lie

1 O me father had a horse
   And me mother she'd a mare
   Sister Susie had a rabbit
   And Johnny he'd a hare
   So we'd a ride from father's horse
   And a gallop from mother's mare
   We'd a pie from Susie's rabbit
   And a course from Johnny's hare
   So the more we have to drink
   And the merrier we shall be
   For we all do belong
   To an Irish familie

3 O me father had a buck
   And me mother she'd a doe
   Sister Susie had a tup
   And Johnny he'd a ewe
   So we'd a horn from father's buck
   And we'd venison from the doe
   We'd mutton from the tup
   And a lamb from Johnny's ewe

2 O me father had a bull
   And me mother she'd a cow
   Sister Susie had a pig
   And Johnny he'd a sow
   So we'd beef from father's bull
   And we'd milk from mother's cow
   We'd pork from Susie's pig
   And a litter from Johnny's sow

4 O me father had a cock
   And me mother she'd a hen
   Sister Susie had a robin
   And Johnny he'd a wren
   So we'd a crow from father's cock
   And we'd eggs from mother's hen
   We'd some chicks from Susie's robin
   And they were fed by Johnny's wren ➔

5 O me father had a rat
 And me mother she'd a mouse
 Sister Susie had a flea
 And Johnny he'd a louse
 So we'd a scratch from father's rat
 And a squeak from mother's mouse
 We'd a nip from Susie's flea
 And a crawl from Johnny's louse

6 O me father had a knife
 And me mother she'd a fork
 Sister Susie had a bottle
 And Johnny he'd a cork
 So we'd a cut from father's knife
 And a pick from mother's fork
 We'd a drink from Susie's bottle
 Johnny bunged it with the cork

276 JOHN BARLEYCORN

1 O three men they did come down from Kent
 To plough for wheat and rye
 And they made a vow and a solemn vow
 John Barleycorn should die
 To me ri-fol-lair-ry, fol-the-diddle-aye
 To me ri-fol-lair-ry O
 To me ri-fol-lair-ry, fol-the-diddle-aye
 To me ri-fol-lair-ry O

2 O they ploughed him in the furrow deep
 Till the clods lay o'er his head
 And these three men were rejoicing then
 John Barleycorn was dead

3 They left him there for a week or so
 And a shower of rain did fall
 John Barleycorn sprung up again
 And he proved them liars all

4 Then they hired men with sickles
 To cut him off at the knee
 And the worst of all they served Barleycorn
 They served him barbarous-ly

5 Then they hired men with pitchforks
 To pitch him onto the load
 And the worst of all they served Barleycorn
 They bound him down with cord

6 Then they hired men with thrashels
 To beat him high and low
 They came smick-smack on poor Jack's back
 Till the flesh bled every blow

7 O the next they put him in the maltin' kiln
 Thinking to dry his bones
 And the worst of all they served Barleycorn
 They crushed him between two stones

8 Then they put him into the mashing-tub
 Thinking to scald his tail
 And the next thing they called Barleycorn
 They called him home-brewed ale

9 So come put your wine into glasses
 Your cider in tin-cans
 But young Barleycorn in the old brown jug
 For he proves the strongest man

277 JOHN BARLEYCORN'S A HERO BOLD

John Bar-ley-corn's a he-ro bold as a-ny in the land
For a-ges good his fame has stood and shall for a-ges stand

The whole wide world re-spect in him, no mat-ter friend or foe

And where they be that makes so free, he's sure to lay them low

Hey, John Bar-ley-corn   Ho, John Bar-ley-corn

Old and young thy praise has sung   John Bar-ley-corn

1 John Barleycorn's a hero bold as any in the land
For ages good his fame has stood and shall for ages stand
The whole wide world respect in him, no matter friend or foe
And where they be that makes so free, he's sure to lay them low
Hey, John Barleycorn
Ho, John Barleycorn
Old and young thy praise has sung
John Barleycorn

2 To see him in his pride of growth, his robes are rich and green
His head is speared with prickly beard, fit nigh to serve the queen
And when the reaping time comes round and Johnny's stricken down
He'll use his blood for England's good and Englishmen's renown

3 The lord in courtly castle and the squire in stately hall
The great of name, of birth and fame, on John for succour call
He bids the troubled hearts rejoice, gives warmth to nature's cold
Makes weak men strong and old ones young and all men brave and bold

4 Then shout for great John Barleycorn, more heed his luscious vine
I have no mind much charm to find in potent draught of wine
Give me my native nut-brown ale, all other drinks I scorn
For true English cheer is English beer, our own John Barleycorn

278 THE JUG OF PUNCH

It was on the twen-ty — fourth of June As I sat wea-ving up-on my loom
I heard a thrush sing-ing in a bush And the song he sang was: A jug of punch
Lad-der-ly fol-the-dee Lad-der-ly fol-the-dee-di-dee-dle-um
Dee-i-dle-doo-i-dle-dee-da-did-dle-um Lad-der-ly fol-the-ding-di-did-dle-um
Dee-dle-i-dle-oo-dle-lad-der-ly-dee-di-dum

1 It was on the twenty-fourth of June
As I sat weaving upon my loom
I heard a thrush singing in a bush
And the song he sang was: A jug of punch
Ladderly fol-the-dee
Ladderly fol-the-dee-di-deedle-um
Dee-idle-doo-idle-dee-da-diddle-um
Ladderly fol-the-ding-di-diddle-um
Deedle-idle-oodle-ladderly-dee-di-dum

2 What more pleasure could a boy desire
Than to sit him down, O, beside the fire?
And in his hand, O, a jug of punch
Aye, and on his knee, O, a tidy wench
Ladderly fol-the-dee

3 What more hardships could a boy endure
Than to sit him down, O, behind the door?
And in his hand, O, no jug of punch
Aye, and on his knee, O, no tidy wench
Ladderly fol-the-dee

4 When I am dead all my drinking's over
I'll drink one glass and I'll drink no more
For fear I mightn't get it on that day
I will drink it now and I'll drink away
Ladderly fol-the-dee

5 When I am dead and left in my mould
At my head and feet place a flowing bowl
And every young man that passes by
He can have a drink and remember I
Ladderly fol-the-dee

279 NANCY WHISKY

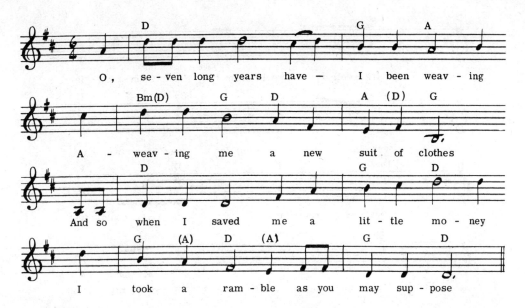

O, se-ven long years have — I been weav-ing
A - weav-ing me a new suit of clothes
And so when I saved me a lit-tle mo-ney
I took a ram-ble as you may sup-pose

1 O, seven long years have I been weaving
A-weaving me a new suit of clothes
And so when I saved me a little money
I took a ramble as you may suppose

2 As I was going up fair London city
Young Nancy Whisky I chanced to smell
So I thought it proper to call and see her
For seven long years I had loved her well

3 I stepped up boldly, knocked at her window
And asked her pardon for being so free
She said: Young man, you are kindly welcome
Come in, sit down and keep me company

4 And when I woke all in the morning
I found myself on some strange bed
I tried to dress but I was not able
For Nancy Whisky had me by the head

5 I boldly call-ed for the waitress
And what's the reckoning I have to pay?
Thirty shillings and a sixpence
Come pay it down and go your way

6 I put my hand all in my pocket
And I paid it down in ready coin
And when I'd paid out all her reckoning
It brought my store down to one half-crown

7 As I went down fair London city
I chanced to meet with a gentleman
Along with him I spent two and tuppence
Which brought me down to one four-pence

8 All I've left now is that one four-pence
The very last of my precious store
I'll go back and see my Nancy
Then I'll go home and work for more

9 Then I'll go back unto my weaving
And there I'll work for seven long years
And if I live for another seven
I'll go back and find my Nancy dear

10 So come all you weavers now take a warning
When you leave off working all at the loom
For of all the girls in London city
Young Nancy Whisky will prove your ruin

280 THE PENNY WAGER

I've tra-velled this world from the North Coun-ter - ie

A - seek-ing, a - seek-ing for good com-pan-ie

Good com — pan - ie ' I ne - ver could find

Nor that which will please me to — my mind

Sing-ing : Whack-fol-the - day   Whack-fol - the - day

And I had in my poc-ket Just one pen - nie

1 I've travelled this world from the North Counterie
A-seeking, a-seeking for good companie
Good companie I never could find
Nor that which will please me to my mind
Singing: Whack-fol-the-day
Whack-fol-the-day
And I had in my pocket
Just one pennie

2 I saddled my horse and away I did ride
Till I came to an alehouse all on the wayside
I boldly got off and sat myself down
And called for a jug of good ale that was brown

3 There were two young men sat playing the dice
And I thought they were playing so gay and so nice
As they were a-playing and I looking on
They took me to be a young nobleman's son

4 One of these young men asked me if I'd play
And I immediately asked him what wagers he'd lay
He sang: Five guineas, and the other: Ten pound
The wager was bet, but no money put down

5 I caught hold of the dice, and I gave them a fling
And it happened to be my good fortune to win
If they had a' won, and I had 'ave lost
I should have to have sold my little black horse

6 I tarried that night, until the next day
When I thought it was time to be joggin' away
I asked the landlady what I had to pay
Come give me a kiss, and go on your way
Singing: Whack-fol-the-day
Whack-fol-the-day
And I had in my pocket
Just ten pounds free

281 ROSIN, THE BEAU

I've tra-velled this wide world all o - ver And now to a-no-ther I'll go ——

For I know that good quar-ters are wait - ing To wel-come old Ro-sin, the beau ——

To wel-come old Ro-sin, the beau —— To wel-come old Ro-sin, the beau ——

For I know that good quar-ters are wait - ing To wel-come old Ro-sin, the beau ——

1 I've travelled this wide world all over
And now to another I'll go
For I know that good quarters are waiting
To welcome old Rosin, the beau
To welcome old Rosin, the beau
To welcome old Rosin, the beau
For I know that good quarters are waiting
To welcome old Rosin, the beau

2 When I'm dead and laid out on the counter
A voice you will hear from below
Crying out for whisky and water
To drink to old Rosin, the beau

3 And when I am dead then, I reckon
My friends will be anxious, I know
Just to lift off the lid of the coffin
And peep at old Rosin, the beau

4 Then get a full dozen young fellows
And stand them all round in a row
And drink out of half-gallon bottles
To the name of old Rosin, the beau

5 Then get four or five jovial fellows
And let them all staggering go
And dig a deep hole in the meadow
And in it toss Rosin, the beau

6 Then get you a couple of tombstones
Put one at my head and my toe
And then don't forget to scratch on it
The good name of old Rosin, the beau

7 I feel that grim tyrant approaching
The cruel impeccable old foe
That spares neither age nor condition
Not even old Rosin, the beau

613

282 ROTHSAY-O

Last Hog-ma-nay, in Gles-ca' Fair — Me an' me-sel' and sev-eral mair — All gaed off to hae a wee tair —— To spend the nicht in Roth-say-O ——

We start-ed off frae the Broom-ie-law — Baith hail and sleet and rain and snaw — For-ty min-utes aif-ter twa —— We got the length of Roth-say-O ——

A dur-rum-a-doo-a-doo-a-day —— A dur-rum-a-doo-a-dad-dy-O ——

A dur-rum-a-doo-a-doo-a-day —— The nicht we went to Roth-say-O ——

ALTERNATIVE CHORUS

A dur-rum-a-doo-a-doo-a-day —— A dur-rum-a-doo-a-dad-dy-O ——

A dur-rum-a-doo-a-doo-a-day —— The nicht we went to Roth-say-O ——

1 Last Hogmanay, in Glesca' Fair
   Me an' mesel' and several mair
   All gaed off to hae a wee tair
   To spend the nicht in Rothsay-O
   We started off frae the Broomielaw
   Baith hail and sleet and rain and snaw
   Forty minutes aifter twa
   We got the length of Rothsay-O
   A-durrum-a-doo-a-doo-a-day
   A-durrum-a-doo-a-daddy-O
   A-durrum-a-doo-a-doo-a-day
   The nicht we went to Rothsay-O

2 There was a lad called Ru'glen Will
   Whose regiment's lying at Barra Hill
   Gaed off wi' a tanner to get a gill
   Before we went to Rothsay-O
   Says he: I think I'd like to sing
   Says I: Ye'll nae dae sicca thing
   I'll clear the room and I'll mak' a ring
   And I'll fecht them all in Rothsay-O

3 In search of lodgings we did slide
   To get a place where we could bide
   There were just eighty-twa of us inside
   In a single room in Rothsay-O
   We all lay doon to get our ease
   When somebody happened for to sneeze
   And they wakened half a million fleas
   In a single room in Rothsay-O

4 There were several different types of bugs
   Some had feet like dyer's clugs
   An' they sat on the bed an' cockit their lugs
   An' cried: Hurrah for Rothsay-O
   O noo, says I, we'll have to 'lope
   So we went and joined the Band o' Hope
   But the pol-is wouldna let us stop
   Another nicht in Rothsay-O

283 TAM BROON

Let the King tak' the Queen and the Queen tak' the Jack ——
And since we're a' to-ge-ther, boys, we are a mer-ry pack ——
Here's to you, Tam Broon Here's to you, my jol-ly loon
Here's to you with a' my hairt —— And we shall have a-no-ther dram
Be-fore that we do pairt Here's to you, Tam Broon

1 Let the King tak' the Queen and the Queen tak' the Jack
And since we're a' together, boys, we are a merry pack
Here's to you, Tam Broon
Here's to you, my jolly loon
Here's to you with a' my hairt
And we shall have another dram
Before that we do pairt
Here's to you, Tam Broon

2 Let the Queen tak' the Jack and the Jack tak' the Ten
And since we're a' together, boys, we'll keep it up like men

3 Let the Jack tak' the Ten and the Ten tak' the Nine
And since we're a' together, boys, we'll drink till call o' Time

4 Let the Ten tak' the Nine and the Nine tak' the Eight
And since we're a' together, boys, we'll drink till it is late

5 Let the Nine tak' the Eight and the Eight tak' the Seven
And since we're a' together, boys, we'll drink till gone eleven

6 Let the Eight tak' the Seven and the Seven tak' the Six
And since we're a' together, boys, we'll hobble home on sticks

7 Let the Seven tak' the Six and the Six tak' the Five
And since we're a' together, boys, we'll drink to keep alive

8 Let the Six tak' the Five and the Five tak' the Four
And since we're a' together, boys, we'll drink and drink some more

9 Let the Five tak' the Four and the Four tak' the Tray
And since we're a' together, boys, we'll drink till break of day

10 Let the Four tak' the Tray and the Tray tak' the Two
And since we're a' together, boys, we'll drink until we're through

11 Let the Tray tak' the Two and the Two tak' the Deuce
And since we're a' together, boys, we'll never cry the truce

12 Let the Two tak' the Deuce and the Deuce tak' them a'
And since we're a' together, boys, we won't go home at a'

284 THOUSANDS OR MORE

1 The time passes over more cheerful and gay
Since we've learnt a new act to drive sorrows away
Sorrows away, sorrows away, sorrows away
Since we've learnt a new act to drive sorrows away

2 Bright Phoebe awakes so high up in the sky
With her red rosy cheeks and her spark-e-ling eye
Spark-e-ling eye, spark-e-ling eye, spark-e-ling eye
With her red rosy cheeks and her spark-e-ling eye

3 If you ask for my credit you'll find I have none
With my bottle and friend you will find me at home
Find me at home, find me at home, find me at home
With my bottle and friend you will find me at home

4 Although I'm not rich and although I'm not poor
I'm as happy as those that's got thousands or more
Thousands or more, thousands or more, thousands or more
I'm as happy as those that's got thousands or more

617

285 TO BE A GOOD COMPANION

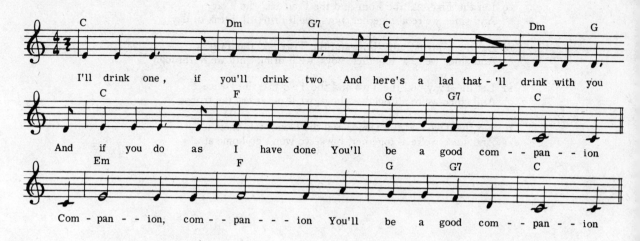

I'll drink one, if you'll drink two And here's a lad that-'ll drink with you

And if you do as I have done You'll be a good com - - pan - - ion

Com - pan - - ion, com - - pan - - - ion You'll be a good com - - pan - - ion

1 I'll drink one, if you'll drink two
And here's a lad that'll drink with you
And if you do as I have done
You'll be a good companion
Companion, companion
You'll be a good companion

2 I'll drink two, if you'll drink three
And here's a lad that'll drink with thee
And if you do as I have done
You'll be a good companion

3 I'll drink three, if you'll drink four
And here's a lad that'll drink for an hour
And if you do as I have done
You'll be a good companion

4 I'll drink four, if you'll drink five
And here's a lad that'll drink till he dies
And if you do as I have done
You'll be a good companion

5 I'll drink five, if you'll drink six
We're the lads that'll drink like bricks
And if you do as I have done
You'll be a good companion

6 I'll drink six, if you'll drink seven
We're the lads that'll drink up eleven
And if you do as I have done
You'll be a good companion

7 I'll drink seven, if you'll drink eight
Here's a lad that'll drink till he's tight
And if you do as I have done
You'll be a good companion

8 I'll drink eight, if you'll drink nine
We're the lads that'll drink any time
And if you do as I have done
You'll be a good companion

9 I'll drink nine, if you'll drink ten
We're the lads that'll drink again
And if you do as I have done
You'll be a good companion

286 TWANKYDILLO

Here's a health to the jol-ly black-smith, the best of all fel-lows

Who works at his an-vil while the boy blows the bel-lows

Which makes his bright ham-mer to rise and to fall ——

There's the Old Cole and the Young Cole and the Old Cole of all

Twan-ky-dil-lo, Twan-ky-dil-lo, Twan-ky-dil-lo - dil-lo -dil-lo - dil-lo

And the roar-ing pair of blow-pipes, made from the green wil-low —

1 Here's a health to the jolly blacksmith, the best of all fellows
Who works at his anvil while the boy blows the bellows
Which makes his bright hammer to rise and to fall
There's the Old Cole and the Young Cole and the Old Cole of all
Twankydillo, Twankydillo, Twankydillo-dillo-dillo-dillo
And the roaring pair of blow-pipes, made from the green willow

2 If a gentleman calls with his horse to be shoed
He will make no denial to one pot or two
Which makes his bright hammer to rise and to fall
There's the Old Cole and the Young Cole and the Old Cole of all

3 Here's a health to that pretty girl, the one I love best
Who kindles a fire all in her own breast
Which makes his bright hammer to rise and to fall
There's the Old Cole and the Young Cole and the Old Cole of all

4 Here's a health from us all, to our sovereign the Queen
And to all the Royal Family, wherever they're seen
Which makes his bright hammer to rise and to fall
There's the Old Cole and the Young Cole and the Old Cole of all

287 WHEN JONES'S ALE WAS NEW

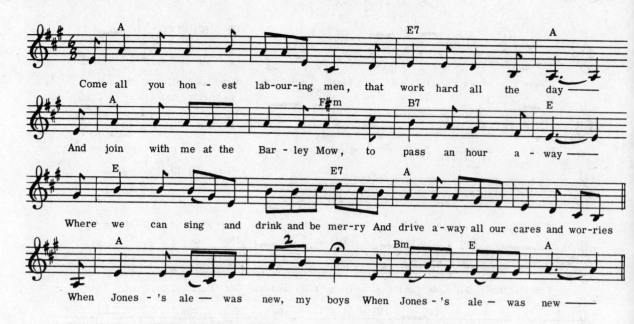

Come all you hon-est lab-our-ing men, that work hard all the day — And join with me at the Bar-ley Mow, to pass an hour a-way — Where we can sing and drink and be mer-ry And drive a-way all our cares and wor-ries When Jones-'s ale — was new, my boys When Jones-'s ale — was new —

1 Come all you honest labouring men, that work hard all the day
And join with me at the Barley Mow, to pass an hour away
Where we can sing and drink and be merry
And drive away all our cares and worries
When Jones's ale was new, my boys
When Jones's ale was new

2 The first to come in was the ploughman, with sweat all on his brow
Up with the lark at the break of day, he guides his speedy plough
He drives his team, how they do toil
O'er hill and valley, to turn the soil

3 The next to come in was the blacksmith, his brawny arms all bare
And with his pint of Jones's ale he has no fear or care
Throughout the day his hammer he's swinging
He sings when he hears his anvil ringing

4 The next to come in was the scytheman, so cheerful and so brown
And with the rhythm of his scythe, the corn he does mow down
He works, he mows, he sweats and blows
And he leaves his swathes laying all in rows

5 The next to come in was the tinker, and he was no small beer drinker
And he was no small beer drinker, to join the jovial crew
He told the old woman he'd mend her old kettle
O Lord, how his hammer and tongs did rattle

6 Now here's to Jones, our landlord, a jovial man is he
Likewise his wife, a buxom lass, who joins in harmony
We wish them happiness and goodwill
While our pots and glasses they do fill

288 WILD ROVER

I have played the wild ro-ver for ma-ny's a year

I've spent all my mo-ney on 'bac-co and beer

I've done it be-fore, but I'll do it no more

I ne-ver will play the wild ro-ver no more

Then I'll say: Nay, no, ne-ver, ne-ver, no more

I ne-ver will play the wild ro-ver no more

1 I have played the wild rover for many's a year
   I've spent all my money on 'bacco and beer
   I've done it before, but I'll do it no more
   I never will play the wild rover no more
   Then I'll say: Nay, no, never, never, no more
   I never will play the wild rover no more

2 I called into an alehouse where I frequently went
   I told the landlady my money I'd spent
   I called for a pot, but she answered me: nay
   We have plenty of custom like yours every day
   And she said: . . .

3 I put me hand in my pocket, so manly and bold
   And up on the counter threw silver and gold
   O stay, sir, O stay, I was only in jest
   I've ale and I've rum and I've brandy the best
   But I said: . . .

4 I'll go home to my parents as I oft ought t'ave done
   And I'll ask them to pardon this prodigal son
   If they will forgive me which they've oft done before
   I never will play the wild rover no more
   Then I'll say: . . .

5 If I'd all the money I'd left in your care
   I would buy a great saddle to ride the grey mare
   I'd save all my money, get it up in great store
   And I'll be a wild rover, wild rover no more
   And I'll say: . . .

6 So now I'll give over and I'll lead a new life
   And I'll stop all my ramblings and look for a wife
   I'll pay up back reckonings, put my money in store
   And I never will play the wild rover no more
   And so I'll say: . . .

265 THE BARLEY MOW

Jack French, The Ship Inn, Blaxhall, Suffolk, *rec.* P. Kennedy, 1953: BBC 19882

Other recorded versions
Unnamed singer (Gloucestershire): BBC 1755
George Spicer, The Cherry Tree, Copthorne, Sussex, *rec.* P. Kennedy, 1956: BBC 23093; *Folk Songs of Britain*, vol. X, CAEDMON TC1225/TOPIC 12T198
Richard Pearce, Exeter, Devon, *rec.* P. Kennedy, 1954: BBC 21478
Gabriel Figg, West Chiltington, Sussex, rec. P. Kennedy, 1958 and J. Hyman, 1964–5: BBC 29821

Printed versions
CHAPPELL: 1938, lxviii, p. 65 (Hertfordshire)
DIXON: 1846 (Suffolk) and BELL: 1857 (West Country)
CHAPPELL: 1858–9, p. 745 (Hertfordshire)
SHARP MS: four variants (Somerset, 1903–9, Kent, 1908 and Essex, 1912)
HAMMOND MS: 1906 (Dorset)
SHARP AND MARSON: 1904–9, vol. V, No. 109, p. 289 (Somerset)
WILLIAMS: 1923, p. 289 (Wiltshire)
MEREDITH AND ANDERSON: 1967, p. 70 (Australia)

All over southern England this was the song to be sung at a Harvest Supper. Here is a typical Cornish description taken from J. C. Tregarthen's *John Penrose: a Romance of the Land's End*:

> That night, as our custom is at 'guldice' [harvest supper], the firstling of the flock was served for supper with fresh-cut vegetables and baked figgy pudding to follow. Supper over, Miss Jenifer took down last year's neck from near the blunderbuss and hump in its place the new neck, bedizened with pink ribbons, while we harvesters upstanding sang *The Barlow Mow*.

The 'neck' is the last sheaf of corn or barley cut at the harvest. In some areas, particularly Somerset, there was a ceremony preceding the harvest supper which was called 'crying the neck'. It was the custom for a young man to run with the last sheaf from the field into the farmhouse while all the women came out and threw buckets of water over him.

266 BILLY JOHNSON'S BALL

Peter Reilly, Cullyhanna, County Armagh, N. Ireland, *rec.* P. Kennedy and S. O'Boyle, 1952: BBC 18309

Other recorded version
Frank Paine, Hambridge, Somerset, *rec.* P. Kennedy, 1957

Compare
Phil the Fluter's Ball (Percy French)

The list of people invited to a dance, a christening or a wedding feast always makes a good tongue-twister and in this case it is a good opportunity for some amusing internal rhyming in the Gaelic tradition. Such a lilting dance ballad as this is frequently to be found among the repertoire of Anglo-Irish and Scots performers, and as 'Irish' songs they were also popular with English folksingers.

Peter Reilly learned the song in the Cullyhanna district of Armagh in 1926 from a travelling fiddler called Sam Rush, who used to visit the farmhouses whenever the gangs gathered for the flax-pulling or the harvest. On these occasions he would play for dancing at a ceili every evening as well as singing this song.

Peter Reilly was born in Cullyhanna in 1893 and after leaving school he went to St Helens in Lancashire to work, first in a colliery outside St Helens, then at a copper works and lastly at Pilkington's glassworks. When he returned home to Cullyhanna he worked for local farmers in the spring and summer and for the harvest, and did cobbling in the winter. His interest in music sprang from his mother, who was well known locally as a traditional singer, and who taught him his first songs. His home had always been a 'ceili house'; neighbours would gather there in the winter, and as he worked at his last they would spend the evening singing and story telling and making music with fiddles and tin whistles.

267 THE BLACK RAM

Bob Copper, Rottingdean, Sussex, *rec.* P. Kennedy, 1955: *The Sheepshearing Song*, BBC 21546

Printed version
BARRETT: 1891, No. 14, p. 26: *Sheep Shearing* (Sussex)

> And there we sit a-drinkin' we smoke and sing and roar
> Till we become far merrier than e'er we were before
> What comes from butt will go to butt, so all you have a care
> Don't lose your head, nor lose your wool, when you the sheep do shear

The strong locally brewed ale known as the 'black ram' or 'hum cap' has been chosen for the title of this Sussex song, which is known locally as *The Sheepshearing Song*. We have avoided this title because there are a number of such songs, and this one is as much concerned with the drink as the work which preceded it.

268 BRING IN THE PUNCH LADLE

Wally Fuller, Laughton, Sussex, *rec.* P. Kennedy, 1952
Printed versions
BARING GOULD: 1889, No. 14, p. 28: *Fathom the Bowl*
(Devon)
BROADWOOD: 1890, p. 40: *Bowl, Bowl* (Sussex)

BARRETT: 1891, p. 71: *The Punch Ladle*
GARDINER MS: 1906–8: two variants (Hampshire)
SHARP MS: 1907 (Somerset)
UDAL: 1922, p. 327: *The Punch Bowl* (Dorset)
WILLIAMS: 1923, p. 88: *Fathom the Bowl* (Oxfordshire)

> From France we do get brandy and from Jamaica comes rum
> Sweet oranges and lemons from Portugal come

The drink known as punch is a mixture of fruit and spirits: rum and brandy are mixed with water to which orange and lemon and spices have been added. It is served hot in a punch bowl and, of course, served with the all-important punch ladle.

Wally Fuller only recorded one verse, which was almost unintelligible in sense, but its tune was obviously of this song, so we have added the verses sung elsewhere in Sussex.

269 CAMPBELL THE ROVER

Joe Heaney, Carna, Galway, Ireland, *rec.* P. Kennedy,
London, 1959: BBC 26311
Other recorded version
Pat Kelly, Newry, County Down, N. Ireland, *rec.* P.
Kennedy and S. O'Boyle, 1953: *Three English Blades*,
BBC 20019

CREIGHTON: 1962, p. 126: *Three English Rovers* (Nova
Scotia, Canada)

> This tumbler of whisky, pour it down your throat
> While we for relief go out into the bog
> They went out of the door and rode quickly away
> Leaving Paddy the Rover the old reckoning to pay

So runs a variant verse of this April Fool's Day piece of drinking trickery. Two or three Englishmen try to play a trick on an Irishman but, as we would expect in an Irish version of the song, Paddy has the last word.

270 DRINK OLD ENGLAND DRY

Rowland Whitehead and Chorus, Haxey, Lindsey,
Lincolnshire, *rec.* P. Kennedy and S. Ennis, 1953:
BBC 23622; *Folk Songs of Britain*, vol. VIII, CAEDMON
TC1164/TOPIC 12T196
Printed versions
BROADWOOD: 1890, p. 46: *He swore he'd drink Old
England dry* (Sussex)
BARRETT: 1891, No. 11, p. 20: *Drink Little England Dry*

GARDINER MS: 1906 (Hampshire)
SHARP: 1912, p. 9 (Worcestershire)
KIDSON AND MOFFAT: 1926, p. 68: similar to Haxey
version (Yorkshire)
JEFDSS: 1937, p. 126, *coll.* Mrs Rudkin and H. H.
Albino at Haxey, notes by Anne Gilchrist. Version *coll.*
C. Sharp, 1911, Worcestershire

This is one of the three songs performed by a group of men known as The Boggens who go round the village of Haxey every evening during the week preceding the day of the Hood Game. The hood is a cylindrical-shaped 'ball' fought for by the young men of the village *very* roughly in the manner of playing Rugby Football. The custom is similar to many other ritual 'football matches' which still take place in other localities in Britain, in which one part of a township is divided against another half. In the case of the Haxey Hood Game, the leading character is a Fool who before the game has to make a speech while he is burned over straw. The Fool has thirteen Boggens to assist him in the conduct of the game.

Anne Gilchrist writes that the song dates from the period of the threatened invasion by Napoleon in about 1800, and was later adapted to suit the Crimean War. She says the song is very characteristic of the Napoleonic period both in its marching air and its anti-Gallic sentiments. A version collected by Cecil Sharp in Worcestershire has a verse about Lord Raglan, who was appointed commander of the British troops in the Crimea in 1854.

When the song was noted in Haxey in 1936 the character was Lord Roberts, a still later substitution who was the star of the third verse, and it was only natural that in the Second World War Winston Churchill should take his place. In the earlier Worcestershire version Russians were the enemy instead of the later substitution of Germans, but in most other versions it is the French who are the opponents.

BARRETT: 1891 for the French has a verse:

> They may come the frogs of France
> But we'll teach them a new dance
> For we'll pepper their jackets most ter-ri-bully

Kidson's version contains a further three verses, not now sung at Haxey, the first of which is about meeting the enemies' ships at sea:

> If we chance for to meet them with their ships upon the sea
> I'll warrant you, my boys, they shall have but little ease
> For we'll take them, or sink them, or cause them to fly
> Before they shall come to drink Old England dry
> Dry boys, dry, before they shall drink old England dry

271 THE EWIE WI' THE CROOKIT HORN

Lucy Stewart, Fetterangus, Aberdeenshire, Scotland, *rec.* P. Kennedy and H. Henderson, 1955: *Folk Songs of Britain*, vol. X, CAEDMON TC1225/TOPIC 12T198

Printed versions
FORD: 1899, p. 87: gives words composed by Rev. John Skinner; no tune
JFSS: 1905, No. 7, p. 79: *T'Owd Yowe wi' One Horn*, coll. F. Kidson and P. Grainger, Lincolnshire
MACCOLL: 1953, p. 86: also gives words composed by Rev. John Skinner

What might appear to be an innocent song about a dead sheep turns out to be one about a raid upon an illicit still. As the singer remarked, 'The ewie was a pot for making whisky, a still-pot'. 'Nickim' is Scots for a gauger or exciseman. In verse four, "carf" means a cut or incision and 'keel' means to mark with ruddle (red ochre). Lucy Stewart learned the song from her father and mother when she was a child, in about 1910.

Frank Kidson and Percy Grainger heard a version of the song at a Folksong Competition held at Brigg in Lincolnshire in 1905. It was printed in the JFSS:

1 There was an old ewe with only one horn
  Fifteen aw me nonny
  And she picked up her living among the green corn
  So turn the wheel round so bonny

2 One day said the pindar to his man
  I prithee go pin the owd yowe if t'a can

3 So off went the men to pin this owd yowe
  She knocked him down among the green corn

4 Then the butcher was sent for to (kill this owd yowe)
                          (Ed: take this yowe's life)
  The butcher comes a-whetting of his knife

5 The owd yowe she started whetting her pegs
  She ran at the butcher and broke both his legs

6 The owd yowe was sent to fight for the king
  She killed horsemen and footmen just as they came in

The end of this version seems almost to develop into *The Ram Song* (No. 304), but it helps to make up gaps in what may have been the original. A. L. Lloyd and Ralph Vaughan Williams, in selecting the song for a book of English folksongs from the Journals (VAUGHAN WILLIAMS AND LLOYD: 1959), felt that 'the shape of verse and classical ring of the tune indicate a noble ancestry', but that 'its former glory had faded out of sight [into] a mild piece of country humour'. The Rev. John Skinner of Longside, Aberdeenshire, felt inclined to rewrite it as a more respectable ode to a stolen sheep without the implication of drink-making:

> A' the claes that we hae worn
> Frae her and hers sae aft was shorn
> The loss o' her we could ha'e born
> Had fair-strae death ta'en her awa'

272 FAREWELL TO WHISKY

Lucy Stewart, Fetterangus, Aberdeenshire, Scotland, *rec.* P. Kennedy and H. Henderson, 1955: *Folk Songs of Britain*, vol. III, CAEDMON TC1144/TOPIC 12T159
Other recorded version
Jessie Murray, Portnockie, Banffshire, Scotland, *rec.* A. Lomax, 1953: BBC 21528

Printed versions
FORD: 1899, p. 327: words only (Scotland)
DUNCAN MS: one variant (Aberdeenshire)
HENRY: 1924, No. 807: *Johnny m' Man* (N. Ireland)
ORD: 1930, p. 367: *O Johnnie My Man*

The tune is popular as a fiddle tune, both as a march and as a Highland schottische.

Ord remarks that this was a favourite street song all over Scotland in the 1860s and 1870s. He gives the last verse:

And Jeannie, my dear, your advice will be taken
I'll leave off the drinkin' and follow thee hame
Live sober and wisely and aye be respected
Nae mair in the alehoose I'll sit down at e'en

273 GOOD ALE

Bob and Ron Copper, Rottingdean, Sussex, *rec.* P. Kennedy, 1955: EFDSS LP 1002

Printed versions
CHAPPELL: 1858–9, p. 660: three verses only, *O Good Ale, Thou Art My Darling*, including a variant of our verse four (from a broadside)
GARDINER MS: 1906: *In Praise of Ale* (Hampshire)

The landlord, he looks very big
With his high cock'd hat and his powder'd wig
Methinks he looks both fair and fat
But he may thank you and me for that
  For tis, O, good ale, thou art my darling
  And my joy both night and morning

The brewer brew'd thee in his pan
The tapster draws thee in his can
Now I wish thee will play my part
And lodge thee next unto my heart

William Chappell includes three verses of this, taken from a broadside with music, in *Popular Music of the Olden Time*, under songs from the reign of Queen Anne to George II. He regarded the tune as being the same as that of *Turpin Hero* (No. 336), but includes the music separately for both songs. He remarks that the first part of his *Good Ale* resembles *John Come Kiss Me Now*, also given in his book.

274 HERE'S TO THE GROG

Bill and Harry Westaway, Belstone, Devon, *rec.* P. Kennedy, 1950

Printed versions
SHARP MS: 1904: *My Jolly, Jolly Tin* (Somerset)
GARDINER MS: 1906: *The Nobby Hat*, with a note about the interesting tune developed by the particular singer (Hampshire)

KIDSON AND MOFFAT: 1929, p. 18: *All for me Grog*: sailor's version (Yorkshire)

CREIGHTON: 1932, p. 133: *Western Ocean* (Nova Scotia, Canada)

After singing *Widdecombe Fair* (*Tom Pearce*: No. 308) for the ciné-camera, Bill Westaway, realising that he had been caught unawares in his old working clothes, burst into a couple of verses of this song. A 'tile' is a hat.

275 THE IRISH FAMILIE

Jim Baldry, Melton, Woodbridge, Suffolk, *rec.* P. Kennedy, 1956: BBC 23100

Other recorded versions
Harold Covill, March, Cambridgeshire, *rec.* P. Kennedy, 1962: *Folk Songs of Britain*, vol. X, CAEDMON TC1225/ TOPIC 12T198: *The Happy Family*

Printed versions
SHARP MS: 1904: *The Irish Family*, no tune (Somerset)
DUNSTAN: 1932, p. 3: *Sporting Song* (Cornwall)
GARDINER MS: 1906: *My father had a horse* (Hampshire)
HAMMOND MS: 1906: *My father had a horse* (Dorset)

This version from Suffolk has an Irish Familie but Harold Colvill, who learned the song from his mother, sang of a *Happy Family*. There is also an unpublished version of the song in the Cecil Sharp manuscript called *The Irish Family*, noted from John Coles at Hambridge in Somerset. Alfred Williams, a collector in the Upper Thames area, received a version of this song from a singer who called it *The Song of the Stock*.

Although the song has apparently enjoyed widespread popularity in many parts of England it has not hitherto appeared in any published collection.

A similar tune is used for a popular Australian sheep-farming song called *Click Go the Shears*.

276 JOHN BARLEYCORN

Bert Edwards, Little Stretton, Shropshire, *rec.* P. Kennedy, 1952: BBC 28698

Other recorded versions
John Biles, Melplash, Dorset, 1943: BBC 6797
Terry Devlin, Dungannon, County Tyrone, N. Ireland, *rec.* P. Kennedy and S. O'Boyle, 1952: BBC 18534
Chorus of 'Boggens', Haxey, Lindsey, Lincolnshire, *rec.* P. Kennedy, 1953: FOLKWAYS FW 8871 (J. Ritchie)
Duncan Burke, Perthshire, Scotland, *rec.* P. Kennedy and H. Henderson, 1955

Printed versions
Pepys Collection (Magdalene Coll., Cambridge), 1, p. 426: printed by Gosson, tune: *Shall I Lie Beyond Thee*
JAMIESON: 1806, vol. II, p. 39: *Alan-O-Maut* (Morayshire)
CHAPPELL: 1838, No. 121, pp. 102–3
DIXON: 1846 and BELL: 1857, p. 80: *Sir John Barleycorn*
CHAPPELL: 1858–9, p. 305: notes about tune: *Stingo* or *Oil of Barley*
ROXBURGHE: 1871–93, vol. II, p. 327
CHRISTIE: 1876–81, vol. I, p. 134: Buchan version (see note about 'crazy man', p. 2) (Banffshire, Scotland)
BARRETT: 1891, No. 8, p. 14
JFSS: 1901, No. 3, p. 81: *coll.* W. Percy Merrick, Surrey
SHARP MS: 1904–9: fourteen unpublished variants (various counties)

BARING GOULD: 1890/1905, No. 14: *coll.* F. W. Bussell, Devon, 1890
GARDINER MS: 1906–9: seven variants (Hampshire)
HAMMOND MS: 1906: four variants (Dorset)
SHARP AND MARSON: 1904–9, vol. III, No. 58, vol. IV, No. 90: collated text (Somerset)
JFSS: 1909, No. 13, p. 255: *coll.* Gardiner and Guyer, Hampshire
GARDINER: 1909, p. 24: arranged by Gustav (von) Holst (Hampshire)
JFSS: 1913, No. 17, p. 294: two verses, *The Queen's Health* with 'Twenty-eighteen' chorus, *coll.* George Butterworth, Sussex
JFSS: 1918, No. 21, p. 27: one verse only, *coll.* Frederick Keel, Surrey notes by Anne Gilchrist about the connection with the Freemen or Three Men's Song *John Dory* (in Ravenscroft's *Deuteromelia*: 1609) and 'three-man songmen' (in Shakespeare's *Winter's Tale*)
WILLIAMS: 1923 (Wiltshire)
JFSS: 1927, No. 31, p. 41: *coll.* C. Sharp, Oxfordshire, 1909
O LOCHLAINN: 1939, No. 89, p. 176: *The Barley Corn* (Dublin)
HAMER: 1967, p. 8 (Bedfordshire)

FLANDERS AND BROWN: 1932, p. 46 (Vermont, USA)
FOWKE: 1965, No. 1, p. 14: *The Barley Grain for Me* (Canada)

See and view this glass of liquor
How inviting it does look
It makes the lawyer prattle quicker
And a scholar burn his book

It makes a dead horse try to caper
And a dumb man try to sing
It makes a coward draw his baton
So here's a health to our good Queen

These verses followed by a 'Twenty eighteen' chorus were collected in Sussex by George Butterworth. Lucy Broadwood was told that the song was used in convivial meetings as a test of sobriety.

At Haxey in Lincolnshire one hears of further effects from the drinking of John Barleycorn:

He'll make a maid dance around this room
Stark naked as ever she was born
He'll make a parson pawn his books
And a farmer burn his corn

He'll turn your gold into silver
Your silver into brass
He'll make a man become a fool
And a fool become an ass

John Barleycorn appears in Chappell's *National English Airs* (1838) where it is probably taken from Evan's *Old Ballads* (1810 edition):

A pleasant new ballad to sing even and morne
Of the bloody murder of Sir John Barley-corn

There are thirty-four verses, of which the first six and last four are concerned with three other 'noblemen', Thomas Good-ale, Richard Beer and Sir William White-wine, who meet John Barley-corn for a 'fray':

Some of them fought in a black jack
Some of them in a can
But the chiefest in a black pot
Like a worthy nobleman

Sir Barley-corn fought in a bowl
Who won the victory
Which made them all to fume and swear
That John Barleycorn should die

However the earliest known copy is in the Pepys Collection (1, p. 426) in black-letter printed by H. Gosson (1607–41) in the reign of James I, and another in the same collection (1, p. 470) is from the reign of Charles II. Robert Burns altered it considerably and added further verses. Jamieson in *Popular Ballads* (1806) tells us that he heard it sung in Morayshire before Burns's songs were published. Dixon in *Songs of the Peasantry* (1846) said it was sung throughout England to the tune of *Stingo* or *Oil of Barley* which occurs in Playford's *English Dancing Master* (1650–90).

Anne Gilchrist (JFSS: 1918, No. 21) makes some interesting comparisons and points:

The grappling hooks were brought at length
The browne bill and the sword-a
John Dory at length, for all his strength
Was clapt fast under board-a

John Dory, a very famous ditty, is amongst the Freeman's (Three Men's) songs in Ravenscroft's *Deuteromelia* (1609). It relates in eight verses an incident belonging apparently to the fourteenth century.

If *John Barleycorn* was originally a three-men's song, this might explain the 'Three Men from the East' (or West) in the first verse of many versions, as the three-men songmen seem often to have announced themselves as a trio. The shearers of Shakespeare's *The Winter's Tale* were 'three-man songmen all, and **very** good ones'. *John Barleycorn* is certainly a very appropriate shearers' song, and it would be interesting if it could be traced back to the musical harvesters of Elizabethan times. Put into the first person, like one of the old sword-dance or pace-egging (calling-on) songs, it suggests an early rustic song with appropriate dramatic action.

The three men, noblemen or kings, in slaying John Barleycorn, may have been reapers competing in the custom of 'crying the mare' (or neck) for the harvest-lordship, when the last patch of corn was left standing and the reapers threw their sickles (held by the point) at the ears of corn to cut them off.

Various tradesmen seem to be brought in to the later verses of some English versions:

> The huntsman he can't hunt the fox
> Nor so loudly blow his horn
> And the tinker he can't mend kettles or pots
> Without a little of Barleycorn

A Scots version in Christie's *Traditional Ballad Airs* (1877) has these verses:

> The browster wife we'll not forget And they have filled it in a cap
> She well her tale can tell And drank it round and round
> She's ta'en the sap out of his bodie And aye the mair they drank o' it
> And made of it good ale The mair did joy abound

> John Barleycorn is the wightest man
> That ever throve on land
> For he could pit a Wallace down
> By the turning of his hand

One Irish singer recorded in County Tyrone believed the song to be the life-cycle of whiskey:

> John Barleycorn is definitely made on whiskey: how it's tilled from the soil, grew up, matured, then it's threshed, cleaned and ground in the mill. Then it goes to the distilleries, it's malted there and then comes out in that great stuff that keeps the world going.

His last verse gave the final note:

> Of all the sins as I came through
> Sure this was the worst of all
> When a big man swallowed me down his throat
> And he pissed me against the wall

277 JOHN BARLEYCORN'S A HERO BOLD

George Attrill, Fittleworth, Sussex, *rec.* R. Copper, 1954: BBC 22738: *Hey John Barleycorn*

Printed version
FORD: 1899, p. 227

Robert Ford printed a Scots version in *Vagabond Songs*, adding: 'For a rattling chorus all round this has few equals'.

278 THE JUG OF PUNCH

Margaret Loughram (and Edward Quinn), Castle-caulfield, County Tyrone, N. Ireland, *rec.* P. Kennedy and S. O'Boyle, 1952: BBC 18532 and 19357; *Folk Songs of Britain*, vol. III, CAEDMON TC1144/TOPIC 12T159

Other recorded version
Frank McPeake, Belfast, N. Ireland, *rec.* P. Kennedy and S. O'Boyle, 1952: BBC 18291

Printed versions
PETRIE: 1903, pp. 352–3
GRAVES AND WOOD: 1897, p. 121: (air: *The Robber*) supplied by Joyce
HENRY: 1924, No. 490: note mentions performance in Buckstone's drama *Green Bushes* (c. 1840)
CREIGHTON: 1932, p. 205: two verse fragment, *Mush a doody* (Nova Scotia, Canada)

Edward Quinn learned this song sixty years ago. It is the matrix on which Alfred Percival Graves based the version in his *Irish Song Book* (London, 1895). Frank McPeake, the Belfast folksinger, has:

1 As I was sittin' with jug and spoon
   On one fine mornin' in the month of June
   A birdy sang on an ivy bunch
   And the song he sang was: A jug of punch
   Toora-loora-loo, toora-loora-loo
   Toora-loora-loo, toora-loora-loo
   A birdy sang on an ivy bunch
   And the song he sang was: A jug of punch

2 What more diversion could a boy desire
   Than to court a girl by a neat turf fire
   With a kerry pippin to crack and crunch
   Aye, and on the table a jug of punch

3 The doctor fails with all his art
   To cure the impression that's on the heart
   Even the cripple he forgets his hunch
   When he's safe outside of a jug of punch

4 All yon mortal lords drink their nectar wine
   And the quality folks drinks their clarets fine
   I'd swap them all the grapes in the bunch
   For a jolly pull at the jug of punch

5 And when I'm dead and in my grave
   No costly tombstone I will crave
   Just lay me down in my native peat
   With a jug of punch at my head and feet

279 NANCY WHISKY

William ('Jinkey') Wells, Bampton, Oxfordshire, *rec.* P. Kennedy, 1952

Printed versions
SHARP MS: 1906–14: two variants (Somerset), two variants (Oxfordshire)
GARDINER MS: 1907: one variant (Hampshire)

DUNCAN MS: W.301; M.90 (Aberdeenshire)
GREIG: 1909–14, No. 90: *The Dublin Weaver* (twelve verses) (nine variants in MS)
HENRY: 1924, No. 745: *Long Cookstown* or *Nancy Whisky* (Ireland)
ORD: 1930, p. 372: words only, *The Calton Weaver*
SEEGER AND MACCOLL: 1960, No. 36, p. 41: tune from MacColl's father (Glasgow)

This song is from the morris dance fiddler William Wells of Bampton-in-the-Bush who in turn learned it from a well-known local singer, Shepherd Haden, who sang many songs to Alfred Williams and Cecil Sharp.
   A fragment of a companion song *Dicky Brandy* was collected by Cecil Sharp in Somerset in 1907:

My name is Dicky Brandy, boys
A man that loves pleasure, a-drinking and a tip-i-ling
He's always at leisure with his mouth at the bung-hole
He'll quickly consume it

And ever after boys
By the strength of the hogshead
Fal the dal the diddle diddle
Diddle all the dee

280 THE PENNY WAGER

George ('Shep') Hawkins, Ebrington, Warwickshire, *rec.* P. Kennedy, 1957: BBC 26368

Other recorded versions
Bob Arnold, Burford, Oxfordshire, *rec.* P. Kennedy, 1952: *The Little Black Horse*, BBC 18687
Ben Baxter, Southrepps, Norfolk, *rec.* S. Ennis, 1956: *The Little Grey Horse*, BBC 23382

Printed versions
BARING GOULD: 1889, No. 26: *The Hearty Good Fellow*
HILL: 1904, No. 1: *Long Time I've Travelled in the North Countrie* (Wiltshire, from a Hampshire man)
SHARP MS: 1904–9: three variants
GARDINER MS: 1907: three variants (Hampshire)
HAMMOND MS: 1906–7: two variants (Dorset)
KIDSON AND MOFFAT: 1926, p. 10: *As I Was Travelling the North Countrie*
PURSLOW: 1965, p. 68: G. Gardiner (Hampshire)

A broadside by Pitts called this song *Adventures of a Penny* and most versions have fairly similar words. However there is considerable variation in the financial calculation of the betting. Most have one player laying a wager of one guinea and the other ten pounds.

281 ROSIN, THE BEAU

Mark Fuller and Luther Hills, East Dean, Sussex, *rec.*
  P. Kennedy, 1952

Printed versions
BARRETT: 1891, No. 53, p. 92: *Old Rosin the Beau*
SHARP MS: 1904: one variant (Somerset)
DUNCAN MS: W. 151: *Rosin de Bow* (Aberdeenshire)
WILLIAMS: 1923, p. 93 (Wiltshire)
HENRY: 1924: No. 698 (N. Ireland)

The tune of this song has enjoyed a separate popularity as a jig-tune for quadrilles and country dances. It is also played more slowly as an old-fashioned waltz.

BARRETT: 1891 regarded the song *Wrap me up in my Tarpaulin Jacket* as an adaptation of this one. Although very similar in theme, we would, I think, now regard them as distinct and separate songs.

282 ROTHSAY-O

Davie Stewart, Dundee, Angus, Scotland, *rec.* P. Kennedy and A. Lomax, 1955; *Folk Songs of Britain*, vol. X, CAEDMON TC1225/TOPIC 12T198

Printed versions
FORD: 1904: *The Tinkler's Waddin'* (William Watt)
SEEGER AND MACCOLL: 1960, No. 89, p. 98: *The Day We Went to Rothsay O*

The tune of this song was published at the beginning of the last century for words composed by the weaver William Watt and called *The Tinkler's Waddin'*:

In June when broom in bloom was seen
And bracken waved fu' fresh and green
And warm the sun wi' silver sheen
The hills and glens did gladden

Ae day upon the Border bent
The tinklers pitch'd their gipsy tent
And auld and young wi' ae consent
Resolved to haud a waddin' O

Dirrim-dey doo-a-dey
Dirrim-doo a-da-dee-O
Dirrim-dey doo-a-dey
Hurrah for the tinkler's waddin' O

The fifth verse of this ballad best describes the wild scene, which has much of the character of the later music hall-type words of our *Rothsay-o*:

The drink flew round in wild galore
And soon upraised a hideous roar
Blythe Comus ne'er a queerer core
Saw seated round his table O

They drank, they danced, they swore, they sang
They quarrell'd and 'greed the hale day lang
And the wranglin' that rang amang the thrang
Wad match'd the tongues o' Babel O

William Watt, who was born in Peebles in 1792, also wrote the well-known Scots ballad *Kate Dalrymple*. It is interesting to note that *The Tinkler's Waddin'* is the first song in Robert Ford's collection of *Vagabond Songs* (1904), put there in order to set the scene.

283 TAM BROON

Jimmy Davidson, Hexham, Northumberland, *rec.* P.
  Kennedy, 1954
Other recorded version
Raymond and John Cantwell, Standlake, Oxfordshire,
  rec. P. Kennedy, 1956: *The Cards*
Printed versions
KIDSON: 1891, p. 159: *Card Song* (Yorkshire)
DUNCAN MS: one variant (Scotland)

RYMOUR: 1911, vol. I, p. 214
KIDSON AND MOFFAT: 1927, p. 8
SEEGER AND MACCOLL: 1960, No. 88, p. 97: *The Card
  Song*, contributed by A. L. Lloyd (his own adaptation
  of the Yorkshire variant)
FMJ: 1969, p. 333: *The Two beats the One* (Oxfordshire)

Frank Kidson collected a Yorkshire version in Teesdale in 1890 from a soldier who had learned it in India thirty years previously. Each member of the company contributed a suitable rhyme as he drained his glass before the whole party joined in the chorus:

Here's to you, Tom Brown
Here's to you with all my heart
We'll have another glass, my boys
At least before we part
Here's to you, Tom Brown

284 THOUSANDS OR MORE

Jim Copper, Rottingdean, Sussex, *rec.* P. Kennedy, 1951
Other recorded versions
Bob and Jim Copper (separate recordings) *rec.* S. Ennis,
  1952: BBC 17989
Bob and Ron Copper, *rec.* P. Kennedy, 1953

This song is one of our finest drinking songs, yet it has not appeared in any of the well-known published collections. It has much in common with and may well be a version of *Drive the Cold Winter Away* which William Chappell included in *National English Airs* (1838), the tune of which appeared in Playford's *English Dancing Master* (1650–90). The song was also published in D'Urfey's *Pills to Purge Melancholy* (1707).

285 TO BE A GOOD COMPANION

Dicky Lashbrook, Kelly, Lifton, Devon, *rec.* P. Kennedy, 1950: BBC 17797 (1952)
Other recorded version
George Belton, Arundel, Sussex, *rec.* T. Wales and S. Davies, 1967: *I have drunk one* (or *The Sussex Toast*): EFDSS LP 1008

Printed version
SHARP MS: 1921: one variant (Herefordshire)

Compare
JEFDSS: 1937, p. 124: *Jack Jintle* (Lancashire)

I'll drink one if you'll drink two
And here's a lad that'll drink with you
And if you do as I have done
You'll be a good companion

Every member of the company in the room of the pub is expected to contribute a verse to this song and to improvise a rhyme to go with the number. The song is not unlike another such drinking song presented as a children's rhyme by Cecil Sharp:

This old man, he played one
He played knick-knack on my drum
Knick-knack, paddy-whack, give a dog a bone
This old man came rolling home

286 TWANKYDILLO

Jim Copper, Rottingdean, Sussex, *rec.* P. Kennedy, 1951
Other recorded versions
Bob and Ron Copper, *rec.* P. Kennedy, 1953: HMV CLP 1327
Gabriel Figg, West Chiltington, Sussex, *rec.* P. Kennedy, 1953, *rec.* J. Hyman, 1965: BBC 29821
Printed versions
BROADWOOD: 1893, p. 138 (Sussex)

SHARP: 1902, No. 27, p. 58, *coll.* Broadwood (Sussex)
HAMMOND MS: 1906, No. 506 (Dorset)
GARDINER MS: 1908: one variant (Hampshire)
SHARP MS: 1907–13: four variants
GILL: 1917, p. 4: *The Blacksmith's Song*
WILLIAMS: 1923, p. 166 (Wiltshire)
REEVES: 1960, No. 135, p. 270: *coll.* Baring Gould, 1889; also gives a version of *The Life of a Shepherd* (*Twanky-dillo* chorus), *coll.* H. H. Hammond, Dorset, 1906

The Blacksmith's Song, as it is sometimes called, seems to have been popular through southern England and the West Country. The best known, *Twankydillo*, published before the turn of the century, was collected as *The Blacksmith's Song* by Lucy Broadwood at Cuckfield in Sussex. This version has for the last line of the chorus:

A roaring pair of bagpipes made of the green willow

In her notes Lucy Broadwood explained that 'bagpipes' was a corruption of ' "blow-pipes" (i.e. bellows) bound round with green willow'. She also pointed out that old 'Cole' was sometimes 'colt', 'foal' or 'goat'. In her piano arrangement she includes the tune of a song about a goose and a shepherd's dog which had the *Twankydillo* chorus and had been used by James Hook. She makes comparison also with *The Goose and the Gander*, a children's song (MASON: 1877) which has 'tangdillo' in a verse about the blacksmith. She also refers to the tune *The Hen and the Blackbird* (BUNTING: 1840).

HAMMOND: 1906 has an interesting variant or parody of *Twankydillo* which is a shepherd's rather than a blacksmith's song:

> The life of a shepherd is a life of great care
> With my crook and my dog, Whitefoot
> I'll drive away all fear
>
> If ever my sheep should go astray on the plain
> I'll send my dog, Whitefoot, to fetch them back again
>
> If ever I should meet with the old shepherd's horse
> I'll cut off his tail right close up to his arse
>
> If ever I should meet with the old shepherd's wife
> I'll make him a cuckold all the days of his life

287 WHEN JONES'S ALE WAS NEW

Bob and Ron Copper, Rottingdean, Sussex, *rec.* P. Kennedy, 1955: BBC 21543; *Folk Songs of Britain*, vol. III, CAEDMON TC1144/TOPIC 12T159

Other recorded versions
Jim Copper, Rottingdean, Sussex, 1951: BBC 16067
Bob Arnold, Burford, Oxfordshire, *rec.* P. Kennedy, 1952: BBC 18686
George Maynard, Copthorne, Sussex, *rec.* P. Kennedy and M. Plunkett, 1953: *Three Jolly Brewers*, BBC 23092
Fred Hewett, Mapledurwell, Hampshire, *rec.* R. Copper, 1955, *Four Jolly Fellows*, BBC 21860

Printed versions
Stationer's Register: 1595 'a ballet intituled Jone's ale is newe', entered by John Danter
D'URFEY: 1707, vol. III, No. 133; 1719, vol. V, No. 61: *The Jovial Tinker* (with tune)

CHAPPELL: 1838–9, No. 167, pp. 131 and 197 (from D'URFEY)
DIXON: 1846, p. 206 and BELL: 1857, p. 197: words only
CHAPPELL: 1858–9, p. 187 (Douce Collection)
BARING GOULD AND SHEPPARD: 1895 (Devon)
FORD: 1900, p. 273
GARDINER MS: 1904–9: two variants (Somerset and Hampshire)
HAMMOND MS: 1906: one variant (Dorset)
JFSS: 1906, No. 9, p. 234: *When John's Sail was New*: Easter 'Jolly Boys' (i.e. Pace-Eggers) coll. Anne Gilchrist, Lancashire
SHARP MS: 1904–11: twelve variants
JFSS: 1918, No. 21, p. 12: coll. Frederick Keel, Surrey
WILLIAMS: 1923, p. 276: E. Warren (Wiltshire)
KIDSON AND MOFFAT: 1926, p. 28 (Yorkshire)
REEVES: 1958, No. 50, p. 133: C. Sharp, Somerset, 1904
STUBBS: 1970, p. 78 (Sussex)
HAMER: 1973, p. 14 (Essex)

> All you that do this merry ditty view
> Taste of Joan's ale, for it is strong and new

This was the introduction given in the copy quoted by William Chappell from the Douce Collection of broadsides in the Bodleian Library, Oxford. The full title was 'Joan's ale is new; or a new, merry medley, shewing the power, the strength, the operation and the virtue that remains in good ale, which is accounted the mother drink of England'. Chappell remarks that the song is included in the list of those printed by W. Thackeray at The Angel, Duck Lane, in the reign of Charles II.

Robert Bell suggests that the song is really a lampoon on Oliver Cromwell. He seems to be the only one to suggest this and it looks as though the origin of the song is earlier. It has much in common with the 'calling-on' songs used by morris dancers (now known as sword dancers) in Durham, Northumberland and Yorkshire. In fact the Easter 'Jolly Boys' (or Pace-Eggers) at Overton, Lancashire, used a version of this song as part of their house-to-house performance.

288 WILD ROVER

Gabriel Figg, West Chiltington, Sussex, *rec.* P. Kennedy, 1953

Other recorded versions
Alec Bloomfield, Framlingham, Suffolk, *rec.* P. Kennedy, 1952: BBC 21150
Amos Beckett, Winslow, Bletchley, Buckinghamshire, *rec.* S. Ennis, 1952: BBC 18139
Jimmy McKee, Tempo, County Fermanagh, N. Ireland, *rec.* P. Kennedy and S. O'Boyle, 1952: BBC 18409
Jack Kelly, Tempo, County Fermanagh, *rec.* P. Kennedy and S. O'Boyle, 1952
George Townshend, Lewes, Sussex, *rec.* P. Kennedy, London, 1956
Sam Larner, Winterton, Norfolk, *rec.* P. Kennedy, 1958

Printed versions
SHARP MS: 1904: two variants (Devon)
SHARP MS: 1911: one variant (Somerset)
HAMMOND MS: 1905: No. 114, one variant (Dorset)
GARDINER MS: 1906–8 (Hampshire)
DUNSTAN: 1932, p. 40 (Cornwall)
SEEGER AND MACCOLL: 1960, No. 45, p. 50: from Sam Larner, Winterton, Norfolk
CREIGHTON: 1932, No. 65, p. 134 (Nova Scotia, Canada)
LOMAX: 1960, p. 257: *Moonshiner* (USA)
MEREDITH AND ANDERSON: 1967, pp. 69, 87 and 127 (Australia)

Although printed on numerous broadsides, as well as being noted down by Cecil Sharp and other English folksong collectors, this song has appeared in few publications. In fact versions which have emigrated to Australia, Canada and the United States and returned as recordings are often more popular in their native country than those which have been recorded in Britain.

In the British versions the rover calls at an alehouse, but in the LOMAX: 1960 collection the American rover is a moonshiner, a man who makes his own liquor with an illicit still. It is interesting to compare this Americanized rye whiskey emigrant with the British tavern original.

Bibliography

This bibliography has been divided into two sections. Books published in Britain and Ireland appear first, followed by those published abroad, both in alphabetical order

BARING GOULD: 1889–1905
Rev. S. Baring Gould and Rev. H. Fleetwood Sheppard, *Songs and Ballads of the West*: Patey & Willis, London (4 parts) 1889–91. Methuen, London (4 parts) 1891–4; (1 vol.) 1895; revised edition 1905. Details are given by E. A. White in JEFDSS: 1937, p. 143, and 1946, p. 67. When reprinted in four parts this collection, mainly from Devon and N. Cornwall, comprised 110 songs 'collected from the mouths of the people'. Texts were modified and in some cases completely re-written and the same applied to tunes. However, in the revised edition, under the musical editorship of Cecil Sharp and with the adding of the name of the Rev. F. W. Bussell, one of the original collectors, many original texts and tunes were restored. For further comment on this publication see Dean-Smith: JEFDSS: 1950, p. 41.

BARING GOULD AND SHEPPARD: 1895
Rev. S. Baring Gould and Rev. H. Fleetwood Sheppard, *A Garland of Country Song*: Methuen, London, 1895. 50 songs with much edited text compounded from various sources; detailed notes about songs, particularly those associated with customs, and comparative texts given. The introduction gives a history of folksong collecting from 1843.

BARRETT: 1891
William A. Barrett, *English Folk Songs*: Novello, London, 1891. 54 songs with piano arrangements. An early publication using the term 'collected folk song'; most of the songs published elsewhere; exact details of origins not given and Barrett not nationally accepted as reputable collector or arranger.

BELL: 1857
See DIXON: 1846 AND BELL: 1857

BROADWOOD: 1843
Rev. John Broadwood, *Old English Songs*: (privately printed) Balls & Co., London, 1843. 16 songs, collected in Surrey and Sussex by the Rev. John Broadwood of Lyne near Horsham. Arrangements by G. A. Dusart of Worthing. Said to be the 'first collection of folksong airs for their own sake'.

BROADWOOD: 1890
Rev. John Broadwood, *Sussex Songs* (*Popular Songs of Sussex*): Stanley, Lucas & Weber, London, 1890. 26 songs (including the 16 in BROADWOOD: 1843) collected by Broadwood and arranged by H. F. Birch Reynardson.

BROADWOOD: 1893
Lucy Broadwood and J. A. Fuller-Maitland, *English County Songs*: Cramer, London, 1893. Important early publication containing 92 songs collected in nearly every county of England. Most have little relevance to their district origins but some are in the dialects of their locality. Scholarly presentation with straightforward piano accompaniments. For article about editor see JEFDSS: 1948, p. 136, and 1950, p. 38.

BUNTING: 1840
Edward Bunting, *The Ancient Music of Ireland*: 1840. Bunting's third collection of folksongs contained 151 tunes.

CHAPPELL: 1838
William Chappell, *National English Airs*: Chappell & Simpkin Marshall, London, 1838. One volume containing 245 tunes arranged for piano and the other historical references, annotations and details of sources. Much of the reference is to printed works and MSS in the library of Edward Rimbault which was later dispersed. This work was superseded twenty years later by *Popular Music of the Olden Time* (1858).

CHAPPELL: 1858/9
William Chappell, *Popular Music of the Olden Time*: Cramer, Beale & Chappell, London, vol. I 1858, vol. II 1859; Dover Publications, New York, 1965. Includes most of material from *National English Airs* (1838) but more has been added from other sources with particular reference to the ballads in the Pepys and Roxburghe collections. For further comment see Dean-Smith's *Guide* and JEFDSS: 1950, p. 38.

CHRISTIE: 1876/81
William Christie, *Traditional Ballad Airs*: Edmonston & Douglas, Edinburgh, vol. I 1876, vol. II 1881. Dean Christie noted down songs mainly in Aberdeenshire. This book combines his own collecting with publication of tunes and words from many other collections, both published and unpublished, including Percy, Scott, Jamieson, Motherwell, Kinloch, Sharpe and Buchan. Also contains a few original compositions.

DEAN-SMITH: 1954
Margaret Dean-Smith, *A Guide to English Folk Song Collections (1822–1952)*: University of Liverpool, 1954. A useful index of published songs under titles, alternative titles and first lines, with some full descriptions of important books with historical annotations and an introduction which traces the development of collecting and publication of folksong in England over a period of 130 years.

DIXON: 1846 AND BELL: 1857
James Henry Dixon, *Ancient Poems, Ballads and Songs of the Peasantry of England*: Percy Society, London, No. 62, 1846. Robert Bell (Title as above): J. W. Parker, London, 1857. By agreement with Dixon, Bell's publication was a revision, enlargement and editing by Bell of Dixon's collection and notes. Most of the material was collected in West Yorkshire and on Tyneside.

DUNCAN MS: 1905–11
James Duncan (1848–1917). MS collected *c.* 1905–11. Aberdeen University Library. Consists of two notebooks, the first containing 800 tunes with words of first verse, and the second giving texts of over 350 songs all supplied by a Mrs Gillespie. For obituary by Lucy Broadwood see JFSS: 1918, No. 21, p. 41.

DUNSTAN: 1929
Ralph Dunstan, *The Cornish Song Book*: A. W. Jordan, Truro and Reid Brothers, London, 1929; Lodenek Press, Padstow, Cornwall, 1974. Contains 11 songs with Cornish words, 72 with English words collected in Cornwall or songs associated with Cornwall, and 48 carols. It is aimed to provide a selection of music for 'community singing wherever Cornishmen (and Cornish women) forgather the world over'.

DUNSTAN: 1932
Ralph Dunstan, *Cornish Dialect and Folk Songs*: A. W. Jordan, Truro and Reid Brothers, London, 1932; Lodenek Press, Padstow, Cornwall, 1972. A sequel to *The Cornish Song Book* containing 37 songs.

D'URFEY: 1698–1720
Thomas D'Urfey, *Wit and Mirth (or Pills to Purge Melancholy)*:

London, 1698–1720. First edition printed with airs was in 2 vols. (1698). Further editions increased to 6 vols (1720). This was the earliest publication to contain both words and music of a large number of English and Scots folksongs.

FMJ: 1965–
Folk Music Journal: English Folk Dance and Song Society, London (from 1965). Continuing the work of JFSS (*Journal of the Folk-Song Society*): 1889–1931 and JEFDSS (*Journal of the English Folk Dance and Song Society*): 1932–64.

FORD: 1899–1904
Robert Ford, *Vagabond Songs and Ballads of Scotland*: Gardiner, Paisley, Scotland, 1899–1901; new edition 1904. A comprehensive collection of songs and ballads, containing a number of 'bothy ballads', but only a few for which he provides the music. Important in that it covers the wide range of songs that were current up to the end of the century, particularly those sung by 'the travellers'.

GARDINER: 1909
George B. Gardiner, *Folk Songs from Hampshire*: Novello, London, 1909. 16 songs collected by Gardiner and his musical associates, Gamblin, Balfour Gardiner and Guyer, and arranged by Gustav (von) Holst.

GARDINER Ms: 1905–9 (see also under HAMMOND)
For further details about Gardiner's work see *The George Gardiner Folksong Collection* in FMJ: 1967, p. 129 and introduction to PURSLOW: 1968.

GILL: 1917
W. H. Gill, *Songs of the British Folk*: Curwen, London, 1917.

GRAVES AND WOOD: 1897
A. P. Graves and Charles Wood, *Irish Folk Songs*: Boosey, London, 1897.

GREIG: 1909/14
Gavin Greig, *Folk Songs of the North-East*: The Buchan Observer, Peterhead, Scotland. Vol. I 1909, vol. II 1914. Folklore Associates, Pennsylvania, USA, 1963. Greig was an Aberdeenshire schoolmaster and an accomplished musician who noted the words and tunes of over 3,000 songs. His manuscripts, extending over 90 volumes, are deposited in the Library of King's College, Aberdeen.

HAMER: 1967
Fred Hamer, *Garners Gay*: EFDS Publications, London, 1967. 50 songs, words and melodies (chord symbols) mainly collected in Bedfordshire but also from other counties of England. No exact locations or dates given of informants or comparative notes to songs, but contains hitherto unpublished local songs and songs connected with local customs.

HAMER: 1973
Fred Hamer, *Green Groves*: EFDS Publications, London, 1973. 38 songs, words and melodies (chord symbols). A further selection published posthumously. As in Hamer's *Garners Gay*, no exact details of locations, dates or comparative notes to songs.

HAMMOND AND GARDINER MSS: 1905–9
H. E. D. Hammond (1866–1910), R. F. F. Hammond (1868–1921) and Dr George Gardiner (1852–1910) collected mainly in Dorset and Hampshire. Their manuscripts, deposited in the Vaughan Williams Memorial Library at Cecil Sharp House, London, have been indexed by Frank Purslow, who has also edited three books drawn from them (see PURSLOW: 1965, 1968 and 1972).

HENRY: 1924
Sam Henry, *Songs of the People*: Northern Constitution, Coleraine, Co. Derry, N. Ireland, 1924. Over 800 songs were published in the local Derry newspaper. Many were contributed by readers but it was Henry's diligent research and background notes that gave interest to each contribution.

HILL: 1904
Rev. Geoffrey Hill, *Wiltshire Folk Songs and Carols*: W. Mate,

Bournemouth, Hants., 1904. 9 songs and carols collected by the Vicar of East and West Harnham, near Salisbury, with music arranged by Walter Barnett of Bournemouth.

JEFDSS: 1932–64
Journal of The English Folk Dance and Song Society: London (32 vols.), 1932–64.

JFSS: 1899–1931
Journal of the Folk-Song Society: London (35 vols.), 1899–1931.

JAMIESON: 1806
Robert Jamieson, *Popular Ballads and Songs from Tradition*: Edinburgh, 1806. A publication, without tunes, mainly of ballads, with the beginnings of comparative study particularly relating to Danish examples, but also containing words of some Scots versions of folk songs.

KIDSON: 1891
Frank Kidson, *Traditional Tunes*: C. Taphouse, Oxford, 1891. Texts and melodies (without accompaniment) mainly from Yorkshire. Later published with piano accompaniment in KIDSON AND MOFFAT: 1926 and 1927. Many texts filled out from broadsides. For article about Frank Kidson see JEFDSS: 1948, p. 127. Reissued by S. R. Publishers, 1970.

KIDSON AND MOFFAT: 1926
Frank Kidson and Alfred Moffat, *A Garland of English Folk Songs*: Ascherberg, Hopwood & Crew, London, 1926. 60 songs collected by Kidson, mainly in Yorkshire, with piano accompaniments by Moffat; most previously published in *Traditional Tunes* (1891). A further 60 songs were selected for a second volume by Kidson and Moffat (1927).

KIDSON AND MOFFAT: 1927
Frank Kidson and Alfred Moffat, *Folk Songs from the North Countrie*: Ascherberg, Hopwood & Crew, London, 1927. A further 60 songs with piano accompaniment, published one year after the collector's death. The foreword by Lucy Broadwood provides information about the collector. See also *Frank Kidson: portrait*, JEFDSS: 1948, pp. 127–35.

KIDSON AND MOFFAT: 1929
Frank Kidson, Ethel Kidson and Alfred Moffat, *English Peasant Songs*: Ascherberg, Hopwood & Crew, London, 1929. 'Third and last Selection of Sixty Folk Songs from the Frank Kidson Collection'. Compiled by his niece with once again piano accompaniments by Moffat. (See KIDSON AND MOFFAT: 1926 and 1927.)

MACCOLL: 1953
Ewan MacColl, *Scotland Sings*: Workers Music Association, London, 1953. 100 songs and ballads divided into 'muckle' (i.e. great songs or ballads), 'Orra' (hero) folk and rebels, Kissin's nae sin, ploo lads, pipes and drums, drinking, shuttle and cage, muckle toons (urban), children's songs and lullabies.

MASON: 1877/1908
Miss M. H. Mason, *Nursery Rhymes and Country Songs*: Metzler, London, 1877. Second edition without illustrations but with additional notes, 1908. Over 50 folksongs of great variety mainly from her own Mitford family in Northumberland, also from Broadwood in Sussex, with piano accompaniments.

O LOCHLAINN: 1939
Colm O Lochlainn, *Irish Street Ballads*: Three Candles, Dublin, 1939. Over 100 songs, words, music and annotations collected in many different parts of Ireland (including the North). All in English and many having equivalents in England and Scotland. Illustrated with woodcuts from the original broadsheets.

ORD: 1930
John Ord, *Bothy Songs and Ballads*: Alexander Gardner, Paisley, Scotland. The standard work on the 'bothy ballads' of N.E. Scotland; 'bothy' meaning farm cottage or hut used by hands, ploughmen, shepherds and farm-servants, and the

ballads, although including folksongs found elsewhere, being mainly those describing, and often complaining about, local farm life.

PETRIE COLLECTION: 1902–5
George Petrie, *The Complete Petrie Collection*: ed. C. V. Stanford, 3 parts, Boosey, London, 1902–5. Full details of the collection are given in JEFDSS: 1946, pp. 1–12 together with a list of tunes appearing in the 1855 and 1882 volumes.

PURSLOW: 1965
Frank Purslow, *Marrowbones*: EFDS Publications, London, 1965. A series of pocket-size publications initiated by Peter Kennedy in order to make available the songs collected by Hammond and Gardiner in the care of the EFDSS library. This selection contains 100 songs, provided with chord symbols over the melodies.

PURSLOW: 1968
Frank Purslow, *The Wanton Seed*: EFDS Publications, London, 1968. A second selection from Hammond and Gardiner again containing 100 songs.

PURSLOW: 1972
Frank Purslow, *The Constant Lovers*: EFDS Publications, London, 1972. A third selection in which the type-size has been increased and the number of songs reduced to 78.

REEVES: 1958
James Reeves, *The Idiom of the People*: Heinemann, London, 1958. Words of 115 folksongs from Cecil Sharp MSS (about 40 printed for the first time) selected as examples of 'English Traditional Verse'. Introduction concerned with the Folk Song Movement in England; Sharp as a collector; text revisions, description of the MSS: the popular idiom; and a detailed consideration of certain songs.

REEVES: 1960
James Reeves, *The Everlasting Circle*: Heinemann, London, 1960. 142 texts from the MSS of Baring Gould, Hammond and Gardiner considered as 'English traditional verse'. Introduction concerned with Baring Gould as a collector and his MSS; Hammond and Gardiner; varieties of folksong; the theme of fertility and a discussion on the *lingua franca* of English traditional song.

ROXBURGHE: 1871–93
Roxburghe Ballads (about 1540–1790): 7 vols. Vols. I–II ed. William Chappell, Ballad Society, London, 1871–80; vols. III–VII ed. J. W. Ebsworth, Hertford, 1883–93.

RYMOUR: 1906–28
Miscellanea of the Rymour Club: Edinburgh, 1906–28. Versions of folksongs and contains nursery rhymes with their tunes collected mainly in the Lowlands by members of the club.

SEEGER AND MACCOLL: 1960
Peggy Seeger and Ewan MacColl, *The Singing Island*: Mills Music, London, 1960. 96 English and Scots folksongs arranged for 'the post-war folk revival' mainly from Scotland under headings: Children, Courting, Men at Work, On the Road, Sailors, Barrack Room, Rovin' Boys and Flash Girls, Historical and Fill up your Glass.

SHARP: 1902
Cecil J. Sharp, *A Book of British Song*: John Murray, London, 1902. 78 songs published before Sharp started collecting. They are listed under National, Soldier and Sailor, Country, Humorous, Old English and Old Scottish, starting with *God Save the King* and *Rule Britannia* and finishing with *Auld Lang Syne*. Only two Welsh and two Irish national songs are included.

SHARP MS 1903–23
Cecil Sharp (1859–1924), foremost collector of English folksongs and folkdances, was the founder of The English Folk Dance Society and for many years a member of The Folk-Song Society. (In 1932 these two societies amalgamated as The English Folk Dance and Song Society.) For a full account of his life-work and publications see *Cecil Sharp* by A. H. Fox-Strangways (Oxford University Press, London, 1933), revised by Maud Karpeles (Routledge & Kegan Paul, London, 1967). Words, songs, tunes and dance notes in Cecil Sharp's autograph are in the Library of Clare College, Cambridge. There are also photostat copies in the Harvard University Library and the New York Public Library, and microfilm copies in the libraries of the University of California and in the library at Cecil Sharp House, London, the headquarters of The English Folk Dance and Song Society. Cecil Sharp's own collection of books was left to the EFDSS and formed the beginnings of the specialist library at Cecil Sharp House.

SHARP AND MARSON: 1904–9
Cecil J. Sharp and Rev. Charles L. Marson, *Folk Songs from Somerset*: Simpkin Marshall, London and Barnicott, Taunton, Somerset. 5 vols. Vol. I 1904, vol. II 1905, vol. III 1906, vol. IV 1908, vol. V 1909. The most important single collection of English folksong, later edited as the *Selected Edition* (1916–21). Introduction concerning singers and style most valuable.

SHARP: 1912
Cecil J. Sharp, *Folk Songs from Various Counties*: Novello, London, 1912. 3 from Worcestershire, 3 from Warwickshire, 2 from Oxfordshire and 1 each from Gloucestershire, Berkshire, Devonshire and Cambridgeshire, arranged with piano accompaniment.

STUBBS: 1970
Ken Stubbs, *The Life of a Man*: EFDS Publications, London, 1970. 50 songs, texts and melodies (chord symbols). Many from our same source singers, but includes a wide variety from Home Counties (Surrey, Sussex mainly and some from Kent) with some important variant versions and some hitherto unpublished songs. Biographical notes about singers.

UDAL: 1922
John Symonds Udal, *Dorsetshire Folk-Lore*: Stephen Austin, Hertford, 1922; J. Stephens-Cox, St Peter Port, Guernsey, 1970. Contains a long 'fore-say' by William Barnes, 'The Dorset Poet'. This is a mixture of material including the words of about 20 songs.

VAUGHAN WILLIAMS AND LLOYD: 1959
Ralph Vaughan Williams and A. L. Lloyd, *The Penguin Book of English Folk Songs*: Penguin Books, Harmondsworth, Middlesex, 1959. Contains words and melody lines only of 70 songs selected by the editors from JFSS and its continuation, JEFDSS.

WILLIAMS: 1923
Alfred Owen Williams, *Folk Songs of the Upper Thames*: Duckworth, London, 1923. Over 300 folksongs (words only) noted mainly in Berkshire, Gloucestershire, Oxfordshire and Wiltshire. Interesting introduction about rural life, more fully covered by Williams in *Round About the Upper Thames* (Duckworth, 1922). Further unpublished texts in Swindon Reference Library. See FMJ: 1969 'Alfred Williams: A Symposium'.

CREIGHTON: 1932
Helen Creighton, *Songs and Ballads from Nova Scotia*: Dent, Toronto, Canada, 1932. Dover Publications Reprint, New York, 1966. 150 songs, gathered mainly in the vicinity of Halifax, written down by the author and afterwards checked with recordings. First of four published collections.

CREIGHTON: 1962
Helen Creighton, *Maritime Folk Songs*: Ryerson Press, Toronto, Canada, 1962. Michigan State University Press, East Lansing, Michigan, USA, 1962. 169 songs which were published with a companion gramophone record (Folkways 4307). There was also an earlier record called *Folk Music from Nova Scotia* (Folkways 4006).

Bibliography

FLANDERS AND BROWN: 1932
Helen Hartness Flanders and George Brown, *Vermont Folk Songs and Ballads*: Stephen Daye, Brattleboro, Vermont, USA, 1932.

FOWKE: 1965
Edith Fowke, *Traditional Singers and Songs from Ontario*: Folklore Associates, Pennsylvania and Burns & MacEachern, Ontario, Canada. 62 songs from 10 traditional singers with musical transcriptions by Peggy Seeger. Songs in the collection are on the following records: Folkways FM 4005, 4018, 4051 and 4052; Folk Legacy FSC 10; Prestige INT 25014; Topic 12T140.

LOMAX: 1960
Alan Lomax, *Folk Songs of North America*: Cassell, London, 1960.

MEREDITH AND ANDERSON: 1967
John Meredith and Hugh Anderson, *Folk Songs of Australia*: Ure Smith, Sydney, 1967.

XIV

Songs of Diversion

Introduction

So I sold me little dog and bought a little goose
He walked so many miles that his legs got loose
Wim-wam-waddles, Jack-stick-swaddles
Rosabow, rosabow, 'way went the broom
Wim-Wam-Waddles: No. 312

In some respects this chapter may be considered almost a continuation of the last, for the cumulative and enumerative type songs have always been a favourite of social occasions in the tavern, when a tongue-twister or a long repeated chorus would be used as a test of a drinking man's ability to keep a clear head.

In Victorian times, such songs were often thought suitable for children and have therefore been included in children's songbooks and labelled as nonsense or animal songs. However, on closer investigation many of them are found to contain unexpected symbolism and inherent social criticism:

O Brian-O-Linn had no watch for to wear
He got a big turnip and scooped it out fair
He put a live cricket then into it then
They'll think it's a ticking, says Brian-O-Linn
Brian-O-Linn: No. 290

Half of the songs in this chapter could also be classed as enumerative. For example, Brian-O-Linn had no coat and no trousers, and the song can be continued by improvising with other articles of clothing. *Soldier, Soldier* (No. 305), *The Frog and the Mouse* (No. 294), *The Hawk and the Crow* (No. 295), and *The Herring Song* (No. 296), are all enumerative songs containing an element of exaggerated fantasy:

My father had an acre of land
He ploughed it with a team of rats
He sowed it with a pepper box
He harrowed it with a small tooth-comb
My Father had an Acre of Land: No. 300

This song probably originates from the ballad *The Elfin Knight* in which there is a set of lover's tasks, one of them being to obtain for his lover an acre of land 'between the salt water and the sea strand' and, when all the cultivation work has been done, she will give him a shirt 'without stitch or seam or needlework'—and this in turn has to be washed and dried in an impossible way. Only when all this is completed can he be her true-love! Which is almost as impossible as the remarkable ram:

This ram he had a horn, sir, that reached up to the sky
The birds went up to build their nests, you could hear the young ones cry
This ram he had another horn, that reached up to the moon
The birds went up in February and didn't come back till June
The Ram Song: No. 304

Another remarkable story is *The Crocodile* (No. 292), the sailor's version of *The Ram Song*. Both songs being of a type which are often described as a song of lies or marvels:

641

Westaway of Belstone, Okehampton,
Devon

Photograph: Peter Kennedy

And now I've sung my little song
Perhaps it has caused you to smile
And perhaps you think I've told a big lie
'Bout that wonderful crocodile?

Eight of the songs in this chapter are of the cumulative type, with each verse growing in length: *A-Going to the Fair* (No. 289); *The Counting Song* (No. 291); *I Bought Myself a Cock* (No. 297); *The Jolly Gos-Hawk* (No. 298); *The Mallard* (No. 299); *Old King Cole* (No. 302); *When I was a Boy* (No. 310); *The Wild Man of Borneo* (No. 311).

Perhaps the best known diversion song is *Tom Pearce* (No. 308). We have given it this title, instead of *Widdecombe Fair*, because the name of the fair varies in different parts of England. In addition, to make things even more involved, we have another similar fair song which is also all about a Widdliecombe Fair, *A-Going to the Fair* (No. 289), the first one in our chapter.

289 A-GOING TO THE FAIR

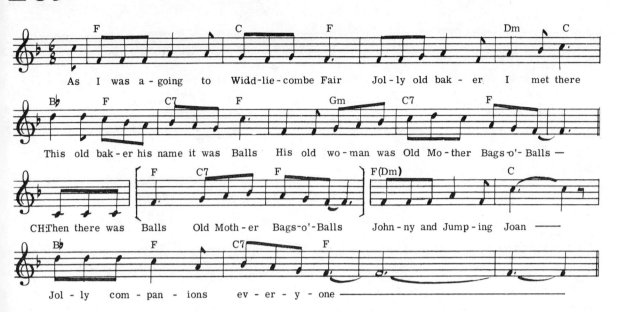

As I was a-going to Widd-lie-combe Fair   Jol-ly old bak-er   I met there

This old bak-er his name it was Balls   His old wo-man was Old Mo-ther Bags-o'-Balls —

CH:Then there was Balls   Old Moth-er Bags-o'-Balls   John-ny and Jump-ing Joan ——

Jol-ly com-pan-ions ev-er-y-one ——————

1 As I was a-going to Widdliecombe Fair
Jolly old baker I met there
This old baker his name it was Balls
His old woman was Old Mother Bags-o'-Balls
Then there was Balls
Old Mother Bags-o'-Balls
Johnny and Jumping Joan
Jolly companions everyone

2 As I was a-going to Widdliecombe Fair
Jolly old cobbler I met there
This old cobbler his name it was Wax
His old woman was Old Mother Balls-o'-Wax
Then there was Wax
Old Mothers Balls-o'-Wax
Balls
Old Mother Bags-o'-Balls
Johnny and Jumping Joan
Jolly companions everyone

3 As I was a-going to Widdliecombe Fair
Jolly old fiddler I met there
This old fiddler his name it was Dicks
His old woman was Old Mother Fiddle-Sticks
Then there was Dicks
Old Mother Fiddle-Sticks
Wax (etc.)

4 As I was a-going to Widdliecombe Fair
Jolly old tailor I met there
This old tailor his name it was Pins
His old woman was Old Mother Prickle-Pins
Then there was Pins
Old Mother Prickle-Pins
Dicks (etc.)

5 As I was a-going to Widdliecombe Fair
Jolly old weaver I met there
This old weaver his name it was Cox
His old woman was Old Mother Shuttle-Cox

6 As I was a-going to Widdliecombe Fair
Jolly old miller I met there
This old miller his name it was Legs
His old woman was Old Mother Shake-a-Legs

7 As I was a-going to Widdliecombe Fair
Jolly old tinker I met there
This old tinker his name it was Pots
His old woman was Old Mother Slipper-Pots

290 BRIAN-O-LINN

O, Brian-O-Linn had an old grey mare Her legs they were long and her sides they were bare

He gal-loped a-way through thick and through thin I'm a won-der-ful beauty, says Brian-O-Linn

With me rant - ing - roar - ing - bor - ing - wedg - ing - sledg - ing

Three-han-dled, ir - on gaug-ing-pin I'm a won-der-ful beau-ty, says Brian-O-Linn

1 O Brian-O-Linn had an old grey mare
Her legs they were long and her sides they were bare
He galloped away through thick and through thin
I'm a wonderful beauty, says Brian-O-Linn

With-me-ranting-roaring-boring-wedging-sledging
Three-handled, iron gauging-pin
I'm a wonderful beauty, says Brian-O-Linn

2 O Brian-O-Linn had no coat to put on
He bought a big buckskin to make him a one
He clamped the two horns right under his chin
They'll answer for pistols, says Brian-O-Linn

3 O Brian-O-Linn had no trousers to wear
He bought a big sheepskin to make him a pair
With the woolly side out and the fleshy side in
There's pleasant and cool, says Brian-O-Linn

4 O Brian-O-Linn had no watch for to wear
He got a big turnip and scooped it out fair
He put a live cricket then into it then
They'll think it's a-ticking, says Brian-O-Linn

5 Brian-O-Linn and his wife and wife's mother
They were all crossing over the bridge together
The bridge it broke down and they all tumbled in
We'll find ground at the bottom, says Brian-O-Linn

291 THE COUNTING SONG

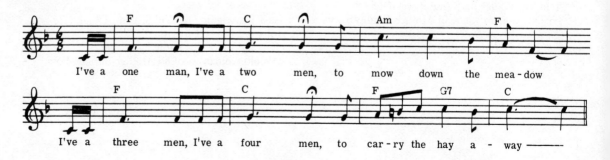

I've a one man, I've a two men, to mow down the mea-dow

I've a three men, I've a four men, to car-ry the hay a-way———

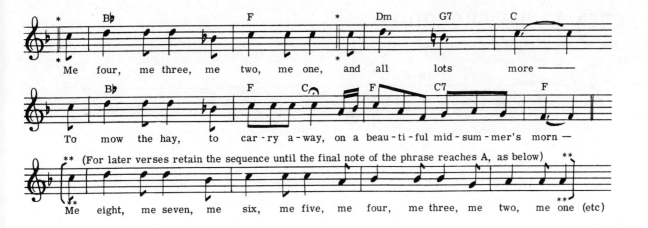

Me four, me three, me two, me one, and all lots more ——————

To mow the hay, to car-ry a-way, on a beau-ti-ful mid-sum-mer's morn ——

** (For later verses retain the sequence until the final note of the phrase reaches A, as below) **

Me eight, me seven, me six, me five, me four, me three, me two, me one (etc)

1 I've a one man, I've a two men, to mow down the meadow
   I've a three men, I've a four men, to carry the hay away
   Me four, me three, me two, me one, and all lots more
   To mow the hay, to carry away, on a beautiful midsummer's morn

2 I've a five men, I've a six men, to mow down the meadow
   I've a seven men, I've an eight men, to carry the hay away
   Me eight, me seven, me six, me five
   Me four, me three, me two, me one, and all lots more
   To mow the hay, to carry away, on a beautiful midsummer's morn

3 I've a nine men, I've a ten men, to mow down the meadow
   I've eleven men, I've a twelve men, to carry the hay away
   Me twelve, eleven, me ten, me nine
   Me eight, me seven, me six, me five
   Me four, me three, me two, me one, and all lots more
   To mow the hay, to carry away, on a beautiful midsummer's morn

4 I've a thirteen men, I've a fourteen men, to mow down the meadow
   I've a fifteen men, I've a sixteen men, to carry the hay away
   Me sixteen, fifteen, fourteen, thirteen (etc.)

5 I've a seventeen men, I've an eighteen men, to mow down the meadow
   I've a nineteen men, I've a twenty men, to carry the hay away

6 I've a thirty men, I've a forty men, to mow down the meadow
   I've a fifty men, I've a sixty men, to carry the hay away

LAST: I've a seventy men, I've an eighty men, to mow down the meadow
       I've a ninety men, I've a hundred men, to carry the hay away
       Me hundred, ninety, eighty, seventy
       Me sixty, fifty, forty, thirty
       Me twenty, nineteen, eighteen, seventeen
       Me sixteen, fifteen, fourteen, thirteen
       Me twelve, eleven, me ten, me nine
       Me eight, me seven, me six, me five
       Me four, me three, me two, me one, and all lots more
       To mow the hay, to carry away, on a beautiful midsummer's morn

292 THE CROCODILE

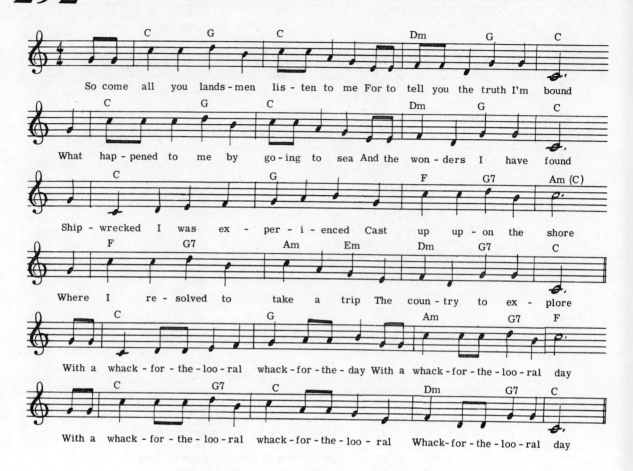

So come all you lands-men lis-ten to me For to tell you the truth I'm bound

What hap-pened to me by go-ing to sea And the won-ders I have found

Ship-wrecked I was ex-per-i-enced Cast up up-on the shore

Where I re-solved to take a trip The coun-try to ex-plore

With a whack-for-the-loo-ral whack-for-the-day With a whack-for-the-loo-ral day

With a whack-for-the-loo-ral whack-for-the-loo-ral Whack-for-the-loo-ral day

1 So come all you landsmen listen to me
For to tell you the truth I'm bound
What happened to me by going to sea
And the wonders I have found
Shipwrecked I was experienced
Cast up upon the shore
Where I resolved to take a trip
The country to explore
With a whack-for-the-looral whack-for-the-day
With a whack-for-the-looral day
With a whack-for-the-looral whack-for-the-looral
Whack-for-the-looral day

2 I had not walked on very very far
   When close alongside the ocean
   I saw something move and my very first thought
   Was all the world in motion?
   But then as I came closer still
   I saw 'twas a crocodile
   And from the end of his nose to the tip of his tail
   He reached ten thousand mile

3 A crocodile I could see quite plain
   He came of a foreign race
   For I had to climb up the nearest tree
   Before I could see his face
   While up aloft I watched all day
   With the wind blowing a gale from the south
   I lost my hold and I dropped straight down
   Right into the crocodile's mouth

4 He quick-e-ly snapped his jaws on me
   For he thought he'd gained a victim
   So I popped down his throat, my boys
   And that's the way I tricked him
   I travelled on for a week or two
   Until I came inside his maw
   And there found rumpsteak not a few
   And fifty bullocks in store

5 While there I banished all my grief
   And thought I wasn't stinted
   And I lived in there for a hundred year
   And very well contented
   The old crocodile was getting old
   At length one day he died
   He was ten year a-getting cold
   He was so long and wide

6 His skin was ten miles thick, I swear
   Or somewhere there about
   For I was just another hundred years
   A-cutting a hole to get out
   And now I've sung my little song
   Perhaps it has caused you to smile
   And perhaps you think I've told a big lie
   'Bout that wonderful crocodile?

293 DAME DURDEN

Dame Dur-den kept five ser-vant maids To car-ry the milk—ing pail——

She al-so kept five lab-our-ing men To use the spade and flail——

'Twas Moll and Bet, and Doll and Kit And Dol-ly to drag her tail——

It was Tom and Dick, and Joe and Jack And Hum-phrey with his flail——

Then Tom kissed Mol-ly, and Dick kissed Bet-ty And Joe kissed Dol-ly, and

Jack kissed Kit-ty And Hum-phrey with his flail——

And— Kit-ty she was a charm-ing girl To car-ry the milk-ing pail——

1 Dame Durden kept five servant maids
To carry the milking pail
She also kept five labouring men
To use the spade and flail
'Twas Moll and Bet, and Doll and Kit
And Dolly to drag her tail
It was Tom and Dick, and Joe and Jack
And Humphrey with his flail
Then Tom kissed Molly, and Dick kissed Betty
And Joe kissed Dolly, and Jack kissed Kitty
And Humphrey with his flail
And Kitty she was a charming girl
To carry the milking pail

2 Dame Durden in the morn so soon
She did begin to call
To rouse her servants, maids and men
She did begin to bawl

3 T'was on the morn of Valentine
When birds began to tweet
Dame Durden and her maids and men
They all together meet

294 THE FROG AND THE MOUSE

There was a frog lived in a well With-a-ring-dum-bull-a-dum-a-coy-me

A mer-ry mouse lived in a mill With-a-ring-dum-bull-a-dum-a-coy-me

Coy - me - ne - ro - kill - to - care - o Coy - me - ne - ro - coy - me

Plim - slin - slam - mer - did - dle, lad - dle bull - a - ring - ting

A - ling - dum - bull - a - me - a - coy - me

1 There was a frog lived in a well
With-a-ring-dum-bull-a-dum-a-coy-me
A merry mouse lived in a mill
With-a-ring-dum-bull-a-dum-a-coy-me
Coy-me-nero-kill-to-care-o
Coy-me-nero-coy-me
Plim-slin-slammer-diddle, laddle-bull-a-ring-ting
A-ling-dum-bull-a-me-a-coy-me

2 This little frog he caught a snail
And rode between its horns and tail

3 He rode up to Miss Mouse's mill
And raised his voice both loud and shrill

4 O Mistress Mouse, are you within?
O yes, kind sir, I sit and spin

5 He took Miss Mouse upon his knee
And said: Miss Mouse, will you marry me?

6 O dear Mister Frog, I can't do that
Without the consent from my Uncle Rat

7 Uncle Rat he soon came home
With a hop and a skip on every stone

8 Uncle Rat, may I marry your niece?
Yes, kind sir, if you pay the lease

9 Then Mister Frog he went to town
To buy Miss Mouse a wedding gown

10 The invitations they were sent out
To all the neighbours round about

11 First to come was the little white moth
She spread out the table-cloth

12 Next to come was the bumble-bee
She danced a jig with the two-legged flea

13 Next to come was a great tom-cat
With his kittens small and fat

14 Last to come was a great big snake
He ate up all the wedding cake

15 Whilst they all at dinner sat
The cat gobbled up poor Uncle Rat

16 The kittens they collared the poor little mouse
Mister Frog he left the house

17 This little frog went down the hill
And swam across the brook to the mill

18 Across the brook came a little white duck
And swallowed him up with a quack-quack-quack

295 THE HAWK AND THE CROW

Said the hawk un-to the crow one day Why do you in mourn-ing stay?

I was once in love and I did-n't prove fact And ev-er since I — wear the black

Sing-ing: Ri-the-did-dle ri-the-did-dle ri-the-did-dley-dum

Sing-ing: Ri-the-did-dle ri-the-did-dle ri-the-did-dley-dum

I was once in love and I did-n't prove fact And ev-er since I — wear the black

1 Said the hawk unto the crow one day
Why do you in mourning stay?
I was once in love and I didn't prove fact
And ever since I wear the black
Singing: Ri-the-diddle ri-the-diddle ri-the-diddley-dum
Singing: Ri-the-diddle ri-the-diddle ri-the-diddley-dum
I was once in love and I didn't prove fact
And ever since I wear the black

2 And next there spoke the Willy Wagtail
I was once in love and I did prevail
I was once in love and I did prevail
And ever since I wag my tail
I was once in love and I did prevail
And ever since I wag my tail

3 And next there spoke the little brown thrush
Who was sitting in yon holly bush
The way to court I've heard them say
Is to court all night and sleep the next day
The way to court I've heard them say
Is to court all night and sleep the next day

4 And last there spoke the Jeannie Wran
Do you know what I'd do if I was a man?
For fear that one would wriggle and go
I would wear two strings upon my bow
For fear that one would wriggle and go
I would wear two strings upon my bow

296 THE HERRING SONG

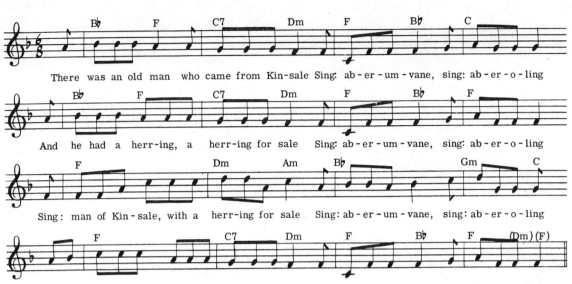

There was an old man who came from Kin-sale Sing: ab-er-um-vane, sing: ab-er-o-ling

And he had a herr-ing, a herr-ing for sale Sing: ab-er-um-vane, sing: ab-er-o-ling

Sing: man of Kin-sale, with a herr-ing for sale Sing: ab-er-um-vane, sing: ab-er-o-ling

And in-deed I have more of my herr-ing to sing Sing: ab-er-um-vane, sing: ab-er-o-ling
I've no

1 There was an old man who came from Kinsale
Sing: aber-um-vane, sing: aber-o-ling
And he had a herring, a herring for sale
Sing: aber-um-vane, sing: aber-o-ling
Sing: man of Kinsale, with a herring for sale
Sing: aber-um-vane, sing: aber-o-ling
And indeed I have more of my herring to sing
Sing: aber-um-vane, sing: aber-o-ling

2 And what do you think they made of his head?
Sing: aber-um-vane, sing: aber-o-ling
The finest griddle that ever baked bread
Sing: aber-um-vane, sing: aber-o-ling
Sing: herring, sing: head, sing: griddle, sing: bread
Sing: aber-um-vane, sing: aber-o-ling
And indeed I have more of my herring to sing
Sing: aber-um-vane, sing: aber-o-ling

3 back: A nice little man and his name it was Jack
     Sing: herring, sing: back, sing: man, sing: Jack

4 eyes: The finest dishes that ever held pies
     Sing: herring, sing: eyes, sing: dishes, sing: pies

5 fins: The finest cases that ever held pins
     Sing: herring, sing: fins, sing: cases, sing: pins

6 scales: The finest ships that ever set sails
     Sing: herring, sing: scales, sing: ships, sing: sails

LAST: And what do you think they made of his hair
     Sing: aber-um-vane, sing: aber-o-ling
     The grandest rope for the seat of a chair
     Sing: aber-um-vane, sing: aber-o-ling
     Sing: herring, sing: hair, sing rope, sing: chair
     Sing: aber-um-vane, sing: aber-o-ling
     And indeed I've no more of my herring to sing
     Sing: aber-um-vane, sing: aber-o-ling

297 I BOUGHT MYSELF A COCK

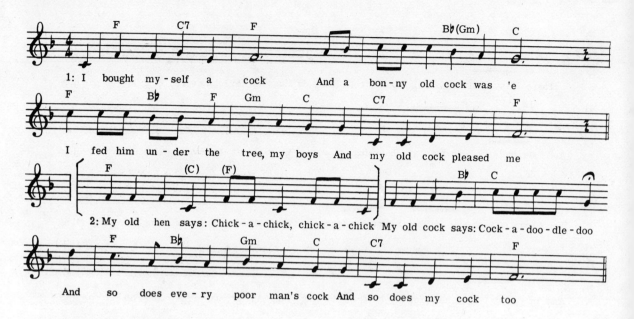

1: I bought my-self a cock And a bon-ny old cock was 'e

I fed him un-der the tree, my boys And my old cock pleased me

2: My old hen says: Chick-a-chick, chick-a-chick My old cock says: Cock-a-doo-dle-doo

And so does eve-ry poor man's cock And so does my cock too

1 I bought myself a cock
And a bonny old cock was 'e
I fed him under the tree, my boys
And my old cock pleased me
My old cock says: Cock-a-doodle-doo
And so does every poor man's cock
And so does my cock too

2 I bought myself a hen
And a bonny old hen was she
I fed her under the tree, my boys
And my old hen pleased me
My old hen says: Chick-a-chick, chick-a-chick
My old cock says: Cock-a-doodle-doo
And so does every poor man's cock
And so does my cock too

3 duck: *Quack-quack*

4 guinea-fowl: *Come-back, come-back*

5 swan: *Whiddy-whack, whiddy-whack*

6 sheep: *Baa-baa*

7 pig: *Urr-urr*

8 cow *Moo-moo*

9 I bought myself a wife
And a bonny old wife was she
I fed her under the tree, my boys
And my old wife pleased me
My old wife says: Hop-picker, hop-picker
My old cow says: Moo-moo
My old pig says: Urr-urr
My old sheep says: Baa-baa
My old swan says: Whiddy-whack, whiddy-whack
My old guinea-fowl says: Come-back, come-back
My old duck says: Quack-quack
My old hen says: Chick-a-chick, chick-a-chick
My old cock says: Cock-a-doodle-doo
And so does every poor man's cock
And so does my cock too

298 THE JOLLY GOS-HAWK

1. I went to my la-dy's the first of May A jol-ly gos-hawk and his wings were grey

O who — will mar-ry my fair la-dy? O who will mar-ry her, you or I ?

2: I went to my la-dy's the se-cond of May Two twit-ty birds

(Repeat this bar for additions in later verses)

A jol ly gos-hawk and his wings were grey

1 I went to my lady's the first of May
A jolly gos-hawk and his wings were grey
O who will marry my fair lady?
O who will marry her, you or I?

2 I went to my lady's the second of May
Two twitty birds
A jolly gos-hawk and his wings were grey
O who will marry my fair lady?
O who will marry her, you or I?

3 third: *Three thrustled-cocks*

4 fourth: *Four-legged pigs*

5 fifth: *Five steers a-stamping*

6 sixth: *Six boars a-bellowing*

7 seventh: *Seven cows a-calving*

8 eighth: *Eight bulls a-roaring*

9 ninth: *Nine cooks a-cooking*

10 tenth: *Ten carpenters sawing*

11 eleventh: *Eleven shepherds yowe-ing*

12 I went to my lady's the twelfth of May
Twelve old women scolding
Eleven shepherds yowe-ing
Ten carpenters sawing
Nine cooks a-cooking
Eight bulls a-roaring
Seven cows a-calving
Six boars a-bellowing
Five steers a-stamping
Four-legged pigs
Three thrustled-cocks
Two twitty birds
A jolly gos-hawk and his wings were grey
O who will marry my fair lady?
O who will marry her, you or I?

299 THE MALLARD

VERSE 1: O I have an ate, O what have I ate? I have an ate the toe of a mal-lard

Toe, toe-ey Nee-mies an' all ——————

O I've a-been to Fea-ther-by Hall So good-a-meat was the mal-lard ——————

2: O I have an ate, O what have I ate? I have an ate the voot of a mal-lard

Voot, voot-ey Toe, toe-ey   Repeat rhythm of preceding bar for additions in later verses.   Nee-mies an all ——————

O I've a-been to Fea-ther-by Hall So good-a-meat was the mal-lard ——————

1 O I have an ate, O what have I ate?
I have an ate the toe of a mallard
Toe, toe-ey
Neemies an' all
O I've a-been to Featherby Hall
So good-a-meat was the mallard

2 O I have an ate, O what have I ate?
I have an ate the voot of a mallard
Voot, voot-ey
Toe, toe-ey
Neemies an' all
O I've a-been to Featherby Hall
So good-a-meat was the mallard

3 *Heel, heel-ey*

4 *Leg, leg-gy*

5 *Knee, knee-ey*

6 *Thigh, thigh-ey*

7 *Romp, romp-ey*

8 *Breast, bress-ey*

9 *Wing, wing-ey*

10 *Back, back-ey*

11 *Neck, neck-ey*

12 *Ear, ear-ey*

13 *Head, head-ey*

14 *Beak, beak-ey*

15 *Eye, eye-ey*

LAST O I have an ate, O what have I ate?
I have an ate the tongue of a mallard
Tongue, tongue-ey
Eye-eye-ey
Beak, beak-ey
Head, head-ey
Ear, ear-ey
Neck, neck-ey
Back, back-ey
Wing, wing-ey
Breast, bress-ey
Romp, romp-ey
Thigh, thigh-ey
Knee, knee-ey
Leg, leg-gy
Heel, heel-ey
Voot, voot-ey
Toe, toe-ey
Neemies an' all
O I've a-been to Featherby Hall
So good-a-meat was the mallard

300 MY FATHER HAD AN ACRE OF LAND

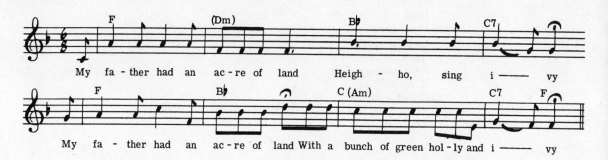

My fa-ther had an ac-re of land Heigh-ho, sing i——vy

My fa-ther had an ac-re of land With a bunch of green hol-ly and i——vy

1 My father had an acre of land
   Heigh-ho, sing ivy
   My father had an acre of land
   With a bunch of green holly and ivy

2 He ploughed it with a team of rats

3 He sowed it with a pepper box

4 He harrowed it with a small-tooth comb

5 He rolled it with a rolling-pin

6 He reaped it with the blade of his knife

7 He wheeled it home in a wheel-barrow

8 He thrashed it with a hazel twig

9 He wimm'd it on the tail of his shirt

10 He measured it up with a walnut shell

11 He sent it to market on a hedgehog's back

12 He sold the lot for eighteen-pence
    Heigh-ho, sing ivy
    He sold the lot for one and six
    With a bunch of green holly and ivy

13 And now the poor old man is dead

14 We buried him with his team of rats
    Heigh-ho, sing ivy
    And all his tools laid by his side
    With a bunch of green holly and ivy

301 OLD DADDY FOX

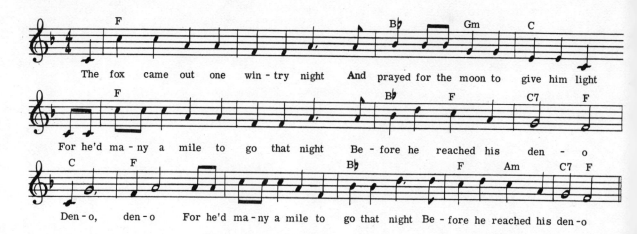

The fox came out one win-try night And prayed for the moon to give him light

For he'd ma-ny a mile to go that night Be-fore he reached his den-o

Den-o, den-o For he'd ma-ny a mile to go that night Be-fore he reached his den-o

1 The fox came out one wintry night
  And prayed for the moon to give him light
  For he'd many a mile to go that night
  Before he reached his den-o
  Den-o, den-o
  For he'd many a mile to go that night
  Before he reached his den-o

2 And when he came to the old park gate
  Where he'd often been both early and late
  It made his poor bones to shiver and shake
  When he heard the full cry of the hounds-o
  Hounds-o, hounds-o
  It made his poor bones to shiver and shake
  When he heard the full cry of the hounds-o

3 At last he came to a farmer's yard
  Where the ducks and the geese to him were barred
  Now the best of you shall grease my beard
  Before I leave the farm-o
  Farm-o (etc.)

4 He grabbed the grey goose by the neck
  And laid the duck across his back
  And heeded not their quack-quack-quack
  With their legs all dangling down-o
  Down-o (etc.)

5 Old mother Slipper-Slopper jumped out of bed
  Down went the window and out popped her head
  Yelling: John, John, John, the grey goose is gone
  And the fox he has gone o'er the moor-o
  Moor-o (etc.)

6 Now John rushed up to the top of the hill
  And blowed his horn both loud and shrill
  Blow on, said the fox, your pretty music still
  Whilst I trot back to my home-o
  Home-o (etc.)

7 At last he reached his cosy little den
  Where sat his young ones, eight, nine, ten
  Quoth they: O Daddy, you must go there again
  For sure 'tis a lucky town-o
  Town-o (etc.)

8 Then the fox and his wife without any strife
  They carved up the goose without fork or knife
  And said: 'Twas the best they'd ever tasted in their life
  And the young ones nibbled the bones-o
  Bones-o (etc.)

302 OLD KING COLE

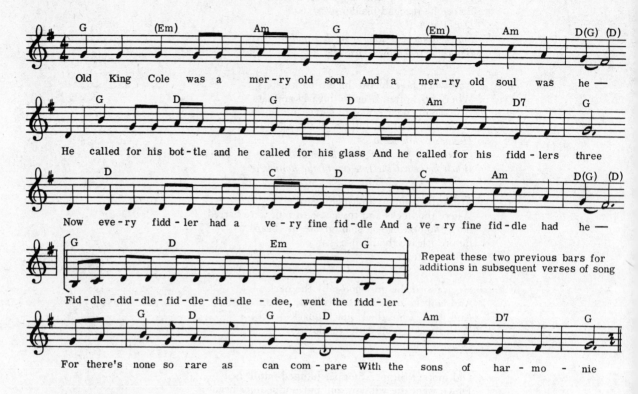

Old King Cole was a mer-ry old soul And a mer-ry old soul was he —

He called for his bot-tle and he called for his glass And he called for his fidd-lers three

Now eve-ry fidd-ler had a ve-ry fine fid-dle And a ve-ry fine fid-dle had he —

Fid-dle-did-dle-fid-dle-did-dle-dee, went the fidd-ler

Repeat these two previous bars for additions in subsequent verses of song

For there's none so rare as can com-pare With the sons of har-mo-nie

1 Old King Cole was a merry old soul
And a merry old soul was he
He called for his bottle and he called for his glass
And he called for his fiddlers three
Now every fiddler had a very fine fiddle
And a very fine fiddle had he
Fiddle-diddle-fiddle-diddle-dee, went the fiddler
For there's none so rare as can compare
With the sons of har-mo-nie

2 Old King Cole was a merry old soul
And a merry old soul was he
He called for his bottle and he called for his glass
And he called for his fifers three
Every fifer had a very fine fife
And a very fine fife had he
Fi-fiddly-aye-fi-fi, went the fifer
Fiddle-diddle-fiddle-diddle-dee, went the fiddler
For there's none so rare as can compare
With the sons of har-mo-nie

3 harpers: harp
Clang-and-a-clang-and-a-clang, went the harper

4 trumpeters: trumpet
Trump-a-trump-a-trump-a-trump-a-trump,
went the trumpeter

5 drummers: drum
Rub-a-a-dub-a-dub-a-dub-a-dub, went the drummer

6 parsons: book
SPOKEN: *Lord have mercy on his soul, on his soul,*
said the parson

7 tailors: needle
SPOKEN: *Stitch it through his coat, through his coat,*
said the tailor

8 cobblers: awl
SPOKEN: *Put it through his foot, through his foot,*
said the cobbler

9 painters: brush
SPOKEN: *Dab him on the wall, on the wall,*
said the painter

LAST: Old King Cole was a merry old soul
And a merry old soul was he
He called for his bottle and he called for his glass
And he called for his p'licemen three
Now every p'liceman had a very fine stick
And a very fine stick had he
SPOKEN: *Hit him on the head, on the head, said the p'liceman*
Dab him on the wall, on the wall, said the painter
Put it through his foot, through his foot, said the cobbler
Stitch it through his coat, through his coat, said the tailor
Lord have mercy on his soul, on his soul, said the parson
SUNG: *Rub-a-dub-a-dub-a-dub-dub, went the drummer*
Trump-a-trump-a-trump-a-trump-a-trump, went the trumpeter
Clang-and-a-clang-and-a-clang, went the harper
Fi-fiddly-aye-fi-fi, went the fifer
Fiddle-diddle-fiddle-diddle-dee, went the fiddler
For there's none so rare as can compare
With the sons of har-mo-nie

303 ON ILKLA MOOR BAH T'AT

Wheear baht thee bahn when I been gone? Wheear baht — thee — bahn when I been gone —?

Wheear baht thee bahn when I been gone? Wheear baht? Wheear baht thee bahn when I been gone?

On Ilk-la Moor bah t'at On Ilk-la Moor bah t'at On Ilk-la Moor bah t'at Bah t'at, bah t'at

1 Wheear baht thee bahn when I been gone?
Wheear baht thee bahn when I been gone?
Wheear baht thee bahn when I been gone?
Wheear baht thee bahn when I been gone?
Wheear baht?
On Ilkla Moor bah t'at
On Ilkla Moor bah t'at
On Ilkla Moor bah t'at
Bah t'at, bah t'at

2 Then thou wilt catch a cold and dee
In Lonnenfuit bah t'buit
In Lonnenfuit bah t'buit
In Lonnenfuit bah t'buit
Bah t'buit, bah t'buit

3 Then we shall cum and bury thee
In Saltruble Docks bah t'socks
In Saltruble Docks bah t'socks
In Saltruble Docks bah t'socks
Bah t'socks, bah t'socks

4 Then worms'll cum and eat up thee
On Ilkla Moor bah t'at (etc.)

5 Then doocks'll cum and eat them worms
In Lonnenfuit bah t'buit (etc.)

6 Then we shall cum and eat them doocks
In Saltruble Docks bah t'socks (etc.)

7 Then we shall catch th'auld cold and dee
On Ilkla Moor bah t'at (etc.)

304 THE RAM SONG

As I went up to Der-by, up-on a Der-by day ——
I bought one of the fin-est rams, sir, that ev-er was fed up-on hay ——
CH: And it's: Aye, me din-gle Der-by, to me Der-by din-gle day ——
It was one of the fin-est rams, sir, that ev-er was fed up-on hay ——

1 As I went up to Derby, upon a Derby day
  I bought one of the finest rams, sir, that ever was fed upon hay
  And it's: Aye, me dingle Derby, to me Derby dingle day
  It was one of the finest rams, sir, that ever was fed upon hay

2 This ram he had a horn, sir, that reached up to the sky
  The birds went up to build their nests, you could hear the young ones cry

3 This ram he had another horn, that reached up to the moon
  The birds went up in February and didn't come back till June

4 This ram was fat behind, sir, this ram was fat before
  And every time his hoof went down, it covered an acre or more

5 This ram he had four legs, sir, that stood incredible wide
  A coach and six could drive right through, with room to spare each side

6 This ram he had a tail, sir, that reached right down to hell
  And this was hung in the belfry to ring the old church bell

7 This ram he had a belly, sir, and so I heard 'em say
  And every time he ate a meal, he swallowed a rick of hay

8 This ram he had a tooth, sir, in the shape of a huntsman's horn
And when they opened it up, sir, they'd a thousand bushel of corn

9 And when this ram was kill-ed sir, there were a terrible flood
Took four and twenty butcher boys to wash away the blood

10 The blood became a river, sir, that flowed down Derby Moor
It turned the biggest mill-wheel that ever was turned before

11 The wool that came from his back, sir, it was both thick and thin
Took all the women in Derby the rest of their lives to spin

12 Then all the boys in Derby, sir, came running for his eyes
To make a pair of footballs for they were of football size

13 All the girls of Derby, sir, came running for his ears
To make them purses and aprons to last them the rest of their years

14 Took all the dogs in Derby, sir, to cart away his bones
And all the horses in Derby to roll away his stones

15 O the owner of this ram, sir, he must be very rich
And the one who's sung this song, sir, must be the lying son of a bitch

305 SOLDIER, SOLDIER

Sol-dier,— sol-dier, will you mar-ry me now?

With a hee, with a hoe, with the sound of a drum

It's — no, fair maid, I — could-n't mar-ry you

For I have no — boots — for to put on

She ran to the shop as quick as she could run

1 Soldier, soldier, will you marry me now?
With a hee, with a hoe, with the sound of a drum
It's no, fair maid, I couldn't marry you
For I have no boots for to put on

She ran to the shop, as quick as she could run
With a hee, with a hoe, with the sound of a drum
And she bought him some boots of the very very best
And here my small man put them on

2 stockings

3 trousers

4 small-clothes

5 jacket

6 waist-coat

7 top-hat

LAST: Soldier, soldier, will you marry me now?
With a hee, with a hoe, with the sound of a drum
It's no, fair maid, I couldn't marry you
For I have my own wife at home

306 THREE MEN WENT A-HUNTING

O three men went a-hunt-ing And no-thing could they find

On-ly a hay-stack in a field, my boys And that they left be-hind

The Eng-lish-man said: That's a hay-stack Scot-tie he says: Nay

Poor old Pat says: Sure and faith

That is an Eng-lish church with the stee-ple blown a-way

1 O three men went a-hunting
And nothing could they find
Only a haystack in a field, my boys
And that they left behind
The Englishman said: That's a haystack
Scottie he says: Nay
Poor old Pat says: Sure and faith   [away
That is an English church with the steeple blown

2 Three men went a-hunting
And nothing could they find
Only a hedgehog in a field, my boys
And that they left behind
The Englishman said: That's a hedgehog
Scottie he says: Nay
Poor old Pat says: Sure and faith   [way
That is a pincushion and the pins stuck in the wrong

3 Three men went a-hunting
And nothing could they find
Only a monkey on a telegraph pole
And that they left behind
The Englishman said: That's a monkey
Scottie he says: Nay
Poor old Pat says: Sure and faith   [turning grey
That is your great grand-father and his whiskers

4 Three men went a-hunting
And nothing could they find
Only a black pig in a field, my boys
And that they left behind
The Englishman said: That's a black pig
Scottie he says: Nay
Poor old Pat says: Sure and faith
That is Old Nick himself and all three ran away

THREE SCAMPING ROGUES

V.1: There lived a man in Lon-don And a vio-lent man was he ——

Three sons on a board and he turned 'em out of doors Be-cause they would not sing

Be - cause they would not sing Be - cause they would not sing

Three sons on a board and he turned 'em out of doors Be-cause they would not sing

V.2: Now the first he was the mil-ler And the se-cond he was the wea-ver

And the third he was the lit-tle tai-lor Three scam-ping rogues to-ge-ther

Three scamp-ing rogues to-ge-ther Three scamp-ing rogues to-ge-ther

And the third he was the lit-tle tai-lor Three scamp-ing rogues to-ge-ther

1 There lived a man in London
And a violent man was he
Three sons on a board and he turned 'em out of doors
Because they would not sing
Because they would not sing
Because they would not sing
Three sons on a board and he turned 'em out of doors
Because they would not sing

2 Now the first he was the miller
And the second he was the weaver
And the third he was the little tailor
Three scamping rogues together
Three scamping rogues together
Three scamping rogues together
And the third he was the little tailor
Three scamping rogues together

3 Now the miller he stole corn
And the weaver he stole yarn
And the little tailor stole broadcloth enough
To keep those three rogues warm
To keep those three rogues warm
To keep those three rogues warm
And the little tailor stole broadcloth enough
To keep those three rogues warm

4 Now the miller was drowned in his pond
And the weaver was hanged in his yarn
And the devil ran away with the little tailor
With the broadcloth under his arm
With the broadcloth under his arm
With the broadcloth under his arm
And the devil ran away with the little tailor
With the broadcloth under his arm

308 TOM PEARCE

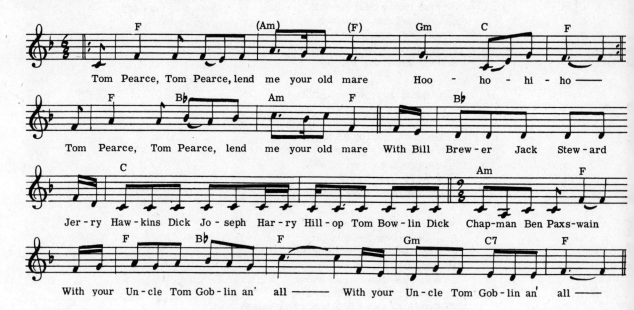

1 Tom Pearce, Tom Pearce, lend me your old mare
   Hoo-ho-hi-ho
   Tom Pearce, Tom Pearce, lend me your old mare
   Hoo-ho-hi-ho
   Tom Pearce, Tom Pearce, lend me your old mare
   With Bill Brewer
   Jack Steward
   Jerry Hawkins
   Dick Joseph
   Harry Hillop
   Tom Bowlin
   Dick Chapman
   Ben Paxswain
   With your Uncle Tom Goblin an' all
   With your Uncle Tom Goblin an' all

2 Tom Pearce's old mare, her's gone to Stow Fair

3 When will Tom Pearce's old mare return?

4 Friday's gone and her hasn't come home

5 Tom Pearce he's gone over to fetch home his mare

6 Tom Pearce's old mare, her's tumbled down dead

7 Tom Pearce's old mare, her'll have to be buried

309 WAS YOU EVER SEE?

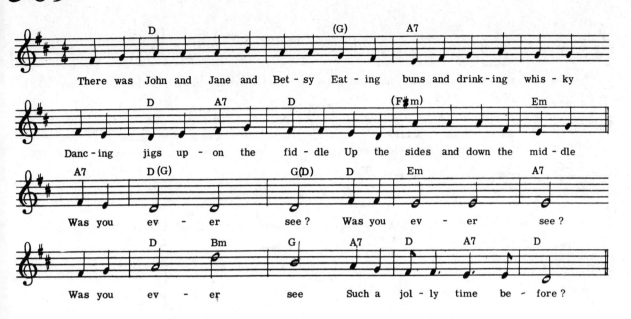

There was John and Jane and Bet-sy Eat-ing buns and drink-ing whis-ky

Danc-ing jigs up-on the fid-dle Up the sides and down the mid-dle

Was you ev - er see? Was you ev - er see?

Was you ev - er see Such a jol-ly time be - fore?

1 There was John and Jane and Betsy
   Eating buns and drinking whisky
   Dancing jigs upon the fiddle
   Up the sides and down the middle
   Was you ever see?
   Was you ever see?
   Was you ever see
   Such a jolly time before?

2 I was got a sister 'Bella
   She was courtin' w'umb-er-ella
   She would think so much about it
   That she was never go without it

3 I was got a brother Joe
   He was came from Calico
   He was go to Chester College
   For to have a bit of knowledge

4 She was strick and strike and whistle
   Making noise just like the devil
   Derby Jones of Pontycellin
   Come to see the open railway

310 WHEN I WAS A BOY

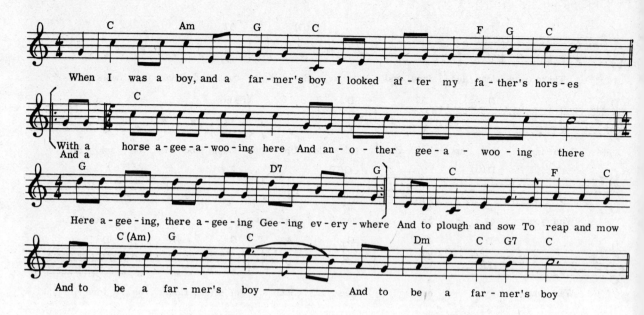

1 When I was a boy, and a farmer's boy
  I looked after my father's horses
  With a horse a-gee-a-woo-ing here
  And another gee-a-woo-ing there
  Here a-gee-ing, there a-gee-ing
  Gee-ing everywhere
  And to plough and sow
  To reap and mow
  And to be a farmer's boy
  And to be a farmer's boy

2 When I was a boy, and a farmer's boy
  I looked after my father's cows
  With a cow a-boo-ing here
  And another a-boo-ing there
  Here a-boo-ing, there a-boo-ing
  Boo-ing everywhere
  And a horse a-gee-a-woo-ing here
  And another gee-a-woo-ing there
  Here a-gee-ing, there a-gee-ing
  Gee-ing everywhere
  And to plough and sow (etc.)

3 sheep: *a-baa-ing*

4 pigs: *a-(snort)-ing*

5 ducks: *a-quack-ing*

6 When I was a boy, and a farmer's boy
  I looked after my father's donkeys
  With a donkey neighing here
  And another neighing there
  Here a-neigh, there a-neigh
  Neighing everywhere
  And a duck a-quacking here
  And another quacking there
  Here a-quack, there a-quack
  Quacking everywhere
  And a pig a-(snort)-ing here
  And another a-(snort)-ing there
  Here a-(snort), there a-(snort)
  (Snort)-ing everywhere
  And a sheep a-baa-ing here
  And another baa-ing there
  Here a-baaing, there a-baaing
  Baa-ing everywhere
  And a cow a-boo-ing here
  And another boo-ing there
  Here a-booing, there a-booing
  Boo-ing everywhere
  And a horse a-gee-a-woo-ing here
  And another gee-a-woo-ing there
  Here a-gee-ing, there a-gee-ing
  Gee-ing everywhere
  And to plough and sow (etc.)

311 THE WILD MAN OF BORNEO

*The wild man of Bor-ne-o has just come to town

*The wild man of Bor-ne-o has just come to town

*The wild man of Bor-ne-o has just come to town

*The wild man of Bor-ne-o has just come to town

CODA: And they've all come to town

Additions in later verses sung to opening note of first bar

1 The wild man of Borneo has just come to town
  The wild man of Borneo has just come to town
  The wild man of Borneo has just come to town
  The wild man of Borneo has just come to town

2 The wife
  of the wild man of Borneo has just come to town

3 The daughter of the wife
  of the wild man of Borneo has just come to town

4 The dog of the daughter of the wife
  of the wild man of Borneo has just come to town

5 The tail of the dog of the daughter of the wife
  of the wild man of Borneo has just come to town

6 The hair in the tail of the dog of the daughter of the wife
  of the wild man of Borneo has just come to town

7 The flea in the hair in the tail of the dog of the daughter of the wife
  of the wild man of Borneo has just come to town

LAST: The left whisker
  of the flea
  in the hair
  in the tail
  of the dog
  of the daughter
  of the wife
  of the wild man of Borneo has just come to town

CODA: And they've all come to town

312 WIM-WAM-WADDLES

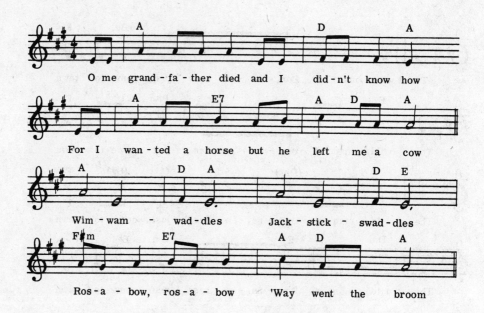

1 O me grandfather died and I didn't know how
For I wanted a horse but he left me a cow
Wim-wam-waddles
Jack-stick-swaddles
Rosabow, rosabow
'Way went the broom

2 So I had a little cow and he had a little calf
Thought I had a bargain, but I lost one half

3 So I sold me little cow and I bought a little dog
A pretty little creature to keep off the mob

4 So I sold me little dog and bought a little goose
He walked so many miles that his legs got loose

5 So I sold me little goose and bought a little cat
A pretty little creature to keep off the rats

6 So I sold me little cat and bought a little mouse
The fire in its tail set fire to me house

7 So me grandfather's died and he's left me alone
I don't know how it is, but I haven't got a home

289 A-GOING TO THE FAIR

Harry Cox, Catfield, Norfolk, *rec.* P. Kennedy, 1953:
EFDSS LP 1004: *Widdliecombe Fair*

Other recorded version
Frank McPeake, Belfast, N. Ireland, *rec.* P. Kennedy and
S. O'Boyle, 1953: BBC 18290: *Monaghan Fair*

Printed versions
CHAMBERS: 1826, p. 197: *The Beggars of Coldingham Fair*
(from *Tait's Magazine*, vol. X, No. 121)
HALLIWELL: 1846, p. 272: *The Beggars of Ratcliffe Fair*
HAYWARD: 1925: *Craigbilly [Crebilly] Fair* (N. Ireland)
JFSS: 1929, No. 33, p. 132: *Donnybrook Fair, coll.*
Thomas Wood, Essex

As I went to Ratcliffe Fair, there I met with a jolly begg-are
Jolly begg-are, and his name was Howell, and his wife's name was Mrs Ap Howell
So there was Howell and Mrs Ap Howell
And there was Shenkyn and Mrs Ap Shenkyn
And there was Lewin and Mrs Ap Lewin
   Owen
   Lloyd
   Jones
   Rice
   Robert
   Richard
   John and Jumping Joan
   Merry companions every one

This early version, *The Beggars of Ratcliffe Fair*, appears in HALLIWELL: 1846. No source is given but the names of the beggars are in this case Welsh names. Ratcliffe could be in Leicestershire or London.

A Scottish version entitled *The Beggars of Coldingham Fair* appears to be the earliest printed version. Coldingham is about twelve miles north of Berwick-on-Tweed:

The first time that I gaed to Coudingham Fair
I there fell in with a jolly beggare
The beggar's name, O, it was Harry
And he had a wife and they ca'd her Mary

O Mary and Harry, and Harry and Mary
And Janet and John
That's the beggars one by one
But now I will give you them pair by pair
All the brave beggars of Coudingham Fair

An Essex version called *Donnybrook Fair*, collected by Thomas Wood, is given in the JFSS: No. 33, p. 132:

The first time I went to Donnybrook Fair
I met an old pal that I knew there
The old pal's name was Ben
And his old woman's name it was Old Mother Bendigo
Hot-ten-ti, hot-ten-ti ad-di-i-o, ad-di
O come and lie close to me now

Anne Gilchrist wrote in JFSS: 1929, No. 33:

This is a modernized relic of an old cumulative song known in Scotland as *The Beggars of Coldingham Fair* (see CHAMBERS: *Popular Rhymes of Scotland*, where it is reprinted from *Tait's Magazine*, X,121) and in the north of Ireland as *Craigbilly* (or *Crebilly*) *Fair* (see Richard HAYWARD: *Ulster Songs and Ballads*, 1925).

The McPeake family in Belfast, Northern Ireland, recorded *Monaghan Fair*, which Frank McPeake learned at a dance in County Antrim at the turn of the century:

1 As I was going to Monaghan Fair
Who did I meet but an old beggar there
Well, this beggar's name it was Nott
And his old wife's name was Old Molly Dopper-dot
Well there was Nott and Old Molly Dopper-dot
And there was Lily and Billy
And Fanny and Sally
And Danny and Manny
And Ratty and Matty
And Rosey and Mosey
And Jenny and Joe
And och but they were a jolly crowd all in a row

2 And I went again to Monaghan Fair
And who did I meet but another beggar there
Well, this beggar's name it was Neil
And his old wife's name it was Old Molly Switcher-tail
Well there was Neil and Old Molly Switcher-tail
And there was Nott and Old Molly Dopper-dot
And there was Lily and Billy, etc.

3 Shake and Old Molly Shake-a-leg
4 Stick and Old Molly Fiddle-sticks
5 Wax and Old Molly Ball-o'-wax
6 Cock and Old Molly Shuttle-cock
7 Nut and Old Molly Funny-nuts

and so on.

290 BRIAN-O-LINN

Thomas Moran, Mohill, County Leitrim, Ireland, *rec.*
S. Ennis, 1954: *Folk Songs of Britain*, vol. X, CAEDMON
TC1225/TOPIC 12T198

Other recorded versions
Seamus Ennis, Dublin, Ireland, 1949: BBC 13770
Wally Fuller (gipsy), Laughton, Lewes, Sussex, *rec.* P.
  Kennedy, 1952: *Briny-o-then* (has chorus: 'Little do')
Bill Williams, Gloucester, *rec.* P. Kennedy, 1957

Printed versions
HALLIWELL: 1849, p. 271
CHRISTIE: 1876–81, vol. I, p. 192: *Tam o' the Lin*
BARING GOULD: 1905, No. 42, p. 84: *Tommy A'Lynn*:
  two Devon singers (full notes about the song given)

WILLIAMS: 1923, p. 181: *Bryan O'Lynn* (has chorus:
  'It'll do') (Gloucestershire)
HENRY: 1924, No. 480 (N. Ireland)
JFSS: 1929, No. 33, p. 137: *Brian O'Lynn* (Lancashire;
  version sung in Buckinghamshire in about 1860) with
  detailed notes by Anne Gilchrist about the early versions
  of the song
OPIE: 1951, pp. 413–15: *Tommy O Lin*: detailed notes
REEVES: 1960, No. 16, p. 65: *Bryan-a-Lynn*, *coll.* Baring
  Gould, Devon, 1889

FLANDERS AND BROWN: 1932, p. 178: *Old Tombolin*
  (Vermont, USA)

> All went over a bridge together
> The bridge was loose, and they all tumbled in
> What a precious concern, cried Bryan O'Lin

Halliwell found this one verse 'in a little black-letter work by W. Wager, printed about the year 1560', which is given in his *Nursery Rhymes of England* (1842), but he admits to its being 'slightly altered'.

Sam Henry, who contributed songs to the *Northern Constitution*, a newspaper in County Derry, Northern Ireland, found some old records about a man of Cashel, Portglenone, which make reference to a Brian O'Lynn who on 18th April 1786 was appointed both Grand Juror and Apprizor. Under the signatures of the Grand Jurors he found the following couplet:

> Brian O'Lynn was a Scotchman bold
> His head it was bald and his beard it was shorn

Sam Henry contributed a version of the song to the well-known Scots tune *Laird o' Cockpen*. It contained the following 'hat' verse:

> Briann O'Lynn had no hat to his head
> He thought that the pot would do him instead
> Then he murdered a cod for the sake of his fin
> Whoo! 'Twill pass for a feather, says Brian O'Lynn

The Rev. Sabine Baring Gould (*Songs of the West*, 1905) quoted from a lecture given on the conditions on Dartmoor in Devonshire in 1837: 'For roughing it on the Moor, warm waterproof coats were made by using a sheepskin, the wool on the inside. Warm caps of rabbitskin were common with lappets over the ears', and remarks upon an old rhyme which was sung locally:

> Old Harry Trewin, no breeches to wear
> He stole a ram's skin to make a new pair
> The shiny side out and the woolly side in
> And thus doth go old Harry Trewin

Anne Gilchrist (JFSS: 1929, No. 33) contributes a Buckinghamshire version which was sung 'amongst the lacemakers and makers of Windsor chairs about 1860 and certainly earlier'. It contains a penultimate verse about Brian O'Lynn's old grey mare:

> Brian O'Lynn went to fetch his wife home
> He'd only one horse that was all skin and bone
> But he seated her on it as neat as a pin
> I think it'll do, said Brian O'Lynn
> *It'll do, it'll do*
> *Said Brian O'Lynn: It'll do*

There are also Scottish versions. *Tam o' the Lin* in Dean Christie's *Traditional Ballad Airs*, 1876, vol. I, has a similar text to the copy printed in Chambers *Scottish Songs*, 1829. 'Thom of Lyn' is a dance of the shepherds in Wedderburn's *Complaynt of Scotland*, 1549, and a 'ballet of Thomalyn' was licensed in 1558.

Anne Gilchrist draws attention to the two types of verse in this song: those in which Brian comments on the various accidents which befall him and his family, whether they fall into the fire or sink into a bog, and those in which he shows his ability at overcoming the poverty of his clothing, adornment, food and bedding: 'It seems to me possible that these latter verses may be the last relics of a song written in derision of the rude habits and scanty clothing of the Celt, whether Scottish or Irish.'

She quotes Newbolt's *Froissart in Britain* and Froissart's *Chronicle* at the time of Richard II, and Edmund Spenser's *View of the Present State of Ireland* written a century and a half later about the Irish 'mantle', which served for 'housing, bedding and clothing'. 'From such evidence it seems possible that the original song was an English satire upon the rude shifts and unruffled complacency of the savage Gael—whether Irish or Scotch.'

She then quotes *The North-Country Chorister*, 1802, where there is not only a version called Tommy Linn (a Scotsman born), but also another ballad called *The Bonny Scot Made a Gentleman*, which derides the clothing worn by the beggarly Scotsman before England transformed him into a gentleman.

291 THE COUNTING SONG

William Rew, Sidbury, Sidmouth, Devon, *rec.* P. Kennedy, 1954: BBC 22321

Other recorded version
Mr Biles, Melplash, Dorset, 1943: *Sheep-Shearing Song*, BBC 6797

Printed versions
HAMMOND MS: 1905–8: three variants (Dorset), one variant (Wiltshire)
SHARP MS: two variants (Somerset)

SHARP 1909 (School Series III): *One Man Shall Mow My Meadow* (Somerset)
WILLIAMS: 1923, p. 288: *Mowing Down The Meadow* (Oxfordshire)
REEVES: 1960, No. 100, p. 200: *One Man Shall Mow my Meadow, coll.* George Gardiner, Hampshire, 1906
PURSLOW: 1965, p. 67: *One Man Shall Shear my Wethers, coll.* H. Hammond, Dorset, 1906
STUBBS: 1970, p. 50: *Mowing Down My Meadow* (Sussex)
CREIGHTON: 1932: *Me One Man* (Nova Scotia, Canada)

> I'll have one man, two men to mow down the meadow
> I'll have three men, four men to carry it away
> With my four, my three, my two, my one; we'll have no more
> To mow the hay and carry it away, for we are all jolly fine fellows

Alfred Williams included this Oxfordshire version in his collection, saying that 'like *The Barley Mow* it was often called for at the harvest-homes and other farm feasts'.

Versions have been collected in the six southern counties of England: Devon, Dorset, Hampshire, Oxfordshire, Somerset and Wiltshire. An almost identical version to ours turns up in Helen Creighton's first collection from Nova Scotia.

292 THE CROCODILE

Harry Cox, Catfield, Norfolk, *rec.* P. Kennedy, 1953

Printed versions
BROADWOOD: 1893, p. 184 (Dorset, 1891)
SHARP: 1902, No. 20, p. 42, *coll.* Broadwood
SHARP MS: 1904: two variants (Somerset)
GARDINER MS: 1906: one variant (Hampshire)
GREIG: 1909–14, No. XIV: as BROADWOOD: 1893
UDAL: 1922, p. 322 (Dorset)
HENRY: 1924, No. 231 (N. Ireland)
PURSLOW: 1965, p. 20: *coll.* G. Gardiner, 1906

FLANDERS AND BROWN: 1932, p. 168: *The Rummy Crocodile* (Vermont, USA)
LOMAX: 1934, p. 498
CREIGHTON: 1932, p. 122 (Nova Scotia, Canada)
CREIGHTON AND SENIOR: 1950, p. 230 (Nova Scotia, Canada)
MEREDITH AND ANDERSON: 1967, p. 134: *The Wonderful Crocodile* (Australia)

> And if my story you should doubt
> If ever you travel the Nile
> Right where he fell you'll find the shell
> Of the Royal Crocodile

So concludes the last verse of the 'Royal' crocodile song collected by Sam Henry in Northern Ireland. The song was popular in the southern counties of England and frequently appeared on broadsides.

An early seventeenth-century ballad about 'a strange and miraculous Fish' appears in *The Pepysian Garland*. The Fish was 'cast up on the sands in the meads' of the Wirral in Cheshire.

> His lower jaw-bone's five yards long
> The upper thrice so much
> Twelve yoke of oxen stout and strong
> The weight of it is such. . . .

293 DAME DURDEN

Bob and Ron Copper, Rottingdean, Sussex, *rec.* P. Kennedy, 1955: *Folk Songs of Britain*, vol. I, CAEDMON TC1142/TOPIC 12T157 (1961); EFDSS LP 1002 (1963)

Other recorded versions
Jim Copper, Rottingdean, Sussex, *rec.* P. Kennedy, 1951
Mark Fuller, Luther Hills, East Dean, Sussex, *rec.* P. Kennedy, 1952: BBC 18714

Printed versions
VOCAL LIBRARY: 1822, No. 1164, p. 435
SHARP MS: 1906: two variants (Somerset)
WILLIAMS: 1923, p. 129 (Wiltshire)
JEFDSS: 1955, p. 250: (words only) 'plough jags', Lincolnshire, 1936

Alfred Williams included a version from Wiltshire in his collection (WILLIAMS: 1923), remarking that the song 'enjoyed great popularity throughout the south of England' at harvest homes and other village festivals.

This is one of the songs that Lincolnshire mummers, known as 'plough jags', who acted a play on Plough Monday at Kirton Lindsey, used to sing outside the farm houses before they collected money from the inhabitants (see *All Jolly Fellows*, No. 241).

Although the song seems to have been well known in England this is, as far as we know, the first time that it has appeared in print with its music.

294 THE FROG AND THE MOUSE

Adolphus Le Ruez, Bonne Nuit, Jersey, Channel Islands, *rec.* P. Kennedy, 1956: BBC 23840

Other recorded versions
Elizabeth Cronin, Ballyvourney, Cork, Ireland, *rec.* A. Lomax, 1951: *Uncle Rat Went Out to Ride*: BBC 11989
Annie Paterson, St Andrews, Mainland, Orkney, *rec.* P. Kennedy, 1955: BBC 22650 (has 'Ah-hum' chorus often found in USA versions)
Albert Beale, Kenardington, Kent, *rec.* P. Kennedy and M. Karpeles, 1954: *A Frog he would a-Wooing Go* (*Anthony Rowley*), BBC 21156
The above four versions are on *Folk Songs of Britain*, vol. X, CAEDMON TC1225/TOPIC 12T198
S. Ennis, Dublin, 1949: BBC 13774: *Uncle Rat*
Cecilia Costello, Birmingham: two verses only, BBC 17034 (1951) and BBC 19929 (1954)
Thomas Moran, Mohill, Co. Leitrim, Ireland, *rec.* S. Ennis, 1954: BBC 21900
Ben Baxter, Southrepps, Norfolk, *rec.* S. Ennis, 1955: fragment *A Frog he would a-wooing Go* (*Anthony Rowley*), BBC 22158
Jack Weafer, Wexford, Ireland, *rec.* S. Ennis, London, 1955: BBC 22373

Printed versions
SHARPE: 1823, p. 86: *There Lived a Puddy in a Well*
CHAMBERS: 1826: quotes Sharpe version and Walter Scott MS, 1830
HALLIWELL: 1842: *Kitty Alone*
CHAPPELL: 1858–9, vol. II, p. 88: *The Marriage of the Frog and the Mouse*; quotes a ballad in *Melismata*, London, 1611
MASON: 1877, pp. 8–9: two variants, *The Frog's Wooing*

BARING GOULD AND SHEPPARD: 1895, No. 13: rewritten as *Kitty Alone*
SHARP MS: 1904–6: four variants (Somerset)
BARING GOULD AND SHARP: 1906: *A Frog he would a-wooing Go*
LEATHER: 1912, p. 209
JWFSS: 1912, vol. I, Pt. 4, p. 178: *Y Broga Bach*
WILLIAMS: 1923, p. 133: *Froggy would a-wooing Go* (Wiltshire)
JFSS: 1906, No. 9, p. 226: *Cuddy Alone* (Midlothians, from the Scott Collection); Anne Gilchrist, 1902
JEFDSS: 1946, p. 38: contains further notes by Anne Gilchrist
JEFDSS: 1953, p. 105: Mrs Costello's version (Birmingham)
GUNDRY: 1966, p. 47: two-part version, 1939 (Cornwall)
WYMAN AND BROCKWAY: 1916, p. 25 (Kentucky, USA)
STURGIS AND HUGHES: 1919, p. 18 (Vermont)
COX: 1925, p. 470 (W. Virginia)
SANDBURG: 1927, p. 143 (Kentucky and Virginia)
WHITE: 1928, p. 218
MACKENZIE: 1928, p. 155 (Nova Scotia, Canada)
CREIGHTON: 1932, p. 194 (Nova Scotia, Canada)
SHARP AND KARPELES: 1932, No. 220, p. 312: fifteen variants (S. Appalachians)
GREENLEAF: 1933, p. 90 (Newfoundland, Canada)
HUDSON: 1936, p. 282 (Mississippi)
SCARBOROUGH: 1937, p. 46
GARDNER AND CHICKERING: 1939, p. 455 (S. Michigan)
LINSCOTT: 1939, p. 199 (New England)
BELDEN: 1940, p. 494 (Missouri)
BREWSTER: 1940, p. 226 (Indiana)

This remarkable wedding was the theme of a song *The Frog Cam to the Myl-dur*, which was sung by shepherds in Wedderburn's *Complaynt of Scotland* (1549). 'A most strange weddinge of the frogge and the mouse' was licensed in 1580 and later reprinted with a tune in *Melismata*. In D'Urfey's *Pills to Purge Melancholy* (1707) there is an early political parody called *A High Amour at St James*.

Anne Gilchrist (JEFDSS: 1946) draws attention to a common characteristic in that all the variant refrains have a strong accent on the first note: it seems to suggest 'an accompanying energetic gesture, or kick, when danced as well as sung—for it has the lilt of the dance'.

A modern form of the song is perhaps better known than other traditional variants. It is Hooks' *A Frog he would a-wooing Go, Heigh Ho, says Rowley*, which has been recorded from traditional singers in Kent and Norfolk, and has appeared in collections by Baring Gould, Cecil Sharp and Alfred Williams.

A Welsh variant, *Y Broga Bach*, recorded in Aberystwyth in 1910, appears in JWFSS: 1912, vol. I, No. 4, p. 178:

Broga bach aeth maes i rodio
Twy-wy-a dio, Am-i-dymda-di-dym-tym-to
Ar gefen ei farch a'i gyfrwy cryno
Am-i-dymda-di-dym-tym-to
Pwy lygadae ond llygoden
Twy-wy-a-dio, Am-i-dymda-di-dym-tym-to

The little frog went forth to ride

On the back of his horse with his neat little saddle

Who eyed him but a mouse

295 THE HAWK AND THE CROW

Liam O'Connor, Pomeroy, County Tyrone, N. Ireland,
  rec. P. Kennedy and S. O'Boyle, 1953

Printed versions
STURGIS AND HUGHES: 1919, p. 40 (Vermont, USA)
SHARP AND KARPELES: 1932, No. 215: *The Bird Song*
  (N. Carolina and Virginia, USA)

Generally known as *The Bird's Courting Song*, this version of the song had not been noted in the British Isles until it appeared in Northern Ireland. It was therefore of great interest to come across a version still being sung in its country of origin before its flight across the Atlantic. In both the United States and in Ireland it was regarded as a children's song.

296 THE HERRING SONG

Seamus Ennis, Dublin, Ireland, *rec.* P. Kennedy, 1959:
  BBC 13775 (1949)

Other recorded versions
Mrs Johns, Kelly, Lifton, Devon, *rec.* P. Kennedy, 1950
Bill Westaway, Belstone, Devon, *rec.* P. Kennedy, 1952:
  BBC 17794
Ted Lambourne, North Marston, Buckinghamshire,
  rec. S. Ennis, 1952: BBC 18139
Harry Knight, Laughton, Sussex, *rec.* P. Kennedy, 1952:
  BBC 17715
Richard Blackman, Arundel, Sussex, *rec.* R. Copper,
  1954: BBC 22736
Edgar Allington, Brandon, Suffolk, *rec.* P. Kennedy,
  1956: BBC 23622 (cumulative variant)
Phoebe Smith, Melton, Woodbridge, Suffolk, *rec.* P.
  Kennedy, 1956
Harry Scott, Eaton Bray, Bedfordshire, *rec.* P. Kennedy,
  1958: BBC 26071
Jack Elliott, Birtley, Durham, 1963: *The Harrin's Heids*,
  BBC 29982 (cumulative variant)

Printed versions
BARING GOULD MS: No. 194: two versions (Devon and
  Cornwall)
GARDINER MS: 1906–9: one variant (Somerset), four
  variants (Hampshire)
HAMMOND MS: 1906: one variant (Somerset)
SHARP: 1909, School Series III: *The Red Herring*
  (Somerset)
JFSS: 1916, No. 20, p. 283: three variants, *coll.* C.
  Sharp, Somerset, followed by a note about the ritual
  origins by Lucy Broadwood, p. 285
WILLIAMS: 1923, p. 167: *The Jolly Red Herring* (various
  sources)
REEVES: 1958, No. 79, p. 179: Louie Hopper version,
  coll. C. Sharp
REEVES: 1960, No. 110, p. 219: *coll.* J. D. Pickman for
  Baring Gould (n.d.), Devon
JEFDSS: 1961, p. 79: Richard Blackman version
GUNDRY: 1966, p. 24, *coll.* Baring Gould, 1890 (Cornwall)
HAMER: 1967, p. 16: Harry Scott version
PURSLOW: 1968, p. 52, *coll.* Gardiner (Somerset)
HAMER: 1973, p. 23 (Bedfordshire)

What'll I do wi' my harrin's heid?
We'll mak' them in tae loaves of breid
Harrin's heid, loaves of breid
And all manner of things
Of all the fish that live in the sea
The harrin' is the one for me
How are ye to-day? How are ye to-day?
How are ye to-day? my hinney O?

I will never forget hearing this song sung, or rather performed, by three ladies in a public house at Powburn in Northumberland in 1953, each of whom in turn asked their audience 'How are ye today?', and then harmonised the final 'my hinney O'. Not only did their audience become hysterical after one verse but the verses went on and on and got longer and longer.

What'll I do wi' my harrin's scales?
We'll make them in tae ships that sail
Harrin's scales, ships that sail
Harrin's belly, a lass called Nelly
Harrin's tail, a barrel of ale,
Harrin's guts, a pair of byutes

Harrin's eyes, puddin's an' pies
Harrin's heid, loaves of breid
And all manners of things
Of all the fish that live in the sea
The harrin' is the one for me

The song is widespread in England. Although many versions are cumulative, with verses getting longer, more commonly the song is non-cumulative with a question and answer chorus in which the solo singer is questioned by another, as in this Sussex version:

> How can you lie, sir?
> So do you as well as I, sir
> Then why ha'n't you told me so?
> So I did long ago
> *Then go, and go with you, and so they come in*
> *Don't you think I done well of my jolly herrin'?*

Lucy Broadwood, writing about *The Herring* and other similar songs like *The Mallard* (No. 299) and *The Ram Song* (No. 304), thought such songs show traces of ritual singing and dancing in connection with sacred and magical animals (see JFSS: 1916, No. 20, p. 285).

297 I BOUGHT MYSELF A COCK

George Blackman, Wisborough Green, Sussex, *rec.* R. Copper, 1954: BBC 22735; *Folk Songs of Britain*, vol. X, CAEDMON TC1225/TOPIC 12T198

Other recorded versions
Frank Rose, Swinbrook, Burford, Oxfordshire, *rec.* P. Kennedy, 1952: BBC 18687
Bill Burnham, Bermondsey, London, *rec.* P. Kennedy, 1954: BBC 21158
Richard Pearse, Exeter, Devon, *rec.* P. Kennedy, 1954: BBC 21478

Printed versions
HALLIWELL: 1849, p. 263: *My Cock Lily-Cock*
GREIG: 1909-14, No. 149: *I Haed a Hennie* (Renfrewshire, Scotland)
SHARP: 1912, School Series VI, p. 14: *coll.* H. Hammond and *arr.* R. Vaughan Williams (Dorset)
WILLIAMS: 1923, p. 284: *Here's Luck to all my Cocks and Hens* (Oxfordshire)
REEVES: 1960, No. 42, p. 111: *Farmyard Song, coll.* H. Hammond, Dorset, 1906
HAMER: 1967, p. 66: *I Had a Little Cock* (Cornwall)

This is one of several songs which go under the generic description of the farmyard song. Another is *When I Was a Boy* (No. 310) with its 'farmer's boy' chorus. This one has variants such as *Up Was I on my Father's Farm*, the well-known version collected by Cecil Sharp. However perhaps the best known are *There Was an Old Farmer Had an Old Sow* and *Old Macdonald Had a Farm*, both of which are more recent remakes on the old theme.

298 THE JOLLY GOS-HAWK

Harry Westaway, Belstone, Okehampton, Devon, *rec.* P. Kennedy, 1950

Printed versions
BARING GOULD: 1889, No. 71: tune only, *coll.* H. Fleetwood Sheppard, from Harry Westaway, father of above singer, Devon
JFSS: 1916, No. 20, p. 282: *coll.* Cecil Sharp, Somerset

JFSS: 1923, No. 27, p. 95: note about the song by Anne Gilchrist
SHARP MS: 1923: variant submitted by Priscilla Wyatt Sopell
REEVES: 1958, No. 51, p. 136: two variants, *Jolly Old Hawk, coll.* Cecil Sharp
REEVES: 1960, No. 78, p. 167: Westaway version noted by J. D. Prickman for Baring Gould (Devon)

The tune of our version from the Westaway family at Belstone was published in *Songs of the West* after it had been noted from our singer's father. Baring Gould, who did not collect the song himself, believed that the tune properly belonged to the words of *The Bonny Bonny Boy* (given as *The Bonny Bird* (No. 106) in *Songs of the West*). He therefore collated various garlands in the British Museum: *The Fond Mother's Garland* (11621 C.S.) and *Beautiful Fanny's Garland*, and from Chappell's *National English Airs* (p. 155):

> I sat on the bank in trifle and play
> With my jolly gos-hawk and her wings were grey
> She flew to my breast and she there built her nest
> I am sure, pretty bird, you with me will stay

At the same time he reported that the song was known in Devonshire as *The Nawden Song*, but Harry Westaway, who only remembered a fragment of the song, had never heard this title. Baring Gould also regarded *The Jolly Gos-Hawk* as a version of *The Twelve Days of Christmas*, and quoted Breton versions; but Cecil Sharp in the JFSS said he preferred to think of it as a distinct and separate song in its own right.

There are therefore to date only the three reported versions of what would appear to be a survival of some antiquity.

299 THE MALLARD

Harry Holland, Exeter, Devon, *rec*. P. Kennedy, 1954: BBC 21490

Other recorded versions
Bunny Palmer (nephew of Harry Holland) at the village Barn Dance, Sidbury, Sidmouth, Devon, *rec*. P. Kennedy, 1950: COLUMBIA SL 206 (1952)
Bob Arnold, Asthall, Burford, Oxfordshire, *rec*. P. Kennedy, 1952: BBC 18687
Richard Pearce, Kingsbridge, *rec*. P. Kennedy, Exeter, Devon, 1954: BBC 21490

Printed versions
BARING GOULD: 1889, No. 79: tune with variable sixth from Devon (noted in revised edition); new words composed by Baring Gould. Reference to Breton version

HAMMOND MS: 1905 (Dorset)
JFSS: 1916, No. 20, p. 286: two variants, *coll*. Sharp, Bridgwater, Somerset, and Devon; one variant (Berkshire), *coll*. Rev. Maunsell Bacon (later published in *The Weekend Book*). Full notes about the song by Lucy Broadwood, who mentions another Mallard song of All Soul's College which is sung annually on 14th January

PEACOCK: 1965, p. 16 (Canada)

We first heard the song from Harry Holland's nephew Bunny Palmer, a newsagent at Sidbury, who recorded it for the BBC in 1950 at a local Barn Dance (his pronunciation of 'Mallard' was 'Mullard'):

> Many years ago, when I was between nine and eleven years of age, I used to go on horseback between Sidmouth and Exeter. My uncle was a carrier. It was a long drag in the hills. When we got to the Cat and Fiddle my uncle he used to take parcels in there for outlying farms. And as soon as ever he got inside there was loud shouts of: 'Good old Harry, let's have a song'. And of course Harry used to sing *The Mullard*. I used to sit out on the wagon, not being old enough to go inside and I learned this song off. And everywhere Harry went: 'Well, let's have *The Mullard*, Harry.'

Bunny always sings 'Featherby Halt' in the chorus, and when questioned he explained that it was probably the name of a stop on the railway. However when we eventually caught up with his uncle we found that he sang 'Featherby Hall', and thought it was a big country house. But if we listen to variants from other parts of the country we hear: 'For I've a'eaten the feathers an' all.'

300 MY FATHER HAD AN ACRE OF LAND

Bob and Ron Copper, Rottingdean, Sussex, *rec*. P. Kennedy, 1955: *Folk Songs of Britain*, vol. IV, CAEDMON TC1145/TOPIC 12T160

Other recorded versions
Jim and Bob Copper, *rec*. S. Ennis, 1952: BBC 17989
Luke Stanley, Barrow-on-Humber, Lincolnshire, *rec*. P. Kennedy, 1953: *Acre of Land*, BBC 19032
William Scarlett, Cranford, Middlesex, *rec*. P. Kennedy, Wick, Sussex, 1953: *The Team of Rats*, BBC 19339
Gabriel Figg, West Chiltington, Sussex, *rec*. P. Kennedy, 1958 and *rec*. Joy Hyman, 1964–5: *Holloman's Ivy*, BBC 29821

Printed versions
HALLIWELL: 1842
JFSS: 1901, No. 3, p. 83: *Sing Ivy, coll*. W. Percy Merrick, Sussex

GARDINER MS: 1906–8: five variants (Hampshire)
HAMMOND MS: 1906: one variant (Dorset)
JFSS: 1906, No. 8, p. 212: *coll*. R. Vaughan Williams, Wiltshire
SHARP MS: 1907: two variants (Somerset)
JFSS: 1909, No. 13, p. 274: *coll*. H. Balfour Gardiner, Hampshire
GARDINER: 1909, No. 8, p. 21: *Sing Ivy, coll*. George B. Gardiner, Wiltshire
WILLIAMS: 1923, p. 221: *Holly and Ivy* (Wiltshire)
KIDSON AND MOFFAT: 1926, p. 48
OPIE: 1951, p. 165
REEVES: 1960, No. 120, p. 243: George Gardiner variant, *Sing Ovy, Sing Ivy*
HAMER: 1973, p. 27: *Evie and Ivy* (Bedfordshire)

Although a farm song in its own right, this certainly seems to owe its origin to the second section of the old classical ballad *The Elfin Knight* (No. 2 in Child's *English and Scottish Popular Ballads*):

1 Now as you are goin' down Strawberry Lane,
   Every rose grows merry betimes
   It's there you will meet a pretty young man
   And tell him that he's a true lover of mine

2 And tell him to get me a Holland shirt
   Without stitch or seam or needlework

3 And tell him to wash it in yon spring well
   Where water ne'er sprung, nor water ne'er fell

4 And tell him to dry it on yonder green thorn
   Where there ne'er grew a thorn since Adam was born

5 Now as you are goin' down Strawberry Lane
   It's there you will meet a pretty young man

6 And tell him to get me an acre of land
   Between the salt water and the sea strand

677

7 Tell him to plough it with yon deer's horn
And sow it all over with one grain of corn

8 Tell him to reap it with shavings o' leather
And bind it all up in a peacock's feather

9 Tell him to tackle a wran and draw it home
And build it all up in a small mouse-hole

10 And tell him to thatch it with midge's claws
And rope it round with pismires' paws

11 And tell him to thresh it on yon church wall
And not let chaff or corn fall

12 And when he has finished and done his work
Send him to me and I'll give him the shirt

301 OLD DADDY FOX

Cyril Biddick, Boscastle, Cornwall, *rec.* P. Kennedy, 1950: COLUMBIA SL 206

Other recorded versions
Bill Westaway, Belstone, Devon, *rec.* P. Kennedy, 1952: BBC 17793
Jim Copper, Rottingdean, Sussex, *rec.* P. Kennedy, 1951
Jim and Bob Copper, *rec.* S. Ennis, 1952: BBC 17990
Bob and Ron Copper, *rec.* P. Kennedy, 1953
Thomas Moran, Mohill, County Leitrim, Ireland, *rec.* S. Ennis, 1953: BBC 22013
Elizabeth Cronin, Ballyvourney, County Cork, Ireland, *rec.* S. Ennis, 1954: BBC 21997
Mary Bennell, Amersham, Buckinghamshire, *rec.* S. Ennis, 1954: BBC 22422

Printed versions
RITSON: 1783: one verse
The Opera or *Cabinet of Song*, Edinburgh, 1832
HALLIWELL: 1842, No. 133, p. 34

NOTES AND QUERIES: 1854, vol. X: *The Fox*, an old Cornish song
LOGAN: 1869, p. 292
BARING GOULD: 1895, p. 10
BARING GOULD: 1905, No. 55, p. 112: Devon, with two other tunes used elsewhere in England in the notes
BARING GOULD AND SHARP: 1906, No. 31
HAMMOND MS: 1906: two variants (Dorset)
GARDINER MS: 1906–7: four variants (Hampshire)
SHARP: 1912, School Series, VI: *coll.* H. Hammond
WILLIAMS: 1923, p. 247: *The Fox and the Grey Goose* (Wiltshire)
HENRY: 1924, No. 38: *The Fox and His Wife* (County Derry, N. Ireland)
DUNSTAN: 1932, p. 46 (Cornwall)
OPIE: 1951, p. 173
GUNDRY: 1966, p. 59, *coll.* P. Kennedy, 1956 (Cornwall)
HAMER: 1967, p. 75 (Cornwall)
PURSLOW: 1968, p. 89, Gardiner (Hampshire)

Although we have heard the song through England and Ireland, it is the first version we heard, from Cornwall, that left the strongest impression. It was sung by a great character, 'The Old King Cole' of Boscastle, who used to gather local musicians around him to sing carols with the harmonium or to play step-dance tunes with Cyril Biddick sawing away on his 'bass viol', as he called his 'cello.

Like the version sung by the Copper family in Sussex, the Cornish version was sung in harmony by Cyril and his 'sons of harmony'.

302 OLD KING COLE

Bill Westaway, Belstone, Okehampton, Devon, *rec.* P. Kennedy, 1952: BBC 17793

Other recorded version
William Wells, Bampton, Oxfordshire, *rec.* P. Kennedy, 1952

Printed versions
King, Dr William (b. 1663): *Useful Transactions*; a version with 'Four and twenty fiddlers' chorus
HERD: 1776: *Old King Coul*
JOHNSON: 1787, vol. V, p. 486
CHAPPELL: 1838, No. 16, p. 40: tune compared to that of *The British Grenadiers*

CHAPPELL: 1858–9, p. 633: version from Gay's *Achilles* (1733) and a traditional version (no source given); notes about person
MASON: 1877–1908, p. 10 (Northumberland)
FORD: 1899, p. 167: *Old King Coul*
HAMMOND MS: 1906 (Dorset)
SHARP MS: 1907–9 (Somerset and Oxfordshire)
DUNCAN MS: (Aberdeenshire, Scotland)
OPIE: 1951, p. 134: background notes to song
REEVES: 1960, No. 45, p. 114: *Four and Twenty Fiddlers*, *coll.* H. Hammond (Dorset)
CREIGHTON: 1932, p. 197: *Old King Coul* (Canada)

The subject of this song, according to twelfth-century chroniclers, is the King Cole after whom the town of Colchester in Essex was named, and who became a British king on the death of Asclepiod in the third century A.D. On the other hand William Chappell, who published three versions of the tune in *National English Airs* (1838) and *Popular Music of the Olden Times* (1858–9), believed the subject to be a Mr Cole-brook, a famous wealthy cloth merchant in Reading. Deloney's *Six Worthy Yeomen of the West* (c. 1598) states that Thomas of Reading was supposed to have had 140 menial servants and about 300 poor people working for him.

The name 'Old Cole' appears in the blacksmith song *Twankydillo* (No. 286), in Dekker's *Satiromastix* (1602), and also in Marston's *The Malcontent* (1604).

For Scotland, Sir Walter Scott put forward the theory that Aul King Coul was the father of the fabled giant Finn McCoul, and Robert Burns contributed one of many versions he had encountered to Johnson's *Musical Museum*.

The tune, in the Northumbrian version (MASON: 1908) was used by Vaughan Williams for his ballet music of the same title. The First World War version was 'There's none so rare as can compare with Kitchener's New Armee'.

303 ON ILKLA MOOR BAH T'AT

Wilfred J. Hall, Ilkley, Yorkshire, *coll.* Douglas Kennedy,
  N. Wales, 1917

Other recorded version
Unnamed singer, Redmire, Wensleydale, Yorkshire,
  1940: BBC 2521

The author of this local dialect song is supposed to have been a Thomas Clark who wrote it in 1805 to the hymn tune *Cranbrook*. Who he was or how the song came to be made are not known. Yorkshire men all over the world regard the song with ritualistic respect and sing what seems to be a shortened version. The song is generally harmonized dolefully and sung slowly with a second verse which is not included in our version:

I've been a'-courting Mary Jane

Our version, which was collected before the song came to be taken up widely in its doleful form, was sung in a more spirited way.

Both places mentioned, Salter Hebble Docks and Luddenden Foot, are canal points on the Hebble and Calder rivers near Halifax. Nowadays this final verse is usually sung:

Then we shall all 'av' etten thee
That's how we get our owen back
This is the moral of this tale
Doan't go a-courtin' Mary Jane

304 THE RAM SONG

William Rew, Sidbury, Sidmouth, Devon, *rec.* P.
  Kennedy, 1950 and 1954: BBC 22321

Other recorded versions
Charlie Wills, Bridport, Dorset, *rec.* P. Kennedy, 1950
  and 1952: BBC 18689
Arthur Lennox (with chorus), Aberdeen, Scotland, *rec.*
  A. Lomax, 1951: *Folk Songs of Britain*, vol. X, CAED-
  MON TC1225/TOPIC 12T198
Ben Baxter, Southrepps, Norfolk, *rec.* S. Ennis, 1955:
  BBC 22022
Robert Cinnamond, Belfast, N. Ireland, *rec.* S. O'Boyle,
  1955: BBC 24841

Printed version
KINLOCH: 1827: *The Ram o' Diram*
JEWITT: 1867, p. 115: 15 stanzas with variants and back-
  ground notes
NOTES AND QUERIES: 1890, 1891 and 1904; DERBY
  N. & Q.: 1932
BROADWOOD: 1893, p. 44 (Derbyshire, Northumberland
  and Yorkshire)
FORD: 1899, p. 135: *Ram o' Bervie* (no tune), note men-
  tions *The Ram o' Diram* (or *Doram*)

GREIG: 1909–14, No. XIV: *The Ram of Derby*
SHARP: 1902, No. 41, p. 88: from Broadwood, 1893
  (Derbyshire)
HAMMOND MS: 1906: three variants (one Somerset, two
  Dorset)
GARDINER MS: 1906: *The Derby Ram* (Somerset)
DUNCAN MS: 1906: *Ram o' Durham* (Scotland)
WILLIAMS: 1923, p. 43: *The Ram* (Berkshire)
JEFDSS: 1946, p. 23: four variants, *The Old Tup*
  (Derbyshire)
OPIE: 1951, No. 129, p. 145: contains notes about early
  versions
REEVES: 1958, No. 26, p. 102: *coll.* Sharp (Somerset)
REEVES: 1960, No. 31, p. 92 from Hammond (Dorset)
WHITE: 1928, p. 201 (USA)
SHARP AND KARPELES: 1932, No. 141: three variants (S.
  Appalachians, USA)
JAFL: xviii, 51; xxxvi, 377; xxxix, 173
MEREDITH AND ANDERSON: 1967, pp. 112 and 120
  (Australia)

Although written for its own sake as a piece of incredibility, this song probably owes its origin to the Old Tup begging custom to which in some areas it is still attached. Like the Welsh *Mari Lwyd*, the Old Oss of the Cheshire Soulcakers, and the May Day Hobby Horses in the West Country, the Old Tup (as it is known in the Midlands) is generally a man covered in a sheepskin, crouching down, holding a pair of ram's horns mounted on a stick. He is generally accompanied by a butcher and a boy to catch the blood. Other characters who sometimes accompany them are an old man, an old woman, Little Devil Doubt (a hump-back), the Fool and old Beelzebub. The old man knocks on the door:

Here comes me and my owd lass
Short of money, short of brass
Fill up your glass, give us a sup
We'll come in and show you the Derby Tup

305 SOLDIER, SOLDIER

Seamus Ennis, Dublin, Ireland, *rec.* P. Kennedy, London, 1958: COLUMBIA KL 204 (World Library of Folk and Primitive Music)

Other recorded versions
Colm Keane, Carna, County Galway, Ireland, 1947: BBC 12489
Walter Hayne, Abbotsbury, Dorset, *rec.* P. Kennedy, 1950. Tune of song (*Not for Joe*) played on melodeon by George Beale, Abbotsbury, Dorset, *rec.* P. Kennedy, 1954: BBC 22437

Printed versions
JEFDSS: 1937, p. 121: *Soldier John, coll.* Anne Gilchrist, Glasgow, Scotland, and version noted by H. H. Albino from father, Gloucestershire. Also version from Virginia, USA, with notes by Anne Gilchrist

NEWELL: 1884–1903, p. 93: children's game version (USA)
POUND: 1922, p. 224 (USA)
COX: 1953, p. 467: well known on Cape Cod (USA)
SHARP AND KARPELES: 1932, No. 90, p. 40: three variants (USA)
EDDY: 1939, p. 211: two variants (Ohio, USA)
JAFL: xxvii, 158; xxxi, 78/161; xxxiii, 92
JAFL: xxvii, 158 78/161; xxxiii, 92
CREIGHTON AND SENIOR: 1950, p. 254: two variants (Nova Scotia, Canada)
KARPELES: 1971, No. 78, p. 234: *Soldier, will you marry me?* (Newfoundland, Canada)

Often sung as a duet between a girl and her soldier, this song probably originates as a children's game, and it has been collected as such in England and America.

Our version is from the west of Ireland, but the song was also known in Scotland, where it was sung to the tune of *The Flowers of Edinburgh*:

> O solgy, O solgy, O won't you marry me?
> With the row and the bow and the sound of the drum
> O no, says the solgy, I canna marry thee
> For I've no shoes to put on

And in the last verse the soldier admits:

> For I've a wife and weans at home

Anne Gilchrist describes the finale of the story as 'the bursting of the bubble of expectation being a climax artfully prepared'.

306 THREE MEN WENT A-HUNTING

Hywel Wood, Bala, Merionethshire, N. Wales, *rec.* P. Kennedy, 1954: BBC 22429; *Folk Songs of Britain*, vol. X, CAEDMON TC1225/TOPIC 12T198

Other recorded version
George Endacott, South Zeal, Devon, *rec.* P. Kennedy, 1952: BBC 17797

Printed versions
ROXBURGHE: 1871–80, vol. 1, p. 105: printed by F. Coles in *A Choice of Inventions* (1632)
HALLIWELL: 1842, No. 290, p. 64
BURNE: 1884, p. 556
BARING GOULD: 1895, p. 7 (Nursery Songs)
SHARP MS: 1903–14: six unpublished versions
BARING GOULD: 1905, No. 75, p. 154: *Three Jovial Welshmen* (Devon)

BARING GOULD AND SHARP: 1906, No. 24: *The Three Huntsmen*
HAMMOND MS: 1906: one variant (Dorset)
GARDINER MS: 1908: one variant (Hampshire)
GRAHAM: 1910, No. 4, p. 6: *Three Jolly Hunters*; words from *Old Cronies* by Edwin Waugh (tune: *The Rose*)
WILLIAMS: 1923, p. 179: *'Twas of Three Jolly Welshmen* (Wiltshire)
OPIE: 1951, p 421: various versions as well as photograph of broadsheet and illustrations from nursery books
HAMER: 1973, p. 37: *The Englishman, Irishman and Scotchman*
LOMAX: 1960, No. 2, p. 12: *Cape Ann*, from *Songs of the Hutchinson Family* (Firth & Hall, New York, 1843)

In the Roxburghe collection there is *A Choice of Inventions Or Several sorts of the figure of three*, printed by F. Coles (1646–74), which includes

> There were three men of Gotham as I've heard say
> That needs would ride a-hunting upon St David's day
> Through all the day they hunting were, yet no sport could they see
> Until they spide an Owle as she sate on a tree

> The first man said 'twas a Goose
> The second man said: Nay
> The third man said 'twas a Hawke
> But his Bells were falne away

Other similar 'three songs' are *Three Scamping Rogues* (the miller, the weaver and the tailor who got turned out of doors because they would not sing; it is also known as *King Arthur's Sons*): No. 307, and *Bold Reynard* (*Beau Rattle*, *Ring Doll* and *Bold Reynolds* were other titles of versions collected by Cecil Sharp). A version of *Bold Reynard* published in *Songs of the West* starts:

There were three jovial Welshmen
They would go hunt the fox
They swore they saw old Reynard
Run over yonder rocks
With a whoop, whoop, whoop
And a blast of my bugle horn
With my twank, twank, twank
And my twank-i-diddle O
And through the woods we'll ride, brave boys
And through the woods we'll ride

All versions have this 'hunting horn' type chorus. Other verses are concerned with a woman (or fair maid), a farmer, a miller, a blind man, a parson, a shepherd, etc.

Three Men Went a-hunting might almost appear to have been written against 'funny Welshmen', so perhaps it was in retaliation that the Welsh introduced the Englishman, the Scotsman and the Irishman into the chorus of contemporary versions.

Here are some verses recorded elsewhere:

South Zeal, Devonshire

Ship in full sail
Wash-tub with the clothes hung out to dry

Camborne, Cornwall

Toad
Granny's duck with the feathers blown away

Armagh, Northern Ireland

Big ship
Part of Ireland that's pinched by Amerikay

307 THREE SCAMPING ROGUES

George Endacott, South Zeal, Okehampton, Devon, *rec.* P. Kennedy, 1950 and 1952: BBC 17797

Other recorded versions
Jack Endacott (nephew of George Endacott), Chagford, Devon, *rec.* P. Kennedy, 1954: BBC 22323
George Maynard, Copthorne, Sussex, *rec.* P. Kennedy, 1955: BBC 23093

Printed versions
MASON: 1877, p. 7: *King Arthur's Servants* (Northumberland)
BROADWOOD: 1893, p. 20: *King Arthur* (Lancashire)
SHARP MS: 1904–9: three variants, two unpublished
HAMMOND MS: 1905 (Dorset)

GARDINER MS: 1906–8: variants (Hampshire), one variant (source unknown)
SHARP: 1909, School Series, III: *The Three Sons* (Somerset)
WHITTAKER: 1921, No. 23, p. 48: version from MASON: 1877
WILLIAMS: 1923, p. 194: *When Arthur Ruled this Land* (Wiltshire)
PURSLOW: 1968, p. 62, *coll.* Gardiner: *King Henry's Three Sons* (Hampshire)
STUBBS: 1970, p. 42: *In Good King Arthur's Days* (Sussex)
LOMAX: 1960, No. 1, p. 1: *In Good Old Colony Times* (USA)

When King Arthur ruled this land
He was a mighty King
Three sons he swore he'd turn out of door
Because they would not sing

This song was widely sung in England, most versions giving the father of the three unscrupulous tradesmen as King Arthur. In a Northumbrian version they are not his sons but servants:

In good King Arthur's days
He was a merry king
He turned three servants out of doors
Because they would not sing

308 TOM PEARCE

Dorothy Pearce, Bourton-on-the-Water, Gloucestershire, *rec.* P. Kennedy, 1952: *Stow Fair*

Other recorded versions
Bill Westaway, Belstone, Devon, *rec.* P. Kennedy, 1950 and 1952: *Widdecombe Fair*, BBC 17783; *Folk Songs of Britain*, vol. X, CAEDMON TC1225/TOPIC 12T198
Bob Arnold, Asthall, Burford, Oxfordshire, *rec.* P. Kennedy, 1952: *Stow Fair*, BBC 18686
George Maynard, Copthorne, Sussex, *rec.* P. Kennedy, 1956: *Lansdown Fair*, BBC 23092; *Folk Songs of Britain* vol. X, CAEDMON TC1225/TOPIC 12T198
La Rena Clark, Ontario, Canada, *rec.* Toronto, 1965: TOPIC 12T140: *The Old County Fair*

Printed versions
BARING GOULD: 1889, No. 16: *Widdecombe Fair* (Devon)
SHARP MS: 1904–7: three unpublished variants (Somerset)
SHARP AND MARSON: 1904–9, No. 49, p. 48: *Midsummer Fair* (Somerset); last verse composed by Sharp
SHARP: 1908, School Series I, p. 4 (same version)
GARDINER MS: 1907: two variants (Hampshire)
REEVES: 1960, No. 75, p. 164: *Illsdown Fair, coll.* G. Gardiner, Hampshire, 1907; another Hampshire variant is similar but has different names in the chorus
HAMER: 1967, p. 10: *Bedford Fair* (Bedfordshire) ('John Jones's old mare')

The Devonshire version, *Widdecombe Fair*, is the one which has become widely known, but the song is not confined to any one locality and several other versions have been collected in England.

Cecil Sharp collected *Lansdown Fair*, *Midsummer Fair* and *Portsdown Fair* in Somerset. This version, *Stow Fair*, came from the aptly named Mrs Pearce of Bourton-on-the-Water, Gloucestershire.

Ralph Dunstan says in the notes to *The Cornish Song Book* (DUNSTAN: 1929) that he knew an old Cornishwoman who told him that her mother knew the Tom Pearce who lived at Truro, and loaned the grey mare to go to Summercourt Fair (Summercourt is between Newquay and St Austell).

Baring Gould, who published the now world-famous Devonshire version in *Songs of the West*, said the original Uncle Tom Cobleigh lived at Spreyton in a house near Yeoford Junction. His will was signed on 20th January 1787 and proved on 14th March 1794; the names in the chorus of the song all belonged to the village of Sticklepath. These two places are on Dartmoor within only a few miles of where Bill Westaway recorded his version. In fact Bill told how Baring Gould had taken down his father's words and then put another tune to it:

> Mr Baring Gould was a parson down Lew Trenchard on the borders of Cornwall and he got Widdecombe Fair from my father in Mr J. D. Prickman's, the solicitor, at Okehampton. He and my father were wonderful great friends and Mr Prickman sent up his coachman to Father that he was to come in to Okehampton as he wanted to see him very particular.
>
> So the day after, Father went into Okehampton. He had a very good time, they fed him well, and paid him very well, and he was given a drop or two, you know, and got a bit merry and they soon got Father singing. Well that's what Baring Gould wanted you see, for Father to sing *Widdecombe Fair*, while he took it in, in shorthand-writing or in notes, you know. And all he done was put a new tune to it.

309 WAS YOU EVER SEE?

Manfrie Wood, Bala, Merionethshire, Wales, *rec.* P. Kennedy, 1954: BBC 22429; *Folk Songs of Britain*, vol. X, CAEDMON TC1225/TOPIC 12T198

The tune of the Welsh folksong *Mochyn Du* is used as a vehicle for amusing improvised verses about local people. In its best-known form it tells of Cosher Bailey, a Monmouth ironmaster who built the Taff Railway along the Aberdare valley in 1846. When Bailey drove the first train along the line the engine got stuck in the tunnel, and as a result there still remains the Cosher Bailey song, which runs to scores of stanzas.

310 WHEN I WAS A BOY

William Rew, Sidbury, Sidmouth, Devon, *rec.* P. Kennedy, 1950 and 1954: *The Farmyard Song*, BBC 22322
Other recorded versions
Mary Bennell, Amersham, Buckinghamshire, *rec.* S. Ennis, 1954: *The Farmyard Song*, BBC 22422
Jack Jones, Cardigan, Wales, *rec.* S. Ennis, 1954: '*As I was a farmer, a farmer, he cried . . .*', BBC 22435

Edgar Allington, Brandon, Suffolk, *rec.* P. Kennedy, 1955: '*When I was a lad, and my brother was a lad . . .*', BBC 23622
Printed version
SHARP: 1909, School Series III, p. 2: *The Farmyard* 'My father keep some very fine sheep in the merry green fields of Ireland.' (London)

Apart from *The Old Sow* and *Old Macdonald Had a Farm*, the best-known version of this farmyard song was the one collected by Cecil Sharp in London:

> Up I was on my father's farm
> On a May day morning early
> A-feeding of my father's cows, etc.
> *Six pretty maids come and gang along o' me*
> *To the merry green fields and the farmyard*

In the three recorded versions we have further chorus variations:

Buckinghamshire

> Come, my bonny fellow, come along with me
> I'm as happy as can be

Cardiganshire

> So now, my bonny lads, come along with me
> To see my grandpa's farmyard

Suffolk

> Say, bonny lass, will you come with me
> To the merry green fields of Ireland

Needless to say the song can be extended indefinitely with other farm animals like horses, hens, turkeys, goats and so on.

311 THE WILD MAN OF BORNEO

Ben Phillips, Lochtwrffin, Mathry, Pembrokeshire, Wales, *rec*. E. Cleaver and S. Ennis, 1952: BBC 19067

Printed version
SHARP MS: 1908: *The Wild Man from Poplar* (Somerset)

CREIGHTON AND SENIOR: 1950, p. 258 (Nova Scotia, Canada)

Cecil Sharp collected a version in 1908 called *The Wild Man from Poplar* from Charles Neville of East Coker, Somerset, of which the last verse ran:

> The wind blew through the whiskers of the flea in the tip of the tail of the dog of the nurse of the child of the wife of the wild man of Poplar just come to town

Like our version from Wales, *The Wild Man of Borneo* from Nova Scotia had a special ending to the song: 'Just come to town'.

A version of the song sung in Welsh is *Dyn Bach o Fangor*. The last verse is as follows:

Chwaren bach y blewyn bach y cynffon bach y ci bach

y wraig bach y dyn bach o Fangor
yn dwad i'r dre

The little blotch on the little hair on the little tail on the little dog
of the little wife of the little man of Bangor
has just come to town

312 WIM-WAM-WADDLES

Harry Greening and chorus of Dorsetshire Mummers, Dorchester, Dorset, 1936: *The Foolish Boy*, BBC 14290; *Folk Songs of Britain*, CAEDMON, vol. X TC1225/TOPIC 12T198

Printed versions
HALLIWELL: 1842, p. 37
MASON: 1877, p. 16: *Wing Wang Waddle O* (Northumberland)
BARING GOULD: 1895–1906, p. 17: *The Foolish Boy*
SHARP MS: three variants
GREIG: 1909–14, No. xliii: *My Fader Deed an' Left Me* (Scotland)

WILLIAMS: 1923, p. 48: *The Bugle Played for Me* (Wiltshire)
HENRY: 1924, No. 732: *My Grandfather Died* (Armagh, N. Ireland)
OPIE: 1951, p. 156: references to several variants
REEVES: 1960, No. 43, p. 112: *coll*. Baring Gould, Devon, 1888
JEFDSS: 1964, p. 270: variant published in *West Sussex Gazette* (1905)
SHARP AND KARPELES: 1932, No. 217, p. 307: three variants (Kentucky, USA)
WYMAN AND BROCKWAY: 1916, p. 6 (Kentucky, USA)

1 When I was a little boy I lived by myself
   All the bread and cheese I had I laid upon the shelf

2 The rats and the mice they gave me such a life
   I had to go to London to get me a wife

3 The roads were so long and the streets were so narrow
  I had to bring her home again in my wheelbarrow

4 My foot slipped and got me a fall
  Down went wheelbarrow, wife and all

5 I swapped my wheelbarrow and got me a horse
  And then I rode from cross to cross

6 I swapped my horse and got me a mare
  And then I rode from fair to fair

This song, known in the United States as *The Swapping Song*, appears in early collections of nursery rhymes as well as in many Scots, Irish and English folksong collections.

Versions collected by Cecil Sharp in the United States in the Southern Appalachians were all given the general title of *The Foolish Boy*.

A Wiltshire version has the last line and title *The Bugle Played for Me*:

> I sold my calf and bought me a mouse
> On purpose to have a pretty thing to run about my house
> In came a neighbour's cat and stole away my mouse
> I flung a fire-stick at his tail which burned down my house

> *Jack stock sliddle uck*
> *Fatty fiddle uck*
> *Ban to the broom*
> *Pick and hack, Jimmy Pack*
> *Ti mi diddle tum tum tay*
> *Hang the day*
> *That the bugle played for me*

Bibliography

This bibliography has been divided into two sections. Books published in Britain and Ireland appear first, followed by those published abroad, both in alphabetical order

Baring Gould: 1889–1905
Rev. S. Baring Gould and Rev. H. Fleetwood Sheppard, *Songs and Ballads of the West*: Patey & Willis, London (4 parts) 1889–91. Methuen, London (4 parts) 1891–4; (1 vol.) 1895; revised edition 1905. Details are given by E. A. White in JEFDSS: 1937, p. 143, and 1946, p. 67. When reprinted in four parts this collection, mainly from Devon and N. Cornwall, comprised 110 songs 'collected from the mouths of the people'. Texts were modified and in some cases completely re-written and the same applied to tunes. However, in the revised edition, under the musical editorship of Cecil Sharp and with the adding of the name of the Rev. F. W. Bussell, one of the original collectors, many original texts and tunes were restored. For further comment on this publication see Dean-Smith: JEFDSS: 1950, p. 41.

Baring Gould: 1895
Rev. S. Baring Gould, *A Book of Nursery Songs and Rhymes*: Methuen, London, 1895. An early collection of diversionary songs for children.

Baring Gould and Sheppard: 1895
Rev. S. Baring Gould and Rev. H. Fleetwood Sheppard, *A Garland of Country Song*: Methuen, London, 1895. 50 songs with much edited text compounded from various sources; detailed notes about songs, particularly those associated with customs, and comparative texts given. The introduction gives a history of folksong collecting from 1843.

Baring Gould and Sharp: 1906
Rev. S. Baring Gould and Cecil J. Sharp, *English Folk Songs for Schools*: Curwen, London, 1906. 53 songs from collections of both editors 'designed to meet the requirements of the Board of Education'—who that year had recommended the inclusion of National or Folk Songs in the school curriculum, and 'dedicated to T. R. H. Prince Edward and Prince Albert of Wales'.

Broadwood: 1893
Lucy Broadwood and J. A. Fuller-Maitland, *English County Songs*: Cramer, London, 1893. Important early publication containing 92 songs collected in nearly every county of England. Most have little relevance to their district origins but some are in the dialects of their locality. Scholarly presentation with straightforward piano accompaniments. For article about editor see JEFDSS: 1948, p. 136, and 1950, p. 38.

Burne: 1884
Charlotte S. Burne, *Shropshire Folk-lore*: Trubner, London, 1884. In addition to local folk-lore there are accounts of Morris dance and Mummers play with song, a number of ballads and carols, wassail songs, some children's games and 'choral games'.

Chambers: 1826/70
Robert Chambers, *Popular Rhymes of Scotland*: Edinburgh, 1826 and 1870. The first collection of Scots nursery rhymes, it contained interesting texts of songs which were connected with annual customs and children's games, but only six tunes were included. (His other important collections were *The Scottish Songs* (1829) and *Twelve Romantic Scottish Ballads with the Original Airs* (1844).)

Chappell: 1838
William Chappell, *National English Airs*: Chappell & Simpkin Marshall, London, 1838. One volume containing 245 tunes arranged for piano and the other historical references, annotations and details of sources. Much of the reference is to printed works and MSS in the library of Edward Rimbault which was later dispersed. This work was superseded twenty years later by *Popular Music of the Olden Time* (1858).

Chappell: 1858/9
William Chappell, *Popular Music of the Olden Time*: Cramer, Beale & Chappell, London, vol. I 1858, vol. II 1859; Dover Publications, New York, 1965. Includes most of material from *National English Airs* (1838) but more has been added from other sources with particular reference to the ballads in the Pepys and Roxburghe collections. For further comment see Dean-Smith's *Guide* and JEFDSS: 1950, p. 38.

Christie: 1876/81
William Christie, *Traditional Ballad Airs*: Edmonston & Douglas, Edinburgh, vol. I 1876, vol. II 1881. Dean Christie noted down songs mainly in Aberdeenshire. This book combines his own collecting with publication of tunes and words from many other collections, both published and unpublished, including Percy, Scott, Jamieson, Motherwell, Kinloch, Sharpe and Buchan. Also contains a few original compositions.

Dean-Smith: 1954
Margaret Dean-Smith, *A Guide to English Folk Song Collections (1822–1952)*: University of Liverpool, 1954. A useful index of published songs under titles, alternative titles and first lines, with some full descriptions of important books with historical annotations and an introduction which traces the development of collecting and publication of folksong in England over a period of 130 years.

Duncan Ms: 1905–11
James Duncan (1848–1917). MS collected *c.* 1905–11. Aberdeen University Library. Consists of two notebooks, the first containing 800 tunes with words of first verse, and the second giving texts of over 350 songs all supplied by a Mrs Gillespie. For obituary by Lucy Broadwood see JFSS: 1918, No. 21, p. 41.

Dunstan: 1929
Ralph Dunstan, *The Cornish Song Book*: A. W. Jordan, Truro and Reid Brothers, London, 1929; Lodenek Press, Padstow, Cornwall, 1974. Contains 11 songs with Cornish words, 72 with English words collected in Cornwall or songs associated with Cornwall, and 48 carols. It is aimed to provide a selection of music for 'community singing wherever Cornishmen (and Cornish women) forgather the world over'.

Dunstan: 1932
Ralph Dunstan, *Cornish Dialect and Folk Songs*: A. W. Jordan, Truro and Reid Brothers, London, 1932; Lodenek Press, Padstow, Cornwall, 1972. A sequel to *The Cornish Song Book* containing 37 songs.

FMJ: 1965–
Folk Music Journal: English Folk Dance and Song Society, London (from 1965). Continuing the work of JFSS (*Journal of the Folk-Song Society*): 1889–1931 and JEFDSS (*Journal of the English Folk Dance and Song Society*): 1932–64.

Ford: 1899–1904
Robert Ford, *Vagabond Songs and Ballads of Scotland*: Gardiner, Paisley, Scotland, 1899–1901; new edition 1904. A compre-

hensive collection of songs and ballads, containing a number of 'bothy ballads', but only a few for which he provides the music. Important in that it covers the wide range of songs that were current up to the end of the century, particularly those sung by 'the travellers'.

GARDINER: 1909
George B. Gardiner, *Folk Songs from Hampshire*: Novello, London, 1909. 16 songs collected by Gardiner and his musical associates, Gamblin, Balfour Gardiner and Guyer, and arranged by Gustav (von) Holst.

GARDINER MS: 1905–9 (see also under HAMMOND)
For further details about Gardiner's work see *The George Gardiner Folksong Collection* in FMJ: 1967, p. 129 and introduction to PURSLOW: 1968.

GRAHAM: 1910
John Graham, *Dialect Songs of the North*: Curwen, London, 1910. 15 songs from Lancashire, Cheshire, Westmorland and Cumberland collected by Graham with piano accompaniments by Percy E. Fletcher.

GREIG: 1909/14
Gavin Greig, *Folk Songs of the North-East*: The Buchan Observer, Peterhead, Scotland. Vol. I 1909, vol. II 1914. Folklore Associates, Pennsylvania, USA, 1963. Greig was an Aberdeenshire schoolmaster and an accomplished musician who noted the words and tunes of over 3,000 songs. His manuscripts, extending over 90 volumes, are deposited in the Library of King's College, Aberdeen.

GUNDRY: 1966
Inglis Gundry, *Canow Kernow*. Federation of Old Cornwall Societies, 1966. Soundpost Publications, Dartington Institute of Traditional Arts, Totnes, Devon, 1972. Over 60 songs, carols, shanties and dance tunes collected in Cornwall. Some songs published with versions in Cornish.

HALLIWELL: 1842/9
J. O. Halliwell, *The Nursery Rhymes of England*: Percy Society Publications, London, 1842. Vol. IV, and several subsequent editions. (It was reissued in 1970 by Bodley Head.) *Popular Rhymes and Nursery Tales*: London, 1849 (a sequel to the above). Words of nursery rhymes 'collected from oral tradition'.

HAMER: 1967
Fred Hamer, *Garners Gay*: EFDS Publications, London, 1967. 50 songs, words and melodies (chord symbols) mainly collected in Bedfordshire but also from other counties of England. No exact locations or dates given of informants or comparative notes to songs, but contains hitherto unpublished local songs and songs connected with local customs.

HAMER: 1973
Fred Hamer, *Green Groves*: EFDS Publications, London, 1973. 38 songs, words and melodies (chord symbols). A further selection published posthumously. As in Hamer's *Garners Gay*, no exact details of locations, dates or comparative notes to songs.

HAMMOND AND GARDINER MSS: 1905–9
H. E. D. Hammond (1866–1910), R. F. F. Hammond (1868–1921) and Dr George Gardiner (1852–1910) collected mainly in Dorset and Hampshire. Their manuscripts, deposited in the Vaughan Williams Memorial Library at Cecil Sharp House, London, have been indexed by Frank Purslow, who has also edited three books drawn from them (see PURSLOW: 1965, 1968 and 1972).

HAYWARD: 1925
H. Richard Hayward, *Ulster Songs and Ballads*: Duckworth, London, 1925. A collection of songs in English mainly from the north of Ireland.

HENRY: 1924
Sam Henry, *Songs of the People*: Northern Constitution, Coleraine, Co. Derry, N. Ireland, 1924. Over 800 songs were published in the local Derry newspaper. Many were contributed by readers but it was Henry's diligent research and background notes that gave interest to each contribution.

HERD: 1769/76
David Herd, *The Ancient and Modern Scots Songs, Heroic Ballads*: Dickson & Elliot, Edinburgh, 1769; (2 vols.) 1776. Paterson, Edinburgh, 1870. New 2-vol. edition, 1973, Scottish Academic Press. Early Scots source material. Herd's original MS, in the British Museum, served as basis for many of Robert Burns's songs as well as for Sir Walter Scott's *Minstrelsy of the Scottish Border*.

JEFDSS: 1932–64
Journal of The English Folk Dance and Song Society: London (32 vols.), 1932–64.

JFSS: 1899–1931
Journal of the Folk-Song Society: London (35 vols.), 1899–1931.

JWFSS: 1909–71
Journal of the Welsh Folk Song Society, ed. J. Lloyd Williams, W. S. Gwynn Williams, 1909–71 (intermittently). The Journal consists of hundreds of songs and variants from aural, MS and published sources, which are given in both staff and sol-fa notation.

JEWITT: 1867
Llewellyn Jewitt, *The Ballads and Songs of Derbyshire*: Bemrose & Lothian, Derby and London, 1867.

JOHNSON: 1787–1853
James Johnson, *The Scots Musical Museum*: 6 vols. Edinburgh, 1787–1803; 4 vols. with notes by William Stenhouse and David Laing, Edinburgh, 1853. This was the beginning of systematic documentation of Scots songs to which Robert Burns contributed material of his own collecting which he restored by re-writing amplifications of the texts.

KIDSON AND MOFFAT: 1926
Frank Kidson and Alfred Moffat, *A Garland of English Folk Songs*: Ascherberg, Hopwood & Crew, London, 1926. 60 songs collected by Kidson, mainly in Yorkshire, with piano accompaniments by Moffat; most previously published in *Traditional Tunes* (1891). A further 60 songs were selected for a second volume by Kidson and Moffat (1927).

KINLOCH: 1827
George R. Kinloch, *Ancient Scottish Ballads*: Longman, London and Edinburgh, 1827. Probably inspired by Sir Walter Scott's collections, this was an important ballad and song publication with tunes.

LEATHER: 1912
Mrs E. M. Leather, *Folk-Lore of Herefordshire*: Jakeman & Carver, Hereford, and Sidgwick & Jackson, London, 1912; S.R. Publishers, E. Ardsley, Wakefield, Yorkshire, 1970. Like Burne's *Shropshire Folk-lore* (1884), this contains mainly folklore, but includes 23 songs, dances, mummers, ballads and carols. For further details about the collector see JFSS: 1928, No. 32, pp. 29–30.

LOGAN: 1869
W. H. Logan, *A Pedlar's Pack*: Paterson, Edinburgh, 1869.

MASON: 1877/1908
Miss M. H. Mason, *Nursery Rhymes and Country Songs*: Metzler, London, 1877. Second edition without illustrations but with additional notes, 1908. Over 50 folksongs of great variety mainly from her own Mitford family in Northumberland, also from Broadwood in Sussex, with piano accompaniments.

OPIE: 1951
Iona and Peter Opie, *The Oxford Dictionary of Nursery Rhymes*: Oxford University Press, London, 1951. 550 rhymes and jingles with literary and historical background information.

PURSLOW: 1965
Frank Purslow, *Marrowbones*: EFDS Publications, London, 1965. A series of pocket-size publications initiated by Peter

Kennedy in order to make available the songs collected by Hammond and Gardiner in the care of the EFDSS library. This selection contains 100 songs, provided with chord symbols over the melodies.

PURSLOW: 1968
Frank Purslow, *The Wanton Seed*: EFDS Publications, London, 1968. A second selection from Hammond and Gardiner again containing 100 songs.

PURSLOW: 1972
Frank Purslow, *The Constant Lovers*: EFDS Publications, London, 1972. A third selection in which the type-size has been increased and the number of songs reduced to 78.

REEVES: 1958
James Reeves, *The Idiom of the People*: Heinemann, London, 1958. Words of 115 folksongs from Cecil Sharp MSS (about 40 printed for the first time) selected as examples of 'English Traditional Verse'. Introduction concerned with the Folk Song Movement in England; Sharp as a collector; text revisions, description of the MSS; the popular idiom; and a detailed consideration of certain songs.

REEVES: 1960
James Reeves, *The Everlasting Circle*: Heinemann, London, 1960. 142 texts from the MSS of Baring Gould, Hammond and Gardiner considered as 'English traditional verse'. Introduction concerned with Baring Gould as a collector and his MSS; Hammond and Gardiner; varieties of folksong; the theme of fertility and a discussion on the *lingua franca* of English traditional song.

RITSON: 1783/1810
Joseph Ritson, *Gammer Gurton's Garland or The Nursery Parnassus*: Durham, 1783; London, 1810.

ROXBURGHE: 1871–93
Roxburghe Ballads (about 1540–1790): 7 vols. Vols. I–II ed. William Chappell, Ballad Society, London, 1871–80; vols. III–VII ed. J. W. Ebsworth, Hertford, 1883–93.

SHARP: 1902
Cecil J. Sharp, *A Book of British Song*: John Murray, London, 1902. 78 songs published before Sharp started collecting. They are listed under National, Soldier and Sailor, Country, Humorous, Old English and Old Scottish, starting with *God Save the King* and *Rule Britannia* and finishing with *Auld Lang Syne*. Only two Welsh and two Irish national songs are included.

SHARP Ms 1903–23
Cecil Sharp (1859–1924), foremost collector of English folksongs and folkdances, was the founder of The English Folk Dance Society and for many years a member of The Folk-Song Society. (In 1932 these two societies amalgamated as The English Folk Dance and Song Society.) For a full account of his life-work and publications see *Cecil Sharp* by A. H. Fox-Strangways (Oxford University Press, London, 1933), revised by Maud Karpeles (Routledge & Kegan Paul, London, 1967). Words, songs, tunes and dance notes in Cecil Sharp's autograph are in the Library of Clare College, Cambridge. There are also photostat copies in the Harvard University Library and the New York Public Library, and microfilm copies in the libraries of University of California and in the library at Cecil Sharp House, London, the headquarters of The English Folk Dance and Song Society. Cecil Sharp's own collection of books was left to the EFDSS and formed the beginnings of the specialist library at Cecil Sharp House.

SHARP AND MARSON: 1904–9
Cecil J. Sharp and Rev. Charles L. Marson, *Folk Songs from Somerset*: Simpkin Marshall, London and Barnicott, Taunton, Somerset. 5 vols. Vol. I 1904, vol. II 1905, vol. III 1906, vol. IV 1908, vol. V 1909. The most important single collection of English folksong, later edited as the *Selected Edition* (1916–21). Introduction concerning singers and style most valuable.

SHARP (School Series): 1908–36
Cecil J. Sharp, *Novello's School Songs*: Novello, London. Sets I and II: *Folk-Songs from Somerset* 1908; Sets III and IV: *Various Counties* 1909; Set V: *Folk-Songs from Somerset* 1910; Set VI: *Folk-Songs for Schools* 1912 (also arranged R. Vaughan Williams); Sets VII and VIII: 1922; IX: 1925; X:1936.

SHARPE: 1823/80
Charles Kirkpatrick Sharpe, *A Ballad Book*: private circulation, Edinburgh, 1823; Blackwood, Edinburgh, 1880.

STUBBS: 1970
Ken Stubbs, *The Life of a Man*: EFDS Publications, London, 1970. 50 songs, texts and melodies (chord symbols). Many from our same source singers, but includes a wide variety from Home Counties (Surrey, Sussex mainly and some from Kent) with some important variant versions and some hitherto unpublished songs. Biographical notes about singers.

UDAL: 1922
John Symonds Udal, *Dorsetshire Folk-Lore*: Stephen Austin, Hertford, 1922; J. Stephens-Cox, St Peter Port, Guernsey, 1970. Contains a long 'fore-say' by William Barnes, 'The Dorset Poet'. Like BURNE: 1884 and LEATHER: 1912–70, this is a mixture of material including the words of about 20 songs.

VOCAL LIBRARY: 1822
The Vocal Library: Sir Richard Phillips, London, 1822. Contains words of nearly 2,000 songs, including many without known authors and described as 'the largest collection of English, Scottish and Irish songs ever printed in one volume selected from the best authors between the age of Shakespeare, Jonson and Cowley and that of Dibdin, Wolcot and Moore'.

WHITTAKER: 1921
W. Gillies Whittaker, *North Countrie Ballads, Songs and Pipe-tunes*: Curwen, London, 1921. 47 songs and 11 pipe-tunes. Although stated to be his own personal collection, most of the material had already appeared in other publications. Further information about the musical traditions of N.E. England is given in his *Collected Essays* (Oxford University Press, 1940).

WILLIAMS: 1923
Alfred Owen Williams, *Folk Songs of the Upper Thames*: Duckworth, London, 1923. Over 300 folksongs (words only) noted mainly in Berkshire, Gloucestershire, Oxfordshire and Wiltshire. Interesting introduction about rural life, more fully covered by Williams in *Round About the Upper Thames* (Duckworth, 1922). Further unpublished texts in Swindon Reference Library. See FMJ: 1969 'Alfred Williams: A Symposium'.

BELDEN: 1940
H. M. Belden, *Ballads and Songs Collected by the Missouri Folklore Society*: University Studies XV (No. 1), Columbia, Missouri, USA, 1940.

BREWSTER: 1940
Paul G. Brewster, *Ballads and Songs of Indiana*: University Folklore Publications No. 1, Bloomington, Indiana, USA, 1940.

COX: 1925
John Harrington Cox, *Folk Songs of the South*: Harvard University Press, Cambridge, Mass., USA, 1925. Dover Publications Reprint, New York, 1967 (released 1968). 185 songs collected in West Virginia (29 with tunes). Introduction describes collecting methods and identifies informants. Notes, references to other versions and other data given with texts of songs.

CREIGHTON: 1932
Helen Creighton, *Songs and Ballads from Nova Scotia*: Dent, Toronto, Canada, 1932. Dover Publications Reprint, New York, 1966. 150 songs, gathered mainly in the vicinity of Halifax, written down by the author and afterwards checked with recordings. First of four published collections.

Bibliography

CREIGHTON AND SENIOR: 1950
Helen Creighton and Doreen Senior, *Traditional Songs from Nova Scotia*: Ryerson Press, Toronto, Canada, 1950. 100 songs and 36 ballads collected in the Maritimes with additional variants of both tunes and texts in many instances. An important and well documented collection with versions of many of the songs in this book.

EDDY: 1939
Mary O. Eddy, *Ballads and Songs from Ohio*: J. J. Augustin, New York, 1939.

FLANDERS AND BROWN: 1932
Helen Hartness Flanders and George Brown, *Vermont Folk Songs and Ballads*: Stephen Daye, Brattleboro, Vermont, USA, 1932.

GARDNER AND CHICKERING: 1939
Emelyn E. Gardner and Geraldine J. Chickering, *Ballads and Songs of Southern Michigan*: University Press, Ann Arbor, Michigan, USA, 1939.

GREENLEAF: 1933
Elizabeth Bristol Greenleaf and Grace Yarrow Mansfield, *Ballads and Sea Songs from Newfoundland*: Harvard University Press, Cambridge, Mass., USA, 1933.

HUDSON: 1936
Arthur Palmer Hudson, *Folksongs of Mississippi*: University of N. Carolina, Chapel Hill, N. Carolina, USA, 1936.

JAFL: 1888–
Journal of American Folklore now published by University of Pennsylvania.

KARPELES: 1934/71
Maud Karpeles, *Folksongs from Newfoundland*: Oxford University Press, London, 1934 (2 vols.); Faber & Faber, London, 1971. 30 songs (with piano accompaniments) were published in 1934 and 90 songs, 150 tunes including variants (with no accompaniments) in 1971. All collected during 1929–30.

LINSCOTT: 1939
E. H. Linscott, *Folk Songs of Old New England*: Macmillan, New York, 1939.

LOMAX: 1934
John and Alan Lomax, *American Ballads and Folk Songs*: Macmillan, New York, 1934.

LOMAX: 1960
Alan Lomax, *Folk Songs of North America*: Cassell, London, 1960.

MACKENZIE: 1928
W. Roy Mackenzie, *Ballads and Sea Songs from Nova Scotia*: Harvard University Press, Cambridge, Mass., USA, 1928.

MEREDITH AND ANDERSON: 1967
John Meredith and Hugh Anderson, *Folk Songs of Australia*: Ure Smith, Sydney, 1967.

NEWELL: 1884/1903
W. W. Newell, *Games and Songs of American Children*: Harper Bros., New York, 1884; new and enlarged edition 1903.

PEACOCK: 1965
Kenneth Peacock, *Songs of the Newfoundland Outports*: National Museum of Canada, Ottawa, 1965. 3 vols.

POUND: 1922
Louise Pound, *American Ballads and Songs*: Charles Scribner's Sons, New York, 1922.

SANDBURG: 1927
Carl Sandburg, *The American Songbag*: Harcourt Brace, New York, 1927.

SCARBOROUGH: 1937
Dorothy Scarborough, *A Song Catcher in the Southern Mountains*: Columbia University Press, New York, 1937.

SHARP AND KARPELES: 1917/32
Olive Dame Campbell and Cecil J. Sharp, *English Folk Songs from the Southern Appalachians*: Putnam, New York, 1917. Cecil J. Sharp and Maud Karpeles (2 vols.), Oxford University Press, London, 1932.

STURGIS AND HUGHES: 1919
Edith B. Sturgis and Robert Hughes, *Songs from the Hills of Vermont*: G. Schirmer, New York, 1919.

WHITE: 1928
Newman I. White, *American Negro Folk Songs*: Harvard University Press, Cambridge, Mass., USA, 1928.

WYMAN AND BROCKWAY: 1916
Loraine Wyman and Howard Brockway, *Lonesome Tunes* (*Folk Songs from the Kentucky Mountains*): H. W. Gray, New York, 1916.

XV

Songs of
Newsworthy Sensation

Introduction

Come all you lovers of the fisticuff, attention to my song
For I'll sing to you a verse or two, and it won't detain you long
It's to describe a champion fight, your time I now employ
Which took place between Tom Sayers and the bold Benicia boy

Heenan and Sayers: No. 321

The songs here feature boxing, burglary, drowning, gambling, ghosts, highwaymen, murder, pickpockets, poison and the like. One might say that in the old days these sort of subjects in local folksong provided the role of today's newsfilm. Before the arrival of the cheap newspapers, particularly in the country districts, people depended on the travelling ballad-singers for coverage of sensational events. The balladmongers sang about them at the markets and fairs and they sold broadsheets which gave all the gory details:

They battled on for an hour or more till Heenan was quite blind
And Sayers with a broken arm, such men you seldom find
The people all around they stood amazed, such a fight they never saw
They rushed the ring and stopped the fight and it ended in a draw

Two other examples of British boxing ballads here are: *Donnelly and Cooper* (No. 317) and *Morrissey and the Russian Sailor* (No. 325). In one of our six murder ballads is the gruesome warning given in the ballad based on the famous murder of a girl at Alton in Hampshire in 1867:

Three halfpence the monster gave the children
To go sweetmeats for to buy
My poor Fanny's hand he dragged bewildered
To the hollow as she bitterly did cry

Sweet Fanny Adams: No. 333

The singer's father heard it being sung at a local fair at the time of the murder, and she heard it from him when she was about ten years old!

When the children came home without my Fanny
The neighbours searched the fields and all around
In the hop-ground the head with the eyes out
And the left ear cut off upon the ground

It is interesting how the name of this little murdered girl has now become part of the English language, and, in the process, undergone a change of meaning. After news of the murder spread through England, sailors started to use the term *Sweet Fanny Adams* for any doubtful-looking stew served up to them in the mess. Gradually the term came to be used for a small helping of food and finally the expression 'Sweet F. A.' came to mean literally nothing at all.

The murder of two teenage sisters in Kent in 1856 also made a strong impression on local people, as they are still heard to frighten their children with tales of the murderer:

Early next morning before the break of day
Maria and Sweet Caroline from Dover town did stray
But before they reached to Folkestone, the villain drew a knife
Maria and Sweet Caroline, he took away their lives

The Folkestone Murder: No. 320

hel and John Findlater of Dounby,
Orkney

Photograph: Peter Kennedy

The whole song is cast objectively in the third person, but the last verse is put into the murderer's mouth as an epitaph:

> The dismal bell is tolling, for the scaffold I must prepare
> I trust in Heaven my soul shall rest and meet dear Caroline there
> Now all young men take warning by this sad fate of mine
> To the memory of Maria Beck and lovely Caroline

Oxford is the location for two of the murder ballads. In one the motive is jealousy of a rival at a dance, and the crime *Poison in a Glass of Wine* (No. 329); in the other, a young man, when his true love does not want to conform to his wishes, takes a stick from the hedge and knocks her down; when he finds that she is dead, he throws her into the river:

> It was about three weeks afterwards
> When that pretty fair maid were found
> Come floating by her own mother's door
> In the river near Oxford town

The Oxford Girl: No. 327

Jealousy was also the motive for a murder which took place near a Stonehenge-type stone circle at Stenness in the Orkneys. Two lovers make their marriage vows by joining hands through a hole in the Lover's Stone; a jealous rival follows and stabs the young man and at the same moment his true love sees a vision of her dead lover standing beside her:

> His hand was pointing to the stars
> And his eyes gazed at the light
> And with a smiling countenance
> He vanished from her sight

The Standing Stones: No. 332

One explanation of the last verse of another murder ballad, *Polly Vaughan* (No. 330), is that Polly herself appeared in the court-house as a ghost, whilst another maintains that she recovered from her wound and came to the trial in order to acquit her lover. The story of the ballad is that Jimmy had been out duck-shooting and mistook her for a swan (our version uses the old form 'in the room of a swan'). Jimmy's uncle persuades him not to flee the country, but to stay and face the proceedings; and that is when Polly comes back onto the scene:

> Now the trial came on and Pretty Polly appeared
> Saying: Uncle, dear Uncle, let Jimmy go clear
> For my apron was wrapped round me when you took me for a swan
> And his poor heart lay bleeding for Polly his own

A vision also appears to the sister of Willie Leonard who was drowned in the deep and false waters of *The Lakes of Shallin* (No. 324).

Three Jolly Sportsmen (No. 335) is probably the finest murder ballad in the collection, containing as it does the most dramatic situations and using the utmost economy of words. Three butchers, Gibson, Johnson and Lipskin, are riding home from market with their takings when they hear the pitiful cry of a woman in distress. The first two butchers ride on, advising Johnson to do the same, but he is too much of a gentleman:

> Now Johnson he got off his horse to search the groves all round
> He found a woman, stark naked, with her hair pinned to the ground

The woman claims she has been stripped and robbed, so the gentlemanly Johnson wraps his coat around her:

> Now Johnson he got on his horse and the woman got on behind
> But she clasped her fingers to her ears and she give three warning cries

At that, three 'swaggelling' young highwaymen appear on the scene:

> Now Johnson he drew his glittering sword, and two of them he slayed
> And while he was killing the other one, the woman stabbed him behind

So the woman turns out to be an accomplice, a female highwayman, and, as the last verse of the ballad says:

> She shall be hung in chains of gold, for the murder she hath done
> She hath killed the finest butcher boy that ever the sun shined on

There are four other songs of highwaymen: first the roving Irish outlaw *Brennan's on the Moor* (No. 315); then the Cornishman from *Newlyn Town* (No. 326) who became a highwayman at the age of seventeen and openly robbed lords and ladies in Grosvenor Square until he was caught while at the theatre with his wife in Covent Garden by the first 'gang' of London policemen; then there is the famous *Dick Turpin* (1705-39) who outwitted the lawyer in *Turpin Hero* (No. 336), and finally the female highwayman, *Sylvia* (No. 334), who became a male impersonator and robbed her own highwayman true love just to put him to the test:

> I only did it for to know whether you were a true-lover or no
> But now I've a contented mind, my heart and all, my dear, are thine

It is interesting to find that it is nothing new for men's hairstyles to give rise to trouble with the police. It happens to Duncan Campbell, the Highlander from Argyllshire. He is mistaken for an Irishman from *Erin-go-Bragh* (No. 319), gets into a tussle with a policeman in Edinburgh and hurriedly has to return to the Highlands.

Pickpocketing is the subject of two songs. Our first victim from Belfast, Northern Ireland, is caught out by *The Black Velvet Band* (No. 313), and the second by the young hussy who clatters her high-heeled boots along the *Knickerbocker Line* (No. 323).

Another charged with stealing and hanged at Tyburn in 1701 was the London chimney-sweep, *Jack Hall* (No. 322). Also in trouble was the broken-down gentleman who gambled his money away at *Epsom Races* (No. 318) and even lost his coach-and-six to the bailiffs, whilst a third is in trouble when he meets a lady in the Strand:

> Now all young men take my advice
> And never take a parcel from a lady
> If you do you'll find your mistake
> In the parcel there'll be a baby
> *The Parcel From a Lady*: No. 328

One of the most effective pieces is a political song from Northern Ireland, clearly based on the classical ballad, *The Maid Freed from the Gallows*. Instead of a maid, a young man is condemned and awaiting execution in *Derry Gaol* (No. 316). As he climbs up to the gallows, he speaks to each of his relations in turn and then to the clergyman who takes confession, in order to drag out the time:

> What keeps my love, she's so long a-coming?
> Or what detains her so long from me?
> Or does she think it a shame or scandal
> To see me die on the gallows tree?
>
> He looked around and he saw her coming
> As she rode swifter than the wynd
> Come down, come down, off that weary gallows
> For I bear pardon all from the Queen

313 THE BLACK VELVET BAND

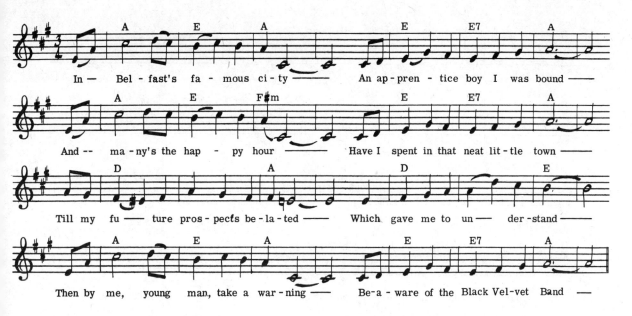

In — Bel-fast's fa - mous ci - ty —— An ap - pren - tice boy I was bound ——

And — ma-ny's the hap - py hour —— Have I spent in that neat lit - tle town ——

Till my fu —— ture pros - pects be - la - ted —— Which gave me to un —— der -stand ——

Then by me, young man, take a war - ning —— Be-a - ware of the Black Vel-vet Band ——

1 In Belfast's famous city
   An apprentice boy I was bound
   And many's the happy hour
   Have I spent in that neat little town
   Till my future prospect's belated
   Which gave me to understand
   Then by me, young man, take a warning
   Be-a-ware of the Black Velvet Band

2 O, one evening late as I rambled
   Not thinking of long for to stay
   Till I met with a gay young deceiver
   Come a-tripping across the pathway
   O, her eyes they shone like diamonds
   And I thought her the pride of the land
   And her hair it hung down o'er her shoulders
   And tied in a black velvet band

3 O, one evening a flash-man, a watch-man
   She happened to meet on the sly
   I could tell that her mind it was altered
   By the roll of her dark eye
   O, that watch she took from his pocket
   She slipped it right into my hand
   Then she gave me in charge to the policeman
   Bad luck to the Black Velvet Band

4 Now before the Lord Mayor I was taken
   My 'guilty' they prov-ed quite plain
   And he said: If I was not mistaken
   I should have to cross the salt main
   Now it's sixteen long years have they gave me
   To plough upon Van Diemen's Land
   And it's far from my friends and relations
   My curse to the Black Velvet Band

314 BLACKBERRY FOLD

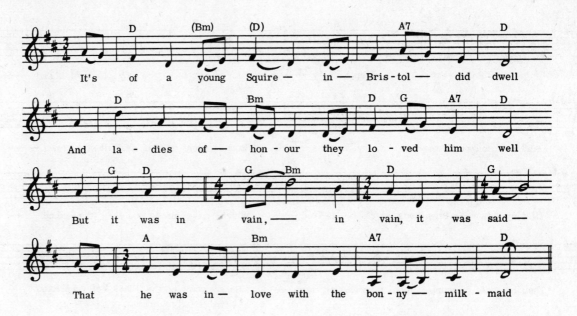

It's of a young Squire — in — Bris-tol — did dwell

And la-dies of — hon-our they lo-ved him well

But it was in vain, — in vain, it was said —

That he was in — love with the bon-ny — milk-maid

1 It's of a young Squire in Bristol did dwell
And ladies of honour they lov-ed him well
But it was in vain, in vain, it was said
That he was in love with the bonny milk-maid

2 As the Squire and his sisters all sat in the hall
And as they sat talking they heard someone call
O hark, said the Squire, to that sweet morning song
Pretty Betsy, the milk-maid, came tripping along

3 Do you want any milk, sir? pretty Betsy did say
O yes, said the Squire, step in, pretty maid
It is your fine body I do so much adore
Such a love as I never endured before

4 Oh no, sir, said Betsy, how can you say so?
In love with the milk-maid and in such poor clothes
For there are fine bodies all built up for you
Not to wed a poor milk-maid from the side of a cow

5 Then the ring from his finger he then instantly drew
And right in the middle he broke it quite through
One part he gave to her, as I have been told
And they both walked together down Blackberry Fold

6 As they were a-walking this Squire did say
There is one thing I must warn you, my sweet pretty
If ever you deny me in this open field   [maid
With my glittering sword I will cause you to yield

7 Oh no, sir, said Betsy, pray let me go free
I will have you now play no such games upon me
I love my sweet virtue as I love my dear life
And out of her bosom drew a long dagger-knife

8 Then out of her bosom this dagger she drew
And into his body she pierced it quite through
Then home to her master with tears in her eyes
Saying: I've wounded the Squire, I'm afraid he will
die

9 A carriage was fetched and the Squire sent home
A doctor was sent for, to heal up his wound
His wound being dressed and in bed he did lay
O Betsy, O Betsy, 'twas all he could say

10 Now Betsy was sent for, and shivering went on
I'm sorry, said Betsy, for what I have done
The wound that you gave me was all my own fault
So don't let such things still remain in your thought

11 Now a parson was sent for this couple to wed
So happy they joined in their sweet marriage bed
So come, maids, prove a virgin, be you ever so poor
For 'twill make you a lady ten thousand times o'er

315 BRENNAN'S ON THE MOOR

It's of a fear-less high-way-man a sto-ry I will tell

His name is Bil-ly Bren-nan, in Ire-land he did dwell

And on the Lim-wood Moun-tains he com-menced his wild car-eer

Where ma-ny a wealth-y gen-tle-man be-fore him shook with fear

Cry-ing: Bren-nan's on the moor, Bren-nan's on the moor

So bold and un-daun-ted stood Bill Bren-nan on the moor

1 It's of a fearless highwayman a story I will tell
   His name is Billy Brennan, in Ireland he did dwell
   And on the Limwood Mountains he commenced his wild career
   Where many a wealthy gentleman before him shook with fear
   Crying: Brennan's on the moor, Brennan's on the moor
   So bold and undaunted stood Bill Brennan on the moor

2 A brace of loaded pistols he carried night and day
   He never robbed a poor man upon the King's highway
   But what he'd taken from the rich like Turpin and Black Bess
   He always would divide it with the widow in distress

3 One day he met a packman, his name was Hillier Brown
   They travelled on together till day began to dawn
   The pedlar seeing his money gone, likewise his watch and chain
   He at once encountered Brennan and robbed him back again

4 Now Brennan seeing the pedlar was as good a man as he
   Engaged him on the highway his companion for to be
   The pedlar threw away his pack without any more delay
   And proved a faithful com-e-rade until his dying day ➝

5 One day as Billy he sat down upon the King's highway
He met the Squire of Cashel a mile outside the town
The Squire he knew his features; I think, young man, said he
Your name is Billy Brennan, you must come along with me

6 Now it happened Billy's wife had gone to town provisions for to buy
And when she met her Billy, she began to sob and cry
He said: Give me the tenpence and as quick as Billy spoke
She handed him a blunderbuss from underneath her clothes

7 Now with this loaded blunderbuss the truth I will unfold
He made the Squire to tremble and robbed him of his gold
One hundred pounds was offered for his apprehension there
And with his horse and saddle to the mountains did repair

8 Now Brennan and his com-e-rades, knowing that they was betrayed
With the mounted cavalry a noble battle made
He lost his foremost finger which was shot off by a ball
So Bill Brennan and his com-e-rade was taken after all

9 Now they was taken prisoners and in irons bound
Conveyed to Clonmel Gaol, strong walls did them surround
They was tried and then found guilty and the judge made this reply
For robbing on the King's highway you're both condemned to die

10 Now farewell unto my wife and to my children three
And to my a-ged father who may shed tears for me
And to my loving mother who tore her grey locks and cried
O I wish, young Billy Brennan, in your cradle you had died

316 DERRY GAOL

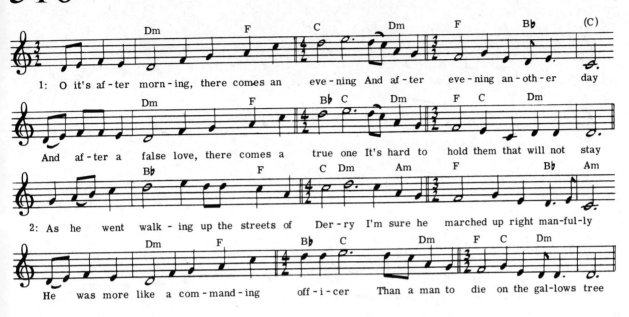

1: O it's af-ter morn-ing, there comes an eve-ning And af-ter eve-ning an-oth-er day

And af-ter a false love, there comes a true one It's hard to hold them that will not stay

2: As he went walk-ing up the streets of Der-ry I'm sure he marched up right man-ful-ly

He was more like a com-mand-ing off-i-cer Than a man to die on the gal-lows tree

1 O it's after morning, there comes an evening
And after evening another day
And after a false love, there comes a true one
It's hard to hold them that will not stay

2 As he went walking up the streets of Derry
I'm sure he marched up right manfully
He was more like a commanding officer
Than a man to die on the gallows tree

3 The very first step he went up the ladder
His blooming colours began to fail
With heavy sighs and with dismal cries
Is there no releasement from Derry Gaol?

4 The very next step he went up the ladder
His a-ged mother was standing by
Come here, come here, my old a-ged mother
And speak one word to me before I die

5 The very next step he went up the ladder
His a-ged father was standing by
Come here, come here, my old a-ged father
And speak one word to me before I die

6 The very next step he went up the ladder
His loving clergyman was standing by
Stand back, stand back, you old prosecutors
I'll let you see that he will not die

7 I'll let you see that you dare not hang him
Till his confession unto me is done
And after that, that you dare not hang him
Till within ten minutes of the setting sun

8 What keeps my love, she's so long a-coming?
Or what detains her so long from me?
Or does she think it a shame or scandal
To see me die on the gallows tree?

9 He looked around and he saw her coming
As she rode swifter than the wynd
Come down, come down, off that weary gallows
For I bear pardon all from the Queen

10 Come down, come down, off that weary gallows
For I bear pardon all from the Queen
I'll let them see that they dare not hang you
And I'll crown my Willie with a bunch of green

317 DONNELLY AND COOPER

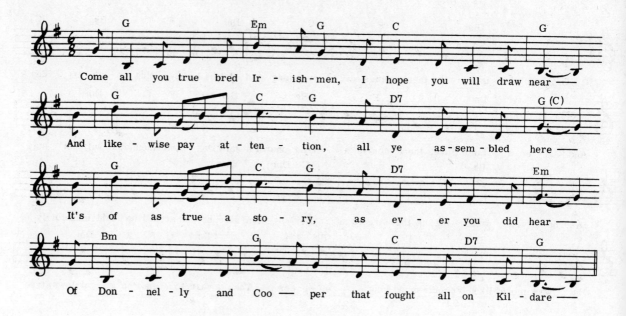

1 Come all you true bred Irishmen, I hope you will draw near
  And likewise pay attention, all ye assembled here
  It's of as true a story, as ever you did hear
  Of Donnelly and Cooper that fought all on Kildare

2 It was on the third of June, me boys, the challenge was sent o'er
  From Britannia to old Grania for to rise their sons once more
  To renew the satisfaction and credit to recall
  For they're all in deep distraction, since Donnelly conquered all

3 The challenge was accepted of the heroes to prepare
  To meet old Captain Kelly on the Curragh of Kildare
  The Englishmen bet ten to one that day against poor Dan
  But such odds as this could not dismiss the blood of our Irishman

4 Now when these two oul' champions were stripped off in the ring
  They were fully determined upon each other's blood to spill
  From six to nine they parried the time, till Donnelly knocked him down
  And now Grania smiled: Well done, my child, you win ten thousand pound

5 The very next round that Cooper fought he knocked down Donnelly
  But Dan likewise being of true game he arose most furiously
  Right active then was Cooper, he knocked Donnelly down again
  Those Englishmen they gave three cheers: The battle's all in vain

6 Long life to brave Miss Kelly, she appeared then on the Plain
  She boldly stepped up to the ring, saying: Dan, what do you mean?
  Ah, Dan, my boy, brave Dan, says she, an Irish lad, says she
  My whole estate is on you bet, to stay brave Donnelly

7 As Donnelly he spoke to her, as he lay on the ground
   And while this English champion kept prancing all around
   Saying: Do not fret, for I am not bate, although I got two falls
   I'll let him know before I go, I'll make him pay for all

8 Then Donnelly got up again and he meeting with great might
   We'll stagnate those nobles too, he continued on the fight
   While Cooper stood his own defence, but exertion proved in vain
   When he soon received a temple-blow which hurled him o'er the rail

9 You sons of old Britannia, your boasting now recall
   Since Cooper now by Donnelly has met his sad downfall
   Of eleven rounds took nine knock-downs besides broke his jaw-bone
   Shake hands, says she, brave Donnelly, the battle is your own

318 EPSOM RACES

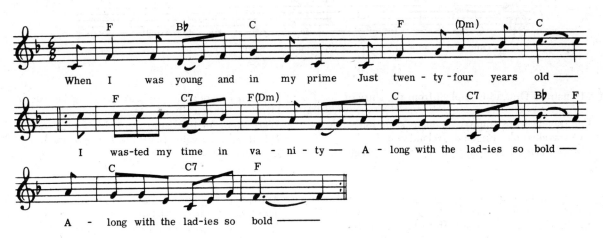

1 When I was young and in my prime
   Just twenty-four years old
   I wasted my time in vanity
   Along with the ladies so bold
   Along with the ladies so bold
   I wasted my time in vanity
   Along with the ladies so bold
   Along with the ladies so bold

2 With silver buckles all round my wrist
   And cane all in my hand
   It's over the nation I did go
   Like a farmer's son so grand
   Like a farmer's son so grand

3 I bought a coach and six bay-horses
   And servants to wait on me
   For I did intend my money to spend
   And that you will plain-lie see

4 I steered my coach to Epsom races
   All on one Derby Day
   'Twas there I lost ten thousand pounds
   All in the delights of one day

5 I brought my coach back home again
   Laden down with grief and woe
   For now I'm a broken-down gentleman
   And that's not the worst of it all

6 The landlord came down for his rent
   And bailiffs he brought three
   They took away my coach and six
   And swore they would have me

7 My wife at home she does lament
   And the children round her cry
   For to think that I in gaol may lie
   Until the day that I die

319 ERIN-GO-BRAGH

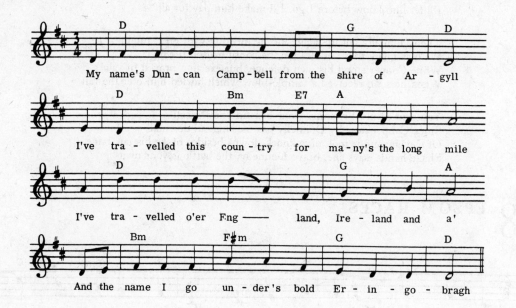

My name's Dun-can Camp-bell from the shire of Ar-gyll

I've tra-velled this coun-try for ma-ny's the long mile

I've tra-velled o'er Eng———land, Ire-land and a'

And the name I go un-der's bold Er-in-go-bragh

1 My name's Duncan Campbell from the shire of
                              Argyll
  I've travelled this country for many's the long mile
  I've travelled o'er England, Ireland and a'
  And the name I go under's bold Erin-go-bragh

2 One night in Auld Reekie as I walked doon the street
  A saucy policeman I chanced for to meet
  He glowered in my face and he gave me some jaw
  Says: When came you over from Erin-go-bragh?

3 I am not a Paddy though through Ireland I've been
  Nor am I a Paddy though Ireland I've seen
  Although I were a Paddy that's nothing ava
  There's many the bold hero from Erin-go-bragh

4 I know you're a Pat by the cut of your hair
  But you all turn to Scotchmen as soon as you're here
  You have left your own country for breaking the law
  We are seizing all strangers from Erin-go-bragh

5 Though I were a Pat and you knew't to be true
  Or were I the devil or what's that to you?
  Were it not for the baton you hold in your paw
  I'll show you a game played in Erin-go-bragh

6 Then with a switch of blackthorn I held in my fist
  Around his big body I made it to twist
  The blood from his knappers I quickly did draw
  He paid stock and interest for Erin-go-bragh

7 The people came round me like a flock of wild geese
  Says: Stop that, you rascal, you'll kill our police
  For every three'n I had, I'm sure he had twa
  It was very tight times for old Erin-go-bragh

8 Then I came to a wee boatie that sailed on the Forth
  I packed up my oars and I steered for the North
  Farewell to Auld Reekie, the policemen and a'
  May the devil be with you, bold Erin-go-bragh

9 Come all you brave fellows that hears o' this song
  I don't care a farthing to where you belong
  For I'm frae Argyllshire in the Highlands sae braw
  But I ne'er tak' it ill being called: Erin-go-bragh

320 THE FOLKESTONE MURDER

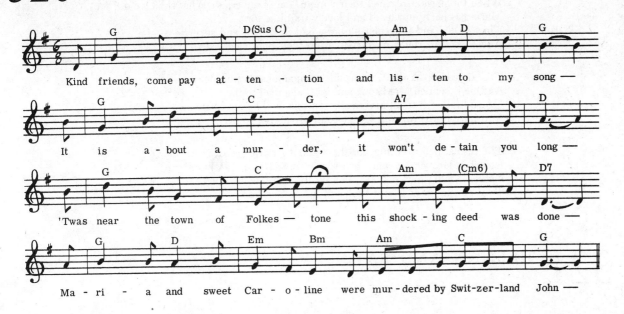

Kind friends, come pay at-ten-tion and lis-ten to my song —
It is a-bout a mur-der, it won't de-tain you long —
'Twas near the town of Folkes-tone this shock-ing deed was done —
Ma-ri-a and sweet Car-o-line were mur-dered by Swit-zer-land John —

1 Kind friends, come pay attention and listen to my song
It is about a murder, it won't detain you long
'Twas near the town of Folkestone this shocking deed was done
Maria and sweet Caroline were murdered by Switzerland John

2 He came unto their parents' house at nine o'clock one night
But little did poor Caroline think he owed her any spite
Will you walk with me, dear Caroline? the murderer did say
And she agreed to accompany him to Shorncliffe Camp next day

3 Said the mother to the daughter: You'd better stay at home
It is not fit for you to go with that young man alone
You'd better take your sister to go along with you
Then I have no objection, dear daughter, you may go

4 Early next morning before the break of day
Maria and sweet Caroline from Dover town did stray
But before they reached to Folkestone, the villain drew a knife
Maria and sweet Caroline, he took away their lives

5 Down on the ground those sisters fell, all in their blooming years
For mercy cried: We're innocent, their eyes were filled with tears
He plunged the knife into their breasts, those lovely breasts so deep
He robbed them of their own sweet lives and left them there to sleep

6 Early next morning their bodies they were found
At a lonely spot called Steady Hole a-bleeding on the ground
And if you go unto that spot these letters you will find
Cut deeply in the grass so green: Maria and Caroline ⟶

7 When the news it reached their parents' ears they cried: What shall we do?
Maria has been murdered and lovely Caroline too
They pulled and tore their old grey hair in sorrow and surprise
And tears they rolled in torrents from their poor aged eyes

8 This murderer has been taken, his companions do him deny
And he is sent to Maidstone and is condemned to die
He said farewell to all his friends: In this world I am alone
And have to die for murder far from my native home

9 The dismal bell is tolling, for the scaffold I must prepare
I trust in Heaven my soul shall rest and meet dear Caroline there
Now all young men take warning by this sad fate of mine
To the memory of Maria Beck and lovely Caroline

321 HEENAN AND SAYERS

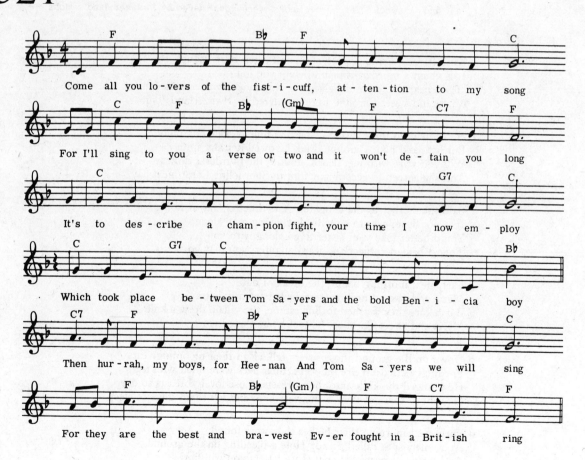

Come all you lo-vers of the fist-i-cuff, at-ten-tion to my song

For I'll sing to you a verse or two and it won't de-tain you long

It's to des-cribe a cham-pion fight, your time I now em-ploy

Which took place be-tween Tom Sa-yers and the bold Ben-i-cia boy

Then hur-rah, my boys, for Hee-nan And Tom Sa-yers we will sing

For they are the best and bra-vest Ev-er fought in a Brit-ish ring

1 Come all you lovers of the fisticuff, attention to my song
   For I'll sing to you a verse or two and it won't detain you long
   It's to describe a champion fight, your time I now employ
   Which took place between Tom Sayers and the bold Benicia boy
   Then hurrah, my boys, for Heenan
   And Tom Sayers we will sing
   For they are the best and bravest
   Ever fought in a British ring

2 There was not a man in Europe with Sayers could contend
   Till Heenan from America a challenge he did send
   Said Heenan: I'll fight any man that stands on England's ground
   For any sum or wager up to a thousand pounds

3 When Tom he heard the challenge he said: O let him come
   For I know he's only boasting for a bit of Yankee fun
   But Erin's son did fearless come across the Atlantic wave
   To battle with our champion, the bravest of the brave

4 It was on the morning of the fight Tom's second he did say
   Remember Evan Jones, my boy, and do your best today
   I'll do my best to win, said Tom, and that you know quite well
   For the man who takes my belt from me, will take my life as well

5 It was hit and stop and jab and cut, till Sayers he let go
   Right on to Heenan's nasal and he made the claret flow
   Then out cried bold Jack Heenan: I owe you many a score
   And I'll pay you back with interest in a couple of moments more

6 The very next round after Jack Heenan gave a spring
   The like was never seen before inside of a British ring
   Our champion drops, though he was shot, and lay there on the ground
   And out cries bold Jack Heenan: I claim the first knock-down

7 They battled on for an hour or more till Heenan was quite blind
   And Sayers with a broken arm, such men you seldom find
   The people all around they stood amazed, such a fight they never saw
   They rushed the ring and stopped the fight and it ended in a draw

8 All honour to Jack Heenan, likewise our champion brave
   And we hope a good subscription to the stranger will be made
   And if these two should battle for the champion belt again
   We want no favours to be shown but let the best man win

322 JACK HALL

O my name it is Jack Hall, chim-ney sweep, chim-ney sweep

O my name it is Jack Hall, chim-ney sweep

My name it is Jack Hall and I've robbed both great and small

And my neck shall pay for all when I die, when I die

And my neck shall pay for all when I die

1 O my name it is Jack Hall, chimney sweep, chimney sweep
O my name it is Jack Hall, chimney sweep
My name it is Jack Hall and I've robbed both great and small
And my neck shall pay for all when I die, when I die
And my neck shall pay for all when I die

2 I have candles, lily-white, hanging high, hanging high
I have candles, lily-white, hanging high
I've candles, lily-white, and I stole them all by night
And they'll fill my room with light till I die, till I die
And they'll fill my room with light till I die

3 I have twenty bullocks in store, that's not all, that's not all
I have twenty bullocks in store, that's not all
I've twenty bullocks in store and I'm up for twenty more
Every rogue shall have his lot, so shall I, so shall I
Every rogue shall have his lot, so shall I

4 I have furnished all my rooms, lot by lot, lot by lot
I have furnished all my rooms, lot by lot
I've furnished all my rooms with black brushes and black brooms
And besides a chimney pot which I stole, which I stole
And besides a chimney pot which I stole

5 They tell me that in gaol I'll go dry, I'll go dry
They tell me that in gaol I'll go dry
They tell me that in gaol I shall drink no more small ale
But be hanged if ever I fail till I die, till I die
But be hanged if ever I fail till I die

6 I rode up Tedburn Hill in a cart, in a cart
I rode up Tedburn Hill in a cart
I rode up Tedburn Hill, there I stopped and made my will
Saying the best of friends must part, so must I, so must I
Saying the best of friends must part, so must I

7 Up the ladder I did grope, that's no joke, that's no joke
Up the ladder I did grope, that's no joke
Up the ladder I did grope and the hangman pulled the rope
But the devil of a word I spoke, coming down, coming down
But the devil of a word I spoke, coming down

323   THE KNICKERBOCKER LINE

O my love she was a stit-cher,—— a tai-lor-ess by trade——

And ma-ny a fan-cy waist-coat for me my love has made——

She gets up in the morn-ing and stit-ches a-way till nine——

Then her high-heeled boots go clat-ter-ing down the Knick-er-bock-er line——

Watch her, trail her, pipe her as she goes With her high-heeled boots and her pa-tent

lea-ther toes That she was one of those flash girls I soon found out in time When her

1 O my love she was a stitcher, a tailoress by trade
And many a fancy waistcoat for me my love has made
She gets up in the morning and stitches away till nine
Then her high-heeled boots go clattering down the Knickerbocker Line

Watch her, trail her, pipe her as she goes
With her high-heeled boots and her patent leather toes
That she was one of those flash girls I soon found out in time
When her high-heeled boots went clattering down the Knickerbocker Line ➞

2 When first I saw this pretty girl, in High Street she did dwell
She really took my breath away, she was such a swell
She'd a dandy hat with feathers in, and didn't she cut a shine
She looked so neat as she clattered her feet on the Knickerbocker Line

3 I took her up to town one day, to the the-ai-ter we did go
To see them all a-staring at her, you'd think she was the show
When coming out she stopped me, and particular asked the time
Then skidaddled with my ticker down the Knickerbocker Line

4 When I found my ticker gone, I raised a hue and cry
I called out to the bobby as she went clattering by
The bobby said: Now come with me, and he marched her off so fine
Saying: For three months you must skiffle off the Knickerbocker Line

324 THE LAKES OF SHALLIN

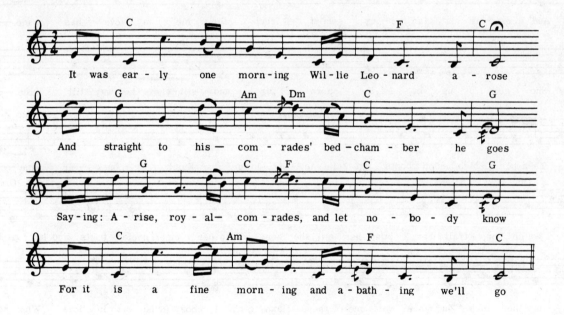

It was ear-ly one morn-ing Wil-lie Leo-nard a-rose
And straight to his — com-rades' bed-cham-ber he goes
Say-ing: A-rise, roy-al— com-rades, and let no-bo-dy know
For it is a fine morn-ing and a-bath-ing we'll go

1 It was early one morning Willie Leonard arose
And straight to his comrades' bed-chamber he goes
Saying: Arise, royal comrades, and let nobody know
For it is a fine morning and a-bathing we'll go

2 They walked and they talked, till they came to a lane
And the first man they met there was the keeper of game
He advised them to turn back and not venture in
For there's deep and false waters on the lakes of Shallin

3 Young Willie stripped naked and he swam the lake round
He swam foreign islands but not for dry ground
Saying: Comrades, royal comrades, I am now getting weak
And these were the last words Willie Leonard did speak

4 It was early that morning his sister arose
And straight to her mother's bed-chamber she goes
Saying: Mother, dear mother, I had a sad dream
That young Willie was floating on a watery main

5 It was early that morning his mother went there
With a-wringing her fingers and a-tearing her hair
Saying: Where was he drowned, was nobody there
That would venture their life for my one only boy?

6 It was early that evening his uncle went there
He rode round the lake like a man in despair
Saying: Where was he drowned or did he fall in?
My cursed life for ever on the lakes of Shallin

7 The day of the funeral it was a sad sight
Four-and-twenty young men and they all dressed in white
They bore him on their shoulders and to rest him did lay
Saying: Farewell to you, Willie, and they all walked away

325 MORRISSEY AND THE RUSSIAN SAILOR

Come — all you gal-lant Ir-ish-men wher-ev-er you may be

I hope you'll pay at-ten-tion and lis-ten un-to me

I'll sing a-bout a bat-tle that took place the oth-er day

Be — tween a Roos-ian sail-or and gal-lant Mor-ris-sey

1 Come all you gallant Irishmen wherever you may be
I hope you'll pay attention and listen unto me
I'll sing about a battle that took place the other day
Between a Roosian sailor and gallant Morrissey

2 'Twas in T'erra del Fuego in South Amerikay
The Roosian challenged Morrissey and these words to him did say
I hear you are a fighting man and wear a belt I see
Indeed I wish you would consent to have a round with me

3 Then out spoke brave Morrissey with heart both brave and true
I am a valiant Irishman that never was subdued
For I can dare the Yankee, the Saxon bull and bear
In honour of old Paddy's land I still the laurel wear

4 Those words enraged the Roosian all upon the Yankee land
To think he should be beaten by any Irish man
Says he: You are too light in frame and that without mistake
I'll have you to resign the belt or else your life I'll take

5 To fight upon the tenth of March those heroes did agree
And thousands came from everywhere this battle for to see
The English and the Russians their hearts were filled with glee
They swore the Roosian sailor would kill brave Morrissey

6 These heroes stepped into the ring most gallant to be seen
  And Morrissey put on the belt bound round with shamrock green
  Full sixty thousand dollars then as you may plainly see
  Was to be the champion's prize for him who'd gain the victory

7 They shook hands and walked around the ring commencing then to fight
  It filled each Irish heart with pride for to behold the sight
  The Roosian he floored Morrissey up to the eleventh round
  With Yankee, Russian, Saxon cheers the valley did resound

8 A minute and a half he lay before that he could rise
  The word went all about the field: He's dead, were all their cries
  But Morrissey worked manfully and rising from the ground
  From then unto the twentieth round the Roosian he put down

9 The Irish offered four to one that day upon the grass
  No sooner said than taken up and down they brought the cash
  They parried away without delay to the twenty-second round
  When Morrissey received a blow that brought him to the ground

10 Up to the thirty-seventh round 'twas fall and fall about
  Which made the foreign tyrants to keep a sharp look-out
  The Roosian called his seconds for to have a glass of wine
  Our Irish hero smiled and said: This battle will be mine

11 The thirty-eighth round decided all, the Roosian felt the smart
  And Morrissey with a dreadful blow struck the Roosian on the heart
  The Doctor he was called in to open up a vein
  He said: It was quite useless for he'll never fight again

12 Our hero conquered Thompson and the Yankee Clipper too
  The Benicia Boy and Sheppard he proudly did subdue
  So let us fill our flowing glass and here is health galore
  To noble Johnny Morrissey and Paddies evermore

326 NEWLYN TOWN

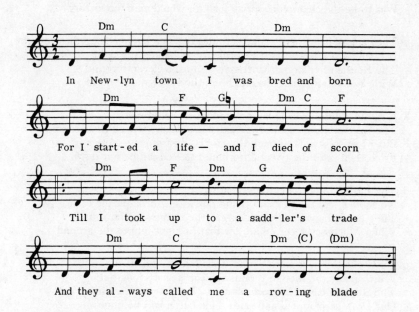

In New-lyn town I was bred and born

For I start-ed a life — and I died of scorn

Till I took up to a sadd-ler's trade

And they al-ways called me a rov-ing blade

1 In Newlyn town I was bred and born
   For I started a life and I died of scorn
   Till I took up to a saddler's trade
   And they always called me a roving blade
   Till I took up to a saddler's trade
   And they always called me a roving blade

2 Now at sweet seventeen I did take a wife
   And I loved her dearly as I love my life
   And to maintain her most bold and gay
   Robbing I went on the King's highway

3 I robbed Lord Golden I do declare
   Lady Mansfield in Grosvenor Square
   For I closed the shutters and bid them: Good night
   Marched home with gold to my heart's delight

4 To Covent Garden I went straight way
   Me and my wife we went to the play
   Till Fieldmen's gang they did me pursue
   Taken I was by that curs-ed crew

5 My father cried he was undone
   My mother she wept for her darling son
   My wife she tore of her golden hair
   Saying: What shall I do now I'm in despair?

6 Now I've six big men to bear my pall
   Give them white gloves and white ribbons all
   I've six highwaymen for to carry me
   Give them broadswords and sweet liberty

7 And now I am dead and in my grave
   The grass grows over me in great big blades
   But now I am dead they can speak the truth
   Here lays a wild and wicked youth

327 THE OXFORD GIRL

I fell in love with an Ox - ford girl
She'd a dark and a roll — ing eye
And I feeled too a - shamed to mar — ry her
She — being too young — and — shy

1 I fell in love with an Oxford girl
   She'd a dark and a rolling eye
   And I feeled too ashamed to marry her
   She being too young and shy

2 I went along to her sister's house
   About eight o'clock that night
   And little did I realize
   I'd show her any spite

3 I asked her if she'd take a walk
   Through the fields and meadows gay
   And there I told her tales of love
   And we fixed the wedding day

4 I catched fast hold of her lily-white hands
   And I kissed both cheek and chin
   And I had no thought of murdering her
   And yet she wouldn't give in

5 I pulled a hedge-stick all from the hedge
   And I gent-lie knocked her down
   And the blood from that poor innocent girl
   Come trickling on the ground

6 I catched fast hold of her curly curly locks
   And I dragged her to the brim
   Until I came to a deep river side
   And I gent-lie flung her in

7 Look how she goes, look how she flows
   She's a-floating by the tide
   And instead of her having a watery grave
   She ought to have been my bride

8 I went all home to my uncle's house
   About ten o'clock that night
   My uncle he jumped out from bed
   And he went to light the light

9 I asked him for a candle
   To light me up to bed
   I asked him for a handkerchief
   To bind my aching head

10 He answered me and he cross-questioned me
   What has stained my hands and clothes
   And the answer that I gave to him
   I'd been bleeding from the nose

11 It was about three weeks afterwards
   When that pretty fair maid were found
   Come floating by her own mother's door
   In the river near Oxford town

12 The judges and the jurymen
   On me they did all agree
   For the murdering of that Oxford girl
   It's hang-ed I must be

328 THE PARCEL FROM A LADY

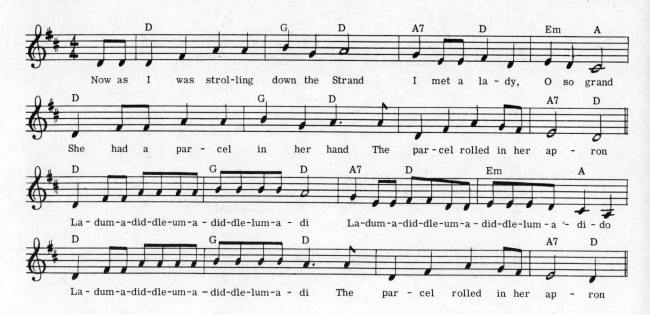

Now as I was strol-ling down the Strand   I met a la-dy, O so grand

She had a par-cel in her hand   The par-cel rolled in her ap-ron

La-dum-a-did-dle-um-a-did-dle-lum-a-di   La-dum-a-did-dle-um-a-did-dle-lum-a-di-do

La-dum-a-did-dle-um-a-did-dle-lum-a-di   The par-cel rolled in her ap-ron

1 Now as I was strolling down the Strand
I met a lady, O so grand
She had a parcel in her hand
The parcel rolled in her apron
La-dum-a-diddle-um-a-diddle-lum-a-di
La-dum-a-diddle-um-a-diddle-lum-a-di-do
La-dum-a-diddle-um-a-diddle-lum-a-di
The parcel rolled in her apron

2 She said: Young man, would you be so kind
As to take this parcel for to mind
While I go my sister for to find?
And she handed me the parcel in her apron

3 Now I waited there for an hour or more
Until my arms grew very sore
So I placed the parcel against the door
A parcel rolled in her apron

4 It was then that I heard something squall
That came from something very small
It came from the parcel against the door
The parcel rolled in her apron

5 I opened the parcel and to my surprise
'Twas there I saw two streaming eyes
And you can imagine my surprise
'Twas a baby rolled in her apron

6 Now all young men take my advice
And never take a parcel from a lady
If you do you'll find your mistake
In the parcel there'll be a baby

329 POISON IN A GLASS OF WINE

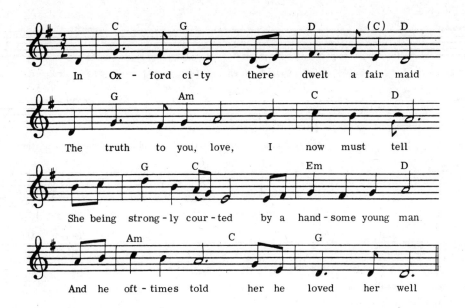

In Ox - ford ci - ty there dwelt a fair maid

The truth to you, love, I now must tell

She being strong - ly cour - ted by a hand - some young man

And he oft - times told her he loved her well

1 In Oxford city there dwelt a fair maid
The truth to you, love, I now must tell
She being strongly courted by a handsome young
And he oft-times told her he loved her well [man

2 He loved her dearly all at a distance
He oft-times told her not to be so fond
And he oft-times told her that he would not leave
Whilst walking down by a shady strand   [her

3 To a dance-house we were invited
And to a dance-house we both did go
When another young man soon followed after
For to prove this young girl's overthrow

4 If she danced all with this young man
Jealousy soon filled his wicked mind
You destroyed the life of a charming young girl
And for that young man she being inclined

5 He went outside, he prepared a poison
He mixed it up with a glass of wine
And he gave it unto his own true-lover
And she drank it up with a willing smile

6 She had not long this liquor taken
Saying: Take me home, my true-love, cried she
O the glass of wine you have lately give me
It has made me feel ill quite inwardly

7 All the same, love, you drank, my darling
All the same, love, as well as thee
In each other's arms we'll die together
Be aware, fair maids, of cruel jealousy

330 POLLY VAUGHAN

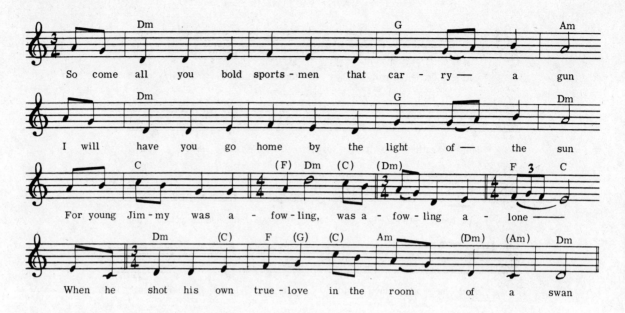

So come all you bold sports-men that car-ry — a gun

I will have you go home by the light of — the sun

For young Jim-my was a-fow-ling, was a-fow-ling a-lone —

When he shot his own true-love in the room of a swan

1 So come all you bold sportsmen that carry a gun
  I will have you go home by the light of the sun
  For young Jimmy was a-fowling, was a-fowling alone
  When he shot his own true-love in the room of a swan

2 So then first he went to her, and found it was she
  He was shaking and tremb-e-ling, his eyes scarce could see
  So now you are dead, love, and your sorrows are o'er
  Fare thee well, my dear Polly, I shall see you no more

3 Then home went young Jimmer with his dog and his gun
  Saying: Uncle, dear Uncle, have you heard what I've done?
  Cur-sed be this old gunsmith that made me this gun
  For I've shot my own true-love in the room of a swan

4 Then out come bold Uncle with his locks hanging grey
  Saying: Jimmer, dear Jimmer, don't you run away
  Don't you leave your own count-e-rie till the trial comes on
  For you ne'er shall be hang-ed for the crime you has done

5 Now the trial came on and Pretty Polly appeared
  Saying: Uncle, dear Uncle, let Jimmy go clear
  For my apron was wrapped round me when he took me for a swan
  And his poor heart lay bleeding for Polly his own

331 SPENCER THE ROVER

These words were com - pos - ed by — Spen - cer the ro — ver

Who tra - velled Great Bri - tain and most parts of Wales

He had been so re — duc — ed which caused great con - fus — ion

And — that was the rea - son he — went on the roam

1 These words were compos-ed by Spencer the rover
Who travelled Great Britain and most parts of Wales
He had been so reduc-ed which caused great confusion
And that was the reason he went on the roam

2 In Yorkshire, near Rotherham, he had been on his rambles
Being weary of travelling, he sat down to rest
At the foot of yonder mountain there runs a clear fountain
With bread and cold water, he himself did refresh

3 It tasted more sweeter than the gold he had wasted
More sweeter than honey and gave more content
But the thoughts of his babies, lamenting their father
Brought tears in his eyes, which made him lament

4 The night fast approaching, to the woods he resorted
With woodbine and ivy, his bed for to make
There he dreamt about sighing, lamenting and crying
Go home to your family and rambling forsake

5 On the fifth of November, I've reason to remember
When first he arriv-ed home to his family and wife
They stood so surpris-ed when first he arriv-ed
To behold such a stranger, once more in their sight

6 His children came around him with their prittle-prattling stories
With their prittle-prattling stories to drive care away
Now they are united, like birds of one feather
Like bees in one hive, contented they'll be

7 So now he is a-living in his cottage contented
With woodbine and roses growing all around the door
He's as happy as those that's got thousands of riches
Contented he'll stay and go a-rambling no more

332 THE STANDING STONES

In one of these lone Ork - ney Isles There dwelled a maid - en fair

Her — cheeks were red and her eyes were blue She had yel - low cur — ling hair

1 In one of these lone Orkney Isles
    There dwelled a maiden fair
    Her cheeks were red and her eyes were blue
    She had yellow curling hair

2 Which caught the eye and then the heart
    Of one who could never be
    A lover of so true a maid
    Or fair a form as she

3 Across that lake in Sandwick
    Dwelled a youth she held most true
    And ever since her infancy
    He had watched those eyes so blue

4 The land runs out into the sea
    It's a narrow neck of land
    Where weird and grim the Standing Stones
    In a circle there they stand

5 One bonny moonlight Christmas Eve
    They met at that sad place
    With her heart in glee and the beams o' love
    Were shining on her face

6 When her lover came and he grasped her hand
    And what loving words they said
    They talked of future's happy days
    As through the Stones they strayed

7 They walked towards the Lovers' Stone
    And through it passed their hands
    They plighted there a constant troth
    Sealed by love's steadfast bands

8 He kissed his maid and he then watched her
That lonely bridge go o'er
For little, little did he think
He wouldn't see his darling more

9 He turned his face toward his home
That home he never did see
And you shall have the story
As it was told to me

10 When a form upon him sprang
With dagger gleaming bright
It pierced his heart and his dying screams
Disturbed the silent night

11 The murderer was the one who wished
That maiden's heart to gain
And unnoticed he had seen them part
And he swore he would give her pain

12 This maid had nearly reached her home
When she was startled by a cry
And she turned to look around her
And her love was standing by

13 His hand was pointing to the stars
And his eyes gazed at the light
And with a smiling countenance
He vanished from her sight

14 She quickly turned and home she ran
Not a word of this was said
For well she knew at seeing his form
That her faithful love was dead

15 And from that day she pined away
Not a smile seen on her face
And with outstretched arms she went to meet him
In a brighter place

333 SWEET FANNY ADAMS

Now, moth-ers dear, who love your lit-tle chil-dren ——

Pray lis-ten a-while — un-to me

I once had a daugh-ter like an an-gel ——

But now from all trou-ble she is free

Shall I ne-ver see thee more, my dear-est Fan-ny? ——

My child that I so fond — ly did love

Was slain and cut to pie-ces by a vil-lain ——

But now she's in Hea — ven a-bove

1 Now, mothers dear, who love your little children
  Pray listen awhile unto me
  I once had a daughter like an angel
  But now from all trouble she is free
  Shall I never see thee more, my dearest Fanny?
  My child that I so fondly did love
  Was slain and cut to pieces by a villain
  But now she's in Heaven above

2 On Saturday the twenty-first of August
  My poor Fanny and her sister went to play
  With another little girl, Minnie Warren
  Little thinking of danger on her way

3 But soon they met young Frederick Baker
  Who's a clerk in solitary we hear
  His parents well-to-do and much respected
  At Alton in the County of Hampshire

4 Three halfpence the monster gave the children
  To go sweetmeats for to buy
  My poor Fanny's hand he dragged bewildered
  To the hollow as she bitterly did cry

5 When the children came home without my Fanny
  The neighbours searched the fields and all around
  In the hop-ground the head with the eyes out
  And the left ear cut off upon the ground

6 Both arms and one leg cut from the body
  Such a cruel deed too strong that man of earth
  Was to hide such a crime so bewildered
  My child cut to pieces dead in dearth

7 She oftentimes would wander with her sister
  In the fields gathering wild flowers gay
  I love her the more when I miss her
  My sorrow I shall never drive away

8 Supposing he so cruelly violate her
  My child, scarcely eight years of age
  Was slain and cut to pieces by a villain
  But now he's lying in the silent grave

334 SYLVIA

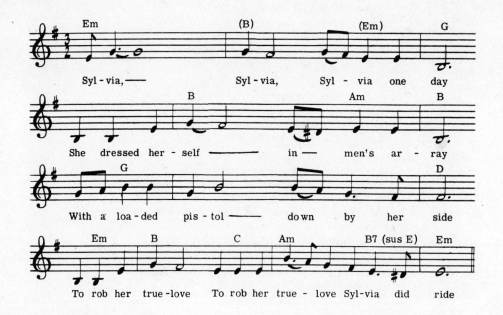

1 Sylvia, Sylvia, Sylvia one day
   She dressed herself in men's array
   With a loaded pistol down by her side
   To rob her true-love
   To rob her true-love
   Sylvia did ride

2 As she rode up to him and she bid him stand
   Stand and deliver all the gold that you have
   Stand and deliver all your gold and store
   Or else this moment
   Or else this moment
   Your life's no more

3 He delivered up all his gold and store
   But yet, she said, there is one thing more
   There's a diamond ring that I know you do wear
   Deliver it
   Deliver it
   And your life I'll spare

4 Now this diamond ring being a token, give o'er
   This ring I'll keep or lose my life
   She was tender-hearted just like a dove
   She rode away
   She rode away
   From her own true-love

5 Now as they were walking the garden green
   He spied his watch hanging from her chain
   He spied his watch hanging through her cloak
   Which made her blush
   Which made her blush
   Like any rose

6 What makes you blush at such a silly thing?
   I fain would have had your diamond ring
   For 'twas I that robbed you on the plain
   So take your watch
   So take your watch
   And gold again

7 Now why did you enter such a silly plot?
   Suppose that pistol you did have shot
   If you had shot me upon that plain
   For ever after
   For ever after
   You'd be put to shame

8 I only did it for to know
   Whether you were a true-lover or no
   But now I've a contented mind
   My heart and all
   My heart and all
   My dear, are thine

9 The match was made without delay
   And soon they fixed the wedding day
   And now they live in joy and content
   In happiness
   In happiness
   Their days are spent

335 THREE JOLLY SPORTSMEN

V.1 & 2: Now it's of three jol-ly sports-men as I have heard peo-ple say

They took five hun-dred guin-eas all on one mar-ket day

TUNE USED FOR SUBSEQUENT VERSES

3: I shall not stop, said Lip-skin, I shall not stop, said he

I shall not stop, said Lip-skin, else rob-bed we shall be

1 Now it's of three jolly sportsmen as I have heard people say
  They took five hundred guineas all on one market day

2 Now as Lipskin was a-riding along the road as fast as they could ride
  Saying: Stop your horse, cried Johnson, for I hear a woman cry

3 I shall not stop, said Lipskin, I shall not stop, said he
  I shall not stop, said Lipskin, else rob-bed we shall be

4 Now Johnson he got off his horse to search the groves all round
  He found a woman, stark naked, with her hair pinned to the ground

5 A woman, a woman, how came you here, fast bound?
  How came you here, stark naked, with your hair pinned to the ground?

6 They strip-ped me, they rob-bed me, both hands and feet they bound
  They left me here, stark naked, with my hair pinned to the ground

7 Now Johnson being a valiant man, of courage man so bold
  He took his coat from off his back, for to keep her from the cold

8 Now Johnson he got on his horse and the woman got on behind
  But she clasp-ed her fingers to her ears and she give three warning cries

9 Now up stepped three young swaggelling young men with swords all in their hands
  They bid him for to stop and stand, and they bid him for to stand

10 I will stop, I will stand, cried Johnson, I will stop, I will stand, cried he
   I never was, in all my life, afraid of any three

11 Now Johnson he drew his glittering sword, and two of them he slain
   And while he was killing the other one, the woman stabbed him behind

12 I must fall, I must fall, cried Johnson, I must fall unto the ground
   It's the cause of the wicked woman, she caused my deadly wound

13 She shall be hung in chains of gold, for the murder she hath done
   She hath killed the finest butcher boy that ever the sun shined on

336 TURPIN HERO

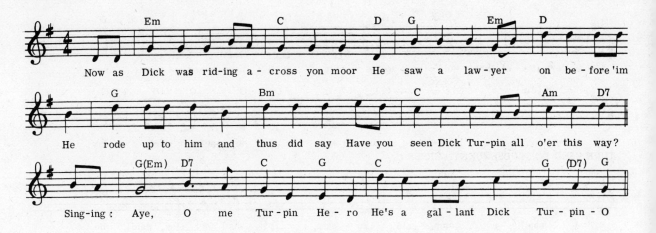

1. Now as Dick was riding across yon moor
   He saw a lawyer on before 'im
   He rode up to him and thus did say
   Have you seen Dick Turpin all o'er this way?

   Singing: Aye, O me Turpin Hero
   He's a gallant Dick Turpin-O

2. The lawyer he answers and thus did say
   I've not seen Dick for many a day
   For if I had, there would be no doubt
   He would turn my pockets inside out

3. O well, says Dick, I'll be his undo'
   I'll fit my money all in my shoe
   The lawyer, he says, he shan't have mine
   For I'll stick it in me top-coat cape behind

4. Now they rode till they came to the bottom of the hill
   Where he bid the lawyer to stand still
   Thy top-coat cape it must come off
   For my bonny Black Bess wants a new saddle cloth

5. And now I've robbed thee of thy store
   Thou can'st boldly go and work for more
   And when you get to the nearest inn
   You can tell them you've been robbed by Dick Turpin

313 THE BLACK VELVET BAND

Bill Cameron, St Mary's, Scilly Isles, *rec.* P. Kennedy, 1956

Other recorded versions
Paddy Doran (tinker), Belfast, N. Ireland, *rec.* P. Kennedy and S. O'Boyle, 1952: BBC 18578
Ben Baxter, Southrepps, Norfolk, *rec.* S. Ennis, 1955: BBC 22158 (fragment)

Printed versions
GARDINER MS: 1907: one variant (Hampshire)
HUGHES: 1936, vol. IV, p. 52: *Black Ribbon Band* (N. Ireland)
SEEGER AND MACCOLL: 1960, No. 75, p. 82 (Norfolk)
MEREDITH AND ANDERSON: 1967, pp. 49, 145 and 192 (Australia)

> Her eyes they shone like diamonds
> I thought her the pride of the land
> Her hair it hung down o'er her shoulders
> And tied in a black velvet band

These words are often sung as a chorus to this song, one of the most popular of the Anglo-Irish broadside ballads. The black velvet band may have been worn by genuine widows to mourn the loss of their husbands, but in this case it was worn by quite another type of lady.

Though also widely sung in England, the song seems to originate in Belfast, Northern Ireland, where it enjoys popularity among sailors. Bill Cameron learned the song from Tommy Crocker, fireman on board the *Lioness*, a mail-boat which sailed between Penzance and the Scilly Isles before the First World War.

314 BLACKBERRY FOLD

Harry Cox, Catfield, Norfolk, *rec.* P. Kennedy, 1953: EFDSS LP 1004 (1965)

Other recorded versions
Willie Brasil (Kent gipsy), Blairgowrie, Perth, Scotland, *rec.* P. Kennedy and H. Henderson, 1954
George Spicer, Copthorne, Sussex, *rec.* P. Kennedy, 1956: BBC 23093
Phoebe Smith, Woodbridge, Suffolk, *rec.* P. Kennedy, 1956

Printed versions
HAMMOND MS: 1905 (Dorset)
GARDINER MS: 1906–8: two variants (Hampshire)
JFSS: 1918, No. 21, p. 35: Lady Ashton of Hyde, Sussex, 1906
JFSS: 1931, No. 35, p. 269: *coll.* E. J. Moeran, Suffolk, 1921
MOERAN: 1932: as JFSS: 1931
PINTO AND RODWAY: 1957, No. 124, p. 351 (Nottingham broadside)
NEELY AND SPARGO: 1938 (Illinois, USA)

Other than in JFSS: 1918, this ballad has not previously been published in full. When Moeran made his arrangement (1932), he only included five of the verses which he had noted in Norfolk, and was thus forced to omit the first verse as well as verses 6–10. Anne Gilchrist regarded the Norfolk tune as having an interesting modal tune, quite distinct from the major tune from Sussex, printed in the earlier *Journal*, which had more kinship to those generally associated with *Spencer the Rover* (No. 331).

315 BRENNAN'S ON THE MOOR

Charlie Wills, Bridport, Dorset, *rec.* P. Kennedy, 1952: BBC 18693

Other recorded versions
Jeannie Robertson, Aberdeen, Scotland, *rec.* A. Lomax and P. Kennedy, 1953
Robert Cinnamond, Belfast, N. Ireland, *rec.* S. O'Boyle, 1955: BBC 24839

Printed versions
KIDSON: 1891, p. 123 (broadside version)
FORD: 1899–1901, vol. II, p. 56: two variants (Scotland)
JOYCE: 1909, No. 379, p. 186 (County Meath, Ireland)
SHARP MS: 1903–7: six variants (Somerset)
SHARP AND MARSON: 1904–9, vol. I, p. 70 (Somerset)
GILLINGTON: 1907: *Brannen on the Moor* (Hampshire)
O LOCHLAINN: 1965: words from JOYCE: 1909
STUBBS: 1970, p. 18 (Sussex)
MACKENZIE: 1928, p. 309 (Nova Scotia, Canada)
FLANDERS AND BROWN: 1932, p. 98: fragment (Vermont, USA)
SHOEMAKER: 1931, p. 242 (Pennsylvania, USA)
SHARP AND KARPELES: 1932, vol. II, p. 170 (Virginia, USA)
BELDEN: 1940, p. 284 (Kansas, USA)
LOMAX: 1941, p. 317 (Oregon via Washington DC, USA)
RANDOLPH: 1947, vol. II, p. 168 (Arkansas, USA)
CREIGHTON AND SENIOR: 1950, p. 236 (Nova Scotia, Canada)

> Brennan being an outlaw upon the mountains high
> With cavalry and infantry to take him they did try
> He laughed at them with scorn, until at length, 'tis said
> By a false-hearted comerade he basely was betrayed

In the County of Tipperary in a place they call Clonmore
Willie Brennan and his comrade that day did suffer sore
He lay amongst the bracken that grew thick upon the field
And nine deep wounds he did receive before that he would yield

These two additional verses appear on the broadsides between verses 7 and 8 (or as verses 8 and 9 of twelve-verse versions) and give the information that the famous Irish highwayman was betrayed in the end by one of his own comrades.

According to JOYCE: 1909, Brennan's career was in the eighteenth century in the Kilworth mountains near Fermoy in County Cork. He cites copies of broadsheets printed by Hay of Cork about 1850, but his version was noted from a ballad singer at Trim in County Meath in about 1860. Colm O Lochlainn (O LOCHLAINN: 1965) informs us that Brennan was finally hanged at Cork in 1804 and that his exploits are still celebrated around Tipperary, Limerick and Cork.

316 DERRY GAOL

Sarah Makem, Keady, County Armagh, Ireland, *rec.* P. Kennedy and S. O'Boyle, 1952: BBC 18476

Other recorded version
Peter Donnelly, Castlecaulfield, County Tyrone, N. Ireland, *rec.* P. Kennedy and S. O'Boyle, 1953: BBC 22336

Printed version
HENRY: 1924, No. 705: *The Dreary Gallows* (N. Ireland)

BARRY: 1929, p. 389: two variants and fragments (Maine, USA)
FLANDERS AND BARRY: 1939, p. 117: one variant (Maine, USA)
CREIGHTON AND SENIOR: 1950, p. 110: four variants, *Gallows* (Nova Scotia, Canada)
JAFL: vol. 26, p. 175: two lines

A young gentleman that fell in love with a rich lady and her parents didn't want him to get her, and she fought hard to get him and she went away to the Queen and got pardon. She took her Willie and she married him and defied her parents—she was right. I didn't blame her one bit. He was the fellow she wanted and she was right to take him.

This was Mrs Makem's own description of the story of a song which she learned from her uncle.

The incident on which the ballad is based probably occurred during the 1798 Rising. It is interesting to note its similarity to *The Maid Freed from the Gallows*, or *The Prickly Bush* (Child Ballads, No. 95). It would seem that it was in fact a parody, but with a man rather than a maid condemned to die.

For a version entitled *The Dreary Gallows* (HENRY: 1924) two tunes are given and it says the song may also be sung to the air of *The True Lovers Discussion* or *The Star of Glenamoyle*. One of the tunes was collected by the Rev. Walter Pitchford, Lamport Rectory, Northamptonshire, the other by a Mrs De Vine in Belfast, Northern Ireland.

Across the Atlantic we find a number of versions of the song noted in Nova Scotia, Canada, and Maine, USA.

317 DONNELLY AND COOPER

Frank ('Wings') Campbell, Armagh, N. Ireland, *rec.* P. Kennedy and S. O'Boyle, 1952: BBC 18485

Printed version
O LOCHLAINN: 1939 (Dublin, Ireland); note says Donnelly was born in Dublin in 1788 and died in 1820; the fight took place in 1815

Old Grania read the challenge and received it with a smile
You'd better haste unto Kildare, my well-beloved child
It is there you'll reign victorious as you often did before
And your deeds will shine most glorious around sweet Erin's shore

This verse, which appears on broadsides between our verses 2 and 3, gives a picture of Old Grania (Ireland), accepting the British challenge for Donnelly to meet Cooper on the Curragh of Kildare under the referee, Captain Kelly. The beautiful Miss Kelly, daughter of the referee, so the ballad tells, had a considerable rallying effect upon the Irishman when he was knocked down.

Other boxing ballads are frequently sung to this same tune. Colm O Lochlainn (O LOCHLAINN: 1939) gives *Heenan and Sayers* (No. 321) as one and *Morrissey and the Russian Sailor* (No. 325) as another.

318 EPSOM RACES

George Attrill, Fittleworth, Sussex, *rec.* R. Copper, 1954: BBC 22737

Other recorded version
Gabriel Figg, West Chiltington, Sussex, *rec.* P. Kennedy, 1958

Printed versions
GARDINER MS: 1906: three variants (Hampshire)
GILLINGTON: 1907: two verses only (Hampshire)
WILLIAMS: 1923, p. 87 (Berkshire)
KIDSON AND MOFFAT: 1929 (Yorkshire)
PURSLOW: 1968, p. 21: from Gardiner (Hampshire)

> I kept a coach and six bay horses
> And hangers all round about
> A golden tassel on each horse's head
> Just ready for me to drive out

This character was a well set-up Fine Old English Gentleman before he took to horse racing. Most versions see him steering his coach to Epsom Races, but Alfred Williams (WILLIAMS: 1923) had Ipswich Town, 'horse racing for to see'. Williams remarked that the song was formerly a favourite throughout the Thames Valley villages.

319 ERIN-GO-BRAGH

John Strachan, Fyvie, Aberdeenshire, Scotland, *rec.* A. Lomax, 1956: *Folk Songs of Britain*, vol. VII, CAEDMON TC1163/TOPIC 12T195

Printed versions
FORD: 1899, vol. I, p. 47 (Scotland)
JOYCE: 1873, p. 86 (Ireland)
GREIG: 1914, cxxvii (Aberdeenshire)
ORD: 1930, p. 387 (Aberdeenshire)
MACKENZIE: 1928, p. 330 (Nova Scotia, Canada)

> Come all you brave fellows that hears o' this song
> I don't care a farthing to where you belong
> For I'm frae Argyllshire in the Highlands sae braw
> But I ne'er tak' it ill being called: Erin-go-bragh

A well-travelled Gaelic-speaking Scotsman from the Highlands, nicknamed Erin-go-bragh, is mistaken for an Irishman by a policeman during the 'No Irish need apply' days in Auld Reekie (Edinburgh). Anyway the young man, Duncan Campbell, beats up the policeman for insulting him and manages to get away home on a boat leaving the Forth.

320 THE FOLKESTONE MURDER

George Spicer, Copthorne, Sussex, *rec.* P. Kennedy and M. Plunkett, 1956: BBC 23093

Printed versions
GARDINER MS: 1908 (Hampshire)
JFSS: 1915, No. 19, p. 138: *coll.* Gilchrist, Sussex

GREENLEAF: 1933, p. 125: *Maria and Caroline* (Newfoundland, Canada)
LEACH: 1965, p. 50 (Canada)

Tedea (or Dedea) Redanies was a British soldier, born in Belgrade, who murdered two sisters, Caroline and Maria Beck (aged nineteen and sixteen) on 3 August 1856. He was hanged at Maidstone on New Year's Day of the following year. The motive for the crime was thought to be jealousy.

The ballad has long been popular with country singers in Kent and east Sussex and also with gipsies in the area. It may also owe its continued existence to the fact that there have always been Army camps in the area, and the song may thus have served as a constant warning to local families.

The song has never been published in English folksong collections except for the version contributed by Gilchrist in 1915 which was included in the JFSS because it was felt that the tune was a good ballad type. However, there is no doubt that in spite of the unpleasantness of the subject there are some very impressive images conveyed by the words.

321 HEENAN AND SAYERS

Frank Hillier, Okeford Fitzpaine, Dorset, *rec*. P.
Kennedy, 1960.

Compare
O LOCHLAINN: 1965, p. 253 (Ireland)

RICKABY: 1926, p. 177: two versions (Minnesota, USA)

> All honour to Jack Heenan, likewise our champion brave
> And we hope a good subscription to the stranger will be made
> And if these two should battle for the champion belt again
> We want no favours to be shown but let the best man win

The fight took place between the Irish–American boxer John Heenan, known as 'The Benicia Boy', and Tom Sayers,
the British and European Champion, at Farnborough, Hampshire, on 17th April 1860. Before the fight Tom Sayers's
second asked Tom to remember a previous champion, the Welshman Evan Jones, and to do his best.

According to the song the fight went on for over an hour until Heenan could no longer see and Sayers had a broken
arm. At this point the crowd rushed the ring and a draw was declared.

322 JACK HALL

Jack Endacott, Chagford, Devon, *rec*. P. Kennedy, 1954:
Tedburn Hill, BBC 22323

Printed versions
KIDSON AND MOFFAT: 1926: one variant (Yorkshire)
SHARP MS: 1903–7: five variants
GARDINER MS: 1907: three variants (Hampshire)
HAMMOND MS: 1906: two variants (Dorset)
SHARP AND MARSON: 1904–9, vol. IV, p. 20: notes
(Somerset)

JEFDSS: 1940, p. 25: article on *The Diggers Song* and
others using this tune pattern, such as *Admiral Benbow*,
Captain Kidd, etc.
REEVES: 1958, p. 132: *coll.* C. Sharp, Somerset
PURSLOW: 1972, p. 42: composite Gardiner–Hammond
LOMAX: 1934, p. 133: *Sam Hall* (California, USA)
FLANDERS AND BROWN: 1932, p. 96 (Vermont, USA)
California Folklore Quarterly: 1942, vol. I, pp. 47–64:
article on Samuel Hall's family tree by Prof. Bronson

Frank Kidson wrote:

> Jack Hall was a notorious burglar. He was sold when a child to a chimney sweep for a guinea, and executed
> in 1701. In the eighteen-fifties a singer named Ross sang a version *Sam Hall*, with a very blasphemous chorus.
> This drew a big audience of a certain kind.

Another song with the same tune and word pattern is *Captain Kidd*, executed for piracy in London in the same year.
While Hall was hanged at Tyburn, Kidd was hanged in chains in Execution Dock, Wapping. The same pattern was used
for *Admiral Benbow*, who was wounded in action off the West Indies the following year.

In the JEFDSS for 1940 there is an article about this pattern of songs, including *The Diggers Song* of 1649. Following
these four songs are others such as *The Moderator's Dream* (anti-Jacobite and anti-Papal), *Ye Jacobites by Name* (which
was improved by Burns), *Aikendrum* (*Ken ye How a Whig Can Fight?*), *A Young Man and a Maid* (a bawdy song in
D'URFEY: 1707), *Admiral Byng* (executed 1757), the American captain *Paul Jones*, *The Praties they are Small* (Irish
famine song) and various Welsh and Methodist hymns.

Tedburn Hill in this song is a local Devonshire adaptation from Tyburn Hill (near Marble Arch in London) where
public hangings took place. Tedburn St Mary is a village not far from Chagford, where the song was recorded.

323 THE KNICKERBOCKER LINE

Stanley Slade, Bristol, *rec*. P. Kennedy, 1950
Printed version
SHARP MS: 1911: one variant (Gloucestershire)

MEREDITH AND ANDERSON: 1967, p. 195 (Australia)

> O I took a trip to Bristol in the train that's run by steam
> The dress my love was wearing was fit for any queen

So run two lines of a broadside version. Stanley Slade learned the song in Bristol and he regarded it as a local song.
Cecil Sharp's version was also collected not far away, from Shipton, outside Cheltenham, in Gloucestershire.

324 THE LAKES OF SHALLIN

Mary Reynolds, Mohill, County Leitrim, Ireland, *rec.*
S. Ennis, 1954: BBC 22028; *Folk Songs of Britain*,
vol. VII, CAEDMON TC1163/TOPIC 12T195

Other recorded versions
Jeannie Robertson, Aberdeenshire, Scotland, *rec.* P.
Kennedy, 1953: *The Loch of Shallin*
Charlie Scamp (gipsy), Kent, *rec.* P. Kennedy, 1954:
Young Leonard, BBC 19964
Joe Moran, Antrim, N. Ireland, *rec.* S. Ennis, 1954:
BBC 21841
Belle Stewart, Blairgowrie, Perthshire, Scotland, *rec.*
P. Kennedy and H. Henderson, 1955
Robert Cinnamond, Belfast, N. Ireland, *rec.* S. O'Boyle,
1955: *The Lake of Coolfinn*, BBC 24838
George Maynard, Copthorne, Sussex, *rec.* P. Kennedy,
1956: *Young Willie*, BBC 23092

Printed versions
JOYCE: 1873, p. 103: *The Lake of Coolfinn* (Ireland)
SHARP MS: 1904–13: eight unpublished variants
GARDINER MS: 1906–7: one variant, *Lake of Colephin*
(Somerset and Hampshire)
HAMMOND MS: 1906: two variants (Somerset)
JOYCE: 1909, p. 227: revised text
GREIG: 1914, No. cxiv: *The Loch o' Shillin* (Scotland)
HENRY: 1924, No. 176: *Willie Lennox* (N. Ireland)
PURSLOW: 1968, p. 65 from Hammond (Somerset): *The
Lake of Colephin*

BARRY: 1929, p. 26 (Maine, USA)
FLANDERS AND BARRY: 1939, p. 32 (Vermont, USA)

The anglicization of what must have been a Gaelic name has resulted in many different names for the lake in which Willie Leonard was drowned, and therefore many different titles of the song. On English broadsides we find *The Lakes of Cold Finn*, and in Scots versions *The Loch of Shallin*, or *Shillin* as it is in GREIG: 1914, where the hero is Billy Henry. In JOYCE: 1873 there is an Irish version from Limerick entitled *The Lake of Coolfinn*, but Joyce had no idea where the lake is situated.

Sam Henry's (HENRY: 1924) version *Willie Lennox*, from County Derry, throws more light on the situation; the lake is Loughinshollin.

It is a most interesting point in topography that the hero of the song was drowned in the lake (no longer on the map) which gives its name to the Barony of Loughinshollin (the lough of the island of the O'Lynns). The O'Lynns (originally O'Flynn's—the F, being aspirated, is not sounded) were a powerful sept who, in the sixth century and from AD 1121 onwards, occupied a territory comprising the modern baronies of Lower Antrim, Lower Toome, Lower Glenarm and Kilconway, on the east side of the river Bann. The Lough was probably an expansion of the river not far north of Lough Beg.

325 MORRISSEY AND THE RUSSIAN SAILOR

Peter Donnelly, Castlecaulfield, County Tyrone, N.
Ireland, *rec.* P. Kennedy and S. O'Boyle, 1952

Other recorded version
Sean McDonagh, Carna, County Galway, Ireland, 1947:
BBC 12500; COLUMBIA KL 204

Printed version
O LOCHLAINN: 1965, p. 255: words only (in Appendix);
also the words of *Morrissey and the Benicia Boy* to the
tune of *Donnelly and Cooper* (No. 317)

RICKABY: 1926, p. 48 (Minnesota, USA)
SANDBURG: 1927, p. 398 (Minnesota, USA)
LEACH: 1965, p. 114: *Morrissey and the Russian Bear*
(Canada)

Carl Sandburg (SANDBURG: 1927) quotes Morrissey's biography, *The Life of John Morrissey, The Irish Boy who Fought his Way to Fame and Fortune*, and tells of a prize fighter, gambler and politician who became a State Senator and a Member of Congress; he gives his dates as 1831–78.

326 NEWLYN TOWN

Bob Scarce, Blaxhall, Suffolk, *rec.* P. Kennedy, 1955:
Folk Songs of Britain, vol. VII, CAEDMON TC1163/
TOPIC 12T195

Other recorded versions
Elijah Bell, Sutton, Norfolk, *rec.* E. J. Moeran, 1947:
Babylon Square, BBC 16415
Harry Cox, Catfield, Norfolk, *rec.* P. Kennedy, 1953:
BBC 21482
Amos Beckett, Winslow, Buckinghamshire, *rec.* S. Ennis,
1952: *The Gallows Tree*, BBC 23930
Sam Larner, Winterton, Norfolk, *rec.* P. Donnellan,
1958: *At Seventeen I took a Wife*, BBC 26076

Printed versions
BARING GOULD MS, No. 142: *The Highwayman:* two
versions (Devon)
BARRETT: 1891, p. 34: *Flash Lad*
JFSS: 1901, No. 3, p. 114: *In Newry Town* (Sussex)
SHARP MS: 1906–9: four variants (Somerset)
GARDINER MS: 1906: two variants (Hampshire and
Somerset)

HAMMOND MS: 1906–7: four variants (Somerset,
Worcestershire and Dorset)
SHARP AND MARSON: 1904–9, vol. V, p. 53: *The Robber*
(Somerset)
KIDSON AND MOFFAT: 1926, p. 96: *The Highwayman*
(Yorkshire)
JFSS: 1930, No. 34, p. 190: *Adieu, Adieu, Hard was my
Fate* (Worcestershire)
JFSS: 1931, No. 35, p. 277: two variants of tune (Nor-
folk)
O LOCHLAINN: 1965, p. 70: *The Newry Highwayman*
(Ireland)
GUNDRY: 1966, p. 30, coll. Baring Gould, 1891 (Cornwall)
PURSLOW: 1972, p. 107 from Hammond: *Wild and
Wicked Youth* (Somerset)

COMBS: 1925, p. 215 (Kentucky, USA)
FUSON: 1931, p. 63: *The Rich Rambler* (Kentucky, USA)
CAMBIARE: 1934, p. 43 (Kentucky, USA)
HENRY: 1938, p. 327 (Tennessee, USA)
BELDEN: 1940, p. 136 (Missouri, USA)
RANDOLPH: 1946–50, vol. II, p. 84 (Missouri and
Arkansas, USA)
BROWN: 1952, p. 355 (N. Carolina, USA)

> I went to London both blithe and gay
> My time I wasted in bowls and play
> Until my cash it did get low
> And then on the highway I was forced to go

This is one of the most popular of the highwaymen ballads, and it has been widely noted in England. It is interesting historically in that there is mention of the first London 'policemen', the Bow Street Runners, who were established in 1751. Below they are called Ned Fielding's gang, referring to Henry Fielding (novelist and playwright) who was appointed a justice of the peace of Westminster in 1748 and started operations from Bow Street Magistrates Court. Later the Runners were also known as Robin Redbreasts, because of their red waistcoats. They were armed and patrolled the streets in order to raid gambling houses and pursue robbers and highwaymen. After his death Fielding's work was carried on by his blind half-brother Sir John Fielding.

Harry Cox also recorded this song, singing these third and fourth verses:

> I robbed Lord Golding I do declare
> And Lady Mansfield in Grosvenor Square
> I robbed them of the gold so bright
> And took it home to my heart's delight

> To Covent Gardens we went straight away
> Me and my wife went to the Play
> Ned Fielding's gang there did me pursue
> Taken I was by that curs-ed crew

A version collected by Cecil Sharp in Somerset contains the following verse:

> I am a wild and a wicked youth
> I love young women and that's the truth
> I love them dearly, I love them all
> I love them better than tongue can tell

327 THE OXFORD GIRL

Phoebe Smith (gipsy), Woodbridge, Suffolk, *rec.* P. Kennedy, 1956: BBC 23099

Other recorded versions

Mary Doran (tinker), Belfast, N. Ireland, *rec.* P. Kennedy and S. O'Boyle, 1952: *Dublin City*, BBC 18581

Harry Cox, Catfield, Norfolk, *rec.* P. Kennedy, 1956: BBC 22915; *The Prentice Boy*, EFDSS LP 1004 (1965)

Jeannie Robertson, Aberdeenshire, Scotland, *rec.* P. Kennedy, 1953: *The Butcher Boy*, BBC 21092

Printed versions

BARING GOULD: 1889, No. 63: tune developed and text rewritten as *The Orchestra*

SHARP MS: 1903–7: nine variants, *The Miller's Apprentice* (Somerset)

GARDINER MS: 1906–7: three variants (Hampshire)

HAMMOND MS: 1905–7: three variants (Dorset)

GREIG: 1914, No. cxxxvii: *The Butcher Boy*; also No. clxxix

JFSS: 1922, No. 26, p. 23: *Hang-ed I shall be* (Norfolk)

JFSS: 1923, No. 27, p. 44: *The Prentice Boy* (Dorset)

MACKENZIE: 1928, p. 293 (Nova Scotia, Canada)

FLANDERS AND BROWN: 1932, p. 88 (Vermont, USA)

SHARP AND KARPELES: 1932, vol. I, p. 407 (Kentucky and Virginia, USA)

HENRY: 1938: two variants, pp. 11, 214 (Tennessee); p. 219 (N. Carolina)

SCARBOROUGH: 1937, p. 160: three variants (N. Carolina and Virginia, USA)

HENRY: 1938, p. 219 (N. Carolina, USA)

HUDSON: 1936, p. 141 (Mississippi, USA)

NEELY AND SPARGO: 1938, p. 150 (Illinois, USA)

GARDNER AND CHICKERING: 1939, p. 77: two variants (Michigan, USA)

BELDEN: 1940, p. 134: two variants (Missouri, USA)

BREWSTER: 1940, p. 204 (Indiana, USA)

LOMAX: 1941, p. 174 (Virginia, USA)

RANDOLPH: 1946–50, vol. II, p. 93: eleven variants (Missouri, Arkansas, N. Carolina and Virginia, USA)

MORRIS: 1950, p. 337 (Florida, USA)

OWENS: 1950, p. 81 (Texas, USA)

BROWN: 1952, p. 240: five variants (N. Carolina, USA)

JAFL: vol. 42, pp. 247 and 290 (N. Carolina, USA)

SFLQ (Southern Folklore Quarterly) III, p. 208: two variants, *The Printer's Boy* (Indiana, USA)

TFLS (Texas Folk Lore Society) VI, p. 213 (Texas, USA)

This is certainly the classic English murder ballad. It goes under many titles, and the towns named are Oxford in England, Wexford in Ireland and Knoxville in the United States. The American ballad *Poor Omie* (or *Omie Wise*) would seem to be a local remake of the ballad. Harry Cox sang his version about Ekefield Town, and the Elk River of the *Omie* ballad could easily derive from this.

A fine six-verse Irish version of the ballad collected from Mary Doran, a tinker, gives the girl as belonging to Dublin:

1 I'm belonging to Dublin city, boys,
And a city you all know well
My parents reared me tenderly
And they brought me up right well

2 'Twas near the town of Limsborough
Where they bound me up to a mill
It was there I beheld a comely girl
With a dark and a rolling eye

3 'Twas with his false and deluding tongue
He coaxed that fair maid out
And from out a ditch he pulled a stick
And he knocked that fair maid down

4 He caught her by the yellow locks
And he drew her along the ground
Till he drew her to the Liffey side
Where her body could not be found

5 Returning to his master's door
At the dead hour of the night
And he asking for a candle
To show himself some light

6 Went into bed and no more he says
No rest or peace could find
For the murder of that fair young maid
Lay heavy on his mind

328 THE PARCEL FROM A LADY

Frank Hillier, Okeford Fitzpaine, Dorset, *rec.* P. Kennedy, 1959: *Rolled in her apron*

Other recorded version

Jumbo Brightwell, Eastbridge, Suffolk, *rec.* P. Kennedy, 1956: *Under her Apron*

Printed versions

JOHNSON: 1787–1803, vol. V, p. 437: *She roun't in her apron* (Scotland)

BARING GOULD: 1889–1905, No. 36, p. 74: *A Sweet Pretty Maiden* (Devon): words of another song substituted

Compare

REEVES: 1958, No. 103, p. 210: *Three Maids a Rushing* from Sharp (Somerset), 1908

REEVES: 1960, No. 132, p. 260: Above and *A Maiden Sweet* from Baring Gould (Devon), 1890

Now all young men take my advice
And never take a parcel from a lady
If you do you'll find your mistake
In the parcel there'll be a baby

Although this song seems to have been popular with singers in many parts of England it does not seem to have been noted by many collectors, or reached the folksong collections published at the turn of the present century. Possibly it was not considered old enough because of the use of the word 'parcel', but in fact it was probably current long before the beginning of the parcel post in England in 1879. Baring Gould did not publish the words: 'it deals with a topic not advisable to be sung about the drawing-room'.

329 POISON IN A GLASS OF WINE

Mary Doran (tinker), Belfast, N. Ireland, *rec.* P. Kennedy and S. O'Boyle, 1952: *Oxford City*, BBC 18581; *Folk Songs of Britain*, vol. VII, CAEDMON TC1163/ TOPIC 12T195

Other recorded versions
Elizabeth Taylor, Saxby-All-Saints, Lincolnshire, *rec.* P. Kennedy, 1953: *Worcester City*
George Attrill, Fittleworth, Sussex, *rec.* R. Copper, 1954; *Oxford City*, BBC 22738
Belle Stewart and Jean Thompson, Blairgowrie, Perthshire, Scotland, *rec.* P. Kennedy, 1961: *In London's Fair City*
Fred Jordan, Wenlock, Shropshire: *Down the Green Groves*, TOPIC 12T150 (1966)

Printed versions
SHARP MS: 1903–9: eleven variants: *Jealousy*
JFSS: 1905, No. 6, p. 37: *Down in the Groves, coll.* Sharp, Somerset
JFSS: 1906, No. 8, p. 157: two variants, *Newport Street* (Essex) and *Oxford City* (Norfolk and Sussex)
GARDINER MS: 1906–7: seven variants (Hampshire), one variant (Wiltshire)
HAMMOND MS: 1905: two variants, No. 275 (Dorset) and No. 317 (Gloucestershire), *In Midfordshire*
GREIG: 1914, No. cxxxvii: *In Oxford Town*
JFSS: 1923, No. 27, p. 41: *Down the Groves, coll.* Hammond, Dorset
REEVES: 1960, p. 186: *Maria and William, coll.* Hammond, Dorset
STUBBS: 1970, p. 59: *Oxford City* (Sussex)
PURSLOW: 1972, p. 46: *Jealousy, coll.* Gardiner (Hampshire)

FLANDERS AND BROWN: 1932, p. 92 (Vermont, USA)
GARDNER AND CHICKERING: 1939, p. 75 (Michigan, USA)
JAFL: vol. 30, p. 356 (England via New Brunswick, Canada)

Come all you young men and pretty maidens
Never let jealousy run in your mind
And never destroy your own true-lover
By giving her poison in a glass of wine

The song has been widely collected in southern England and it appears on many broadsides. For the Gavin Greig version (GREIG: 1914), called *In Oxford Town*, the collector says,

> The tragedy here is rendered more bearable through certain redeeming features. The sad fate of the girl does not exhaust our pity. We have some to spare for the poor fellow who elected to share the fate of the victim. Jealousy was indeed cruel—but cruel to both.

330 POLLY VAUGHAN

Harry Cox, Catfield, Norfolk, *rec.* P. Kennedy, 1953: *The Fowler*, BBC 13864 (1947)

Other recorded versions
John Connell, Ballyvourney, Cork, Ireland, *rec.* S. Ennis, 1952: *Molly Bawn*, BBC 19024
Phoebe Smith, Woodbridge, Suffolk, *rec.* P. Kennedy, 1956: *Molly Varden*, BBC 23099

Printed versions
JAMIESON: 1806, vol. i, p. 194: *Peggy Bawn*
BARING GOULD: 1889, No. 62: *At the Setting of the Sun* (Devon)
SHARP AND MARSON: 1904–9, vol. I, No. 16, p. 32: *The Shooting of his Dear* (Somerset)
JFSS: 1905, No. 6, p. 59: two variants, *coll.* Sharp, Somerset, Kent
GARDINER MS: 1906–8: four variants (Hampshire)
HAMMOND MS: 1906: three variants (Dorset)
JOYCE: 1909, p. 220 (Ireland)
JFSS: 1922, No. 26, pp. 17–21: *The Fowler coll.* Moeran, Sutton, Norfolk, with notes by Anne Gilchrist about the supernatural elements
HENRY: 1924, No. 114: *Molly Bawn Lowry* (N. Ireland)
MOERAN: 1924, p. 20: *The Shooting of his Dear*, Sutton, Norfolk
JIFSS: III, p. 25 (Ireland)
O LOCHLAINN: 1939, No. 29, p. 58: *Young Molly Bán* (Ireland)
JEFDSS: 1955, p. 241: John Connell version (Ireland)
PURSLOW: 1965, p. 70, from Gardiner (Hampshire)

POUND: 1922, p. 78 (Kentucky, USA)
COX: 1925, p. 339 (Ohio via W. Virginia, USA), p. 529 (W. Virginia, USA)
SHARP AND KARPELES: 1932, vol. I, p. 328: six variants (N. Carolina, Tennessee, Kentucky and Virginia, USA)
HUDSON: 1936, p. 145 (Mississippi, USA), thirteen lines (Kentucky, USA)
SCARBOROUGH: 1937, p. 116 (Virginia, USA)
CHAPPELL: 1939, p. 101 (N. Carolina, USA)
EDDY: 1939, p. 194 (Ohio, USA)
GARDNER AND CHICKERING: 1939, p. 66 (Michigan, USA)
LINSCOTT: 1939, p. 274: *Polly Van* (Massachusetts, USA)
RANDOLPH: 1946–50, vol. I, p. 254: four variants (Missouri and Arkansas, USA)
KORSON: 1949, p. 46: *Molly Banding* (Pennsylvania, USA)
MORRIS: 1950, p. 398 (Georgia and Florida, USA)
BROWN: 1952, p. 263 (N. Carolina, USA)
FSSNE, Bulletin No. 10, p. 12 (Maine, USA)
JAFL: vol. 22, p. 387 (Maine, USA)
JAFL: vol. 30, p. 359 (Massachusetts, USA)
JAFL: vol. 52, p. 32 (Kentucky via Wisconsin, USA)
JAFL: vol. 52, p. 56 (New Jersey, USA)
MEREDITH AND ANDERSON: 1967, p. 196; *Molly Bawn Lavery* (Australia)
KARPELES: 1971, p. 113: *Molly Bond* (Newfoundland, Canada)

When the ballad was printed in *Popular Ballads* (JAMIESON: 1806), Jamieson commented that 'This is indeed a silly ditty, one of the very lowest description of vulgar English ballads which are sung about the streets in country towns and sold four or five for a halfpenny.' However, subsequent collectors have found the theme of the greatest interest as being in all probability a modern rationalization of the extremely ancient myth of animal transformation, in particular the transformation of maidens into birds.

There are good notes about the song in JFSS: 1922, and the animal metamorphosis is discussed in Wimberly's *Folklore in the English and Scottish Ballads* (University of Chicago Press, 1928), p. 54.

A version collected by Cecil Sharp was called *The Shooting of his Dear*, where the idea of transformation into a hind (which figures so much in Danish balladry) is not implied. This is borne out by a version in JOYCE: 1909 in which *Molly Bawn* is mistaken for a 'fawn'.

Cecil Sharp said (JFSS: 1905) that:

> The supernatural element enters so rarely into the English ballad that one is inclined to see in its occurrence an indication of Celtic origin. In the present case this suspicion is perhaps strengthened by the presence of certain Irish characteristics. . . . The incidents related in the song are a strange admixture of fancy with matter of fact. I would hazard the suggestion that the ballad is the survival of a genuine piece of Celtic or, still more probably, of Norse imagination, and that the efforts made to account for the tragedy without resorting to the supernatural . . . are the work of a more modern and less imaginative generation of singers.

Lucy Broadwood said she had noted a tune in the Western Highlands of Scotland, 'The Gaelic text of which turns on the same subject as this'.

331 SPENCER THE ROVER

Bob and Ron Copper, Rottingdean, Sussex, *rec.* P.
  Kennedy, 1955: EFDSS LP 1002 (1963)

Other recorded version
Jim Barratt, North Waltham, Hampshire, *rec.* R.
  Copper, 1955: BBC 21861

Printed versions
MASON: 1877, p. 44 (Derbyshire)
KIDSON: 1891, p. 154 (Yorkshire)

SHARP MS: 1904: one variant (Somerset)
GARDINER MS: 1906–9: five variants (Hampshire), one
  variant (Surrey)
HAMMOND MS: 1906: one variant (Worcestershire)
WILLIAMS: 1923, p. 130 (Oxfordshire)
JEFSS: 1918, No. 21, p. 22: *coll.* Frederick Keel,
  Surrey; p. 24: *coll.* Anne Gilchrist, Sussex
STUBBS: 1970, p. 66 (Sussex)

These words were compos-ed by Spencer the rover
Who travelled Great Britain and most parts of Wales

Anne Gilchrist believed the song to be of Irish origin, particularly because of its Gaelic assonances. She compared it to other Anglo-Irish 'ornate productions' and suggested that Spencer was a 'roving hero' like the character in the ballad *Rambler from Clare*. However, neither she nor any other collector to date has encountered the song in Ireland, or indeed outside England.

332 THE STANDING STONES

John and Ethel Findlater, Dounby, Orkney, *rec.* P.
  Kennedy, 1955: BBC 22645 and BBC 22647; *Folk Songs
  of Britain*, vol. VII, CAEDMON TC1163/TOPIC 12T195

Compare
The Cappabinee Murder: Elizabeth Cronin, Cork, Ireland, *rec.* A. Lomax, 1951; *rec.* S. Ennis, 1952: BBC
  19022

This local Orkney murder ballad may or may not be founded on fact, but to the singers it has a very strong feeling of reality. It was recorded within sight of the prehistoric stone circles at Stenness on Orkney.

One of the stones, now no longer in position, is an Odin Stone, which was regarded as a betrothal altar. In 1814 a farmer was fined £40 for breaking it up and building it into a cow byre. Lovers plighted their troth by grasping each other's hands through 'the round hole' and then dividing between them a broken sixpenny piece.

The church at Stenness had a door at each end, and in order to sever their bond the lovers could turn their backs and walk out in opposite directions. If one lover died the other could be freed from his or her vows by touching the dead hand.

The words of the song were published in John Mooney's *Songs of the Norse* (Calder, Kirkwall, 1883) where it is en-titled *The Lovers—a West Mainland Legend* (Mainland, in Orkney, means the largest or main island). The ballad is sung to the tune of the well-known bothy ballad *The Ploughboy's Dream*.

333 SWEET FANNY ADAMS

Vashti Vincent, Sixpenny Handley, Wiltshire, *rec.* P. Kennedy, 1954: *Folk Songs of Britain*, vol. VII, Caedmon TC1163/Topic 12T195

Printed version
1867 broadside announcing execution: Curtis Museum, Alton, Hampshire

The murder described in this song took place at Alton in Hampshire on 27th August 1867. Fanny Adams, aged eight, was murdered by Frederick Baker, a solicitor's clerk, who was sentenced at the Winter Assizes, held at the Castle, Winchester, to be hanged. Local inhabitants heard the details of the murder sung by ballad singers at the markets and fairs, as Mrs Vincent said:

> Years ago, it didn't used to be like it is now, when a murder was on. My father used to be shepherd and used to go to Wilton Fair years ago—drive his sheep up there—and when he come home he told us that men were walking about up there with a placard and on it about Fanny Adams. He heard the song sung up there at the Fair, brought it home, and we learned it. I was about ten years old at the time.

The expression 'Sweet Fanny Adams', still used in popular speech in England, shows what a strong impression the murder made on the public at that time. The meaning of this phrase has shifted as the incident has been forgotten. At first any suspicious-looking meat stew served in the Royal Navy was called 'Sweet Fanny Adams', but now, by popular usage, the term has come to mean 'nothing at all'. For example, if one receives no payment for a job, one would say 'I got Sweet Fanny Adams'.

It is reputed that the words of the ballad were written by Carel Jaeger (information from John Brune).

334 SYLVIA

Tim Walsh, Devonport, *rec.* C. Tawney, 1960: *Folk Songs of Britain*, vol. VII, Caedmon TC1163/Topic 12T195; BBC 26310

Other recorded version
Kitty Harvey, Thaxted, Essex, *rec.* P. Kennedy, 1958

Printed versions
Baring Gould MS: 1890, No. 163: *The Lady turned Highwayman* (Dorset)
Sharp MS: 1904–11: five variants
Gardiner MS: 1905–9: eight variants (Hampshire)
Sharp and Marson: 1904–9, vol. II, p. 10: *Sovay Sovay* (Somerset)
JFSS: 1907, No. 11, p. 127: three variants (Dorset)
Henry: 1924, No. 35: *The Female Highwayman* (N. Ireland)

Kidson and Moffat: 1926, p. 4: *The Female Highwayman* (*Sylvia*)
JFSS: 1930, No. 34, p. 225 (Sussex, England and Ontario, Canada)
JEFDSS: 1932, p. 52 (Australia)
Purslow: 1968, p. 42 from Hammond, 1906 (Dorset)
Mackenzie: 1928, p. 318: two variants (Nova Scotia, Canada, references)
Flanders and Brown: 1932, p. 133 (Vermont, USA)
Shoemaker: 1931, p. 180 (Pennsylvania, USA)
Creighton: 1932, p. 51 (Nova Scotia, Canada)
Greenleaf: 1933, p. 61: *Wexford City*, (Newfoundland)
Peacock: 1965, p. 342: *Gold Watch and Chain* (Newfoundland)

This song is usually classified as *The Female Highwayman* since the young lady's name varies from Sylvia to Sovie, Sovay, Shillo, Sally, Silvery, and so on; on broadside copies the title is sometimes given as *Sylvia's Request and William's Denial*.

335 THREE JOLLY SPORTSMEN

Bob Scarce, Blaxhall, Suffolk, *rec.* P. Kennedy and A. Lomax, 1953: BBC 19884; *Folk Songs of Britain*, vol. VIII, CAEDMON TC1164/TOPIC 12T196

Other recorded versions
Elijah Bell and Harry Cox, Sutton, Norfolk: BBC 16416
George Fosbury, Axford, Hampshire, *rec.* R. Copper, 1955: *Young Butcher Boy*: two verses, BBC 21858
Ben Baxter, Southrepps, Norfolk, *rec.* S. Ennis, 1955: *Two Jolly Butchers*, BBC 22158
Joe Thomas, Constantine, Cornwall, *rec.* P. Kennedy, 1956: *The Three Butchers*, fragment, BBC 23654

Printed versions
JFSS: 1902, No. 4, p. 174, *coll.* Broadwood (Sussex): chorus version
SHARP MS: 1903–9: nine variants
BROADWOOD: 1908, p. 42: from JFSS: 1902 (Sussex)
HAMMOND MS: 1905–6: four variants (Dorset), one variant (Somerset)
GARDINER MS: 1905–8: three variants (Hampshire), one variant (Somerset)
GREIG: 1909–14, No. xxxvi (Scotland)
WILLIAMS: 1923, p. 275: two variants, *The Two Jolly Butchers* (Wiltshire)

HENRY: 1924, No. 185: *Three Huntsmen* (N. Ireland)
JFSS: 1927, No. 31, p. 2 (Somerset)
PURSLOW: 1965, p. 89, from Hammond (Dorset)
COX: 1925, p. 302 (W. Virginia, USA)
SHARP AND KARPELES: 1932, vol. I, p. 370: three variants (Tennessee, Kentucky and a fragment from N. Carolina, USA)
CREIGHTON: 1932, p. 208 (Nova Scotia, Canada)
GREENLEAF: 1933, p. 82: two variants (Newfoundland, Canada)
FLANDERS AND BARRY: 1939, p. 238: notes and references: *Three Jovial Huntsmen* (Vermont, USA)
RANDOLPH: 1946, vol. I, p. 375 (Arkansas, USA)
CREIGHTON AND SENIOR: 1950, p. 120: two variants (Nova Scotia, Canada)
MORRIS: 1950, p. 385 (Florida, USA)
BROWN: 1952, p. 270: two variants (N. Carolina, USA)
LEACH: 1965, p. 160: *Three Boocher Lads* (Labrador, Canada)
PEACOCK: 1965, p. 817: *The Jolly Butcherman* (Newfoundland, Canada)
KARPELES: 1971, p. 132: two versions (Newfoundland, Canada)

J. Russell Smith's *Catalogue of English Broadside Ballads* (1856) gives a comprehensive title:

A new ballad of three merry butchers and ten highwaymen, how three butchers were to pay 500 pounds away, and hearing a woman crying in the wood went to relieve her and was there set upon by these ten highwaymen; and how only stout Johnson fought with them all; who killed eight of the ten and at last was killed by the woman he went to save in the wood. To an excellent new tune printed for J. Bissel at the Bible and Harp in W. Smithfield.

In *The Roxburghe Ballads*, vol. III (Reeves and Turner, London, 1873), there is a black-letter broadside printed about 1678 called *The Three Worthy Butchers of the North*. Such and Catnach printed ballad sheets called *Ips, Gips and Johnson* or *The Three Butchers*.

It was Ips, Gips and Johnson as I've heard many say
They had 5000 guineas on a market day
As they rode over Northumberland as hard as they could ride
O hark, O hark, says Johnson, I hear a woman cry

Bob Scarce's recording is, we believe, a classic of traditional singing with a remarkable story-telling technique in which the singer works his audience into a frenzy of excitement. The whole sequence of colourful images is brought out with control and subtle changes of tempo and modality. Verse 1, for instance, is sung in the major key, verse 2 somewhere between the major and minor, and verse 3, in the minor.

336 TURPIN HERO

George Messenger, Blaxhall, Suffolk, *rec.* P. Kennedy, 1956

Printed versions
CHAPPELL: 1858–9, p. 661: *O Rare Turpin, Hero*, from a pamphlet entitled *The Dunghill Cock*
LOGAN: 1869, pp. 115–18: gives an account of Turpin's career
SHARP: 1902, No. 69, p. 146
SHARP MS: 1904–8: nine variants
GARDINER MS: 1904–7 (Somerset and Hampshire)

JFSS: 1906, No. 9, p. 279 (Somerset and Yorkshire); note by Cecil Sharp says that 'some of Turpin's exploits were supposed to have taken place in the neighbourhood of South Petherton and this may account for the popularity of the song in Somerset'
WILLIAMS: 1923, p. 99: *Dick Turpin* (Wiltshire); p. 100: *Turpin and the Lawyer* (Somerset)
KIDSON AND MOFFAT: 1926, p. 60: *Turpin Hero*
HAMER: 1967, p. 6 (Bedfordshire)

POUND: 1922, p. 157: from MACKENZIE
MACKENZIE: 1928, p. 311: reference (Nova Scotia, Canada)

Bold Dick Turpin was his name
He brought himself to grief and shame
It was his slight and nimble hand
Caused him to be a highwayman

Turpin, the son of an innkeeper, was born at Hempstead, near Thaxted, Essex, on 21st September 1705. At one time he and his accomplice Robert King lived in a cave in Epping Forest and for a time he was a butcher at Thaxted.

No facts seem to support his ride to York, and the same alibi is said to have been used by two other highwaymen. Nor is it known for certain that he had a horse called Black Bess, and much that is attributed to Turpin may be legendary, or composed about the exploits of a number of highwaymen. In fact the robbing of the lawyer may well have been the work of William Page, the gentleman highwayman.

It was when he had retired from highway robbery and was living at Welton, near Beverley, Yorkshire, that Turpin was finally arrested for shooting his landlord's cockerel after imbibing too much drink, and it was for this insignificant incident that he was caught and hanged at York on 7th April 1739.

Bibliography

This bibliography has been divided into two sections. Books published in Britain and Ireland appear first, followed by those published abroad, both in alphabetical order

BARING GOULD: 1889–1905
Rev. S. Baring Gould and Rev. H. Fleetwood Sheppard, *Songs and Ballads of the West*: Patey & Willis, London (4 parts) 1889–91. Methuen, London (4 parts) 1891–4; (1 vol.) 1895; revised edition 1905. Details are given by E. A. White in JEFDSS: 1937, p. 143, and 1946, p. 67. When reprinted in four parts this collection, mainly from Devon and N. Cornwall, comprised 110 songs 'collected from the mouths of the people'. Texts were modified and in some cases completely re-written and the same applied to tunes. However, in the revised edition, under the musical editorship of Cecil Sharp and with the adding of the name of the Rev. F. W. Bussell, one of the original collectors, many original texts and tunes were restored. For further comment on this publication see Dean-Smith: JEFDSS: 1950, p. 41.

BARING GOULD MS: 1889–95
Rev. S. Baring Gould. Manuscript in Plymouth City Library.

BARRETT: 1891
William A. Barrett, *English Folk Songs*: Novello, London, 1891. 54 songs with piano arrangements. An early publication using the term 'collected folk song'; most of the songs published elsewhere; exact details of origins not given and Barrett not nationally accepted as reputable collector or arranger.

BROADWOOD: 1908
Lucy Broadwood, *English Traditional Songs and Carols*: Boosey, London, 1908. 39 songs mainly from Surrey–Sussex border with informative preface and brief notes about singers with comparative transcriptions made by phonograph cylinder recordings.

CHAPPELL: 1858/9
William Chappell, *Popular Music of the Olden Time*: Cramer, Beale & Chappell, London, vol. I 1858, vol. II 1859; Dover Publications, New York, 1965. Includes most of material from *National English Airs* (1838) but more has been added from other sources with particular reference to the ballads in the Pepys and Roxburghe collections. For further comment see Dean-Smith's *Guide* and JEFDSS: 1950, p. 38.

DEAN-SMITH: 1954
Margaret Dean-Smith, *A Guide to English Folk Song Collections (1822–1952)*: University of Liverpool, 1954. A useful index of published songs under titles, alternative titles and first lines, with some full descriptions of important books with historical annotations and an introduction which traces the development of collecting and publication of folksong in England over a period of 130 years.

DUNCAN MS: 1905–11
James Duncan (1848–1917). MS collected c. 1905–11. Aberdeen University Library. Consists of two notebooks, the first containing 800 tunes with words of first verse, and the second giving texts of over 350 songs all supplied by a Mrs Gillespie. For obituary by Lucy Broadwood see JFSS: 1918, No. 21, p. 41.

D'URFEY: 1698–1720
Thomas D'Urfey, *Wit and Mirth* (or *Pills to Purge Melancholy*): London, 1698–1720. First edition printed with airs was in 2 vols. (1698). Further editions increased to 6 vols. (1720). This was the earliest publication to contain both words and music of a large number of English and Scots folksongs.

FMJ: 1965–
Folk Music Journal: English Folk Dance and Song Society, London (from 1965). Continuing the work of JFSS (*Journal of the Folk-Song Society*): 1889–1931 and JEFDSS (*Journal of the English Folk Dance and Song Society*): 1932–64.

FORD: 1899–1904
Robert Ford, *Vagabond Songs and Ballads of Scotland*: Gardiner, Paisley, Scotland, 1899–1901; new edition 1904. A comprehensive collection of songs and ballads, containing a number of 'bothy ballads', but only a few for which he provides the music. Important in that it covers the wide range of songs that were current up to the end of the century, particularly those sung by 'the travellers'.

GARDINER: 1909
George B. Gardiner, *Folk Songs from Hampshire*: Novello, London, 1909. 16 songs collected by Gardiner and his musical associates, Gamblin, Balfour Gardiner and Guyer, and arranged by Gustav (von) Holst.

GARDINER MS: 1905–9 (see also under HAMMOND)
For further details about Gardiner's work see *The George Gardiner Folksong Collection* in FMJ: 1967, p. 129 and introduction to PURSLOW: 1968.

GILLINGTON: 1907
Alice E. Gillington, *Eight Hampshire Songs*: Curwen, London, 1907. Songs arranged by Miss Gillington with piano accompaniments. No preface or notes to songs.

GREIG: 1909/14
Gavin Greig, *Folk Songs of the North-East*: The Buchan Observer, Peterhead, Scotland. Vol. I 1909, vol. II 1914. Folklore Associates, Pennsylvania, USA, 1963. Greig was an Aberdeenshire schoolmaster and an accomplished musician who noted the words and tunes of over 3,000 songs. His manuscripts, extending over 90 volumes, are deposited in the Library of King's College, Aberdeen.

GUNDRY: 1966
Inglis Gundry, *Canow Kernow*. Federation of Old Cornwall Societies, 1966. Soundpost Publications, Dartington Institute of Traditional Arts, Totnes, Devon, 1972. Over 60 songs, carols, shanties and dance tunes collected in Cornwall. Some songs published with versions in Cornish.

HAMER: 1967
Fred Hamer, *Garners Gay*: EFDS Publications, London, 1967. 50 songs, words and melodies (chord symbols) mainly collected in Bedfordshire but also from other counties of England. No exact locations or dates given of informants or comparative notes to songs, but contains hitherto unpublished local songs and songs connected with local customs.

HAMMOND AND GARDINER MSS: 1905–9
H. E. D. Hammond (1866–1910), R. F. F. Hammond (1868–1921) and Dr George Gardiner (1852–1910) collected mainly in Dorset and Hampshire. Their manuscripts, deposited in the Vaughan Williams Memorial Library at Cecil Sharp House, London, have been indexed by Frank Purslow, who has also edited three books drawn from them (see PURSLOW: 1965, 1968 and 1972).

HENRY: 1924
Sam Henry, *Songs of the People*: Northern Constitution, Coleraine, Co. Derry, N. Ireland, 1924. Over 800 songs were published in the local Derry newspaper. Many were contributed by readers but it was Henry's diligent research and background notes that gave interest to each contribution.

HUGHES: 1909–36
Herbert Hughes, *Irish Country Songs*: Boosey, London, 1909–36. 4 vols. Vol. I 1909, vol. II 1915, vol. III 1935, vol. IV 1936. About 20 songs in each album collected in the northern counties of Ireland.

JEFDSS: 1932–64
Journal of The English Folk Dance and Song Society: London (32 vols.), 1932–64.

JFSS: 1899–1931
Journal of the Folk-Song Society: London (35 vols.), 1899–1931.

JIFSS: 1904–37
Journal of the Irish Folk-Song Society: London, 1904–37.

JAMIESON: 1806
Robert Jamieson, *Popular Ballads and Songs from Tradition*: Edinburgh, 1806. A publication, without tunes, mainly of ballads with the beginnings of comparative study particularly relating to Danish examples, but also containing words of some Scots versions of folk songs.

JOHNSON: 1787–1853
James Johnson, *The Scots Musical Museum*: 6 vols. Edinburgh, 1787–1803; 4 vols. with notes by William Stenhouse and David Laing, Edinburgh, 1853. This was the beginning of systematic documentation of Scots songs to which Robert Burns contributed material of his own collecting which he restored by re-writing amplification of the texts.

JOYCE: 1873/1906
P. Weston Joyce, *Ancient Music of Ireland*: McGlashan & Gill, Dublin, 1873. Longmans Green, Dublin and New York, 1906.

JOYCE: 1909
P. Weston Joyce, *Old Irish Folk Music and Songs*: University Press, Dublin, 1909. 842 Irish airs and songs, edited with annotations for the Royal Society of Antiquaries of Ireland of which Joyce was the President. Most of the music previously unpublished but some are versions of songs already in *Ancient Music of Ireland* (1873) and *Irish Peasant Songs in the English Language* (1906).

KIDSON: 1891
Frank Kidson, *Traditional Tunes*: C. Taphouse, Oxford, 1891. Texts and melodies (without accompaniment) mainly from Yorkshire. Later published with piano accompaniment in KIDSON AND MOFFAT: 1926 and 1927. Many texts filled out from broadsides. For article about Frank Kidson see JEFDSS: 1948, p. 127. Reissued by S. R. Publishers, 1970.

KIDSON AND MOFFAT: 1926
Frank Kidson and Alfred Moffat, *A Garland of English Folk Songs*: Ascherberg, Hopwood & Crew, London, 1926. 60 songs collected by Kidson, mainly in Yorkshire, with piano accompaniments by Moffat; most previously published in *Traditional Tunes* (1891). A further 60 songs were selected for a second volume by Kidson and Moffat (1927).

KIDSON AND MOFFAT: 1927
Frank Kidson and Alfred Moffat, *Folk Songs from the North Countrie*: Ascherberg, Hopwood & Crew, London, 1927. A further 60 songs with piano accompaniment, published one year after the collector's death. The foreword by Lucy Broadwood provides information about the collector. See also *Frank Kidson: portrait*, JEFDSS: 1948, pp. 127–35.

KIDSON AND MOFFAT: 1929
Frank Kidson, Ethel Kidson and Alfred Moffat, *English Peasant Songs*: Ascherberg, Hopwood & Crew, London, 1929. 'Third and last Selection of Sixty Folk Songs from the Frank Kidson Collection.' Compiled by his niece with once again piano accompaniments by Moffat. (See KIDSON AND MOFFAT: 1926 and 1927.)

LOGAN: 1869
W. H. Logan, *A Pedlar's Pack*: Paterson, Edinburgh, 1869.

MASON: 1877/1908
Miss M. H. Mason, *Nursery Rhymes and Country Songs*: Metzler, London, 1877. Second edition without illustrations but with additional notes, 1908. Over 50 folksongs of great variety mainly from her own Mitford family in Northumberland, also from Broadwood in Sussex, with piano accompaniments.

MOERAN: 1924
E. J. Moeran, *Six Folk Songs from Norfolk*: Augener, London, 1924. A selection with piano accompaniments of songs contributed to JFSS: 1922, No. 26.

MOERAN: 1932
E. J. Moeran, *Six Suffolk Folk Songs*: Curwen, London, 1932. Collected and arranged with piano accompaniments by Moeran, who also collected songs in his own native Kerry, in Ireland. The two areas are compared in JEFDSS: 1948, pp. 152–4 'Some Folk Singing of To-day'.

O LOCHLAINN: 1939
Colm O Lochlainn, *Irish Street Ballads*: Three Candles, Dublin, 1939. Over 100 songs, words, music and annotations collected in many different parts of Ireland (including the North). All in English and many having equivalents in England and Scotland. Illustrated with woodcuts from the original broadsheets.

O LOCHLAINN: 1965
Colm O Lochlainn, *More Irish Street Ballads*: Three Candles, Dublin, 1965. A further 100 songs, all again in the English language.

ORD: 1930
John Ord, *Bothy Songs and Ballads*: Alexander Gardner, Paisley, Scotland. The standard work on the 'bothy ballads' of N.E. Scotland; 'bothy' meaning farm cottage or hut used by hands, ploughmen, shepherds and farm-servants, and the ballads, although including folksongs found elsewhere, being mainly those describing, and often complaining about, local farm life.

PINTO AND RODWAY: 1957
V. de Sola Pinto and A. E. Rodway, *The Common Muse*: Chatto & Windus, London, 1957; Penguin Books, London, 1965. An anthology of Popular British Ballad Poetry from the 15th to the 20th century. In two parts: the first 'Amatory' and the second 'General'. 245 texts from England, Ireland and Scotland with an introduction mainly about street balladry.

PURSLOW: 1965
Frank Purslow, *Marrowbones*: EFDS Publications, London, 1965. A series of pocket-size publications initiated by Peter Kennedy in order to make available the songs collected by Hammond and Gardiner in the care of the EFDSS library. This selection contains 100 songs, provided with chord symbols over the melodies.

PURSLOW: 1968
Frank Purslow, *The Wanton Seed*: EFDS Publications, London, 1968. A second selection from Hammond and Gardiner again containing 100 songs.

PURSLOW: 1972
Frank Purslow, *The Constant Lovers*: EFDS Publications, London, 1972. A third selection in which the type-size has been increased and the number of songs reduced to 78.

REEVES: 1958
James Reeves, *The Idiom of the People*: Heinemann, London, 1958. Words of 115 folksongs from Cecil Sharp MSS (about 40 printed for the first time) selected as examples of 'English

Bibliography

Traditional Verse'. Introduction concerned with the Folk Song Movement in England; Sharp as a collector; text revisions, description of the MSS; the popular idiom; and a detailed consideration of certain songs.

REEVES: 1960
James Reeves, *The Everlasting Circle*: Heinemann, London, 1960. 142 texts from the MSS of Baring Gould, Hammond and Gardiner considered as 'English traditional verse'. Introduction concerned with Baring Gould as a collector and his MSS; Hammond and Gardiner; varieties of folksong; the theme of fertility and a discussion on the *lingua franca* of English traditional song.

SEEGER AND MACCOLL: 1960
Peggy Seeger and Ewan MacColl, *The Singing Island*: Mills Music, London, 1960. 96 English and Scots folksongs arranged for 'the post-war folk revival' mainly from Scotland under headings: Children, Courting, Men at Work, On the Road, Sailors, Barrack Room, Rovin' Boys and Flash Girls, Historical and Fill up your Glass.

SHARP: 1902
Cecil J. Sharp, *A Book of British Song*: John Murray, London, 1902. 78 songs published before Sharp started collecting. They are listed under National, Soldier and Sailor, Country, Humorous, Old English and Old Scottish, starting with *God Save the King* and *Rule Britannia* and finishing with *Auld Lang Syne*. Only two Welsh and two Irish national songs are included.

SHARP MS 1903–23
Cecil Sharp (1859–1924), foremost collector of English folksongs and folkdances, was the founder of The English Folk Dance Society and for many years a member of The Folk-Song Society. (In 1932 these two societies amalgamated as The English Folk Dance and Song Society.) For a full account of his life-work and publications see *Cecil Sharp* by A. H. Fox-Strangways (Oxford University Press, London, 1933), revised by Maud Karpeles (Routledge & Kegan Paul, London, 1967). Words, songs, tunes and dance notes in Cecil Sharp's autograph are in the Library of Clare College, Cambridge. There are also photostat copies in the Harvard University Library and the New York Public Library, and microfilm copies in the libraries of the University of California and in the library at Cecil Sharp House, London, the headquarters of The English Folk Dance and Song Society. Cecil Sharp's own collection of books was left to the EFDSS and formed the beginning of the specialist library at Cecil Sharp House.

SHARP AND MARSON: 1904–9
Cecil J. Sharp and Rev. Charles L. Marson, *Folk Songs from Somerset*: Simpkin Marshall, London and Barnicott, Taunton, Somerset. 5 vols. Vol. I 1904, vol. II 1905, vol. III 1906, vol. IV 1908, vol. V 1909. The most important single collection of English folksong, later edited as the *Selected Edition* (1916–21). Introduction concerning singers and style most valuable.

STUBBS: 1970
Ken Stubbs, *The Life of a Man*: EFDS Publications, London, 1970. 50 songs, texts and melodies (chord symbols). Many from our same source singers, but includes a wide variety from Home Counties (Surrey, Sussex mainly and some from Kent) with some important variant versions and some hitherto unpublished songs. Biographical notes about singers.

WILLIAMS: 1923
Alfred Owen Williams, *Folk Songs of the Upper Thames*: Duckworth, London, 1923. Over 300 folksongs (words only) noted mainly in Berkshire, Gloucestershire, Oxfordshire and Wiltshire. Interesting introduction about rural life, more fully covered by Williams in *Round About the Upper Thames* (Duckworth, 1922). Further unpublished texts in Swindon Reference Library. See FMJ: 1969 'Alfred Williams: A Symposium'.

*

BARRY: 1929
Phillips Barry, Fanny Hardy Eckstorm and Mary Winslow Smyth, *British Ballads from Maine*: Yale University Press, New Haven, Conn., USA, 1929.

BELDEN: 1940
H. M. Belden, *Ballads and Songs Collected by the Missouri Folklore Society*: University Studies XV (No. 1), Columbia, Missouri, USA, 1940.

BREWSTER: 1940
Paul G. Brewster, *Ballads and Songs of Indiana*: University Folklore Publications No. 1, Bloomington, Indiana, USA, 1940.

BROWN: 1952–62
Frank C. Brown, *Collection of North Carolina Folklore*: vol. II Ballads; vol. III Songs; vols. IV and V Tunes. Duke University Press, Durham, N. Carolina, USA, 1952–62.

CAMBIARE: 1934
Celestin Pierre Cambiare, *East Tennessee and Western Virginia Mountain Ballads*: Mitre Press, London, 1934.

CHAPPELL: 1939
Louis W. Chappell, *Folk-Songs of Roanoke and the Albemarle*: Ballad Press, Morgantown, W. Virginia, USA, 1939.

COMBS: 1925
Josiah H. Combs, *Folk Songs du Midi des États-Unis*: Les Presses Universitaires de France, Paris, 1925. *Folk Songs of the Southern United States* edited by D. K. Wilgus (annotated English edition) as 19th volume of American Folklore Society's Bibliographical Special Series. University of Texas Press, Austin, Texas, USA, 1967.

COX: 1925
John Harrington Cox, *Folk Songs of the South*: Harvard University Press, Cambridge, Mass., USA, 1925. Dover Publications Reprint, New York, 1967 (released 1968). 185 songs collected in West Virginia (29 with tunes). Introduction describes collecting methods and identifies informants. Notes, references to other versions and other data given with texts of songs.

CREIGHTON: 1932
Helen Creighton, *Songs and Ballads from Nova Scotia*: Dent, Toronto, Canada, 1932. Dover Publications Reprint, New York, 1966. 150 songs, gathered mainly in the vicinity of Halifax, written down by the author and afterwards checked with recordings. First of four published collections.

CREIGHTON AND SENIOR: 1950
Helen Creighton and Doreen Senior, *Traditional Songs from Nova Scotia*: Ryerson Press, Toronto, Canada, 1950. 100 songs and 36 ballads collected in the Maritimes with additional variants of both tunes and texts in many instances. An important and well documented collection with versions of many of the songs in this book.

EDDY: 1939
Mary O. Eddy, *Ballads and Songs from Ohio*: J. J. Augustin, New York, 1939.

FLANDERS AND BROWN: 1932
Helen Hartness Flanders and George Brown, *Vermont Folk Songs and Ballads*: Stephen Daye, Brattleboro, Vermont, USA, 1932.

FLANDERS AND BARRY: 1939
Helen Hartness Flanders, Elizabeth Flanders Ballard, George Brown and Phillips Barry, *The New Green Mountain Songster: Traditional Folksongs of Vermont*: Yale University, New Haven, Conn., USA, 1939.

FUSON: 1931
Harvey H. Fuson, *Ballads of the Kentucky Highlands*: Mitre Press, London, 1931.

GARDNER AND CHICKERING: 1939
Emelyn E. Gardner and Geraldine J. Chickering, *Ballads and Songs of Southern Michigan*: University Press, Ann Arbor, Michigan, USA, 1939.

Bibliography

GREENLEAF: 1933
Elizabeth Bristol Greenleaf and Grace Yarrow Mansfield, *Ballads and Sea Songs from Newfoundland*: Harvard University Press, Cambridge, Mass., USA, 1933.

HENRY: 1938
Mellinger E. Henry, *Folksongs from the Southern Highlands*: J. J. Augustin, New York, 1938.

HUDSON: 1936
Arthur Palmer Hudson, *Folksongs of Mississippi*: University of N. Carolina, Chapel Hill, N. Carolina, USA, 1936.

JAFL: 1888–
Journal of American Folklore now published by University of Pennsylvania.

KARPELES: 1934/71
Maud Karpeles, *Folksongs from Newfoundland*: Oxford University Press, London, 1934 (2 vols.); Faber & Faber, London, 1971. 30 songs (with piano accompaniments) were published in 1934 and 90 songs, 150 tunes including variants (with no accompaniments) in 1971. All collected during 1929–30.

KORSON: 1949
George Korson, *Pennsylvania Songs and Legends*: University Press, Philadelphia, Penn., USA, 1949.

LEACH: 1965
MacEdward Leach, *Folk Ballads and Songs of the Lower Labrador Coast*: National Museum of Canada, Ottawa, 1965.

LINSCOTT: 1939
E. H. Linscott, *Folk Songs of Old New England*: Macmillan, New York, 1939.

LOMAX: 1934
John and Alan Lomax, *American Ballads and Folk Songs*: Macmillan, New York, 1934.

LOMAX: 1941
John and Alan Lomax, *Our Singing Country*: Macmillan, New York, 1941.

MACKENZIE: 1928
W. Roy Mackenzie, *Ballads and Sea Songs from Nova Scotia*: Harvard University Press, Cambridge, Mass., USA, 1928.

MEREDITH AND ANDERSON: 1967
John Meredith and Hugh Anderson, *Folk Songs of Australia*: Ure Smith, Sydney, 1967.

MORRIS: 1950
Alton C. Morris, *Folksongs of Florida*: University of Florida, Gainesville, Florida, USA, 1950.

NEELY AND SPARGO: 1938
Charles Neely and John W. Spargo, *Tales and Songs of Southern Illinois*: George Banta, Menasha, Wisconsin, USA, 1938.

OWENS: 1950
William A. Owens, *Texas Folk Songs*: Texas Folk-Lore Society, Dallas, Texas, USA, 1950.

PEACOCK: 1965
Kenneth Peacock, *Songs of the Newfoundland Outports*: National Museum of Canada, Ottawa, 1965. 3 vols.

POUND: 1922
Louise Pound, *American Ballads and Songs*: Charles Scribner's Sons, New York, 1922.

RANDOLPH: 1946–50
Vance Randolph and Floyd C. Shoemaker, *Ozark Folk Songs*: State Historical Society, Columbia, Missouri, USA, 1946–50. 4 vols.

RICKABY: 1926
Frank Rickaby, *Ballads and Songs of the Shanty-boy*: Harvard University Press, Cambridge, Mass., USA, 1926.

SFLQ: 1937–
Southern Folklore Quarterly: University of Florida, Gainesville, Florida, USA, 1937–.

SANDBURG: 1927
Carl Sandburg, *The American Songbag*: Harcourt Brace, New York, 1927.

SCARBOROUGH: 1937
Dorothy Scarborough, *A Song Catcher in the Southern Mountains*: Columbia University Press, New York, 1937.

SHARP AND KARPELES: 1917/32
Olive Dame Campbell and Cecil J. Sharp, *English Folk Songs from the Southern Appalachians*: Putnam, New York, 1917. Cecil J. Sharp and Maud Karpeles (2 vols.), Oxford University Press, London, 1932.

SHOEMAKER: 1931
Henry W. Shoemaker, *Mountain Minstrelsy of Pennsylvania*: Newman F. McGirr, Philadelphia, USA, 1931.

XVI

Songs of the
Travelling People

Introduction

The people described here as 'Travellers' have been variously classified according to their trades and professions, their particular form of dwelling—such as tent-dwellers, horse-wagon dwellers, and so on—and according to their ethnic antecedents. The last is the most interesting for our purpose, and in some areas it is still relevant today.

The Travellers (Gipsies, Tinkers, Potters and Hawkers) of Great Britain and Ireland are descended from at least three different races, and possibly from four or five. Originally there were just the itinerant metalworkers and other craftsmen of Celtic and pre-Celtic stock. Their languages were Pictish, Welsh, Gaelic, Shelta and Gamon, the last two being made-up code languages. Shelta, according to John Sampson (SAMPSON: 1926), is a systematic perversion of the pre-aspirated Gaelic spoken before the eleventh century; but according to Dr Kuno Meyer, writing in 1908, Shelta is based on an ancient secret language called Ogam; quite a number of terms, however, have no known etymology. Gamon is apparently an Anglo-Irish derivation of Shelta.

The Celtic and pre-Celtic travellers, generally referred to nowadays as Tinkers, Hawkers and Potters, were joined in Anglo-Saxon to Tudor times by the English Rogues, first described by Awdeley, Harman, Dekker and others in the sixteenth and seventeenth centuries. Their secret language, known as Cant, may well have derived from a *lingua franca* of the Crusades. One theory is that the Rogues were the descendants of returned Crusaders who found the free-booting life in the Middle East more to their taste than an ordered life at home and hence continued 'crusading' on the King's Highway. Many of the original cant words, mixed with a surprisingly large number of Romany words, are still in use today among Scots tinkers, basket-makers, hawkers, and other travellers.

The third strain, the Romanies, were originally a low-caste Indian people, speaking a modi-fied form of Sanskrit, mixed with Prakrit, tenth century North Indian, Persian, medieval Greek, Slavonic, German, French, and odd words from other languages. The early history of their wanderings, as well as the relative length of their stay in any one country, can only be conjectured from their vocabulary; but from the fourteenth century onward their history is increasingly well-documented in Europe since an alarming number of them terrorized the length and breadth of the Continent, and they were outlawed in all but a handful of countries. In England, almost at their first appearance in the early part of the sixteenth century, the penalty just for being a Romany, a 'gipsy', was death or banishment.

These three main types of travellers were joined from time to time by successive waves of 'refugees' from political, social and economic upheavals—particularly the Irish potato famine and the Highland clearances when English and Lowland Scots landlords evicted the original cattle-raising and grain-farming Gaelic inhabitants of the Scottish Highlands and put the land to sheep. In mid-nineteenth-century literature the non-Romany travellers were frequently referred to as 'Pikies' or 'Pikers'. In George Borrow's *Romano Lavo-Lil* (1874):

> The people called in Acts of Parliament sturdy beggars and vagrants, in the old cant language Abraham men, and in the modern Pikers . . . roam about like the gipsies, and, like them, have a kind of secret language. But the gipsies are a people of Oriental origin, whilst the Abrahamites are the scurf of the English body corporate. . . . The speech of the Abrahamites is a horrid jargon, com-posed for the most part of low English words used in an allegorical sense—a jargon in which a stick

is called a crack; a hostess, a rum necklace; a bar-maid, a dolly-mort; brandy, rum, booze; a constable, a horny. But enough of these Pikers, these Abrahamites. . . .

Eric Partridge in his *Dictionary of the Underworld* gives Pikey as '*a tramp; a gipsy*'; and Piker as '*2. a tramp; a vagrant; occ. a gipsy. . . . 5. a hobo.*' These extracts are quoted, even though the term is no longer in general use, because according to some of the Smiths of Essex and to some of the Lees of Kent as well as to Fred Wood of Box Hill in Surrey the definition is wrong. The correct term for this kind of vagrant is 'hedgemumper'. A piker is a man who has been cast out from gipsy society.

From a Romany point of view there are four classifications of people on the road:

> *Pure Romanies*: Fairly pure-blooded Romanies who follow the Romany way of life or code. This code is not fully explained to outsiders but might on occasion be acquired instinctively by non-gipsy people who have constant dealings with the Romanies. Any unusual non-gipsy who does adopt the Romany code in this manner might become an acceptable adopted member of the tribe and eventually even marry into it. He will never be considered a Romany, but his children, growing up with the tribe, though technically half-breeds will be referred to as pure Romanies.
>
> *Posh-rats* (literally 'half-bloods'): These may be regarded as Romanies if their parents were married with the consent of the head of the tribe; if they married without this consent they are called *Didikais*.
>
> *Pikers* or *Pikies*: Romanies expelled from a tribe for breaking the code.
>
> *Needies*, *Mumpers* or *Hedgemumpers*: Travellers with no Romany blood at all.

From a Scots tinker point of view the classification is as follows:

> *Tinkers, Hawkers, Potters, Basketmakers*: All trade classifications, lumped together under the group-terms *nokems, nahkens* or *nackers*.
>
> *Gipsies, screeves*: Many of the first three Romany classes listed.
>
> *Bucks, Blue-bucks* or *Buck-men*: Town-dwellers or country people who have drifted onto the road and live among the travellers.

Until recent times the different races of travellers did not normally intermarry; even today there are still some tribes whose members will only marry close blood relations with the same family name and preferably only those who have travelled constantly with the tribe.

There was an 'armed truce' between the various tribes. They all kept to their own territories in which they travelled in well-defined circular routes from which they never strayed; the idea being that since they all followed similar trades—such as potmending, horse-breeding and doctoring, knife sharpening—for which there was only a limited demand in any one district, more than one itinerant tradesman covering the same route would have reduced the earnings of each below subsistence level.

It is often said that travellers do not take to organization or to any kind of discipline; this may occasionally be true when said with reference to some hedgemumpers, but the various Celtic and pre-Celtic tinkers, as well as the Romanies, have always travelled in highly organized clans and tribes. No kind of society could possibly have survived constant persecution through the centuries without a high degree of discipline and organization. Each clan or tribe can be considered as a small autonomous Republic or Kingdom which is in loose contact with other clans and tribes and has binding verbal treaties with all its neighbouring tribes and clans. Every member observes the laws of the road—laws of custom—which are in many ways more terrible than any statutory laws.

These laws, sometimes referred to as 'The Gipsy Code', have often had to be adjusted to changing conditions or even abandoned under harassment by the local police, as for instance the Romany ritual of erecting maternity tents in which a woman will bear her child and live with it for several days before moving back to the family wagon or tent. Also worthy of mention is the gradual change from a largely criminal way of life to one of useful labour in agriculture, building, and so on, the sort of work which was almost taboo among Romanies only two centuries ago. Such changes in the mode of living are decided on at secret meetings, and those who do not comply with major tribal decisions of this kind become outcasts in every sense of the word.

A Romany tribe is headed by the oldest man or woman. All money earned by any member of the tribe is handed over to the head, who is the tribe's banker. The banker pays each back a certain amount for food and other necessities and keeps the rest for the common purse. Apart from being the banker, the head of a Romany tribe makes all major decisions; he or she decides who will go to work at which jobs from day to day; who will go poaching; which of the women will go out hawking and which will stay behind for chores around the wagons; when to break camp and which new camping place to aim for. The only real freedoms that members of the tribe have are freedoms of execution and time-keeping—that is that within reason they can start and finish their daily work at any time they please and they are not watched over while they do their work. They are, however, judged on performance—and woe betide any habitual shirkers.

Any member of the tribe who wants, say, some new tool, a new horse, or a new wagon, for which he has not enough money, goes to the head of the tribe to ask for a grant to buy what he needs. Normally, if the funds are available, the head will grant such a request, but if it is turned down, the head's decision is final and no more is heard about the matter. If the money is granted, the member of the tribe can use it only for the purpose for which it was granted, and any surplus has to go back into the common purse. The item bought with the tribe's money in this way is considered the private property of the member who bought it. He can exchange it for something else without consulting anyone—but if he sells it, the money he gets for it must go back into the common purse.

The same social structure and system of the common purse also exists among some of the itinerant Celtic and pre-Celtic clans, except that it is always the oldest male who is accepted as the head of the clan.

Any member of a Romany tribe who consistently offends against the Romany code of behaviour is ceremoniously expelled from the brotherhood. Within weeks of such an expulsion every Romany in Great Britain would know that such-and-such a person is no longer considered a Romany. This is final and there is no appeal.

The differences between Romanies and other travellers are not merely differences of race and language; there are also differences of marriage, funeral and other customs, as well as differences of standards of cleanliness (in hygiene and ritual cleanliness) and minimum standards of honesty. For instance, among Romanies, a woman in her menstrual periods is considered unclean; and when a woman is in labour, a maternity tent is supposed to be pitched for her away from the main camp. In some areas this is still the custom. When she moves back, the maternity tent is burned with all its contents.

Centuries ago, according to Fred Wood, when a Romany died he was cremated with his caravan; but when this sort of cremation became illegal, the funeral customs had to be modified. In the more recent past, when a Romany died, his dogs and horses were shot, his crockery smashed, his wagon with everything in it burned—except money and jewellery (which, however, was frequently buried with him)—and the kettle-cranes, kettles, pots, pans and cutlery as well as any tools, guns, snares, slings and musical instruments were buried either with him or in some auspicious place. A flint cross laid out on the verge of the highway generally marked the spot where a Romany died. Nowadays only the burning of wagons, clothes and bedding, and the smashing of crockery are sometimes observed.

When a Romany fancied a girl for his wife he gave her his 'dickler' (neckscarf) and if she wore it on her head when next he saw her, he knew they were engaged. They then went off together for a few days to see if they suited each other. What happened if they were incompatible remains a mystery, but normally they went back to the tribe after this honeymoon and a marriage ceremony was held in which the bride's and groom's right wrists were pricked and pressed together for the mingling of their blood, and they were told to be kind to each other. After that, they either lived together in a tent until they could afford a wagon or, if they were lucky, they moved straight into a wagon of their own which someone might have given them as a wedding present. There were slight variations to all these customs from tribe to tribe; Fred Wood underwent the blood-mingling ceremony, Jasper Smith did not. . . .

There are hundreds of customs and traditions which together constitute a distinct Romany way of life, quite different from, say, the Scottish tinker's customs and traditions. The tinkers, for example, do not burn the wagons of their deceased; but they 'wake' their dead—sometimes keeping a wake for as long as a whole week—and if the deceased was a musician, will have someone playing his favourite instrument at the head of the funeral procession, while often the coffin is carried by all the male members of the clan of the deceased in turn.

The decline of the traditional tribal and clan systems began in the middle of the nineteenth century, accelerated in the First World War and was almost completed in the Second World War, when a large number of gipsies and other travellers were drafted into the Army and acquired a lot of the habits of thought and action of their non-gipsy comrades. When they returned to civilian life most of them married, often outside their own kind, and started out on their own without even considering paying anything into their tribe's common purse. Further blows to the traditional life on the road came through new legislation—particularly the Highways Act, 1959, which closed most of the traditional stopping places. Since then gipsies and other travellers, who before the War would not have consented to camp in the same field together, have increasingly found themselves herded together by the hundreds. Another contributing factor towards the decline of the old way of life is that most of the traditional gipsy trades have become obsolete and have had to be replaced by other occupations; and whereas a traditional hand-carved, brightly painted wooden gipsy caravan with some well-groomed horses and a group of handsome, brightly dressed gipsies doing a traditional job rarely offended anyone, a group of dirty people pulled on to a field with their ramshackle vehicles and trailer caravans surrounded by an assortment of rusty old bicycle frames, car-bodies, prams, bedsprings and other garbage is a different matter.

*

The traveller's style of singing is quite distinctive. The singer will stand or sit up stiffly, throw back his head and sing flat out—generally in a nasal tone. The voice of the singer is, more often than not, modified by acute bronchitis, which has undoubtedly been brought on by travellers living in overheated caravans which they will come into and go out of in their shirt-sleeves in all weathers.

Many singers tend to add simple decorations to insipid tunes, and rhythmically their singing style is interesting because they tend to experiment, having an uncanny feel for *rubato*, often modifying the basic rhythm of an air from one verse to the next; whether these characteristics are part of an old native tradition is a matter for argument. In any case, some of the best-known travelling singers deviate from the general *gipsy* style of singing in one or more details.

As a rule, gipsies and travellers look upon any activity as a possible source of income and, while they certainly enjoy singing, making music and dancing around their campfires, they almost invariably think of these private sessions as practice for possible public performance. Generally speaking, they will not make up their own songs and tunes and will concentrate on whatever is most popular in the areas in which they travel. This is not to say that they have no distinctive style of performance, but the material is on the whole common. The most popular types of song among gipsies in England today are nineteenth-century music hall songs, Victorian tear-jerkers, a number of popular songs of the twenties and early thirties and the odd latest pop number. Fiddles, squeeze-boxes, harmonicas, jews harps, tambourines, clappers, spoons and various types of whistles all occasionally figure in the English gipsies' music. If they do give a sideshow when a travelling circus passes through their area, it is frequently a performance of traditional tap-dances to harmonica and tambourine music.

In Scotland the repertoire is somewhat different. The Scots have always been proud of their traditional music, and the travellers there have preserved a great many old songs and ballads which would never have survived otherwise. Such singers as Belle Stewart, Jeannie Robertson, Davie Stewart and Jimmy McBeath are known to folk music enthusiasts all over the English-speaking world. There are also some fine instrumentalists among the Scots travellers who play bagpipes, mouth-organs and button accordions, and here and there in England and Scotland one does come across the odd traveller who makes up songs on the travelling life. As for traditional English gipsy ballad singers, there are some fine performers such as the Scamp family in Kent and Phoebe Smith of Woodbridge, Suffolk.

Apart from Gavin Greig (GREIG: 1914), few collectors of folksongs before the Second World War paid attention to the collection of travellers' material, although most collectors seem to have jotted down a handful of minor songs from odd tinkers and gipsies they chanced to meet. And even Gavin Greig did not himself collect material from the travellers, but received it by mail from other house-dwellers.

Much credit for the belated recognition of the travellers' important place in folksong must go to Hamish Henderson and the School of Scottish Studies in Edinburgh, whose collectors have gone to great trouble to track down traditional song-carriers, storytellers and musicians all over Scotland.

In England the only songbook completely given over to songs collected from gipsies was GILLINGTON: 1911. Other odd songs are scattered here and there through other British folksong collections, but the gipsy tradition is in the main buried in a few specialist publications such as the *Journal of the Gypsy Lore Society* (JGLS).

The first thing that strikes anyone in search of older traditional gipsy song is the paucity of the material, and when met, its fragmentary character. In England and Wales most old gipsy songs have only one verse consisting of four short lines, and frequently the first two lines in such a stanza have absolutely no connection with the other two lines. It has no parallel in other British song tradition. With few exceptions these songs have no fixed text or meaning and they even include occasional meaningless lines. Collectors generally dismiss these fragments as too short to be noted, and if asked about gipsy folksong tradition say that it does not exist.

It is true that the words of most old gipsy songs are not verse in the accepted sense of the word. This is perhaps the reason for their almost total omission from folksong books. A text may consist of just one word or one line which may or may not set the mood for the song. Sometimes a set of such single words and lines may be woven into a melody—which may be in an unsuitable rhythm in relation to the metre of the words—the resultant improvised text being entirely incomprehensible. Even when a text has been well thought out it rarely comes to more than four lines in the older gipsy tradition. These may be ad-libbed or followed by mouth music.

Typical examples of single-line texts are:

Mangen mas y moro	Begging meat and bread
Purdilo baval	Blow wind
Ballovas an' yarrers	Bacon and eggs
Poove the groi, chav	Let the horse into the field, mate

and a common introductory line is:

Mandi jalled to poove the gry	I went to put the horse to graze in the farmer's field without his consent

An example of a two-liner is:

Mandi jilled to the rakli's ken	I went to the lady's house
To mang a pair o' chockers	To beg a pair of shoes

In Britain the single-line song has ceased to be part of gipsy tradition. To find this, one has to go to Hungary, where the older traditions are still strong.* But a number of four-line stanzas are still in current use in Britain. For example, to the tune of *Bobby Shaftoe* there are a number of well-known Romany and cant children's songs, notably *Oko Vela o Chavo* (No. 352), and this, recorded from some children playing at the side of the A2 trunk road near Stone, in Kent, in 1962:

Dick akai, Didikai	Look here, Didikai
Daddy's jalled to poove the gry	Daddy's gone to graze the horse
Off the drom into the tan	Off the road into the camp
At five o'clock torarty	At five o'clock tonight

And from children skipping near Colney Heath, Hertfordshire, in 1962:

O ballovas an' yarrers	O the bacon and eggs
An' ballovas an' yarrers	And the bacon and eggs
An' the rye an' the rawny	And the gentleman and the lady
Come jillin' up the drom	Come going up the road†

Another four-line survivor is *Can you Rocker Romany?*, which must either have some secret significance or owe its survival to a fluke. It was published with music (GILLINGTON: 1911), but nowadays it is a recitation only. Solomon Smith of west Kent gave a version in May 1960 in which the four questions are identical with those quoted in BORROW: 1874, although his wording is somewhat more archaic. However, Solomon Smith was unable to translate the phrase 'kil the bosh'. He said that originally his version was that in general use, but that nowadays everybody quotes it differently:‡

Can you rocker Romany	Can you speak Romany?
Can you kil the bosh?	Can you play the fiddle?
Can you jall the sturraben?	Can you go to prison?
An' can you chin the kosh?	And can you carve wood [carve clothes pegs]?
Now can you rocker Romany?	Can you speak Romany?
An' can you lel a mush?	Can you do a chop?
An' can you chor a cannie?	And can you steal a chicken?
And a bittie kosh?	And a bit of firewood?

John Smith, Birmingham, August, 1962

---

* The single-line song has been exhaustively treated in VEKERDI: 1967, in which all types of current Hungarian gipsy songs are analysed.
† *Dick akai, Didikai*, see WEBB: 1960. *O ballovas an' yarrers*, see LELAND: 1875, a book which contains mainly rye-songs by Leland, Palmer and Tuckey, and a handful of genuine Romany jingles. 'Ballovas an' yarrers', incidentally, is traditionally always linked with 'the rye an' the rawny come jillin' up the drom'.
‡ See also McEVOY: 1938.

Can you rocker Romany?	Can you speak Romany?
Can you pook a kosh?	Can you read a road sign?
Can you mor a gavmush?	Can you beat a policeman?
With a knobbly kosh?	With a knobbly stick?

Frank Smith, A2 trunk road, August, 1963

Can you pooker Romany?	Can you speak Romany?
Can you Didikai?	Can you Didikai?
Can you chor a cannie	Can you steal a chicken
While the mush is jallin' by?	While the man is walking by?

Wally Fuller

Fred Wood of Box Hill, Surrey, said that in his family very short nonsensical songs were frequently made up on the spur of the moment after nocturnal poaching expeditions. When the men got back to the waggons the women had stayed up to brew some tea for them, and while the men were waiting they made up little songs about the night's exploits. The women made up hawking songs and songs about 'scrapes' (encounters) they had with local people and the police. These songs rarely came to more than four to six lines, and very few of them became part of the permanent repertoire.

In recent years the tradition has changed somewhat, especially in areas where Romany has been replaced by cant. On the one hand whole ballads and songs from British tradition have been taken over and slightly changed in mood by getting a traveller's setting and becoming obscure through cantification of the words; on the other hand a more comprehensible new style of traveller's song has evolved under the influence of British tradition. These new songs, both in English and in cant, are gradually ousting the bulk of traditional gipsy song described above—including the four-line verses which at best float amid the newer material.*

An early example of an English ballad verse together with its cantified form appeared in JFSS: 1901, No. 3, p. 110, collected by W. P. Merrick:

If you diks up a fun'ychel that's bukalo and shel	When you meets with a poor traveller who is hungry and dry
Lel lesti to a kitchema . . .	And if he craves for charity, his wants I will supply
Del les tatti-panni, levina . . .	Here's ale, wine, and brandy, till I've spent all my store
And when the loovo is saw jalled	And when my money is all gone I'll boldly rob for more
Go a-looring for bootidair	

Captain Grant (verse 2)

Apart from these modified versions of traditional songs and ballads there is very little in the repertoire that can be described as specifically gipsy or tinker, except street cries and hawkers' jingles which appear to be known to travellers all over England and Scotland. These cries and jingles are of little interest musically, their main purpose being to attract attention. But they do give an insight into the everyday life of the people who sing or, rather, shout them.

Street cries have been amply covered in JFSS and JEFDSS: Baskets, Chairs, JFSS: 1910, No. 15, p. 99, which were sung by travellers. Others are: Bottles and Rags, JFSS: 1919, No. 22, p. 66; Brooms, JEFDSS: 1944, p. 189; Chairs to mend, JFSS: 1919, No. 22, pp. 70–1;

---

* Other songs in this collection sung by travellers: *Old Grey Beard* (No. 139); *The Ploughboy* (No. 140); *The Queen Among the Heather* (No. 141); *A Blacksmith Courted Me* (No. 146); *Down by Blackwaterside* (No. 151); *The False Bride* (No. 152); *Going to Mass Last Sunday* (No. 155); *The Bold English Navvy* (No. 171); *The Coachman's Whip* (No. 172); *The Lady o' the Dainty Doon-by* (No. 179); *The Little Ball of Yarn* (No. 180); *The Overgate* (No. 187); *She Was a Rum One* (No. 190); *Grat for Gruel* (No. 202); *Never Wed a' Auld Man* (No. 207); *Rocking the Cradle* (No. 212); *Rue the Day* (No. 213); *Needlecases* (No. 233); *Poor Wee Jockie Clarke* (No. 236); *The Barnyards o' Delgaty* (No. 242); *Van Diemen's Land* (No. 262); *The Ewie wi' the Crookit Horn* (No. 271); *Farewell to Whisky* (No. 272); *Rothsay-O* (No. 282); *Three Men Went a-Hunting* (No. 306); *Was You Ever See?* (No. 309); *The Oxford Girl* (No. 327); *Poison in a Glass of Wine* (No. 329).

Clothes-props, JFSS: 1910, No. 15, p. 101; Flowers, JFSS: 1915, No. 19, p. 216; Knives to grind, JFSS: 1919, No. 22, pp. 63, 76 with note; Lumber and old Iron, JFSS: 1919, No. 22, p. 64; Rags and Bones, JFSS: 1919, No. 22, p. 64.

The most remarkable street cry or trade jingle is a long inventory which has wide currency among travellers of the 'general dealer' class who select the lines applicable to their own business and forget the rest. Nobody outside the travelling community appears to use it, so one can fairly assume that it was composed by a traveller. The most remarkable thing about this long trade jingle is that a class of mainly illiterate people should be able to memorise and select from it at will.

Trade rhymes, sir, we still use 'em, so we remember them. There's a long one—you shout it when you slowly walk yer 'orse an' cart up a residential street an' you don't reckon anybody will listen to what you say—they just know you an' they listen for your bell an' the rhyme, an' they'll call out for you:

I beg with most respectful feeling	Old roping, sacking and old rags
Leave to inform you what I deal in	Any bottles, horsehair and old glass
I have not come your purse to try	Old copper, pewter and old brass
Yourself shall sell and I will buy	Old saucepans, boilers, copper-kettles
So please look out that useless lumber	Pewters, spoons and other metals
Which long you may have left to slumber	Old coins, old silver, ancient buttons
I'll buy old boots, old shoes, old socks	Clothing, in fashion, or old-style cut 'uns
Jackets, trousers, and smock frocks	Skins—whether worn by hare or rabbit
Towels, cloths and cast-off linen	However small your stock, I'll have it
Cords, cashmeers, and worn-out women's	I'll buy old rags, however rotten
Old gowns, caps, bonnets torn to tatters	If made of woollen, hemp, or cotton
If fine or coarse, it never matters	I'll buy old iron, cast or wrought
Bed ticking, fustians, velveteens	And pay the money when it's bought
Stuffs, worsted cords and bombazines	If you have any bones to sell
Old worn-out handkerchiefs and shawls	Their value in a trice I'll tell
Likewise umbrellas and parasols	So over your dwelling give a glance
Bicycles, parts, spokes and old tyres	You'll never have a better chance
And rolls of plain and of barbed wire	My price is good, my weight is just
Sheep-netting, canvassing and carpeting	And mind, I never ask for trust
And whatever else you have to bring	So just look up if just a handful
And the weight I'll very soon tell you	And for the same I shall be thankful
For which I'll pay the utmost value	If you find it too late—keep it in a sack
I'll purchase dirty, fat dusty bags	And I'll buy it off you next time I'm back

You start the rhyme anywhere you please and you cast out things you can't sell. I know one dealer that had the whole thing printed. He left the printed card one day and made his rounds the next—collected all the junk an' got most of 'is cards back the same time. But I reckon myself the best street cry is the shortest yelp you can think of what nobody can understand—makes women curious and chase arter you an' you get a lot o' things for nothing. You get a bell, tinkle it an' shout 'Maheeeeup! Maheeeeup!' Nother tinkle an' 'Maheeeeup! Maheeeeup!' an' that's as much as I'll record for you for nothin', sir.—SOLOMON SMITH, west Kent, 1960.

Finally there is the most recent type of traditional gipsy song with the sure imprint of the last hundred years on it. This is the romantic type of song dealing with the carefree life under the open sky, such as *I'm a Romany Rye* (or *I'm no Romany Rye*). The first version by John Smith, Birmingham, 1962:

I'm no Romany Rye, I'm a real Didikai
I bide in a bender beneath the blue sky
In a van or a tent where I don't pay no rent
That's why the locals calls me a Romany Rye

And I'm thinking of getting married
With a mort or two of me own
And move around all over England like the ones fully blown

A 'bender' is a bow tent made up of branches and potato sacks (see *The Atching Tan Song*, No. 337). A 'mort' is a woman, and 'fully blown' means 'like a proper Romany'. A Romany version from Fred Wood goes:

I want no gilded mansion
I want no gilded hall
O, give to me the open sky
And the song of the lark that is flying high
I'm a Romany, everyone knows
And that's good enough for me

I would travel all round this country
With a heart that's ever willing
And I will cry
Why you can buy
Three pots for a shilling

This version was sung by Fred's mother when she went out hawking.

Finally we have the version of Wally Fuller and the Smith family of Woodbridge, Suffolk:

I will roam all around the country
This life will just suit me
I am a Romany, everyone knows
And a Romany I will be

But I'm determined to marry the girl I love
Take a waggin and tent on my own
I want no gilded mansion
I want no lovely home

I was born in an old gipsy's waggon
I were brought from these commons, you know
All our troubles begin in the winter
That's when we've nowhere to go

I'm a Romany Rye, a poor Didikai
Born in a tent underneath the blue sky
You give to me the open sky
And the song of the lark as it flies so high

Roamin' around the country
That life will just suit me
For I am a Romany, everyone knows
And a Romany I shall be

The bulk of the Romany vocabulary is derived from Indian languages. A few words, such as 'paanii' for 'water' and 'tshurii' (knife), are identical with their modern Indian equivalents; others are only vaguely similar to their modern Indian equivalents—like 'grai' (horse) which in modern Indian form is 'ghora'. Only by seeing a number of words side by side does the connection between Romany and its roots become obvious.

Here are some Sanskrit words with their Romany counterparts: 'antare' (inside) and 'andre', 'adre', ''dre'; 'vala' (hair) and 'bal'; 'vata' (stone) and 'bar'; 'cora' (thief) and 'tshor'; 'danta' (tooth) and 'dand'; 'agni' (fire) and 'yog'.

From the Persian 'beysha' (wood, forest) we have the Romany 'wesh'.

From the Turkish 'baht' comes the Romany 'bock'.

From the Greek come most of the words to do with metalwork, as well as the names of most of the actual metals; also from 'dromos' (road, way) we have the Romany 'drom'.

Various books have been written on Romany, all of them treating the language as a normal form of speech with a standard pronunciation and a standard intonation. To do this the authors had to select which of their sources they preferred or thought most knowledgeable in the subject. SMART AND CROFTON: 1875 were probably the only authorities to note the variations in the Romany vocabulary of their time. But even they ruled on what they considered the 'correct' pronunciation of Romany. In fact Romany takes on the phonetic characteristics of the dialect spoken in the area in which a tribe travels. When Frank Smith of Edenbridge was asked how far he had travelled, he replied, 'Broitn, oi been that fur.' ('I've been to Brighton.') He will call a horse a 'groi', a Didikai a 'Didikoi', and the gipsy word 'stariben' (prison) becomes 'sturriben' in his speech. In the North of England 'stariben' is sometimes pronounced 'stardipen', at other times it is abbreviated into 'stardi' (which in south-east England is the word for a hat), and in Wales, near the Shropshire border, it has been called 'strickapen'. In Wales the language sounds superficially Welsh, everywhere else like an archaic local dialect, and if anybody wishes to pronounce either Romany or tinker's cant correctly he should study the dialect of the area in which a vocabulary was collected.

The cantification of Romany has gone on for many years. Not only has the entire grammar gone overboard in most parts of England, but the actual vocabulary has changed considerably; a considerable number of English cant words have been admitted into the language and many Romany words have been abbreviated, particularly words ending in -engero. 'Gavengero' becomes 'gavver', 'Yogengero' 'yogger', and so on, and the whole vocabulary is grafted on to a purely English sentence in true canting fashion.

A number of Scots tinker words have an interesting etymology. The word 'pooskie', for instance, is derived from Romany 'pushca', a gun; a gamekeeper used to be called a 'pooskie-cowal', in tinker's cant, but as the word 'pooskie' ceased to be used for a gun, it is now used for a gamekeeper.

Gipsies and travellers are fully aware that their various vocabularies have been published and are readily available, so in emergencies it is necessary to speak in coded messages. As an example, a gipsy tribe has been shifted by the police from a spot where there was some honest work to another spot fifty miles away. They are out of money and have no food. They are not entitled to public assistance. All they can do in their plight is to go poaching and stealing from farms until they are back on home ground. One man is sent off to steal a dozen chickens from a farm five miles away. When he comes back there is a stranger in the encampment. Here are two coded Romany cant conversations:

'You chopped the groi, mush?'	'Did you swap the horse, man?'
'Arvah.'	'Yes.'
'Khushti chop?'	'Did you make a good deal?'
'Maw; gi'e'm five bar.'	'No, I had to give him five pounds with the horse.'
'Dordie! Dordie!'	'O, my God!'
'You kair the morts?'	'Did you do the women?'
'Arvah.'	'Yes.'
'Which keir you jalled?'	'Which house did you go to?'
'Number seven.'	'Number seven.'

Either conversation is coded cant for:

'You chored the kannies?'	'Did you steal the chickens?'
'Arvah.'	'Yes.'
''ow many you get?'	'How many did you get?'
'Seven.'	'Seven.'

In different circumstances an identical conversation might mean something quite different—'A farmer wants us to work for him—he only wants seven of us and he doesn't want any other gipsies to get wind of it so keep it under your hat.'

Welsh Romany Glossary

adre	in, inside
arey	at
bal	hair
balano kosht	fiddle bow—lit. hairy stick
bar	stone
barri	big
beshtas	sat
bosh	fiddle
bosh-kelomengero (usually boshomengro)	fiddle maker or player
chavi	girl
chavo	boy
chindilo	cut (past action)
chindyas	the one who cut it
dand	tooth
dicklo	neck scarf
doodah	sweetmeat
drey (adre)	in, inside
drom	road
gad	shirt
gooi	pudding
grai, gry	horse
i	the (*f.*)
keck	no, not
kedas	he made
kertsheema	inn

kon	who
kosht	stick
koshtenengo	wooden
kushti	good, fine
les, leske, leskee, lesko	his (endings vary according to number and gender)
miri	my (f.)
miro	my (n.)
nai	a negative
nai man (keck)	I have not got any
o	the (m.)
o bawrey choreskero	Father Christmas
paanii	water
pesko	his
petalo	horseshoe
poov	field
potchee	pocket
pushka	gun
rinkeni	pretty, attractive (usually refers only to people)
shee	is
shero	head
staadi	hat
top	on
tshor	thief
tshurii	knife
vela (avela)	came
wesh	wood (forest)
y	and
yog	fire
zigaira	tent (archaic)

English and English Gipsy Cant Glossary

(c)=Cant

akai	(c) here
arter	after
arvah	(c) yes
atch	(c) stop
atchin tan	(c) stopping place
avree	(c) away
bar	(c) pound (£)
beebee	(c) aunt
bender	bow tent
candyman	rag-and-bone man
cha(h)vi	(c) child
chop	exchange
chor	(c) a thief, to steal
dick	(c) to see, to look
dickin	(c) looking
dickler	(c) neck scarf
Diddies	(c) Didikais

dinilo	(c) crazy, deranged, mad
dordie	(c) an exclamation, usually *dordie dordie*!
drom	(c) road
gavver	(c) policeman
ghel	girl
groi, gry, grai	(c) horse
gry's chockers	horseshoes
jall, jawl, jil	(c) to go
jilling	(c) going
kair	(c) to do
kanny	(c) chicken
keir	(c) house
kek	(c) no
kharveesaster	(c) kettle crane, kettle prop
khushti	(c) good
lav	(c) word, name
lel	(c) to take, catch, arrest
lil	(c) book
Mandi	(c) I
mang	(c) to beg
ma, maw	(c) an exclamation
mas	(c) meat
monashay, mollisher	(c) woman, wife
moro	(c) bread
mort	(c) woman
mulla	(c) corpse, ghost
mulla, the old	the devil
muller'd	(c) killed, dead
mush	(c) man
nacker	horse ready for slaughter
nail	(c) to catch, surprise
narkey	(c) bad, unpleasant, risky
oprey	(c) up
orf	off
pooker	(c) to ask, to talk
poove	field
pound, in pound, in the pound	impounded
prey	(c) on, up, upon
public mansion	prison
rakli	(c) girl
rarti	(c) night
rawnie	(c) lady
rocka, rockra	(c) to speak
rye	(c) gentleman
scran	(c) food
shav, sherp	push, shove, go
stariben, sturraben, stardipen, strickapen	(c) prison
stuggers	(c) haystacks
tan	(c) stopping place
tit (*pl.* titties)	(c) old mare recently in foal
tooti	(c) you

torarti	(c) tonight
wavver	(c) other
yogengro	(c) gun, firearm

Scots and Scottish Cant Glossary

(c) = Cant

a'	all
ablaw	from all over the place
ain	one
airms	arms
annee	(c) in
aroon	around
a troachtan (*the* ch *pron. as in* loch)	abroad
avah	at all
avree	(c) away
awaft lo	(c) out of the way
awfi	awful
baith	both
baren	(c) case
barld heid	bald head
barrie	(c) good, gentle
beerie	(c) boat
belliment	(c) front door
bellum	(c) town
bene	(c) fine, gentle, classy, elegant
bene pahtren	(c) minister of the church
beneship	(c) pretty, handsome, fine
beneyerrum	(c) blood
bing	(c) come, go, put
binged	(c) went
bingen	(c) coming, going
bivvies	bivouac tents
blackie	(c) pot
blanchin	a clean out
blasswark	(c) bag, shopping bag
blink	twinkle
blyth	glad
bocht (*the* ch *pron. as in* loch)	bought
bothy	a shared cottage or hut for several farm servants
Brae	hillside, steep road
braxie (ham)	cured flesh of sheep (or other animal) that has died a natural death
breid	bread
brickets	(c) trousers
brig	bridge
broskin	(c) bicycle, any horseless vehicle
bruckler	(c) bowl
buck, blue-buck, buckman, half-buck	(c) non-travellers who have drifted on to the road
cairt	cart

carnish	(c) beef, meat
casro	(c) a greeting
chackers	(c) face
chet	(c) a thing
chetries	green vegetables
chiel	child, person near and dear to the speaker
choorie	(c) knife
chor	(c) to steal
chorin, choring	(c) stealing
chover	(c) shop
clach (*the* ch *pron. as in* loch)	(c) stone
cleestie, cleespie	(c) soldier, policeman
cleestie ken	(c) prison
cleg	gadfly
clippie	donkey
clochter (*the* ch *pron. as in* loch)	(c) doctor
clye	(c) to steal
cowal	(c) man
culyach (*the* ch *pron. as in* loch)	woman
dae	do
darkie	(c) night
dauntonly	courageously
dee	die
deek	(c) look
dick	(c) look
dicked	(c) looked
digger	machine to dig up potatoes
dilly	(c) girl
dinna	do not
divvies	clods of earth
dodder	(c) doctor
doon	down
duff	dullard
een	eyes
fae	from
faezum	(c) hay, grass, hair
fairm	farm
fat	what
faunie	ring
fee, to	to hire oneself out to a farmer
feek	(c) take, fetch, give, get
feekie	(c) policeman
felshies	(c) sticks, firewood
femmel	(c) finger, hand, arm
femmeltree	(c) hand and arm
fent	(c) vulva
fichels (*the* ch *pron. as in* loch)	(c) rags, old clothes
flatren	(c) fish
fordrum	(c) lady's apron
frae	from
gaffer	overseer

gahjee	(c) man
gaird (*more usually* gaed)	came, went
gairt, let	done away with
gallant (*more usually* callan)	a fine fellow
gan, gang	go, going
gat	got
ghahnee	(c) chicken, fowl
gheddi	(c) a youth
ginned	went
glimmer	(c) fire, light
gloored	glowered, glared
gowl	(c) stomach
granzie	(c) barn
grass-gruttin	cropping
grenum	(c) corn
grib	(c) to work, play
grinder	knife sharpener
gry	(c) horse
habben	(c) food
habbish	(c) hungry
hae	have
hah	to eat
hairt	heart
hanger	(c) ladies' dress, kilt
hantle	(c) people
har	(c) to hit
harld	(c) trouble
harnchets	(c) berries
harrie	harrow
hawkers, hawkies	people who go from door to door buying and selling
heid	head
hog	(c) shilling
hollifers	(c) socks, stockings
horny	(c) policeman
hotchets	(c) onions
ithers	others
jaun, jan, jin	(c) to know
jockey	kettle crane, kettle prop
joogal	(c) dog
kadik	(c) stone
ken	(c) house
kenchin	(c) child, baby
khaesum	(c) cheese
klooashes	(c) ears
koanyach (*the* ch *pron. as in* loch)	a haunting air
koories	(c) blankets
kranshers	(c) apples
krimush	(c) shirt
langer	longer
lav	(c) name
lenum	(c) earth, soil, field

lig	(c) road
loss	lose
lour	(c) money
lowie, lowdie, rowdie, luggie	(c) money
mackram	(c) hare
mahzee	(c) small, dish, cup
mairk	mark
mang	(c) to speak
manishi, manashi	(c) woman
meal	oatmeal
megget	(c) sheep, lamb
mind	to think about, remember
mither	mother
moolin	(c) killing, dying
mootch	(c) to beg
morakins	(c) stomach
morgen	(c) morning
morgen, the	(c) tomorrow
mort	(c) woman
moss	moorland
mowd	(c) hit, kill
mowded	(c) dead, fed up
muckle	great, big, large
mun	(c) mouth, month
mun	must
musker	(c) policeman
muytyi	(c) rabbit
na, nae	no, not
naeyisser	'no user', a worthless person
naggis	(c) self
nahkens, nackers, nokums	(c) travellers
naiscowal, naiskel	(c) father, priest
naismort	(c) mother
nane	none
nante	(c) no
nax	(c) night
neb	(c) nose
neddies	(c) potatoes
neist	next
nicht (*the* ch *pron. as in* loch)	night
niowenchet	(c) cat
nitchels	(c) not, nothing, none
no	not
noo	how
o'erflow	overtaken, unnecessary
oor, waur	our
oot	out
ora(man)	odd job man
Paddy's lan'	Ireland
pagger	(c) to beat, break
pahnee	(c) water, rain

759

pairt	part
paplers	(c) porridge
peeve	(c) drink, whisky, beer
peeven ken	(c) public house, ale house, saloon
peevie	(c) drunk
penum	(c) bread
percherie	(c) fish pond, fish farm
persteejie	(c) horse waggon, coach
plock	bag
ploffan	(c) tobacco
ploo	plough
ploop	(c) policeman
pooskie—(cowal)	(c) gun, gamekeeper
poovers	(c) apples
porris	(c) pocket
pottach	(c) man
pourin'	(c) water
prokhans	(c) shoes
pruskies	(c) broken biscuits
pub	public house, ale house, bar
puckle	a small quantity
pud	(c) to bed down
pudden ken	(c) lodging house
puddin	(c) lodging
pyre	(c) to look
quarker	(c) duck
rantonly	full of glee
rasps	raspberries
rattlers	(c) beans
ringle	(c) beer
rised	arose
rooble	(c) bottle
rowdie	(c) money
rowtler	(c) cow
rudli	(c) girl
ruffie	(c) the devil
ruskie	(c) basket
sae	so
salum	(c) salt
sa'nt	saint
saplers	(c) soap
scabed	crowned
shach (*the* ch *pron. as in* loch)	(c) cabbage, kale, soup
shan	(c) bad
shanish shanish	(c) an exclamation
shannas	(c) badness
shannas, O my	(c) an exclamation
shelt, sheltie	shetland pony
sic	such
singlin'	sorting out
skaldie	(c) a town person

skipper	(c) a barn
skroof	(c) hat
slob, slahp	(c) tea
slum	(c) to sleep on straw
slummed	hit
smout	(c) butter
snyeps	(c) turnips
sprach (*the* ch *pron. as in* loch)	(c) to beg
sprachan (*the* ch *pron. as in* loch)	(c) begging
sprachet (*the* ch *pron. as in* loch)	(c) begged
spurnie	(c) a match
stal	(c) stop
stane	stone
stardie	(c) prison
steemers, stewmers	(c) bagpipes
stewmerry cowal	(c) bagpiper
strammel	(c) straw
strawn	(c) nose
straws	strawberries
strelum	(c) hay, grass, hair
strods	(c) shoes
sweetnie, sweetnum	(c) sugar
syët	(c) yes
tae	to, too
tanner	sixpence
tattie	potato
tellum	(c) spoon
test	(c) head
thackit hoosie	thatched cottage
tiknie	(c) small, little
tilleypan	a skillet, a pan for lifting water
tippence	twopence
tober	(c) road
toggery	(c) clothes
toon	town
tramplers	(c) feet
trangle	(c) to fight, to pick a fight
trash	(c) afraid
trine	(c) to hang
trummel	trouble
turnip-shawin	to cut leaves from turnips
twa	two
vile	(c) town
wain	child
wattle	(c) encampment
wavver	(c) other, more
weed	(c) tea
weel	well
wha	who
whar	where
whims, whins	furze

whomlin	(c) boiling
wid	would
widdera, widder	window
winklers	(c) eyes
wis	know
wrang	wrong
yag	(c) fire, coal
yahfen	(c) dog
yaik	(c) one
yaks	(c) eyes
yarrers	(c) eggs
yerrum	(c) milk
yin	one
you, thon	that, those

337 THE ATCHING TAN SONG

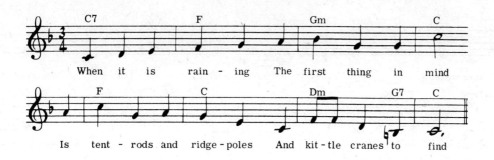

When it is rain - ing The first thing in mind

Is tent - rods and ridge - poles And kit - tle cranes to find

1 When it is raining
   The first thing in mind
   Is tent-rods and ridge-poles
   And kittle-cranes to find

2 Up in the morning
   The first thing to find
   They find the old pony
   In pound for a pound

3 They pooker to the farmer
   And him they do find
   They cob that old tit
   For a half a dollar

4 Then they shav off
   On the drum the next day
   The first thing they find
   Is pannum for the chavvies

338 THE BEGGAR WENCH

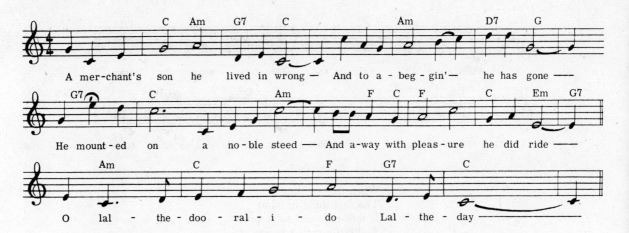

A mer-chant's son he lived in wrong — And to a-beg-gin'— he has gone — He mount-ed on a no-ble steed — And a-way with pleas-ure he did ride — O lal-the-doo-ral-i-do Lal-the-day —

1 A merchant's son he lived in wrong
And to a-beggin' he has gone
He mounted on a noble steed
And away with pleasure he did ride
O lal-the-doo-ral-i-do
Lal-the-day

2 A beggar wench he chance to meet
A beggar wench with low degree
He took pity on her distress
And says: My lass, you've got a pretty face

3 They both inclined noo to have a drink
Into a public-house they both went
They both drunk ale and brandy too
Till the both of them they got rollin' fu'

4 They both inclined noo to go to bed
Soon under cover they were laid
Strong ale and brandy went to their head
And both now slept as they were dead

5 Later on, this wench she rose
And putting on noo the merchant's clothes
With her hat so high and her sword so clear
And she's awa' with the merchant's gear

6 Early next morning the merchant rose
And looking round for to find his clothes
There was nothing left into the room
But a ragged petticoat and a winsey goon

7 The merchant being a stranger to the town
So he put on the old coat and gown
And down the street he solemnly swore
He would never lie with a beggar no more

339 THE BERRYFIELDS OF BLAIR

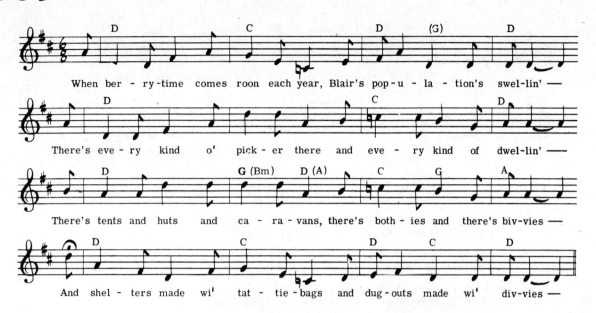

When ber - ry-time comes roon each year, Blair's pop - u - la - tion's swel-lin' —

There's eve - ry kind o' pick - er there and eve - ry kind of dwel-lin' —

There's tents and huts and ca - ra - vans, there's both - ies and there's biv-vies —

And shel - ters made wi' tat - tie - bags and dug - outs made wi' div-vies —

1 When berry-time comes roon each year, Blair's population's swellin'
There's every kind o' picker there and every kind of dwellin'
There's tents and huts and caravans, there's bothies and there's bivvies
And shelters made wi' tattie-bags and dug-outs made wi' divvies

2 Noo, there's cornerboys fae Glescae, kettleboilers fae Lochee
And miners fae the pits o' Fife, millworkers fae Dundee
And fisherfolk fae Peterheid and tramps fae everywhere
All lookin' for a livin' at the berryfields o' Blair

3 Noo, there's travellers fae the Western Isles, fae Arran, Mull and Skye
Fae Harris, Lewis and Kyles o' Bute, they come their luck to try
Fae Inverness and Aiberdeen, fae Stornoway and Wick
All flock to Blair at the berry-time, the straws and rasps to pick

4 Noo, there's some wha earn a pound or twa, some canna earn their keep
And some would pick fae morn tae nicht, and some would raither sleep
There's some wha has to pick or stairve, and some wha dinna care
There's some wha bless and some wha curse the berryfields o' Blair

5 There's families pickin' for one purse and some wha pick alane
There's men wha share and share alike wi' wives that's no their ain
There's gladness and there's sadness tae, there's happy hearts and sair
O, there's comedy and tragedy played on the fields o' Blair

6 But afore I put my pen awa' it's this I would like to say
You'll travel far before you'll meet a kinder lot than they
I've mixed wi' them in fields and pubs, and while I've breath to spare
I'll bless the hand that led me to the berryfields o' Blair

340 BOGIE'S BONNY BELLE

As I gaed doon tae Hunt-ly's toon, ain morn-ing for to fee —
I met Bog-heid o' Cair - nie, wi' him I did a-gree —

1 As I gaed doon tae Huntly's toon, ain morning for to fee
   I met Bogheid o' Cairnie, wi' him I did agree

2 To work his twa best horses, cart, or harrie, or ploo
   Or onything aboot farmwork I very weel could do

3 Aul' Bogie had a daughter, her name was Isabel
   The lily of the valley and the primrose of the dell

4 When she went a-walkin', she choosed me for her guide
   Doon by the burn o' Cairnie to watch the fishes glide

5 I throwed my arms aroon her waist, frae her her feet did slide
   And there she lay contented on Cairnie's burnie side

6 The first three months were scarcely o'er, the lassie lost her bloom
   The red fell frae her bonny cheeks and her een begin to swoon

7 The neist nine months was passed and gone, she brought forth to me a son
   And I was quickly sent for, to see what could be done

8 They said that I should marry her, but oh that would-na dee
   Said: You're nae match for my bonny Belle and she's nae match for thee

9 But noo she's married wi' a tinker lad, he comes frae Huntly toon
   He mends pots and pans and paraffin lamps, and he scours the country roon'

10 May-be she's gotten a better match, aul' Bogie canna tell
   Farewell, ye lads o' Huntly side, and Bogie's Bonny Belle

341 CASRO, MANISHI-O

Cas - ro, man-i-shi - O — As I rode oot in the dar-kie - O —

And I binged av - ree to the hel-lum — One fine day

1 Casro, manishi–O
  As I rode oot in the darkie-O
  And I binged avree to the hellum
  One fine day

2 I dicked a geddie playin' steemers
  O my shannas* how he binged avree
  I spied a young dillie bingen doon the hellum
  And some pourin' and nothing to eat

3 As I binged near this dillie
  She dicked and gloored at me
  I said: Shanish-shanish, manishi
  Can you bing avree wi' me?

4 I took my steemers out o' my baren
  And me 'n her binged avree
  So one dark nax we ginned a-campin'
  Noo I hae binged her avree

5 For us binged tae the fairm in the darkie
  And puddin' we did slum
  But three four years are over
  And four bonny children she bring

6 So all ye travellers an' hawkies
  And nackers ae dick at me
  I binged avree wi' a manishi
  O pottachs a avree

7 I bing o'er hame to the hellum
  And I played some tunes, you see
  And I loved my bonny wee manishi
  And a wee kenchin on her knee

8 The culyach says to the pottach
  Bing avree, gheddie, get some peeve
  There's nackers in their own campin'
  My shannas bing avree

9 Doon to the peeven-ken I binged wi' him
  Wi' my kenchin on my knee
  I've 'ome rowdie from the pottach
  Playin' the steemers, you see

10 So a' ye tramps an' hawkers
  Come listen to fat ye have heard
  I binged avree wi' a young manishi
  And back wi' her I gaird

11 So a' ye tramps an' hawkers
  Listen unto me
  A bonny wee manishi
  And three kenchins she bore to me

1 Greetings, woman-O
  As I rode through the night-O
  I went away to the town
  One fine day

2 I saw a lad playing bagpipes
  O my goodness
  I spied a young girl going down the town
  I had some water but nothing to eat

3 As I went near this girl
  She looked and glared [glowered] at me
  I said: O my God, woman
  Can you go away with me?

4 I took my pipes out of the bag
  And I and she went away
  So one dark night we went a-camping
  Now I have taken her away

5 We went to the farm in the night
  And we bedded down in the barn
  But three, four years are over
  And four bonny children she bore me

6 So all you travellers and hawkers
  And tinkers all look at me
  I went away with a woman
  O men all away

7 I go home over to the town
  And I played some tunes, you see
  And I loved my bonny wee woman
  And a small child on her knee

8 The woman said to the man
  Go away, lad, get some beer
  There are tinkers in their own camping†
  O my God, get away

9 Down to the public house I went with him
  With my child on my knee
  I've some money from the man
  Playing the pipes, you see

10 So all you tramps and hawkers
  Come listen to what you have heard
  I went away with a woman
  And back with her I came

11 So all you tramps and hawkers
  Listen unto me
  A pretty wee woman
  And three children she bore to me

* 'shannas' actually means 'badness'

† place reserved in the field for the tinkers

342 THE CHORING SONG

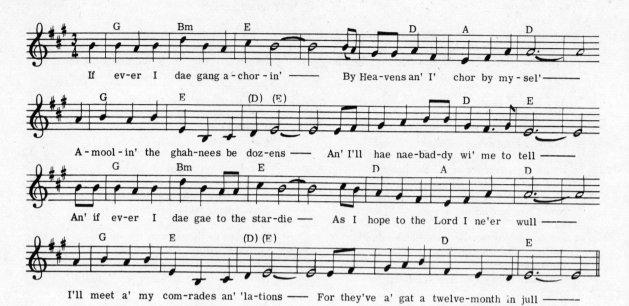

1 If ever I dae gang a-chorin'
By Heavens an' I' chor by mysel'
A-moolin' the ghahnees be dozens
An' I'll hae nae-baddy wi' me to tell
An' if ever I dae gae to the stardie
As I hope to the Lord I ne'er wull
I'll meet a' my comrades an' 'lations
For they've a' gat a twelve-month in jull

2 An' if ever I dae gae to the stardie
As I hope to the Lord I ne'er wull
I'll go back to my wife and my family
As true as there's Erin's Green Isle

343 HUSH, LITTLE BABBIE

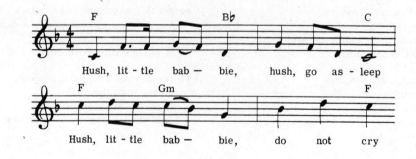

1 Hush, little babbie, hush, go asleep
Hush, little babbie, do not cry
O then hush, little babbie, and go asleep
For your mammy and daddy will be home by an' by
With me ho-hi-hey-hi-ho

2 Where are you going, my old man?
Where are you going, my honey?
O then hush, little babbie, do not cry
For your daddy and mammy will be home by an' by
Musha ho-hi-hi-ho-hi-ho
Ho-ho-hi-ho-di-hill-de-ho-ri-am

344 I BINGED AVREE

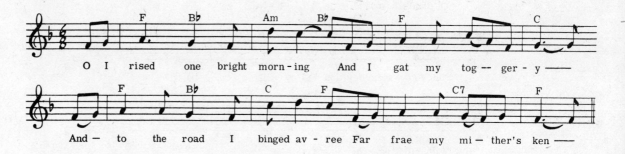

O I rised one bright morn-ing And I gat my tog — ger-y —
And — to the road I binged av - ree Far frae my mi — ther's ken —

1 O I rised one bright morning
And I gat my toggery
And to the road I binged avree
Far frae my mither's ken

2 I binged a troachtan
Far frae auld Aiberdeen
Tae the north o' Scotland I roved
And, aye, slummed on many a green

3 I bingèd one dark darkie
Into a pudden ken
Twa shan gahjees near me
And they asked me: Did I come frae hame?

4 O the twa cowals neist darkie
They got peevie in the peeven ken
They come that nicht tae the pudden ken
And tried tae trangle wi' me

5 One gahjee put his prokhans on
And tried tae kick at me
I slummed the pottach in the gowl, boys
Then I binged avree

6 I got that day me awaft lo
As far I could bing avree
Tae the hellum next darkie
And far frae hame d'ye see

1 O I rose one bright morning early
Put on my clothes
And I took to the road
Far from my mother's house

2 I went abroad
Far from old Aberdeen
To the north of Scotland I roved
And I did sleep on many a green

3 I went one dark night
Into a lodging house
Two bad men near me
Asked me if I came from home

4 O those two men the next night
They got drunk in the public house
They came that night to the lodging house
And tried to pick a fight with me

5 One man put his shoes on
And tried to kick at me
I hit the man in the stomach, boys
Then I went away

6 I fled that day
As far away as I could get
To the town the next night
And far from home, you see

7 I binged into a chover
   And a gadget I did take
   O all the lowie I sprachet
   A gadget I bocht to my naggis

8 Next morning I rose wi' content
   To the wee hellum doon the brae
   I got me slob frae a manishi
   In a wee thackit hoosie, you see

9 Her pottach was avree workin'
   This manishi says to me
   Here's twa hogs fae me, gheddie
   And ye better bing avree

10 I binged avree over to Ireland
   Far across the sea
   To meet wi' some Irish nackers
   In a place called Tralee

11 Noo these nackers they dicked at me
   Saying: Gheddie, why did you bing avree
   Frae the place they call bonny Scotland
   Far across the sea?

---

7 I went into a [music] shop
   And a gadget [accordion] I did take
   O all the money I begged
   A gadget I bought to myself

8 Next morning I rose with content
   To the little town down the hill
   I got my tea from a woman
   In a little thatched cottage, you see

9 Her man was away working
   This woman says to me
   Here's two shillings from me, lad
   And you'd better get away

10 I went away over to Ireland
   Far across the sea
   To meet with some Irish tinkers
   In a place called Tralee

11 Now these tinkers looked at me
   Saying: Laddie, why did you go away
   From the place they call Bonny Scotland
   Far across the sea?

345 THE LITTLE BEGGARMAN

Well, I am a lit-tle beg-gar-man an' beg-gin' I have been

Three-score years and more — in this lit-tle Isle of Green

I'm — known from the Lif — fey, way down to Kill-al-oe

And the name — that I'm known by is Old — John-ny Dhu

Of — all the trades an' cal — lin's, sure, beg-gin' is the best

For when a man is wea-ry, he can aye sit down and rest

He can beg — for his din-ner, he has no-thing else to do

On-ly tod-dle a-round the cor-ner with his old — rig-a-doo

1 Well, I am a little beggarman an' beggin' I have been
  Threescore years and more in this little Isle of Green
  I'm known from the Liffey, way down to Killaloe
  And the name that I'm known by is Old Johnny Dhu
  Of all the trades an' callin's, sure, beggin' is the best
  For when a man is weary, he can aye sit down and rest
  He can beg for his dinner, he has nothing else to do
  Only toddle around the corner with his old rigadoo
  (*Chorus: Mouth music improvised to tune of verse*)
  Dal-di-diddle-towdle-tiddle-rowdle-diddly-idle-dum (etc.)

2 Well, I slept in a barn way down by Killavone
  On a dark and stormy night and sleepin' all alone
  With holes in the roof and the rain a-comin' through
  And the rats and mice they were playin' at peek-a-boo
  O then, who did waken but the woman of the house
  With her white spotty apron and her calico blouse
  She began to cry and when I said: Boo
  O now don't you be afraid o' me, 'tis only Johnny Dhu

3 Well, I met a little flaxen-haired girl the other day
  Good morning to you, flaxen-haired girl, I did say
  Good morning, Johnny Beggarman, there's how do ye do?
  With your rags and your bags and your old rigadoo
  Well, I'll buy ye a pair o' trousers, a collar and a tie
  And a nice little lassie then I'll fetch her by an' by
  I'll buy a pair of goggles and I'll paint them up so blue
  And that nice little lassie, I'll be her lover too

4 Well, it's over the road, wi' me bag upon me back
  It's over the fields wi' me big haver-sack
  With holes in me shoes and me toes peepin' through
  Singing: Tithery-ump-a-daddy, sure, I'm old Johnny Dhu
  So now my song is ended and I'll bid you's all good night
  The fires are all raked and it's out with the light
  And now you've heard the story of the old rigadoo
  It's good luck and God be wid you's and to old Johnny too

346 THE LITTLE GIPSY GIRL

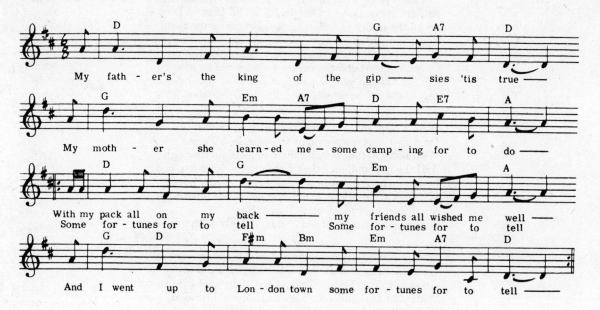

1 My father's the king of the gipsies 'tis true
  My mother she learn-ed me some camping for to do
  With my pack all on my back my friends all wished me well
  And I went up to London town some fortunes for to tell
  Some fortunes for to tell
  Some fortunes for to tell
  And I went up to London town some fortunes for to tell

2 As I was a-walking through fair London's streets
  A wealthy young Squire the first I chanced to meet
  He view-ed my brown cheeks and he lik-ed them so well
  Said he: My little gipsy girl, can you my fortune tell?
  Can you my fortune tell?
  Can you my fortune tell?
  Said he: My little gipsy girl, can you my fortune tell?

3 O yes, replied the gipsy girl, pray give to me your hand
  'Tis you that have good riches both houses and good land
  The fairer girls are dainty but you must cast them by
  For it is the little gipsy girl that is to be your bride
  That is to be your bride (etc.)

4 He took me to his palace, there were carpets on the floor
  And servants there a-waiting for to open every door
  There were ladies there of honour and the music it did play
  And all were there to celebrate the gipsy's wedding day
  The gipsy's wedding day (etc.)

5 It's farewell to the gipsy world and a-camping on the green
  No more with my brothers or my sisters I'll be seen
  For I was a gipsy girl but now I'm a Squire's bride
  With servants for to wait on me and in my carriage ride
  And in my carriage ride (etc.)

347 THE LOST LADY FOUND

1 Down in a valley a damsel did dwell
 She lived with her uncle we all know full well
 Down in a valley where violets grew gay
 Three gipsies betrayed her and stole her away
 Down in a valley where violets grew gay
 Three gipsies betrayed her and stole her away

2 Long time she'd been missing but could not be found
 Her uncle he search-ed the country all round
 Till he came to the Trustees between hope and fear
 Why the Trustees made answer: She has not been here

3 Now the Trustees spake up with their courage so bold
 We'll see she's not lost for the sake of her gold
 We will have life for life now, the Trustees did say
 We'll put you to prison and there you shall lay

4 Now there was a young Squire who lov-ed her so
 Oft-times to the school-house together would go
 I'm afraid she's been murdered, so great is my fear
 If I'd wings like a dove, I would fly to my dear

5 Now he travelled through England, through France
 and through Spain
 He ventured his life on a watery main
 Till he came to a house where he lodg-ed one night
 And in that same house lived his own heart's delight

6 Now soon as she saw him she flew to his arms
 She told him her grief whilst he gazed on her charms
 How came you in Dublin, in Dublin, my dear
 Three gipsies they stole me and then brought me here

7 Now your uncle in England in prison do lie
 He's now for your sweet sake condemned to die
 O take me to England, to England, she cried
 Ten thousand I'll give you and then be your bride

8 Now they went to England her uncle to see
 When the cart it stood under a high gallows tree
 O pardon, O pardon, O pardon, she craved
 Why you see I'm alive, his dear life for to save

9 Now as soon as they heard her, they led him away
 And the drums they did beat and the musicks did play
 Every house in the valley with mirth it did resound
 As soon as they heard that lost lady was found

348 MACPHERSON'S LAMENT

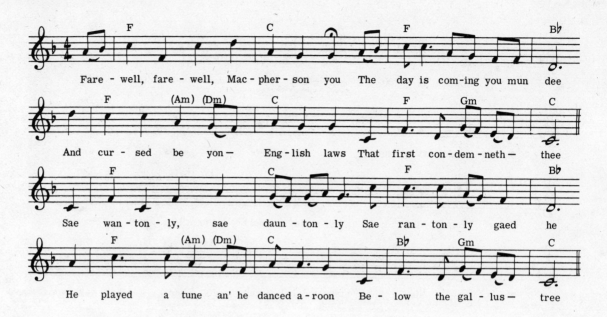

1 Farewell, farewell, Macpherson you
   The day is coming you mun dee
   And curs-ed be yon English laws
   That first condemneth thee
   Sae wanton-ly, sae daunton-ly
   Sae ranton-ly gaed he
   He played a tune an' he danced aroon
   Below the gallus tree

2 It was by a lady's treacherous hand
   That I'm condemned to dee
   It was in below her window-sill
   They threw a blanket over me

3 The laird o' Grant, that highlan' Sa'nt
   That first laid hands on me
   He pleyed the cause o' Peter Broon
   But he let Macpherson dee

4 Untie those bands from off my hands
   And bring tae me a sword
   There's not a man in a' Scotland
   But I'll brave him at his word

5 There's some come here tae see me hang
   And some tae buy my fiddle
   But before that I do pairt wi' her
   I'll brak' her through the middle

6 He took the fiddle into baith his hands
   And he brak' it o'er a stane
   There nae body will play on her
   While I lay dead and gone

7 Fare thee well, my ain dear highlan' hame
   Fare thee well, my wife an' my bairns
   There's nae fa'nting at the hairt
   While the fiddle was in my airms

8 The reprieve was coming o'er the brig o' Banff
   When they stood on the Galla' Hill to see
   They put the clock three-quarters fast
   And hanged him tae the tree

349 MANDI WENT TO POOVE THE GRYS

Man - di went to poove the grys In a - mong the stug-gers a - kai

The gav-vers are ar - ter man - di To lel o' me op - rey

1 Mandi went to poove the grys
In among the stuggers akai
The gavvers are arter mandi
To lel o' me oprey

2 Ma, says the rakli
Dickin' at the gavvers
'Tis like our dear ol' daddy say
We can't jawl avree

3 Up comes the farmer
Wi' the titties in the pound
If mandi doesn't want a charge
I'll have to find three pounds

4 Then all around the stuggers
A tittie my beebee chased
The gavver said: Now move along
And don't atch 'ere again

1 I went to put the horses in a field
In among the haystacks there
The policeman, he's after me
To take me away

2 Damn, says the girl
Looking at the policeman
Just as our father used to say
We can't get away

3 The farmer comes up
Saying the mares* are impounded
If I don't want to be charged
I'll have to find three pounds

4 Then all around the haystacks
My aunt chased a mare
The policeman said: Now move on
And don't stop here again

* titties are mares recently in foal

350 ME BROTHER'S 'ORSE

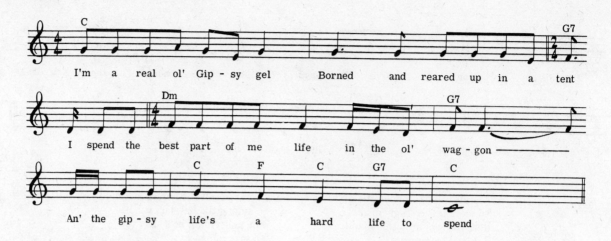

I'm a real ol' Gip-sy gel Borned and reared up in a tent

I spend the best part of me life in the ol' wag-gon ——

An' the gip-sy life's a hard life to spend

1 I'm a real ol' gipsy gel
Borned and reared up in a tent
I spend the best part of me life in the ol' waggon
An' the gipsy life's a hard life to spend
CHORUS SPOKEN: *O dordi, dordi*
Dick at the muller's gry prey the drom
mush*

2 Me brother's 'orse was killed on the A2
And it wasn't me brother's 'orse's fault
'E was a bright one and 'e thought 'e'd be a'right
If 'e crossed over the road
O dordi, dordi
Dick at the gry, mush, dick at gry

3 And that's when the car 'it 'im
And 'e was all me brother 'ad to make 'is livin' with
'E was a smart 'orse, a real good cart 'orse
Gord, I wish 'e 'adn't tried to cross the road
O dordi, dordi
Dick at the gavver, dick at the gavver

4 We was charged with causing an obstruction
And when ol' gavver 'eard me brother's pleas
'E thought 'e was a-startin' orf of a big eruption
An' then 'e charged 'im for a breachin' o' the peace
O dordi, dordi
The ol' gavver's nine part dinilo

5 It's a good job we can always change our name-like
And scarper orf away to some other verge
Course as how me brother's 'orse weren't really to
blame-like
We ain't gorn to court cause we just don't feel the
O dordi, dordi [urge
Why don't they leave us-like people alone?

6 Me brother's 'orse was killed on the A2
An' 'e's all me brother 'ad to make 'is livin' with
And I reckon meself we'll never get another 'orse just
like 'im
And then the gavver comed along and breached the
O dordi, dordi [peace
Dick at the gavver! Come along chavies
We'll 'ave to sherp orf a wavver drom or we be lell'd†

* O, my God
Look at the dead horse on the road, mate

† Pull off onto another roadside or we'll be charged by the police

351 THE MOSS O' BURRELDALE

1 Have ye ever seen a tinkler's camp upon a summer's night
  A night before a market when all things goin' right
  When a' the tramps and hawkers they come from hill and dale
  To gather in the gloamin' in the Moss o' Burreldale?

Man, the ale was only tippence and a tanner bought a gill
A besom or a tilley-pan, a shelt we aye could sell
Aye, we a' forgot our troubles o'er a forty o' smal' ale
As we gathered in the gloamin' in the Moss o' Burreldale

2 The time was ne'er long that day when muckle Jock McQueen
  He started tuning up his pipes he bought in Aberdeen
  He blew so hard, the skin was thin, the bag began to swell
  And awa' flew Jock wi' his sheepskin piock o'er the Moss o' Burreldale

3 Now our Jock swore he'd ha'e a fight and tore his jacket off
  But squeakin' Annie settled him, we a' got such a laugh
  Heaved him o'er amang the tilley-pans wi' a wee bit iron pail
  An' she scabed him like a swarm of bees on the Moss o' Burreldale

4 Noo little Jimmy Docherty, a horseman great was he
  He jump-ed on a sheltie's back, some tricks to let us see
  But a gallant shoved some prickly whims beneath the sheltie's tail
  He cast a shot in a mossy pot in the Moss o' Burreldale

5 By this time Stewart got the pail torn off his achin' heid
  An' kick-ed up an a'fu' sound, enough to wak' the deid
  When Annie said: Come on, my duff, now I shall get a gill
  Put them up, my manny, ye're nae fit for Annie, the Rose o' Burreldale ➤

6 O the dogs they started barkin' an' the clippie roared hee-haw
The tramps and hawkers a' stood roond and sic a sight we saw
It was Docherty as black as nicht, the bairns were told to yiel'
We showed them for packs, we a' made tracks from the Moss o' Burreldale

7 O the spring-cairt is let gairt, the shelty is o'er-flow
The tramps and hawkers noo-a-days they've langer roads to go
They a', man, hae a motor-car their winter goods for sale
I'll ne'er forget the nicht we spent in the Moss o' Burreldale

352 OKO VELA O CHAVO

1: O - ko ve - la o cha - vo   Kon chin - di - lo pe - ta - lo

Chind-yas shee mi - ro chav - lo   Drey i bar - ri kert - shee - ma

2: O baw - ley chor - es - ko ve - la   Top pes kosh - ten - en - go gry —

Lesk' doo-dah 'ree les - ki po - chee   Top - ler she - ro gooii shee - lo

3: O - ko ve - la a cha - vo   Kon pe - ta - lo chin - di - lo

Chind-yas shee mi - ro chav - lo   Drey i bar - ri kert - shee - ma

1 Oko vela o chavo	2 O bawley choresko vela	3 Oko vela a chavo
Kon chindilo petalo	Top pes koshtenengo gry	Kon petalo chindilo
Chindyas shee miro chavlo	Lesk' doodah 'ree leski po-chee	Chindyas shee miro chavlo
Drey i barri kertsheema	Topler shero gooii sheelo	Drey i barri kertsheema

1 Here comes the lad	2 Father Christmas is coming	3 The lad came by
Who cut the horse-shoe	On his wooden horse	Who cut the horse-shoe
My boy cut the horse-shoe	With sweetmeat in his pocket	My boy cut the horse-shoe
In the big inn	And a pudding on his head	In the big inn

353 THE ROVING JOURNEYMAN

I am a rov-ing jour-ney-man, I roam from town to town ——
And when I get a job of work, I'm wil-ling to sit down ——
With my bun-dle on — my shoul-der and my stick all in my hand ——
And it's round the coun-try I will go, I'm a rov — ing jour-ney-man ——

1 I am a roving journeyman, I roam from town to town
  And when I get a job of work, I'm willing to sit down
  With my bundle on my shoulder and my stick all in my hand
  And it's round the country I will go, I'm a roving journeyman

2 Now when I get to Brighton town, the girls they jump for joy
  Saying one unto the other: O there comes a roaming boy
  One hands to me the bottle and the other the glass in me hand
  And the toast goes round the table: Here's good luck to the journeyman

3 They took me to a big hotel, was there to spend the night
  The landlord's wife and daughter, 'twas me their great delight
  She never took her eyes off me, when on the floor I'd stand
  And she shouted to her mother: I'm in love with the journeyman

4 It's now that we are married and we're settled down for life
  As happy as two turtle doves, meself and my little wife
  I'll work for her, I'll toil for her, I'll do the best I can
  She'll never say that she rued the day she married the journeyman

5 I cannot think the reason why my love she looks so sly
  I never had any false heart to any young female kind
  I never had any false heart to any young female kind
  But I always went a-roaming for to leave my girl behind

354 ROW-DOW-DOW

If you will lis-ten for a while, a sto-ry I will tell you
And if you don't at-ten-tion pay, I'm sure I can't com-pel you
But as you've asked me for to sing, I'd bet-ter start at once —
And I'll tell you how I got six weeks, and my mate got two months —
With me: Row-dow-dow   Fol-the-rid-dle-lod-die With me:Row-dow-dow

1 If you will listen for a while, a story I will tell you
And if you don't attention pay, I'm sure I can't compel you
But as you've asked me for to sing, I'd better start at once
And I'll tell you how I got six weeks, and my mate got two months
With me: row-dow-dow fol-the-riddle-loddie
With me: row-dow-dow

2 Now it happened on one Monday night, two more, myself and Clarkie
Went out pheasant-shooting, in a place we knew was narkey
Three keepers rushed upon the spot, when the guns began to rattle
And our two mates they done a bunk, and left us to the battle

3 We tried our best to get away, but vain was our endeavour
We should not have been taken if we had all stuck together
But me and Clarkie was captured and taken to the lock-ups
And charged before the magistrate, for shooting Goschen's cock-ups

4 At ten o'clock next morning, to the Town Hall we was taken
We thought our case would settled be, but we were quite mistaken
We was put back upon remand, till the fourteenth of November
And, if you'd read the Croydon Times, I expect you will remember

5 Now when our remand was at an end, for Croydon we came steering
And soon before the magistrate, we stood to have our hearing
Our case it was so very clear, it didn't want much trying
When our time it was note down to us, our wives they started crying

6 Now we asked them to propose a fine, but that they would not sanction
Then soon we knew our residence would be in a public mansion
The magistrates to me I own, they acted like a neighbour
They let me off with but six weeks, but Clarkie two months' hard labour

7 At four o'clock that afternoon for Wandsworth Gaol we started
Our friends were there to see us off, they all seemed broken-hearted
Whilst rattling up to Wandsworth Gaol our minds seemed so bewild'ring
Upon the future situation of our wives and little children

8 At Holloway our clothes were searched and everything was taken
Away from us the warders thought, but they were quite mistaken
For, as I paced my lonely cell, it caused me for to smile
To think I had been stealing, I'd got my 'baccy all the while

9 Now the first four weeks I was in gaol, they put me grinding flour
Likewise pumping water, boys, into some lofty tower
My mate he looked around and said: O don't you think it cruel
To make a man work hard all day on dry bread, water and gruel?

10 The twenty-fourth of December, my time it did expire
When I got out I had some scran, that's what I did require
And, when I had a drink of beer, I really felt quite merry
But my mate he don't come out until the middle of January

355 THE SQUIRE AND THE GIPSY

One spring morn - ing ear - ly a young squire — was stray - ing

Ov - er the beau - ty that na - ture gave birth

The old folks were blown far, the young ones were play - ing

And there he be - held such a dark gip - sy lass

Struck with such beau - ty, he seemed most de - light - ed

He for - got his des - cend - ing and fam - i - ly pride

But let her be what she may, eith - er wealth - y or low - ly

He — swore by the pow - ers he would make her his bride

1 One spring morning early a young squire was straying
  Over the beauty that nature gave birth
  The old folks were blown far, the young ones were playing
  And there he beheld such a dark gipsy lass
  Struck with such beauty, he seemed most delighted
  He forgot his descending and family pride
  But let her be what she may, either wealthy or lowly
  He swore by the powers he would make her his bride

2 Now here's to your horses, your carriage and splendours
  Here's to your horses in green-wooded dells
  Behind the camp-fires two bright eyes were shining
  And that's where he first saw his own gipsy girl
  Stay with me now: In a few months I will marry you
  The smoke shall be your descending and shall be your guide
  May I tell your fortune? My dearie, I know it
  The fortune I crave for is you for my bride

3 Do you wish to insult me by your grand proposal?
  Do you wish a poor girl in misery be seen?
  Through dirt and through mires and I am light-hearted
  You may ride upon my mead that stands on the green
  I'm a poor gipsy girl and you are a squire
  With wealth and great beauty it is your command
  And there's more honest such in the poor and lowly
  Than all those proud ladies that walks through our land

356 SWEET BLOOMING LAVENDER

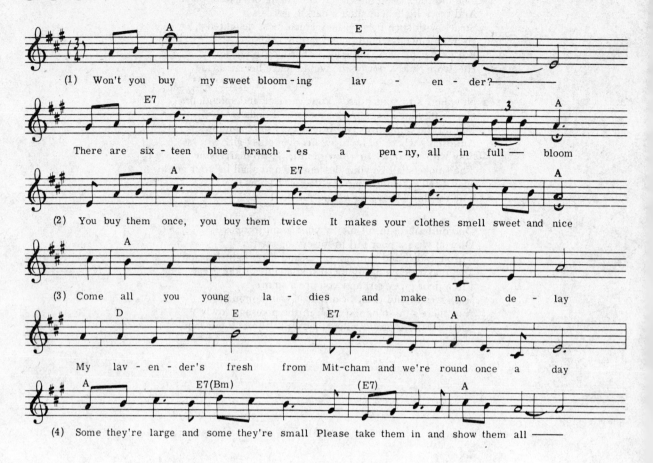

(1) Won't you buy my sweet bloom-ing lav - en - der?

There are six-teen blue branch-es a pen-ny, all in full — bloom

(2) You buy them once, you buy them twice It makes your clothes smell sweet and nice

(3) Come all you young la - dies and make no de - lay

My lav - en - der's fresh from Mit-cham and we're round once a day

(4) Some they're large and some they're small Please take them in and show them all ———

1 Won't you buy my sweet blooming lavender?
There are sixteen blue branches a penny, all in full bloom

2 You buy them once, you buy them twice
It makes your clothes smell sweet and nice

3 Come all you young ladies and make no delay
My lavender's fresh from Mitcham and we're round once a day

4 Some they're large and some they're small
Please take them in and show them all

(5) 'Twas ear-ly this morn-ing, when the dew was a-fall-ing

I ga-thered my sweet la-ven-der from the val-ley, all in full bloom

(6) Now's the time to scent your clothes and pock-et hand————ker-chiefs————

And to keep those moths a-way

(7) Won't you buy my sweet bloom-ing la-ven-der?————

There are six-teen blue bran-ches a pen-ny, all in full—bloom

5 'Twas early this morning, when the dew was a-falling
   I gathered my sweet lavender from the valley, all in full bloom

6 Now's the time to scent your clothes and pocket handkerchiefs
   And to keep those moths away

7 Won't you buy my sweet blooming lavender?
   There are sixteen blue branches a penny, all in full bloom

357 THE TATTIE TIME

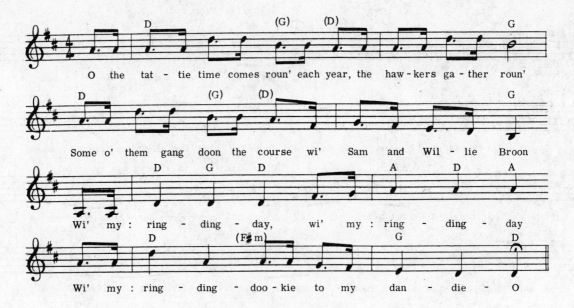

O the tat - tie time comes roun' each year, the haw-kers ga - ther roun'

Some o' them gang doon the course wi' Sam and Wil - lie Broon

Wi' my : ring - ding - day, wi' my : ring - ding - day

Wi' my : ring - ding - doo - kie to my dan - die - O

1 O the tattie-time comes roun' each year, the hawkers gather roun'
   Some o' them gang doon the course wi' Sam and Willie Broon
   Wi' my: ring-ding-day, wi' my: ring-ding-day
   Wi' my: ring-ding-dookie to my dandie-o

2 O the cairt has gone to fetch the squad they're working at Kinross
   For the digger it goes in the field an' time is dear tae loss

3 Noo some o' them dae awfi' weel, like Deacon an' big Tam
   But some o' them's still in the dirt an' has to push a pram

4 Ye've heard o' Eppie Townsley, she's liftin' near Gateside
   I'd advise ye no to work for them for she has never been paid

5 Ye'll easy ken the gaffer, for he is never wrang
   Ye'll easy ken the gaffer, he's the yin wi' the leggin's on

6 Noo there's auld Mary Townsley, she's left in her wee tent
   For her nose is gi'en her trummel and she's clamps in her fent

7 An' then there's Wullie Johnson glowerin' oot o' his tent
   For the digger worked too fast for him an' he's aye doubled up an' bent

8 An' then there's curly Andra' wi' a barld heid like an egg
   And it's aye gettin' bitten by horsefly, midge and cleg

9 He keeps rubbin' in hair-oil to try get back some hair
   An' when he looks in the shavin'-mirror he canna see nothin' there

10 Noo the money it is comin' and wi' the greatest speed
   An' when the gaffer sees it, he's abt tae lose his heid

11 Noo some o' us has caravans, but some ithers has got nane
   For them that spent it a' on drink hae pished it doon the drain

12 When the tattie-time is come an' gone, we scatter far an' wide
   Some o' us return to the North and some tae the Glesca-side

13 We're turnin' tae oor ither trades, sic as scrap an' rags
   Some gan ðot wi' sacks an' bills, some wi' cars an' paper-bags

788

358 TRAMPS AND HAWKERS

O come a' ye tramps and haw-ker-lads an' gai-the-rers o' bla' ——

That tramp the coun-try roun' and roun', come lis-ten one and a' ——

I'll tell tae you a ro-vin' tale, an' plac-es I hae been ——

Far up in-to the snow-y north or sooth by Gret-na Green ——

1 O come a' ye tramps and hawker-lads an' gaitherers o' bla'
That tramp the country roun' and roun', come listen one and a'
I'll tell tae you a rovin' tale, an' places I hae been
Far up into the snowy north or sooth by Gretna Green

2 I've seen the high Ben Nevis that gangs towerin' tae the moon
I've been roun' by Crieff an' Callander and by Bonny Doon
I've been by Nethy's silvery tide and places ill to ken
Far up into the stormy north lies Urquart's fairy glen

3 Sometimes noo I laugh to mysel' when dodgin' alang the road
Wi' a bag o' meal slung upon my back, my face as broun's a toad
Wi' lumps o' cheese an' tattie-scones or breid an' braxie ham
Nae thinkin' whar' I'm comin' frae nor thinkin' whar' I'm gang

4 I'm happy in the summer-time beneath the dark blue sky
Nae thinkin' in the mornin' at nicht where I'm gang to lie
Bothies or byres or barns, or oot amangst the hay
And if the weather does permit, I'm happy a' the day

5 Loch Katrine and Loch Lomond, they've oft been seen by me
The Dee, the Don, the Devron, that a' flows tae the sea
Dunrobin Castle, by the way, I nearly had forgot
And the reckless stanes o' cairn that mairks the hoose o' John o' Groat

6 I've been by bonny Gallowa', an' often roun' Stranraer
My business leads me anywhere, I travel near an' far
I've got that rovin' notion I wouldna like tae loss
It's a' for my daily fare an' as much'll pay my doss

7 I think I'll gang to Paddy's Lan', I'm making up my mind
For Scotland's greatly altered noo, I canna raise the wind
But if I can trust in providence, if providence should prove true
I'll sing ye's a' of Erin's Isle when I come back to you

359 THE TRAVELLING CANDYMAN

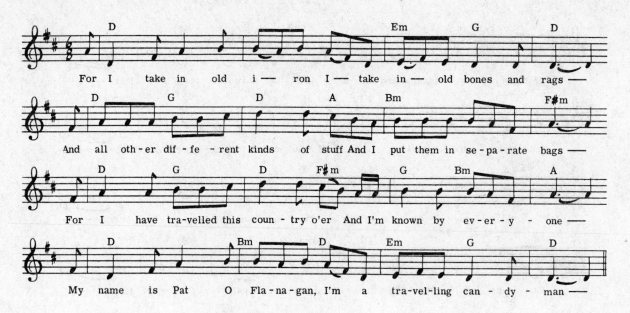

For I take in old i-ron I take in old bones and rags —

And all oth-er dif-fe-rent kinds of stuff And I put them in se-pa-rate bags —

For I have tra-velled this coun-try o'er And I'm known by ev-er-y-one —

My name is Pat O Fla-na-gan, I'm a tra-vel-ling can-dy-man —

For I take in old iron
I take in old bones and rags
And all other different kinds of stuff
And I put them in separate bags
For I have travelled this country o'er
And I'm known by everyone
My name is Pat O Flanagan
I'm a travelling candyman

1 For I'm sailed over from Belfast
The work it was very slack
And when I landed in Glasgow
I was wishing that I was back
I searched for work but no work could I find
So I struck on another plan
I came to the conclusion that
I would be a candyman
Chorus

2 A woman came up the other day
And she said she had lost her frock
Said she: My good man, come and tumble it out
For I know it is in your stock
Says I: My good woman, your frock is not here
And no more of your lip I will stand
Bedad, she up with her ug-e-ly fists
And she nailed the candyman
Chorus

360 THE YELLOW HANDKERCHIEF

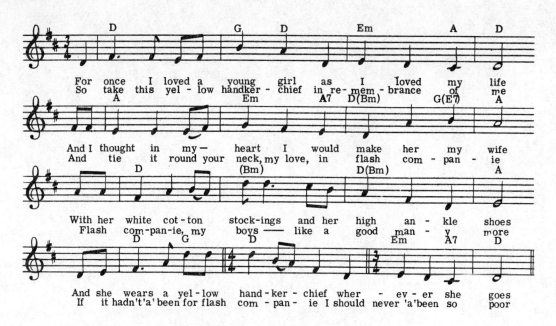

1 For once I loved a young girl as I loved my life
  And I thought in my heart I would make her my wife
  With her white cotton stockings and her high ankle shoes
  And she wears a yellow handkerchief wherever she goes

  So take this yellow handkerchief in remembrance of me
  And tie it round your neck, my love, in flash companie
  Flash companie, my boys, like a good many more
  If it hadn't 'a' been for flash companie I should never 'a' been so poor

2 For with fiddling and dancing 'twas all my delight
  In keeping such company it has ruined me quite
  It has ruined me quite, my boys, like a great many more
  If it hadn't 'a' been for flash companie I should never 'a' been so poor

3 For once I had a colour as red as the rose
  But now I'm as pale as the lily that grows
  Like a flower in the garden all my colour has gone
  So you see what I'm coming to through loving that one

337 THE ATCHING TAN SONG

Charlie Scamp, Chartham Hatch, near Canterbury,
Kent, *rec.* P. Kennedy, 1954: BBC 19966
Other recorded version
Frank Copper, Kent, *rec.* John Brune, 1960

1 We pulls in by the roadside
An' first thing in mind
Is tent-rods and ridge-poles
We quickly must find

2 We tie up the old pony's legs
But away he will go
And where shall we find him?
The old mulla may know

3 We get up next morning
And search all around
It's a hundred to one
We will find him in pound

4 We jall to the old mush
And what will 'e say?
Pay a bar and pack up
And clear out right away

I were came-ing up one day—travellin' with a load of horses up through, and I fell in with some caravan-dwellers (which you commonly call 'gipsies'), and I stayed there with 'em the night. They were making up a song with 'Romanish' in their own language, and whilst I was there I asked them the meaning of it, and quite learned the song.—FRANK COPPER.

Tent rods are rods they cut out of a wood, they put felt over it, and put a canvas over the top of that—that was the tent what they laid into. They put their tits [horses] in a field, and next day morning they're found in Court, and the answer is: that the farmer wants a bar [pound] for him. So they pooker [talk] to the farmer in their way and they cop the tit for half a dollar. They shav [move] off, shav to the next drum [road] and they'd better get scran [food] and panum [bread] for the chavvies [kiddies or children] the next day morning.—CHARLIE SCAMP.

An 'atchin' tan' is a stopping place, preferably an authorized one with a running stream or even a standpipe, plenty of dead wood for the picking and a field for grazing the horses. The first thing the gipsies do when they reach any stopping place is to pull their waggon to the highest, flattest piece of hard ground, away from any trees if possible but ideally not too far away from high trees: in a storm they are thus safe from both lightning and falling trees. If they intend to stop for some time they might extend their dwelling by putting up a bow-tent (also known as a 'bender'). For this they must find tent rods and ridgepoles—long branches of the springiest wood available, larch and yew are very suitable. The ridgepole—a strong, straight stick—determines the length of the tent, the rods its height and width. An equal number of sticks are stuck into the ground in two parallel rows as far apart as the intended width of the tent. While the thick ends of the sticks are rammed into the ground at an angle towards the interior of the tent they are steadied, and the ground is kept firm, with the instep of the right foot. There may be four or five such sticks opposite each other, as well as three or more to form a back wall. The thin ends of the sticks are tied together and to the ridge-pole which runs along the whole length of the tent. Potato sacks, canvas or any other woven fabric sheets are thrown over this structure and anchored to the ground with stones. Where springy tent rods are unavailable, a differently shaped tent is constructed with a number of rigid straight sticks. Both types of tent are occasionally referred to as 'sticks and rags'.

A fire is made and the kettle crane, a long iron rod with a double bend hook at the top, is rammed into the ground over it. The women get busy with the cooking while the men see about catching some food, look for casual employment and see to the horses.

Normally the 'atchin' tan' is in an unauthorized place in a hostile neighbourhood. There is nowhere for grazing the horses (as far as the local people are concerned) so that they are tied up by the roadside until dusk, when the gipsies lead them to a likely field and let them in for the night with the intention of getting them out before dawn. But as often as not the plan misfires, the gipsies oversleep or the farmer has walked round his land during the night, found the horses and impounded them. He now charges the gipsies a ransom for their horses—and has them moved on by the police.

338 THE BEGGAR WENCH

Davie Stewart, Dundee, Angus, Scotland, *rec.* P. Kennedy and A. Lomax, 1956: *Folk Songs of Britain*, vol. II, CAEDMON TC1143/TOPIC 12T158: *The Merchant's Son*
Other recorded version
John Strachan, Fyvie, Aberdeenshire, Scotland, *rec.* A. Lomax, 1951

Printed versions
A Collection of Old Ballads (London): 1723
LOGAN: 1869: *Merchant's Son and Beggar Wench of Hull*
GREIG MS: Aberdeenshire (one version also has Hull as location)
CHRISTIE: 1876, vol. II, p. 122: *The Beggar Wench of Wales*: first verse and tune only: rest 'unsuited to his collection' (Banffshire)

I learned it from my sisters and brothers. My old father used to sing it. It's a real tinker's song. There's no much tinkers, bar the Stewarts and the Hutchinsons, has that song. There was some of those tinker girls was very good looking. They'd go away all day with a basket hawking, and one girl would say, 'We'll have a little drop before we go home.' And there would be a ploughman sitting in the pub, and he would buy something, studs or bootlaces, and then the girl would get a cigarette from him, or a few shillings to have a drink— and they'd rob him of his money. And he couldn't say anything about it because he shouldn't be there along with the tinker girls. In them days it wasn't wrong for her to go and put her hands round his back and rob him. They were two distinct classes then—the ploughman and the tinkers—and if she'd marry him she'd always have the inclination to be away on the road like. . . . The ploughboys were afraid that if they got a child with a farm-girl they'd have to pay for it. But the tinker girl would be away. There was a lot of carry-on between the two of them all over Scotland and Ireland, and I suppose England too. . . . This man was out for a good time, and he had a lot of money with him, and he met the tinker-woman and tried her, but he rued the day he did.—DAVIE STEWART.

339　THE BERRYFIELDS OF BLAIR

Belle Stewart, Blairgowrie, Perthshire, Scotland, *rec*. P. Kennedy, 1955

Printed version
BRUNE: 1965, p. 21

Other recorded version
John MacDonald, Elgin, Morayshire, *rec*. P. Kennedy, 1955

The berrypicking season is one of the main earning periods of the Scots travellers' calendar, the other two being the potato and turnip harvests. The song is quite remarkable for its perfect rhymes and scansion. Belle Stewart, like most Scots in the travelling community, is literate, which gives her a great advantage over the English gipsy song writers, and the fact that she is, in the main, a house dweller gives her more leisure to work up her songs.

The raspberries are grown in straight lines or drills. The pickers are given a large and a small pail each and a length of string for tying the small pail round their waists. Each picker is assigned one side of a drill and works up to the end, dropping the berries into the small pail until it is full, when the contents are poured into the large pail, which is always left standing a little way ahead. When the large pail is full it is taken for weighing at a loading platform by the side of the road. At one side of the platform is a gallows with a spring-scale. The bucket is hung on the hook of the scale and the weigher shouts the weight to the cashier, who pays out so much a pound to the picker. The contents of the bucket go into a barrel which is shut tight as soon as it is full. The barrels are taken to a pulping station where they are emptied into vats and pulped with a preservative, an ammonium compound which turns the berries and juice white. Later, when the pulp is made into jam, another chemical compound neutralizes the ammonium compound, largely evaporating it, and almost restores the original colour.

Travellers have been engaged in the whole process up to the pulping stage, but the picking is the main job employing men, women and children for several weeks every year. Some fields produce high quality fruit suitable for eating raw. These are packed more carefully into baskets, and payment is so much a full basket.

From Belle Stewart's song it is evident that not every picker is a traveller. The ratio of travellers among the pickers in Blairgowrie would appear to be roughly forty-five per cent, which is considerable. But the travellers are on the whole faster pickers than the rest, and they stay on for the whole of the berry season, so the ratio is perhaps misleading.

340　BOGIE'S BONNY BELLE

Davie Stewart, Dundee, Angus, Scotland, *rec*. P. Kennedy and A. Lomax, 1956: *Folk Songs of Britain*, vol. I, CAEDMON TC1142/TOPIC 12T157

Other recorded version
Jimmie McBeath, Elgin, Morayshire, Scotland, *rec*. S. Ennis, 1952: BBC 18130; *rec*. A. Lomax, London, 1953, with three additional verses

The powers above protect this girl
And keep her right and fine
And keep her from all danger
Who has this heart of mine

And keep her aye contented
And always free from pride
But I'll return to Bogie's land
On Carnie's burnie-side

These are Jimmy McBeath's two concluding stanzas; they were not on his original recording made for the BBC in 1952 but were sung for Alan Lomax the following year.

A literary version of the song, called *Bogieside*, was supposed to have been composed by John Riddel of New Deer, Aberdeenshire, and appears in FORD: 1900, p. 265 and GREIG: 1909–14, Nos. xxviii and xxx.

A sprightly ploughboy goes to the feeing market in Huntly, Aberdeenshire. The feeing market was an annual event, where farmworkers and servants left the farm at which they were employed the previous year to find employment on other farms in the district. This is referred to as 'the feeing time' or 'the term' and the annual move from farm to farm was the common working tradition right up to the beginning of this century in many areas of rural Scotland, particularly the north-east.

Our ploughboy agrees to work for a farmer who has a very lovely daughter called Isabelle. They fall in love and nine months later she has a son. The farmer is furious and gives the ploughboy a dressing-down. The ploughboy offers to marry the girl but the farmer turns him down because of his low social status. She ends up by marrying a tinker and they go all over the country.

341 CASRO, MANISHI-O

Davie Stewart, Dundee, Angus, Scotland, *rec.* J. Brune, 1960

It's all about a young man with a kilt and a set of bagpipes who met a young girl coming down the road one day and he spoke to her—and of course, they fell in love with one another.

One time the travellers didn't really marry. They went away with one another in old-fashioned times.

And of course he bide the years with this girl. First they went into a barn, 'slumming', that's sleeping with straw, and after that they went away down to a public house and the husband started to play the bagpipes. He was getting lowie [money] fae the ghajees [men] and the three kenchins, the three bonny bairns.

Of course, all the travelling people in Scotland mostly knows this language, but I'm just giving you a small includation of it.—DAVIE STEWART.

The existentialist quality of the lyric is characteristic of this type of traveller's improvisation in which a singer sings the thoughts and feelings of two separate people without ever indicating which line reflects the sentiments of which character. The confusion is further increased by the constant switching of tense, and by the odd lines that do not appear to mean anything. In the cant it has great lyrical force which is almost completely lost in translation.

In the travelling community marriage was frequently the result of a snap decision. This was particularly the case among the non-Romany travellers. There was no solemn marriage ceremony: the couple just lived together and produced a family, but it was generally a highly successful marriage which was respected by other travellers and by local people as well. There are many traveller's songs on the subject, the best known, *Bogie's Bonny Belle* (No. 340), being of a romance that failed, but they are all used as a basis for improvisation only and no two travellers apparently sing the same version of any of these songs. Indeed the same singer would vary both words and tune at each performance. Davie Stewart at his best has produced a number of improvisations of great lyrical quality. *Casro, Manishi-O* and *I Binged Avree* (No. 344) are both good examples of Scots travellers' improvised song.

342 THE CHORING SONG

Travellers at St Fillans, Loch Earn, Perthshire, Scotland, *rec.* J. Brune, 1956

'Choring' means 'stealing', and it is an old word derived from the Sanskrit 'chur'. It is a desperate means of making a living when all other ways have failed. Generally it is the livelihood of didikais and pikies, but in emergencies other travellers, including Romanies, will stoop to it. 'Choring' is women's work, poaching a man's. 'Kannie-chorin'—stealing poultry, 'kannies' are chickens—is normally done with a dog specially trained to bring the chickens out alive without injury and not a feather out of place. It is difficult to see how anybody can secretly train a dog for this, but it must be every lower class traveller's dream to own such an animal.

The Choring Song is a nonsense song with a surprisingly wide distribution, having been noted all over the British Isles with only slight local alteration in the words. In the south of England it is normally sung to a tune of the *Botany Bay* family.

343 HUSH, LITTLE BABBIE

Winnie Ryan (of Kerry), Belfast, N. Ireland, *rec.* P. Kennedy and S. O'Boyle, 1952: BBC 18580

Printed version
HAMER: 1973, p. 53: *Lullaby* (Lancashire)

This is probably a traveller's version of an English translation or a remake of an Irish-Gaelic original. Winifred Ryan spent her young life in the Gaelic-speaking districts of Kerry and Connemara, where she first heard the song.

344 I BINGED AVREE

Davie Stewart, Dundee, Angus, *rec.* J. Brune, Aberdeen,
Scotland, 1961

Now this is a song . . . oh, it happened when I was a young boy—well, a young man in fact. I was about eighteen years of age and I took to the travelling around the country, and going here and going there. 'Course I used to go round and work to the farmers now and then, but me being a traveller I had the language.

Now I've travelled all over Scotland and England, Wales and many years in Ireland, and my wife is an Irishwoman and we speak our cant well-mixed. We use what we like best of the language and a bit o' the Gaelic thrown in, and when I sing in the cant I just change the song a bit to suit myself. So there may be a word like 'vile' for a town. Well that's Scots tinkers' cant, but I always say 'hellum', that's an old Irish word— and so I'll sing it that way. So here is an old ballad fae the north of Scotland the way I sing it.—DAVIE STEWART.

This song, Davie Stewart's masterpiece for lyrical content, loses very little in translation, and as a cant song it is in fact somewhat less effective, probably because there are fewer variations in the music. It belongs to a song group peculiar to the travelling musician, a busker or street singer, and is his private improvisation, sung for his own pleasure. The song invariably purports to be autobiographical. It tells of the singer first running away from home, then making or buying an instrument, begging food from a farmer's wife, who gives it to him saying 'you had better be gone before my man comes home', and of the fight in a lodging house or a whisky camp followed finally by a trip to Ireland where the welcome is lukewarm. Another singer, from Wiltshire, has been heard to tell an identical story in a more rambling way with an account of how he stole his first musical instrument from a shop and 'chopped' (swapped) it for one more to his liking with a black gipsy called Ebenezer Boswell. In passing he mentions that the gipsies are a strange bunch who own their individual possessions but must hand over their cash to their head man, which gives them a taste for 'chopping' rather than buying or selling—a good thing for a poor busker who can swap a rubbishy instrument for an extremely good one.

In its older form the busker's song was in the third person only. Thus in an archaic words Welsh Romany version the setting is said to be in a field at a place called Ackerlo, and the hero is introduced as the only Romany ever to build proper fiddles of the normal shape. His name was Lucas Petulengero and he lived about 1660–1740. Fragments of his fiddles, some of them branded with his name and the date when they were made, still exist, but none of his instruments have come down to us intact because they all went to gipsy fiddlers, at whose death and burial the fiddles were smashed up, burned or buried.

O Bosh-kelomengero beshtas	The fiddle maker sat
Oprey o poov arey Ackerlo	Upon the field at Ackerlo
Kedas o bosh y balano kosht	He made the fiddle and the bow
Adrey i kushti zigaira*	In his fine tent
Nai man keck dicklo	I have no neck-scarf
Nai man gad	I have no shirt
Nai man keck pushka	I have no gun
Nai man staadi	I have no hat
Nai man keck rinkeni vongustrin	I have no pretty ring on my finger
Y nai man bosh y balano kosht	And I have neither fiddle nor bow

* This word, 'zigaira', was noted by SAMPSON: 1926, but is now unknown to most gipsies.

345 THE LITTLE BEGGARMAN

Paddy Doran and others, N. Ireland, *rec.* P. Kennedy
and S. O'Boyle, 1952; BBC 18550; *Folk Songs of
Britain*, vol. III, CAEDMON TC1144/TOPIC 12T159

Printed versions
HENRY: 1924, No. 751: *The Oul' Rigadoo*
O LOCHLAINN: 1965, No. 26, p. 52: *The Beggarman's
Song* (from a ballad sheet)

This ballad is sung to the tune of the Gaelic song *The Red-haired Boy*, which is also played as an instrumental in reel-time. The tune is not unlike that of the Scots ballad *Gilderoy*.

346 THE LITTLE GIPSY GIRL

Louise Holmes, Dinedor, Herefordshire, *rec.* P. Kennedy, 1952: BBC 18691

Other recorded versions
Elizabeth Taylor, Brigg, Lincolnshire, *rec.* P. Kennedy, 1953
Isabel Kelby, Blairgowrie, Perthshire, Scotland, *rec.* P. Kennedy and H. Henderson, 1955
Ben Baxter, Southrepps, Norfolk, *rec.* S. Ennis, 1956: BBC 23382

Printed versions
ROXBURGHE: 1871–99, VIII, p. 853 (Lincolnshire)
SHARP MS: 1904–6: two variants (Somerset and Devon)
GARDINER MS: 1904–9: one variant (Somerset), two variants (Hampshire)

JFSS: 1904, No. 5, p. 231: *coll.* Frank Kidson, Yorkshire
JFSS: 1908, No. 12, p. 220: Joseph Taylor, Brigg, Lincolnshire, 'phonographed by Percy Grainger': *The Gipsy's Wedding Day*
LEWIS: 1914, p. 36: Jane Williams, Holywell, Flintshire (N. Wales)
FMJ: 1972, p. 174: *The Squiyers Bride, coll.* D. P. Spratley (Nottinghamshire)

COX: 1925, p. 335 (W. Virginia, USA)
EDDY: 1939, p. 224 (Ohio, USA)
RANDOLPH: 1946–50, I, p. 437 (Missouri, USA)

Cecil Sharp was doubtful of the folk-origin of this song, while Anne Gilchrist regarded it as being of the same vintage as *The Nutting Girl* (No. 186). Broadside versions such as that printed by Jackson of Birmingham call the song *The Little Gipsy Lass*.

347 THE LOST LADY FOUND

Harry Cox, Catfield, Norfolk, *rec.* P. Kennedy, 1953

Other recorded versions
Charlie Chettleburgh, 1947: BBC 13866
Edwin Thomas, Allerford, Somerset, *rec.* P. Kennedy and Maud Karpeles, 1952: *Three Gipsies*, BBC 23622
George Maynard, Copthorne, Sussex, *rec.* P. Kennedy and M. Plunkett, 1955

Printed versions
BROADWOOD: 1843: *Gipsy Song* (squire finds lady in Flanders)
MASON: 1877–1908, p. 56: *'Tis of a Young Damsel* (that was left all alone)
BROADWOOD: 1890, p. 20: *Gipsy Song* (Sussex)
BARRETT: 1891, No. 43, p. 74 (Cheshire), note says that in the London neighbourhood it is sung to a variant of the tune of the nursery song *Little Bo-Peep*

SHARP MS: 1905–21: eleven unpublished variants (mainly Somerset)
GARDINER MS: 1904–9 (Somerset, Wiltshire, Hampshire and Sussex)
HAMMOND MS: 1905–7: one variant (Somerset), one variant (Dorset)
JFSS: 1905, No. 7, p. 99: from an old cook who danced as she sang, *coll.* Lucy Broadwood, Isle of Wight, 1893, from Mrs Hill, Lincolnshire; three tunes *coll.* R. Vaughan Williams, Essex
GILLINGTON: 1907 (Hampshire)
BROADWOOD: 1908 (Lincolnshire)
VAUGHAN WILLIAMS: 1908, p. 12 (Essex)
UDAL: 1922, p. 325: *The Lost Lady* (Dorset)

When a young damsel who lived with her uncle disappeared, her uncle went in search of her all over the country. He could find no trace of her, so he went to the authorities to report her missing. They suspected him of having murdered her for the sake of her money and put him in prison. A young squire who had been the girl's lover travelled all over England, France and Spain. One day in Dublin he took up a night's lodging, where he saw the young damsel. She flew into his arms and told him that she had been abducted by three gipsies. They quickly made their way to England to rescue her uncle and they arrived in the nick of time—he was on the cart under the gallows about to be hanged.

There are various songs and ballads to do with gipsies bewitching and abducting ladies of quality; there are also similar songs and ballads telling of the abduction of children. While it is quite likely that some ladies of quality (perhaps the wife in *The Wraggle Taggle Gipsies*) did run off with gipsies, it is not proven that abductions of 'gorgio' women ever occurred. As to the charge that gipsies are child stealers, they usually have too many children of their own to bother about increasing their problems.

348 MACPHERSON'S LAMENT

Davie Stewart, Dundee, Angus, Scotland, *rec.* P. Kennedy and A. Lomax, 1956

Other recorded versions
Lucy Stewart, Fetterangus, Aberdeenshire, Scotland, *rec.* P. Kennedy and H. Henderson, 1955
John Strachan, Fyvie, Aberdeenshire, *rec.* A. Lomax, 1951
Jimmy McBeath, Banffshire, Scotland, *rec.* A. Lomax, 1951: BBC 21533

Printed versions
JOHNSON: 1787–1803, II, p. 117: Robert Burns, *McPherson's Farewell*
DUNCAN MS: two variants (W. 524 and 569; M. 169)
ORD: 1930, p. 443: *McPherson's Farewell* (words only)
SEEGER AND MACCOLL: 1960, No. 82, p. 89: *MacPherson's Lament*, from J. McBeath
COLLINSON: 1966, pp. 210–12: full description of story and illustrations

> Farewell, ye dungeons dark and deep
> Farewell, farewell to thee
> MacPherson's time will nae be long
> Below the gallows tree

Jimmy McBeath's alternative opening verse is not unlike *Macpherson's Farewell*, the ballad reconstruction of the song by Robert Burns.

Lucy Stewart, for her opening, sang:

> O, a gipsy band I did command
> With courage better by far
> Than any British soldier (lad)
> That ever fought in war

James Macpherson, Lucy told us, was a freebooter. He was captured in Turriff, Aberdeenshire, and hanged at Banff on November 16th, 1700, only eight days after his capture. She described his capture:

> Shepherds wearing tartan plaids pinned them together and circled round him. That is the story but the song says differently.
> He was head of the gipsies. His mother was a gipsy, his father was a lord, an Earl, in the Highlands. His father brought him up. A minister took a liking to him, to teach him music. He taught him the fiddle and he became a great fiddler.
> Well then he found out he was an illegitimate son, when he was fifteen. And he went and followed the gipsy clans because his mother was a gipsy. These gipsies were Jacobites and held out for the old Stewart house and so they had to take to the roads. He went all over Banffshire robbing the rich to give to the poor.
> The shepherds who captured him were under the orders of the Laird o' Grant, of Rothiemurchus, the Highland Sa'nt. And when he was arrested and sent up for trial, his girl, his sweetheart, tried for a pardon for him. She got a pardon but they put the clock up quarter of an hour in Banff and hanged him before his time. He was supposed to have played this tune on his fiddle on the way to the gallows tree.

The remains of his fiddle are now on exhibition in the Macpherson Clan Museum at Newtonmore, Inverness-shire.

349 MANDI WENT TO POOVE THE GRYS

Frank Copper, W. Kent, *rec.* J. Brune, 1960
Other recorded version
Caroline Hughes, Blandford, Dorset, *rec.* P. Kennedy, 1968

Printed versions
GILLINGTON: 1911, No. 12, p. 24: *Mandi Jalled to Puv a Grai*; No. 14, p. 28: *Ovva Tshavi (Mandi Well'd to Puv the Grai)* from New Forest, Hampshire

Probably because its words are generally idioms in everyday use on the road, this song is more common in gipsy tradition than in any other. 'Mandi went to poove the grys' was an obvious floating line, starting off dozens if not hundreds of improvised songs. It was also frequently used as a one-line song right up to the years between the World Wars. The line would be repeated twice, followed by 'mouth music' syllables which were used for singing improvisations on the theme.

350 ME BROTHER'S 'ORSE

Minty Smith, Stone, Kent, *rec.* J. Brune, 1962

> Now I was squatting out in these woods at Darenth for years, and the vicar in charge of the land did not really mind me or any of the other gipsies staying there, but the local council requisitioned the land and had us evicted on to the side of this trunk road.

My brother had a very clever horse—the finest horse that ever was seen on the road. The grass was a bit more lush on the other side of the road; a car ran into him and there he was lying dead. Along came a policeman and took down our names and postal addresses and we gave him a lot of wrong information.—MINTY SMITH.

This is a typical Romany improvisation referring to an actual happening. The Smiths, together with about a hundred other families, had been evicted from Darenth Wood during the winter of 1961–2 to a verge on the main A2 trunk road half-way between London and Rochester. Norman Dodds, known as the 'gipsy MP' because he was a campaigner for gipsy rights of several years' standing, camped out among the gipsies to attract public attention to their plight. The gipsies who camped out by the side of the road for several months gave a number of impromptu 'concerts' in his honour, and *Me Brother's 'orse* was one item improvised at one of these sessions. The horse belonged to Levi Smith.

351 THE MOSS O' BURRELDALE

Jimmy McBeath, Elgin, Morayshire, Scotland, *rec.* S. Ennis, Banffshire, 1952: BBC 18130

Other recorded versions
Mark McAllister, *rec.* S. Ennis, Banffshire, Scotland, 1952: BBC 18778
Belle Stewart, Blairgowrie, Perthshire, Scotland, *rec.* P. Kennedy and H. Henderson, 1955

Davie Stewart, Dundee, Angus, Scotland, *rec.* P. Kennedy, London, 1956

Printed version
BRUNE: 1965, p. 18: from Davie Stewart and Robert Brodie, Glasgow, Scotland

There is always a lot of atmosphere inside a tinker's 'whisky camp' of a summer's night—this is the night before the market when all the tramps and hawkers come from hill and dale to gather in the gloaming in the moss of Burreldale. I well remember years ago, when the ale and the whisky were cheap, when there was a great fight in which 'Squeaking Annie' went for big Jock Stewart who was out to pick a fight, and she crowned him with a pail, heaving him among the ironmongery. And there was Piper McQueen who at that time had a terrible accident, when the warpipes he had just bought were blocked up. The bag began to swell and Jock flew away. O, the jokes we played that time, and the laughs we had! But these days are almost over now, most of the spring-carts and ponies are gone now, and we have to travel further afield to make ends meet. The tramps and hawkers all have to have motors now—but still, I'll never forget that night we spent on the Moss of Burreldale.—JIMMY McBEATH.

352 OKO VELA O CHAVO

Welsh gipsy children, Rorrington, Shropshire, *rec.* J. Brune, 1962

Other recorded version
Hungarian version, *rec.* D. Kenrick, 1967

Printed version
SAMPSON: 1926, Pt. IV, Vocabulary, p. 70

There was once an innkeeper who also traded in horses, donkeys and mules. One year the Romans conquered the land and built roads. As a result of being constantly forced on the roads the horses' hooves suffered a great deal of wear and tear. The innkeeper's son sat up one night brooding over the problem, and it struck him that just as he was wearing wooden clogs on his feet it should be possible to fit wooden shoes on to the horses' hooves. So he cut some wooden horseshoes out of cedar wood, but these were not very durable. The innkeeper's son thought again, and the idea of forging iron shoes came to him in a dream. Within a month the first smithy in the world was built and the innkeeper's son shoed horses and made nails for the whole world.

One day, when the smith was already very old, a man came to him and ordered the three nails with which Christ was nailed to the cross. After the Crucifixion the citizens of the town were so enraged that they chased the smith and all his friends and relations from their land, and they have been hounded from place to place ever since.

The smith was apparently condemned to eternal life. On bright nights you can see him sitting on the moon with his hammer in his hand, his anvil by his side and other implements of his trade scattered around him.

One of the smith's sons managed to conceal his identity and marry a princess. Her father, the king of Romania, went blind because of the curse on the smith's family. The smith's son went in search of a magic herb grown by a magician belonging to his tribe, but he was waylaid by the king's three sons who nailed a red hot horseshoe on his backside. However the boy recovered from the torture inflicted on him and procured the magic herb. The king was cured of his blindness, but when the princess told him of the brand mark on her husband's backside he banished him from the country.

This is the traditional gipsy tale of *The Man Who Invented The Horseshoe*, and it would certainly be the origin from which was derived the short Romany song recorded from Welsh gipsy children in Shropshire. The words of the second verse appeared in John Sampson's book (SAMPSON: 1926):

O bawrey choresk(er)o 'vela	Father Christmas is coming
Top pes(ko) koshtenengo gry	On his wooden horse
Lesk(e) doodah(a)ree leskee potchee	With sweets in his pocket
Top lesko shero shee les gooi	And a pudding on his head

Whereas for the last line the children in Shropshire sang:

Topler shero gooi shee-lo

The words of the first verse have been recorded on tape from a Hungarian gipsy by Donald Kenrick, and they are quoted here by permission:

The gipsy woman introduced and concluded her verse with a few minutes of mouth dance music in true gipsy fashion, the words coming out differently each time. She then dictated the correct wording which was different again:

1st line	Kodo avla o shavo	Here comes the lad
Variant 1	Kodo av' lako shav'	Here comes her lad
Variant 2	Kodo avelas o shav'	The lad came by
2nd line	Kon petalo chinela	Who cut the horseshoe
3rd line	Chineles muro shav	The one who cut it (present tense)
Variant	Chinelas muro shavo	The one who cut it (past tense)
4th line	Ande bari kirtshema	In the big inn

353 THE ROVING JOURNEYMAN

Chris and Tom Willett, Paddock Wood, Kent, *rec.* P. Kennedy, 1961

Other recorded versions
Mary Doran, Belfast, N. Ireland, *rec.* P. Kennedy and S. O'Boyle, 1952: *The Rambling Irishman*, BBC 18552
'Jim' Harold Swain, Angmering, Sussex, *rec.* R. Copper, 1964: *William Riley*, BBC 22763

Printed versions
BARING GOULD: 1889–1905, No. 8, p. 16: *Roving Jack*; title substituted in the revised edition was collected from two singers in Devon
SHARP MS: 1905: four variants (Somerset)
HAMMOND MS: 1905: one variant (Dorset)
GARDINER MS: 1906: one variant (Hampshire)
WILLIAMS: 1923: *The Roving Navigator*
REEVES: 1958, No. 84, p. 186: *coll.* Cecil Sharp, 1905 (Somerset)

This song seems to have been particularly popular in southern England and in Ireland, where with a few variations it is basically the same song, except that the hero is a rambling Irishman instead of a roving journeyman. These are the verses as recorded from Mary Doran:

I am a rambling Irishman I travelled the country o'er
In search of an occupation like I never done before
I turned across the ocean and I thought it a very good plan
To take a trip to Amerikay unto your happy land

When I landed in Philadelphie all the girls all jumped with joy
Says one unto the other here comes an Irish boy
They wanted me to join with them and took me by the hand
They took me merrily around the room, long life to the Irish man

They took me to a big hotel was there to spend the night
The landlord's wife and daughter 'twas me to great delight
She never took her eyes off me 'twas on the floor I stand
And she shouted to her mother I'm in love with the Irishman

It's daughter, dear daughter, what's this you are going to do
To fall in love with an Irishman, a laddie you never knew
With his knapsack on his shoulder, his shillelagh in his hand
Saying: Mother dear, I'd roam the world with a rambling Irishman

It's now that we are married and we're settled down for life
As happy as a turtle dove, meself and my wee wife
I'll work for her, I'll toil for her, I'll do the best I can
But she'll never say she rued the day that she married the Irishman

One broadside version in the Williams collection from Swindon, Wiltshire, concerns a roving 'navigator', a navvy, one of the men who dug the canals and railways that criss-crossed the British Isles. It has the concluding verse:

Now we'll go down to Oxford Town and there we'll wed with speed
The bells shall ring so merrily and the bride shall dance indeed
We'll spend the night in dancing and drinking from a can
Now she's happy and contented with her roving navvy man

354 ROW-DOW-DOW

George Maynard, Copthorne, Sussex, *rec.* P. Kennedy and M. Plunkett, 1955: *Shooting Goschen's Cock-ups*

Other recorded version
Wally Fuller, Laughton, Sussex, *rec.* P. Kennedy, 1952: *Bold Poachers*, BBC 18719

Printed version
JEFDSS: 1963, p. 189: George Maynard version

Compare (tune)
CHAPPELL: 1858, p. 717: *The Barking Barber*: tune usually known as *Bow Wow Wow* used for political lampoons such as *Guy Fawkes Song*

Goschen was probably a local placename or the name of a local family who had a game preserve. Though both recorded versions were heard in Sussex, this local poaching song would seem to come from the area around Croydon in Surrey.

After being convicted the poachers were sent to Wandsworth Gaol and then to Holloway in north London (now a woman's prison). In this prison they had to grind flour and pump water, and the verse which described this left a strong impression on Wally Fuller the gipsy, who only remembered a few verses of the song.

George Maynard's faultless performance of the song probably contained all the verses; he had them from Fred Holman of Copthorne.

355 THE SQUIRE AND THE GIPSY

Harry Cox, Catfield, Norfolk, *rec.* P. Kennedy, 1953:
DTS LFX 4 (1965)

This song does not seem to appear in any collections, although the theme is common (see *The Little Gipsy Girl*, No. 346). A similar story is told in *The Laird o' Cockpen*, a song which has been (probably erroneously) ascribed to Lady Nairne, who wrote under the pseudonym BB (Mrs Brogan of Bogan). It was included posthumously in a collection of her Scottish songs.

356 SWEET BLOOMING LAVENDER

Janet and Florrie Penfold, Battersea, London, *rec.* P. Kennedy, 1958

Other recorded version
Ben Baxter, Southrepps, Norfolk, *rec.* S. Ennis, 1955: BBC 22022

Printed versions
Addison: *The Spectator*, 18th December 1711: *The Cries of London*
BROADWOOD: 1893, p. 105: Kensington (1880), three variants (1884)

GARDINER MS: 1898: *coll.* Dr Gardiner, Surrey
JFSS: 1910, No. 15, p. 97: *coll.* Frederick Keel, Marylebone, 1899; Lucy Broadwood, Westminster, 1903; Frederick Austin, Kennington, 1907; Cecil Sharp, Camden Town, 1908
JFSS: 1919, No. 22, p. 61: Juliet Williams, Chelsea, 1912–16 (two versions selected from twenty Lavender cries noted in Chelsea)
JFSS: 1919, No. 22, p. 73: note on Lavender and other cries by Anne Gilchrist, including two Lavender cries noted in Brighton, Sussex

This was recorded from a mother and daughter who were possibly the last to use the lavender street cry in London. In the mother's time the lavender was grown at Mitcham in Surrey, and from the end of July to the end of August she used to get up at four o'clock in the morning to walk from Battersea to Mitcham. The lavender was picked when the dew was still on it, then tied up in little bunches to be sold, hawked in large rectangular baskets through Chelsea, Pimlico, Sloane Square to 'all up in London'.

> It was my grandmother learned us. They done it all their life and it sort of come through from generation to generation. It's because they like the smell of it and the people like to hear the London cry.—FLORRIE PENFOLD.

> People, particularly old people, like to hear 'em, it brings back memories and brings 'em sort of comfort. Not like now; all they want to hear is rock and roll just to please the young people, but we've not only got to study the young but look after the old people.—JANET PENFOLD.

Mrs Florrie Penfold was seventy when she assisted her daughter Janet to record the song. She also knew the cries *Fire Winter Log O* and *Roses and Carnations*, but she particularly liked the lavender cry because it was 'more of a song'. There was little money in it, she said, but it was useful, because as people got to know the seller she could offer other wares such as laces and pins.

357 THE TATTIE TIME

Ronnie White, Blairgowrie, Perthshire, Scotland, *rec.* J. Brune, 1961

Printed version
BRUNE: 1965, p. 25

The potato time—the tattie time—is probably the most important season in the Scots traveller's calendar. First thing in the morning the 'digger' is driven into the potato field, then a truck is sent to the camps to pick up the potato gangs. In the meantime the digger turns over the soil, leaving the potatoes at the surface ready for lifting and putting into sacks. When the gang arrives on the field each person is assigned a stretch or a square portion of land from which to lift potatoes. They are paid so much per sack.

The song probably has as many authors as verses, more verses being added from year to year. It is generally sung flat out and at the fastest possible speed the singer can manage. The final verse by John Cameron of Blairgowrie goes:

> An' if ye want anither verse, compose it for yersel'
> For I'm no awfi gude at it, as ye can easy tell

But a more traditional verse is often preferred:

> An' if ye want the author an' composer of this song
> Ye'll find him in a herrin' boat at the pier o' Foggie Loan

358 TRAMPS AND HAWKERS

Davie Stewart, Dundee, Angus, Scotland, *rec.* P. Kennedy, London, 1956

Printed version
SEEGER AND MACCOLL: 1960, No. 46, p. 50: four verses from a MS; contributed by Mary Brookbank of Dundee

> I heard it from a traveller called 'Thumby' Mathieson—they called him 'Thumby' 'cause he had two thumbs on each hand. I couldn't tell you where he is now, but he went off to America. At the time he kept a big rag-store in Peterhead and he was a big metal merchant too. I used to go around hawking with him and that's how I learned *Tramps and Hawkers*, but all the travellers know it now. It really tells you how it is when you're on the road.—DAVIE STEWART.

In the third verse 'braxie ham' is mentioned. Braxie ham is meat from an animal, usually a sheep, that has died naturally —perhaps one that has choked itself eating a turnip. If its throat is slit while the body is still warm the blood will drain off and you have mutton, but if it is not found until it is cold and stiff it is braxie: you remove the skin, the gall and the guts and then slice the remaining meat and blood into a small barrel, keeping the bones for marrow soup. The braxie meat is stored for a few months in salt and saltpetre, which gradually neutralizes the poisons of putrefaction. When this is matured you have braxie ham which can be stewed with vegetables and herbs.

359 THE TRAVELLING CANDYMAN

Jennie Davison, Antrim, N. Ireland, *rec.* S. Ennis, 1954:
BBC 21839

Pat O'Flanagan, the Irish hero of this traveller's composition, came over to Scotland and turned to rags as a last resort. In fact although dealing in rags is often regarded as the last, desperate occupation, some of the wealthiest travellers in Britain have made their money as dealers in rags 'and all other different kinds of stuff'. Within the branches of a tinker family there will be those who specialize in all the different kinds of materials. Many articles of clothing discarded by house-dwellers can, with a bit of touching up, became serviceable; the rest must be sorted into sacks according to the ways they can be used for furnishings or by paper manufacturers and others. A candyman today must know quite a bit about man-made fibres as well as conventional animal wool cloths, and as much of his time will be spent in sorting as in going round the houses collecting the rags.

360 THE YELLOW HANDKERCHIEF

Eli Sterry, Blaxhall, Suffolk, *rec.* P. Kennedy, 1957
Other recorded versions
Phoebe Smith, Woodbridge, Suffolk, *rec.* P. Kennedy, 1957
Jasper Smith, Edenbridge, Kent, *rec.* J. Brune, 1967

Printed versions
GARDINER MS: 1906–7: three variants, *Flash Company*; *Once I loved Thomas*; *Bonny Blue Handkerchief* (Hampshire)
JFSS: 1915, No. 19, p. 174: *First I Loved Thomas*, 'phonographed by Walter Ford', Surrey, 1907; note by Frank Kidson
PURSLOW: 1968, p. 43: *Flash Company, coll.* Gardiner (Hampshire)

First I loved Thomas and then I loved John
And then I loved William, he's a clever young man
With his white cotton stockings and his low ankle shoes
And he wears a blue jacket wherever he goes

The rocks shall run to water, and the sea shall run dry
If ever I prove false, my love, to the girl that loves I
In the middle of the ocean there shall grow a myrtle tree
If ever I proves false, my love, to the girl that loves me

Two of the verses sung by a Surrey singer recorded by Walter Ford in 1907. The tune used was a variant of *Green Bushes* (No. 156). When the song was published in the *Folk Song Journal*, Frank Kidson added a note that he had heard a very similar version of the air and words sung at the Retford Music Competition in Nottinghamshire a few years previously under the title of *Flash Company*.

Phoebe Smith, who learned her version in the Kent and Surrey area, had a moralizing concluding verse:

Come all you pretty flash girls take warning by me
And never build your nest in the top of any tree
For the leaves they will wither and the roots they will decay
And the beauty of a young girl will soon fade away

Bibliography

ACTON: 1972

Thomas Acton (ed.), *The Romano Drom Song Book I*: Romanestan Publications, T. A. Acton, Nuffield College, Oxford, 1972. A collection of songs contributed by gipsies and other travellers for use by their own community. Includes 5 songs in very deep Romany from Eastern Europe and Spain, 5 English gipsy songs, *The Ballad of Brownhills*, by the Irish traveller Johnny Connors, and *We shall not be Moved*.

BARING GOULD: 1889–1905

Rev. S. Baring Gould and Rev. H. Fleetwood Sheppard, *Songs and Ballads of the West*: Patey & Willis, London (4 parts), 1889–91; Methuen, London (4 parts), 1891–94; (1 vol.), 1895; revised ed., 1905. Details are given by E. A. White in JEFDSS: 1937, p. 143 and 1946, p. 67. When reprinted in four parts this collection, mainly from Devon and N. Cornwall, comprised 110 songs 'collected from the mouths of the people'. Texts were modified and in some cases completely rewritten, and the same applied to tunes. However, in the revised edition, under the musical editorship of Cecil Sharp and with the adding of the name of the Rev. F. W. Bussell, one of the original collectors, many original texts and tunes were restored. For further comment on this publication see Dean-Smith, JEFDSS: 1950, p. 41.

BARRERE AND LELAND: 1889–97

Albert Barrère and C. G. Leland, *A Dictionary of Slang, Jargon and Cant*: Ballantyne Press, Edinburgh, 1889–90. Bell & Sons, London, 1897. (Gale Research Company, Detroit, Michigan, USA, 1967, with new introduction by Eric Partridge.) Contains 'English, American, Anglo-Indian Slang, Pidgin English, Tinker's Jargon and Other Irregular Phraseology', which includes most of Leland's Romany and Shelta vocabulary.

BARRETT: 1891

William A. Barrett, *English Folk Songs*: Novello, London, 1891. 54 songs with piano arrangements. An early publication using the term 'collected folk song'; most of the songs published elsewhere; exact details of origins not given and Barrett not nationally accepted as reputable collector or arranger.

BLACK: 1914

G. Black, *A Gypsy Bibliography*: Gypsy Lore Society, Monograph No. 1., Bernard Quaritch, London, for the Edinburgh University Press, 1914. The best bibliographical guide up to 1913.

BORDE: 1547

Andrew Borde, *The Fyrst Boke of the Introduction of Knowledge*: William Copland, London, 1547 and 1550. Whole work reprinted by R. A. Taylor, London, 1814. Early English Text Society, London, 1870 and 1919. Ch. 38 reproduced in JGLS, 2nd series, pp. 163 ff. The first known description of gipsies in English literature; also contains earliest specimens of Romany speech.

BORROW: 1843

George Borrow, *The Zincali*, 2nd ed., London, 1843. Deals mainly with gipsies in Spain on whom he was a great authority, but gives some good examples of English speech and song. Borrow's only reliable work. Extensive vocabulary.

BORROW: 1874

George Borrow, *Romano Lavo-Lil*: John Murray, London, 1874. Frequently reprinted. As a dictionary inferior to SMART AND CROFTON: 1875, and glossary in LELAND: 1875 but does contain a collection of English gipsy songs, some of which are probably Borrow's own compositions.

BOSWELL: 1970

Silvester Gordon Boswell (ed. John Seymour), *The Book of Boswell*: Gollancz, London, 1970. One of the very rare books actually written by an English Romany, giving his account of 'the life'. There are a number of references to singing and also to step-dancing. Rambling gipsy songs of the Boswells reproduced in the book are: *On the Road again, Appleby Fair in the Nineteen-Fifties*, and *I would like to Travel the Roads Again*.

BREPOHL: 1911

F. W. Brepohl, *Die Zigeuner als Musiker* ('The gipsies as musicians') in JGLS, 2nd series, iv, p. 241. Adds more on the subject to that given earlier by LISZT: 1861.

BROADWOOD: 1843

Rev. John Broadwood, *Old English Songs*: (privately printed) Balls & Co., London, 1843. 16 songs, collected in Surrey and Sussex by the Rev. John Broadwood of Lyne near Horsham. Arrangements by G. A. Dusart of Worthing. Said to be the 'first collection of folksong airs for their own sake'.

BROADWOOD: 1890

Rev. John Broadwood, *Sussex Songs* (*Popular Songs of Sussex*): Stanley, Lucas & Weber, London, 1890. 26 songs (including the 16 in BROADWOOD: 1843) collected by Broadwood and arranged by H. F. Birch Reynardson.

BROADWOOD: 1893

Lucy Broadwood and J. A. Fuller-Maitland, *English County Songs*: Cramer, London, 1893. Important early publication containing 92 songs collected in nearly every county of England. Most have little relevance to their district origins but some are in the dialects of their locality. Scholarly presentation with straightforward piano accompaniments. For article about editor see JEFDSS: 1948, p. 136 and 1950, p. 38.

BROADWOOD: 1908

Lucy Broadwood, *English Traditional Songs and Carols*: Boosey, London, 1908. 39 songs mainly from Surrey–Sussex border. Informative preface and brief notes about singers with comparative transcriptions made by phonograph cylinder recordings.

BROCKIE: 1884

William Brockie, *Gipsy Sketches: Historical, Traditional, Philological and Humorous*: J. & J. H. Rutherfurd, Kelso, 1884. A good sociological study of gipsies, mainly on the English–Scottish border.

BRUNE: 1965

John A. Brune, *The Roving Songster*: Gillian Cook, London, 1965. This collection includes 9 songs and ballads collected from Scots travellers, 3 songs by Belle Stewart and 5 songs on the travelling life by John Brune; the latter were all composed 'on the road'. There are 31 songs in the book.

BUCHAN: 1962

Norman Buchan, *101 Scottish Songs*: William Collins & Son, Ltd., Glasgow and London, 1962. Contains the largest selection of traveller's material in a popular song book. Some of these are apparently in no other collection.

CHAPPELL: 1858/9

William Chappell, *Popular Music of the Olden Time*: Cramer, Beale & Chappell, London, vol. I 1858, vol. II 1859; Dover Publications, New York, 1965. Includes most of material from *National English Airs* (1838) but more has been added from other sources with particular reference to the ballads in the

Pepys and Roxburghe collections. For further comment see Dean-Smith's *Guide* and JEFDSS: 1950, p. 38.

CHRISTIE: 1876/1881
William Christie, *Traditional Ballad Airs*: Edmonston & Douglas, Edinburgh, vol. I 1876; vol. II 1881. Dean Christie noted down songs mainly in Aberdeenshire. This book combines his own collecting with publication of tunes and words from many other collections, both published and unpublished, including Percy, Scott, Jamieson, Motherwell, Kinloch, Sharpe and Buchan. Also contains a few original compositions.

CLEBERT: 1963
Jean-Paul Clébert, *The Gypsies*: Vista Books, London, 1963. Translated by Charles Duff from the French *Les Tziganes*: B. Arthaud, Paris, 1961; Penguin Books, London, 1967. Clébert's aim is to show the richness of gipsy folklore; he covers much the same ground as Jules Bloch's *Les Tsiganes*, which served as the main source. Translator provides further valuable original material including bibliography and data on English and American gipsies. 69 excellent illustrations make up for much 'doubtful' material.

COLLINSON: 1966
Francis Collinson, *The Traditional and National Music of Scotland*: Routledge & Kegan Paul, London, 1966. Not a music collection but a general discussion on the music of both Gaelic and Lowland Scotland. A useful background study to all types of Scots music.

COX: 1925
John Harrington Cox, *Folk Songs of the South*: Harvard University Press, Cambridge, Mass., USA, 1925. Dover Publications Reprint, New York, 1967 (released 1968). 185 songs collected in West Virginia (29 with tunes). Introduction describes collecting methods and identifies informants. Notes, references to other versions and other data given with texts of songs.

CROFT-COOKE: 1948
Rupert Croft-Cooke, *The Moon in my Pocket*: Sampson Low, Marston & Co. Ltd., London, 1948. Croft-Cooke's chief contribution is the list (pp. 186–98) of words in common usage among Southern English gipsies; the first half of the book is an account of a journey in a gipsy horse-waggon with Ted Scamp —brother of Phoebe Smith of Woodbridge, Suffolk, and of Charlie Scamp (see No. 337). This makes good reading, as does the chapter 'The Rais and their Books', which is more than just a bibliography. The rest of the book is inclined to be over-romantic.

DEAN-SMITH: 1954
Margaret Dean-Smith, *A Guide to English Folk Song Collections (1822–1952)*: University of Liverpool, 1954. A useful index of published songs under titles, alternative titles and first lines, with some full descriptions of important books with historical annotations and an introduction which traces the development of collecting and publication of folksong in England over a period of 130 years.

DODDS: 1966
Norman Dodds, *Gypsies, Didikois and Other Travellers*: Johnson Publications Ltd., London, 1966. History of the author's gipsy campaign and from the point of the present work useful, if not indispensable. It gives a full account of the circumstances in which such songs as *Me brother's 'orse* (No. 350) were improvised. See also CLEBERT: 1963 for an illustration showing Norman Dodds at an improvised party in Darenth Wood, Kent, early in 1962.

DUNCAN Ms: 1905–11
James Duncan (1848–1917). MS, collected 1905–11, in Aberdeen University Library. Consists of two notebooks, the first containing 800 tunes with words of first verse, and the second giving texts of over 350 songs all supplied by a Mrs Gillespie. For obituary by Lucy Broadwood see JFSS: 1918, No. 21, p. 41.

EDDY: 1939
Mary O. Eddy, *Ballads and Songs from Ohio*: J. J. Augustin, New York, 1939.

FMJ: 1965–
Folk Music Journal: English Folk Dance and Song Society, London (from 1965). Continuing the work of JFSS (*Journal of the Folk-Song Society*), 1889–1931 and JEFDSS (*Journal of the English Folk Dance and Song Society*), 1932–64.

FORD: 1899–1904
Robert Ford, *Vagabond Songs and Ballads of Scotland*: Gardiner, Paisley, Scotland, 1899–1901; new edition 1904. A comprehensive collection of songs and ballads, containing a number of 'bothy ballads', but only a few for which he provides the music. Important in that it covers the wide range of songs that were current up to the end of the century, particularly those sung by 'the travellers'.

GARDINER Ms: 1905–9
For further details about Gardiner's work see *The George Gardiner Folksong Collection* in FMJ: 1967, p. 129 and introduction to PURSLOW: 1968. (See also under HAMMOND.)

GILLINGTON: 1907
Alice E. Gillington, *Eight Hampshire Songs*: Curwen, London, 1907. Songs arranged by Miss Gillington with piano accompaniments. No preface or notes to songs.

GILLINGTON: 1911
Alice E. Gillington, *Songs of the Open Road*: Williams, London, 1911. The earliest English publication devoted to gipsy songs and dance tunes. 16 songs and 9 dances collected in Hampshire and the New Forest mostly from a family called Lee. Music arranged for piano by Dowsett Sellars. Includes 4 songs in Romany.

GREIG: 1909/14
Gavin Greig, *Folk Songs of the North-East*: The Buchan Observer, Peterhead, Scotland. Vol. I 1909, vol. II 1914. Folklore Associates, Pennsylvania, USA, 1963. Greig was an Aberdeenshire schoolmaster and an accomplished musician who noted the words and tunes of over 3,000 songs. His manuscripts, extending over 90 volumes, are deposited in the Library of King's College, Aberdeen.

GRELLMANN: 1783
Heinrich M. G. Grellmann, *Historischer Versuch über die Zigeuner*: 2nd edition, Göttingen, 1787. English translation *Dissertation on the Gypsies*, London, 1787. The earliest serious study of the gipsies and their origins. Has never been challenged by informed people except in minor details and had no equal for over a century. Main source for HOYLAND: 1816.

HAMER: 1973
Fred Hamer, *Green Groves*: EFDS Publications, London, 1973. 38 songs, words and melodies (chord symbols). A further selection published posthumously. As in Hamer's *Garners Gay*, no exact details of locations, dates or comparative notes to songs.

HAMMOND AND GARDINER Mss: 1905–9
H. E. D. Hammond (1866–1910), R. F. F. Hammond (1868–1921) and Dr George Gardiner (1852–1910) collected mainly in Dorset and Hampshire. Their manuscripts, deposited in the Vaughan Williams Memorial Library at Cecil Sharp House, London, have been indexed by Frank Purslow, who has also edited three books drawn from them.

HOYLAND: 1816
John Hoyland, *The Gypsies*: York, 1816. A historical survey of the customs, habits and present state of the gipsies. The first serious English book on the subject. The early portion of the work is based on Grellmann but sections V, VI, IX, X, XI and XII are the result of original research and independent thought. Much of the original work consisted of correspondence; a statement by Sir Walter Scott, the then Sheriff of Selkirkshire, appears on p. 93.

JAFL: 1888–
Journal of American Folklore now published by University of Pennsylvania. April 1890, pp. 157–9; July 1890, pp. 238–9.

JEFDSS: 1932–64
Journal of The English Folk Dance and Song Society: London (32 vols.), 1932–64. See also STARKIE: 1935.

JFSS: 1899–1931
Journal of the Folk-Song Society: London (35 vols.), 1899–1931. W. P. Merrick, JFSS: 1901, No. 3, p. 110. Romany paraphrase of the second verse of *Captain Grant*.

JGLS: 1888–
Journal of the Gypsy Lore Society, 1st series 1888–92, 2nd series 1907–16, 3rd series 1922 onwards: The Gypsy Lore Society, The University Library, Liverpool. The source of most serious gipsy scholarship, covering gipsy problems from all possible points of view and giving extensive Romany, Shelta and Cant vocabularies, Romany and Cant song versions, tales, proverbs, traditions and practical features of gipsy life. The main stress is on the Romany section of the Travelling Community. JGLS: 1908–9, pp. 241ff., Kuno Meyer, 'The Secret Languages of Ireland.' See also SAMPSON: 1933 and SMITH: 1889.

JIFLS
Journal of the Irish Folk Lore Society: Dublin. Article in 1931 issue 'Irish Tinkers', by Padraig MacGraine, contains extensive list of Shelta and Gamon terms.

JOHNSON: 1787–1853
James Johnson, *The Scots Musical Museum*: 6 vols. Edinburgh, 1787–1803; 4 vols. with notes by William Stenhouse and David Laing, Edinburgh, 1853. This was the beginning of systematic documentation of Scots songs to which Robert Burns contributed material of his own collecting which he restored by re-writing and amplification of the texts.

JUDGES: 1930
A. V. Judges, *The Elizabethan Underworld*: Routledge & Kegan Paul Ltd., London, 1930, 3rd impression, May 1965. The most comprehensive study on the English Rogues available. Contains all the main early works except Chapter 38 of Andrew Borde's *First Book of the Introduction of Knowledge*, 1547. Includes some canting songs and an extensive glossary.

KING: 1972
Charles King, *Men of the Road*: Frederick Muller Ltd., London, 1972. This book is a summary of all the most important statements made on gipsy life and traditions in this century in English up to 1969. Twelve pages of gipsy music and 3 song texts are given as well as some traditional stories.

LEEDS UNIVERSITY
Catalogue of the Gipsy Collection in Leeds University Library.

LELAND: 1874
Charles G. Leland, *The English Gipsies and their Language*: Trübner & Co., London, 1874. Leland's main contribution; possibly the best introduction to the corrupted form of the language currently spoken in the South of England; most of Leland's original theories are doubtful but his facts are unimpeachable.

LELAND: 1875
Charles G. Leland, Professor E. H. Palmer and Janet Tuckey, *English Gipsy Songs, In Romany with Metrical English Translations*: Trübner & Co., 1875. The preface gives a good account of Romany song as experienced by Leland. The book contains 47 rye songs and 9 genuine gipsy songs. Extensive glossary.

LELAND: 1880
Charles G. Leland, 'The Gipsies', article in *The New Quarterly Review*, 1880, iii, pp. 136–41. The earliest account of Shelta as a distinct language.

LEWIS: 1914
Mrs Herbert Lewis, *Folk Songs collected in Flintshire and the Vale of Clwyd*: Hughes, Cardiff and Wrexham, 1914. Contains 12 songs in Welsh only (with no translations into English) and 2 songs in English. Arranged for voice and piano with comparative notes and details of sources.

LISZT: 1861
Franz Liszt, *Die Zigeuner und ihre Musik in Ungarn* ('The Gipsies and their music in Hungary'). Cornelius, Pest, 1861. Description of the influence of the gipsies on the music of Hungary.

LIVERPOOL UNIVERSITY
Catalogue of the Gipsy Collection in Liverpool University Library.

LOGAN: 1869
W. H. Logan, *A Pedlar's Pack*: Paterson, Edinburgh, 1869.

MACALISTER: 1937
R. A. S. MacAlister, *The Secret Languages of Ireland*: University Press, Cambridge, 1937. The only really full description of Shelta to date.

MACCOLL: 1965
Ewan MacColl, *Folk Songs and Ballads of Scotland*: Oak Publications, New York, 1965. An unusually good collection of Scots songs and ballads built up around the repertory of MacColl's parents.

MACCOLL/SEEGER: 1968
Ewan MacColl and Peggy Seeger, *I'm a Freeborn Man*: Oak Publications, New York, 1968. A collection of songs written and composed by Ewan MacColl and Peggy Seeger. Contains rye songs compiled from tape-recordings made around travellers' encampments in various parts of Britain, also a good selection of transcribed actuality and illustrations. One of the songs, *I'm a Freeborn Man*, has since gone into the repertory of travelling folk up and down the country.

McCORMICK: 1906
Andrew McCormick, *The Tinkler Gypsies of Galloway*: J. Maxwell & Son, Dumfries, 1906. The most important work on the Scots travellers with an extensive glossary of tinker's cant fragments and songs.

McEVOY: 1938
Patrick A. McEvoy, *The Gorse and the Briar*: George Harrap & Co. Ltd., London, 1938. A good factual account of travelling with Romanies before World War II with delicate drawings by Christopher C. McEvoy. There are several pages on gipsy singing and dancing scattered throughout the book.

MacKENZIE: 1883
Alexander MacKenzie, *The History of the Highland Clearances*: 2nd revised edition 1946: Alex. MacLaren & Sons, Glasgow. Gives great insight into the movements of an evicted population, with many accounts of evictions.

MacRITCHIE: 1894
David MacRitchie, *Scottish Gypsies under the Stewarts*: Edinburgh, 1894. Good background to Scottish tinkers.

MacRITCHIE: 1911
David MacRitchie, 'The Speech of the Roads', article in *Nineteenth Century*, 1911, vol. 70, pp. 545–54.

MASON: 1877/1908
Miss M. H. Mason, *Nursery Rhymes and Country Songs*: Metzler, London, 1877. Second edition without illustrations and with additional notes, 1908. Over 50 folksongs of great variety mainly from her own Mitford family in Northumberland, also from Broadwood in Sussex, with piano accompaniments.

O LOCHLAINN: 1939
Colm O Lochlainn, *Irish Street Ballads*: Three Candles, Dublin, 1939. Over 100 songs, words, music and annotations collected in many different parts of Ireland (including the North). All in English and many having equivalents in England and Scotland. Illustrated with woodcuts from the original broadsheets.

O LOCHLAINN: 1965
Colm O Lochlainn, *More Irish Street Ballads*: Three Candles, Dublin, 1965. A further 100 songs, all again in the English language.

ORD: 1930
John Ord, *Bothy Songs and Ballads*: Alexander Gardner, Paisley, Scotland. The standard work on the 'bothy ballads' of N.E. Scotland; a 'bothy' is a farm cottage or hut used by hands, ploughmen, shepherds and farm-servants. It also includes folksongs found elsewhere, being mainly those describing, and often complaining about, local farm life.

PARTRIDGE: 1949
Eric Partridge, *A Dictionary of Slang and Unconventional English*, 3rd ed. much enlarged: Routledge & Kegan Paul, London, 1949. Covers English-speaking world from 16th century.

PARTRIDGE: 1950
Eric Partridge, *A Dictionary of the Underworld*: Routledge & Kegan Paul, London, 1950. Vocabulary of criminals, tramps, prostitutes, white slavers, drug-pushers and includes tinkers and hawkers. Again from the 16th century.

PURSLOW: 1965
Frank Purslow, *Marrowbones*: EFDS Publications, London, 1965. A series of pocket-size publications initiated by Peter Kennedy in order to make available the songs collected by Hammond and Gardiner in the care of the EFDSS Library. This selection contains 100 songs, provided with chord symbols over the melodies.

PURSLOW: 1968
Frank Purslow, *The Wanton Seed*: EFDS Publications, London, 1968. A second selection from Hammond and Gardiner again containing 100 songs.

RANDOLPH: 1946–50
Vance Randolph and Floyd C. Shoemaker, *Ozark Folk Songs*: (4 vols.) State Historical Society, Columbia, Missouri, USA, 1946–50.

REEVE: 1958
Dominic Reeve, *Smoke in the Lanes*: Constable, London, 1958. Quotes a number of songs and trade jingles and describes a singing session. Provides good contemporary background description of gipsy life in England.

REEVES: 1958
James Reeves, *The Idiom of the People*: Heinemann, London, 1958. Words of 115 folksongs from Cecil Sharp MSS (about 40 printed for the first time) selected as examples of 'English Traditional Verse'. Introduction concerned with the Folk Song Movement in England; Sharp as a collector; text revisions, description of the MSS; the popular idiom; and a detailed consideration of certain songs.

ROXBURGHE: 1871–93
Roxburghe Ballads (about 1540–1790): Vols. I–II ed. William Chappell, Ballad Society, London, 1871–80; vols. III–VII ed. J. W. Ebsworth, Hertford, 1883–93.

SAMPSON: 1923
John Sampson, 'The Origin and Early Migrations of the Gypsies', article in JGLS, Series 3, ii, p. 156.

SAMPSON: 1926
John Sampson, *The Dialect of the Gypsies of Wales*: Oxford University Press, 1926. A landmark in linguistics and philology. The author devised a practical phonetic alphabet for the Welsh Romany dialect as spoken by the Wood family, whose speech he took down in long-hand and from it evolved a very full grammar and an archaic vocabulary. Both the grammar and the vocabulary are painstakingly compared with the root languages. Indispensable to serious students of Romany.

SAMPSON: 1930
John Sampson, *The Wind on the Heath*: Chatto & Windus, London, 1930. Comprehensive anthology on English gipsies.

SAMPSON: 1931
John Sampson, *Romane Gilia*: Oxford University Press, London, 1931. A number of Sampson's own poems rendered into deep Welsh romany. A few of his lines appear to have remained in the tradition.

SAMPSON: 1933
John Sampson, *Welsh Gypsy Folk Tales* (in English): Gregynog Press, Newton, Monmouthshire, 1933. A collection of most of the tales which appeared in the JGLS.

SEEGER AND MACCOLL: 1960
Peggy Seeger and Ewan MacColl, *The Singing Island*: Mills Music, London, 1960. 96 English and Scots folksongs arranged for 'the post-war folk revival' mainly from Scotland under headings: Children, Courting, Men at Work, On the Road, Sailors, Barrack Room, Rovin' Boys and Flash Girls, Historical and Fill up your Glass.

SHARP MS: 1903–23
Cecil Sharp (1859–1924), foremost collector of English folksongs and folkdances, was the founder of The English Folk Dance Society and for many years a member of The Folk-Song Society. (In 1932 these two societies amalgamated as The English Folk Dance and Song Society.) For a full account of his life-work and publications see *Cecil Sharp* by A. H. Fox-Strangways (Oxford University Press, London, 1933), revised by Maud Karpeles (Routledge & Kegan Paul, London, 1967). Words, songs, tunes and dance notes in Cecil Sharp's autograph are in the Library of Clare College, Cambridge. There are also photostat copies in the Harvard University Library and the New York Public Library, and microfilm copies in the libraries of the University of California and in the library at Cecil Sharp House, London, the headquarters of The English Folk Dance and Song Society. Cecil Sharp's own collection of books was left to the EFDSS and formed the beginnings of the specialist library at Cecil Sharp House.

SMART AND CROFTON: 1875
B. C. Smart and H. T. Crofton, *The Dialect of the English Gipsies*, 2nd enlarged edition: Asher, London, 1875. The most extensive vocabulary of English gipsy dialect with examples of grammatical Romany as well as the more corrupted forms that were current at the time.

SMITH: 1889
Laura Alexandrine Smith, *Through Romany Songland*: London, 1889. An important book containing a number of gipsy songs. Twelve of these songs are quoted in English translation in JGLS, Series 1, ii, 1891, pp. 5 ff. in an article titled 'Romany Songs Englished'.

STARKIE: 1935
Walter Starkie, *Gypsy Folklore and Music*, article in JEFDSS: 1935, pp. 83–91. In the main a study of gipsy music and its characteristics in Hungary, Rumania and Spain.

UDAL: 1922
John Symonds Udal, *Dorsetshire Folk-Lore*: Stephen Austin, Hertford, 1922; J. Stephens-Cox, St Peter Port, Guernsey, 1970. Contains a long 'fore-say' by William Barnes, 'The Dorset Poet', and is a mixture of material including the words of about 20 songs.

VAUGHAN WILLIAMS: 1908
Ralph Vaughan Williams, *Folk Songs from the Eastern Counties*: Novello, London, 1908. 15 songs from Essex, Norfolk and Cambridgeshire most already in JFSS: 1906, No. 8.

VEKERDI: 1967
J. Vekerdi, *Gypsy Folk Songs*: Acta Orient, Hung. Tomux XX, Budapest, 1967. A complete analysis of gipsy song types.

VESEY-FITZGERALD: 1944
Brian Vesey-Fitzgerald, *Gypsies of Britain*: Chapman & Hall, London, 1944. This is probably the best general introductory

work on Romanies, based on a life-long experience of gipsy ways. The author checked all his own findings against those of other authorities, in particular contributors to JGLS. He also drew freely from the pages of the Journal—in fact this book can be described as a synopsis of all the most vital facts (apart from linguistics, which he leaves severely alone) connected with the gipsy way of life.

WEBB: 1960

G. E. C. Webb, *Gypsies, The Secret People*: Herbert Jenkins, London, 1960. Strong in gipsy lore and good illustrations.

WILLIAMS: 1923

Alfred Owen Williams, *Folk Songs of the Upper Thames*: Duckworth, London, 1923. Over 300 folksongs (words only) noted mainly in Berkshire, Gloucestershire, Oxfordshire and Wiltshire. Interesting introduction about rural life, more fully covered by Williams in *Round About the Upper Thames* (Duckworth, 1922). Further unpublished texts in Swindon Reference Library. See FMJ: 1969 'Alfred Williams: A Symposium'.

INDEX OF SONG TITLES, TRANSLATIONS AND VARIANT SONG TITLES

Roman numerals indicate chapters, figures in **bold** *type song numbers. The letter 't' after a song number stands for translation, 'v' before a number indicates a variant title.*

INDEX OF FIRST LINES in original language and translation

*Roman numerals indicate chapters, figures in **bold** song numbers.*

INDEX OF FOLKSINGERS

The Roman numerals and figures indicate chapters and song numbers. The names of the folksingers are given in the song-notes.

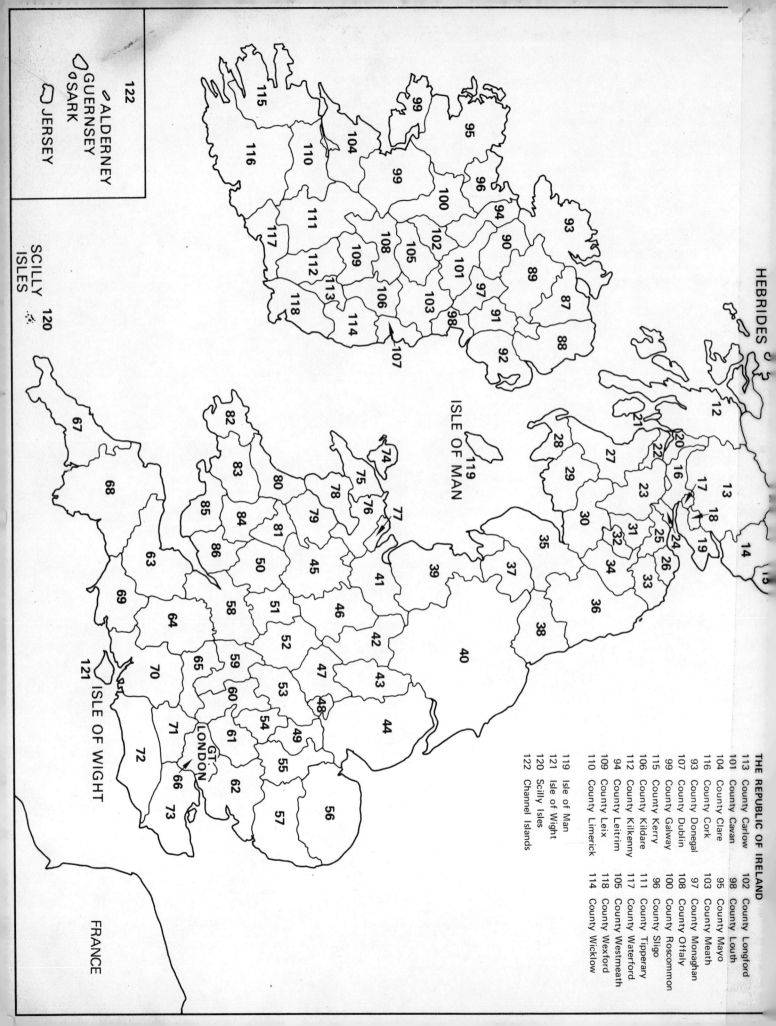

HEBRIDES

ISLE OF MAN

GT. LONDON

ISLE OF WIGHT

FRANCE

SCILLY ISLES

ALDERNEY
GUERNSEY
SARK
JERSEY